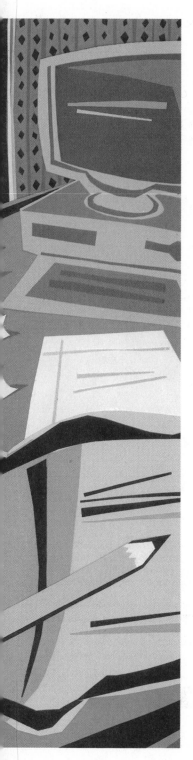

Fifth Edition

THE BEDFORD GUIDE FOR COLLEGE WRITERS

with Reader, Research Manual, and Handbook

X. J. Kennedy, Dorothy M. Kennedy, and Sylvia A. Holladay

Bedford/St. Martin's   Boston   New York

FOR BEDFORD/ST. MARTIN'S

Developmental Editors: Denise B. Wydra, Leasa Burton, Michelle M. Clark
Production Editor: Karen S. Baart
Production Supervisor: Joe Ford
Marketing Manager: Karen Melton
Editorial Assistants: Amanda J. Bristow, Nicole R. Simonsen
Production Assistants: Coleen O'Hanley, Edward R. Tonderys
Copyeditor: Rosemary Winfield
Text Design: Claire Seng-Niemoeller
Cover Design: Donna Lee Dennison
Cover Art: Original art by Tina Vey
Composition: Monotype Composition Company, Inc.
Printing and Binding: RR Donnelley & Sons Company

President: Charles H. Christensen
Editorial Director: Joan E. Feinberg
Director of Editing, Design, and Production: Marcia Cohen
Managing Editor: Elizabeth M. Schaaf

Library of Congress Catalog Card Number: 98–87532

Manufactured in the United States of America.

3   2   1   0   9   8
f   e   d   c   b   a

For information, write: Bedford/St. Martin's, 75 Arlington Street, Boston, MA 02116
(617-426-7440)

ISBN: 0-312-19608-3 (Instructor's Annotated Edition)
      0-312-17156-0 (hardcover Student Edition)
      0-312-20184-2 (paperback Student Edition)

ACKNOWLEDGMENTS

Russell Baker, "The Art of Eating Spaghetti." Reprinted from *Growing Up* by Russell Baker, © 1982. Used with permission of NTC/Contemporary Publishing Group, Inc.

Judy Brady, "I Want a Wife." From *Ms.*, December 1971. Reprinted by permission of the author.

Stephanie Brail, "The Price of Admission." From *Wired Women* (1996). Copyright 1996 by Stephanie Brail. Reprinted with permission.

Rachel Carson, "A Fable for Tomorrow." From *Silent Spring* by Rachel Carson. Copyright © 1962 by Rachel L. Carson, renewed 1990 by Roger Christie. Reprinted by permission of Houghton Mifflin Co. All rights reserved.

Bruce Catton, "Grant and Lee: A Study in Contrasts." From *The American Story,* edited by Earl Schenck Miers. © 1956 by United States Capitol Historical Society.

Thomas F. Cawsey, Gene Deszca, and Maurice Mazerolle, "The Portfolio Career as a Response to a Changing Job Market." From *Journal of Career Planning and Employment* (November 1995). Copyright © 1995 by National Association of Colleges and Employers. Reprinted with permission.

Veronica Chambers, "The Myth of Cinderella." From *Newsweek* (November 3, 1997). Copyright © 1997 Newsweek, Inc. All rights reserved. Reprinted by permission.

Stephanie Coontz, "Remarriage and Stepfamilies." From *The Way We Really Are* (1997). Copyright 1997 by Stephanie Coontz. Reprinted by permission of HarperCollins.

Meghan Daum, "Virtual Love." From *The New Yorker* (August 25 and September 1, 1997). Copyright © 1997 by Meghan Daum. Reprinted by permission of International Creative Management, Inc.

Acknowledgments and copyrights are continued at the back of the book on pages R-45–46, which constitute an extension of the copyright page. It is a violation of the law to reproduce these selections by any means whatsoever without the written permission of the copyright holder.

Preface:
To the Instructor

No one ever learned to swim or play a musical instrument by reading a book. Similarly, no one ever learned to write by reading or talking about writing. If a student is to learn to write well, practice and feedback are more valuable than theory and prescriptions. The emphasis in *The Bedford Guide for College Writers* is on students' own writing, not on reading and talking about writing. Pressed immediately into the act of writing, students learn by doing, without being burdened by a lot of preliminary advice. *The Bedford Guide* is based on our belief that writing is the lively, usually surprising, often rewarding art of thinking while working with language.

The fifth edition of *The Bedford Guide*, like the fourth, offers four coordinated composition books integrated into one convenient text. A single volume offers a process-oriented rhetoric, a thematically arranged reader, a full research manual, and a comprehensive reference handbook—all the textbooks you and your students will need for a thorough writing course. (*The Bedford Guide* is available in two other versions as well: as three books in one, without a handbook; and as two books in one, a rhetoric and a reader.) For the fifth edition, we have revised the book to give students more support and guidance in the crucial areas of critical reading and thinking, computers and technological literacy, and support for underprepared students.

Overview of The Bedford Guide

BOOK ONE: A WRITER'S GUIDE

This first book is a process-oriented rhetoric with readings; it addresses all traditional assignments and topics typically covered in the first-year writing course. For convenience, the rhetoric is divided into four parts.

Parts One and Two contain the main assignment chapters, which are structured according to a typical writing process. Part One, "A Writer's Resources," focuses on four major resources that writers draw on: recall (Chapter 1), observation (Chapter 2), conversation (Chapter 3), and imagination (Chapter 4). Part Two, "Thinking Critically," moves students into the rigorous analytical writing that will comprise most of the writing they do in their college careers: writing from critical reading (Chapter 5), analyzing (Chapter 6), comparing and contrasting (Chapter 7), explaining causes and effects (Chapter 8), taking a stand (Chapter 9), proposing a solution (Chapter 10), and evaluating (Chapter 11).

Each of these first eleven chapters begins with "Learning from Other Writers" — two model essays, one by a professional and one by a student writer. Next, students are whisked into an assignment in "Learning by Writing." As they draw on the chapter's resource or deploy its critical strategy to write an essay, students are guided by suggestions for generating ideas, planning, drafting, developing, revising, and editing. "Learning by Writing" also features checklists for discovery, revision, and peer response, as well as tips for writing with a computer and for collaborative learning. After students learn by writing, "Applying What You Learn" links the resource or critical strategy with other courses across the curriculum and with on-the-job situations. Each chapter ends with a "Making Connections" section that points the student toward relevant selections in Book Two, *A Writer's Reader.*

Part Three, "Special Writing Situations," supports students' efforts in three additional common writing situations: writing about literature, writing for assessment, and writing for business.

Chapter 12, "Writing about Literature," guides students through writing an analysis of a literary work, using samples of student writing about both fiction and poetry. It also illustrates how to compare and contrast two literary selections. This chapter includes a glossary of terms for analyzing the elements of literature and a section on specific strategies for writing about literature — synopsis and paraphrase.

Chapter 13, "Writing for Assessment," discusses essay examinations and timed competency exams and includes a new section on portfolios.

Chapter 14, "Writing for Business," guides students in their personal and professional business writing — letters, memoranda, electronic mail, and résumés. To clarify the role of purpose and audience, the chapter presents sample documents in the context of typical sequences of events: a customer writes a letter of complaint, which is answered and is passed along to others in the company; a candidate applies for a job in response to a real ad.

Part Four, "A Writer's Strategies," is a convenient resource that gives students strategies for approaching all aspects of writing. The first five chapters explain and exemplify the stages of the writing process: generating ideas (Chapter 15), planning (Chapter 16), drafting (Chapter 17), developing (Chapter 18), and revising and editing (Chapter 19). Part Four also includes strategies for working with other writers (Chapter 20) and for writing with a computer (Chapter 21). Several chapters in Part Four contain "Making Connections" sections, which refer students to specific selections in the reader that exemplify the writing strategies covered in the chapters.

BOOK TWO: A WRITER'S READER

A Writer's Reader provides interesting content and clear models, accompanied by apparatus that moves students smoothly from reading to writing. Thirty-eight brief prose selections — twenty-two new — are arranged according to five themes: families (Chapter 22), men and women (Chapter 23), American diversity (Chapter 24), popular culture (Chapter 25), and the interaction of technology and society (Chapter 26). The thematic arrangement, which helps students find something to write about, is unique in a textbook of this kind. The reader mixes the works of both new and familiar writers who are culturally and professionally diverse. Here you can find perennial favorites like E. B. White's "Once More to the Lake" and Judy Brady's "I Want a Wife" alongside essays by engaging contemporary writers such as Toi Derricotte, Richard Rodriguez, Stephen King, and Amy Tan. Readings are also coordinated with *A Writer's Guide* and serve as models of the types of writing assigned there; cross-references to the reader from the assignment chapters (under the heading "Making Connections") and a new rhetorical index help students see the connection. Introduced by a biographical headnote, each reading is followed by questions — on meaning, writing strategies, critical thinking, vocabulary, and connections to other selections; journal prompts; and suggested writing assignments, one personal and one analytical. These move students from careful reading for both thematic and rhetorical elements to applying new strategies and insights in their own writing.

BOOK THREE: A WRITER'S RESEARCH MANUAL

A Writer's Research Manual is the most comprehensive research guide in a combination textbook. All of the essential information that students involved in research need to have is here, in chapters reorganized and updated since the previous edition: conducting research in the library, on the Internet, and in the field (Chapter 27), critically evaluating sources (Chapter 28), writing from sources (Chapter 29), and documenting sources (Chapter 30). It is the only research section in a combination textbook to include three complete annotated student papers in a variety of formats and so extensive a selection of documentation models — sixty-nine MLA and forty-three APA. In fact, this book within a book can hold its own against research guides offered separately.

BOOK FOUR: A WRITER'S HANDBOOK

With thorough coverage of all standard handbook topics, reference tabs, highlighted rules, boxed charts, and ESL guidelines, *A Writer's Handbook* looks and works like a conventional handbook. The handbook includes sixty-six exercise sets (one-third of them new) for practice in and out of class. Answers to the first five questions in each set are provided in the back of the book so that students can check their understanding.

New to the Fifth Edition

The revisions in this new edition, incorporating current findings of composition research, strengthen each of the four books. We have focused on the goal of giving students more help where they need it most.

MORE HELP WITH CRITICAL READING AND THINKING

The ability to think actively and analytically is essential to the development of college writers. Students must be able to scrutinize the written texts they encounter — whether these pieces serve as topical springboards, rhetorical models, or research sources — and to turn the same level of critical scrutiny on their own work in order to mature as writers and thinkers. For the fifth edition of *The Bedford Guide,* we have made improvements throughout the text that give students additional tools and opportunities for critical reading and thinking. Changes include the following:

- In *A Writer's Guide,* a new assignment chapter, "Reading Critically" (Chapter 5), leads students through the process of reading a text actively and analytically and then writing a paper based on their critical analysis.
- In *A Writer's Reader,* new prereading questions — labeled "As You Read" — for each selection help students focus their active reading; new critical reading questions after each selection help them bring their analytical skills to bear on the piece. In addition, each chapter now contains a pair of selections by different writers on the same topic, to give students an opportunity to compare and evaluate writing strategies.
- In *A Writer's Research Manual,* Chapter 28, "Evaluating Sources and Taking Notes," now focuses exclusively on the critical evaluation of research sources found in the library, on the Internet, and in the field, and on the taking of effective notes.

MORE HELP WITH COMPUTERS AND TECHNOLOGICAL LITERACY

With the growth of computers and the rapid expansion of the Internet and the World Wide Web into all areas of our lives, technological literacy — the ability to use computer skills effectively to navigate and benefit from the tide of digital information surrounding us — is becoming an essential ability in our society. In the fifth edition of *The Bedford Guide,* we have given students more guidance on acquiring and using computer-related skills, whether for drafting, revising, editing, reading, or researching.

- In *A Writer's Guide,* an updated and expanded chapter on writing with computers (Chapter 21) helps students master the computer both as a tool and as a medium for writing. New sections cover writing for the Internet and the principles of netiquette.

- In *A Writer's Reader,* the last chapter now focuses on technology and society, exploring such timely topics as privacy in a digital world and the unequal access to computers in our society. Several of the readings are taken from Internet sources, illustrating the growing importance of the Internet as a unique and valuable source of written texts. Throughout the reader, activities at the beginning of each chapter and after many selections encourage students to use the World Wide Web to explore questions related to the chapter's theme and to writing strategies covered in *A Writer's Guide.*
- In *A Writer's Research Manual,* expanded coverage of the Internet in all chapters guides students through searching online, evaluating online sources, writing a paper incorporating Internet sources, and documenting electronic media.
- In *A Writer's Handbook,* new "Editing with a Computer" tips help students use the computer effectively as an editing tool. The tips give special attention to the capabilities and limitations of spell checkers and grammar checkers so that students can use these tools wisely.

MORE HELP FOR UNDERPREPARED STUDENTS

First-year composition students at many schools increasingly need more help with basic writing and thinking skills. In this edition of *The Bedford Guide,* we have added features that will help underprepared students grow as writers.

- In *A Writer's Guide,* new "Facing the Challenge" boxes in assignment chapters alert students to the most complex part of each assignment and give them strategies for coping effectively with it. New "Editing Checklists" in each assignment chapter help students identify and correct common grammar problems.
- In *A Writer's Reader,* new vocabulary glosses at the bottom of the page help students read actively and increase their comprehension.
- Following *A Writer's Handbook,* a new "Quick Editing Guide" — which is included in all three versions of *The Bedford Guide* — gives special attention to the most troublesome grammar and editing problems. (These are also highlighted in *A Writer's Guide*). A concise "Editing Checklist" is included for each topic.

Ancillaries

As before, *The Bedford Guide for College Writers* is accompanied by a full ancillary package that gives instructors a wide array of resources. Providing flexibility and support for experienced and beginning instructors alike, this package includes a variety of supplements that help you tailor your course to your students' needs.

FOR INSTRUCTORS

NEW

- *Instructor's Annotated Edition of* THE BEDFORD GUIDE FOR COLLEGE WRITERS, by X. J. Kennedy, Dorothy M. Kennedy, and Sylvia A. Holladay, puts information busy instructors need right where they need it: on the page of the book itself. The marginal annotations offer teaching tips, last-minute activities, vocabulary glosses, quick assignments, and cross-references to other ancillaries.

- *Practical Suggestions,* Volume One of *Teaching with* THE BEDFORD GUIDE FOR COLLEGE WRITERS, by Dana Waters of Dodge City Community College, Sylvia A. Holladay, and Phillip Sipiora of the University of South Florida, helps instructors plan and teach composition. The text includes practical advice on designing an effective course, sample syllabi, pop quizzes, and suggestions for using the resources in the text, as well as chapter-by-chapter support (including answers to all exercises).

- *Background Readings,* Volume Two of *Teaching with* THE BEDFORD GUIDE FOR COLLEGE WRITERS, is an anthology of articles on composition and rhetoric, covering theory, research, and pedagogy. Revised and updated by T. R. Johnson of Boston University from the fourth edition by Shirley Morahan, *Background Readings* now includes thirty-three articles chosen to provide novice instructors professional resources to help them get the most out of this textbook and to develop their own teaching techniques. Introductions and suggested activities connect the background readings to *The Bedford Guide for College Writers* and to the classroom.

- *Online,* Volume Three of *Teaching with* THE BEDFORD GUIDE FOR COLLEGE WRITERS, by David Hartman of St. Petersburg Junior College, is a comprehensive booklet for both novice and experienced computer users. It acquaints instructors with networks and the Internet and offers concrete suggestions for introducing students to a variety of the computer's capacities: for word processing, for collaboration, for research, and for distance education. The comprehensive appendices and glossary also make it an indispensable reference tool.

- *Supplemental Exercises,* Volume Four of *Teaching with* THE BEDFORD GUIDE FOR COLLEGE WRITERS, by Mitchell Evich of Northeastern University, is an ample set of exercises for students who require practice beyond that supplied in *A Writer's Handbook;* it also includes a set of exercises for ESL students.

- *Transparencies,* Volume Five of *Teaching with* THE BEDFORD GUIDE FOR COLLEGE WRITERS, by Sylvia A. Holladay, provides supplemental examples of writing strategies, visual representations of rhetorical and grammatical concepts, and other materials useful for classroom discussion.

NEW

- *Audiotape,* Volume Six of *Teaching with* THE BEDFORD GUIDE FOR COLLEGE WRITERS, contains experts' ideas on key pedagogical issues such as how to teach the writing process and how to respond to student writing, along with concrete suggestions for classroom activities; the format allows busy instructors to listen to these ideas while commuting.

ELECTRONIC MEDIA

NEW
- *Interactive Writing Software for THE BEDFORD GUIDE FOR COLLEGE WRITERS*, by X. J. Kennedy, Dorothy M. Kennedy, and Sylvia A. Holladay, is writing-process software that guides students through the completion of each assignment in the book. Students have access to the rich array of explanations, examples, and other support available in the book itself in a clean, intuitive format. (Available on CD-ROM for both Windows and Macintosh.)

NEW
- *Interactive Grammar Exercises for THE BEDFORD GUIDE FOR COLLEGE WRITERS*, by Mitchell Evich, is a set of interactive editing exercises that can be used for either study or assessment. The network-compatible version allows you to diagnose the needs of the class as a whole and simplifies the task of record keeping. (Available on CD-ROM for both Windows and Macintosh.)

NEW
- *Grammar Diagnostics for THE BEDFORD GUIDE FOR COLLEGE WRITERS* contains diagnostic grammar tests that can be distributed on paper, on disk, or online. The networked version provides convenient reports on both individual and classwide results. (Available on disk for both Windows and Macintosh.)

NEW
- The Web site for *The Bedford Guide for College Writers*, at www.bedfordstmartins.com/bedguide, is a developing resource for both students and instructors. Topics include exploring the World Wide Web, conducting online research, teaching composition with computers, and connecting with other teachers and students via the Internet.

Thanks and Appreciation

Working on the fifth edition of *The Bedford Guide for College Writers* has been a giant collaborative writing project, different only in scope from those assigned to the students for whom we write. Many individuals have contributed significantly to our project, and we extend our thanks to all of them. Two members of the Bedford/St. Martin's staff deserve special recognition. President Charles H. Christensen and Editorial Director Joan E. Feinberg have provided unstinting encouragement and inspiration from the beginnings of the book. We deeply appreciate their creative suggestions and perceptive advice; their continuing faith in our work has buoyed us through long hours at the computer screen.

The editorial effort behind this edition was truly a team endeavor. Senior Editor Denise B. Wydra coordinated all aspects of the project and kept us on track and on schedule. She patiently read, reread, and cogently edited our manuscript, spotting the problems and coming up with sound solutions. Leasa Burton edited and refreshed *A Writer's Reader*, coordinated the ancillaries, and skillfully developed and edited the *Instructor's Annotated Edition* and *Practical Suggestions*. Michelle Clark judiciously edited the research manual. Amanda Bristow edited the rhetoric, the handbook, and the supplemental exercises booklet with great care. Nicole Simonsen assisted with the reader, cleared permissions, and edited both *Online* and the transparencies. Karen Henry, Executive Editor, was largely responsible for guiding this team through the many twists and turns of the development process.

Other members of the Bedford staff contributed greatly to the fifth edition. Many thanks and heartfelt appreciation go to Karen Baart, whose exacting eye, careful hand, and immense patience shepherded the book through production. Dawn Skorczewski oversaw development of the audiotape, and Jennifer Rush contributed her expertise to the rhetoric. Joanne Diaz brought her fine editorial sense to *Background Readings*. Jill Chmelko assisted with editing the annotations in the *Instructor's Annotated Edition*. Marcia Cohen, Elizabeth Schaaf, and John Amburg were immensely helpful in overseeing production, as was Production Supervisor Joe Ford. Coleen O'Hanley and Edward Tonderys gave essential production assistance. Deborah Baker, Helaine Denenberg, Arthur Johnson, and Coleen O'Hanley guided the production of the ancillaries. Donna Dennison and Persis Barron oversaw the impressive redesign of the book's cover, giving us a new look that still preserves the integrity of *The Bedford Guide*. Karen Melton and Joanne Hinkel coordinated the marketing of the book, while its promotion was ably handled by Jeannie Tarkenton, Susan Pace, and Terry Govan. Tony Perriello cleared permissions. We are grateful for Rosemary Winfield's copyediting and for Claire Seng-Niemoeller's design of the book's interior. Thanks are also due to proofreaders Melissa Cook and Mary Lou Wilshaw.

The fifth edition could not have been completed without the help of numerous other individuals. Andrea Kaston and Matthew Stratton contributed focused editorial apparatus for both the reader and the rhetoric; Andrea also assisted greatly with *Practical Suggestions*. Matthew Parfitt (Boston University) revised the chapter on writing with computers, and the suggestions of Ted Johnston (El Paso Community College) immensely improved the chapter on taking a stand. Nedra Reynolds (University of Rhode Island) lent her expertise to the new material on portfolios. Diane Reese (St. Petersburg Junior College) helped refine the critical thinking chapters. Michael Palmquist (Colorado State University) and Keith Dorwick (University of Illinois at Chicago) both assisted with the revision of the research manual, and Fred W. Wright Jr. (St. Petersburg Junior College) assisted with the instructor's annotations in the research manual. Katherine Finch (North Shore Community College) helped with material for the *Instructor's Annotated Edition*. Dana Waters (Dodge City Community College) revised *Practical Suggestions* for the fifth edition. David Hartman (St. Petersburg Junior College) revised his excellent booklet explaining how the textbook can be used in the electronic environment of computers and cyberspace. Mitchell Evich prepared the exercises for the supplemental exercises ancillary.

Special thanks to all the students who have challenged us over the years to find better ways to help them learn. In particular we would like to thank those who granted us permission to use their essays in the fifth edition. Focused as this textbook is on student writing, student essays are the linchpin of *A Writer's Guide*. The writings of Robert Schreiner, Sandy Messina, Betsy Buffo, Tim Chabot, Yun Yung Choi, Heather Colbenson, Geoffrey Fallon, Jonathan Burns, Lionel Prokop, Maria Halloran, and Chris Robinson were included in earlier editions as well as this one. New to the fifth edition are the writings of Ron Larsen, Kelly Grecian, Lillian Tsu, Thaddeus Watulak, and Mark Sanchez.

Many thanks to our colleagues across the country who took time and care to review the fourth edition, to respond to our questionnaires, and to send us their suggestions gleaned from experience with students. For this we thank Patricia Allen, Cape Cod Community College; David Auchter, San Jacinto Junior College; Pamela J. Behrens, Alabama A&M University; Carmine J. Bell, Pasco Hernando Community College; Kay Berg, Sinclair Community College; Dr. Carolyn Craft, Longwood College; Mary Cullen, Middlesex Community College; Fred D'Astoli, Ventura College; Patricia Ann Delamar, University of Dayton; Robert Grindy, Richland Community College; Irene Duprey-Gutierrez, University of Massachusetts, Dartmouth; Sherry F. Gott, Danville Community College; Johnnie Hargrove, Alabama A&M University; Marita Hinton, Alabama A&M University; Patricia Hunt, Catonsville Community College; Jean L. Johnson, University of North Alabama; Ted Johnston, El Paso Community College; Cynthia Kellogg, Yuba College; Norman Lanquist, Eastern Arizona College; Colleen Lloyd, Cuyahoga Community College; Jennifer Madej, Milwaukee Area Technical College; Janice Mandile, Front Range Community College; Dr. Elizabeth Metzger, University of South Florida; Sandra Moore, Mississippi Delta Community College; Sheryl A. Mylan, Stephen F. Austin State University; Peggy J. Oliver, San Jacinto College South; Mike Palmquist, Colorado State University; Laurel S. Peterson, Norwalk Community Technical College; Kenneth E. Poitras, Antelope Valley College; Michael Punches, Oklahoma City Community College; Patrice Quarg, Cantonsville Community College; Jeanie Randall, Austin Peay State University; Kira Roark, University of Denver; Dr. Susan Schurman, Ventura College; Patricia C. Schwindt, Mesa Community College; Elizabeth Smart, Utah State University; Scott R. Stankey, Anoka-Ramsey Community College; Leroy Sterling, Alabama A&M University; Dean Stover, Gateway Community College; Darlene Summers, Montgomery College; Dana Waters, Dodge City Community College; Ann Westmoreland Runsick, Gateway Technical College; Patricia South White, Norwich University; and Dr. Valerie P. Zimbaro, Valencia Community College.

We remain grateful to our mentors and colleagues in universities and colleges across the country, who prompted us to reexamine our positions and defend our assertions. We thank our friends and families for their unstinting patience, understanding, and encouragement. For the fifth edition, Sylvia Holladay sends special thanks to Thomas E. Hicks Sr.

Contents

A WRITER'S READER   485

Introduction: Reading to Write 487

A WRITER'S GUIDE

Introduction:
A Writing Process

You are already a writer with long experience. In school you have taken notes, written book reports, essays, and term papers, answered exam questions, perhaps kept a journal. In clubs you have kept minutes, and on the job you've composed memos. You've written letters and postcards to family and friends, made shopping lists, maybe even tried your hand at writing stories and poetry. All this experience is about to pay off for you.

In college you will combine what you already know about writing with the new techniques you will learn, and you will perform writing tasks more challenging than most you have faced before. To write a psychology or economics paper, you'll find that your mind has to stretch more than it did in writing a report on the solar system or a letter of application. From now on, you will find yourself working in complex disciplines, writing reports based on information from many sources, and above all thinking critically about the information — not just reading articles and stacking up facts but analyzing what you discover, deciding what it means, weighing its value, taking a stand, proposing solutions. College instructors will expect you to question what they say and what you read, to form your own judgments, and to put them to use.

Unlike parachute jumping, writing for a college course is something you go ahead and try without first learning all there is to know. In truth, nothing anyone can tell you about writing can help you as much as learning by doing. In this book we suggest various writing situations and say, "Go to it!" We also recommend specific strategies that will make your writing go smoother than it has in the past. In this introduction, we give you an overview of the central issues that concern most writers, and we point out how each section in the following chapters supports you in making decisions about one or more of these issues.

Critical Thinking, Creativity, and Writing

Effective writing is both critical and creative. Each writing task can be viewed as a problem to solve — one that requires both *creative thinking* (making) and *critical thinking* (judging). According to Richard W. Paul, director of the Center for Critical Thinking,

> "Criticality" and "creativity" have an intimate relationship to the ability to figure things out. There is a natural marriage between them. Indeed, all thinking that is properly called "excellent" combines these two dimensions in an intimate way.[1]

When you write, you create, making something out of nothing, bringing order out of chaos. Of necessity you begin to shape the information before you know clearly what you will include or where you are going with it.

Simultaneously with your creating or making when you write, you think critically. You think purposefully and judge your ideas and your processes. As a writer you not only assess *what* you create; you also assess *how* you create *as* you create. You use criteria — models, conventions, principles, standards — to help you determine whether you are fulfilling your purpose and are approaching the end you have in mind. As you compose, you monitor and evaluate what you are doing by asking yourself specific questions based on your criteria for effective written communication: Have I made my point clear? Are my ideas arranged in a logical order? Does each thought follow from and support or add to the preceding thought? Are the connections clear to the reader? Have I provided sufficient evidence or proof to make my point clear? To convince my readers? Is my tone appropriate for my readers?

Thus, thinking creatively and thinking critically are integral and interrelated parts of writing well. In large measure, learning to write well is learning what questions to ask yourself as you write. Throughout *A Writer's Guide*, we include questions and suggestions designed to help you think creatively and critically about your own writing tasks and processes. In addition, Part Two, "Thinking Critically," focuses exclusively on writing assignments that challenge you to use your critical thinking skills to the fullest.

The Process of Writing

Writing can seem at times an overwhelming drudgery, worse than scrubbing floors; at other moments, a sport full of thrills and excitement — like whizzing downhill on skis, not knowing what you'll meet around a bend. Surprising and unpredictable though the writing process may seem, you can understand what happens in it. Nearly all writers do similar things:

---

[1] Richard W. Paul, *Critical Thinking: What Every Person Needs to Survive in a Rapidly Changing World*, rev. 2nd ed. (Rohnert Park, CA: Foundation for Critical Thinking, 1992) 17.

They generate ideas.
They plan, draft, and develop their papers.
They revise and edit.

These activities aren't lockstep stages: you don't always proceed in a straight line. You can skip around, taking up parts of the process in whatever order you like, or work on several parts at a time, or circle back over what you have already done. Gathering material, you may feel an urge to play with a sentence until it clicks. Writing a draft, you may decide to stop writing and look for more material. You may find yourself dashing off, crossing out, leaping ahead, backtracking, correcting, adjusting, questioning, trying a fresh approach, not being satisfied, trying still another approach, breaking through, tinkering a bit more, polishing — and then in the end checking unfamiliar punctuation and looking up the spellings of tricky words.

These three activities form the basis of most effective writing processes. Each chapter in Part One, "A Writer's Resources," and Part Two, "Thinking Critically," has this basis at its heart. Let's look briefly at what each activity entails and how the chapters in *A Writer's Guide* help you approach it.

GENERATING IDEAS

The first activity in writing — finding a topic to write about and finding something to say about it — is often the most challenging and least predictable. Each chapter in Parts One and Two has a section entitled "Generating Ideas" filled with examples, questions, and checklists that will trigger ideas and associations about the specific writing assignment studied in that chapter. (For an example, see p. 22). In addition, Chapter 15, "Strategies for Generating Ideas," is a storehouse of useful discovery techniques that you can apply to this part of the writing process for any writing assignment.

Discovering What to Write About.   Finding a topic you honestly want to pursue, one about which you really have something to say, is half the task: find it, and words will flow. Although finding the topic is not always easy, often it lies near home. Stephen Dunn in "Locker Room Talk" (p. 545), remembers a conversation in the school yard; Brent Staples in "Black Men and Public Space" (p. 561), an evening walk; Judith Ortiz Cofer in "The Myth of the Latin Woman: I Just Met a Girl Named María" (p. 564), a bus trip — all ordinary occurrences. In college, of course, an instructor may give you a writing assignment that seems to hold no personal interest for you. In that case, you face the challenge of making it your own by finding a slant that does interest you.

Discovering Material.   You'll need information to back up your ideas — facts and figures, reports and opinions, examples and illustrations. How do you find this material to support your ideas and make them clear and convincing to your readers? Luckily you have endless resources at your fingertips.

You can *recall* your own experience and knowledge, you can go out and *observe* things around you, you can *converse* with others who are knowledgeable on your topic, and you can *imagine* possibilities and results.

These four resources are covered in depth in Part One; the four chapters there explore each resource in turn and give you some practice in applying it.

PLANNING, DRAFTING, AND DEVELOPING

Having discovered a burning idea to write about (or at least a smoldering one) and material to back it up with (maybe not enough yet, but some), you sort out what matters most and decide on an order for your ideas. If right away you can see one main point you want to make in your paper, you're lucky. Try to state that point in writing; try various ways of expressing it. Next, you can arrange your ideas and material in what seems a clear and sensible order that will make your one point clear. To discover that order, you might group and label the ideas you have generated, or you might analyze the main idea. But if no one main point emerges quickly, never mind: you may find one while you draft — that is, while you write an early version of your paper. At least by the time you finish the paper, you should focus everything in it on a main point.

Usually your first version of a draft will be rough and preliminary. Writing takes time: a paper usually needs several drafts and perhaps a revision of your plan, especially if your subject is unfamiliar or complicated. You may decide to throw out your first attempt and start all over because a stronger idea or a better arrangement hits you. Include explanations, definitions, illustrations, and evidence to make your ideas clear. If, as you draft, you realize you don't have enough specific evidence, work through your four resources again (recall, observe, converse, imagine). You can expect to keep discovering ideas, having insights, and drawing conclusions while you draft. By all means, welcome them, and work them in if they fit.

Each chapter in Parts One and Two has a section entitled "Planning, Drafting, and Developing," designed to help you through this part of the writing process for the specific writing assignment studied in that chapter. (For an example, see p. 24.) Each chapter also contains a tip called "Writing with a Computer" in this section, intended to help you find new ways of integrating computers with your writing process. (See p. 26.) Finally, three chapters in Part Four contain a wealth of general strategies appropriate to this part of the writing process: Chapter 16, "Strategies for Planning"; Chapter 17, "Strategies for Drafting"; and Chapter 18, "Strategies for Developing."

REVISING AND EDITING

Revising — both reseeing and rewriting — occurs throughout the process of composing, not only after you have finished. It is part of your critically monitoring *what* you are creating and *how* you are creating. In an apt comparison, Chinese American writer Maxine Hong Kingston likens writing to gardening in Hawaii — a little time spent in planting, much more time spent in "cutting and pruning and hacking back." Novelist Ernest Hemingway, when asked what made him revise the ending of *A Farewell to Arms* thirty-nine times, replied, "Getting the words right." Usually most of your revision will occur after you have completed a draft. At that time you might think that your work is done, but very few writers can get their ideas across to others by doing only one draft. For most writers the time of revising is the time when work begins in earnest. Each chapter in Parts One and Two has a section entitled "Revising and Editing," which focuses on this part of the writing process; each section contains at least one revision checklist and one suggestion for working with a peer editor. (For examples, see pp. 26 and 28.) In Part Four, Chapter 19, "Strategies for Revising and Editing," comprises a trove of revision, editing, and proofreading techniques.

Revising.   Revision — the word means "see again" — is more than a matter of just revising words: you sometimes revise what you know and what you think. Such changes may take place at any time while you're writing or at any moment when you pause to reread or to think. You can then shift your plans, decide to put in or leave out, move sentences or paragraphs around, connect ideas differently, or express them better. If you put aside your draft for a few hours or a day, you can reread it with fresh eyes and a clear mind.

When you revise, as humorist Leo Rosten has said, "you have to put yourself in the position of the negative reader, the resistant reader, the reader who doesn't surrender easily, the reader who is alien to you as a type, even the reader who doesn't like what you are writing." However, you should probably sit in the seat of the scornful only when your paper is well along. When your ideas first start to flow, you want to welcome them — lure them forth, not tear them apart — or they might go back into hiding. Get something on paper before you begin major rewriting. Don't be afraid to take risks: you'll probably be surprised and pleased at what happens.

Editing.   Near the end of your labors, you'll edit what you have written: you'll correct any flaws that may stand in the way of your readers' understanding and enjoyment. Don't edit too early, though, because you may waste time on some part that you later revise out. In editing, you usually accomplish these repairs:

Get rid of unnecessary words.

Choose better words.

Rearrange words into a stronger, clearer order.

Use more subordination in sentences.

Add accurate transitions for continuity of thought.

Check usage.

Check grammar (make subjects agree with verbs, pronouns with what they stand for; make verb tenses consistent).

The "Quick Editing Guide" located near the very end of *The Bedford Guide for College Writers* (look for the pages at the back with blue edges) contains useful explanations, examples, and suggestions for tackling the most troubling and common editing problems college writers face.

Proofreading.   A final activity in the writing process, proofreading is giving your paper one last look, with a dictionary at your elbow, checking doubtful spellings and fixing any typing mistakes.

Audience and Purpose

A big part of learning to write well is learning what questions to ask yourself. At any moment in the writing process, two questions are worth asking: Whom do I write for? And why?

Writing for Readers.   In fulfilling most of the assignments for a college composition course like this one, you'll know who your readers are — yourself, your classmates, and your instructor. Writing for these readers will give you practice that will benefit you in writing for less sympathetic audiences in other settings.

As reading specialist Frank Smith says, "The writer is always the first reader." As your own first reader, you'll want to step back from a draft and reread it as though you weren't the writer but were someone else, detached and objective — and not too easy to please. You'll have to get outside yourself and see where you need explanations, examples, and bridges between thoughts. You'll also want to comb your writing for weak spots and errors before you turn it in. That is merely to follow the Golden Rule of Writing: do unto your other readers as you trust other writers will do unto you.

In fulfilling some relatively straightforward assignments — say, recalling an experience or reporting a conversation — you won't need to keep asking, Who besides myself is reading me? If, as you write a paper, you believe it is going well, chances are that your readers will think so too. But in tackling complex writing tasks, you'll write more effectively if you consider your audience. Say you wish to persuade your readers to take a certain action — to ban (or approve) a law regulating the hiring of illegal aliens or the sale of pornography. At some point you might ask, What do my readers know already about this subject? What do they need to be told? What do they probably believe? Where are my statements likely to offend them? What objections are they likely to raise? How can I keep from alienating them? You should analyze your readers carefully and know a great deal about them (what they know and don't know, what they believe, what they value) to aim your writing toward them and hit your mark. As you write, keep the uninformed reader, the reluctant reader, and the resistant reader in mind, and write for all three. Among your classmates you'll find all three types of readers, and in responding to your writing, your instructor will assume all three roles.

Writing for a Reason.   Usually a college writing assignment has a clear-cut purpose. Every assignment in this book asks you to write for a definite reason. For example, in Chapter 1 you'll be asked to recall a memorable experience in order to explain how it changed you; in Chapter 9, to take a stand on a controversy that interests you, to argue for your position, and to evaluate.

Be careful not to confuse the resources and strategies you are asked to apply in these assignments with your ultimate purpose for writing. "To compare and contrast two things" is not a very interesting purpose; "to compare and contrast *in order to explain* the differences between two things" implies a real reason for writing. In most college writing, your ultimate purpose will be to explain something to your readers or to convince your readers of something.

Aware that you write for a reason, you can concentrate on your task. From the start you can ask yourself, What do I want to do? And, in revising, Did I do what I meant to do? You'll find that these are very practical questions. They'll help you cut the irrelevant that wanders into your writing, anything that hinders your paper from getting where you want it to go.

The readers you write for and the reason you write will always deserve consideration. Throughout this book we'll remind you of these two points.

What Matters Most

In *The Bedford Guide for College Writers,* we too have a purpose. It is to help you write better, deeper, clearer, more interesting, and more satisfying papers than you have ever written before and to learn to do so by actually writing. Throughout the book we'll give you a lot of practice — in writing processes, patterns, and strategies — to help you build your confidence.

How This Book Is Built.   As you already know, writing and learning to write are complex and many-faceted tasks. Each part in *A Writer's Guide* is devoted to a different aspect of writing. We hope, though, that as you work through the chapters and become adept at using them, you will come to feel they are all parts of a seamless whole, much like the writing process itself.

Part One, "A Writer's Resources." This part encourages you to write papers that draw on the four essential resources for generating ideas and material — recalling, observing, conversing, and imagining.

Part Two, "Thinking Critically." Part Two asks you to write papers using critical thinking strategies. You'll develop the skills of reading critically, analyzing, comparing and contrasting, explaining causes and effects, taking a stand, proposing a solution, and evaluating.

Part Three, "Special Writing Situations." This part leads you through three special situations that most students encounter at one point or another — writing about literature, writing for assessment, and writing for business.

Part Four, "A Writer's Strategies." Part Four is packed with advice, tips, and exercises that you can unpack whenever you are hunting for ways to generate ideas, plan, draft, develop, revise, edit, and proofread your papers. You will also find strategies for working with other writers and for using computers for writing. Browse through these chapters at your leisure, study them as you need to, or refer to them in a pinch.

Taking It to the Hoop. Like a hard game of basketball, writing a college paper is strenuous. Without getting in your way, we want to lend you all possible support and to provide guidance and direction for your efforts. So, no doubt, does your instructor, someone closer to you than any textbook writers. Still, like even the best coaches, instructors and textbook writers can improve your game only so far. Advice on how to write won't make you a better writer. You'll learn more and have more fun when you take a few sentences to the hoop and make points yourself. After you make a few baskets, you will increase your confidence in your ability and find the process of writing a bit easier.

As you know, other students can also help you — sometimes more than a textbook or an instructor. This book suggests opportunities for you to learn from your classmates and for them to learn from you. If your instructor asks you to exchange your work with other students, to give and receive reactions, you'll face a challenge: Just how do you go about commenting on another student's writing? Throughout the book are useful hints for ways that you and other students can help one another discover ideas as you write and rewrite your papers. In Chapter 20, "Strategies for Working with Other Writers: Collaborative Learning," you will find multiple suggestions and illustrations for collaborating with your classmates. As you respond to your classmates' papers, you will learn to judge your own writing better.

Part One

A Writer's Resources

Introduction

As a college writer you probably wrestle with the question What should I write? You may feel you have nothing to say or nothing worth saying. Sometimes your difficulty lies in finding a topic, sometimes in uncovering enough information about the topic you have chosen. Perhaps you, like many other college writers, have convinced yourself that professional writers are different in some way, that they have some special way of thinking or looking at the world or discovering ideas for writing. But they have no magic. In reality you already possess the major resources of a writer.

None of the resources are new to you. Already you are adept at *recalling* your own experience and knowledge and *observing* the world around you. You're accustomed to *conversing* with people. And you've had experience with the richest resource of all—*imagining*. If you learn to use these four tremendous resources, you need never find yourself at a loss for words. The purpose of Part One is to explore each resource in turn and give you some practice in applying it.

At the start of each chapter, we offer illustrations of good writing by two writers—a professional and a college student—who draw on the same resource. Then we suggest a writing assignment—a broad one that leaves you room to discover a specific topic you care about. Immediately following the assignment you'll find suggestions to guide you in writing it. We pose questions that, if you like, you can ask yourself. Some of these questions will remind you of your audience and your purpose. Sometimes we report the experience of other students. We offer you guidance throughout the whole shifting, tentative, surprise-filled process of writing. But if, instead of reading our suggestions, you'd rather go ahead and write, please do. Our only aim in offering suggestions is to provide you with a trusty support system for whenever you feel the need for it. "Applying What You Learn" shows you how writers typically use the same kind of writing in other college courses and in careers. Finally, "Making Connections" points out selections in *A Writer's Reader* that use these very same resources.

Chapter 1

Writing from Recall

Writing from recall is writing from memory, the richest resource a writer has and the handiest. Novelist William Saroyan said that a writer observes — and then remembers having observed. This is clearly the case in an English course when you are asked to write of a personal experience, a favorite place, a memorable person. But even when an instructor hands you a subject that at first glance seems to have nothing to do with you, your memory is the first place to look. Suppose you have to write a psychology paper about how advertisers play on consumers' fears. Begin with what you remember. What ads have sent chills down your back? (We recall a tire ad that showed the luckless buyer of an inferior product stuck with a blowout on a remote road on a stormy night while the Frankenstein monster bore down on him.)

You may also need to observe, read more, talk with someone, and imagine. All by itself, memory may not give you enough to write about. But whenever you need to start writing, you will rarely go wrong if you start by jotting down something remembered.

Learning from Other Writers

In this chapter you will be invited to write a whole paper from recall. Here are two samples of good writing — one by a professional writer, one by a college student. We begin with an essay from columnist Russell Baker's autobiography, *Growing Up*, because autobiographical writing so clearly demonstrates the uses of memory. Baker recalls what it was like to be sixteen in urban Baltimore, wondering what to do with his life.

The second essay was written by a student, Robert G. Schreiner, in response to an assignment asking him to recall a significant event from his childhood. As you read his essay, notice the vivid details that help bring the incident alive.

Russell Baker   The Art of Eating Spaghetti

The only thing that truly interested me was writing, and I knew that sixteen-year-olds did not come out of high school and become writers. I thought of writing as something to be done only by the rich. It was so obviously not real work, not a job at which you could earn a living. Still, I had begun to think of myself as a writer. It was the only thing for which I seemed to have the smallest talent, and, silly though it sounded when I told people I'd like to be a writer, it gave me a way of thinking about myself which satisfied my need to have an identity.

The notion of becoming a writer had flickered off and on in my head since the Belleville days, but it wasn't until my third year in high school that the possibility took hold. Until then I'd been bored by everything associated with English courses. I found English grammar dull and baffling. I hated the assignments to turn out "compositions," and went at them like heavy labor, turning out leaden, lackluster paragraphs that were agonies for teachers to read and for me to write. The classics thrust on me to read seemed as deadening as chloroform.

When our class was assigned to Mr. Fleagle for third-year English I anticipated another grim year in that dreariest of subjects. Mr. Fleagle was notorious among City students for dullness and inability to inspire. He was said to be stuffy, dull, and hopelessly out of date. To me he looked to be sixty or seventy and prim to a fault. He wore primly severe eyeglasses, his wavy hair was primly cut and primly combed. He wore prim vested suits with neckties blocked primly against the collar buttons of his primly starched white shirts. He had a primly pointed jaw, a primly straight nose, and a prim manner of speaking that was so correct, so gentlemanly, that he seemed a comic antique.

I anticipated a listless, unfruitful year with Mr. Fleagle and for a long time was not disappointed. We read *Macbeth*. Mr. Fleagle loved *Macbeth* and wanted us to love it too, but he lacked the gift of infecting others with his own passion. He tried to convey the murderous ferocity of Lady Macbeth one day by reading aloud the passage that concludes

> ...I have given suck, and know
> How tender 'tis to love the babe that milks me.
> I would, while it was smiling in my face,
> Have plucked my nipple from his boneless gums....

The idea of prim Mr. Fleagle plucking his nipple from boneless gums was too much for the class. We burst into gasps of irrepressible snickering. Mr. Fleagle stopped.

"There is nothing funny, boys, about giving suck to a babe. It is the — the very essence of motherhood, don't you see." 5

He constantly sprinkled his sentences with "don't you see." It wasn't a question but an exclamation of mild surprise at our ignorance. "Your pronoun needs an antecedent, don't you see," he would say, very primly. "The purpose of the Porter's scene, boys, is to provide comic relief from the horror, don't you see." 6

Late in the year we tackled the informal essay. "The essay, don't you see, is the. . . ." My mind went numb. Of all forms of writing, none seemed so boring as the essay. Naturally we would have to write informal essays. Mr. Fleagle distributed a homework sheet offering us a choice of topics. None was quite so simpleminded as "What I Did on My Summer Vacation," but most seemed to be almost as dull. I took the list home and dawdled until the night before the essay was due. Sprawled on the sofa, I finally faced up to the grim task, took the list out of my notebook, and scanned it. The topic on which my eye stopped was "The Art of Eating Spaghetti." 7

This title produced an extraordinary sequence of mental images. Surging up out of the depths of memory came a vivid recollection of a night in Belleville when all of us were seated around the supper table — Uncle Allen, my mother, Uncle Charlie, Doris, Uncle Hal — and Aunt Pat served spaghetti for supper. Spaghetti was an exotic treat in those days. Neither Doris nor I had ever eaten spaghetti, and none of the adults had enough experience to be good at it. All the good humor of Uncle Allen's house reawoke in my mind as I recalled the laughing arguments we had that night about the socially respectable method for moving spaghetti from plate to mouth. 8

Suddenly I wanted to write about that, about the warmth and good feeling of it, but I wanted to put it down simply for my own joy, not for Mr. Fleagle. It was a moment I wanted to recapture and hold for myself. I wanted to relive the pleasure of an evening at New Street. To write it as I wanted, however, would violate all the rules of formal composition I'd learned in school, and Mr. Fleagle would surely give it a failing grade. Never mind. I would write something else for Mr. Fleagle after I had written this thing for myself. 9

When I finished it the night was half gone and there was no time left to compose a proper, respectable essay for Mr. Fleagle. There was no choice next morning but to turn in my private reminiscence of Belleville. Two days passed before Mr. Fleagle returned the graded papers, and he returned everyone's but mine. I was bracing myself for a command to report to Mr. Fleagle immediately after school for discipline when I saw him lift my paper from his desk and rap for the class's attention. 10

"Now, boys," he said, "I want to read you an essay. This is titled 'The Art of Eating Spaghetti.'" 11

And he started to read. My words! He was reading *my words* out loud to the entire class. What's more, the entire class was listening. Listening atten- 12 tively. Then somebody laughed, then the entire class was laughing, and not in contempt and ridicule, but with openhearted enjoyment. Even Mr. Fleagle stopped two or three times to repress a small prim smile.

I did my best to avoid showing pleasure, but what I was feeling was pure ecstasy at this startling demonstration that my words had the power to make people laugh. In the eleventh grade, at the eleventh hour as it were, I had discovered a calling. It was the happiest moment of my entire school career. When Mr. Fleagle finished he put the final seal on my happiness by saying, "Now that, boys, is an essay, don't you see. It's — don't you see — it's of the very essence of the essay, don't you see. Congratulations, Mr. Baker."   13

For the first time, light shone on a possibility. It wasn't a very heartening possibility, to be sure. Writing couldn't lead to a job after high school, and it was hardly honest work, but Mr. Fleagle had opened a door for me. After that I ranked Mr. Fleagle among the finest teachers in the school.   14

Questions to Start You Thinking

Meaning

1. In your own words, state what Baker believes he learned in the eleventh grade about the art of writing. What incidents or statements help identify this lesson for readers of the essay? Tell what lesson, if any, you learned from the essay.
2. Why do you think Baker included this event in his autobiography?
3. Have you ever changed your mind about something you had to do, as Baker did about writing? Or about a person, as he did about Mr. Fleagle?

Writing Strategies

4. What is the effect, in paragraph 3, of Baker's many repetitions of the words *prim* and *primly*? What other devices does Baker use to make vivid his characterization of Mr. Fleagle? Why do you think the author uses so much space to portray his teacher?
5. What does the quotation from *Macbeth* add to Baker's account? Had the quotation been omitted, what would have been lost?
6. How does Baker organize the essay? Why does he use this order?

STUDENT ESSAY

Robert G. Schreiner   **What Is a Hunter?**

What is a hunter? This is a simple question with a relatively straightforward answer. A hunter is, according to Webster's New Collegiate Dictionary, a person who hunts game (game being various types of animals hunted or pursued for various reasons). However, a question that is just as simple but without such a straightforward answer is What character-   1

istics make up a hunter? As a child, I had always considered
the most important aspect of the hunter's person to be his
ability to use a rifle, bow, or whatever weapon was appropriate to the type of hunting being done. Having many relatives
in rural areas of Virginia and Kansas, I had been exposed to
rifles a great deal. I had done extensive target shooting and
considered myself to be quite proficient in the use of
firearms. I had never been hunting, but I had always thought
that since I could fire a rifle accurately I would make a
good hunter.

One Christmas holiday, while we were visiting our grand-   2
parents in Kansas, my grandfather asked me if I wanted to go
jackrabbit hunting with him. I eagerly accepted, anxious to
show off my prowess with a rifle. A younger cousin of mine
also wanted to come, so we all went out into the garage,
loaded two .22 caliber rifles and a 20-gauge shotgun, hopped
into the pickup truck, and drove out of town. It had snowed
the night before, and to either side of the narrow road swept
six-foot-deep powdery drifts. The wind twirled the fine crystalline snow into whirling vortexes that bounced along the
icy road and sprayed snow into the open windows of the
pickup. As we drove, my grandfather gave us some pointers
about both spotting and shooting jackrabbits. He told us that
when it snows, jackrabbits like to dig out a hollow in the
top of a snowdrift, usually near a fencepost, and lie there
soaking up the sunshine. He told us that even though jackrabbits are a grayish brown, this coloration is excellent camou-
flage in the snow, for the curled-up rabbits resemble rocks.
He then pointed out a few rabbits in such positions as we
drove along, showing us how to distinguish them from exposed
rocks and dirt. He then explained that the only way to be
sure that we killed the rabbit was to shoot for the head and,
in particular, the eye, for this was on a direct line with
the rabbit's brain. Since we were using solid point bullets,
which deform into a ball upon impact, a hit anywhere but the
head would most likely only wound the rabbit.

My grandfather then slowed down the pickup and told us   3
to look out for the rabbits hidden in the snowdrifts. We
eventually spotted one about thirty feet from the road in a

snow-filled gully. My cousin wished to shoot the first one, so
he hopped out of the truck, balanced the .22 on the hood, and
fired. A spray of snow erupted about a foot to the left of the
rabbit's hollow. My cousin fired again, and again, and again,
the shots pockmarking the slope of the drift. He fired once
more and the rabbit bounced out of its hollow, its head rocking from side to side. He was hit. My cousin eagerly gamboled
into the snow to claim his quarry. He brought it back holding
it by the hind legs, proudly displaying it as would a warrior
the severed head of his enemy. The bullet had entered the
rabbit's right shoulder and exited through the neck. In both
places a thin trickle of crimson marred the gray sheen of the
rabbit's pelt. It quivered slightly and its rib cage pulsed
with its labored breathing. My cousin was about to toss it
into the back of the pickup when my grandfather pointed out
that it would be cruel to allow the rabbit to bleed slowly to
death and instructed my cousin to bang its head against the
side of the pickup to kill it. My cousin then proceeded to
bang the rabbit's head against the yellow metal. Thump,
thump, thump, thump; after a minute or so my cousin loudly
proclaimed that it was dead and hopped back into the truck.

The whole episode sickened me to some degree, and at the
time I did not know why. We continued to hunt throughout the
afternoon, and feigning boredom, I allowed my cousin and
grandfather to shoot all of the rabbits. Often, the shots
didn't kill the rabbits outright so they had to be killed
against the pickup. The thump, thump, thump of the rabbits'
skulls against the metal began to irritate me, and I was
strangely glad when we turned around and headed back toward
home. We were a few miles from the city limits when my grandfather slowed the truck to a stop, then backed up a few
yards. My grandfather said he spotted two huge "jacks" sitting in the sun in a field just off the road. He pointed them
out and handed me the .22, saying that if I didn't shoot
something the whole afternoon would have been a wasted trip
for me. I hesitated and then reluctantly accepted the rifle. I
stepped out onto the road, my feet crunching on the ice. The
two rabbits were about seventy feet away, both sitting upright in the sun. I cocked and leveled the rifle, my elbow

4

held almost horizontal in the military fashion I had learned to employ. I brought the sights to bear on the right eye of the first rabbit, compensated for distance, and fired. There was a harsh snap like the crack of a whip and a small jolt to my shoulder. The first rabbit was gone, presumably knocked over the side of the snowdrift. The second rabbit hadn't moved a muscle; it just sat there staring with that black eye. I cocked the rifle once more and sighted a second time, the bead of the rifle just barely above the glassy black orb that regarded me so passively. I squeezed the trigger. Again the crack, again the jolt, and again the rabbit disappeared over the top of the drift. I handed the rifle to my cousin and began making my way toward the rabbits. I sank into powdery snow up to my waist as I clambered to the top of the drift and looked over.

On the other side of the drift was a sight that I doubt   5
I will ever forget. There was a shallow, snow-covered ditch on the leeward side of the drift and it was into this ditch that the rabbits had fallen, at least what was left of the rabbits. The entire ditch, in an area about ten feet wide, was spattered with splashes of crimson blood, pink gobbets of brain, and splintered fragments of bone. The twisted corpses of the rabbits lay in the bottom of the ditch in small pools of streaming blood. Of both the rabbits, only the bodies remained, the heads being completely gone. Stumps of vertebrae protruded obscenely from the mangled bodies, and one rabbit's hind legs twitched spasmodically. I realized that my cousin must have made a mistake and loaded the rifle with hollowpoint explosive bullets instead of solid ones.

I shouted back to the pickup, explaining the situation,   6
and asked if I should bring them back anyway. My grandfather shouted back, "No, don't worry about it, just leave them there. I'm gonna toss these jacks by the side of the road anyway; jackrabbits aren't any good for eatin'."

Looking at the dead, twitching bodies I thought only of   7
the incredible waste of life that the afternoon had been, and I realized that there was much more to being a hunter than knowing how to use a rifle. I turned and walked back to the pickup, riding the rest of the way home in silence.

**Questions to Start
You Thinking**

Meaning

1. Where in the essay do you first begin to suspect the nature of the writer's feelings toward hunting? What in the essay or in your experience led you to this perception?

2. How would you characterize the writer's grandfather? How would you characterize his cousin?

3. How did the writer's understanding of himself change as a result of this hunting experience?

Writing Strategies

4. How might the essay be strengthened or weakened if the opening paragraph were cut out? How would your understanding of the author and how he changed be different if this paragraph were not included?

5. Would Schreiner's essay be more or less effective if he explained in the last paragraph what he means by "much more to being a hunter"?

6. What are some of Schreiner's memorable images?

Learning by Writing

THE ASSIGNMENT: RECALLING A PERSONAL EXPERIENCE

Write about one specific experience that changed how you acted, thought, or felt. Use your experience as a springboard for reflection. Your purpose is not merely to tell an interesting story but to show your readers the importance that that experience has had for you. Your audience is your instructor and your classmates.

We suggest you pick an event that is not too subjective. Something that happened to you or something that you observed, an encounter with a person who greatly influenced you, a decision that you made, or a challenge or an obstacle that you faced will be easier to recall (and to make vivid for your readers) than a subjective, interior experience like a religious conversion or falling in love.

Some memorable student papers we have read have recalled experiences like those that follow — some heavy, some light:

A man recalled guitar lessons with a teacher who at first seemed harsh but who turned out to be a true friend.

A woman recalled how, as a small girl, she sneaked into a nun's room, out of curiosity stole some rosary beads, and discovered that crime does not pay.

A man recalled meeting an American Indian who taught him a deeper understanding of the natural world.

To help you fulfill this assignment, let's consider the question What does writing from personal experience call for?

Facing the Challenge: Writing from Recall

The major challenge writers confront when they write from recall is to focus their essays. When writing about a familiar — and often very powerful — personal experience, writers often have difficulty making objective decisions about the most effective method of presenting that experience to readers. On the one hand, it is tempting to include every detail that comes to mind. On the other hand, because the experience is so familiar, they may overlook details that would make the story's relevance clearer to the reader. Writers may also find it difficult to decide what details to include, where to begin their narrative, what order to use in recounting events, and how to conclude their essay.

If you are not certain what your purpose is in writing about a particular event — what you want to *show* readers about your experience — your narrative is likely to read like a laundry list of details, with no clear connections between events and no main idea. To focus your ideas for a personal narrative, begin by freewriting or brainstorming to put all the details you remember about your experience down on paper. Then review this writing, circling connected ideas in your freewriting or drawing lines between related items on your brainstorming list — to highlight threads that run throughout your experience. To help you to decide what you want to show your readers, state your response to each of the following questions in a nutshell (no more than two or three sentences): What was important to you about the experience? What did you learn from it? How did it change you?

Once you have decided on the main point you want to make about your experience, you should select those details that will best illustrate that point. Review the way Russell Baker in "The Art of Eating Spaghetti" uses details that reinforce his changing perceptions of Mr. Fleagle's abilities as a teacher and his own abilities as a writer. Baker doesn't mention every book he read in his eleventh-grade English class or every paper he wrote. He describes the class on *Macbeth* to establish his initial perceptions of Mr. Fleagle, and he describes the particular experience that led him to see Mr. Fleagle as one of "the finest teachers in the school." Remember that in your essay you must do more than just describe your experience. You must use details that show readers why the experience was so important to you that you chose to write about it.

GENERATING IDEAS

You may find that the minute you are asked to write about a significant experience in your life, the very incident will flash to mind. Most writers, though, will need a little time to shake down their memories.

Probably what will come to you first will be recent memories, but give long-ago memories time to surface, too. Be ready for any recollections that well up unexpectedly. Often, when you are busy doing something else — observing the scene around you, talking with someone, reading about someone else's experience — the activity can trigger a recollection from the past.

When a promising one surfaces, write it down. It may be the start of your paper. Perhaps, like Russell Baker, you found success only when you ignored what you thought you were supposed to do in favor of what you really wanted to do. Perhaps, like Robert Schreiner, you learned from a painful experience. If nothing much surfaces, you might want to try the following strategies for generating ideas. (For more suggestions on using each of these strategies, see Chapter 15.)

Try brainstorming. Brainstorming is a good way to jog your memory. When you brainstorm, you try to come up with as many ideas as you can without any thought for their form or their practical applications. You just jot down ideas for a certain amount of time and see where your thoughts lead you. You can start with a suggestive word or phrase — *disobedience, painful lesson, childhood, peer pressure* — and list under that word or phrase as many ideas as occur to you through free association. You can also try asking yourself the questions in the following discovery checklist:

 DISCOVERY CHECKLIST

Searching Your Memory

- Did you ever break an important rule or rebel against authority? Did you learn anything from your actions?
- Did you ever succumb to peer pressure? What were the results of going along with the crowd? What did you learn?
- Did you ever regard a person in a certain way and then have to change your opinion of him or her?
- Did you ever have to choose between two equally attractive alternatives? How might your life have been different if you had chosen differently?
- Have you ever been appalled by witnessing an act of prejudice or insensitivity? What did you do? Do you wish you had done something different?
- Did you ever, as Robert Schreiner did, have a long-held belief or assumption shattered? Can you trace the change to one event or a series of events?
- Was there ever a moment in your life when you decided to reform, to adopt a whole new outlook? How would you characterize your attempt? (Successful? Unsuccessful? Laughable? Painful?)

Try freewriting. If you still have difficulty recalling a meaningful experience, spend ten or fifteen minutes freewriting — simply writing without stopping whatever comes into your head. If you think you have nothing to say, write "I have nothing to say" over and over, until ideas come. They will come. Don't worry about spelling, punctuation, or coherence. When you read over what you have written, you may be surprised to find the germ of a good paper.

Try a reporter's questions. Once you recall an experience you want to write about, ask the reporter's questions, "the five *W*'s and an *H*" that journalists find useful in their work:

Who was involved?
What happened?
Where did it take place?
When did it happen?
Why did it happen?
How did the events unfold?

Any one of these questions can lead to further questions — and to further discovery. Take, for instance, Who was involved? If people besides you were involved in the incident, you might also ask, What did they look like? What did the people do? What did they say? (Might their words supply a lively quotation for your paper?) What information about them would a reader have to know to appreciate their importance to you and the story? Or take the question What happened? You might also ask, What were your inmost thoughts as the event took place? At what moment did you become aware that the event was no ordinary, everyday experience? Or weren't you aware of that until later — perhaps only now that you are writing about it? (For more advice about putting these questions to work for you, see p. 368.)

Check other sources of information.   As we find out from psychology, the memory drops as well as retains. So it may be that you will want to check your recollections against those of anyone else who shared the experience. If possible, talk to a friend or family member who was there. Did you keep a diary or a journal at the time? If so, you might glance into it and refresh your memory. Was the experience public enough (such as a riot or a blizzard) to have been recorded in a newspaper or a magazine? If so, perhaps you can read about it in a library. In doing these things, you will probably discover details or angles that you had forgotten about — which will, in turn, open up new areas for exploring through writing.

PLANNING, DRAFTING, AND DEVELOPING

Now, how will you tell your story? If the experience you want to write about is still fresh in your mind, you may be able to begin by writing a draft, writing and planning simultaneously, following the order of occurrence of events, shaping your story as you go along. Even if you choose not to plan as a separate stage before drafting, you'll find it reassuring to have at your elbow any jottings you made as you searched your memory. If you decide to plan before you write, here are some additional suggestions. (For more advice on planning, drafting, and developing college papers, see Chapters 16, 17, and 18.)

Establish a chronology.   Retelling an experience is called *narration*, and the simplest way to organize the information is chronologically — relating events in the order in which they occurred. In doing so, you take the King's advice to the White Rabbit in *Alice's Adventures in Wonderland*: "Begin at the beginning, and go on till you come to the end: then stop."

But sometimes because all experience flows together, you may not know just when to start or stop. If that occurs, stick to the essentials, and write in chronological order.

Sometimes you can start an account of a personal experience in the middle and then, through *flashback*, fill in whatever background a reader needs to know. Richard Rodriguez, for instance, begins *Hunger of Memory*, a memoir of his bilingual childhood, with an arresting sentence:

> I remember, to start with, that day in Sacramento, in a California now nearly thirty years past — when I first entered a classroom, able to understand about fifty stray English words.

The opening hooks our attention. In the rest of his essay, Rodriguez fills us in on his family history, on the gulf he came to perceive between the public language (English) and the language of his home (Spanish).

Show what happened.   How can you best make your recollections come alive for your readers? Look again at Russell Baker's account of Mr. Fleagle teaching *Macbeth* and at the way Robert G. Schreiner depicts his cousin putting the wounded rabbits out of their misery. These two writers have done what good novelists and story writers do: they have not merely told us what happened but have *shown* us, by creating scenes that we can see in our mind's eye. As you tell your story, include at least two or three such specific scenes. Show your readers exactly what happened, where it occurred, what was said, who said it. Use details and words that appeal to all five senses — sight, sound, touch, taste, and smell.

REVISING AND EDITING

After you have written an early draft, put it aside for a day or two if possible (for a few hours if your deadline is looming) before revising it. Then read it over carefully. Try to see everything through the eyes of one of your readers, noting both the pleasing parts and the confusing spots. Revise to ensure that you've expressed your thoughts and feelings clearly and strongly in a way that will reach your readers; edit to ensure that no distracting weaknesses in grammar or expression remain. (For more on revising and editing, see Chapter 19.)

As you read over the essay to revise it, ask yourself: What was so important about this experience? Why is it so memorable? Ask whether that importance will be clear to your readers; if nothing else, they should be able to discern why this experience was a crucial one in your life. Ask again the question you asked yourself when you began: How has your life been different ever since? Be sure that the difference is genuine and specific. Don't ramble on insincerely about "significances" that don't reflect the incident's real impact on you. In other words, be sure that your essay is focused on a single main idea or thesis.

Also ask whether you have succeeded in making the events come alive for your readers by recalling them in sufficient concrete detail. Be specific enough that your readers can see, smell, taste, hear, and feel what you experienced. Notice again Robert Schreiner's focus in his second paragraph on the world outside his own skin: his close recall of the snow, of the pointers his grandfather offered about the habits of jackrabbits and the way to shoot them. As you draft and revise, you may well recall more and more vivid details to include.

Finally, consider whether the story you tell will be easy for readers to follow. Have you consistently followed a logical sequence of events? Have you indicated transitions clearly? Readers will follow you through your essay more readily if you give them a good idea of where they're going.

Revise and rewrite until you know you've related your experience and its impact as well as you know how. Here are some questions to ask yourself as you go over your paper to revise it:

REVISION CHECKLIST

- Have you fulfilled your purpose by showing why this experience was important and by demonstrating how it changed your life?
- Will readers want to keep reading? Have you paid enough attention to what is most dramatic, instructive, or revealing? Can readers see and feel what you experienced?
- Why do you begin your narration as you do? Is there another place in the draft that would make a better beginning?
- If the events are not in chronological order, is it easy to follow the organization?
- Does the ending provide a sense of finality?

WRITING WITH A COMPUTER

A word processor can help you set down your recollections rapidly, an advantage for this assignment. You might begin by making, as fast as you can, a simple on-screen list of the events you wish to record. This done, go back and flesh out the skeleton. Add any exact details that might make the experience real to your reader. Have you recalled a person? If so, add a sentence or two that will make him or her come alive ("a gray-haired gentleman who wore old white shirts with frayed collars, fond of consulting his gold pocket watch"). Did a certain locale shape your experience? (A shallow, snow-covered ditch is central to Schreiner's memoir; see p. 20.) What made that place so unforgettable? Keep recalling, dropping in memorable details. Before your eyes, your bare list will start becoming a meaty draft.

If your list remains bare and you need more material, save your list, and create a fresh document. Ask yourself a reporter's questions (the five W's and an H), and jot down your replies. With the power of word processing to lift the contents of one document to another, you can transfer to your draft all or any of the material you generate and work it in wherever it best fits.

You can also try out different patterns of organization to see which chronology works best with your story. Move your statement of what your story means to the end, or try a flashback to start. If you don't like the changes, with word processing you can easily move the parts back or delete them.

- Do you stick to the point? Is everything that is included relevant to your main idea or thesis?
- Do you portray any people? If so, is their importance clear? Do you provide enough detail to make them seem real, not just shadowy figures?
- If there is dialogue, does it have the ring of real speech? Read it aloud. Try it on a friend.

After you have revised your recall essay, proofread and edit it. Check carefully for problems with grammar, word choice, punctuation, and mechanics — and then correct any problems you find. A comprehensive reference handbook is an indispensable tool for this task; the "Quick Editing Guide" at the end of *The Bedford Guide for College Writers* (see the pages with the colored edges) will get you started.

When editing a recall paper, pay particular attention to verb form and verb tense: Have you juggled a sequence of events that happened in the past and created confusing constructions? Also make sure that the transitions you've introduced to connect these events are properly punctuated; most introductory elements will need a comma after them. Finally, don't rely on your memory to supply the correct spelling and capitalization for the names of people and places you include in your story: check them thoroughly.

Here are some questions to get you started when proofreading and editing your story:

EDITING CHECKLIST

- Have you used correct verb tenses throughout? Is it clear what happened first and what happened next? Have you used the correct form for all verbs? (See A1 in the "Quick Editing Guide.")
- Is your sentence structure correct? Have you avoided writing fragments and run-on sentences? (See A6 and A7 in the "Quick Editing Guide.")
- Do your transitions and other introductory elements have commas after them, if these are needed? (See C1 in the "Quick Editing Guide.")
- Have you spelled everything correctly, especially the names of people and places? Have you capitalized names correctly? (See D1 and D2 in the "Quick Editing Guide.")
- Have you used the proper paper format, including special requirements for your instructor and course? (See D3 in the "Quick Editing Guide.")

When you have made all the changes you need to make, retype or print out a clean copy of your paper — and hand it in.

OTHER ASSIGNMENTS

1. Choose a person outside your immediate family who had a marked effect on your life, either good or bad, and jot down ten details about that person that might help a reader understand what he or she was like. In searching your memory for details, consider the person's phys-

ical appearance, way of talking, and habits as well as any memorable incidents. When your list is finished, look back to "The Art of Eating Spaghetti" to identify the kinds of detail Baker uses in his portrait of Mr. Fleagle, paying particular attention to the kinds of detail you might have included in your list but didn't. Then write a paper in which you portray that person and explore the nature of his or her impact on you. Include those details that help explain the effect the person had on you.

2. Write a paper in which you remember a place you were once fond of — your grandmother's kitchen, a tree house, a library, a locker room, a clubhouse, a vacation retreat. Emphasize why this place was memorable. What made it different from every other place? Why was it important to you? What do you feel when you remember it?

3. Write a paper in which, from memory, you inform your readers about some traditional ceremony, ritual, or observation familiar to you.

FOR PEER RESPONSE

You may also find it helpful during the revising stage to call on a classmate to read and respond to your draft. Your instructor may pair you with a classmate; if not, you may choose a friend. See Chapter 20 for advice on working with other student writers and for general questions you should always ask a peer editor to address. For a paper in which you write from recall, you'll also want to ask your peer editor to answer these specific questions.

- What do you think the writer's main idea or message is? Do you understand why this experience was important to him or her?
- What emotions do the people (especially the main character) in the narration feel? How did *you* feel while reading the essay?
- Where does the essay come alive? Underline any sensory images or descriptions that seem particularly effective.
- If this were your paper, what is the one thing you would be sure to work on before handing it in?

FOR GROUP LEARNING

Learning to Be a Peer Editor

To gain dry-run practice in peer response before trying your skills on a classmate's paper, select from this book's table of contents any student-written paper, and write a detailed response to it. Write it in the form of a short letter to the writer. Tell the writer what is effective and what is ineffective about the essay and explain why. Get together with others in your class who chose the same paper, and compare comments. What did you notice in the paper? What did you miss that others noticed? If you have any doubts that comparing your responses with other people's is worth your time, this activity will show you that several people can notice far more than one individual can.

Such a tradition can pertain to a holiday, a rite of passage (confirmation, bar or bat mitzvah, graduation), a sporting event, a family custom. Explain the importance of the tradition to you, making use of whatever information you recall. How did the observation or custom originate? Who takes part? How has the tradition changed through the years? What does it add to the lives of those who observe it?

4. Narrate an experience in which you felt like an outsider, someone who didn't belong. Explore why you felt this way, and explain what you did as a result of this feeling.

Applying What You Learn: Some Uses of Writing from Recall

Autobiographers and writers of informal essays rely extensively on recall. All of us depend on recall in much of our informal, everyday writing—when we pen a letter to friends or family members, when we write out directions for someone who doesn't know where we live, when we make a diary entry. Recall is an important resource for the kind of paper in which you are asked to explain how to do something—train a puppy, drive a car, build a coffee table, make a speech.

Recall also plays a role in writing for classes other than English. Even when you are asked to investigate, to analyze, to explain, or to argue, you can sometimes use personal experience as support for exposition and argument. Rebecca Shriver, a student who had spent a year living and working in St. Thomas, added life and verisimilitude to her sociology research paper analyzing cultural differences between the Virgin Islands and the United States by including not only material gathered from books and periodicals but also this telling recollection:

Among the first things an American in the Virgin Islands will notice are the driving and the drivers. St. Thomas retains the custom, a carryover from Danish rule, of driving on the left-hand side of the road. Drivers are extremely aggressive, vocal, and heedless of others. West Indians, especially the cabdrivers, virtually own the road. They stop for minutes at a time at the bottom of steep hills to chat with friends or to pick up hordes of workers. The streets resound with honks and screams as drivers yell obscenities at each other. Hitchhikers, too, are aggressive. Often a West Indian jumps into the back of one's truck, or schoolchildren tap on one's window, soliciting a ride.

```
       The mind-set of left-hand driving surfaces in an un-
  usual way--walking habits. Since St. Thomians are so used
  to driving on the left, they also walk on the left, and
  an American who is unused to this will bump into a lot of
  West Indians on the sidewalk.
```

The writer used this recollection to make an important point — that recognizing and understanding cultural differences provide the keys to understanding. In an article called "Sex and Size," paleontologist Stephen Jay Gould makes effective use of recollection to ease his readers into a seven-page essay on a challenging subject. (Linnaeus [1707–1778], a Swedish botanist, originated the system of classifying organisms in established categories.)

As an eight-year-old collector of shells at Rockaway Beach, I took a functional but non-Linnaean approach to taxonomy, dividing my booty into "regular," "unusual," and "extraordinary." My favorite was the common slipper limpet, although it resided in the realm of the regular by virtue of its ubiquity. I loved its range of shapes and colors, and the pocket underneath that served as a protective home for the animal. My appeal turned to fascination a few years later, when I both entered puberty and studied some Linnaean taxonomy at the same time. I learned its proper name, *Crepidula fornicata* — a sure spur to curiosity. Since Linnaeus himself had christened this particular species, I marveled at the unbridled libido of taxonomy's father.

When I learned about the habits of *C. fornicata*, I felt confident that I had found the key to its curious name. For the slipper limpet forms stacks, smaller piled atop larger, often reaching a dozen shells or more. The smaller animals on top are invariably male, the larger supporters underneath always female. And lest you suspect that the topmost males might be restricted to a life of obligate homosexuality by virtue of their separation from the first large female, fear not. The male's penis is longer by far than its entire body and can easily slip around a few males to reach the females. *Crepidula fornicata* indeed: a sexy congeries.

Then, to complete the disappointing story, I discovered that the name had nothing to do with sex. Linnaeus had described the species from single specimens in museum drawers; he knew nothing of their peculiar stacking behavior. *Fornix* means "arch" in Latin, and Linnaeus chose his name to recognize the shell's smoothly domed shape.

Disappointment finally yielded to renewed interest a few years later when I learned the details of *Crepidula*'s sexuality and found the story more intriguing than ever, even if the name had been a come-on. *Crepidula* is a natural sex changer, a sequential hermaphrodite in our jargon. Small juveniles mature first as males and later change to female as they grow larger. Intermediate animals in the middle of a *Crepidula* stack are usually in the process of changing from male to female.

For an academic writing assignment, you usually have to research your subject in some depth before you can write about it. You need to rely on resources other than memory. Yet even as you approach such an assignment, you can *begin* by writing down your own relevant experiences. Whether or not you use them in your finished paper, they can help direct your research. Often you *will* use them, as Shriver and Gould did, in conjunction with more academic sources. A student who has worked in a day-care center can add vigor and authority to a sociology paper on day care in the United States by including a few pertinent illustrations based on that experience. An economics paper about the recent growth of the fast-food industry could benefit immeasurably from an incident remembered from harried days behind the counter at a McDonald's. If you grew up in the inner city, your recollections might lend enormous impact to a paper arguing for or against a particular city planning proposal.

Virtually every paper, no matter what it sets out to accomplish, stands to benefit from vivid examples and illustrations. And when you plan to include such examples and illustrations in your writing, your memories can prove as valuable as hidden treasure.

Making Connections: Writing from Recall in A Writer's Reader

Recall is probably the major resource for writers in all professions and from all walks of life. In *A Writer's Reader*, some of the writers recall and respond to events from childhood, others to events from adulthood. For example, in "Shades" (p. 505), professor and fiction writer William Henry Lewis recalls the details of a particular summer in his childhood as he examines the impact of meeting his father for the first time. On the other hand, social commentator Marion Winik in "Visiting Steven" (p. 511) recalls incidents from throughout her adult life as she explores her emotional connection to her former brother-in-law and tries to cope with his impending death from AIDS. These two writers, like Russell Baker (p. 15) and Robert G. Schreiner (p. 17), not only recall and report significant events in their lives but also reflect on these experiences and explain how they shaped their thoughts, feelings, and actions.

Some of the writers from various fields who use the resource of recall include essayist E. B. White, "Once More to the Lake" (p. 490); poet and screenwriter Joy Harjo, "Three Generations of Native American Women's Birth Experience" (p. 540); journalist and editor Brent Staples, "Black Men and Public Space" (p. 561); poet and professor Toi Derricotte, "Early Memory: The *California Zephyr*" (p. 573); essayist Nancy Mairs, "Freeing Choices" (p. 579); and editor and essayist Richard Rodriguez, "Does America Still Exist?" (p. 583). These writers look back over important events in their lives and interpret how the experiences have influenced them. As you read these essays, consider the role that recall plays in them. For each essay, answer the following questions:

1. Does the author recall events from childhood or from adulthood?
2. Is the perspective of the essay that of a child or an adult? How do you know? What does the author realize after reflecting on the events? Does the realization come soon after the experience or later, when he or she examines the events from a more mature perspective?
3. How does the realization change the individual?
4. How do you think recall is useful to the author in his or her field of work or study?

Chapter 2

Writing from Observation

Most writers begin to write by recalling what they know. Then they look around themselves and add what they see. A very handy resource for them — and for you as a writer — is observation.

Some writing consists almost entirely of observation — a news story by a reporter who has witnessed a fire, a clinical report by a doctor or nurse detailing a patient's condition, a scientist's account of a laboratory experiment. So does any writing — fiction or nonfiction — in which the writer describes a person, place, or thing. In other writing, observation provides supporting details to make the primary ideas clear or convincing. Indeed, we can hardly think of a kind of writing that doesn't call for a writer to describe his or her observations.

Sometimes when you sit down to write, you look around the storehouse of your brain only to find empty shelves. Not enough to write about? In such a case, use the resource of observation. Open your eyes — and your other senses. Take in not only what you can see but also what you can hear, smell, touch, and taste. Then when you write, draw on your sensory observations, and report your experiences in concrete detail. Of course, you can't record everything your senses bring you. You must be selective. Keeping in mind your purpose in writing and your audience will help you to choose the important and relevant details. To make a football game come alive for readers of your college newspaper, you might briefly mention the overcast cold weather and the buttery smell of popcorn. But if your purpose is primarily to explain which team won and why, you might stress the muddy condition of the playing field, the most spectacular plays, and the players who scored.

Learning from Other Writers

Let's read two essays by writers who write from observation — a professional writer and a college student. In both essays, the authors observe their surroundings, and both reflect on their observations to draw conclusions about human behavior. The first selection, "The Shock of Teapots," is by Cynthia Ozick, a professional novelist, short story writer, and essayist. Ozick uses vivid details to describe the quality of strangeness that familiar objects take on when we see them far away from home — the shock to the traveler of meeting everyday objects in a strange setting.

Sandy Messina, a student, submitted the second essay for an assignment in both freshman composition and environmental biology. She looks closely at the desert and its inhabitants.

Cynthia Ozick   The Shock of Teapots

One morning in Stockholm, after rain and just before November, a mysteriously translucent shadow began to paint itself across the top of the city. It skimmed high over people's heads, a gauzy brass net, keeping well above the streets, skirting everything fabricated by human arts — though one or two steeples were allowed to dip into it, like pens filling their nibs with palest ink. It made a sort of watermark over Stockholm, as if a faintly luminous river ran overhead, yet with no more weight or gravity than a vapor. 1

This glorious strangeness — a kind of crystalline wash — was the sunlight of a Swedish autumn. The sun looked *new*: it had a lucidity, a texture, a tincture, a position across the sky that my New York gape had never before taken in. The horizontal ladder of light hung high up, higher than any sunlight I had ever seen, and the quality of its glow seemed thinner, wanner, more tentatively morning-brushed; or else like gold leaf beaten gossamer as tissue — a lambent skin laid over the spired marrow of the town. 2

"Ah, yes, the sun *does* look a bit different this time of year," say the Stockholmers in their perfect English (English as a second first language), but with a touch of ennui. Whereas I, under the electrified rays of my whitening hair, stand drawn upward to the startling sky, restored to the clarity of childhood. The Swedes have known a Swedish autumn before; I have not. 3

Travel returns us in just this way to sharpness of notice; and to be saturated in the sight of what is entirely new — the sun at an unaccustomed slope, stretched across the northland, separate from the infiltrating dusk that always seems about to fall through clear gray Stockholm — is to revisit the enigmatically lit puppet-stage outlines of childhood: those mental photographs and dreaming woodcuts or engravings that we retain from our earliest years. What we remember from childhood we remember forever — permanent ghosts, 4 stamped, imprinted, eternally seen. Travelers regain this ghost-seizing bright-ness, eeriness, firstness.

They regain it because they have cut themselves loose from their own so-   5
ciety, from every society; they are, for a while, floating vagabonds, like astro-nauts out for a space walk on a long free line. They are subject to preternat-ural exhilarations, absurd horizons, unexpected forms and transmutations: the matter-of-fact (a battered old stoop, say, or the shape of a door) appears beautiful; or a stone that at home would not merit the blink of your eye here arrests you with its absolute particularity — just because it is what your hand already intimately knows. You think: a stone, a stone! They have stones here too! And you think: how uncannily the planet is girdled, as stone-speckled in Sweden as in New York. For the vagabond-voyeur (and for travelers voyeurism is irresistible), nothing is not for notice, nothing is banal, nothing is ordinary: not a rock, not the shoulder of a passer-by, not a teapot.

Plenitude assaults; replication invades. Everything known has its spooky   6
shadow and Doppelgänger. On my first trip anywhere — it was 1957 and I landed in Edinburgh with the roaring of the plane's four mammoth pro-pellers for days afterward embedded in my ears — I rode in a red airport bus to the middle of the city, out of which ascended its great castle. It is a fairy-book castle, dreamlike, Arthurian, secured in the long-ago. But the shuddery red bus — hadn't I been bounced along in an old bus before, perhaps not so terrifically red as this one? — the red bus was not within reach of plain sense. Every inch of its interior streamed with unearthliness, with an undivulged and consummate witchery. It put me in the grip of a wild Elsewhere. This unex-ceptional vehicle, with its bright forward snout, was all at once eclipsed by a rush of the abnormal, the unfathomably Martian. It was the bus, not the phantasmagorical castle, that clouded over and bewildered our reasoned hu-manity. The red bus was what I intimately knew: only I had never seen it be-fore. A reflected flicker of the actual. A looking-glass bus. A Scottish ghost.

This is what travelers discover: that when you sever the links of normality   7
and its claims, when you break off from the quotidian, it is the teapots that truly shock. Nothing is so awesomely unfamiliar as the familiar that discloses itself at the end of a journey. Nothing shakes the heart so much as meeting — far, far away — what you last met at home. Some say that travelers are infor-mal anthropologists. But it is ontology — the investigation of the nature of being — that travelers do. Call it the flooding-in of the real.

There is, besides, the flooding-in of character. Here one enters not land-   8
scapes or streetlit night scenes, but fragments of drama: splinters of euphoria that catch you up when you are least deserving. Sometimes it is a jump into a pop-up book, as when a cockney cabdriver, of whom you have asked direc-tions while leaning out from the curb, gives his native wink of blithe good-will. Sometimes it is a mazy stroll into a toy theater, as when, in a museum, you suddenly come on the intense little band following the lecturer on Mesopotamia, or the lecturer on genre painting, and the muse of civilization alights on these rapt few. What you are struck with then — one of those men-tal photographs that go on sticking to the retina — is not what lies somno-

lently in the glass case or hangs romantically on the wall, but the enchantment of a minutely idiosyncratic face shot into your vision with indelible singularity, delivered over forever by your own fertile gaze. When travelers stare at heads and ears and necks and beards and mustaches, they are — in the encapsuled force of the selection — making art: portraits, voice sonatinas, the quick haiku of a strictly triangular nostril.

Traveling is seeing; it is the implicit that we travel by. Travelers are fantasists, conjurers, seers — and what they finally discover is that every round object everywhere is a crystal ball: stone, teapot, the marvelous globe of the human eye.

9

Questions to Start You Thinking

Meaning

1. In simple terms, what does Ozick observe in the first three paragraphs of her essay?

2. What does Ozick mean when she says that travel creates a "sharpness of notice" and leaves us "saturated in the sight of what is entirely new" (paragraph 4)?

3. According to Ozick, when are teapots shocking? Why?

Writing Strategies

4. Give some examples of specific images Ozick uses in the first three paragraphs of her essay that bring her experience of the autumn morning alive for readers by showing them what she has seen.

5. How does Ozick use the example of the Scottish bus (paragraph 6) to help explain her idea that travel makes the familiar unfamiliar?

6. Locate as many places as you can where Ozick uses images that describe a vision that is partially obscured — as though in a fog. Does the repetition of such images help to reinforce her point about what travel does to the senses? Why, or why not?

STUDENT ESSAY

Sandy Messina   Footprints: The Mark of Our Passing

No footprints. No tracks. No marks. The Navajo leave no footprints because their shoes have no heels to dig into the earth's womb. They have a philosophy--walk gently on mother earth; she is pregnant with life. In the spring, when the earth is ready to deliver, they wear no shoes at all.

1

As I walk across the desert, I look at my shoes etch the sand dune. There they are following me: the telltale prints left on the brown earth. Each footprint has a story to tell, a story of change, a story of death. Many lives are marked by our passing. Our steps can bring death to the life of a

2

flower, the life of a forest, the life of a friendship. Some
of our passages can bring death to the life of a nation.

I see my prints dug deeply into the spawning grounds of   3
the desert lavender, the evening primrose, the desert sun-
flower, and the little golden gilia. Life destroyed. Birth
aborted. There under each mark of my passing is death. The
fetuses--seeds of desert color, spring glory, trapped just
below the surface waiting parturition--crushed into lifeless-
ness. Man walks heavily on the earth.

He tramples across America, leaving giant footprints   4
everywhere he goes. He fills swamps, furrows hillsides, forms
roads, fells trees, fashions cities. Man leaves the prints
of his lifelong quest to subdue the earth, to conquer the
wilderness. He pushes and pulls and kneads the earth into a
loaf to satisfy his own appetites. He constantly tugs at the
earth, trying to regulate it. Yet man was not told to regulate, restrict, restrain the Garden of Eden but to care for
it and allow it to replenish itself.

I look at my own footprints in the sand and see nearby   5
other, gentler tracks. Here on the sandy hummock I see
prints, soft and slithery. The snake goes softly on the
earth. His willowy form causes no tyranny. He has no need to
prove his prowess: he graciously gives warning and strikes
only in self-defense. He doesn't mar the surface of the earth
by his entrance, for his home is found in the burrows of the
other animals.

The spidery prints of the roadrunner, as he escapes with   6
a lizard dangling from his beak, show that he goes mercifully
on the earth. He does not use his power of flight to feed off
wide distances but instead employs his feathers to insulate
his body from high temperatures. He takes sustenance from the
earth but does not hoard or store it.

The wood rat scrambles over the hillock to burrow beneath   7
the Joshua tree. His clawed plantigrade feet make sensitive
little marks. He is caring of the earth. He doesn't destroy
forage but browses for food and eats cactus, food no other animal will eat. His home is a refuge of underground runways. It
even provides protection for his enemy the snake, as well as
for himself, from the heat of the day. He never feels the com-

pulsion to be his own person or have his own space but lives
in harmony with many other animals, under the Joshua tree.

The Joshua tree, that prickly paragon that invades the   8
desolation of desert, welcomes to its house all who would
dwell there. Many lives depend on this odd-looking creature,
the Joshua tree. It is intimately associated with the moth,
the lizard, the wood rat, the snake, the termite, the woodpecker, the boring weevil, the oriole. This spiky fellow is
hospitable, tolerant, and kind on the earth. He provides a
small world for other creatures: a world of pavilion, provision, protection from the harsh desert.

Unlike the Navajo's, my prints are still there in the   9
sand, but not the ruthless furrows I once perceived. My mus-
ings over nature have made my touch on the earth lighter,
softer, gentler.

Man too can walk gently on the earth. He must reflect   10
on his passing. Is the earth changed, bent and twisted, because he has traveled there, or has he considered nature as
a symphony he can walk with, in euphony? He need not walk
heavily on the earth, allowing the heat of adversity and the
winds of circumstance to destroy him. He can walk gently on
the earth, allowing life to grow undisturbed in seeming
desert places until it springs forth.

Questions to Start You Thinking	*Meaning*

Meaning

1. According to Messina, how is her way of walking across the earth different from the Navajo way?

2. How has the process of observing her own footprints changed the writer's behavior? How would she change the behavior of the rest of us?

Writing Strategies

3. Why doesn't Messina plunge right in and immediately start to report her observations? Of what use to her essay is her first paragraph?

4. Paragraph 3 isn't observation, but what does Messina accomplish in it? With paragraphs 4, 5, and 6, the writer returns to observing — for what purpose? What is the function of paragraphs 7–8? Of 9–10?

5. What specialized words suggest that this essay was written for readers familiar with biology (her instructor and other students)? Would any of the *jargon*, or technical terminology, interfere with Messina's communication of her ideas to general readers?

Learning by Writing

THE ASSIGNMENT: OBSERVING A SCENE

Observe a place near your campus or your home or your job and the people who frequent this place. Station yourself where you can mingle with the people there. Then write a paper in which you describe the place, the people, and their actions so as to convey the spirit of the place and offer some insight into the impact of the place on the people. Write for your instructor and class-mates. Fill at least two typewritten or three handwritten pages.

This assignment asks you to use observation as your primary resource for writing. It is meant to start you observing closely, so we suggest you don't write from long-ago memory. Go somewhere nearby, and open your senses — all of them. Jot down what you can immediately see and sense. No-tice the atmosphere of the place and how it affects the people there. Take notes in which you describe the location, the people, and the actions and events you see. After you have set down your observations in detail, use them to form a general impression of the place and the people there. What conclu-sions can you draw about this place? What is your main impression of the place? Of the people there? What is the relationship of the people to the place? Remember, your purpose is not only to describe what you see but also to express thoughts and feelings connected with those sights.

Three student writers wrote about these observations:

One student, who works nights in the emergency room of a hospital, ob-served the scene and the community of people that abruptly forms on the arrival of an accident victim (doctors, nurses, orderlies, the patient's friends or relatives, the patient himself or herself).

Another observed a bar mitzvah celebration that reunited a family for the first time in many years.

Another observed the bleachers in a baseball stadium before, during, and after a game.

GENERATING IDEAS

Setting down observations might seem a cut-and-dried task, not a matter of discovering anything. But to reporter and essayist Joan Didion it is true dis-covery. "I write," she says, "entirely to find out what I'm thinking, what I'm looking at, what I see and what it means." Here are some ways to generate the observations you'll need for your final paper.

Do some brainstorming. First, you need to find a subject to observe. What places interest you? Which are memorable? Get out your pencil, and start brainstorming — listing rapidly and at random any ideas that come to mind.

Facing the Challenge: Writing from Observation

The major challenge writers face when they write from observation is to include compelling details that allow their readers to fully share an experience and grasp its importance. As we experience the world, we are constantly bombarded by sensory details — sights, sounds, textures, smells, tastes, and feelings. Our task as writers is to choose details that will engage the readers and make a subject come alive for them. Describing a tree as "a big tree with green leaves and two brown birds on a low branch" is too vague to help readers envision the tree by showing them what is unique about it. The description does not contain sufficient sensory details.

As writers, we must create the illusion of life with black ink on white paper. Using details that arouse the senses makes a piece of writing more vivid for the reader. Using details that evoke thoughts and emotions makes an essay engaging. Notice how Cynthia Ozick in "The Shock of Teapots" uses details to paint a picture of the autumn light in Sweden: "One morning in Stockholm, after rain and just before November, a mysteriously translucent shadow began to paint itself across the top of the city. It skimmed high over people's heads, a gauzy brass net, keeping well above the streets, skirting everything fabricated by human arts — though one or two steeples were allowed to dip into it, like pens filling their nibs with palest ink." Ozick does not simply *tell* us that the sun was coming through a haze, which, in and of itself, is an uninteresting detail. Instead, she *shows* us textures and shapes, color and movement. She refers to the shadow as mysterious and describes its actions as if it were a living creature. She awakens our imaginations to picture the scene.

When writing from observation, choose a subject that has significance for you. When you're bored with a subject, your senses wander, and your writing becomes vague and unengaging. When you are interested in a subject, you are better able to write about it in a way that will interest your readers. So if describing a tree sounds boring, write about something that interests you — a football stadium, a hot-fudge sundae, your boyfriend or girlfriend, your car, your grandma's porch.

If you're having trouble coming up with ideas, try putting yourself in the position of a tourist by going someplace where you've never been or haven't been in a while. Your destination doesn't have to be far, but it should be unfamiliar enough to give you the heightened awareness of your surroundings that can make ideas come more easily and details stand out. Ozick's essay on traveling revels in the newness of Swedish sunshine: "I, under the electrified rays of my whitening hair, stand drawn upward to the startling sky, restored to the clarity of childhood. The Swedes have known a Swedish autumn before; I have not. . . . Travel returns us in just this way to sharpness of notice."

Such "sharpness of notice" is exactly what you want to achieve when you write from observation. To determine whether you have used details effectively, ask a peer to read your draft and then tell you what he or she sees, hears, smells, tastes, and feels. Before calling an essay complete, be sure your reader can understand the situation and share in your experience. If you have presented compelling sensory details in a significant and evocative way, then the relationship between writer and reader will be a dynamic one.

(Brainstorming is often a useful technique for getting started; for more advice about it, see p. 360.) Here are a few questions to help you start your list:

DISCOVERY
CHECKLIST

Finding a Scene to Observe

- Where do people get together to take in some event or performance? (a stadium, a theater, an auditorium)
- Where do people get together to participate in some activity? (a church, a classroom)
- Where do people form crowds while they are obtaining something or receiving a service? (a shopping mall, a dining hall or student union, a dentist's waiting room)
- Where do people gather for recreation or relaxation? (a party, a video arcade, a ballpark)
- What events do people gather at? (a fire, a wedding, a graduation)

Get out and look. After you make your list, read it, and put a check mark next to any subject that appeals to you. If no subject strikes you as compelling, plunge into the world, and see what you will see. You might go to a city street or a hillside in the country, a college building or a campus lawn, a furiously busy scene — a shopping mall, an airport terminal, a fast-food restaurant, a student hangout — or one in which only two or three people are idling — sunbathers, dog walkers, anglers, Frisbee throwers. Move around within a group of people, if possible. Stand off in a corner for a while, and then mix in again with the throng to obtain different viewpoints on the place and the people.

Record your observations. Sandy Messina's essay "Footprints: The Mark of Our Passing" began as a journal entry. In her biology course, Sandy was asked to keep a *specialized* journal in which to record her thoughts and observations on environmental biology. When she looked back over her observations of a desert walk, a subject stood out — one deep enough for a paper that she could submit to her English course as well. As you can see from her final version, keeping such a journal or notebook, occasionally jotting down thoughts and observations, creates a trove of material ready and waiting for use in more formal writing. (For further thoughts on journal keeping, see p. 366.)

The notes you take on your subject — or tentative subject — can be taken in any old order or methodically. One experienced teacher of writing, Myra Cohn Livingston, urges her students to draw up an "observation sheet" to organize their note taking. To use one yourself, fold a sheet of paper in half lengthwise. On the left make a column (which might be called "Objective") and list exactly what you saw, in an impartial way, like a zoologist looking at a new species of moth. Then on the right make a column (called "Subjective") and list your thoughts and feelings about what you observed. An observation sheet inspired by a trip to observe people at a beach might begin in the following way:

Objective	Subjective
Two kids toss a red beach ball while a spotted dog runs back and forth trying to intercept it.	Reminds me of when I was five and my beach ball rolled under a parked car. Got stuck crawling in to rescue it, cried, had to be calmed down, dragged free. Never much liked beach balls after that.
College couples on dates, smearing each other with suntan lotion.	Good way to get to know each other!
Middle-aged man eating a foot-long hot dog. Mustard drips on his paunch. "Hell! I just lost two percent!"	Guy looks like a business executive: three-piece suit type, I bet. But today he's a slob. Who cares? The beach brings out the slob in everybody.

For this writing assignment, an observation sheet seems an especially useful device. The notes in column one will trigger more notes in column two. As your list grows, it may spill over onto a fresh sheet. Write on one side of your paper only: later you can more easily organize your notes if you can spread them out and look at them all in one glance. Even in the sample observation sheet made at the beach, some sense is starting to take shape. The second and third notes both suggest that the beach is where people come to let their hair down. That insight might turn out to be the main impression the paper conveys.

The quality of your finished paper will depend in large part on the truthfulness and accuracy of your observations. If possible, while you write keep looking at your subject. Sandy Messina is a good, exact observer of nature: the details of the snake's "soft and slithery" print in the sand, the wood rat's "clawed plantigrade feet" (a technical word: *plantigrade* means walking with both sole and heel touching the ground).

Include a range of images. Have you captured not just sights but sounds, touches, odors? A memorable *image,* or evocation of a sense experience, can do wonders for a paper. In his memoir *Northern Farm,* naturalist Henry Beston observes a remarkable sound: "the voice of ice," the midwinter sound of a whole frozen pond settling and expanding in its bed.

> Sometimes there was a sort of hollow oboe sound, and sometimes a groan with a delicate undertone of thunder. . . . Just as I turned to go, there came from below one curious and sinister crack which ran off into a sound like the whine of a giant whip of steel lashed through the moonlit air.

Apparently, Beston's purpose in this passage is to report the nature of ice from his observations of it, and yet he uses accurate language that arrests us by the power of its suggestions.

When British journalist and fiction writer G. K. Chesterton wrote of ocean waves, he was tempted at first to speak of the "rushing swiftness of a wave" — a usual phrase. But instead, as he tells us in his essay "The Two Noises," he dusted off his glasses and observed a real wave toppling.

> The horrible thing about a wave is its hideous slowness. It lifts its load of water laboriously. . . . In front of me that night the waves were not like water: they were like falling city walls. The breaker rose first as if it did not wish to attack the earth; it wished only to attack the stars. For a time it stood up in the air as naturally as a tower; then it went a little wrong in its outline, like a tower that might some day fall.

PLANNING, DRAFTING, AND DEVELOPING

Having been writing, however roughly, all the while you've been observing, you will now have some rough stuff to organize. Spread out your notes and look them over. If you have made an observation sheet, circle whatever looks useful. Maybe you can rewrite your preliminary notes into a draft, throwing out details that don't matter, leaving those that do. Maybe you'll need some kind of plan to help you organize all the details you have gathered from observing. In either case, you'll need to employ a sensible method of organization and select details that help convey your main impression. (For more on these writing strategies, see Chapters 16 and 18.)

Use a sensible method of organization. How do you map out a series of observations? One simple way is to proceed *spatially.* You can lay out your observations graphically or in a simple scratch outline. In observing a landscape, you might move from left to right, from top to bottom, from near to far, from center to periphery. Your choice will depend on your purpose in writing.

You might instead see a reason to move *from the most prominent feature to the least prominent.* If you are writing about a sketch artist at work, the most prominent and interesting feature might be the artist's busy, confident hands. If you are describing a basketball game, you might start with the action under a basket.

Or you might move *from specific details to a general statement of an overall impression.* In describing Fisherman's Wharf in San Francisco, you might start with sellers of shrimp cups and souvenir fishnets, tour boats loading passengers, and the smell of frying fish and go on to say: "In all this commotion and commerce, a visitor senses the constant activity of the area."

Or you could move *from common, everyday features to the unusual features you want to stress.* After starting with the smell of frying fish and the cries of gulls, you might go on: "Yet this ordinary scene attracts visitors from afar: the Japanese sightseer, perhaps a fan of American prison films, making a pilgrimage by tour boat to Alcatraz."

Consider your purpose.   Perhaps your most important planning will take place as you answer the question What main insight or impression do I want to get across? Answering this question will help you decide which details to include and which to omit. Focusing on purpose will also help you avoid writing a dry recitation of observed facts. Remember that you want to *tell* readers something about what you have seen.

REVISING AND EDITING

Your revising, editing, and proofreading will all be easier if you have taken accurate notes on your observations. Clearly, Sandy Messina did. But what if, when you look over your draft, you find that in observing you skimped and now you don't have enough detail? If you have any doubts, go back to the scene and check more closely. Do you see any details you overlooked before? Did you miss anything? Take more notes to flesh out your draft. Professional journalists often make such follow-ups.

Not all writers rewrite in the same way. Some start tinkering early, perfecting little bits here and there. Even in her original version of "Footprints," a few sheets of rough notes, Sandy Messina started making small improvements. In her first draft, she had written the following:

> *Each of us must learn to walk gently on the earth. We must quit pushing and pulling and kneading it into a loaf to be our own bread.*

WRITING WITH A COMPUTER

If you find a second, follow-up trip to the scene necessary, word processing will allow you to amplify your draft easily. You can simply reopen your draft on the computer to insert further details wherever they will make your paper more vivid and lifelike.

Making your observations crackle with life, by the way, isn't just a matter of trying to intensify things with adverbs such as *very*. William Allen White, author and Kansas newspaper editor, hated such modifiers, which he believed are usually unnecessary. He once instructed his reporters to change every *very* they wrote to a *damn*, then cross out all the *damns*; they would then have stronger prose. Thanks to word processors, you can easily imitate William Allen White's technique of searching for one term and replacing it with another. Many writers benefit from keeping a list of problems they tend to make over and over. White's list includes only the word *very*, but you should put on your list any words you tend to overuse when trying to write a vivid description. You can then use the word processor's Search or Find command to locate each instance of each word on your list and replace or delete all but the most effective. (You can also use the Search function to find every instance of a grammar, spelling, or punctuation problem.) This technique will help you not only to edit more thoroughly but also to focus on recurring problems so that you can eventually eliminate them altogether.

Right away, she realized that by calling the earth "a loaf" she had already likened it to bread. So she crossed out "be our own bread" and substituted "suit our own appetites." She also crossed out verbs one at a time, as they occurred to her, until a strong verb came along.

We ~~moved marched~~ trooped across America, leaving our giant ~~footsteps~~ footprints.

To see what parts of your draft still need work when you rewrite, you might ask yourself these questions:

REVISION CHECKLIST

- Have you accomplished your purpose—to convey clearly your overall impression of your subject and to share some telling insight about it?
- What can you assume your readers already know? What do they need to be told?
- Have you gathered enough observations to make your subject understandable? Have you observed with *all* your senses? (Smell isn't always useful, but it might be.)
- Do any of your observations need to be checked for accuracy?
- Is the organizational pattern you have used the most effective pattern for your subject? Would another pattern be more effective?

After you have revised your observation essay, proofread and edit it. Check carefully for problems with grammar, word choice, punctuation, and mechanics—and then correct any problems you find. A comprehensive reference handbook is an indispensable tool for this task; the "Quick Editing Guide" at the end of *The Bedford Guide for College Writers* (see the pages with the colored edges) will get you started.

When editing a paper written from observation, pay particular attention to the modifiers—adjectives and adverbs—you used to describe your subject in detail. Make sure you have used the most precise and evocative words possible, given your purpose. Check to see that you have used adjective and adverb forms properly. And if you have added more details in the revising stage, consider whether they have been sufficiently blended in with the ideas that were already there.

Here are some questions to get you started when proofreading and editing your observation paper:

EDITING CHECKLIST

- Have you used the exact words you need to convey your meaning to your reader?
- Have you used an adjective whenever describing a noun or pronoun? Have you used an adverb whenever describing a verb, adjective, or adverb? Have you used the correct form when comparing two or more things? (See A5 in the "Quick Editing Guide.")
- Is your sentence structure correct? Have you avoided writing fragments and run-on sentences? (See A6 and A7 in the "Quick Editing Guide.")

- Is it clear what each modifier in a sentence modifies? Have you created any dangling or misplaced modifiers? (See B1 in the "Quick Editing Guide.")
- Have you used parallel structure wherever needed, especially in lists or comparisons? (See B2 in the "Quick Editing Guide.")
- Have you spelled everything correctly? (See D2 in the "Quick Editing Guide.")
- Have you used the proper paper format, including special requirements for your instructor and course? (See D3 in the "Quick Editing Guide.")

(For more on revising and editing, see Chapter 19.)

OTHER ASSIGNMENTS

1. To develop your powers of observation, follow Sandy Messina's example. Go for a walk, recording your observations in two or three detailed paragraphs. Let your walk take you either through an unfamiliar scene or through a familiar scene perhaps worth a closer look than you normally give it (such as a supermarket, a city street, an open field). Avoid a subject so familiar that it would be difficult for you to see it from a fresh perspective (such as a dormitory corridor or a parking lot). Sum up your impression of the place, including any opinion you form by your close observations.

2. Here is a short, spontaneous writing exercise that might serve as a warmup for a long assignment. Lin Haire-Sargeant of Tufts University, whose students enjoy the exercise, calls it "You Are the Detective."

FOR PEER RESPONSE

Once you've accurately recorded your observations, you may find it useful to seek another writer's reactions to your draft. See Chapter 20 for advice on working with other student writers and for general questions you should always ask a peer editor to address. For a paper in which you write from observation, you'll also want your peer editor to answer these specific questions:

- What is the main insight or impression you carry away from this piece of writing?
- Which sense does the writer use particularly well? Are any senses neglected that could be used?
- Can you see and feel what the writer experienced? Would more details make this writing more compelling? Put check marks on the manuscript wherever you want more details.
- How well has the writer used the evidence from his or her senses to build a dominant impression? Which sensory impressions contribute most strongly to the overall picture? Which seem superfluous?
- If this were your paper, what is the one thing you would be sure to work on before handing it in?

She asks her students to begin the assignment immediately after the class in which it is given and to turn it in the same afternoon.

> Go to a nearby public place — burger joint, library, copy center, art gallery — and select a person who catches your eye, who somehow intrigues you. Try to choose someone who looks as if she or he will stay put for a while. Settle yourself where you can observe your subject unobtrusively. Take notes, if you can do so without being observed yourself.
>
> Now, carefully and tactfully (we don't want any fistfights or lawsuits) notice everything you can about this person. The obvious place to start would be with physical characteristics, but focus on other things too. How does the person talk? Move? What does the person's body language tell you?
>
> Write a paragraph describing the person. Pretend that the person is going to hold up a bank ten minutes from now, and the police will expect you to supply a full and accurate description of him or her.

3. The perspective of a tourist, an outsider alert to details, often reveals the distinctive character of places and people. Think of some place you have visited as an outsider or a visitor in the past year, and jot down from memory any details you noticed that you haven't been able to forget. Or spend a few minutes as a tourist right now. Go to a busy spot on or off campus and record your observations of anything you find amusing, surprising, puzzling, or intriguing. Then write an essay on the unique character of the place.

4. From among the photographs that open Chapters 22 through 26, select one to observe. In a paragraph or two, capture in words its most memorable features. Does the photograph have any center that draws your attention? What main impression or insight does that picture convey to you? See if you can put a sense of the picture into the mind of a reader who hasn't seen it at all. What do you see that your classmates missed? What do they see that you missed?

FOR GROUP LEARNING

Reading Your Writing Aloud

Instead of soliciting written comments about your work, try reading aloud to your group the draft you have written for an assignment in this chapter. Prepare your reading beforehand, and try to deliver it with some feeling. Ask others to stop you when something isn't clear. Have pencil in hand to mark any such problem. After you've finished reading aloud, ask for reactions. If these are slow in coming, ask your listeners any of the questions in the peer response checklist on page 46. Have your group's secretary record the most vital suggestions and reactions that your draft provokes.

Applying What You Learn:
Some Uses of Writing from Observation

Many college courses designed to prepare students for a professional career involve field trips. In such courses, you are often expected to observe closely and later to write your observations in a report. A sociology or a prelaw class might visit a city police court to hear the judge trying spouse abusers, drug pushers, and streetwalkers. Criminology or anatomy students might observe an autopsy. A journalism class might visit the newsroom of a daily newspaper to see how journalists work at deadline. History students can share their first-hand impressions of a nearby historic site. A class in early childhood education might visit a day-care center to observe and write about children's behavior. After a visit to the coastal wetlands, biology students may be asked to describe the various forms of marine life they have observed. For a language development course, students might be asked to report on the way in which a particular child communicates.

Practitioners in the helping professions often write case studies, sometimes for publication, sometimes for reference. Here, in *A Career in Speech Pathology* (1979), C. Van Riper describes his initial observations of three severely deprived rural children in need of treatment.

> As I watched through the screen I saw the three children huddled in a corner like kittens in a cold barn, silent and not moving for almost five minutes. Then the oldest one separated from the tangle and tiptoed all around the edge of the room, listening and watching. Then he motioned the other two to come with him to the door which he found was locked. Then he spied a little blue truck which had been placed under the table (with a ball and other toys), made a dive for it, and suddenly the room was full of wild animals, fighting, snarling, making animal noises of every kind, barking, mewing, shrieking. I knocked on the door and they fled again to huddle in the corner, human again but silently frozen with terror. I sat down in a chair and played with the truck and talked to myself about what I was doing, occasionally giving them a slow smile. I held out a piece of candy but none of them would reach for it. It was an eerie first session.

Much writing in scientific and technical courses involves observation. In a report for a chemistry or biology course, students might be asked to report their observations of a laboratory experiment, in zoology to observe and report on the behavior of animals. Here is a good illustration of scientific reporting from *Gorillas in the Mist*, written by Dian Fossey, a zoologist who for many years studied mountain gorillas in Rwanda, Africa.

> The body skin color of a newly born gorilla is usually pinkish gray and may have pink concentrations of color on the ears, palms, or soles. The infant's body hair varies in color from medium brown to black and is sparsely distributed except on the dorsal surfaces of the body. The head hair is often

jet black, short, and slick, and the face wizened, with a pronounced protrusion of the nasal region, giving a pig-snouted appearance. Like the nose, the ears are prominent, but the eyes are usually squinted or closed the first day following birth. The limbs are thin and spidery, and the digits typically remain tightly flexed when the baby's hands are not grasping the mother's abdominal hair. The extremities may exhibit a spastic type of involuntary thrusting movement, especially when searching for a nipple. Most of the time, however, a gorilla infant appears asleep.

Making Connections: Writing from Observation in A Writer's Reader

Observation is a major resource for writers, one that often goes hand in hand with *recall*. Authors in *A Writer's Reader* use observation for a variety of purposes. Essayist E. B. White in "Once More to the Lake" (p. 490) reports his carefully juxtaposed observations of a lake in Maine as it was when he visited it as a child and as it is when he returns as an adult. White uses observation to convey the feeling that there has been no passage of time — the place, the people, even the dragonfly seem to be the same. In "Year of the Blue-Collar Guy" (p. 570), construction worker Steve Olson uses observation not just to paint a vivid picture for his readers but to support his claim that we should give more credit to those who work hard at blue-collar jobs. He mixes details of the impressive feats of blue-collar guys with observations of other people's reactions to these men to help us see how we might need to change our own attitudes. Essayist Phyllis Rose, in "Shopping and Other Spiritual Adventures in America Today" (p. 610), takes a more light-hearted approach, using observations of people's shopping styles (including her own) to comment on the "spiritual" satisfaction Americans gain from consumerism. All of these writers, like Cynthia Ozick (p. 34) and Sandy Messina (p. 36), record their observations with fresh, authentic details and also use observation as a method for developing a larger message.

Other writers in various fields who use observation as a resource include novelist Amy Tan, "Mother Tongue" (p. 496); writer and professor Scott Russell Sanders, "The Men We Carry in Our Minds" (p. 531); poet and essayist Stephen Dunn, "Locker Room Talk" (p. 545); and editor and essayist Richard Rodriguez, "Does America Still Exist?" (p. 583). As you read these essays, consider the role that observation plays in them. For each essay, answer the following questions:

1. Specifically, what does the author observe? People? Behavior? Nature? Things?
2. What senses does he or she rely on and appeal to? What sensory images does this author develop? Is this effective, given the subject being

observed? Find some striking passages in which the author reports his or her observations. What makes these passages memorable to you?

3. Why does the author use observation? How would the essay be weakened without the reported observations?

4. What conclusion does the author draw from reflecting on his or her observations?

Chapter 3

Writing from Conversation

Don't know what to write about? Go talk with someone. When you exchange facts, thoughts, and feelings with people, you both give and receive. Not only do you find out things from others that you didn't know, but you have a chance to shape and define your own ideas in words. Listen closely to an hour's discussion between students and an anthropology professor, and you may get material for a paper. Just as likely, you can get a paper's worth of information from a five-minute exchange with a mechanic who relines brakes. Both the mechanic and the professor are experts. But even people who aren't usually considered experts may provide you with material.

As this chapter suggests, you can direct a conversation by asking questions to elicit what you want to find out. You do so in that special kind of conversation called the *interview*. An interview is a conversation with a purpose — usually to help you understand the other person or to find out what the other person knows.

Learning from Other Writers

Here are two essays whose writers talked to someone and reported their conversations. The first is by Melina Gerosa, the entertainment editor for *Ladies' Home Journal*. It is based on an interview with movie star Jodie Foster, but Gerosa adds her own observations and conclusions to enrich her conversation with Foster.

Betsy Buffo, a student at St. Petersburg Junior College, wrote the second essay in response to an assignment asking her to interview and report on someone representing a segment of society with which she was unfamiliar but found interesting. Buffo was originally apprehensive about interviewing a stranger but "was surprised to find it a pleasant experience" and pleased at her own success in capturing her subject's personality and conveying his "intensity of purpose."

Some things you might not know about Jodie Foster: Her toenails are always painted fire-engine red. She goes to the movies to cry. She still writes letters to her first love. And she doesn't always know where she's going.

In fact, right now, Jodie Foster is lost. A four-letter word sails from her lips like a dart, a rare blush spreads across her cheekbones, and the actress most noted for her calm and cool jerks her station wagon into reverse. A pair of little red boxing gloves swings mockingly from the rearview mirror as Foster backs away from the dead end that has taken her totally by surprise.

All this, and we haven't even left the parking garage.

That Foster has lost her way so easily is surprising, considering that she has a reputation for knowing exactly where she's going, both in the car and in her career. At thirty-two, she's arguably the most, well, driven and focused actress in Hollywood, and her penchant for being in control is no more evident than how she handles interviews. There are some things she doesn't want to talk about. One subject that is automatically off-limits: John Hinckley Jr. (the warped fan who became obsessed with the actress's performance in *Taxi Driver* and tried to assassinate President Reagan in 1981 to impress her). And she will *not* discuss her much-speculated-about lovelife. But the real secret about Jodie Foster is that beneath that icy exterior lurks a surprisingly vulnerable soul, at once uncertain and romantic.

After a few more false turns, Foster finally escapes the garage and heads toward Los Angeles's Hancock Park, where she wants to spend this morning driving around looking at the houses. Perhaps the preoccupation with homes has to do with the fact that Foster is currently homeless. Sort of, anyway. She owns a house in the San Fernando Valley, but since it's too far from her production company, she wound up moving into a hotel.

Foster isn't house hunting; cruising around the quiet streets is like a nostalgic trip to the childhood she never had. With its manicured lawns and family homes, the area is everything that the more bohemian section where Foster grew up, in Hollywood, isn't. As a kid, she used to be dropped off in Hancock Park to trick-or-treat on Halloween; her mother also pretended that the family lived there so that Foster, from the age of nine to eleven, could attend cotillion, the stuffy dancing and manners school tradition where she was taught decorum and the fox-trot.

"Now every time I go to one of those Oscar things, I'm the first one on the dance floor, because it's the only time I get to use my incredible ballroom-dancing skills," says Foster, looking surprisingly kidlike in red jeans, a black top, and wire-rimmed glasses, her hair wet from her shower.

When she speaks about her mother, her tone is a mixture of humor, respect, and affection. It's clear that Brandy Foster gave her daughter a lot more than dance lessons: She gave Jodie a strong heart, an independent spirit, and a firm belief in her own talent. "When you think about what in your parenting has allowed you to achieve excellence, if winning an Oscar is about excellence," says Foster, "it's not her telling me to wear my raincoat. It was the side of her that encouraged me to *fly*. And that told me to not hesitate."

A single mom of four children, Brandy Foster did this without the help 9 of her husband, an air force pilot, who left home before Jodie was born. And Brandy started the encouragement early. At three years old, Jodie bared her bottom as the Coppertone girl, and a star was born. Thanks to Brandy's shrewd management, Jodie was able to land enough movie parts to support her entire family over the years, literally growing up before the public's eyes.

Yet once she was old enough to choose her own roles, Foster had to make 10 some awkward decisions about her mom. And judging by how difficult mother-daughter relationships can be under normal, everyday circumstances, this transition of Brandy from business partner to mom must have been tricky. "I always get really careful around this line of questioning because she reads these things and the inference is, 'Yeah, when she was sixteen, she didn't need her ever again.' And that's not true," says Foster, a protective edge to her voice. "She has a different capacity now in my life. There was a time when I only wanted her in the professional and I didn't want her in the personal, and now it's just the opposite."

Foster hasn't hesitated to make other tough decisions as well. "I've walked 11 away from enormous amounts of money when no one would walk away from that. I went to college when, if I wanted to have a career, it was the stupidest thing I could have done," says Foster of her stint at Yale. "I directed [*Little Man Tate*] right when I was about to win an Academy Award, when in terms of earning power as an actress you'll never be as high." Since then she's continued to forge into uncharted terrain; *Sommersby* was her first romantic lead, *Maverick* her first comedic turn, and later this year Foster will direct Holly Hunter in the drama *Home for the Holidays.*

But *Nell*, the first offspring hatched from her company, Egg Pictures, is her 12 riskiest role to date. In the drama, released nationwide in January, Foster plays a woman raised in the Appalachian Mountains, completely isolated from society. The actress wails, dances, and speaks an indecipherable language with such passion that she is literally unrecognizable. She is playing a part that's a 180-degree turn away from the steely characters she brought to life in *The Accused* and *The Silence of the Lambs*. "It's as bold as anyone's ever been on film," says *Nell*'s director, Michael Apted. "It's one of those performances that if you don't get it right, it's laughable. . . . And she managed to give a great performance without your ever realizing that it's Jodie Foster. She doesn't implant her fingerprints all over it."

Renée Missel, who coproduced *Nell* with Foster, admits it was a stretch to 13 cast the actress even though she is a two-time Oscar winner. "Most agents saw someone more vulnerable [in the role]," says Missel. "But I've always seen Jodie's pain in all of her films, the vulnerability in her eyes, and I thought, If that could just come to the forefront."

The thought of getting that emotion to the forefront made *Nell* the most 14 terrifying role Foster has ever undertaken.

"I was scared to death because I play people that have four different lay-   15
ers, and she doesn't have any," she says. "She doesn't have any protection." For
Foster, who's used to hiding behind a coolly cerebral mask both on-screen
and off, to show what is in her heart would make her feel psychologically
nude.

Yet taking calculated chances has paid off. Considering her A-list status as   16
an actress and her clout as a producer, Foster may be the most powerful thir-
tysomething woman in Hollywood. But that only exacerbates the pressure to
reach all her goals while she's still hot. "I have a very short burst of time to be
as effective as possible," Foster says. "This is a 'What was your last gig?' industry, and I'm sure at some point I'm going to have a movie that's a complete
bomb."

So far, the buzz on *Nell* is more Best Actress than bomb, and with that, of   17
course, comes another sort of pressure. Does she think she will get nominated? "I try not to think about it because I don't want to get too weirded out,"
says Foster. "[The pressure isn't] necessarily coming from everyone else, it's really coming from me. But I thrive on that, because I don't let the ball drop."

But no one, not even Foster, can stay cool and focused all the time, so she   18
unwinds by going to the movies — not as a professional but as an unabashed
fan. "I go to cry," Foster says simply. She's seen both *The Piano* (a romantic
melodrama) and *Fearless* (a story of recovery from tragedy) four times for this
very reason.

Movies aren't the only thing that moves Foster to tears. "Every time I see   19
men and women ballroom dancing, I start weeping uncontrollably," she says.
"It's romantic, and it's about opposites and celebrating the difference."

As we drive around looking at moldings and architectural detail in Han-   20
cock Park, Foster suddenly blurts, "I *love* this song!," turns up her tape deck
and hums along with Chrissie Hynde's pop love ballad "I'll Stand by You."
When the song ends, her hand immediately hits the rewind button. "I want
to hear my *favorite* song, on my *favorite* street, in front of my *favorite* house,"
says Foster, with all the enthusiasm of a teenage girl. As we pull up to a stone
Tudor, her thin lips stretch into a smile. "It looks like it has a great mahogany
library with a big green leather chair," Foster says. She cranes her neck to get
a better view. "It looks *warm*."

The actress's ability to fantasize about romantic ideals stretches far be-   21
yond Hancock Park: She wears the male cologne Vetiver — a memento, she
says, of a long-ago love. "My first boyfriend wore it when I was fifteen," she
says, breaking her own cardinal rule never to talk about her private life. "He
was French and in the military service when I met him at a New Year's Eve
party in Tahiti. I always wonder what happened to him. Every once in a while
I send a letter to his parents [to forward to him], and I look him up in the
French phone book," says Foster. She admits, sheepishly, that she doesn't
know if he gets the letters. "It's a funny thing; it's been so many years since I
knew him, but I can still remember absolutely every way that he smiled."

But when asked if she is dating anyone these days, her sentimental mood   22
evaporates almost instantly. "You have to ask it," she says with a forced laugh,

"and I get to answer that it's none of your business." In any case, her romanticism does not include children. "There is nothing that annoys me more than all of my friends who are over forty who desperately want to have children by fifty because basically they want someone to love them," she says. "It's too desperate. If I have kids, I have them. If I don't, I don't." Once she's settled in a new home in Los Angeles, she says she would like to get a dog— "a big slobbery one."

In the meantime, the actress feels as if she's still growing up herself, and as we drive around the streets where she used to trick-or-treat, she sums up where she is right now. "You hit a certain age, and then you realize that you're intent on changing; I've gotten more fragile as I've gotten older. I thought it would be the opposite; I thought I'd get stronger. It has completely changed the course of my relationships because I can't be in friendships with people who are antagonistic—Oh, *damn*," says Foster. Once again, she realizes she's lost her way—except this time, we're on the freeway.   23

As Foster tries to find the right exit, she keeps talking. "I finally realized that I didn't have to act like I knew everything, and like everything was okay. It was a revelation because people didn't recoil in horror—by giving them a little bit of power, it helped me out. And I didn't get as hateful and crazy. It's an interesting change, especially with my family. We're starting to have a different relationship, with my mom especially. Parents don't realize what they're talking about any more than you do. So why do you keep getting mad at them?"   24

Given this newly tolerant perspective, it's not surprising that Foster is able to acknowledge her own shortcomings, like the fact that once again she has managed to get herself lost. So, after several trips up and down a stretch of road, Foster admits defeat, picks up her car phone, and calls for directions. Lo and behold, it turns out that she was right smack where she was supposed to be. It's just a little hard to see the address from behind the black tinted windows that shield her from the rest of the world.   25

Questions to Start You Thinking

Meaning

1. What does the title of this essay— "Jodie Loses Her Cool"—mean?
2. What is the thesis of Gerosa's article?
3. How has Jodie Foster's relationship with her mother changed?
4. After reading this article, how would you describe Jodie Foster's personality? What did you learn about Foster that is surprising?

Writing Strategies

5. Gerosa frames the information from her interview with Jodie Foster in a narrative of driving around Los Angeles with Foster. Why does she do this instead of setting up the information in a question-and-answer format?
6. From evidence in the essay, what proportion of the conversation with Foster would you say the author has included? Why did she select the details she included? For what reasons do you think she omitted the rest?
7. What information did Gerosa use that did not come from the conversation with Foster?

Betsy Buffo   Interview with an Artist

The Ovo Café in the heart of Ybor City seems like the   1
perfect place to interview an avant-garde artist, but the
nouvelle cuisine holds no interest for painter Derek Washington. He wants nothing but coffee. He tells me that this is
the fuel that powers his creative activities. Often he will
exist on gallons of it, and little else, while involved in
his artistic endeavors.

It's obvious that I've caught him at one of those times.   2
Although he answers my questions patiently and politely, his
thoughts are elsewhere. His dark eyes look through me occasionally, and my guess is that he's concentrating on the unfinished project that I called him away from. His lean body
vibrates with tension, and his fingers search aimlessly on the
tabletop when he's not holding his cup.

If my eager questions seem inane to him, he doesn't show   3
it. His answers are articulate, delivered in a soft, almost
shy voice that belies the anger that screams from his vibrant
canvases. His paintings are large, caustic, often filled with
images of pornography or racism meant to shock and disturb.
He hopes to make a change with his work by portraying the
anxiety and frustration of an African American male in
today's society.

"I want my work to make a difference," he says, stran-   4
gling his coffee cup, "but I get so discouraged sometimes
that I think I want to quit. I don't know if I'll ever be
able to make people see, but I guess I really can't stop trying."

Experiencing his intensity, I'm surprised to learn that   5
Derek has been painting seriously for only about five years.
A casual interest in art became much more when he was laid up
at home with back problems for six months. "I thought it
would be a good way to pass the time." He smiles and shrugs.
"Instead it's become my life's passion."

Now he lives with his mother to save money, his bedroom   6
turned into a makeshift studio. The income from part-time

work and from the sale of his paintings is used for only one thing--paint. "When I have paint, I work every day; when I don't have it, I'm trying to find ways to get it," he confides.

Financial necessity created a unique style that has become Derek's hallmark. He rarely works on conventional canvas but uses a wide array of material--cardboard boxes carefully opened flat, old pieces of sail, yards of burlap, old wooden boards nailed together, whatever comes to hand. Besides his precious paint, these found canvases are filled with more found objects--magazine cutouts, plastic dolls or other knickknacks, rope, cloth, paper. His medium is anything that meets his needs.   7

When he began his new career, about fifty percent of his work had a social message, but the rest was more conventional fare, still lifes and such. These were never for public consumption but were simply completed for perfection of technique and individual style. Now this type of painting makes only an occasional appearance among the brash and blatant pieces that he exhibits.   8

Derek is straightforward when asked about how his work is received in the local community: "My work is outside the mainstream. Because it's controversial, it's not easy for me to get exposure. I've had favorable reviews from the newspaper critics, but this area doesn't have much to offer me as an artist. I have an abrasive personality, and I'm much too outspoken. My contemporaries respect my work, but the avant-garde artists are white, and we have nothing in common socially, while local black artists are not interested in the avant-garde and so we have nothing in common artistically. Most of the people who can afford to collect art are the very ones that I castigate in my paintings, so there's not much of a market for me here."   9

He is considering several options for his future, all of them designed to take him far away. Since he is finishing his last class at the University of South Florida, he's investigating several scholarships or grants that could enable him to work in New York City or perhaps even in Europe.   10

Presently Derek is engrossed in preparations for the opening of his first St. Petersburg exhibition, which will   11 be held in the middle of July. Prior to this show, his work was always exhibited in Tampa, most often in Ybor City. St. Pete is not known for an appreciation of experimental or controversial artists, so it will be interesting to see the outcome. Whatever it may be, it's clear that Derek Washington will not be content. He's after something more, a chance to make a statement that will affect as many people as possible. He still intends to make a difference.

Questions to Start You Thinking

Meaning

1. What is the main point of this essay?

2. Summarize what you think the artist's words reveal about his values, his goals, and his outlook on life.

3. What is the writer's attitude toward the artist? How do you know?

Writing Strategies

4. How does Buffo interweave description of Derek Washington with information and quotations from her interview with him? What is the effect of this integration of description and dialogue?

5. What specific details of his appearance and his gestures help you to understand the artist? Does Buffo provide sufficient detail to characterize Washington clearly?

6. Besides conversing, which resources (recalling, observing, imagining) does Buffo draw on?

7. Why does Buffo organize the information on Derek Washington as she does? Is the order of ideas easy to follow? Could any of the parts be put in a different location?

8. If you were Buffo's peer editor, what suggestions would you give her to strengthen the essay?

Learning by Writing

THE ASSIGNMENT: INTERVIEWING

Write a paper about someone who interests you and base the paper primarily on a conversation with that person. Write about any acquaintance, friend, relative, or someone you have heard about, whose traits, interests, activities, background, or outlook on life you think will interest your readers. Your purpose is to show as thoroughly as you can this person's character and personality as revealed through his or her conversation — in other words, to bring your subject alive for your readers.

Among student papers we have read that grew out of a similar assignment were the following:

A man wrote about a high school science teacher who had quit teaching for a higher-paying job in the computer industry, only to return three years later to the classroom.

A man wrote about an acquaintance who had embraced the hippie lifestyle in the 1960s by "dropping out" of mainstream society.

A woman recorded the thoughts and feelings of a discouraged farmer she had known since childhood.

A man learned about adjustment to life in a new country by talking to a neighbor from Vietnam.

If you would prefer not to write about a person but rather would like to interview someone for information *about* something, see "Other Assignments" (p. 69).

GENERATING IDEAS

Brainstorm for possible subjects. It may be that the minute you read the assignment, an image of the perfect subject flashed into your mind. If that's the case, consider yourself lucky, and set up an appointment with that person at once. If, however, you drew a blank at first, you'll need to spend a little time casting about for a likely interview subject. Try brainstorming for a few minutes, seeing what pops into your mind. (For more advice about brainstorming, see p. 360.) As you begin examining the possibilities, you may find it helpful to consider the following questions:

DISCOVERY CHECKLIST

Finding an Interview Subject

- Of the people you know, whom do you most enjoy talking with?
- Are you acquainted with anyone whose life has been unusually eventful, stressful, or successful? It does not have to be a spectacular or unusual person. Ordinary lives can make fascinating reading.
- Are you curious about why someone you know made a certain decision or how he or she got to the point in life where he or she is now?
- Is there an expert or leader whom you admire or are puzzled by?
- Do you know someone with a job or a hobby that interests you?
- Do you know a younger person or an older person who has values and attitudes different from yours?
- Do you know an older person who can tell you what life was like thirty or even fifty years ago?
- Among the people you know, who has passionate convictions about society, politics, sex, or childrearing? A likely person may be someone actively engaged in a cause.

- Is there anyone whose background and life history you would like to know more about?
- Do you know someone whose lifestyle is utterly different from your own and from that of most people you know?
- Do you have an older relative who can tell you about your family and his or her relationship to other members of the family?

Set up your interview. First find out whether your prospective source will grant you an interview. Make sure that the person can talk with you at some length — an hour, say. Make sure, too, that the person has no objections to appearing in your paper. If you sense any reluctance on the person's part, probably your wisest course is to find another subject.

Don't be timid about asking for an interview. When you interview a subject, you acknowledge that person as someone with valuable things to say. Most people will be flattered by your interest in them.

Try to schedule the interview on your subject's own ground — his or her home or workplace. As you can see in Buffo's essay, an interviewer can learn a great deal from the physical surroundings of an individual, and the interview becomes more realistic and the essay more vivid because of the details the writer can observe and include.

Prepare questions. The interview will go better if you have prepared some questions to ask. Give these careful thought. What kinds of questions will encourage your subject to open up? Questions about the person's background, everyday tasks, favorite leisure-time activities, hopes, and aspirations are likely to bring forth answers that you'll want to record. Sometimes a question that asks your subject to do a little imagining will elicit a revealing response. (If your house were on fire, what are the first objects you'd try to save from the flames? If you were stranded on a desert island, what books would you like to have with you? If you had your life to live over, what would you do differently?)

You can't find out everything there is to know about the person you're interviewing, but you should focus on whatever aspect of that person's life you think will best reveal his or her personality. Good questions will enable you to lead the conversation where you want it to go and get it back on track when it strays too far. Such questions will also help you avoid awkward silences. Here are some of the questions Betsy Buffo scribbled down before going to see Derek Washington, a man with whom she had only a slight acquaintance:

How long have you been painting?

How did you get involved in painting?

Has your involvement/commitment to painting changed your life in any way? Has it changed where you live? How you live? What you do?

What do you hope to do in your art?

What does success mean to you? Have you had a lot of success?

What are your plans for the future?

Probably Buffo didn't have to use all those questions. One good question can get some people talking for hours. Some experts insist that four or five are enough to bring to any interview, but we believe it's better to err on the side of too many than too few. If, as you're actually talking with your subject, some of your questions strike you as no longer relevant, you can easily skip them. Some of Buffo's questions would have elicited very brief answers. Others — like "How did you get involved in painting?" — clearly inspired Washington to respond with enthusiasm.

Be flexible and observant. If the discussion is moving in a worthwhile direction, don't be a slave to your questions. Betsy Buffo was willing to let the conversation stray down interesting byways. Sometimes the question that takes the interview in its most rewarding direction is the one the interviewer didn't write down in advance but that simply grew out of something the subject said. Buffo allowed Washington to answer some questions she hadn't even asked, and she really *listened* to what he was saying. Melina Gerosa in the account of her conversation with Jodie Foster demonstrates both the same flexibility and the same genuine interest in her subject. Of course, if the conversation heads toward a dead end, you can always steer it back: "But to get back to what you were saying about . . . ."

During the interviews, both Gerosa and Buffo do something else that will later add vividness to their characterization: they use their eyes as well as their ears. Buffo observes what's in the café — food, coffee — and the way the artist looks while they are talking. When you conduct your interview, try to notice and ask about distinctive items in the subject's environment. Your interest may encourage your subject to reveal unexpected facets of his or her personality. Gerosa reports Foster's physical appearance: her toenails are "painted fire-engine red" (paragraph 1); "her thin lips stretch into a smile" (paragraph 20); she is "surprisingly kidlike in red jeans, a black top, and wire-rimmed glasses, her hair wet from her shower" (paragraph 7). From her observations, she also indicates Foster's emotional reactions: "the enthusiasm of a teenage girl" (paragraph 20); "her sentimental mood evaporates almost instantly" (paragraph 22). (For more on using the resource of observation, see Chapter 2.)

Sometimes a question won't interest your subject as much as you'd hoped it would. Or the person may seem reluctant to answer, especially if you're unwittingly trespassing into private territory, such as Foster's love life or John Hinckley, Jr. Don't badger. If you have the confidence to wait silently for a bit, you might be rewarded. But if the silence persists, just go on to the next question.

Decide how to record the interview. Many interviewers approach their subjects with only paper and pen or pencil so that they can take notes unobtrusively as the interview proceeds. However, you won't be able to write down everything the person says as he or she is talking. It's more important to look your subject in the eye and keep the conversation lively than to scribble down everything the person says. But be sure to record on the scene whatever you

Facing the Challenge: Writing from Conversation

The major challenge writers face when they write from conversation is to find a clear focus for their paper. They must first sift through the enormous amount of information that can be generated in an interview and then come up with an organizing idea — an angle they wish to pursue in their essay. Then they must determine which observations and quotations gathered during their interview will best illustrate and support the main point they want to make about their interviewee.

Once you have completed an interview, distilling the material you have gathered into a focused, overall impression of your interviewee may seem to be an overwhelming task. As a writer, you have the responsibility to organize your material for your readers — by picking out the different angles, or possible themes, suggested by your notes and then determining which of these organizational options you will use. You cannot simply hand in a transcription of your interview notes as a first draft of your interview essay.

To pinpoint the different angles suggested by your interview notes, jot down answers to the following questions: What did you find most interesting about the interview? What topics did your interviewee talk about the most? What topics did he or she become most excited or animated about? What topics generated the most interesting quotes? The answers to these questions should help you to determine a focus for your paper — the aspect of your interviewee that you want to emphasize for your readers.

Once you have determined a focus, your challenge will be to pick the details and direct quotations from the interview that best illustrate the points you want to make about your subject. Merely recording a volley of questions and answers will not help you to make your points, and it is an uninteresting and uninventive way to present an interview. To engage your readers, you must include your own observations as well as actual quotations. Note how Melina Gerosa includes descriptions of Jodie Foster's actions and appearance that work to elucidate the actress's character. In her second paragraph, she tells us that "right now, Jodie Foster is lost. A four-letter word sails from her lips like a dart, a rare blush spreads across her cheekbones, and the actress most noted for her calm and cool jerks her station wagon into reverse." In addition to hooking the reader with this compelling detail, Gerosa uses her description of the incident to reinforce her overall point that Foster, though perceived to be "calm and cool" and directed in her life and her art, *can* lose her way. And she establishes this point without relying on direct quotations from her interview.

You can and should use direct quotations to make the subject of your interview come alive for your readers, but you should use them strategically and sparingly. Choose comments that reveal the aspects of your interviewee's character that you wish to emphasize, and choose colorful quotations that allow readers to "hear" the distinctive voice of your interviewee. Make sure that the quotations — long or short — are accurate. The combination of colorful quotations with narration captures the dynamic of conversation and makes an interview essay vivid for its readers.

want to remember in exact detail—names and dates, numbers, addresses, surroundings, physical appearance, whatever. If the person you're interviewing says anything that is so memorable that you want to record it exactly, take time to jot down the speaker's words just as he or she says them. Put quotation marks around them so that when you transcribe your notes later, you know that they are a direct quotation.

A telephone interview may sound like an easy way to work, but it is often less valuable than talking with the subject in person. You won't be able to duplicate by phone the lively interplay you can achieve in a face-to-face encounter. You'll be unable to observe the subject's possessions and environment, which so often reveal a person's personality, or see your subject's smiles, frowns, or other body language. Think of the important details that would be missing from Gerosa's article and from Buffo's paper if they had not met the individual in person. Meet with your subject if at all possible.

Many professionals advise against bringing a tape recorder to an interview because sometimes it inhibits the subject and makes the interviewer lazy about concentrating on the subject's responses. Too often, the objections go, it tempts the interviewer simply to quote the rambling conversation as it appears on the tape without shaping it into good writing. If you do bring a tape recorder to your interview, be sure that the person you're talking with has no objections. Arm yourself with a pad of paper and a pen or pencil just in case the recorder malfunctions or the tape runs out before the interview ends. And don't let your mind wander.

Perhaps the best practice is to tape-record the interview but at the same time take notes. Write down in your notes the main points of the conversation, and use your tape as a backup to check or expand an idea or quotation.

As soon as the interview ends, rush to the nearest available desk or table and write down everything you remember but were unable to record during the conversation. Do this while the conversation is still fresh in your mind. The questions you took with you into the interview will guide your memory, as will any notes you took while your subject talked.

PLANNING, DRAFTING, AND DEVELOPING

Now that you have gathered information on your subject, you are ready to start planning and writing your first draft. You probably have a good notion of what information to include, what to emphasize, what to quote directly, what to summarize. But if your notes seem a confused jumble, you may need to approach your first draft more slowly. What are you to do with the bales of material you have amassed during the interview? Inevitably, much of what you collected will be garbage, useless information. Should you have collected less? No, but as you plan, you have to identify what is most valuable and throw out the rest. How do you do this?

Evaluate your material. Remember that your purpose in this assignment is to show as thoroughly as possible your subject's character and personality as revealed through his or her conversation. Start by making a list of those details you're already pretty sure you want to include. To guide you as you sift and evaluate your material, you may find it useful to ask yourself a few questions.

What part of the conversation gave you the most insight into your subject's character and circumstances?

Which direct quotations that you wrote down reveal the most about your subject? Which are the most amusing, pithy, witty, surprising, or outrageous?

Which objects that you observed in the subject's environment provide you with valuable clues about his or her interests?

What, if anything, did your subject's body language reveal? Did it give evidence of discomfort, pride, self-confidence, shyness, pomposity?

Did the tone of voice or gestures of the person tell you anything about his or her state of mind?

How can you summarize your subject's personality?

Is there one theme that runs through the material you have written down? If so, what is it?

If you have a great deal of material and if, as often happens, your subject's conversation tended to ramble, you may want to emphasize just one or two things about him or her—a personality trait, the person's views on one particular topic, the influences that shaped the views he or she holds today. If such a focus is not immediately evident, try grouping your details to help you discover a focus. (For more on grouping ideas, see Chapter 16.)

Focus on a dominant impression. Most successful portraits focus on a single dominant impression of the interview subject. If you had to characterize your subject in a single sentence, how would you describe him or her? Betsy Buffo's main impression of Derek Washington is that he's an idealistic, ambitious

---

FOR PEER RESPONSE

Interviewing

Share with a classmate the questions you plan to use in your interview. Ask your classmate to respond to the following points about your questions:

- Are the questions appropriate for the person to be interviewed?
- Will the questions help the writer gather the information he or she is seeking?
- Are any of the questions unclear? How would you rephrase them?
- Do any of the questions seem redundant? Irrelevant?
- Is there anything you would add to these questions?

artist who's channeling his creative energies and financial resources in a sincere attempt to make a difference; everything in her paper supports this view, even though she never states it in so many words. See if you can find a single main impression that you want to convey about your subject. Then look through your material, and eliminate anything that doesn't contribute to this view.

Bring your subject alive. At the beginning of your paper, can you introduce the person you interviewed in a way that will frame him or her immediately in your reader's mind? A quotation, a bit of physical description, a portrait of your subject at home or at work can bring the person instantly to life.

From time to time you'll want to quote your subject directly. Be as accurate as possible, and don't put into quotation marks something your subject didn't say. Sometimes you may want to quote a whole sentence or more, sometimes just a phrase. Throughout Gerosa's article she moves gracefully back and forth between direct quotation and summing up.

In *Reporting*, a collection of interviews, noted reporter Lillian Ross suggests that when you quote directly the person you have interviewed, you work

---

 **FOR PEER RESPONSE**

If you find it hard to criticize your own work, ask a classmate or a friend to read your draft and suggest how to make the portrait more vivid, clear, and honest. See Chapter 20 for advice on working with other student writers and for general questions you should always ask a peer editor to address. For a paper in which you write from conversation, you'll also want your peer editor to answer these specific questions:

- What is the main insight or impression you carry away from this piece of writing?
- Look at the beginning of the essay. Did the writer make you want to get to know the person? If so, how? If not, what got in your way?
- What seems to make the person interviewed interesting to the writer? What do you understand to be the writer's dominant impression of or insight into the person?
- Does the writer tell you anything about the person that seems unconnected to his or her dominant impression or insight?
- Do the quoted words of the person interviewed "sound" real to you? Has the writer quoted anything that seems at odds with the general impression you now have of the person?
- Star the places where you have questions about the subject that aren't answered in the paper.
- Would you leave out any of the conversation the writer used? Underline anything you would omit.
- If this were your paper, what is the one thing you would be sure to work on before handing it in?

hard to "find the quotations that get to the truth of what that person is. That does not mean that you make up quotations. Somewhere along the line, in the time you spend with your subject, you will find the quotations that are significant—that reveal the character of the person, that present as close an approximation of the truth as you can achieve." Keep evaluating and selecting until you believe you have come close to that truth. (For more on selecting and using examples and details, see Chapter 18.)

Double-check important information. You may find yourself unable to read your hasty handwriting, or you may discover you need some crucial bit of information that somehow escaped you when you were taking notes. In such a case, telephone the person you interviewed to check out what you need to know. Have specific questions ready so that you will not take much of your subject's time. You may also want to read back to your subject any direct quotations you intend to use in your final paper, so that he or she can confirm their accuracy.

REVISING AND EDITING

Wait a few hours or a few days before you look again at your first draft. As you read it over, keep in mind that your purpose was to bring alive for your reader the person you interviewed. Your main task now is to make sure you have succeeded in this goal. Remember, too, that most successful papers of this kind focus on a single dominant impression and that readers will be interested in your observations and insights. This checklist may help you in reviewing your work.

REVISION CHECKLIST

- Should your paper have a stronger beginning? Is your ending satisfactory?
- Are some quotations better suited to summarizing or indirect quotation? Should some of what you summed up be given greater prominence by adding specific quotations?
- When the direct quotations are read out loud, do they sound as if they're coming out of the mouth of the person you're portraying?
- Have you included revealing details about the person's surroundings, personal appearance, or mannerisms?
- Have you put in a few of your own observations and insights?
- Are the details focused on a dominant impression you want to emphasize? Are all the details in your paper relevant to this impression?
- Do the parts of the conversation you've reported reveal the subject's personality, character, or mood? Is his or her individuality clear from the details you've selected?
- Have you included details that show what your subject cares most about?
- Does any of the material in your paper strike you now as irrelevant or uninteresting?
- Have you revealed a unique individual worth paying attention to?

If you find that your portrayal still lacks life and focus, you may want to skim over your interview notes or listen again to selected parts of your tape recording for material whose significance may not have struck you earlier. Do additional details now seem worth putting in after all? Do you need to do a little reading to expand on your comments? Is there anything you now wish you had asked your interview subject? It may not be too late to find new material and add it to your paper.

After you have revised your essay, proofread and edit it. Check carefully for problems with grammar, word choice, punctuation, and mechanics — and then correct any problems you find. A comprehensive reference handbook is an indispensable tool for this task; the "Quick Editing Guide" at the end of *The Bedford Guide for College Writers* (see the pages with the colored edges) will get you started.

When editing a paper written from conversation, pay particular attention to quotations. Make sure that all direct quotations are enclosed in quotation marks and that commas, periods, and other punctuation are used correctly with quotations. Be sure that where you have omitted words from a direct quotation, you have substituted an ellipsis mark (. . .) — three dots to show

WRITING WITH A COMPUTER

One problem with turning conversation into writing is that the results may not make easy reading. When people talk, their facial expressions, voice inflections, and gestures can lend interest and emphasis to their words. But sometimes the conversation of even a lively speaker, transcribed word for word, will sound dull and long-winded. And almost no one speaks in complete thoughts and sentences.

A word processor can help you counter this problem. If you used a tape recorder, transcribe the conversation (or a selected portion of it) word for word; if you took notes, transcribe the conversation as fully as you can. Then scroll through the results on your computer screen. Since you can delete with a couple of keystrokes, keeping the best material and cutting the rest will be easy. While working on-screen, you can readily replace any comment that seems rambling with a terse summary; remember to use quotation marks only around words and sentences that your interviewee actually said, not around your summaries or paraphrases. You may choose to revise this transcript into grammatically correct sentences (be careful not to change the words so much that you distort the meaning or tone), or if you are trying to capture more of the personal flavor of the conversation, you can leave it exactly as it sounds.

Now read the transcript, and ask yourself which parts stand out. Where does the interviewee's personality or tone shine through? Which quotations would be the most useful for supporting your overall message or point? Can you combine comments that came out at different times in the conversation but that seem to be on a common theme? Can you highlight troubling ideas by juxtaposing two conflicting statements? Once you've reworked the conversation itself, you can easily copy the best portions of it into your paper.

where omissions have occurred — and that the sentence containing the omission makes sense with the sentences that come before and after it. If you quote your subject quoting someone else (a quotation within a quotation), put your subject's words in quotation marks and the words he or she is quoting in single quotation marks. You should also take some time to scrutinize your pronouns; in writing done from interviews, the *he*'s and *she*'s can sometimes become vague and confusing.

Here are some questions to get you started when proofreading and editing your paper:

EDITING CHECKLIST

- Is it clear what each pronoun refers to? Does each pronoun agree with (match) its antecedent? (See A4 in the "Quick Editing Guide.")
- Have you used the correct case for all your pronouns (*he* versus *him*)? (See A3 in the "Quick Editing Guide.")
- Is your sentence structure correct? Have you avoided writing fragments and run-on sentences? (See A6 and A7 in the "Quick Editing Guide.")
- Have you spelled everything correctly? (See D2 in the "Quick Editing Guide.")
- Have you used the proper paper format, including special requirements for your instructor and course? (See D3 in the "Quick Editing Guide.")

FOR GROUP LEARNING

Conducting a Collective Interview

Let your whole class or just your writing group interview someone who has some special knowledge or who represents a walk of life that you want to learn more about. Public figures such as writers, who occasionally visit schools, are used to facing the questions of a whole class. Or perhaps someone on campus will be willing to be interviewed about a problem your group is interested in.

Before your subject arrives, let your group take time to plan the discussion: What do you want to find out? What questions or lines of questioning do you wish to pursue? What topic will each student ask about? We suggest that when the interviewee is present, each questioner be allowed (as far as time permits) to ask all of his or her main questions before yielding the floor to the next questioner. This way each person can pursue a complete line of thought. Preview each student's questions before the interview so that there will be no duplication. Later, students can write individual papers based on the group interview, showing what they have learned not only from their own questions but from everybody's.

An alternative plan is to collaborate on the paper, to produce one group-written paper. The group might appoint two members to act as reporters or recording secretaries and take notes. After the interview the group might meet to sift what you learned. The two reporters who took notes during the interview might show (or read aloud) their notes to the group to check the accuracy of both questions and answers. To parcel out the project fairly, designate two or three others to write what the group has learned.

OTHER ASSIGNMENTS

1. Interview someone from whom you think you can learn a lot, possibly someone in a career you are considering or someone who can help you solve a problem or make a decision. Your purpose in this paper will be to gather and communicate information, not to characterize the subject you interview.

2. Write a paper based on an interview with at least two members of your extended family about some incident that is part of your family lore. You may notice that different people's accounts of the same event don't always agree. If you can't reconcile them, combine them into one vivid account, noting that some details may be more trustworthy than others. Give credit to your sources. The paper that results might be worth saving for younger relatives.

3. Interview a mother or father about her or his reactions to a child's birth and how the child has changed the family's life.

4. After briefly questioning fifteen or twenty students on your campus to find out what careers they are preparing for, write a short essay summing up what you find out. What are their reasons for their choices? Are most students more intent on earning money than on other pursuits? How many are choosing lucrative careers because they have to pay back college loans? Provide some quotations to flesh out your survey. From the information you have gathered, characterize your classmates. Are they materialists? Idealists? Practical people?

5. Interview an older person in your family or neighborhood about what life was like when he or she was a child. Gather enough information to re-create in an essay that person's past world.

Applying What You Learn: Some Uses of Writing from Conversation

Interviewing is a familiar tool for many writers in the world beyond college. Biographers who write about someone living often conduct extensive interviews with their subject to guarantee accuracy. Usually they interview friends, relatives, and other associates to round out their picture of the person. Likewise, news reporters and commentators often rely on interviews with "informed sources" to give their readers the complete story. Another familiar kind of interview is that in which an author, actor, or political figure airs his or her views on a variety of subjects. Such interviews are written by people who have talked with their subjects, usually face to face. James Dickey, the poet and novelist, has even published self-interviews to present his opinions.

Often in college writing you find yourself interviewing people not because you are interested in their personalities but because they can contribute valuable insights to what you are studying. Students of human development often interview people at various stages of the life cycle. They talk to men and women about the transition from student life to the working world, to mothers about the experience of giving birth, to older people about widowhood or retirement. In recent years historians, acknowledging that "ordinary" people matter, have shown increasing interest in gathering and publishing oral histories and in uncovering those from the past. One such collection that throws vivid light on the civil rights movement is Howell Raines's *My Soul Is Rested* (New York: Putnam, 1977). In the following excerpt the author records the words of Franklin McCain, who participated in the now famous sit-in at Woolworth's in Greensboro, North Carolina, on February 1, 1960:

> Once getting there . . . we did make purchases of school supplies and took the patience and time to get receipts for our purchases, and Joseph and myself went over to the counter and asked to be served coffee and doughnuts. As anticipated, the reply was, "I'm sorry, we don't serve you here." And of course we said, "We just beg to disagree with you. We've in fact already been served; you've served us already and that's just not quite true. . . . We wonder why you'd invite us in to serve us at one counter and deny service at another. If this is a private club or private concern, then we believe you ought to sell membership cards and sell only to persons who have a membership card. If we don't have a card, then we'd know pretty well that we shouldn't come in or even attempt to come in." That didn't go over too well. . . . And the only thing that an individual in her case or position could do is, of course, call the manager. [Laughs].

In professional scholarly research, dozens of interviews may be necessary. The five sociologists who wrote the much-acclaimed *Habits of the Heart: Individualism and Commitment in American Life* (Berkeley: U of California P, 1985) used as their sources not only books and periodicals but also extensive interviews with both ordinary citizens and professionals in various fields. Note how this example from a chapter written by Ann Swidler enlivens its discussion with pointed, informative quotations that read like spoken words:

> Asked why she went into therapy, a woman summed up the themes that recur again and again in accounts by therapists and their clients: "I was not able to form close relationships to people, I didn't like myself, I didn't love myself, I didn't love other people." In the therapeutic ideology, such incapacities are in turn related to a failure fully to accept, fully to love, one's self.
>
> As the therapist Margaret Oldham puts it, many of the professionally trained, upper-middle-class young adults who come to her, depressed and lonely, are seeking "that big relationship in the sky — the perfect person." They want "that one person who is going to stop making them feel alone." But this search for a perfect relationship cannot succeed because it comes from a self that is not full and self-sustaining. The desire for relatedness is really a reflection of incompleteness, of one's own dependent needs.

Making Connections: Writing from Conversation in A Writer's Reader

Conversation is a resource used in nonfiction to make an essay realistic and interesting, much the way dialogue is used in fiction. Writers may use conversation as a springboard for their reflections on an idea or may report conversation within the essay to support a point. For example, in "Mother Tongue" (p. 496), novelist Amy Tan uses direct and indirect quotation to show us the contrast between the standard English she learned in school and the expressive, but less accepted, English spoken by her Chinese American mother. Her use of quotation enlivens her analysis of the role these two Englishes have played in her own life and work. In "The Men We Carry in Our Minds" (p. 531), Scott Russell Sanders, a writer and professor, uses conversation to add a ring of truth to his arguments. In his essay's introduction, he uses direct conversation, but in other parts of the essay he uses indirect quotations, summarizing what he has learned from talking with other people. This technique is appropriate to his background as a literature professor.

Just as Sanders, Tan, Melina Gerosa (p. 52), and Betsy Buffo (p. 56) use conversation as a resource for writing, so do professor of African American studies Gerald Early in "Black like . . . Shirley Temple?" (p. 502); social commentator Marion Winik in "Visiting Steven" (p. 511); reporter Matthew Futterman in "The Gender Gap" (p. 547); and freelance writer Meghan Daum in "Virtual Love" (p. 623). As you read these essays, consider the role that conversation plays in them. For each essay, answer the following questions:

1. Does the writer report conversation directly or indirectly?
2. Were the reported conversations the result of recall of informal discussions or of planned interviews?
3. What do the conversations show about the personality of the individual speaking? About the author/listener?
4. Why do you think the writer draws on conversation as a resource for writing?

Chapter 4

Writing from Imagination

"Imagination," said Albert Einstein, "is more important than knowledge." Coming from a theoretical physicist who widened our knowledge of the universe, the remark is striking. Although "imaginative writing" usually suggests stories, poems, or plays, storytellers, poets, and playwrights have no monopoly on imagination. Scientists and economists, historians and businesspeople need imagination just as much. The astronomer Copernicus *imagined* the earth revolving around the sun; he didn't see and report it. Economist John Maynard Keynes imagined the theory of aggregate demand before he set about proving it, and engineer and architect Buckminster Fuller conceived the geodesic dome before he could build one. Freud never saw the id; he imagined it. Anyone who comes up with a theory to explain a strange event or a hypothesis to account for a mysterious phenomenon uses imagination. College students will do well to call on the resource of imagination to strengthen and enliven their writing.

In one familiar sense of the word, imagining is nothing but daydreaming — imagining yourself wafted from a cold and rainy city street to a sunny beach in the tropics. Enlarging that definition a little, the *Shorter Oxford Dictionary* calls imagination "forming a mental concept of what is not actually present to the senses."

That definition is all right as far as it goes, but imagination is a far greater resource. According to mathematician Jacob Bronowski, "*To imagine* means to make images and to move them about inside one's head in new arrangements. When you and I recall the past, we imagine it in this direct and homely sense. . . . With the same symbolic vocabulary we spell out the future — not one but many futures, which we weigh one against another." He added that imagination and reason work together, beginning in childhood.

When a child begins to play games with things that stand for other things, with chairs or chessmen, he enters the gateway to reason and imagination together. For the human reason discovers new relations between things not by deduction, but by that unpredictable blend of speculation and insight that scientists call induction, which — like other forms of imagination — cannot be formalized.

In the view of Samuel Taylor Coleridge, imagination is nothing less than a "magical power" that can reveal in familiar objects "novelty and freshness." Sometimes it brings new things into existence by combining old things that already exist. Instead of creating out of thin air, imaginative writers often build from materials they find at hand. Lewis Carroll, whose Alice books seem remote from actual life, drew the stuff of his fantastic adventures from his friendship with a real child and some of his fantastic characters from real persons in England.

Yet, as many writers have testified, imagining is often playful — a fruitful kind of fooling around. Ursula K. Le Guin, writer of science fiction, calls imagination "the free play of the mind." In her essay "Why Are Americans Afraid of Dragons?" she explains:

> By "free" I mean that the action is done without an immediate object of profit — spontaneously. That does not mean, however, that there may not be a purpose behind the free play of the mind, a goal; and the goal may be a very serious object indeed. Children's imaginative play is clearly a practicing at the acts and emotions of adulthood; a child who did not play would not become mature. As for the free play of an adult mind, its result may be *War and Peace,* or the theory of relativity.

Though the result of the free play of your imagination may not be Leo Tolstoy's classic novel or Einstein's theory, you will find that such free play with language and ideas can be valuable and productive — and fun besides.

Learning from Other Writers

To be a whole writer and a whole human being, each of us needs both a logical, analytical mind and what Shakespeare called "the mind's eye" — the faculty of imagining. In this chapter, we don't presume to tell you how to imagine. We only suggest how you may use your imagination. Here are two examples of imaginative writing, the first by a professional writer and the second by a student.

Rachel Carson was a scientist who through observation and research became concerned about the environment. In 1962 she wrote *Silent Spring,* a deeply moving indictment of chemical pesticides in which she set forth the position that pesticides, especially DDT, were destroying the reproductive systems of birds, wildlife, and wild vegetation and would lead to a "silent spring." This work raised the public consciousness and prompted the federal government to limit the use of pesticides. In "A Fable for Tomorrow," the introduction to this important work, Carson combines imagination and reason, imaginative fiction and scientific exposition.

The student essay "Put Me Out of My Misery, Shoot Me!" was written by Ron A. Larsen at the University of Nebraska. The assignment was to write a persuasive essay about a current problem of significance to the writer. Larsen wanted to explore the issue of euthanasia, or mercy killing. He used his imagination to write an essay from the point of view of an elderly, terminally ill patient to convince his readers that allowing such a patient to die could be an act of compassion.

Rachel Carson   A Fable for Tomorrow

There was once a town in the heart of America where all life seemed to live in harmony with its surroundings. The town lay in the midst of a checkerboard of prosperous farms, with fields of grain and hillsides of orchards where, in spring, white clouds of bloom drifted above the green fields. In autumn, oak and maple and birch set up a blaze of color that flamed and flickered across a backdrop of pines. Then foxes barked in the hills and deer silently crossed the fields, half hidden in the mists of the fall mornings.

Along the roads, laurel, viburnum and alder, great ferns and wildflowers delighted the traveler's eye through much of the year. Even in winter the roadsides were places of beauty, where countless birds came to feed on the berries and on the seed heads of the dried weeds rising above the snow. The countryside was, in fact, famous for the abundance and variety of its bird life, and when the flood of migrants was pouring through in spring and fall people traveled from great distances to observe them. Others came to fish the streams, which flowed clear and cold out of the hills and contained shady pools where trout lay. So it had been from the days many years ago when the first settlers raised their houses, sank their wells, and built their barns.

Then a strange blight crept over the area and everything began to change. Some evil spell had settled on the community: mysterious maladies swept the flocks of chickens; the cattle and sheep sickened and died. Everywhere was a shadow of death. The farmers spoke of much illness among their families. In the town the doctors had become more and more puzzled by new kinds of sickness appearing among their patients. There had been several sudden and unexplained deaths, not only among adults but even among children, who would be stricken suddenly while at play and die within a few hours.

There was a strange stillness. The birds, for example—where had they gone? Many people spoke of them, puzzled and disturbed. The feeding stations in the backyards were deserted. The few birds seen anywhere were moribund; they trembled violently and could not fly. It was a spring without voices. On the mornings that had once throbbed with the dawn chorus of robins, catbirds, doves, jays, wrens, and scores of other bird voices there was now no sound; only silence lay over the fields and woods and marsh.

On the farms the hens brooded, but no chicks hatched. The farmers com- 5
plained that they were unable to raise any pigs — the litters were small and the
young survived only a few days. The apple trees were coming into bloom but
no bees droned among the blossoms, so there was no pollination and there
would be no fruit.

The roadsides, once so attractive, were now lined with browned and with- 6
ered vegetation as though swept by fire. These, too, were silent, deserted by all
living things. Even the streams were now lifeless. Anglers no longer visited
them, for all the fish had died.

In the gutters under the eaves and between the shingles of the roofs, a 7
white granular powder still showed a few patches; some weeks before it had
fallen like snow upon the roofs and the lawns, the fields and streams.

No witchcraft, no enemy action had silenced the rebirth of new life in this 8
stricken world. The people had done it themselves.

This town does not actually exist, but it might easily have a thousand coun- 9
terparts in America or elsewhere in the world. I know of no community that
has experienced all the misfortunes I describe. Yet every one of these disasters
has actually happened somewhere, and many real communities have already
suffered a substantial number of them. A grim specter has crept upon us almost unnoticed, and this imagined tragedy may easily become a stark reality
we all shall know.

What has already silenced the voices of spring in countless towns in 10
America? This book is an attempt to explain.

| **Questions to Start You Thinking** | *Meaning* |

Meaning

1. What is a *fable*? Why do you think Carson titled this introduction to her book *Silent Spring* "A Fable for Tomorrow"? What does her title mean? Is it an appropriate title?

2. Specifically what does Carson fantasize about? On what does she base her fantasies?

3. Can you think of any substances or practices that are threatening our world today?

Writing Strategies

4. The eye of the scientist is evident in Carson's use of specific detail. Which of the descriptive details is particularly memorable?

5. How does Carson organize the details?

6. What is the effect of her ending with a question?

7. Aesop ended his fables with a moral. State a moral that could be used to end Carson's fable.

Ron A. Larsen   Put Me Out of My Misery, Shoot Me!

Hello out there. Let me introduce myself. My name is Martha and I'm ninety-nine years old. I'm composing this letter in my head. I do that often--it's the only real form of stimulation left to me.

I would very much like to die.

I've existed here at the Spring Valley Manor since 1985. I came here after my husband, Emil, died in the spring of that year. I could walk back then. Well, with an aluminum walker, anyway. And I'm using the term walk loosely. It was more of a totter. Yet I would love to totter again. Or read a newspaper. Or hear Vivaldi, or rain on a rooftop, or children playing.

You see, I'm a prisoner in my own body. I haven't left this bed on my own for five years, and I haven't been able to speak for the past three. I hear as if through layers of wet blankets; my eyes discern only degrees of darkness and shadow; my taste buds resigned long ago; my nose has betrayed me. I retain only the sense of touch. I feel cold, heat, dampness, and pain. Lots of pain.

You've no real idea what time and gravity do to the human body. Those two thieves have stolen mine. For decades I was a beautiful woman--vibrant, charming, athletic, and sexy. Men stared and whistled at me on the street from my teens until I was past sixty. They wanted to mate with me, to possess me.

I now weigh perhaps seventy pounds. I lie curled in a rigid fetal position, my stringy arms crossed over my flaccid breasts, a clawed hand on either side of my chin. I can't move from this position on my own. I have no teeth. Not that it matters. My jaws don't function anyway.

If memory serves, the hair on my head is sparse and the color of spent charcoal. My skin resembles rice paper--dry, thin, and translucent. It tears at the slightest pressure. Spidery blue veins play hide-and-seek with the purplish hematomas that cover my arms and legs. Sores and scabs cover

my upper forehead. Pus collects and crusts in the corner of
my eyes.

No one wants me now except the mortician.   8

I spend my days and nights in an isolated twilight, al-   9
ternating between intervals of fitful sleep and excruciating
bouts of consciousness. Every two hours or so, around the
clock, nursing aides come in and flip me from one side to the
other--presumably to alleviate bedsores. They also change my
dirtied cloth diaper, hospital gown, and bedclothes. I'm totally incontinent, you see. Sometimes they forget, or are too
busy, and I'll lie in my own waste for hours.

Three times a day, the aides attempt a feeding. They   10
puree the meals in a blender and squirt this tasteless goo
between my gums with a syringe. I'm trying to starve myself
to death, so I gag, and dribble most of it back up over my
chin. Even if I wanted to, I couldn't swallow much.

The slightest touch shoots bolts of searing pain   11
throughout my body, pain that transcends the "normal" agony I
constantly endure. I believe I have some sort of metastasized
cancer. The aides, who must think me a total vegetable,
handle me roughly, and I don't blame them. Cleaning my body
is an unappetizing assignment. I try to whine or groan since
I can't speak, but I don't know if they hear or care. I'm
just another mouth to feed, another rear end to wipe.

Do you know what it's like to be unable to scratch an   12
itch or pull up a blanket? Do you know the horror of "living"
with no sensory stimulation other than torturous pain for
days upon days, weeks upon weeks, months upon months and
years upon years?

Please don't judge my death wish harshly until you've   13
spent a year in this bed with me--bound into a fetal ball,
ears cotton-stuffed, blindfolded, and gagged. And please do
not speak to me of the sanctity of life, for this is not
life.

I ask you: What kind of society mercifully puts beloved   14
Scout or Boots to sleep when they're ancient, broken, and
suffering, yet denies such compassion to humans?

Marooned inside this rotted ship--sails tattered and   15
useless, mast snapped in half--I compose these mental letters

as if they were messages in a bottle. I dream that one will
find its way to a friendly shore, to a reader who may provide
me with a soft asylum. Push a needle into my veins; press a
pillow to my face; put a bullet to my head--as an act of
love.

**Questions to Start
You Thinking**

Meaning

1. What does the imagined speaker, Martha, mean when she describes herself as "a prisoner in my own body" (paragraph 4)?

2. Why does Larsen have Martha say that the reader would need to spend a year with "ears cotton-stuffed, blindfolded, and gagged" (paragraph 13) in order to judge her desire to die?

3. How harshly does Larsen seem to judge the people who take care of Martha? Explain your response.

Writing Strategies

4. What details does Larsen use to make the imaginary character of Martha come alive for readers? Where do we get a sense of what her personality was like before she came to Spring Valley Manor?

5. What is the effect of the paragraph in which Martha describes herself as a younger woman (paragraph 5)? Why does Larsen choose to have Martha include these details?

6. What effect does Larsen create by having Martha ask the reader direct questions, as in paragraph 12?

7. Larsen's essay makes a case for euthanasia without ever directly engaging the political debates about this issue. How effective is his strategy of writing from imagination to make his point? What are the drawbacks of using such an approach to make a point about a serious issue? What other topics can you think of that might be treated in a similar manner?

Learning by Writing

THE ASSIGNMENT: EXPLORING THROUGH IMAGINATION

Write an essay of imaginative nonfiction, one in which you use your imagination as a resource for examining, analyzing, evaluating, or solving a current problem. It may be a social problem, an economic problem, a medical problem, an educational problem, a governmental or legal problem, or a personal problem. Your treatment of the problem may be lighthearted, but the root of your concern should be serious. You may take an ironic position, but be sure that your attitude toward the problem is clear to your readers.

Unless your instructor encourages you to do so, don't write a story. To be sure, you could conceivably write this paper as science fiction. If you were writing about the spread of unknown viruses, you might begin: "As I walked into Montopolis in 2500 A.D., the mayor rushed up to me. 'A terrible plague of headaches has struck our city! We don't know what is causing this plague,' he shouted. Luckily, I had had some experience with tracking down mysterious viruses when I lived before in the twentieth century." Instead, write imaginative *nonfiction* in the essay form you are familiar with.

To help you start imagining, here are some topics that students generated for this assignment. Some may reveal interesting dimensions of your possible major field of study.

A single parent, concerned about the problem of budgeting time, imagined what life would be like if a day were thirty hours instead of twenty-four.

A budding scientist imagined new crops to help feed the hungry.

A pacifist imagined the next war being fought only by men over fifty.

An education major wrote a fable about an animal school.

In a research paper about future space law, a student used both existing documents and his power of imagination to propose answers to the question of who should control the natural resources of the moon and other planets.

For a paper in economics, a man looked at government aid to disadvantaged people in the inner city, thinking and writing first as a liberal (his own conviction) and then — by an act of imagination — as a conservative.

GENERATING IDEAS

Although there are no fixed rules to follow in imagining, all of us tend to imagine in familiar ways. Being acquainted with these ways may help you fulfill your assignment. Here we first give you some suggestions to help you locate a subject through brainstorming. Then we describe three forms of imagination that may already be familiar to you — shifting perspective, envisioning, and synthesizing.

Try brainstorming.   In making your own list of possible topics, you may find it helpful to brainstorm, either by yourself or with the aid of a group. Sometimes two or three imaginations are better than one. (For helpful tips on brainstorming, see p. 360.) To help you generate, here are a few questions:

**DISCOVERY
CHECKLIST**

Imagining Possibilities

- What common assumption — something we all take for granted — might be questioned or denied? (It might be a scientific opinion, such as the widely accepted knowledge that the ultraviolet rays of the sun are harmful to the skin.)
- What present-day problem or deplorable condition do you wish to see remedied?
- What problems do you foresee as happening in the future if we don't change current policies, practices, or attitudes?
- What different paths in life might you take? What problems might occur with each path? How might your life be different with each path?

Jot down as many questions as you can think of, do some trial imagining, and then choose the topic that seems most promising. Say you pick as your topic "What if the average North American life span were to lengthen to more than a century?" You might begin by reflecting on some of the ways in which society would have to change. When ideas start to flow, start listing them. No doubt a lengthened life span would mean that a greater proportion of the populace would be old. Ask questions: How would that fact affect doctors and nurses, hospitals, and other medical facilities? How might city planners respond to the needs of so many more old people? What would the change mean for retail merchants? For television programming? For the social security system? For taxes?

Facing the Challenge: Writing from Imagination

The major challenge writers face when they write from imagination is to have the courage to be original and to explore realms and ideas outside their real-life experience. They may find it unsettling to reach into the imagination for details that will help to make a point.

While some people may associate a lively imagination with young children, using the imagination to write a forceful essay that is intended to change the way readers think about a topic is *not* child's play: it's hard work. Rachel Carson, in her depiction of an imaginary town "in the heart of America," uses intricate details to persuade her readers of the dangers of pesticides. Ron A. Larsen knew that to convince his readers to sympathize with his imagined character's plea to be euthanized, he needed to practice thinking and writing like a ninety-nine-year-old woman. He found that several sessions of focused freewriting helped him feel comfortable writing in Martha's voice. Both of these authors use their imaginations to influence their readers. Their writing is as critical as it is creative.

If you need convincing that imaginative writing can also be critical writing — that the imagination is a useful tool for making a serious point or trying to persuade an audience — spend some time listening to the lyrics of your favorite songs. The lyrics of much popular music, from the Beatles to Queen Latifah, present alternative points of view and argue for social change at the same time that they entertain audiences with imaginative imagery.

There is no set formula for writing from your imagination, but remember that you're writing an essay rather than a story, and keep your goal — the effect you want to have on your reader — in mind. However, if you haven't practiced using your imagination as a resource in writing, doing a few warm-up exercises before you decide on a topic will help you get started. To practice seeing the world from a different perspective, try freewriting from the point of view of a character very different from you — a supermodel, the CEO of a cigarette company, or a first-grader. Then move on to the tips for generating ideas and determining a focus for your essay (pp. 79–81).

Shifting perspective. In imagining, a writer sometimes thinks and perceives from a point of view other than the usual one. This new perspective could be a preexisting one that another person or group already has (how would you argue about an issue if you were on the opposite side?) or it could be one that you make up (what would the situation look like to a Martian?). You can also try shifting perspective by shifting the debate to a somewhat different arena: What if, instead of trying to decide whether *teenagers* should be allowed to drink alcohol, the debate were about whether *people over the age of sixty-five* should be allowed to drink?

Envisioning. Imagining what might be, seeing in the mind's eye and in graphic detail, is the process of envisioning or imaging. A writer might imagine a utopia or ideal state, as did Thomas More in *Utopia* (1516), or an anti-utopia, as did George Orwell in his 1949 novel of a grim future, *Nineteen Eighty-Four,* or as Rachel Carson did in *Silent Spring.* By envisioning, you can conceive of other possible alternatives — to imagine, say, a different and better way of treating illness, of electing a president.

Sometimes in envisioning, you will find a meaningful order in what had seemed a chaotic jumble. Leonardo da Vinci, in his notebooks, tells how, when starting to conceive a painting, he would gaze at an old stained wall made of various stones until he began to see "landscapes adorned with mountains, rivers, rocks, trees, plains, . . . combats and figures in quick movement, and strange expressions of faces, and outlandish costumes, and an infinite number of things." Not everyone might see that much in a wall, but Leonardo's method is familiar to writers who also have looked into a confused and random array of stuff and envisioned in it a meaningful arrangement.

Synthesizing. Synthesizing (generating new ideas by combining previously separate ideas) is the opposite of analyzing (breaking down into component parts). In synthesizing, a writer brings together materials, perhaps old and familiar materials, and fuses them into something new. A writer makes fresh connections. Surely Picasso achieved a synthesis when, in making a metal sculpture of a baboon and needing a skull for the animal, he clapped on the baboon's neck a child's toy car. With its windshield like a pair of eyes and its mouthlike bumper, the car didn't just look like a baboon's skull: it *became* one. German chemist Friedrich August Kekulé rightly guessed the structure of the benzene molecule when, in reverie, he imagined a snake swallowing its own tail. In a flash he realized that the elusive molecule was a ring of carbon atoms, not a chain, as earlier chemists had believed. Surely to bring together the benzene molecule and a snake was a feat of imaginative synthesis.

Some things cannot be totally reduced to rule and line, and imagination is one of them. But we hope you will accept that imagining is a practical activity of which you are fully capable. The more words you put on paper, the more often you will find that you can discover surprising ideas, original examples, unexpected relationships. The more you write, the more you involve yourself with language, that fascinating stained glass window that invites you to find fresh shapes in it.

PLANNING, DRAFTING, AND DEVELOPING

We trust we haven't given you the impression that all imagining takes place *before* you write. On the contrary, you'll probably find yourself generating more ideas — perhaps more imaginative and startling ideas — in the act of writing.

Find a method of organization. Though in writing a piece of imaginative non-fiction you are freely imagining, you'll still need to lay out your ideas in a clear and orderly fashion. Some writers prefer to outline. However, you might find that in fulfilling this assignment all the outline you will need is a list of points not to forget. If in writing your paper you enjoy yourself and words flow read-ily, by all means let the flow carry you along. In that happy event, you may be able to plan at the same time that you write your first draft. (For more on or-ganizing ideas and using outlines, see Chapter 16.)

Hook readers with your opening. To help your readers envision and share your imagined world just as vividly as you do, your essay needs an engaging (and convincing) opening. Rachel Carson's "A Fable for Tomorrow" (p. 74) has such a beginning. The author arrests our interest with an opening sentence reminiscent of childhood fairy tales: "There was once a town in the heart of America where all life seemed to live in harmony with its surroundings." With this basis in shared reality, we are then willing to share her fantasy as well. Ron A. Larsen draws readers into his essay by directly addressing them ("Hello out there") in the voice of the ninety-nine-year-old woman from whose imag-ined perspective he writes. (For more on openings, see Chapter 17.)

Use interesting details. As in any essay, you also need specific concrete details and evidence to support and clarify your assertions. Carson, in relying on con-crete specifics (such as her details about the deserted feeding stations, the birds trembling violently and not being able to fly, the white powder lying on roofs and lawns), makes her description of her imaginary American town ring true. Larsen roots his imaginative argument in reality by creating an authen-tic voice for the imagined "Martha," who uses vivid details such as "My skin resembles rice paper — dry, thin, and translucent. It tears at the slightest pres-sure." Like Carson and Larsen, use your imagination to come up with specific details and concrete examples for your writing. You'll need to make your vi-sion appear tangible, as if it really could exist. (For more on selecting and using details, see Chapter 18.)

Carry through in your conclusion. The endings of Carson's fable and of Larsen's imagined monologue work well. Carson pushes to a believable con-clusion the details of destruction and death — "The people had done it them-selves" — and turns the meaning back on the readers and alludes to their re-sponsibility for what happens to the environment. Larsen concludes with Martha's plea to the reader to put her out of her misery — to "put a bullet to my head." Your ending should have an imaginative thrust, but it should be logically based on the details you have provided. (For more on conclusions, see Chapter 17.)

Consider your imagery. Often imaginative writing appeals to the mind's eye. For some accessible picture-filled writing, see the sports pages of a daily newspaper. Sports writer Bugs Baer once wrote of fireball pitcher Lefty Grove: "He could throw a lambchop past a wolf." Dan Shaughnessy in the *Boston Globe* described pitcher Roger Clemens: "Watching the Mariners try to hit Clemens was like watching a stack of waste paper dive into a shredder." Such language isn't mere decoration: it points to a truth and puts vivid pictures in the reader's "mind's eye." (For more about writing with *images* — language that evokes sense experiences, not always sight — look back through Chapter 2.)

Be patient. Imagination isn't a constant flame: sometimes it flickers and wavers. If in shaping your draft you get stuck and words don't flow, you may find it helpful to shift your perspective. Try imagining the past, present, or future as if you were somebody else or an alien or an animal or a plant. Perhaps you will then see fresh possibilities in your topic. Also helpful may be what all writers do now and then: take a walk, relax, do something else for a while. Then return to your draft and try to look at it with a *reader's* eyes.

REVISING AND EDITING

As Ron A. Larsen reread his first draft on the screen of his computer, he thought of additional details, such as Martha's memories of the way that she used to look and feel as a younger woman. He incorporated them into his final version. Do you need more detail in places to make your vision clear and convincing? Then make yourself comfortable and do some more imagining.

In beginning to write his imaginative essay, Larsen found that his biggest challenge was to make readers of all ages identify with the plight of a terminally ill ninety-nine-year-old woman. He realized that he would have to use details that would help the reader to experience Martha's pain and loss of dignity. In revising, he was able to go back through his paper and strengthen it by adding compelling examples, such as the comparison between Martha's sensory-deprived condition and the experience of being bound, blindfolded, and gagged in a fetal position. The addition of specific details also helped

 **WRITING WITH A COMPUTER**

Did you ever try "invisible writing"? This is a technique to make yourself less self-conscious while you write — as you'll especially need to be when you're imagining. Turn off just the monitor so that you can't see any words appearing on your screen; either twist down the contrast control or turn off the monitor's switch if it is independent from the computer's power source. Then write. Do you feel slightly at sea? Don't worry — keep writing. Then bring the screen back up and behold what you have written. The advantage of this trick is that you won't be fussing over particular words (and spelling errors); you'll be able to devote your full attention to imagining.

Larsen to create a more believable voice for the imaginary Martha in his revised draft.

> *existed here at the Spring Valley Manor*
> I've ~~been at the nursing home~~ since 1985. I came here
>   *, Emil,*   *in the spring of*
> after my husband died that year. I could walk back
>   *It was more of a totter.*
> *Well, with an aluminum walker, anyway.*
> then. And I'm using the term <u>walk</u> loosely /. ~~because I~~
>
> ~~couldn't really get around very well on my own~~. Yet I
>   *totter*   *a newspaper*
> would love to ~~walk even a little bit~~ again. Or read.
>   *hear Vivaldi, or rain on a rooftop,*
> Or ~~listen to music~~ or children playing.

The belief of poet William Butler Yeats that inspiration can come in rewriting as well as in writing may hold true when you write your essay drawing on the resource of imagination. As you revise, you may find fresh and imaginative ideas occurring for the first time. While you review your paper, you might consider the following points:

REVISION CHECKLIST

- Is your vision consistent? Do all the parts of your vision agree with all the others? Or is some part discordant, needing to be cut out?
- Does your paper at any point need more information about the real world? If so, where might you find it: What can you read, whom can you talk with, what can you observe?
- Is your imaginative solution plausible? Could the solution you imagine possibly exist? What physical details, vivid description, and images can you add that will help make your vision seem real?
- Have you used any facts that need verifying, any words that need checking?
- What difficulties did you run into in writing your paper? Did you overcome them? Are any still present that bother you? If you can't come up with solutions, ask your instructor or classmates to help you.

After you have revised your imaginative essay, proofread and edit it. Check carefully for problems with grammar, word choice, punctuation, and mechanics — and then correct any problems you find. A comprehensive reference handbook is an indispensable tool for this task; the "Quick Editing Guide" at the end of *The Bedford Guide for College Writers* (see the pages with the colored edges) will get you started.

When editing a paper written from imagination, pay close attention to verbs, word choice, and sentence structure. In this type of essay, writers sometimes find themselves slipping around between the future tense ("you *will* notice something unusual"), the past tense ("he *did* not *believe* what was happening"), and the conditional ("the problem *would continue* to grow"). Check to make sure you have used verbs consistently and logically. Also pay attention to correct word choice, especially as it affects your tone. You may have used unusual or unfamiliar words and expressions to create a special effect in your paper, but be sure that they do not sound affected, trite, or odd. Finally, be especially careful that all your sentences are complete: imaginative papers are often heavily reworked throughout the writing process, a practice that sometimes leads to sentence fragments (incomplete sentences) and to comma splices and run-ons (two sentences incorrectly joined).

Here are some questions to get you started when proofreading and editing your paper written from imagination:

EDITING CHECKLIST

- Have you used the correct verb tense to convey your meaning in each sentence? Have you used the correct form for every verb, so that your meaning will be clear? (See A1 in the "Quick Editing Guide.")
- Have you avoided writing fragments, comma splices, or run-ons, especially where you have added new ideas or details? (See A6 and A7 in the "Quick Editing Guide.")
- Have you used the best possible words to create the effect you intend?
- Have you spelled everything correctly, especially unusual or unfamiliar words included to create a special effect? (See D2 in the "Quick Editing Guide.")
- Have you used the proper paper format, including special requirements for your instructor and course? (See D3 in the "Quick Editing Guide.")

(For more on revising and editing, see Chapter 19.)

OTHER ASSIGNMENTS

1. Write a fable about a problem in modern life, similar to the fable by Rachel Carson. Aesop and James Thurber also wrote fables about the

---

FOR PEER RESPONSE

Ask a classmate to let you know if he or she has any doubts about what you've written. Here is a list of questions for your peer editor to answer. See Chapter 20 for advice on working with other student writers and for general questions you should always ask a peer editor to address. For a paper in which you write from imagination, you'll also want your peer editor to answer these specific questions:

- Has the writer chosen a topic that you consider significant? What point is he or she trying to make?
- What do you like best about the writer's imaginative thinking?
- What did you find hardest to follow or imagine or accept? Is it difficult because of the ideas themselves or the way the writer presents them or both? List your problems with the essay and explain why they are problems.
- Is what the writer imagines sufficiently rooted in reality to be believable? Plausible?
- Where should the writer add details, examples, description, or images to make the imagined reality seem more plausible? Star the places where the writer needs to be more specific.
- If this were your paper, what is the one thing you would be sure to work on before handing it in?

human condition. Check them out if you want to see how someone else uses fable.

2. Think of a law or government policy or educational practice that you think should be changed, and write an ironic argument for or against it. A classic ironic argument is the well-known "A Modest Proposal" in which Jonathan Swift proposes solving the Irish food shortage, caused by famine, by eating babies.

3. Have you ever observed some people in a public place, perhaps on a bus or plane, and imagined who they are and why they are in that place at that time? What problems might they be facing? Have you imagined the conversation they are having? What clues do you have to what they are saying? Try this kind of fantasizing the next time you go to the airport, the mall, or a restaurant. Use your imagination as Ron A. Larsen does in his essay, and share your imagined situation with your classmates. (This experience could also provide information for a paper.)

4. Write an essay in answer to a question that begins "What if . . . ?" You might imagine a past that unfolded differently: What if the airplane had never been invented? What if the Equal Rights Amendment had become law? What if the South had won the Civil War? What if John F. Kennedy or Martin Luther King Jr. had not been assassinated? You might imagine a reversal of fact: What if men had to bear children? How would life be different? What problems would result? What other problems might be solved? Or you might imagine an event in the future: What if there were no more wars? Or what if you were elected president of the United States? Envision in specific detail a world in which the supposition is true. Your purpose is to make the supposition seem credible and convincing to your readers.

5. Imagine an ideal — a person (such as a teacher or boss), place (college or theme park), or thing (automobile or computer) that to your mind would be virtually perfect. Shape this ideal to your own desires. Then put it in writing. Perhaps this ideal might combine the best features of two or three real people, places, or things. You will have to decide whether what you imagine could exist today or in a more nearly perfect future — and how far into the future? You may be tempted to build up to a surprise ending. It might seem a great trick to reveal at the end that your ideal city is really good old Topeka or that your ideal mother is your own real-life mother after all. But it probably won't be a convincing way to write your paper. Nothing that exists is ideal. Simply to describe what exists won't take any imagining.

6. Imagine two alternative versions of your own future, say, ten years down the road — the worst possible future you could have and the best possible. Describe each in detail. If you would prefer not to limit your vision to your own future, imagine the future of your hometown or city, your region, or your country, perhaps taking one current problem, such as violence or drug abuse, to a logical conclusion.

7. Recall the way you envisioned something before you experienced it; then describe the reality you found instead. Your expectations, of course, might be good or bad; the reality might be a disappointment or a pleasant surprise. But, if possible, pick something about which your ideas changed drastically.

8. Draw a connection between two things you hadn't ever thought of connecting before. Start with something that interests you — running, moviegoing, sports cars — and try relating it to something remote from it: running to writing or cars to clothes. See what both have in common, and explain their similarities in two or three paragraphs.

Applying What You Learn: Some Uses of Writing from Imagination

Imagination, we have suggested, is tremendously useful as a resource in many fields, not only in a creative writing course. In scholarly thinking and writing, imagination is essential. French philosopher of history Paul Veyne points out that a historian has to infer the motives of persons long dead. Understanding the past, Veyne argues, is often a matter of imaginatively "filling in" what cannot be completely documented. In the field of geography, according to Robert W. Durrenberger in *Geographical Research and Writing,* a student who wishes to do research needs most of all to develop imagination. "Admittedly, an individual cannot be taught how to be creative," Durrenberger concedes. "But he can observe those who are creative and be on the lookout for new and original approaches to the solutions of problems."

Similarly, imagination can be valuable to you as a college student. To show you how you can usefully apply the ways of imagining to your writing in college and beyond, let's consider them one at a time.

FOR GROUP LEARNING

Brainstorming in a Group

Try a brainstorming session with your writing group to generate ideas for an imaginative paper. When you brainstorm as a group, appoint a recording secretary to write down the ideas as fast as they are called out. Or your instructor may choose to do this exercise with the whole class, with the ideas being written on the blackboard. Don't be surprised if this activity seems wild and chaotic; order can emerge from it. Limit your initial brainstorming session to ten or twelve minutes; then stop to discuss the results, circling any items that draw strong reactions from the group. These may be the seeds that will grow a memorable paper. If nothing much comes out of this first session, brainstorm again. (For further advice on how to brainstorm, see p. 360.)

Shifting perspective. The next time you are given an assignment in another course, try looking at the entire topic through someone else's eyes — someone unlike yourself — as Ron A. Larsen does in writing on euthanasia. This way of imagining is often at work in specialized and professional writing. Philosophers and science writers challenge us, as Dr. Peter Saltzstein of Northeast Missouri State University puts it, to "step outside of received opinion or commonly held beliefs and examine those beliefs through the use of alternative perspectives." In the following passage from *Naked Emperors: Essays of a Taboo-Stalker,* science writer Garrett Hardin shifts perspectives. He imagines that an economist asks an ecologist, "Would you plant a redwood tree in your backyard?" When the ecologist says that he would, the economist charges him with being a fool — in economic terms.

> The economist is right, of course. The supporting economic analysis is easily carried out. A redwood tree can hardly be planted for less than a dollar. To mature [it] takes some two thousand years, by which time the tree will be about three hundred feet high. How much is the tree worth then? An economist will insist, of course, on evaluating the forest giant as lumber. Measured at a man's height above the ground, the diameter of the tree will be about ten feet, and the shape of the shaft from there upward is approximately conical. The volume of this cone is 94,248 board feet. At a "stumpage" price of 15[c] a board foot — the approximate price a lumberer must pay for a tree unfelled, unmilled, untransported — the tree would be worth some $14,000.
>
> That may sound like a large return on an investment of only one dollar, but we must not forget how long the investment took to mature: 2,000 years. Using the exponential formula to calculate the rate of compound interest we find that the capital earned slightly less than one-half of 1 percent per year. Yes, a man would be an economic fool to put his money into a redwood seedling when so many profitable opportunities lie at hand.

Hardin, of course, is being unfair to economists, many of whom are undoubtedly capable of feeling awe before a giant redwood. But his momentary shift to the strict dollars-and-cents point of view enables him to conclude that, if we care for the future and for our descendants, we sometimes need to act without regard for economics.

Envisioning. Some challenging assignments you'll meet in a college course will set forth a problem and ask you to envision a solution. The following question, from a final examination in an economics course, asks the student to imagine a better procedure:

> As we have seen, methods of stabilizing the dollar have depended on enlisting the cooperation of large banks and foreign governments, which has not always been forthcoming. Propose a better, alternative way for our own government to follow in protecting the value of its currency from severe fluctuations.

An effective answer to that question would be based on facts that the student has learned. What the exam question tries to provide is not just practice in recalling facts but also training in envisioning — in bringing the facts together and applying them.

Students in family science courses may be asked to envision ideal situations, play devil's advocate, even take a stand opposed to their own when learning to debate issues informatively. In envisioning an ideal, a writer sets up an imagined goal and perhaps also begins thinking about how to achieve it. In his epoch-making speech in Washington, D.C., on the 1963 centennial of Lincoln's Emancipation Proclamation, Martin Luther King Jr. set forth his vision of an unsegregated future.

> I have a dream that one day on the red hills of Georgia the sons of former slaves and the sons of former slave owners will be able to sit down together at the table of brotherhood . . . . I have a dream that my four little children will one day live in a nation where they will not be judged by the color of their skin but by the content of their character.

Synthesizing. Combining unlike things and drawing unexpected conclusions may result in a lively and revealing paper. But in explaining almost anything, an imaginative writer can make metaphors and draw connections. Sylvan Barnet, in *A Short Guide to Writing about Art* (Boston: Little, 1989), questions whether a period of art can be entirely "Gothic" in spirit. To make a highly abstract idea clear, he introduces a brief *analogy,* a metaphor that likens the unfamiliar thing to something familiar.

> Is there really an all-embracing style in a given period? One can be skeptical, and a simple analogy may be useful. A family often consists of radically different personalities: improvident husband, patient wife, one son an idler and the other a go-getter, one daughter wise in her choice of a career and the other daughter unwise. And yet all may have come from the same culture.

To be sure, imagining has practical applications beyond the writing of college papers and scholarly articles. Asked why World War I took place, Franz Kafka, one of the most influential writers of our century, gave a memorable explanation: the war was caused by a "monstrous lack of imagination." Evidently if we are to survive, we would do well to imagine both World War III and its alternatives — not only the consequences of the problems we now face but also the solutions.

Making Connections: Writing from Imagination in A Writer's Reader

Imagination can be the fount of powerful nonfiction. Various writers in *A Writer's Reader* effectively use this resource to convey their ideas and enhance their stands. Professor and writer William Henry Lewis in "Shades" (p. 505) lets us into the mind of a boy longing for a relationship with the father he's never met, as he imagines what their interactions might be like. In "I Want a Wife" (p. 529), satirist Judy Brady imagines what a wife would do for her —

the same things that the traditional wife does for her husband — and concludes, "My God, who *wouldn't* want a wife?"

Besides Lewis, Brady, Rachel Carson (p. 74), and Ron A. Larsen (p. 76), other writers who use imagination in their nonfiction include professor Noel Perrin, "A Part-Time Marriage" (p. 518); construction worker Steve Olson, "Year of the Blue-Collar Guy" (p. 570); essayist Nancy Mairs, "Freeing Choices" (p. 579); and political thinker and professor James Q. Wilson, "In Praise of Asphalt Nation" (p. 606). As you read these essays, consider the role that imagination plays in them. For each essay, answer the following questions:

1. Which "What if?" question does the author ask? What is the author's answer to the question?
2. How does the writer use imagination as a resource? What does it add to this piece of nonfiction?
3. How does the imagined world differ from the real world as presented in the essay?

Part Two

Thinking Critically

Introduction:
Critical Strategies for
Reading and Writing

Critic, from the Greek word *kritikos*, means "one who can judge and discern" or one who can think critically. College will have given you your money's worth if it leaves you better able to judge and discern — to determine what is more important and less important, to make distinctions and recognize differences, to generalize from specifics, to draw conclusions from evidence, to grasp complicated concepts and get to the bottom of things, to judge and choose wisely. The effective thinking that you will need in college and on the job is active and purposeful, not passive and ambling. It is critical thinking. Part Two of this textbook gives you the critical thinking strategies you need for efficient reading and effective writing.

What Is Critical Thinking?

Critical thinking is not new to you. You use critical strategies daily to solve problems and make decisions. For example, you may not have enough money both to pay your college tuition and to buy the car you need, so you have to decide what you are going to do about this situation. First, you *identify the causes* of your lack of funds to see whether you can resolve the problem by eliminating one of its causes. Have you had a medical emergency or lost your job? Have you spent a lot of money on renting a fancy apartment or paying for a trip to the Bahamas? Has tuition increased? You decide that the cause is higher tuition and realize you cannot control the cost of tuition, so you *analyze* the problem, exploring it from all angles. You discern right away that you have three options: you can do without the car you need, you can decrease the amount of your tuition, or you can get more money. To analyze further, you ask yourself more questions to explore each of these possibilities. To eliminate the need to buy a car, can you catch rides with a friend or relative? Can you use public transportation? To decrease your tuition, can you take fewer courses? Can you get a loan from the bank, the college, or a family member? (If so, can you repay it without sacrificing other things you need?) Can you get another job to bring in more money? (If so, can you still keep up your studies?) You *evaluate* each of your choices and *compare and contrast* them so that you can choose the most feasible way to solve your problem of not having enough money. Finally, you reach a conclusion and *propose a solution:* because you need money for both the new car and tuition, the most logical thing to do is to get a short-term loan from your college to pay your tuition and use the money you have to buy a car. You visit the financial aid officer and *take a stand* that you should be granted a loan, presenting your reasons to support your position — that you are a serious student who has maintained a B average in your college courses, that you have a job that pays you sufficient salary so that you can repay the loan, and that you have proven that you can work and go to college at the same time. Your arguments convince the officer, so you receive the loan and your problem is solved. You have used critical thinking to explore your problem step by step and to arrive at a reasonable solution.

You have already used critical thinking in high school writing assignments and in other college courses. You analyzed causes and effects when you traced the development of labor unions in the United States on your history exam. You compared and contrasted two poems for a literature paper. You evaluated a book that you read for your science class when you wrote a book report that ended with a statement like "I would recommend this book highly to anyone interested in bioengineering". For an effective paper in college, however, you must go deeply into the subject, analyzing it thoroughly and providing convincing evidence for your claims.

Critical thinking is not a specialized, isolated activity. It is part of a continuum of thinking strategies that thoughtful people use every day to grapple with new information and to solve problems. To explain the thinking strategies necessary for purposeful reading and writing, educational expert Benjamin S. Bloom[1] identified six levels of cognitive activity — knowledge, comprehension, application, analysis, synthesis, and evaluation. Each level becomes more complex and demands higher thinking skills than the previous one. The first three levels are *literal* thinking skills. When you show that you *know* a fact, *comprehend* its meaning, and can *apply* it to a new situation, you demonstrate your mastery over information, the building blocks of thought. The other three levels — analysis, synthesis, and evaluation — are *critical* thinking skills. When you use these skills, you go beyond the literal level of thinking: you *break apart* the building blocks to see what makes them work, *recombine* them in new and useful ways, and *judge* their worth or significance. *Analysis* is the breaking down of information into its elements. As a

---

[1] Benjamin S. Bloom, et al., *Taxonomy of Educational Objectives, Handbook I: Cognitive Domain* (New York: McKay, 1956).

reader, you will analyze articles, reports, and books to comprehend the information they contain. As a writer, you will analyze events, processes, structures, and ideas to understand them fully and explain them to readers. *Synthesis* is putting together elements and parts to form new wholes. As a researcher you will synthesize information from several sources you have read, integrate this synthesized material with your own thoughts, and convey the unique combination to others through writing. Finally, *evaluation* means judging according to standards or criteria. When you evaluate something you have read, you determine standards for judging, apply them to the passage, and arrive at a conclusion about the significance or value of the information. When you as a critic evaluate something in writing, you must convince readers that your standards are reasonable and that the subject being evaluated either does or does not meet those standards.

These three cognitive activities — analysis, synthesis, and evaluation — are the core of critical thinking. They are not new to you, but applying them rigorously in college-level reading and writing may be. The writing assignments in Part Two are designed to help you focus on each of these thinking skills in turn and give you some practice in applying them.

Thinking Critically While Reading and Writing

In Part Two, we present a sequence of writing assignments that require you to use critical thinking strategies. The seven writing assignments — reading critically, analyzing, comparing and contrasting, explaining causes and effects, taking a stand, proposing a solution, and evaluating — are arranged roughly in order of increasing complexity — that is, according to the level of critical thinking required. The first four are basically forms of analysis, breaking something down into its components to understand it better. The next two — taking a stand and proposing a solution — require synthesis of information from various sources with your own ideas and conclusions. You analyze all the information, reflect on it, and present a new perspective. The last one — evaluating — is the most complex and can incorporate several of the other critical strategies. Let's look at these seven writing tasks in more detail.

Reading Critically. Reading critically means applying critical reading strategies to a written passage in order to understand it at both a literal level and an analytical level. A paper based on critical reading explains what is going on in the text and then goes on to make a point based on the ideas in the piece. Reading critically is an essential college-level skill that can be part of the other assignments in Part Two. For example, you may need to read a newspaper critically to take a stand effectively on the topic it covers, and you need to read critically any text that you evaluate. Critical reading is also important in other courses. For example, in a sociology course you may be asked to analyze a research report on children who kill; to scrutinize not only the soundness of the argument in the piece but also the assumptions and implications behind the explicit meaning. The writing task of writing from critical reading is covered in Chapter 5.

Analyzing.   Analyzing is breaking an idea, event, or item into parts to explain it. In a history class you may be asked to explain the federal government. To do so, you would analyze it — breaking it into its three branches, identifying the functions of each, and demonstrating how they work together as a whole. In an English course you may be required to parse a sentence, analyze a poem, or outline an essay to explain how each part functions within the whole. The writing task of analyzing is covered in Chapter 6.

Comparing and Contrasting.   Comparing and contrasting focuses on the similarities and differences of two (or more) items or groups. First you analyze each item, and then you line up the characteristics of each, side by side, to determine how they are alike and how they are different. But an effective comparison and contrast analysis goes beyond merely pointing out likenesses and differences; it has a more significant purpose. You may explain how each alternative operates, or you may determine which alternative is preferable. In a government class you may compare and contrast two or more laws; in a nursing course, treatments of a disease; in a psychology course, two people in case studies; in a literature course, two or three fictional characters. The writing task of comparing and contrasting is covered in Chapter 7.

Explaining Causes and Effects.   Explaining causes and effects focuses on the causes and effects of an action, event, or situation. Identifying causes means ferreting out roots and origins. Determining effects is figuring out results. Often in thinking, the two are integrated; often in writing, they are combined. In a history course, you may identify the multiple causes of World War I to help readers understand why this military struggle started and why it was so difficult to end. Or you may trace the several effects of slavery on the African American family through the last four hundred years to try to understand some of the problems of African Americans today.

Sometimes as you analyze, you will find a chain of causes and effects: a situation causes specific effects, which in turn cause other results. For example, through investigating the effects of overpopulation for an economics course, you may discover that one effect is filling and building on tidal water basins. This causes depletion of plankton and other small sea life, which in turn decreases the supply of fish in the bays and oceans. That decrease may result in fewer fish for commercial fishers to catch, less money for the families of these workers, and higher prices of seafood for all of us in grocery stores and restaurants. The writing task of explaining causes and effects is covered in Chapter 8.

Taking a Stand.   Taking a stand means arguing for one side or another of an issue. You may come to the debate with strong beliefs and opinions, or you may develop a position while looking into the matter. In either case, you need to analyze the situation and the available information, reach a firm conclusion, and present your case persuasively to your readers. To be persuasive, you must support your claims with more than personal opinion, memories, and anecdotes; you must provide solid evidence — facts, statistics, expert opinion, and direct observation. In an ethics course, you might argue that abortion should be a woman's choice or that all abortion should be illegal or that abortion should be allowed only in the case of rape or incest or threat to the mother's life. In a biology course, you may assert that the use of large nets for fishing needlessly destroys much sea life or that these nets are necessary for commercial anglers to make a living. The writing task of taking a stand is covered in Chapter 9.

Proposing a Solution.   Proposing a solution requires not only taking a stand but also presenting a feasible solution to the problem at hand. You need to identify a problem and analyze it to determine the probable causes and possible solutions. Then you need to analyze each solution to see whether it is workable and compare and contrast all the solutions to determine which one is best. Finally, you need to argue persuasively that your solution is the best one possible. A civics professor may ask you to propose a way to involve more students in student elections on your college campus. For a biology class, you may be asked to write a paper proposing a solution to the problem of increased air pollution or setting forth a proposal to solve the problem of the depletion of the ozone layer above the earth. The writing task of proposing a solution is covered in Chapter 10.

Evaluating.   Evaluating is a complex task that usually requires a combination of critical thinking and writing strategies. You must propose — implicitly or explicitly — specific criteria for judging the subject, whether it is a system, an idea, or a work of art. You usually determine these criteria by studying what experts in the field have to say as well as by consulting your own personal preferences; sometimes you must take a stand and defend these criteria themselves. You must also analyze the subject to see how it works, in particular to see how well it matches the criteria you propose. Finally you must make a judgment — is the subject good or bad? effective or not? — and persuade your readers that your view is correct.

You may be asked to write a review of a book or movie for a humanities course; your criterion might be plausibility of plot and character. A psychology professor may request that you evaluate Howard Gardner's theory of multiple intelligence. You might research what experts consider necessary characteristics in a theory of intelligence, apply the ones you consider valid to Gardner's theory, and compare and contrast his theory with other theories to arrive at a conclusion about the value of Gardner's theory. The writing task of evaluating is covered in Chapter 11.

Taken together, these seven forms of writing represent most of the writing you will do in the rest of your college courses and in your career. The resources that you explored in Part One are still important, of course, but in the chapters in Part Two they serve as sources of background information or as evidence rather than as the focus for an entire essay. When you approach these seven writing tasks, instructors will expect you (and you should expect yourself) to do the following:

1. *Think* through a topic or problem critically to understand it thoroughly,
2. *Read* relevant sources of information critically to comprehend them thoroughly,
3. *Write,* presenting information and arguments that will stand up to critical scrutiny, and, to succeed at all three of these,
4. *Think critically*—about your own thinking, reading, and writing skills.

In other words, you should learn to apply the same sort of critical scrutiny to your writing that you do to the subjects that you are writing about and to the information you are reading. This kind of careful examination does not mean forever criticizing what you've written. It *does* mean analyzing your current thoughts on a topic and possible weaknesses in your position, analyzing your thinking and reading and writing processes, analyzing your methods for drafting and developing a paper, and analyzing your expression of ideas in writing—to determine what is effective and what might be changed and improved. Richard Paul, the internationally known expert on critical thinking, described that responsibility this way: "We must continually monitor and assess how our thinking is going, whether it is plausibly on the right track, whether it is sufficiently clear, accurate, precise, consistent, relevant, deep, or broad for our purposes."[2] Such self-examination is a necessary ingredient for thinking critically in reading and writing.

Supporting Critical Thinking with Evidence

When writers use the critical strategies we have described here, they provide sound evidence from a credible stance to convince critical readers. They use evidence to clarify, explain, and support assertions. Using clear reasoning, they weave the evidence and assertions together into a cohesive explanation or argument. These standards apply to you when you write an essay using critical strategies. You should also apply them to evaluation of the work of other writers whom you read, both when you are conducting research for a specific paper and when you are reading more widely for knowledge and information. Indeed, one of the most important ways you can apply your critical thinking skills will be to analyze and evaluate the evidence and reasoning of the materials you read for your courses and career.

[2] Richard Paul, *Critical Thinking: What Every Person Needs to Survive in a Rapidly Changing World,* 2nd ed. (Santa Rosa: Foundation for Critical Thinking, 1992) 17.

TYPES OF EVIDENCE

What is evidence? It is anything that demonstrates the soundness of a claim — facts and figures, observations, opinions, illustrations. The four writers' resources presented in Part One of this book — recall, observation, conversation, and imagination — are four sources of evidence, four fruitful places to look for convincing examples and details. Remember, though, that in many critical writing tasks some kinds of evidence weigh in more heavily than others: readers might discount your memories of livestock care on the farm where you spent your summers as a child unless you can demonstrate that your memories are representative or you can establish yourself as an expert on the subject. In effective analytical and argumentative writing, writers often use personal experience or imagination to bolster their arguments but usually avoid relying on it for their sole support. The four most reliable forms of evidence are *facts, expert testimony, statistics,* and *firsthand observation.*

Facts.   Facts are statements that can be verified by objective means, such as by observing or by reading a reliable account. Of course, we take many of our facts from the testimony of others. Facts are usually agreed on by all parties in a dispute or by all reasonable people. We believe that the Great Wall of China exists although we have never seen it with our own eyes. A fact is usually stated in an impersonal way: "Algonquin Indians still live in Old Orchard Beach"; "If you pump the air out of a five-gallon varnish can, it will collapse."

Sometimes people say that *facts* are *true* statements, but what is truth? Sometimes writers confuse *truth* and *soundness of evidence.* Take care that you do not do so. Truth is an ambiguous concept. Consider the truth of the following statements:

The tree in my yard is ten feet tall.	*True* because it can be verified
Over 50 percent of the students who enter college in the United States today take freshman composition in two-year colleges.	*True* according to statistics
A kilometer is 1,000 meters.	*True* in the metric system of measurement
A football team can have eleven players on the field at one time.	*True* according to the rules of football
The speed limit on the highway is fifty-five miles per hour.	*True* according to law
Fewer fatal highway accidents have occurred since the fifty-five mph speed limit became law.	*True* according to research studies
I went to the football game last night.	*True* according to memory

My favorite food is pizza.	*True* as an opinion
More violent criminals should receive the death penalty.	*True* as a belief
Murder is wrong.	*True* according to value judgment
Nirvana, a divine state of release from earthly pain and desire, can be reached by right living, right thinking, and self-denial.	*True* according to Buddhist religious belief

Some individuals would claim each of the statements in this list to be true. When you are thinking critically for writing or about reading, use the word *true* very cautiously, and avoid treating statements of opinion, judgment, belief, or personal experience as true in the same sense that verifiable facts and events are true.

Statistics.   Statistics are facts expressed in numbers. What are the odds that an American child is on welfare? According to statistics compiled by the U.S. Department of Health and Human Services and the Census Bureau in 1991, the chances are one in eight. (A student cited that statistic in an essay arguing that politicians should put themselves in the shoes of single mothers before denouncing "welfare handouts.")

Most writers, without trying to be dishonest, interpret statistics to help their causes. The statement "Fifty percent of the populace have incomes above the poverty level" might be used to back the claim that the government of an African nation is doing a fine job. Putting the statement another way — "Fifty percent of the populace have incomes below the poverty level" — might use the same statistic to show that the government's efforts to aid the disadvantaged are inadequate. A writer, of course, is free to interpret a statistic; and it is only human to present a case in a favorable light. But statistics should not be used to mislead. On the wrapper of a peanut candy bar, we read that one one-ounce serving contains only 150 calories and 70 milligrams of sodium. The claim is true, but the bar weighs 1.6 ounces. Eat the whole thing, as you are more likely to do than to consume 62 percent of it, and you'll ingest 240 calories and 112 milligrams of sodium — a heftier amount than the innocent statistic on the wrapper leads you to believe.

Such abuses make some readers automatically distrust statistics. Use figures fairly, and make sure they are accurate. If you doubt a statistic or a fact, why not check it out? Compare it with facts and statistics reported by several other sources. Distrust a statistical report that differs from every other report unless it is backed by further evidence.

Testimony of Experts.   By *experts*, we mean people with knowledge gained from study and experience of a particular field. The test of an expert is whether his or her expertise stands up to the scrutiny of others who are knowledgeable in that field. An essay by basketball player Michael Jordan explaining how to play offense or by economist John Kenneth Galbraith setting forth the causes of inflation carries authority, while a piece by Galbraith on how to play basketball would not be credible. But consider whether the expert has any bias that would affect his or her reliability. Statistics on cases of lung cancer attributed to smoking might be better taken from government sources than from a representative of the tobacco industry.

Firsthand Observation.   Firsthand observation is persuasive. It adds life to any writing and can lend concrete reality to abstract or complex points. Perhaps in supporting the claim "The Meadowfield waste recycling plant fails to meet state safety and sanitation guidelines" you might recall your own observations of the site: "When I visited the plant last January, I was struck by the number of open waste canisters and by the lack of protective gear for the workers who handle these toxic materials daily."

As readers, most of us tend to trust the writer who declares, "I was there. This is what I saw." Sometimes that trust is misplaced, though, and you should always be wary of a writer's claim to have seen something that no other evidence supports. Ask yourself, Is this writer biased? Is he or she an expert? Is there any possibility that the writer has (intentionally or unintentionally) misinterpreted what he or she saw? Be aware, too, that your own firsthand observations will be subjected to similar scrutiny; take care to reassure your readers that your observations are unbiased and accurate.

TESTING EVIDENCE

As both a reader and a writer, you should always be thinking critically about evidence, testing it to see whether it is strong enough to carry the weight of the writer's claims. Evidence is useful and trustworthy when it satisfies the following requirements:

It is accurate. A writer assumes all responsibility for facts and figures in an essay. Are the facts and figures accurate? If you doubt a piece of information, try to check it against published sources. See reports by others and facts given in reference works. When you are writing, be sure to copy correctly and proofread carefully.

It is reliable. To decide whether you can trust the evidence, you'll need to evaluate its source and check the credentials of the writer. Whenever possible, do some reading. Compare information given in one source with information given in another. If an important point rests on an opinion or information from an expert, check to see that the person is respected in the field. What are his or her credentials as an authority?

It is up-to-date. Facts and statistics from ten-year-old encyclopedias, such as population figures or scientific research, are probably out of date. Use information from the latest sources in what you write, and be sure that what you read contains up-to-date source material, as well.

It is to the point. Evidence must back the exact claim a writer makes. This point may seem too obvious to deserve mention, but you'd be surprised how many writers present interesting facts or opinions that have nothing to do with what they're trying to demonstrate. Sometimes a writer will leap from evidence to conclusion without reason, and the result is a *non sequitur* (Latin for "it does not follow"): "Benito Mussolini made the trains run on time. He was one of the world's leading statesmen." The evidence about trains doesn't support a judgment on Mussolini's statesmanship. (For more about errors in reasoning, see "Recognizing Logical Fallacies," p. 104.)

It is representative. Any examples should be typical of all the things included in the claim. If a writer wants to support the claim that, in general, students on campus are well informed about their legal rights, she should not talk just to prelaw majors but should talk to an English major, an engineering major, a biology major, and others. Probably most writers, in the heat of persuading, can't help unconsciously stacking the evidence in their own favor, but the best writers don't deliberately suppress evidence to the contrary. The writer for an airline magazine who tried to sell package tours to India by declaring "India is an attractive land of sumptuous wealth and splendor" might give for evidence the Taj Mahal and a luxury hotel while ignoring the slums of Bombay and Calcutta. The result might be effective advertising but hardly a full and faithful view and not critically sound.

It is not oversimplified. Some writers fall into the error of *oversimplification*, supplying a too-easy explanation for a phenomenon that may be vast and complicated: "Of course our economy is in trouble. People aren't buying American-made cars." Both statements may be true, but the second is insufficient to account for the first: there is much more to the economy than the auto industry alone. More information is called for. Whenever in doubt that you've given enough evidence to convince your readers, you are probably well advised to come up with more.

It is sufficient and strong enough to back the claim and persuade your readers. How much evidence a writer should use depends on the claim. It will take less evidence to claim that a downtown park needs better maintenance than to claim that the Department of the Interior needs reorganizing.

How much evidence a writer needs may depend, too, on how much readers already know. Who will be reading the piece? A group of readers all from Washington, D.C., and vicinity will not need much evidence to be persuaded that the city's modern Metro transit system is admirable in its efficiency, but more evidence may be needed to convince readers from out of town. When writing, try to comprehend another person's beliefs and feelings, and try to imagine yourself in that person's place and anticipate questions he or she would ask. If you do, you will probably think of more ideas — points to make, objections to answer — than if you think only of presenting your own view. But mere quantity is not enough. One piece of vivid and significant evidence — such as the firsthand testimony of a reliable expert, given in that person's memorable words — may be more valid and persuasive than a foot-high stack of statistics.

USING EVIDENCE TO SUPPORT AN APPEAL

As a writer, you must determine what evidence is appropriate to support your main point or thesis according to your purpose, your audience, and your position as a writer; as a reader, you need to determine when writers have adequately supported their points. One way to select evidence and to judge whether it is appropriate and sufficient is to consider the types of appeal — *logical appeal, emotional appeal,* and *ethical appeal*. Most effective arguments work on all three levels, using all three types of appeals. As a writer, you will usually want to make sure that you have evidence that supports all three. As a reader, you will want to make sure that the author has not relied too heavily on any one type of appeal.

Logical Appeal.   When writers use a logical appeal, they appeal to the mind or the intellect. The logical appeal relies on evidence that is factual, objective, clear, and relevant. For example, if a writer were arguing for term limits for legislators, she wouldn't want to base her argument on the evidence that some long-term legislators weren't reelected last term (irrelevant) or that the current system is unfair to young people who want to get into politics (not logical). Instead, she might argue that a lack of term limits encourages corruption and then use evidence of legislators becoming indebted to lobbyists or special-interest committees by taking campaign contributions from them and then siding automatically with these groups in key legislative votes. Critical readers, such as college professors, demand logical evidence to support major claims and important statements; you should, too, when you read the writing of someone who claims to be an authority on a subject.

Emotional Appeal.   When writers use an emotional appeal, they appeal to the reader's heart and emotions. They choose language, facts, quotes, examples, and images that will evoke emotional responses. To be convincing, every piece of writing must hit readers in their hearts as well as their minds. A strict logical appeal may seem cold and dehumanized if not combined with an emotional appeal. If a writer were arguing against the hunting of seals for their fur, he might combine statistics on the factual evidence of how many seals are killed each year and how the population is decreasing with a vivid description of baby seals being slaughtered. Be aware that some writers use emotional appeals to manipulate readers — to arouse their sympathy, pity, or anger in order to bring them over to the position of the writer without any logical evidence. Such emotional appeals are couched in emotionally laden words and overly sentimental examples and images. Modern readers don't like to feel used. When writing, take care not to alienate your readers by using a dishonest emotional appeal; instead of arguing against a vote for a particular candidate on the basis of pity for ill-nourished children living in roach-infested squalor, report his or her voting record on welfare reform issues. When reading, be wary of anyone who tugs on your heartstrings without giving you some hard facts as well.

Ethical Appeal.   When writers use an ethical appeal, they appeal to readers' sense of fairness and trust. They choose evidence and present it in a manner that will make the audience trust them, respect their judgment, and believe what they have to say. The best logical argument in the world falls flat when readers don't take the writer seriously. To use an ethical appeal, a writer can establish his credentials in the field. He can indicate any experience, such as a job or travel, that helped him learn about the subject. He can refer to relevant reading and interviews. Also, he can demonstrate his knowledge of the subject by the information he generates and gathers, the experts and the sources he chooses to cite, and the depth of understanding of the topic that he conveys in his writing. Further, he can establish a meeting of the minds with his readers by indicating values and attitudes that he shares with them and by responding to the arguments of the opposition. Finally, he can demonstrate his credibility by using language that is precise, clear, and appropriate in tone. When writing, you should do all these things to establish your credibility with your readers. When reading, you'll probably find that you're most swayed by authors who have managed to do all these things successfully. Be careful, however, not to let a strong ethical appeal manipulate you into believing an author who doesn't offer any hard evidence for the claims he or she makes.

RECOGNIZING LOGICAL FALLACIES

Logical fallacies are common mistakes in thinking — often, the making of statements that lead to wrong conclusions. By mistakes in thinking, writers may distort evidence. Good writers avoid logical fallacies: although they seem persuasive on the surface, critical readers will recognize them as weaknesses in an argument. Here are a few of the most familiar logical fallacies, to help you recognize them when you see or hear them and so guard against them when you write. If when you look back over your draft you discover any of these, cut them, think again, and come up with a different argument. If you come across them in a source you are considering, you should seriously doubt the validity of the writer's case.

Non sequitur (from the Latin, "It does not follow"). This fallacy is the error of stating a claim that doesn't follow from your first premise (the statement you begin with): "Marge should marry Jergus. Why, in high school he got all A's." Come up with stronger reasons for your recommendation — reasons that have to do with getting good grades *as a husband.*

Oversimplification. This fallacy is evident when a writer offers neat and easy solutions for large, complicated problems: "If we want to do away with drug abuse, let's get tough. Let's sentence every drug user to life imprisonment." (Even users of aspirin?)

Post hoc ergo propter hoc *("after this, therefore because of this").* This fallacy assumes a cause-and-effect relationship where there is none. We assume that when one event precedes another in time, the first is the cause of the second.

Many superstitions result from *post hoc* reasoning: neither seeing a black cat nor strolling under a ladder causes misfortune. (In a way, this is another form of oversimplification — attributing huge effects to just one simple cause.)

Allness. The allness fallacy means stating or implying that something is true of an entire class of things. There are exceptions to every rule, and your readers are likely to find them. Instead of saying "Students enjoy studying" (which implies that *all* students enjoy *all* types of studying *all* the time), qualify: "Some students enjoy studying math." Be wary of *allness* words — *all, everyone, no one, always, never.*

Proof by example (or too few examples). An example illustrates or helps to clarify, but it does not prove: "Armenians are great chefs. My next-door neighbor is Armenian, and, boy, can he cook!" This type of overgeneralizing is the basis of much prejudice. Be sure you have sufficient evidence — enough examples, a large enough sampling — to draw a conclusion.

Begging the question. The writer who sets out to prove a statement already taken for granted begs the question. For instance, the argument that rapists are menaces because they are dangerous doesn't prove a thing: "menaces" are "dangerous" people. Beggars of questions just repeat in different words what they have already stated. Sometimes this fallacy takes the form of "circular reasoning": "He is a liar because he simply isn't telling the truth." Sometimes it takes the form of defining a word in terms of itself: "Happiness is the state of being happy."

Either/or reasoning. This logical fallacy is a special brand of oversimplified thinking — assuming that there are only two sides to a question, that all statements are either true or false, that all questions demand either a yes or a no answer. An either/or reasoner assumes that a problem has only two possible solutions, only one of which is acceptable. "What are we going to do about acid rain? Either we shut down all the factories that cause it, or we just forget about acid rain and learn to live with it. We've got no choice, right?" Realize that there are more than two choices or more than two causes.

Argument from dubious authority. An unidentified authority can be used unfairly to shore up a quaking argument: "According to some of the most knowing scientists in America, smoking two packs a day is as harmless as eating a couple of oatmeal cookies. So let's all smoke." A reader should also doubt an authority whose expertise lies outside the subject being considered: "TV personality Pat Sajak says this insurance policy is the lowest-priced and most comprehensive available."

Argument ad hominem *(from the Latin, "against the man").* This fallacy consists of attacking an individual's opinion by attacking his or her character. This fallacy is widespread in politics: "Sure candidate Smithers advocates this tax plan. It will put money in his pocket!" Judge the tax proposal on its merits, not on the character of its originator. Or "Carruthers may argue that we need to save the whales, but Carruthers is the kind of person who always gets excited over nothing." His characteristic of being easily excited is not relevant to the argument to save whales. Joining these two ideas implies that his attempt to save the whales is not important. A person's circumstances can also be turned against him or her: "Carruthers would have us spend millons to save whales, but I happen to know that he owns a yacht from which he selfishly enjoys watching whales." His circumstances are irrelevant to any argument he may make concerning the whales. Again, judge the proposal to save the whales on its merits, not on the proposer's character.

Argument from ignorance. This fallacy involves maintaining that because a claim has not been disproved, it has to be accepted: "Despite years of effort, no one has conclusively proved that ghosts don't exist; therefore, we should expect to see them at any time." Don't accept the existence of ghosts merely on the basis that their existence has not been disproved. The converse is also an error — that because a conclusion has not been proved, it should be rejected: "No one has ever shown that there is life on any other planet. Evidently the notion of other living things in the universe is unthinkable." Demand other evidence of the lack of plausibility of life on other planets.

Argument by analogy. The writer who makes this mistake uses a *metaphor* (a figure of speech that points to a similarity: "Her speech was a string of firecrackers") as though it were evidence to support a claim. In explanation, an analogy may be useful. It can set forth a complex idea in terms of something familiar and easy to imagine. For instance, shooting a spacecraft to a distant planet is like sinking a golf ball with uncanny accuracy into a hole a half mile away. But if used to convince, an analogy will be logically weak, though it may sound neat and clear. Dwelling only on similarities, a writer doesn't consider differences — since to admit them would only weaken the analogy: "People were born free as the birds. It's cruel to expect them to work." Hold on: human society and bird society have more differences than similarities. Because they are alike in one way doesn't mean they're alike in *every* way.

Bandwagon argument. The writer who uses this technique tries to persuade the reader to jump on the bandwagon, appealing to the human desire to belong. The argument suggests that everyone is joining the group and if the readers don't join also, they will be left out. Often the bandwagon technique is used in arguments related to happiness, success, or reward. An advertiser may suggest that if readers don't drive a certain car or drink a certain soda, they won't be part of the "in" crowd. If readers identify with a specific group or if they aspire to a certain group (political, social, financial, or educational), a political pamphlet may imply that a particular candidate is the choice of the people in that group. A writer may argue that any readers who disagree with the position set forth, for example, in favor of more funding for education, are misinformed and should change their opinions to jump on the bandwagon with all the other well-informed taxpayers.

RECOGNIZING MISUSES OF LANGUAGE

The effectiveness of a writer's position may also be weakened by misuse of language, either intentional or unconscious. Pitfalls that you should avoid when writing and be sensitive to when reading are lifting words out of context, equivocation, weasel words, and doublespeak.

Lifting words or statements out of context. Doing so changes the original meaning and is often used purposefully to distort evidence. For example, a drama critic writes, "The new play is a tremendous flop, with the only real suspense being whether the audience would stay until the end." But an advertiser selectively quotes, "According to a well-known drama critic, the new play is . . . 'tremendous' with 'real suspense,' " purposefully distorting the original review in order to sell tickets.

Equivocating. Equivocating is using a word in more than one sense in the same context. Poetry is enriched by the ambiguity of multiple meaning. Poet Robert Frost ends "The Road Not Taken" with the lines "Two roads diverged in a wood, and I — / I took the one less traveled by. / And that has made all the difference." He does not specify "all the difference," a purposefully ambiguous phrase, but leaves the interpretation to readers. Puns (plays on words) turn on ambiguity: "Try a Sound Sleeper mattress for the *rest* of your life" or "No noose is good news." However, when a conclusion is drawn by using a word whose meaning has been deliberately or inadvertently shifted in the discussion, distortion of evidence occurs: "As you can see, Johnson's statistics do not fairly represent the real situation. And if he is unfair, why should we trust his judgment?" (In the first sentence, *fair* means "accurate"; in the second sentence, it means "just.") You can avoid distortion through equivocation by carefully and consciously defining your terms.

Weasel words. These are used to evade or retreat from a direct or forthright statement or opinion. According to Paul Stevens, a writer of advertising copy, weasel words "can make you hear things that aren't being said, accept as truths things that have only been implied, and believe things that have only been suggested. . . . When *you* hear a weasel word, you automatically hear the implication. Not the real meaning, but the meaning *it* wants *you* to hear."[3] One of the most commonly used weasel words is *help*, as in "helps keep you healthy" or "helps prevent cavities." Notice that these statements don't claim anything very risky: they don't say the product *will* keep you healthy or prevent cavities, only that it will *help*, which isn't saying very much at all. (Breathing probably helps, too.) When you hear or read phrases like these, you are unaware of the word *help* and process only the strong language that follows it. Other weasel words are *like* ("these changes are like a complete overhaul of the system"); *virtual* or *virtually*, which means "in essence or effect, but not in fact" ("education is virtually a right

---

[3] Paul Stevens, "Weasel Words: God's Little Helpers," in *I Can Sell You Anything,* by Carl P. Wrighter (New York: Ballantine, 1972).

of every American"); and *up to,* which can mean none at all ("this measure guarantees improvement for up to twenty percent of the population"). When you come across these words in your own writing or in something you are reading, stop and read the sentence again: What does the sentence *really* say?

Doublespeak or obfuscating.   This means using language to hide the truth, either by using a series of meaningless generalities or by using terms and phrases unfamiliar to readers. Doublespeak is language that appears to be legitimate but is actually used purposefully to distort meaning. William Lutz in the book *Doublespeak*[4] cites as an example the Pentagon's attempt to avoid unpleasant associations by referring to bombs and artillery shells that fall on civilian targets as "incontinent ordnance" and by calling the neutron bomb a "radiation enhancement device." He also cites an incident during the investigation into the *Challenger* disaster in 1986. When Jesse Moore of NASA was asked if the performance in the shuttle program had improved, he answered:

> I think our performance in terms of the liftoff performance and in terms of the orbital performance, we knew more about the envelope we were operating under, and we have been pretty accurately staying in that. And so I would say the performance has not by design drastically improved. I think we have been able to characterize the performance more as a function of our launch experience as opposed to it improving as a function of time.

Take care that you do not fall victim to doublespeak, either when you are reading or when you are writing.

---

[4] William Lutz, *Doublespeak: From "Revenue Enhancement" to "Terminal Living," How Government, Business, Advertisers, and Others Use Language to Deceive You* (New York: Harper, 1989).

Chapter 5

Reading Critically

"A shut book," according to a saying, "is only a block of paper." So is an open book, until a reader interacts with it. Like flints that strike against one another and cause sparks, readers and writers provoke one another. Did you ever observe someone truly involved with a book? From time to time that reader may put down the book to ponder, to dream, or to doubt, may pick it up again, jot notes, underline, highlight, leaf backward for a second glance, sigh, mutter, fidget, nod approvingly, frown, perhaps laugh aloud, or disgustedly slam the book shut. Such a reader interacts visibly with the printed page. But not all readers are demonstrative. Some sit quietly, hardly moving a muscle, and yet they too may be interacting, deeply involved. Effective reading is active, not passive, reading.

Do all readers extract the same things from the same reading? Surely they don't. The act of reading is highly personal. What readers take away from reading is as varied as their interactions with the printed page. *The Divine Comedy,* said T. S. Eliot, has as many versions as it has readers. The point is not that a book can mean any old thing you want it to, but that each reader, like each visitor to a city, has different interests and experiences and so comes away with different responses and insights. Listening to a class discussion of an essay or a poem that all your classmates have read, you may be surprised by the range of insights reported by those other readers. If you missed some of their insights when you read alone, don't feel crestfallen. Other students may be equally surprised by what you see — something they missed entirely. Through using critical reading strategies, all of you can go beyond personal response to interpret more analytically and objectively.

You read for various reasons and in various ways. Often you look to other writers — in books or magazines — to stimulate your ideas. Sometimes you read in search of a topic to write about. Sometimes when you already have a topic, you seek information about it. Sometimes when you have an idea, you turn to other writers to help you explain it or back it up with examples and

109

evidence. Sometimes you read because you have ideas you want to test; sometimes reading can change your ideas. Often when you read, you respond, carrying on a mental conversation with the writer, agreeing or disagreeing with what you have read. Sometimes you analyze what a writer says to understand it better or to explain it to other people. In your college classes you will read for several reasons, but most of your reading should be focused and analytical—in other words, critical.

You will read critically to complete the assignments in this course and in other college courses. You need the skills of thinking critically about an idea or issue and using critical writing strategies and also the skill of approaching whatever you read in an active, questioning manner. You will think critically about sources for research papers and about pieces of literature for essays of analysis, interpretation, and evaluation. Often your instructors will ask you to read something critically and carefully and then to write about what you have read. This chapter provides you examples of and practice in writing from critical reading.

Learning from Other Writers

Let's look at two examples of writing based on critical reading. Each of these writers read a magazine article that he or she thought contained significant information, analyzed the ideas in the article in order to understand it fully, and wrote an essay incorporating analysis, response, and evaluation. The first essay is by George Will, a well-known contemporary newspaper columnist, television commentator, and political scientist. Commenting on an article from the *Atlantic Monthly* by Elijah Anderson, he analyzes the views of Professor Anderson on two social orientations—"decent" and "street,"—in the inner-city African American community. Through his analysis of Anderson's article, Will implies his own views on the worries of young inner-city black men.

Kelly Grecian, a student at Colby Community College, wrote her critique on an article in *Ms.* magazine for her English Composition I class. She analyzes the article point by point and adds her personal comments to each point. Grecian includes her personal views more explicitly than does George Will.

George Will The "Decent" against the "Street"

All at once Sherman was aware of the figure approaching him on the sidewalk, in the wet black shadows of the townhouses and the trees. Even from fifty feet away in the darkness, he could tell. It was that deep worry that lives in the base of the skull of every resident of Park Avenue south of Ninety-sixth Street—a black youth, tall, rangy, wearing white sneakers.
— Tom Wolfe, *The Bonfire of the Vanities*

But in real life the black youth probably would be worried more often   1
than Sherman McCoy. In inner cities, where life is a slow-motion riot, young
black men live worried, which is one reason why they often live briefly. Elijah
Anderson understands why they worry.

Anderson, a black professor of urban sociology at the University of Penn-   2
sylvania, and a superb reporter of real life, says the inner-city black community is divided, socially, between two orientations, "decent" and "street." The
street code is a quest for "respect" by people who are apt to have thin skins
and short fuses because they feel constantly buffeted by forces beyond their
control. Writing on "The Code of the Streets" in the *Atlantic Monthly*, Anderson says respect in the streets is hard won and easily lost, and losing it leaves
the individual naked to the aggression of others seeking to acquire or preserve
respect.

Amid the congenial academic clutter of an office overlooking the campus,   3
itself an island of calm in urban turmoil, Anderson says lack of confidence in
the police and criminal justice system produces a defensive demeanor of aggression. This demeanor expresses a proclivity for violent self-help in a menacing environment. A readiness to resort to violence is communicated by "facial expressions, gait, and verbal expressions — all of which are geared mainly
to deterring aggression" and to discouraging strangers "from even thinking
about testing their manhood."

Inner-city youths are apt to construct identities based precariously on   4
possessions — sneakers, jackets, jewelry, girlfriends. The taking and defense of
them is part of a tense and sometimes lethal ritual. It has, Anderson says, a
"zero-sum quality" because raising oneself requires putting someone down.
Hence the low threshold of violence among people who feel they have no way
of gaining or keeping status other than through physical displays.

The street is the alternative source of self-esteem because work experi-   5
ences are so often unsatisfactory, partly because of demeanors and behaviors
acquired in the streets. A prickly sensitivity about "respect" causes many
black youths to resent entry-level jobs as demeaning. And, Anderson says,
employers, black as well as white, react with distrust to a young black man
"with his sneakers, 'gangster cap,' chain necklace, and portable radio at his
side."

For such a person, work becomes a horizontal experience of movement   6
from one entry-level job to another. And the young person's "oppositional
culture" is reinforced by the lure of the underground economy of drugs. Furthermore, says Anderson, some young people develop "an elaborate ideology
in order to justify their criminal adaptation" to their situation, an ideology
portraying " 'getting by' without work as virtuous."

Anderson's father brought his family north from Arkansas to do war work   7
in the Studebaker plant in South Bend, Indiana (making fighter planes that
anticipated the look of postwar Studebaker cars), and by 1948 was making
$5,500 a year, equivalent to more than $30,000 today. Such jobs are scarce
now in cities, even for youths who have not adopted the demeanors, or succumbed to the temptations, of the street.

Also, says Anderson, many inner-city parents who love their children nev- 8
ertheless parent harshly to prepare their children for the harsh world beyond
the front stoop. A child who comes home from a losing fight may be sent out
to refight it, and parents yell at and strike their children for small infractions
of rules. As a result, says Anderson, children "learn that to solve any kind of
interpersonal problem one must quickly resort to hitting or other violent
behavior."

Anderson is not censorious of the black middle class which could have 9
leavened the ghetto with role models and encouragement, but which instead
has produced what Anderson calls "a kind of diaspora." However, Anderson,
who lives where gunfire occasionally disturbs his family's sleep, has various
family experiences with the violent possibilities of urban life.

During the 1992 rioting in South Central Los Angeles, his brother's 10
restaurant was burned down because it was sandwiched between two Korean
shops targeted by black rioters. Elijah Anderson and his brother both know
that the fictional worries of Sherman McCoy are as nothing next to the real-
life worries the decent black majority has about the minority that lives by the
code of the streets.

Questions to Start You Thinking

Meaning

1. How does Professor Elijah Anderson define the "street" code? What does he say are the causes of the street code?
2. What is the thesis of Will's essay?
3. What does Anderson mean when he says that the black middle class has produced "a kind of diaspora" (paragraph 9)?
4. According to Will, what do "decent" blacks have to fear from those who live by the street code?

Writing Strategies

5. What does the opening quotation from Tom Wolfe's *The Bonfire of the Vanities* add to Will's essay? Is this technique of beginning with a quotation effective? Why, or why not?
6. Why does Will end with an image from the 1992 Los Angeles riot? What point is he making here?
7. Why does Will describe Anderson's office? What do these details add to the essay?
8. Is Anderson a credible person to write and talk about inner-city blacks? Why, or why not? Is George Will qualified to write about Anderson's views? Why, or why not?
9. Why does Will use so many quotations from Anderson? Would Will's essay have been as effective if he had put Anderson's ideas in his own words instead?

Kelly Grecian   **Playing Games with Women's Sports**

In the January-February 1991 issue of <u>Ms</u>. magazine, Kate
Rounds, author of "Why Men Fear Women's Teams," casts a very
critical eye on the many reasons that women sports teams have
never reached the same prominence that men's sports have. She
believes this phenomenon is rooted in deep gender biases in
American society and economics. I agree with her that women's
sports have not been given the same recognition as men's
sports, even with the push for gender equality.

Rounds's first point is that women's teams have simply
not been given equal attention by fans or the media. Professional men's teams have the "big-name corporate sponsors,
television exposure, arenas, fan support," while the women's
sports are rarely televised and very rarely even known. A
women's team could be playing the same high-intensity game as
a men's team, but it doesn't matter because no one sees it.

In my own high school, boys' sports teams were catered
to and given priority. First, there was the matter of scheduling, which in turn affected fan turnout. Girls's volleyball
games were scheduled on Tuesday nights and Saturday after-
noons, which took away from our crowds. A lot of people hate
to make the trip to school on a work or school night "just to
watch volleyball," and most people have to work or have other
scheduled activities on Saturdays. The boys' football games
were on Friday nights, a great time for a lot of people to
turn out and watch. Although many of the girls at my school
thought this situation was unfair, we still made it a priority to be at all the football games--including those played
out of town--to lend support for our team. I rarely saw even
one of the boys from the high school at the away games of our
volleyball team. Second, there were big differences in media
coverage. Radio coverage or at least the final score is given
for many high school football games, but when was the last
time you heard how the area's girls' volleyball teams were
doing? Or when have you seen a major feature story in your
local newspaper about the high school girls' volleyball team?

1

2

3

At times the middle segment of the <u>Hill City Times</u> has devoted the entire spread to the Palco Rooster Football Team.

Rounds makes a very good point about the nature of some
of the successful women's sports, such as beach volleyball.
"The importance of what women athletes wear can't be underestimated," Rounds claims. "Beach volleyball, which is
played in the sand by bikini-clad women, rates network coverage while traditional court volleyball can't marshal any
of the forces that would make a women's pro league succeed."
She also considers it bizarre that a strange television
spectacle, called <u>American Gladiators</u>, is as popular as it
is: "Women stand on pastel pedestals, wearing Lycra tights
and brandishing weapons that look like huge Q-Tips. The attraction obviously has something to do with the 'uniforms.'"   4

Women in basic two-piece beach gear definitely are alluring to much of the male population. But I also love to
watch beach volleyball, and it is not because I think the
women look really sexy. I find it incredible that two women
can work together to play all the roles that a whole six-
member volleyball team would traditionally play. Regardless of
your sex, it seems to me that the beach, the surf, the sand,
and the sun create a very unique sports setting that is unparalleled in the sports world. I support the attention women
now get in beach volleyball--but I also agree with Rounds
that women in other sports also deserve more recognition.   5

According to Rounds, the fear of perceived lesbianism is
still another reason that the general public shies from
women's teams. She captures her point in a quote from Major
League Volleyball executive director Lindy Vivas: "The United
States in general has problems dealing with women athletes
and strong, aggressive females. Women athletes are looked at
as masculine and get the stigma of being gay." Rounds agrees
with Vivas and notes, "People in women's sports spend a lot of
time dancing around the 'L' word, and the word 'image' pops up
in a way it never does in men's sports. Men can spit tobacco
juice, smoke, and even scratch their testicles on national television and get away with it."   6

In my opinion, lesbianism is just a scapegoat, a way to
stigmatize women's sports. Many boys and men have trouble ac-   7

cepting that girls and women can be just as aggressive, if
not more so, than they are. They would rather believe that
female athletes are "weak" or "prissy"--as if all sports depend completely on brute strength--and that any strong, aggressive, and mean women players are strangely unfeminine--
that is, lesbians. The fact is, sexual preference has little
to do with the performance of female (or male) athletes, and
both gay and straight female athletes can be tough, skilled
opponents.

The final reason that Rounds gives for the failure of   8
professional women's sports teams is that too often athletes
have been taken advantage of by men looking for a fast
profit. "There's no doubt that many athletes in the women's
sports establishment are leery of fast-talking guys who try
to make a buck off women's pro sports, especially when the
women themselves don't profit from those ventures," says
Rounds. She then supports this claim by providing the example
of the first Women's Basketball League. The owners routinely
overestimated profits, received less than they anticipated,
and then failed to pay their players. Of course, they still
managed to pay arena owners what they had promised.

Past mismanagement of women's sports obviously discour-   9
ages a lot of female athletes from participating in professional women's sports. These kinds of financial practices
cause me to question the integrity of the men who were supposedly opening up opportunities for these women. I really
begin to doubt that they were in the business for anything
other than a quick profit at the expense of some very vulnerable athletes trying to make a place in the sports world for
themselves. If women's sports teams continue to be handled in
the manner that they have in the past, they are threatened
with losing any foothold they have already secured.

I am far from being a feminist, which is a label often   10
pinned on those of us who would like to see women's sports
given a little more credit. I think, however, that there
still are a lot of issues that need to be addressed when discussing the so-called equality of men's and women's sports.
Kate Rounds just happened to be bold enough to address some
of these issues.

Questions to Start You Thinking	*Meaning*

Meaning

1. What is the thesis of Kate Rounds's article? What is the thesis of Grecian's essay? How are they similar, and how are they different?

2. How many reasons does Grecian give for gender inequality in sports? State each one briefly.

3. In your opinion, for which reason does Grecian provide the most convincing evidence? Which reason has the weakest evidence?

4. In the last paragraph, why does Grecian deny that she is a feminist? Do you agree she is not a feminist? What is your definition of *feminism*? Is Rounds a feminist?

Writing Strategies

5. Is Grecian's introductory paragraph effective? Why, or why not? Can you think of any way she might strengthen the introduction?

6. How does Grecian organize her essay? Is this organization effective for her purpose?

7. An essay written for a freshman composition class is usually written for classmates as audience. Would Grecian's essay, especially the tone and the evidence, effectively convince you and your classmates? Why, or why not?

Learning by Writing

THE ASSIGNMENT: READING CRITICALLY

This assignment invites you to do some reading that will expand your knowledge on an interesting topic, to analyze the text you read by using critical reading strategies, and then to write an essay based on your critical analysis. To read critically, you will look for passages that stimulate what you think, actively engage with the text on both a literal level and an analytical level, and arrive at a well-reasoned conclusion about both the text and the points that it makes. In your paper, you will then present to your readers the text itself, your analysis, and your conclusion.

Critical reading is different from other types of reading you may do. When you read a telephone book, you quickly read down a list of names to find the one whose phone number you need. When you read the sports page in the newspaper, you read to find out about the key plays of a football game or a tennis match. When you read a novel for pleasure, you read to find out what happens to the characters in the story. But reading critically to study a text requires critical thinking skills. First, you must read on the *literal level*: you must be aware of, comprehend, and be able to apply the information in a passage. Then you must go further and read on an *analytical level*: you must analyze, synthesize, and evaluate what you read. Both levels are necessary for a thorough critical reading.

We have seen many thoughtful papers written in response to this assignment; for example:

A man read and analyzed George Orwell's classic essay "Shooting an Ele-phant" and agreed with Orwell that governments can act unwisely simply to save face. He wrote an essay in which he analyzed Orwell's view, agreed with Orwell's position, and drew parallels between imperial Great Britain and contemporary governments.

A woman found an interesting article on the working conditions of work-fare recipients. She analyzed the article point by point and wrote an essay in which she refuted the arguments of the author.

A woman read an article in which the author took the stand that the fu-neral profession is a reflection of our culture. At first she was startled by this claim, but after analyzing the article, she discovered she agreed with the author. She wrote an essay explaining the author's position in order to share her new insights with others.

A man read an editorial on the need for reform of the way political cam-paigns are funded. He was so convinced by the editorial's argument and so outraged by the evidence provided that he wrote an essay to share the significant information with his classmates and to try to convince them that campaign reform is necessary.

GENERATING IDEAS

How will you find ideas for this assignment? First you need to find interest-ing and challenging reading material, and then you need to fully engage with it. Try reading a variety of materials first — maybe one essay, one book chapter, one magazine article, one Internet source — and see what piques your interest or looks promising for a meaty analysis. Don't worry if you find an interesting piece that you don't fully comprehend because this as-signment will guide you to understand the article more fully by analyzing it. Here are some suggestions for unlocking some of the potential hidden in a good text.

Keep a journal of your reading. For several days keep a log of articles that you read in newspapers or magazines. If you do not find any likely pieces, visit the library to go through some essay collections, or search the Internet. Try read-ing a variety of pieces first — whatever engages your interests and challenges you to think seriously. Then your journal will contain a variety of possibilities for a paper topic.

At this point you are skimming, not reading, possible pieces, so you will need to return later to the one you choose for analytical reading. Record the author, title source, and a brief notation of the subject and point of view of each article that you think contains significant ideas. Be sure that you record enough information about the articles so that you can easily find them again.

Your journal entries should not be just a record of what you read; they should also include your response to your reading. The questions in the fol-lowing checklist will help you get started with your own reading journal. If you write in your journal the answers to at least some of these questions for the articles you find, you'll have valuable thoughts on hand when you start reading critically. (For more suggestions about keeping a journal, see Chapter 15.)

Facing the Challenge: Critical Reading

The major challenge writers face when they write essays based on critical reading is to understand all the points made in the articles or books they are analyzing, so that they can summarize the author's points clearly and accurately and explain whether they agree or disagree. If you don't do the active reading necessary to arrive at a clear understanding of the main points made in an article, you won't be able to explain those points to your readers. Worse still, you are likely to misrepresent your sources in your paper—attacking authors for beliefs they never expressed.

In addition, your instructors will expect you to move beyond a mere summary of an article's main points to a critical analysis of them—to provide your own opinions and evidence rather than simply reporting someone else's argument. In "Playing Games with Women's Sports," Kelly Grecian does more than just summarize Kate Rounds's article "Why Men Fear Women's Teams." For example, while Grecian agrees with Rounds's assertion that beach volleyball is popular with men because it is played by women in bikinis, she defends network coverage of the sport, stating that "I also love to watch beach volleyball, and it is not because I think the women look really sexy. I find it incredible that two women can work together to play all the roles that a whole six-member team would traditionally play." This opinion comes from Grecian's personal knowledge of the sport and thus constitutes reliable evidence.

To make sure that you understand an article and can move from explaining its main points to analyzing them, complete the following five-part exercise in your journal:

1. Locate the author's thesis, or main point, and state it in your own words, in a sentence or two.
2. Go through the article, paragraph by paragraph, and summarize or "nutshell" the main point made in each paragraph in a sentence or two, leaving several lines of blank space after each of your summaries.
3. Locate the author's conclusion and summarize it.
4. In the blank space after your summary of the main point made in each paragraph, note any evidence the author provides to support that point.
5. Finally, write out your own response to each main point, clarifying whether you agree or disagree with the author's interpretation.

As a college student you must begin questioning the authority and opinions of established thinkers. Don't be afraid to challenge the opinions expressed in an article or a book: skepticism is often the foundation of critical thinking and reading. But remember to remain respectful of the opinions of others by not rushing to judgment until you have taken the time to fully understand the points they have made and the arguments and evidence they have provided to support those points.

DISCOVERY
CHECKLIST

Keeping a Reading Journal

- What is the subject of the article? What stand does the author take concerning the subject?
- What does the writer take for granted? What assumptions — stated or unstated — does he or she begin with?
- Do the writer's assertions rest on evidence? What kind of evidence?
- Do you agree with what the writer has said? Do his or her ideas clash with any ideas you hold dear? Does he or she question anything you take for granted?
- From any facts the writer presents, what inferences can you draw? Might any conflicting evidence be mustered? Has the writer failed to tell you anything you wish you knew?
- Has anything you read opened your eyes to new ways of looking at the world?

Skim and sample. As you begin your search for promising material, keep in mind that you can't afford the luxury of reading every possibility word for word, especially at this stage in the process. Skim, skip, and sample ideas. Try reading just the first two and the last two paragraphs of articles. Those paragraphs will probably alert you to the writers' main points. When you look into books, skim through the first chapter and the last chapter, and study the table of contents. Then, if an article or a book looks interesting, you can spend more time analyzing it critically.

Look for meaty pieces. Start in the library, and browse through several current magazines to spur your thinking, such as the *Atlantic, Harper's, New Republic, Commentary, Ms.,* and *Esquire.* Check special-interest magazines — such as the *New England Journal of Medicine, Architectural Digest,* or *Black History Monthly* — on subjects of interest to you. Check the editorials and op-ed columns in your local newspaper or in the *New York Times* or the *Wall Street Journal.* Avoid *People, Life,* the *National Enquirer,* or other periodicals written primarily to entertain. You want good, meaty articles conducive to reflection and analysis. If the essays are a bit difficult to understand and need to be read more than once, so much the better. They will give you the opportunity to apply critical reading strategies and strengthen your reading ability. Try not to look only for confirmation of ideas you already have. Instead, stay open to fresh ideas that you may unexpectedly encounter in your readings.

Also check the Internet. Type a subject of interest to you (such as the effects of poverty on children, computer addiction, street talk, Asian American authors) into an Internet search engine such as Yahoo! or Excite, and locate some articles on your subject. Be sure that the articles you find are meaty, not superficial, and are written to inform and convince, not to entertain or amuse.

Recall something you have already read. What have you read lately that started you thinking and wondering? Classic books like Sigmund Freud's *The Interpretation of Dreams* and Rachel Carson's *The Sea Around Us* or classic essays such as Ralph Waldo Emerson's "Self-Reliance" make a clear point and bristle with challenging ideas. Consider drawing on some readings you have done for your composition course or for another course — a chapter in a humanities textbook, an article in a professional journal assigned for outside reading in a sociology course, a research study for a biology course.

Choose a promising piece. Once you have spent a few days sampling various pieces, look back over your reading journal, and choose a promising lead. Faced now with several days' worth of journal entries, how do you decide which essay to focus on in a paper? First, ask yourself which entry most interests you. Second, ask which of your reflections would most interest your possible readers — your classmates and your instructor. Which entry most clearly seems to say something? Which arrives at or points toward a conclusion, however tentative? For which one do you clearly have some ideas of your own to add, either in agreement or disagreement? That's the one to develop. You may want to discuss your possible choices with your classmates or your instructor before you proceed.

Read critically. Once you select a thought-provoking article, essay, or chapter, return to it, and read it slowly and carefully, giving yourself plenty of time to think between the lines. Read on the analytical level as well as the literal level. Try to discern the writer's opinions, even if they are unstated. But don't just soak up opinions and information. Carry on a mental dialogue with the writer. Criticize. Question. Wonder. Argue back. Dare to differ with the author. Demand evidence to be convinced. Most printed pages are not holy writ. You can doubt them; you can disagree with them. Opinions you don't agree with can be valuable if they set your own thoughts in motion.

To read critically, you must engage with a piece on both a literal level and an analytical level. To **read on the literal level**, you must first *be aware* of the information the text is presenting—that is, you must notice the fact or idea presented. Second, you must *comprehend* what the fact or idea means. Third, you must be able to *apply* it. For example, you read in your history book a passage that asserts that Franklin Delano Roosevelt is the only American president who was elected to four consecutive terms of office. You now are aware of this fact, but to comprehend it, you need to know that a term for a U.S. president is four years and that *consecutive* means continuous. Thus, FDR was elected to serve sixteen years as president of the United States. To apply this knowledge, you think of other presidents — George Washington, who served two terms; Theodore Roosevelt, who served two terms but not consecutively; Ronald Reagan, who served two terms; George Bush, who served one; and Bill Clinton, who in 1996 was reelected to a second term. Then you realize that being elected to four terms is quite unusual. To read literally, you decode the words in the passage to figure out the meaning, bringing to bear related information that you already know. Clearly, even a good literal reading of a passage requires active reading and thinking.

After mastering a fact or passage on the literal level, you need to **read on the analytical level**, probing deeply into the meaning beneath the surface. First you *scrutinize* the fact, looking at it and its implications from various angles.

Then you gather more information related to the fact and *synthesize* all of it, recombining it into new insights. Finally, you *evaluate* the significance of the fact. To return to the example above, once you have literally understood the fact that Franklin Delano Roosevelt was elected to four terms of office as president, you ask yourself questions about it to scrutinize it from various angles. Why is FDR the only president who has been elected to serve four terms? What circumstances during his terms of office contributed to three reelections? How is FDR different from other presidents? To answer some of these questions, you may have to do additional reading, and what you discover may lead you to ask even more questions. After you have gathered sufficient information about FDR and his reelections, you examine all the facts and opinions and draw some inferences and conclusions about this fact. You need to ask yourself what logical inferences may be drawn from the information you have collected, and you need to have sufficient evidence to support whatever conclusions you draw. It would be logical to conclude that the special circumstances of the Depression and World War II contributed to Roosevelt's four terms. It would not be logical to conclude that Americans reelected him out of pity because he was a victim of polio. Finally, you evaluate your newly found knowledge to determine its significance, both to your understanding of Depression-era politics and to the soundness of the textbook author's message. At this point, you might ask yourself, Why has the author chosen to make this point? How does it affect the rest of the author's message? Should I trust this author? And you may also form your own opinion based on the evidence you have gathered. Based on a good critical reading of the facts in the preceding example, for instance, it might be reasonable to conclude that FDR's four-term presidency is understandable in light of the events of the 1930s and 1940s, that the author has mentioned this fact to highlight the unique political atmosphere of that era, and that in your opinion it is evidence neither for nor against FDR's excellence as a president.

Critical readers ask questions as they read. These questions help them to stay alert to important points and to monitor their processes of reading. You can think of it as a conversation with the author of the piece you are reading or as a conversation with yourself, if that makes more sense. The following checklist includes questions designed to improve your reading:

 **CRITICAL READING CHECKLIST**

- *What are the key concepts or ideas of the text? What problems and issues does the author raise?* The problems and issues in the article are the main points that the writer sets forth. He or she may present only one main issue (expressed in the thesis sentence or main idea) or several points unified by the thesis.
- *Is the author credible?* What are his or her credentials? Is the writer an expert in the field? Can you trust him or her to verify information presented? Can you rely on the author to know what he or she is talking about?
- *What is the author's purpose?* Is it to explain or inform? To convince or persuade? To amuse? In addition to the obvious purpose of the piece, is there some other agenda the author is trying to accomplish?
- *How is the text organized?* To understand the piece fully on the literal level, you should understand how it is put together. Note where one point ends and an-

other begins; notice how ideas are sequenced and connected. Is it easy to follow? Does it seem appropriate?

- *Do you understand every important word and idea?* Sometimes the key to a thorough literal understanding is just slowing down and asking this question. If you don't understand something, it may be that the author has not explained it sufficiently. Or it could mean that you need to read more carefully or go to an outside source (such as a dictionary or reference book) to find more information.

- *Where do you agree, and where do you disagree?* Make a note of every point you strongly agree or disagree with. Start talking back to the piece, whether that's to say "yeah, right!" or "I don't think so!"

- *What does this remind you of in your own life?* Try to connect the piece somehow to your own experiences or thoughts. Have you encountered anything similar to the situation described? Is any aspect of the discussion personally intriguing to you?

- *What is the author assuming or taking for granted?* You will need to be aware of the author's implicit assumptions to understand what he or she is saying on an explicit level. Even more important, ferreting out an author's assumptions can help you see where his or her argument is weak or biased.

- *What is the author's tone?* Tone reveals the author's attitude toward the topic of the piece; it is generally conveyed through the choice of words and examples. It may be objective or biased, amused or serious, satiric or straightforward, liberal or conservative. By paying attention to tone, you may be able to detect the author's biases or assumptions.

- *What evidence, information, and data are presented? Is the evidence accurate, relevant, and sufficient?* Evidence is the information used to support and clarify the general assertions that the author makes. The evidence may be facts, statistics, expert opinions, or personal experiences and observations. Always ask whether there is enough good evidence to convince you of the author's points: try arguing back. (For more on evaluating evidence, see pp. 101–02.)

- *Which statements are fact? Which are opinions? Does one or the other dominate the piece?* A fact is a statement that can be verified by observation or firsthand testimony or research in credible sources. An opinion is someone's personal response to a fact or person or situation. Do not confuse the two, and make sure that the writer does not either. (For more on facts and opinions, see pp. 99–101.)

- *Does the author make logical fallacies or misuse language?* Make note of any "fighting words," leaps of logic, or other signs that the author's case is not as sound as it should be. Misused language and shoddy reasoning should lead you to question the author's credibility, if not the soundness of his or her ideas. (For more on logical fallacies and misused language, see pp. 104–08.)

- *What would you ask the author if she or he were here?* Go back to the passages that you strongly agreed with and disagreed with, and try to capture the thoughts and questions these evoke. Why do you agree or disagree? What further questions do you have? What other lines of thought do these passages suggest?

Annotate the text.   One of the best ways to engage fully with a piece is to "talk back" by writing notes directly on the page. Obviously, if the piece appears in a book or periodical that you don't own, you'll need to make a photocopy; if it's an Internet source, you'll need to make a printout. As you pose and answer the questions in the Critical Reading Checklist, make notes to yourself. You can underline key points, make checks and stars by ideas you agree with or disagree with, and jot down questions or comments in the margins. The exact system doesn't matter: just try to come up with one that you'll understand later. When Kelly Grecian started to analyze on the *Ms.* article by Kate Rounds, she annotated a key passage in the article like this:

different case from individual sports

By contrast, women's professional (team) sports have failed spectacularly. Since the mid-seventies, every professional league — softball, basketball, and volleyball — has gone belly-up. In 1981, after a four-year struggle, the Women's Basketball League (WBL), backed by sports promoter Bill Byrne, folded. The league was drawing fans in a number of cities, but the sponsors weren't there, TV wasn't there, and nobody seemed to miss the spectacle of a few good women fighting for a basketball.

bitter tone

Something I know about!

our team never got these either

Or a (volleyball,) for that matter. Despite the success of (bikini) volleyball, an organization called MLV (Major League Volleyball) bit the dust in March of 1989 after nearly three years of struggling for sponsorship, fan support, and television exposure. [As with pro basketball, there was a man behind women's professional volleyball,] real estate investor Robert (Bat) Batinovich. Batinovich admits that, unlike court volleyball, beach volleyball has a lot of "visual T&A mixed into it."

Why does she call it this?

She's suspicious of men

oh, great

seems like these are only two options

What court volleyball does have, according to former MLV executive director Lindy Vivas, is strong women athletes. Vivas is assistant volleyball coach at San Jose State University. "The United States in general," she says, "has problems dealing with women athletes and strong, aggressive females. The perception is you have to be more aggressive in team sports than in golf and tennis, which aren't contact sports. Women athletes are looked at as masculine and get the stigma of being gay."

good quote

credential

Why do guys always think we're weak and prissy?

PLANNING, DRAFTING, AND DEVELOPING

Decide what point you want to make. Before you begin writing, backtrack for a while, and take some time to reflect. Read the article again. Look over your journal entry to review your critical analysis of the passage. Do more thinking. What conclusions have you drawn so far? What point do you want to make? Do you have what you need to make that point?

One strength of both Will's essay and Grecian's essay is the examples from real life: Will draws from Professor Anderson's experiences, and Grecian draws from her own. After Grecian annotated the passage from Rounds's article, she decided her material was still a little skimpy. She brainstormed about her high school experiences, jotting down specific examples. Then Grecian discussed her article and her experiences with three other students. She told them of her assignment, shared her preliminary thoughts, and asked, "Do you know of other examples?" This conversation helped her think of other specifics, including the notion that males still like to think of women as weak creatures and not as strong, aggressive individuals. As Grecian began to draft, looking over the notes from her brainstorming session and from her conversation, she discarded examples that didn't work and thought of new ones. (For more on individual brainstorming, see p. 360; for more on working with other student writers, see Chapter 20.)

Determine an order for your ideas. As you plan your essay, you must not only select the ideas to include but also begin to organize the information. You may start your draft with a quotation from your reading, as George Will does in "The 'Decent' against the 'Street'," or with a summary of your reading followed by a statement of your agreement or disagreement with what you have read, as Kelly Grecian does in "Playing Games with Women's Sports." You may decide to use a relevant anecdote, a comment about the author, or a personal account of the article's effect on you to establish a basis for your own reflections and insights.

WRITING WITH A COMPUTER

Try sitting at your word processor with the book you are reading in your lap, so you can read and take notes at the same time. If you use electronic note cards instead of paper ones, you won't have to transcribe any material more than once. You can copy portions of your notes into your paper or leave them where they are and write *around* them. Remember that immediately after transcribing a passage, you should carefully record all the information you will need to acknowledge your source in your final paper — and to find it again, if necessary.

If you have long quotations that require extended proofreading, try this. Enlarge a long quotation using a large font size to give your writing a different look. If your screen displays the page as it appears coming off the printer, edit it on screen; if not, print out a copy. A long passage like this might be more fun to proofread:

Benvenuto Cellini, the celebrated sculptor of the Italian Renaissance, designed for Francis I a famous saltcellar of enamel and gold, preserved in the Vienna Art Museum.

Errors in an exaggerated font size will stand out readily. But remember to return your fonts to a standard size after you finish proofreading.

Then you need to decide on an arrangement of ideas for the body of your essay. Grecian first states Rounds's three reasons in the order Rounds uses, and then Grecian follows each reason with her own opinion, experiences, and observations. If you are not sure how to organize your ideas, try several ways. To discover a satisfactory order, you might jot down your ideas and number them, write a formal outline, or write several drafts, each organized differently. (A computer makes this last method easy.) The strategy that works for you may not work for your classmates. The important thing is that you think and plan as you work.

Finally, you'll conclude your piece by referring to your main point, not by introducing a new idea. Look again at how both Will and Grecian allude to the main idea in the conclusion of the essays. (For more about organizing ideas, see Chapter 16; for more on openings and conclusions, see Chapter 17.)

Borrow honestly. The first law of writing from reading is to acknowledge fully and honestly your debt to the writer from whom you borrowed anything—a quotation, information, an idea. Not to do so is to lay yourself open to the charge of ***plagiarism***. In both the academic and professional worlds, using someone else's words or ideas and failing to cite the source is considered a grave offense akin to theft. In college, it can be the grounds for a failing grade or even for expulsion. Therefore, you should identify any source of an idea or quotation right away, as soon as you write it in your journal, and carry that acknowledgment to your first draft and subsequent drafts. Notice how Will and Grecian work the citations of their sources right into the text of their essays. You can use information from your sources in any of three ways.

Quoting. When an author expresses an idea in a way that is so incisive, so brilliant, or so memorable that you want to reproduce his or her words exactly, quote them word for word. Direct quotations add life and color and the sound of an authoritative speaking voice. If you quote, be sure to quote exactly, including punctuation and capitalization. If you leave out part of a quotation, indicate the omission with an ellipsis mark—three dots (. . .). If the ellipsis mark occurs at the beginning or end of a sentence within the quotation, use four dots. You don't need an ellipsis mark at the beginning or end of the quotation. Why leave anything out? Usually material is omitted because, if left in, it would be too boring or cumbersome or would add information that mattered to the author but doesn't matter to your point. But be careful that omitting words does not distort the author's meaning. For example, if a reviewer calls a movie "a perfect example of poor directing and inept acting," you cannot quote this comment as "perfect . . . directing and . . . acting."

In paragraph 2 of "Playing Games with Women's Sports," Grecian quotes Kate Rounds's list of necessary components for the success of professional women's sports teams: "big-name corporate sponsors, television exposure, arenas, fan support." She used a direct quotation here because Rounds's words were precise, authoritative, and powerful.

Nutshelling. Also called *summarizing,* nutshelling is a useful way to deal with a whole paragraph or section of a work when you're interested in only the section's general point. Rather than quoting word for word, and without doing violence to an idea, you put it in a nutshell: you express its main sense in your own words and tell where you got the idea. A summary or nutshell is generally much shorter than the original; it expresses only the most important ideas in the original. Be sure you understand the passage before you attempt to summarize it, and take care not to distort the meaning.

In paragraph 6, Grecian summarizes one of Rounds's points this way: "According to Rounds, the fear of perceived lesbianism is still another reason that the general public shies from women's teams."

Paraphrasing. The technique of paraphrasing involves restating an author's ideas in your own words. Unlike a nutshell or summary, a paraphrase is generally about the same length as the original; it expresses every idea in the original but in your words. You have to be careful not to let the author's words slip in. If a source says, "President Wilson called an emergency meeting of his cabinet to discuss the new crisis," and you say, "The president called his cabinet to hold an emergency meeting to discuss the new crisis," your words aren't far enough removed from the original. You have paraphrased too close to the source. You could put quotation marks around the original sentence, although it seems not worth quoting word for word. Or, better, you could write: "Summoning his cabinet to an emergency session, Wilson laid out the challenge before them." If you comprehend the material you are reading, think through it, and deal carefully with it, you will be able to find words of your own to express the ideas.

In paragraph 8, Grecian uses a direct quote about women being taken advantage of, followed by a paraphrase of the situation in the first Women's Basketball League. Without using Rounds's exact language, Grecian produces a new version true to the writer's ideas.

ROUNDS'S ORIGINAL PASSAGE

In the old league, finances were so shaky that some players claim they were never paid.

"We weren't getting the gate receipts," says Lieberman-Cline. "They'd expect 2,000, get only 400, and then they'd have to decide whether to pay the arena or pay the girls, and the girls were the last choice."

GRECIAN'S PARAPHRASE

She then supports this claim by providing the example of the first Women's Basketball League. The owners routinely overestimated profits, received less than they anticipated, and then failed to pay their players. Of course, they still managed to pay arena owners what they had promised.

How do you paraphrase another writer's thoughts? We suggest you do the following:

1. Read the original passage over a couple of times to comprehend it. Underline key parts, or jot them down.
2. Without looking at the passage, try to state its gist—the main point it makes, the main sense you remember, and the major supporting points.
3. Then go back and reread the original passage one more time, making sure you stated its meaning faithfully. Revise your paraphrase as necessary.
4. Check your paraphrase to be sure that you have not slipped in a few words from the original author and that you have not paraphrased too closely to the source.

REVISING AND EDITING

Perhaps as you look over your draft, you will feel the need to read the text again to check what you have said about it. As you discover new insights while rereading or think of other conclusions or examples while drafting, you may find your views changing. If you find yourself rearranging your ideas drastically after starting to write, cosmetic changes may not be enough: you may have to revise thoroughly. To see how much your ideas have changed since you first wrote your journal entry, you might try to state (to yourself or in writ-

FOR PEER RESPONSE

Once you have a preliminary draft that you like, ask a friend or classmate to read your paper and answer the following questions before you make your final revisions. See Chapter 20 for advice on working with other student writers and for general questions you should always ask a peer editor to address. For a paper in which you write from reading, you'll also want your peer editor to answer these specific questions:

- Can you restate or quote the major insight the writer shares from his or her reading?
- Does this paper make you want to read the original source?
- Do you see evidence of critical reading strategies in the essay?
- How useful and how interesting are the quotations the writer uses? Does the writer introduce them smoothly?
- Has the writer shared enough of his or her own ideas?
- Are there parts of the essay where you're not sure whether you are reading the writer's ideas or the source's ideas? Underline any such places.
- Are there any long quotations that would be more effective as nutshells or paraphrases?
- At any point, do you need additional examples or explanations? Put a check by such places.
- If this were your paper, what is the one thing you would be sure to work on before handing it in?

ing) what insight you had then and what insight you have now after applying critical reading strategies to the article. This exercise will help you to focus in on your main idea for your final draft. In looking back over your paper, you might ask the following questions:

REVISION CHECKLIST

- Have you emphasized the significant and relevant points in the work you read?
- Have you gone on to develop your own ideas and insights?
- Do you see any place where a good, lively direct quotation might interrupt a monotonous passage?
- Have you used any direct quotations where a nutshell or a paraphrase would serve better?
- Have you checked direct quotations for accuracy?
- Do you identify clearly any information or ideas you have borrowed from another source?
- Is the order and flow of your ideas easy to follow?
- Do you have enough details and examples to clarify and back up your assertions?

Kelly Grecian found that the hardest part of writing her paper was making it coherent. Some of the transitions from Rounds's ideas to her own opinions were jerky, some connections between ideas were unclear, and other transitions seemed mechanical and repetitious. There were also places where she had included interesting but irrelevant information that did not belong in the paper. As she set about revising, she spent a lot of time rewriting transition sentences and deleting unnecessary and irrelevant information. Below are paragraphs 2 and 3 from Grecian's first draft marked up for her final draft. As you revise, remember that you have to put the ideas that are in your head on paper in a logical manner so that readers can follow the thoughts easily. Also, you have to be selective; you can't use everything you have read or everything you think.

Rounds ~~says~~ *'s first point is* that women's teams have simply not been given equal ~~coverage.~~ *attention by fans or the media.* Professional men's teams have the "big-name corporate sponsors, television exposure, arenas, fan support, and a critical mass of well-trained players/" While women's sports are rarely televised and very rarely even known. Women could be playing the same high-intensity game. *as men, but it doesn't matter because no one sees it.* ~~People underestimate their talent and capability.~~

^{own}
^{were}
In my ^high school, boys' sports teams ^are catered to
First, there was the matter of   *volleyball games were*
and given priority. ~~Think about~~ scheduling. Girls' ~~are~~
                                              which took away from
scheduled on Tuesday nights and Saturdays. ~~when not many~~
our crowds.
~~people attend.~~ A lot of people don't want to come out ~~to~~
                                   "just to watch volleyball."
~~watch volleyball~~ on a school night/ People have to work
or have other scheduled activities.   *, a great night for a lot of*
^~~at those times.~~ Football is on Fridays/ ~~Lots of people~~
people to turn out and watch.
~~turn out then.~~

After you have revised your essay written from critical reading, proofread
and edit it. Check carefully for problems with grammar, word choice, punctuation, and mechanics—and then correct any problems you find. A comprehensive reference handbook is an indispensable tool for this task; the "Quick
Editing Guide" at the end of *The Bedford Guide for College Writers* (see the pages
with the colored edges) will get you started.

When editing a paper written from critical reading, pay particular attention to quotations. Make sure that all direct quotations are enclosed in
quotation marks and that commas, periods, and other punctuation are used
correctly with quotations. Be sure that where you have omitted words from
a direct quotation, you have substituted an ellipsis mark (. . .)—three dots
to show where omissions have occurred—and that the sentence containing
the omission makes sense, given the sentences before and after it. If you
quote your source quoting someone else (a quotation within a quotation),
make sure to put your source's words in quotation marks and the words he
or she is quoting in single quotation marks. You should also take some time
to scrutinize your verb tense, especially if the text you are reading critically
is written in a tense different from the one you are using for most of your
paper.

Here are some questions to get you started when proofreading and editing your paper.

**EDITING
CHECKLIST**

- Have you used the present tense where you need it? Have you used the past
  tense where you need it? Are all tenses conveyed with the proper verb forms?
  (See A1 in the "Quick Editing Guide.")
- Do you know what the subject of each sentence is? Does each verb agree with
  its subject? (See A2 in the "Quick Editing Guide.")
- Is your sentence structure correct? Have you avoided writing fragments and
  run-on sentences? (See A6 and A7 in the "Quick Editing Guide.")

- Have you spelled and capitalized everything correctly, especially the names of the writer and the text you are analyzing? (See D1 and D2 in the "Quick Editing Guide.")
- Have you used the proper paper format, including special requirements for your instructor and course? (See D3 in the "Quick Editing Guide.")

(For more on revising and editing, see Chapter 19.)

OTHER ASSIGNMENTS

1. Write a letter to the editor of your local newspaper in which you criticize an editorial or a commentary that the newspaper printed recently. (You will find meaty commentaries on the editorial page, op-ed page, sports pages, and local news pages.) Summarize the newspaper passage, and refer to it sufficiently so that someone who hasn't read the article you're criticizing will know what you're talking about. Then go beyond summarizing what you have read, and include your own ideas and observations.

2. Using the critical reading strategies discussed in this chapter, analyze one of the essays in *A Writer's Reader* in this textbook. Write an essay in which you first give the reader an account of the information in the essay (through quotation, nutshell, or paraphrase) and then add your

FOR GROUP LEARNING

Discussing Your Reading

When your instructor assigns a paper for which all students in the class are to analyze a specific reading selection, first meet with your writing group—in class if your instructor provides time for this discussion or outside of class. Appoint a moderator to run a discussion of everyone's reaction to the reading. To start the discussion, here are some questions you might ask each group member:

- What problems did you have with this reading? What didn't you understand that someone else might explain?
- What do you take to be the author's purpose?
- What main point does the author make?
- Where do you disagree with or doubt the author?
- What does the author do especially well? What do you wish the author might have done better?
- What did you find out from this reading that you didn't know before?

The goal of this discussion is to give you a better understanding of critical reading strategies and appreciation of your reading so that you can come up with more ideas for your own paper.

own insights and ideas. Or you may organize the essay as Grecian does, point by point.

3. Use Will's or Grecian's ideas as a springboard for an essay.

4. Instead of analyzing something you have read, apply the critical strategies to analyze something that you hear — a lecture, a television or radio commentary, or a conversation.

5. Analyze an advertisement. You may use an ad that you have seen on television, on a billboard, in a magazine, or on the Internet. Quote the ad or announcement, analyze it according to critical strategies for thinking and reading, and then add your own insights and evaluation of the ad.

6. Analyze two history books' or two newspapers' accounts of a celebrated event — the writing of the Declaration of Independence, the bombing of Hiroshima, a natural disaster, a recent political event, or any event you wish to read more about. Try to find one recent source and one at least thirty years old. Write an essay in which you explain the differences between the two versions and how you account for those differences.

Applying What You Learn: Some Uses of Writing from Critical Reading

In college, you'll write from your reading almost daily. Many instructors, to encourage you to read and write, will ask you to keep a notebook of your reading and may ask you to turn it in for inspection. Writing about your reading on tests and examinations allows you to demonstrate your mastery of the course material. (For advice about writing essay examinations, see Chapter 13.) Knowing how to read critically will increase your comprehension and help you make good grades.

For other college writing assignments, reading will be just one of your resources. An education course, for instance, might ask you to combine reading and observing — to watch a toddler for an hour a day for a week, keep a detailed record of her actions, compare them with what is average for a child her age (information you would find by reading), and then draw some conclusions about her behavior. In the field of human development, students are constantly asked to make informed judgments on current issues (abortion, day care, joint custody) by learning to understand the differing views presented in books and articles.

You may be used to reading general magazines like *Newsweek* and *National Geographic*, which most literate readers enjoy. But later in college, many of your courses will require you to read journals written and read by trained specialists. Many specialists, from physicists to zoologists, write articles for others in their field, sharing what they know. Doctors and other health professionals report on new diseases or new treatments; scientists and technicians advance new theories; literary critics make fresh ventures into literary criticism; historians enlarge on and reinterpret knowledge of the past. As part of your training in a special discipline, you may be introduced to the *Journal of Comparative Behavior, Nature, Educational Research, American Journal of Sociology, PMLA,* or *Foreign Affairs.* You will often be asked to report on an article, reading it critically, perhaps summarizing or paraphrasing its essentials, and finally adding a thoughtful comment. Doing so, you will absorb the vocabulary and habits of thought of your chosen field and make them your own. You will see how skilled writers prove, demonstrate, evaluate, explain, select useful details, assert, affirm, deny, try to convince.

Many learned articles begin with a short review of previous research, which the writer then dashes to pieces. In some professional journals, though, summary or paraphrase of other writing may be an end in itself. Attorney Peter L. Knox, who writes articles about pension tax laws for professional legal journals, says that writing for him is often a matter of reading difficult writing (such as rulings of the Tax Court and the *Internal Revenue Manual*) and condensing it in plainer prose — "expressing in an organized, somewhat literary form a set of complex rules." You can see how Knox's articles might greatly help taxpayers and beginning tax lawyers struggling to understand legal prose such as the following, from *Final and Temporary IRS Regulations:*

§ 1.401(b)-1 **Certain retroactive changes in plan** [TD 7437, filed 9-23-76].

(a) *General rule.* Under section 401(b) a stock bonus, pension, profit-sharing, annuity, or bond purchase plan which does not satisfy the requirements of section 401(a) on any day solely as a result of a disqualifying provision (as defined in paragraph (b) of this section) shall be considered to have satisfied such requirement on such date if, on or before the last day of the remedial amendment period (as determined under paragraphs (c), (d) and (e) of this section) with respect to such disqualifying provision, all provisions of the plan which are necessary to satisfy all requirements of sections 401(a), 403(a), or 405(a) are in effect and have been made effective for all purposes for the whole of such period.

The entry goes on like that for three and a half pages of fine print. Yet thousands of a client's dollars may be riding on an attorney's ability to interpret that entry correctly. In an article explaining the passage to his fellow pension plan professionals, Knox helpfully begins, "Section 401(b) provides a way for retirement plans to be retroactively corrected" and goes on to tell how the law is generally applied. Besides being a challenging exercise in critical reading, Knox's brand of specialized nutshelling and paraphrasing calls for hard, even imaginative, thought.

We have been viewing books and articles as *immediately* useful sources of ideas and information. But sometimes there is a time lag: you read Melville's novel *Moby-Dick* or Thorstein Veblen's *The Theory of the Leisure Class*, and although your reading isn't useful for the paper you are writing this week, something from it remains with you—a phrase, a stray idea, a way of constructing a sentence. Perhaps months later, when you are writing another paper, it returns to the forefront of your mind. In truth, writing from reading is useful to you in ways we haven't begun to indicate. We hold this truth to be self-evident: that the better you read—the more alertly, critically, questioningly—the better you will write.

Making Connections: Writing from Critical Reading in A Writer's Reader

Some writers use critical reading as a springboard for writing, analyzing the points made in an article or book in order to clarify and present their own ideas on an issue; others rely on critical reading as a source of evidence for their writing. In *A Writer's Reader*, historian Stephanie Coontz in "Remarriage and Stepfamilies" (p. 522) uses her substantial reading on divorce and remarriage to support her discussion of their effects on family dynamics. In building her argument, she is careful to cite broadly from the sources she has read, including work by therapists, psychology researchers, and administrators whose projects target families undergoing change. Editor and writer Cynthia Joyce in "Six Clicks from Death" (p. 646) evaluates the articles and other reading material on medical issues available online, using specific examples to illustrate the importance of learning to read Internet sources critically.

Like Coontz, Joyce, George Will (p. 110), and Kelly Grecian (p. 113), writers from various backgrounds in *A Writer's Reader* use critical reading as a springboard for writing, including science writer Nicholas Wade, "How Men and Women Think" (p. 556); science and psychology writer Michael Shermer, "Abducted! Encounters with Aliens" (p. 596); conservative thinker James Q. Wilson, "In Praise of Asphalt Nation" (p. 606); columnist Ellen Goodman, "How to Zap Violence on TV" (p. 613); and freelance writer Mike Males, "Public Enemy Number One?" (p. 616). As you read these essays, consider the role that critical reading plays in them. For each essay, answer the following questions:

1. Is the information discovered in the reading a result of careful selection, or is it an unexpected discovery?
2. How is the author's reading related to her or his occupation or area of study?

3. What does the author learn from reading? How does she or he use that information in the essay?
4. What original insight does the author arrive at as a result of reflecting on what she or he has read?

Chapter 6

Analyzing

Many times in college you will be asked to understand some matter that seems complicated — an earthquake, the metabolism of a cell, the Federal Reserve Bank, the Protestant Reformation. Viewed as a whole, such a subject may look intimidating. But often you can simplify your task by *analyzing* your subject — by dividing it into its parts and then dealing with it one part at a time.

Analysis is already familiar to you. If you took high school chemistry, you probably analyzed water: you separated it into hydrogen and oxygen, its two elements. You've heard many a television commentator analyze the news. Did a riot break out in Bombay? Trying to help us understand what happened, the commentator tells us what made up the event — who the protesters were, whom they protested to, what they were protesting. Analyzing a news event may produce results less certain and clear-cut than analyzing a chemical compound, but the principle is similar — to take something apart for the purpose of understanding it better. In a college writing assignment you might analyze anything from a contemporary subculture (What social groups make up the homeless population of Los Angeles?) to an ecosystem (What animals, plants, and minerals coexist in a rainforest?) in order to explain it to readers. Whenever you analyze a subject, you'll be dividing it into its components, the more readily to make sense of it.

Learning from Other Writers

Let's look first at two examples of written analyses. James Fallows is a defense reporter, economic theorist, and media critic. In the following article from the *Atlantic Monthly*, he explains the reasons why so many women "throw like a girl."

The second essay is by Lillian Tsu, a government major at Cornell University. Tsu analyzes the elections of three women who came to power in Great Britain, the Philippines, and Pakistan in the 1980s and tries to determine the implications of their political success for female politicians in the United States.

135

Most people remember the 1994 baseball season for the way it ended — 1
with a strike rather than a World Series. I keep thinking about the way it
began. On opening day, April 4, Bill Clinton went to Cleveland and, like
many Presidents before him, threw out a ceremonial first pitch. That same day
Hillary Rodham Clinton went to Chicago and, like no First Lady before her,
also threw out a first ball, at a Cubs game in Wrigley Field.

The next day photos of the Clintons in action appeared in newspapers 2
around the country. Many papers, including the *New York Times* and the *Washington Post*, chose the same two photos to run. The one of Bill Clinton showed
him wearing an Indians cap and warm-up jacket. The President, throwing
lefty, had turned his shoulders sideways to the plate in preparation for delivery. He was bringing the ball forward from behind his head in a clean-
looking throwing action as the photo was snapped. Hillary Clinton was pictured wearing a dark jacket, a scarf, and an oversized Cubs hat. In preparation
for her throw she was standing directly facing the plate. A right-hander, she
had the elbow of her throwing arm pointed out in front of her. Her forearm
was tilted back, toward her shoulder. The ball rested on her upturned palm.
As the picture was taken, she was in the middle of an action that can only be
described as throwing like a girl.

The phrase "throwing like a girl" has become an embattled and offensive 3
one. Feminists smart at its implication that to do something "like a girl" is to
do it the wrong way. Recently, on the heels of the O. J. Simpson case, a book
appeared in which the phrase was used to help explain why male athletes, especially football players, were involved in so many assaults against women.
Having been trained (like most American boys) to dread the accusation of
doing anything "like a girl," athletes were said to grow into the assumption
that women were valueless, and natural prey.

I grant the justice of such complaints. I am attuned to the hurt caused by 4
similar broad-brush stereotypes when they apply to groups I belong to —
"dancing like a white man," for instance, or "speaking foreign languages like
an American," or "thinking like a Washingtonian."

Still, whatever we want to call it, the difference between the two Clintons 5
in what they were doing that day is real, and it is instantly recognizable. And
since seeing those photos I have been wondering, Why, exactly, do so many
women throw "like a girl"? If the motion were easy to change, presumably a
woman as motivated and self-possessed as Hillary Clinton would have
changed it. (According to her press secretary, Lisa Caputo, Mrs. Clinton spent
the weekend before opening day tossing a ball in the Rose Garden with her
husband, for practice.) Presumably, too, the answer to the question cannot be
anything quite as simple as, Because they *are* girls.

A surprising number of people think that there is a structural difference 6
between male and female arms or shoulders — in the famous "rotator cuff,"

perhaps — that dictates different throwing motions. "It's in the shoulder joint," a well-educated woman told me recently. "They're hinged differently." Someday researchers may find evidence to support a biological theory of throwing actions. For now, what you'll hear if you ask an orthopedist, an anatomist, or (especially) the coach of a women's softball team is that there is no structural reason why men and women should throw in different ways. This point will be obvious to any male who grew up around girls who liked to play baseball and became good at it. It should be obvious on a larger scale this summer, in broadcasts of the Olympic Games. This year, for the first time, women's fast-pitch softball teams will compete in the Olympics. Although the pitchers in these games will deliver the ball underhand, viewers will see female shortstops, center fielders, catchers, and so on pegging the ball to one another at speeds few male viewers could match.

Even women's tennis is a constant if indirect reminder that men's and women's shoulders are "hinged" the same way. The serving motion in tennis is like a throw — but more difficult, because it must be coordinated with the toss of the tennis ball. The men in professional tennis serve harder than the women, because they are bigger and stronger. But women pros serve harder than most male amateurs have ever done, and the service motion for good players is the same for men and women alike. There is no expectation in college or pro tennis that because of their anatomy female players must "serve like a girl." "I know many women who can throw a lot harder and better than the normal male," says Linda Wells, the coach of the highly successful women's softball team at Arizona State University. "It's not gender that makes the difference in how they throw."

So what is it, then? Since Hillary Clinton's ceremonial visit to Wrigley Field, I have asked men and women how they learned to throw, or didn't. Why did I care? My impetus was the knowledge that eventually my sons would be grown and gone. If my wife, in all other ways a talented athlete, could learn how to throw, I would still have someone to play catch with. My research left some women, including my wife, thinking that I am some kind of obsessed lout, but it has led me to the solution to the mystery. First let's be clear about what there is to be explained.

At a superficial level it's easy to tick off the traits of an awkward-looking throw. The fundamental mistake is the one Mrs. Clinton appeared to be making in the photo: trying to throw a ball with your body facing the target, rather than rotating your shoulders and hips ninety degrees away from the target and then swinging them around in order to accelerate the ball. A throw looks bad if your elbow is lower than your shoulder as your arm comes forward (unless you're throwing sidearm). A throw looks really bad if, as the ball leaves your hand, your wrist is "inside your elbow" — that is, your elbow joint is bent in such a way that your forearm angles back toward your body and your wrist is closer to your head than your elbow is. Slow-motion film of big-league pitchers shows that when they release the ball, the throwing arm is fully extended and straight from shoulder to wrist. The combination of these three elements — head-on stance, dropped elbow, and wrist inside the elbow — mechanically dictates a pushing rather than a hurling motion, creating the familiar pattern of "throwing like a girl."

It is surprisingly hard to find in the literature of baseball a deeper explanation of the mechanics of good and bad throws. Tom Seaver's pitching for the Mets and the White Sox got him into the Hall of Fame, but his book *The Art of Pitching* is full of bromides that hardly clarify the process of throwing, even if they might mean something to accomplished pitchers. His chapter "The Absolutes of Pitching Mechanics," for instance, lays out these four unhelpful principles: "Keep the Front Leg Flexible!" "Rub Up the Baseball." "Hide the Baseball!" "Get It Out, Get It Up!" (The fourth refers to the need to get the ball out of the glove and into the throwing hand in a quick motion.)   10

A variety of other instructional documents, from *Little League's Official How-to-Play Baseball Book* to *Softball for Girls and Women*, mainly reveal the difficulty of finding words to describe a simple motor activity that everyone can recognize. The challenge, I suppose, is like that of writing a manual on how to ride a bike, or how to kiss. Indeed, the most useful description I've found of the mechanics of throwing comes from a man whose specialty is another sport: Vic Braden made his name as a tennis coach, but he has attempted to analyze the physics of a wide variety of sports so that they all will be easier to teach.   11

Braden says that an effective throw involves connecting a series of links in a "kinetic chain." The kinetic chain, which is Braden's tool for analyzing most sporting activity, operates on a principle like that of crack-the-whip. Momentum builds up in one part of the body. When that part is suddenly stopped, as the end of the "whip" is stopped in crack-the-whip, the momentum is transferred to and concentrated in the next link in the chain. A good throw uses six links of chain, Braden says. The first two links involve the lower body, from feet to waist. The first motion of a throw (after the body has been rotated away from the target) is to rotate the legs and hips back in the direction of the throw, building up momentum as large muscles move body mass. Then those links stop — a pitcher stops turning his hips once they face the plate — and the momentum is transferred to the next link. This is the torso, from waist to shoulders, and since its mass is less than that of the legs, momentum makes it rotate faster than the hips and legs did. The torso stops when it is facing the plate, and the momentum is transferred to the next link — the upper arm. As the upper arm comes past the head, it stops moving forward, and the momentum goes into the final links — the forearm and wrist, which snap forward at tremendous speed.   12

This may sound arcane and jerkily mechanical, but it makes perfect sense when one sees Braden's slow-mo movies of pitchers in action. And it explains why people do, or don't, learn how to throw. The implication of Braden's analysis is that throwing is a perfectly natural action (millions and millions of people can do it), but not at all innate. A successful throw involves an intricate series of actions coordinated among muscle groups, as each link of the   13 chain is timed to interact with the next. Like bike riding or skating, it can be learned by anyone — male or female. No one starts out knowing how to ride a bike or throw a ball. Everyone has to learn.

Readers who are happy with their throwing skills can prove this to them- 14 selves in about two seconds. If you are right-handed, pick up a ball with your left hand and throw it. Unless you are ambidextrous or have some other odd advantage, you will throw it "like a girl." The problem is not that your left shoulder is hinged strangely or that you don't know what a good throw looks like. It is that you have not spent time training your leg, hip, shoulder, and arm muscles on that side to work together as required for a throw. The actor John Goodman, who played football seriously and baseball casually when he was in high school, is right-handed. When cast in the 1992 movie *The Babe*, he had to learn to bat and throw left-handed, for realism in the role of Babe Ruth. For weeks before the filming began, he would arrive an hour early at the set of his TV show, *Roseanne*, so that he could practice throwing a tennis ball against a wall left-handed. "I made damn sure no one could see me," Good-man told me recently. "I'm hard enough on myself without the derisive laugh-ter of my so-called friends." When *The Babe* was released, Goodman told a newspaper interviewer, "I'll never say something like 'He throws like a girl' again. It's not easy to learn how to throw."

What Goodman discovered is what most men have forgotten: that if they 15 know how to throw now, it is because they spent time learning at some point long ago. (Goodman says that he can remember learning to ride a bicycle but not learning to throw with his right hand.) This brings us back to the roots of the "throwing like a girl" phenomenon. The crucial factor is not that males and females are put together differently but that they typically spend their early years in different ways. Little boys often learn how to throw without noticing that they are learning. Little girls are more rarely in environments that encourage them to learn in the same way. A boy who wonders why a girl throws the way she does is like a Frenchman who wonders why so many Americans speak French "with an accent."

"For young boys it is culturally acceptable and politically correct to de- 16 velop these skills," says Linda Wells, of the Arizona State softball team. "They are mentored and networked. Usually girls are not coached at all, or are coached by Mom — or if it's by Dad, he may not be much of an athlete. Girls are often stuck with the bottom of the male talent pool as examples. I would argue that rather than learning to 'throw like a girl,' they learn to throw like poor male athletes. I say that a bad throw is 'throwing like an old man.' This is not gender, it's acculturation."

Almost any motor skill, from doing handstands to dribbling a basketball, 17 is easier to learn if you start young, which is why John Goodman did not re-alize that learning to throw is difficult until he attempted it as an adult. Many girls reach adulthood having missed the chance to learn to throw when that would have been easiest to do. And as adults they have neither John Goodman's incentive to teach their muscles a new set of skills nor his confidence that the feat is possible. Five years ago Joseph Russo, long a baseball coach at St. John's University, gave athletic-talent tests to actresses who were trying out for roles in *A League of Their Own*, a movie about women's baseball. Most of them were "well coordinated in general, like for dancing," he says. But those who had not happened to play baseball or softball when they were young had a problem: "It sounds silly to say it, but they kept throwing like girls." (The best ball-field talents, by the way, were Madonna, Demi Moore, and the rock singer Joan Jett, who according to Russo "can really hit it hard." Careful viewers of *A League of Their Own* will note that only in a fleeting instant in one scene is the star, Geena Davis, shown actually throwing a ball.)

I'm not sure that I buy Linda Wells's theory that most boys are "mentored" or "networked" into developing ball skills. Those who make the baseball team, maybe. But for a far larger number the decisive ingredient seems to be the hundreds of idle hours spent throwing balls, sticks, rocks, and so on in the playground or the back yard. Children on the playground, I think, demonstrate the moment when the kinetic chain begins to work. It is when a little boy tries to throw a rock farther than his friend can, or to throw a stick over a telephone wire thirty feet up. A toddler's first, instinctive throw is a push from the shoulder, showing the essential traits of "throwing like a girl." But when a child is really trying to put some oomph into the throw, his natural instinct is to wind up his body and let fly with the links of the chain. Little girls who do the same thing — compete with each other in distance throwing — learn the same way; but whereas many boys do this, few girls do. Tammy Richards, a woman who was raised on a farm in central California, says that she learned to throw by trying to heave dried cow chips farther than her brother could. It may have helped that her father, Bob Richards, was a former Olympic competitor in the decathlon (and two-time Olympic champion in the pole vault), and that he taught all his sons and daughters to throw not only the ball but also the discus, the shotput, and the javelin. [18]

Is there a way to make up for lost time if you failed to invest those long hours on the playground years ago? Of course. Adults may not be able to learn to speak unaccented French, but they can learn to ride a bike, or skate, or throw. All that is required for developing any of these motor skills is time for practice — and spending that time requires overcoming the sense of embarrassment and futility that adults often have when attempting something new. Here are two tips that may help. [19]

One is a surprisingly valuable drill suggested by the Little League's *How-to-Play* handbook. Play catch with a partner who is ten or fifteen feet away — but do so while squatting with the knee of your throwing side touching the ground. When you start out this low, you have to keep the throw high to get the ball to your partner without bouncing it. This encourages a throw with the elbow held well above the shoulder, where it belongs. [20]

The other is to play catch with a person who can throw like an athlete but 21
is using his or her off hand. The typical adult woman hates to play catch with
the typical adult man. She is well aware that she's not looking graceful, and
reacts murderously to the condescending tone in his voice ("That's more like
it, honey!"). Forcing a right-handed man to throw left-handed is the great
equalizer. He suddenly concentrates his attention on what it takes to get hips,
shoulder, and elbow working together. He is suddenly aware of the strength
of character needed to ignore the snickers of onlookers while learning new
motor skills. He can no longer be condescending. He may even be nervous,
wondering what he'll do if his partner makes the breakthrough first and he's
the one still throwing like a girl.

Questions to Start You Thinking

Meaning

1. What does Fallows mean by "throwing like a girl" (paragraphs 2 and 9)?
2. What are the arguments of those who believe that biology explains why men and women throw differently? Why does Fallows reject these arguments?
3. What does Fallows conclude is the reason that so many females "throw like a girl"?
4. According to Fallows, what are the major differences between learning a motor skill as a child and learning one as an adult?

Writing Strategies

5. Fallows opens his essay with a description of photos of Bill and Hillary Clinton. How does he use a comparison and contrast of these photos to draw the reader into his essay?
6. How do the various analyses of the steps involved in good and bad throws (paragraphs 8–13) contribute to the overall point Fallows makes in his essay?
7. Locate the examples of people throwing that Fallows includes throughout his essay. Taken together, how do these examples support his point that being able to throw well is not a gender-specific trait?
8. Why does Fallows repeatedly use the phrase "throwing like a girl" even though he admits, early in his essay, that many people find it offensive? Does his use of the phrase weaken his argument in any way?

STUDENT ESSAY

Lillian Tsu   A Woman in the White House

The past twenty years have witnessed the rise of several 1
powerful female leaders in world politics. In 1979, Margaret
Thatcher became the first female prime minister of Great
Britain; in 1986, Corazon Aquino ended a twenty-year
dictatorship in the Philippines; and in 1988, Benazir Bhutto

became the first woman to head a modern Muslim state when she
became the Prime Minister of Pakistan. However, the success
of these women may not translate into the future success of
prospective female presidential candidates in the United
States. Though these women rose to the top of their respective political ladders, their successes can be categorized as
political anomaly or the result of a highly unusual set of
circumstances. Although traditionally paternalistic societies
like the Philippines and Pakistan and socially conservative
states like Great Britain have elected female leaders, particular characteristics of the United States' own electoral
system make it unlikely that this country will follow suit
and elect a female president. Despite social modernization
and the progress of the women's movement, the voters of the
United States still lag far behind other nations in their
willingness to trust in the leadership of a female executive.
While the women's movement has succeeded in changing Americans' attitudes as to what roles are socially acceptable for
women, female candidates still face a more difficult task in
U.S. elections than their male counterparts face. Three factors are responsible for this situation--political socialization, lack of experience, and open discrimination.

Political Socialization

One obstacle that politically oriented women in the United   2
States face is that the characteristics deemed necessary to
demonstrate leadership ability and thus win the confidence of
voters do not correlate with the values and behaviors American women are conditioned to possess. According to Susan Carroll, author of Women as Candidates in American Politics,
"Although socialized to exhibit values and behaviors considered appropriate for females, in running for office, women
enter into a sphere of life dominated by masculine values and
behavior patterns."[1] In order to compete with males, female
candidates must exhibit such traditionally masculine characteristics as self-confidence, ambition, and assertiveness.
Yet unlike their male counterparts, female candidates must
then appease voters by demonstrating those feminine qualities
"that make up the social definition of reality and 'appropriate' gender roles."[2]

Image becomes a key issue during a female candidate's   3
campaign. To succeed, a woman running for office must find the
right balance of traditional feminine behavior and strong,
masculine leadership qualities. Thus, "the extent to which
women candidates can overcome conflict between their socialization into female behavior patterns and the need to cultivate masculine traits may affect their election outcomes."[3]
Candidates "must appear strong and assertive at the same time
that they look and sound feminine; they must be tough with the
opposition, but avoid seeming strident."[4]

Lack of Experience

A second obstacle for women candidates in the United States is   4
that while today's female candidates possess educational backgrounds that are similar to their male rivals' backgrounds,
they are perceived as lacking the practical experience of their
male counterparts. According to Carroll, "Women candidates are
perceived not only to lack the non-political accomplishments
and credentials necessary for public officeholding, but also
to lack political experience."[5] Thus, female candidates are
less attractive to many voters than male candidates.

The lack of qualifications among female candidates may,   5
however, be attributed to structural flaws in the U.S. electoral system. Women tend to have a difficult time breaking
into the political arena because the electoral system impedes
their progress. Studies indicate that, while incumbents tend
to win elections at a much higher rate than nonincumbents,
very few women candidates are incumbents. Candidates who run
against incumbents rarely win elections, and sizable numbers
of women candidates confront such situations.[6] In such a system, women will necessarily be seen as underqualified because
they cannot break the structural barriers.

Active Discrimination against Women

A third obstacle that may hinder the political success of fe-   6
male candidates is voter discrimination because of a double
standard for men and women in American society. Many American
voters still believe that "the 'right image' for a state senator or any other public official is male."[7] A female candidate must first struggle to convince the electorate that, as a

woman, she is capable of handling the responsibilities of the
office she is seeking and then convince the electorate that she
is better qualified for the position than her male opponent is.

Women candidates may also be encumbered by American sex-   7
ual double standards. The bachelorhood of male candidates has
been less of an issue during U.S. campaigns than the marital
status of female candidates. According to Ruth Mandel,

> the public assumption about a young single male who runs
> for office may be that he is an ambitious go-getter whose
> personal agenda prioritizes domesticity and family life
> as less important. However, the young single woman seek-
> ing office frequently is questioned and criticized for
> her unmarried status.[8]

The issue of family life is a double-edged sword in most   8
female candidates' campaigns, for while voters find family-
oriented candidates more appealing, choosing to have a family
may deter the progress of a woman's political career. While
male candidates are rarely censured for neglecting family duties in order to serve the public, "political women are expected to defer to their roles as mothers and homemakers. If
women run for office themselves, the question of whether they
are fulfilling their responsibilities as parents immediately
arises."[9] Because women are faced with the greater responsibility in parenting, they tend to begin their political careers later than their male counterparts, opting to wait
until their children are grown before running for office.

Clearly, women candidates face more challenges than   9
their male opponents, but these obstacles can be overcome. In
the 1980s Benazir Bhutto of Pakistan, Corazon Aquino of the
Philippines, and Margaret Thatcher of Great Britain managed
to win leadership positions in their respective countries.
Does the success of these women mean that it is possible for
a female candidate in the United States to win the presidency
in the near future?

Implications of Women's Political Success
Benazir Bhutto's election as Prime Minister of Pakistan was ex-   10
traordinary, considering the obstacles she had to overcome.

Bhutto, a female candidate in a paternalistic society, was forced to contend with the active discrimination of many Pakistanis against women. In addition, Bhutto lacked political experience. What circumstances made it possible for her to win the election for Prime Minister?

Though politically inexperienced, Benazir Bhutto won   11
credibility through association with her father, Zulfikar Bhutto, who ruled as Prime Minister of Pakistan from 1971 until 1977. In 1977, Zulfikar Bhutto's government was overthrown by a military coup led by General Mohammed Zia ul-Haq, and he was executed by the Zia government in 1979. During her election, Benazir Bhutto "campaigned on the appeal of the memory of her martyred father."[10] Through her association with her father, Bhutto managed to overcome the gender bias of the male-dominated society of Pakistan. According to Nancy Anderson, "Despite the ethos of male-domination in Pakistan, which confined women to a familial role, it was generally not considered inappropriate for a woman to take the political role of an imprisoned or dead male family member."[11] Thus, Bhutto appealed to voters because she was seen as representing not her own ideals but those of her dead father. In campaigning for Prime Minister, Bhutto was merely doing her duty of continuing the political legacy of her father.

Bhutto's political success can also be attributed to the   12
political situation in Pakistan during her campaign. General Zia's government was noted for its many human rights violations against civilians who opposed the oppressive government. Bhutto's candidacy offered Pakistanis an alternative to the rule of a tyrannical leader. She was able to overcome the obstacles that face female candidates by riding on the success of her father and by providing the Pakistani people with a more promising government than the despotic system of the incumbent prime minister.

The path taken by Corazon Aquino toward national leader-   13
ship was similar to that of Benazir Bhutto. In 1986, the global community was astounded when a shy, gentle, former housewife won the presidential election in the Philippines, ending the twenty-year dictatorship of Ferdinand Marcos. Aquino seemingly lacked the "masculine" leadership qualities required by those running for political office, and her can-

didacy was also threatened by her lack of professional or political experience. How did this former housewife achieve
such incredible political success?

Like Benazir Bhutto, Corazon Aquino's credibility and   14
subsequent political success can be attributed to familial
ties. As a child, Aquino "had been tutored in politics . . .
first in a 'politically oriented' family and later by a husband with considerable political instinct, ambition, and accomplishment."[12] When her husband was jailed numerous times
for criticizing the Marcos regime, Aquino developed her political acumen by acting as a liaison between her incarcerated husband and the people of the Philippines. Following the
assassination of her husband, Aquino "was in great demand as
a speaker, and was increasingly consulted during negotiations
among opposition leaders."[13] Corazon Aquino was embraced by
voters not for her own ideals but because she was seen as
merely carrying on the legacy and ideals of her husband.

Like Bhutto, Aquino benefited from the unpopularity of   15
the incumbent regime. During her campaign, economic problems
plagued the nation. In the 1980s the economic situation in
the Philippines worsened and was "characterized by capital
flight, factory closings, rising unemployment, bank closings,
devaluation of the peso by 38%, rising prices, and the collapse of world prices for sugar and coconut oil."[14] Marcos's
negative image in the eyes of Filipinos became one of
Aquino's assets. Aquino was viewed by the Catholic Philippines as "almost a Madonna, a saint in contrast to the wily,
corrupt Marcos."[15] Corazon Aquino's election as president of
the Philippines was the result of factors and circumstances--
such as her association with her slain husband's policies and
the unpopularity of the Marcos regime--that made the question
of gender inconsequential.

The circumstances present in the developing countries of   16
Pakistan and the Philippines that led to the election of female national leaders would be difficult to recreate in the
United States, but in Great Britain, a country more similar
to the United States, Margaret Thatcher wrestled with the active discrimination of some of the electorate during her 1979
campaign. Thatcher was often criticized for being too ambi-

tious and neglecting her family in her pursuit of political success.[16] Without the reputation of a male family member to campaign behind, Thatcher was vulnerable to the harsh gender bias of society. How, then, did Thatcher manage to become Prime Minister of Great Britain?

Surprisingly, Margaret Thatcher's gender was both her greatest liability and her greatest asset. The British women's movement of the 1970s benefited Thatcher's career tremendously, for in order to appease the growing demand that women be represented among their leadership, the members of the Conservative party promoted her faster than they might have promoted a man. According to Michael Genovese, "The Conservative party was overwhelmingly male, and in the early days of the women's liberation movement, [Conservative party leader Edward] Heath felt compelled to appoint women to shadow roles."[17] Her gender actually opened many doors for Thatcher. [17]

Like Bhutto's and Aquino's, Thatcher's election was also aided by the poor standing of the current regime during her campaign. By the late 1970s, the electorate of Great Britain had realized that big government was not working. High inflation, low economic growth, and high unemployment had weakened the encumbent Labour party, and strengthened Thatcher's candidacy. Margaret Thatcher became the alternative that British voters were seeking. They disregarded the issue of gender, choosing instead to vote for any alternative to the failing Labour party. [18]

A comparison of the elections of Benazir Bhutto, Corazon Aquino, and Margaret Thatcher points to several general conclusions. Each leader's election was aided by difficult political and economic circumstances facing her country, which undermined the popularity of the incumbent regime. In addition, both Bhutto's and Aquino's success relied heavily on the reputation of slain male relatives. It can be assumed that the circumstances leading to these elections would be unlikely to be duplicated in the United States. [19]

Margaret Thatcher's successful election as Prime Minister of Great Britain may be as unlikely as the elections of Bhutto and Aquino to be duplicated in the United States' political arena. Thatcher's success in the late 1970s was the [20]

culmination of numerous promotions within the Conservative
party prompted by the women's movement. While women in the
United States also began to infiltrate once male-dominated
political parties during this period, the respective electoral systems of the United States and Great Britain are
quite different. In the British parliamentary system, Margaret Thatcher was appointed as the Prime Minister because
she was the leader of the majority party in Parliament. The
electorate of Great Britain did not directly select her; that
duty was left to the party itself. Thatcher needed only to
win the support of her party to become the political leader
of the United Kingdom. Relying on the success of her party on
election day, she could win the seat of the Prime Minister.
In contrast, a prospective female president of the United
States must win both her party's nomination at the national
convention and the support of the general public on election
day.

Thus, despite the successes of Bhutto, Aquino, and   21
Thatcher, it still seems unlikely that the United States will
elect a female president in the near future. American female
candidates must contend with greater obstacles than these
three national leaders did in the 1980s. Bhutto, Aquino, and
Thatcher all came to power under circumstances that are unlikely to be reproduced in the United States.

Endnotes
1. Susan J. Carroll, Women as Candidates in American Politics
   (Bloomington: Indiana UP, 1985), 94.
2. Michael Genovese, "Margaret Thatcher and the Politics
   of Conviction," Women as National Leaders. ed. Michael
   Genovese (London: Sage, 1993), 3.
3. Carroll, 94.
4. Ruth B. Mandel, In the Running (New Haven: Ticknor and
   Fields, 1981), 38.
5. Carroll, 65.
6. Carroll, 119.
7. Mandel, 66.
8. Ibid.

9. Frank P. LeVeness and Jane P. Sweeney, "Women in the Political Arena," Women Leaders in Contemporary U.S. Politics (Boulder: Lynne Rienner, 1987), 5.

10. Nancy Fix Anderson, "Benazir Bhutto and Dynastic Politics: Her Father's Daughter, Her People's Sister," Women as National Leaders, op cit., 41.

11. Ibid., 55.

12. Jeanne-Marie Col, "Managing Softly in Turbulent Times: Corazon C. Aquino, President of the Philippines," Women as National Leaders, op cit., 13.

13. Ibid.

14. Ibid., 19.

15. Ibid., 24.

16. Genovese, 183.

17. Ibid., 184.

Questions to Start You Thinking

Meaning

1. In your own words, explain the three major obstacles that Tsu claims American women face when trying to enter politics.

2. What are the primary reasons Tsu cites for the successes of Bhutto, Aquino, and Thatcher in winning elections to become national leaders?

3. Why does Tsu conclude that the successes of Bhutto, Aquino, and Thatcher do not suggest it is likely that an American woman might win the presidency in the near future?

Writing Strategies

4. How does Tsu draw on other sources she's read to support her analysis of the difficulties women in this country face when trying to break into politics?

5. Where do you find Tsu's thesis statement and her topic sentences? What are the advantages of locating them where she does?

6. What is Tsu's purpose in posing questions periodically throughout her essay? Do you find this writing strategy effective? Why, or why not?

7. Do you agree with Tsu's conclusion that the elections of Bhutto, Aquino, and Thatcher constitute "political anomalies" (paragraph 1) rather than a trend in world politics toward women taking more leadership roles? Why, or why not?

Learning by Writing

THE ASSIGNMENT: ANALYZING

Write an essay analyzing a subject — a thing, an idea, or a system — that you know well or want to find out about. Make the subject clear to an audience of your classmates. You will develop a larger purpose as well, some further point that you want to make, like Tsu's point that we are unlikely to have a female president in the United States anytime soon. Here are instances of college writers who successfully responded to this type of assignment:

A woman who plans a career as a consultant in time and motion study divided a typical day in the life of a college student into the segments that compose it (class time, study time, feeding time, grooming time, recreation time, social time, waste time) and suggested ways for a student to make more efficient use of time.

A student of psychology divided the human brain into its parts and explained the function of each to illustrate the brain's intricate complexity.

A musician analyzed the behavior of the audience at a rap concert to demonstrate his theory that rap concerts cause various types of people to act in an uninhibited manner.

GENERATING IDEAS

To complete this assignment, you will need to find a subject you care about, determine what you want to say about it, and devise a method for explaining it.

Find a subject. The paper topics just listed may help start your own ideas flowing. Do some idle, relaxed thinking with pencil and paper at hand. Or do some fast scribbling (see "Brainstorming" and "Freewriting," pp. 360–65). Try to come up with something complicated that you understand and would really like to explain to someone else or something you would like to understand more clearly yourself.

Determine your reason for analyzing. You want to explain your subject, but what about it do you want to explain? For example, you might want to analyze New York City for the purpose of showing its ethnic composition, or you might want to focus on its social classes. As you develop your paper, you may also find that you have a stronger point to make — that New York City's social hierarchy is oppressive and unstable, for example. Make sure before you begin that your analysis has a purpose — that it will demonstrate something or tell your readers something they didn't know before. Have a reason for analyzing.

Decide on a principle of division. Right away, decide on the principle you will follow in your analysis. Just as you can slice a carrot in many ways, you can find many ways to analyze a subject. If you want to explain New York City's

Facing the Challenge: Analyzing

The major challenge writers face when they analyze a given topic is to deter-mine a logical principle of division and to stick to it. If the division of thought is unclear, the essay will not be clear to readers. For example, a writer should not divide college students into students eighteen to twenty-one years old, adults retraining for a new job, and international students. A writer who did so would be using three different principles of analysis for the three classifi-cations of students. The first classification is based on age, the second on the reason for attending college, and the third on the place where the students live. Such an analysis would lead to a confusing essay. A writer could produce a clear essay based on age classifications, such as eighteen to twenty-one years old, twenty-one to thirty-five years old, thirty-five to fifty years old, fifty to sixty-five years old, and over sixty-five years old (or any age groups the writer chooses to use). Alternatively, the essay-writer could classify students based on their reasons for attending college or on their nationality.

Successful analytic writers must be able to illuminate a subject for read-ers by dividing it into discrete parts following a clear principle of division. When writing an analytical essay, choose a topic that you can divide into clear subtopics for your essay. If you cannot think of a series of distinct ideas or subtopics, you should consider another subject that you can easily divide into parts. Think of your topic as an open umbrella, divided into clearly defined but interconnected parts, each of which contributes to the whole.

The principle of division for an analytical topic guides a writer in deter-mining the organizational framework for an analytical essay. The clearer the organization, the more likely your explanation will be clear to your readers. Because most topics can be arranged in a number of ways, you should inves-tigate several organizational plans for your analysis. Experiment with several outlines and choose the one that allows you to present the best support for your thesis, the overall point that you want to make in your essay. Remember that the different sections of your essay should reflect the different parts into which you have divided your topic and that each subsection should be clearly related to your overall point. If you have difficulty determining an appropri-ate principle of division for your analysis, try presenting an outline or a rough draft to your peer writing group. Such an audience can often prevent you from deviating from your principle of division.

ethnic composition, you might divide the city geographically into neighbor-hoods — Harlem, Spanish Harlem, Yorkville, Chinatown, Little Italy. If you want to explain its social classes, you might start at the bottom with homeless people and work your way up to the cream of society. The way you slice your subject into pieces will depend in part on the point you want to make about it — and the point you end up making will depend in part on how you've sliced it up. In other words, expect to do some tinkering in the early stages as you come up with the right purpose and method for your analysis. (For more on the strategy of division, see p. 421.)

- Have you found a subject that interests you and that seems worthwhile to analyze?
- Exactly what will you be trying to achieve in your essay?
- What is the principle of division you will follow in your analysis?
- Is your subject clear to you, so that you can make it clear to your readers?
- Can you generate enough details about each aspect of your analysis to write an interesting, informative essay?

PLANNING, DRAFTING, AND DEVELOPING

Many college assignments call for analysis, and a paper that analyzes a subject often turns out to be among the best essays that a college student writes. The secret is to care about what you say and to organize your essay so that it won't look (and read) like a lifeless stack of blocks. Organize your material in logical, easy-to-follow order. Some kind of outline — whether extremely detailed or rough — will save you time and avoid confusion.

The outline for a subject analysis might be a pielike circle with the slices labeled. If you make the sizes of the slices correspond to their relative importance, the sketch might give you some notion of how much time to spend explaining each part. The pie outline for a paper analyzing the parts of a radio station's twenty-four-hour broadcast day might look like the illustration below. Another

Pie outline of a radio station's broadcast day

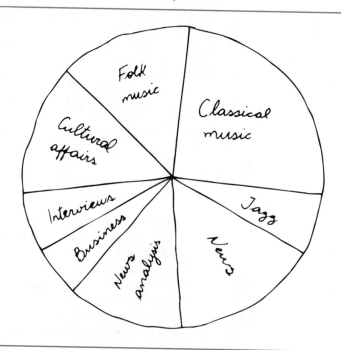

way to plan your paper is to arrange your subdivisions from smallest to largest or from least important to most important — or any other order that makes sense to you. (For more on organizing and outlining, see Chapter 16.)

Some writers like to start a subject analysis by telling their readers the subdivisions into which they are going to slice their subject ("A typical political party has these components . . ." or "The federal government has three branches"). Julius Caesar opens his *Commentaries on the Gallic War* with a famous division: "All Gaul is divided into three parts." That is one clear-cut way to go. Indicate the divisions and subdivisions in your writing so that your readers won't get lost. If you haven't already done so, invent a name or label for each part you mention to distinguish it from all the others. This device will help you keep your material clearly in mind and also help your readers keep the divisions straight. As you draft your essay, provide definitions of unfamiliar words, explain anything your readers may misunderstand, and clarify with examples.

REVISING AND EDITING

As you revise, concentrate on making sure that your essay is meaty. If you find places that are thin, expand them with additional details and examples. Look, for instance, at each paragraph of Fallows's analysis to see how many details and examples from experience, conversation, and reading he has marshaled to support his points. Also, if on rereading your paper you find any sentence that now strikes you as awkward or murky, perhaps it needs a second try, or perhaps you can do without it altogether.

How can you make sure that your readers will be able to follow your thinking as you analyze? You can make your essay as readable as possible by using transitions, those valuable words and phrases that introduce and connect ideas. Lillian Tsu, for example, begins each of her first three sections with

WRITING WITH A COMPUTER

Analysis involves breaking a subject down into its essential parts in order to understand and explain it better. The computer itself is a good example of a subject that makes for a fairly straightforward analysis. If you were analyzing a computer you could begin by typing the name of each of the computer's major components on a different line, creating a vertical list that includes *central processing unit, monitor, drives, mouse,* and *keyboard.* Each of these terms could then serve as a heading for a couple of sentences or even a paragraph that describes that component in more detail.

Now try the same technique to help you analyze your subject, regardless of whether the subject is a physical object like a computer or an abstract concept like the political atmosphere of the 1990s. By using a word processor to enter headings first and then filling in description and detail, you establish a logical and methodical framework from which you can construct an analysis.

a transition phrase emphasizing the difficulties U.S. female candidates face: "One obstacle," "A second obstacle," "A third obstacle." This listing gives readers clear direction in a complicated essay. (For more on transitions, see p. 407.)

As you revise, you should also make sure that you have applied your principle of division consistently. In other words, the parts you use in your analysis to explain your subject should be similar to one another and equal in importance. If in an analysis of your campus, you have used the categories *students, instructors, service staff,* and *foreign students,* you should probably consider folding *foreign students* in with the other students. You should also ask yourself whether you have left out any obvious parts that a reader might expect to find. Some readers might object to an analysis dividing pop music into rap, rock, and jazz fusion on the grounds that it has a few holes.

As you prepare to write your final draft, ask yourself the following questions. Until you can answer them all to your complete satisfaction, you probably still have more work to do on your analysis.

REVISION CHECKLIST

- Does your introduction engage the reader?
- Have you explained each part completely enough that a reader will understand it?
- Have you shown how each part functions and how it relates to the whole?
- Have you made clear your basis for dividing — the principle on which you sliced?
- Is the purpose of your analysis clear?
- Does your concluding paragraph bring all the separate parts back together and affirm what your dividing has explained?

FOR PEER RESPONSE

Once you have a legible draft, call on the services of a trustworthy peer editor. See Chapter 20 for advice on working with other student writers and for general questions you should always ask a peer editor to address. For a paper in which you analyze, you'll also want your peer editor to answer these specific questions:

- What seems to be the writer's purpose in this essay? Is the writer successful in achieving that purpose?
- Is the logic behind the writer's principle of division clear to you? Can you make an outline or pie chart that represents the analysis?
- If the writer subdivided, has she or he clearly situated the subdivisions within the larger division? Tell the writer where he or she needs to be clearer.
- Is the paper easy to follow? Are there places where more (or better) transitions are needed?
- Did you learn something from this paper? Is there something important that the writer has left unsaid?
- If this were your paper, what is the one thing you would be sure to work on before handing it in?

After you have revised your analytical essay, proofread and edit it. Check carefully for problems with grammar, word choice, punctuation, and mechanics — and then correct any problems you find. A comprehensive reference handbook is an indispensable tool for this task; the "Quick Editing Guide" at the end of *The Bedford Guide for College Writers* (see the pages with the colored edges) will get you started.

When editing a paper written from analysis, look carefully for passages with choppy, monotonous sentences. When writers break up their subjects in an analysis, they sometimes break up their sentences as well. Try combining sentences. Aim for a varied but clear style. Don't make things more complex than they need to be. If you find some passages that are not clear, you may need to straighten out problems with pronoun reference, pronoun agreement, and subject-verb agreement.

Here are some questions to get you started when proofreading and editing your paper:

**EDITING
CHECKLIST**

- Is it clear what subjects and verbs go together? Do all subjects and verbs agree (match)? (See A2 in the "Quick Editing Guide.")
- Is it clear what each pronoun refers to? Does each pronoun agree with (match) its antecedent? (See A4 in the "Quick Editing Guide.")
- When breaking your subject up into its parts, have you avoided creating sentence fragments? (See A6 in the "Quick Editing Guide.")
- When combining choppy sentences, have you avoided creating run-ons? (See A7 in the "Quick Editing Guide.")
- Have you spelled everything correctly? (See D2 in the "Quick Editing Guide.")
- Have you used the proper paper format, including special requirements for your instructor and course? (See D3 in the "Quick Editing Guide.")

(For more on revising and editing, see Chapter 19.)

OTHER ASSIGNMENTS

1. In an essay, analyze one of the following subjects by dividing it into its basic parts or elements and explaining the purpose and function of each part. Be sure to have a purpose beyond analyzing.

   A college
   A newspaper
   A TV talk show
   A symphony orchestra
   A computer or other technological device
   A basketball, football, baseball, or hockey team
   An essay, short story, novel, or play
   Education
   A family
   A belief or opinion

2. What point would you want to make in an analysis of each of the following? Write an informative essay analyzing one of them.

The techniques of effective teaching
The aspects of true love
One candidate's political campaign
The gap between generations
The elements of good nutrition
Things to consider in choosing an exercise plan
Excellence
Literacy
Leadership
Individualism
Civil disobedience

3. Analyze the elements of a TV commercial, a political ad, a magazine ad, or a popular device used to manipulate viewers and listeners. What is the purpose of the manipulation?

Applying What You Learn: Some Uses of Analysis

As you have no doubt seen already, many different college courses will give you an opportunity to analyze a subject. In explaining for a political science course how the power structure in Iraq works, you might divide the government into its branches, explain each branch, and then factor in the influence of religion. In a nutrition class, you might submit an essay analyzing the components of a healthy diet. In a paper for a course on art history, you might single out each element of a Rembrandt painting: perhaps its human figures, their clothing, the background, the light.

You won't always write papers entirely devoted to analyzing. But you may often find analysis useful in writing *part* of an explanatory paper — a paragraph or a section. In the middle of his essay "Things Unflattened by Science," Lewis Thomas pauses to divide biology into three parts.

We can imagine three worlds of biology, corresponding roughly to the three worlds of physics: the very small world now being explored by the molecular geneticists and virologists, not yet as strange a place as quantum mechanics

FOR GROUP LEARNING

Collaborating on an Analysis

As a group, write a paper in which you analyze one of the topics suggested in the assignments in this section. Working together, choose a subject for analysis, a purpose for the analysis, and a principle of division. Each member of the group should then take one of the parts to explain independently. Reconvene as a group to work the sections written by individuals into a single paper. As you revise and edit the final draft, consider the advantages and disadvantages of working in a group.

but well on its way to strangeness; an everyday, middle-sized world where things are as they are; and a world of the very large, which is the whole affair, the lovely conjoined biosphere, the vast embryo, the closed ecosystem in which we live as working parts, the place for which Lovelock and Margulis invented the term "Gaia" because of its extraordinary capacity to regulate itself. This world seems to me an even stranger one than the world of very small things in biology: it looks like the biggest organism I've ever heard of, and at the same time the most delicate and fragile, exactly the delicate and fragile creature it appeared to be in those first photographs taken from the surface of the moon.

Analysis helps readers understand something complex: they can more readily take in the subject in a series of bites than in one gulp. For this reason, college textbooks do a lot of analyzing: an economics book divides a labor union into its component parts, an anatomy text divides the hand into the bones, muscles, and ligaments that make it up. In *Cultural Anthropology: A Perspective on the Human Condition* (1987), authors Emily A. Schultz and Robert H. Lavenda briefly but effectively demonstrate by analysis how a metaphor like "the Lord is my shepherd" makes a difficult concept ("the Lord") easy to understand.

> The first part of a metaphor, the *metaphorical subject,* indicates the domain of experience that needs to be clarified (e.g., "the Lord"). The second part of a metaphor, the *metaphorical predicate,* suggests a domain of experience which is familiar (e.g., sheep-herding) and which may help us understand what "the Lord" is all about.

You will also find yourself from time to time being called on to set forth an informative analysis, tracing the steps by which something takes place — the formation of a star, a mountain, or a human embryo; the fall of Rome, the awarding of child custody in a divorce case, or the election of a president. Here is an example from a professional writer of an informative analysis — a passage from *The Perceptual World of the Child* by T. G. R. Bower. The author finds it necessary to stop partway through the chapter he calls "Some Complex Effects of Simple Growth" to explain in brief the workings of the human eye.

> Finally we come to the most complex sensory system, the eye and its associated neural structures. The eye is an extremely intricate and complex organ. Light enters the eye through the cornea, passes through the anterior chamber and thence through the pupil to the lens. The lens is a soft transparent tissue that can stretch out and get thinner or shorten and thicken, thus focusing the rays of light and enabling images of objects at different distances to be seen clearly. The lens focuses the light on the retina, which is the thin membrane covering the posterior surface of the eyeball. The nerve cells in the retina itself are sensitive to spots of light. Each nerve cell at the next level of analysis in the brain receives inputs from a number of these retinal nerve cells and responds best to lines or long edges in particular orientations. Numbers of these nerve cells feed into the next level, where nerve cells are sensitive to

movement of lines in particular orientations in particular directions. There are other levels that seem sensitive to size, and still others that respond to specific differences in the signals from the two eyes.

As you enter the world of work, you will probably find yourself called on any number of times to analyze — in lab reports, technical writing of all sorts, business reports and memos, case studies, nursing records, treatment histories, and a host of other kinds of writing, depending on your career. You'll find knowing how to analyze and explain to help readers understand better immensely useful.

Making Connections:
Analysis in A Writer's Reader

Writers often use the strategy of *analysis* to help them achieve their purposes, sometimes alone and sometimes in combination with other writing techniques. Analysis is perhaps the most frequently used critical thinking strategy, as illustrated by the authors in *A Writer's Reader*. In "The Myth of Cinderella" (p. 603), writer and editor Veronica Chambers analyzes the differences between white and black women's interpretations of the Cinderella myth to demonstrate the ways in which past experience influences and shapes individual responses to the story. Management and organizational development experts Thomas F. Cawsey, Gene Deszca, and Maurice Mazerolle, in "The Portfolio Career as a Response to a Changing Job Market" (p. 635), explain why a portfolio career will be the best option for many people in the future and analyze the potential risks that portfolio careerists must learn to manage.

Similar to James Fallows (p. 136), Lillian Tsu (p. 141), Chambers and Cawsey, Deszca, and Mazerolle, a number of other authors use analysis in the process of exploring their topics and making their arguments. They include satirist Emily Prager, "Our Barbies, Ourselves" (p. 537); poet and professor Judith Ortiz Cofer, "The Myth of the Latin Woman: I Just Met a Girl Named María" (p. 564); columnist Paul Varnell, "The Niceness Solution" (p. 576); writer and professor Phyllis Rose, "Shopping and Other Spiritual Adventures in America Today" (p. 610); and freelance writer Mike Males, "Public Enemy Number One?" (p. 616). As you read these essays, consider the role that analysis plays in each. For each essay, answer the following questions:

1. What idea does the author analyze? For what purpose?
2. How is the analysis related to the writer's occupation or field of interest?
3. What devices does the writer use to make the analysis clear and easy to follow?

Chapter 7

Comparing and Contrasting

Which city — Dallas or Atlanta — has more advantages and more drawbacks for a young single person thinking of settling down to a career? How does the IBM personal computer stack up against a Macintosh for word processing? As songwriters, how are Bruce Springsteen and Bob Dylan similar and dissimilar? Such questions invite answers that set two subjects side by side.

When you compare, you point out similarities; when you contrast, you discuss differences. In writing assignments that ask you to deal with two complicated subjects, usually you will need both to compare *and* contrast. Taking Mozart and Bach, you might find that each has traits the other has — or lacks. In writing about the two, you wouldn't have to conclude that one is great and the other inferior. You might look at their differences and similarities and then conclude that they're two distinct composers, each with an individual style. Of course, if you have a preference for either Bach or Mozart, you'll want to voice it. In a paper whose main purpose is to judge between two subjects (as when you'd recommend that a young single person move either to Dallas or to Atlanta), you would look especially for positive and negative features, weigh the attractions of each city and its faults, and then stick your neck out and make your choice. In daily life all of us frequently compare and contrast as when we decide which menu selection to choose or which car (or other product) to buy. Though in everyday thinking we do not usually commit our reasoning to paper, comparing and contrasting are familiar habits of thought.

Learning from Other Writers

In this chapter you will be asked to write a paper setting two subjects side by side, comparing and contrasting them. Let's see how other writers have used these familiar habits of thought in writing. First is an essay by historian Bruce Catton about two great American generals, Ulysses S. Grant and Robert E. Lee.

The second essay is by Tim Chabot, a student at the University of Virginia. Chabot compares and contrasts the sports of baseball and basketball and asks us to consider which should hold the honor of being our national pastime.

Bruce Catton   Grant and Lee: A Study in Contrasts

When Ulysses S. Grant and Robert E. Lee met in the parlor of a modest house at Appomattox Court House, Virginia, on April 9, 1865, to work out the terms for the surrender of Lee's Army of Northern Virginia, a great chapter in American life came to a close, and a great new chapter began.

These men were bringing the Civil War to its virtual finish. To be sure, other armies had yet to surrender, and for a few days the fugitive Confederate government would struggle desperately and vainly, trying to find some way to go on living now that its chief support was gone. But in effect it was all over when Grant and Lee signed the papers. And the little room where they wrote out the terms was the scene of one of the poignant, dramatic contrasts in American history.

They were two strong men, these oddly different generals, and they represented the strengths of two conflicting currents that, through them, had come into final collision.

Back of Robert E. Lee was the notion that the old aristocratic concept might somehow survive and be dominant in American life.

Lee was tidewater Virginia, and in his background were family, culture, and tradition . . . the age of chivalry transplanted to a New World which was making its own legends and its own myths. He embodied a way of life that had come down through the age of knighthood and the English country squire. America was a land that was beginning all over again, dedicated to nothing much more complicated than the rather hazy belief that all men had equal rights and should have an equal chance in the world. In such a land Lee stood for the feeling that it was somehow of advantage to human society to have a pronounced inequality in the social structure. There should be a leisure class, backed by ownership of land; in turn, society itself should be keyed to the land as the chief source of wealth and influence. It would bring forth (according to this ideal) a class of men with a strong sense of obligation to the community; men who lived not to gain advantage for themselves, but to meet the solemn obligations which had been laid on them by the very fact that they were privileged. From them the country would get its leadership; to them it could look for the higher values — of thought, of conduct, of personal deportment — to give it strength and virtue.

Lee embodied the noblest elements of this aristocratic ideal. Through him, the landed nobility justified itself. For four years, the Southern states had fought a desperate war to uphold the ideals for which Lee stood. In the end, it almost seemed as if the Confederacy fought for Lee; as if he himself was the Confederacy . . . the best thing that the way of life for which the Confederacy stood could ever have to offer. He had passed into legend before Appomattox. Thousands of tired, underfed, poorly clothed Confederate soldiers, long since past the simple enthusiasm of the early days of the struggle, somehow considered Lee the symbol of everything for which they had been willing to die. But they could not quite put this feeling into words. If the Lost Cause, sanctified by so much heroism and so many deaths, had a living justification, its justification was General Lee.

Grant, the son of a tanner on the Western frontier, was everything Lee was   7
not. He had come up the hard way and embodied nothing in particular except the eternal toughness and sinewy fiber of the men who grew up beyond the mountains. He was one of a body of men who owed reverence and obeisance to no one, who were self-reliant to a fault, who cared hardly anything for the past but who had a sharp eye for the future.

These frontier men were the precise opposites of the tidewater aristocrats.   8
Back of them, in the great surge that had taken people over the Alleghenies and into the opening Western country, there was a deep, implicit dissatisfaction with a past that had settled into grooves. They stood for democracy, not from any reasoned conclusion about the proper ordering of human society, but simply because they had grown up in the middle of democracy and knew how it worked. Their society might have privileges, but they would be privileges each man had won for himself. Forms and patterns meant nothing. No man was born to anything, except perhaps a chance to show how far he could rise. Life was competition.

Yet along with this feeling had come a deep sense of belonging to a na-   9
tional community. The Westerner who developed a farm, opened a shop, or set up in business as a trader, could hope to prosper only as his own community prospered — and his community ran from the Atlantic to the Pacific and from Canada down to Mexico. If the land was settled, with towns and highways and accessible markets, he could better himself. He saw his fate in terms of the nation's own destiny. As its horizons expanded, so did his. He had, in other words, an acute dollars-and-cents stake in the continued growth and development of his country.

And that, perhaps, is where the contrast between Grant and Lee becomes   10
most striking. The Virginia aristocrat, inevitably, saw himself in relation to his own region. He lived in a static society which could endure almost anything except change. Instinctively, his first loyalty would go to the locality in which that society existed. He would fight to the limit of endurance to defend it, because in defending it he was defending everything that gave his own life its deepest meaning.

The Westerner, on the other hand, would fight with an equal tenacity for   11
the broader concept of society. He fought so because everything he lived by was tied to growth, expansion, and a constantly widening horizon. What he lived by would survive or fall with the nation itself. He could not possibly stand by unmoved in the face of an attempt to destroy the Union. He would combat it with everything he had, because he could only see it as an effort to cut the ground out from under his feet.

So Grant and Lee were in complete contrast, representing two diametri-   12
cally opposed elements in American life. Grant was the modern man emerging; beyond him, ready to come on the stage, was the great age of steel and machinery; of crowded cities and a restless burgeoning vitality. Lee might have ridden down from the old age of chivalry, lance in hand, silken banner

fluttering over his head. Each man was the perfect champion of his cause, drawing both his strengths and his weaknesses from the people he led.

Yet it was not all contrast, after all. Different as they were — in background, in personality, in underlying aspiration — these two great soldiers had much in common. Under everything else, they were marvelous fighters. Furthermore, their fighting qualities were really very much alike.   13

Each man had, to begin with, the great virtue of utter tenacity and fidelity. Grant fought his way down the Mississippi Valley in spite of acute personal discouragement and profound military handicaps. Lee hung on in the trenches at Petersburg after hope itself had died. In each man there was an indomitable quality . . . the born fighter's refusal to give up as long as he can still remain on his feet and lift his two fists.   14

Daring and resourcefulness they had, too; the ability to think faster and move faster than the enemy. These were the qualities which gave Lee the dazzling campaigns of Second Manassas and Chancellorsville and won Vicksburg for Grant.   15

Lastly, and perhaps greatest of all, there was the ability, at the end, to turn quickly from war to peace once the fighting was over. Out of the way these two men behaved at Appomattox came the possibility of a peace of reconciliation. It was a possibility not wholly realized, in the years to come, but which did, in the end, help the two sections to become one nation again . . . after a war whose bitterness might have seemed to make such a reunion wholly impossible. No part of either man's life became him more than the part he played in this brief meeting in the McLean house at Appomattox. Their behavior there put all succeeding generations of Americans in their debt. Two great Americans, Grant and Lee — very different, yet under everything very much alike. Their encounter at Appomattox was one of the great moments of American history.   16

Questions to Start You Thinking

Meaning

1. Catton in this essay describes two very different men. In what ways were Grant and Lee different? How were they similar?

2. How do the two personalities symbolize the struggle of the American Civil War?

3. Do the ways of thinking and living represented by Grant and Lee still exist today?

Writing Strategies

4. What techniques does Catton use to describe Grant and Lee?

5. The author ends the essay by showing how Grant and Lee were comparable. Why does he place their differences first? In your opinion, which are stronger — the similarities or the differences of the two men? Does Catton give proper proportion to both the similarities and the differences?

6. Catton compares and contrasts the two men, but he does not judge who was the better general. What, then, is his purpose in the essay, if not to say one general was better than the other?

Tim Chabot   Take Me Out to the Ball Game, but Which One?

For much of the twentieth century, baseball has been
considered the national pastime of the United States. Hank
Aaron, home runs, and hot dogs seem as American as Thanksgiv-
ing. Many American presidents, from Eisenhower to Clinton,
have participated in the tradition of a celebrity throwing
out the first ball on opening day of a new baseball season.
But in the 1990s, baseball stars are being eclipsed by the
stars of another game invented in America--basketball.
Michael Jordan and Shaquille O'Neal, basketball greats and
household names, have become more famous than any current
pitcher or home run king. In addition, the 1994 to 1995 baseball strike has pushed the sport further out of the lime-
light, since the public has become disillusioned with the
greed of both players and managers. The strike has raised a
question in the minds of many: Should baseball continue to be
considered our national pastime, or should basketball take
its place?

Both sports are very popular with American sports fans.
In addition, both games attract fans of all races--white,
African American, Asian American, Hispanic--and all classes,
rich and poor, educated and uneducated. Baseball has become a
national treasure through its appeal to a wide, wide audience. At a Saturday afternoon game, men, women, grandparents,
and kids of all ages wait to catch a fly ball. The appeal of
basketball is growing, the sport having become popular in
urban and rural areas, on high school and college campuses.
Both sports are played in quite a variety of locations. Baseball games occur on neighborhood sandlots as well as official
diamonds. Basketball requires little space and equipment, so
pickup basketball games occur in almost every neighborhood
park and virtually anywhere that a hoop can be rigged up.

Although both sports are popular with American fans, attending a baseball game is quite different from attending a
basketball game. Baseball is a family-oriented spectator
sport. Because of the widely diverse baseball fans with var-

163

ied interests and attention spans, the experience of going to
a baseball game can be compared to that of an open-air carni-
val, in which the game itself is only one of the many spec-
tacles. If fans are bored with the game, they can listen to
the vendors hawking ice cream, watch a fight brewing in the
bleacher seats, stand in line to buy peanuts or hot dogs,
participate in "the wave," or just bask in the sun. Only
diehard fans keep a constant eye on the game itself since
there are frequent breaks in the play.

In contrast, the central spectacle of any basketball   4
arena is definitely the game itself. Few distractions to entertain a casual fan occur, except for cheerleaders for college teams. Basketball arenas are always indoors, and the
games are usually at night, creating an atmosphere that is
urban and adult. The constant motion of the sport rivets attention to the game itself. Attending a basketball game can
be compared to an exciting night on the town, while watching
a baseball game is like relaxing with the family in the backyard.

The pace of the two games is also quite different. The   5
leisurely pace of a baseball game contributes to its popularity because it offers relaxation to harried Americans. Each
batter may spend several minutes at the plate, hit a few foul
balls, and reach a full count of three balls and two strikes
before getting on base, hitting a routine pop fly, or striking out. While batters slow things down by stepping out of
the box to practice their swing, pitchers stall the play by
"holding the runners on" to prevent stolen bases. The substitution of relief pitchers suspends the game and gives spectators an opportunity to purchase junk food or memorabilia. In
games in which star pitchers duel, the audience may see only
a few men on base in nine innings and a very low score. Also,
the tradition of the seventh-inning stretch underscores baseball's appeal to a person who wants to take it easy and
relax.

On the other hand, the quick pace of basketball has con-   6
tributed to its popularity in our fast-paced society. Players
run down the court at sometimes exhausting speed for a "fast
break," successful baskets can occur merely seconds apart,

each team may score as many as one hundred points a game, and the ball changes sides hundreds of times, as opposed to every half-inning in baseball. Games can be won or lost in the few seconds before the final buzzer. Basketball players are always in motion, much like American society. The pounding excitement of basketball appeals to people who play hard as well as work hard.

These two sports require different athletic abilities from the players. Although baseball games are slow-paced, the sport places a premium on athletic precision and therefore showcases strategy and skill rather than brute physical strength. The choice of a pitch, the decision to bunt or to steal a base, and the order of batters are all careful strategic moves that could affect the outcome of the whole game. Baseball has been called the "thinking person's game" because of its emphasis on statistics and probabilities. Although mental strategy and dexterity are emphasized, physical strength is not unimportant to the sport. A strong arm obviously increases the power of a player's throw or of his swing, and speed is essential in running bases. But intimidating physical ability is not necessarily a required element to become a major league player, and even out-of-shape players can become stars if their bats are hot. The importance of skill over brawn has contributed to baseball's popularity not merely as a spectator sport but also as a sport in which millions of Americans participate, from Little League to neighborhood leagues for adults.

Unlike baseball, basketball emphasizes physical power, stamina, and size since jumping high, running fast, and just being tall with long legs and big hands usually contribute to a player's success. Skill and dexterity, however, are certainly necessary in executing a slam dunk or dribbling past a double team, but these skills are usually combined with physical strength. In order to be a successful rebounder, a player needs to be extremely aggressive and occasionally commit fouls. Many more injuries occur on basketball courts than on baseball fields. Perhaps the physical power and intimidation required in basketball have led to the media's focus on individual players' star qualities. Magic, Bird, Jordan, and

7

8

Shaq are icons who have taken the place of baseball stars of previous generations like Joe DiMaggio, Ted Williams, and Babe Ruth. Furthermore, in the international arena of the Olympics, basketball came to be seen as a symbol of American strength and power, as the 1992 Dream Team demolished all of its opponents.

If the rest of the world now equates basketball with America, should we consider it to be our true national pastime? The increasing popularity of basketball seems to reflect the change in American society in the past few decades, a change to a more fast-paced and aggressive culture. But basketball doesn't yet appeal to as diverse an audience as does baseball, and thus it doesn't seem to deserve to be called a national phenomenon--yet. Until kids, women, and grandparents are as prevalent at a Lakers game as are young males, baseball will retain its title as the national pastime. But when the leisurely pace of the baseball game grinds to a halt because of players' strikes, impatient fans may turn to the exciting speed of basketball to rejuvenate their faith in American sports.

9

Questions to Start You Thinking

Meaning

1. In what specific ways does Chabot claim that baseball and basketball are similar? In what ways are these two sports different? Do the similarities outweigh the differences, or vice versa?
2. Can you think of other ways these two sports are similar and different?
3. As a result of comparing and contrasting baseball and basketball, what conclusion does Chabot arrive at? Does he convince you of his conclusion?
4. Would you nominate another sport, say football or ice hockey, for the national pastime? Why?

Writing Strategies

5. What is Chabot's thesis? Where does he state it? Why there?
6. How does Chabot organize his essay?
7. What transitional devices does Chabot use to indicate when he is comparing and when he is contrasting?

Learning by Writing

THE ASSIGNMENT: COMPARING AND CONTRASTING

Write a paper in which you compare and contrast two items for the general purpose of enlightening readers about both subjects. The specific points of similarity and difference will be important, but you will go beyond just comparing and contrasting to draw a conclusion from your analysis of the similarities and differences. This conclusion will be your thesis, and it will be more than "point A is different from point B" or "I prefer subject B to subject A." You will need to explain why you have drawn the conclusion you have and to provide sufficient specific supporting evidence to explain your position to your readers and to convince them of the soundness of your conclusion. You may choose two people, two kinds of people, two places, two things, two activities, or two ideas. Be sure to choose two subjects you care about. Like Bruce Catton, you might write an impartial paper that distinctly portrays both subjects, or like Tim Chabot, you might demonstrate why you favor one over the other.

Although the subjects should differ enough to throw each other into sharp relief, be sure they have enough in common to compare. A comparison of sports cars and racing cars might reveal much, but a comparison of sports cars and oil tankers would probably reveal little.

Among the most engaging and instructive recent student papers we've seen in response to similar assignments are these:

An American woman compared and contrasted her home life with that of her roommate, a student from Nigeria. Her goal was to understand more deeply Nigerian society and her own.

A man who had read some articles and books about comets contrasted the spectacular fly-by of Halley's comet in 1910 with its less spectacular return in 1985 and 1986. He also compared and contrasted public responses to the comet's two twentieth-century appearances. He concluded that the comet's latest performance had not really been a flop.

For an economics course that asked for an explanation of a major idea of influential economist John Maynard Keynes, a woman compared and contrasted Keynes's views of the causes of monetary inflation with those of Karl Marx on the same subject, concluding that Keynes's theories are more relevant today.

A man compared the differences between traveling by airline and traveling by train. His purpose was to make a case for continuing intercontinental passenger rail service.

GENERATING IDEAS

Find two subjects. Pick subjects you can compare and contrast purposefully. An examination question may give them to you, ready-made: "Compare and contrast ancient Roman sculpture with that of the ancient Greeks" or "Discuss the main differences between the British system of higher education and the American system." But suppose you have to find your subjects for yourself. You'll need to choose things that can sensibly be compared and contrasted. Find a basis for comparison, a common element. There is probably no point in comparing and contrasting moon rocks and stars, but it will make sense to bring together Springsteen and Dylan *as songwriters,* Dallas and Atlanta *as cities to consider settling in,* or Karl Barth and Søren Kierkegaard *as religious thinkers.*

Try generating a list of what you might like to compare and contrast. Try a little *brainstorming* (see p. 360). Let your mind skitter around in search of pairs that go together. Write them down in two columns as you think of them. Consult your trusty writer's resources: Have you experienced, seen, or read anything lately that suggests a suitable subject? Have you talked to someone who reminds you of someone else or imagined a possibility that contrasts starkly with reality? You might find it useful to ask yourself the following questions:

DISCOVERY CHECKLIST

- Do you know two people who are strikingly different in attitude or behavior? (Perhaps your parents, or two brothers, two friends, two teachers)
- Can you think of two groups of people who are both alike and different? (Perhaps two football teams or two clubs)
- Have you taken two courses that were both valuable to you although they were quite different?
- Can you describe two places you have lived or two places you have visited? Do you prefer one over the other?
- Can you recall two events in your life that shared some similar aspects but turned out to be quite different? (Perhaps two sporting events or two romances or the birth of two children)
- Can you compare and contrast two holidays or two family customs that you are familiar with? What would be your point in setting this pair side by side?
- Are you familiar with two writers, two artists, or two musicians who seem to have similar goals but quite different accomplishments?
- Have you studied two interesting historical figures whom you can understand better by comparing and contrasting them? (If you choose this topic for writing, you will probably have to do some review and additional reading about the two people.)
- Are you familiar with two ideas or schools of thought ("-isms") that seem strikingly different in basic principles or in effects? (Perhaps two economic theories such as capitalism and communism, two literary movements such as classicism and romanticism, or two religious groups such as Christians and Buddhists)

You can also play the game of *free association,* jotting down whatever comes to mind as you think. Write down a word, and then write down whatever comes to mind when you think of that word. What comes to mind when you write *mothers? Fathers* perhaps. *Democrats? Republicans. New York? Los Angeles. King Kong? Godzilla. High school? College.* Or whatever.

Once you have a list of pairs, go through the list and put a star by those pairs that seem promising. Ask yourself what similarities immediately come to mind. What differences? Can you think of several of each? If not, move on to another pair. As you think, write down the points of comparison for the two subjects. Then write down the points of contrast. (You may have the beginnings of a useful outline.) Review your list, and ask yourself if these are striking, significant similarities and differences. If not, keep on thinking and jotting until you discover a pair you think will work.

Find a purpose. You need a reason to place two subjects side by side — a reason that you and most of your readers will find compelling and worthwhile. After you have selected your pair, ask yourself if you prefer one subject in the pair over the other. And ask yourself why you have this preference. What reasons can you give for your preference? It's all right not to have a preference. Bruce Catton isn't arguing that Robert E. Lee is superior to Ulysses S. Grant, or vice versa. Instead, he shows how each throws the other into sharp relief and helps us understand both generals as well as the effects of their personalities and actions better. You may take either approach for your paper.

You also need to determine what point you want to make by your comparison and contrast of the two subjects. Bruce Catton wanted to show how the meeting of these two great men made a peace of reconciliation possible after such a bitter civil struggle between the states. Tim Chabot wanted to explore the question of whether we should continue to consider baseball our national pastime. In his freshman writing course, Eli Kavon, who had spent some time studying at an Israeli military seminary, wrote an account of his experience for the information of his instructor and classmates. In part of this account, he compared and contrasted himself (and the other American Jewish students in Israel) with Israeli students.

> We — the foreigners — had much in common with our Israeli contemporaries: a history dating back thousands of years, a belief in one God, a love of Judaism and the land of Israel. However, we would be in the country only for a year or two and would not be drafted with the Israelis, who devote two of five years in the seminary to military service. Unlike the average Israeli, none of us had grown up in a household where real weapons rested in closets and on top of refrigerators, ready for use. American teenagers know of war either as a childhood game with plastic weapons or as a memory of the battles and the body bags of a "television war." Israelis, on the other hand, have been forced to live a life of drafts, weapons, and fear. In Israel preparation for war is the norm.

As you can see from this passage, Kavon's comparing and contrasting is no meaningless exercise. It is a way to think clearly and pointedly in order to explain an idea about which the writer cares deeply.

Limit the scope of your paper. If you propose to write a comparison and contrast between Japanese literature and American literature in 750 words, probably you will be tackling an impossible task. To explore this topic thoroughly, you might need to write a whole book. But to cut down the size of this promising subject, you might propose to compare and contrast, say, a haiku of Bashō about a snake with a short poem about a snake by Emily Dickinson. You would then be dealing with a topic you could cover adequately in 750 words. Of course, the larger and more abstract topic might be manageable — if you had much time to read and more space to develop the ideas.

Explore each member of your pair. Now that you have a pair of subjects and a purpose in mind and have limited your scope, you'll need to examine in depth each of your two subjects. Your goal is twofold: you want to analyze each subject using a similar approach so that you have a reasonable basis for comparison and contrast, and you want to find the details and examples that you'll need to support your points.

If you are considering writing about two events, procedures, or processes, try asking yourself a reporter's questions — the five *W*'s and an *H* that journalists use. (See p. 368). Make two columns, and write your answers to the following questions opposite each other:

Who was there?
What happened?
Where did the event take place?
When did it happen?
Why did the event occur?
How did the event or events happen?

If you are considering writing about two events from the past, try using the resource of *conversation* to generate material: discuss what happened at each event with someone else who was there. Or if you want to write about what goes on behind the scenes in the locker rooms of two professional football teams, talk to someone who has been there. When you talk to these people, go prepared with specific questions you want answers to, and ask both people the same questions so that you can compare and contrast the same points. If you don't, you will have some gaps in your information, and you may need to go back to talk to one or both at a later time. What will you do if they don't have time to talk to you again? (For more on using the resource of conversation, see Chapter 3.)

You can also try *reading*. Perhaps you can think of two possible subjects to compare and contrast, but you are not sure that the pair will work or you may not know quite enough about them to write a full essay. Go to the library and read a few articles about the subjects to test the possibility of your potential pair.

If your immediate answers to the reporter's questions are skimpy, or if you're less interested in your subjects than you thought you'd be, you may want to pick a new pair and start again. Or it may be that with a little more imagination, some reading, observing, conversing, or recalling, you'll find you've made a good choice after all.

PLANNING, DRAFTING, AND DEVELOPING

Now that you are about to start writing your whole paper, remind yourself once more that in comparing and contrasting two subjects, you have a goal. What is it you want to demonstrate, argue, or find out?

When you write a draft, an outline isn't always necessary. If you are setting forth something you can hold clearly in mind (such as a personal experience, written from recall), you may find you work best by just taking off and letting words flow. You may find you can compare and contrast without outlining. But in comparing and contrasting, most writers find that some planning helps speed the job. For one thing, an outline — even a rough scratch outline — enables you to keep track of all the points you want to make, which so easily may be lost or confused as you glance from side to side. You can make an outline in your head, of course, but it is probably easier to keep track of things on paper. (For more on outlines, see p. 384.).

In comparing and contrasting, two ways of organizing are possible. The first way is the *opposing pattern* of *subject by subject*. You state all your observations about subject A and then do the same for subject B. The book *Educational Policies in Crisis: Japanese and American Perspectives* (New York: Praeger, 1986) is a collection of essays analyzing and evaluating the Japanese and American educational systems. In Chapter 15, "Learning from Each Other," William K. Cummings and others, the editors of the book, use the opposing pattern to compare and contrast how the two countries think about education.

> More salient, however, than these structural characteristics is the way that the two nations think about education. The United States fosters a myth of limitless opportunity. Football players can earn more than corporation presidents, and the local shoe store of today has the possibility of becoming one of *Fortune*'s Top 100 in 20 years. School is but one of several routes to success. For the individual who seeks the educational route, being a late bloomer is not necessarily an obstacle to upward mobility. Thus even when they enter college, many Americans have poorly developed intellectual skills. Most Americans are also relaxed about choosing their educational institutions, believing that what happens outside school and later in life may have more influence on their chances for success than what takes place in school. In contrast with the American belief in limitless opportunity, the Japanese assign great importance to a small number of career choices in the central government bureaucracy and the top corporations. They rank other careers in descending order and assume that an individual's educational performance will determine where he or she ends up in this hierarchy. Most Japanese parents seek to manage the lives of their children, from a surprisingly young age, so that the children will have the best chances of entering the top careers. Because admission to a prestigious university is known to be essential for gaining access to these attractive careers, parents are deeply concerned with the educational performance of their children. They exert every effort to ensure that their children earn good grades and enter the best schools. The large number of parents sharing this common belief results in severe academic competition. In contrast to Americans, Japanese children develop from an early age a realistic sense of the opportunities they can expect as they grow up.

In this paragraph, following the first sentence, the editors discuss the American attitude toward education (subject A), beginning with the sentence "The United States fosters a myth of limitless opportunity." Then they explain the American attitude toward the relationship of education to career opportunities and toward choice of educational institutions. In the middle of the paragraph, they announce a shift with the phrase "In contrast" and present information about the Japanese attitude toward education. Using the same order as for subject A, they discuss first the attitude toward career opportunities and then toward educational institutions. This pattern of organization is a workable method for writing a single paragraph or a short essay, but for a long essay or a more complicated subject, it has a drawback. Readers might find it difficult to remember all the separate information about subject A while reading about subject B.

There's a better way to organize most longer papers: the *alternating pattern* of *point by point*. Working by this method, you take up one point at a time, applying it first to one subject and then to the other. Tim Chabot uses this pattern of organization. It is often the more appropriate method for complicated subjects and fully developed essays. Looking at each subject before moving on to the next point, Chabot leads the reader along clearly and carefully. His outline might have looked like the one on the next page.

FOR PEER RESPONSE   You may find it helpful to ask a classmate to read and respond to your draft. See Chapter 20 for advice on working with other student writers and for general questions you should always ask a peer editor to address. For a paper in which you compare and contrast, you'll also want your peer editor to answer these specific questions:

- Does the introduction make you want to read the entire essay?
- Is the point of the comparison and contrast of the two subjects clear to you? What is that point? Does the writer state it in the essay, or is it implied?
- Is the essay organized by the opposing pattern or by the alternating pattern? Would the other pattern work better for the topic, or is the pattern used the more appropriate?
- Are the same categories discussed for each item? If not, should they be?
- Are there sufficient details to allow you to understand the comparison and contrast? Put a check mark anywhere that more details or examples would be useful.
- Does the paper avoid falling into a tedious singsong pattern? Are the transitions varied and helpful?
- If this were your paper, what is the one thing you would be sure to work on before handing it in?

Thesis: Despite the popularity of basketball in the 1990s, baseball should continue to be considered our national pastime.

I. Similarities of fans
    A. Appeal to diverse groups
        1. Baseball
        2. Basketball
    B. Varied locations
        1. Baseball
        2. Basketball
II. Difference in atmosphere at game
    A. Baseball as a diverse family-oriented spectator sport
        1. Many distractions
        2. Frequent breaks in play
    B. Basketball as game-focused sport
        1. Few distractions
        2. Constant game activity
III. Difference in pace of game
    A. Leisurely pace of baseball
        1. Slow batters
        2. Stalling pitchers
        3. Substitution of relief pitchers
        4. Low score
        5. Seventh-inning stretch
    B. Quick pace of basketball
        1. Fast players
        2. High scores
        3. Frequent changes of sides
        4. Constant motion
IV. Different athletic abilities of players
    A. Baseball as a mental game
        1. Emphasis on athletic precision
            a. Strategy
            b. Skill
            c. Decision-making
        2. Physical strength less important
    B. Basketball as a physical game
        1. Emphasis on physical power
            a. Jumping high
            b. Running fast
            c. Being tall and big
            d. Being aggressive
        2. Importance of skill and dexterity

Facing the Challenge: Comparing and Contrasting

The major challenge writers face when they compare and contrast two subjects is to determine what method of organization will best help them make
their overall point. The purpose of the essay is not simply to show the similarities and differences in two subjects; it is to use comparison and contrast
to make a point. A writer should choose an organizational method that will
enable readers to easily follow the differences and similarities of the subjects
and to see the relationship of the comparisons and contrasts to the main
point or thesis.

Once you have selected a topic with which you can work, choose the organizational method that will enable readers to easily follow the differences
and similarities of the subjects. Two methods for organizing a comparison-
contrast essay are the opposing (subject-by-subject) pattern and the alternating (point-by-point) pattern. When using the opposing pattern, you make all
of your points about Subject A before moving on to Subject B. When using
the alternating pattern, you discuss each point in relation to both subjects before moving on to the next point.

In his essay "Take Me Out to the Ball Game, but Which One?" Tim
Chabot organizes by using the point-by-point pattern, alternating paragraphs
on baseball with paragraphs on basketball as he compares and contrasts various categories of the two sports. If he had adhered to the opposing, or
subject-by-subject, pattern, his readers probably would have forgotten much
of what he'd said about baseball by the time he'd finished telling them about
basketball and would have missed his overall aim in comparing and contrasting the two sports.

Although a strict use of the subject-by-subject pattern is not advisable in
a long essay, it is possible to use this approach in a *portion* of your paper.
Bruce Catton, for example, in his essay on Grant and Lee, deliberately shifts
between the opposing and alternating patterns. In the first portion of his
essay, he uses the opposing method — presenting the whole of his evidence
and assertions about Lee as an aristocratic Southern gentleman and then contrasting it with the whole of his evidence and assertions about Grant as a
democratic Northern frontiersman. In the latter portion of his essay, he
switches to the alternating method to illustrate three points of similarity between the two generals. Catton's switch in organizational method works to
emphasize the shift in his essay from a discussion of the differences between
Grant and Lee to a discussion of their similarities.

Both Catton and Chabot bring cohesion to their complex essays through
their use of effective transitional words and phrases — *on the other hand, in
contrast, also, both, yet, although, lastly, unlike* (for more transitional phrases,
see p. 407). Your choice of transitional phrases will depend on the content of
your paragraphs, but check to make sure that your transitions are varied and
smooth. Jarring, choppy transitions will distract attention from your main
point. Remember that while your task is to compare and contrast two distinct
subjects, your ultimate goal is to produce a unified essay, each part of which
works to support a meaningful thesis.

Even without outlining, you can sometimes follow the point-by-point method informally. Mystery writer Raymond Chandler, for an essay comparing and contrasting English people and Americans (which he left unfinished in his notebooks), wrote this opening paragraph. It probably didn't require any outline at all.

> The keynote of American civilization is a sort of warm-hearted vulgarity. The Americans have none of the irony of the English, none of their cool poise, none of their manner. But they do have friendliness. Where an Englishman would give you his card, an American would very likely give you his shirt.

In its blast-off sentence, the paragraph announces its main idea. Then Chandler proceeds to compare the English and the Americans in two ways — (1) in manner, cool or friendly, and (2) in generosity. Like all generalizations about groups of people, this one can be shot full of holes; but Chandler's paragraph states a memorable insight. A comparison and contrast can explain things neatly and intelligently, even though (like a one-paragraph description of Japanese and American literature) it might stereotype the particulars.

In developing a meaty essay that compares and contrasts, an outline, however sketchy, will be your trusty friend. Keep your outline simple, and don't be ruled by it. If excellent thoughts come to you in writing your first draft, by all means let them in.

Before you begin to draft your essay, you may need to do a bit more thinking to come up with enough details about your two subjects to write a good essay of comparison and contrast. If so, try brainstorming (p. 360) or freewriting (p. 363) again, this time specifically about the pair of subjects you have selected. Then go back over the details you have generated to eliminate any weak points (perhaps those that force the comparison or contrast) and to add

---

WRITING WITH A COMPUTER

In Chapter 6, on analyzing, you focused on breaking a subject down into its component parts. Comparison and contrast is a type of analysis, only now you are examining a number of things instead of just one subject — and a word processor can help immensely with this complex type of writing. Begin by writing on a word processor an analysis of one of the items you will compare. For example, to begin a comparison between surfing and badminton using this approach, first write an analysis of surfing. Describe each of the major components of surfing by using headings such as *equipment, technique, fashion, rules, environment,* and *attitude.* Add thorough descriptions beneath each of the headings, leaving lots of white space between divisions. Then go back and add descriptions of badminton under the same headings so that you generate contrasting pictures. At first, your comparison may not be balanced, and some of your original divisions may need to be rearranged or discarded if they don't produce revealing contrasts. But the beauty of word processing is that it encourages you to try different configurations and make sweeping changes.

specifics in any sections that might be underdeveloped. You may also draw on a writer's resources again here — recall, observation, conversation, and imagination — to flesh out your ideas.

REVISING AND EDITING

As you look over your early draft, you'll want to be sure that each comparison or contrast you include discusses similar elements. You'll only confuse your readers if, in considering the merits of two cities, you contrast New York's public transportation with Milwaukee's tree-lined streets; or if, in setting Springsteen and Dylan side by side, you deal with Springsteen's fondness for pizza and Dylan's politics. Go through your draft with a fine-tooth comb to make sure that at every point you compare or contrast, you are looking at the same feature.

If your purpose in writing is to illuminate two subjects impartially, you can ask yourself if you have given your reader a balanced view. Although you might well have more to say about one than about the other, obviously it would be unfair to set forth all the advantages of Oklahoma City and all the disadvantages of Honolulu and then conclude that Oklahoma City is superior to Honolulu on every count. If you haven't been fair, you may need to re-plan — perhaps make a new outline — and do some more discovering. (One useful way to tell whether you have done a thorough job of comparing and contrasting is to make an outline of your first draft and then give the outline a critical squint. See p. 171.)

Of course, if you love Oklahoma City and can't stand Honolulu, or vice versa, go ahead: don't be balanced; take a stand. Even so, you will want to include the same points about each city and to admit, in all honesty, that Oklahoma City, unlike Eden, has its faults.

Make sure, too, as you go over your draft, that you have escaped falling into a monotonous drone: A does this, B does that; A looks like this, B looks like that; A has these advantages, B has those. Comparison and contrast is a useful method, but it needn't result in a paper as symmetrical as a pair of sneakers. Revising and editing gives you a chance to add any lively details, varied transitions, interesting later thoughts, dashes of color, finishing touches that (with any luck) may occur to you.

FOR GROUP LEARNING

Comparing and Contrasting Yourself with a Partner

Work with a partner to develop a single comparison and contrast essay for assignment 4 in this section. Decide together what the focus of your essay will be: Your family backgrounds? Your hobbies? Your career goals? Your study habits? Your taste in music or clothes? Your political beliefs? Then each partner should work alone to generate a detailed analysis of himself or herself, given this focus. Come together again to compare your analyses; to decide what shape the essay should take; and to draft, revise, and edit the paper.

In critiquing your draft as you rewrite, this checklist may prove handy:

REVISION CHECKLIST

- Have you chosen the *major* similarities and differences to write about?
- Is your reason for doing all the comparing and contrasting unmistakably clear? If not, your paper will seem an arbitrary exercise conducted in outer space. Do you need to reexamine your goal? What is it you want to demonstrate, argue for, or find out?
- Have you used the same categories for each item? In discussing each feature, do you always look at the very same thing?
- Have you come to a conclusion about the two? Do you prefer one over the other? If so, is this preference (and your reasons for it) clear?
- If you are making a judgment between your subjects, do you feel you have treated both fairly?
- Does your draft look thin for lack of evidence? If so, from which resources might you draw more?
- Have you avoided a boringly mechanical, monotonous style ("On one hand, . . . now on the other hand")?
- Have you given some attention to your introduction? Does it introduce your topic and main point clearly? Is it interesting enough to make you want to read the whole essay?

After you have revised your comparison and contrast essay, proofread and edit it. Check carefully for problems with grammar, word choice, punctuation, and mechanics — and then correct any problems you may find. A comprehensive reference handbook is an indispensable tool for this task; the "Quick Editing Guide" at the end of *The Bedford Guide for College Writers* (see the pages with the colored edges) will get you started.

When editing a comparison and contrast paper, pay close attention to the sentences that actually contain the comparisons or contrasts. To make them as effective as possible, you should use a parallel structure that balances the two elements you are examining. Also make sure you have used the correct form for any adjectives and adverbs you use: you should use the *comparative* form when placing two things side by side but the *superlative* form when writing about three or more things. Finally, you have probably already integrated transitions that move the reader smoothly between the two subjects of your analysis. At this stage, check once more to be sure that the transitions are not only clear but that they avoid a tedious ping-pong quality, as if you were bouncing back and forth between one thing and another.

Here are some questions to get you started when proofreading and editing your paper:

EDITING CHECKLIST

- Have you used comparative and superlative forms of adjectives and adverbs correctly? (See A5 in the "Quick Editing Guide.")
- Is your sentence structure correct? Have you avoided writing fragments and run-on sentences? (See A6 and A7 in the "Quick Editing Guide.")
- Have you used parallel structure in your comparisons and contrasts? Are your sentences as balanced as your ideas? (See B2 in the "Quick Editing Guide.")

- Have you used commas correctly after introductory phrases and other transitions? (See C1 in the "Quick Editing Guide.")
- Have you spelled everything correctly (See D2 in the "Quick Editing Guide.")
- Have you used the proper paper format, including special requirements for your instructor and course? (See D3 in the "Quick Editing Guide.")

(For more on revising and editing, see Chapter 19.)

OTHER ASSIGNMENTS

1. Choose two historical or literary figures, and write an essay in which you compare and contrast them as Catton did in his essay "Grant and Lee." Be sure to bring the two into sharp relief and have a purpose other than merely recounting the similarities and differences.

2. Listen to two different recordings of the same piece of music as performed by two different orchestras (or groups or singers). What elements of the music does each performer stress? What contrasting attitudes toward the music do you detect? In an essay, compare and contrast these versions.

3. Write an essay in which you compare and contrast the subjects in any of the following pairs, for the purpose of throwing light on both. In a short paper, you can hope to trace only a few similarities and differences, but don't hesitate to use your own recall or observation, go to the library, or converse with a friendly expert if you need material.

    Women and men as single parents

    Living at home and living away from home

    Japanese and American workers

    The coverage of a world event on a television newscast and in a newspaper

    The state of AIDS research at two moments in time — ten years ago and today

    Alexander Hamilton and Thomas Jefferson — their ideas of the role of the federal government

    The playing styles of two major league pitchers (or two quarterbacks or two basketball players)

    Cubist painting and abstract expressionist painting

    English and another language

    Your college and a rival college

    Two differing views of a current controversy

    Classic French cooking and nouvelle cuisine

    The Odyssey and *The Iliad* (or F. Scott Fitzgerald's *The Great Gatsby* and Ernest Hemingway's *The Sun Also Rises,* or Walt Whitman's poem "To a Locomotive in Winter" and Emily Dickinson's poem about a locomotive "I like to see it lap the Miles," or two other comparable works of literature)

Northern California and southern California (or two other regions)

The experience of watching a film on a VCR and in a theater

Euclidean and non-Euclidean geometry

Two similar works of architecture (two churches, two skyscrapers, two city halls, two museums)

4. In an essay either serious or nonserious, for the purpose of introducing yourself to other members of your class, compare and contrast yourself with someone else. You and this other person should have much in common: avoid comparing and contrasting yourself with someone like Napoleon ("I admit to having less skill on the battlefield"). You might choose either a real person or a character in a film, a TV series, a novel, or a comic strip. Choose a few points of comparison (an attitude, a habit, or a way of life), and deal with each. Feel free to draw on your recall, your own observations, your conversation with him or her (or with a mutual friend), and your imagination (what might it be like to be the other person?).

Applying What You Learn: Some Uses of Comparing and Contrasting

Because comparing and contrasting show a reader how closely writers observe and how hard they think, comparison and contrast questions are great favorites on college essay exams of many kinds. In a nursing course you might be asked to compare and contrast earlier methods of treating heart attack victims with those that prevail today. At times, the examiner won't even mention the method of comparison and contrast by name. But when you get a request such as "Evaluate the relative merits of Norman Rockwell and Andrew Wyeth as realistic painters" (for a course in American art history) or "Consider the tax consequences of doing business as a small corporation and doing business as a partnership. How are they different, or similar?" (in a course in business law), then you can bet your bottom dollar that to compare and contrast is what the examiner hopes you will do.

Sometimes, in an exam or paper, you are asked to describe a person, a thing, or a scene. One good way to approach your response is to recall the useful method of comparison and contrast and to portray your subject by setting it next to something else, something similar but a little different. If asked to describe, for instance, a Cape Cod–style house, you might most clearly reveal its distinctive features by comparing and contrasting it with a Dutch colonial. Or you might explain the protagonist of a literary selection by comparing or contrasting him or her to a contrasting foil character (for example, Othello and Iago in the Shakespearean play, or Tessie Hutchinson and Old Man Warner in "The Lottery" by Shirley Jackson; see p. 272).

When you're called on to analyze, define, or argue in your college writing, you'll often find it useful, as Catton does, to use comparison, contrast, or both to make a point, even though your paper's main purpose may be other than comparing and contrasting. Although Bruce Catton in his essay compares and contrasts throughout, he also has another purpose. He is trying to explain how both of these great generals contributed to American history. In an essay called "How to Make People Smaller Than They Are," Norman Cousins's purpose is to deplore "the increasing vocationalization of our colleges and universities." But in one paragraph in that essay, Cousins introduces a series of contrasts to strengthen his argument:

> The irony of the emphasis being placed on careers is that nothing is more valuable for anyone who has had a professional or vocational education than to be able to deal with abstractions or complexities, or to feel comfortable with subtleties of thought or language, or to think sequentially. The doctor who knows only disease is at a disadvantage alongside the doctor who knows at least as much about people as he does about pathological organisms. The lawyer who argues in court from a narrow legal base is no match for the lawyer who can connect legal precedents to historical experience and who employs wide-ranging intellectual resources. The business executive whose competence in general management is bolstered by an artistic ability to deal with people is of prime value to his company. For the technologist, the engineering of consent can be just as important as the engineering of moving parts. In all these respects, the liberal arts have much to offer. Just in terms of career preparation, therefore, a student is shortchanging himself by shortcutting the humanities.

In the sentence about the business executive, for variety's sake the contrast is implied rather than stated. Readers armed with the contrasts Cousins has already imagined have no difficulty inferring that this ideal business executive, like the liberally educated doctor and lawyer before him, has a less desirable counterpart — a business executive whose schooling has given him nothing more than job training.

Cousins directs his argument to a general audience. In contrast, let's look at two brief illustrations of comparing and contrasting found in writing more specialized and scholarly. William Broad and Nicholas Wade, in *Betrayers of the Truth: Fraud and Deceit in the Halls of Science* (New York: Simon, 1982), a book-length study of scientists who have faked evidence in order to claim fictitious discoveries, contrast two influential opinions of what it is that keeps most scientists honest.

> The renowned German sociologist Max Weber saw science as a vocation. The individual scientist's devotion to the truth, in Weber's view, is what keeps science honest. His French contemporary Emile Durkheim, on the other hand, considered that it is the community of science, not the individual, that guarantees scientific integrity. Weber's view that scientists are innately honest is still sometimes heard. "The scientists I have known . . . have been in certain respects just perceptibly more morally admirable than most other groups of

intelligent men," said the scientist and novelist C. P. Snow. . . . But the opinion that scientists are somehow more honest than other people is not particularly fashionable. The prevailing view is that laid out by Robert Merton, the leading American sociologist of science, who like Durkheim attributes honesty in science to institutional mechanisms, not the personal virtue of scientists. The verifiability of results, the exacting scrutiny of fellow experts, the subjection of scientists' activities to "rigorous policing, to a degree perhaps unparalleled in any other field of activity" — these are features, says Merton, that ensure "the virtual absence of fraud in the annals of science."

Howard Gardner, in *Artful Scribbles* (New York: Basic, 1980), an inquiry into what children's drawings mean, makes a sharp contrast between the drawings of younger children and those of older children.

When drawings made by eight- or nine-year-olds are juxtaposed to those produced by younger children, a striking contrast emerges. There is little doubt about which came from which group: works by the older children feature a kind of precision, a concern for detail, a command of geometrical form which are lacking in the attempts by younger artists. Schemas for familiar objects are readily recognized, and attempts at rendering less familiar objects can initially be decoded. And yet one hesitates to call the drawings by the older children "better" — indeed, most observers and sometimes even the youngsters themselves feel that something vital which is present at the age of six or seven has disappeared from the drawings by the older children. A certain freedom, flexibility, *joie de vivre* [zest for life], and a special fresh exploratory flavor which mark the childlike drawings of the six-year-old are gone; and instead of being replaced by adult mastery, this loss has merely been supplanted by a product that is at once more carefully wrought yet also more wooden and lifeless.

As you'll notice, Gardner, while giving the strong points of each age group of artists, apparently favors the work of the young, for all its faults.

These brief examples may suggest to you that comparing and contrasting aren't just meaningless academic calisthenics. Critical thinking strategies and explaining devices, they appeal to writers who have a passion for making things clear.

Making Connections: Comparing and Contrasting in A Writer's Reader

Writers often use the critical thinking strategy of *comparing and contrasting* to arrive at a fuller understanding of two or more items being discussed. Various authors in *A Writer's Reader* use this strategy in their writing. Linguist Deborah Tannen in "Women and Men Talking on the Job" (p. 550) uses her comparison and contrast of gender differences in conversation to support and illustrate the different ways men and women make decisions. Science writer Nicholas Wade in "How Men and Women Think" (p. 556) compares and contrasts the thinking processes of males and females to support his rather controversial position that "the test of equal opportunity, when all unfair barriers to women have fallen, will not necessarily be equal outcomes."

Like Bruce Catton (p. 160), Tim Chabot (p. 163), Wade, and Tannen, other writers who use comparing and contrasting are writer and professor Scott Russell Sanders, "The Men We Carry in Our Minds" (p. 531); poet and screenwriter Joy Harjo, "Three Generations of Native American Women's Birth Experience" (p. 540); journalist Matthew Futterman, "The Gender Gap" (p. 547); freelance writer Meghan Daum, "Virtual Love" (p. 623); and journalism professor and editor LynNell Hancock, "The Haves and the Have-Nots" (p. 631). As you read these essays, consider the role that comparison and contrast plays in them. For each essay, answer the following questions:

1. Does the writer use comparison only? Contrast only? A combination of the two? Why?
2. What two (or more) items are compared and contrasted? What does the comparison-contrast reveal about the items?
3. What is the purpose of the comparison-contrast? What idea does the information support or refute?
4. Does the writer use the opposing or alternating pattern of organization? Why?

Chapter 8

Explaining Causes and Effects

When a house burns down, an insurance company assigns a claims adjuster to look into the disaster and answer the question Why? He or she investigates to find the answer — the *cause* of the fire, whether lightning, a forgotten cigar, or a match that someone deliberately struck — and presents it in a written report. The adjuster also details the *effects* of the fire — what was destroyed or damaged, what repairs will be needed, how much they will cost.

Often for assignments and exams in college you are asked to act and think like the insurance adjuster, tracing causes or identifying effects. To do so, you have to think about a subject critically, to gather information and ideas, to marshal evidence, to analyze and evaluate the evidence logically. Effects, by the way, are usually easier to identify and demonstrate than causes. The results of a fire are apparent to an onlooker the next day, although its cause may be obscure.

Seeking causes and effects is an uncertain pursuit. In assigning you to write a paper of cause and effect, an instructor will not expect you to set forth a definitive explanation with absolute certainty. "Causality," says French philosopher of history Paul Veyne, "is always accompanied by mental reservation." However, in the process of your ferreting out, probing, and detailing causes and effects, both you and your readers learn a good deal and understand the subject more clearly.

Learning from Other Writers

The following two essays explore causes and effects. The first is by David L. Evans, an engineer and college admissions officer. Evans begins his essay by commenting on a disturbing fact he has observed: black men are underrepresented in the pool of college applicants at his college. Evans asks what the causes of this situation are and explores one possibility.

Yun Yung Choi, a native of Seoul, Korea, wrote "Invisible Women" when she was a student at Harvard College. In her essay, Choi looks at one cause of women's subordinate status in Korea's traditional culture — the introduction of a new state religion — and traces the subtle but important effects of that change.

David L. Evans   The Wrong Examples

As a college admissions officer I am alarmed at the dearth of qualified black male candidates. Often in high schools that are 90 percent black, *all* the African American students who come to my presentation are female! This gender disparity persists to college matriculation where the black male population almost never equals that of the female.

What is happening to these young men? Who or what is influencing them? I submit that the absence of male role models and slanted television images of black males have something to do with it.

More than half of black children live in homes headed by women, and almost all of the black teachers they encounter are also women. This means that most African American male children do not often meet black male role models in their daily lives. They must look beyond their immediate surroundings for exemplary black men to emulate. Lacking in-the-flesh models, many look to TV for black heroes.

Unfortunately, TV images of black males are not particularly diverse. Their usual roles are to display physical prowess, sing, dance, play a musical instrument, or make an audience laugh. These roles are enticing and generously rewarded. But the reality is that success comes to only a few extraordinarily gifted performers or athletes.

A foreigner watching American TV would probably conclude that most successful black males are either athletes or entertainers. That image represents both success and failure. Success, because the substantial presence of blacks in sports, music, and sitcoms is a milestone in the struggle begun almost 50 years ago to penetrate the racial barriers of big-league athletics and television. It is a failure because the overwhelming success of a *few* highly visible athletes, musicians, and comedians has typecast black males. Millions see these televised roles as a definition of black men. Nowhere is this more misleading than in the inner city, where young males see it as "the way out."

Ask a random sample of Americans to identify Michael Jordan, Bo Jackson, Magic Johnson, Hammer, Prince, Eddie Murphy, or Mike Tyson. Correct responses would probably exceed 90 percent. Then ask them to identify Colin Powell, August Wilson, Franklin Thomas, Mike Espy, Walter Massey, Earl Graves, or the late Reginald Lewis and I doubt that 10 percent would respond correctly. The second group contains the chairman of the Joint Chiefs of Staff, a Pulitzer Prize–winning playwright, the president of the Ford Foundation, the secretary of agriculture, the director of the National Science Foundation, the publisher of *Black Enterprise* magazine, and the former CEO of a multi-million-dollar business.

The Democratic National Convention that nominated Bill Clinton [in 1992] brought Ron Brown, Jesse Jackson, David Dinkins, Kurt Schmoke, and Bernard Shaw into living rooms as impressive role models. Their relative numbers at the convention were in noticeable contrast to the black baseball players who made up nearly half of the All-Star teams on the Tuesday night of the convention.

This powerful medium has made the glamour of millionaire boxers, ballplayers, musicians, and comedians appear so close, so tangible that, to naive young boys, it seems only a dribble or dance step away. In the hot glare of such surrealism, schoolwork and prudent personal behavior can become irrelevant.

Impressionable young black males are not the only Americans getting this potent message. *All* TV viewers are subtly told that blacks are "natural" athletes, they are "funny," and all of them have "rhythm." Such a thoroughly reinforced message doesn't lie dormant. A teacher who thinks every little black boy is a potential Bo Jackson or Eddie Murphy is likely to give his football practice a higher priority than his homework or to excuse his disruptive humor.

Neck Jewelry

Television's influence is so pronounced that one seldom meets a young black man who isn't wearing paraphernalia normally worn by athletes and entertainers. Young white men wear similar attire but not in the same proportion. Whites have many more televised role models from which to choose. There are very few whites in comparison to the number of blacks in the NBA. Black males are 12 1/2 percent of the American male population but constitute 75 percent of the NBA and are thereby six times overrepresented. That television presents poor role models for *all* kids doesn't wash.

These highly visible men's influence is so dominant that it has redefined the place of neck jewelry, sneakers, and sports apparel in our society. The yearning to imitate the stars has sometimes had dire consequences. Young lives have been lost over sneakers, gold chains, and jackets. I dare say that many black prison inmates are the flotsam and jetsam from dreamboats that never made it to the NBA or MTV.

Producers of TV sports, popular music, and sitcoms should acknowledge these "side effects" of the American Dream. More important are the superstars themselves. To a man, they are similar to lottery winners and their presence on TV is cruelly deceptive to their electronic protégés. Surely they can spend some of their time and resources to convince their young followers that even incredible talent doesn't assure fame or fortune. An athlete or performer must also be amazingly lucky in his quest for Mount Olympus.

A well-trained mind is a surer, although less glamorous, bet for success. Arthur Ashe spent his whole life teaching precisely this message. Bill Cosby and Jim Brown also come to mind as African American superstars who use their substantial influence to redirect young black males. At this time, when black men are finally making some inroads into the upper echelons of American society, we need more than ever to encourage the young to look beyond the stereotypes of popular culture.

Questions to Start You Thinking

Meaning

1. What is Evans's thesis? Where does he state it?

2. What does the author state are the causes that so few qualified black male candidates apply for admission to college? Can you suggest additional causes that Evans has not included?

3. What does *surrealism* (paragraph 8) mean? According to Evans, in what way is the situation he describes surreal? Do you agree?

Writing Strategies

4. Is Evans trying to be exhaustive in his analysis? In other words, is he trying to identify every possible cause for the problem he identifies? How do you know?

5. Trace the chain of causes and effects that Evans sets forth in this essay. Explain how television is both a cause and an effect in this chain of causal relationships.

6. Where does Evans use specific examples? Find two examples that you think are especially effective. What makes them so?

7. Do you find Evans's cause and effect analysis effective? Why, or why not?

STUDENT ESSAY

Yun Yung Choi   Invisible Women

For me, growing up in a small suburb on the outskirts of Seoul, the adults' preference for boys seemed quite natural. All the important people that I knew--doctors, lawyers, policemen, and soldiers--were men. On the other hand, most of the women that I knew were either housekeepers or housewives whose duty seemed to be to obey and please the men of the family. When my teachers at school asked me what I wanted to be when I grew up, I would answer, "I want to be the wife of the president." Since all women must become wives and mothers, I thought, becoming the wife of the president would be the highest achievement for a woman. I knew that the birth of a boy was a greatly desired and celebrated event, whereas the birth of a girl was a disappointing one, accompanied by the frequent words of consolation for the sad parents: "A daughter is her mother's chief help in keeping house."

These attitudes toward women, widely considered the continuation of an unbroken chain of tradition, are, in fact, only a few hundred years old, a relatively short period considering Korea's long history. During the first half of the Yi dynasty, which lasted from 1392 to 1910, and during the Koryo period, which preceded the Yi dynasty, women were treated almost as equals, with many privileges that were denied them during the latter half of the Yi dynasty. This turnabout in women's place in Korean society was brought about by one of the greatest influences that shaped the government, literature, and thoughts of the Korean people--Confucianism.

Throughout the Koryo period, which lasted from 918 to 1392, and throughout the first half of the Yi dynasty, according to Laurel Kendall in her book View from the Inner Room, women were important and contributing members of the society and not marginal and dependent as they later became. Women were, to a large extent, in command of their own lives. They were permitted to own property and receive inheritances from their fathers. Wedding ceremonies were held in the bride's house, where the couple lived, and the wife retained her surname. Women were also allowed freedom of movement-- that is, they were able to go outside the house without any feelings of shame or embarrassment.

With the introduction of Confucianism, however, the rights and privileges that women enjoyed were confiscated. The government of the Yi dynasty made great efforts to incorporate into the society the Confucian ideologies, including the principle of agnation, which, according to Kendall, made men the important members of society and relegated women to a dependent position. The government succeeded in its attempt at Confucianizing the country and at encouraging the acceptance of Confucian proverbs such as the following: "Men are honored, but women are abased." "A daughter is a 'robber woman' who carries household wealth away when she marries."

The unfortunate effects of this Confucianization in the   5
lives of women were numerous. The most noticeable was the
virtual confinement of women. They were forced to remain un-
seen in the anbang, the inner room of the house. This room
was the women's domain, or, rather, the women's prison. Outside, a woman was carried through the streets in a closed
sedan chair. Walking outside, she had to wear a veil that
covered her face and could travel abroad only after nightfall. Thus, it is no wonder that Westerners traveling through
Korea in the late nineteenth century expressed surprise at
the apparent absence of women in the country.

Women received no formal education. Their only schooling   6
came from government textbooks. By giving instruction on the
virtuous conduct of women, these books attempted to fit women
into the Confucian stereotype--meek, quiet, and obedient.
Thus, this Confucian society acclaimed particular women not
for their talent or achievement but for the degree of perfection with which they were able to mimic the stereotype.

A woman even lost her identity in such a society. Once   7
married, she became a stranger to her natal family, becoming a
member of her husband's family. Her name was omitted from the
family chokpo, or genealogy book, and was entered in the chokpo
of her in-laws as a mere "wife" next to her husband's name.

Even a desirable marriage, the ultimate hope for a woman,   8
failed to provide financial and emotional security for her.
Failure to produce a son was legal grounds for sending the
wife back to her natal home, thereby subjecting the woman to
the greatest humiliation and to a life of continued shame.
And because the Confucian ideology stressed a wife's devotion
to her husband as the greatest of womanly virtues, widows
were forced to avoid social disgrace by remaining faithfully
unmarried, no matter how young they were. As women lost their
rights to own or inherit property, these widows, with no
means to support themselves, suffered great hardships. Thus,
as Sandra Martielle says in Virtues in Conflict, what the
government considered "the ugly custom of remarriage" was
slowly eliminated at the expense of women's happiness.

This male-dominated system of Confucianism is one of the   9
surviving traditions from the Yi dynasty. Although the Con-

stitution of the Republic of Korea proclaimed on July 17, 1948, guarantees individual freedom and sexual equality, these ideals failed to have any immediate effect on the Korean mentality that stubbornly adheres to its belief in the superiority of men. Women still regard marriage as their prime objective in life, and little girls are still wishing to become the doctor's wife, the lawyer's wife, and even the president's wife. But as the system of Confucianism is slowly being forced out of existence by new legal and social standards, perhaps a day will come, after all, when a little girl will stand up in class and answer, "I want to be the president."

Questions to Start You Thinking

Meaning

1. What effect does Choi observe? What cause does she attribute it to?

2. What specific changes in Korean culture does Choi attribute to the introduction of Confucianism?

3. What evidence do you find of the writer's critically rethinking an earlier belief and then revising it? What do you think may have influenced her to change her belief?

Writing Strategies

4. What does Choi gain by beginning and ending with her personal experience?

5. Where does Choi use the strategy of comparing and contrasting? Do you think this is effective?

6. What resources for writing does the author draw on?

7. Do you find Choi's cause and effect analysis persuasive? Why, or why not?

Learning by Writing

THE ASSIGNMENT: EXPLAINING CAUSES AND EFFECTS

Pick a disturbing fact or situation that you have observed, and seek out the causes and effects to help you and your readers understand the issue better. When you actually write your essay, you may limit your ideas to the causes *or* the effects, or you may include both but emphasize one more than the other. Yun Yung Choi uses this approach when she briefly identifies the cause of the status of Korean women (Confucianism) but spends most of her essay detailing the effects of this cause.

Facing the Challenge: Causes and Effects

The major challenge writers face when they explore causal relationships is to limit their subject. In exploring a given phenomenon — from teenage drug use to the success of your favorite rock band — it is impossible to devote equal space to all possible causes and effects without either overwhelming your readers or putting them to sleep. You must decide what you want the main point of your paper to be — what you want to show your readers — and then emphasize the causal relationships that will help you to support your overall argument.

If you are writing an essay about your parents' divorce, for example, you may be tempted to discuss all the possible *causes* for their separation that you can think of in addition to analyzing all the *effects* it has had on you. However, both you and your readers will have a much easier time if you make some decisions about your focus before drafting. First, you must decide whether you want to focus on the *causes* of the divorce or its *effects* on you. Next, you will need to narrow your focus still further by ranking the different points you plan to discuss so you can emphasize those that are most important to you and omit those that are relatively insignificant or irrelevant. You don't want to list every single argument your parents had in an essay that explores the causes of their divorce.

In "The Wrong Examples," college admissions officer David L. Evans begins by describing a situation that troubles him: his office gets few applications from qualified black male students. He then focuses the body of his essay on the *causes* of this situation, and he further limits his discussion by focusing on one cause in particular: television's portrayal of black men. In contrast, Yun Yung Choi identifies Confucianism as the cause of women's inferior position in Korean society but chooses to focus her essay on the *effects* of the discriminatory teachings.

Before deciding how to focus your paper, you must be certain that you can state your main point in a single sentence that clearly expresses a cause-and-effect relationship. Choi, for example, wrote the following sentence when asked to summarize the main point she wanted to make in her essay: "The inherent sexism of Confucianism has led to discrimination against women in Korean society." Once you can articulate your thesis as a cause-and-effect relationship, you are ready to decide which part of the relationship — cause or effect — to stress and how to limit your ideas to strengthen your overall point.

The situation you choose might be one that may have affected you and people you know well, such as the limited number of scholarships available for college students, the pressure to get good grades, the difficulty of working while going to school, or divorce in the family. It might have affected people in your city or region — pollution of a lake or river near you, only a small percentage of eligible voters voting in a city or county election, decaying bridge supports, or pet owners not using pooper-scoopers. It may affect society at large — the high rate of inflation in central Europe, apathy, drunk driving, or the high cost of health care. It might be gender or racial stereotypes on television, unsavory language in music lyrics, spouse abuse, teenage suicide, the difficulty of getting admitted to law school, the shortage of male elementary school teachers, the unwillingness of businesses to hire college graduates with liberal arts degrees, or the effects of using dragnets for ocean fishing.

Don't think you must choose an earthshaking topic to write a good paper. On the contrary, you will do a better job on a subject you are personally familiar with.

Write for your classmates. If you write about a situation you have observed in your own life, assume that your readers will care to know more about you. If you write about an issue in a region or in society, assume that they will want to compare their impressions of this situation with yours.

Papers written in response to this assignment have included the following:

A woman recollected her observations of the deplorable plight of Indians in rural Mexico and cited this as one cause of the recent rebellions there.

A woman analyzed the negative attitudes of men toward women in the company where she worked and the resulting tension among workers. She identified some of the effects as inefficiency and low production.

A man contended that buildings constructed in Miami are not built to withstand hurricane force winds. One reason he cited is the inadequate city inspection system.

A woman observed that popular interest in space travel has declined in the United States. She cited evidence to support this claim and then detailed causes for the decline, including decreased funding for the space program and the *Challenger* disaster.

GENERATING IDEAS

Find a topic. What situation with which you are familiar would be informative or instructive to explore? This assignment leaves you the option of writing either from personal experience or from what you know or can find out, or a combination of the two.

Begin by searching your memory. You might let your thoughts wander over the results of an undesirable situation that you have witnessed. Has the situation always been this way? Or have things changed in the last few years? Have things gotten better or worse?

The ideas in the following list may help you search your memory:

DISCOVERY CHECKLIST

- An unpleasant situation caused by a change in your life (a new job; a fluctuation in income; personal or family upheaval following death, divorce, accident, illness, or good fortune; a new school)
- An undesirable change in the environment (caused by air pollution, a flood or a storm, a new industry, the failure of an old industry)
- A disturbing situation caused by an invention (the automobile, the computer, the VCR, the television, the ATM)

- Employment opportunities that cause you concern (for women in management, for blacks in the military, for white males in nursing)
- A situation in your neighborhood, city, or state that is causing problems for you (traffic, pollution, population, health care)

When a few thoughts begin to percolate, reach for a pencil and brainstorm: jot down a list of likely topics that come to mind. (For more tips on brainstorming, see p. 360). Then choose the idea that you care most about and that promises to be neither too large nor too small. A paper that confined itself to the causes of a family's move from New Jersey to Montana might be only one sentence long: "My father's company transferred him." But the subsequent effects of the move on the various members of the family might form the basis of an interesting essay. So the writer might choose to focus on the effects. Unless you are writing a long term paper, however, an exhaustive study of the effects of gangs in urban high schools is likely to prove too wide-ranging even to sketch in fewer than ten thousand words. Instead, you might consider just one unusual effect of this situation, such as gang members staking out territory in the parking lot of a local school.

List causes and effects. Your choice tentatively made, write for ten or fifteen minutes, identifying likely causes and effects. In looking for causes, look first for *immediate causes* — those evident and close at hand that clearly led to the situation. Then look for *remote causes* — underlying, more basic reasons for the situation, perhaps causes that came earlier. The immediate cause of unemployment in a town might be the closing of a factory. But the more remote cause might be competition from a foreign business, against which the local company couldn't survive. When looking for effects, too, consider both the *immediate* consequences of your situation and the longer-range *remote* effects it might have, even if you're not sure yet what these might be.

Whether you're looking for causes or effects, you can make separate lists of causes and effects and, next to each item on each list, insert your evidence for it. Does your evidence seem substantial? You can tell from a glance at your list exactly where you need to generate more material. Highlight (with a star or an underline) any causes and effects that stand out. A way to rate the items on your list is to ask, Is this an *essential* cause? Would the situation not exist without it? (Then it deserves a big star.) Or would the situation have arisen without it, for some other reason? (It might still matter but be less important.) Is this a significant effect? Has it had a resounding impact? Is it something that is necessary to include to adequately explain the results?

If you haven't figured out enough causes and effects to explain the situation to your satisfaction, you need to do some more digging. Remember, you have four major resources — recall, observation, conversation, and imagination.

If your topic calls on you to account for people's behavior, consider some suggestions from Kenneth Burke (see p. 371). A literary critic and philosopher, Burke has proposed a set of questions designed to discover the deep-down causes of a person's actions. For a writer, Burke's questions often generate insights, observations, and hunches worth pursuing.

PLANNING, DRAFTING, AND DEVELOPING

Yun Yung Choi's "Invisible Women" follows a clear plan. In the first two paragraphs Choi establishes the role of women in modern-day Korea, posits that the current attitudes toward women are relatively new, and asserts that Confucianism is the cause of this turnabout. In paragraphs 3 and 4 she contrasts the status of women before and after Confucianism. Beginning in paragraph 5 she explains the numerous adverse effects of Confucianization in the lives of women. She concludes her essay in paragraph 9 by indicating that change is again on the horizon. The essay was written from a brief scratch outline that simply lists the effects of the change:

Intro—Personal anecdote

> *— Tie with Korean history*

> *— State thesis: This turnabout in women's place in Korean society was brought about by one of the greatest influences that shaped the government, literature, and thoughts of the Korean people — Confucianism.*

Comparison and contrast of status of women before and after Confucianism
Effects of Confucianism on women
1) Confinement
2) Little education
3) Loss of identity in marriage
4) No property rights
Conclusion: Impact still evident in Korea today but some hints of change

The paper makes its point: it shows Confucianism as the reason for the status of Korean women and details four specific effects of Confucianism on women in Korean society. And it shows that cause and effect are closely related: Confucianism is the cause of the change in the status of Korean women, and Confucianism has had specific effects on Korean women.

You can begin planning your paper by assigning relative importance to the causal relationships: classify the causes, and then the effects, as major or minor ones. If, for example, you are writing about the reasons why more married women hold jobs now than they did twenty years ago, you might make a list that includes (1) economic necessity, (2) wanting to get out of the house, and (3) more jobs now open to women. On reflection you might decide that economic necessity — the need for both husband and wife to contribute to family expenses — is a major cause and that desire to get out of the house is a minor one. You could then plan to give the economic cause more space and place it last in your essay to emphasize it. You would organize the causes from least important to most important — (1) desire to get out of house, (2) more jobs open, (3) economic necessity.

Once you have a tentative order for the causes or effects, draft the first part of your paper: describe the situation you want to explain. Then make clear to your readers which one of the three tasks — to explain the causes of the change, to explain the effects, or to explain both — you intend to accomplish. You can do this subtly, not in a flat, mechanical fashion: "Now I am going to explain the causes of this situation." You can announce your task casually, naturally, as if you were talking to someone: "At first, I didn't realize that keeping six pet cheetahs in our back yard would bother the neighbors." Or, as one writer did in a paper about her father's sudden move to a Trappist monastery: "The real reason for Father's decision didn't become clear to me for a long while."

Using your list of causes and effects, you are now ready to draft the main part of your paper. In the first section of your paper — taking no more than two or three paragraphs — describe the situation. Then show how the situation came about (the causes) or what followed as a result (the effects) or both. More than likely, the organization of your ideas will follow one of these patterns:

I. The situation	I. The situation	I. The situation
II. Its causes	II. Its effects	II. Its causes
		III. Its effects

REVISING AND EDITING

As you know by now, ascertaining causes and effects takes hard thought. You'll want to set aside an especially generous amount of time to look back over, ponder, and rewrite this paper. Yun Yung Choi wrote several drafts of "Invisible Women." As she approached the paper's final version, one of the

---

WRITING WITH A COMPUTER

Whether you're looking for causes or effects, word processing can simplify your job. In setting forth causes, you can make a list of them and, next to each item on the list, insert your evidence for it. In writing a paper determining effects, you can make a similar list and flesh it out with evidence. ("The lowering of the tariff on Japanese-made cars worked havoc in the automotive industry": that statement of an effect calls for evidence — a few facts to back it up.)

Does your evidence seem substantial? You can tell from a glance at your screen exactly where you might need to generate more material. Highlight any skimpy parts with **boldface** so you won't forget these needy places when you revise. With a couple of keystrokes or mouse clicks, you can boldface a whole long passage. Later, after you've revised and strengthened the passage, you can delete the highlighting.

problems she faced was making a smooth transition from recalling her own experience to probing causes.

(emphasize that everyone thinks that) ——→ *widely*

These attitudes toward women, ~~which I once~~ believed

, a relatively short time, considering Korea's long history

to be the continuation of an unbroken chain of tradition, are, in fact, only a few hundred years old. During the first half of the Yi dynasty, which lasted from 1392 to

[tell when]

1910, and during [the Koryo period,] women were treated almost as equals, with many privileges that were denied them during the latter half of the Yi dynasty. This up-heaval in women's place in Korean society was brought about by one of the greatest influences that shaped the government, literature, and thoughts of the Korean people: Confucianism. Because of Confucianism, my birth was not greeted with joy and celebration but rather with these words of consolation: "A daughter is her mother's chief help in keeping house." *(Belongs in opening paragraph)*

In revising a paper that traces causes, effects, or both, you might ask yourself some or all of the questions in the following checklist:

REVISION CHECKLIST

If you are tracing causes,

- Have you made it clear that you are explaining causes?
- Have you left out any essential causes?
- Have you given enough evidence to convince readers that the causal relationships are valid?
- Have you claimed remote causes you can't begin to prove? Or made assertions but offered no proof?
- Have you stated the causes with swaggering certainty, when in all honesty you might admit that you're only guessing?
- Have you fallen into any logical fallacies, such as *oversimplification* (assuming that there was only one small cause for a large phenomenon) or the *post hoc* fallacy (assuming that one thing caused another just because the one preceded the other). (For more on fallacies, see p. 104.)
- Have you shown your readers your point in demonstrating causes?

If you are determining effects,

- Have you made it clear that you are explaining effects?
- What possible effects have you left out? Are any of them worth adding?
- Have you given sufficient evidence that these effects have occurred?
- Could any effect you mention have resulted not from the cause you describe but from some other cause?

Remember, unless you are writing a paper that sets forth exact scientific findings, your instructor won't expect you to write a definitive explanation. You'll be expected only to write an explanation that is thoughtful, searching, and reasonable.

After you have revised your cause-and-effect essay, proofread and edit it. Check carefully for problems with grammar, word choice, punctuation, and

 **FOR PEER RESPONSE**

Before you type a final draft, let a peer reader check over your paper and answer the questions on one of the following checklists. See Chapter 20 for advice on working with other student writers and for general questions you should always ask a peer editor to address. For a paper in which you explain causes and effects, you'll also want your peer editor to answer the following specific questions.

If the writer explains causes,

- Does he or she do more than merely list causes? Does the writer explain the causes that he or she identifies?
- Does the writer present causes that seem logical and possible?
- Did other causes occur to you that you think the writer should consider? If so, list them.

If the writer explains effects,

- Do all the effects seem to be the result of the change he or she describes?
- Has the writer overlooked some effects that should be added? List any that occurred to you as you read the paper.

For all cause and effect papers,

- What point is the writer trying to make? What is the purpose of the essay? Does the explanation of causes or effects help the writer accomplish this purpose?
- Is the order of the points in the paper clear and useful? Can you suggest a better organization?
- Are you convinced by the logic used in the paper? Do you see any logical fallacies (see p. 104)?
- Point out any causes or effects you found hard to accept.
- Does the writer give you enough detail? Enough evidence to convince you? Put stars where more evidence is needed.
- If this were your paper, what is the one thing you would be sure to work on before handing it in?

mechanics — and then correct any problems you find. A comprehensive reference handbook is an indispensable tool for this task; the "Quick Editing Guide" at the end of *The Bedford Guide for College Writers* (see the pages with the colored edges) will get you started.

When editing a paper written about causes and effects, pay attention to sentences describing things that happened in the past, whether these were causes or effects. Has juggling a sequence of past events led to any confusing constructions? You will want to make sure that you have used the correct verb tense and verb form in each case. You may also need to be on the alert for fragments: many writers create fragments in the revision stage when they insert one more idea starting *"Because . . ."* or *"Causing . . ."*

Here are some questions to get you started when proofreading and editing your paper:

EDITING CHECKLIST

- Have you used correct verb tenses throughout? Is it clear what happened first and what happened next? Have you used the correct form for all verbs? (See A1 in the "Quick Editing Guide.")
- Is your sentence structure correct? Have you avoided creating fragments when filling in additional causes or effects? Have you avoided writing run-ons when trying to integrate additional ideas smoothly? (See A6 and A7 in the "Quick Editing Guide.")
- Do your transitions and other introductory elements have commas after them, if these are needed? (See C1 in the "Quick Editing Guide.")
- Have you spelled everything correctly? (See D2 in the "Quick Editing Guide.")
- Have you used the proper paper format, including special requirements for your instructor and course? (See D3 in the "Quick Editing Guide.")

(For more on revising and editing, see Chapter 19.)

OTHER ASSIGNMENTS

1. Pick a definite change that has taken place during your lifetime, and seek out the causes and effects to help you and your readers understand that change better. By "change" we mean a noticeable, lasting transformation produced by an event or series of events. The change might be one that has affected only you, such as a move to another location, a decision you made that changed the course of your life, or an alteration in a strong personal opinion or belief. It might be a change that has affected not only you but also other people in your neighborhood or city (a new zoning law), in a region (the growth of high technology in the Silicon Valley of California), or in society at large (the arrival of the personal computer or the fall of communism in Europe). It might be a new invention, a medical breakthrough, or a deep-down shift in the structure or attitudes of society.

198   Part Two • Thinking Critically   A WRITER'S GUIDE

2. Explore your own motives and explain your reasons for taking some
    step or for doing something in a routine way. (If you need help in pin-
    ning down reasons for your own behavior, some of Kenneth Burke's
    suggestions on pp. 371–72 may be useful.)

3. In an introductory philosophy course at Loyola College in Maryland,
    Frank J. Cunningham asks his students to write, instead of a tradi-
    tional research paper, a short original essay exploring their own ideas
    and opinions. Below is his assignment: Try it yourself.

    Over the years, in the process of growing up and growing civilized,
    all of us have developed certain opinions about the way things hap-
    pen, about what works and what doesn't work, about how things are.
    We have also developed certain expectations toward our world based
    on these opinions.

    Under ordinary circumstances, we live with these opinions and ex-
    pectations unquestioningly, and, on the whole, we manage quite well
    with our lives. But . . . in philosophy we look at things we don't nor-
    mally look at, question things we normally take for granted, analyze
    what we accept from day to day.

    As preparation for this somewhat unusual (some would say per-
    verse) activity, I would like you to think about your own opinions.
    Think about your views of the world, your expectations, your cer-
    tainties, and decide on something of which you are absolutely cer-
    tain. It may be a part of your normal life, a truth derived from your
    education, something that you have learned through your years of ex-
    perience, something you were told, something you figured out on
    your own. Now write a short essay (no more than two pages) de-
    scribing the one thing about which you are absolutely certain and
    why this thing commands such certainty.

    Remember that an essay such as this requires thought as prepara-
    tion. You should not expect to sit down immediately at the typewriter
    and produce it. Remember too that there are at least two separate
    thinking tasks to be performed. First you must consider your stock of
    truths to find one in which you have utmost confidence. This will
    probably take some time and effort since we are willing to let a lot of
    truths pass without putting them to the test. Second, you must con-
    sider the reason for your certainty. In working out this part of the
    essay it might be useful to pretend that you are trying to convince a
    very reasonable but thoroughly doubting person of the truth of your
    position.

4. Read one newspaper or magazine article that probes the causes of some
    contemporary problem: the shortage of reasonable day-care options,
    for instance, or the low academic scores of American students com-
    pared with those of students in other developed countries. Can you sug-
    gest additional causes that the article writer seems to have ignored?
    Write an essay in which you argue either that the author has done a good
    job of explaining the causes of this problem or that he or she has not.

Applying What You Learn:
Some Uses of Explaining Causes and Effects

Examination questions often pose a problem in causality: "Trace the causes of the decline of foreign sales of American automobiles." Equally familiar is the exam question that calls for a survey of effects: "What economic effects of the repeal of Prohibition were immediately evident in the early 1930s?" Problems of that very same sort, you'll find, will frequently turn up as paper topics. In a child development course, you might be asked to research what makes some people become child abusers. In a speech pathology course you might be called on to investigate the causes and effects of head trauma, fetal alcohol syndrome, learning disabilities, or Down's syndrome — all of which are relevant to impaired communication skills.

But in fulfilling any kind of college writing assignment, even one that doesn't ask you to look for causes or effects, you may wish to spend *part* of your paper exploring one or the other or both. In a paper that deals with any phenomenon — say, a sociology assignment to write about an increase in teenage pregnancies among middle-class suburbanites — a paragraph or two that explores the causes of that phenomenon or its effects might add depth to your paper.

In a book or article that deals with some current phenomenon, the writer may ask why — in only a paragraph or a few paragraphs. In an article titled "Propaganda Techniques in Today's Advertising," Ann McClintock analyzes the methods advertisers, corporations, and politicians use so effectively to persuade consumers to do whatever they want us to do, anything from buying a product to voting for a candidate. She exemplifies seven types of propaganda — name calling, glittering generalities, transfer, testimonial, plain folks, card stacking, and bandwagon. She concludes her article asking *why* these propaganda devices work:

FOR GROUP LEARNING

Explaining the News

Together in class or in your writing group, tell aloud a two-minute story that you invent to explain the causes behind any surprising event reported in this morning's news. Either realistic explanations or tall tales are acceptable. You'll need to prepare your story carefully in advance. Invite the others to comment on it, and, with their reactions in mind, set down your story on paper to turn in at the next class. In writing it down, embellish and improve on your story as much as you desire.

Before you write *any* paper setting forth causes or effects, talk over with other students what you plan to say. Ask for their comments. Invite them to add to your list of causes or effects if they can.

Why do these propaganda techniques work? Why do so many of us buy the products, viewpoints, and candidates urged on us by propaganda messages? They work because they appeal to our emotions, not to our minds. Often, in fact, they capitalize on our prejudices and biases. For example, if we are convinced that environmentalists are radicals who want to destroy America's record of industrial growth and progress, then we will applaud the candidate who refers to them as "treehuggers." Clear thinking requires hard work: analyzing a claim, researching the facts, examining both sides of an issue, using logic to see the flaws in an argument. Many of us would rather let the propagandists do our thinking for us.

In his article "Causation of Terror," social historian Feliks Gross seeks to explain a difficult, complex, and vitally important matter — the reasons for political assassinations and terrorism in Europe and Russia in the nineteenth and twentieth centuries. Gross recalls cases of political parties that have used terrorist tactics to overthrow moderate and democratic governments; he remembers the victims of oppressive rule who have used terrorist tactics to fight back — the Armenians and Bulgarians under Turkish rule, the Serbs under the Croatian Ustashe, the Polish underground fighters who resisted Nazi occupation. Tentatively generalizing, Gross finds that ethnic tensions and clashes of political ideology, not economic hardship, cause the victims of terrorism to respond with terrorist tactics and political assassination.

"It is of paramount significance," Gross concludes, "to understand the conditions that are conducive to political assassination." By controlling such conditions, perhaps we might even prevent terrorism. Applied to such an end, exploring causes and effects is no mere game, but a way of seeking peace and ensuring it.

Making Connections: Explanations of Causes and Effects in A Writer's Reader

As human beings we often try to understand why something occurs by identifying causal relationships — determining *causes* and analyzing *effects*. Writers do much the same thing; in fact, they often use the critical thinking skill of identifying and explaining causes and effects to help readers understand a person, an idea, or a process. An author's explanation of causes and effects is often interwoven with analyzing, taking a stand, investigating a problem, proposing a solution, and evaluating. Novelist Amy Tan in "Mother Tongue" (p. 496) explores the effects her mother's limited English have had on her personal life. Freelance writer Mike Males in "Public Enemy Number One?" (p. 616) argues against critics who suggest that violence on television is the main cause of violence among teenagers by carefully analyzing a number of other more direct causes of teenage violence. David L. Evans (p. 184) and Yun Yung Choi (p. 186) explain both causes and effects in their essays.

Some of the other writers in *A Writer's Reader* who explain causal relationships include historian Stephanie Coontz, "Remarriage and Stepfamilies" (p. 522); journalist and editor Brent Staples, "Black Men and Public Space" (p. 561); horror fiction writer Stephen King, "Why We Crave Horror Movies" (p. 593); publisher and historian of science Michael Shermer, "Abducted! Encounters with Aliens" (p. 596); author and editor Veronica Chambers, "The Myth of Cinderella" (p. 603); columnist Ellen Goodman, "How to Zap Violence on TV" (p. 613); and journalist Jeffrey Obser, "Privacy Is the Problem, Not the Solution (p. 657). As you read these essays, consider the role that explanations of cause and effect plays in them. For each essay, answer the following questions:

1. Does the writer explain causes? Or effects? Or both? Why? Does the writer perceive and explain a chain or series of causal relationships?
2. Is the evidence sufficient to clarify the causal relationships and to provide credibility to the essay?
3. How is the subject relevant to the writer's occupation or field of interest?

Chapter 9

Taking a Stand

In college, both in class and outside of class, you'll hear controversial issues discussed — the baseball strike, television talk shows, prayer in the schools, welfare reform, health care, gun control. In some fields of study, experts don't always agree, and issues remain controversies for years. In response to these issues, in your college writing, you will often find yourself taking up pen (or typewriter or word processor). Taking a stand on an issue will help you understand the controversy and clarify what you believe.

Writing of this kind has a twofold purpose — to state an opinion and to win your readers' respect for it. A reader's opinion might alter from reading what you say; then again, it might not. But if you fulfill your purpose, your readers at least will see good reasons for your thinking the way you do. In taking a stand, you do three things:

You state what you believe and give reasons with evidence to support your position.

You enlist your readers' trust.

You consider and respect what your readers probably think and feel.

Learning from Other Writers

Let's look at two essays in which the writers take a stand effectively. The first is an article by Suzan Shown Harjo entitled "Last Rites for Indian Dead," first published in the Los Angeles Times on September 16, 1989. In it, Harjo, president of the Morning Star Institute, takes a stand about an issue of great importance to her as a Native American of Cheyenne and Creek heritage. As a result of persuasive efforts such as hers to gain public support for this Native American cause, the federal law known as the NAGPRA — the Native American Graves Protection and Repatriation Act—was passed in 1990. Effective persuasion, then, is not an empty academic exercise but a powerful force that can bring about significant change.

Thaddeus Watulak, a student at Johns Hopkins, wrote the second essay, "Affirmative Action Encourages Racism." It was published as an opinion piece in the university's online newsletter on March 26, 1998.

Suzan Shown Harjo   Last Rites for Indian Dead

What if museums, universities and government agencies could put your dead relatives on display or keep them in boxes to be cut up and otherwise studied? What if you believed that the spirits of the dead could not rest until their human remains were placed in a sacred area?   1

The ordinary American would say there ought to be a law—and there is, for ordinary Americans. The problem for American Indians is that there are too many laws of the kind that make us the archeological property of the United States and too few of the kind that protect us from such insults.   2

Some of my own Cheyenne relatives' skulls are in the Smithsonian Institution today, along with those of at least 4,500 other Indian people who were violated in the 1800s by the U.S. Army for an "Indian Crania Study." It wasn't enough that these unarmed Cheyenne people were mowed down by the cavalry at the infamous Sand Creek massacre; many were decapitated and their heads shipped to Washington as freight. (The Army Medical Museum's collection is now in the Smithsonian.) Some had been exhumed only hours after being buried. Imagine their grieving families' reaction on finding their loved ones disinterred and headless.   3

Some targets of the Army's study were killed in noncombat situations and beheaded immediately. The officer's account of the decapitation of the Apache chief Mangas Coloradas in 1863 shows the pseudoscientific nature of the exercise. "I weighed the brain and measured the skull," the good doctor wrote, "and found that while the skull was smaller, the brain was larger than that of Daniel Webster."   4

These journal accounts exist in excruciating detail, yet missing are any records of overall comparisons, conclusions or final reports of the Army study. Since it is unlike the Army not to leave a paper trail, one must wonder about the motive for its collection.   5

The total Indian body count in the Smithsonian collection is more than 19,000, and it is not the largest in the country. It is not inconceivable that the 1.5 million of us living today are outnumbered by our dead stored in museums, educational institutions, federal agencies, state historical societies and private collections. The Indian people are further dehumanized by being exhibited alongside the mastodons and dinosaurs and other extinct creatures.   6

Where we have buried our dead in peace, more often than not the sites have been desecrated. For more than two hundred years, relic-hunting has been a pop-   7 ular pursuit. Lately, the market in Indian artifacts has brought this abhorrent activity to a fever pitch in some areas. And when scavengers come upon Indian burial sites, everything found becomes fair game, including sacred burial offerings, teeth and skeletal remains.

One unusually well-publicized example of Indian grave desecration occurred   8
two years ago in a western Kentucky field known as Slack Farm, the site of an Indian village five centuries ago. Ten men — one with a business card stating "Have Shovel, Will Travel" — paid the landowner $10,000 to lease digging rights between planting seasons. They dug extensively on the forty-acre farm, rummaging through an estimated 650 graves, collecting burial goods, tools and ceremonial items. Skeletons were strewn about like litter.

What motivates people to do something like this? Financial gain is the first   9
answer. Indian relic-collecting has become a multimillion-dollar industry. The price tag on a bead necklace can easily top $1,000; rare pieces fetch tens of thousands.

And it is not just collectors of the macabre who pay for skeletal remains. Sci-   10
entists say that these deceased Indians are needed for research that someday could benefit the health and welfare of living Indians. But just how many dead Indians must they examine? Nineteen thousand?

There is doubt as to whether permanent curation of our dead really benefits   11
Indians. Dr. Emery A. Johnson, former assistant Surgeon General, recently observed, "I am not aware of any current medical diagnostic or treatment procedure that has been derived from research on such skeletal remains. Nor am I aware of any during the thirty-four years that I have been involved in American Indian . . . health care."

Indian remains are still being collected for racial biological studies. While the   12
intentions may be honorable, the ethics of using human remains this way without the full consent of relatives must be questioned.

Some relief for Indian people has come on the state level. Almost half of the   13
states, including California, have passed laws protecting Indian burial sites and restricting the sale of Indian bones, burial offerings and other sacred items. Rep. Charles E. Bennett (D-Fla.) and Sen. John McCain (R-Ariz.) have introduced bills that are a good start in invoking the federal government's protection. However, no legislation has attacked the problem head-on by imposing stiff penalties at the marketplace, or by changing laws that make dead Indians the nation's property.

Some universities — notably Stanford, Nebraska, Minnesota, and Seattle —   14
have returned, or agreed to return, Indian human remains; it is fitting that institutions of higher education should lead the way.

Congress is now deciding what to do with the government's extensive collec-   15
tion of Indian human remains and associated funerary objects. The secretary of the Smithsonian, Robert McC. Adams, has been valiantly attempting to apply modern ethics to yesterday's excesses. This week, he announced that the Smithsonian would conduct an inventory and return all Indian skeletal remains that could be identified with specific tribes or living kin.

But there remains a reluctance generally among collectors of Indian remains   16
to take action of a scope that would have a quantitative impact and a healing qual-

ity. If they will not act on their own — and it is highly unlikely that they will —
then Congress must act.

The country must recognize that the bodies of dead American Indian people   17
are not artifacts to be bought and sold as collector's items. It is not appropriate to
store tens of thousands of our ancestors for possible future research. They are our
family. They deserve to be returned to their sacred burial grounds and given a
chance to rest.

The plunder of our people's graves has gone on too long. Let us rebury our   18
dead and remove this shameful past from America's future.

Questions to Start You Thinking

Meaning

1. What is the problem Harjo identifies? How extensive does she show it to be?

2. What is Harjo's position on this issue? Where does she first state her position?

3. What evidence does Harjo present to refute the claim that housing skeletal remains of Native Americans in museums is necessary for medical research and may benefit living Indians?

Writing Strategies

4. What assumptions do you think Harjo makes about her audience?

5. What types of evidence does Harjo use to support her argument? How convincing is the evidence to you?

6. How does Harjo use her status as a Native American to enhance her position? Would her argument be as credible if it were written by someone of another background?

7. How does she appeal to the emotions of the readers in the essay? In what ways do these strategies strengthen or detract from her logical reasons?

8. How would you describe the tone of this essay? Can you find places where specific words or phrases help set this tone? Do you think this tone is appropriate? Effective? Why, or why not?

9. Why does Harjo discuss what legislatures and universities are doing in response to the situation?

STUDENT ESSAY

Thaddeus Watulak   Affirmative Action Encourages Racism

Racism: discrimination or prejudice based on race. That's   1
the dictionary definition of the word. By that, or any other
reasonable definition, affirmative action is easily the most
racist institution in America today. From its inception affirmative action was at best misguided, and it is today the single
largest obstacle to good race relations in this country.

How is affirmative action racist? Let's say a firm sees   2
two almost equally qualified candidates for the same position, one white and one black. If the white guy is hired because he's white, then the company has broken the law and is
considered terribly immoral. If the black guy is hired because he's black, not only is the firm considered morally
righteous, but it will probably qualify for some kind of government subsidy. Let's go back to the dictionary for a second. Discrimination: action or policies based on prejudice or
partiality. Both possibilities in this imaginary scenario
clearly show partiality based on race; both are clearly
racist. Yet one is the official policy of our government, a
government supposedly founded on the principle that all men
are created equal.

Not only does affirmative action require discrimination   3
based on race; it also ignores our status as individuals. The
notion that the white race should be punished for, or at
least forced to make amends for, supposed racial crimes
against minority races is as racist a proposition as anything
from the darkest days of Jim Crow. No one alive today has
ever been a slave or owned a slave; there are no legitimate
parties for reparations there. The people of our generation
have grown up in a society utterly devoid of legal discrimination against minorities of any kind.

Just what crimes are we supposed to be making amends   4
for? The usual answer is that it's our racial crimes of the
past. Well, frankly, I feel responsible only for actions
that I have taken or directly sanctioned. When the city of
Rome starts granting preferential treatment to Tunisians to
make up for the razing of Carthage, I'll think about recon-
sidering. Even then I don't think I'll quite understand
why a dirt-poor, just naturalized Australian immigrant
should legally be discriminated against in favor of the
scion of an old-money American family who happens to be
Hispanic.

Affirmative action also has some rather unpleasant   5
racist assumptions hiding behind it. The clear implication
that minorities could not adequately get ahead without special considerations seems just a touch bigoted. Personally,

I'd be a bit insulted if an employer said they understood
since I grew up in Vermont I couldn't possibly do as well as
those cosmopolitan New Yorkers and that they'd take that into
consideration when they decided whether or not to give me a
job. I'd also be a bit upset if I applied to law school and
was told that since I have brown hair I wasn't expected to
have a high LSAT score. All that kind of treatment does is
make the recipients question whether or not they really
earned their accomplishments.

    I honestly believe that all people, whether they are in   6
the majority or the minority in their particular region, have
the same inherent capacity to succeed given a level playing
field. A white kid in inner-city L.A. is just as disadvantaged as his black and Latino neighbors. The minority student
at Harvard who had a tutor as a child before going off to a
top-rated prep school is just as much a member of the privileged elite as any of her classmates. Using the term minority
as a kind of shorthand for poor and disadvantaged is not only
terribly insulting, but it also obscures the real problems in
this country.

    Finally, not only is affirmative action essentially   7
racist, and not only does it rely on racial stereotypes, but
it also reinforces racist attitudes in our society that are
based on these stereotypes. First, as already noted, the debate on affirmative action tends to portray minorities as
kind of poor and disadvantaged second-class citizens. This
trend can't help but boomerang by reinforcing the ghetto
stereotypes held about minority groups. Second, nothing can
further embitter the closet racist more than the belief, encouraged by the existence of affirmative action programs,
that minorities promoted above him have not really earned
their positions. Perhaps most significant for the continuance
of racist attitudes, affirmative action polarizes society
along racial lines and encourages an "us versus them"
attitude.

    Affirmative action is an essentially racist policy that   8
generates only more racism. It is past time that society
moved beyond this stumbling block and took the next halting
steps toward Dr. King's dream of a truly colorblind society.

Questions to Start You Thinking

Meaning

1. What claims does Watulak make to support his general position that affirmative action is racist in both its premises and its effects?

2. What does Watulak claim are "unpleasant racist assumptions" hiding behind the policy of affirmative action?

3. What does Watulak's concluding allusion ("Dr. King's dream of a truly colorblind society") mean?

Writing Strategies

4. What impression of Watulak do you get from reading his paper? What kind of person do you think he is? Would you like to meet him?

5. How does Watulak use the issue of class to support his argument that affirmative action promotes racist attitudes and practices?

6. What kind of support does Watulak use to back up his claims about affirmative action? Do you find his argument effective? Is his evidence sufficient and appropriate for this kind of paper? Why, or why not?

7. Where and how does Watulak consider the attitudes of readers who might be the beneficiaries of affirmative action? Does he do enough to reach out to them?

8. What is Watulak's tone? What are the benefits and drawbacks of the tone he uses? How effective is it when he includes personal anecdotes and opinions such as "Personally, I'd be a bit insulted . . ."?

Learning by Writing

THE ASSIGNMENT: TAKING A STAND

Find a controversy that rouses your interest. It might be an issue currently in the news, or it might be a long-standing one, such as "In our public schools, should the teaching of creationism, the Biblical explanation for the origin of species, be given the same amount of classroom time as Darwin's theory of evolution?" or "Do intercollegiate sports on campus enhance the educational purpose of college or detract from it?" Your purpose in this paper isn't to try to solve a large social or moral problem but to make clear where you stand on an issue of importance to you and to persuade your readers to respect your position and perhaps even to accept it. To do so effectively, you must first know exactly where you stand and why. As you reflect on your topic and write your paper, you may change your position, but don't shift positions in the middle of your essay. Assume that your readers are people who may or may not be familiar with the controversy, so provide some background or an overview to give them a clear understanding of the situation you are concerned about. Furthermore, your readers may not have taken sides yet or may hold a position different from yours. To be effective, then, you must

Facing the Challenge: Taking a Stand

The major challenge writers face when they take a stand on an issue is to gather sufficient evidence to support their position. To encourage readers to respect your opinions even if they don't entirely agree with you, you must do enough research to anticipate their objections to your argument. By becoming aware of possible counterarguments, you'll better understand the kind of evidence you'll need to support your position. Otherwise, the only readers you'll convince will be those who agreed with you in the first place—not a very meaningful goal for an argumentative essay.

If you rave hysterically about an issue—insulting people whose opinions differ from yours by dismissing their concerns as ignorant—you will convince no one. Probably anyone who disagrees with you will not bother to finish reading your paper. To write a successful argumentative essay that gets readers to take your opinion seriously and understand your concerns (even if they don't ultimately agree with you), you must win your audience's respect by demonstrating a knowledge of and respect for opposing viewpoints. This approach does not mean that you should write a wishy-washy essay in which your own position isn't strongly expressed. Rather, it means that a careful consideration of your opponents' viewpoints will enable you to strengthen your own argument by finding evidence that addresses their concerns.

In "Last Rites for Indian Dead," Suzan Shown Harjo strengthens her argument against the violation of American Indian burial grounds and the collection of Indian skeletal remains and artifacts by predicting and addressing opposing viewpoints. For example, she anticipates scientists' counterarguments that "deceased Indians are needed for research that someday could benefit the health and welfare of living Indians" and addresses such concerns by quoting former assistant Surgeon General Dr. Emery A. Johnson's statement that "I am not aware of any current medical diagnostic or treatment procedure that has been derived from research on such skeletal remains. Nor am I aware of any during the thirty-four years that I have been involved in American Indian . . . health care." Harjo quotes this respected medical professional to provide evidence that strengthens and supports her position.

To understand the range of viewpoints readers may have on the issue you've chosen to tackle, so that you can anticipate and find evidence to refute possible counterarguments, brainstorm a list of the various groups of people who might have strong opinions on your topic. (Thaddeus Watulak's list might have included liberals, conservatives, inner-city African American teenagers, white college applicants from poor backgrounds, African American and white professionals, guidance counselors in the New York City public school system, and employers.) Then try putting yourself in the shoes of a member of each of these groups by writing a paragraph on the issue from *her* point of view. What would her opinion be, and on what grounds might she object to your argument? How can you best address her concerns and overcome her objections? This exercise will help you to demonstrate a knowledge of opposing viewpoints in your paper and will show you where you need to find additional evidence to support your claims.

also consider your readers' views and choose strategies that will enlist their support.

Here are brief summaries of a few good papers that take a stand, written by students at several colleges:

A woman who pays her own way through college countered the opinion that working full- or part-time during the school year provides a college student with valuable knowledge. Citing her own painful experience, she maintained that a student who can devote full time to her studies is far better off than a student who must work.

A man attacked his history textbook's portrayal of Joan of Arc on the grounds that the author had characterized Joan as "an ignorant farm girl subject to religious hysteria."

A man, citing American history and Christian doctrine, gave his reasons for preferring to keep prayer out of public school classrooms.

A woman in an education course disputed the claim of E. D. Hirsch Jr. in his book *Cultural Literacy* that we must give schoolchildren a grounding in facts common to the majority culture, including American history, literature, mythology, science, geography, and sports. Children, she affirmed, should first study their own cultural backgrounds.

A man on the wrestling team argued that the number of weight categories in competitive wrestling should be increased because athletes who overtrain in a desperate effort to qualify for the limited number of existing weight categories often suffer detrimental health effects and even death.

GENERATING IDEAS

For this assignment, you will need to find an issue on which to take a stand, develop a clear position, and assemble evidence that supports your view. If you don't have a rock-solid opinion and a ready-made argument when you start, don't worry. In fact, that's part of the challenge of an assignment like this: as you explore the topic more deeply, sifting through all the implications and information, you may find that the evidence supports a view different from one you might have started out with. Or you may find that the issue intersects with strongly held beliefs in ways you couldn't have predicted. Try to remain flexible while you are generating a topic and materials for your paper, and be prepared for a bit of backtracking when unexpected twists appear.

Find an issue. The topic for this paper should be an issue or controversy that's interesting to both you and your readers. Try brainstorming a list of possible topics (see p. 360). If you can't get started, look at the headlines of a newspaper or news magazine or Web site, review the letters to the editor, consult the indexes to the *CQ Researcher* or *Opposing Viewpoints* series in the library, listen to a news broadcast on television or radio, or talk with some of your friends. You might also consider topics that you have covered in this class and others. If you keep a journal, look over past entries to see what has perplexed or angered you in the past months.

At this stage, many writers find it useful to think of the issue in terms of a question — a question that then will be answered through the position they take in their papers. Remember that you need to find a topic on which rational, reasonably educated individuals can take different stands. The question "Is sexism bad?" is probably not going to lead to a strong paper because most rational, reasonably educated readers would agree that sexism is a bad thing. And what does *bad* really mean in this context? It's too vague a word to provide you with clear direction. However, a question like "Should we fight sexism by eliminating sexist stereotypes in advertising?" is more fruitful because it focuses on a clearly debatable topic.

Once you have a list of possible topics, go through your list, and delete those that are too broad or complex for a paper that is to be completed in about two weeks. Strike also those that you don't know much about. Finally, weed out anything that on second thought looks as if it might not hold your interest or that of your readers. From your new, shorter list, pick one issue or controversy to write about. Choose the one for which you think you can make the strongest argument to your classmates.

Do some preliminary exploring. Once you have an issue in mind, you may need to do a little investigating — both to understand the topic better and to make sure that this is a topic you really can and want to take a stand on. Turn to some of your trusty resources. Recall how this issue has affected your own life. Observe, if you can. Converse. What do others think? Do some reading in a library. Imagine other possibilities. In gathering material, you will discover more exactly where you stand.

As he strove to discover ideas for his paper, Thaddeus Watulak kept a free-flowing journal in which he recorded thoughts as they came to him and as he read them or heard them. His notes reveal interesting facets of his writing process. Many of the ideas he wrote down never actually made it into his final draft. Still, when he began writing, he had more than enough material to choose from.

10/18/98

　　Topic:　Effectiveness of affirmative action
　　　　　　　— Has it really helped racism in this country?
　　　　　　　— What have been the real consequences of this policy?

10/22/98

　　Those students talking about affirmative action in the cafeteria sounded really angry. "Another way white people are discriminated against." "Punishing us for something we didn't do." What do most people think about when they hear about a.a.? Can a.a. possibly be fair?

10/23/98

  Why do people only care about race? What about the difference between poor and rich? Someone could be black but have loads of resources — money, good schools, caring parents. Someone else could be white but have almost nothing. Why should race be the only consideration?

State your position. You can help focus your view by stating it in a sentence — a thesis, or statement of the stand you are taking. If you phrased your topic as a question, answer that question in your position statement. Just as your topic had to be a debatable issue, your position needs to be one that invites continued debate. In other words, you're going to have to stick your neck out a little; if you try to play it too safe, then there isn't really any point to what you are writing. "Minority students constitute 3 percent of our school's population" isn't really a stand; it's a fact. "Minority students are underrepresented at our school" or — even better — "Our school should increase its minority population" is a strong position that can be argued.

Make your thesis narrow. For a paper due a week from now, "The city's waterfront has become a run-down disgrace" can probably be supported by your own observations. But the claim "The welfare program in this country has become a disgrace" would take much digging, perhaps the work of years. (For more advice on developing a thesis, see Chapter 16.)

Consider the types of claims you can use. If you're having trouble pinning down a position, or if you're unsure what sort of evidence your position would need, consider the issue in terms of the three general types of claims — claims that require substantiation, claims that provide evaluation, or claims that endorse policy. (Be aware that these categories overlap somewhat and that different types of claims can usually be made about the same topic.) Given your issue and the question you have asked about it, think about what sort of claim you need to make.

Claims of substantiation require examining and interpreting information in an effort to resolve disputed facts or circumstances, the applicability of definitions, the extent of a problem, or contested causes or effects, as in these examples:

  Certain types of cigarette ads, such as the once-popular Joe Camel ads, significantly encourage smoking among teenagers.

  Rather than being a major problem, police brutality in this country is a distorted perception based on a few well-publicized exceptions to the rule.

  On the whole, bilingual education programs actually help students learn English faster than total immersion.

Claims of evaluation consider the rightness or wrongness, appropriateness or inappropriateness, worth or lack of worth involved in certain issues, as seen in these examples:

Research using fetal tissue is unethical in a civilized society.

English-only legislation promotes cultural intolerance in our society.

Allowing gays and lesbians to adopt children is immoral.

Claims of policy challenge or defend approaches for achieving generally agreed on goals, as in the following:

The federal government should support the distribution of clean needles to reduce the rate of HIV infection among intravenous drug users.

Denying illegal immigrant children enrollment in American public schools will reduce the illegal immigration problem.

Underage teenagers accused of murder should be tried as adults.

The nature of your audience might influence the type of claim you choose to make. For example, if you wish to promote the distribution of free condoms in high school and your audience consists of conservative parents, this claim of evaluation might make them unnecessarily angry: "Because it saves lives and prevents unwanted pregnancies, distributing free condoms in high school is our moral duty." Because it can be presumed that most conservative parents believe free condom distribution will promote immoral sexual behavior, while the writer might be perceived as implying that the parents themselves are immoral for not supporting free condom distribution, this claim seems counterproductive. Although you shouldn't back away from your pro-condom position if you're convinced of it, always remember that your purpose is to persuade, not alienate.

A claim of substantiation might work better with these parents by using the issue of effectiveness as a common ground. Most parents, after all, want to protect their children from harmful consequences, no matter what. This thesis might gain a more receptive response: "Distributing free condoms in high school is an effective way of reducing the pregnancy rates and the incidence of STDs, especially the spread of AIDS, without necessarily leading to a substantially higher rate of sexual activity among teenagers." Notice that this claim also attempts to deflate the main fear parents probably have about free condom distribution in high school.

School administrators, on the other hand, might be better swayed with a claim endorsing policy. Most of them want to do what's right, but they don't want hordes of outraged parents banging down the school doors. They might be more inclined to consider your position if you stated it thus: "Distributing free condoms in high school to prevent unwanted pregnancies and the spread of STDs, including AIDS, is best accomplished in the context of a voluntary sexual education program that strongly emphasizes abstinence as the primary preventative."

These three types of claims may also be used as support for a position. For example, in "Last Rites for Indian Dead," Suzan Shown Harjo uses claims of substantiation and of evaluation to support her larger claim of policy calling for a strong federal law to remedy the shameful situation she addresses in her article: the desecration of Native American remains and artifacts is a problem of overwhelming proportions that has produced no valid scientific results (supporting claim of substantiation), and the rampant accumulation of such remains and artifacts is immoral because it dehumanizes Native Americans (supporting claim of evaluation). Stating your supporting points as supporting claims can provide topic sentences to help your reader to follow your line of reasoning without confusion. In "Affirmative Action Encourages Racism," for example, Thaddeus Watulak uses topic sentences that are claims; these help the reader see the subpoints he's trying to make through his examples. "Affirmative action also has some rather unpleasant racist assumptions hiding behind it" and "I honestly believe that all people, whether they are in the majority or the minority in their particular region, have the same inherent capacity to succeed given a level playing field" are two such topic sentences.

Assemble evidence.   Your claim stated, you'll need evidence to support it. What is evidence? It is anything that demonstrates the soundness of your position and the points you make in your argument — facts and figures, observations, opinions, illustrations, examples, and case studies. Of course, evidence must be used carefully to avoid defending logical fallacies — common mistakes in thinking — and making statements that lead to wrong conclusions. (See p. 104.)

One logical fallacy that often crops up in position papers is the misuse of examples (proof by example or too few examples — see p. 105). You can't claim that two professors you know are dissatisfied with state-mandated testing programs and therefore that all or even most professors are. You would have to survey more professors at your school, but even then you could speak only of your general impression concerning "many professors." Depending on how formal your paper is, you might need to conduct scientific surveys, access reliable statistics in the library or on the Internet, or solicit the views of a respected expert in the area.

If you are having trouble thinking of types of evidence, the four writer's resources — recall, observation, conversation, and imagination — are a good place to start. Even if they don't provide you with definitive evidence, they may suggest other avenues for exploration, perhaps a book or article you might benefit from reading. Ask yourself the following questions:

DISCOVERY
CHECKLIST

- What incidents or periods of time can you recall from your own life that shed light on this issue? What experiences have led you to have the opinions on it that you do?
- What have you observed, or what might you observe, that would support your stand?
- What expert might you converse with?
- Can you imagine hypothetical situations that could illustrate some aspect of the situation you are taking a stand on? Though not real, hypothetical examples should nevertheless be realistic — that is, they *could* happen. In "Affirmative Action Encourages Racism," Watulak effectively uses several such examples, such as contrasting the poor white kid from the L.A. inner city with the minority student at Harvard who had a tutor and went to a prep school but was still considered disadvantaged.

As with most critical thinking tasks, this paper will require you to assemble evidence beyond your own personal memories and beliefs. The three most important sources of evidence are these:

1. *Facts, including statistics* Facts are statements that can be verified by objective means; statistics are facts expressed in numbers. Facts usually form the basis of a successful argument.
2. *Expert testimony* By experts, we mean people with knowledge of a particular field gained from study and experience.
3. *Firsthand observation* Your own observations can be a persuasive source of evidence, if you can assure your readers that your account is accurate.

For more about each of these forms of evidence, see "Types of Evidence" on page 99.

For this assignment, you will need to assemble evidence in written form. Take notes, in a notebook, on 4-by-6-inch or 5-by-7-inch index cards, or on the computer. Be sure to record exactly where each piece of information comes from. Keep the form of your notes flexible so that you can easily arrange and rearrange them as you order your thoughts in drafting your paper.

Test and select evidence. Now that you've collected some evidence to support your position, you need to sift through it to decide which pieces of information you will use in your paper. Evidence is useful and trustworthy when it is

Accurate,
Reliable,
Up to date,
To the point,
Representative,
Not oversimplified, and
Sufficient and strong enough to back the claim and persuade your readers.

For more on each of these criteria for testing evidence, see "Testing Evidence" (p. 101).

You may find that your evidence supports a position different from the one you intended to state in your paper. Take a moment to think things through: Is it possible that you could find some facts, testimony, and observations that would support your original position after all? Is it possible that you should rethink your original position? If you need to approach the paper from a completely different angle, this is a good time to do so.

Most effective arguments take opposing viewpoints into consideration and refute them whenever possible. Do you know the arguments on the other side of the issue? Do you know who supports these arguments? Do you have evidence or reasons that you can use to show why these arguments are weak, only partially true, misguided, or just plain wrong? In your final paper, you will probably want to address these counterarguments and rebut them to make headway with readers who disagree with you; make sure you have the necessary evidence on hand.

As you look over your evidence and begin to put together your argument, consider things from your readers' point of view. What are their attitudes, interests, and priorities? What do they already know about the topic? What do they expect you to say? Imagine your readers, and ask yourself whether the evidence you now have in front of you is appropriate and sufficient to convince them.

PLANNING, DRAFTING, AND DEVELOPING

Reassess your position. Now that you have looked into the matter, what is your current position on the issue? If necessary, revise the thesis that you formulated at the beginning of this assignment. After stating your position, summarize your reasons for holding this view. List your supporting evidence.

Organize your material. Once you have clarified your position and sifted through your evidence, you will probably find your argument falling into shape. Organize your notes into the order you think you'll follow in writing your draft. You may decide to make an outline (for methods, see p. 384). One useful pattern is the classical form of argument:

1. Introduce the subject to gain the readers' interest.
2. State your main point or thesis.
3. If useful, give the historical background or an explanatory overview of the situation.
4. Provide evidence to support your position.
5. Refute the opposition.
6. Reaffirm your main point.

In some situations, especially when you expect readers to be hostile to your position, you may want to take the opposite approach: refute the opposition to weaken it first, then replace those views by building a logical chain

FOR GROUP LEARNING

Getting a Response to Your Position

Allow a day or two for members of your writing group to decide, at least tentatively, the positions they wish to take in their individual papers. Then hold a meeting at which each member takes a few minutes to set forth his or her position and to support it. Invite other members of the group to suggest useful supporting evidence or to argue with counterevidence. Ask your group's recorder to list all the objections so that you'll have them when writing your paper. Of course, this group discussion might cause you to alter your whole stand. If so, give thanks: it will be easier to revise your ideas now than to revise your paper later.

of evidence that leads to your main point, and finally state your position. If you state your position too early, you might alienate resistant readers; if so, they will become defensive and not open up to what you have to say. Of course, you can always try both organizational approaches to see which one works better (a fairly easy process if you are working with word-processed files). Note also that, depending on the topic, some papers will be mostly based on refutation and some mostly on confirmation (that is, direct support for your position). Others might even alternate refutation and confirmation rather than separating them.

Define your terms. Make clear any unfamiliar or questionable terms used in your thesis. If your position is "Humanists are dangerous," give a short definition of what you mean by *humanists* and by *dangerous* early in the paper. Clearly defined terms will prevent misunderstanding and will help keep your argument on track.

Attend to logical, emotional, and ethical appeals. The logical appeal engages readers' intellect; the emotional appeal touches their hearts; the ethical appeal draws on their sense of fairness and reasonableness. A persuasive argument usually operates on all three levels. (For more on the three forms of appeal, see pp. 103–04.)

To use the *logical appeal*, you need to make sure that your reasoning is clear and your evidence is sound. Don't claim more than you can demonstrate, and do demonstrate everything that you claim. (Much of the advice we've given so far on testing and selecting evidence will help you construct a sound logical appeal (see pp. 98–108).

To use the *emotional appeal*, select examples and language that will influence how your readers feel about the issue. In some cases, a well-chosen image can win more support than a truckload of statistics. For instance, statistics on accidental killings involving guns in homes may establish that there is a problem, but the example of a father who accidentally shot a son who came home early from college in the middle of the night to surprise his family makes the reader care. Be careful not to overdo it, though: your argument

---

WRITING WITH A COMPUTER

If in taking your stand you'll be disputing the view of some other writer, start by creating a document into which you type those passages from the book, magazine article, newspaper column, or editorial that have provoked you to dissent. Then, on the same disk create a second document in which you'll write your paper.

When you want to cite the other writer's exact words, just use your word processor to copy the text from the first document into the document with your paper. (Different word processors have different names for "copying" — some will use COPY and PASTE; others use MOVE or INSERT. As you incorporate the other writer's words, blend them in with your text, but avoid plagiarism by acknowledging the original source properly.

will fall flat if you tug too hard on readers' heartstrings. Emotions should support the logical appeal but never replace it.

To use the *ethical appeal* in a paper taking a position, you must spell out your beliefs and give attention to beliefs opposing yours. If you declare, "I am against eating red meat because it contains fats and chemicals known to be harmful," you assert a position and then provide evidence for it. The reader who responds, "That's right. I'm a vegetarian myself," is likely to see the soundness of your position. But even the reader who responds, "Oh, I don't know. A hamburger never killed anyone!" may warm to your view if you consider his or her assumptions. These might include the beliefs that a burger is delicious, that vegetables aren't, that red meat supplies needed protein, and that the chemicals haven't been proved dangerous. You should show that you are aware of these assumptions and that you have considered them seriously. You might even agree with some of them. But then you must set forth in a reasonable way your own view. By spelling out your assumptions and by imagining those of a dissenting reader, you will win respect, if not conversion to your ideas.

As part of the ethical appeal, you should establish your credentials, if you have any, and those of your experts. Let your readers know who you are and why the things you say about the subject are trustworthy. If you are writing about environmental pollution, tell your readers that your allergies have been irritated by chemicals in the air. If you are writing about euthanasia, establish the fact that you have witnessed the lingering death of a grandparent. By sharing with us her perceptions and feelings as a Native American, Suzan Shown Harjo in "Last Rites for Indian Dead" makes us care more about the disrespect shown Native Americans through the violation of their remains and cultural artifacts.

However, whether or not you have personal experience with your topic, you must always demonstrate that you are a rational and caring individual who can be trusted — not just by saying you are but by expressing yourself, relating to your reader, and handling your topic respectfully. The reader who doesn't agree with you will not consider you trustworthy if you stoop to name-calling, misrepresentations of the other side, logical fallacies, and emotional excess, and you will certainly never persuade them to take your position seriously.

If you quote an expert who has outstanding credentials, you may easily be able to insert a brief citation of those credentials: "Lewis Thomas, former chancellor of the Memorial Sloan-Kettering Cancer Center . . . " If you have talked to experts and are convinced of their authority, state why you believe that they can be trusted: "From conversation with Mr. Dworshak, who showed me six model wind tunnels he has built, I can testify to his extensive knowledge of aeronautics."

Credit your sources. As you write, make your sources of evidence clear. The simplest way to do so is to incorporate your source into the text: "According to an article in the December 10, 1995, issue of *Time*" or "When I talked with my history professor, Dr. Harry Cleghorn, he said. . . ."

REVISING AND EDITING

When you're writing a paper taking a stand, you may be tempted to fall in love with the evidence you have gone to such trouble to collect. One of the hardest things for a writer to do is to take out information, but you must do so if it is irrelevant, redundant, or weak. Some of it won't help your case; some may just seem boring and unlikely to persuade anybody. If so, pitch it. Sometimes you can have too much evidence, and if you throw some out, a stronger argument will remain. Sometimes you can become so attached to old evidence that, when new evidence or new thoughts come along, you won't want to discard what you have on hand. But in taking a stand, as in any other writing, second thoughts often surpass first thoughts. Be willing to revise not only your words but your view.

Make sure that your main point is clear and that your paper doesn't drift away from it into a contradiction. The process of arriving at a defensible position and conveying it through writing is a complicated and sometimes ambiguous one. But the final paper should be as clear and straightforward as possible.

When you're taking a last look over your paper, proofread with care. Wherever you have given facts and figures as evidence, check for errors in names and numbers. This advice may seem trivial, but there's a considerable difference between "10,000 people" and "100,000 people."

As you revise, here are some points to consider:

REVISION CHECKLIST

- Does your view convince you? Or do you think you need still more evidence?
- Have you tried to keep in mind your readers and what would appeal to them? Have you answered what you think their major objections will be?
- Have you defined all necessary terms and explained all your points clearly?

FOR PEER RESPONSE

Enlist some other students to read your draft critically and tell you whether they accept your arguments. For a paper in which you take a stand, you'll also want your peer editors to answer these specific questions:

- Can you state what you understand the writer's claim to be?
- Do you have any problems following or accepting the reasons for the writer's position? Would you make any changes in the reasoning?
- How persuasive is the writer's evidence? Do you have any questions about that evidence? Can you suggest some good evidence the writer has overlooked?
- Has the writer provided sufficient transitions to guide you through his or her argument?
- Has the writer made a good case for his or her position? Are you persuaded to his or her point of view? If not, is there any point or objection that the writer could address that would make the argument more compelling?
- If this were your paper, what is the one thing you would be sure to work on before handing it in?

- Is your tone suitable for your readers? Do you say anything in a way that may alienate them, or, at the other extreme, does your writing sound weak or apologetic?
- Might the points in your argument seem stronger if arranged in a different sequence?
- Have you unfairly omitted any evidence that would hurt your case?
- In rereading your paper, do you have any excellent, fresh thoughts? If so, make room for them.

After you have revised your argument, proofread and edit it. Check carefully for problems with grammar, word choice, punctuation, and mechanics — and then correct any problems you find. A comprehensive reference handbook is an indispensable tool for this task; the "Quick Editing Guide" at the end of *The Bedford Guide for College Writers* (see the pages with the colored edges) will get you started.

When editing a paper in which you take a stand, look carefully at transitions and at words you have used in order to highlight or comment on a point: "The proposal, *obviously*, will fail." In many cases, introductory words and interrupters need to be set off with commas to help clarify their relationship to the surrounding ideas. Also take the time to double-check sentences in which you make broad claims about *everyone, no one, some, a few,* or some other group identified by an indefinite pronoun. Because you may have difficulty remembering whether these pronouns are grammatically singular or plural, be sure to check agreement between verbs and subjects or between pronouns and antecedents.

Here are some questions to get you started when proofreading and editing your paper:

EDITING CHECKLIST

- Is it clear what subjects and verbs go together? Do all subjects and verbs agree (match)? (See A2 in the "Quick Editing Guide.")
- Is it clear what each pronoun refers to? Does each pronoun agree with (match) its antecedent? (See A4 in the "Quick Editing Guide.")
- Have you used the precise and forceful words you need to convince your readers?
- Have you used an adjective whenever describing a noun or pronoun? Have you used an adverb whenever describing a verb, adjective, or adverb? Have you used the correct form when comparing two or more things? (See A5 in the "Quick Editing Guide.")
- Is your sentence structure correct? Have you avoided writing fragments and run-on sentences? (See A6 and A7 in the "Quick Editing Guide.")
- Do your transitions and other introductory elements have commas after them, if these are needed? (See C1 in the "Quick Editing Guide.")
- Have you spelled and capitalized everything correctly, especially names of people and organizations? (See D1 and D2 in the "Quick Editing Guide.")
- Have you used the proper paper format, including special requirements for your instructor and course? (See D3 in the "Quick Editing Guide.")

(For more on revising and editing, see Chapter 19.)

OTHER ASSIGNMENTS

1. Write a letter to the editor of your local newspaper or of a national newsmagazine in which you agree or disagree with the publication's editorial stand on a current question or with the recent words or actions of some public figure. Be sure to make clear your reasons for holding your view.

2. Write a short paper in which you express your view on one of the following topics or another that comes to mind. Make clear your reasons for believing as you do.

Bilingual education	Raising the minimum wage
Nonsmokers' rights	Protecting the rainforests
Dealing with date rape	Controlling terrorism
Salaries of professional athletes	Prayer in public schools

3. Write one claim each of substantiation, of evaluation, and of policy for or against gun control, and indicate an audience each claim might work best with. Then list reasons and types of evidence you might need to support one of these claims. Finally, for the same claim, indicate what opposing viewpoints you would need to refute and how you could best do so.

Applying What You Learn: Some Uses of Taking a Stand

As you may have found out by now, writing assignments and college examination questions sometimes ask you to take a stand on a controversy:

Criticize this statement: "There's too much science and not enough caring in the modern practice of medicine."

Respond to the view that "there's no need to be concerned about carbon dioxide heating up the earth's atmosphere because a warmer climate, by increasing farm production, would be preferable to the one we have now."

Your answers to such exam questions indicate clearly to your instructor how firm a grasp you have on the material.

In your daily life, too, you'll sometimes feel the need to advance a view in writing. You may be called on to represent the tenants of your apartment building by writing a letter of protest to a landlord who wants to raise your rent, or you may feel moved to write to a store manager complaining about the treatment you received from a salesperson. As an active citizen, you'll wish from time to time to write a letter to the editor of your local newspaper or to your senator.

When you enter the working world, you'll need to be able to state your views clearly in writing. There is hardly a professional position you can hold — lawyer, teacher, nurse, business manager, journalist — in which you won't be invited to state and support your views about some important matter, often for the benefit of others in your profession or the general public. Here is a sample of such writing, in which Mary Anne Raywid, in the *Journal of Teacher Education* (Sept.–Oct. 1978), defends professors of education against the charge that they use jargon when ordinary English would do:

> This is not to deny that educators speak a language of their own. Indeed they do; and it is very much a part of their specialized knowledge. These words become a way first to select out certain qualities, events, and phenomena for attention; and they expedite communication via shorthand references to particular combinations of these. To cite a familiar example, when an educationist talks about a meaningful learning experience, s/he is not just spouting jargon, but distinguishing out of all the events and phenomena of a given time and place, a particular set. Moreover, a substantial list of things is being asserted about what is going on — e.g., the words *learning experience* suggest that it is, or it is meant to be, an episode from which learning results. The term *meaningful* is not superfluous but does a specific job: it adds that it is likely to be or was (depending on temporal perspective) a successful exercise in learning — which not all learning experiences proffered by teachers can claim. To qualify as meaningful in advance — in other words, well calculated to succeed — a number of conditions must be met, ordinarily including learner comprehension, interest, motivation, capacity, and likely retention.

Scientists who do original research face the task of persuading the scientific community that their findings are valid. They write and publish accounts of their work in scientific journals for evaluation by their peers. In such articles they report new facts as well as state opinions. Some also write for general readers as well. Here, for instance, is Gerald Weissmann, in an essay called "Foucault and the Bag Lady" from *The Woods Hole Cantata: Essays on Science and Society* (New York: Dodd, 1985), airing his views on the recent trend to deinstitutionalize the mentally ill:

> It has always seemed to me to constitute a fantastic notion that the social landscape of our large cities bears any direct relationship to that kind of stable, nurturing community which would support the fragile psyche of the mentally ill. Cast into an environment limited by the welfare hotel or park bench, lacking adequate outpatient services, prey to climatic extremes and urban criminals, the deinstitutionalized patients wind up as conscripts in an army of the homeless. Indeed, only this winter was the city of New York forced to open temporary shelters in church basements, armories, and lodging houses for thousands of half-frozen street dwellers. A psychiatrist of my acquaintance has summarized the experience of a generation in treating the mentally deranged: "In the nineteen-fifties, the mad people were warehoused in heated public hospitals with occasional access to trained professionals. In the sixties and seventies, they were released into the community and permitted to wander the streets without access to psychiatric care. In the eighties,

we have made progress, however. When the mentally ill become too cold to wander the streets, we can warehouse them in heated church basements without supervision."

Weissmann's statement is a good illustration of a specialist writing for the rest of us — and forcefully taking a stand.

Making Connections: Taking a Stand in A Writer's Reader

The issues of concern in our society — ranging from the significance of a particular song to our relationships with foreign nations — are debated most often in the forum of public writing. In fact, presenting one's position on an issue and giving the reasons and evidence supporting that position may be one of the most common uses of writing in our culture. Not surprisingly, *A Writer's Reader* provides a variety of examples of a writer taking a stand on an issue. Columnist Anna Quindlen in "Evan's Two Moms" (p. 516) argues the controversial position that gay marriage should be legalized. Conservative thinker James Q. Wilson in "In Praise of Asphalt Nation" (p. 606) enters what he describes as "a debate between private benefits and public goods" to argue in defense of the automobile as the best means of transportation for our modern society. Both writers make their arguments with the aid of hard facts, personal experience and observation, and clear reasoning.

Besides Quindlen, Wilson, Suzan Shown Harjo (p. 203), and Thaddeus Watulak (p. 205), other writers in a variety of professions in *A Writer's Reader* take a clear, forceful stand — columnist Paul Varnell, "The Niceness Solution" (p. 576); essayist Nancy Mairs, "Freeing Choices" (p. 579); science psychology writer Michael Shermer, "Abducted! Encounters with Aliens" (p. 596); freelance writer Mike Males, "Public Enemy Number One?" (p. 616); and computer consultant and Web expert Stephanie Brail, "The Price of Admission" (p. 651). As you read these essays, consider how each writer takes a stand. For each essay, answer the following questions:

1. What stand does the writer take? Is it a popular opinion, or does it break from commonly accepted beliefs?
2. How does the writer use the logical, emotional, and ethical appeals? Does the writer achieve the right balance for the audience and the nature of the topic?
3. How does the writer support his or her position? Is the evidence sufficient to gain your respect? Why, or why not?
4. How does the writer's occupation or expertise contribute to the credibility of his or her stand?

Chapter 10

Proposing a Solution

Sometimes when you learn of a problem such as acid rain, homelessness, or famine, you say to yourself, "Something should be done about that." You can do something constructive yourself — by the powerful and persuasive activity of writing. This chapter gives you some tips on how to be convincing.

Your purpose in such writing, as political leaders and advertisers well know, is to rouse your audience to action. Thomas Jefferson and his associates who wrote the Declaration of Independence accomplished as much, and even in your daily life at college you will find chances to demonstrate this effect often. Does some policy of your college administrators irk you? Would you urge students to attend a rally for a cause or a charity? You can write a letter to your college newspaper or to someone in authority and try to stir your readers to action.

The uses of such writing go far beyond these immediate applications. A college course will sometimes ask you to write a *proposal* — a recommendation that an action be taken. In Chapter 9, you took a stand and backed it up with evidence. Now go a step further. If, for instance, you have made the claim "Our national parks are in sorry condition," you might urge readers to write to their representatives in Congress or visit a national park and pick up trash. Or you might want to suggest that the Department of the Interior be given a budget increase to hire more park rangers, purchase additional park land to accommodate increased visitors, and buy more cleanup equipment. You might further suggest that the department could raise funds for this increase through sales of videos of individual parks as well as through increased revenues from visitors who come to the parks because of the videos. The first paper would be a call to immediate action on the part of your readers; the second, an attempt to forge a consensus about what needs to be done.

In making a proposal, you set forth a solution and urge action by using words like *should, ought,* and *must:* "This city ought to have a Bureau of Missing Persons"; "Small private aircraft should be banned from flying closer than

224

one mile to a major commercial airport." Take care that you don't become preachy with your *should*s and *must*s. Explain the problem fully, and lay out, clearly and concisely, all the reasons you can muster to persuade your readers that your proposal deserves to be implemented.

Learning from Other Writers

The writers of the following two essays propose sensible solutions for pressing problems. One of the most controversial problems today is control of crime. What is the best treatment for criminals — punishment, rehabilitation, or a combination of both? And how are we going to pay for the continually increasing number of inmates in our prisons? Politicians, lawyers, and ordinary citizens have made suggestions about how to solve this major problem. One voice seldom heard in this controversy is that of the criminals themselves. The first essay is written by Wilbert Rideau, editor of the *Angolite*, the Louisiana State Penitentiary newsmagazine.

The second essay is by Heather Colbenson, who wrote the essay for a course at the University of Minnesota, where she was studying agricultural business. Her proposal addresses a problem she had encountered personally — the lack of funds to support agricultural programs in rural high schools. "I wrote about something close to my heart," states Colbenson, "and I was excited because I felt that the solutions presented could really work."

Wilbert Rideau   Why Prisons Don't Work

I was among thirty-one murderers sent to the Louisiana State Penitentiary in 1962 to be executed or imprisoned for life. We weren't much different from those we found here, or those who had preceded us. We were unskilled, impulsive, and uneducated misfits, mostly black, who had done dumb, impulsive things — failures, rejects from the larger society. Now a generation has come of age and gone since I've been here, and everything is much the same as I found it. The faces of the prisoners are different, but behind them are the same impulsive, uneducated, unskilled minds that made dumb, impulsive choices that got them into more trouble than they ever thought existed. The vast majority of us are consigned to suffer and die here so politicians can sell the illusion that permanently exiling people to prison will make society safe.

Getting tough has always been a "silver bullet," a quick fix for the crime and violence that society fears. Each year in Louisiana — where excess is a way of life — lawmakers have tried to outdo each other in legislating harsher mandatory penalties and in reducing avenues of release. The only thing to do with criminals, they say, is get tougher. They have. In the process, the purpose of prison began to change. The state boasts one of the highest lockup rates in the country, imposes the most severe penalties in the nation, and vies to execute more criminals per capita than anywhere else. This state is so tough that last year, when prison authorities here wanted to punish an inmate in solitary confinement for an infraction, the most they could inflict on him was to deprive him of his underwear. It was all he had left.

If getting tough resulted in public safety, Louisiana citizens would be the **3** safest in the nation. They're not. Louisiana has the highest murder rate among states. Prison, like the police and the courts, has a minimal impact on crime because it is a response after the fact, a mop-up operation. It doesn't work. The idea of punishing the few to deter the many is counterfeit because potential criminals either think they're not going to get caught or they're so emotionally desperate or psychologically distressed that they don't care about the consequences of their actions. The threatened punishment, regardless of its severity, is never a factor in the equation. But society, like the incorrigible criminal it abhors, is unable to learn from its mistakes.

Prison has a role in public safety, but it is not a cure-all. Its value is lim- **4** ited, and its use should also be limited to what it does best: isolating young criminals long enough to give them a chance to grow up and get a grip on their impulses. It is a traumatic experience, certainly, but it should be only a temporary one, not a way of life. Prisoners kept too long tend to embrace the criminal culture, its distorted values and beliefs; they have little choice — prison is their life. There are some prisoners who cannot be returned to society — serial killers, serial rapists, professional hit men, and the like — but the monsters who need to die in prison are rare exceptions in the criminal landscape.

Crime is a young man's game. Most of the nation's random violence is **5** committed by young urban terrorists. But because of long, mandatory sentences, most prisoners here are much older, having spent fifteen, twenty, thirty, or more years behind bars, long past necessity. Rather than pay for new prisons, society would be well served by releasing some of its older prisoners who pose no threat and using the money to catch young street thugs. Warden John Whitley agrees that many older prisoners here could be freed tomorrow with little or no danger to society. Release, however, is governed by law or by politicians, not by penal professionals. Even murderers, those most feared by society, pose little risk. Historically, for example, the domestic staff at Louisiana's Governor's mansion has been made up of murderers, handpicked to work among the chief-of-state and his family. Penologists have long known that murder is almost always a once-in-a-lifetime act. The most dangerous criminal is the one who has not yet killed but has a history of escalating offenses. He's the one to watch.

Rehabilitation can work. Everyone changes in time. The trick is to influ- **6** ence the direction that change takes. The problem with prisons is that they don't do more to rehabilitate those confined in them. The convict who enters prison illiterate will probably leave the same way. Most convicts want to be better than they are, but education is not a priority. This prison houses 4,600 men and offers academic training to 240, vocational training to a like number. Perhaps it doesn't matter. About 90 percent of the men here may never leave this prison alive.

The only effective way to curb crime is for society to work to *prevent* the   7
criminal act in the first place, to come between the perpetrator and crime. Our
youngsters must be taught to respect the humanity of others and to handle
disputes without violence. It is essential to educate and equip them with the
skills to pursue their life ambitions in a meaningful way. As a community, we
must address the adverse life circumstances that spawn criminality. These
things are not quick, and they're not easy, but they're effective. Politicians
think that's too hard a sell. They want to be on record for doing something
now, something they can point to at reelection time. So the drumbeat goes on
for more police, more prisons, more of the same failed policies.

Ever see a dog chase its tail?   8

Questions to Start You Thinking

Meaning

1. Does Rideau convince you that the belief that "permanently exiling people to prison will make society safe" is an "illusion" (paragraph 1)?

2. According to Rideau, why don't prisons work?

3. What does he propose as solutions to the problem of escalating crime? What other solutions can you think of?

Writing Strategies

4. How does Rideau organize his essay? Is his organization easy to follow?

5. What evidence does the author provide to support his assertion that Louisiana's "getting tough" policy has not worked? Does he provide sufficient evidence to convince you? Does he persuade you that action is necessary?

6. What evidence does Rideau give to support his proposals? Does he convince you that they would work? What would make his argument more persuasive?

7. Other than himself, what authorities does Rideau cite? Why do you think he does this?

8. Does the fact that the author is a convicted criminal strengthen or weaken his argument? Why do you think he mentions this fact in his very first sentence?

STUDENT ESSAY

Heather Colbenson   Missed Opportunities

A terrible problem is occurring within some small high   1
schools in Minnesota: the agriculture classes are being reduced or even cut from the curriculum. By cutting the agriculture classes, the FFA program is also cut because a student must take an ag class to be in the FFA. At one time the
FFA stood for the Future Farmers of America; however, the or-

ganization has grown to encompass things other than farming,
so it is now called the National FFA Organization, and it has
become the largest youth organization in the United States.
This is an important organization because it helps students
develop leadership skills that they will use to be successful
in business and in life. Therefore, the FFA programs in small
schools should be saved.

Why would high schools in farming communities drop agri-   2
culture classes and the FFA program? One reason is that many
colleges require that high school students take specific
courses for entry into college. When funding decreases, these
courses for college-bound students are seldom cut. Also, students must choose between general education college-prep
courses and elective courses such as agriculture. For example, Minnesota colleges now require two years of foreign
language. In small schools, like my own, the students could
take either foreign language or ag classes. Most students
choose the language classes to fulfill the college requirement. When the students leave the ag classes to take foreign
language, the ag enrollment declines, making it easy for
school administrators to cut ag classes.

The main reason that small schools are cutting ag pro-   3
grams is that the state has not provided significant funding
for the schools to operate. When schools have to make cuts,
some decide that the agriculture classes are not as important
as other courses--basic education courses such as English,
math, and science and college-prep courses such as foreign
language, calculus, and physics. When there is not enough
money, something has to go, and ag often gets cut.

If cuts have to be made, why should schools keep their   4
ag courses and the FFA programs? If schools do cut these programs, students lose many opportunities. The FFA and ag
classes are not just about cows and corn; they teach leadership, teamwork, and self motivation. The FFA provides many
different ways for a student to develop skills in these areas
through holding offices, competing in contests, and making
friends.

The main goal of the FFA is leadership development, and   5
one significant benefit of the FFA is the opportunity for

high school students to develop leadership skills. This opportunity is lost if ag classes and FFA organizations are cut
in the schools. Through FFA projects students learn to identify problems, to research solutions, to formulate plans to
solve problems, and to direct and guide other people in implementing the plans. Through these activities, they develop
self-confidence and self-motivation. This organization definitely helped me develop leadership and confidence. When an
FFA program is cut from a school, a major resource of leadership development is gone because students may never find out
that they can develop the ability to lead. George Bush, former president of the United States and a former member of the
FFA, praises this organization for its leadership opportunities. If FFA programs are cut, students may not have other
avenues to help them develop these skills.

Learning teamwork is another benefit of the FFA, and the   6
chance to work as a team is also lost when an ag program is
cut. Of course, students learn teamwork from sports, but what
sport has a team that consists of seventy people, as my FFA
did? When FFA programs are cut, students have fewer opportunities to learn to work cooperatively with other people.

A third advantage of FFA programs is that students dis-   7
cover that they can compete successfully against other students outside of the sports arena. The FFA has competitions
at the local, district, and state levels. If the FFA is cut,
a student may never know the pride of representing his or her
school at all these levels and might never experience the
thrill of competing with people from all over the nation at a
national contest.

A fourth advantage is that FFA offers opportunities for   8
students to explore various careers. FFA activities and competitions deal with livestock, business, sales, horticulture,
floriculture, and public speaking. Cutting the program would
result in the lost opportunity of trying different possible
career areas. I might never have found my desire to be a
business major had I not been in the FFA.

A fifth benefit from the FFA is meeting other people. If   9
I had not been in the FFA, one of the greatest losses for me
would be missing the opportunity to meet other people. I

gained friends from many different schools and states. Now
many of those same friends attend the University of Minnesota
with me. The loss of ag classes and an FFA program would result in a lot of missed opportunities for the students. I believe that there is no other student organization that can
provide the opportunities the FFA does.

With all of these benefits from FFA programs for stu-   10
dents in small high schools, these programs definitely
should be saved. But what can be done to save them? Consolidation of programs, fundraising, education, and support
are all things that can very easily keep a program going
strong. First, schools that are having financial trouble
can consolidate FFA programs. Small schools that have con-
solidated have been able to save their ag program, making
the chapter stronger and dividing the cost. A second activity that can help the financial situation is local
fundraising. This is a great way to keep an FFA program. My
chapter sells fruit and raffle tickets every year to raise
money. The school doesn't pay for any of the activities.
Third, the FFA members themselves must educate the administration, teachers, younger students, and businesspeople of
the town as to how the FFA supports and helps students beyond their increased knowledge of agriculture. If these
people realize the range of benefits that students receive
from the FFA, then they will ensure that the program remains in the local school. Fourth, FFA members must support
their own program from within. If even one FFA member says
negative things about the FFA, it will hurt the program;
people always remember negative things. Instead, members
should share their concerns with other members and work
within the group to change the situation.

I believe that ag classes and the FFA should remain   11
available for the benefit of students. Small schools do have
financial trouble and do have to make cuts, yet the FFA is
the wrong place to cut because many students would miss out
on opportunities that could very easily change their lives. I
want other students to be members of this great organization
from which I have benefited so much.

Meaning

1. What problem does Colbenson identify? Does she convince you that this is an important problem? Why, or why not?

2. What solutions does she propose? Which is her strongest suggestion? Her least convincing? Can you think of any other suggestions she might have included?

Writing Strategies

3. What kinds of transitions does Colbenson use to lead readers through the points she makes in her paper? How effective do you find them?

4. Is her argument easy to follow? Does she provide sufficient evidence?

Learning by Writing

THE ASSIGNMENT: PROPOSING A SOLUTION

In this essay you're going to accomplish two things. First, you'll carefully analyze and explain a specific social, economic, political, civic, or environmental problem — a problem you care about and strongly wish to see resolved. The problem may be large or small, but it shouldn't be trivial. (No comic essays about the awful problem of ketchup that squirts from Big Macs or the problems of eating peanut butter, please.) The problem may be one that affects the whole country, or it may be one that affects mainly people in your city, campus, or classroom. Show your readers that this problem really exists and that it matters to you and to them. Write for an audience who, once made aware of the problem, may be expected to help do something about it. After setting forth the problem, you may want to include the reasons that the problem exists, similar to Colbenson's approach in her essay "Missed Opportunities."

The second thing you are to accomplish in the essay is to propose one or more ways to solve the problem or at least alleviate it. You will supply evidence that your solution is reasonable and that it can work. Remember that your purpose is to convince your readers that something should be done about the problem.

Some recent papers in which students cogently argued for actions include the following:

Using research studies and statistics, a man argued that the practice of using the scores from standardized tests such as the SAT and the ACT as criteria for college admissions or placement is a problem because it favors aggressive students from affluent families. He further argued that the practice of using the scores in this way should be abolished.

A woman argued that one solution to vacation frustration is to turn everything — planning, choosing a location, arranging transportation, reserving lodging — over to a travel agent.

A man identified the problem of the exposure of nonsmokers to a haze of cigarette smoke as they enter buildings on college campuses, and he proposed that to protect nonsmokers, outdoor smoking on college campuses be limited to restricted areas away from building entrances.

A woman argued that the best solution to the problem of her children's poor education is home schooling.

GENERATING IDEAS

Identify a problem. In selecting a topic, brainstorming is a good way to begin. Write down all the possible writing topics that come to mind. Then go back over the list and star those that seem to have the most potential for your paper. (See p. 360 for more advice on this useful strategy.) Your four familiar resources — recall, observation, conversation, and imagination — may supply you with knowledge of a problem that needs to be cured. Here are a few questions to help ideas start flowing:

 **DISCOVERY CHECKLIST**

- Can you *recall* any problem you have encountered that you think needs a solution? Ask yourself what problems you meet every day or occasionally or what problems concern people near you. Can you think of a better way for your college to run course registration? A better way for your state to control dangerous drugs?
- What conditions in need of improvement have you *observed* on television or in your daily activities? What action is called for?
- What problems have you heard discussed recently in *conversation* on campus or in the classroom?
- By *imagining* yourself in the position of another person, perhaps someone of a different economic or ethnic background, can you imagine a problem of importance to that person?

Also try scanning the news. One of the most convenient sources of information about real and current problems is a daily newspaper or a newsmagazine such as *Time, Newsweek,* or *U.S. News & World Report.* In a single newspaper published on the morning we wrote these words, we found discussions of the problems of gang violence, teenage pregnancy, the high school dropout rate, overfishing in the oceans, the threat of extinction of the panda bear, overregulation by the government, the national debt, the results of floods and earthquakes in California, terrorist cults, declining academic skills of high school students, the devaluation of the American dollar, obesity, illegal Chinese aliens on a tanker off the coast of the United States, people addicted to gambling, cuts in school lunch programs, attention deficient syndrome among crack babies, the difficulty of apprehending parents suspected of child abuse, children falsely accusing parents of child abuse, traffic congestion, and the failure of a new drug to control AIDS.

Facing the Challenge: Proposing a Solution

The major challenge writers face when they propose a solution to a problem is to develop a detailed and convincing solution. Finding problems is much easier than finding solutions. One way to generate a viable solution is first to spend time and energy analyzing a problem to understand how it might affect different groups of people (conservatives and liberals, parents and children, or men and women, for example).

Do some freewriting or brainstorming to help you understand the *range* of concerns your readers have, so that you can propose a solution that addresses *all* aspects of the problem. If you don't anticipate the questions a particular group might have, you will fail to convince a portion of your audience. For example, suppose you've decided to propose the combination of a rigorous exercise program and a low-fat diet as a solution for obesity. While these solutions may make perfect sense to you, readers who have lost weight on strict regimen and then gained it back might point out that their main problem is coming up with realistic goals they can maintain over time.

Once you are aware of the concerns your readers may have about a particular problem, you are able to propose more realistic solutions. And demonstrating a knowledge of such concerns enhances your credibility with readers. In the above example, you might revise your solution to focus on the importance of defining realistic goals and developing strategies for sticking to an exercise program. You might recommend that friends join a health club together, so that they can encourage each other to participate, or that they make plans to take a brisk walk together two or three times a week. Finally, you would probably mention the importance of seeking a doctor's advice to target appropriate goals for weight loss and explore any medical reasons for severe obesity.

Wilbert Rideau's essay "Why Prisons Don't Work" illustrates the importance of anticipating concerns and questions that readers may have about a proposed solution. Rideau writes an informative essay on the prison system, the problem of crime in America, and how he feels as a "lifer." His proposed solution for curbing crime is to rehabilitate prisoners and educate potential criminals through programs that give them a sense of purpose and self-worth. But Rideau fails to anticipate a number of questions that some of his readers are likely to ask: How do we fund this rehabilitation? How can we effectively revamp our current public education system to educate at-risk young people "to pursue their life ambitions in a meaningful way"? How will we convince inmates and "emotionally desperate or psychologically distressed" youths that education is the solution? Rideau's argument would be more persuasive had he anticipated and addressed such questions.

Before you draft your essay, take some time to brainstorm a list of the different groups of people who have an interest in the problem you are proposing to solve (Rideau's list might have included prisoners, law enforcement officials, teachers, gang members, and adults and young people who live in neighborhoods with high crime rates). Then, for each of these groups, do some focused freewriting on the kinds of concerns each group might have. In planning and drafting your paper, try to come up with a solution that addresses as many of these concerns as possible.

Think about solutions.   Once you've chosen a problem, come up with possible solutions. Some problems — such as reducing international tensions — present no easy solutions. Still, give some thought to any problem that you feel seriously concerned about. You can't be expected to solve, in one college writing assignment, a problem that may have thwarted teams of experts. But sometimes a solution to a problem will reveal itself to a novice thinker. And for some problems, even a small contribution to a partial solution is worth offering. Brainstorming — alone or with classmates — can be a valuable strategy for finding solutions (see p. 360).

When thinking critically about the problem, try to *analyze* it by breaking it into smaller pieces — subproblems that can be solved one at a time perhaps. You should also try to understand the *causes* of the problem and project the *effects* of not solving the problem; both of these can contribute to a persuasive paper. When you come across a promising solution, try a little *comparison and contrast* to gain a sense of how effective and useful this solution would be: Has this solution been tried before? How well did it work then? Is it more or less likely to be successful now? Finally, *evaluate* how urgent this problem is. Does something need to be done about it immediately, or should you look for long-range solutions, which may take more time to implement?

Consider your readers.   Think of your audience — the readers you seek to persuade. For your proposal to be successful, readers need to believe that the problem is real and that your solution is feasible. Often the most difficult part is convincing readers that you're addressing a legitimate and significant problem — one that should concern them, too. If you are addressing your classmates, maybe they haven't thought about the problem before. Try to discover any way to make it personal for them, to show that it affects them and deserves their attention. To attract readers to your side, you need to consider things from their point of view. Here are some questions to ask yourself about your readers:

DISCOVERY
CHECKLIST

Understanding Your Audience

- Who are your readers? How would you describe them?
- Why should your readers care about this problem? Why should it concern them personally? Does it affect their health, conscience, or pocketbook?
- Have they ever expressed any interest in the problem?
- Do they belong to any organization or segment of society that makes them especially susceptible to — or uninterested in — this problem?
- What attitudes about the problem and your proposal do you have in common with your readers?
- Do you and your readers already agree on anything? Do they have assumptions or values different from yours that will affect how they view your proposal?

Gather evidence. To show that the problem really exists, you'll need evidence and examples. Draw on your four familiar resources — recall, observation, conversation, and imagination. While you think, scribble notes to yourself. If you feel that further reading in the library will help you know more about the problem you're proposing to solve, now is the time to do it. (For more advice on assembling, testing, and selecting evidence, see pp. 99–108.)

PLANNING, DRAFTING, AND DEVELOPING

Start with your proposal. A basic way to approach your paper is to state your proposal in a sentence: "A law should be passed enabling couples to divorce without having to go to court"; "The United States should secede from the United Nations." From such a statement, the rest of the argument may start to unfold. Usually a paper of this kind falls naturally into a simple two-part shape:

1. *A claim that a problem exists* This part explains the problem and supplies evidence to suggest that it is intolerable.
2. *A claim that something ought to be done about it* This part presents the proposal for a solution to the problem.

You can make your proposal more persuasive by including some or all of the following elements:

Knowledge or experience you have that qualifies you to propose a solution (your experience as a player or a coach for example, can help establish your credibility as an authority on Little League);

Values, beliefs, or assumptions that have caused you to feel strongly about the need for action;

An estimate of the resources — money, people, skills, material — required to implement the solution (this part might include a list of what is readily available now and what else has to be obtained);

Step-by-step actions that need to be taken to achieve your solution;

An estimate of the time needed to implement the solution;

Possible obstacles or difficulties that may need to be overcome;

Reasons that your solution is better than others that have been proposed or tried already;

Controls or quality checks that can be used to ensure that your solution is proceeding as expected;

Any other evidence that shows that your suggestion is practical, reasonable in cost, and likely to be effective.

Following is the informal outline that Heather Colbenson used as she wrote her essay "Missed Opportunities." Note the kinds of evidence she chose to include and the order she chose for organizing that evidence.

Thesis: FFA programs in small schools should be saved.

1. Reasons FFA programs are being cut
   – College requirements
   – Decreased funds

2. Reasons FFA programs should not be cut: benefits of FFA
   – Leadership training
   – Teamwork
   – Competition
   – Career exploration
   – Meeting people

3. Suggestions for saving FFA programs
   – Consolidation
   – Fundraising
   – Education
   – Support from within

When you state your proposal by claiming that a problem exists, you will increase the likelihood that the proposal will be accepted if your claim that something should be done about it begins with a simple and inviting suggestion. A claim that national parks need better care might begin by suggesting that readers head for such a park and personally size up the situation.

If at some point you find you don't know enough about a certain issue, don't hesitate to backtrack to the library or to one of your four resources.

Imagine your readers' objections. Perhaps you can think of possible objections your readers might raise — reservations about the high cost, the complexity, or the workability of your plan, for instance. It is persuasive to anticipate an objection that might occur to your readers and to lay it to rest. Jonathan Swift, in *A Modest Proposal,* is aware of this rhetorical strategy. After arguing that it will greatly help the poor of Ireland to sell their babies to rich landlords for meat (he's being ironic, savagely condemning the landlords' lack of feeling), Swift goes on:

> I can think of no one objection that will possibly be raised against this proposal, unless it should be urged that the number of people will be thereby much lessened in the kingdom. This I freely own, and it was indeed one principal design in offering it to the world.

Cite sources carefully. When you collect ideas and evidence from outside sources, you need to document your evidence — that is, tell where you found everything. Check with your instructor on the documentation method he or she wants you to use. For a short paper like the one assigned here, introducing brief lines and phrases to identify sources will be enough.

> According to <u>Newsweek</u> correspondent Josie Fair . . .
>
> As 1990 census figures indicate . . .
>
> In his biography <u>FDR: The New Deal Years</u>, Kenneth S.
>
> Davis reports . . .
>
> While working as a Senate page in the summer of 1994, I
> observed . . .

REVISING AND EDITING

Revising this paper will require you truly to *re-see* or *re-vision* the problem and your proposed solution. As you revise, concentrate on a clear explanation of the problem and solid supporting evidence for the solution. Keep your purpose of convincing your readers uppermost in your thoughts. Be sure to use the necessary connections to make the parts of your essay clear for your readers.

In drafting her essay, Heather Colbenson encountered problems with organization and coherence. Following are paragraphs 2 and 3 from her first draft:

> Why would high schools in farming communities drop
> agriculture classes and the FFA program? Small schools
> are cutting ag programs because the state has not pro-
> vided significant funding for the small schools to oper-
> ate. The small schools have to make cuts, and some small
> schools are deciding that the agriculture classes are not
> as important as other courses. Some small schools are
> consolidating to receive more aid. Many of these schools
> have been able to save their ag program.
>
> Many colleges are demanding that students have two
> years of foreign language. In small schools, like my own,

WRITING WITH A COMPUTER Your word processor's ability to lift and move blocks of words is especially useful for this assignment. It gives you the power to play around, arranging the points of your argument in whatever sequence seems most effective. You might first try beginning with what you expect to be your readers' most powerful objection to your proposal and your answer to it. Then you'd present and answer the second strongest objection and so on. Try different sequences until you find the one that works best. Try reversing that order, putting the strongest objection last so that your most convincing point would come last — for an effective clincher.

the students could take either foreign language or ag
classes. Therefore, students choose language classes to
fill the college requirement. When the students leave the
ag classes to take foreign language, the number of students declines, which makes it easier for school administrators to cut ag classes.

As she read over her draft, Colbenson realized that she was really talking about the two primary reasons FFA programs are being cut. That was clear in her mind, but she had not made it clear on paper for her readers. She decided to use transitional phrases to make her point clear and to tie her ideas together explicitly, so she added "One reason" and "The main reason." Then she decided to place the main reason, decreased funds, last for emphasis. As she worked with her draft further, she realized that her first reason was not actually college requirements, as she had stated, but the competition between college-prep courses and other courses in the high school curriculum when money is limited. She further revised her second paragraph to make this point clear. As she looked at her comment about consolidation, she realized it did not fit at the end of the paragraph explaining cuts made because of inadequate funding. This point was a way to save ag programs, not a reason they were being cut. For unity, she moved the point about consolidation to the last section of her essay, which consists of suggestions to save FFA programs. She found similar problems with coherence in her section on the benefits of FFA programs. She thought through this information in a similar manner, rearranged it, and added key words for transition: "one significant benefit," "another benefit," "A third advantage," "A fourth advantage," "A fifth benefit" (see paragraphs 5–9).

With the corrections, the paper was more forcefully organized and more tightly coherent, making it easier for readers to follow and understand. The bridges between ideas in the writer's mind were now on paper. In going over her draft, Colbenson was also able to eliminate unnecessary words and, in general, improve the style. As she re-viewed her ideas for unity and coherence, she also found more precise words and more effective sentences to express her ideas. Adding those made her essay even stronger.

Be reasonable. Exaggerated claims for your solution will not persuade your readers. Don't be afraid to express your own reasonable doubts about the completeness of your solution. If you have ended your draft with a horrific vision of what will happen if your idea should go untried, ask yourself whether you have exaggerated.

In writing a paper that proposes a solution, you may be tempted to simplify the problem so that the solution seems very likely to apply. Looking back over your draft, consider whether perhaps you have fallen into *oversimplification*. (For help in recognizing this and other errors in reasoning, see p. 104.) You may need to rethink both the problem and the solution.

In looking back over your draft once more, review these points:

**REVISION
CHECKLIST**

- Does your introduction invite the reader into the discussion?
- Have you made the problem clear? Have you made it relevant to your readers?
- Have you clearly outlined the steps that must be taken to solve the problem?
- Have you demonstrated the benefits of your solution?
- Have you considered other possible solutions to the problem before rejecting them in favor of your own?
- Have you anticipated the doubts readers may have about your solution?
- Do you come across as a well-meaning, reasonable writer willing to admit that you don't know everything?
- Have you avoided promising that your solution will do more than it can possibly do? Have you made believable predictions for the success of your plan?

After you have revised your proposal, proofread and edit it. Check carefully for problems with grammar, word choice, punctuation, and mechanics — and then correct any problems you find. A comprehensive reference handbook is an indispensable tool for this task; the "Quick Editing Guide" at the end of *The Bedford Guide for College Writers* (see the pages with the colored edges) will get you started.

When editing a paper in which you propose a solution, make sure your sentence structure helps you make your points clearly and directly. Don't let yourself slip into the passive voice, a grammatical construction that represents things as happening without any obvious agent: "The problem should be remedied by spending more money on prevention." It should be obvious in every sentence who should take action: "The dean of students should remedy the problem by spending more money on prevention." Also beware of ambiguous *this*'s and *that*'s. Make sure that every pronoun clearly refers to something (its antecedent) and that it agrees with (matches) its antecedent.

Here are some questions to get you started when proofreading and editing your paper:

**EDITING
CHECKLIST**

- Have you avoided using the passive voice where a more direct structure would be clearer?
- Is it clear what each pronoun refers to? Does each pronoun agree with (match) its antecedent? (See A4 in the "Quick Editing Guide.")
- Is your sentence structure correct? Have you avoided writing fragments and run-on sentences? (See A6 and A7 in the "Quick Editing Guide.")
- Do your transitions and other introductory elements have commas after them, if these are needed? (See C1 in the "Quick Editing Guide.")
- Have you spelled and capitalized everything correctly, especially names of people and organizations? (See D1 and D2 in the "Quick Editing Guide.")
- Have you used the proper paper format, including special requirements for your instructor and course? (See D3 in the "Quick Editing Guide.")

(For more on revising and editing, see Chapter 19.)

OTHER ASSIGNMENTS

1. If in Chapter 9 you followed the assignment and took a stand, now write a few additional paragraphs extending that paper, going on to propose a solution that argues for action. You may find it helpful to brainstorm with classmates first (see p. 360).

2. Write an editorial for a newspaper in which you propose to your town officials an innovation you think would benefit the whole community. Here are a few suggestions to help you begin:

FOR GROUP LEARNING

Exchanging Written Reactions

Here is a one-on-one activity. Exchange with another student the papers you both have written for an assignment in this chapter. Then instead of writing the brief comments that you ordinarily might write on another student's paper, write each other at least a few hundred words of reactions and suggestions. Exchange comments, and then sit down together to discuss your experiences. What did you find out about proposing a solution? About writing? About peer editing?

FOR PEER RESPONSE

For this type of writing in particular, try your draft on other students. You will find your readers' feedback invaluable as you revise and edit your paper. See Chapter 20 for advice on working with other student writers and for general questions you should always ask a peer editor to address. For a paper in which you propose a solution, you'll also want your peer editor to answer these specific questions:

- What is your overall reaction to this proposal? Does it make you want to go out and do something about the problem?
- Are you convinced that the problem is of vital concern to you? If not, why don't you care?
- Are you persuaded that the writer's solution is workable?
- Restate what you understand to be the proposal's major points —

> Problem:
> Proposal:
> Explanation of proposal:
> Procedure:
> Advantages:
> Disadvantages:
> Response to other solutions:
> Recommendation:

- Has the writer argued persuasively against other solutions? List any additional solutions you think the writer should refute.
- Describe what you think makes the writer trustworthy as a proposer.
- Has the writer paid enough attention to readers?
- If this were your paper, what is the one thing you would be sure to work on before handing it in?

Instituting a drug and alcohol education program in the schools
Building a network of bicycle paths
Establishing after-school programs for children of working parents
Involving people in neighborhood programs for crime prevention
Lowering college tuition

3. Write a letter to your congressional representative or senator in which you object to some government policy. End your letter with a proposal for righting the wrong that concerns you.

4. Choose from the following list a practice that seems to you to represent an inefficient, unethical, unfair, or morally wrong solution to a problem. In a few paragraphs, give reasons for your objections. Then propose a better solution:

Censorship
Corporal punishment for children
Laboratory experiments on animals
Surrogate motherhood
State lotteries
Dumping of wastes in the ocean

5. What activities in your high school or your college (similar to the agriculture classes and the FFA described in Heather Colbenson's paper) are in jeopardy of being cut because of decreased funding? Music classes? Art? Foreign language? School dances? If you don't know, talk to some of your instructors to find out. What solutions can you propose to save these important activities? Write an essay in which you present a solution to this problem.

Applying What You Learn: Some Uses of Proposals

In college a proposal is often a written plan submitted to someone in authority who must approve it before the proposer goes ahead with implementing a solution. Students embarking on a research project may be required to submit a proposal to an adviser or a committee that sets forth what they intend to investigate and how they will approach their topic. Students who object to a grade can file a grievance to try to get the grade changed. Like writers of persuasive essays, they state a claim and supply evidence in support of it.

In business, too, proposals for action are often useful — for persuading a prospective customer to buy a product or service, for solving a personnel problem, for recommending a change in procedure, for suggesting a new project, or for urging a purchase of new equipment. An office manager might use a proposal as a means to achieve harmony with co-workers — first discussing with the staff a certain problem (such as poor morale or a conflict between smokers and nonsmokers) and then writing a proposal to outline the solution on which the group has agreed.

Every day in the world around us, we encounter proposals for solutions — on the editorial pages of newspapers and magazines, in books, in public service announcements on television, in legislative proposals and responses to proposed bills. In a 1995 "Random Access" column in *Newsweek*, Steven Levy laments the legislation proposed by Jim Exon, Democratic senator from Nebraska, to protect children by censoring information on the Internet. Exon's bill would clean up language and visuals on the Internet by levying fines and imposing jail terms on those who post obscene messages and pornographic documents on the information highway. Levy argues that censorship is not the answer and then offers his own proposal for solution:

> So how do we protect our children from the pictures of naked ladies, the discussions of bestiality, and the rough language that currently characterize the Net? Even Exon has admitted that his bill probably won't stop the smut he so urgently wants to eliminate. There are high-tech dodges around anything that the simple minds of the Senate can concoct. We would have better results by implementing some newly proposed technological solutions, ranging from software that filters out possibly objectionable material to special services that present only a bowdlerized version of the Net to junior web-surfers. And then, there's always that remedy in which censorious legislators never seem to have confidence: parental guidance.

Sometimes an entire article or essay is devoted to arguing for an action. In other cases, a writer's chief purpose may be to explain something or perhaps to express an opinion and then to end with a proposal. In a 1983 article for the *New York Times Magazine*, Lewis Thomas, a distinguished physician and writer, laments the way science has been perceived as the key to understanding the universe and blames teaching from this perspective for the widespread dislike and ignorance of science. Then he proposes a drastic change in how science is taught.

> I suggest that the introductory courses in science, at all levels from grade school through college, be radically revised. Leave the fundamentals, the so-called basics, aside for a while, and concentrate the attention of all students on the things that are not known. You cannot possibly teach quantum mechanics without mathematics, to be sure, but you can describe the strangeness of the world opened up by quantum theory. Let it be known, early on, that there are deep mysteries and profound paradoxes revealed in distant outline by modern physics. Explain that these can be approached more closely and puzzled over, once the language of mathematics has been sufficiently mastered.
>
> At the outset, before any of the fundamentals, teach the still imponderable puzzles of cosmology. Describe as clearly as possible, for the youngest minds, that there are some things going on in the universe that lie still beyond comprehension, and make it plain how little is known.

Like many proposals that you will read during your college years and beyond, Thomas's is controversial. Whether Thomas persuades or fails to persuade his readers, he performs a useful service. By giving us a thoughtful proposal on this crucial issue, he challenges us to think.

In time, some calls to action that at first are controversial become generally accepted. This is certainly true of Dr. Elisabeth Kübler-Ross's views about how dying patients and their loved ones have been treated. Before she wrote her landmark book *On Death and Dying* (1969), terminally ill patients in hospitals were seldom told when they were close to death, and little was done to help them die with dignity. Their families felt uncomfortable about the silences and deceptions imposed on the dying. After studying the problem, Kübler-Ross evolved a number of suggestions that would ease a patient's transition into death — easing pain for the caregivers as well as for the patient. Among them is this one:

> There is a time in a patient's life when the pain ceases to be, when the mind slips off into a dreamless state, when the need for food becomes minimal and the awareness of the environment all but disappears into darkness. This is the time when the relatives walk up and down the hospital hallways, tormented by the waiting, not knowing if they should leave to attend the living or stay to be around for the moment of death. This is the time when it is too late for words, and yet the time when the relatives cry the loudest for help — with or without words. It is too late for medical interventions (and too cruel, though well meant, when they do occur), but it is also too early for a final separation from the dying. It is the hardest time for the next of kin as he either wishes to take off, to get it over with; or he desperately clings to something that he is in the process of losing forever. It is the time for the therapy of silence with the patient and availability for the relatives.
>
> The doctor, nurse, social worker, or chaplain can be of great help during these final moments if they can understand the family's conflicts at this time and help select the one person who feels most comfortable staying with the dying patient. This person then becomes in effect the patient's therapist. Those who feel too uncomfortable can be assisted by alleviating their guilt and by the reassurance that someone will stay with the dying until his death has occurred. They can then return home knowing that the patient did not die alone, yet not feeling ashamed or guilty for having avoided this moment which for many people is so difficult to face.

At their best, like Kübler-Ross's pioneering recommendations for facing death and dying, proposals are often the advance guard that comes before useful action.

Making Connections: Proposals in A Writer's Reader

Whenever we encounter a problem, we search for solutions. When we find an answer that satisfies us, we *propose a solution* to share our excitement with other people. We move from trying to convince readers of the soundness of our position to trying to persuade them to do something — to act or change their behavior. Some writers in *A Writer's Reader* present proposals for solutions to problems. In "A Part-Time Marriage" (p. 518), professor and writer

Noel Perrin, after experiencing the problems that come with divorce, proposes part-time marriages. In "The Price of Admission" (p. 651), computer consultant and Web expert Stephanie Brail analyzes the harassment that women may face while using the Internet and proposes that the solution to this problem is not regulation of Internet participation but a greater presence online of women who have been educated to use Internet "tools" — a philosophy she calls "tools not rules."

Like Perrin, Brail, Wilbert Rideau (p. 225), and Heather Colbenson (p. 227), other writers from a variety of professions propose solutions to problems they identify: professor and writer Stephanie Coontz, "Remarriage and Stepfamilies" (p. 522); poet and professor Judith Ortiz Cofer, "The Myth of the Latin Woman: I Just Met a Girl Named María" (p. 564); Republican politician Jack Kemp, "Affirmative Action: The 'Radical Republican' Example" (p. 588); and editor and essayist Leonce Gaiter, "Is the Web Too Cool for Blacks?" (p. 642). As you read these essays, consider the role that proposals play in them. For each essay, answer the following questions:

1. What problem does the writer identify? What solution does she or he propose?
2. How is the writer qualified to write on this subject?
3. What evidence for the proposed solution does the writer present? Does the writer convince you to agree with her or him? Does the writer rouse you to want to do something about the problem?

Chapter 11

Evaluating

Evaluating means judging. You do it when you decide what candidate to vote for, pick which camera to buy from among several on the market, watch a game and size up a team's prowess, recommend a new restaurant to your friends. All of us find ourselves passing judgments continually as we move through a day's routine.

Often in everyday situations we make snap judgments. A friend asks, "How was that movie you saw last night?" and you reply, "Terrific — don't miss it" or maybe "Pretty good, but it had too much blood and gore for me." Those off-the-cuff opinions are necessary and useful. But to *write* an evaluation calls for you to think more critically. As a writer you first decide on *criteria*, or standards for judging, and then come up with evidence to back up your judgment.

A written evaluation zeroes in on a definite subject. You inspect the subject carefully and come to a considered opinion. The subject might be a film, a book, a piece of music, a restaurant, a sports team, a group of performers, a product, a scientific theory, a body of research: the possibilities are endless.

Learning from Other Writers

Here are two evaluations — the first by a professional writer, the second by a student. Michiko Kakutani is a Pulitzer Prize–winning senior book critic for the *New York Times*, where this book review first appeared. In the review, Kakutani evaluates bestselling author and Nobel Prize winner Toni Morrison's novel, *Paradise*.

Geoffrey Fallon wrote his evaluative essay "Hatred within an Illustrated Medium: Those Uncanny X-Men" for a composition class at Santa Fe Community College in Florida. Fallon enjoyed writing this paper because he was

able to show how the genre of comics can be used to send important messages. "I also am proud of the way the paper sounds," he states. "It sounds very
academic, even though it is discussing a comic book. I hope that helps get my
point across."

Michiko Kakutani   *Paradise*: Worthy Women, Unredeemable Men

Paradise, Toni Morrison's latest novel — and her first since winning the   1
Nobel Prize for Literature in 1993 — addresses the same great themes of her
1987 masterpiece, *Beloved*: the loss of innocence, the paralyzing power of ancient memories, and the difficulty of accepting loss and change and pain.

It, too, deals with the blighted legacy of slavery. It, too, examines the emo-   2
tional and physical violence that human beings are capable of inflicting upon
one another. And it, too, suggests that redemption is to be found not in ob-
sessively remembering the past but in letting go.

Unfortunately, *Paradise* is everything that *Beloved* was not: it's a heavy-   3
handed, schematic piece of writing, thoroughly lacking in the novelistic
magic Ms. Morrison has wielded so effortlessly in the past. It's a contrived,
formulaic book that mechanically pits men against women, old against
young, the past against the present.

The basic dynamic of *Paradise* will vaguely remind Morrison fans of her   4
powerful 1974 novel *Sula*, which also looked at conformity and rebellion
within an insular community. In the case of *Paradise*, the story, briefly, goes
like this: a small all-black Oklahoma town that has been reeling from the
racial, generational and political confusions of the 1960s and '70s finds a
scapegoat in an all-female household occupying a former convent on the
edge of town. There are rumors of abortions and witchcraft and complaints
against "this new and obscene breed of female" that dares to be self-
sufficient.

One morning, we're told in the opening pages of *Paradise*, the men of   5
Ruby decide to take matters into their own hands, and they descend upon the
convent with guns, handcuffs, and Mace. "God at their side, the men take
aim," Ms. Morrison writes, "for Ruby."

The remainder of *Paradise* is devoted to explaining who these men are and   6
what brought their intended victims to the convent in the first place. We learn
that the townsmen have never been able to move past their village's history:
its traumatic founding by former slaves, who were ostracized by both whites
and lighter-skinned blacks, and the determination of its current elders to keep
the community isolated and pure, wary of strangers detached from politics,
and skeptical of the idealism and anger of the young.

As for the convent women, they are a motley assortment of misfits and   7
fugitives: Connie, a former ward of the nuns, who ran the convent when it was
a boarding school for Indian girls; Mavis, a paranoid woman who has fled her
domineering husband in the East; Gigi, a seductive young woman whose

boyfriend is in jail; Seneca, a hitchhiker who has survived abandonment and sexual exploitation; Pallas, a wealthy lawyer's daughter whose lover left her for her mother.

Nearly every one of these characters is a two-dimensional cliché, thin and papery and disposable. Unlike the heroine of *Beloved*, who was strong, desperate, loving, vulnerable, and angry all at once, almost all the women in this novel are victims: they have spent years grappling with economic hardship, romantic disappointment, social inequity, and the stupid misdeeds of men.

The men, on the other hand, are almost uniformly control freaks or hotheads, eager to dismiss independent women as sluts or witches and determined to make everyone submit to their will. The real battles in Ruby, a character observes, were "about disobedience, which meant, of course, the stallions were fighting about who controlled the mares and their foals."

Whereas earlier Morrison novels like *Beloved, Song of Solomon*, and *Sula* fused the historical and the mythic, the mundane and the fantastic into a seamless piece of music, this novel remains an earthbound hodgepodge, devoid of both urgency and narrative sleight of hand. It's neither grounded in closely observed vignettes of real life, nor lofted by the dreamlike images the author has used so dexterously in the past to suggest the strangeness of American history; the novel's one surreal set-piece feels like a hasty afterthought, clumsily grafted on to try to kick the story to another level.

Although *Paradise* employs familiar Morrison techniques — cutting back and forth from one character's point of view to another, back and forth from the past to the present — the novel's language feels closer to the hectoring, didactic voice that warped her 1992 essay "Playing in the Dark."

As a result, Ms. Morrison's efforts to endow the story with a symbolic subtext tend to feel hokey. There are gratuitous biblical allusions (like comparing the story of Ruby's founders to the story of the Holy Family, turned away from the inn) and even more gratuitous suggestions that the women at the convent are feminist martyrs, like the witches of Salem.

Plot developments are also contrived. Although the convent is supposedly a mansion in the middle of nowhere, a steady stream of women conveniently arrive there to continually add new drama, and other anomalous events, like the appearance of some lost white people on the eve of a blizzard in Ruby, are similarly orchestrated to keep the novel's story line ticking along. These events do not tumble together neatly to create a sense of inevitability; they remain a series of random dominoes, falling over noisily, one by one by one.

To make matters worse, Ms. Morrison is constantly having her characters spell out the meaning of her story. "They think they have outfoxed the whiteman when in fact they imitate him," she writes toward the end of the novel. "They think they are protecting their wives and children, when in fact they are maiming them. And when the maimed children ask for help, they look elsewhere for the cause. Born out of an old hatred, one that began when one kind of black man scorned another kind and that kind took the hatred to another level, their selfishness had trashed two hundred years of suffering and triumph in a moment of such pomposity and error and callousness it froze the mind."

Ruby, she adds, was "a backward noplace ruled by men whose power to   15
control was out of control and who had the nerve to say who could live and
who not and where; who had seen in lively, free, unarmed females the mutiny
of the mares and so got rid of them."

Had Ms. Morrison persuasively dramatized her story, had she managed to   16
make the reader feel her characters' plight, she might have realized that such
blunt announcements were unnecessary, indeed annoying. As it is, they stand
as portentous footnotes in what is a clunky, leaden novel.

Questions to Start You Thinking

Meaning

1. What is Kakutani's thesis in this review? In which paragraph do you find it?

2. Like all writers of evaluations, Kakutani relies on words that imply judgment. What specific words or phrases does she choose to reinforce her negative evaluation of *Paradise*?

3. What does Kakutani mean when she calls "every one" of the characters in *Paradise* a "two-dimensional cliché, thin and papery and disposable," and refers to the plot as "contrived" (paragraphs 8 and 13)?

4. Reread paragraph 10. In your own words, explain what Kakutani is praising in Morrison's earlier work and what problems she has with *Paradise*.

Writing Strategies

5. Based on the first two paragraphs of this essay, what would you expect Kakutani's evaluation of *Paradise* to be? Why does she begin her essay by leading you to think that she will continue to find similarities between the two novels?

6. What is the main point Kakutani is trying to make by comparing and contrasting *Paradise* with Morrison's earlier works?

7. What aspects of *Paradise* does Kakutani critique in her analysis of the novel? Why does she choose to focus on these elements to support her evaluation?

8. Note the places where Kakutani uses examples and direct quotations from *Paradise* to support her critique of Morrison's novel. Does she provide sufficient evidence to convince you to agree with her opinion? Why, or why not?

STUDENT ESSAY

Geoffrey Fallon   **Hatred within an Illustrated Medium: Those Uncanny X-Men**

His arms raised majestically over his head, his cape   1
flowing behind him like an emperor's robes, the mutant called
Magneto speaks to his self-proclaimed children--mutants like
himself, scorned by those who fear them for being different.
With fatherly undertones he defends his terrorist actions

with the following address: "All my life, I have seen people
slaughtered wholesale for no more reason than the deity they
worshiped, or the color of their skin--or the presence in
their DNA of an extra, special gene. I cannot change the
world, but I can and will ensure that my race will never
again suffer for its fear and prejudice."

The year was 1976, and while the country was still re-   2
covering from the aftereffects of the Vietnam conflict, the
problems of civil rights and racial unrest began to rear
their heads after lying dormant for almost a decade. Activists once again began to speak out as minority groups witnessed blatant disregard for the rights their predecessors
had fought for in the mid-sixties. In the midst of this political strife, a young comic book writer named Chris Claremont decided to incorporate this unfortunate trend of continued minority inequality into his comic book The Uncanny
X-Men. The series tells the story of a team of superheroes
who have banded together to help others like themselves, humans with a genetic quirk, an "X-Factor," that gives them su-
perhuman characteristics. These mutants are feared and hated
by many normal humans. In his stories Claremont is quite deliberate in his attempt to educate readers about the dangers
and the consequences of racism. While comic books are generally thought of as a child's medium not worth serious attention, Claremont uses his series to speak out on a serious
topic, bigotry, in a form that is accessible to a variety of
readers.

The story of the X-Men is a story of how people of di-   3
verse ethnic and racial backgrounds can come together in the
spirit of harmony but encounter widespread prejudice because
they are different. Originally, the X-Men are a team of
superheroes who battle evil and use their powers to serve
humanity. However, humans without an X-Factor--the genetic
quirk that makes a human exhibit mutant powers--begin to show
prejudice against mutated humans. The very people the X-Men
have sworn to protect regard the team with anger and fear.
They cry out for special laws for mutant control and set up
Human Liberation Organizations. These acts of aggression
cause other mutant groups to band together. Now, however,

their goal is not to protect the human race but to protect
themselves from the hatred beginning to form in the normal
human population. As these new groups form, humans become
even more frightened, thinking that these mutants will someday take over the world, forcing normal humans underground.
Mutant Registration Acts are passed, forcing mutants to register with special government offices so they can be monitored. The final phase of this new trend toward slavery is
inaugurated by the creation of an entire nation, Genosha,
dedicated to the advancement of humankind and the persecution
of mutants.

The entrance of Genosha into the world market prompts an   4
ultrapowerful mutant by the name of Magneto (who possesses
control over the electromagnetic spectrum) to create a nation
of his own. Floating over Earth's atmosphere, Magneto creates
an asteroid with everything that would be needed for an entire race of mutants to make it their home. He calls it Asteroid M and invites any mutant to settle there, away from
the hate that is building on the planet below. The asteroid
is systematically destroyed by a joint task force of the most
powerful nations on Earth, who fear that the mutants will use
it as a base for terrorist actions against Earth. Magneto is
apparently killed in the explosion, while diverting all of
his vast power toward saving as many mutants as possible.
Thus, he becomes a martyr for other mutants, who vow to fight
on to reclaim their place on Earth.

The Uncanny X-Men is the best-selling comic book series   5
in the history of the industry. Tales of the mutants Cyclops,
Gamit, Rogue, Wolverine, Psylocke, Beast, Storm, Archangel,
Forge, Marvel Girl, Banshee, Ice-Man, Jubilee, Colossus, and
Professor X have propelled the Marvel Comic Series to the
front of every top ten list available. What are the messages
in this widely read story? First and foremost, there is the
utopian ideal of people of different races and backgrounds
living together in harmony. The fifteen mutants who make up
the X-Men form a loving family, with Professor X as their
parental figure. The respect and consideration they show for
one another--despite their differences--is a perfect model
for a better world. In the series, the need for harmonious

diversity is not limited to the X-Men. Almost every type of cultural background is represented here--African, Russian, Japanese, Canadian, Irish, and American. Different cultures are brought together by fate and can continue to survive only through the realization that they are really all the same. In this respect, Claremont's vision corresponds to that of Martin Luther King Jr., who spoke of a "world house" in which we must all learn to live together because we can never again live apart.

Second, we are also introduced to the darker side of human nature--discrimination and the drive for supremacy--within the unfolding story line of Claremont's comic book. Hatred, prejudice, oppression, and the maddening spiral of ever-increasing militancy and aggression are all present. Genosha is perhaps the ultimate symbol for the supposed superiority of one race over another. Claremont quite deliberately links the fictional oppression of the mutants to similar moments in human history. Magneto's family, for instance, died in the concentration camps in Nazi Germany. The name of Nimrod, a hunter of mutants in the series, comes from Genesis 10:8-9 of the Bible; the biblical Nimrod was a mighty hunter whose skill was unparalleled. Claremont's Nimrod is similar. He is the ultimate killing machine with one primary mission-- to destroy mutants. The idea of complete genocide is a topic too heinous to speak about in a straightforward manner, so Claremont uses X-Men to bring it to the attention of his readers.

Claremont's third message is that activism is needed to combat this terrorism and hatred, and he provides clear models for activism. Just as is the case in the real world, there are those who try to make a difference. Magneto is portrayed as a villain, and in many cases he does indeed act like one, dealing in hatred and aggression himself. Nonetheless, Magneto makes an admirable effort to bring about change. Perhaps the real-life figure he resembles most is Malcolm X: though some may condemn his hatred for his oppressors, which motivates his actions, few can fault his passionate devotion to improving the lives of his people. It is this passion to create change that propels activists into action, and it is these activists that instill the very same passion into the people they lead.

What is to become of these powerful messages? Are they doomed to remain in the never-never land of a child's illustrated fairy tale? In actuality, comic books are much more than fantasy adventure placed in a thirty-page magazine. They have become a viable source for social commentary, and publishers both in the United States and abroad are now using the medium to express ideas for change. Pagan Kennedy makes this point in her essay "P.C. Comics" (The Nation, 19 Mar. 1990):

> Like film, comic books are far more sensual than pure language, and therefore have the potential to appeal to a large popular audience, as they do in Europe and Japan. . . . As visceral as film, as silent as a book, and as easy to produce as finding an idle photocopier, the comic book is inherently subversive.

The comic book has indeed found its way into the hands of some of the most aggressive proponents for social change. The Uncanny X-Men is one example. It sold over eight million copies in the last few months, and it is improbable that this many people are introduced to a socially correct way of thinking through any other medium each and every month. The Uncanny X-Men is a stellar forum in which to talk about the dangers of hate-mongers and supremacists.

Perhaps the stereotype is correct. Perhaps comic books are just for kids. If this is true, maybe it is a blessing, for children can gain enlightenment from the illustrated medium even if the minds of adults are too shrouded in prejudice and ignorance. Children, at least, have a chance to start anew with fresh dreams of equality, untainted by those who refuse to see every man and woman as equal.

As Asteroid M cracks in half, as its core explodes in a fiery cloud of intense heat, a regal figure floats in its midst, protected by a field of magnetic energy. With a flick of his gloved hand, the X-Men's craft is hurled toward Earth, away from danger. Magneto lowers his arm, and, looking upward to the stars, he opens his mind to Professor X, leader of the

8

9

10

11

X-Men and his utter enemy, who telepathically listens to the
last words of the man he has fought for so many years:

> I save you X-Men because that is my task in life:
> to safeguard my people Homo sapiens superior-mutant
> kind from those that would do us harm. And those
> forces are legion. I have survived one holocaust, I
> could not tolerate another. . . . Perhaps it is best
> it end this way, Charles [Professor X]. Best for my
> dream to end in flames and glory, here far above
> Earth. . . . I give you your dream, Charles. But I
> fear, in time, your heart will break, as you real-
> ize it has ever been a fool's hope. Farewell, my
> friend.

Questions to Start You Thinking

Meaning

1. What is Fallon's main point, his thesis? Why do you agree or disagree with it?

2. Why does Fallon consider this comic book series worthwhile and significant? What criteria does he use in evaluating the comic book?

3. Can you think of other books, stories, or television shows considered children's entertainment that are really commentaries on the adult world?

Writing Strategies

4. How convincing is the evidence the writer marshals to support his evaluation? What could make it more convincing?

5. How does Fallon organize his essay? How could this organization be improved?

6. What resources does Fallon draw on in the essay? What critical strategies?

7. Fallon begins and ends his essay with descriptions of scenes from the X-Men series. Why do you think he uses this technique?

Learning by Writing

THE ASSIGNMENT: WRITING AN EVALUATION

Pick a subject to evaluate. It should be one that you have some personal experience with and that you feel reasonably competent to evaluate. This might be a movie, a TV program, a piece of music, an artwork, a new product, a government agency, or anything else you can think of. Then in a thoughtful essay, evaluate your subject. In both your preparation for writing and in the essay itself, you will need to analyze the subject before you attempt to evaluate it. You will also need to determine specific criteria for evaluation and make them clear to your readers. In writing your evaluation, you will have a twofold purpose — (1) to set forth your assessment of the quality of your subject and (2) to convince your readers that your judgment is reasonable.

Among the lively and instructive student-written evaluations we've seen recently are these:

A music major evaluated several works by American composer Aaron Copland and found Copland a trivial and imitative composer "without a tenth of the talent or inventiveness that George Gershwin or Duke Ellington had in his little finger."

A man planning a career in business management evaluated a computer firm in which he had worked one summer. His criteria were efficiency, productivity, appeal to new customers, and employee satisfaction.

A woman from Brazil, who had seen firsthand the effects of industrial development in the Amazon rainforest, evaluated the efforts of the U.S. government to protect the ozone layer, comparing them with the efforts of environmentalists in her own country.

A student of history, assigned to evaluate the long-term effects of Prohibition, found in favor of the maligned Volstead Act, passed to enforce Prohibition.

For an English course, a man evaluated *Going after Cacciato*, Tim O'Brien's novel of American soldiers in Vietnam (1978), favorably comparing it with Ernest Hemingway's World War I novel *A Farewell to Arms*.

GENERATING IDEAS

Find something to evaluate. Try using *brainstorming* to find a suitable topic. List as many possible topics as you can think of that you might evaluate. Look over your list, and select the ones that seem to have the most potential — the ones that you are most familiar with or that you can easily find out more about. Then combine your brainstorming with a little *freewriting*, setting down ideas about the topics as fast as they come to mind. (These strategies are discussed in detail on pp. 360 and 363.) From the results of these two techniques for generating ideas, choose one subject for your essay.

Gather information. You'll want to spend time finding material to help you develop a judgment. Consult your four writer's resources. You probably will *recall* (for example, a performance you have seen on television or an article you have read); you might *observe* (if you are evaluating a performance or the prowess of a sports team); you might *converse* to see what others think; or you might *imagine* what a friend or relative would think of your subject.

Establish your criteria. In evaluating, you will find it helpful to establish and jot down criteria, standards to apply to your subject. Think of the features of the subject worth considering: in the case of a popular entertainer such as Puff Daddy or Michael Jackson, perhaps onstage manner, rapport with the audience, musicianship, selection of material, originality. How well does the performer score on these points? In evaluating the desirability of Atlanta as a home for a young careerist, you might ask: Does it provide an ample choice of decent-paying entry-level positions in growth firms? Any criterion you use to evaluate has to fit your subject, your audience, and your purpose. Ample entry-level jobs might not matter to the writer of an article addressing an audience of retirees. Or in a review of a new automobile for *Car & Driver*, addressed to car buffs, a writer might use criteria such as styling and design, handling, fuel efficiency, safety features, and quality of the ride.

Try comparing and contrasting. Comparing and contrasting may be useful, although they're not essential, for evaluating. (When you *compare*, you point to similarities; when you *contrast*, you note differences.) Often you can readily size up the worth of a thing by setting it next to another of its kind. Michiko Kakutani uses this technique effectively in her review of Toni Morrison's *Paradise* when she compares the novel to earlier works by Morrison. To be comparable, of course, your two subjects need to have plenty in common. The quality of a Harley Davidson motorcycle might be judged by contrasting it with a Honda but not by contrasting it with a Sherman tank.

When you decide on something that is comparable to your subject, make a list of points you wish to compare. What similarities and differences leap to mind? Your list might turn into a scratch outline you can use in drafting your paper. For example, if you are writing a paper for a film history course, you might compare and contrast the classic German horror movie *The Cabinet of Dr. Caligari* with the classic Hollywood movie *Frankenstein*, concluding that *Caligari* is the more artistic film. In your planning of the paper, you might make two columns in which you list the characteristics of each film:

	CALIGARI	FRANKENSTEIN
Sets and lighting	Dreamlike and impressionistic	Realistic, but with heavy Gothic atmosphere
	Sets deliberately angular and distorted	Gothic sets
	Deep shadows that throw figures into relief	In climax: a night scene, torches highlighting monster's face

And so on, point by point. By jotting down each point and each bit of evidence side by side, you can outline your comparison and contrast with great efficiency. Once you have listed them, decide on a possible order for the points. (For more on using comparing and contrasting, see Chapter 7.)

Try defining your subject. Another technique for evaluating is to define your subject, indicating its nature so clearly that your readers can easily distinguish it from others of its kind. In defining, you help your readers understand your subject — its structure, its habitat, its functions. In evaluating a classic television show such as *Roseanne* or *The Mary Tyler Moore Show*, you would want to do some *extended* defining, discussing the nature of sitcoms over the years, their techniques, their views of women, their effects on the audience. This kind of defining isn't the same as writing a *short definition*, such as you'd find in a dictionary. (For how to do that, see "Defining," p. 419.) Your purpose is to judge. You might ask, What is the nature of my subject? Or, What qualities make my subject unique, unlike others of its sort? Scribble down any qualities that occur to you. In writing out your answer, you may find that you have written most of your paper and have formed an opinion of your subject.

Develop a judgment. In the end, you will have to come to a decision: Is your subject good, worthwhile, significant, exemplary, preferable — or not? Most writers find themselves coming to a judgment gradually as they explore their subjects. If you haven't developed one yet, look back over your criteria and any comparing and contrasting or defining you've done to see whether a judgment becomes apparent. If not, you may have to do some more investigating.

To help you to close in on a promising subject and some likely material, you might ask yourself a few questions:

DISCOVERY CHECKLIST

- What criteria, if any, do you plan to use in making your evaluation? Are they clear and reasonably easy to apply?
- What evidence can you recall to back up your judgments? If not from memory, from what other resource might you draw evidence?
- Would comparing or contrasting help in evaluating your subject? If so, with what might you compare or contrast your subject?
- What specific qualities set your subject apart from all the rest of its class?

PLANNING, DRAFTING, AND DEVELOPING

Remember your purpose. Reflect a moment: What is your purpose in this evaluation? What main point do you wish to make? Geoffrey Fallon asked himself these questions and answered them by writing a purpose statement for his project:

> In my evaluation, I plan to examine the messages about racial prejudices present in the Marvel comic book series The Uncanny X-Men. I will show how the writer Chris Claremont uses his characters to tell a compelling story of how ignorance and fear can inspire hatred. In the series, the X-Men are looked at as freaks and "gene-jokes" simply because their genetic pattern is different from the norm. This bigotry is quite apparent in all of Claremont's scripts, and the writer's purpose is to il-

lustrate a parallel to the hate-mongers present in real
life. The story line is very complex and not the type of
plot you would expect in a comic book format. In the
story, the archvillain, Magneto, decides to take it on
himself to create a world in which bigotry does not
exist. He could almost be thought of as a tragic hero in
one sense. I believe it is through this particular character that Claremont explains the frustrations of oppressed races and cultures. In my conclusion, I plan to
prove that The Uncanny X-Men is a direct attempt to show
children the horrors of racism in a format they can relate to. While comic books are usually geared toward a
younger audience, I feel this particular one has something meaningful to say to any one of a number of older
generations, and through my essay I will make this point
clear.

Through this exploration of his early thoughts on the comic book series and
his intentions in his paper, Fallon was able to focus his thinking before he
began to draft his paper.

Consider your criteria. Some writers like to apply specific criteria to whatever
they're evaluating. Many find that a list of criteria gives them confidence and
provokes ideas. But to be a good evaluator, you don't absolutely have to have
foreordained criteria. T. S. Eliot said that, in criticizing literature, criteria, standards, and touchstones (great works to hold lesser works up to) don't help all
that much. In a statement that sounds snobbish but isn't when you think
about it, he declared that all a good critic needs is intelligence.

Develop an organization. To organize your paper, you might want to make
your main point at the beginning of your paper, then demonstrate it by
looking at specific evidence (possibly comparison and contrast but definitely specific examples and details), and finally return to it in your closing
lines. Organizing your paper differently, you might open by wondering,
"How good a film is *Rain Man*?" or "Is Keynes's theory of inflation still valuable, or is it hopelessly out of date?" — raising a question about your subject that your paper will answer. You then consider the evidence, one piece
at a time, and conclude with your overall judgment. You might try both
patterns of organization and see which works better for your subject and
purpose. Or you might discover a different pattern that works better for
your ideas.

Most writers find that an outline — even a rough list — facilitates writing
a draft. An outline will help you keep track of points to make. Following is Fallon's scratch outline for his paper on the X-Men:

Thesis: While comic books are generally thought of as a child's medium, Clare-mont in the X-Man series speaks out against bigotry in any form, using the genre as a tool to allow a wide variety of readers to relate easily to his point.
Issue of racism in the 1970s
C. C. chose medium of comic books
Overview of story
Messages in the series
   – Possibility of peaceful coexistence
   – Reality of hatred and discrimination
   – Activism
Comics as a serious social commentary

If you intend to compare and contrast your subject with something else, one way to arrange the points is *subject by subject*: discuss subject A, and then discuss subject B. This method is workable for a short essay of two or three paragraphs, but for a longer essay it has drawbacks. In an essay of, say, a thousand or two thousand words, your readers might find it hard to remember all your points about subject A, ten paragraphs ago, while reading about subject B. A better way to organize a long comparison is *point by point*. You take up one point at a time and apply it first to one subject and then to the other. (For more on organizing an essay that uses comparing and contrasting, see Chapter 7.)

Keep your outline simple, and don't be ruled by it. If, while you write your draft, good thoughts come to you, by all means let them in. (If you need a quick refresher in outlining, see p. 384.)

REVISING AND EDITING

Be fair. Make your judgments reasonable, not extreme. Few things on earth are all good or all evil. A reviewer can find fault with a film and conclude that nevertheless it is worth seeing. There's nothing wrong, of course, with passing

WRITING WITH A COMPUTER

This chapter opens with the declaration "Evaluating means judging." Weak evaluations are usually the result of a lack of specific support and evidence. Writing with a word processor can help strengthen your evaluation by allowing you to focus on the connections between your judgments and the evidence you use. After you have written an early draft of your evaluation, scroll through the text, and highlight every *opinion* or *subjective judgment* with boldface or a different font size. Then scroll through the text again, highlighting all *facts* or *evidence* in italics or underlining. Can you identify a fairly direct correlation between your judgments and the evidence you provide? Do you need to move sentences or paragraphs around so that your support is linked more closely to your opinions? Do you need to provide additional facts or narrow the scope of your judgments?

a fervent judgment ("This is the trashiest excuse for a play I have ever suffered through"), but consider your readers and their likely reactions. Read some reviews in your local newspaper, or watch some movie critics on television to see how they balance their judgments.

In thinking critically about your draft, you might find this checklist handy:

REVISION CHECKLIST

- Is the judgment you pass on your subject unmistakably clear?
- Have you given your readers evidence to support each point you make?
- Have you been fair? If you are championing something, have you deliberately skipped over any of its disadvantages or faults? If you are condemning your subject, have you omitted any of its admirable traits?
- Have you anticipated readers' objections to your views and provided answers to their possible objections?
- If you compared one thing with another, do you look consistently at the same points in both?

After you have revised your evaluation, proofread and edit it. Check carefully for problems with grammar, word choice, punctuation, and mechanics — and then correct any problems you find. A comprehensive reference handbook is an indispensable tool for this task; the "Quick Editing Guide" at the end of *The Bedford Guide for College Writers* (see the pages with the colored edges) will get you started.

When editing an evaluation paper, pay attention to sentences in which you describe the subject of your evaluation. Make your descriptions as precise and useful as possible, and see that you have not used any dangling or misplaced modifiers. If you have used comparisons or contrasts within your evaluation, make sure these are clear: don't lose your readers in a thicket of vague pronouns or confusing references. You should also use parallel structure

FOR PEER RESPONSE

Enlist the help of a peer editor. See Chapter 20 for advice on working with other student writers and for general questions you should always ask a peer editor to address. For a paper in which you evaluate, you'll also want your peer editor to answer these specific questions:

- What is your overall reaction to this essay? Does the writer make you agree with his or her evaluation?
- When you finish reading the essay, can you tell exactly what the writer thinks of the subject?
- Does the writer give you sufficient evidence for his or her judgment? Put stars wherever more evidence is needed.
- What audience does the writer seem to have in mind?
- Would you recommend any changes in how the essay is organized?
- If this were your paper, what is the one thing you would be sure to work on before handing it in?

Facing the Challenge: Evaluating

The major challenge writers face when they write evaluations is to make clear to their readers the criteria they have used to arrive at their opinion of the subject. When writing a review of a movie, for example, you may tend toward simply summarizing the story of the entire film and saying whether you like it or not. However, for your review to be useful to readers who are wondering whether to see the movie, you must go beyond these comments. You must analyze the relevant elements of the film — acting, special effects, costumes, for example — and use your evaluation of these elements to arrive at a clear judgment of the movie's overall effectiveness.

While you may not be an expert in any field, you should never underestimate your powers of discrimination. Once you've chosen a topic, clarify the criteria or standards you will apply in evaluating it — the features that you want to consider. This explanation will ensure that you move beyond a mere summary of your topic to an opinion or judgment that you can justify to your readers.

Let's imagine that you've decided to write a review of the movie *Titanic*. Instead of overwhelming your readers with detailed descriptions of every scene, express your opinions, explain how you came to think the way you do, and provide examples that support your point of view. Brainstorming a list of possible features to consider and doing some focused freewriting on each of those features should help you to clarify both your criteria for judging the film and your overall opinion.

In the case of the *Titanic* review, your brainstorming list might include such elements as plot, dialogue, characters, acting, historical accuracy of sets and costumes, and special effects. In freewriting on each of these topics, you might discover that you thought the movie's special effects and the reconstruction of the *Titanic* were effective but that you wished that the characters had seemed more believable. As a result of your freewriting, you might come up with the thesis, or overall opinion, that *Titanic* is an extremely entertaining movie that your readers should be sure to see. To clarify the criteria you used in making this judgment, you could point to the historical accuracy of the set designs, the terrific use of special effects, and the engaging personas of the main actors — giving a few specific examples to support your opinion.

Rather than simply explaining what happens in *Paradise*, in her review, Michiko Kakutani forcefully presents her opinion of the novel and clarifies the criteria she has used in making her negative evaluation. Note that Kakutani devotes just seven sentences to summarizing the novel, giving readers only the essential background they will need to make sense of her evaluation. What Kakutani does provide is a sharp negative opinion of the book, tempered by her admiration for its Nobel Prize–winning author. She uses a comparison with an earlier novel by Morrison to clarify her thesis: "Unfortunately, *Paradise* is everything that *Beloved* was not: it's a heavy-handed, schematic piece of writing, thoroughly lacking in the novelistic magic Ms. Morrison has wielded so effortlessly in the past. It's a contrived, formulaic book that mechanically pits men against women, old against young, the past against the present." She then includes specific examples that illustrate her standards of judgment and support her point of view.

wherever it is appropriate in comparisons and contrasts: balanced grammatical structures give balanced ideas more force and clarity.

Here are some questions to get you started when proofreading and editing your paper:

EDITING CHECKLIST

- Is your sentence structure correct? Have you avoided writing fragments and run-on sentences? (See A6 and A7 in the "Quick Editing Guide.")
- Is the reference of each pronoun clear? Does each pronoun agree with (match) its antecedent? (See A4 in the "Quick Editing Guide.")
- Is it clear what each modifier in a sentence modifies? Have you created any dangling or misplaced modifiers? (See B1 in the "Quick Editing Guide.")
- Have you used parallel structure wherever needed, especially in lists or comparisons? (See B2 in the "Quick Editing Guide.")
- Have you spelled everything correctly? (See D2 in the "Quick Editing Guide.")
- Have you used the proper paper format, including special requirements for your instructor and course? (See D3 in the "Quick Editing Guide.")

(For more on revising and editing, see Chapter 19.)

OTHER ASSIGNMENTS

1. After reading Michiko Kakutani's review of Toni Morrison's *Paradise*, write your own judgment of another book published in the last ten years.

2. Write an evaluation of a college course you have taken or are now taking. (So that you can be completely objective, we suggest you select some course other than your writing course.) Analyze its strengths and weaknesses. Does the instructor present the material

FOR GROUP LEARNING

Developing a Consensus

Before you write a paper evaluating a subject, get together with your writing group. Discuss the subject you plan to evaluate, and see whether the group can help you arrive at a sound judgment of it. The other group members will need to see what it is you're evaluating or hear your detailed report about it. If you are evaluating a short literary work or an idea expressed in a reading, you might want to read that work aloud so that the group members may become familiar with it. Ask your listeners to supply reasons for their own evaluations. Maybe they'll suggest reasons that hadn't occurred to you.

clearly, understandably, and interestingly? Can you confer with the instructor if you need to? Is there any class discussion or other feedback? Are the assignments pointed and purposeful? Is the textbook helpful, readable, and easy to use? Does this course give you your money's worth?

3. If you analyze a story, poem, or play (as we discuss in Chapter 12), you will be in a good position to evaluate it. Here are two poems on a similar theme. Read them critically, seeing what you find in them, and decide which seems to you the better poem. Then, in a brief essay, set forth your evaluation. Some criteria to apply might be the poet's choice of concrete, specific words that appeal to the senses and his awareness of his audience.

Putting in the Seed
ROBERT FROST (1874–1963)

You come to fetch me from my work tonight
When supper's on the table, and we'll see

If I can leave off burying the white
Soft petals fallen from the apple tree
(Soft petals, yes, but not so barren quite,
Mingled with these, smooth bean and wrinkled pea),
And go along with you ere you lose sight
Of what you came for and become like me,
Slave to a springtime passion for the earth.
How Love burns through the Putting in the Seed
On through the watching for that early birth
When, just as the soil tarnishes with weed,
The sturdy seedling with arched body comes
Shouldering its way and shedding the earth crumbs.

Between Our Folding Lips
T. E. BROWN (1830–1897)

Between our folding lips
God slips
An embryon life, and goes;
And this becomes your rose.
We love, God makes: in our sweet mirth
God spies occasion for a birth.
Then is it His, or is it ours?
I know not — He is fond of flowers.

4. Visit a restaurant, a museum, or a tourist attraction, and write an evaluation of it for others who might be considering a visit to the place. Be sure to specify your criteria for evaluation.

5. Analyze and evaluate a magazine you do not often read.

6. Analyze and evaluate one of the essays in this textbook, using the criteria for effective writing you have learned in this course.

Applying What You Learn:
Some Uses of Evaluating

In your college writing you'll be called on over and over to evaluate. On an art appreciation exam, you might be asked to evaluate the merits of Andrew Wyeth as a realistic painter. Speech pathology students, after considering the long-standing controversy that rages in education for the deaf, might be called on to describe and then evaluate three currently disputed teaching methods — oral/aural, signing, and a combination of the two. Students of language and linguistics might be asked to evaluate Skinner's behaviorist theory of articulation therapy. Outside class, students on some campuses are invited to write comments for a student-run survey to evaluate their college courses.

In life beyond campus, every executive or professional needs to evaluate. An editor accepts and rejects manuscripts. A personnel director selects people to hire. A doctor evaluates a patient's symptoms. A lawyer sizes up the merits of a case and decides whether to take it. A retailer chooses the best product to sell. A speech pathologist evaluates the speech and language skills of prospective patients. You can think of endless other examples of evaluating, a kind of critical thinking we do every day of our lives. This kind of thinking is the basis of evaluative writing.

Familiar kinds of written evaluation abound. Daily newspapers and weekly or monthly magazines contain reviews of films, books, TV programs, records, and videos. Many sportswriters, columnists, and political commentators evaluate. The magazine *Consumer Reports* contains detailed evaluations of products and services, like this one from "Is There a DAT [digital audio tape] in Your Future?" (Jan. 1989).

> While prices will surely decline over time, we don't think DATs are going to make CDs obsolete anytime soon. First, while DAT players are much faster than conventional cassette decks at locating song tracks, they'll never be able to hop from track to track as quickly as a CD player.
>
> Second, digital audio tapes aren't as impervious to wear as compact discs. The tape comes into physical contact with a rotating recording head similar to a VCR's, and that will eventually degrade sound quality on the tape.
>
> Finally, recording quality might not be quite as close to perfect as DAT makers have implied — and record companies feared. When we tried out the *Sony DTC 1000 ES* DAT recorder last year, we found that it didn't match the low background noise performance of CD players. Unless that noise was a problem unique to our tested machine, DAT sound doesn't equal the quality of CD sound.
>
> For all of those reasons — price, durability, convenience, quality of sound, and the reluctance of the recording industry — we think that DAT will coexist with, rather than supplant, the compact disc in the years ahead.

Like many general magazines, professional journals contain book reviews that not only give a brief rundown of a book's contents but also indicate whether the reviewer considers the book worth reading. In *Chemical and Engineering News* (13 Mar. 1989), Deborah C. Andrews reviews the second edition of a textbook by H. J. Tichy called *Effective Writing for Engineers, Managers, Scientists.* Included in the review is an evaluation:

> What this text does well is to use words to talk about words. Pages are heavy with text, and visuals are exceedingly rare. Tichy writes within the framework of English (and French) literature as well as the literature of science, often calling upon the masters for clever phrases and telling anecdotes, some of them somewhat arcane — like a reference to an address before the French Academy by the eighteenth-century naturalist Count Georges-Louis Leclerc de Buffon. In a section on figures of speech, she includes mention of some, like metonymy and litotes, that would stymie many English majors.

Making Connections: Evaluations in A Writer's Reader

To be effective, evaluating — the highest level of critical thinking — must be based on sound comprehension and analysis. Several writers in *A Writer's Reader* successfully evaluate ideas, people, and media. They establish criteria for their evaluation and end by expressing their personal opinions based on the evaluation. Columnist Ellen Goodman, in "How to Zap Violence on TV" (p. 613), evaluates the portrayal of violence on television and the usefulness of the V-chip as a means of controlling children's access to programs with destructive plots. She concludes that lack of creativity is an even bigger problem than violence in television programming. In "Six Clicks from Death" (p. 646), editor and author Cynthia Joyce evaluates the usefulness of the Internet as a source for medical information and concludes that "too much information can sometimes be a real health hazard."

Just as Goodman, Joyce, Michiko Kakutani (p. 246), and Geoffrey Fallon (p. 248) use evaluation for writing from their individual perspectives, so do writer Emily Prager, "Our Barbies, Ourselves" (p. 537); horror writer Stephen King, "Why We Crave Horror Movies" (p. 593); editor and writer Veronica Chambers, "The Myth of Cinderella" (p. 603); conservative thinker James Q. Wilson, "In Praise of Asphalt Nation" (p. 606); and editor Leonce Gaiter, "Is the Web Too Cool for Blacks?" (p. 642). As you read these essays, consider the role that evaluation plays in them. For each essay, answer the following questions:

1. Do you consider the writer qualified to evaluate the subject he or she chose? What biases and prejudices might the writer bring to the evaluation?

2. What criteria for evaluation does the writer establish? Are these reasonable standards for evaluating the subject?
3. Is the writer's assessment of the subject clear?
4. Does the writer provide sufficient evidence to convince you of his or her evaluation?

Part Three

Special Writing Situations

Introduction

Most of the writing you'll do while you are in college will fall into one of the categories covered in the preceding eleven chapters. However, three common situations that you're likely to encounter will call for specialized forms of writing — writing about literature, writing for assessment, and writing for business. In the next three chapters you'll find suggestions for responding to each of these special writing situations.

In college English and humanities classes you'll write papers about literature. You may need to write a personal response, a synopsis, a paraphrase, a review, or — most common in college — a literary analysis. Professors will often ask you to write literary analyses and comparison and contrast papers about literature because they reveal how well you understand the literature; how perceptively you use critical thinking skills (see Part Two); and how effectively you adapt the strategies for planning, drafting, developing, and revising (see Part Four). To write an effective analysis, you must thoroughly analyze the piece of literature, develop a coherent interpretation, and present your interpretation persuasively. You may need to write a synopsis or paraphrase as an intermediate step in one of these two complex assignments, either because the professor requires it or because you find it useful. Chapter 12 provides guidance for writing literary analyses, comparison and contrast papers, synopses, and paraphrases about literature.

Furthermore, as a student you'll often find yourself in testing situations in which you must demonstrate your knowledge of a subject as well as your proficiency in writing; more than likely, you will be constrained by a time limit. The writing in these situations usually takes the form of essay examinations, short-answer quizzes, impromptu themes, and writing portfolios. To do this type of writing well requires you to use special skills — reading carefully, planning globally, composing quickly, and proofreading independently. Chapter 13 gives valuable tips on how not only to survive but also to thrive on such writings.

Finally, sometimes you'll want to respond in writing to a business situation. You may need to write a business letter to an organization with which you've had business dealings, perhaps to straighten out a bill or lodge a complaint. You may need to write memos and e-mail as part of a job that you hold while you are attending school. And you may need to write a résumé and letter of application to a company when you apply for a new position. Because time means money, business writing is concise and direct. Chapter 14 offers recommendations and samples for business writing, whether personal or corporate.

Chapter 12

Writing about Literature

In your college career you might take one or more literature courses: literary study has long been recognized as an essential in most college curricula. Reading and understanding a literary masterpiece offer you rewards beyond those measurable in dollars and cents.

As countless readers know, reading fiction gives pleasure and delight. Whether you are reading Dante or Danielle Steele, Stephen King or Stephen Crane, you can be swept up into an imaginative world where you can do and see things you can't in real life. You're held spellbound as you journey to distant lands and meet exotic people.

Literature also increases your understanding of life. Late-nineteenth-century American writer and editor William Dean Howells said that literature "widens the bounds of human sympathy"; contemporary novelist Ursula K. Le Guin, that it deepens "your understanding of your world, and your fellow men, and your own feelings, and your destiny." As you read, you meet characters similar to and different from yourself, and you encounter familiar as well as new ideas and ways of viewing life. By sharing the experiences of literary characters, you gain insight into your own problems and become more tolerant of others.

More often than not, a writing assignment in a literature or humanities course will require you to read a literary work (short story, novel, play, or poem) closely, divide it into its elements, explain its meaning, and support your interpretation with evidence from the work. The analysis is not an end in itself; the purpose is to illuminate the meaning of the work, to help you and others understand it better. You may also be asked to evaluate what you read and to compare and contrast individual selections with other pieces you have read.

Reading closely a work such as Shakespeare's great play *Hamlet* or Kate Chopin's classic American novel *The Awakening,* Shirley Jackson's short story "The Lottery" or Amy Lowell's poem "Patterns" will help you develop critical thinking skills useful in the academic world as well as in the job market. As you develop these skills, you will truly become a *critic* in the sense of the Greek *kritikos,* "one who can judge and discern." (See "Introduction: Critical Strategies for Reading and Writing," p. 93.)

There are certain basic ways of writing about literature, each with its own purpose. We emphasize the *literary analysis,* which requires you to analyze, interpret, and evaluate what you read. We also offer an example of comparing and contrasting, another basic way of writing about literature, and examples of synopsis and paraphrase, two strategies for writing about literature. Assignments throughout the chapter give you practice with these basic forms. We also provide an introduction to literary terms.

Literary Analysis

LEARNING FROM OTHER WRITERS

In a composition course, Jonathan Burns was given an assignment to write a literary analysis of "The Lottery," a short story by the American writer Shirley Jackson. "The Lottery" caused a sensation when it was published in the *New Yorker* in 1948. In this story, Shirley Jackson simultaneously conceals and reveals meaning. Students, teachers, and professional critics have offered varied interpretations of the work. Read it with care; try to figure out what it means. Then read on to see what Jonathan Burns made of it.

Shirley Jackson   The Lottery

The morning of June 27th was clear and sunny, with the fresh warmth of   1
a full-summer day; the flowers were blossoming profusely and the grass was richly green. The people of the village began to gather in the square, between the post office and the bank, around ten o'clock; in some towns there were so many people that the lottery took two days and had to be started on June 26th, but in this village, where there were only about three hundred people, the whole lottery took less than two hours, so it could begin at ten o'clock in the morning and still be through in time to allow the villagers to get home for noon dinner.

The children assembled first, of course. School was recently over for the   2
summer, and the feeling of liberty sat uneasily on most of them; they tended to gather together quietly for a while before they broke into boisterous play, and their talk was still of the classroom and the teacher, of books and reprimands. Bobby Martin had already stuffed his pockets full of stones, and the other boys soon followed his example, selecting the smoothest and roundest stones; Bobby and Harry Jones and Dickie Delacroix — the villagers pronounced his name "Dellacroy" — eventually made a great pile of stones in

one corner of the square and guarded it against the raids of the other boys. The girls stood aside, talking among themselves, looking over their shoulders at the boys, and the very small children rolled in the dust or clung to the hands of their older brothers or sisters.

Soon the men began to gather, surveying their own children, speaking of 3 planting and rain, tractors and taxes. They stood together, away from the pile of stones in the corner, and their jokes were quiet and they smiled rather than laughed. The women, wearing faded house dresses and sweaters, came shortly after their menfolk. They greeted one another and exchanged bits of gossip as they went to join their husbands. Soon the women, standing by their husbands, began to call to their children, and the children came reluctantly, having to be called four or five times. Bobby Martin ducked under his mother's grasping hand and ran, laughing, back to the pile of stones. His father spoke up sharply, and Bobby came quickly and took his place between his father and his oldest brother.

The lottery was conducted — as were the square dances, the teenage club, 4 the Halloween program — by Mr. Summers, who had time and energy to devote to civic activities. He was a round-faced, jovial man and he ran the coal business, and people were sorry for him, because he had no children and his wife was a scold. When he arrived in the square, carrying the black wooden box, there was a murmur of conversation among the villagers, and he waved and called, "Little late today, folks." The postmaster, Mr. Graves, followed him, carrying a three-legged stool, and the stool was put in the center of the square and Mr. Summers set the black box down on it. The villagers kept their distance, leaving a space between themselves and the stool, and when Mr. Summers said, "Some of you fellows want to give me a hand?" there was a hesitation before two men, Mr. Martin and his oldest son, Baxter, came forward to hold the box steady on the stool while Mr. Summers stirred up the papers inside it.

The original paraphernalia for the lottery had been lost long ago, and the 5 black box now resting on the stool had been put into use even before Old Man Warner, the oldest man in town, was born. Mr. Summers spoke frequently to the villagers about making a new box, but no one liked to upset even as much tradition as was represented by the black box. There was a story that the present box had been made with some pieces of the box that had preceded it, the one that had been constructed when the first people settled down to make a village here. Every year, after the lottery, Mr. Summers began talking again about a new box, but every year the subject was allowed to fade off without anything's being done. The black box grew shabbier each year; by now it was no longer completely black but splintered badly along one side to show the original wood color, and in some places faded or stained.

Mr. Martin and his oldest son, Baxter, held the black box securely on the 6 stool until Mr. Summers had stirred the papers thoroughly with his hand. Because so much of the ritual had been forgotten or discarded, Mr. Summers had been successful in having slips of paper substituted for the chips of wood that had been used for generations. Chips of wood, Mr. Summers had argued, had been all very well when the village was tiny, but now that the population was more than three hundred and likely to keep on growing, it was necessary to use something that would fit more easily into the black box. The night before the lottery, Mr. Summers and Mr. Graves made up the slips of paper and put them in the box, and it was then taken to the safe of Mr. Summers's coal company and locked up until Mr. Summers was ready to take it to the square next morning. The rest of the year, the box was put away, sometimes one place, sometimes another; it had spent one year in Mr. Graves's barn and another year underfoot in the post office, and sometimes it was set on a shelf in the Martin grocery and left there.

There was a great deal of fussing to be done before Mr. Summers declared   7
the lottery open. There were the lists to make up — of heads of families, heads of households in each family, members of each household in each family. There was the proper swearing-in of Mr. Summers by the postmaster, as the official of the lottery; at one time, some people remembered, there had been a recital of some sort, performed by the official of the lottery, a perfunctory, tuneless chant that had been rattled off duly each year; some people believed that the official of the lottery used to stand just so when he said or sang it, others believed that he was supposed to walk among the people, but years and years ago this part of the ritual had been allowed to lapse. There had been, also, a ritual salute, which the official of the lottery had had to use in addressing each person who came up to draw from the box, but this also had changed with time, until now it was felt necessary only for the official to speak to each person approaching. Mr. Summers was very good at all this; in his clean white shirt and blue jeans, with one hand resting carelessly on the black box, he seemed very proper and important as he talked interminably to Mr. Graves and the Martins.

Just as Mr. Summers finally left off talking and turned to the assembled   8
villagers, Mrs. Hutchinson came hurriedly along the path to the square, her sweater thrown over her shoulders, and slid into place in the back of the crowd. "Clean forgot what day it was," she said to Mrs. Delacroix, who stood next to her, and they both laughed softly. "Thought my old man was out back stacking wood," Mrs. Hutchinson went on, "and then I looked out the window and the kids was gone, and then I remembered it was the twenty-seventh and came a-running." She dried her hands on her apron, and Mrs. Delacroix said, "You're in time, though. They're still talking away up there."

Mrs. Hutchinson craned her neck to see through the crowd and found her   9
husband and children standing near the front. She tapped Mrs. Delacroix on the arm as a farewell and began to make her way through the crowd. The people separated good-humoredly to let her through; two or three people said, in voices just loud enough to be heard across the crowd, "Here comes your Missus, Hutchinson," and "Bill, she made it after all." Mrs. Hutchinson reached her husband, and Mr. Summers, who had been waiting, said cheerfully, "Thought we were going to have to get on without you, Tessie." Mrs.

Hutchinson said, grinning, "Wouldn't have me leave m'dishes in the sink, now, would you, Joe?" and soft laughter ran through the crowd as the people stirred back into position after Mrs. Hutchinson's arrival.

"Well, now," Mr. Summers said soberly, "guess we better get started, get 10 this over with, so's we can go back to work. Anybody ain't here?"

"Dunbar," several people said. "Dunbar, Dunbar." 11

Mr. Summers consulted his list. "Clyde Dunbar," he said. "That's right. 12 He's broke his leg, hasn't he? Who's drawing for him?"

"Me, I guess," a women said, and Mr. Summers turned to look at her. 13 "Wife draws for her husband," Mr. Summers said. "Don't you have a grown boy to do it for you, Janey?" Although Mr. Summers and everyone else in the village knew the answer perfectly well, it was the business of the official of the lottery to ask such questions formally. Mr. Summers waited with an expression of polite interest while Mrs. Dunbar answered.

"Horace's not but sixteen yet," Mrs. Dunbar said regretfully. "Guess I gotta 14 fill in for the old man this year."

"Right," Mr. Summers said. He made a note on the list he was holding. 15 Then he asked, "Watson boy drawing this year?"

A tall boy in the crowd raised his hand. "Here," he said. "I'm drawing for 16 m'mother and me." He blinked his eyes nervously and ducked his head as several voices in the crowd said things like "Good fellow, Jack," and "Glad to see your mother's got a man to do it."

"Well," Mr. Summers said, "guess that's everyone. Old Man Warner make it?" 17

"Here," a voice said, and Mr. Summers nodded. 18

A sudden hush fell on the crowd as Mr. Summers cleared his throat and 19 looked at the list. "All ready?" he called. "Now, I'll read the names — heads of families first — and the men come up and take a paper out of the box. Keep the paper folded in your hand without looking at it until everyone has had a turn. Everything clear?"

The people had done it so many times that they only half listened to the 20 directions; most of them were quiet, wetting their lips, not looking around. Then Mr. Summers raised one hand high and said, "Adams." A man disengaged himself from the crowd and came forward. "Hi, Steve," Mr. Summers said, and Mr. Adams said, "Hi, Joe." They grinned at one another humorlessly and nervously. Then Mr. Adams reached into the black box and took out a folded paper. He held it firmly by one corner as he turned and went hastily back to his place in the crowd, where he stood a little apart from his family, not looking down at his hand.

"Allen," Mr. Summers said. "Anderson. . . . Bentham." 21

"Seems like there's no time at all between lotteries anymore," Mrs. 22 Delacroix said to Mrs. Graves in the back row. "Seems like we got through with the last one only last week."

"Time sure goes fast," Mrs. Graves said. 23

"Clark. . . . Delacroix." 24

"There goes my old man," Mrs. Delacroix said. She held her breath while   25
her husband went forward.

"Dunbar," Mr. Summers said, and Mrs. Dunbar went steadily to the box   26
while one of the women said, "Go on, Janey," and another said, "There she goes."

"We're next," Mrs. Graves said. She watched while Mr. Graves came   27
around from the side of the box, greeted Mr. Summers gravely, and selected a
slip of paper from the box. By now, all through the crowd there were men
holding the small folded papers in their large hands, turning them over and
over nervously. Mrs. Dunbar and her two sons stood together, Mrs. Dunbar
holding the slip of paper.

"Harburt. . . . Hutchinson."   28

"Get up there, Bill," Mrs. Hutchinson said, and the people near her   29
laughed.

"Jones."   30

"They do say," Mr. Adams said to Old Man Warner, who stood next to   31
him, "that over in the north village they're talking of giving up the lottery."

Old Man Warner snorted. "Pack of crazy fools," he said. "Listening to the   32
young folks, nothing's good enough for *them*. Next thing you know, they'll be
wanting to go back to living in caves, nobody work anymore, live *that* way for
a while. Used to be a saying about 'Lottery in June, corn be heavy soon.' First
thing you know, we'd all be eating stewed chickweed and acorns. There's *always* been a lottery," he added petulantly. "Bad enough to see young Joe Summers up there joking with everybody."

"Some places have already quit lotteries," Mrs. Adams said.   33

"Nothing but trouble in *that*," Old Man Warner said stoutly. "Pack of   34
young fools."

"Martin." And Bobby Martin watched his father go forward. "Overdyke. . . .   35
Percy."

"I wish they'd hurry," Mrs. Dunbar said to her older son. "I wish they'd   36
hurry."

"They're almost through," her son said.   37

"You get ready to run tell Dad," Mrs. Dunbar said.   38

Mr. Summers called his own name and then stepped forward precisely   39
and selected a slip from the box. Then he called, "Warner."

"Seventy-seventh year I been in the lottery," Old Man Warner said as he   40
went through the crowd. "Seventy-seventh time."

"Watson." The tall boy came awkwardly through the crowd. Someone   41
said, "Don't be nervous, Jack," and Mr. Summers said, "Take your time, son."

"Zanini."   42

After that, there was a long pause, a breathless pause, until Mr. Summers,   43
holding his slip of paper in the air, said, "All right, fellows." For a minute, no
one moved, and then all the slips of paper were opened. Suddenly, all the
women began to speak at once, saying, "Who is it?" "Who's got it?" "Is it the
Dunbars?" "Is it the Watsons?" Then the voices began to say, "It's Hutchinson.
It's Bill." "Bill Hutchinson's got it."

"Go tell your father," Mrs. Dunbar said to her older son. 44

People began to look around to see the Hutchinsons. Bill Hutchinson 45
was standing quiet, staring down at the paper in his hand. Suddenly, Tessie
Hutchinson shouted to Mr. Summers, "You didn't give him time enough to
take any paper he wanted. I saw you. It wasn't fair!"

"Be a good sport, Tessie," Mrs. Delacroix called, and Mrs. Graves said, "All 46
of us took the same chance."

"Shut up, Tessie," Bill Hutchinson said. 47

"Well, everyone," Mr. Summers said, "that was done pretty fast, and now 48
we've got to be hurrying a little more to get done in time." He consulted his
next list. "Bill," he said, "you draw for the Hutchinson family. You got any
other households in the Hutchinsons?"

"There's Don and Eva," Mrs. Hutchinson yelled. "Make *them* take their 49
chance!"

"Daughters draw with their husbands' families, Tessie," Mr. Summers said 50
gently. "You know that as well as anyone else."

"It wasn't *fair*," Tessie said. 51

"I guess not, Joe," Bill Hutchinson said regretfully. "My daughter draws 52
with her husband's family, that's only fair. And I've got no other family except
the kids."

"Then, as far as drawing for families is concerned, it's you," Mr. Summers 53
said in explanation, "and as far as drawing for households is concerned, that's
you, too. Right?"

"Right," Bill Hutchinson said. 54

"How many kids, Bill?" Mr. Summers asked formally. 55

"Three," Bill Hutchinson said. "There's Bill, Jr., and Nancy, and little 56
Dave. And Tessie and me."

"All right, then," Mr. Summers said. "Harry, you got their tickets back?" 57

Mr. Graves nodded and held up the slips of paper. "Put them in the box, 58
then," Mr. Summers directed. "Take Bill's and put it in."

"I think we ought to start over," Mrs. Hutchinson said, as quietly as she 59
could. "I tell you it wasn't *fair*. You didn't give him time enough to choose.
*Every*body saw that."

Mr. Graves had selected the five slips and put them in the box, and he 60
dropped all the papers but those onto the ground, where the breeze caught
them and lifted them off.

"Listen, everybody," Mrs. Hutchinson was saying to the people around her. 61

"Ready, Bill?" Mr. Summers asked, and Bill Hutchinson, with one quick 62
glance around at his wife and children, nodded.

"Remember," Mr. Summers said, "take the slips and keep them folded until 63
each person has taken one. Harry, you help little Dave." Mr. Graves took the hand
of the little boy, who came willingly with him up to the box. "Take a paper out of
the box, Davy," Mr. Summers said. Davy put his hand into the box and laughed.
"Take just *one* paper," Mr. Summers said. "Harry, you hold it for him." Mr. Graves
took the child's hand and removed the folded paper from the tight fist and held
it while little Dave stood next to him and looked up at him wonderingly.

"Nancy next," Mr. Summers said. Nancy was twelve, and her school   64
friends breathed heavily as she went forward, switching her skirt, and took a
slip daintily from the box. "Bill, Jr.," Mr. Summers said, and Billy, his face red
and his feet overlarge, nearly knocked the box over as he got a paper out.
"Tessie," Mr. Summers said. She hesitated for a minute, looking around defiantly, and then set her lips and went up to the box. She snatched a paper out
and held it behind her.

"Bill," Mr. Summers said, and Bill Hutchinson reached into the box and   65
felt around, bringing his hand out at last with the slip of paper in it.

The crowd was quiet. A girl whispered, "I hope it's not Nancy," and the   66
sound of the whisper reached the edges of the crowd.

"It's not the way it used to be," Old Man Warner said clearly. "People ain't   67
the way they used to be."

"All right," Mr. Summers said. "Open the papers. Harry, you open little   68
Dave's."

Mr. Graves opened the slip of paper and there was a general sigh through   69
the crowd as he held it up and everyone could see that it was blank. Nancy and
Bill, Jr., opened theirs at the same time, and both beamed and laughed, turning around to the crowd and holding their slips of paper above their heads.

"Tessie," Mr. Summers said. There was a pause, and then Mr. Summers   70
looked at Bill Hutchinson, and Bill unfolded his paper and showed it. It was
blank.

"It's Tessie," Mr. Summers said, and his voice was hushed. "Show us her   71
paper, Bill."

Bill Hutchinson went over to his wife and forced the slip of paper out of   72
her hand. It had a black spot on it, the black spot Mr. Summers had made the
night before with the heavy pencil in the coal-company office. Bill Hutchinson held it up, and there was a stir in the crowd.

"All right, folks," Mr. Summers said. "Let's finish quickly."   73

Although the villagers had forgotten the ritual and lost the original black   74
box, they still remembered to use stones. The pile of stones the boys had
made earlier was ready; there were stones on the ground with the blowing
scraps of paper that had come out of the box. Mrs. Delacroix selected a stone
so large she had to pick it up with both hands and turned to Mrs. Dunbar.
"Come on," she said. "Hurry up."

Mrs. Dunbar had small stones in both hands, and she said, gasping for   75
breath, "I can't run at all. You'll have to go ahead and I'll catch up with you."

The children had stones already, and someone gave little Davy Hutchin-   76
son a few pebbles.

Tessie Hutchinson was in the center of a cleared space by now, and she   77
held her hands out desperately as the villagers moved in on her. "It isn't fair,"
she said. A stone hit her on the side of the head.

Old Man Warner was saying, "Come on, come on, everyone." Steve   78
Adams was in the front of the crowd of villagers, with Mrs. Graves beside him.

"It isn't fair, it isn't right," Mrs. Hutchinson screamed, and then they were   79
upon her.

Questions to Start You Thinking

Meaning

1. Where does this story take place? When?

2. How does this lottery differ from what we usually think of as a lottery? Why would people conduct a lottery such as this?

3. What does this story mean to you?

Writing Strategies

4. Can you see and hear the people in the story? Do they seem real, or fantastic? Who is the most memorable character to you?

5. Are the events believable? Does the ending shock you? Is it believable?

6. Is this story realistic, or is Jackson using these events to represent something else?

As Jonathan Burns read "The Lottery," he was carried along quickly to the startling ending. After the immediate impact of the story wore off, Burns reread it, this time to savor some of the details he had missed during his first reading. Then, knowing he had to write a literary analysis for his composition course, he wrote a summary or *synopsis* of "The Lottery" to get a clear fix on the literal events in the story. (We reprint his synopsis on p. 307.)

But Burns knew that he could not write a good analysis without reading the story repeatedly and closely, marking key points in the text. Students who read a complex work of literature only once, thinking that is enough, are mistaken. Even if you are trying to understand only the literal level — what happens in a story or what a poet says — you'll need to read the work more than once. If your purpose is to comprehend, interpret, and evaluate, you'll find that several close readings are necessary.

For close critical reading, read the text *at least* three times, each time for a different reason. In all readings, read purposefully.

Read to comprehend. Read for the literal meaning, an overall idea of what the work contains — what happens to whom, where, when, and why. Get all the facts straight — the setting, the events of the plot, the characters and what they say and do. Be sure you understand all the vocabulary, especially in titles and in poems.

Read to interpret. Read to understand the meaning of the story or poem beyond the literal level. Read between the lines. Mark the sections and analyze the parts. Read with an eye for what you seek in the work — theme, character, style, symbol, form. Read with pencil in hand, and make notes. Is there an especially hard part? Try putting it into your own words. Is it a difficult piece? Try reading it aloud to yourself; that may help you make sense of it. What does the literary work mean? What does it imply? What does it help you understand about the human condition? What insights can you apply to your own life?

Read to evaluate. Read to assess the soundness and plausibility of what the author says. Are the words appropriate for the purpose and audience? What is the author's tone? Is it appropriate for the audience? Does the author achieve his or her purpose? Is it a worthwhile purpose? Synthesize what you have discovered from your analysis through all your readings in order to determine the effectiveness and significance of the piece of literature. As you are evaluating, be sure that you use definite criteria beyond personal or whimsical likes and dislikes.

Later, as you draft your literary analysis, you will discover, just as Jonathan Burns did, that you have to reread specific sections over and over to check your interpretations and to be sure the evidence from the story supports your claims.

Jonathan Burns knew he had to analyze the important elements in "The Lottery" to understand the story well enough to write about it. He thought about what he had learned in class about the different elements of a literary work and the terms used to describe them. (For a description of the basic elements of literature, see the glossary on pp. 284–88.) His analysis of these elements — setting, character, tone, and others — helped him think about a topic for his paper, some point on which he could focus his thoughts and comments. He immediately thought of the undertone of violence in the story but decided that the undertone was so subtle that it would be difficult to write about it. Then he considered writing about the characters in the story. Mr. Summers and Old Man Warner were especially memorable. And then there was Tessie Hutchinson; he could hear her screams as the stones hit her. But he decided not to write about the characters because he could not think of much to say about them except that they were memorable, and he knew that that was too vague a statement. He considered other elements — language and symbols, foreshadowing and ambiguity — and dismissed each in turn. All of a sudden he hit on the surprise ending. How did Jackson manipulate all the details to generate such a shock?

To begin to focus his thinking, he brainstormed titles having to do with the ending, some serious, others flippant: Death Comes as a Surprise; The Unsuspected Finish; Patience of the Devil; An Inquiry into the Implementation of Pure Reason; The Wrath of Grapes; Bob Dylan Was Right. He chose the straightforward title "The Hidden Truth."

After reviewing his notes from his analysis of the story, Burns realized that Jackson uses characterization, symbolism, and ambiguous description to prepare readers for the ending. Writing about how the author shocks readers at the end of the story would allow him to discuss several elements that interested him, and focusing on the techniques she uses to build up to the ending would help him unify the aspects of his interpretation.

He listed details from the story under three headings — characters, symbols, and language. Following is the informal plan he made for his paper:

Title: *The Hidden Truth*
Thesis: *In "The Lottery" Shirley Jackson effectively crafts a shock ending.*
1. *Characterization that contributes to the shock ending*
    —The children of the village
    —The adults of the village
    —Conversations among the villagers

  2. *Symbols that contribute to the shock ending*
     —*The stones*
     —*The black box*
  3. *Language that contributes to the shock ending*
     —*The word "lottery"*
     —*Comments*
        —*"clean forgot"*
        —*"wish they'd hurry"*
        —*"It isn't fair."*
     —*Actions*
        —*Relief*
        —*Suspense*

Then he drafted the following introduction:

> Unsuspecting, the reader follows Shirley Jackson's softly flowing tale of a rural community's timeless ritual, the lottery. Awareness of what is at stake--the savage murder of one random member--comes slow, only becoming clear toward the last fraction of the story. No sooner does the realization set in than the story is over. It is a shock ending.
>
> What created so great a shock as the reader experiences after reading "The Lottery"? Shirley Jackson takes great care in producing this effect, using elements such as language, symbolism, and characterization to lure the reader into not anticipating what is to come.

With his synopsis (p. 307), his plan, his copy of the story, and this beginning of a draft, he revised the introduction and wrote the following essay.

STUDENT ESSAY

Jonathan Burns   ## The Hidden Truth: An Analysis of Shirley Jackson's "The Lottery"

It is as if the first stone thrown strikes the reader as well as Mrs. Hutchinson. And even though there were signs of the stoning to come, somehow the reader is taken by surprise at Tessie's violent death. What factors contribute to the

shock ending to "The Lottery"? On closer examination of the
story, the reader finds that through all events leading up to
the ending, Shirley Jackson has used unsuspicious character-
izations, unobtrusive symbolism, and ambiguous descriptions
to achieve so sudden an impact.

By all appearances, the village is a normal place with
normal people. Children arrive at the scene first, with
school just over for the summer, talking of teachers and
books, not of the fact that someone will die today (272).
And as the adults show up, their actions are just as stereotypical: the men talk of farming and taxes, while the women
gossip (273). No trace of hostility, no sense of dread in
anyone: death seems very far away here.

2

The conversations between the villagers are no more ominous. As the husbands draw slips of paper for their families,
the villagers make apparently everyday comments about the
seemingly ordinary event of the lottery. Mr. Summers is regarded as a competent and respected figure, despite the fact
that his wife is "a scold" (273). Old Man Warner brags about
how many lotteries he's seen and rambles on criticizing other
towns that have given up the tradition (276). The characters'
comments show the crowd to be more a closely knit community
than a murderous mob.

3

The symbols of "The Lottery" seem equally ordinary. The
stones collected by the boys (272) are unnoticed by the
adults and thus seem a trivial detail. The reader thinks of
the "great pile" (272) as children's entertainment, like a
stack of imaginary coins rather than an arsenal. Ironically,
no stones are ever thrown during the children's play, and no
violence is seen in the pile of stones.

4

Similarly, Jackson describes the box and its history in
great detail, but there seems nothing unusual about it. It is
just another everyday object, stored away in the post office
or on a shelf in the grocery (274). Every other day of the
year, the box is in plain view but goes virtually unnoticed.
The only indication that the box has lethal consequences is
that it is painted black (273), yet this is an ambiguous detail, as a black box can also signify mystery or magic, mysti-
cal forces that are sometimes thought to exist in any lottery.

5

In her ambiguous descriptions, Jackson refers regularly   6
to the village's lottery and emphasizes it as a central ritual for the people. The word lottery itself is ironic, as it
typically implies a winning of some kind, like a raffle or
sweepstakes. It is paralleled to square dances and to the
teenage club, all under the direction of Mr. Summers (272),
activities people look forward to. There is no implied difference between the occurrences of this day and the festivities of Halloween: according to Jackson, they are all merely
"civic activities" (272). Equally ambiguous are the people's
emotions: some of the villagers are casual, such as Mrs.
Hutchinson, who arrives late because she "clean forgot" what
day it is (274), and some are anxious, such as Mrs. Dunbar,
who repeats to her son, "I wish they'd hurry," without any
sign of the cause of her anxiety (276). With these descriptive details the reader finds no threat or malice in the villagers, only vague expectation and congeniality.

Even when it becomes clear that the lottery is something   7
no one wants to win, Jackson presents only a vague sense of
sadness and mild protest. The crowd is relieved that the
youngest of the Hutchinsons, Davy, doesn't draw the fatal
slip of paper (278). One girl whispers that she hopes it
isn't Nancy (278), and when the Hutchinson children discover
they aren't the winners, they beam with joy and proudly display their blank slips (278). It's like a theatrical scene,
with growing suspense and excitement apparent only when the
victim is close to being identified. And when Tessie is revealed to be the winner of the lottery (278), she merely
holds her hands out "desperately" and repeats, "It isn't
fair'" (278).

With a blend of character, symbolism, and description,   8
Shirley Jackson paints an overall portrait of a gentle-
seeming rural community, apparently no different from any
other. The tragic end is sudden only because there is no
recognition of violence beforehand, despite the fact that
Jackson has provided the reader with plenty of clues in the
ample details about the lottery and the people. It is a
haunting discovery that the story ends in death, even though
such is the truth in the everyday life of all people.

Questions to Start You Thinking

Meaning

1. What is Burns's thesis?

2. What major points does he use to support his thesis? What specific elements of the story does he include as evidence to support his interpretation?

Writing Strategies

3. How does this essay differ from a synopsis, a summary of the events of the plot? (For a synopsis of "The Lottery," see p. 307.)

4. Does Jonathan Burns focus on the technique of the short story or on its theme?

5. Is his introduction effective? Compare and contrast it with the first introduction he drafted (p. 281). What did he change? Which version do you prefer?

6. Why does he explain characterization first, symbolism second, and description last? Would discussing these elements in a different order have made much difference in his essay?

7. Is his conclusion effective?

8. How does he tie his ideas together as he moves from paragraph to paragraph? How does he keep the focus on idea and technique instead of plot?

ANALYZING THE ELEMENTS OF LITERATURE: A GLOSSARY OF TERMS

Every field — scuba diving, football, gourmet cooking, engineering, business — has its own vocabulary. If you are going to play football, you should know the difference between a blitz and a quarterback sneak. Before you start cooking, you'd better know the difference between basting and shirring. Literary analysis is no different. Before you can analyze and interpret a piece of literature or write a successful literary analysis, you must be familiar with the elements of fiction, poetry, and drama and with the specialized terms critics and scholars use to talk about those elements. We list a few of the elements here — a handy glossary of terms that you can use to discuss any piece of literature.

Setting.   Setting is the time and place where events occur. The season, the weather, the atmosphere, and people in the background may be part of the setting. Jonathan Burns recognized that Shirley Jackson describes the setting in the first sentence of "The Lottery": "The morning of June 27th was clear and sunny, with the fresh warmth of a full-summer day; the flowers were blossoming profusely and the grass was richly green" (paragraph 1). That description is precise: Burns could almost feel the sun and smell the flowers. But he did not know the period of time — eighteenth century, nineteenth century, twentieth century? And he did not know where Jackson's village is located.

Characters.   Characters are imagined people. The author lets you know what they are like through their actions, speech, thoughts, attitudes, and background. Sometimes a writer also tells you about physical characteristics or names or relationships with other people.

Jonathan Burns reread the initial description of Mr. Summers: he "had time and energy to devote to civic activities. He was a round-faced, jovial man and he ran the coal business, and people were sorry for him, because he had no children and his wife was a scold" (paragraph 4). These details introduce this official of the lottery. Burns also learned about him through what he says: "'Little late today, folks'" (paragraph 4); "'Thought we were going to have to get on without you, Tessie'" (paragraph 9); "'Well, now, . . . guess we better get started, get this over with, so's we can go back to work'" (paragraph 10). Burns decided that Mr. Summers is in charge of the situation and doesn't want any slip-ups. What does Mr. Warner's speech in "The Lottery" tell you about him?

In addition, Burns learned about the characters through what they do, as when the Watson boy "blinked his eyes nervously and ducked his head" at the lottery (paragraph 16) or when the villagers "only half listened to the directions; most of them were quiet, wetting their lips, not looking around" (paragraph 20). What does Tessie do that gives you some insight into what she is like?

Plot.   Plot is the arrangement of the events of the story — what happens to whom, where, when, and why. If the events follow each other logically and if they are in keeping with what the author tells us about the characters, the plot is **plausible**, or believable. Although the ending of "The Lottery" at first shocked Burns, when he looked back through the story he found **foreshadowing**, hints that the author provides to help readers understand future events or twists in the plot. Looking back, Burns saw numerous clues that Tessie and the other villagers are nervous and hesitant about the lottery, not the usual reaction of people who expect someone to win a desirable prize of money, a car, or a vacation. See how many of these clues you can find.

The **protagonist,** or main character, is placed in a dramatic situation of **conflict** with some other person or group of people, the **antagonist.** In "The Lottery," Burns identified Tessie Hutchinson as the protagonist, the villagers as the antagonist, and the dramatic situation as Tessie's joining the group waiting for the lottery. **Conflict** consists of two forces attempting to conquer each other or resisting being conquered. It is not merely any vaguely defined turmoil in a story. **External conflicts** are conflicts outside an individual — between two people, between a person and a group (Tessie Hutchinson versus the villagers), between two groups (those who support the lottery and those who want to do away with it), or even between a character and his or her environment. **Internal conflicts** are those within an individual, between two opposing forces or desires (such as reason versus emotion or fear versus hope in each villager as the slips of paper are drawn). The **central conflict** of a story is the primary conflict for the protagonist that propels and accounts for the action of the story. What is the central conflict for Tessie?

Events of the plot **complicate** the conflict (Tessie arrives late, Bill Hutchinson draws the slip with the black spot for his family, Tessie claims it wasn't fair) and lead to the **climax,** the moment at which the outcome is inevitable (Tessie draws the slip with the black dot). The outcome itself is the **resolution,** or conclusion (the villagers stone Tessie Hutchinson). Some contemporary stories let events unfold without any apparent plot — action and change occur inside the characters.

Point of view.   Point of view is the angle from which a story is told. Who is the **narrator:** who tells the story? Through whose eyes are the events perceived? It might be the author, or it might be some character in the story. If a character, what part does he or she play, and what limits does the author place on that character's knowledge? Is the character aware of everything that is going on, or is he or she an outsider? Jonathan Burns tried to answer these questions to determine the point of view in "The Lottery." Three often-used points of view are those of a **first-person narrator** (*I*), a **third-person narrator** (*he* or *she*) who is a major participant in the action (often the protagonist), and a **third-person narrator** who is an observer, not a participant. The point of view may be **omniscient** (told through several characters' eyes), **limited omniscient** (told through one character's eyes), or **objective** (not told through any character's eyes). Burns realized that the point of view in "The Lottery" is that of a third-person objective narrator seemingly looking on and reporting what occurs without knowing what any of the characters are thinking. Why do you think Shirley Jackson chose this point of view for "The Lottery"? How would the story be different if it were told from Tessie's point of view? From Mr. Summers's? From Old Man Warner's?

Theme.   Theme is a main idea or insight a work contains. It is the author's observations about life, society, or human nature. Sometimes you can sum up a theme in a sentence: "Honesty is the best policy," "Human beings cannot live without illusion."

In a complex work, a theme may be implied and difficult to discern. Some works have more than one theme, and they may be stated in various ways. In an analysis of "The Lottery," the critics Cleanth Brooks and Robert Penn Warren assert, "We had best not try to restrict the meaning to some simple dogmatic statement. The author herself has been rather careful to allow a good deal of flexibility in our interpretation of the meaning, yet surely a general meaning does emerge."

To state a theme, find an important subject in the story and ask yourself, What does the author say about this subject? Details from the story itself should support your statement of theme, and your theme should account for all the details in the story. Be careful not to confuse a subject or topic of a story with a theme. To find the theme, Jonathan Burns first listed some of the important subjects of "The Lottery" — the unexpected, scapegoating, people's inhumanity to one another, outmoded rituals, victims of society, hostility, violence, death. What other subjects do you see in this story? Then Burns focused on Tessie's claim that the lottery wasn't fair and on the reaction of the Hutchinson children and the other villagers when the children did not draw the black dot, believing these to be significant occurrences leading to Jackson's meaning. From this interpretation, he stated the theme as "People are selfish, always looking out for number one."

Images.   Images are words or groups of words that refer to any sense experience:

Seeing. In his analysis of "The Lottery," Burns determined that Shirley Jackson uses many images of sight to help readers visualize what happens. The flowers bloom "profusely" and the grass is "richly green" (paragraph 1). Jackson describes the black box so precisely that Jonathan — and we — can see it clearly: it has grown "shabbier each year" and is "no longer completely black but splintered badly along one side to show the original wood color, and in some places faded or stained" (paragraph 5). When Mr. Graves drops all the slips of paper except the five for the Hutchinson family, "the breeze [catches] them and [lifts] them off" (paragraph 60).

Hearing. Burns found several images of sound in Jackson's story. The children engage in "boisterous play" (paragraph 2). When Mr. Summers arrives in the square, a "murmur of conversation" (paragraph 4) spreads among the villagers; a "hush" comes over the crowd when he speaks (paragraph 19). Nancy's friends breathe "heavily" as Nancy goes forward to draw a slip of paper (paragraph 64). Mrs. Dunbar is "gasping for breath" as the villagers move toward Tessie (paragraph 75).

Smelling. Although Jackson doesn't include any smells in her story, Burns himself imagined the musty smell of Mr. Summers's coal company where the black box was locked away the night before the lottery and Mr. Graves's barn where the dusty black box had been stored for a year since the last lottery.

Tasting. What do you think the villagers tasted when they wet their lips?

Touching. The stones the children gather are smooth and round (paragraph 2), and Tessie taps Mrs. Delacroix on the arm as she makes her way toward her husband (paragraph 9).

Feeling. Do the characters feel heat or cold, fear or joy, pain or thirst? Jonathan saw that the villagers feel "the fresh warmth of a full-summer day" (paragraph 1). Then he realized that because of the point of view in "The Lottery," he wasn't told much more about what the villagers feel.

Figures of speech.   Figures of speech are defined by William Thrall and Addison Hibbard as "intentional departures from the normal order, construction, or meaning of words in order to gain strength and freshness of expression" (*A Handbook to Literature*, 4th ed. [Indianapolis: Bobbs-Merrill, 1980]). Some of the most common types of figurative language are the

simile, a comparison using *like* or *as*; the **metaphor,** an implied comparison; and **personification,** the attribution of human qualities to inanimate or nonhuman creatures or things. Burns found several metaphors in "The Lottery." Bobby Martin, Harry Jones, and Dickie Delacroix *guard* their pile of stones "against the *raids* of the other boys" (paragraph 2). Tessie *cranes* her neck to find her family (paragraph 9). Old Man Warner says that the young people who want to give up the lottery will next " 'be wanting to go back to living in caves' " (paragraph 32).

Symbols.   Symbols are tangible objects or visible actions or characters that hint at meanings beyond themselves. In "The Lottery," a story filled with symbols, Burns decided that the black box suggests outdated tradition, the mysteriously inexplicable, the past, resistance to change, evil, cruelty, and more. What does Old Man Warner suggest? In this story, as in others, if you can identify a central symbol and figure out what it suggests, you are well on your way to stating the theme.

Irony.   Irony results from readers' sense of some discrepancy. A simple kind of irony, **sarcasm,** occurs when you say a thing but mean the opposite: "I just love scrubbing the floor" or "Of course, I don't want a Mercedes." In literature, an **ironic situation** sets up a wry contrast or incongruity. In "The Lottery," actions of evil cruelty and horror take place on a bright sunny June day in an ordinary village. **Ironic dialogue** occurs when a character says one thing but the audience or reader is aware of another meaning. When someone mentions that some people in the north village are talking of giving up the lottery, Old Man Warner snorts, " 'Next thing you know, they'll be wanting to go back to living in caves, nobody work anymore, live *that* way for a while. . . . First thing you know, we'd all be eating stewed chickweed and acorns" (paragraph 32). He implies that doing away with the lottery would cause the villagers to return to a more primitive way of life. His comment is ironic because the reader is aware that this lottery is a primitive ritual. A story has an **ironic point of view** when we sense a difference between the author and the character through whose eyes the story is perceived or between the author and the narrator. Burns realized that Shirley Jackson does not condone the actions of the villagers, no matter what the reason. Find some other ironic events and comments in this story.

As you read literary criticism and discuss literature in your classes, you will discover other literary terms, but the basic ones listed here give you a foundation for analyzing literature.

LEARNING BY WRITING

The Assignment: Analyzing a Literary Work.   A literary critic analyzes, interprets, and evaluates a work of literature. The critic sees and understands deeply not because he or she has some special inspiration or power but because he or she has studied the piece of writing very carefully. For this assignment, you are to be a critic — analyzing, interpreting, and evaluating a literary selection for your classmates. You will deepen their understanding because you will have devoted time and effort to digging out the meaning and testing it with evidence from the work itself. Even if they too have studied the work carefully, you will try to convince them that your interpretation is valid.

Write an essay interpreting one or more aspects of a literary work that intrigues you or that you think expresses a worthwhile meaning. Probably your instructor will want to approve your selection. After careful analysis of the literary work, you will become the expert critic, explaining the meaning you discern, supporting your interpretation with evidence from the work itself as well as from your own experience, and evaluating the effectiveness of the literary elements used by the author and the significance of the theme. You may draw from any of your four resources — recall, observation, conversation, imagination. Probably you'll use several critical thinking skills — analyzing the parts of the work; comparing and contrasting characters in the story, or comparing and contrasting the work with other works you know; identifying causal relationships in the action of the work; taking a stand on your interpretation; proposing a solution to a puzzling part of the work or to a problem posed by the author (perhaps as a theme); and evaluating the quality of the work. Refer to Parts One and Two of this book to remind yourself about these resources and critical thinking skills.

You cannot attempt to include everything about the work in your paper, so you should focus on one element (such as character, setting, or theme) or the interrelationship of two or three elements (as Jonathan Burns did when he analyzed characterization, symbolism, and ambiguity in his interpretation of the surprise ending of "The Lottery"). The purpose of your essay is to help your classmates — who have read but not studied the selection as thoroughly as you have — to understand the meaning of the work and to gain insight into their own lives just as you have through your careful study.

Your assignment is to analyze, to interpret, and to evaluate the work, not just to retell the story. Although a summary, or *synopsis,* of the plot and characterization is a good beginning point for your ideas, it is not a satisfactory literary analysis. Notice, for example, how Jonathan Burns uses details from the plot in the second and third paragraphs of his essay (282) but then moves beyond events of the plot to an analysis of character, symbol, and description.

Here are instances of college writers who successfully responded to this type of assignment:

A man who was a musician analyzed the credibility of Sonny as a musician in James Baldwin's "Sonny's Blues" — his attitudes, actions, struggles, relationship with his instrument and with other musicians — and concluded that Sonny is a believable character.

A woman analyzed the plot of the short story "The Necklace" by Guy de Maupassant and concluded that the change in the protagonist Mathilde Loisel at the end of the story is unrealistic.

A man demonstrated how the rhythm, rhymes, and images of Adrienne Rich's poem "Aunt Jennifer's Tigers" mesh to convey the poem's theme of tension between a woman's artistic urge and the constraints placed on her by society.

A man explained how Carson McCullers in the short story "A Tree, a Rock, a Cloud" uses characterization to reveal the theme that severe emotional hurt caused by rejection in love can predispose an individual toward emotional detachment in subsequent relationships.

A woman analyzed the reasons why the protagonist Charles Woodruff does what he does in the short story "Witness" by Ann Petry. She analyzed Woodruff's background, beliefs, and relationship to the community, the position and attitudes of the boys, and the attitudes of the community. She concluded that Woodruff's motivation is sufficient and his actions, although tragic, are plausible.

A woman majoring in psychology concluded that the relationship between Hamlet and Claudius in Shakespeare's *Hamlet* is in many ways representative of the tension, jealously, and misunderstanding between stepsons and stepfathers.

A woman explained how Walter Van Tilburg Clark uses symbols in "A Portable Phonograph" to reveal and intensify the theme of humans' inhumanity to others because of selfishness.

Finding a Subject.   Read several literary works until you find two or three you like. Perhaps one makes you nod your head in agreement as you read, or sends a chill up your spine when you finish, or leaves you puzzled at the end, or even makes you angry. Do you have a favorite author? A favorite short story among those you have read for this course? Any of these might make a suitable selection for your analysis.

Next, slowly and carefully reread the two or three works that tweak your interest to decide which one you want to concentrate on. Choose the one that strikes you as especially significant — realistic or universal, moving or disturbing, believable or shocking. Choose the one that seems to have a meaning that you wish to share with your classmates.

Generating Ideas.   Analyzing a literary work is the first step in interpreting meaning and evaluating literary quality. Your analysis of the work will give you ideas to write about and will help you find evidence in the work to support your interpretation. As you read the work you have selected, see it as divisible into its elements and analyze those elements as Jonathan Burns did in his paper on "The Lottery." Then focus on *one* significant element. When you write your interpretation, restrict your discussion to that element and possibly its relationship to other literary elements.

We provide checklists to guide you in studying different types of literature. Each analytical model is an aid to understanding; it is *not* an organizational outline for writing about literature. (See pp. 284–88 for a glossary of the literary terms used in the checklists.) The following checklist focuses on short stories and novels, but because thinking about your reaction to the work and about setting, characters, and theme is important whether you are analyzing a short story, a poem, or a play, some of the questions can help you analyze almost any kind of literary work. Checklists focusing specifically on poetry and plays follow.

DISCOVERY CHECKLIST

Analyzing a Short Story or a Novel

- What is your reaction to the story? Jot it down.
- Who is the *narrator* — not the author but the one who tells the story?
- What is the *point of view*?
- What is the *setting* (time and place)? What is the *atmosphere* or *mood*?
- How does the *plot* unfold? Write a synopsis, or summary, of the events in time order, including relationships among those events.
- What are the *characters* like? Describe their personalities and traits. Who is the *protagonist*? The *antagonist*? Do any characters change, and are the changes plausible or believable?
- How would you describe the story's *style*, or use of language? Is the style informal or conversational? Is it formal? Is there any dialect? Are there any foreign words?
- What are the *conflicts* in the story? Determine the *external conflicts* and the *internal conflicts*. What is the *central conflict*? Express the conflicts using the word *versus*, such as "dreams versus reality" or "the individual versus society."
- What is the *climax* of the story? Is there any *resolution*?
- Are there important *symbols*? What might they mean?
- What does the *title* of the story mean?
- Does the story have more than one *level of meaning*?
- What are the *themes* of the story? State your interpretation of the main theme. How is this theme related to your own life?
- What other literary works or experiences from life does the story make you think of? Jot them down.

When looking at a poem, you should consider the elements specific to poetry — for example, the importance of word choice, rhythm, and rhyme — and the elements poetry has in common with other genres. The following checklist provides both general and specific questions to ask yourself when reading a poem.

DISCOVERY CHECKLIST

Analyzing a Poem

- What is your reaction to the poem? Jot it down.
- Who is the *speaker* — not the author, but the one who narrates?
- Is there a *setting*? What is the *mood*?
- Can you put the poem into your own words — paraphrase it?
- What is striking about the language of the poem? Identify any unusual words or words used in an unusual sense. Look for *archaic* words (words no longer

commonly used) and *repetition* of words. Consider the *connotations* of important words (the suggestions conjured by the words: *house* has a different connotation from *home,* although both may refer to the same place). Is the level of language colloquial or formal? What kind of figurative language is used: *imagery, metaphor, irony*?

- Is the poem *lyric* (expressing emotion) or *narrative* (telling a story)?
- What is the structure of the poem? How is it divided? Does it consist of *couplets* (two consecutive rhyming lines) or *quatrains* (units of four lines)? Notice especially how the beginning and the end relate to each other and to the poem as a whole.
- Does the poem use *rhyme* (words that sound alike)? If so, how does the rhyme contribute to the meaning?
- Does the poem have *rhythm* (regular meter or beat, patterns of accented and unaccented syllables)? How does the rhythm contribute to the meaning?
- What does the *title* of the poem mean?
- What is the major *theme* of the poem? How does this underlying idea unify the poem? How is it related to your own life?
- What other literary works or experiences from life does the poem make you think of? Jot them down.

A play is written to be seen and heard, not read. When you analyze a play, you may ask what kind of play it is and how it would appear onstage. The questions in the following checklist will help you understand a play.

DISCOVERY CHECKLIST

Analyzing a Play

- What is your reaction to the play? Jot it down.
- How does the play differ from a short story or a novel? Can you visualize the action? Can you hear the words of the characters? If you were an actor, how would you interpret the stage directions and say the words? If you were the casting director, whom would you cast in the major roles of the play?
- Is the play a *tragedy* (a serious drama that arouses pity and fear in the audience and usually ends unhappily with the death or downfall of the *tragic hero*) or a *comedy* (drama that aims primarily to amuse and that usually ends happily)?
- What is the *setting* of the play? What is its *mood*?
- In brief, what happens? Summarize each act of the play.
- What are the characters like? Who is the *protagonist*? What *antagonist* opposes the main character? Are there *foil characters* (those who contrast with the main character and reveal his or her traits)? Which characters are in conflict? Do any of the characters change?
- Which speeches seem especially significant?
- What is the plot? Identify the *exposition,* the background information needed to understand the story. Determine the main *external* and *internal conflicts.* What is the *central conflict*? What events *complicate* the central conflict? How are these elements of the plot spread throughout the play?
- What is the *climax* of the play? Is there a *resolution* to the action?
- What does the *title* mean?

- Can you identify any *dramatic irony*, words or actions of a character that carry meaning unperceived by the character but evident to the audience?
- What is the major *theme* of the play — a universal idea that underlies it? How is this theme related to your own life?
- What other literary works or experiences from life does the play make you think of? Jot them down.

As you write your analysis, don't worry about impressing your readers with your brilliance. Though you need a critical vocabulary, use only terms that you understand. The writer who writes "The ironic symbolism in 'The Lottery' is portrayed as highly symbolic in theme" is about as clear as corned beef hash. Assume that your readers have read the work you're analyzing but that they have not studied it as carefully as you have. This assumption will help you determine how much evidence from the story you need to include and will save you a lot of wordy summarizing ("On the next page they bring out a black box, sit it on a three-legged stool, and put slips of paper in it"). We suggest that you regard your readers as friends in whose company you are discussing something already familiar to all of you. Your purpose is to explain the deeper meaning of the story, meaning that they may not be aware of after only a cursory reading.

DISCOVERY
CHECKLIST

Finding Ideas

- Have you known people similar to those in the literary work? Are the characters believable? Is their motivation sufficient to cause them to act as they do? How do you know what they are like (through their actions, speech, habits, and so on)?
- Have similar things happened to you? Can you use some information from your experience to explain the meaning of the work?
- Are there any significant images that help illuminate the meaning? Any important symbols? Any irony? What about the setting and the atmosphere?
- Are the characters universal (representative of all human beings)? Are they stereotypes?
- What ideas do the characters and the author consider? Do these ideas imply themes? Can you generalize about them to state some of the themes the author intends? Are the main themes in the literary work universal (applicable to all people everywhere at all times)?
- What is the main point you want to make about this work? Does the evidence that you have gathered through your close reading and analysis of the work itself support this point?
- Have you selected a major element in the work to focus on? Have you avoided focusing on a minor element simply because it strikes your fancy?

Planning, Drafting, and Developing.   After you have determined the element or the related elements of the work that you intend to focus on to interpret meaning, go through the work again to find all the passages that relate to your main point, marking them or taking notes as you find them. It's a good idea to put these relevant passages on note cards or in a computer file, just as you do when you are conducting library research. Remember to note the page references for the details you select, and if you use any quotations, quote them exactly.

Begin writing by trying to express the main point you want to convey in your analysis — your thesis. Suppose you start with a tentative thesis on the theme of "The Lottery" (note that the thesis statement identifies the literary work and the author):

```
In "The Lottery," Shirley Jackson reveals the theme.
```

But this statement is too vague, so you decide to rewrite it to be more precise:

```
In "The Lottery" by Shirley Jackson, the theme is tradi-
tion.
```

This thesis is better, but still unsatisfactory. The statement of the theme of the story is not yet clear or precise: In her narrative, what does Jackson imply about tradition? You try several other ways of expressing your idea.

```
In "The Lottery" by Shirley Jackson, one of the major
themes is that outmoded traditions can be harmful.
```

You used the qualifier *one of* to indicate that this theme is not the only one in the story, but the rest of the thesis is vague. What does "outmoded" mean? How are the traditions harmful?

```
In "The Lottery" by Shirley Jackson, one of the major
themes is that traditions that have lost their meaning
can cause otherwise normal people to act abnormally by
rote.
```

This is a better thesis, one you might start writing from, but keep in mind that it may change as you develop the analysis. You might decide to go beyond interpretation of Jackson's ideas to an evaluation of what she says. If so, you could write the following thesis:

```
In "The Lottery," Shirley Jackson reveals the tragic
theme that traditions that have lost their meaning can
cause otherwise normal people to act abnormally by rote.
```

In this thesis the word *tragic* reveals your evaluation of Jackson's observation of the human condition. Or you might say this:

```
In "The Lottery," Shirley Jackson effectively uses sym-
bolism and irony to reveal the theme that traditions that
have lost their meaning can cause otherwise normal people
to act abnormally by rote.
```

When planning and organizing your essay, focus on ideas, not events; take care not to merely retell the story. One way you might maintain that focus is to analyze your thesis. The thesis just presented could be divided into (1) use of symbolism to reveal theme and (2) use of irony to reveal theme. If you are writing about character change — say, that of Mrs. Mallard in Kate Chopin's "The Story of an Hour" (p. 311) — you might divide the information into her original character traits or attitudes, the events that cause the change, and her new traits or attitudes.

To start your analysis, you might relate a personal experience that parallels that of the protagonist (for "The Story of an Hour," for instance, how you felt when someone close to you died) and tie your experience to that of the character in the work. Or you might focus on the universality of the character (pointing out that most people would feel as Tessie in "The Lottery" did and would probably shout "It isn't fair, it isn't right" if their name were drawn in the village lottery) or of the theme (discussing briefly how traditions seem to be losing their meaning in modern society). You might quote a striking line from the work ("and then they were upon her" or "'Lottery in June, corn be heavy soon'" or "'we'd all be eating stewed chickweed and acorns'"). More simply, you can start with a statement of what the work is about, or with your reaction to the work when you read it, or with a comment about a technique that the writer uses. You might begin with a "Have you ever?" question to draw the reader into your interpretation. Be sure your beginning is tied to your main point.

As you write the body of your literary analysis, include information that supports your interpretation — descriptions of setting and character, summaries of events, quotations of important comments of the characters, and other specific evidence from the story. Cite the page numbers (for prose) or line numbers (for poetry) where details can be found in the work. (See "A Note on Documenting Sources," p. 298.) Look again at how student writer Jonathan Burns used and documented information from "The Lottery" (p. 281). Integrate details from the story with your own comments and ideas.

Use transitions to keep the focus on ideas, not events. Use transition markers that refer to character traits and personality change, not those that refer to time. Say "Although Mr. Summers was . . ." instead of "At the beginning of the story Mr. Summers was . . . ." Write "Tessie became . . ." instead of "After that Tessie was . . . ." State "The protagonist in 'The Lottery' realized . . ." or "The villagers in 'The Lottery' changed . . . ," not "On the next page . . ." or "In the following paragraph . . ." or "At the end of the story she. . . . " (See pp. 407–10 on using transitions effectively.)

Provide a conclusion for your essay; don't just stop writing. Use the same techniques you use for introductions — anecdote, personal experience, comment on technique, quotation — to provide a sense of finality and closing for the readers. Refer to or reaffirm your thesis. Often an effective conclusion ties in directly with the introduction. Notice how Jonathan Burns tied his conclusion (p. 281) to his introduction (p. 283).

In an essay for her writing class, Cindy MacDonald analyzed the change in the protagonist in a story by Meg Campbell. See how she starts and ends her essay.

INTRODUCTION

All many people think about is the good old days.
They live in the past instead of living in the present.
The character of Anne in the short story "Just Saying
You Love Me Doesn't Make It So" by Meg Campbell is
revealed as a young woman who lives in the past but changes
to a person who is concerned with the present and
the future.

CONCLUSION

When most people are forced to take an honest look at
what they think of as the good old days, they sometimes
realize that the good old days were not so good after
all. If they start living in the present and making the
future into what they want it to be, instead of dreaming
of what might have been, they will find, as Anne did, that
their lives are much happier.

In an analysis of the theme in "A Tree, a Rock, a Cloud" by Carson McCullers, student Diana Ward concludes her comments:

Carson McCullers brings out the universal capacity to
be deeply hurt by rejection in a close relationship and the
necessity to overcome the adverse effects of this rejection. Without exception, inherent in love is its capacity
to inflict the most intense kind of pain that a human being may experience. Unless a human being is able to control this pain, the pain will control the person.

Here are some questions you can ask yourself as you shape your draft:

**REVISION
CHECKLIST**

Developing a Draft

- Are your interpretations supported by evidence from the literary work?
- Are the passages and details from the work integrated smoothly into your comments and interpretations?
- Do the transitions focus on ideas and guide your readers easily from one section or sentence to the next?
- Is the essay unified, with everything related to your main point? Do you need to refine your thesis statement to fit what you have actually written?
- Do you use words you understand? Are any sentences not clear because of your use of literary terms?
- Are any of your sentences wordy or unnecessary?
- Have you tried to share your insights into the meaning of the work with your readers, or have you slipped into trying to impress them with your profound perceptions?

You may find that you need to recast problem areas; rephrase unclear passages, using words you understand; cut out deadwood; add or change transitions. Just keep your readers in mind.

**FOR PEER
RESPONSE**

To determine how well you have succeeded in communicating with your readers, ask one of your classmates to read your draft. See Chapter 20 for advice on working with other student writers and for general questions you should always ask a peer editor to address. For a paper in which you analyze a literary work, you'll also want your peer editor to answer these specific questions:

- What is your first reaction to the literary analysis?
- Does the analysis add to your understanding of the literary work? Add to your insights into life?
- Does the introduction make you want to read the rest of the analysis?
- Is the main point clear? Does the writer provide sufficient evidence from the work to back up that point? Put stars wherever additional evidence is needed. Is there anything in the analysis that does not belong? Put a check mark by any irrelevant information.
- Does the writer go beyond synopsis to analysis of elements, interpretation of meaning, and evaluation of literary merit?
- Is the analysis organized by ideas instead of events?
- Do the transitions guide you smoothly from one point to the next? Do the transitions focus on ideas, not on time or position in the story?
- Is the writer's use of literary terminology clear and appropriate?
- If this were your paper, what is the one thing you would be sure to work on before handing it in?

Before you write and proofread your final draft, answer the following questions about your paper. Answer them honestly, and if your evaluation of your writing indicates that the piece needs more work, take the time to make the necessary changes.

REVISION CHECKLIST

Testing the Evidence

- Have you clearly identified the literary work and the author near the beginning of the analysis?
- Have you gone beyond synopsis? Have you organized your analysis according to ideas, not events? Do your transitions focus on ideas, not on plot or time sequence?
- Is your main point clear?
- Have you focused on one element or a limited number of related elements in your analysis?
- Have you used literary terms properly?
- Have you avoided lifting language and sentence structure from the work itself without properly using quotation marks and citations?
- Have you found all the details in the work that support your interpretation? Is there any additional dialogue you can use? Any action? Any description? Are the details that you use really relevant to the points of analysis, or are they just interesting sidelights?
- Have you woven the details from the work smoothly into your text? Have you cited the correct page or line numbers for the details from the work?
- Have you sincerely tried to add to your classmates' understanding of this work?
- After you read your introduction, do you want to read the rest of the analysis?

A NOTE ON DOCUMENTING SOURCES

If, when writing an analysis of a literary work, you quote directly from the work or paraphrase parts of the work, you should cite your source. Correctly and systematically documenting your sources indicates your intellectual honesty. It also helps readers who want to find out more information about assertions in your paper or who want to look at one of your sources — perhaps so they can write a paper on a related topic. A documentation system provides a way to acknowledge your sources.

The style recommended by the Modern Language Association (MLA) is the style most often used when writing about literature. If you are not sure this is the style you should use for your class, check with your instructor.

If you use the MLA style, you put page or line numbers in parentheses immediately after each paraphrase of an event, detail, or description and after each direct quotation from the literary work. Referring to the precise location helps your readers find a particular detail or section in context. The following MLA-style models will help you deal with some of the most common situations.

When you use only one source in your paper, just give page or line numbers in parentheses immediately following a direct quotation from or a paraphrase of the source.

```
The reader thinks of the "great pile" (272) as children's
entertainment, like a stack of imaginary coins rather
than an arsenal.
```

When you use two or more sources in your paper, you must indicate the author's name as well as the page or line numbers. You can do this in your own sentence leading in to the quotation from, or paraphrase of, the source.

```
The speaker in Amy Lowell's poem "Patterns" views life
from a pleasant garden where "daffodils / Are blowing"
(2-3).
```

When the author's name does not appear in your sentence, you can give the author's name in the parentheses with the page or line numbers.

```
The speaker in the poem views life from a pleasant garden
where "daffodils / Are blowing" (Lowell 2-3).
```

```
The speaker in the poem tries to ease his pain by visual-
izing the girl with "wings" (Weigl 30).
```

A reader who wants more information about your source or about a particular detail or quotation can go from the in-text citation to the other part of this system of documentation — the list of works cited. On a page at the end of your paper, you list each of the sources you have used, giving information about the author, title, edition, publisher, and year of publication. (Some sources will require more complicated citations. For these, consult a research or documentation manual.) The following are two examples that might appear on a typical "Works Cited" page of a paper about literature.

When your source is a book, use the following format:

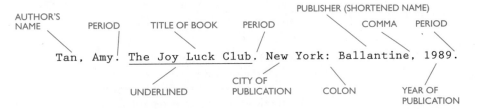

When your source is a short story or poem that appears in an anthology, use this format:

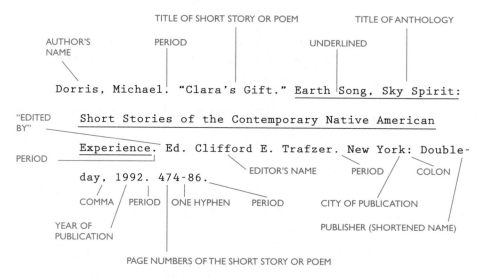

Comparison and Contrast

LEARNING FROM OTHER WRITERS

One way to increase your understanding of the meaning of a piece of literature is to compare and contrast it with another work. As you identify similarities and differences, you deepen your knowledge of the technique and the meaning of both pieces. (For a complete discussion of comparison and contrast analyses, see Chapter 7.)

Lionel Prokop identified similarities and differences and thereby deepened his understanding in a comparison and contrast of two poems, "Patterns" by Amy Lowell and "Song of Napalm" by Bruce Weigl. Amy Lowell (1874–1925) was a poet and a critic from a prominent New England family. Bruce Weigl (b. 1949) is a Vietnam veteran, professor, and author of several collections of poetry. His most recent collections include *Sweet Lorain* (1996) and *Song of Napalm* (1988), which contains the poem Prokop analyzed. The authors of these poems come from very different times and places, but, as Prokop points out in his essay, the poems have similar themes.

Patterns

AMY LOWELL

I walk down the garden paths,
And all the daffodils
Are blowing, and the bright blue squills.
I walk down the patterned garden paths

In my stiff, brocaded gown.   5
With my powdered hair and jewelled fan,
I too am a rare
Pattern. As I wander down
The garden paths.

My dress is richly figured,   10
And the train
Makes a pink and silver stain
On the gravel, and the thrift
Of the borders.
Just a plate of current fashion,   15
Tripping by in high-heeled, ribboned shoes.
Not a softness anywhere about me,
Only whale-bone and brocade.
And I sink on a seat in the shade
Of a lime tree. For my passion   20
Wars against the stiff brocade.
The daffodils and squills
Flutter in the breeze
As they please.
And I weep;   25
For the lime tree is in blossom
And one small flower has dropped upon my bosom.

And the plashing of waterdrops
In the marble fountain
Comes down the garden paths.   30
The dripping never stops.
Underneath my stiffened gown
Is the softness of a woman bathing in a marble basin,
A basin in the midst of hedges grown
So thick, she cannot see her lover hiding,   35
But she guesses he is near,
And the sliding of the water
Seems the stroking of a dear
Hand upon her.
What is Summer in a fine brocaded gown!   40
I should like to see it lying in a heap upon the ground,
All the pink and silver crumpled up on the ground.

I would be the pink and silver as I ran along the paths,
And he would stumble after
Bewildered by my laughter.   45
I should see the sun flashing from his sword hilt and the buckles on his
        shoes.
I would choose
To lead him in a maze along the patterned paths,
A bright and laughing maze for my heavy-booted lover,
Till he caught me in the shade,   50
And the buttons of his waistcoat bruised my body as he clasped me,

Aching, melting, unafraid,
With the shadows of the leaves and the sundrops,
And the plopping of the waterdrops,
All about us in the open afternoon —   55
I am very like to swoon
With the weight of this brocade,
For the sun sifts through the shade.

Underneath the fallen blossom
In my bosom,   60
Is a letter I have hid.
It was brought to me this morning by a rider from the Duke.
"Madam, we regret to inform you that Lord Hartwell
Died in action Thursday se'n-night."°
As I read it in the white, morning sunlight,   65
The letters squirmed like snakes.
"Any answer, Madam," said my footman.
"No," I told him.
"See that the messenger takes some refreshment.
No, no answer."   70
And I walked into the garden,
Up and down the patterned paths,
In my stiff, correct brocade.
The blue and yellow flowers stood up proudly in the sun
Each one.   75
I stood upright too,
Held rigid to the pattern
By the stiffness of my gown.
Up and down I walked,
Up and down.   80

In a month he would have been my husband.
In a month, here, underneath this lime,
We would have broke the pattern;
He for me, and I for him,
He as Colonel, I as Lady,   85
On this shady seat.
He had a whim
That sunlight carried blessing.
And I answered, "It shall be as you have said."
Now he is dead.   90

In Summer and in Winter I shall walk
Up and down
The patterned garden paths
In my stiff, brocaded gown.
The squills and daffodils   95
Will give place to pillared roses, and to asters, and to snow.
I shall go

se'n night: A week ago (seven nights ago).

Up and down,
In my gown.
Gorgeously arrayed,   100
Boned and stayed.
And the softness of my body will be guarded from embrace
By each button, hook, and lace.

For the man who should loose me is dead,
Fighting with the Duke in Flanders,   105
In a pattern called a war.
Christ! What are patterns for?

Song of Napalm

BRUCE WEIGL

—FOR MY WIFE

After the storm, after the rain stopped pounding,
We stood in the doorway watching horses
Walk off lazily across the pasture's hill.
We stared through the black screen,
Our vision altered by the distance   5
So I thought I saw a mist
Kicked up around their hooves when they faded
Like cut-out horses
Away from us.
The grass was never more blue in that light, more   10
Scarlet; beyond the pasture
Trees scraped their voices into the wind, branches
Criss-crossed the sky like barbed wire
But you said they were only branches.

Okay. The storm stopped pounding.   15
I am trying to say this straight: for once
I was sane enough to pause and breathe
Outside my wild plans and after the hard rain
I turned my back on the old curses. I believed
They swung finally away from me . . .   20

But still the branches are wire
And thunder is the pounding mortar,
Still I close my eyes and see the girl
Running from her village, napalm
Stuck to her dress like jelly,   25
Her hands reaching for the no one
Who waits in waves of heat before her.

So I can keep on living,
So I can stay here beside you,
I try to imagine she runs down the road and wings   30
Beat inside her until she rises
Above the stinking jungle and her pain
Eases, and your pain, and mine.

But the lie swings back again.
The lie works only as long as it takes to speak   35
And the girl runs only as far
As the napalm allows
Until her burning tendons and crackling
Muscles draw her up
Into that final position   40
Burning bodies so perfectly assume. Nothing
Can change that; she is burned behind my eyes
And not your good love and not the rain-swept air
And not the jungle green
Pasture unfolding before us can deny it.   45

STUDENT ESSAY

Lionel Prokop   **Love and War: Images of Nature in Two Poems by Bruce Weigl and Amy Lowell**

Amy Lowell wrote "Patterns" during World War I from a   1
woman's viewpoint, while Bruce Weigl wrote "Song of Napalm"
about the Vietnam War from a male veteran's viewpoint. Although the poems were written approximately fifty years
apart, they still contain similar themes concerning the effects of war on people's lives.

Both poems relate experiences involving love and war. In   2
"Song of Napalm," Weigl illustrates how a man has been unable
to forget the painful memories of war despite his desire to
love his wife and despite the seemingly peaceful setting
where he now lives. In "Patterns," Lowell explains a woman's
feelings after war took the man she was to marry. Both authors use images from nature to help express some of the in-
tricacies of love and war and to contrast with the pain both
love and war can bring.

Weigl places the Vietnam veteran and his wife in the   3
doorway of their home looking out into the pasture after a
storm has passed through. Although the scene depicted following the rain appears to be one of freshness and perfection,
Weigl changes the tone as he introduces branches that "Criss-
crossed the sky like barbed wire" (line 13), bringing back
the painful memories of war, the "old curses" (19). The image

of nature becomes even less peaceful as the thunder makes him
think of "pounding mortar" and "see[ing] the girl / Running
from her village" (22-24). The napalm is "Stuck to her dress
like jelly," and she reaches "for the no one / Who waits in
waves of heat before her" (25-27). The speaker in the poem
tries to ease his pain by visualizing the girl with "wings"
(30), able to rise "Above the stinking jungle and her pain"
(32). This is his attempt to block out the memory that continues to return, yet he comes to realize that "Nothing /
Can change" the image because "she is burned behind my eyes"
(41-42). He concludes that neither nature--"the rain-swept
air" and "the jungle green / Pasture unfolding"--nor his
wife's "good love" has the ability to "deny" his painful memories (43-45).

The speaker in Lowell's poem views life from a pleasant   4
garden where "daffodils / Are blowing" (2-3) and "squills /
Flutter in the breeze" (22-23). She walks and wanders "down
the patterned garden paths" in her "stiff, brocaded gown"
(4-5) and comments that her "passion / Wars against" her restrictive dress (20-21). Perhaps she refers to the stiffness
or unfairness of life and of the events of war and how her
soul fights against what is happening. Images from nature express the sadness she feels. She sits beneath a lime tree and
weeps. The "waterdrops" that drip unceasingly in the fountain
are like her tears. She relates the "sliding of the water" to
the "stroking of a dear / Hand" in an image that is both sad
and happy (37-39).

The woman is brought back to reality when a small blossom   5
drops from the lime tree, landing on her chest, where a letter
is hidden. The letter informed her this morning that her lover
had died in battle. She declares that her love for him will
never die and that she will continue to "walk / Up and down /
The patterned garden paths" (91-93). In the poem, the peaceful
garden is patterned with paths and different plants, and the
woman's dress is rich with patterned decoration. The woman realizes that war is a pattern too, in which people leave their
loved ones, then fight, then die. The beauty of the first patterns do not make up for the pain of the second, and the woman
is left asking, "What are patterns for?" (107).

In both of these poems, images from nature are beauti-   6
ful, but sad. Even when its images are beautiful, nature is
not enough to protect the speakers in the two poems from the
pain of war and loss. Walking through the many patterns of
life that have come my way, I can identify with feelings of
being left alone and with a broken heart. The dreams and memories that return bring with them fears of going on in this
world. But because of my upbringing, I must, like the woman
in "Patterns," go on with life and struggle with the memories. Like the speaker in "Song of Napalm," we all must deal
with the painful realities that often overshadow love. We
must not let that pain defeat us.

Works Cited

Lowell, Amy. "Patterns." Understanding Poetry. Ed. Cleanth
    Brooks and Robert Penn Warren. New York: Holt, 1950.
    55-58.

Weigl, Bruce. "Song of Napalm." The Morrow Anthology of
    Younger American Poets. Ed. Dave Smith and David Bot-
    toms. New York: Quill, 1985. 760-61.

Questions to Start You Thinking

Meaning

1. What is the main point that Prokop makes about the two poems?

2. What memorable images does Prokop cite from the poems? How are these images related to the themes of the poems?

3. Why do you think two such different poets use nature in similar ways?

Writing Strategies

4. What other poems have you read that contain memorable images from nature?

5. Is Prokop's introduction effective? Is his conclusion?

6. Why does Prokop use the alternating pattern of organization for his essay of comparison and contrast? (For more on this method of organization, see Chapter 7.)

7. Does he provide sufficient evidence from the poems to support and clarify his main point?

8. If you were Prokop's peer editor, what suggestions would you make to help him improve his paper?

Strategies for Writing about Literature: Synopsis and Paraphrase

LEARNING FROM OTHER WRITERS

Earlier in this chapter we mentioned that Jonathan Burns wrote a synopsis of "The Lottery" as part of his preparation for writing a literary analysis of the story. A *synopsis* is a summary of the plot of a work of narrative literature — a short story, a novel, a play, or a narrative poem. It describes the first level of meaning, the literal layer. It condenses the story to only the major events and the most significant details. You do not include your own interpretation in a synopsis but rather limit your comments to what the author has written. You summarize the work in your own words, taking care not to lift language or sentence structure from the work itself. Writing a synopsis is valuable to you as a writer because it requires you to get the chronology straight and to pick out the significant events and details. It also allows you to see the relationship of the parts to each other and to the themes of the work.

In your literature courses you will often be asked to write synopses of short stories and novels but to paraphrase poems. Like a synopsis, a *paraphrase* is a summary of the original piece of literature, showing understanding of meaning and relationships of the parts. Both assignments require you to dig out the literal level of the work.

In preparation for writing his literary analysis of "The Lottery" — to make sure he had the sequence of events clear — Jonathan Burns wrote the following synopsis of the story.

STUDENT EXAMPLE

Jonathan Burns   A Synopsis of "The Lottery"

Around ten o'clock on a sunny June 27, the villagers gathered in the square for a lottery, expecting to be home in time for lunch. The children came first, glad that school was out for the summer. The boys romped and gathered stones, the girls talked quietly in small groups, and the little ones hovered near their brothers and sisters. Then the men came, followed by the women. When parents called, the children came reluctantly.

Mr. Summers, who always conducted the town lottery, arrived with the black wooden box and set it on the three-legged stool that Mr. Graves had brought out. The villagers

remained at a distance from these men and didn't respond
when Mr. Summers asked for help. Finally, Mr. Martin and his
son held the shabby black box as Mr. Summers mixed the papers in it. Although the townspeople had talked about replacing the box, they never had, but they had substituted
paper slips for the original wooden chips. To prepare for
the drawing, they listed the members of every household and
swore in Mr. Summers. Although they had dropped many aspects
of the original ritual, the official still greeted each person individually.

Tessie Hutchinson rushed into the square, telling her   3
friend Mrs. Delacroix she had almost forgotten what day it
was. Then she joined her husband and children.

When Mr. Summers asked if everyone was present, he was   4
told that Clyde Dunbar was absent because of a broken leg but
that his wife would draw for the family. Summers noted that
the Watson boy was drawing for his mother and checked to see
if Old Man Warner had made it.

The crowd got quiet. Mr. Summers reminded everybody of   5
what they were to do and began to call the names in alphabetical order. People in the group joked nervously as the names
were called. Mrs. Delacroix and Mrs. Graves commented on how
fast time had passed since the last lottery, and Old Man
Warner talked about how important the lottery was to the villagers. When Mr. Summers finished calling the roll, there was
a pause before the heads of households opened their slips.
Everybody wondered who had the special slip of paper, who had
won the lottery. They discovered it was Bill Hutchinson. When
Tessie complained that the drawing hadn't been done fairly,
the others told her to be a good sport.

Mr. Graves put five slips into the box, one for each   6
member of Bill Hutchinson's family. Tessie kept charging that
it wasn't fair. The children drew first, then Tessie, then
Bill. The children opened their slips, smiled broadly, and
held blank pieces of paper over their heads. Bill opened his
and it was blank too. Tessie wouldn't open hers; Bill had to
do it for her. Hers had a black spot on it.

Mr. Summers urged the villagers to finish quickly. They   7
picked up stones, even little Davy Hutchinson, and started

throwing them at Tessie, as she kept screaming, "It isn't
fair, it isn't right." Then they stoned her.

**Questions to Start
You Thinking**

Meaning

1. Does this synopsis help you understand the story better?

2. Why isn't a synopsis as interesting as a short story?

3. Can you tell from this synopsis whether Burns understands Jackson's story beyond the narrative level?

Writing Strategies

4. Does Burns retell the story accurately and clearly? Does he get the events in correct time order? Does he show the relationships of the events to each other and to the whole? How?

5. Does Burns select the details necessary to indicate what happened in "The Lottery"? Why do you think he omits certain details?

6. Are there any details, comments, or events that you would add to his synopsis? Why, or why not?

7. Why doesn't Burns include his own interpretation and responses to the story in this synopsis?

8. How does this synopsis differ from Burns's literary analysis (p. 281)?

In his composition course Lionel Prokop was asked to write a paraphrase of the poem "Patterns" by Amy Lowell (p. 300). His instructor wanted to know if Prokop could comprehend the poem on his own. First Prokop read the poem several times to be sure he understood it, marking important parts. He checked the definitions of words he was not sure of: *squills* (line 3), *brocaded* (line 5), *pillared* (line 96). He also looked up words that seemed familiar but were used in unfamiliar ways: *figured* (line 10), *thrift* (line 13), *stayed* (line 101). Then he divided the poem into sections and briefly summarized each in the margin of the text. Finally he drafted the paraphrase, connecting the parts of the paraphrase with transitions.

STUDENT EXAMPLE

Lionel Prokop   A Paraphrase of "Patterns"

On a breezy afternoon, dressed in a brocaded gown and   1
carrying a fan, I walk down a worn garden path lined with
daffodils and blue herbs. As I walk, my long, patterned dress
dusts the pebbles and the herbs along the edge of the path. I
sit down in the shade of a blossoming lime tree and struggle

with my feelings. I observe the freedom of the wind-blown daffodils and squills and begin to cry as a lime blossom falls on my chest. I hear the ceaseless dripping of the water in the marble fountain and yearn for my soft body to be set free from the stiffness of the gown.

My body is as soft as the body of a woman washing her-self in a marble basin concealed behind thick hedges. She cannot see her lover, but she knows he is there. The water feels like his hand stroking her. I would like to see the dress in a pile on the ground. Laughing and naked, I would run down the path with my lover in pursuit. He would be clad in soldier's attire with a sword and boots as I would lead him in a mazelike path. He would catch me under a tree and hold me passionately against him.   2

I return to the awareness of the hot summer day and of the weight of my gown. The fallen lime blossom brings my at-tention back to the letter I hid in my bosom this morning. It informed me that Lord Hartwell had died in battle. As my eyes filled with tears, I returned no answer with the messenger.   3

Standing straight and tall like the bordering flowers, I continue to walk along the familiar worn path of the garden. I think about the event that had been planned: my marriage to Lord Hartwell in one month under that special lime tree. I remember when he proposed. That day the sun brought blessing. If we had married, the patterns of our lives would have been broken.   4

I vow to continue walking the path in summer and winter in my fine brocaded gown as the squills and daffodils fade, the roses and asters bloom, and the snow falls. My dress will protect me from any further embraces because the man who would undo its laces has been killed in war. War is a pat-tern. What is the point of all these patterns?   5

LEARNING BY WRITING

The Assignment: Writing a Synopsis of a Story by Kate Chopin.   Whenever you are having trouble understanding a story or if you have a lot of stories to read and are afraid you won't remember the specifics of each one, you will benefit from writing a synopsis to refer to later. Condensing five pages to 300 words forces you to isolate the most important details in the story and allows you to see clearly the sequence of events. This focus often leads you to a statement of theme.

Kate Chopin was a nineteenth-century American writer whose female characters search for their own identity and for freedom from domination and oppression. For practice, write a synopsis of 200 to 300 words of Chopin's short story "The Story of an Hour."

REVISION CHECKLIST

Writing a Synopsis of a Story

- Is your summary of the plot of the story true to the original? Are the details accurate? Are they in correct time order?
- Did you include only the major events and details of the story?
- Did you show the relationships of the parts without giving your opinions and interpretations?
- Did you use quotation marks to indicate any of the author's words you used?

Kate Chopin   The Story of an Hour

Knowing that Mrs. Mallard was afflicted with a heart trouble, great care was taken to break to her as gently as possible the news of her husband's death. 1

It was her sister Josephine who told her, in broken sentences, veiled hints that revealed in half concealing. Her husband's friend Richards was there, too, near her. It was he who had been in the newspaper office when intelligence of the railroad disaster was received, with Brently Mallard's name leading the list of "killed." He had only taken the time to assure himself of its truth by a second telegram, and had hastened to forestall any less careful, less tender friend in bearing the sad message. 2

She did not hear the story as many women have heard the same, with a paralyzed inability to accept its significance. She wept at once, with sudden, wild abandonment, in her sister's arms. When the storm of grief had spent itself she went away to her room alone. She would have no one follow her. 3

There stood, facing the open window, a comfortable, roomy armchair. Into this she sank, pressed down by a physical exhaustion that haunted her body and seemed to reach into her soul. 4

She could see in the open square before her house the tops of trees that were all aquiver with the new spring life. The delicious breath of rain was in the air. In the street below a peddler was crying his wares. The notes of a distant song which someone was singing reached her faintly, and countless sparrows were twittering in the eaves. 5

There were patches of blue sky showing here and there through the clouds that had met and piled one above the other in the west facing her window. 6

She sat with her head thrown back upon the cushion of the chair, quite   7
motionless, except when a sob came up into her throat and shook her, as a
child who has cried itself to sleep continues to sob in its dreams.

She was young, with a fair, calm face, whose lines bespoke repression and   8
even a certain strength. But now there was a dull stare in her eyes, whose gaze
was fixed away off yonder on one of those patches of blue sky. It was not a
glance of reflection, but rather indicated a suspension of intelligent thought.

There was something coming to her and she was waiting for it, fearfully.   9
What was it? She did not know; it was too subtle and elusive to name. But she
felt it, creeping out of the sky, reaching toward her through the sounds, the
scents, the color that filled the air.

Now her bosom rose and fell tumultuously. She was beginning to recog-   10
nize this thing that was approaching to possess her, and she was striving to
beat it back with her will — as powerless as her two white slender hands
would have been.

When she abandoned herself a little whispered word escaped her slightly   11
parted lips. She said it over and over under her breath: "Free, free, free!" The
vacant stare and the look of terror that had followed it went from her eyes.
They stayed keen and bright. Her pulses beat fast, and the coursing blood
warmed and relaxed every inch of her body.

She did not stop to ask if it were not a monstrous joy that held her.   12
A clear and exalted perception enabled her to dismiss the suggestion as
trivial.

She knew that she would weep again when she saw the kind, tender   13
hands folded in death; the face that had never looked save with love upon her,
fixed and gray and dead. But she saw beyond that bitter moment a long procession of years to come that would belong to her absolutely. And she opened
and spread her arms out to them in welcome.

There would be no one to live for during those coming years; she would   14
live for herself. There would be no powerful will bending her in that blind
persistence with which men and women believe they have a right to impose
a private will upon a fellow creature. A kind intention or a cruel intention
made the act seem no less a crime as she looked upon it in that brief moment
of illumination.

And yet she had loved him — sometimes. Often she had not. What did it   15
matter! What could love, the unsolved mystery, count for in face of this possession of self-assertion which she suddenly recognized as the strongest impulse of her being.

"Free! Body and soul free!" she kept whispering.   16

Josephine was kneeling before the closed door with her lips to the key-   17
hole, imploring for admission. "Louise, open the door! I beg; open the
door — you will make yourself ill. What are you doing, Louise? For heaven's
sake open the door."

"Go away. I am not making myself ill." No; she was drinking in a very   18
elixir of life through that open window.

Her fancy was running riot along those days ahead of her. Spring days,   19
and summer days, and all sorts of days that would be her own. She breathed
a quick prayer that life might be long. It was only yesterday she had thought
with a shudder that life might be long.

She arose at length and opened the door to her sister's importunities.   20
There was a feverish triumph in her eyes, and she carried herself unwittingly
like a goddess of Victory. She clasped her sister's waist, and together they descended the stairs. Richards stood waiting for them at the bottom.

Someone was opening the front door with a latchkey. It was Brently Mal-   21
lard who entered, a little travel-stained, composedly carrying his gripsack and
umbrella. He had been far from the scene of the accident, and did not even
know there had been one. He stood amazed at Josephine's piercing cry; at
Richards's quick motion to screen him from the view of his wife.

But Richards was too late.   22

When the doctors came they said she had died of heart disease—of joy   23
that kills.

The Assignment: Writing a Paraphrase of a Poem by Bruce Weigl.   When
you study poetry, you can benefit from paraphrasing—that is, expressing the
content of a poem in your own words. You may write your paraphrase in the
margin of the poem or in a notebook. Writing a paraphrase forces you to
divide the poem into logical sections, to figure out what the poet says in each
section, and to discern the relationships of the parts.

To practice this way of writing about literature, write a paraphrase of
"Song of Napalm" by Bruce Weigl (pp. 303–04).

 **DISCOVERY CHECKLIST**

Writing a Paraphrase of a Poem

- How are the sections of the poem related?
- Are there any words whose meanings you don't know? Are there any words
  that seem to be used in a special sense, a sense in which the usual meanings
  do not fit? What do those words mean in the context of the poem?
- Does the poet use any important images or pictures? Any metaphors? How
  do these contribute to the meaning?
- Do you leave your personal opinions out of your paraphrase?
- After you have completed the paraphrase, can you express the theme of the
  poem in one or two sentences?

Papers written in response to literature are often some of the most enjoyable and interesting essays you will write in college. Interpreting literature is
a rewarding activity. You see yourself and your friends and family in the works
you read, and the best writers provide you with insights into yourself and your

relationships. As you read and analyze, solutions to problems you have struggled with may become clear, or you may just enjoy figuring out why a character does such crazy things or enjoy ferreting out the techniques an author uses to make you respond as you do. Once you understand the literary selection you are interpreting, you have the pleasure of sharing your insights with your readers and thus increasing their insights as well.

Other Assignments for Writing about Literature

1. Use a poem, a play, or a novel instead of a short story to complete the literary assignment analysis in this chapter (p. 288).
2. Write an essay comparing and contrasting a literary element in two or three short stories or poems, as Lionel Prokop did for the poems by Amy Lowell and Bruce Weigl (p. 304).
3. Analyze and write a critical essay on a song, a movie, or a television program. Because you won't have a written text in front of you, you probably will need to hear the work or view it more than once to pull out the specific evidence necessary to support your interpretation.
4. Read the following poem by Robert Frost. Then write an essay in which you use a paraphrase of this poem as a springboard for your thoughts on a fork in the road of your life — a decision that made a big difference for you.

The Road Not Taken

Two roads diverged in a yellow wood,
And sorry I could not travel both
And be one traveler, long I stood
And looked down one as far as I could
To where it bent in the undergrowth;

Then took the other, as just as fair,
And having perhaps the better claim,
Because it was grassy and wanted wear;
Though as for that the passing there
Had worn them really about the same,

And both that morning equally lay
In leaves no step had trodden black.
Oh, I kept the first for another day!
Yet knowing how way leads on to way,
I doubted if I should ever come back.

I shall be telling this with a sigh
Somewhere ages and ages hence:
Two roads diverged in a wood, and I —
I took the one less traveled by,
And that has made all the difference.

5. Read the following poem by Edwin Arlington Robinson. Have you known and envied someone similar to Richard Cory, someone who everyone else thought had it all? What happened to him or her? Did you discover that your impression of this individual was wrong? Write a personal response essay in which you compare and contrast the person you knew with Richard Cory. This assignment requires you to analyze the poem as well as draw on your own experience and knowledge.

Richard Cory

Whenever Richard Cory went down town,
We people on the pavement looked at him:
He was a gentleman from sole to crown,
Clean favored, and imperially slim.

And he was always quietly arrayed,
And he was always human when he talked;
But still he fluttered pulses when he said,
"Good-morning," and he glittered when he walked.

And he was rich — yes, richer than a king —
And admirably schooled in every grace:
In fine, we thought that he was everything
To make us wish that we were in his place.

So on we worked, and waited for the light,
And went without the meat, and cursed the bread;
And Richard Cory, one calm summer night,
Went home and put a bullet through his head.

Chapter 13

Writing for Assessment

Most college writing is done for assessment — that is, most of the papers you complete and hand in are eventually evaluated and graded. But some college writing tasks exist *only* as methods of assessment: they are designed not to help you explore and expand your writing skills (or content knowledge, in courses other than composition) but to allow you to demonstrate that you have mastered them.

We've considered how you write when *you* control your writing circumstances. We've assumed that you can write (anything from a brief account of a remembered experience to a hefty research paper) lying down or standing up, in the quiet of a library or in a clattering cafeteria. You can think, plan, draft, revise, and recopy. Although an instructor may have handed you a deadline, you usually have a week or more for the assignment. But in college you often need to write on the spot — a quiz to finish in twenty minutes, a final exam to complete in three or four hours, an impromptu essay to dash off in one class period. How do you discover and shape your ideas in a limited time?

In this chapter we discuss three types of in-class writing that are commonly used for assessment — the essay exam, the short-answer exam, and the timed writing. The thinking and composing processes that these types of writing require are different from those used for writing a paper over a period of several days or several weeks. You have probably done all three before, but the tips provided in this chapter will help you write better under pressure.

We also discuss an assessment tool that is becoming more common on college campuses these days — the writing portfolio. A portfolio is simply a collection of writing samples, but it takes careful thinking and effective writing to create and present one that adequately demonstrates your strengths as a writer.

Essay Examinations

In many courses an essay exam is the most important kind of in-class writing. Although lately multiple-choice tests, scored by computer, have been whittling down the number of essay exams that college students write, the tradition of the essay exam endures. Instructors believe that such writing shows that you haven't just memorized a batch of material but that you understand it, have examined it critically, can see connections in it, and can clearly communicate your thoughts about it to someone else.

PREPARING FOR THE EXAM

The chief resource for most essay exams is your memory. What you remember may include observations, conversation, reading, and perhaps some imagination. The days before an examination offer you a chance to review what you have learned, to fill in any blank spots in your understanding, and to fix these ideas firmly in your memory. Such review enables you to think deeply about your course work and see how its scattered parts fit together.

As you review your reading and your notes from lectures and class discussion, it's a good idea — if the exam will be closed book — to fix in memory any vitally important names, dates, and definitions. We said "vitally important" — you don't want to clutter your mind with a lot of spare parts selected at random. But preparation isn't merely a matter of decorating a vast glacier of ignorance with a few spring flowers of dates and quotations. When you review, look for the main ideas or themes in each textbook chapter. Then ask yourself: What do these main ideas have to do with each other? How might they be combined? What conclusions can I draw from all the facts?

Some instructors favor open-book exams, in which you bring your books and perhaps your notes to class for reference. In an open-book exam, ability to memorize and recall is less important than ability to reason and to select what matters most. In such a writing situation, you have more opportunity than in a closed-book exam to generate ideas and to discover material on the spot.

A good way to prepare in advance for any exam, whether the books are to be closed or open, is to imagine questions you might be asked and then plan answers. We don't mean to suggest that you should try to psyche out your instructor. You're only slightly more likely to guess all the questions in advance than you are to clean out a slot machine in Las Vegas. But by thinking up your own questions, you review much material, imaginatively bring some of it together, and gain valuable experience in shaping answers. Sometimes, to help you prepare for an exam, the instructor will supply a few questions that he or she asked in former years. If you are given such examples, you can pattern new questions after them.

As you probably don't need to be told, trying to cram at the eleventh hour, going without sleep and food, consuming gallons of coffee or cola, and reducing yourself to a wreck is no way to prepare. You can learn more in little bites than in huge gulps. Psychologists testify that if you study something for fifteen minutes a day for eight days, you'll remember far more than if you study the same material in one unbroken sprint of two hours.

LEARNING FROM ANOTHER WRITER

To start looking at techniques of answering *any* exam question, let's take one concrete example. A final exam in developmental psychology posed this question:

> What evidence indicates innate factors in perceptual organization? You might find it useful to recall any research that shows how infants perceive depth and forms.

In response, David Ian Cohn sat back in his chair for five minutes and thought over the reading he'd done for the course. What perception research had he heard about that used babies for subjects? He spent another five minutes jotting down ideas, crossed out a couple of weak ones, and drew lines connecting ideas that went together. (For an illustration of this handy technique, see "Linking," p. 381.) Then he took a deep breath and, without revising (except to cross out a few words of a sentence that seemed a false start), wrote this straightforward grade A answer:

> Research on infants is probably the best way to demonstrate that some factors in perceptual organization are innate. In the cliff box experiment, an infant will avoid what looks like a drop-off, even though its mother calls it and even though it can feel glass covering the drop-off area. The same infant will crawl to the other end of the box, which appears (and is) safe. Apparently, infants do not have to be taught what a cliff looks like.
>
> Psychologists have also observed that infants are aware of size constancy. They recognize a difference in size between a 10 cm box at a distance of one meter and a 20 cm box at a distance of two meters. If this phenomenon is not innate, it is at least learned early, for the subjects of the experiment were infants of sixteen to eighteen months.
>
> When shown various patterns, infants tend to respond more noticeably to patterns that resemble the human face than to those that appear random. This seemingly innate recognition helps the infant identify people (such as its mother) from less important inanimate objects.
>
> Infants also seem to have an innate ability to match sight with sound. When simultaneously shown two television screens, each depicting a different subject, while being played a tape that sometimes matched one screen and sometimes the other, infants looked at whichever screen matched what they heard—not always, but at least twice as often.

**Questions to Start
You Thinking**

Meaning

1. What is the main idea of Cohn's answer?

2. If you were the psychology instructor, how could you immediately see from this answer that Cohn had thoroughly dealt with the question and only with the question?

Writing Strategies

3. In what places is Cohn's answer concrete and specific, not vague and general?

4. Suppose he had tacked on a concluding sentence: "Thus I have conclusively proved that there are innate factors in perceptual organization, by citing much evidence showing that infants definitely can perceive depth and forms." Would that sentence have strengthened his answer?

GENERATING IDEAS

When, seated in the classroom, you begin your race with the clock, resist the temptation to start scribbling away frantically. First read over all the questions on the exam carefully. Notice whether you are expected to make any choices, and decide which questions to answer. Choices are luxuries: they let you ignore questions you are less prepared to answer in favor of those you can tackle with more confidence. If you are offered a choice, just cross out any questions you are *not* going to answer so you don't waste time thinking about them by mistake. And if you don't understand what a question calls for, ask your instructor right away.

Few people can dash off an excellent essay exam answer without first taking time to discover a few ideas and plan an answer. So take a deep breath, get comfortable, sit back, and spend a few moments in thought. Instructors prefer answers that are concrete and specific rather than those that stay up in the clouds of generality. David Cohn's answer to the psychology question cites evidence all the way through—particular experiments in which infants were subjects. A little time taken to generate concrete examples—as Cohn did—will be time wisely spent.

Instructors also prefer answers that are organized and coherent rather than rambling. Some people have a rare talent for rapidly putting their thoughts in order. Most of us, however, need to plot some direction to follow before we begin. Your pen will move more smoothly if you have a few thoughts in mind. These thoughts don't have to be definitive—only something to start you writing. You can keep thinking and shaping and adding your thoughts as you write.

Often a question will suggest a way to start your answer. Many questions contain directive words that help you define your task: *evaluate, compare, discuss, explain, describe, summarize, trace the development of.* You can put yourself on the right track if you incorporate a form of such a word in your first sentence. See examples on the next page.

QUESTION   Define romanticism, citing its major characteristics and giving examples of each.

ANSWER   Romanticism is defined as . . .

ANSWER   Romanticism is a complex concept, difficult to define. It . . .

PLANNING: RECOGNIZING TYPICAL EXAM QUESTIONS

Most exam questions fall into recognizable types, and if you can recognize them, you will know how to organize them and begin to write. Here are examples.

The Cause and Effect Question.   In general, these questions usually mention *causes* and *effects*.

What were the immediate causes of the stock market crash of 1929?

Set forth the principal effects on the economy commonly noticed as a result of a low prime rate of interest.

For specific advice on writing to show cause or effect, see Chapter 8.

The Compare or Contrast Question.   This is one of the most popular types of examination questions. It calls on you to point out similarities (comparing) or discuss differences (contrasting), and in the process you explain not one subject but two.

Compare and contrast *iconic memory* and *eidetic imagery*. (1) Define the two terms, indicating the ways in which they differ, and (2) state the way or ways in which they are related or alike.

After supplying a one-sentence definition of each term, a student proceeded first to contrast and then to compare, for full credit.

Iconic memory is a picturelike impression that lasts for only a fraction of a second in short-term memory. Eidetic imagery is the ability to take a mental photograph, exact in detail, as though its subject were still present. But iconic memory soon disappears. Unlike an eidetic image, it does not last long enough to enter long-term memory. IM is common; EI is unusual: very few people have it. Both iconic memory and eidetic imagery are similar, however: both record visual images, and every sighted person of normal intelligence has both abilities to some degree.

A question of this kind doesn't always use the words *compare* and *contrast*. Consider this question from a midterm exam in basic astronomy:

Signal at least three differences between Copernicus's and Kepler's models of the solar system. In what respects was Kepler's model an improvement on that of Copernicus?

That question is nothing more than good old contrasting (citing three differences and showing that Kepler's model was superior).

Distinguish between *agnosia* and *receptive aphasia*. In what ways are the two conditions similar?

Again, without using the words *comparison* and *contrast*, the question asks for both. When you distinguish, you contrast, or point out differences; when you tell how two things are similar, you compare.

Briefly explain the duplex theory of memory. What are the main differences between short-term memory and long-term memory?

In this two-part question, the second part calls on the student to contrast (but not compare):

Which bryophyta resemble vascular plants? In what ways? How do these bryophyta *differ* from the vascular plants?

Writers of comparison and contrast answers sometimes fall into a trap: in this case, they might get all wound up about bryophyta and fail to give vascular plants more than a few words. When you compare and contrast two things, pay attention to both, paralleling the points you make about each, giving both equal space.

For more on comparing and contrasting, see Chapter 7.

The Demonstration Question.   In this kind of question, you are given a statement and asked to back it up.

Demonstrate the truth of Freud's contention that laughter may contain elements of aggression.

In other words, you are asked to explain Freud's claim and supply evidence to support it. You might refer to crowd scenes you have experienced, perhaps quote and analyze a joke, perhaps analyze a scene in a TV show or film, or use examples from your reading.

The Discussion Question.   A discussion question may tempt an unwary writer to shoot the breeze.

Name and discuss three events that precipitated Lyndon B. Johnson's withdrawal from the 1968 presidential race.

This question looks like an open invitation to ramble about Johnson and Vietnam, but it isn't. Whenever a question says "discuss," you will be wise to plan your discussion. Try rewording the question to help you focus your discussion: "Why did President Johnson decide not to seek another term? Analyze the causes and explain each a little."

Sometimes a discussion question won't announce itself with the word *discuss*, but with *describe* or *explain* or *explore*.

> Describe the national experience following passage of the Eighteenth Amendment. What did most Americans learn from it?

Provided you know that the Eighteenth Amendment (Prohibition) banned the sale, manufacture, and transportation of alcoholic drinks and that it was finally repealed, you can discuss its effects — or perhaps the reasons for its repeal.

The Divide or Classify Question.   Sometimes you are asked to slice a subject into sections or sort things into kinds. You will analyze the idea, place, person, or process into its parts.

> Enumerate the ways in which each inhabitant of the United States uses, on the average, 1,595 gallons of water a day. How and to what degree might each person cut down on this amount?

To answer this two-part question, for a start, you would divide up water use into several parts — drinking, cooking, bathing, washing cars, and so on. Then after that division, you would give tips for water conservation and tell how effective each is.

> What different genres of film did King Vidor direct? Name at least one outstanding example of each kind.

In this classification question, you sort things into categories — films into general kinds — possibly comedy, war, adventure, mystery, musical, western.
For more on division and classification, see Chapter 18.

The Definition Question.   You'll often be asked to write an extended definition on an essay exam.

> Explain the three dominant styles of parenting — *permissive, authoritarian-restrictive,* and *authoritative.*

This question calls for a trio of definitions. Illustrating each definition with an example, whether recalled or imagined, will strengthen your response.

> Define the Stanislavsky method of acting, citing outstanding actors who have followed it.

Here, you would explain the meaning of the method and give examples to make your answer clear.
For more on definition, see Chapter 18.

The Evaluation Question.   This is another favorite kind of question because it calls on students to think critically and to present an argument.

> Set forth and evaluate the most widely accepted theories to account for the disappearance of the dinosaurs.

> Evaluate *two* of the following suggestions, giving reasons for your judgments:
> a. Cities should stop building highways to the suburbs and instead build public monorail systems.
> b. Houses and public buildings should be constructed to last no longer than twenty years.
> c. Freeways leading to the core of the city should have marked express lanes for buses and carpooling drivers and narrow lanes for individual commuters who drive their cars.

This last three-part question calls on you to argue for or against. Other argument questions might begin "Defend the idea of . . ." or "Show weaknesses in the concept of . . ." or otherwise call on you to take a stand. For more on taking a stand and evaluating, see Chapters 9 and 11.

The Respond to the Comment or Quotation Question.   A question might begin "Test the validity of this statement" and then supply a statement for close reading and evaluation.

> Discuss the following statement: high-minded opposition to slavery was only one cause, and not a very important one, of the animosity between North and South that in 1861 escalated into civil war.

The question asks you to test the writer's opinion against what you know. You would begin by carefully reading that statement a couple of times and then seeing whether you can pick a fight with it. Jot down any contrary evidence you can think of. If you end up agreeing with the statement, supply evidence to support it. Sometimes the passage is the invention of the instructor, who hopes to provoke you to argument.

> Was the following passage written by Gertrude Stein, Kate Chopin, or Tillie Olsen? On what evidence do you base your answer?
>
> > She waited for the material pictures which she thought would gather and blaze before her imagination. She waited in vain. She saw no pictures of solitude, of hope, of longing, or of despair. But the very passions themselves were aroused within her soul, swaying it, lashing it, as the waves daily beat upon her splendid body. She trembled, she was choking, and the tears blinded her.

The passage is taken from a story by Kate Chopin. If you were familiar with Chopin, who specializes in physical and emotional descriptions of impassioned women, you would know the answer to the examination question, and you might point to language (*swaying, lashing*) that marks it as hers.

The Process Analysis Question.   In brief, you divide the process into steps and detail each step. Often you can spot this kind of question by the word *trace*:

> Trace the stages through which a bill becomes a federal law.

> Trace the development of the medieval Italian city-state.

Both questions want you to tell how something occurs or occurred. The other familiar type of process analysis, the "how-to" variety, is called for in this question:

> An employee has been consistently late for work, varying from fifteen minutes to a half hour daily. This employee has been on the job only five months but shows promise of learning skills that your firm needs badly. How would you deal with this situation?

For more on process analyses, see Chapter 18.

The Far-Out Question.   Sometimes, to invite you to use your imagination, an instructor will throw in a question that at first glance might seem bizarre. On second glance, you may see that the question reaches deep.

> Imagine yourself to be a trial lawyer in 1921, charged with defending Nicola Sacco and Bartolomeo Vanzetti, two anarchists accused of murder. Argue for their acquittal on whatever grounds you can justify.

This question calls on a prelaw student to show familiarity with a famous case (which ended with the execution of the defendants). In addition, it calls for knowledge of the law and of trial procedure. Such a question might be fun to answer; moreover, in being obliged to imagine a time, a place, and dramatic circumstances, you might learn something. The following is another far-out question, this time from a philosophy course:

> What might an ancient Roman Stoic philosopher have thought of Jean-Paul Sartre's doctrine of anguish?

In response, you might try to remember what the Stoics had to say about enduring suffering, define Sartre's view and define theirs, compare their views with Sartre's, and imagine how they would agree (or, more probably, differ) with him. For more on imagining, see Chapter 4.

DRAFTING: THE ONLY VERSION

When the clock on the wall is ticking away, generating ideas and shaping an answer are seldom two distinct, leisurely processes: they often take place at the same time, and on scratch paper. Does your instructor hand you your own copy of the exam questions? If so, see if there's room in the margins to jot down ideas and put them in rough order. If you can do your preliminary work right on the exam sheet, you will save time: annotate questions, underline points you think important, scribble short definitions. Write reminders that you will notice while you work: TWO PARTS TO THIS QUES.! or GET IN EX-AMPLE OF ABORIGINES. To make sure that you include all necessary information without padding or repetition, you might jot down a brief, informal outline before setting pen to paper. This was David Cohn's outline for his answer on his psychology exam (p. 318):

Thesis: Research on infants is probably the best way to demonstrate that some factors in perceptual organization are innate
Cliff box — kid fears drop despite glass, mother, knows shallow side safe
Size constancy — learned early if not intrinsic
Shapes — infants respond more/better to face shape than nonformed
Match sound w/ sight — 2 TVs, look twice as much at right one

Budget Your Time.   When you have two or more essay questions to answer, block out your time at least roughly. Sometimes your instructor will suggest how many minutes to devote to each question or will declare that one question counts twenty points, another ten, and so on. Obviously, a twenty-point question deserves twice as much time and work as a ten-pointer. If the instructor doesn't specify, then after you have read the questions, decide for yourself how much time each question is worth. Make a little schedule so that you'll know that at 10:30 it's time to wrap up question 2 and move on. Allot extra minutes to a complicated question (such as one with several parts) or to one that counts more points than the other questions. Otherwise, give every answer equal time. Then pace yourself as you write. A watch with an alarm you can set to buzz at the end of twenty or thirty minutes, alerting you that it's time to move on, might help — unless it would distract your classmates.

Begin with the Easy Questions.   Many students find that it helps their morale to start with the question they feel best able to answer. Unless your instructor specifies that you have to answer the questions in their given order, why not skip around? Just make sure you clearly number the questions on your answer sheet or booklet and begin each answer in such a way that the instructor will immediately recognize which question you're answering. If the task is "Compare and contrast the depression of the 1930s with the recession of the 1970s," an answer might begin

Compared to the paralyzing depression that began in 1929, the recession of the 1970s seems a bad case of measles.

The instructor would recognize that question, all right, whether you answered it first or last. If you have a choice of questions, label your answer to correspond to the instructor's labels or restate the question at the start of your essay so that your instructor will have no doubt which alternative you have chosen.

QUESTION

Discuss *one* of the following quotations from the writings of Voltaire:

a. "The truths of religion are never so well understood as by those who have lost the power of reasoning."
b. "All roads lead to Rome."

ANSWER

When in September 1750 Voltaire wrote in a letter to Mme. de Fontaine, "All roads lead to Rome," his remark referred to more than the vast network of roads the ancient Romans had built—and built so well—throughout Europe. . . .

Try Stating Your Thesis at the Start.   Some students make their opening sentence a thesis statement—a sentence that makes clear right away the main point they're going to make. Then they proceed in the rest of the answer to back that statement up. This method often makes good sense. With a clear thesis statement to begin with, you will be less likely to ramble into byways that carry you miles away from your main point. A clear thesis statement also lets your instructor know right away that you know what you're talking about. (See "Stating and Using a Thesis," p. 375). That's how David Cohn opens his answer to the psychology question (p. 318). An easy way to get started is to begin with the question itself. You might turn the question around, make it into a declarative statement, and transform it into the start of an answer.

QUESTION

Can adequate reasons for leasing cars and office equipment, instead of purchasing them, be cited for a two-person partnership?

ANSWER

I can cite at least four adequate reasons for a two-person partnership to lease cars and office equipment. For one thing, under present tax laws, the entire cost of a regular payment under a leasing agreement may be deducted. . . .

Stick to the Point of the Question.   You may be tempted to throw into your answer everything you have learned in the course. But to do so defeats the purpose of the examination—to put your knowledge to use, not to parade your knowledge. So when you answer an exam question cogently, you select *what matters* from what you know, at the same time shaping it.

Answer the Whole Question.   Often a question will have two parts. It will ask you, say, to name the most common styles of contemporary architecture and then to evaluate one of them. Or

List three differences between the landscape paintings of Monet and those of Van Gogh. Which of the two shows the greater influence of eighteenth-century neoclassicism?

When the dragon of a question has two heads, make sure you cut off both.

Stay Specific.   Pressed for time, some harried exam takers think, "I haven't got time to get specific here. I'll just sum up this idea in general." That's a mistake. Every time you throw in a large, general statement ("The industrial revolution was a beneficial thing for the peasant"), take time to include specific examples ("In Dusseldorf, as Taine tells us, the mortality rate from starvation among displaced Prussian farmworkers now dropped to nearly zero, although once it had reached almost ten percent a year").

Leave Room to Revise.   Give yourself room for second thoughts and last-minute inspirations by writing on only one side of the page in your examination booklet and skipping every other line. Then later, should you wish to add words or sentences or even a whole paragraph, you can do so with ease. As you write and as you revise, you may well do further discovering.

REVISING: REREADING AND PROOFING

If you have paced yourself, you'll have at least a few minutes left at the end of your examination period when, while some around you are frantically trying to finish, you can relax a moment and look over your work with a critical eye.

Even if you happen to stop writing with an hour to spare, don't spend your time recopying your whole exam. Use any time you have left not to improve your penmanship and the appearance of the paper but to check how clear your ideas are and how well they hang together.

Your foresight in skipping every other line will now pay off. You can add sentences wherever you think new ones are needed. Cross out any hopelessly garbled sentences and rewrite them in the blank lines. If you recall an important point you forgot to put in, you can add a paragraph or two on a blank left-hand page. Just draw an arrow indicating where it goes. If you find that you have gone off on a big digression or have thrown in knowledge merely to show it off, boldly X out that block of wordage. Your answer may look sloppier, but your instructor will think the better of it.

Naturally, errors occur oftener when you write under pressure than when you have time to edit and proofread carefully. Most instructors will take into consideration your haste and your human fallibility. On an exam, what you say and how forcefully you say it matter most. Still, getting the small details right will make your answer look all the sharper. No instructor will object to careful corrections. You can easily add words with carets:

foreign
Israeli ∧ policy

Or you can neatly strike out a word by drawing a line through it. Some students like to use an erasable pen for in-class writing, but most instructors prefer cross-outs to the smears of erasable ink.

We don't expect you to memorize the following questions and carry them like crib notes into an examination. But when you receive your paper or blue book back and you look it over, you might learn more about writing essay exams if you ask these questions of yourself:

 **DISCOVERY CHECKLIST**

Evaluating Your Performance

- Did you answer the whole question, not just part of it?
- Did you stick to the point, not throw in information the question didn't call for?
- Did you make your general statements clear by citing evidence or examples?
- Does your answer sprawl, or is it focused?
- Does your answer show a need for more knowledge and more ideas? Did you inflate your answer with hot air, or did you stay close to earth, giving plenty of facts, examples, and illustrations?
- Did you proofread for omissions and lack of clarity?
- On what question or questions do you feel you did a good job that satisfies you, no matter what grade you received?
- If you had to write this exam over again, how would you now go about the job?

Short-Answer Examinations

Requiring answers much terser than those expected on an essay exam, the *short-answer exam* may call on you to identify names or phrases from your reading, in a sentence or a few words.

Identify the following: Clemenceau, Treaty of Versailles, Maginot line, Dreyfus affair.

You might answer the question as follows:

Georges Clemenceau — This French premier, nicknamed The Tiger, headed a popular coalition cabinet during World War I and at the Paris Peace Conference demanded stronger penalties against Germany.

Writing a short identification is much like writing a short definition. Be sure to mention the general class to which a thing belongs.

Clemenceau — French premier who . . .
Treaty of Versailles — pact between Germany and the Allies that . . .
Maginot line — fortifications that . . .

If you do so, you won't lose points for an answer like this, which fails to make clear the nature of the thing being identified:

Maginot line — The Germans went around it.

Timed Writings

At some point in college you may need to prove your writing expertise on a competency exam (maybe at the end of a course or at the completion of a program). Most composition instructors, to give you experience in writing on demand, assign impromptu essays to be written in class. For such writings, your time is limited (usually forty-five minutes to an hour), the setting is controlled (usually you're sitting at a desk and you're not allowed to use a dictionary or a spell checker), and you can't choose your own subject. The purpose of timed writings is to test your writing skills, not to see how much information you can recall.

At first, this rapid-fire type of writing may cause you some anxiety — sweaty palms and a blank mind. It seems a lot different from the leisurely think-plan-draft-revise method of composing. It does require you to think and recall much faster, yet the way you write a timed essay doesn't differ greatly from the way you write anything else. Your usual methods of writing can serve you well, even though you have to use them in a hurry. With a few tips and a little practice, you can produce a top-notch piece that will please even the toughest readers.

Budget Your Time Wisely.   For an in-class essay, if you have forty-five minutes to write, a good rule of thumb is to spend ten minutes preparing, thirty minutes writing, and five minutes rereading and making last-minute changes. In the act of writing, you may find new ideas occurring to you and perhaps these exact proportions of time will change. Or you may know from past experience that you need longer to plan or to proofread and check what you have written. Even so, a rough schedule like that will help you to allocate your time. The worst mistake you can make is to spend so much time thinking and planning that you must rush through getting your ideas down on paper in an essay — the part you will be graded on.

Choose Your Topic Wisely.   For extemporaneous writing, you're given little choice of topic — usually one, two, or three. The trick is to make the topic your own. If you have a choice at all, choose the one you know the most about, not the one you think will impress your readers. They'll be most impressed by logical argument and solid evidence. If you have to write on a broad abstract subject (say, a world problem that affects many people), don't choose something you can't quickly recall much about. You'll only end up being vague and general, while your readers will be expecting specifics to back up your claims. Instead, bring it down to something personal, something you have observed or experienced. Have you witnessed traffic jams, brownouts, or condos ruining beaches? Then write about increased population. If your doctor's and dentist's fees have gone up, if your insurance rates have increased, if you have put off a medical checkup because it's so expensive, then write about the increasing costs of health care.

Think and Plan before You Write. With limited time, your tendency will probably be to jump right in and start writing. However, as with all effective writing, you need to think and plan before you start putting ideas into sentences and paragraphs. You should read the instructions and the topics or questions carefully, choose your topic thoughtfully, restrict it to something you know about, form a main idea for focus, and jot down the major divisions for development. While you're thinking, if a good hook for the introduction or conclusion occurs to you, make a note of it. Just don't spend so much time on this planning part of the process that you can't finish the essay.

Don't Try to Be Perfect. No one expects extemporaneous essays to be as polished as reports written over several weeks. Realize that you may not be able to do everything you would like to do in so brief a time. Turn off your internal monitor. You can't polish every sentence or remember the exact word for every spot. You may not include as many details as you would if you had more time, but do include some specifics. And never waste time recopying. A little messiness won't hurt, and you should devote your time to the more important parts of writing.

Save Time to Proofread. The last few minutes you leave yourself to read over your work and correct glaring errors may be the best-spent minutes of all. Cross out and make corrections neatly. Use asterisks (*), arrows, and carets (∧). (See more suggestions on how to make corrections on p. R-27.) Especially check for the following:

> Omitted letters (*-ed* or *-s*)
> Added letters (develop*e*)
> Inverted letters (rec*ie*ve)
> Wrong punctuation (a comma instead of a period)
> Omitted apostrophes (*dont* instead of *don't*)
> Omitted words ("She going" instead of "She *is* going")
> Wrong words (*except* instead of *accept*)
> Misspelled words (*mispelled*)

TYPES OF TOPICS

Often you can expect the same types of questions or topics for in-class writings as for essay exams. If you are familiar with those recognizable types (discussed on pp. 320–24) and know how to organize them, you can do well. Just remember to look for the key words and do what they suggest.

> What were the *causes* of World War I?
> *Compare and contrast* the theories of capitalism and socialism.
> How did the metaphysical poets of the seventeenth century *influence* the work of T. S. Eliot?
> *Define* civil rights.

Another type of topic for timed writings is a general subject on which thousands of diverse students can write. Give this type of question your own personal twist. But again, you should pay attention to key words.

A problem in education that is *difficult to solve.*
Ways to cope with stress.

A type of question you may be familiar with from the standardized tests is one in which you are given a short passage to read and then asked to respond to it. This type of question tests not only your writing ability but also your reading comprehension.

In one of his most famous sonnets, Wordsworth claimed, "The world is too much with us." *Explain* what he meant by that line, and *discuss* whether his assessment of the world still applies today.

Thomas Jefferson stated, "If a nation expects to be ignorant and free, in a state of civilization, it expects what never was and never will be." *How* is his comment *relevant* to education today?

Writing for Portfolio Assessment

The writing portfolio has become a popular method for assessment for college classes. In a portfolio course, you generally are asked to submit a collection of your best writing — pieces that you have revised the most expertly or in which you have invested a lot of time and energy. Portfolio courses typically emphasize revision and reflection — the ability to identify and discuss your choices, strengths, or learning processes. In a portfolio writing course, you'll need to save all your drafts and notes, keep track of your choices and changes, and make some important selection decisions near the end of the term.

Writing teachers who use portfolios want students to think critically about their writing and to present final projects in a polished form. Even if you haven't encountered portfolios before in other classes, you may still recognize the term from art or investing. Artists transport their work in a portable case or folder; they show their portfolios of pieces that represent their inter-

FOR GROUP LEARNING

Brainstorming Ideas

For practice in thinking and planning quickly, brainstorm with your classmates how you might approach writing on the sample topics provided for essay exams and timed writings in this chapter. Include in your discussions possible thesis sentences, various patterns of organization, and specific evidence you might use. Don't expect everybody to come up with the same ideas.

ests, potential, or progress over time to teachers, gallery owners, employers, or juries of other artists. Financial managers keep records of clients' stocks, bonds, mutual funds, or investments and periodically review and update these investment portfolios as needed. In fact, even faculty members sometimes compile portfolios of work products to apply for promotions or to change positions. In every version, the portfolio is not static but changes according to recent achievements, expanded ideas, or new interests. A writing portfolio, then, is a collection of pieces of writing that represent the writer's best work. Collected over time and across projects or interests, a portfolio showcases a writer's talent and hard work and demonstrates an ability to make thoughtful choices about content and presentation. It is a final product meant to be shared with others — perhaps to be evaluated by a teacher or trained rater or to be enjoyed by friends or family.

Ideally, the contents of a college student's writing portfolio would be collected over several terms and from different types of courses, since most educators believe that measurable growth happens most clearly over months and in different subject areas. Some colleges and universities are using portfolios for long-term assessment or to test students for competency (perhaps as an exit examination to the composition courses). Much of the advice in this section applies if you are preparing a portfolio for either a single class or a wider assessment program. In portfolio assessment for a single course, the portfolio is usually due at the end of the course, includes pieces you have written and revised for that course, and ends with the completion of the course. With some variations, most portfolios ask for some kind of accompanying introduction (usually some form of self-assessment or rationale) addressed to readers, who might be teachers, supervisors, evaluators, parents, or classmates.

UNDERSTANDING PORTFOLIO ASSESSMENT

The portfolio is more than one big assignment that comes at the end of the course; it is, instead, a method of evaluation and teaching that shapes the whole course from beginning to end. For example, your portfolio course will probably emphasize responses to your writing — from your classmates and your instructor — but not necessarily grades on your papers. In other words, the portfolio is graded at the end of the term, but your separate papers or drafts may not be. The portfolio method attempts to deemphasize grades in an effort to shift the attention to the writing process itself — to discovery, planning, drafting, peer response, revision, editing — and to give time for your skills to develop before the writing "counts."

The portfolio method is very flexible, but you will need to read your instructor's syllabus and assignment sheets carefully and listen well in class to determine what kind of portfolio you'll be expected to keep. Below are a few of the typical types of portfolios. Not all of them are mutually exclusive, and more than one might be used in a single course. Consider which of the following descriptions fit with your instructors' assignment or expectations.

A writing folder. Students are asked to submit all drafts, notes, outlines, scribbles, doodles, and messy pages — in short, all writing done for the course, whether finished or unfinished. Everything is saved, if only for simple record keeping, but students may also be asked to select from the folder two or three of their most promising pieces to revise for a "presentation portfolio." The folder is usually not accompanied by a reflective introduction or cover letter.

A learning (or open) portfolio. Students are free to submit a variety of materials that have contributed to their learning of the course material or subject matter. In this approach, the instructor may give students considerable freedom to determine the contents, organization, and presentation of the portfolio. A learning portfolio for composition class might include photos or other nonprint objects collected to demonstrate learning.

A closed portfolio. Students must turn in assignments that are specified by the instructor, or their options for what to include may be limited. For example, the instructor may ask for a "writing from recall" assignment, a "writing from imagination" assignment, and a "writing from sources" assignment.

A midterm portfolio. The portfolio is given a trial run at midterm, or the midterm grade is determined by one or two papers that are submitted for evaluation, perhaps accompanied by a brief self-assessment.

A final or presentation portfolio. The portfolio is due and is evaluated at the end of the course, after it has been revised, edited, and polished to presentation quality.

A modified or combination portfolio. The student has some choice, but not unlimited choice, in what to include. For example, the instructor may ask for three entries that demonstrate certain features or parts of the course.

Find out as soon as possible after the course begins what kind of portfolio your instructor has in mind and what the final result of your portfolio assessment will be. Here's one likely scenario. You are required to submit a modified or combination portfolio — one that contains, for example, three revised papers (out of the five or six papers written to fulfill the course requirements). You decide, late in the term, which three papers to include or where to concentrate on revision and editing. It's also likely that you will be asked to reflect on what those choices say about you as a writer, to demonstrate your own learning in the course, or at least to explain the decisions you made in the process of writing a paper.

To find out more about the type of portfolio expected in your course, you might find out answers to the following questions from your instructor, the syllabus, or assignment sheets:

How many papers should you include in the portfolio?

Do all the papers you include need to be revised?

If so, what level of revision is expected?

How much of the final grade for the course is determined by the portfolio grade?

Are the portfolio entries graded separately, or does the entire portfolio receive one grade?

May you include papers written for other courses?

May you include entries other than texts or documents — such as photographs, videos, maps, diskettes with downloaded Web pages, or other visual aids?

Must you preface the portfolio with a cover letter?

Does each entry need a separate cover sheet?

Is reflection or self-assessment expected, or are description and explanation adequate?

TIPS FOR KEEPING A PORTFOLIO

Keep Everything, and Stay Organized.   Don't throw anything away! Keep all your notes, lists, drafts, outlines, clusters, responses from readers, photocopied articles, and references for works cited. If you have your own computer, *back up everything* to a diskette or an external tape drive. If you use campus or community computers, save your work to a diskette, and keep an extra blank diskette in your bag or backpack. Use a system to organize everything. Invest in a good folder with pockets, and label the contents of each pocket with the drafts, notes, outlines, and peer review forms included for each assignment.

Manage Your Time.   The portfolio isn't due until the end of the course (or at midterm), but planning ahead will save you time and frustration. For example, as your instructor returns each of your assignments with comments or suggestions for revision, make some changes in response to those suggestions while the ideas are fresh. In addition, if you don't understand one of your instructor's comments or don't know how to approach the suggestion, ask right away — at the end of class or during office hours that same week. Then, after you are clear about the comment and have one or two ideas for revision, make notes of what you think you want to do, put the paper away, and let it simmer. When you're ready to work on it again, you will have both a plan and some fresh insight.

Practice Self-Assessment.   For writing and other complex activities, it's important to your improvement to step back and evaluate your own performance — to keep track of what you do well and what you need to work on. Maybe you have great ideas but find it hard to organize them. Maybe you write powerful thesis statements but run out of things to say in support of them. Maybe you hate the part of writing that insists on correctness and perfection — parts like the final editing and the "Works Cited" pages. Don't wait until the portfolio cover letter due date to begin tracking your learning or assessing your strengths, weaknesses, or preferences.

You can practice self-assessment from the first day of class. For example, after receiving the course syllabus from your instructor, and after picking up your books at the bookstore, review your class syllabus carefully, especially the course policies, procedures, assignments, and expectations. After reviewing these materials, write one or two paragraphs about how you think you will do in this course. What assignments or activities do you think you will do well on and why? What assignments or activities do you think will be hard for you and why? In addition, for each paper you share in peer response groups or for each paper your instructor collects, write a journal entry to yourself about what you think the paper does well and what it still needs. Keep track, in a log or journal, of the process you go through to plan, research, or draft each paper — where you get stuck and where things click.

Choose the Entries Carefully.   If your instructor has not assigned each entry and you have choices about what to include, consider your choices in light of the course as a whole and what it has emphasized about good writing. Of course, you want to include your best pieces and select those your instructor or evaluator will think are "the best," but also consider which ones show the most promise or potential. Keep in mind that more work must be done to prepare them for the final presentation, so be sure you have ideas and energy for revisiting these assignments. Which ones do you want to continue working on or have the most interest in revising? As you look through the pile, which drafts show creativity, insight, or an unusual approach to the assignment? Instructors will appreciate seeing some variety in your portfolio — pieces with different purposes, audiences, or voices. They also may appreciate evidence of depth, so show your ability to do thorough research or stay with a topic for several weeks. As you make your choices and prepare to revise and edit them, consider the order of the entries — which piece might work best first or last and how the placement of each entry affects the whole.

Write a Strong Reflective Introduction or Cover Letter.   Practicing self-assessment and tracking your writing process and your good decisions or successes will be useful when it's time to write your introduction. This piece — usually a self-assessment piece or rationale in the form of a cover letter, a statement, or a description for each of your entries — could be the most important text you write all semester. As your evaluator opens your portfolio and begins reading, first impressions are crucial. The introduction or cover letter introduces readers to your collection of writing and portrays you as a student writer. It explains your choices in putting the portfolio together and demonstrates that you can evaluate the strengths and weaknesses of your work and your writing process. For many portfolio-based courses, the reflective introduction or cover letter is the "final exam" or the ultimate test of what you've learned about the qualities of good writing, about the anticipation of readers' needs, and about the importance of details — in this case, the details of a careful self-presentation. The self-assessment piece does not have to be the first entry in the portfolio, but it often is because of its role in establishing a relationship with your reader or evaluator. Check with your instructor if the placement is not specified.

If your instructor has not assigned a reflective introduction or cover letter, it could be that you've been asked to keep a writing folder and not a portfolio. Folders hold the materials assembled for the course but don't ask for self-assessment or reflective learning. But it also could be that descriptions of your process or your choices are expected to appear throughout the portfolio — perhaps at the end or perhaps in brief introductions to each portfolio entry.

DISCOVERY
CHECKLIST

Writing a Reflective Introduction or Cover Letter

- Who will read the cover letter in this portfolio?
- What qualities of writing will your reader value?
- Is the reader reading it to suggest changes or to evaluate your work and assess your effort and talent?
- What will the outcome of the reading be? How much can you influence the outcome?
- What do you want to emphasize about your writing? What are you proud of? What have you learned? What did you have trouble with?
- How can you present your writing ability in the best light?

If your reader or evaluator is also your classroom instructor, look back over the comments and responses on your returned papers, and review the course syllabus and assignment sheets. What patterns do you see in your instructor's concerns or directions? Imagine that a friend has asked you whether she should enroll in your instructor's section. What information can you give your friend about your instructor's expectations — or pet peeves? Use what you've learned about your instructor's values as a reader to compose a convincing, well-developed introductory statement or cover letter for your portfolio. It's doubtful that your instructor is looking to be flattered, and asking for an *A* is probably not very diplomatic, but some humor, lively writing, or a charming anecdote might be effective.

If your readers or evaluators are unknown, ask your instructor to give you as much information as possible about your readers so that you can decide which logical, ethical, or emotional appeals (see p. 103) might be most effective for your audience. In this scenario, you won't know your readers personally (and they won't know you, either). Still, it's safe to assume that your evaluators will be trained in portfolio assessment and that they share with your instructor many of the same ideas about good writing. If your college writing program has a set of guidelines or policies and grading criteria, consult it for information as you begin composing.

How long should your introduction or cover letter be? Check with your instructor for these types of details, but regardless of length, you need to develop your ideas or support your claims, as you do in any effective piece of writing. In this situation, you are trying to convince your reader that you have chosen wisely, revised judiciously, and edited carefully. If you are asked to write a letter, follow the format for a business letter: include the date, a salutation, and a closing, and remember how important first impressions are.

In the reflective introduction, you might try some of the following (but don't try to use all of them):

Discuss your best entry and why it is your best.

Detail the revisions you've done — the improvements and changes that you want readers to notice.

Discuss everything included, touching on the strengths of each.

Outline the writing and revising process that you used for one or more of your entries.

State what the portfolio illustrates about you as a writer, student, researcher, or critical thinker.

Acknowledge your weaknesses, but show how you've worked to overcome them.

Acknowledge your reader-respondents and how they have influenced your portfolio pieces.

Reflect on what you've learned about writing, reading, and other topics of the course.

Lay the groundwork for a positive evaluation of your work.

Polishing the Final Portfolio.   From the first page to the last, your portfolio should meet high standards. It should be a set of documents ready for public presentation and a product you can take pride in or show to others. Taking pride in your work should begin with careful editing and proofreading, but think too about creative ways to give your portfolio a final distinctive feature. For example, consider having the portfolio bound at your local copy shop, adding a colorful cover or illustrations, or including a table of contents or a running header. Although a cheerful cover or photographs will not make up for weak writing or careless editing, readers will value the extra time and effort you put into the final product.

Chapter 14

Writing for Business

Most of the world's business communication takes place in writing. The reasons are easy to understand. Although a conversation or telephone message may conveniently be forgotten or ignored, a letter or memorandum is a physical thing that sits on a desk, calling for some action. Written documents also provide a permanent record of an individual's or organization's business dealings: they can be kept on file and checked for details later.

Personnel managers of large corporations, the people who do the hiring, tend to be keenly interested in applicants who can write clearly, accurately, and effectively. A survey conducted at Cornell University asked business executives to rate in importance the qualities they would like their employees to possess. Skill in writing was ranked in fourth place, ahead of managerial skill and skill in analysis. This fact is worth recalling if you ever wonder what practical good you can do your career by taking a writing course.

In this chapter, we first outline some general guidelines for business writing and then show you four kinds of business writing likely to prove useful — letters, memoranda, electronic mail, and résumés.

Guidelines for Business Writing

The types of writing generated in the business world are even more varied in their form and content than the types of writing you will encounter in college. Nonetheless, certain principles apply to almost all of them. Good business writing has a clear purpose and succeeds in achieving that purpose. To be effective, you need to know your purpose, remember your audience, use an appropriate tone, and present your information carefully. Perhaps most important, you need to remember that when you write to a business, your writing represents you; when you write as part of your job, your writing represents your company as well.

KNOW YOUR PURPOSE

To write effectively for business, you first need to determine your purpose in writing. This helps you select and arrange information; it gives you a standard against which to measure your final draft. Most likely, you will want to inform your readers about something or motivate them to take a specific action. In other words, a large part of the purpose in any business writing is to create a certain response in your readers.

DISCOVERY CHECKLIST

Purpose in Business Writing

- Do you want to inform? (For example, do you want to make an announcement, keep your readers posted on a developing situation, explain a specialized piece of knowledge, or reply to a request?)
- Do you want to motivate some action? (For example, do you want a question answered, a wrong corrected, a certain decision to be made, or a personnel director to hire you?)
- When your readers are finished reading what you've written, what do you want them to think? What do you want them to do?
- What is your ultimate goal? What do you want to be the final outcome of writing this piece of business correspondence?

KEEP YOUR AUDIENCE IN MIND

Consider everything in your business writing from your readers' point of view. After all, the purpose of business communication is not to express your ideas but to have your readers act on them, even if the action is simply to notice that you are well informed and on top of the situation.

Sometimes you will be acquainted with the person to whom you are writing; in such cases, you already know a great deal about that person's expertise, priorities, and attitudes. At other times, you may never have met the person. Still, if you brainstorm for a few minutes, you'll probably find that you can make some educated guesses about the person based on what you know about her or his position or company. Here are some questions to ask yourself about your readers:

DISCOVERY CHECKLIST

Audience in Business Writing

- What do your readers already know about the subject? Are they experts in the field? Have they been kept up to date on the situation? Avoid telling people what they already know: it only frustrates and annoys them.
- What do your readers need to know about the subject? If your purpose is to inform, what information do they expect you to provide? If your purpose is to motivate, what information do they need before they can take action? Be sure to include this information.
- What can you assume about your readers' priorities and expectations? Are they busy executives, with stacks of mail to weed through? Are they careful,

conscientious administrators who will appreciate your attention to detail? Tailor your writing to meet your readers' expectations.
• What is most likely to motivate your readers to take the action you want? Sometimes it may be acknowledging a shared interest in a social cause; sometimes it may be stating that prompt action will avoid a lawsuit. Whatever the motivating factor is, be sure to include and emphasize it.

In most business writing—especially in letters and memoranda where the purpose is to motivate—it's useful to adopt a "you" attitude. In other words, instead of focusing on what "I, the writer" would like, focus on how "you, the reader" will benefit.

"I" ATTITUDE	Please send me the form so that I can process your order.
"YOU" ATTITUDE	So that you can receive your shipment promptly, please send me the form.

Another technique is to picture your reader in your mind as concretely as possible. Even if you have no idea who, exactly, will be reading your writing, make up someone—and supply her or him with a personality, an office, and a wardrobe. Then imagine this reader looking over your writing and reacting to it, line by line.

USE AN APPROPRIATE TONE

Tone is the quality of writing that reveals your attitude toward your topic and your readers. Whether or not you are aware of it, everything you write has a tone, and much of your readers' impression of you depends on the tone of your writing. If you show your readers that you respect them, their intelligence, and their feelings, they in turn are far more likely to view you and your message favorably.

Most business writing today ranges from the informal to the slightly formal. Gone are the extremely formal phrases that once dotted business correspondence: *enclosed herewith, be advised that, pursuant to the stated request.* That sort of language is considered stuffy and pompous today. At the other extreme, however, slang, overfriendliness, and any other marks of a casual style might cast doubts on your seriousness or credibility. Strive for a relaxed and conversational style, using simple sentences, familiar words, and the active voice. As you gain more experience, you may find that for certain people and certain situations a casual manner is comfortable and effective. The safest route, though, is to be somewhat more restrained.

TOO CASUAL	I hear that thing with the new lackey is a definite go.
TOO FORMAL	This office stands informed that the administration's request for supplementary personnel has been honored.
APPROPRIATE	I've learned that a new office assistant has been hired.

In all your business writing, be courteous, polite, and considerate. If you are writing to complain, remember that the person reading your letter may not be the one who caused the problem — and even if he or she is, you are more likely to win your case with courtesy than with sarcasm or insults. When delivering bad news, you might be tempted to hide behind a impersonal bureaucratic facade, but remember that your reader will probably interpret this as coldness and lack of sympathy. And try to avoid language that makes it seem as if you're avoiding responsibility; if you have made a mistake or done something wrong, acknowledge it. "Too often," notes a professor of business English, "inexperienced writers in the corporate world equate 'professional' with 'bureaucratic,' forgetting that every good writer — in or out of business — writes as one human being to another."

Having someone else read your writing to check for tone or setting it aside for a "cooling off" period is always a good idea. This will help you catch impersonal phrases such as "your claim for damaged goods is acknowledged" and transform them into the far more effective "I have received your request for a replacement part." When you reread your writing to check for tone, here are some things you can ask yourself:

REVISION CHECKLIST

Tone in Business Writing

- Have you avoided slang terms and extremely casual language?
- Have you avoided excessively formal or unnecessarily sophisticated words?
- Are your sentences of a manageable length? (Try reading a questionable sentence out loud in a single breath; if it sounds too long and complicated, it is.)
- Have you used the active voice ("I am sending it") rather than the passive voice ("It is being sent")?
- Is there anything in what you've written that might sound blaming or accusatory?
- When you read your writing, do you hear a friendly, considerate, competent person behind the words?
- Have you asked someone else to read your writing to check for tone?

PRESENT INFORMATION CAREFULLY

In business, time is money: time wasted reading irrelevant material or trying to comprehend poorly written documents is money wasted. To be effective, the information you present in your business writing should be concise, clear, and well organized.

Concise writing shows that you respect your readers' time. In most cases, if a letter, memo, or résumé is longer than a page or two, it's too long. You might need to find a better way to present the information (long lists can be placed in separate documents, for example), or you might need to cut information or details that your readers don't really need. Go through your writing sentence by sentence and delete any wordy or unnecessary expressions.

Clear writing ensures that the correct message will reach your readers. If the readers of your business correspondence misinterpret what you've said, you may not have the chance to correct their misunderstanding. First, make sure the information you convey is accurate and complete. Then make your writing so clear and unambiguous that no possibility of misinterpretation exists. Scrutinize each word and phrase to make sure that it means exactly what you want it to mean. Avoid jargon, as it can cloud meaning. Emphasize the most important information by putting it in a prominent spot (usually at the beginning). Let your readers know exactly what you want them to do — politely, of course. If you have a question, ask it. If you want something, request it.

Well-organized writing helps readers move through it quickly and easily. Every piece of business correspondence should be written so that it can be skimmed. Although you want your readers to consider carefully what you've written, in reality many of them will glance over it quickly; if a reader spends fifteen seconds looking over what you've written, you want to be sure that she or he comes away with an accurate impression. Make sure the topic of the document is absolutely clear from the very beginning. In a letter, you should usually state your topic in the first paragraph; in a memorandum, you should put it in the subject line. Use a conventional format that your readers will expect (see Figures 14.1, 14.2, and 14.4 later in this chapter). Break information into easily processed chunks: in letters and memoranda, use paragraphs of no more than seven or eight lines. Order the chunks of information logically and consistently. Finally, use topic sentences and headings (when each is appropriate) to label each chunk of information and give your readers an overview of your document.

Crafting a concise, clear, and well-organized piece of business writing takes skill and patience — but so does all good writing. Take a look at the examples in the next sections to see how the principles described here can be put into action. As you work on your own business writing, here are some questions you can ask yourself:

REVISION CHECKLIST

Conciseness, Clarity, and Organization in Business Writing

- Have you kept your letter, memo, or résumé to a page or two?
- Have you cut all deadwood and wordiness?
- Have you scrutinized every word and phrase to ensure that it can't be misinterpreted? Have you supplied all the background information readers need to understand your points?
- Have you emphasized the most important part of your message? Will readers know what you want them to do?
- Have you used a consistent and logical order? Have you followed a conventional format?
- If appropriate, have you included the labels and headings your readers will need to make their way through your writing quickly and easily?

Business Letters

Knowing how to draft a good business letter is a skill that can serve you well in any job and in your personal business dealings. Organizations use business letters to correspond with outside parties — either individual people or other organizations. (Most correspondence within an organization is conveyed through memoranda; see p. 347.) Business letters are used to request and provide information, motivate action, respond to requests, and sell goods and services. Letters rather than phone calls are used for most important transactions because a letter writer has the opportunity to craft a clear, thorough statement — and a letter reader has the opportunity to review and scrutinize the facts and make a considered decision. Letters are also more convenient because a busy person can respond whenever he or she has an opportunity. Finally, letters are useful because they become part of the permanent record; they can be referred to later to determine exactly who said what and when. You should keep a copy of every letter you write; if you write on a computer, keep a printout as well as a backup on disk.

An effective business letter is straightforward, forceful (but polite and considerate), concise, neat, and legible. Letters are usually written person to person (or at least read as if they were written this way), so the tone you use is very important. A good business letter is brief — limited to one page if at all possible. It supplies whatever information the reader needs, no more. Because they are so brief, business letters are often judged on the basis of small but important details — grammar, punctuation, format, appearance, and openings and closings. In general, business letters tend to be conservative and conventional: this is not the place to try out nifty new typefaces on your word processor or experiment with stream-of-consciousness writing.

(Letters written to apply for a job are covered in "Résumés and Application Letters"; see p. 350.)

FORMAT FOR BUSINESS LETTERS

Although there are few absolute rights and wrongs, the format of business letters is fairly well established by convention. Listed here are the elements of a standard business letter followed by two examples of business letters using these elements (Figures 14.1 and 14.2). Except where noted, leave one line of extra space between elements; in very short letters, it's acceptable to leave additional space before the inside address.

Return address. This is your address or the address of the company for which you are writing. Use no abbreviations except the two-letter postal abbreviation for the state. (Note: You do not have to type a return address on preprinted letterhead stationery that already provides this information.)

Date. This goes on the first line after the return address, without an extra line of space above. Spell out the name of the month, and follow it by the day, a comma, and the year.

Inside address. This is the address of the person to whom you are writing. The first name should be the full name of the person, with his or her title (*Mr., Ms., Dr., Professor*); when addressing a woman who does not have a professional title, use *Ms.* unless you know for certain that she prefers *Miss* or *Mrs.* The second line should identify the position the person holds (if any), and the third line should be the name of the organization (if you are writing to one). If you don't know the name of the person who will read your letter, it is acceptable to start with the name of the position, department, or organization. When writing the address, use no abbreviations except the two-letter postal abbreviation for the state.

Salutation. Skip a line of space, and then type *Dear* followed by the person's title and last name; end the line with a colon. If you don't know the name of the person who will read your letter, it is acceptable to word your salutation *Dear Editor* or *Dear Angell's Bakery.* The salutation *Gentlemen* has become too sexist for contemporary usage. You can also omit the salutation altogether.

Body. This is your message. Leave one line of space between paragraphs, and begin each paragraph even with the left margin (no indentations). Paragraphs should generally be no longer than seven or eight typed lines.

Closing. Leave one line of space after the last paragraph, and then use a conventional closing followed by a comma: *Sincerely, Sincerely yours, Respectfully yours, Yours truly.*

Typed name with position. Leave four lines of space after the closing, and type your name in full, even if you will sign only your first name. Do not include a title before your name. If you are writing on behalf of an organization, you can include your position on the next line.

Signature. After you have finished typing or printing out the letter, be sure to sign your name in the space between the closing and the typed name. Unless you have established a personal relationship with the person to whom you are writing, use both your first and last names. Do not include a title before your name.

Abbreviations at end. In some cases, abbreviations after your typed name communicate additional information about the letter. If you send a copy of the letter to someone other than the person addressed, use *cc:* followed by the name of the person or organization who will receive a copy. If the letter is accompanied by another document in the same envelope, use *Enc.* or *Enclosure.* If the letter has been typed by someone other than the person who wrote and signed it, the writer's initials are given in capital letters, followed by a slash and the initials of the typist in lowercase letters: *VW/dbw.* Leave at least two lines of extra space between the typed name and any abbreviations; put each abbreviation on a separate line.

Two standard formats specify the placement of these elements on the page. To correctly align a letter using *modified block style* (see Figure 14.1), you need to

FIGURE 14.1.   Letter Using Modified Block Style

                                                1453 Illinois Avenue
                                                Miami, FL 33133
                                                January 26, 1999

Customer Service Department
Fidelity Products, Inc.
1192 Plymouth Avenue
Little Rock, AK 72210

Dear Customer Service Representative:

I recently purchased a VCR stand (Model XAR) from your company. I
have been unable to assemble it because the instructions are unclear. These
instructions not only are incomplete (step 6 is missing) but are accompanied
by diagrams so small and dark that it is impossible to distinguish the numbers
for the different pieces.

Please send me usable instructions. If I do not receive improved instructions
in the next fourteen days, I will return my VCR stand to the store where I
purchased it and request a full refund.

I have used your TV and video equipment for more than ten years and have
been very satisfied, so I was particularly surprised and disappointed to find
that you produce such an inferior item. If you continue to pay little attention
to the needs of your customers, I will consider purchasing the products of
other companies.

Thank you for your attention to these concerns.

                                                Sincerely,

                                                James Winter

                                                James Winter

imagine a line running down the center of the page from top to bottom. The return address, date, closing, signature, and typed name are placed to align at the
left side with this line. The *full block style* is generally used only on letterhead stationery that includes the name and address of the organization. Omit typing the
return address, and align all the elements at the left margin. (See Figure 14.2.)
    There are also two standard formats for envelopes. The U.S. Postal Service
recommends a format that uses all capital letters, standard abbreviations, and

FIGURE 14.2.   Letter Using Full Block Style

Fidelity Products, Inc.
1192 Plymouth Avenue · Little Rock, AK 72210 · 501–555–0100

February 2, 1999

Mr. James Winter
1453 Illinois Avenue
Miami, FL 33133

Dear Mr. Winter:

Thank you for your letter expressing concern about the instructions for assembling the Model XAR VCR stand. We always appreciate honest feedback from our customers. Enclosed you will find a corrected and legible copy of the instructions. You can also call one of our technicians at 1-800-555-1234 for assistance in assembling the stand. If you are still unsatisfied, we will be more than happy to refund the cost of the stand or to exchange the stand for another of our products.

We were sorry to hear that the original instructions for Model XAR were not helpful. We are working to improve them and the instructions for other products we offer. I have forwarded a copy of your letter to our director of product support, who is responsible for strengthening our instruction packages.

Thank you again for helping us improve our products. I hope you will continue to purchase and enjoy Fidelity's products. Please feel free to contact me if I can be of any further assistance.

Sincerely yours,

Maria Solis

Maria Solis
Customer Service Supervisor

cc: Edward Copply
Enc.

no punctuation; this style makes the information on the envelope easier for the Postal Service to scan and process. However, this format may not be acceptable in all situations; it is always safe to use a conventional envelope format. See Figure 14.3 for examples of both formats.

Finally, remember that the physical appearance of a business letter is very important. Observe these guidelines:

FIGURE 14.3.   Envelope Formats

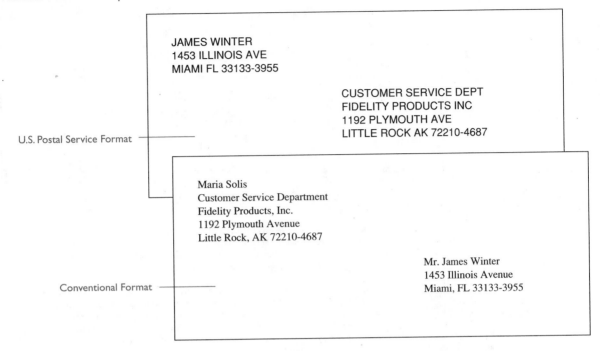

U.S. Postal Service Format

JAMES WINTER
1453 ILLINOIS AVE
MIAMI FL 33133-3955

CUSTOMER SERVICE DEPT
FIDELITY PRODUCTS INC
1192 PLYMOUTH AVE
LITTLE ROCK AK 72210-4687

Conventional Format

Maria Solis
Customer Service Department
Fidelity Products, Inc.
1192 Plymouth Avenue
Little Rock, AK 72210-4687

Mr. James Winter
1453 Illinois Avenue
Miami, FL 33133-3955

Use 8-½-by-11-inch bond paper, with matching envelopes.

If you use a typewriter, make sure the ribbon is dark and the keys are clean; if you use a word processor, use a letter-quality or laser printer.

Single-space and use an extra line of space to separate paragraphs and the different elements of the letter. Use only one side of the page.

Leave margins of at least one inch on the right and left sides; try to make the top and bottom margins fairly even, although you may have to have a larger bottom margin if your letter is very short.

Pay extremely careful attention to grammar, punctuation, and mechanics. Your readers will.

Memoranda

A *memorandum* (*memo* for short) is a form of communication used within a company to request or exchange information, to make announcements, and to confirm what has passed in conversation. Generally, the topic is quite narrow and should be apparent to the reader in a single glance. Memos tend to be written in the first person (*I* or *we*) and can range from the very informal (if written to a peer) to the extremely formal (if written to a high-ranking

FIGURE 14.4.   Memorandum

memorandum

Date: February 8, 1999

To: Edward Copply, Director, Product Support

cc: Justin Blake

From: Maria Solis, Customer Service Supervisor   *MS*

Subject: Customer dissatisfaction with instructions for Model XAR

As I mentioned in our conversation of January 30, the Customer Service Department has recently received many letters and phone calls regarding the instructions for assembling our new VCR stand, Model XAR. Customers find these instructions confusing and often ask us to arrange a refund. (A copy of the instructions is attached.)

After examining the letters in our files, I've concluded that customers have two specific concerns. The first concern is that the written instructions skip words and entire steps. If you look at the attached copy, you will notice that there is no step 6 and that step 3 reads "Connect the to leg one." The second concern is that the drawings are too dark. Customers complain that dark shading obscures the numbers and makes it difficult to determine where one sections begins and the other ends.

The number of calls and letters we're getting suggests that these poor instructions are creating frustration and resentment among both our loyal customers and first-time buyers. In most cases, the customers who contact us are satisfied when we send them a photocopied set of the corrected instructions we've created here in Customer Service, but I feel strongly that the instructions sent out with the product should be improved.

I know that you're planning to review and revise the entire line of product information sheets and instructions, Ed. I recommend that the instructions for Model XAR be put at the top of the list.

Please let me know if I can provide further information.

Enclosure

superior on an important matter). Memos are frequently used to convey information to large groups — an entire team, department, or organization. Most memos are short, but the memo format can also be used to convey proposals and reports; when they are long, good memos make free use of headings, subheadings, lists, and other features that make information easy to scan.

FORMAT FOR MEMORANDA

Every organization has its own format for memos; some organizations even have preprinted forms with spaces to fill in the appropriate information. In general, the heading consists of a series of lines with clear labels (followed by colons), each line conveying a key piece of information about the memo and its distribution.

Date:	(date on which memo is sent)
To:	(person or persons to whom it is primarily addressed)
cc:	(names of anyone else who receives a copy)
From:	(name of the writer)
Subject: *or* Re:	(concise, accurate statement of the memo's topic)

The most important line of a memo may be the subject line, as this often determines whether the memo is read or not. (The old-fashioned abbreviation *Re:* for *regarding,* is still used, but we recommend the more common *Subject.*) State the topic in very few words, but provide the details needed to make it an accurate summary ("Agenda for 12/10 meeting with Ann Kois," "Sales estimates for new product line"). Usually, instead of signing a memo, the writer simply initials it in the space after his or her name. (For an example of a memo, see Figure 14.4.)

Electronic Mail

Electronic mail (e-mail for short) is a message sent directly from one computer to another by means of a network. E-mail is becoming more popular in business settings because it is easy (the writer needs only type a message and send it without printing a copy, typing an envelope, putting on postage, and so on), speedy (messages usually arrive the same day they are sent), and convenient (writers can send messages at any time, and readers can read and respond to them at their convenience). E-mail combines the immediacy of a telephone conversation with the permanence of letters and memoranda. It is commonly used both within organizations and between organizations and outside parties. However, letters and memos are usually still preferred for formal, official correspondence.

Because it seems so conversational, e-mail is rarely scrutinized and polished like other written correspondence. Much of it is neither printed out before it is sent nor reviewed by anyone other than the writer. Obviously, the likelihood for errors and omissions is much higher than it is for letters and memos. People who correspond regularly through e-mail tend to forgive one another's spelling mistakes and infelicities; however, you should remember that your e-mail messages are a part of the official record. Remember, too, that there is no guarantee of privacy with e-mail. You may feel that you are having a confidential chat with a trusted friend or colleague, but the chat can be intercepted, recorded on other computers, and distributed either in print or over a network.

FIGURE 14.5.   Electronic Mail

Subject: Improving Product Instructions
Date: 99-02-08 10:11:31 EST
To: JMANDALA_INTSALES (Jeannie Mandala, Institutional Sales)
From: ECOPPLY_PRODSUP (Edward Copply, Product Support)

Jeannie,
As you know, we're planning to review and revise our entire line of product info.
sheets and instructions. The goal will be to make the instructions more useful and to
present a consistent image for FIDELITY PRODUCTS.

Could you please fill me in on any complaints you've been receiving from our institutional customers? Let me know which products are causing difficulties, how many
complaints you've received, and what the specific criticisms are.

Thanks for your help on this, Jeannie. I'll keep you posted on our plans.

Ed

FORMAT FOR E-MAIL

The headings for e-mail are predetermined by the systems that generate and transmit it; these almost universally use a standard memo format. The computer will prompt you to enter information in the header lines: *To:*, *cc:*, and *Subject:*, for example. Then you simply type your message. The person receiving your message sees your header information as well as a *From* line that gives your name.

E-mail is a developing and flexible form, so there are fewer conventions and a wider range of acceptable practices than with other business correspondence. Keep in mind that many e-mail messages will be read and responded to while displayed on the computer screen. If possible, keep the messages short, no more than a couple of screens. If a message is longer, make it easy to navigate by stating at the beginning what it covers and by using clear, obvious headings and visually noticeable dividers (extra space or a line of asterisks between sections, for example). If you send long messages or messages with important information, it's likely that they'll be printed out; consider what your writing will look like in this format, as well. (For an example of an e-mail message, see Figure 14.5.)

For more about e-mail and writing with computers, see Chapter 21.

Résumés and Application Letters

The most momentous business correspondence you write may be the résumé and letter you use to apply for a job. It's wise to take great pains with both. They will enable a busy personnel manager to decide quickly whether your application deserves any follow-up. To write a good résumé and application letter, you will need to draw on many of the skills and strategies for clear and persuasive writing that you have learned about and practiced elsewhere in this book. Direct, persuasive, correct prose can help you stand out above the crowd.

RÉSUMÉS

In a résumé, you present yourself as someone who has the qualifications needed to excel at a job, someone who will be an asset to the organization to which you are applying. You will want to consider every word and format decision carefully, revising and revising again until the finished product gleams like a jewel. Because of the time and expense spent in crafting a good résumé, job seekers often have multiple copies of a single résumé on hand to include with all their applications; any relevant information not highlighted in the résumé can be discussed in the accompanying application letter. However, if you have access to a word processor and can easily print out attractive copies, you may want to customize your résumé for each job you apply for.

A résumé is a highly formatted document, but also one that allows a wide variety of decisions about style, organization, and appearance. In this section, we describe a typical résumé, but you should know that there are many acceptable formats. Unless you have a great deal of relevant work experience, your résumé should be no longer than one page long. The standard résumé consists of a heading and labeled sections that detail your experience and qualifications in a number of areas. (For an example of a résumé, see Figure 14.6.)

Heading. Put your name on the first line; street address on the second; city, state, and zip code on the third; and phone number on the fourth. The heading is generally centered on the page.

Employment objective. Although this section is optional, we recommend it because it allows personnel officers to see at a glance what your priorities and goals are. Try to sound confident, ambitious, and eager but not pompous or presumptuous.

Education. This is generally the first section and is almost always included. For each postsecondary school you've attended, specify the name of the institution, your major, your date of graduation (or expected graduation), and your grade point average (if it reflects well on you). You can also mention any awards or honors or any course work that may be relevant to the job.

Experience. This is the most important section of the résumé. List each job separately, starting with the most recent one first. You can include both full-time and part-time jobs. For each job, give the name of the organization, your position, your responsibilities, and the dates you held the job. If you were involved in any unusual projects or were responsible for any important developments, describe them. Remember that the point of the résumé is to show your prospective employer that you are well qualified for the position you want. Highlight details that show relevant work experience and leadership ability. Minimize information about jobs or responsibilities that are unconnected to the job for which you're applying.

FIGURE 14.6.   Résumé

Sheryl W. Fitzgerald
266 Castrodale Ave., Apt. 4
Falmouth MA 02541
508-555-9876

Objective	An editorial position with a publication at a nonprofit organization
Education	**Ohio State University**, Columbus, OH. Bachelor's degree in journalism, June 1995. Grade point average: 3.6.
	Oakland Community College, Bloomfield Hills, MI. Associate degree in public relations, May 1992. Course work in communications, business writing.
Experience	
9/93 to 6/95	**The Lantern** (circulation 30,000), Ohio University's daily student newspaper. Reporter, copyeditor, layout chief.
6/94 to 9/94	**Cincinnati Enquirer** (circulation 350,000), Cincinnati, OH. General assignment reporter.
6/92 to 8/93	**Cape Cod Times** (circulation 50,000), Hyannis, MA. Business reporter. Covered local stocks, real estate, and business issues and trends.
5/91 to 8/91	**Dow Jones News Service**, New York City. Editing intern under the Dow Jones Newspaper Fund program. Edited stories from *Wall Street Journal* reporters, corporate sources, and wire services.
Skills	Word processing (WordPerfect 5.1 for DOS, Word for Windows), layout, copyediting, proofreading.
Interests	Volunteer tutor for the Cape Cod Literacy Council, 9/92 to 8/93. Founding member of the Cape and Islands News Association.
References	Available upon request.

Skills. If you have special skills that your prospective employer might find attractive (data processing, technical drawing, knowledge of a foreign language) but that aren't obvious from the descriptions of your education and work experience, you can list them.

Interests. You can either specify professional interests and activities (*Member of Birmingham Bricklayers Association*) or personal pursuits (*skiing, hiking, needlepoint*). In either case, this section should show that you are a dedicated and well-rounded individual.

References. If you are answering a job advertisement that requests references, give them. Always contact your references in advance to make sure they will be willing to give you a good recommendation. For each person, give the name, his or her organization and position, and the organization's address and phone number. If references have not been requested, you can simply note "Available on request."

Keep your résumé brief and pointed by using phrases and clauses rather than complete sentences. Use action verbs (*supervised, ordered, maintained*) and the active voice whenever possible. Highlight labels with underlining, boldface, or a larger type size. And remember that a neat, attractive, professional appearance is extremely important. Arrange information on the page so that it is pleasing to the eye, use the best paper you can, and either print your résumé on a laser printer or have it typeset.

FIGURE 14.7.   Job Advertisement

Editor
Bloomfield College Magazine
Bloomfield College seeks an energetic, innovative, and experienced editor to join its staff. The successful candidate will join and help lead a team that promotes College interests, programs, and alumni through the *Bloomfield College Magazine*. Specific responsibilities include
- Conceptualizing themes and developing story ideas
- Writing feature articles
- Assigning writing and editing to in-house and freelance writers
- Editing copy
- Helping manage advertising and distribution

The ideal candidate will understand and enjoy working in a college atmosphere. He or she will have outstanding written and oral communication abilities as well as excellent proofreading, editing, and computer skills. Two to four years' experience in editing a magazine or other periodical is desired. Bachelor's degree or equivalent combination of education and experience is required.

Salary is commensurate with experience. Deadline is August 15, 1998. Send cover letter with résumé and three writing samples to Search Committee, *Bloomfield College Magazine*, Office of Human Resources, 101 Glengarry Ave., Bloomfield, MI 48301.

APPLICATION LETTERS

When writing a letter applying for a job, you should follow all the guidelines for writing other business letters (see pp. 343–47). In addition, remember that you are trying to sell yourself to your prospective employer and that your immediate objective is to obtain an interview. Remember, too, that you are competing against other candidates and that your letter and résumé are all the employer has to judge you on.

If you're responding to an advertisement, read it critically. What qualifications are listed? Ideally, you should have all the required qualifications for any job you're applying for, but if you lack one, try to find something in your

FIGURE 14.8.   Application Letter

266 Castrodale Avenue, Apartment 4
Falmouth, MA 02541.
August 2, 1998

Emma Kinsella
Search Committee
Bloomfield College Magazine
Office of Human Resources
101 Glengarry Avenue
Bloomfield, MI 48301

Dear Ms. Kinsella:

I would like to apply for the job of editor at *Bloomfield College Magazine*, which I saw advertised recently in *The Chronicle of Higher Education.* My extensive journalism experience and my recent degree in journalism, I believe, make me highly qualified for the position.

The time I spent as a reporter at *Cape Cod Times* was so rewarding that I decided to return to college to pursue a degree in journalism. While at Ohio State University, I continued my work in the field of publications not only in my studies but also in the role of reporter and editor for *The Lantern*, Ohio State University's daily student newspaper. One of the most interesting of my responsibilities was to coordinate the coverage of university events with the staff of *Alumni*, the university's alumni magazine. My résumé and three writing samples are enclosed.

I believe I would be a strong addition to the team at *Bloomfield College Magazine*, and I would like to discuss my qualifications with you further in an interview. Please write to me or call me at 508-555-9876. Thank you for your consideration.

Sincerely,

Sheryl W. Fitzgerald

Sheryl W. Fitzgerald

Enclosures

background that compensates, something that gives you similar experience in a different form. What else can you tell about the organization or position from the ad? How does the organization represent itself? Creative? Prestigious? The new kid on the block? (If you're unfamiliar with the organization and you can't glean much about it from the ad, it's usually wise to do some research.) How does the ad describe the ideal candidate? A team player? A dynamic individual? If you feel that you are the person this organization is looking for, you'll want to portray yourself this way in your letter. (For an example of a job advertisement, see Figure 14.7.)

In your letter, you want to catch your readers' attention, convince them that you're a qualified and attractive candidate, and motivate them to grant you an interview. Whenever possible, address your letter to the person responsible for screening applicants and setting up interviews; you may need to call the organization to find out this person's name. In the first paragraph, you should identify the job, indicate how you heard about it, and summarize your qualifications. Try to spark some interest in your readers. In the second paragraph, you should expand on your qualifications, highlighting key information on your résumé and supplementing it with additional details, if necessary. At this point, you need to establish superiority, show your readers that you're a better candidate than the other people applying. In the third paragraph, you should restate your interest in the job, ask for an interview, and let your prospective employer know how you can be reached. (For an example of an application letter, see Figure 14.8.)

Every time you write an application letter, you'll want to draft it, ponder it, cut out unnecessary words, rephrase it, correct spelling, and check grammar and punctuation. Ask a friend to read it over for you. If you have time, set it aside for a day before printing out the final version. If you sound qualified, eager, and interesting, chances are that the prospective employer will be interested in you.

Part Four

A Writer's Strategies

Introduction

The following seven chapters constitute a manual offering in-depth advice on writing strategies. The word *strategy* may remind you of warfare: in the original Greek sense of the word, it is a way to win a battle. Writing a college paper, you'll probably agree, is a battle of a kind. In this manual you'll find an array of small weapons to use — and perhaps some heavy artillery.

Here are techniques you can learn, methods you can follow, good practices you can observe in writing effectively. The first five chapters offer a wealth of suggestions for approaching each of the stages of the writing process: generating ideas, planning, drafting, developing, and revising and editing. You're already familiar with this writing process from the chapters in Part One and Part Two. There, each stage was covered briefly for each assignment, and relevant strategies were mentioned briefly. Here, each stage of the writing process gets a full chapter, and the strategies belonging to each are explained and illustrated more fully. The last two chapters here offer advice on two writing strategies that writers may or may not choose to integrate into their writing process for a particular assignment — working collaboratively with other writers and writing with a computer.

No strategy will appeal to every writer, and no writer uses every one for every writing task. Outlining has rescued many a writer from getting lost, but we know writers who never outline except in their heads. Consider this part of the book a reference guide or instruction manual. Turn to it when you need more help, when you're curious, or when you'd like to enlarge your repertoire of writing skills. We can't tell you which of the ideas and techniques covered in these pages will work for you, but we can promise that if you try some of them, you'll be rewarded.

Chapter 15

Strategies for Generating Ideas

For most writers, the hardest part of writing comes first — the moment when they confront a blank sheet of paper. Fortunately, you can do much to get ready for it. Experienced writers have many tested techniques to get moving. Many of the suggestions that follow may strike you as far-out, even silly, but all have worked for some writers — both professionals and students — and some may work for you. This chapter suggests two types of devices — methods you can try to find ideas for your writing and strategies you can use to get ready to write.

Finding Ideas

Learning to write is learning what questions to ask yourself. When you begin to write, no matter what the source of information — recall, observation, conversation, imagination — you need to start the ideas flowing. Sometimes ideas appear quickly on the paper or screen. But if at other times you find yourself staring at a blank, you needn't throw up your hands in frustration. Instead, you can try one of the strategies in this chapter for getting ideas started. These strategies are useful not only when you are thinking and planning but also at any point in the writing process when you find your flow of ideas drying up or when you find that you need additional evidence. If one doesn't work for a particular writing task, try another. Seldom will you use all of them on one writing task. Think of these strategies as your arsenal of idea generators, techniques that you can call on at any point in the writing process.

BRAINSTORMING

A *brainstorm* is a sudden insight or inspiration, and *brainstorming* is free association for stimulating a chain of ideas. When you brainstorm, you start with a word or phrase to launch your thoughts in some direction. For a set length of time — say, ten or fifteen minutes — put the conscious, analytical part of your mind on hold as you scribble a list of ideas as rapidly as possible, writing down whatever comes to mind with no editing or going back. Then you look over the often surprising results.

For a college writing assignment, you might brainstorm to find a specific topic for a paper. Or if you need to generate some material, such as an illustration or example, as you are writing your paper, you can brainstorm. If you have already written your paper, you can brainstorm to come up with a title for it.

Brainstorming can be a group activity. In the business world, brainstorming is a common strategy to fill a specific need — a name for a product, a corporate emblem, a slogan for an advertising campaign. You can try group brainstorming with a few other students or your entire class. Members of the group sit facing one another. They designate one person as the recorder to take down on paper or a blackboard whatever suggestions the others offer. If the suggestions fly too thick and fast, the secretary jots down the best one in the air at that moment. For several minutes, people call out ideas. Then they look over the recorder's list in hopes of finding useful results.

You may find solo brainstorming helpful when you need to shake an idea out of your unconscious. Here is how one student did just that. On the opening day of a writing course, Martha Calbick's instructor assigned a paper from recall: "Demonstrate that the invention of the computer has significantly changed our lives." Following the instructor's advice, Calbick went home and brainstormed. First, she wrote the word *computer* at the top of a sheet of paper. Then she set her alarm clock to sound in fifteen minutes and began to scribble single words or phrases. The first thing she recalled was how her kid brother sits by the hour in front of a home computer playing *Wizardry*, a *Dungeons and Dragons* kind of game. The first recollection quickly led, by free association, to several more.

Wizardry
My kid bro. thinks computers are for kids
Always trading games with other kids — software pirates
Mother says it's too bad kids don't play Wiffle ball anymore
In 3rd grade they teach programming
Hackers
Some get rich
Ed's brother-in-law — wrote a program for accountants
Become a programmer? big future?
Guided missiles
Computers in subway stations — print tickets
Banks — shove in your plastic card
A man lucked out — deposited $100 — computer credited him with $10,000
Sort mail — zip codes
Computers print out grades
My report card showed a D instead of a B — big fight to correct it
Are we just numbers now?

When her alarm clock rang, Calbick dropped her pencil and took a coffee break. When she returned to her desk, she was pleased to find that a few of her random thoughts suggested directions that interested her. First she went through her list with a pencil, discarding ideas that did not interest her. She didn't know much about *Wizardry* or about missiles. She circled the question "Are we just numbers now?" It looked promising. Maybe some of the other ideas she had listed might express that very idea, such as the mindlessness of the computer that had credited the man with $10,000. As she looked over the list, she continued brainstorming, jotting down more thoughts, making notes on the list, and adding to it. "Dealing with computers isn't dealing with people," she wrote next to the circled question. From her rough list, an idea was beginning to emerge.

Calbick later wrote a paper on the effect of computer errors, focusing on the simple computer error in her high school office that had momentarily robbed her of a good grade. She recalled how time-consuming it had been to have that error corrected. She mentioned a few other cases of computer error, including that of the man who had struck it rich at the bank. Her conclusion was a wry complaint about computerized society: "A computer knows your name and number, but it doesn't know who you are."

You can see how brainstorming typically works and how it started one student going. It is valuable because it helps you personalize a topic and break it down into specifics. Whenever you try brainstorming, you might follow these bits of advice:

1. *Start with a key word or phrase* — one that will head your thoughts in the direction you wish to pursue. If you are trying to find a topic, begin with a general word or phrase. If you are searching for an example to fill out a paragraph in progress, use a specific word or phrase.

2. *Set a time limit.* Ten to fifteen minutes is long enough: brainstorming can be strenuous.

3. *Write rapidly.* List any words, thoughts, phrases, fragments, or short sentences that surface in connection with your key word. Keep your entries brief. Put them in a list so that you can scan them quickly later.

4. *Don't stop.* Don't pause. While you're brainstorming, don't worry about misspelling, repetition, absurdity, or irrelevance. Write down whatever comes into your head, as fast as your pen will go. Now is not the time to analyze or discard any suggestion. Never mind if you come up with ideas that seem crazy or far out. Don't judge, don't arrange: just produce. If your mind goes blank, keep your pencil moving, even if you are only repeating what you've just written.

When you finish, look over your list. Circle or check anything that suggests interesting directions you may wish to pursue. If anything looks useless or uninteresting, scratch it out.

You can now do some conscious organizing. Look over your edited list. If you are brainstorming to find a topic for a paper, notice whether any of the thoughts are related. Can you group them? If so, maybe such a group of ideas will suggest a topic. (Once you have a topic, you might try another technique — *freewriting*, the next strategy we discuss.)

If you need an example or some details for a paper you've already started, you can brainstorm at any time. In writing her paper on computers, Martha Calbick couldn't think of a name for a typical computer store. She wrote down some real names she knew, and those triggered a few imaginary ones. Within three minutes, she hit on one she liked — Byte City.

Whether you brainstorm at your desk or in a classroom with your writing group, you will find this strategy calling up a rich array of thoughts from knowledge, memory, and imagination.

EXERCISE

Brainstorming

From the following list, choose a subject that interests you, that you know something about, and that you'd like to learn more about — in other words, a subject that you might like to write a paper on. Then brainstorm for ten minutes.

travel	fear	exercise
dieting	dreams	automobiles
family	television	sports
advertisements	animals	education

Now look over your brainstorming list, and circle anything that looks as if it might work well as a topic for a paper. How well did this brainstorming exercise work for you? Can you think of any variations that would make it more useful?

FREEWRITING

Like brainstorming, *freewriting* is a way to fight writer's block by tapping your unconscious. To freewrite, you simply begin writing in the hope that good ideas will surface. You write without stopping for fifteen or twenty minutes, trying to keep words pouring forth in a steady flow. In freewriting, unlike brainstorming, you write a series of sentences, not a list. The sentences don't have to be grammatical or coherent or stylish; just let them leap to the paper and keep them flowing. When you have just the beginning of an idea, freewriting can help open it up and show you what it contains. When you have an assignment that looks difficult, freewriting can get you under way.

Generally, freewriting is most productive if it has an aim. It's best to have in mind — at least roughly — a topic, a purpose, or a question you want answered. Before you begin, you write a sentence or two summing up the idea you're starting out with. Martha Calbick, who found a topic by brainstorming (p. 361), wrote her topic at the head of sheet of paper — "How life in the computer age seems impersonal" — and then, exploring some of her rough brainstorming ideas, she let words flow rapidly.

> *Computers — so how do they make life impersonal? You push in your plastic card and try to get some cash. Just a glassy screen. That's different — not like looking at a human teller behind a window. When the computer tells you you have no money left in your account, that's terrible, frightening. Worse than when a person won't cash your check. At least the person looks you in the face, maybe even gives you a faint smile. Computers make mistakes, don't they? That story in the paper about a man — in Utica, was it? — who deposited $100.00 to his account and the computer misplaced a decimal point and said he had put in $10,000.*

The result, as you can see, wasn't polished prose. It was full of false starts and little asides to herself. Still, in twenty minutes she produced a paragraph that served (with much rewriting) as the basis for her finished essay.

If you want to try freewriting, here's what you do.

1. *Write a sentence or two at the top of your page or computer screen* — the idea you plan to develop by freewriting.

2. *For at least ten minutes, write steadily without stopping.* Expressing whatever comes to mind, even "I don't want to write a paper because I have nothing at all to say about any subject in the universe." If your mind goes blank, write "My mind is blank, I don't know where to go next," and keep at it until some new thought floats into view.

3. *Don't censor yourself.* Don't cross out false starts, misspellings, or grammatical errors. If your ideas have gaps between them, later, when you look them over, some of the gaps may close. If you can't think of the word that perfectly expresses your meaning, use a substitute. (You might draw a squiggly line under it to remind yourself to search for a better word or phrase later.) Keep your pencil moving.

4. *Feel free to explore.* The sentence or sentences you start with can serve as a rough guide, but they shouldn't be a straitjacket. If you find yourself straying from your original idea, a change in direction may be valuable.

FOR GROUP LEARNING

Group Brainstorming

Here's another way to use the brainstorming exercise on page 363. Working with a small group of your classmates — or with the entire class — choose a subject from the list that everyone knows something about. After you've agreed on a subject, everyone in the group should brainstorm about it individually for ten minutes.

Then compare and contrast the brainstorming lists of everyone in the group. Notice especially the differences — how each individual's list reflects his or her personal experiences. Although several writers may start with the same subject, each writer's treatment will be unique because of differences in experience and perspective. What does this exercise tell you about the advantages or disadvantages of group brainstorming as a technique for generating topics for writing?

5. *Prepare yourself* — if you want to. Some writers prepare for freewriting by spending a few minutes in thought. While you wait for the moment when your pencil starts racing, it may be worth asking yourself some of these questions:

What interests you about this topic? What aspects of it do you most care about?

What do you recall about this topic from your own experience? What do you know about it that the next person doesn't?

What have you read about it? Observed about it? Heard about it from someone else?

How might you feel about this topic if you were someone else (a parent, an instructor, a person from another country)?

At the very least, your freewriting session may give you something to expand and develop. You can poke at the parts that look most interesting to see if they will further unfold. In developing the ideas produced by freewriting, here are a few questions you might ask:

What do you mean by that?
If that is true, what then? So what?
What other examples or evidence does this statement call to mind?
What objections might your reader raise to this?
How might you answer them?

EXERCISE

Freewriting

Edit one of your brainstorming lists by circling interesting ideas, deleting irrelevant or repetitious items, and grouping related ideas. Select one significant idea you can explore further, put that idea at the top of a piece of paper or your computer screen, and freewrite about it for fifteen minutes. Are you further along in generating ideas for a paper? Share your freewriting with some of your classmates.

WRITING WITH A COMPUTER

Invisible Writing

Invisible writing is a kind of freewriting done on a word processor. After typing your topic at the top of the screen, turn off your monitor so that you cannot read what's on the screen. (You can either turn down the contrast on your monitor or turn it off altogether.) Then freewrite. Not being able to see the words and the punctuation, you can relax and concentrate on the ideas. If you feel somewhat uneasy, just keep typing and let the ideas flow through your fingers. After ten minutes of invisible writing, turn the monitor back on, scroll to the beginning, and read what you have written.

KEEPING A JOURNAL

If you are already in the habit of keeping a journal, consider yourself lucky. If not, now is a good time to begin. Journal writing offers rich rewards to anyone who engages in it every day or several times a week. All you need is a notebook, a writing implement, and a few minutes for each entry; and you can write anywhere. For the faithful journal keeper, a journal is a mine studded with priceless nuggets — thoughts and observations, reactions and revelations that are yours for the taking. When you have an essay to write, a well-stocked journal is a treasure indeed. Rifle it freely — not only for writing topics, but for insights and material. "This book is my savings bank," wrote Ralph Waldo Emerson in his journal. "I grow richer because I have somewhere to deposit my earnings."

What do you write? The main thing to remember is that a journal is not a diary. When you make a journal entry, the emphasis is less on recording what happened than on *reflecting* about what you do or see, hear or read, learn or believe. A journal is a record of your thoughts, for an audience of one: yourself. In a journal you can explore dreams, try out ideas, vent fears and frustrations.

Poet Sylvia Plath found keeping a journal quite worthwhile. The following passage, from *The Journals of Sylvia Plath* (New York: Doubleday, 1982), was written in the early 1950s when she was a college freshman. Uncommonly sensitive and colorful, her entries exhibit the freedom and frankness of a writer who was writing for only her own eyes. In this entry Plath contrasts the happy fantasy world she inhabited as a child with the harsher realities of college life.

After being conditioned as a child to the lovely never-never land of magic, of fairy queens and virginal maidens, of little princes and their rosebushes, of poignant bears and Eeyore-ish donkeys, of life personalized as the pagans loved it, of the magic wand, and the faultless illustrations — the beautiful dark-haired child (who was you) winging through the midnight sky on a star-path . . . of the Hobbit and the dwarves, gold-belted with blue and purple hoods, drinking ale and singing of dragons in the caverns of the valley — all this I knew, and felt, and believed. All this was my life when I was young. To go from this to the world of grown-up reality. . . . To feel the sex organs develop and call loud to the flesh; to become aware of school, exams (the very words as unlovely as the sound of chalk shrilling on the blackboard), bread and butter, marriage, sex, compatibility, war, economics, death, and self. What a pathetic blighting of the beauty and reality of childhood. Not to be sentimental, as I sound, but why the hell are we conditioned into the smooth strawberry-and-cream Mother Goose world, Alice-in-Wonderland fable, only to be broken on the wheel as we grow older and become aware of ourselves as individuals with a dull responsibility in life? To learn snide and smutty meanings of words you once loved, like "fairy." To go to college fraternity parties where a boy buries his face in your neck or tries to rape you if he isn't satisfied with burying his fingers in the flesh of your breast. To learn that there are a million girls who are beautiful and that each day more leave behind the awkward teenage stage, as you once did, and embark on the adventure of being loved. . . . To be aware that you must compete somehow, and yet that wealth and beauty are not in your realm.

Like Plath, to write a valuable journal you need only the honesty and the willingness to set down what you *genuinely think and feel.* When you first face that blank journal page, plunge boldly into your task by writing down whatever observation or reaction comes to mind. No one will criticize your spelling or punctuation, the way you organize your ideas or the way you express yourself. A journal entry can be a list or an outline, a paragraph or a full-blown essay, a poem or a letter you don't intend to send.

Reflective Journal Writing.   In this kind of entry, you have only to *un*cover, *re*cover, *dis*cover what is happening both inside and outside your head. Describe a person or a place. As accurately as you can, set down a conversation you have heard, complete with slang or dialect or colloquialisms. Record any insights you have gained into your actions or those of others. Make comparisons. Record images. Make analogies. Play with language. Respond to something you have read or to something mentioned in a class. Do you agree with it? Disagree? Why? What was wrong with the last movie or television show you watched? What was good about it? Have you or has someone you know faced a moral dilemma? Was it resolved? If so, how? Perhaps you have some pet peeves. List them. What do you treasure? Have you had an interesting dream or daydream? What would the world be like if you were in charge? What are your religious convictions? What do you think about the current political scene or about this nation's priorities? Have you visited any foreign countries? Did you learn anything of worth from your travels? On days when your mind is sluggish, when you can come up with no observations or insights to record, do a stint of freewriting or of brainstorming. This may at least result in a few good thoughts to follow up in future entries.

Responsive Journal Writing.   In this type of entry, you *respond* to something in particular — to the reading you've been doing for class or for an assignment, to classroom discussions or lectures, to a movie or television program, to a conversation or observation. This type of journal entry is more focused than the reflective entry. If your instructor assigns a journal, he or she will most likely want at least some responsive entries. Faced with a long paper to write and weeks or months to do it, you might assign *yourself* a response journal. Then when the time comes to write your paper, you will have plenty of material to quarry. In *A Writer's Reader* we have included some *responsive journal prompts* to help you focus some of your entries. These prompts are located at the end of each selection. We hope you'll find them stimulating and thought-provoking.

Warm-up Journal Writing.   You can also use your journal to collect and explore your thoughts in preparation for an assignment. You can group ideas, scribble outlines, sketch beginnings, try out introductions, capture stray thoughts, record relevant material from any one of your four resources (recalling, observing, conversing, imagining).

There's a fine line between responsive journal writing and warm-up journal writing: what starts out as a quick comment on one puzzling aspect of an essay you've read or a lecture you've heard may turn into the draft of a paper. Similarly, the responsive journal entries you write based on the prompts following the essays in *A Writer's Reader* can easily turn into warm-up journal entries for the writing suggestions that follow. (In fact, we hope they do.) In other words, don't let the categories and descriptions we've given discourage or straitjacket you. Remember: a journal can be just about anything you want it to be, and the best journal is the one that's most useful to *you*.

EXERCISE

Journal Writing

Keep a journal for at least a week. Each day record your thoughts, feelings, and reactions. You may include some events, but go beyond what happens, and include your reflections on what happens and your responses to what you read. Some of your entries may be free — on anything that comes to your mind. Try at least one of the responsive prompts following one of the selections in *A Writer's Reader*. At the end of the week, bring your journal to class, select the entry you like best, and read it aloud to your classmates.

ASKING A REPORTER'S QUESTIONS

Journalists, assembling facts to write the story of a news event, ask themselves six simple questions — the five *W*'s and an *H*:

Who?	When?
What?	Why?
Where?	How?

In the *lead*, or opening paragraph, of a good news story, where the writer tries to condense the whole story into a sentence or two, you will find simple answers to all six questions.

> The ascent of a giant homemade fire balloon [*what*] startled residents of Costa Mesa [*where*] last night [*when*] as Ambrose Barker, 79, [*who*] in an attempt to set a new altitude record [*why*], zigzagged across the sky at a speed of nearly 300 miles per hour. [*how*]

Later in the news story, the reporter will relate the details of the event, using the six basic questions to generate more information about what happened and why.

For your college writing you can use these six questions in a similar manner to generate specific details for your essays. Your topic in a college writing assignment may not be the spectacular narrative of a fire balloon's ascent, but you will find these questions just as helpful as the reporter does. The five *W*'s and an *H* can help you get started exploring the significance of an experience from childhood, analyzing what happened at some moment in history, or investigating a problem on campus or in your neighborhood.

The six basic questions can help you not only discover what to write about but also generate specific details to use as evidence in your essays. These questions can lead to further questions, providing you more to write about than space and time will allow. If you are using the five *W*'s and an *H* to explore a topic that is not based on your personal experience, you'll find that you have to do some research — reading or interviewing — to answer some of the questions. Take, for example, the topic of the assassination of John F. Kennedy.

Who was John F. Kennedy? What kind of person was he? What was his background? What kind of president was he? What were his goals? Who else was with him when he was killed? Who do most people believe shot him? What kind of person was the killer? Who was nearby?

What happened to Kennedy — exactly? What was he doing? What was his purpose in being where he was? What events led up to the assassination? Describe the assassination itself. Describe his wounds. Was anyone else hurt? What happened immediately after the shots to Kennedy? What did the people around him do? How did his wife react? What did the police do? What did the Secret Service agents do? What did the media representatives do? What did everyone across the country do? What happened in the next forty-eight

WRITING WITH A COMPUTER

Keeping a Journal on a Word Processor

Consider keeping your journal on a computer. If you're more comfortable writing at a keyboard than with pen and paper or if you already do most of your writing with a word processor, it will be quite easy for you. If you don't already use word processing, keeping a personal journal will be a good way to practice using a word processor.

Keeping a journal on a computer allows you to explore topics easily and to expand ideas by inserting material at any point. Later you'll be able to move text from your journal to your papers (and vice versa) quickly and easily. Sometimes the word processor's ability to search comes in handy. For example, if you're assigned a paper on the homeless, you might want to search through your journal entries for the terms *homeless, shelters, street people,* and so on to see if you've already done some preliminary thinking and writing on the topic.

There will still be times when you want to use means other than a computer for your journal entries. Notebooks and pens are perfectly portable and unobtrusive, making them ideal for jotting down sudden inspirations whenever and wherever they occur, whether in the dining hall or at the bus stop. If you have to wait until you get back to your computer to record your fleeting insights, many of them may never get recorded at all.

hours? Ask someone who remembers this event what he or she did on hearing about the assassination.

Where was Kennedy assassinated? The city? The street? From where to where was he going? Did he follow the planned route? Was the route announced beforehand? What kind of vehicle was Kennedy riding in? Where was he sitting? Where were the other passengers in the vehicle sitting? Where did the shots likely come from? What path did they likely follow? Where did the shots hit Kennedy? Where did Kennedy die? How did he get there?

When was he assassinated — the day, month, year, time? When did Kennedy decide to go to this city? When — precisely — were the shots fired? When did he die? When was a suspect arrested?

Why was Kennedy assassinated? What are some of the theories of the assassination? What solid evidence is available to explain the assassination? Why was a suspect arrested so soon? Why has Kennedy's assassination caused so much controversy? Why are most of the records related to his assassination still sealed?

How was Kennedy assassinated? What kind of weapon was used? How many shots were fired? How did he die? Specifically what caused his death? How can we get at the truth of how and why he was assassinated?

Don't worry if some of the questions lead nowhere or don't seem relevant or if some lead to repetitious answers. Just jot down any thoughts and information that come to you. You are trying to gather ideas and material. Later, before you start to write, you'll want to weed out the frivolous and irrelevant ones, keeping only those that look promising for your topic.

EXERCISE

Asking a Reporter's Questions

Choose one of the following topics, or use one of your own:

A memorable event in history
An unforgettable event in your life
A concert that you have seen
An accomplishment on campus
An occurrence in your city
An important speech
A proposal for change
A questionable stand someone has taken

Answer the six reporter's questions about the topic. Then write a thesis in which you synthesize the answers to the six questions into one sentence. Incorporate that thesis sentence into an introductory paragraph for an essay that you might write later.

SEEKING MOTIVES

In a surprisingly large part of your college writing, you will try to explain human behavior. In a paper for history, you might show why Lyndon Baines Johnson decided not to seek a second full term as president. In a report for a psychology course, you might try to explain the behavior of people in an experimental situation. In a literature course, you might analyze the motives of Hester Prynne in *The Scarlet Letter*. Because people, including characters in fiction, are so complex, this task is challenging. But here is a strategy useful in seeking out human motives.

If you want to understand any human act, according to philosopher–critic Kenneth Burke, you can break it down into five basic components and ask questions about each one.

1. The *act:* What was done?
2. The *actor:* Who did it?
3. The *agency:* What means did the person use to make it happen?
4. The *scene:* Where and when did the act happen and in what circumstances?
5. The *purpose or motive* for acting: What could have made the person do it?

As you can see, Burke's *pentad,* or set of five components, covers much the same ground as the reporter's questions. But Burke's method differs in that it can show how the components of a human act affect one another. This line of thought can take you deeper into the motives for human behavior than most reporters' investigations ever go.

How might you apply the method? If you are writing a paper on Lyndon Johnson's decision not to run for a second term, the five components might be these:

Act: Announcing the decision to leave office without standing for re-election.

Actor: President Johnson.

Agency: A televised address to the nation.

Scene (including circumstances at the time): Washington, D.C., March 31, 1968. Protesters against the nation's involvement in Vietnam were gaining in numbers and influence. The press was increasing its criticism of the president's escalation of the war. Senator Eugene McCarthy, an antiwar candidate for president, had made a strong showing against Johnson in the New Hampshire primary election.

Purpose: Possible purposes might include to avoid a probable defeat, to escape further personal attacks, to spare his family, to make it easier for his successor to pull the country out of the war, and to ease bitter dissent among Americans.

To further apply Burke's method, you can begin fruitful lines of inquiry by asking questions that pair the five components:

actor to act	act to scene	scene to agency
actor to scene	act to agency	scene to purpose
actor to agency	act to purpose	agency to purpose
actor to purpose		

For the paper about Lyndon Johnson, you might ask, "What did the actor [Johnson] have to do with the agency [his televised address]?" Your answer might be something like "Commanding the attention of a vast audience, Johnson must have felt he was in control — even though his ability to control the situation in Vietnam was slipping."

The value of Burke's questions is that they can start you writing. Not all the questions will prove fruitful, and some may not even apply. But one or two individual questions or pairs might reveal valuable answers.

EXERCISE

Seeking Motives

Choose an action that puzzles you. It may be one of the following:

Something you have done
An action of a family member or a friend
A decision of a historical or current political figure
Something in a movie or television program
An occurrence in a literary selection

Then apply Burke's pentad to this action to try to determine the individual's motives. If Burke's five basic categories do not go far enough to help you understand the human act, team up the components (see p. 371) to perceive deeper relationships. When you believe you understand the individual's motivation, write a paragraph explaining the action, and share it with your classmates.

Getting Ready

Once you have generated a suitable topic and some ideas related to that topic, you are ready to get down to the job of actually writing. Sometimes at this point, your mind goes blank or you just don't know what to do next. Here are some suggestions that we hope will help you.

SETTING UP CIRCUMSTANCES

Get Comfortable.   We don't just mean turn on a bright light because it's good for your eyes. Why not create an environment? If you can write only with your shoes off or with a can of Orange Crush, set yourself up that way. Some writers need a radio blaring heavy metal; others need quiet. Circumstances that put you in the mood for writing can encourage you.

Devote One Special Place to Writing.   When you go to your special place, your mind and body will be ready to settle in and get to work. Your place may be a desk in your bedroom, the dining room table, or a lap board on a den sofa. It may be a quiet cubicle in a corner of the library. It should be a place where no one will bother you when you are working. It should have good lighting and plenty of space to spread out. If it's at home or in your dorm, try to make it a place where you can leave projects you are working on, where you can keep your pens, paper, typewriter or word processor, dictionary, and other reference materials.

Establish a Ritual.   Many writers follow certain routines to get themselves in the mood for writing. You might get a drink, turn the radio on (or off), sharpen your pencils, turn on the computer, check your paper supply, and straighten the things on your desk. Some writers find that following a writing ritual relaxes them enough to think clearly and write effectively.

Relocate.   If you're not getting anywhere with your writing, change places. If you usually write in the college library, try writing at home. If you usually write at a desk in the den, relocate to your bedroom. Try writing in an unfamiliar place—a bowling alley, a restaurant, an airport, a mall. The noises around you and the curiosity of passersby might cause you to concentrate hard on your writing.

Reduce Distractions.   Most of us can't prevent interruptions when we are trying to concentrate, but we can reduce them. If you are expecting your boyfriend to call, call him before you start writing. If you have small children, write when they are asleep or at school. Turn on the answering machine for the telephone. Do all you can to let people around you know you are serious about writing and allow yourself to give your full attention to it.

Exhaust Your Excuses.   Most writers are born experts at coming up with reasons not to write; if you are one of those writers, you might find that it helps to run out of reasons. Is your room annoyingly jumbled? Straighten it. Drink that can of soda, sharpen those pencils, throw out that trash, and make that phone call. Then, with your room, your desk, and your mind swept clean, you can sit down and write.

Yield to Inspiration.   Classical Greek and Roman critics held that a goddess called a Muse would gently touch a poet and leave him inspired. Whether or not you believe in divine inspiration, sometimes ideas, images, metaphors, or vague but powerful urges to write will arrive like sudden miracles. When they come, even if you are taking a shower or getting ready to go to a movie, yield to impulse and write. At these times you will probably find that words will flow with little exertion. If going to that movie is irresistible, jot down enough notes beforehand to rekindle your ideas later when you can go back to writing.

Write at the Time Best for You.   Some people think best early in the morning, others in the afternoon or late at night. Try writing in the small hours when the world is still. Before you are wholly awake, your stern self-critic might not be awake yet either. (When you edit and proofread, though, you want to be fully awake.) Or take a nap in the afternoon and write from 10:00 P.M. until 2:00 or 3:00 A.M. Writing at dawn or the wee hours, you also will have fewer distractions from other people.

Write on a Schedule.   Many writers find that it helps to have a certain predictable time of day to write. This method won't work for all, but it worked marvels for English novelist Anthony Trollope. Each day Trollope would start at 5:30 A.M., write 2,500 words before 8:30 A.M., and then go to his job at the General Post Office. (He wrote more than sixty books.) Even if you can't write at the same time every day, it may help to decide, "Today from four to five, I'll sit down and write."

Defy a Schedule.   If you write on a schedule and your work isn't going well, break out of your usual time frame. If you are an afternoon writer, write at night, and vice versa.

PREPARING YOUR MIND

Discuss Your Plans.   Collar any nearby listener — roommate, student down the hall, spouse, parent, friend. Tell the other person why you want to write this particular paper, what you're going to put into it, how you're going to lay out your material. If the other person says, "That sounds good," you'll be encouraged; but even if the reaction is a yawn, at least you will have set your own thinking in motion.

Keep a Notebook Handy.   Always have some paper in your pocket or purse or on the night table to write down those good ideas whenever they pop into your mind. Imagination may strike in the checkout lane of the supermarket, in the doctor's waiting room, or during a lull on the job. Take advantage of those calm times, and write down your ideas so that you won't forget them.

Keep a Daily Journal.   Use a journal to record your experiences as a writer. Scribbling in a journal for fifteen minutes a day can nourish your writing. You might note writing problems you run into (and overcome), ideas for things you'd like to write, reactions to your writing from other people, writing strategies that work well. You can record your reading and your reactions to it, track your progress in any course, or save stray thoughts. (For more detailed suggestions about journals, see p. 366.)

Read.   The step from reading to writing is a short one. Read whatever you feel like reading. Read for fun. Even when you're just reading for kicks, you start to involve yourself with words. Who knows? You might also hit on something useful for your paper. Or read purposefully. If you have a specific topic or a general notion for one, set out to read and take notes.

Chapter 16

Strategies for Planning

Starting to write often seems a chaotic activity, but you can use the strategies in this chapter to reduce the chaos and create order. For most papers you write — and certainly for all papers that rely on critical thinking — you will want to focus your writing around a central point. For help with this, see the first section in this chapter, "Stating and Using a Thesis." In nearly any kind of writing task, you can make better use of your material if it is sensibly arranged. For more help with this, see "Organizing Your Ideas" (p. 380), which includes advice on grouping ideas and on outlining.

Stating and Using a Thesis

Most pieces of effective writing make one main point. All ideas in an essay or article are unified around that point; that is, all the subpoints and details are relevant to the point. In "What Is a Hunter?" (p. 17), student Robert G. Schreiner maintains that there is more to being a hunter than knowing how to use a rifle. In "The Myth of the Latin Woman: I Just Met a Girl Named María" (p. 564), Judith Ortiz Cofer claims that Latinas cannot escape misconceptions about the Latin woman. After you have read such an essay, you can sum up the writer's main point in a sentence, even if the author has not stated it explicitly. We call this summary statement a *thesis*.

Often the thesis — the writer's main point — will be *explicit*, plainly stated, in the piece of writing itself. Ortiz Cofer states her thesis in the last sentence of the first paragraph of her essay — "You can leave the Island, master the English language, and travel as far as you can, but if you are a Latina, especially one like me who so obviously belongs to Rita Moreno's gene pool, the Island travels with you" — and rephrases it in paragraph 14: "For them [most Latin women] life is a struggle against the misconceptions perpetuated

by the myth of the Latina as whore, domestic or criminal." Such clear statements strategically placed as well as her title help readers see her main point
unmistakably.

In some writing, a thesis may be *implicit*, implied rather than directly
stated. In "Once More to the Lake," E. B. White (p. 490) clearly focuses on the
realization of his own mortality. All the descriptive and narrative details from
the past and the present, the references to time, and the allusions to his relationships with his father and his son culminate in the final sentence: "As he
[the son] buckled the swollen belt, suddenly my groin felt the chill of death."
Although White does not state his main point in one concise sentence, after
you have read his essay you know that he is keenly aware that one generation
is quickly and inevitably replaced by the next.

The purpose of most academic and business writing is to inform, to explain, or to convince, and to achieve any of these purposes you must make
your main point crystal clear. A thesis sentence helps you clarify your main
idea in your own mind, and it helps you stay on track as you write. If your thesis is clear in your final paper, it also helps your readers readily see your point
and follow your discussion. Sometimes you may want to imply your thesis as
E. B. White does in his essay, but for most of your writing you will communicate more effectively with your readers if you state your thesis explicitly so that
readers cannot miss it. In either case, for almost every essay you write, discovering and stating a thesis is a useful planning strategy.

DISCOVERING YOUR THESIS

Don't be dismayed if your thesis does not come to you early in the writing
process. In fact, it's rare for a writer to develop a clear thesis statement early in
the process and then write an effective essay that fits it exactly. What you should
aim for is a *working thesis* — a statement that can guide you in your writing but
that you will ultimately refocus and refine. Trying to discover and state a working thesis is far less intimidating (and less likely to cause writer's block) than
trying to find the perfect sentence before you've even written a first draft.

Look back over your notes or your brainstorming or freewriting results,
and see if you can generalize from them. Write several tentative thesis sen-

FOR GROUP LEARNING

Identifying Theses

Working in a small group, select five essays from Part One and Part Two of this
book to analyze (or your instructor may choose the essays for your group). Then,
individually, write out the thesis for each essay. Some thesis sentences are stated
outright (explicit), but others are implied (implicit). Compare and contrast the
thesis statements that you identified with the statements of your classmates, and
discuss the similarities and differences. How can you account for the differences?
Try to agree on a thesis statement for each essay.

tences. Try some of the strategies for generating ideas or for getting started. Brainstorm titles: the title is usually a shortened form of the thesis. Freewrite the introduction or conclusion. Write a one-paragraph summary of your paper. Often during the interplay among a writer's mind, the English language, and a piece of paper or a computer screen, an insight will occur. Talk your ideas over with a friend, or tape-record your rambling thoughts about your topic. Whenever such a discovery appears to you, set it down and try it out on your peer group or your instructor.

A useful thesis contains not only the *topic* you're writing about but also the *point* you want to make or the *attitude* you intend to take. If you decide to write on the topic "the decline of old-fashioned formal courtesy toward women," you've indicated the area to be explored, but that topic doesn't tell you the point of your paper. If you say, "Old-fashioned formal courtesy toward women is a thing of the past," you are talking in circles. But a *working thesis* might be "As the roles of men and women have changed in our society, old-fashioned formal courtesy toward women has declined." Then you could focus on how changing attitudes in society have caused many men to stop exercising the old-fashioned courtesies toward women. What other thesis sentences might you come up with for this topic?

In some college writing it's easy to let the formal requirements of the assignment distract you from the purpose of writing and the point you should be making in the paper. For example, when you write a comparison and contrast paper, don't fall into the trap of thinking that the point of your paper is to compare and contrast. If you are going to compare and contrast two local newspapers in their coverage of a Senate election, ask yourself what is the point of that comparison and contrast. A suitable thesis would *not* be "The coverage of the Senate elections by the *Herald* was different from that of the *Courier*." A more satisfactory thesis sentence might be "The *Herald*'s coverage of the Senate elections was more thorough than the *Courier*'s."

EXERCISE

Discovering a Thesis

Generalize about each of the following groups of details to find a working thesis for each group. Then compare and contrast your theses with those of your classmates. What other information would you need to write a good paper on each of these topics? How might the thesis statement change as you write the paper?

1. Cigarettes are expensive.
   Cigarettes can cause fires.
   Cigarettes cause unpleasant odors.
   Cigarettes can cause health problems to the smoker.
   Secondhand smoke from cigarettes can cause health problems.
2. Clinger College has a highly qualified faculty.
   Clinger College has an excellent curriculum in my field.
   Clinger College has a beautiful campus.
   Clinger College is expensive.
   Clinger College has offered me a scholarship.

3. Crisis centers report that date rape is increasing.
   Most date rape is not reported to the police.
   Often the victim of date rape is not believed.
   Sometimes the victim of date rape is blamed.
   Sometimes the victim of date rape blames herself.
   The effects of date rape stay with a woman for years.

HOW TO STATE A THESIS

Once you have a notion of what your thesis might be, you should try to state it in a way that will be useful to you as you plan and draft the essay. Here are four suggestions for writing a workable thesis statement.

1. *State the thesis sentence exactly.* Use concise, detailed, and down-to-earth language. The statement "There are a lot of troubles with chemical wastes" is too general. Are you going to deal with all chemical wastes, through all of history, all over the world? Are you going to list all the troubles they can cause? Make the statement more specific: "Careless dumping of leftover paint is to blame for a recent skin rash in Atlanta." Now you have a concise, restricted statement that you can use as the basis for a brief essay.

2. *State just one central idea in the thesis sentence.* If your paper is to focus on one point, your thesis should state only one main idea. This statement has one idea too many: "Careless dumping of leftover paint has caused a serious problem in Atlanta, and a new kind of biodegradable paint now looks promising." Either the first half or the second half of the statement would suffice and lead you to a unified essay.

3. *State your thesis positively.* You can usually find evidence to support a positive statement, but you can't prove a negative one. Write "The causes of breast cancer remain a challenge for medical scientists" instead of "Medical scientists do not know what causes breast cancer." The former statement might lead to a paper about an exciting quest. But the latter statement seems to reflect a halfhearted attitude by the writer. Besides, to demonstrate that some medical scientists are still working on the problem would be relatively easy: you could show that after an hour of research in a library. To prove that not one medical scientist knows the answer would be a very difficult task.

4. *Limit your thesis sentence to a statement that is possible to demonstrate.* A thesis sentence should stake out enough territory for you to cover thoroughly within the assigned word length and the time available, and no more. To maintain throughout a 700-word paper the thesis "My favorite piece of music is Beethoven's Fifth Symphony" would be a difficult task because you would need to explain how and why it is your favorite and contrast it with *all* the other musical compositions you know. The statement "For centuries, popular music has been indicative of vital trends in Western society" wouldn't do for a 700-word paper either: that thesis would be enough to inform a whole encyclopedia of music. "In the past two years, a rise in the number of

preteenagers has resulted in a comeback for heavy metal on our local concert scene": that thesis idea sounds much more likely. You could cover it in a brief 500- to 800-word essay.

Let's try a few more examples of thesis sentences:

"Indian blankets are very beautiful." That statement is too vague and hard to demonstrate for a usual college writing assignment of 500 to 800 words.

"American Indians have adapted to modern civilization." That sounds too large, too unrestricted, unless you plan to write a 5,000-word paper in sociology.

"Members of the Apache tribe are skilled workers in high-rise construction." You could probably find support for that thesis by spending a couple of hours in a library.

EXERCISE

Examining Thesis Statements

Discuss each of the following thesis sentences with your classmates. Answer these questions for each:

Is the thesis stated exactly?
Does the thesis state just one idea?
Is the thesis stated positively?
Is the thesis sufficiently limited for 500 to 800 words?
How might the thesis be improved?

1. Teenagers should not get married.
2. Cutting classes is like a disease.
3. Going to college prepares a person for the future, and it is increasingly expensive.
4. Students have developed a variety of techniques to conceal inadequate study from their instructors.
5. Older people often imitate teenagers.
6. There are many different types of students in college today.
7. Violence on television can be harmful to children.
8. Teachers have influenced my life.
9. I don't know how to change the oil in my car.
10. My hobbies are scuba diving, playing the guitar, and motocross racing.

HOW TO USE A THESIS

Often a good, clear statement of a thesis will suggest an organization for your ideas. Say you plan to write a paper with the thesis "Despite the several disadvantages of living in a downtown business district, I wouldn't live anywhere else." That thesis sentence suggests how to organize your essay. You could start with several paragraphs discussing disadvantages of living in the business district, move on to a few paragraphs discussing the advantages, and then close with an affirmation of your fondness for downtown city life. (For more on using a thesis to develop an outline, see "Outlining," p. 384.)

A clear statement of the main idea in your thesis will also help keep you on track as you write. Just putting your trial thesis into words can help you stake out the territory you need to know better. You can refer to it as you select details and as you make connections between sections of the essay.

As you write, however, you don't have to cling to a thesis for dear life. If some facts or notions don't seem to fit, you can change your thesis as you write. You might think that you want to write a paper on the thesis "Because wolves are a menace to people and farm animals, they ought to be exterminated." If further investigation doesn't support that statement, your thesis isn't chiseled in marble. You can change it to "The wolf, a relatively peaceful animal useful in nature's scheme of things, ought to be protected," if that is the idea your investigation has led you to. The purpose of a thesis statement is to guide you on a quest, not to limit your ideas and put your thinking in a straitjacket. You can restate it at any time: as you write, as you revise, as you revise again.

MAKING CONNECTIONS: THESIS STATEMENTS IN *A WRITER'S READER*

Experienced writers use the strategies for planning that we have suggested in this chapter. They work from statements of their main idea — *thesis statements* — to focus and unify their writings, and they purposefully select an organizational pattern for each piece, often constructing an outline to guide them. The results of these techniques are evident in the selections in *A Writer's Reader*.

Explicit thesis sentences are generally present in essays in which the writer takes a stand or proposes a solution, such as Anna Quindlen's "Evan's Two Moms" (last paragraph, p. 517) and Paul Varnell's "The Niceness Solution" (paragraph 13, p. 577). Writers of other types of essays also include explicit theses, such as Nicholas Wade in the comparison and contrast essay "How Men and Women Think" (end of paragraph 11, p. 558) and Mike Males in his cause-and-effect essay "Public Enemy Number One?" (second sentence of paragraph 8, p. 617). Other writers imply the thesis: Gerald Early, "Black like . . . Shirley Temple?" (p. 502); Emily Prager, "Our Barbies, Ourselves" (p. 537); and Richard Rodriguez, "Does America Still Exist?" (p. 583).

Organizing Your Ideas

After you have generated and gathered ideas on your topic by using the four resources of a writer — recall, observation, conversation, and imagination — and employing the strategies for generating ideas (see Chapter 15), and after you have focused your ideas by stating a working thesis, you next need to determine how you might organize the information. Each of the chapters in Part

One and Part Two of this book discusses possible organizational patterns for the particular assignment, but the following sections give you some general advice on organizing and discuss two strategies to help you — grouping ideas and outlining.

When you organize the information in an essay, you select an order for the parts that makes sense and shows your readers how the ideas are connected. If you are describing a place, you might use spatial organization, moving from left to right or bottom to top. You want to choose an order for the details that will make it easy for readers to visualize. Mark Twain describes a scene on the Mississippi River by beginning with the dock and moving to the steamboat coming in to the landing, over the broad expanse of the river to the shore on the other side, and finally up through the trees to the clouds in the sky. If you are narrating an event or explaining the steps in a procedure, you would use chronological or time order — what happens first, next, and next until the end. If you are explaining an idea or trying to persuade readers, you would use some variation of logical order — for example, general to specific, specific to general, least important to most important, cause to effect, or problem to solution. In writing an essay on the results of the 1997 El Niño, you might select four major effects and arrange them in ascending order, placing the most important one last for emphasis. Following are some techniques to help you select an order for your ideas.

GROUPING YOUR IDEAS

In the scribblings you have made while exploring a topic, you will usually find a few ideas that seem to belong together — two facts on New York traffic jams, four actions of New York drivers, three problems with New York streets. But similar ideas are seldom together in your list because you did not discover them all at the same time. As you look over your preliminary notes, indicate to yourself any connections you find among your materials. You'll need to sort your notes into groups, arrange them in sequences. Here are five common ways to work.

1. *Rainbow connections.* List on a sheet of paper all the main points you're going to express. Don't recopy all the material: just list each main point briefly, not worrying about order. Then, taking colored pencils, circle with the same color any points that go together. When you write, follow the color code, and deal with similar ideas at the same time.

2. *Linking.* Start by making a list of major points, and then draw lines that link related ideas. Number each linked group to remember in what sequence to deal with the ideas. Figure 16.1 is an illustration of a linked list produced by one writer in a brainstorming session for an essay to be called "Manhattan Driving." The writer has drawn lines connecting points that go together and has supplied each linked group with a heading. When he writes his draft, each heading will probably inspire a topic sentence or a few lines to introduce each major division of his essay. One point failed to relate to

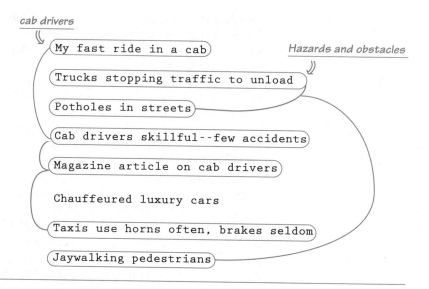

cab drivers

My fast ride in a cab   Hazards and obstacles

Trucks stopping traffic to unload

Potholes in streets

Cab drivers skillful--few accidents

Magazine article on cab drivers

Chauffeured luxury cars

Taxis use horns often, brakes seldom

Jaywalking pedestrians

FIGURE 16.1.   The Linking Method for Grouping Ideas

any other: "Chauffeured luxury cars." In the finished paper, he will leave it out.

3. *Solitaire.* Collect notes and ideas on roomy (5-by-8-inch) file cards. To organize, spread out the cards and arrange and rearrange them, as in a game of solitaire. When the order looks worth keeping, when each idea seems to lead to the next, gather all the cards into a deck once more. Then when you write, deal yourself a card at a time and translate its contents into sentences. This technique is particularly helpful when you write about literature or when you write from research.

4. *Scissors and tape.* Lay out your rough notes and group the ones that refer to the same point and that probably belong in the same vicinity. With scissors, separate items that don't belong together. Shuffle the pieces around, trying for the most promising order. After throwing out any ideas that don't belong anywhere, lock up the material into a structure and join all the parts with tape. If you find places in the grand design where ideas and information are lacking, make a note of what's missing, and tape that note into place. This taped-together construction of cards or slips of paper serves as a workable outline.

You may use this strategy for planning and drafting simultaneously. Tape together not just notes but separate passages you have written. Write whatever part you want to write first, then the next most tempting part, and so on until you have enough rough stuff to arrange into a whole piece of writing. Then add missing parts and supply transitions (discussed on pp. 407–09).

5. *Clustering.* Clustering is useful for coming up with ideas, but it is just as valuable as a visual method of grouping those ideas. For clustering, in the middle of a piece of paper write your topic in a word or a phrase. Then think of the major divisions into which this topic might be organized. For an essay called "Manhattan Drivers," the major divisions might be the *types* of Manhattan drivers: (1) taxi drivers, (2) bus drivers, (3) truck drivers, (4) drivers of private cars — New Yorkers, and (5) drivers of private cars — out-of-town visitors. Arrange these divisions around your topic on your page and circle them too. Draw lines out from the major topic to the subdivisions. You now have the beginning of a rough plan for an essay.

Around each division, make another cluster of points you're going to include — examples, illustrations, facts, statistics, bits of evidence, opinions.

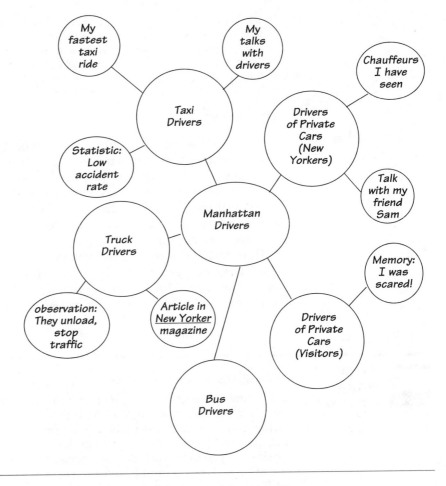

FIGURE 16.2. The Clustering Method for Generating Ideas.

Circle each specific item, and connect it to the appropriate type of driver. When you write your paper, you can expand the details into one paragraph for each type of driver. Figure 16.2 presents a cluster for "Manhattan Drivers."

This technique lets you know where you have enough specific information to make your paper clear and interesting — and where you don't. If one of your subtopics has no small circles around it (such as "bus drivers" in Figure 16.2), you should think of some specific examples to expand it; if you can't, drop it.

EXERCISE

Clustering

Generate idea clusters for three of the following topics. Share them with your classmates or writing group. Discuss which one of the three would probably help you write the best paper.

teachers	U.S. presidents
television programs	civil rights
my favorite restaurants	drug abuse
fast food	good health
leisure-time activities	technology

OUTLINING

In the previous section, we set forth ways to bring related thoughts together. Another, perhaps more familiar means to organize ideas is to outline. A written outline, whether brief or detailed, shouldn't say *everything* you plan to write in your paper. Think of it as a map that you make before setting out on a journey. It shows where to leave from, where to stop along the way, and where at last to arrive. If you forget where you are going or what you are trying to say, you can consult it to get back on track.

How detailed an outline will you need? The answer depends in part on the kind of writer you are and in part on the kind of writing you are doing. Some writers like to lay out the job very carefully in advance; others prefer to lay it out more loosely. Sometimes college writers find an *informal outline* —

WRITING
WITH A
COMPUTER

Arranging Ideas On-Screen

Many writers arrange their rough notes into groups right on the computer screen, moving items from place to place until they like the resulting plan. Cutting and pasting is quicker and easier with a word processor than with scissors and tape, and the word processor's ability to create and store multiple versions makes it possible for you to try out different schemes of organizing before deciding on any one of them. Using a word processor, you can also move smoothly from grouping ideas to creating an outline without having to rewrite your notes.

perhaps just a list of points to make — is enough. If you are working with familiar material, such a brief outline will probably be sufficient. If you are dealing with complex, unfamiliar information, you'll probably need a more detailed *formal outline* to keep from getting lost. Do people tell you your writing isn't well organized and that they can't follow you? Then probably you would benefit from using a more detailed plan. Do they tell you your writing sounds mechanical? Maybe your outline is constricting you. Once you complete your essay, your outline and the essay should go hand in hand. Often instructors require that you turn in an outline with the final essay so that readers can have a skeletal summary of what your essay contains in the order you have arranged the information.

Informal Outlines.   For in-class writing and for brief essays, often a *short* or *informal outline,* also called a *scratch outline,* will serve your needs. It is just a brief list of points to make, in the order you plan to make them. The short outline is only for your eyes. When the writing job is done, you pitch the outline along with your preliminary drafts into the trash basket.

The following is an informal outline for a 600-word paper contrasting city drivers with small-town drivers. Its thesis sentence is "City drivers are quite different from small-town drivers." One obvious way to proceed is to think of and list the specific areas of contrast (perhaps physical fitness, skill, and consideration). Then, for each quality, the writer would discuss first city drivers and then small-town drivers — how they do or don't exhibit the characteristic. The writer could put this plan in scratch form like this:

Introduction: Different driving habits
1. *Physical fitness*
    – City drivers: little time and space in which to exercise
    – Small-town drivers: lifestyle conducive to physical ease
2. *Skill at the wheel*
    – City drivers: small, crowded streets
    – Small-town drivers: narrow streets
3. *Consideration for others*
    – City drivers: tendency to vent their aggressions at the wheel
    – Small-town drivers: laid-back attitude toward life reflected in driving habits
Conclusion: I'd rather drive in a small town

A simple outline like that could easily fall into a five-paragraph essay. If you have a great deal to say, though, the essay might well run to perhaps eight paragraphs — introduction, conclusion, and three pairs of paragraphs in between. You probably won't know until you write the paper exactly how many paragraphs you'll need.

An informal outline can be even briefer than the preceding one. If you were writing an in-class essay, an answer to an examination question, or a very short paper, your outline might be no more than an *outer plan* — three or four phrases jotted down in a list:

> *Physical fitness*
> *Skill*
> *Consideration for others*

Often a clear thesis statement (see p. 378) will suggest a way to outline. If the thesis contains a plural word (such as *benefits* or *advantages* or *teenagers*), you can make a list of outline headings related to the plural word. If one part of the thesis sentence is subordinate to another (beginning with *because* or *since* or *although*, for instance), you can analyze according to the parts of the sentence. Let's say you are assigned, for an anthropology course, a paper on the people of Melanesia. You decide to focus on the following idea:

> *Thesis: Although the Melanesian pattern of family life may look strange to Westerners, it fosters a degree of independence that rivals our own.*

Laying out ideas in the same order as they follow in that thesis statement, you might make a short, simple outline like this:

> 1. *Features that appear strange to Westerners*
>   – *A woman supported by her brother, not her husband*
>   – *Trial marriages usual*
>   – *Divorce from her children possible for any mother*
> 2. *Admirable results of system*
>   – *Wives not dependent on husbands for support*
>   – *Divorce between mates uncommon*
>   – *Greater freedom for parents and children*

This informal outline might result in an essay that naturally falls into two parts — features that seem strange and admirable results of the system. In writing and thinking further, you will need to flesh out that outline with more details.

Say you plan to write a "how-to" essay analyzing the process of buying a used car. Your thesis statement might read:

> *Thesis: Despite traps that lie in wait for the unwary, you can get a good deal in a used car if you prepare yourself before you shop.*

The key word in this sentence is *prepare*, and you ask yourself *how* the buyer should prepare himself or herself. What should he or she do before shopping for a used car? You think of several things, and you analyze the key word *prepare* into those parts:

> – *Read car magazine and Consumer Reports.*
> – *Check ads in the newspapers.*
> – *Make phone calls to several dealers.*
> – *Talk to friends who have bought used cars.*
> – *Know what to look and listen for when you test drive.*
> – *Have a mechanic check it out.*

Follow this sequence of ideas in your paper. You can start your paper with some horror stories about people who got taken by car sharks and then proceed to list and discuss, point by point, your bits of advice. Of course, you can always change the sequence, add an idea or take one out, or revise your thesis sentence if you find it makes sense to do so as you go along.

Formal Outlines.   A *formal outline* is an elaborate job built with time and care. It is probably more than you need for brief writings. As a guide for long, complex papers, it can help you express your ideas in an orderly manner.

In college, a formal outline is usually used for ambitious projects. Because long reports, research papers, and honors theses require so much work, some academic professors and departments ask a writer to submit a formal outline at an early stage of the project before proceeding and to include it in the final draft.

A formal outline offers the greatest amount of guidance that an outline can give. In a clear, logical way, it spells out where you are going. It shows how ideas relate one to another. It shows which ideas are equal and important (*coordinate*) and which are less important (*subordinate*).

When you make a formal outline, you place your thesis sentence at the beginning. Then you list your major points and label them with roman numerals (I, II, III). These points support and develop the main idea of your whole paper. Then you break down these points into divisions with capital letters, indenting them (A, B, C). You subdivide those into divisions with arabic numerals (1, 2, 3) indenting further, and then subdivide those into divisions with small letters (a, b, c) indenting yet again. Align like-numbered or -lettered headings under one another. As indentations go farther in, ideas become more specific.

```
Thesis:

  I.
     A.
        1.
           a.
           b.
        2.
           a.
           b.
     B.
        1.
        2.
 II.
```

The outline would continue until fully developed. If you have so much material that you have to subdivide still further, arabic numerals and small letters in parentheses are commonly used, but only hugely complicated writing projects need that much subdivision. Be sure to cast all headings in parallel grammatical form: phrases or sentences, but not both in the same outline.

A *formal topic outline* for a long paper about city and small-town drivers might be constructed as follows. Notice that the writer decided to drop the subdivision "physical fitness" because it is not directly related to the subject of driving habits.

```
                 Drivers in Cities and Small Towns
Thesis: Different lifestyles cause city drivers to be more
aggressive than small-town drivers.
  I. Lifestyles of drivers
     A. Fast-paced, stress-filled lifestyle of city drivers
        1. Aggressive
        2. Impatient
        3. Tense
        4. Often frustrated
     B. Slow-paced lifestyle of small-town drivers
        1. Laid back
        2. Patient
        3. Relaxed
        4. Not easily upset
 II. Resulting behavior as drivers
     A. City drivers
        1. Little consideration for other drivers
           a. Horn blowing
           b. Shouting
           c. Not using proper signals
              (1) Turning across lanes
              (2) Stopping without warning
        2. Disregard for pedestrians
        3. Speeding
           a. Running red lights
           b. Having many accidents
     B. Small-town drivers
        1. Considerate of other drivers
           a. Driving defensively
           b. Less yelling
           c. Signaling
```

```
(1) For turning
(2) For stopping
2. Regard for pedestrians
3. Driving within speed limits
   a. Observing traffic lights
   b. Fewer accidents
```

If a topic outline is not thorough enough to help you know what you want to say or how to say it or to indicate to you how ideas relate, you should consider a *sentence outline,* using complete sentences for the topic headings. Some people use a topic outline as a step in developing a full-blown sentence outline. The following is a sentence outline on types of drivers. When the headings are changed to sentences, relationships between ideas are clearer, and changes in wording are needed, even in the thesis. Truly, the sentence outline can be a step in clarifying what you intend to say in the essay, but you cannot be sure how the ideas will fit together until you write the draft itself. Although you may not need to use a sentence outline for all of the papers you write in college, knowing how to construct such a complete outline will prove valuable for long, complex papers.

```
              Drivers in Cities and Small Towns
Thesis: Because of more stressful lives, city drivers are
more aggressive drivers than small-town drivers.
  I. The lives of city drivers are more stress-filled than are
     the lives of small-town drivers.
     A. City drivers are always in a hurry.
        1. They are impatient.
        2. They are often frustrated.
     B. Small-town drivers live slower-paced lives.
        1. They are relaxed.
        2. They are seldom frustrated on the streets.
 II. As a result of the tension they live with constantly,
     city drivers are more aggressive than are small-town
     drivers.
     A. City drivers are aggressive.
        1. They show little consideration for other
           drivers.
           a. They blow their horns often.
           b. They shout at other drivers frequently.
        2. They show little respect for pedestrians.
        3. They do not obey traffic laws.
```

       a. They do not use proper signals.

       b. They turn across lanes.

       c. They stop without warning.

       d. They speed.

    4. They have many accidents.

  B. Small-town drivers are laid back.

    1. They are considerate of other drivers.

       a. They drive carefully.

       b. They rarely yell or honk at other
          drivers.

    2. They show concern for pedestrians.

    3. They obey traffic laws.

       a. They use proper signals.

       b. They turn properly.

       c. They stop slowly.

       d. They speed less.

    4. They have fewer accidents.

Caution.   Some readers and instructors disapprove of categories that contain only one subpoint, reasoning that you can't divide anything into one part (and that's what an outline does — divide or analyze ideas). Let's say that in an outline on earthquakes you list a 1 without a 2:

    D. Probable results of an earthquake

      1. Houses stripped of their paint

Logically, if you are going to discuss the *probable results* of an earthquake, you need to include more than one result. If you can't think of more than one subpoint, then just combine your categories:

**FOR
GROUP
LEARNING**

Outlining

Discuss the formal topic outline on pages 388–89 with some of your classmates or the entire class. Answer the following questions:

1. Would this outline guide a student writer in organizing an essay? Is the organization logical? Is it easy to follow? Try to think of other possible arrangements for the ideas.
2. Does this outline indicate sufficient details to develop a paper? About how many words would an essay developed from this outline be?
3. What possible pitfalls would the writer using this outline need to avoid?

D. Houses stripped of paint during an earthquake

Often, your use of only one subpoint indicates that you need to do more thinking, to discover more evidence. With a little more thought or reading, you might write this:

D. Probable results of an earthquake
   1. Houses stripped of their paint
   2. Cracks in foundations
   3. Gaps in road surfaces
   4. Collapsed bridges
   5. Broken water mains

Not only have you now come up with more points, but you have also arranged them in an order of increasing importance, placing the most important last for emphasis. This careful planning will save you some decisions when you write ("Now, which of these results do I deal with first?").

EXERCISE

Outlining

1. Select one of your groups of ideas from the exercises in Chapter 15. Using those ideas, construct a formal topic outline that might serve as a guide for an essay.
2. Now turn that topic outline into a formal sentence outline.
3. Discuss both outlines with your classmates and your instructor, bringing up any difficulties you encountered. If you get any better notions for organizing your ideas, change the outline.
4. Write an essay based on your outline.

Chapter 17

Strategies for Drafting

Learning to write well involves learning what questions to ask yourself. Some key questions are: How can I begin this draft? What should I do if I get stuck? How can I flesh out the bones of my paper? How can I begin and end my paper effectively? How can I keep my readers with me? In this chapter we offer advice to get you going and keep you going on your draft, from the first paragraph to the last.

Making a Start Enjoyable

Some writers find that if they can just make the art of writing start out playfully, like a game, they will be hard at work before they know it.

Time Yourself.   Try setting your watch, alarm clock, or egg timer, and vow to finish a page of your draft before the buzzer sounds. Don't stop for anything. If you find yourself writing drivel, just push on. You can cross out later.

Slow to a Crawl.   If speed quotas don't work for you, time yourself to write with exaggerated laziness, completing, say, not a page but a sentence every fifteen minutes.

Begin Badly — on Purpose.   For fun, begin by writing a deliberately crummy sentence, full of mistakes and misspellings and fuzzy-headedness. Then cross it out and write another, better sentence. This technique may help you clear out the false starts all at once.

Begin on Scrap Paper.   Some writers feel reluctant to mess up a blank white sheet of paper that may have cost two or three cents. John Legget, novelist, biographer, and former director of the Writers' Workshop at the University of

Iowa, uses the back of an old envelope or other scrap paper to get started, so he avoids feeling guilty about "spoiling a nice piece of paper with my thoughts."

Begin Writing the Part You Find Most Appetizing.   Start in the middle or at the end. Novelist Bill Downey points out that writing is different from childhood, "when we were forced to eat our vegetables first and then get our dessert. Writers are allowed to have their dessert first." When you begin a draft, try skipping the tough-looking steak and start with the brownie. Set down first the thoughts that come most easily to mind.

State Your Purpose.   In a sentence or a few lines, set forth what you want your paper to achieve. Are you trying to tell a story? To explain something? To win a reader over to your way of thinking? (For more about stating your purpose, see "Stating and Using a Thesis," p. 375.)

Nutshell It.   Write a very terse summary of the paper you want to write. Condense all your ideas into one small, tight paragraph. Later you can go back and expand each sentence until the meaning is clear and all points are adequately supported.

Shrink Your Immediate Job.   Break the writing task into several smaller parts, and do only the first one. Writing a 750-word paper, you might get going faster if you vow to turn out, say, just the first two paragraphs.

Seek a Provocative Title.   Write down ten or twenty possible titles for your paper, and then decide if any one sounds strikingly good. You can't let such a promising title go to waste, can you?

Tape-Record Yourself.   Talk a first draft of your paper into a tape recorder. Then play it back. Then write. You may find it hard to transcribe your spoken words, but this technique may set your mind in motion.

Imagine You're Giving a Speech.   On your feet, in front of an imaginary cheering crowd, spontaneously utter an opening paragraph. Then — quick! — write it down. Or tape it so you can get it down exactly.

Write in a Role.   Pretend you are someone else, and write in that person's voice. Or invent an imaginary character, and write as that character would.

Try the Great Chef Method.   According to legend, the great French chef Escoffier, by smelling a dish of food, could analyze its ingredients and then duplicate it in his kitchen. Analyze a paragraph you admire by another writer and cook up a new paragraph of your own from its ingredients. Take care to avoid plagiarism.

Write with Excessive Simple-Mindedness.   Do a whole paragraph or a whole draft the way a six-year-old talks — in plain, short, simple sentences. Karin Mack and Eric Skjei, in *Overcoming Writing Blocks* (Los Angeles: Tarcher, 1979), call this technique "Dick-and-Janing," from those first-grade readers featuring Dick and Jane doing simple things in simple sentences. Of course, you won't want to turn in a paper written like that; but for the first draft you have something down on paper that you can retool.

Restarting

When you have to write a long or demanding essay that you can't finish at one sitting, you may return to it only to find yourself stalled. You tromp your starter and nothing happens. Your engine seems reluctant to turn over. Try the following suggestions for getting back on the road.

Take Regular Short Breaks.   Even if you don't feel tired, take a regular break every half hour or so. Get up, walk around the room, stretch, get a drink of water, or refill your coffee cup. Two or three minutes should be enough to refresh your mind.

Change Activities.   When words won't come, do something quite different from writing for a while. Run, take your dog for a walk, or work out at the gym. Sometimes it helps to eat lunch, cook your favorite meal, take in a movie, listen to music, or take a nap. Or reward yourself — after you arrive at some predetermined point in your labors — with a trip to the vending machine, a phone call to a friend, or a TV show. Even while you're not thinking about your writing task, your unconscious mind will be working on it.

Switch Instruments.   Change the way your writing feels, looks, and sounds when it hits paper. Are you a typist? Try writing in longhand. If you are a pen user, type for a change. Try writing on note cards or on colored paper. Try composing directly on a computer screen. Perhaps you'll discover a new medium you'll enjoy more than your usual one.

Reread What You Have Written.   When you return to work, spend a few minutes rereading what you have already written. This method was a favorite of Ernest Hemingway, who, even when writing a novel, would begin a day's work by rereading his manuscript from page 1. (Just don't let rereading become a way to evade the writing itself.)

Try Snowplowing.   *Snowplowing* is the term invented by Jacqueline Jackson in her book *Turn Not Pale, Beloved Snail* (Boston: Little, Brown, 1979). When you reach a point that stops you cold — an obstinate passage or paragraph that won't come right — you imitate a snowplow and charge ahead through the difficulty.

> The plow gets to the bank and can't push it any farther. Then it goes back, revs up, comes barreling along the plowed snow, hits the bank and goes through — or at least a little farther.
> I reread the earlier paragraphs . . . and approach the impasse pretending it isn't there. I want to take it by surprise. Then when I'm suddenly upon it, I swerve. I don't reread it, for this would keep me in the same old rut. Instead I start writing madly, on the strength of the new thrust. This often gets me a few sentences farther, sometimes right through the bank.

Pause in Midstream.   End a writing session by breaking off in midsentence or midparagraph. Just leave a sentence trailing off into space, even if you know what its closing words should be. When you return to your task, you can sit down and start writing again immediately.

Leave Yourself Hints for How to Continue.   If you're ready to quit, but your head still holds some ideas you have not yet expressed, jot them down briefly. Tell yourself what you think might come next or write the first sentence of the next section. When you come back to work, you will face not a blank wall but some rich and suggestive graffiti.

Paragraphing

An essay is written not in large, indigestible lumps, but in *paragraphs* — small units, each more or less self-contained, each contributing some new idea in support of the thesis or main point of the essay. Writers dwell on one idea at a time, stating it, developing it, illustrating it with one or more examples or with a few facts. Paragraphing effectively means taking your readers by the hand and not only telling but also *showing* them, with plenty of detailed evidence, exactly what you mean. It means providing signposts to guide your readers through what you say.

Finished with one idea, you indent and start making a further point in a fresh paragraph. A paragraph indentation signifies a pause, as if you are taking a breath before moving on to another point. Readers assume that when you begin a new paragraph, you're moving on to a new idea, a new aspect of your thesis — and that you're going to ask them to think only about that idea for the rest of that paragraph.

Paragraphs can be as short as one sentence or as long as a page. Sometimes the length is governed by the audience for whom the paragraph is written, sometimes by the purpose of the writing, sometimes by the medium in which the paragraph appears. News writers, for instance, tend to write in brief, one- or two-sentence paragraphs. Newspaper readers, consuming facts like popcorn, find that the short paragraphing allows them to skim an article quickly. College writers, in contrast, should assume some willingness on the part of their readers to read through well-developed paragraphs.

The following sections give you some advice on using topic sentences to focus and control *body paragraphs* within an essay. You will also find advice on paragraphs that do special jobs — *opening paragraphs* that draw the reader in and *concluding paragraphs* that wrap up the discussion. You can use much of the advice on writing topic sentences for paragraphs when you are writing thesis sentences for essays. For more on filling out the main ideas within paragraphs, see Chapter 18, "Strategies for Developing."

Using Topic Sentences

A *topic sentence* spells out the main idea of a paragraph in the body of an essay. When you read clear prose, especially writing that explains or argues, you can easily pick out the topic sentence of a body paragraph, and you know what to expect next. When you write, you should provide topic sentences to guide you in your writing and to help direct readers through your prose.

One tried-and-true way to write an effectively focused paragraph is to write a topic sentence first. It then becomes the foundation on which to build the rest of the paragraph. If you have written a sentence outline for your essay, you can convert the heading for each major subdivision (marked with roman numerals in a formal outline) into the topic sentence of a body paragraph in your essay. Even if you've written a topic outline, you may be able to expand each major subdivision heading into a topic sentence. (For more on topic outlines and sentence outlines, see pp. 388–91.)

Good topic sentences hook readers and give them a way to interpret the rest of the paragraph. An effective topic sentence is *interesting, accurate,* and *limited.* The more pointed and lively your topic sentence is, the more *interesting* it will be to your readers. "There are many things wrong with television" is dull and vague, but it's a start. Zero in on one specific flaw, and your topic sentence might become "Of all television's faults, the one I dislike most is melodramatizing the news." You can then illustrate your point with two or three melodramatic newscasts that you remember. A topic sentence should be *accurate* because it serves as a guide to the rest of the paragraph: if, after reading the topic sentence, readers think you mean one thing but then think you mean something else after reading the rest of the paragraph, you've got a problem. A topic sentence should be *limited* for the same reason: you don't want to mislead readers about what you intend to cover in a paragraph. If you start off by saying "Seven factors have contributed to the increasing obesity of the average American" but then introduce only one or two of them, you're going to frustrate your readers.

KINDS OF TOPIC SENTENCES

Topic Sentence as First Sentence.   Usually, as in the following example from James David Barber's *The Presidential Character: Predicting Performance in the White House*, 3rd ed. (Englewood Cliffs: Prentice, 1985), the topic sentence appears first in the paragraph, followed by sentences that clarify, illustrate, and support what it says. (In all the following examples, we have put the topic sentences in *italics*.)

> *The first baseline in defining Presidential types is activity-passivity.* How much energy does the man invest in his Presidency? Lyndon Johnson went at his day like a human cyclone, coming to rest long after the sun went down. Calvin Coolidge often slept eleven hours a night and still needed a nap in the middle of the day. In between, the Presidents array themselves on the high or low side of the activity line.

This paragraph moves from the general to the specific. The topic sentence clearly states at the outset what the paragraph is to be about. The second sentence defines *activity-passivity*. The third and fourth sentences, by citing extremes at either end of the baseline, supply illustrations — active Johnson, passive Coolidge. The final sentence makes a generalization that reinforces the central point.

Topic Sentence near the Beginning of Paragraph.   Sometimes the first sentence of a new paragraph functions as a transition, linking what is to come with what has gone before. In such a paragraph the *second* sentence might be the topic sentence. The paragraph quoted here, from "On Societies as Organisms" in *The Lives of a Cell* (New York: Viking, 1974) by science writer and physician Lewis Thomas, follows one about insects that ends "and we violate science when we try to read human meanings in their arrangements." The first sentence is transition, and the second is the topic sentence.

> It is hard for a bystander not to do so. *Ants are so much like human beings as to be an embarrassment.* They farm fungi, raise aphids as livestock, launch armies into wars, use chemical sprays to alarm and confuse enemies, capture slaves. The families of weaver ants engage in child labor, holding their larvae like shuttles to spin out the thread that sews the leaves together for their fungus gardens. They exchange information ceaselessly. They do everything but watch television.

Topic Sentence at End of Paragraph.   Occasionally a writer, especially one attempting to persuade the reader to agree, piles detail on detail throughout a paragraph. Then, with a dramatic flourish, the writer *concludes* with the topic sentence. You can see this technique in the following paragraph, from student Heidi Kessler's paper giving an opinion about a contemporary social problem:

> A fourteen-year-old writes to an advice columnist in my hometown newspaper that she has "done it" lots of times and sex is "no big deal." At the

neighborhood clinic where my aunt works, a hardened sixteen-year-old requests her third abortion. A girl-child I know has two children of her own, but no husband. A college student in my dorm now finds herself sterile from a "social disease" picked up during casual sexual encounters. Multiply these examples by thousands. *It seems clear to me that women, who fought so hard for sexual freedom equal to that of men, have emerged from the battle not as joyous free spirits but as the sexual revolution's walking wounded.*

This paragraph moves from the particular to the general — from four examples about individuals to one large statement about American women at the end. By the time you come to the general statement at the end of the paragraph, you might be ready to accept the conclusion in the topic sentence.

Topic Sentence Implied.   It is also possible to find a perfectly unified, well-organized paragraph that has no topic sentence at all, like the following from "New York" by Gay Talese:

> Each afternoon in New York a rather seedy saxophone player, his cheeks blown out like a spinnaker, stands on the sidewalk playing "Danny Boy" in such a sad, sensitive way that he soon has half the neighborhood peeking out of windows tossing nickels, dimes, and quarters at his feet. Some of the coins roll under parked cars, but most of them are caught in his outstretched hand. The saxophone player is a street musician named Joe Gabler; for the past thirty years he has serenaded every block in New York and has sometimes been tossed as much as $100 a day in coins. He is also hit with buckets of water, empty beer cans and eggs, and chased by wild dogs. He is believed to be the last of New York's ancient street musicians.

No one sentence neatly sums up the writer's idea. Like most effective paragraphs that lack a topic sentence, Talese's paragraph contains something just as good — a *topic idea.* The author doesn't allow his paragraph to wander aimlessly. He knows exactly what he wants to achieve — a description of how Joe Gabler, a famous New York street musician, plies his trade. Because Talese succeeds in keeping this main purpose firmly in mind, the main point — that Gabler meets both reward and abuse — is clear to the reader as well.

Question to Answer.   Not all topic sentences are statements. Sometimes a question can effectively alert your reader to the topic of the paragraph without giving away the punchline. Here, for example, is such a paragraph by psychoanalyst Erik Erikson:

> Is the sense of identity conscious? At times, of course, it seems only too conscious. For between the double prongs of vital inner need and inexorable outer demand, the as yet experimenting individual may become the victim of a transitory extreme identity consciousness, which is the common core of the many forms of "self-consciousness" typical for youth. Where the processes of identity formation are prolonged (a factor which can bring creative gain), such preoccupation with the "self-image" also prevails. We are thus most aware of our identity when we are just about to gain it and when we (with

that startle which motion pictures call a "double take") are somewhat surprised to make its acquaintance; or, again, when we are just about to enter a crisis and feel the encroachment of identity confusion.

For more specific suggestions on developing your ideas in paragraphs and essays, see Chapter 18, "Strategies for Developing."

EXERCISE

Topic Sentences

Discuss each of the following topic sentences with your peer group, answering these questions:

Will it catch readers' attention?
Is it accurate?
Is it limited?
How might you develop the idea in the rest of the paragraph?
Can you improve it?

1. Television commercials stereotype people.
2. Teenagers face many problems growing up.
3. Living away from home for the first time is hard.
4. Violence in movies can be harmful.
5. I have been influenced by teachers.
6. It's good for a child to have a pet.
7. A flea market is a good place to buy jewelry.
8. Pollution should be controlled.
9. Everybody should recycle wastes.
10. *Casablanca* is my favorite movie.

MAKING CONNECTIONS: TOPIC SENTENCES IN *A WRITER'S READER*

Experienced writers use topic sentences to strengthen their drafts as they write. The essays in *A Writer's Reader* contain many examples of the various kinds of topic sentences described in this section. Here is a small sampling:

AS FIRST SENTENCE OF PARAGRAPH
Stephanie Coontz, "Remarriage and Stepfamilies" (p. 522, paragraphs 2, 6–7, 10–12)
Stephen King, "Why We Crave Horror Movies" (p. 593, paragraphs 8–12)

NEAR BEGINNING OF PARAGRAPH
Jack Kemp, "Affirmative Action: The 'Radical Republican' Example" (p. 588, paragraphs 3, 5, 9)
Brent Staples, "Black Men and Public Space" (p. 561, paragraphs 2, 11)

AT END OF PARAGRAPH
Michael Shermer, "Abducted! Encounters with Aliens" (p. 596, paragraph 6)

Joy Harjo, "Three Generations of Native American Women's Birth Experience" (p. 540, paragraphs 9, 15, 18)

IMPLICIT
Emily Prager, "Our Barbies, Ourselves" (p. 537, paragraphs 5, 7)
Amy Tan, "Mother Tongue" (p. 496, paragraphs 4–7, 14)

AS A QUESTION
Mike Males, "Public Enemy Number One?" (p. 616, paragraphs 3, 4, 8, 22–23)
Scott Russell Sanders, "The Men We Carry in Our Minds" (p. 531, paragraphs 10, 17, 21)

Writing an Opening

Even writers with something to say find it hard occasionally to begin. Often they are so intent on writing a brilliant opening paragraph that they freeze, unable to write anything at all. When you sit down to draft an essay, you can ease your way into the job by simply deciding to set words — any words — on paper, without trying at all for an arresting or witty opening.

A time-honored approach to the opening paragraph is to write it *last*, after you have written the body of your essay and know exactly in what direction it is headed. Some writers like to write a long, meandering beginning in the first draft and then in rewriting cut it down to the most dramatic, exciting, or interesting essentials. Others use the introduction as a summary guide for themselves and their readers. At whatever point in the writing process you fashion an opening paragraph, remember that your chief aim is to persuade your readers to lay aside their preoccupations and enter the world set forth in your essay.

KINDS OF OPENINGS

Begin with a Story.   Often a simple anecdote can capture your readers' interest and thus serve as a good beginning. Here is how writer Harry Crews opens his essay "The Car" in *Florida Frenzy* (Gainesville: U Presses of Florida, 1982):

> The other day, there arrived in the mail a clipping sent by a friend of mine. It had been cut from a Long Beach, California, newspaper and dealt with a young man who had eluded police for fifty-five minutes while he raced over freeways and through city streets at speeds up to 130 miles per hour. During the entire time, he ripped his clothes off and threw them out the window bit by bit. It finally took twenty-five patrol cars and a helicopter to catch him. When they did, he said that God had given him the car and that he had "found God."

Most of us, reading such an anecdote, want to read on. What will the writer say next? What has the anecdote to do with the essay as a whole? Crews has aroused our curiosity.

Introduce Your Subject and Comment on It.   In some essays, the writer introduces a subject and then expands on it, bringing in vital details, as in this opening paragraph by David Morris, from an article entitled "Rootlessness":

> Americans are a rootless people. Each year one in six of us changes residences; one in four changes jobs. We see nothing troubling in these statistics. For most of us, they merely reflect the restless energy that made America great. A nation of immigrants, unsurprisingly, celebrates those willing to pick up stakes and move on: the frontiersman, the cowboy, the entrepreneur, the corporate raider.

After first stating his point baldly, Morris goes on to supply some interesting statistics that back up his contention and offer a partial explanation of the phenomenon he focuses on.

Ask a Question.   A well-written essay can begin with a question and answer, as writer James H. Austin begins "Four Kinds of Chance":

> What is chance? Dictionaries define it as something fortuitous that happens unpredictably without discernible human intention. Chance is unintentional and capricious, but we needn't conclude that chance is immune from human intervention. Indeed, chance plays several distinct roles when humans react creatively with one another and with their environment.

Beginning to answer the question in the first paragraph leads readers to expect the rest of the essay to continue the answer.

State an Opinion.   To challenge readers, a writer may begin with a controversial opinion, as writer Wade Thompson did.

> Unlike any other sport, football is played solely for the benefit of the spectator. If you take the spectator away from any other game, the game could still survive on its own. Thus tennis players love tennis, whether or not anyone is watching. Golfers are almost churlish in their dedication to their game. Ping-Pong players never look around. Basketball players can dribble and shoot for hours without hearing a single cheer. Even baseball might survive the deprivation, despite the lack of parks. Softball surely would. But if you took away the spectators, if you demolished the grandstands and boarded up the stadium, it is inconceivable to think that any football would be played in the eerie privacy of the field itself. No football team ever plays another team just for the fun of playing football. Army plays Navy, Michigan plays Purdue, P.S. 123 plays P.S. 124, only with the prospect of a loud crowd on hand.

After his first, startling remark, Thompson generalizes about games unlike football, backing up his generalization with examples of such games. Finally he returns to his original point, emphasizing the direction his essay will take.

End with the Thesis Sentence.   An effective opening paragraph can end with a statement of the essay's main point. After first capturing your readers' attention with an anecdote or with gripping details or examples, you take your readers by the hand and lead them in exactly the direction your essay is to go. Such a thesis statement can be brief, as in this powerful opening of an essay by educator George B. Leonard called "No School?":

> The most obvious barrier between our children and the kind of education that can free their enormous potential seems to be the educational system itself: a vast, suffocating web of people, practices and presumptions, kindly in intent, ponderous in response. Now, when true educational alternatives are at last becoming clear, we may overlook the simplest: no school.

If you find writing an opening paragraph difficult, don't worry *too* hard about capturing and transfixing your readers; just introduce your idea. Keep it simple. Open with an anecdote, a description, a comparison, a definition, a quotation, a question, or some vital background. Be sure that what you say is relevant to your main point. And don't forget to set forth your thesis (as discussed on p. 375).

MAKING CONNECTIONS: OPENINGS IN *A WRITER'S READER*

Professional writers use the same kinds of openings discussed in this chapter. *A Writer's Reader* contains many useful examples; here are a few. Deborah Tannen in "Women and Men Talking on the Job" (p. 550) and Cynthia Joyce in "Six Clicks from Death" (p. 646) both begin with stories. Veronica Chambers in "The Myth of Cinderella" (p. 603) introduces the subject and comments on it. Joy Harjo in "Three Generations of Native American Women's Birth Experience" (p. 540) and Thomas F. Cawsey, Gene Deszca, and Maurice Mazerolle in "The Portfolio Career as a Response to a Changing Job Market" (p. 635) open with a question. Stephen King in "Why We Crave Horror Movies" (p. 593) opens by expressing a dramatic opinion. Judith Ortiz Cofer in "The Myth of the Latin Woman: I Just Met a Girl Named María" (p. 564) ends her introduction with the thesis statement for her essay.

Writing a Conclusion

The final paragraphs of an essay linger longest in readers' minds. E. B. White's conclusion to "Once More to the Lake" (p. 490) certainly does so. In the essay, White describes his return with his young son to a vacation spot he had known and loved as a child. At the end of the essay, in an unforgettable image, he remembers how old he really is and realizes the inevitable passing of generations.

> When the others went swimming my son said he was going in, too. He pulled his dripping trunks from the line where they had hung all through the shower and wrung them out. Languidly, and with no thought of going in, I watched him, his hard little body, skinny and bare, saw him wince slightly as he pulled up around his vitals the small, soggy, icy garment. As he buckled the swollen belt, suddenly my groin felt the chill of death.

White's concluding paragraph is a classic example of an effective ending. It begins with a sentence that points back to the previous paragraph and at the same time looks ahead. Then White leads us quickly to his final, chilling insight. And then he stops.

KINDS OF CONCLUSIONS

It's easy to suggest what *not* to do at the end of an essay: Don't leave your readers suspended in midair, half expecting you to go on. Don't restate everything you've already said. Don't introduce a brand-new topic that leads away from the point of your essay. And don't feel you have to introduce your final paragraph with an obvious signal that the end is near. Avoid ending an essay with words and phrases like "In conclusion," "As I have said," or "So, as we see." In a long, complicated paper, a terse summation of your main points right before your concluding sentences may help your reader grasp your ideas; but a short paper usually requires either no summary at all or little more than a single sentence or two.

"How *do* you write an ending, then?" you might well ask.

End with a Quotation. An apt quotation can neatly round out an essay, as literary critic Malcolm Cowley demonstrates at the end of an essay in *The View from Eighty* (New York: Viking, 1980), his discussion of the pitfalls and compensations of old age.

> "Eighty years old!" the great Catholic poet Paul Claudel wrote in his journal. "No eyes left, no ears, no teeth, no legs, no wind! And when all is said and done, how astonishingly well one does without them!"

State or Restate Your Thesis. In a sharp criticism of American schools, humorist Russell Baker in "School vs. Education" ends by stating his main point, that schools do not educate.

> Afterward, the former student's destiny fulfilled, his life rich with Oriental carpets, rare porcelain, and full bank accounts, he may one day find himself with the leisure and the inclination to open a book with a curious mind, and start to become educated.

End with a Brief Emphatic Sentence. For an essay that traces causes or effects, analyzes, evaluates, or argues, a deft concluding thought can reinforce your main idea. Notice the definite click with which former heavyweight champion Gene Tunney (*The Long Count* [New York: Atheneum, 1969]) closes the door on "The Long Count," an analysis of his two victorious fights with Jack Dempsey, whose boxing style differed markedly from Tunney's own.

> Jack Dempsey was a great fighter — possibly the greatest that ever entered a ring. Looking back objectively, one has to conclude that he was more valuable to the sport or "The Game" than any prizefighter of his time. Whether you consider it from his worth as a gladiator or from the point of view of the

box office, he was tops. His name in his most glorious days was magic among his people, and today, twenty years after, the name Jack Dempsey is still magic. This tells a volume in itself. As one who has always had pride in his profession as well as his professional theories, and possessing a fair share of Celtic romanticism, I wish that we could have met when we were both at our unquestionable best. We could have decided many questions, to me the most important of which is whether "a good boxer can always lick a good fighter."
   I still say yes.

Introduce Some Ideas Implied by Your Essay.   You don't want to introduce new topics at the end of your essay, but you might mention a few new *implications* concerning the topic you have covered. As you draw to a close, ask yourself, "What now?" "What is the significance of what I have said?" Leave your readers with one or two provocative thoughts to ponder. Obstreperous 1920s debunker H. L. Mencken uses this technique in "The Libido for the Ugly," an essay about the ugliness of American cities and towns.

   Here is something that the psychologists have so far neglected: the love of ugliness for its own sake, the lust to make the world intolerable. Its habitat is the United States. Out of the melting pot emerges a race which hates beauty as it hates truth. The etiology of this madness deserves a great deal more study than it has got. There must be causes behind it; it arises and flourishes in obedience to biological laws, and not as a mere act of God. What, precisely, are the terms of those laws? And why do they run stronger in America than elsewhere? Let some honest *Privat Dozent*° in pathological sociology apply himself to the problem.

Stop When the Story Is Over.   Even a quiet ending can be effective, as long as it signals clearly that the essay is finished. Sometimes the best way to conclude a story, for instance, is simply to stop when the story is over. This is what journalist Martin Gansberg does in his true account of the fatal beating of a young woman, Kitty Genovese, in full view of residents of a Queens, New York, apartment house. The residents, unwilling to become involved, did nothing to interfere. Here is the last paragraph of his account, "Thirty-eight Who Saw Murder Didn't Call Police":

   It was 4:25 A.M. when the ambulance arrived to take the body of Miss Genovese. It drove off. "Then," a solemn police detective said, "the people came out."

EXERCISE

Openings and Conclusions

Openings and conclusions frame an essay, contributing to the unity of the whole. The opening sets up the subject and the main idea; the conclusion reaffirms the thesis and rounds off the ideas. Discuss the following with your classmates.

Privat Dozent: A lecturer at a German university.

I. Here are two possible beginning paragraphs from a student essay on the importance of children learning how to swim.

    A. Humans inhabit a world made up of over 70 percent water. In addition to these great bodies of water, we have built millions of swimming pools for sports and leisure activities. At one time or another most people will be faced with either the danger of drowning or the challenge of aquatic recreation. For these reasons, it is essential that we learn to swim. Being a competitive swimmer and a swimming instructor, I fully realize the importance of knowing how to swim.

    B. Four-year-old Carl, curious like most children, last spring ventured out onto his pool patio. He fell into the pool and, not knowing how to swim, helplessly sank to the bottom. Minutes later his uncle found the child and brought him to the surface. Since Carl had no pulse, his uncle immediately administered CPR on him until the paramedics arrived. Eventually he was revived. During his stay in the hospital, his mother signed him up for beginning swimming classes. Carl was a lucky one. Unlike thousands of other children and adults, he got a second chance.

    1. Which introduction is more effective? Why?
    2. What would the body of this essay consist of? What kinds of evidence would be included?
    3. Write a suitable conclusion for this essay.

II. If you were to read each of the following introductions from professional essays, would you want to read the entire essay? Why?

    A. During my ninth hour underground, as I scrambled up a slanting tunnel through the powdered gypsum, Rick Bridges turned to me and said, "You know, this whole area was just discovered Tuesday." (David Roberts, "Caving Comes into Its Golden Age: A New Mexico Marvel," *Smithsonian* Nov. 1988: 52)

    B. From the batting average on the back of a George Brett baseball card to the interest rate fluctuations that determine whether the economy grows or stagnates, Americans are fascinated by statistics. (Stephen E. Nordlinger, "By the Numbers," *St. Petersburg Times* 6 Nov. 1988: 11)

    C. "What does it look like under there?"
       It was always this question back then, always the same pattern of hello and what's your name, what happened to your eye and what's under there. (Natalie Kusz, "Waiting for a Glass Eye," *Road Song* [New York: Farrar, 1990], rpt. in *Harper's* Nov. 1990)

III. Evaluate the effectiveness of each of the following introductions from student essays.

    A. On June 4, 1985, Los Angeles police arrested Jerald Curtis Johns. Police believe he may have raped as many as 100 women, ranging in age from 24 to 71, living in a ten block radius (*Time* 5 Sept. 1985). But of those 100 women, only 13 reported rape. This situation is commonplace: most rapes are not reported.

B. Is it possible for a young girl of twelve or so who has been sexually and mentally abused to recover her self-worth and have a productive and happy life? The movie *The Color Purple* attempts to answer that question.

IV. How effective are the following introductions and conclusions from student essays? Could they be improved? If so, how? If they are satisfactory, explain why. What would be an eye-catching yet informative title for each essay?

A. Recently a friend down from New York astonished me with stories of several people infected — some with AIDS — by stepping on needles washed up on the New Jersey beaches. This is just one incident of pollution, a devastating problem in our society today. Pollution is increasing in our world because of greed, apathy, and Congress's inability to control this problem. . . .

Wouldn't it be nice to have a pollution-free world without medical wastes floating in the water and washing up on our beaches? Without garbage scattered on the streets? With every corporation abiding by the laws set by Congress? In the future we can have a pollution-free world, but it is going to take the cooperation of everyone, including Congress, to ensure our survival on this Planet Earth.

B. The divorce rate has risen 700 percent in this century and continues to rise. More than one out of every two couples who are married end up in divorce. Over one million children a year are affected by divorce in the family. From these statistics it is clear that one of the greatest problems concerning the family today is divorce and the adverse effects it has on our society. . . .

Divorce causes problems that change people for life. The number of divorces will continue to exceed the 700 percent figure unless married couples learn to communicate, to accept their mates unconditionally, and to sacrificially give of themselves.

V. Choose one of the topics from your brainstorming or freewriting in Chapter 15, and write several — at least three — different introductions with conclusions. Ask your classmates which is the most effective.

MAKING CONNECTIONS: CONCLUSIONS IN *A WRITER'S READER*

Professional writers use the strategies discussed in this chapter to close their essays. William Henry Lewis simply stops "Shades" (p. 505) when the narration is over. Nicholas Wade concludes "How Men and Women Think" (p. 556) with a brief discussion of some of the ideas implied by his essay. Judy Brady in "I Want a Wife" (p. 529) ends with a pithy statement. Steve Olson in "Year of the Blue-Collar Guy" (p. 570) restates his thesis. LynNell Hancock in "The Haves and the Have-Nots" (p. 631) relies primarily on quotations in her final paragraph.

Achieving Coherence

Effective writing is well organized. It proceeds in some sensible order, each sentence following naturally from the one before it. Yet even well-organized prose can be hard to read unless it is *coherent*. To make your writing coherent, you can use various devices that tie together words in a sentence, sentences in a paragraph, paragraphs in an essay.

DEVICES THAT CREATE COHERENCE

Transitional Words and Sentences.   You already use transitions every day, in both your writing and your speech. Instinctively you realize that certain words and phrases help your readers and listeners follow your train of thought. But some writers, in a rush to get through what they have to say, omit important links between thoughts. Mistakenly, they assume that because a connection is clear to them it will automatically be clear to their readers. Often just a word, phrase, or sentence of transition inserted in the right place will transform a seemingly disconnected passage into a coherent one.

Time markers are transitions that make clear *when* one thing happens in relation to another. Time markers include words and phrases like *then, soon, the following day,* and *in a little while.*

Not all transitions mark time. The English language contains many words and phrases that make clear other connections between or within sentences. Consider choosing one of the following commonly used *transitional markers* to fit your purpose. They are grouped here by purpose or the kind of relation or connection they establish.

TO MARK TIME	then, soon, first, second, next, recently, the following day, in a little while, meanwhile, after, later, in the past
TO MARK PLACE OR DIRECTION	in the distance, close by, near, far away, above, below, to the right, on the other side, opposite, to the west, next door
TO SUMMARIZE OR RESTATE	in other words, to put it another way, in brief, in simpler terms, on the whole, in fact, in a word, to sum up, in short, in conclusion, to conclude, finally, therefore
TO RELATE CAUSE AND EFFECT OR RESULT	therefore, accordingly, hence, thus, for, so, consequently, as a result, because of
TO ADD OR AMPLIFY OR LIST	and, also, too, besides, as well, moreover, in addition, furthermore, in effect, second, in the second place, again, next

TO COMPARE	similarly, likewise, in like manner
TO CONCEDE	whereas, on the other hand, with that in mind, still, and yet, even so, in spite of, despite, at least
TO CONTRAST	on the other hand, but, or, however, unlike, nevertheless, on the contrary, conversely, in contrast, instead
TO INDICATE PURPOSE	to this end, for this purpose, with this objective
TO EXPRESS CONDITION	although, though
TO GIVE EXAMPLES OR SPECIFY	for example, for instance, in this case, in particular, to illustrate
TO QUALIFY	for the most part, by and large, with few exceptions, mainly, in most cases, some, sometimes
TO EMPHASIZE	it is true, truly, indeed, of course, to be sure, obviously, without doubt, evidently, clearly, understandably

Occasionally a whole sentence serves as a transition. Often, but not always, it is the first sentence of a new paragraph. When the transitional sentence appears in that position, it harks back to the contents of the previous paragraph while simultaneously hinting at the direction the new paragraph is to take. Here is a sample, excerpted from an essay by Marsha Traugot about adopting older and handicapped children, in which the transitional sentence (in *italics*) begins a new paragraph.

> Some exchanges hold monthly meetings where placement workers looking for a match can discuss waiting children or families, and they also sponsor parties where children, workers, and prospective parents meet informally.
> *And if a match still cannot be made?* Exchanges and other child welfare organizations now employ media blitzes as aggressive as those of commercial advertising. . . .

By repeating the key word *match* in her transitional sentence and by inserting the word *still*, Traugot makes clear that in what follows she will build on what has gone before. At the same time, by making the transitional sentence a rhetorical question, Traugot promises that the new paragraph will introduce fresh material, in this case answering the question.

Transition Paragraphs. Transitions may be even longer than sentences. When you write an essay, especially one that is long and complicated, you'll find that to move clearly from one idea to the next will sometimes require an entire paragraph of transition.

```
     So far, we have been dwelling on the physical and
psychological effects of driving nonstop for more than
two hundred miles. Now let's reflect on causes. Why do
people become addicted to their steering wheels?
```

Usually, such a paragraph will be shorter than other body paragraphs, but you'll want to allow it whatever space it may require. Often, as in the preceding example, it makes a comment on the structure of the essay, looking back and pointing forward.

A transition paragraph can come to your aid when you go off on one branch of argument and then return to your main trunk. Here's an example from a masterly writer, Lewis Thomas, in an essay, "Things Unflattened by Science, from *Late Night Thoughts on Listening to Mahler's Ninth Symphony* (New York: Viking, 1983)." A medical doctor, Thomas has been complaining in his essay that biologists keep expecting medical researchers to come up with quick answers to intractable problems — cancer, schizophrenia, stress. He takes most of a paragraph to explain why he doesn't think medical science can solve the problem of stress: "Stress is simply the condition of being human." Now, to turn again to the main idea of his essay — what biological problems he would like to see solved — Thomas inserts a transition paragraph.

> But I digress. What I wish to get at is an imaginary situation in which I am allowed three or four questions to ask the world of biomedical science to settle for me by research, as soon as possible. Can I make a short list of top-priority puzzles, things I am more puzzled by than anything else? I can.

In a new paragraph, he continues: "First, I want to know what goes on in the mind of a honeybee." He wonders if a bee is just a sort of programmed robot or if it can think and imagine, even a little bit. Neatly and effectively, the transition paragraph has led to this speculation and to several further paragraphs that will come.

Use a transition paragraph only when you sense that your readers might get lost if you don't patiently lead them by the hand. If you can do without transition paragraphs, do. If the essay is short, one question or statement at the beginning of a new paragraph will be enough.

Repetitions. As we see in Traugot's passage about adoption, another way to make clear the relationship between two sentences, two paragraphs, or two ideas is to *repeat* a key word or phrase. Such repetition, purposefully done, almost guarantees that readers will understand how all the parts of even a complicated passage fit together. Note the repetition of the word *anger* in the following paragraph (italics ours) from *Of Woman Born* (New York: Norton,

1976) by poet Adrienne Rich, in which the writer explores her relationship with her mother. The repetition holds all the parts of this complex paragraph together and makes clear the unity and coherence of its ideas.

> And I know there must be deep reservoirs of *anger* in her; every mother has known overwhelming, unacceptable *anger* at her children. When I think of the conditions under which my mother became a mother, the impossible expectations, my father's distaste for pregnant women, his hatred of all that he could not control, my *anger* at her dissolves into grief and *anger for* her, and then dissolves back again into *anger* at her: the ancient, unpurged *anger* of the child.

Pronouns.   Because they always refer back to nouns or other pronouns, pronouns serve as transitions by making readers refer back as well. Note how certain pronouns (indicated by *italics*) hold together the following paragraph by columnist Ellen Goodman:

> I have two friends who moved in together many years ago. *He* looked upon this step as a trial marriage. *She* looked upon it as, well, moving in together. *He* was sure that in a matter of time, after *they* had built up trust and confidence, *she* would agree that marriage was the next logical step. *She,* on the other hand, was thrilled that here at last was a man *who* would never push *her* back to the altar.

Goodman's paragraph contains transitions other than pronouns, too: time markers like *many years ago, in a matter of time,* and *after;* the transitional marker *on the other hand,* which indicates that what follows will contrast with what has gone before; and repetition of synonyms like *trial marriage, marriage,* and *the altar.* All serve the main purpose of transitions — keeping readers on track.

EXERCISE

Identifying Transitions

Go over one of the papers you have already written for this course, and circle all the transitional devices you can detect. Then share your paper with a classmate. Can the classmate find additional transitions? Does the classmate think you need transitions where you don't have any?

MAKING CONNECTIONS: COHERENCE IN
A WRITER'S READER

The essays in *A Writer's Reader* demonstrate how professional writers use the devices discussed in this chapter to create a sense of coherence within and among their paragraphs. For example, E. B. White uses transitions denoting place or direction in "Once More to the Lake" (p. 490) and Gerald Early uses transitions denoting time in "Black like . . . Shirley Temple?" (p. 502). Scott Russell Sanders in "The Men We Carry in Our Minds" (p. 531) and Stephen Dunn in "Locker Room Talk" (p. 545) use clear transitional words and sentences, repetition, and pronouns throughout their essays. In paragraph 5 of "Freeing Choices" (p. 580), Nancy Mairs uses the repeated pronoun *she* and a repeated sentence structure to create a sense of rhythm and unity. Jeffrey Obser uses paragraph 8 in "Privacy Is the Problem, Not the Solution" (p. 658) as a transition between an extended example and his next point. Can you identify all the types of transitions used by Meghan Daum in "Virtual Love" (p. 623) and Jeffrey Obser in "Privacy Is the Problem, Not the Solution" (p. 657)?

Chapter 18

Strategies for Developing

In Parts One and Two of this book, you learned a lot about writing, you had a lot of practice, and we hope you improved your writing. In those sections, you saw specifically how a writer can use resources that are always available (such as recall and conversation) and critical thinking strategies (such as analyzing and evaluating) to focus and develop an entire essay. In this chapter you will look at methods for supporting and clarifying your ideas in individual paragraphs and parts of essays. Some of these methods are the same as the writer's resources and critical thinking strategies you've already seen. Others, such as defining, have not been discussed in this book before—although you've no doubt already used them in your writing, perhaps without even knowing it.

In this chapter we cover giving examples, providing details, defining, dividing and classifying, analyzing a process, comparing and contrasting, and showing cause and effect. You'll find these seven methods of development to be indispensable, whether your purpose in a particular essay is to relate a personal experience, to explain, or to persuade. Although you may choose to use only one method within a single paragraph, a strong essay will almost always require a combination of developmental strategies.

Here are some questions to ask yourself when looking for places in your essay to develop your ideas more fully:

DISCOVERY CHECKLIST

Developing Ideas

- Are any paragraphs in your essay only one or two sentences long? Could these paragraphs benefit from being developed more fully?
- Are your longer paragraphs solid and stout, meaty and interesting to read? Or are they just filled with generalizations, mindless repetitions, and wordy phrasings?
- Is there any point in your essay where you think your readers might have difficulty following you or understanding your meaning? Would more evidence help?
- If you've shown your draft to a peer editor, has he or she pointed out ideas that need to be developed more fully?

412

Giving Examples

METHODS OF GIVING EXAMPLES

An example — the word comes from the Latin *exemplum,* meaning "one thing chosen from among many" — is a typical instance that illustrates a whole type or kind. Giving examples to support a generalization is probably the most often used means of development. Here's an example, from *In Search of Excellence* (New York: Harper and Row, 1982) by Thomas J. Peters and Robert H. Waterman Jr. explaining why America's top corporations are so successful:

> Although he's not a company, our favorite illustration of closeness to the customer is car salesman Joe Girard. He sold more new cars and trucks, each year, for eleven years running, than any other human being. In fact, in a typical year, Joe sold more than twice as many units as whoever was in second place. In explaining his secret of success, Joe said: "I sent out over thirteen thousand cards every month."
>
> Why start with Joe? Because his magic is the magic of IBM and many of the rest of the excellent companies. It is simply service, overpowering service, especially after-sales service. Joe noted, "There's one thing that I do that a lot of salesmen don't, and that's believe the sale really begins *after* the sale — not before. . . . The customer ain't out the door, and my son has made up a thank-you note." Joe would intercede personally, a year later, with the service manager on behalf of his customer. Meanwhile he would keep the communications flowing.

Notice how Peters and Waterman focus on the specific, Joe Girard. They don't write *corporation employees* or even *car salespeople,* but zero in on one particular man to make the point come alive.

America's top corporations
corporation employees
car salespeople
Joe Girard

This ladder of abstraction moves from the general — America's top corporations — to a specific person — Joe Girard. Peters and Waterman's use of the specific example of Joe Girard makes their point about the importance of closeness to the customer *concrete* to readers: he is someone readers can relate to.

Another instance of a writer moving from a broad generalization to recognizable individual examples is found on page 397, where James David Barber discusses presidential types. Barber illustrates the main idea of his paragraph (that presidents can be located on an "activity-passivity" spectrum) with two examples — the drowsy Coolidge and the energetic Johnson. Like Peters and Waterman, Barber moves several levels down the ladder of abstraction to make his idea specific.

```
| presidents of the United States
  | presidential types
     | active presidents
        | Lyndon Johnson
  | passive presidents
        | Calvin Coolidge
```

To check the level of specification in one of your paragraphs or outlines, draw a ladder of abstraction for it. If you haven't gone down to the fourth or fifth level, you are probably being too general and need to add examples. This strategy is also a way for you to restrict a broad subject to a topic manageable in a short essay.

An example doesn't always have to be a specific individual. Sometimes you can create a picture in your readers' minds of something that they have never encountered before (and that may not actually exist), or you can make an abstraction come alive by giving it a recognizable personality and identity. Using this strategy, writer Jonathan Kozol makes real the plight of illiterate people in our bureaucratized health care system. The following paragraph is from *Prisoners of Silence: Breaking the Bonds of Adult Illiteracy in the United States* (New York: Continuum, 1980).

> Illiterates live, in more than literal ways, an uninsured existence. They cannot understand the written details on a health insurance form. They cannot read waivers that they sign preceding surgical procedures. Several women I have known in Boston have entered a slum hospital with the intention of obtaining a tubal ligation and have emerged a few days later after having been subjected to a hysterectomy. Unaware of their rights, incognizant of jargon, intimidated by the unfamiliar air of fear and atmosphere of ether that so many of us find oppressive in the confines even of the most attractive and expensive medical facilities, they have signed their names to documents they could not read and which nobody, in the hectic situation that prevails so often in those overcrowded hospitals that serve the urban poor, had ever bothered to explain.

Examples aren't trivial doodads you add to a paragraph for decoration; they are what holds your readers' attention and shows them that your writing makes sense. By using examples, you make your ideas more concrete and tangible. To give plenty of examples is one of the writer's chief tasks. We can't stress this truth enough.

You may generate examples at any point in the writing process. To find your own examples, do a little brainstorming or thinking. Begin with your own experience, with whatever is near you, even if you're working with a topic about which you think you know nothing. With such a topic — say, the psychology of gift giving — think it over slowly. Did you ever know a person who gave large gifts people didn't want and felt uncomfortable accepting? Why do you suppose the gift giver behaved that way? Was he or she looking for gratitude? A feeling of importance? Power over the recipients?

Draw on your other resources as well. With any topic, you might discover examples from conversing with others, from reading, from digging in the library. You can observe examples for your writing all around you. If you are writing a paper on bumper stickers, take a stroll through any parking lot, pen and notepad in hand. After you have gathered a few examples on your topic, share them with your classmates or writing group, and they'll probably think of some to add to your list.

Here are some questions to ask yourself when you use examples in your writing:

DISCOVERY
CHECKLIST

Using Examples to Develop Ideas

- Are your examples relevant to the point you are making?
- Are your examples the best ones you can think of?
- Are your examples really specific? Or do they just repeat generalities?
- From each paragraph, can you draw a ladder of abstraction to at least the fourth level?

EXERCISE

Giving Examples

To help you get in the habit of thinking specifically, fill in a ladder of abstraction for five of the following general subjects. Then share your ladders with your classmates or writing group and compare and contrast your specifics with theirs. Examples:

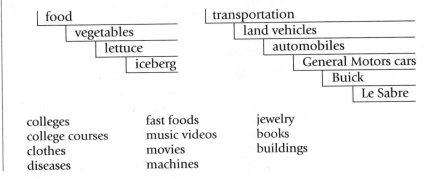

colleges   fast foods   jewelry
college courses   music videos   books
clothes   movies   buildings
diseases   machines

MAKING CONNECTIONS: EXAMPLES IN
A WRITER'S READER

Professional writers often use the same strategies you are studying in this chapter to develop their ideas in writing. Here we list a few clear examples of essays from *A Writer's Reader* in which authors *give examples* to particularly good effect, so that you can see this strategy at work. As you read the essays in *A Writer's Reader*, try to identify other essays that use this strategy.

E. B. White in "Once More to the Lake" (p. 490) gives examples to show how the lake has and hasn't changed over the years. In "Mother Tongue" (p. 496), Amy Tan uses examples of "different Englishes" to illustrate her points (see especially paragraphs 3, 4, and 6). Steve Olson's "Year of the Blue-Collar Guy" (p. 570) presents brief examples of the specific feats of working men, while Stephanie Brail's "The Price of Admission" (p. 651) uses the extended examples of Sandy's story to illustrate both the hazards women might face on the Internet and the steps they should (and shouldn't) take to avoid them.

Providing Details

METHODS OF PROVIDING DETAILS

In addition to giving examples, you can make your generalizations in your writing more convincing by providing details. A *detail* is any specific, concrete bit of information. Writers usually use details to make the scenes and images they're creating more realistic and vivid for their readers or to convince their readers that they have the facts they need to make broad assertions with authority. Often details and examples work together. Besides pointing to the example of President Coolidge, James David Barber (p. 397) gives a little evidence or specific detail to show that Coolidge was sleepy — the report that he slept eleven hours a night and then took a nap in midday besides. To back up your general statements, you need to supply such statements of fact, bits of historical record, or your own observations.

Mary Harris "Mother" Jones in old age published the story of her life as a labor organizer, *The Autobiography of Mother Jones* (Chicago: Kerr, 1980). In this view of a Pennsylvania coal miner's lot at the turn of the century, she makes a general statement and then lends conviction to her words with ample evidence from her own experience.

> Mining at its best is wretched work, and the life and surroundings of the miner are hard and ugly. His work is down in the black depths of the earth. He works alone in a drift. There can be little friendly companionship as there is in the factory; as there is among men who build bridges and houses, working together in groups. The work is dirty. Coal dust grinds itself into the skin, never to be removed. The miner must stoop as he works in the drift. He becomes bent like a gnome.
>
> His work is utterly fatiguing. Muscles and bones ache. His lungs breathe coal dust and the strange, damp air of places that are never filled with sunlight. His house is a poor makeshift and there is little to encourage him to make it attractive. The company owns the ground it stands on, and the miner feels the precariousness of his hold. Around his house is mud and slush. Great mounds of culm [the refuse left after coal is screened], black and sullen, surround him. His children are perpetually grimy from playing on the culm mounds. The wife struggles with dirt, with inadequate water supply, with small wages, with overcrowded shacks.

> The miner's wife, who in the majority of cases worked from childhood in the nearby silk mills, is overburdened with childbearing. She ages young. She knows much illness. Many a time I have been in a home where the poor wife was sick in bed, the children crawling over her, quarreling and playing in the room, often the only warm room in the house.

Mother Jones, who was not a learned writer, wrote these memoirs in her mid-nineties. Her style may be heavy with short, simple sentences ("She ages young. She knows much illness."), but her writing is clear and powerful because of the specific details she uses. She knows the strength of a well-chosen verb: "Coal dust *grinds* itself into the skin." Notice how she opens her description by making two general statements: (1) "Mining is wretched work," and (2) the miner's life and surroundings are "hard and ugly." Then she supports these generalizations with an overwhelming barrage of factual evidence from her own experience. The result is a moving, convincingly detailed portrait of the miner and his family.

Writer N. Scott Momaday ("To the Singing, to the Drums" [*Natural History* Feb. 1975]) uses many interesting details to describe the scene of the Kiowa celebration of the Gourd Dance on the Fourth of July at Carnegie, Oklahoma.

> The celebration is on the north side. We turn down into a dark depression, a large hollow among trees. It is full of camps and cars and people. At first there are children. According to some centrifugal social force, children function on the periphery. They run about, making festival noises. Firecrackers are snapping all around. We park and I make ready; the girls help me with my regalia. I am already wearing white trousers and moccasins. Now I tie the black velvet sash around my waist, placing the beaded tassels at my right leg. The bandoleer of red beans, which was my grandfather's, goes over my left shoulder, the V at my right hip. I decide to carry the blanket over my arm until I join the dancers; no sense in wrapping up in this heat. There is deep, brick-red dust on the ground. The grass is pale and brittle here and there. We make our way through the camps, stepping carefully to avoid the pegs and guy lines that reach about the tents. Old people, imperturbable, are lying down on cots and benches in the shadows. Smoke hangs in the air. We smell hamburgers, popcorn, gunpowder. Later there will be fried bread, boiled meat, Indian corn.

Momaday arranges his vivid details both spatially and chronologically. Notice his spatial transitions: *on the north side, turn down, on the periphery, all around, on the ground, here and there, through the camps, in the shadows, in the air.* Look also at the time markers: *At first, Now, until, Later.* These transitions guide readers through the experience.

Quite different from Momaday's personal details are Paula Gunn Allen's hard facts and objective statistics. She heaps statistic on statistic to convince readers that ever since American Indians began making pacts with the U.S. government, their survival has been threatened.

Some researchers put our pre-contact population at more than 45 million, while others put it at around 20 million. The U.S. government long put it at 450,000 — a comforting if imaginary figure, though at one point it was put at around 270,000. If our current population is around one million; if, as some researchers estimate, around 25 percent of Indian women and 10 percent of Indian men in the United States have been sterilized without informed consent; if our average life expectancy is, as the best-informed research presently says, 55 years; if our infant mortality rate continues at well above national standards; if our average unemployment for all segments of our population — male, female, young, adult, and middle-aged is between 60 and 90 percent; if the U.S. government continues its policy of termination, re-location, removal, and assimilation along with the destruction of wilderness, reservation land, and its resources, and severe curtailment of hunting, fishing, timber harvesting and water-use rights — then existing tribes are facing the threat of extinction which for several hundred tribal groups has already become fact in the past five hundred years.

Providing details is one of the simplest yet most effective ways of developing ideas. All it takes on your part is close observation and attention and then precise words to communicate the details to readers. Begin with the senses (combined with a bit of imagination, if you can't actually observe firsthand). If readers were on the scene or encountering your example themselves, what would be the first thing they'd see? What would they hear, smell, or feel? Would there be any tastes involved? If you're explaining a historical account, think about which small details were most meaningful to you in your reading: your readers will probably find them interesting, too. If you haven't encountered any details that make the point as strongly as you'd like, you may need to do a bit of research to find just the right fact or statistic. Remember that effective details have a specific purpose: they must help make your images more evocative or your point more convincing. In your final draft, you'll want to make sure that every detail supports — in some way — the main idea of your paragraph.

Here are some questions to ask yourself when you use details in your writing:

DISCOVERY CHECKLIST

Using Details to Develop Ideas

- Do all your details support your point of view or main idea?
- Do you have details of sights? Sounds? Tastes? Touch? Smells?
- Have you included enough details to make your writing clear? To make it interesting?
- Have you arranged your details in an order that is easy to follow?

EXERCISE

Providing Details

To practice generating and using specific details, brainstorm with your group or alone on one of the following subjects. Be sure to include details that appeal to all five senses. Group the details in your list (see p. 381), and write a paragraph or two using your specific details. Start off with a statement of the main idea that conveys an interesting message about the subject you choose (not "My grandmother's house was in Topeka, Kansas" but "My grandmother's house was my childhood haven").

the things in my room	an unforgettable game
my grandmother's house	an unusual person
the haunted house	my favorite pet
my graduation	a hospital room
my old car	a high school dance

MAKING CONNECTIONS: DETAILS IN *A WRITER'S READER*

Professional writers often use the same strategies you are studying in this chapter to develop their ideas in writing. Here we list a few clear examples of essays from *A Writer's Reader* in which authors *provide details* to particularly good effect, so that you can see this strategy at work. As you read the essays in *A Writer's Reader*, try to identify other essays that use this strategy.

Marion Winik, in "Visiting Steven" (p. 511), relies on details of her relationship with Steven in the past to help explain her present feelings. Joy Harjo, in "Three Generations of Native American Women's Birth Experience" (p. 540), uses details to show how the experience of giving birth has (and hasn't) changed over time for her family. Other authors who write with lots of details include William Henry Lewis, in "Shades" (p. 505), and Richard Rodriguez, in "Does America Still Exist?" (p. 583).

Defining

METHODS OF DEFINING

Often in a paper that calls for critical thinking, you'll need to do some defining. *Define*, from the Latin, means "to set bounds to." You define a thing, a word, or a concept by describing it in such a way that it is distinguished from all similar things.

If writers and thinkers don't agree on the meaning of a word or an idea, they can't share knowledge. Scientists in particular take special care to define their terms precisely and accurately. In his article "A Chemist's Definition of pH," Gessner G. Hawley makes his subject clear to readers who can follow him. Though he goes on to write an extended definition, he begins with a brief definition:

> pH is a value taken to represent the acidity or alkalinity of an aqueous solution; it is defined as the logarithm of the reciprocal of the hydrogen-ion concentration of a solution:

$$pH = 1n \frac{1}{[H^+]}$$

If you use a word in a special sense or if you coin a word, you have to explain it or your readers won't know what you're talking about. Prolific word coiner and social prophet Alvin Toffler in *The Third Wave* (New York: Morrow, 1980) invents (among many others) the word *techno-sphere*, which he defines as follows:

> All societies — primitive, agricultural, or industrial — use energy; they make things; they distribute things. In all societies the energy system, the production system, and the distribution system are interrelated parts of something larger. This larger system is the *techno-sphere*.

In his later book *PowerShift* (New York: Bantam, 1990), Toffler picks up the word *screenie* from Jeffrey Moritz, president of National College Television, and adds his own boundaries to this coined term:

> Moritz uses the term *screenie* to describe this video-drenched generation, which has digested thousands of hours of television, imbibing its "video-logic." To that must be added, for many of them, more hours of interactive video games and, even more important, of work on their own personal computers. They not only follow a different logic, but are accustomed to make the screen do things, thus making them good prospects for the interactive services and products soon to hit the market. Above all, they are accustomed to choice.

Sometimes in writing you stop to define a standard word not often used, to save your readers a trip to the dictionary. Or you may define a concept that is familiar but often misunderstood. What is equality, intelligence, socialism, HMO, minimum wage, a holding corporation? Whenever in your writing you need to indicate the nature of an idea, a thing, a movement, a phenomenon, an organization, you'll find defining a helpful strategy. The more complex or ambiguous the subject, the longer the definition you need to clarify the term for your readers.

Here are some questions you can ask yourself when you use definitions in your writing:

DISCOVERY CHECKLIST

Using Definitions to Develop Ideas

- Have you used definitions to help your readers understand the subject matter, not to show off your knowledge?
- Have you tailored your definition to the needs of your audience?
- Is your definition specific, clear, and accurate?
- Would your definition benefit from an example or from details?

EXERCISE

Defining

Write an extended definition (a paragraph or so in length) of one of the following words. Begin with a one-sentence definition of the word. Then, to expand and clarify your ideas, use some of the strategies discussed in this chapter — examples, details, division and classification, process analysis, comparison and contrast, and identifying causes or effects. You may also use *negation* (explaining what something is by stating what it is not). Don't get most of your definition from a dictionary or textbook. Then share your definition with your classmates or writing group.

education	abuse	exercise	literacy
privacy	jazz	dieting	success
taboo	rock music	gossip	fear
prejudice	AIDS	ecology	gender

MAKING CONNECTIONS: DEFINITIONS IN *A WRITER'S READER*

Professional writers often use the same strategies you are studying in this chapter to develop their ideas in writing. Here we list a few clear examples of essays from *A Writer's Reader* in which authors *define terms* to particularly good effect, so that you can see this strategy at work. As you read the essays in *A Writer's Reader*, try to identify other essays that use this strategy.

Judy Brady, in "I Want a Wife" (p. 529), plays with the traditional definition of a wife in order to critique it. Thomas F. Cawsey, Gene Deszca, and Maurice Mazerolle offer an extended definition of a portfolio career in "The Portfolio Career as a Response to a Changing Job Market" (p. 635). Leonce Gaiter, in "Is the Web Too Cool for Blacks?" (p. 642), defines what it means for the Web to be cool.

Dividing and Classifying

METHODS OF DIVIDING AND CLASSIFYING

To divide is to break something down into its components. It's far easier to take in a subject, especially a complex subject, one piece at a time. The thing divided may be as concrete and definite as Manhattan (which a writer might divide into neighborhoods) or as abstract as a person's knowledge of art (which the writer might divide into knowledge of sculpture, painting, drawing, and other forms). To classify is to make sense of a complicated and potentially bewildering array of things—works of literature, this year's movies—by sorting them into categories (*types* or *classes*) that you can deal with one at a time. Literature is customarily arranged by genre or class—novels, stories, poems, plays. A discussion about movies might sort them by audience (children's movies, movies for teenagers, movies for mature audiences).

These two methods of development are like two sides of the same coin. In theory, any broad subject can be *divided* into components, which can then be *classified* into categories. In practice, it's often difficult to tell where division stops and classification begins. And if you think the definitions of division and classification we've just given sound familiar, you're not imagining things: *analyzing*, the critical thinking task we discuss in Chapter 6, requires the writer to first break an item down into its component parts (and perhaps organize them into categories) to better understand, explain, or evaluate it.

In the following paragraph from his college textbook *Wildlife Management* (San Francisco: Freeman, 1978), Robert H. Giles Jr. uses division to simplify an especially large, abstract subject: the management of forest wildlife in America. To explain which professional environmentalists in America assume which duties and responsibilities, Giles divides forest wildlife management into six levels or areas of concern, arranged roughly from large to small. To a nonspecialist, this subject may seem head-stoppingly complicated. But see how neatly Giles divides it and explains it in a paragraph of fewer than 175 words.

> There are six scales of forest wildlife management: (1) national, (2) regional, (3) state or industrial, (4) county or parish, (5) intra-state region, management unit, or watershed, and (6) forest. Each is different. At the national and regional levels, management includes decisions on timber harvest quotas, grazing policy in forested lands, official stance on forest taxation bills, cutting policy relative to threatened and endangered species, management coordination of migratory species, and research fund allocation. At the state or industrial level, decision types include land acquisition, sale, or trade; season setting; and permit systems and fees. At the county level, plans are made, seasons set, and special fees levied. At the intra-state level, decisions include what seasons to recommend, what stances to take on bills not affecting local conditions, the sequence in which to attempt land acquisition, and the placement of facilities. At the forest level, decisions may include some of those of the larger management unit but typically are those of maintenance schedules, planting stock, cutting rotations, personnel employment and supervision, road closures, equipment use, practices to be attempted or used, and boundaries to be marked.

In a textbook lesson on how babies develop, Kurt W. Fischer and Arlyne Lazerson (writing in *Human Development* [New York: Freeman, 1984]) take a paragraph to describe a research project that classified individual babies into three types according to temperament.

> The researchers also found that certain of these temperamental qualities tended to occur together. These clusters of characteristics generally fell into three types — the easy baby, the difficult baby, and the baby who was slow to warm up. The *easy infant* has regular patterns of eating and sleeping, readily approaches new objects and people, adapts easily to changes in the environment, generally reacts with low or moderate intensity, and typically is in a cheerful mood. The *difficult infant* usually shows irregular patterns of eating and sleeping, withdraws from new objects or people, adapts slowly to changes, reacts with great intensity, and is frequently cranky. The *slow-to-warm-up infant* typically has a low activity level, tends to withdraw when presented with an unfamiliar object, reacts with a low level of intensity, and adapts slowly to changes in the environment. Fortunately for parents, most healthy infants — 40 percent or more — have an easy temperament. Only about 10 percent have a difficult temperament, and about 15 percent are slow to warm up. The remaining 35 percent do not easily fit one of the three types but show some other pattern.

When you divide and classify, your point is to make order out of a complex or overwhelming jumble of stuff. Take care that your divisions and classifications really do make the jumble easier for you and your readers to understand. Make sure the components and categories you identify are sensible, given the purpose of your paragraph or essay. Use the same principle of classification or analysis for all categories. For example, if you're trying to discuss campus relations, it makes sense to divide the school population into *instructors, students,* and *support staff;* it would make less sense to divide it into *people from the South, people from the rest of the United States,* and *people from overseas.* Also, try to group apples with apples, not with oranges. In other words, make sure all the components or categories you use are roughly equivalent. For example, if you're classifying television shows and you've come up with *sitcoms, dramas, talk shows, children's shows, news,* and *cartoons,* then you've got a problem: the last category is probably part of *children's shows.* Finally, check that your final division or classification system is simple and easy for your readers to understand. Most people can handle only about seven things at once. If you've got more than six or seven components in your division, perhaps you need to use classification to assemble the individual components into groups. If you've got more than six or seven categories in your classification, perhaps you need to combine or eliminate some.

Here are some questions to ask yourself when you use division or classification in your writing:

DISCOVERY CHECKLIST

Using Division and Classification to Develop Ideas

- Do you use the most logical principle of division or classification for your purpose?
- Do you stick to one principle throughout?
- Have you identified components or categories that are comparable?
- Have you used the best order for your components or categories?
- Have you given specific examples for each of your components or categories?
- Have you succeeded in making a complex subject more accessible to your readers?

EXERCISE

Dividing and Classifying

To practice dividing and classifying, choose one or two of the following subjects, and brainstorm for five minutes on each, trying to come up with as many components as you can. Then compare your lists with those of your classmates. For each subject, create one large list by combining items from all students who chose that subject. Working as a group, take the largest list and try to classify the items on it into logical categories. Feel free to add or change components or categories if you find you've overlooked something.

students	customers	sports	families
teachers	automobiles	vacations	drivers

MAKING CONNECTIONS: DIVISION AND
CLASSIFICATION IN *A WRITER'S READER*

Professional writers often use the same strategies you are studying in this
chapter to develop their ideas in writing. Here we list a few clear examples of
essays from *A Writer's Reader* in which authors *divide and classify* to particularly
good effect, so that you can see this strategy at work. As you read the essays in
A Writer's Reader, try to identify other essays that use this strategy.

Deborah Tannen's "Women and Men Talking on the Job" (p. 550) classi-
fies talking styles according to gendered influences on these styles. James Q.
Wilson's "In Praise of Asphalt Nation" (p. 606) divides the debate over automobiles into those who favor individual freedoms versus those who support
public good. Other authors who use division and classification include Ellen
Goodman, in "How to Zap Violence on TV" (p. 613), and LynNell Hancock,
in "The Haves and the Have-Nots" (p. 631).

Analyzing a Process

METHODS OF ANALYZING A PROCESS

Analyzing a process — telling step by step how something is or was done or
how to do something — is one of the most useful kinds of writing. An entire
essay can be built on analysis of a process, but here we look at ways process
analysis can be used in paragraphs to develop an idea within an essay.

You can analyze an action or a phenomenon — how a skyscraper is built,
how a political revolution begins, how sunspots form on the sun's surface.
This strategy will be familiar if you have ever followed directions in a cookbook, but it can also explain large, long-ago happenings that a writer couldn't
possibly have witnessed. Here, for instance, is a paragraph by a team of
botanists, Peter H. Raven, Ray F. Evert, and Helena Curtis (from their college
textbook *Biology of Plants* [New York: Worth, 1992]), analyzing the process of
continental drift.

> About 127 million years ago — when angiosperm pollen first appears in the
> fossil record — Africa and South America were directly linked with one an-
> other and with Antarctica, India, and Australia in a great southern supercontin-
> nent called Gondwanaland. Africa and South America began to separate at
> about this time, forming the southern Atlantic Ocean, but they did not move
> completely apart in the tropical regions until about 90 million years ago. India
> began to move northward at about the same time, colliding with Asia about
> 45 million years ago and thrusting up the Himalayas in the process. Australia
> began to separate from Antarctica about 55 million years ago, but their sepa-
> ration did not become complete until about 40 million years ago.

Notice the writers' use of time markers — *about 127 million years ago, at about
this time, until about 90 million years ago.* This paragraph illustrates the kind of
process analysis that sets forth how something happens — an *informative*
process analysis.

Another familiar kind is the *directive* or "how-to" process analysis, which instructs readers how to do something — how to box, invest for retirement, clean a painting — or how to make something — how to draw a map, blaze a trail, put together a simple computer. In the following example (from *The Little Windows Book, 3.1 Edition* [Berkeley: Peachpit, 1992]), technical writer Kay Yarborough Nelson uses a directive process description to teach her readers how to use a computer mouse.

> You can use the mouse in three basic ways: by clicking, double-clicking, and dragging.
> To select an item on the screen, you can move the mouse pointer to it and click once with the left mouse button. (If you're left-handed, you can change it to the right mouse button, as you'll see in the chapter on customizing Windows.) Selecting an item makes it active, so that you can work with it. For example, you might click on a document's icon so that you could copy or move it.
> You can also double-click on an item to make it active and actually start it. To double-click, quickly click twice with the left mouse button. For example, double-clicking on a program's icon will open a window and start the program. . . .
> A third way of using the mouse is dragging. To drag, put the mouse pointer on what you want to drag, press and hold the left mouse button down, and then move the mouse.

Notice the care Nelson takes to make each step seem as simple and logical as possible. Her clear divisions (*three basic ways*), unambiguous commands (*move . . . , click . . . , put . . .*), concrete examples (*For example . . .*), and helpful transitions (*a third way, and then*) help guide readers through an unfamiliar process step by step.

A process analysis is a wonderful way to show your readers the inside workings of an event or system, even if they're never going to participate directly in it themselves. Process analyses can be difficult to follow, though, so make sure you do everything possible to guide your readers along the way. Be sure to divide the process into logical steps or stages and to put the steps in a sensible chronological order. Add details or examples wherever your description may become too ambiguous or abstract, and use transitions to mark the end of one step and the beginning of the next.

Here are some questions to ask yourself when you use process analysis in your writing:

DISCOVERY CHECKLIST

Using Process Analysis to Develop Ideas
- Do you thoroughly understand the process you are analyzing?
- Do you have a good reason to use process analysis at this point in your essay?
- Have you broken the process down into logical and useful steps?
- Is the order in which you present these steps the best one possible?
- Have you used transitions to guide your readers from one step to the next?

Analyzing a Process

Analyze one of the following processes or procedures and use your analysis as the basis of a paragraph or short essay. Then share your analysis with your peer group. Can members of your group follow your analysis easily? Do they spot anything you left out?

registration for college classes   falling in love
studying for a test   buying a used car
influenza (or another disease)   cloud formation

MAKING CONNECTIONS: PROCESS ANALYSES IN *A WRITER'S READER*

Professional writers often use the same strategies you are studying in this chapter to develop their ideas in writing. Here we list a few clear examples of essays from *A Writer's Reader* in which authors *analyze a process* to particularly good effect, so that you can see this strategy at work. As you read the essays in *A Writer's Reader*, try to identify other essays that use this strategy.

Phyllis Rose, in "Shopping and Other Spiritual Adventures in America Today" (p. 610), analyzes people's shopping processes. Cynthia Joyce's "Six Clicks from Death" (p. 646) takes the reader on a journey through the somewhat hazardous process of searching for information on the Internet. Other authors who analyze a process include Toi Derricotte, in "Early Memory: The *California Zephyr*" (p. 573), and Meghan Daum, in "Virtual Love" (p. 623).

Comparing and Contrasting

METHODS OF COMPARING AND CONTRASTING

Often you can develop a paragraph effectively by setting a pair of subjects side by side and comparing and contrasting them. When you compare, you point out similarities; when you contrast, you discuss differences. Working together, these twin strategies use one subject to clarify another. The dual method works well for a pair of things similar in nature — two cities, two films, the theories of two economists. It can show that a writer has clearly observed and thoroughly understood both. For this reason, college instructors will often ask you on exams to compare and contrast ("Discuss the chief similarities and differences between nineteenth-century French and English colonial policies in West Africa").

An entire essay can be focused around a central comparison and contrast. This type of assignment is covered in Chapter 7. Here we will look at ways comparing and contrasting — or either one of them used alone — can be used to develop an idea within an essay.

In daily life, all of us frequently compare and contrast: we decide which menu selection to choose, which car (or other product) to buy, which magazine to read in a waiting room, which college course to sign up for. A comparison and contrast can lead to a final evaluation and a decision about which thing under consideration is better (as in these cases), but it doesn't have to. In a travel essay, "Venezuela for Visitors" from *Hugging the Shore* (New York: Knopf, 1983), written for the readers of the *New Yorker,* novelist John Updike sees Venezuelan society as polarized: it consists of rich people and Indians. In the following paragraph, Updike compares and contrasts the two classes without choosing between them:

> Missionaries, many of them United States citizens, move among the Indians. They claim that since Western civilization, with all its diseases and detritus, must come, it had best come through them. Nevertheless, Marxist anthropologists inveigh against them. Foreign experts, many of them United States citizens, move among the rich. They claim they are just helping out, and that anyway the oil industry was nationalized five years ago. Nevertheless, Marxist anthropologists are not mollified. The feet of the Indians are very broad in front, their toes spread wide for climbing avocado trees. The feet of the rich are very narrow in front, their toes compressed by pointed Italian shoes. The Indians seek relief from tension in the use of *ebene,* or *yopo,* a mind-altering drug distilled from the bark of the ebene tree and blown into the user's nose through a hollow cane by a colleague. The rich take cocaine through the nose, and frequent mind-altering discotheques, but more customarily imbibe cognac, *vino blanco,* and Scotch, in association with colleagues.

Updike simply sets the two side by side: the feet of the poor, the feet of the rich; how the poor get high, how the rich do. By doing so, he throws the two groups of people into sharp relief.

You can use two basic methods of organization for comparison and contrast — the opposing pattern and the alternating pattern. Using the *opposing pattern,* you discuss all of the characteristics or subdivisions of the first subject in the first half of the paragraph or essay and then discuss all the characteristics of the other subject. Using the *alternating pattern,* you move back and forth between the two subjects. This pattern places the specifics close together for immediate comparison and contrast. For example, a writer using the opposing pattern to compare and contrast the brothers Jim and Jack would discuss Jim's physical appearance, his personality traits, and his interests and would then discuss Jack's appearance, his personality, and his interests — discussing in both parts the same characteristics in the same order. A writer using the alternating pattern would discuss Jim's physical appearance, then Jack's physical appearance; Jim's personality, then Jack's; Jim's interests, then Jack's. Whichever pattern of order you choose, be sure to cover the same subpoints under each item and do so in the same order in all parts.

In the paragraph above about Venezuelan society, John Updike uses the alternating pattern to compare and contrast rich people and Indians. In the following paragraph, Jacquelyn Wonder and Priscilla Donovan, management consultants, use the opposing pattern of organization to explain the differences in the brains of females and males.

At birth there are basic differences between male and female brains. The female cortex is more fully developed. The sound of the human voice elicits more left-brain activity in infant girls than in infant boys, accounting in part for the earlier development in females of language. Baby girls have larger connectors between the brain's hemispheres and thus integrate information more skillfully. This flexibility bestows greater verbal and intuitive skills. Male infants lack this ready communication between the brain's lobes; therefore, messages are routed and rerouted to the right brain, producing larger right hemispheres. The size advantage accounts for males having greater spatial and physical abilities and explains why they may become more highly lateralized and skilled in specific areas.

After the topic sentence, "At birth there are basic differences between male and female brains," the authors first explain the development of the female brain and how it accounts for specific thinking styles in females, and then in the last part of the paragraph they explain the development of the male brain and the effects on males' abilities.

These brief examples may suggest that comparing and contrasting aren't just meaningless academic calisthenics. They are explaining devices that appeal to writers who have a passion for making things clear.

Here are some questions to ask yourself when you use comparison and contrast in your writing:

**DISCOVERY
CHECKLIST**

Using Comparison and Contrast to Develop Ideas

- Is your reason for comparing and contrasting unmistakably clear?
- Have you chosen the *major* similarities and differences to write about?
- Have you used the same categories for each item? In discussing each feature, do you always compare or contrast like things?
- Have you used the best possible arrangement, given your subject and the point you're trying to make?
- If you are making a judgment between your subjects, have you treated both fairly?
- Have you avoided a boringly mechanical, monotonous style ("On one hand, . . . now on the other hand")?

EXERCISE

Comparing and Contrasting

Write a paragraph or two in which you compare and contrast the subjects in one of the following pairs. Use your own recall or observation, go to the library, or converse with an expert if you need material.

baseball and football (or basketball)
living in an apartment and living in a house
two cities or towns you are familiar with
two musicians
two poems
watching a sports event on television and in person

MAKING CONNECTIONS: COMPARISONS AND
CONTRASTS IN *A WRITER'S READER*

Professional writers often use the same strategies you are studying in this
chapter to develop their ideas in writing. Here we list a few clear examples of
essays from *A Writer's Reader* in which authors *compare and contrast* two or
more things to particularly good effect, so that you can see this strategy at
work. As you read the essays in *A Writer's Reader*, try to identify other essays
that use this strategy.

Scott Russell Sanders compares and contrasts types of men in his essay
"The Men We Carry in Our Minds" (p. 531). Veronica Chambers, in "The
Myth of Cinderella" (p. 603), compares and contrasts different women's in-
terpretations of this myth. Other authors who rely on comparison and con-
trast include Nicholas Wade, in "How Men and Women Think" (p. 556), and
Michael Shermer, in "Abducted! Encounters with Aliens" (p. 596).

Identifying Causes and Effects

METHODS OF IDENTIFYING CAUSES AND EFFECTS

From the time we are children, we ask why. Why can't I go out and play? Why
is the sky blue? Why do pickles taste sour? Why did my goldfish die? Our seeking causes and effects continues into adulthood. We try to understand our
often puzzling world by searching for causes and identifying effects. So it's
natural that explaining causal relationships is one of the most used methods
of development in writing.

To use cause and effect successfully, you must think about the subject critically, gather evidence, draw judicious conclusions, and show relationships
clearly. Chapter 8 gives you detailed information about how to write a complete essay identifying causes and effects, but let's look at a couple of brief examples of how this technique for development can be used in one paragraph
of a longer essay.

Thomas McKeown, in a chapter called "The Diseases of Affluence" in his
book *The Origins of Human Disease* (New York: Blackwell, 1988), speculates
on the *causes* of the attention that ill effects of smoking have received.

> There is probably no other hazard whose ill effects on health have been,
> or perhaps could be, charted as meticulously as those of tobacco. There are
> several reasons why it has received so much attention. First, it has been under
> investigation for almost exactly the period — the last four decades — in which
> the origins of non-communicable diseases have been seriously considered;
> until the end of the Second World War interest in the relation of behavior
> and environment to disease was almost confined to the infections. Second,
> the large increase in the frequency of smoking has occurred in the present
> century, when evidence from national statistics and other sources was much
> better than that available for diet and reproduction, in which some of the

major changes occurred in the nineteenth century. And third, the effects of smoking on health are so large and so obvious that they are accepted even by people who dismiss other features of behavior as scarcely worth attention.

Notice how McKeown clearly marks his *reasons: First, Second, And third.*

Instead of focusing on causes *or* effects, often writers trace a *chain* of cause and effect relationships, as Charles C. Mann and Mark L. Plummer do in "The Butterfly Problem" (*Atlantic* Jan. 1992).

> More generally, the web of species around us helps generate soil, regulate freshwater supplies, dispose of waste, and maintain the quality of the atmosphere. Pillaging nature to the point where it cannot perform these functions is dangerously foolish. Simple self-protection is thus a second motive for preserving biodiversity. When DDT was sprayed in Borneo, the biologists Paul and Anne Ehrlich relate in their book *Extinction* (1981), it killed all the houseflies. The gecko lizards that preyed on the flies ate their pesticide-filled corpses and died. House cats consumed the dying lizards; they died too. Rats descended on the villages, bringing bubonic plague. Incredibly, the housefly in this case was part of an intricate system that controlled human disease. To make up for its absence, the government was forced to parachute cats into the area.

As these examples show, an effective use of cause and effect can help you present a complex situation or chain of events to your readers.

Here are some questions to ask youself when you identify causes and effects in your writing:

DISCOVERY CHECKLIST

Using Cause and Effect to Develop Ideas

- Is your use of cause and effect clearly tied to the overall message or point you're trying to make?
- Are the causes you have identified actual causes? Can you find evidence to support them?
- Are the effects you have identified actual effects, or are they merely conjecture? If conjecture, are they logical results? Can you find evidence to support them?
- Have you judiciously drawn conclusions concerning causes and effects? Have you avoided fallacies of thinking, such as hasty generalization and stereotyping (see p. 104)?
- Have you presented things clearly and logically, so that your readers can follow and understand them easily?

EXERCISE

Identifying Causes and Effects

1. Identify some of the *causes* of *five* of the following. Discuss possible causes with your classmates.

failing an exam	stage fright	losing a job
an automobile accident	losing or winning a game	losing weight
poor health	stress	going to college
good health	getting a job	getting a scholarship

2. Identify some of the *effects* of *five* of the following. Discuss possible effects with your classmates.

an insult	dieting	divorce
a compliment	speeding	increase in taxes
poor attendance in class	smoking cigarettes	
a child's running away from home	drinking while driving	

3. Identify some of the *causes and effects* of *one* of the following. You may need to do a little research in the library or in a textbook to identify the chain of causes and effects for the event. How might you use what you have discovered as part of an essay? Discuss your findings with your classmates.

the Civil War	the AIDS virus
the Vietnam War	recycling
Bill Clinton's tenure as president	smoking crack cocaine
the discovery of atomic energy	the uses of solar energy
a U.S. Supreme Court decision	the hole in the ozone layer
on abortion	racial tension

MAKING CONNECTIONS: CAUSES AND EFFECTS IN *A WRITER'S READER*

Professional writers often use the same strategies you are studying in this chapter to develop their ideas in writing. Here we list a few clear examples of essays from *A Writer's Reader* in which authors *identify causes and effects* to particularly good effect, so that you can see this strategy at work. As you read the essays in *A Writer's Reader*, try to identify other essays that use this strategy.

Stephanie Coontz, in "Remarriage and Stepfamilies" (p. 522), examines the effects of divorce and remarriage on families by focusing on how not to cause more problems than necessary throughout these events. In "Black Men and Public Space" (p. 561), Brent Staples identifies a chain of causes and effects that help explain racial stereotypes and people's responses to them. Other authors whose arguments depend on explaining causes and effects include Stephen King, in "Why We Crave Horror Movies" (p. 593); Mike Males, in "Public Enemy Number One?" (p. 616); and Jeffrey Obser, in "Privacy Is the Problem, Not the Solution" (p. 657).

Chapter 19

Strategies for Revising and Editing

Good writing is rewriting. When Ernest Hemingway was asked why he rewrote the last page of the novel *A Farewell to Arms* thirty-nine times, he replied, "Getting the words right." His comment reflects the care that serious writers take in revising their work. You will do well to follow Hemingway's lead and take care with your revising.

In this chapter we provide strategies for revising and editing what you write. We suggest ways to rethink muddy ideas and emphasize important ideas, to rephrase obscure passages and restructure garbled sentences. Our advice applies not only to reseeing and rewriting whole essays but also to rewriting sentences and paragraphs. In addition, we give you tips for proofreading and editing.

Re-viewing, Revising, and Editing

Revision is much more than mere correction of grammar and spelling. *Revision* actually means "seeing again" — discovering again, conceiving again, shaping again. It is not something you do only after you complete a paper. Rather, it is an integral aspect of the total writing process; it may occur at any and all stages of the process.

Most writers do a lot of rewriting. Sometimes it's general — reordering ideas or finding additional information to develop an idea. Other times it's more particular, just tinkering with sentence structure or playing around with word choice. You will be doing both types of revision. *Macro revising* is making large, global, or fundamental changes that affect the overall direction or impact of writing. Macro revising involves the rhetorical aspects of writing —

purpose, voice, audience, unity, organization, development, coherence, clarity. We'll focus on techniques for revising for purpose, organization, development, and audience. *Micro revising* is paying attention to the details. It involves the language aspects of writing—sentences, words, punctuation, grammar. We'll focus on techniques for creating emphasis and eliminating wordiness. We'll also provide techniques for editing (rewriting to make the use of language more effective) and for proofreading (checking the correctness of spelling, grammar, and mechanics).

In the "Revising and Editing" sections of previous chapters, you found specific advice for making decisions about revising. Here now are some general guidelines for revising, accompanied by three *general* checklists of questions you might ask yourself as you reread and revise. You can use these questions for almost every writing task, but they will prove useful only if you allow time to give your work a thorough going-over. Allow your ideas to incubate. When you have time to spare, these questions will guide you to make not just slight, cosmetic touch-ups but major improvements.

REVISING FOR PURPOSE

When you revise for purpose, you make sure that your writing really accomplishes whatever it is that you want it to do. If your goal is to create an interesting profile of a person you know, have you done that? If you want to persuade your readers to take a certain course of action, have you succeeded? If you want to voice your opinion of recent legislative acts, have you done so? To revise for purpose, you'll have to take a step back from your writing and try to see it as other readers will see it. Concentrate on what's actually in your paper.

Remember that the purpose of your final essay may be different from the purpose you had in mind when you began writing. Such a change may be especially true for long, complex writing projects that usually evolve over time or for writing assignments that you begin without a clear direction.

At this point you'll probably want to either review and revise your working thesis statement (if you've developed one) or create a thesis sentence (if you haven't). (See "Stating and Using a Thesis," p. 375.) Scrutinize your tentative statement of main idea, considering whether each part of the essay is directly related to it, whether each part develops and supports it, and whether everything promised in the working thesis is carried out in the essay. If you find passages that are not related to the thesis, or if you find contradictions between your thesis and the information in the essay, or if you find gaps between your thesis and the information in the essay, you have two options: revise the thesis, or revise the essay. As an exercise, develop a comprehensive, detailed, and precise thesis statement that covers every major point in your essay. Then ask yourself if that thesis really makes sense. Even if you don't include the detailed thesis in your essay—and it's quite likely that you won't—

the thesis will help you to see where your essay works effectively to fulfill your purpose and where it doesn't.

Here are some questions you can ask yourself when revising for purpose:

REVISION CHECKLIST

Achieving Your Purpose

- Do you know exactly what you want your essay to accomplish? Can you express it clearly to yourself? Can you put it in one sentence: "In this paper I want to . . . ."
- Is your thesis stated outright anywhere in the essay? If not, have you provided clues so that your readers will know precisely what it is?
- Does every part of the essay work to achieve the same goal?
- Have you tried to take in too much territory, with the result that your coverage of your topic seems too thin? If so, how might you reduce the scope of your essay?
- Does your essay say everything that needs to be said? Is everything — ideas, connections between ideas, supporting evidence — on paper, not just in your head?
- Do you still believe everything you say? In writing the essay, have you changed your mind, rethought your assumptions, made a discovery? Do any of your interpretations or statements of opinion now need to be recast?
- Do you have enough evidence? Is every point developed fully enough to be clear? To be convincing? If not, try recalling, observing, conversing, and imagining. Try some of the strategies for generating ideas (Chapter 15) or for developing paragraphs (Chapter 18).

REVISING FOR STRUCTURE

When revising for structure, you make sure that the order of your ideas and the arrangement of material is as effective as possible. You may have put down on paper all the ingredients of a successful essay — but in a hugely jumbled, confusing mess. What you want to do now is make sure that you've set up your essay in a way that your readers can easily follow where you want to lead them and end up at the destination you have in mind.

In a well-structured essay each paragraph, sentence, and phrase fulfills a clear function. Scrutinize opening and closing paragraphs to ensure that they are relevant, concise, and interesting. Look at each paragraph to make sure everything in it is on the same topic and that all ideas are adequately developed. Consider the paragraphs as a group to decide whether they're in the best possible order; have a reason for putting them in the order you select. Finally, review each place where you lead readers from one idea to the next to be absolutely certain that the transition is clear and painless. (For more on paragraphs, topic sentences, and transition, see Chapter 17, "Strategies for Drafting.")

An outline can be useful for diagnosing a draft that you suspect doesn't quite make sense. You may have already used outlining as a planning technique (see p. 384); now you want to create an outline that shows what you've succeeded in getting down on paper. If you can't easily make an outline of what you have written, then probably your readers will have a hard time following your writing. Start by finding the topic sentence of each paragraph in your draft (or creating one, if necessary) and listing them in order. Label the sentences *I.*, *II.*, *A.*, *B.*, and so on, according to logical patterns of coordination and subordination to indicate the relationships of ideas in your essay. Do the same with the supporting details under each topic sentence, labeling them also with letters and numbers and indenting appropriately. Now look at the outline. Does it make sense on its own, without the essay to explain it? Would any different order or arrangement be more effective? Is there any section that looks thin, where more evidence might be needed? Maybe the sequence of ideas needs rearranging. Maybe the connections between parts are in your head but not on paper. Maybe too many ideas are jammed into too few paragraphs. Maybe you don't have as many specific details and examples as you need. It is often easier and quicker to operate on your outline than on your ailing draft because the outline includes only the main points. Work on the outline until you get it into strong shape, and then rewrite the essay to follow it.

Here are some questions to ask yourself when you are revising for structure:

REVISION CHECKLIST

Testing Structure

- Does the introduction set up the whole essay? Does it both grab readers' attention and hint at what is to follow? (See p. 400.)
- Does the essay fulfill all the promises that you make in your opening?
- Is there any passage later in the essay that would make a better beginning?
- Is the thesis clear early in the essay? If explicit, is it given a position of emphasis?
- Do the paragraph breaks seem logical? Does each paragraph begin a new idea? (See p. 395.)
- Is the main idea of each paragraph clear? Have you used a topic sentence in every paragraph? (See p. 396.) If not, try putting one in every paragraph to try to strengthen clarity and coherence.
- Is the main idea of each paragraph fully developed? Can you see any places where you might need more details or evidence to be convincing? (See p. 416.)
- Within each paragraph, is each detail or piece of evidence relevant to the topic sentence? If you find a stray bit, should you omit it altogether or move it to another paragraph?
- Are all the ideas directly relevant to the main point of the essay?
- Would any paragraphs make more sense or follow better if arranged in a different order?
- Does everything follow clearly? Does one point smoothly lead to the next? If connections aren't clear, would transitions help? (See p. 407.)
- Does the conclusion follow from what has gone before? Does it avoid seeming arbitrarily tacked on? (See p. 402.)

REVISING FOR AUDIENCE

An essay is successful only if it succeeds with its particular audience, and what works with one audience of readers can fall flat with another. Take the time to think about who your readers are and to reread your essay with your intended readers in mind. Visualize one of your readers poring over the essay, sentence by sentence, reacting to what you have written. What expressions do you see on his or her face? Where does he or she have trouble understanding? Where have you hit the mark? Your organization, your selection of details, your word choice, and your tone all affect your readers, so you should pay special attention to these aspects of your writing.

Of course, there's no substitute for having another person go over your writing. Most college assignments ask you to write for an audience of your classmates, but even if your essay is written for a different group (the town council or readers of the *New Yorker*, for example), having a classmate read over your essay is a worthwhile revision technique. (See Chapter 20, "Strategies for Working with Other Writers: Collaborative Learning.")

Here are some questions you can ask yourself when you are revising with your audience in mind:

REVISION
CHECKLIST

Considering Your Audience

- Who will read this essay?
- Does the essay tell them what they will want to know? Or does it tell them only what they probably know already?
- Are there any places where readers might go to sleep? If so, can such passages be shortened or deleted or livened up?
- Does the opening of the essay mislead your readers by promising anything that the essay never delivers?
- Do you take ample time and space to unfold each idea in enough detail to make it both clear and interesting? Would more detailed evidence help? (See p. 416.)
- Have you anticipated questions the readers might ask?
- Are there any long-winded explanations or examples that really don't contribute to your main point?
- Are there places where readers might raise serious objections? How might you anticipate these objections and answer them?
- Have you used any specialized or technical language that your readers might not understand? Have you used any familiar words in a technical sense? If so, work in brief definitions.
- What attitude toward your readers do you seem to take? Are you chummy, angry, superior, apologetic, condescending, preachy? Should you revise to improve your attitude? Ask your peers for an opinion.
- From your conclusion and from your essay as a whole, will your readers be convinced that you have told them something worth knowing?

Stressing What Counts

A boring writer writes as though every idea is no more important than any other. An effective writer cares what matters, decides what matters most, and shines a bright light on it. You can't emphasize merely by <u>underlining</u> things, by putting them in "quotation marks," or by throwing them into CAPITAL LETTERS. Such devices soon grow monotonous, and a writer who works them hard ends up stressing nothing at all. This section offers suggestions for how to emphasize things that count.

STATING FIRST OR LAST

The most emphatic positions in an essay, in a paragraph, or in a single sentence are the beginning and the end. Let's consider each.

Stating First.   In an essay, you might state in your opening paragraph what matters most. Writing a paper for an economics course in which students had been assigned to explain the consequences of import quotas (such as a limit on the number of foreign cars allowed into a country), Donna Waite began by summing up her findings.

```
     Although an import quota has many effects, both for
the nation imposing the quota and for the nation whose
industries must suffer from it, I believe that the most
important effect is generally felt at home. A native in-
dustry gains a chance to thrive in a marketplace of less-
ened competition.
```

Waite's paper goes on to illustrate her general observation with evidence. Summing up the most important point right at the start is a good strategy for answering a question in an essay examination. It immediately shows the instructor that you know the answer.

A paper that takes a stand or makes a proposal might open with a statement of what the writer believes.

```
     Our state's antiquated system of justices of the
peace is inefficient.
```

```
     For urgent reasons, I recommend that the United
States place a human observer in temporary orbit around
the planet Mars.
```

The body of the paper would set forth the writer's reasons for holding the view, and probably the writer would hammer the claim or thesis again at the end.

That advice refers to whole essays. Now let's see how in a single sentence you can stress things at the start. Consider the following unemphatic sentence:

```
When Congress debates the Hall-Hayes Act removing
existing legal protections for endangered species, as now
seems likely to occur on May 12, it will be a consider-
able misfortune if this bill should pass, since the ex-
tinction of many rare birds and animals would certainly
be the result.
```

The coming debate and its probable date take up the start of the sentence. The writer might have made better use of this emphatic position.

```
The extinction of many rare birds and animals would
follow passage of the Hall-Hayes Act.
```

Now the writer stresses what he most fears — dire consequences. (In a further sentence, he might add the date of the coming debate in Congress and his opinion that passage of the legislation would be a misfortune.)

Consider these further examples:

DRAFT   It may be argued that the best way to choose software for a small business is to call in a professional consultant, who is likely to be familiar with the many systems available and can give helpful advice.

REVISED   The best way to choose software for a small business is to call in a professional consultant.

Notice that in the revision, the two most important ingredients of the idea are placed first and last. *Best way* is placed up front, and *professional consultant*, standing last in the sentence, is also emphasized.

Stating Last.   To place an idea last can throw weight on it. One way to assemble your ideas in an emphatic order is to proceed from least important to most important. This order is dramatic: it builds up and up.

Not all writing assignments call for drama, of course. In the papers on import quotas and justices of the peace, any attempt at a big dramatic buildup might look artificial and contrived. Still, this strategy is worth considering. Perhaps in an essay on how city parks lure shoppers to the city, the thesis sentence — summing up the whole point of the essay — might stand at the very end: "For the inner city, to improve city parks will bring about a new era of prosperity." Giving all the evidence first and leading up to the thesis at the end is particularly effective in editorials and informal persuasive essays. Ask yourself: Just where in my essay have I made my one main point, the point I most want to make? Once you find it, see if you can place it last by cutting or shifting what comes after it.

This climactic order works not only in essays but also in sentences. A sentence that suspends its main point until the end is a *periodic* sentence. Waiting for someone to finish readying for a trip, you might say, "Now that you've packed your toothbrush and a change of clothing, let's roll!" By placing "let's roll" at the end of the sentence, you emphasize it. Notice how novelist Julian Green builds to his point of emphasis.

> Amid chaos of illusions into which we are cast headlong, there is one thing that stands out as true, and that is — love.

REPEATING

In general, it's economical to say a thing once. But at times repetition can be valuable. One such time is when repetition serves as a transition: it recalls something said earlier. (We discuss such repetition on p. 409.)

Repetition can be valuable, too, when it lends emphasis. When Robert Frost ends his poem "Stopping by Woods on a Snowy Evening" by repeating a line, he does so deliberately.

> The woods are lovely, dark and deep,
> But I have promises to keep,
> And miles to go before I sleep,
> And miles to go before I sleep.

The device of repeating the words that matter most is more often heard in a speech than found in writing. Recall Lincoln's Gettysburg Address, with its promise that "government of the people, by the people, and for the people" will endure; and Martin Luther King Jr.'s famous speech with the insistent refrain "I have a dream." Repetition is a powerful device for emphasis. Break it out only when the occasion calls for it.

Cutting and Whittling

Like pea pickers who throw out dirt and pebbles, good writers remove needless words that clog their prose. One of the chief joys of revising is to watch 200 paunchy words shrink to a svelte 150. To see how saving words helps, let's first look at some wordiness. In what she imagined to be a gracious, Oriental style, a New York socialite once sent this dinner invitation to Hu Shi, the Chinese ambassador:

> O learned sage and distinguished representative of the numerous Chinese nation, pray deign to honor my humble abode with your noble presence at a pouring of libations, to be followed by a modest evening repast, on the forthcoming Friday, June Eighteenth, in this Year of the Pig, at the approximate hour of eight o'clock, Eastern Standard Time. Kindly be assured furthermore, O most illustrious sire, that a favorable reply at your earliest convenience will be received most humbly and gratefully by the undersigned unworthy suppliant.

In reply, the witty diplomat sent this telegram:

CAN DO. HU SHI.

Hu Shi's reply disputes a common assumption — that the more words an idea takes, the more impressive it will seem. Most good contemporary writers know that the more succinctly they can state an idea, the clearer and more forceful it will be.

Some writers may begin by writing a long first draft, putting in every scrap of material, spelling out their every thought in detail. To them, it is easier to trim away the surplus than to add missing essentials. In their revising habits, such writers may be like sculptor Auguste Rodin, who when an admirer asked, "Oh, Monsieur Rodin, is sculpture difficult?" answered lightly, "Not at all! I merely behold the statue in the block of stone. Then I chip away everything else." Let us see how writers chip away.

Cut the Fanfare.   Why bother to announce that you're going to say something? Cut the fanfare. We aren't, by the way, attacking the usefulness of transitions that lead readers along (see p. 407).

> WORDY   As far as getting ready for winter is concerned, I put antifreeze in my car.
>
> REVISED   To get ready for winter, I put antifreeze in my car.
>
> WORDY   The point should be made that . . .
> I might hasten to add that . . .
> Let me make it perfectly clear that . . .
> In this paper I intend to . . .
> In conclusion I would like to say that . . .

Be Direct.   The phrases *on the subject of, in regard to, in terms of, as far as . . . is concerned,* and their ilk often lead to wind.

> WORDY   He is more or less a pretty outstanding person in regard to good looks.
>
> REVISED   He is strikingly handsome.

Here's an especially grim example of corporate prose (before cutting and after):

> WORDY   Regarding trainees' personal life in relation to domestic status, it is not the intention of the management to object to the marriage of any of its trainees at their own individual discretions.
>
> REVISED   Trainees may marry if they like.

Words can also tend to abound after *There is* or *There are.*

> WORDY   There are many people who dislike flying.
>
> REVISED   Many people dislike flying.

```
WORDY    There is a lack of a sense of beauty in Wallace.

REVISED  Wallace lacks a sense of beauty.
         Wallace is insensitive to beauty.
```

Use Strong Verbs.   Forms of the verb *be* (*am, is, are, was, were*) can make a statement wordy when a noun or an adjective follows it. Such weak verbs can almost always be replaced by active verbs.

```
WORDY    The Akron game was a disappointment to the fans.

REVISED  The Akron game disappointed the fans.
```

Use Relative Pronouns with Caution.   Often, when a clause begins with a relative pronoun (*who, which, that*), you can whittle it to a phrase.

```
WORDY    Venus, which is the second planet of the solar
         system, is called the evening star.

REVISED  Venus, the second planet of the solar system, is
         called the evening star.

WORDY    Bert, who is a prize-winning violist, played a
         work of Brahms.

REVISED  Bert, a prize-winning violist, played a work of
         Brahms.
```

Cut Out Deadwood.   The more you revise, the more shortcuts you'll discover. The following sentences have words that can just be cut (indicated in *italics*). Try reading each sentence without them.

Howell spoke for the sophomores, and Janet *also spoke* for the seniors.

Professor Lombardi is *one of the most* amazing *men.*

He is *something of* a clown but *sort of the* lovable *type.*

As a major in *the field of* economics, I plan to concentrate on *the area of* international banking.

The decision as to whether *or not* to go is up to you.

Cut Descriptors.   Adjectives and adverbs are often dispensable. Consider the difference between these two versions:

```
WORDY    Johnson's extremely significant research led to
         highly important major discoveries.

REVISED  Johnson's research led to major discoveries.
```

Be Short, Not Long.   While sometimes a long word conveys a shade of meaning that a shorter synonym doesn't, in general it's a good idea to shun a long word or phrase when you can pick a short one. Instead of *the remainder,* write *the rest;* instead of *activate, start* or *begin;* instead of *expedite, rush;* instead of *adequate* or *sufficient, enough*. Long-windedness, to be sure, doesn't always come from slinging overlarge words. Sometimes it comes from not knowing a right word — one that wraps an idea in a smaller package. The cumbersome expression *persons who are new to the sport of skiing* could be replaced by *novice skiers*. Consider these two remarks about a boxer:

WORDY   Andy has a left fist that has a lot of power in it.

REVISED Andy has a potent left.

By the way, it pays to read. From reading, you absorb words like *potent* and *novice* and set them to work for you.

Here is a list of questions to use in slimming your writing:

**REVISION
CHECKLIST**

Cutting and Whittling

- Are you direct and straightforward?
- Do you announce an idea before you utter it? If so, consider chopping out the announcement.
- Can you recast any sentence that begins *There is* or *There are*?
- Can you substitute an active verb wherever you use a form of the verb *be* (*is, was, were*)?
- Can you reduce to a phrase any clause beginning with *which, who,* or *that*?
- Have you used too many adjectives and adverbs?
- Do you see any long words where short words would do?

John Martin, a business administration major, wrote the following economics paper to fulfill the assignment "Set forth and briefly discuss a current problem in international trade. Venture an opinion or propose a solution." You can see the thoughtful cuts and condensations that Martin made with the help of his English instructor and his peer editor. Following the edited draft you'll find the paper as he resubmitted it — in fewer words.

**WRITING
WITH A
COMPUTER**

Revising and Editing with a Word Processor

The tasks of revising and editing are usually more fruitful — and more fun — if you view them as opportunities to explore new options and to tinker with words and phrases. Computers are ideally suited to such exploration. The word processor can't think for you or tell you how to revise and edit, but it can make turning your thoughts into reality a bit easier. Locating, moving, and changing specific bits and pieces of text — key processes in revising and editing—are all immensely easier on a word processor than with pen and paper. And because you can save multiple versions of your work, you can try out a new introduction or rewrite a troublesome sentence without sacrificing the old one. (For more on using computers for revision and editing, see Chapter 21, "Strategies for Writing with a Computer.")

FIRST DRAFT

Japan's Closed Doors: Should the U.S. Retaliate?

There ~~is currently~~ a serious problem ~~is~~ brewing in ~~the world of~~ international trade, *a cliché to cut* ~~which may turn out to be a real tempest in a teapot, so to speak.~~ According to the latest National Trade Estimates report, several ~~of the countries that the~~ U.S. *trading partners* ~~has been doing business with~~ deserve to be condemned for ~~what the report has characterized as~~ "unfair trade practices." The government has said it will use the report to single out ~~specific~~ countries ~~which it is then going to go ahead and~~ *to* punish under the Super 301 provisions of the trade law.

The Super 301 section ~~of the trade law~~ requires Carla Hills, ~~who is~~ the U.S. trade representative, to *attack* ~~try to get rid of~~ what she *calls* ~~has officially designated to be~~ "priority unfair practices." She will ~~be~~ slashing at the *same as impediments* ~~whole~~ web of impediments ~~and obstacles~~ that have ~~slowed down or~~ denied *American* ~~the various products of the many United States~~ firms ~~much~~ *fast* access to Japanese markets.

~~It is important for the reader to note here that for a long time, longer than anyone can remember,~~ Japan *long* has ~~been the~~ been ~~leading~~ prime candidate for a dose of Super 301. Over the past decade, ~~there have been many years of negotiations and battering by different~~ industry groups *have battered* at the unyielding doors of ~~the~~ Japanese markets, *with* ~~which have yielded~~ some successes, but have ~~pretty much~~

make them swing wide.

failed ~~miserably~~ to ^dent ~~the invisible trade barriers~~ ~~that stand looming between us and the Japanese markets,~~ ~~preventing the free access of U.S. goods to Japanese con-~~ ~~sumers. As far as the~~ *The* U.S. trade deficit with Japan, ~~is concerned, it was somewhat~~ more than $50 billion last year,~~and it~~ shows ~~very~~ little sign of ^*improving* ~~getting signif-~~ ~~icantly much better~~ this year.

Some American businesspeople would ~~like to~~ take aim at Japan immediately. However, Clyde Prestowitz, ~~who is~~ a former Commerce Department official, ~~seriously~~ doubts that ~~in the last analysis~~ it would be ^*wise to* ~~a good idea to come~~ ~~out and~~ name Japan ~~to feel the terrible effects of~~ ^*for* retaliation under Super 301 ~~in view of the fact that in his~~ ~~opinion,~~ "It's hard to negotiate with guys you are calling cheats." No doubt ~~there are~~ many other observers ~~who~~ share his view.

~~Evidently it is the task of the~~ *The* administration ^*has* to try to ^*help* ~~pave the way for~~ U.S. exports ~~to~~ wedge their way into ~~the~~ protected Japanese markets while keeping ~~it~~ ~~firmly~~ in mind that the interests of both ^*nations* ~~the United~~ ~~States and Japan~~ call for ^*stronger* ~~strengthening of the~~ economic and military ties.~~that bind both countries into a sphere~~ ~~of friendly relationship. It is my personal conclusion~~ ~~that if~~ *If* the administration goes ahead,~~with this,~~ it will ~~certainly~~ need to plan ~~ahead for the future~~ carefully.

REVISED VERSION

```
     Japan's Closed Doors: Should the U.S. Retaliate?
     A serious problem is brewing in international trade.
According to the latest National Trade Estimates report,
several U.S. trading partners deserve to be condemned for
"unfair trade practices." The government has said it will
use the report to single out countries to punish under the
Super 301 provisions of the trade law.
     The Super 301 section requires Carla Hills, the U.S.
trade representative, to attack what she calls "priority un-
fair practices." She will slash at the web of impediments that
have denied American firms fast access to Japanese markets.
     Japan has long been the prime candidate for a dose of
Super 301. Over the past decade, industry groups have bat-
tered at the unyielding doors of Japanese markets, with some
success, but have failed to make them swing wide. The U.S.
trade deficit with Japan, more than $50 billion last year,
shows little sign of improving this year.
     Some American businesspeople would take aim at Japan im-
mediately. However, Clyde Prestowitz, a former Commerce De-
partment official, doubts that it would be wise to name Japan
for retaliation under Super 301: "It's hard to negotiate with
guys you are calling cheats." No doubt many other observers
share his view.
     The administration has to try to help U.S. exports wedge
their way into protected Japanese markets while keeping in
mind that the interests of both nations call for stronger
economic and military ties. If the administration goes ahead,
it will need to plan carefully.
```

Proofreading and Editing

Proofreading is checking for correctness of grammar, spelling, punctuation, and mechanics, and editing is fixing those errors. In college, good proofreading and editing can make the difference between a C and an A. On the job, it may help you get a promotion. Readers, teachers, and bosses like careful writers who take time to proofread.

Don't proofread and edit too soon. In your early drafting, don't fret over the correct spelling of an unfamiliar word; the word may be revised out in a later version. If the word stays in, you'll have time to check it later. Turn your internal monitor or editor off until you have the ideas right.

Most errors in writing occur unconsciously. Some result from faulty information in your memory. If you have never learned the difference between *its* and *it's,* you'll probably misuse these words without realizing you're making a mistake. If you have never looked closely at the spelling of *environment,* you may never have seen the second *n,* and so you'll habitually spell it *enviroment.* Such errors easily become habits and reinforce themselves every time you write them.

Split-second inattention or a break in concentration can also cause errors. Because the mind works faster than the pen or the pencil (or the typewriter or word processor), when you are distracted by someone's voice or a telephone ring, you may omit a letter or a whole word or you may put in the wrong punctuation.

The very way our eyes work leads to errors. When you read normally, you usually see only the shells of words — the first and last letters. You fix your eyes on the print only three or four times per line or less. To proofread effectively, you must look at the individual letters in each word and the punctuation marks between words and not slide over the individual symbols. Proofreading requires time and patience.

The skill of proofreading does not come naturally, but it is a skill you can develop. It is your responsibility as a writer to break old habits and develop this skill. It will pay off in the long run.

Tips for Proofreading

1. Turn off your internal monitor until you get the ideas right.
2. Realize that *all* writers make mistakes in their haste to put ideas on paper and must proofread to find and correct their errors.
3. Realize that you are human and you will make mistakes. Develop a healthy sense of doubt because mistakes are so easy to make. Making mistakes isn't bad — but not taking time to find and correct them is.
4. Budget enough time to proofread thoroughly.
5. Let a paper "get cold." Let it sit several days, or overnight, or at least a few hours before proofreading it.
6. Learn the grammar conventions you don't understand so you can spot and eliminate problems in your own writing. Practice until you easily recognize major errors such as fragments and comma splices. Learn how to correct your own common problems. Ask for assistance from a peer editor or a tutor in the writing center if your campus has one.
7. Read what you have written very slowly, looking at every word and every letter.
8. Read your paper aloud. Speaking forces you to slow down and see more, and sometimes you will hear a mistake you haven't seen.
9. Read what you have actually written, not what you think is there. Don't let your mind play tricks on you. Developing the objectivity to

see what is really on the page or screen is one of the most difficult aspects of proofreading.

10. Use a dictionary or a spell checker whenever you can. (But be aware that a spell checker is not foolproof. It will not know if you've typed *own* when you meant to type *won*, for instance.)

11. Double-check for habitual errors (such as leaving off *-s* or *-ed* or putting in unnecessary commas).

12. Read the essay backward. This will force you to look at each word because you won't get caught up in the flow of ideas.

13. Read the essay several times, focusing each time on a specific area of difficulty (once for spelling, once for punctuation, once for a problem you know is recurrent in your writing).

14. Ask someone else to read your paper and tell you if it is free of errors. But *don't* let someone else do your work for you.

15. Take pride in your work.

Whenever you are in doubt as to whether a word or construction is correct, you should consult a good reference handbook. The "Quick Editing Guide" at the end of *The Bedford Guide for College Writers* will get you started (look for the pages with blue edges). It provides a brief overview of the most troubling grammar, style, punctuation, and mechanics problems typically found in college writing. For each problem covered, there are definitions, examples, a checklist to help you tackle the problem, and a tip that will come in handy if you are editing with a computer. Here is a checklist to give you an overview; the letter and numbers in parentheses direct you to the relevant section in the "Quick Editing Guide":

EDITING CHECKLIST

Common and Serious Problems in College Writing

- Have you used the correct form for all verbs in the past tense? (See A1.)
- Do all verbs agree with their subjects? (See A2.)
- Have you used the correct case for all pronouns? (See A3.)
- Do all pronouns agree with their antecedents? (See A4.)
- Have you used adjectives and adverbs correctly? (See A5.)
- Have you avoided writing sentence fragments? (See A6.)

WRITING WITH A COMPUTER

Proofreading

Most grammar checkers aren't very reliable or useful, but computerized spell checkers are handy tools. Remember, though, that they aren't foolproof. They can't tell you that you've used *you're* when you meant to write *your* or *affect* when you meant *effect*. For more on spell checkers and on other computer techniques for proofreading, see p. 473.

- Have you avoided writing comma splices or fused sentences? (See A7.)
- Do all modifiers clearly modify the appropriate sentence element? (See B1.)
- Have you used parallel structure where necessary? (See B2.)
- Have you used commas correctly? (See C1.)
- Have you used apostrophes correctly? (See C2.)
- Have you used capital letters correctly? (See D1.)
- Have you spelled all words correctly? (See D2.)
- Have you used correct manuscript form? (See D3.)

Proofreading and Editing

Proofread the following passage carefully. Assume that the organization of the paragraph is satisfactory. You are to look for mistakes in sentence structure, grammar, spelling, punctuation, and capitalization and correct them. There are ten errors in the paragraph. After you have completed your editing of the passage, discuss with your classmates the changes you have made and your reasons for making those changes.

Robert Frost, one of the most popular American poets. He was born in San Francisco in 1874, and died in Boston in 1963. His family moved to new England when his father died in 1885. There he completed highschool and attended colledge but never graduate. Poverty and problems filled his life. He worked in a woolen mill, on a newspaper, and on varous odd jobs. Because of ill health he settled on a farm and began to teach school to support his wife and children. Throughout his life he dedicated himself to writing poetry, by 1915 he was in demand for public readings and speaking engagements. He was awarded the Pulitzer Prize for poetry four times — in 1924, 1931, 1937, and 1943. The popularity of his poetry rests in his use of common themes and images, expressed in everyday language. Everyone can relate to his universal poems, such as "Swinging on Birches" and "Stopping by Woods on a Snowy Evening." Students read his poetry in school from seventh grade through graduate school, so almost everyone recognize lines from his best-loved poems. America is proud of it's son, the homespun poet Robert Frost.

Chapter 20

Strategies for Working with Other Writers: Collaborative Learning

Some people imagine the writer all alone in an ivory tower, toiling in perfect solitude. But in the real world, writing is often a collaborative effort. In business firms, reports are sometimes written by teams and revised by committees before being submitted to top-level managers. People sit around a table throwing out ideas, which a secretary transcribes and someone else writes up. A crucial letter, an advertisement, or a company's annual report embodies the thinking and writing of many. Research scientists and social scientists often work in teams of two or more and collaborate on articles for professional journals. Even this book is the result of collaborative writing.

Student writers are often pleasantly surprised to find how genuinely helpful other students can be. When you are the writer, working with your classmates and friends gives you a very real sense of having a living, breathing, supportive audience. Asked to read an early draft, peers can respond to a paper, signal strengths in it, and offer constructive suggestions. Asked to read a later draft, they can help pinpoint problems with word choice and let you know where you need more evidence. Many instructors today encourage students to form groups and write essays collaboratively. That is why, throughout this book, we include peer response checklists and suggest activities for group learning.

If your instructor does not require peer editing or collaborative writing, you can arrange it on your own. Enlist one or more classmates or friends to read your work and comment on it. You can provide the same service in return. Before you show a draft to a friend, take a few minutes to write down two or three questions you'd like him or her to answer. If you are reading a classmate's work, ask the writer to give you a few specific questions.

449

If you don't know someone who is willing to respond to your writing for you, go to the writing center on campus. Here you can get help from special instructors and work with trained, experienced peer tutors. The lab staff will not do your work—planning, drafting, revising, proofreading—for you but will help you fulfill your assigned task.

Serving as a Reader

What does it take to be a helpful, supportive peer editor? Here are a few tips for you.

Look at the Big Picture.   Your job isn't merely to notice misspelled words or misused semicolons (although it can't hurt to signal any that you see). Bend your mind to deeper matters—the writer's primary point, the sequence of ideas, the apparent truth or falsity of the observations, the quantity and quality of the evidence, the coherence or unity of the paper as a whole.

Be Specific.   Vague blame or praise won't help the writer. Don't say, "It's an interesting paper" or "I liked this essay a lot because I can relate to it." Such a response might make the writer feel good, but statements like "That example in paragraph 9 clarified the whole point of the paper for me" will make the writer feel good for good reason.

Be Tactful.   Approach the work in a friendly way. Remember, you aren't out to pass godlike judgment on your peer's effort. Your purpose as a reader is to give honest, intelligent comments—to help make the other writer aware of what he or she has written right, not only what he or she has written wrong. When you find fault, you can do so by making impartial observations—statements nobody can deny. A judgmental way to criticize might be "This paper is confused. It keeps saying the same thing over and over again." But a more useful comment might be more specific: "Paragraph 5 makes the same point as paragraphs 2 and 3," suggesting that two of the three paragraphs might be eliminated.

Answer Any Questions the Writer Has Asked You.   If the writer has indicated that he or she has questions about a specific spot or issue in the paper, take the time to address his or her concerns.

Ask Yourself Questions.   For help in looking for worthwhile, specific, tactful responses, skim the following checklist of readers' questions. Not all these points will apply to every paper.

FIRST QUESTIONS

What is your first reaction to this paper?

What is this writer trying to tell you? What does he or she most want you to learn?

What are this paper's greatest strengths?

Does it have any major weaknesses?

QUESTIONS ON MEANING

Do you understand everything? Is there any information missing from this draft that you still need to know?

Is what this paper tells you worth saying, or does it only belabor the obvious? Does it tell you anything you didn't know before?

Is the writer trying to cover too much territory? Too little?

Does any point need to be more fully explained or illustrated?

When you come to the end, do you find that the paper hasn't delivered something it promised?

Could this paper use a down-to-the-ground revision? Would it be better on a different topic altogether — one the writer perhaps touches but doesn't deal with in this paper?

QUESTIONS ON ORGANIZATION

Has the writer begun in a way that grabs your interest? Are you quickly drawn into the paper's main idea? Or can you find, at some point later in the paper, a better possible beginning?

Does the paper have one main idea, or does it struggle to handle more than one? Would the main idea stand out better if anything were removed?

Might the ideas in the paper be more effectively rearranged in a different order? Do any ideas belong together that now seem too far apart?

Does the writer keep to one point of view — one angle of seeing?

Does the ending seem deliberate, as if the writer meant to conclude at this point? Or does the writer seem merely to have run out of gas? If so, what can the writer do to write a stronger conclusion?

QUESTIONS ON LANGUAGE AND WRITING STRATEGIES

Do you feel that this paper addresses you personally?

At any point in the paper, do you find yourself disliking or objecting to a statement the writer makes, to a word or a phrase with which you're not in sympathy? What is the problem here? Is it the writer's tone? Does the writer provide inadequate support to clarify or convince you? Should the writer keep this part, or should he or she change it?

Does the draft contain anything that distracts you, that seems unnecessary, that might be struck?

Do you get bored at any point and want to tune out? What might the writer do to make you want to keep reading?

Can you follow the writer's ideas easily? Does the paper need transitions? If so, at what places?

Does the language of this paper stay up in the clouds of generality? If so, where and how might the writer come down to earth and get specific?

Do you understand all the words the writer uses, or are there any specialized words whose meaning needs to be made clearer?

LAST QUESTION

Now that you have spent some time with this paper and looked at it closely, how well does it work for you?

Write Comments.   To show the writer just where you had a reaction, write notations in the margins of the paper. Then at the end write an overall comment, making major, general suggestions. Sum up the paper's strong and weak points: it can hardly be all good or all bad.

Here is a helpful comment by Maria Mendez on a draft of a paper by Jill Walker that ended up being titled "Euthanasia and the Law":

> Jill—
>
>   The topic of this paper interested me a lot because we had a case of euthanasia in our neighborhood. I didn't realize at first what your topic was — maybe the title "Life and Death" didn't say it to me. Your paper is full of good ideas and fact — like the Hemlock Society to help mercy-killing. I got lost when you start talking about advances in modern medicine (paragraph 6) but don't finish the idea. To go into modern medicine thoroughly would take a lot more room. Maybe euthanasia is enough to cover in five pages. Also, I don't know everything you're mentioning ("traditional attitudes toward life and death"). I could have used an explanation there — I'm from a different tradition. On the whole, your paper is solid and is going to make us agree with you.
>
>   Maria

Learning as a Writer

You, the writer whose work is in the spotlight, will probably find that you can't just sit back and enjoy your fans' reactions. To extract all the usefulness from the process of peer reviewing, you'll need to play an active part in discussing your work.

Ask Your Readers Questions.   Probably your readers will give you more helpful specific reactions if you provide them with questions such as those in the previous section. As the writer, however, you may already suspect that something is wrong with your early draft, so you should add your own questions. Direct the peer readers' attention to places in your paper where you especially want insights. Express any doubts you have. Point out parts you found difficult to write. Ask what your readers would do about any weak spots.

Ask pointed questions like these *in writing* for your readers to think about:

> When you read my conclusion, are you convinced that I'm arguing for the one right solution to this problem? Can you imagine any better solution?
>
> Paragraph 4 looks skimpy — only two short sentences. What could I do to make it longer?

How clear is my purpose? Can you sum up what I'm trying to say? What steps can I take to make my point hit home to you?

Throughout Parts One and Two of this book, we have provided brief checklists that writers can give to their peer editors to help them focus on the most important elements in that specific type of writing.

Encourage Your Readers to Be Sympathetic but Tough.   Ask your peer editors not to be too easy on you. Let them know that you are willing to make deep structural changes, not merely cosmetic repairs, in what you have written.

Be Open to New Ideas.   You might get completely new ideas — for focus, for organization, for details — from the readers' reactions. They may also have some tips about where to find more, and more valuable, relevant material.

Take What's Helpful.   Occasionally students worry that asking another student, no wiser or brighter or more experienced than they, to criticize their work is a risk not worth taking. You have to accept such help judiciously. You want to be wary about following all the suggestions you receive. While some of them may help, others may lead to a dead end.

Realize You're the Boss.   The important thing in taking advice and suggestions is to listen to your readers but not be a slave to them. Trust yourself. Let your instincts operate. Make a list of the suggestions you receive. Do any of

---

 **WRITING WITH A COMPUTER**

Peer Editing on Screen

If the writer wrote with a word processor, ask to work with an electronic copy of the draft in addition to a paper copy. The easiest way for you to enter your comments and suggestions is to turn on the Caps Lock feature (the Caps Lock button is usually on the left side of the keyboard). You can then type away at whatever places in the draft you would like. Your comments, now in all capital letters, will remain clearly distinguishable from the original text. The writer should make backup copies (both electronic and paper) of this file before turning it over to you: computer accidents can happen too easily. Here's an example of what a brief passage might look like:

> Harry S. Truman had a folksy way of expressing himself, which makes us remember many of his sayings. CAN YOU GIVE AN EXAMPLE? He was a folksy speaker CUT THIS REPETITION and developed his style in the rough-and-tumble of Mississippi politics. MISSOURI?

them cancel out others? Does any suggestion seem worth trying? If so, give it a try, but drop it if it doesn't work.

It takes self-confidence to sift through criticism with profit. The final decision about whether to act on the advice you receive from your fellow students is solely up to you. If you feel that one person's suggestions have not helped at all, you would be wise to ask for a second and even a third opinion. When several of your readers disagree, only you can decide what direction to follow.

Learn to Evaluate Your Own Writing.   As your writing skills continue to develop, you will find yourself relying less on your peers and more on your own ability to analyze and revise your early drafts. You can ask yourself the same questions you use in evaluating other writers' papers. And when you learn to answer those questions searchingly, you'll become your own most valuable reader.

Peer Editors in Action

The following brief histories point out how effectively classmates can help a revision. First, consider this early draft of an opening paragraph for the essay "Why Don't More People Donate Their Bodies to Science?" by Dana Falk, written in an interdepartmental course in English and sociology.

```
     The question of why more organs and body parts are
not donated "to science"--that is, for the use of organ
transplants, medical research, and college education--is
a puzzling one. As I have learned through my research, it
is also a multidetermined one. There are a plethora of
```

Using E-Mail to Collaborate

E-mail offers another way for writers and readers to work together, since drafts and comments can be sent back and forth quickly and easily from almost anywhere, at almost any time. If you find arranging a meeting between writer and reader difficult, have the writer send the reader a copy of the draft over e-mail. The draft will sit in the reader's electronic mailbox until he or she has time to respond to it. Most e-mail can be easily answered with the Reply command, and the original draft (or passages from it) can be incorporated into this reply.

Some writers find e-mail exchanges particularly helpful in getting started. The conversational, personal nature of e-mail helps some writers to relax and to direct their writing to a tangible audience. (For more on e-mail, see p. 349.)

```
reasons that prevent there from being enough organs to go
around, and in this paper I shall examine a number of the
reasons I have uncovered, trying to evaluate the effec-
tiveness of efforts to alleviate the shortage and suggest
possible alternate approaches myself. Primarily, though,
we will simply look at the factors that prevent health
professionals from being able to supply body parts each
and every time a donor is needed.
```

Falk showed the paper to a classmate, Pamela Kong, who commented first on the opening sentence. "This could be rephrased as a question," she suggested, and she wrote "AWKWARD" next to the sentence that begins "There are a plethora of reasons. . . . " "That sentence was pretty bad!" Falk later realized. Kong zeroed in on the stilted word *multidetermined* (apparently meaning "having several causes") and called for a clearer announcement of where the paper was going. After reading Kong's comments and doing some hard thinking, Falk recast the opening paragraph.

```
    The gap between the demand for human organs and
their current supply is ever-widening. Although the suc-
cess rate of transplants is way up because of the intro-
duction of cyclosporine, an immunosuppressant, many po-
tential donors and their families resist giving away
their body parts, creating an acute shortage. Why is it
that people so fear giving their bodies to science? Let's
examine the causes of the shortage of transplantable or-
gans and review some possible solutions.
```

In the second version Falk's language becomes more concrete and definite. He uses a figure of speech — a "gap" that is "ever-widening" — and the vivid phrase "giving away their body parts." The added detail about the newly successful drug lends the paper fresh authority. Kong's suggestion to turn the question into an actual one (with a question mark) lends life to the sentence that now begins "Why is it that people so fear. . . . " The announced plan for the rest of the paper, now placed at the end of the paragraph, points toward everything that will follow.

Now let's see how a peer editor helped another student strengthen an entire paper. Kevin Deters wrote the following short essay for an English composition course. The assignment asked for a reflective essay in response to his own reading. Even in this early draft, you'll find that Deters's paper treats a challenging subject and comes to a thoughtful conclusion. But as the paper stands, what does it lack? For practice, try to critique the paper yourself before you look at the peer editor's comments.

FIRST DRAFT

Where Few Men Have Gone Before

Space: the final frontier. This is the subject addressed   1
by the renowned writer Isaac Asimov in "Into Space: The Next
Giant Step," a short piece published in the St. Louis Post-
Dispatch. Asimov, the author of over four hundred science and
science fiction books, writes about the space station that
will be built in orbit around the earth in the near future.
He examines the advantages and numerous possibilities of
space travel that such a station would allow. This space station will give people the opportunity to be explorers, help
conserve resources on earth, and unite the nations of the
world as they forge the common goal of discovering knowledge
of outer space.

"It is absolutely necessary that we build a base other   2
than earth for our ventures into space. . . . The logical beginning is with a space station," Asimov says. The space station would serve as a stepping-stone to future permanent
bases on the moon and Mars. Adventurous settlers would pave
the spaceways just as Daniel Boone and his followers blazed
trails through the Kentucky wilderness. It is these space
travelers "who will be the Phoenicians, the Vikings, the
Polynesians of the future, making their way into the 21st
century through a space-ocean far vaster than the water-ocean
traversed by their predecessors."

These spacefarers will also find ways to help conserve   3
valuable energy on earth. Asimov suggests that, using the
space station as a base, lunar materials could be excavated
from the moon to construct power stations to direct solar
energy toward the earth. Thus, energy and money are saved,
and this conservation could serve as a deterrent to the use
of nuclear energy.

With this new surplus of energy, nuclear energy and   4
all its applications such as power plants and missiles would
become unnecessary. A major threat to world safety would
be removed. The sun's never-ending supply of solar energy
could be harnessed to become the chief energy source on
earth, and dangerous forms of energy could be done away with.

As a result, expensive heating bills and the like would   5
be unheard of. Energy costs would plummet as earth's populace
took advantage of the sun's plentiful rays. The price decrease would snowball, affecting other aspects of life, eventually resulting in a cheaper cost of living.

The construction of such a space station could also   6
help unify the countries of the world. A massive project
like this enterprise would cost billions of dollars and take
a massive amount of time and hard work. Asimov suggests that
if the United States and Russia were to work together, costs
and time could be considerably lessened. Such joint
U.S./Russia missions are not unheard of. The Apollo-Soyuz
venture and the space shuttle Mir hookup, projects that
linked a spacecraft from each nation, were successful examples of cooperation.

This joint effort could help promote global togetherness   7
as well. If the world's nations could unite to explore space,
surely problems back home on earth could be easily solved.
Such quibbles as the nuclear arms race and foreign trading
disputes seem trivial and inconsequential when compared to
the grandeur of space exploration.

And so this space station will serve as a valuable tool   8
for humanity. Man must now reach for the heavens above him
because if the earth's population keeps increasing, the
planet will soon be too small to accommodate everyone. Space
exploration is the only logical answer. Space is indeed the
final frontier that lies before us. We only have to take advantage of it.

Kevin Deters's classmate Jennifer Balsavias read his reflective essay and
filled out a peer editing questionnaire. Here are the questions and her responses to them.

PEER RESPONSE CHECKLIST

1. First, sit on your hands and read the essay through. Then
describe your first reaction.

*This was a well-written report. The only time I really noticed any reflection on the
reading was in the last paragraph.*

2. What is "reflective" about this essay? What is the purpose of the essay and the major reflection?

The purpose of the essay was to show the importance of space to humans and their expansion into that final frontier. In the last paragraph, he lets us know his feelings on the information given. He doesn't reflect about the reading throughout the paper.

3. How skillfully has the writer used reading? Look at the way quotations or paraphrases are inserted. Is it clear when the writer is using reading and when the ideas are the writer's? Comment on any areas that were problematic to you.

He uses quotes and information from the reading very well. (By the way, where's the second quote in the second paragraph from?) The writer is definitely using the reading and adds only a few thoughts of his own. Needs to reflect more!

4. Is the paper informed enough by reading? Where could the paper improve by more careful or detailed use of "secondary" (not personal) materials?

It's not very personal. His own feelings and reflections should be involved. There is enough about the reading. Maybe he shouldn't expand so much on the subject. Maybe stop after the first or second paragraph and REFLECT!

5. Who is the essay written to? Describe the audience.

I feel it is written to those interested in space and the new space programs. I found it interesting.

6. List any terms or phrases that are too technical or specialized or any words that need further definition.

None

7. If you were handing the essay in for a grade, what would you be sure to revise?

I'd put some of my reflections in, not just facts.

8. Circle on the manuscript any problems with spelling, punctuation, grammar, or usage.

> *He should correct his sexist usage — for example, in the title and in paragraph 8, where "man" is used to mean "people."*

In reading Jennifer Balsavias's evaluation, Deters was struck by her main criticism: "The only time I really noticed any reflection on the reading was in the last paragraph." "Needs to reflect *more!*" Deters's paper seemed more like a report on an article than an essay analyzing the article with some original thinking. It was difficult for the reader to tell Isaac Asimov's opinions from Deters's own. Perhaps Deters needed to express his views more clearly and not shun the first-person *I*. He reworked his draft, trying to set forth his own opinions, trying also to tighten and sharpen his prose. His revised essay follows.

REVISED VERSION

Where Few Have Gone Before

Space: the final frontier. The renowned writer Isaac Asimov addresses this subject in "Into Space: The Next Giant Step," a short piece published in the <u>St. Louis Post-Dispatch</u>. Asimov, the author of over four hundred science and science fiction books, writes about the space station that will be built in orbit around the earth in the near future. He examines the advantages and numerous possibilities of space travel that such a station would allow. From this article, I gathered that this space station will give people the opportunity to be explorers, help conserve resources on earth, and unite the nations of the world as they forge the common goal of discovering knowledge of outer space. I'm intrigued by each of these possibilities.

"It is absolutely necessary that we build a base other than earth for our ventures into space," Asimov tells us. "The logical beginning is with a space station." A space station would serve as a stepping-stone to future permanent bases on the moon and Mars. I can imagine adventurous settlers who would pave the spaceways just as Daniel Boone and his followers blazed trails through the Kentucky wilderness. These space travelers Asimov describes as "the Phoenicians, the Vikings, the Polynesians of the future, making their way into the twenty-first century through a space-ocean far vaster than the water-ocean traversed by their predecessors."

The spacefarers will also find ways to help conserve valuable energy on earth. Asimov suggests that, with the space station as a base, they could construct power stations to direct solar energy toward the earth. Thus, lessening our use of fossil fuels, conserving energy and saving money. I believe that this conservation could also serve as a deterrent to the use of nuclear energy. With a new surplus of energy, nuclear energy and all its applications such as power plants and missiles would become unnecessary. The sun's never-ending supply of solar energy could be harnessed to become the chief energy source on earth, and dangerous forms of energy could be done away with.   3

As a result, I suggest that expensive heating bills and the like would be unheard of. Energy costs would plummet as earth's populace would take advantage of the sun's plentiful rays. The price decrease would snowball, affecting other aspects of life, eventually resulting in a cheaper cost of living.   4

The construction of the space station that Asimov discusses could also help unify the countries of the world. A project like this would cost billions of dollars and take a massive amount of time and hard work. No one country could afford the project. Asimov suggests that if the United States and Russia were to work together, costs and time could be considerably lessened. I believe that this joint effort could help promote global togetherness as well. Joint missions of the United States and other countries have been conducted. For example, the Apollo-Soyuz venture linked spacecrafts from the United States and Russia. If the world's nations can unite to explore space, surely problems back home could be easily solved. Such quibbles as the nuclear arms race and foreign trading disputes seem trivial when compared to the grandeur of space exploration.   5

Asimov suggests that the space station will serve as a valuable tool for humanity. I concur, for I believe that the human race must now reach for the heavens. Space is indeed the final frontier that lies before us. We can all be Daniel Boones.   6

You'll notice that, as Jennifer Balsavias suggested, Deters seems to reflect harder in his revised version. And by speaking out in his own voice, he makes clear (as he didn't do in the earlier version) that many of his thoughts are his own, not Asimov's. Notice, too, Deters's smaller but effective alterations. At the end, he returns to his earlier, original comparison between pioneers in space and Daniel Boone. All his changes produce a more concise, readable, and absorbing paper, one that goes a little deeper — thanks in part to the services of an honest, helpful peer editor.

Chapter 21

Strategies for Writing with a Computer

"I love being a writer," declares novelist Peter De Vries. "What I can't stand is the paperwork."

If you have ever felt this impatience with writing and revising, you probably can appreciate the modern miracle of the word processor—a computer with the software necessary for writing. Some writers think word processing is the greatest thing since movable type was invented by Gutenberg. Others find computers to be complicated and intimidating machines and would like to return to the days of pen and typewriter. But some of those who object to computer-assisted writing may misunderstand technology and think of computers as tools designed for scientists, mathematicians, and programmers but not really for writers. In fact, word processing is by far the most commonly used computer application, and in many ways the personal computer is primarily a writing machine.

Learning to use word-processing software does not mean that you'll have to use a computer for every phase of your writing process. Some enthusiastic computer writers find that the traditional pencil and paper method works better for some phases of composing and revising, and so they combine the old method and the new in a way that proves enjoyable and productive for them. Most computer users find that if they take just a few hours to learn how their software works, they can prevent a great deal of frustration and turn their computers into powerful and helpful writing tools.

Even though you may eventually decide against using computers extensively in your writing process, to do so without giving them a serious try would be unwise. Computer skills, especially computer writing skills, are a tremendous advantage in both writing college papers and applying for jobs. In today's business world, technological literacy—integrating computers effectively in thinking and writing tasks — is a valuable asset and, in some fields, a common requirement. You may not have another opportunity to improve your computer skills in an environment as supportive as your college, so take advantage of it.

On most campuses you will find open-access laboratories where you can use a computer and a variety of programs. These facilities are frequently staffed with people who can help you get started. Asking for help from a friend who knows about word processing is another great way to learn. In addition, this chapter contains advice and practical tips for those who are new to word processing (see especially the first two sections, pp. 463–74). If you are a practiced veteran who already writes with a computer, you can skip over to page 474 for some hints that can make word processing work more effectively for you. You may also find some useful advice in "Formatting Your Manuscript" (p. 469).

This chapter also discusses some recent developments in the world of computer-assisted writing, particularly those made possible by the Internet (see "Writing on Computer Networks," p. 476). Finally, you've probably already noticed the suggestions for completing specific assignments in the "Writing with a Computer" features placed throughout the chapters of this book. (For a complete list, see the index.)

What Word Processing Can and Cannot Do

Computers have been oversold as "miracle machines" and lead some new users to expect too much from them. You must approach learning word processing with patience, flexibility, and a positive attitude. Computers can eventually save you enormous amounts of time, but you will not fully realize these savings until you have learned how to take advantage of the program's most useful features.

Don't be intimidated. Computer programs are increasingly "user friendly" — meaning easy to learn and use. Remember, though, that all word-processing programs have certain limitations. A computer does not really think on its own or do things for you. It performs only as it is told. So if you want to use a word processor effectively, you must understand what it can and cannot do. No computer has yet been marketed that can write an essay for you or accurately check your grammar or even your spelling, although some programs have limited grammar and spell checkers. The writer is still in control; a word processor is merely a powerful writing tool.

ADVANTAGES

By enabling your work-in-progress to take shape on screen instead of on paper and by storing what you write, word processing helps do away with much of the mechanical work of rewriting. Instead of typing and retyping draft after draft, with word processing you can do all the following:

Rearrange swiftly

Insert short sentences or long sections

Delete unwanted words, sentences, or passages

Search for and replace a word or phrase

Correct mistakes easily

Format and reformat quickly

Check your spelling

Number pages automatically

Put headings on each page

Print multiple copies

Store several hundred pages on a small disk

Supplemental programs — such as grammar checkers, spell checkers, and other writing tools — can provide still greater assistance. Sometimes their features are built right into a word-processing program; sometimes you can buy them as separate programs. Such programs can do the following:

Feed you questions or prompts to generate ideas

Help you organize material

Produce detailed, readable outlines

Help you choose better words

Review grammar rules

Help you edit

Help you proofread

Detect clichés

Count the number of words

Correctly format endnotes and bibliographies

Produce tables and graphs

The basic features of word processors — such as the ability to save, delete, paste, and print — can free your mind for the more essential work of writing. But writers have also discovered some additional advantages to using a word processor, benefits that don't necessarily correspond to specific commands or features that the manufacturers included in their software packages. Here are a few.

Ease of Drafting.   Word processors let you throw down thoughts in whatever order they come to mind and then later move them around and arrange them as seems best. Of course, you can do this kind of thinking and revising with paper and scissors, too, but word processors encourage it and make it easy. Word processors enable you to write an outline, add to each outline section on the screen, and shape a list of headings into a finished essay. A separate outlining program, or an outlining module within a word processor, lets you arrange and rearrange ideas under headings and subheadings. Word processors let you start with seemingly chaotic writing — messy freewriting, brainstormed lists, meandering journal entries — and build them bit by bit into solid chunks for your final paper.

Ease of Revising.   Earlier we wrote that "the personal computer is primarily a writing machine." To be more specific, it is primarily a revision machine. A willingness to undergo a number of revisions is often the key to successful writing, and as a revision machine a word processor can be tremendously helpful. You can experiment freely by making a duplicate of your current document. You can rearrange sentences and paragraphs, try out new material, and play around with the sequence of ideas. You can edit on the screen or make a printout to annotate by hand. Try three different versions of a short paper or of a section of an essay (such as the introduction or the conclusion), starting a separate document for each. Then combine the best parts from all three versions.

Ease of Formatting.   Formatting a college paper correctly on your first try may not seem particularly easy, but once you have learned a few basic techniques, you will be able to format your papers quickly and painlessly. Almost all word processors let you format — adjust margins, number pages, place headers, center text, indent block quotations — with just a couple of keystrokes or mouse clicks. Personal computers are now sophisticated enough to create magazine-quality page designs, and formatting the typical college paper is well within their capabilities. With a word processor you can also do things that you could never have done on a typewriter, such as use boldface, select a specific type font and type size, and create sophisticated tables and graphs. And you can create a blank, preformatted document called a *template* to make formatting tasks even easier (see "Formatting Your Manuscript," p. 469).

DISADVANTAGES

Just as word processors offer some advantages that software manufacturers did not intentionally design, these programs can also cause some problems, which we would be remiss not to mention.

No Substitute for the Human Mind.   The so-called mind of a computer remains relatively simple compared with the human mind. In reality, the computer has no actual mind, no power to originate thought, no imagination at all — even though we call its spacious storage capacity a *memory*. Computer applications such as word processors can help you only with the mechanical aspects of writing, allowing you to focus more on generating ideas and crafting language. These machines cannot actually write. Some programs claim to check your spelling, word choice, clichés, or style for you, but they actually have serious limitations. In fact, it's questionable whether you should use any checker other than one for spelling. English grammar is far too complicated to be checked accurately by any software, despite what some programs promise. (For more on spell checkers and grammar checkers, see p. 473 and the computer tips placed throughout the "Quick Editing Guide" at the end of *The Bedford Guide for College Writers*.)

Possible Loss of Data.   If you use a computer to write, you will almost certainly lose some of your data accidentally at some point — a frustrating experience. If, say, your roommate plugs in a hair dryer and blows a fuse or there is a power surge in the computer lab while you are word processing — poof! there goes your unsaved work. If you have not used the Save command to store your document on a disk, your work remains highly vulnerable to any interruption in the power source. Unsaved work exists only temporarily in the computer's memory chips and disappears if the computer is turned off even for a moment. But saved work exists on a disk from which it can be easily retrieved — as long as no one accidentally damages the disk or erases the document file. In practice, power outages and surges cause less trouble than people cause. The most common way to lose data is to mismanage — by deleting, losing, or miscopying — your files, and you can also easily damage or misplace your storage disks. Experienced computer users always make backup copies of their work. But, believe it or not, the best safety measure is to print out a hard (paper) copy. (For more on file management and making backup copies, see p. 474.)

Alienation and Discomfort.   Since almost all of us learned to write and read with ink and paper, writing with a keyboard and a monitor can seem disorienting and unnatural at first. Some writers miss the action of the typewriter or the feel of the pen and paper. According to author William Zinsser, others miss the satisfaction of being able to rip a page out of the typewriter and "crumble it in a fit of frustration or rage." Computers can also be physically uncomfortable. Staring at a monitor will fatigue your eyes faster than reading from paper. Most screens display only about twenty-four lines at a time, some as few as sixteen; so scrolling through text on screen can be tedious compared with flipping back and forth through a stack of paper.

Long hours working with a keyboard and a mouse can also cause inflammation in the tendons of the wrist, a condition known as *carpal tunnel syndrome* or *repetitive stress syndrome*. This problem can be painful and even debilitating, but avoiding it is not difficult if you take precautions. Take frequent breaks to stretch your fingers (about five minutes to each hour of steady work); keep your wrist straight (a wrist rest pad can help); and type with a soft touch.

Lack of Access.   You can carry a pen and paper with you anywhere, but you can't easily carry a computer around with you in your pocket. Computers are certainly more expensive to own and operate than conventional writing tools, and many writers don't have easy access to one.

Information Overload.   Computers have the potential to present enormous amounts of information to the writer, and this glut of information may be overwhelming. If you use a computer to gather information off the Internet, CD-ROMs, or electronic library databases, you can become stymied by the oceans of information at your fingertips. A word processor might also free you to compose volumes of your own material — a generally beneficial feature. But you may then be faced with a new problem — having to sort through piles of your own writing.

An Introduction to Word Processing

To get the most out of word-processing software, you must become familiar with your program's features, tools, and commands. Software designers try to make programs easy to use, but they must also try to meet the needs of as many customers as possible. The result is that a program's *interface* — the manner in which the program interacts with the user — can at first seem cluttered and confusing. Most beginners need someone to help them learn how to use a word-processing program, but others just pick up an instruction manual and ferret out the directions for themselves, finding what works by trial and error. A combination of personal advice and going it alone is probably the best approach. Do whatever feels comfortable for you, but prepare yourself for obstacles and frustrations.

Learning to use new products takes time and patience, and at times we may feel that the hours we save by using computer technology are offset by the hours we spend learning how to operate the software. In fact, many computer users find that over the long run they gain more from thoroughly understanding their current software than from trying to keep up with all the latest upgrades and gadgets being produced by the computer industry.

As computers have become faster and more powerful, they have also become easier to operate. Computer and software manufacturers want to make using their products easy for everyone so that the computer revolution can keep growing. Word processors in particular have become easy to operate. Now is a good time to catch up with the swiftly advancing technology. Most recent versions of major word-processing programs employ a common set of user-friendly commands and functions. Once you learn some of the basic commands, you should be able to transfer your knowledge easily from one word-processing program to another.

The purpose of this introduction to word processing is both to present the basic operations of word processors and to describe how these operations can help you to draft and format a college paper. Within the space of this textbook, we cannot provide you with all the information necessary to master all the word-processing software programs on the market today. But we can describe those things that most computers, word processors, and software programs have in common. The best way to start is to ask someone to guide you while you are actually sitting with your hands on a computer. This section will help you make the most of such tutoring sessions and will be of great help if you can't find anyone to lend assistance.

NOTE: Please keep in mind that although this section describes word processors in general, you should be able to apply these descriptions to most word processors. Be aware that word processors have many more features than you need to produce most college papers; explore these other features when you find the time and are feeling adventurous.

BASIC WORD-PROCESSING CONCEPTS

Word processors operate according to instructions known as *commands*. Some of these commands are named in association with typewriter operations. For instance, the terms *tabs, margins, single spacing,* and *double spacing* — which are associated primarily with typewriters — are still used in word-processing programs. But even though the computer's keyboard resembles a typewriter's, you shouldn't make the mistake of thinking that you can treat the computer like a glorified typewriter. Doing so will cause some problems. For example, to center text horizontally with a typewriter, you use the tab key or space bar until you reach the middle of the page. But imitating this technique on a word processor may not give you the results you want; you should use the Center command instead. In other words, word processors have a logic and a terminology all their own.

Understanding Computers.   If you are new to word processing, the definitions below will help you to avoid mistakes that could result in the loss of your work. The physical objects that make up a computer — such as the disks, keyboard, central processing unit, monitor, mouse, and cables — constitute its *hardware*. In contrast, applications, files, and operating systems are known as *software*. Storing and managing files safely will be easier if you become familiar with the most common types of disk and understand how hardware and software work together.

Disk. A disk is used to record and store data. *Floppy disks* are the small, portable disks used in floppy drives. The 3½-inch micro floppy is currently the most popular computer disk. It comes in a square plastic case designed to protect the disk inside. A hard disk is the larger and faster disk inside a hard drive. A cartridge is a small, removable hard disk; it has a much larger capacity than a floppy.

Floppy drive and removable disk drive. On the front of most computers, you will find a narrow slot into which you can insert floppy disks. This device, which reads information from the disks, is known as a *floppy drive*. Some computers also have drives for removable cartridges. The slots on these drives are slightly wider, but they perform the same function as floppy drives.

Hard drive. A *hard drive* is a device similar to a floppy drive, except that you cannot remove its disk. A hard disk resides permanently inside the computer and is therefore a more secure and permanent place to store information than a floppy — and it usually has a far larger storage capacity.

CD drive. Many newer computers also contain a CD drive that can read multimedia and audio compact discs. Most of these drives are *read-only* drives, meaning that you cannot save work onto a compact disc.

Program and application. A *program* is an extensive set of instructions that tell the computer what to do. An *application* is a computer program designed to do a certain job, like word processing, drawing, or sending electronic mail. Applications are also known as *software*.

File or document. A *file* or a *document* is a new software item that an application has created. Think of it as a tiny packet of information stored under a particular name. In word processing, a file is generally any text or manuscript that exists in electronic form instead of on paper. For example, the file "My research paper" might hold the entire contents of your twenty-page research paper. Some word-processing programs refer to files as documents because this term sounds a little more like something from the world of writing than computing; the two words are used almost interchangeably.

Operating system. The *operating system* (for example, Windows 98 or the Macintosh OS) is a complicated set of smaller programs that enables the computer to run applications. Usually the operating system is stored permanently on the hard disk and starts up automatically when you turn on the computer. The operating system determines the "look and feel" of what appears on the screen of the computer. Much of it is stored in something called a *system folder*. If you decide to modify the operating system in any way, be sure that you understand what you are doing because the computer uses the operating system to function properly.

Formatting Your Manuscript. The following operations are invaluable for creating attractive, effective papers. See Figure 21.1 for a visual representation of many of the important terms discussed here.

Fonts. A *font* is a particular design of the letters and other characters that make up printed text. Fonts come in all sizes and shapes; some are flowery, and others look like what you would get from a typewriter. For college papers you should use conventional fonts. Courier is the name of the most widely accepted font. Helvetica, Times Roman, and Palatino are other fonts that give a paper a serious academic appearance. Generally, college papers are not the place to experiment with different type sizes: 12-point type is the standard, although some instructors accept the smaller 10-point type.

Italics, Underline, Bold. Most word processors make changing the style of your text easy. Italic type looks *like this*. To make text italic, first choose Italics from the appropriate menu, then type, and then choose Italics again to turn off the function. Or you can type first, select the text you want to italicize, and then select the Italics function. In college writing, text styles are used accord-

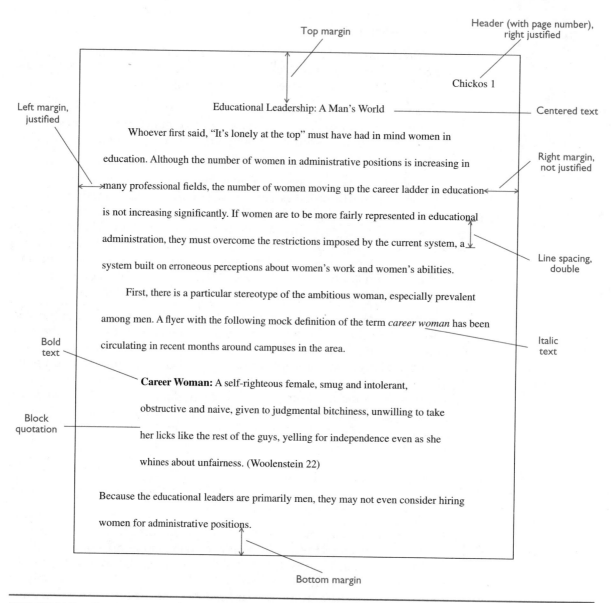

FIGURE 21.1.   Format Concepts for Word Processing

ing to conventions and not generally for the purpose of decoration or expression. Underlining evolved as a way to format manuscripts when typists were unable to produce italics. Therefore, italicizing is generally preferable to underlining if you have the choice. College papers do not usually require **bold type**: headings and subheadings are the only widely accepted uses of boldface.

Line spacing. This term refers to the amount of space between lines of type. College papers almost always require double spacing. Make sure a document is set to double line spacing before you begin entering text. You can also select a block of text and set the line spacing for that particular block only.

Page numbers, headers, footers. Almost all word processors will automatically number pages for you. If you need to place your last name or a brief title adjacent to the page number, you should use a header or a footer. A *header* is writing that is preset to appear at the top of every page in a document. A *footer* is similar — only it appears at the bottom of every page. Automatic page numbers, headers, and footers can be tricky if you don't want them to appear on the first page, or if you want the first page numbered to be something other than 1. Using these functions can require a little practice, so don't try to figure out how to use them at the last minute.

Centering and justification. If you want text centered horizontally in the middle of your page (as on a title page), use the Center function. You may either turn the Center function on and then type, or select already typed text and then center it. Normal text is *left justified* — that is, aligned so that it is even with the left margin. Page numbers and headers are usually the only things that require alignment with the right margin. *Full justification* stretches lines of text so that each line touches both the left and right margins, like the text in this book and most books. Using full justification on word-processed papers is not a good idea because it can result in awkward spacing between letters and words.

Margins. Most word processors allow you to change the margins by entering measurements into a dialog box that appears when you choose the appropriate item within the Format menu. Top and bottom margins are usually preset to 1 inch. Different instructors have different standards for left and right margins, but 1 to 1½ inches is typical. If you have specific guidelines for your papers, be sure to practice setting margins well before your deadline.

First-line indentation and tabs. In most word processors, you can set first-line indentation in two ways: you can either enter a measurement in a dialog box that appears within the Format menu, or you can drag the indent markers on the ruler. In some word-processing systems, the left indent marker on the ruler is actually two markers, which you can move separately; dragging the upper marker a few spaces to the right will indent the first line only of each new paragraph. You can sometimes set tabs by dragging a tab marker onto the ruler.

Creating block quotations. If you need to format an indented block quotation for your paper, don't use tabs (as you would on a typewriter). Some word processors have commands that can automatically set block quotations for you. In general, use the following three steps: first, type the quotation as a separate paragraph; second, select the quote; third, change the left margin for this block of text only.

Style sheets. A *style sheet* or *style* is a set of formatting commands that you can apply to text all at once. For example, you can create a style sheet for block quotations and apply it to all the block quotations in your essay so that each has the same appearance. You can create another for your bibliography, so that each entry in the "Works Cited" list has the same appearance. This technique saves you time and effort: it takes only one or two commands to apply a group of eight or ten characteristics instantly.

Creating a template or master document. As you advance through college courses, you may find yourself using one or two formats again and again. If so, a template can simplify the work of formatting considerably. A *template* (sometimes called a *master document*) is a document that contains only brief sample text that has already been set up with the formatting commands that a typical essay or report requires. By using the Save As command to make a duplicate of the template under a new name, you can use this document again and again. For example, for a research paper that needs to be formatted in MLA style, you might open a template entitled "MLA template" and use the Save As function to save it as "EN 102 research paper." Such a template might include these elements:

> A header with your last name and the page number at the right, positioned one-half inch from the top of the page
>
> One-inch margins at the top, bottom, left, and right
>
> A sample of body text in 12-point Courier, left-justified, double-spaced, and indented on the first line only
>
> A sample of block quotation text, indented ten spaces from the left margin
>
> A sample "Works Cited" page that includes a sample entry with the second line indented five spaces

Once you have made a duplicate of the template under a new name, you are free to replace sample text with the text of your new paper, making use of the preset formats.

Getting Help.   Word processors usually contain online information that can help you solve many computer problems. Some Help programs are better than others, but all are valuable. Help programs are especially useful for finding commands and features that you know your word processor has but that you can't locate—a common problem. The Help function is organized according to the names of these commands and features, and it includes an alphabetical index. The descriptions and definitions that you have just read about should give you a sense of what to look for when using Help.

Using Writing Tools.   Most modern word-processing systems come with a set of writing tools, such as spell checkers, grammar checkers, or style checkers. If yours does not, such applications are usually readily available at low or no cost. However, like all tools, writing tools work best in the hands of someone who uses them wisely. You cannot rely on them to revise or edit your paper for you. At the best, they can highlight areas that may need improvement and can provide a limited set of possible options; at the worst, they can mislead the uncritical writer and even lead to the introduction of new errors. Master these tools and use them wisely: don't let them use you.

Spell checker. A spell checker locates a word it thinks is misspelled; it highlights the word and prompts you for a response. The spell checker works by matching what you type against words in a dictionary stored electronically in the computer's memory. You may retype the word yourself, select a substitution from the suggestions that the checker provides, or make no change to the word. Spell checkers can be tricky; be sure you understand yours before relying on it. None of these programs is a substitute for human proofreading. Even the cleverest spell checker won't point out certain errors. For example, if you accidentally type *her* instead of *here*, the program won't see the error as a mistake because in its dictionary *her* is a perfectly good word. Spell checking should be the last thing you do before printing your document.

Grammar checker and style checker. Grammar checkers and style checkers search for certain word patterns in your writing and alert you to usages that may be incorrect or awkward. These writing tools can be useful, but they must be used with caution. The checkers do not understand the meanings of words, and so they cannot do the work of an attentive and knowledgeable human reader. At best, these tools make suggestions for revision — suggestions that writers need to consider carefully for themselves. When you use these tools, you need to have a basis for making such decisions and to know enough about grammatical correctness and the principles of good style to know whether to accept the suggestions these tools offer. If you don't have this basis, these tools could actually work against you.

Nevertheless, you do not need to memorize all the rules of grammar before you write with a word processor. Instead, keep your reference handbook open on your desk as you run through your document with the grammar checker or style checker. Whenever the computer makes a suggestion that you are unsure about, use your handbook to help you decide what to do. Several of the computer tips included in the "Quick Editing Guide" found at the back of *The Bedford Guide for College Writers* are particularly useful for this method. They give detailed information about the accuracy of grammar or style checkers when identifying specific problems. Used in this way, grammar and style checkers can become powerful learning tools — but they cannot do the work of revision for you.

Thesaurus. Many word processors include a thesaurus that provides an efficient way to search for the exact word you need without turning away from your computer. Use it as you would use any thesaurus, to find the exact word, not to find fancy words that might have inappropriate connotations. Be aware that the thesaurus that comes with a word processor may offer fewer word choices than a book version.

Outliners. Some word processors contain a special module or a set of commands that makes constructing an outline composed of headings and subheadings easy. Outliners are also available as separate, stand-alone programs. Any outliner can help you to arrange your ideas and design an effective structure for your paper.

A Few Practical Tips for Word Processing

Even after you have become familiar with a word processor, try to learn from mistakes that others have made. The following list of practical tips can help you avoid some of the classic pitfalls of word processing.

Count to Five.   Before quitting, closing, exiting, or deleting, pause for a count of five, and be sure you're not about to make a mistake. Use this technique before you leave your workstation, especially if it is an open-use, on-campus computer. Did you save everything? Did you make the necessary printouts? Did you eject your disk and then leave the station in proper order? Taking five before leaving your computer is especially important if you use an e-mail account; you must be sure that you are completely disconnected so that others cannot access your account.

Don't Get Carried Away.   Word processors offer amazing features: you can import graphics, create tables, and incorporate dozens of elaborate fonts in different sizes and even twisted shapes. Use advanced design features whenever they help clarify your writing. However, strange fonts, full justification, and an abundance of text styles tend to distract readers of academic work. You should resist the temptation to make your document look like a three-ring circus. A laser or ink-jet printer will produce crisp, black copy and can enhance the readability of what you write. If you have access to one, you won't need anything fancy to create an attractive manuscript.

Plan for Glitches.   Computer systems are more complicated than pens, pencils, or typewriters; therefore, they provide a much greater chance of something going wrong. If you rely on computers and you flirt with deadlines, eventually you're going to get burned. The old excuse "the dog ate my homework" has been replaced with "the computer ate my file." Instructors have, by now, heard this new excuse so many times that they are less sympathetic than ever. Glitches are simply part of the territory, so prepare for them.

Practice Careful File Management.   Name your files in consistent patterns, and use numbers and dates in your filenames to keep track of which versions are most recent. Make backup copies of everything. You should have one working disk and one backup disk, which you should update weekly; if you want to be extra careful, keep one backup disk with you or at school and another one at home. Label your disks carefully, and buy a plastic case to store them in. Don't let the disks melt or be exposed to something that might demagnetize them (such as a strong magnet or an airport security device). In addition to electronic backups, you should make hard-copy (paper) backups. You can always retype from paper, but a damaged disk, deleted file, or broken computer can leave you with nothing to work from. A good rule of thumb is that if you spent thirty solid minutes or more working on a document, print out that work before quitting for the day. Print or photocopy two copies of a file that you absolutely can't afford to lose. (If you are printing out something just for security, you can use single spacing and a small font to save paper.) Put the date on the printout so that you can separate one version from another.

Don't Fall into the Twilight Zone.   Some writers become so absorbed with writing on a computer that they lose track of time. You also want to avoid CRT (cathode ray tube) fatigue: staring at a monitor for extended periods of time is more of a strain on your eyes than reading print on paper. For reading comfort, adjust the angle of your monitor and also its level of brightness. Take breaks now and then to stretch your wrists and back, exercise, and take light refreshments.

Keep Reference Materials within Reach.   If these resources aren't nearby, you probably won't use them when you really need to. Keep computer manuals, a dictionary, and your reference handbook handy. These books still provide the kind of help that a computer can't offer, and they can save you time and frustration.

Try Revising, Editing, and Proofreading on a Hard (Paper) Copy.   Because a typical screen displays only about twenty-four lines at a time, you may have difficulty holding in mind an entire piece of writing while working online. In a long composition, large changes that involve several paragraphs may be harder to envision on screen than on several pages spread across a table. Because word processors make tinkering with a draft at the level of the sentence and the paragraph easy, they can make us reluctant to begin those extensive, deep revisions that a first draft often requires. Keep in mind that printing out a draft and then rewriting from scratch in a new file is sometimes the most effective way to make progress. Printing out a draft can be equally useful in the later stages of revision. One of the secrets of editing is to look at a paper from a different perspective. If you composed online, editing and proofreading from paper makes mistakes stand out.

Change the Look of Your Text.   Changing the look of your text is one of the best ways to gain a fresh perspective on it so that mistakes are easier to notice. Enlarging your text using a big, bold font is one good way to shake things up. Or try inserting two returns after each sentence, so that each sentence is surrounded by white space. This last technique is especially effective if you then scroll backward from the end of the document to read and edit one sentence at a time. But save a backup copy of your file before trying either of these techniques: you'll want to be sure that you can restore the document to its proper formatting after you have finished editing.

Don't Think of a Word Processor as a Typewriter.   Computer users who are making a transition from the typewriter to the word processor sometimes treat the two the same. But they need to bear in mind that these writing machines actually function very differently. For example, to move text away from the left margin using a word processor, you should use the Center function or the Tab key instead of the space bar. You should not use the Return or Enter key at the end of every line of text; almost all word processors have a function known as Word Wrap or Line Wrap that will break your lines properly. If you've been using a typewriter for a long time, it may be hard to break these habits, but if you don't, you'll end up with some odd-looking printouts. More important, if you impose the rigid framework of typewriting conventions on the fluid text stored in a computer, you won't be able to take advantage of the full power and flexibility of word processing, which allows you to make sweeping changes and minor revisions with a few simple keystrokes.

Writing on Computer Networks

Computer networks — especially the Internet and the World Wide Web — are part of a dramatic revolution in communications that is redefining our world. Using personal computers, inexpensive software, and ordinary phone lines, people on a campus or around the world can now talk — and send pictures and sounds — to one another with amazing speed and ease. Instructors are experimenting with new ways to teach many college courses, and students are finding they have a wealth of new research sources at their fingertips. Every day there are new developments — new places to visit online and new features that make the old places more useful.

Knowing about these changes is important for you. If your instructor teaches a course in a networked classroom, corresponds with students over e-mail, or expects you to incorporate Internet research in your papers, you need to become acquainted with computer networks to do well in class. But even if you don't, take advantage of whatever computer access or training you have available on your campus. Not only will computer skills make you more attractive to future employers, but they will prove to be valuable tools in your everyday life. Whether as consumers or scholars, you all can benefit from becoming a more sophisticated consumer and a more discriminating user of computer technology.

You will find more information on computer networks and some useful links to Internet resources at the Bedford/St. Martin's Web site at <http://www.bedfordstmartins.com/bedguide>; click on *The Bedford Guide for College Writers*.

UNDERSTANDING NETWORKS

A *computer network* is simply a connection of two or more computers that can communicate with each other. Networks come in different sizes and varying degrees of complexity, but they all follow the same basic principles.

LANs (Local-Area Networks).   One of the simplest computer networks is known as a LAN, or local-area network. More and more writing courses are being taught in computer labs and computer classrooms, and most of these facilities link their computers through a LAN so that the computers in the room can communicate. With the proper software, students in networked classrooms can write to others in their class in real time — that is, as soon as they send their words into the network, classmates can read what they have written. Unlike many class discussions in which the instructor or one or two students do all the talking, real-time interchanges allow everyone in the class to participate on an equal basis. If you feel nervous about speaking publicly or prefer a few moments to fine-tune what you have to say, you may enjoy such a computer-mediated discussion.

If your class participates in real-time interchanges, you should be aware that instructors can and often do print transcripts of these conversations. You are, therefore, more accountable for what you say than in most conventional class discussions. Some people can be misled into thinking that computers are toys for playing games, but classroom discussions are generally serious business, requiring a mature attitude.

WANs (Wide-Area Networks).   Computers can also be linked through networks much larger than a LAN. A small network of computers within a lab can easily be connected to a larger network of computers throughout an entire school, and your schoolwide network can then be connected to other schoolwide networks. In fact, schools that are externally networked form an important segment of the Internet.

The Internet.   The Internet is almost exactly what it sounds like — an international network of computers. It is literally a network of networks that links together computers belonging to educational institutions, governments, corporations, and private individuals from around the world. So if the workstation you use in a campus computer lab is connected to the Internet, and you have an account to access the Internet, you have the power to send messages to almost anyone else in the world who also has an account. In a matter of minutes, through your keyboard, you can send a message to the White House or to Buckingham Palace.

The Internet has been growing at a breathtaking pace for several years, and this growth may continue for another decade. In 1994, just three million people used the Internet, the majority of them in the United States. Today, over a hundred million people, all over the world, are using the Internet. According to *The Emerging Digital Economy*, published by the U.S. Department of Commerce, by 2005 a billion people may be connected to the Internet (<http://www.ecommerce.gov>). The Internet's nickname — "the information superhighway" — emphasizes its ability to give computer users quick access to an enormous and expanding fund of information. But not only information (in the narrow sense) travels across the Internet. Virtually every form of human expression from the most serious to the most trivial — ideas, gossip, music, jokes, business transactions, games, reports, music, maps, art reproductions — can circulate between computers as a sequence of electronic pulses on the Net. The bigger the Internet becomes, the more vital it becomes as a means of communicating, doing business, and learning.

World Wide Web.   The World Wide Web has now become the way most users access the Internet's resources. The World Wide Web is not a network separate from the Internet; rather, it is a special way of using the Internet that requires the assistance of a program called a *browser,* such as Netscape Navigator or Microsoft Explorer. The browser makes it possible to receive and view *Web pages* that can incorporate text, images, sound, and video. With a Web browser, exploring the Internet becomes a lively multimedia experience. Clicking on a *link* (a highlighted phrase or button) in a Web page takes you directly to a new page or area, even if that page is located on a computer hundreds or thousands of miles away. Navigating freely among Web sites in different locations is often described as *surfing the Web.* Many of the expressions used to describe the Web — *surfing, navigating, cyberspace* — relate to the sensation of traveling, almost in a different dimension, that comes from browsing the Web.

Because the World Wide Web is so easy and exciting to use, it has grown rapidly during the 1990s. You may have noticed that Web site addresses or Uniform Resource Locators (URLs) have begun to appear everywhere — notably in advertisements and on packaging. We cited a URL above — <http://www.ecommerce.gov> — as the source for our information about the rate of the Internet's growth. The Web is becoming increasingly useful to businesses as a way to advertise and sell products. But this use has not diminished the importance of the Web as a research and communication tool; in fact, it has only widened the circle of users.

The Web has allowed users to become familiar with a new mode of computer writing that lets readers follow links at will, instead of requiring them to read pages in sequence like printed text. This system of organizing ideas and information is known as *hypertext,* and effective Web pages generally use this approach to present their content. You can create your own hypertext documents by marking up a text file with the special set of codes, known as Hypertext Markup Language (HTML), that browsers use to interpret Web pages.

WRITING ON NETWORKS

Computer networks have the capacity to join dozens, hundreds, or even thousands of people in a "virtual" conversation — the global village come to life. This section gives you a brief overview of the different formats that conversation can take.

Sending and receiving information through a global network of computers gives the writer awesome powers but also awesome responsibilities. Regardless of whether you write on a local-area network or the World Wide Web, you must be aware of the following point: *Any writing that you send out over a computer network should be considered public discourse — as public as if you were reading your words aloud in a crowded hallway.* Do not be misled into thinking that something you wrote in the seemingly quiet, private space of your room or a lab will not be read and reacted to by others. You are legally and ethically responsible for what you post to a network; you could even be expelled from school or arrested for the things you write. And any research information you take from the Internet should be documented just as you document evidence from books, periodicals, and interviews.

E-Mail. E-mail (electronic mail) serves as the most basic — and most common — form of writing on networks. E-mail works like conventional mail in that you can write letters or messages and send them to other people if you know their addresses. But instead of street addresses that correspond to actual physical locations, e-mail addresses represent electronic storage places on computers.

The format of e-mail is fairly standard, regardless of the specific software used. It is based on a time-tested format from the nonvirtual (paper) world — the memorandum. When sending e-mail, you usually are asked to type in the address of one or more recipients in a *field* (area where you can type) designated "To"; you usually can send copies of the message to still more people by putting their addresses in the "cc" field. The topic of the message is typed into the "Subject" field. The computer inserts a date on the final message. The largest field is the one where you type your message. (See Figure 21.2.) When the message is sent to the person or people identified in the "to" and "cc" fields, the information you entered under "to," "cc," and "subject" is assembled with the date at the top of the message in a *header,* sometimes joined by other information about how and when the message was sent and where it went on its trip across the Internet. (See Figure 21.3.) The recipient of an e-mail can easily respond to it, forward it to other people, print it out, file it, or delete it altogether.

Newsgroups. Writing on the Internet can involve much more than just sending letters back and forth to one correspondent at a time. A *newsgroup* is an ongoing discussion among many participants on some particular subject — hobbies, politics, sports, technologies, and many other subjects. One of the richest sources of information on the Internet is Usenet, a special network

FIGURE 21.2.   Writing
an E-Mail Message

New Message — E-mail program

| File   Edit   Insert   Tools   Help |

To: alicesmith@university.edu

cc:

Subject: Your ideas on our proposal

Dear Alice:

Thanks for looking at our proposal and offering your
comments. I think the idea of creating a daycare here on
campus for parents attending classes is a feasible one, but
I appreciate the obstacles you've pointed out. I think I
can supply statistics supporting my claim that the number
of students--and potential students--affected is
surprisingly large. But I

FIGURE 21.3.   E-Mail
Message as Received

Return-Path: <steveortega@university.edu>
From: Steve Ortega
To: Alice Smith <alicesmith@university.edu>
Subject: Your ideas on our proposal
Date: 8 Sept 1999 14:11:55 -0500

Dear Alice:

Thanks for looking at our proposal and offering your comments.
I think the idea of creating a daycare here on campus for parents
attending classes is a feasible one, but I appreciate the
obstacles you've pointed out. I think I can supply statistics
supporting my claim that the number of students--and potential
students--affected is surprisingly large. But I don't know how
I could really prove that the university will gain more money
(through new tuitions) than it loses (by offering daycare). Do
you think that the example of another university that has
successfully started a daycare program would be convincing
enough? I also want to add some of the quotations we collected in
our informal survey. I'll send you the revised proposal next
week.

Thanks,
Steve

that provides access to thousands of newsgroups. Anyone can join in the electronic conversation by using a newsreader program (often incorporated within a Web browser) to read and post messages. Newsgroups are open to the public but must be subscribed to, which is simply a matter of telling the newsreader the names of the newsgroups that you'd like to keep an eye on.

The democratic culture of these forums is both the greatest strength of newsgroups and their greatest weakness. They bring together opinions and ideas from the well-informed and the uninformed alike, and in some instances assessing the quality of the information you find there may be difficult. But as in most conversations, strong, well-informed ideas usually emerge clearly in the long run, and the exchange of views is usually illuminating.

Mailing Lists.   A mailing list is like a newsgroup, except that the discussion is restricted to subscribers who agree to receive messages to the list in their e-mail boxes. Subscribers send messages from their own e-mail accounts to a program that automatically distributes incoming messages to all the list's subscribers. No one knows exactly how many lists exist, but they number in the tens of thousands. You can find out more about these lists on the World Wide Web (<http://www.liszt.com>). Be aware, however, that while a newsgroup is something like an open town meeting, a mailing list is more like a private club. Some mailing lists are meant to serve only a select group of experts; others are intended for a much wider readership. Before you decide to subscribe to a list, monitor the discussion for a while to understand its tone and standards. When you do contribute for the first time, introduce yourself to the other participants on the list.

Internet Real-Time Discussions.   You can also participate in conversations that take place almost as fast as you can input your words. MOOs, MUDs, and IRCs are three of the most common Internet programs that allow people to join in imaginary conference rooms to conduct real-time interchanges. These real-time programs are somewhat controversial because they are often misused as ways to waste time. But some of these imaginary rooms serve as online writing centers staffed with instructors who can help you with your writing.

THE BASICS OF NETIQUETTE

The word *netiquette* combines the words *net* and *etiquette* to describe the principles of good behavior for writing on computer networks. Here are some principles you should observe, whether you are sending an e-mail to a single correspondent or posting a message to a public forum such as a newsgroup.

1. Always use a greeting at the beginning of a message and a salutation at the end. Include your name and e-mail address at the end, as you cannot assume that the routing information in the header of the message will clearly identify you.

2. Always fill in the subject line of an e-mail message. In private e-mail, this information helps your correspondent to identify and file your message. On newsgroups and mailing lists, the subject line helps readers decide whether your message is of interest to them.

3. Although the ease and speed of e-mail makes firing off messages instantly very tempting, e-mail is a form of writing, so you should express your thoughts clearly, economically, and completely to avoid confusing or misleading your readers. Always take a moment to proofread and polish your message before you send it.

4. Try to limit important ideas to one per paragraph, and indicate each main topic near the beginning of the paragraph. Keep paragraphs short. An e-mail that looks uncluttered and is easy to skim stands a better chance of being read and responded to than one that isn't.

5. Avoid writing in all capital letters (a habit known as *shouting*) or all lowercase letters. You can use asterisks around a word to emphasize it, but do so sparingly.

6. Avoid using special characters, such as accented characters, super-scripted numerals, and "curly quotes" (or smart quotes). Although word processors can type and print a great many special characters, e-mail programs recognize only the basic alphabet (both upper and lower case), numerals, and punctuation marks.

7. Avoid overlong signature files. A signature file in your e-mail account contains text you put at the end of every e-mail message you send. Most people use them to store their full name, affiliation, contact information, and perhaps a brief quotation or quip. Signature files that are too long (usually because the quotation or quip is too long) cause on-screen clutter, eat up storage space, and lead to unnecessarily long printouts.

8. When participating in a mailing list, consult the FAQ (frequently asked questions) file first if you have a question about procedure or protocol. If you can't find a FAQ file, send a brief inquiry to the list for directions. The FAQ file will provide instructions on how to handle routine requests or activities, such as corresponding with a contact person.

9. When responding to someone else's e-mail message, be sure what you are referring to is clear. Most programs let you click a Reply button so that the original post is automatically duplicated in your message. If the original message is lengthy, you may want to omit the extraneous passages.

10. Don't use academic mailing lists for commercial purposes.

11. Cite all quotations and references, and give complete (and accurate) URLs when appropriate.

12. Never forward chain letters because they can quickly grow into monstrosities that clog e-mail servers and prevent important messages from getting through.

13. Do not send unwanted junk e-mail to others (a practice known as *spamming*).

14. Forward private mail to others only when you have the author's permission.

15. Be respectful and courteous. Do not participate in *flaming* — rude, hostile, or impolite writing that is exchanged over a computer network. Flaming occurs when writers erroneously feel protected from being responsible for their words because of the illusion of anonymity that the computer provides. You should certainly express your views, but continue to consider how others might react to what you say. Remember that everything you write can easily be forwarded to someone else.

16. Use sarcasm and humor with care. On the screen, they often can be misinterpreted as hostile remarks or flaming.

A WRITER'S
READER

Contents

Introduction:
Reading to Write

A Writer's Reader is a collection of professional essays that you will find worthwhile. We have carefully selected these thirty-eight essays for specific reasons. We hope, first of all, that you will read these pieces simply for the sake of reading — enjoying, comprehending, responding to the ideas presented. Good writers read widely, and in doing so, they increase their knowledge of the English language and of the craft of writing. Second, we hope you will actively study these essays as solid examples of the resources and strategies explored in *A Writer's Guide* and of effective writing in general. The authors represented in this reader, experts from varied fields, have faced the same problems and choices you do when you write. You can learn from studying their decisions, structures, and techniques. Finally, we hope that you will find the content of the essays intriguing and that the information presented in the selections and the questions posed at the ends of the essays will give you some ideas to write about.

Each chapter in *A Writer's Reader* concentrates on a broad theme that will be familiar and interesting to you — families, men and women, American diversity, popular culture, and technology and society. Within each chapter you'll find a variety of voices and perspectives, including four new essays from the Internet. In some essays the writers focus on the inner world and write personal experience and opinion papers. In others the authors turn their attention to the outer world and write informational, analytical, and persuasive essays. Some of the writers — Stephen King and Amy Tan, for example — may already be familiar to you. Many of the others we hope will become new friends. Some of the messages and arguments presented here will have you nodding in agreement, some will have you strongly disagreeing, and perhaps others will lead you to pause and reconsider long-held beliefs. Within each chapter, the last two selections are a pair of essays on the same subject. We've provided these pairs so that you can see how different writers use different strategies to address similar issues.

Each section in the reader begins with a picture and a Web search activity, which are intended to stimulate you to begin to think and write. Each essay is preceded by biographical information about the author, placing him or her — and the essay itself — into a cultural and informational context. Following each essay is a set of discussion questions and writing suggestions. The five "Questions to Start You Thinking" cover the same ground for every selection: meaning, writing strategies, critical reading, vocabulary, and comparison or contrast of this selection with one or more of the other selections in *A Writer's Reader*. After these questions come a couple of journal prompts designed to get your writing juices flowing (for more about journal writing, see p. 366). Each paired essay is also followed by a question that asks you about a connection between the essays. Finally, two possible composition assignments are designed with specific suggestions for writing. The first assignment is directed toward your inner world, asking you to draw generally on your personal experience and your understanding of the essay. The second is outer directed, asking you to look outside yourself and write an analytical or argumentative paper, one that may require further reading or research.

A Writer's Reader, an integral part of *The Bedford Guide for College Writers*, is directly connected to *A Writer's Guide*. The essays in the reader illustrate various uses of the four resources of writers from Part One in *A Writer's Guide* — recall, observation, conversation, and imagination. They exemplify the critical thinking skills for writing from Part Two of *A Writer's Guide* — reading critically, analyzing, comparing and contrasting, explaining causes and effects, taking a stand, proposing a solution, and evaluating. They also illustrate many of the writing strategies explained in Part Four. In addition, at the end of each chapter in Part One and in many of the chapters in Part Four, you will find "Making Connections," a brief passage that draws your attention to essays in the reader that use the resource, the critical thinking skill, or the strategies explained in the chapter.

Chapter 22

Families

Web Search

Search the Library of Congress online archive called American Memory (<http://memory.loc.gov/ammem/>) by entering a subject related to your family's history, such as a state or city where your ancestors or family have lived, an industry a relative has worked in, or a historical event or natural disaster that affected your family in some way. Locate and study a specific photograph or document on this subject. Imagine that your family has a direct connection to the photo or document you have found. Write an imaginary narrative about one or more members of your family based on your finding.

E. B. (Elwyn Brooks) White *(1899–1985) was born in Mount Vernon, New York. After serving in the army, he graduated from Cornell University and moved to Seattle to work as a reporter. His career led him back to the East Coast, where he joined the staff of the recently established* New Yorker *magazine in 1927. For half a century his satires, poems, and essays helped define that magazine's distinctive style of elegant wit and social comment. He moved to Maine in 1933, and his widely read books for children,* Stuart Little *(1945),* Charlotte's Web *(1952), and* The Trumpet of the Swan *(1970), draw on his life in the country to celebrate life's blend of sadness, happiness, love, and loss. In the following essay, first published in* Harper's *magazine in 1941, White reflects on the experience of returning with his son to a favorite scene from his own childhood.*

AS YOU READ: *Notice what, according to White, changes a person's perspective from childhood to adulthood.*

E. B. White   Once More to the Lake

August 1941

One summer, along about 1904, my father rented a camp on a lake in Maine and took us all there for the month of August. We all got ringworm from some kittens and had to rub Pond's Extract on our arms and legs night and morning, and my father rolled over in a canoe with all his clothes on; but outside of that the vacation was a success and from then on none of us ever thought there was any place in the world like that lake in Maine. We returned summer after summer—always on August 1 for one month. I have since become a salt-water man, but sometimes in summer there are days when the restlessness of the tides and the fearful cold of the sea water and the incessant wind that blows across the afternoon and into the evening make me wish for the placidity of a lake in the woods. A few weeks ago this feeling got so strong I bought myself a couple of bass hooks and a spinner and returned to the lake where we used to go, for a week's fishing and to revisit old haunts.

I took along my son, who had never had any fresh water up his nose and who had seen lily pads only from train windows. On the journey over to the lake I began to wonder what it would be like. I wondered how time would have marred this unique, this holy spot—the coves and streams, the hills that the sun set behind, the camps and the paths behind the camps. I was sure that the tarred road would have found it out, and I wondered in what other ways it would be desolated. It is strange how much you can remember about places like that once you allow your mind to return into the grooves that lead back. You remember one thing, and that suddenly reminds you of another thing. I guess I remembered clearest of all the early mornings, when the lake was cool and motionless, remembered how the bedroom smelled of the lumber it was made of and of the wet woods whose scent entered through the screen. The partitions in the camp were thin and did not extend clear to the top of the rooms, and as I was always the first up I would dress softly so as not to wake the others, and sneak out into the sweet outdoors and start out in the canoe, keeping close along the shore in the long shadows of the pines. I remembered being very careful never to rub my paddle against the gunwale° for fear of disturbing the stillness of the cathedral.

The lake had never been what you would call a wild lake. There were cottages sprinkled around the shores, and it was in farming country although the shores of the lake were quite heavily wooded. Some of the cottages were owned by nearby farmers, and you would live at the shore and eat your meals at the farmhouse. That's what our family did. But although it wasn't wild, it was a fairly large and undisturbed lake and there were places in it that, to a child at least, seemed infinitely remote and primeval. 3

I was right about the tar: it led to within half a mile of the shore. But when I got back there, with my boy, and we settled into a camp near a farmhouse and into the kind of summertime I had known, I could tell that it was going to be pretty much the same as it had been before — I knew it, lying in bed the first morning smelling the bedroom and hearing the boy sneak quietly out and go off along the shore in a boat. I began to sustain the illusion that he was I, and therefore, by simple transposition, that I was my father. This sensation persisted, kept cropping up all the time we were there. It was not an entirely new feeling, but in this setting it grew much stronger. I seemed to be living a dual existence. I would be in the middle of some simple act, I would be picking up a bait box or laying down a table fork, or I would be saying something and suddenly it would be not I but my father who was saying the words or making the gesture. It gave me a creepy sensation. 4

We went fishing the first morning. I felt the same damp moss covering the worms in the bait can, and saw the dragonfly alight on the tip of my rod as it hovered a few inches from the surface of the water. It was the arrival of this fly that convinced me beyond any doubt that everything was as it always had been, that the years were a mirage, and that there had been no years. The small waves were the same, chucking the rowboat under the chin as we fished at anchor, and the boat was the same boat, the same color green and the ribs broken in the same places, and under the floorboards the same fresh water leavings and debris — the dead hellgrammite, the wisps of moss, the rusty discarded fishhook, the dried blood from yesterday's catch. We stared silently at the tips of our rods, at the dragonflies that came and went. I lowered the tip of mine into the water, tentatively, pensively dislodging the fly, which darted two feet away, poised, darted two feet back, and came to rest again a little farther up the rod. There had been no years between the ducking of this dragonfly and the other one — the one that was part of memory. I looked at the boy, who was silently watching his fly, and it was my hands that held his rod, my eyes watching. I felt dizzy and didn't know which rod I was at the end of. 5

We caught two bass, hauling them in briskly as though they were mackerel, pulling them over the side of the boat in a businesslike manner without 6

gunwale: Upper edge of the side of a boat.

any landing net, and stunning them with a blow on the back of the head. When we got back for a swim before lunch, the lake was exactly where we had left it, the same number of inches from the dock, and there was only the merest suggestion of a breeze. This seemed an utterly enchanted sea, this lake you could leave to its own devices for a few hours and come back to, and find that it had not stirred, this constant and trustworthy body of water. In the shallows, the dark, water-soaked sticks and twigs, smooth and old, were undulating in clusters on the bottom against the clean ribbed sand, and the track of the mussel was plain. A school of minnows swam by, each minnow with its small individual shadow, doubling the attendance, so clear and sharp in the sunlight. Some of the other campers were in swimming, along the shore, one of them with a cake of soap, and the water felt thin and clear and unsubstantial. Over the years there had been this person with the cake of soap, this cultist, and here he was. There had been no years.

Up to the farmhouse to dinner through the teeming dusty field, the road   7
under our sneakers was only a two-track road. The middle track was missing, the one with the marks of the hooves and the splotches of dried, flaky manure. There had always been three tracks to choose from in choosing which track to walk in; now the choice was narrowed down to two. For a moment I missed terribly the middle alternative. But the way led past the tennis court, and something about the way it lay there in the sun reassured me; the tape had loosened along the backline, the alleys were green with plantains° and other weeds, and the net (installed in June and removed in September) sagged in the dry noon, and the whole place steamed with midday heat and hunger and emptiness. There was a choice of pie for dessert, and one was blueberry and one was apple, and the waitresses were the same country girls, there having been no passage of time, only the illusion of it as in a dropped curtain — the waitresses were still fifteen; their hair had been washed, that was the only difference — they had been to the movies and seen the pretty girls with the clean hair.

Summertime, oh, summertime, pattern of life indelible° with fade-proof   8
lake, the wood unshatterable, the pasture with the sweetfern and the juniper forever and ever, summer without end; this was the background, and the life along the shore was the design, the cottages with their innocent and tranquil design, their tiny docks with the flagpole and the American flag floating against the white clouds in the blue sky, the little paths over the roots of the trees leading from camp to camp and the paths leading back to the outhouses and the can of lime for sprinkling, and at the souvenir counters at the store the miniature birchbark canoes and the postcards that showed things looking a little better than they looked. This was the American family at play, escaping the city heat, wondering whether the newcomers in the camp at the head of the cove were "common" or "nice," wondering whether it was true that the people who drove up for Sunday dinner at the farmhouse were turned away because there wasn't enough chicken.

plantains: Common wild plants.   **indelible:** Unable to be removed.

It seemed to me, as I kept remembering all this, that those times and those summers had been infinitely precious and worth saving. There had been jollity and peace and goodness. The arriving (at the beginning of August) had been so big a business in itself, at the railway station the farm wagon drawn up, the first smell of the pine-laden air, the first glimpse of the smiling farmer, and the great importance of the trunks and your father's enormous authority in such matters, and the feel of the wagon under you for the long ten-mile haul, and at the top of the last long hill catching the first view of the lake after eleven months of not seeing this cherished body of water. The shouts and cries of the other campers when they saw you, and the trunks to be unpacked, to give up their rich burden. (Arriving was less exciting nowadays, when you sneaked up in your car and parked it under a tree near the camp and took out the bags and in five minutes it was all over, no fuss, no loud wonderful fuss about trunks.)

Peace and goodness and jollity. The only thing that was wrong now, really, was the sound of the place, an unfamiliar nervous sound of the outboard motors. This was the note that jarred, the one thing that would sometimes break the illusion and set the years moving. In those other summertimes all motors were inboard; and when they were at a little distance, the noise they made was a sedative, an ingredient of summer sleep. They were one-cylinder and two-cylinder engines, and some were make-and-break and some were jump-spark, but they all made a sleepy sound across the lake. The one-lungers throbbed and fluttered, and the twin-cylinder ones purred and purred, and that was a quiet sound, too. But now the campers all had outboards. In the daytime, in the hot mornings, these motors made a petulant, irritable sound; at night in the still evening when the afterglow lit the water, they whined about one's ears like mosquitoes. My boy loved our rented outboard, and his great desire was to achieve single-handed mastery over it, and authority, and he soon learned the trick of choking it a little (but not too much), and the adjustment of the needle valve. Watching him I would remember the things you could do with the old one-cylinder engine with the heavy flywheel,° how you could have it eating out of your hand if you got really close to it spiritually. Motorboats in those days didn't have clutches, and you would make a landing by shutting off the motor at the proper time and coasting in with a dead rudder. But there was a way of reversing them, if you learned the trick, by cutting the switch and putting it on again exactly on the final dying revolution of the flywheel, so that it would kick back against compression and begin reversing. Approaching a dock in a strong following breeze, it was difficult to slow up sufficiently by the ordinary coasting method, and if a boy felt he had complete mastery over his motor, he was tempted to keep it running beyond its time and then reverse it a few feet from the dock. It took a cool nerve, because if you threw the switch a twentieth of a second too soon you would catch the flywheel when it still had speed enough to go up past center, and the boat would leap ahead, charging bull-fashion at the dock.

flywheel: A heavy wheel revolving on a shaft to regulate machinery.

We had a good week at the camp. The bass were biting well and the sun ‖ shone endlessly, day after day. We would be tired at night and lie down in the accumulated heat of the little bedrooms after the long hot day and the breeze would stir almost imperceptibly outside and the smell of the swamp drift in through the rusty screens. Sleep would come easily and in the morning the red squirrel would be on the roof, tapping out his gay routine. I kept remembering everything, lying in bed in the mornings — the small steamboat that had a long rounded stern like the lip of a Ubangi,° and how quietly she ran on the moonlight sails, when the older boys played their mandolins° and the girls sang and we ate doughnuts dipped in sugar, and how sweet the music was on the water in the shining night, and what it had felt like to think about girls then. After breakfast we would go up to the store and the things were in the same place — the minnows in a bottle, the plugs and spinners disarranged and pawed over by the youngsters from the boys' camp, the Fig Newtons and the Beeman's gum. Outside, the road was tarred and cars stood in front of the store. Inside, all was just as it had always been, except there was more Coca-Cola and not so much Moxie and root beer and birch beer and sarsaparilla. We would walk out with the bottle of pop apiece and sometimes the pop would backfire up our noses and hurt. We explored the streams, quietly, where the turtles slid off the sunny logs and dug their way into the soft bottom; and we lay on the town wharf and fed worms to the tame bass. Everywhere we went I had trouble making out which was I, the one walking at my side, the one walking in my pants.

One afternoon while we were at that lake a thunderstorm came up. It was ₁₂ the revival of an old melodrama that I had seen long ago with childish awe. The second-act climax of the drama of the electrical disturbance over a lake in America had not changed in any important respect. This was the big scene. The whole thing was so familiar, the first feeling of oppression and heat and a general air around camp of not wanting to go very far away. In midafternoon (it was all the same) a curious darkening of the sky, and a lull in everything that had made life tick; and then the way the boats suddenly swung the other way at their moorings with the coming of a breeze out of the new quarter, and the premonitory° rumble. Then the kettle drum, then the snare, then the bass drum and cymbals, then crackling light against the dark, and the gods grinning and licking their chops in the hills. Afterward the calm, the rain steadily rustling in the calm lake, the return of light and hope and spirits, and the campers running out in joy and relief to go swimming in the rain, their bright cries perpetuating the deathless joke about how they were getting simply drenched, and the children screaming with delight at the new sensation of bathing in the rain, and the joke about getting drenched linking the generations in a strong indestructible chain. And the comedian who waded in carrying an umbrella.

Ubangi: People who live near the Ubangi River in the Central African Republic and Zaire. The women traditionally pierce and stretch their lips around flat wooden disks.   **mandolins:** Small stringed instruments often used in ballads and folk music.   **premonitory:** A warning.

When the others went swimming my son said he was going in, too. He   13
pulled his dripping trunks from the line where they had hung all through the
shower and wrung them out. Languidly, and with no thought of going in, I
watched him, his hard little body, skinny and bare, saw him wince slightly as
he pulled up around his vitals the small, soggy, icy garment. As he buckled the
swollen belt, suddenly my groin felt the chill of death.

Questions to Start You Thinking

1. CONSIDERING MEANING: How have the lake and the surrounding community, as White depicts them, changed since he was a boy?

2. IDENTIFYING WRITING STRATEGIES: Notice the details White uses to describe life at the lake. How many different sense experiences do his images evoke? Identify and then analyze at least four memorable images from the essay, explaining what makes each memorable.

3. READING CRITICALLY: White compares the past with the present to show that "there had been no years" since his childhood at the lake (paragraph 5). How does this comparison shape the tone of White's essay? How does the tone change at the end? What is the effect of this sudden change?

4. EXPANDING VOCABULARY: Define *primeval* (paragraph 3), *transposition* (paragraph 4), *hellgrammite* (paragraph 5), *undulating, cultist* (paragraph 6), and *petulant* (paragraph 10). What is White's purpose in using adult words rather than a child's words to look back on his childhood experience?

5. MAKING CONNECTIONS: Both White and Gerald Early in "Black like . . . Shirley Temple?" (p. 502) describe their efforts to please and to draw closer to their children. Whose attempt seems more successful? Why?

Journal Prompts

1. Describe a place that has special meaning for you. Why is it special?

2. Use White's description of a thunderstorm (paragraph 12) as a model to describe a natural event that you have witnessed.

Suggestions for Writing

1. Think of a place you knew as a child and then visited again as an adult. Write an essay explaining how the place had changed and not changed. Use observation and recall to make the place as memorable for your readers as it was for you.

2. How do you think nostalgia — the desire to return to an important and pleasant time in the past — influences the way we remember our own experiences? Use examples from White's essay and from your experience to illustrate your explanation.

Amy Tan *was born in 1952 in Oakland, California, a few years after her parents
immigrated to the United States from China. After receiving a B.A. in English and
linguistics and an M.A. in linguistics from San Jose State University, Tan worked as
a specialist in language development for five years before becoming a freelance business writer in 1981. Tan wrote her first short story in 1985; it became the basis for
her first novel,* The Joy Luck Club *(1990), which was a phenomenal best-seller and*

was made into a movie. Tan's second novel, The Kitchen God's Wife *(1991), was equally popular. She has also written children's books,* The Moon Lady *(1992) and* The Chinese Siamese Cat *(1994). With* The One Hundred Secret Senses *(1995), Tan's ambitious third novel, she returned to familiar themes of familial relationships, loyalty, and ways of reconciling the past with the present. "Mother Tongue" first appeared in* Threepenny Review *in 1990; in this essay, Tan explores the effect her mother's "broken" English — the language Tan grew up with — has had on her life and writing.*

AS YOU READ: *Identify the difficulties Tan says exist for a child growing up in a family that speaks nonstandard English.*

Amy Tan   Mother Tongue

I am not a scholar of English or literature. I cannot give you much more   1
than personal opinions on the English language and its variations in this
country or others.

I am a writer. And by that definition, I am someone who has always loved   2
language. I am fascinated by language in daily life. I spend a great deal of my
time thinking about the power of language — the way it can evoke an emotion, a visual image, a complex idea, or a simple truth. Language is the tool of
my trade. And I use them all — all the Englishes I grew up with.

Recently, I was made keenly aware of the different Englishes I do use. I was   3
giving a talk to a large group of people, the same talk I had already given to
half a dozen other groups. The nature of the talk was about my writing, my
life, and my book, *The Joy Luck Club.* The talk was going along well enough,
until I remembered one major difference that made the whole talk sound
wrong. My mother was in the room. And it was perhaps the first time she had
heard me give a lengthy speech, using the kind of English I have never used
with her. I was saying things like, "The intersection of memory upon imagination" and "There is an aspect of my fiction that relates to thus-and-thus" —
a speech filled with carefully wrought° grammatical phrases, burdened, it
suddenly seemed to me, with nominalized° forms, past perfect tenses, conditional phrases, all the forms of Standard English that I had learned in school
and through books, the forms of English I did not use at home with my
mother.

Just last week, I was walking down the street with my mother, and I again   4
found myself conscious of the English I was using, and the English I do use
with her. We were talking about the price of new and used furniture and I
heard myself saying this: "Not waste money that way." My husband was with
us as well, and he didn't notice any switch in my English. And then I realized
why. It's because over the twenty years we've been together I've often used that
same kind of English with him, and sometimes he even uses it with me. It has

wrought: Crafted.   **nominalized:** Made into a noun from a verb.

become our language of intimacy, a different sort of English that relates to family talk, the language I grew up with.

So you'll have some idea of what this family talk I heard sounds like, I'll quote what my mother said during a recent conversation which I videotaped and then transcribed.° During this conversation, my mother was talking about a political gangster in Shanghai who had the same last name as her family's, Du, and how the gangster in his early years wanted to be adopted by her family, which was rich by comparison. Later, the gangster became more powerful, far richer than my mother's family, and one day showed up at my mother's wedding to pay his respects. Here's what she said in part:

"Du Yusong having business like fruit stand. Like off the street kind. He is like Du Zong — but not Tsung-ming Island people. The local people call putong, the river east side, he belong to that side local people. That man want to ask Du Zong father take him in like become own family. Du Zong father wasn't look down on him, but didn't take seriously, until that man big like become a mafia. Now important person, very hard to inviting him. Chinese way, came only to show respect, don't stay for dinner. Respect for making big celebration, he shows up. Mean gives lots of respect. Chinese custom. Chinese social life that way. If too important won't have to stay too long. He come to my wedding. I didn't see, I heard it. I gone to boy's side, they have YMCA dinner. Chinese age I was nineteen."

You should know that my mother's expressive command of English belies° how much she actually understands. She reads the *Forbes* report, listens to *Wall Street Week*, converses daily with her stockbroker, reads all of Shirley MacLaine's books with ease — all kinds of things I can't begin to understand. Yet some of my friends tell me they understand fifty percent of what my mother says. Some say they understand eighty to ninety percent. Some say they understand none of it, as if she were speaking pure Chinese. But to me, my mother's English is perfectly clear, perfectly natural. It's my mother tongue. Her language, as I hear it, is vivid, direct, full of observation and imagery. That was the language that helped shape the way I saw things, expressed things, made sense of the world.

Lately, I've been giving more thought to the kind of English my mother speaks. Like others, I have described it to people as "broken" or "fractured" English. But I wince when I say that. It has always bothered me that I can think of no way to describe it other than "broken," as if it were damaged and needed to be fixed, as if it lacked a certain wholeness and soundness. I've heard other terms used, "limited English," for example. But they seem just as bad, as if everything is limited, including people's perceptions of the limited English speaker.

I know this for a fact, because when I was growing up, my mother's "limited" English limited *my* perception of her. I was ashamed of her English. I believed that her English reflected the quality of what she had to say. That is, be-

transcribed: Made a written copy of what was said.   **belies:** Shows to be false.

cause she expressed them imperfectly her thoughts were imperfect. And I had plenty of empirical evidence to support me: the fact that people in department stores, at banks, and at restaurants did not take her seriously, did not give her good service, pretended not to understand her, or even acted as if they did not hear her.

My mother has long realized the limitations of her English as well. When I was fifteen, she used to have me call people on the phone to pretend I was she. In this guise, I was forced to ask for information or even to complain and yell at people who had been rude to her. One time it was a call to her stockbroker in New York. She had cashed out her small portfolio and it just so happened we were going to go to New York the next week, our very first trip outside California. I had to get on the phone and say in an adolescent voice that was not very convincing, "This is Mrs. Tan." 10

And my mother was standing in the back whispering loudly, "Why he don't send me check, already two weeks late. So mad he lie to me, losing me money." 11

And then I said in perfect English, "Yes, I'm getting rather concerned. You had agreed to send the check two weeks ago, but it hasn't arrived." 12

Then she began to talk more loudly. "What he want, I come to New York tell him front of his boss, you cheating me?" And I was trying to calm her down, make her be quiet, while telling the stockbroker, "I can't tolerate any more excuses. If I don't receive the check immediately, I am going to have to speak to your manager when I'm in New York next week." And sure enough, the following week there we were in front of this astonished stockbroker, and I was sitting there red-faced and quiet, and my mother, the real Mrs. Tan, was shouting at his boss in her impeccable broken English. 13

We used a similar routine just five days ago, for a situation that was far less humorous. My mother had gone to the hospital for an appointment, to find out about a benign brain tumor a CAT scan had revealed a month ago. She said she had spoken very good English, her best English, no mistakes. Still, she said, the hospital did not apologize when they said they had lost the CAT scan and she had come for nothing. She said they did not seem to have any sympathy when she told them she was anxious to know the exact diagnosis, since her husband and son had both died of brain tumors. She said they would not give her any more information until the next time and she would have to make another appointment for that. So she said she would not leave until the doctor called her daughter. She wouldn't budge. And when the doctor finally called her daughter, me, who spoke in perfect English — lo and behold — we had assurances the CAT scan would be found, promises that a conference call on Monday would be held, and apologies for any suffering my mother had gone through for a most regrettable mistake. 14

I think my mother's English almost had an effect on limiting my possibilities in life as well. Sociologists and linguists probably will tell you that a person's developing language skills are more influenced by peers. But I think that the language spoken in the family, especially in immigrant families which are more insular, plays a large role in shaping the language of the child. 15

And I believe that it affected my results on achievement tests, IQ tests, and the SAT. While my English skills were never judged as poor, compared to math, English could not be considered my strong suit. In grade school I did moderately well, getting perhaps B's, sometimes B-pluses, in English and scoring perhaps in the sixtieth or seventieth percentile on achievement tests. But those scores were not good enough to override the opinion that my true abilities lay in math and science, because in those areas I achieved A's and scored in the ninetieth percentile or higher.

This was understandable. Math is precise; there is only one correct an- 16
swer. Whereas, for me at least, the answers on English tests were always a judgment call, a matter of opinion and personal experience. Those tests were constructed around items like fill-in-the-blank sentence completion, such as, "Even though Tom was _____ , Mary thought he was _____ ." And the correct answer always seemed to be the most bland combinations of thoughts, for example, "Even though Tom was shy, Mary thought he was charming," with the grammatical structure "even though" limiting the correct answer to some sort of semantic° opposites, so you wouldn't get answers like, "Even though Tom was foolish, Mary thought he was ridiculous." Well, according to my mother, there were very few limitations as to what Tom could have been and what Mary might have thought of him. So I never did well on tests like that.

The same was true with word analogies, pairs of words in which you were 17
supposed to find some sort of logical, semantic relationship — for example, "*Sunset* is to *nightfall* as _____ is to _____ ." And here you would be presented with a list of four possible pairs, one of which showed the same kind of relationship: *red* is to *stoplight, bus* is to *arrival, chills* is to *fever, yawn* is to *boring*. Well, I could never think that way. I knew what the tests were asking, but I could not block out of my mind the images already created by the first pair, "*sunset* is to *nightfall*" — and I would see a burst of colors against a darkening sky, the moon rising, the lowering of a curtain of stars. And all the other pairs of words — *red, bus, stoplight, boring* — just threw up a mass of confusing images, making it impossible for me to sort out something as logical as saying: "A sunset precedes nightfall" is the same as "a chill precedes a fever." The only way I would have gotten that answer right would have been to imagine an associative situation, for example, my being disobedient and staying out past sunset, catching a chill at night, which turns into feverish pneumonia as punishment, which indeed did happen to me.

I have been thinking about all this lately, about my mother's English, 18
about achievement tests. Because lately I've been asked, as a writer, why there are not more Asian Americans enrolled in creative writing programs. Why do so many Chinese students go into engineering? Well, these are broad sociological questions I can't begin to answer. But I have noticed in surveys — in fact, just last week — that Asian students, as a whole, always do significantly better on math achievement tests than in English. And this makes me think

semantic: Relating to the meaning of language.

that there are other Asian American students whose English spoken in the home might also be described as "broken" or "limited." And perhaps they also have teachers who are steering them away from writing and into math and science, which is what happened to me.

Fortunately, I happen to be rebellious in nature and enjoy the challenge of disproving assumptions made about me. I became an English major my first year in college, after being enrolled as pre-med. I started writing non-fiction as a freelancer the week after I was told by my former boss that writing was my worst skill and I should hone my talents toward account management.   19

But it wasn't until 1985 that I finally began to write fiction. And at first I wrote using what I thought to be wittily crafted sentences, sentences that would finally prove I had mastery over the English language. Here's an example from the first draft of a story that later made its way into *The Joy Luck Club*, but without this line: "That was my mental quandary in its nascent° state." A terrible line, which I can barely pronounce.   20

Fortunately, for reasons I won't get into today, I later decided I should envision a reader for the stories I would write. And the reader I decided upon was my mother, because these were stories about mothers. So with this reader in mind — and in fact she did read my early drafts — I began to write stories using all the Englishes I grew up with: the English I spoke to my mother, which for lack of a better term might be described as "simple"; the English she used with me, which for lack of a better term might be described as "broken"; my translation of her Chinese, which could certainly be described as "watered down"; and what I imagined to be her translation of her Chinese if she could speak in perfect English, her internal language, and for that I sought to preserve the essence, but neither an English nor a Chinese structure. I wanted to capture what language ability tests can never reveal: her intent, her passion, her imagery, the rhythms of her speech, and the nature of her thoughts.   21

Apart from what any critic had to say about my writing, I knew I had succeeded where it counted when my mother finished reading my book and gave me her verdict: "So easy to read."   22

Questions to Start You Thinking

1. CONSIDERING MEANING: What are the Englishes that Tan grew up with? What other Englishes has she used in her life? What does each English have that gives it an advantage over the other Englishes in certain situations?

2. IDENTIFYING WRITING STRATEGIES: What examples does Tan use to analyze the various Englishes she uses? How has Tan been able to successfully synthesize her Englishes into her present style of writing fiction?

3. READING CRITICALLY: Although Tan explains that she writes using "all the Englishes" she has known throughout her life (paragraph 21), she doesn't do that in this essay. What are the differences between the English Tan uses in

nascent: Beginning; only partly formed.

this essay and the kinds she says she uses in her fiction? How does the language she uses here fit the purpose of her essay?

4. EXPANDING VOCABULARY: In paragraph 9, Tan writes that she had "plenty of empirical evidence" that her mother's "limited" English meant that her mother's thoughts were "imperfect" as well. Define *empirical*. What does Tan's use of this word tell us about her present attitude toward the way she judged her mother when she was growing up?

5. MAKING CONNECTIONS: Tan says that her mother's presence at a speech Tan was giving suddenly made her talk sound "wrong" (paragraph 3). In William Henry Lewis's selection ("Shades," p. 505), how does the sudden appearance of the father affect the son? How are Tan's and Lewis's responses similar?

Journal Prompts

1. Describe one of the Englishes you use to communicate. When do you use it, and when do you avoid using it?

2. In what ways are you a "translator," if not of language, then of current events and fashions, for your parents or other members of your family?

Suggestions for Writing

1. In a personal essay explain an important event in your family's history, using your family's various Englishes or other languages.

2. Take note of and, if possible, transcribe one conversation you have had with a parent or other family member, one with a teacher, and one with a close friend. Write an essay comparing and contrasting the "languages" of the three conversations. How do the languages differ? How do you account for these differences? What do you think would happen if someone used "teacher language" to talk to a friend or used "friend language" in a class discussion or paper?

Gerald Early, *born in 1952 in Philadelphia, attended the University of Pennsylvania and earned his M.A. and Ph.D. degrees at Cornell University. He now teaches English and directs the African and Afro-American Studies Program at Washington University in St. Louis. Early writes prolifically about various aspects of American culture, from literature to family to sports. Some of his many books include* Tuxedo Junction: Essays on American Culture *(1989),* The Culture of Bruising: Essays on Prizefighting *(1991),* Daughters: On Family and Fatherhood *(1994), and the autobiographical* How the War in the Street Is Won: A Black Poet's Journey into Himself *(1995). He has also edited several books, including* Lure and Loathing: Essays on Race, Identity, and the Ambivalence of Assimilation *(1993) and* The Mohammed Ali Reader *(1998). In this excerpt from an essay entitled "Life with Daughters, or the Cakewalk with Shirley Temple," which was first published in the Winter 91–92 issue of* Hungry Mind Review, *Early describes a dilemma he faced when his attempt to influence his daughters backfired.*

AS YOU READ: *Ask yourself whose opinions seem to influence Early's daughters the most in making decisions about their appearances. Why?*

Gerald Early   Black like . . . Shirley Temple?

It was two years ago, the summer that my daughters gave up their Afros   1
and had their hair straightened, that I decided to watch every Shirley Temple
film available on video with them. This included nineteen Twentieth Century-
Fox films that were made during her heyday° — 1934 to 1938 — and several
short Baby Burlesks.

I am not quite sure why I did this. I do not like Shirley Temple movies. I   2
did not like them much as a child. But my daughters — Linnet, then age ten,
and Rosalind, then age seven — after having seen a colorized version of *Our
Little Girl*, a perfectly wretched Temple vehicle (even Temple herself admits
this in her autobiography), on the Disney channel one evening, very much
wanted to do this summer project. We watched each of the films at least three
times. The project appealed to me because I felt I could share something with
my children while exercising parental control. I would seem to be a kid while
retaining my status and authority as father.

Perhaps I associate my children's change in hairstyle with our Shirley   3
Temple phase because so much was made of Temple's hair, her curls, during
her years of stardom. My daughters liked Temple's hair very much.

During the summer that we watched these films together, my relationship   4
with my daughters changed. At first I saw the films merely as vehicles for
parental instruction — black parental instruction, I should say, for I had prepared to give a history of black actors in Hollywood in the 1930s and provide
information on the lives of the black dancer Bill "Bojangles" Robinson, the
actress Hattie McDaniel, and some of the other blacks who appeared in
Temple films. I was never given much of an opportunity.

"I don't want to hear your old lectures, Daddy," Linnet said. "We want to   5
watch the movies. This isn't school. You make being black seem like a lesson."

When they laughed uproariously at some graceless thing that Stepin   6
Fetchit or Willie Best did, Rosalind turned to me, knowing that I was aghast,
and said:

"Don't worry, we know they aren't real black people."   7

"But do you know what you're laughing at?" I asked, chagrined.°   8

"Yeah," Rosalind said, "clowns, not black people."   9

Eventually, I was told that if all I wanted to do was talk about the movies   10
or analyze them, then I would not be permitted to watch. Besides, they were
more than capable of judging the films themselves. So I grew quiet as the summer went on. I did not want to be banished.

It was during this summer that they abandoned their Afro hairstyles for   11
good. They had had a hard time of it in school the previous year; their hair
had been the subject of jokes and taunts from both black and white children.
Moreover, I suppose they wanted straightened hair like their mother.

When they both burst through the door that evening with their hair   12

---

heyday: Height of success.   chagrined: Dismayed and embarrassed.

newly straightened, beaming, looking for all the world like young ladies, I was so taken aback in a kind of horror that I could only mutter in astonishment when they asked, "How do you like it?" It was as if my children were no longer mine, as if a culture that had convinced them they were ugly had taken them from me. I momentarily looked at my wife as if to say, "This is your doing. If only you would wear your hair as you did when we first met, this would not have happened."

My wife's response was, "They wanted their hair straightened and they 13 thought they were old enough for it. Besides, there is no virtue in wearing an Afro. I don't believe in politically correct hair. Who was the last white woman you saw who didn't have something done to her hair? Most white women don't wear their hair the way God put it on their heads. It's been dyed, moussed, permed, teased, spiked, shagged, curled, and coiffed. What do you think, Shirley Temple was born with those curls? I've got news for you. Her mom had to work like heck to get those curls set just right. I want the same privilege to do to my hair what white women can do to theirs. It's my right to self-expression."

Right after this happened, late in the summer, I began to find excuses not 14 to watch the Shirley Temple movies. After about two or three weeks, Linnet, who was particularly upset by my lack of approval, asked me why I would not watch the movies with them anymore. I said that I thought the films were for children, not adults; that I was, in effect, intruding. Besides, I had work to do. Eventually, we got around to her new hairstyle.

"I like my hair like this," she said. "This is the way I want to wear it." 15

"Do you care if I like it?" I asked. 16

She paused for a moment. "No," she said, bravely. "I want to wear my hair 17 the way I like."

"To get the approval of other people?" I asked unkindly. 18

"Well," she said, "a little. I don't like to be called dumb. I don't like to be 19 called ugly. I want to be like everybody else. I wear my hair some for me and some for other people. I don't think I'm Shirley Temple or a white girl, but I want to look like a girl, not like a boy. When you write, Daddy, don't you want approval from other people, too?"

Before the discussion ended, she said, "I wish you would watch the 20 movies with us. It's more fun when you watch, too."

About two weeks later, the weekend before the start of school, I received 21 in the mail a Shirley Temple video we hadn't seen, some early shorts that mimicked adult-genre movies, in which she and the other children went around dressed in diapers. I thought this might make a good truce, and so I brought it to my daughters' room and offered to watch it with them. Just before the video started I made a gesture that surprised even me: I stood above Linnet, bent over, and smelled her hair. It had just been washed and freshly straightened ("touched up," my wife said), and it smelled a bit like shampoo, a bit like pressing oil, and very slightly burned, much like, during my childhood, my mother's, my sisters', my aunts' hair smelled. It was a smell that I had, in some odd way, become fond of because, I suppose, it was so familiar, so distressingly familiar, like home.

Questions to Start You Thinking

1. CONSIDERING MEANING: Why does Early's wife object to "politically correct hair" (paragraph 13)?

2. IDENTIFYING WRITING STRATEGIES: Where in the essay does Early use comparison and contrast? How does the essay's final comparison reveal the author's feelings of ambiguity?

3. READING CRITICALLY: What is Early's purpose in writing this essay? Are the conversations with his children that he includes appropriate to his purpose? Why, or why not?

4. EXPANDING VOCABULARY: What is your definition of *politically correct* (paragraph 13)? Do you think that something like hair can be politically correct or incorrect?

5. MAKING CONNECTIONS: In what ways do both Early and Joy Harjo ("Three Generations of Native American Women's Birth Experience," p. 540) feel powerless to shape their children's lives? Where in each essay does the narrator realize that part of his or her family's history is being repeated?

Journal Prompts

1. Describe some of the hairstyles you have had. What or who influenced those styles?

2. What do you think your current hairstyle "says" about you?

Suggestions for Writing

1. Write an essay narrating a time when you rebelled against your parents with a style of dress or hair. What was the nature of your rebellion? How did your parents react? Was your rebellion "successful"? What is your opinion now of that style?

2. Were you ever influenced by a movie or television show to change your appearance or behavior? Tell the story of this change, and then use examples from your own experience to defend or rebut the notion that movies and television shows have too much influence over viewers.

William Henry Lewis *was born in 1967 in Denver and spent many of his growing up years in Washington, D.C., and Chattanooga, Tennessee. He received his M.F.A. from the University of Virginia and has taught English at the high school level as well as creative writing and literature at the University of Virginia, Denison University, Mary Washington College, and Trinity College in Connecticut, where he currently serves as the Allan K. Smith Assistant Professor of Creative Writing in Fiction. He has published nonfiction, plays, poetry, and fiction and is the author of a collection of short stories,* In the Arms of Our Elders *(1995). The following selection, which appeared in* Speak My Name: Black Men on Masculinity and the American Dream *(1996), is an account of events that lead to a boy meeting his father for the first time.*

AS YOU READ: *What comes to mind when you first read the title of Lewis's piece? What other ways do you interpret the title?*

I was fourteen that summer. August brought a heat I had never known,   1
and during the dreamlike drought of those days I saw my father for the first
time in my life.

The tulip poplars faded to yellow before September came that year. There   2
had been no rain for weeks and the people's faces along Eleventh Street wore
a longing for something cool and wet, something distant, like the promise of
a balmy October. Talk of weather was of the heat and the dry taste in their
mouths, and they were frustrated at having to notice something other than
the weather in their daily pleasantries. Sometimes, in the haven of afternoon
porch shade or in the still and cooler places of late night, they drank and
laughed, content because they had managed to make it through the day.

What I noticed was the way the skin of my neighbors glistened as they   3
toiled in their backyards, trying to save their gardens or working a few more
miles into their cars. My own skin surprised me each morning in the mirror,
becoming darker and darker, my hair lightening, dispelling my assumption
that it had always been a curly black, the whole of me a new and stranger
blend of browns from day after day of basketball on asphalt courts or racing
the other boys down the street after the Icee truck each afternoon.

I came to believe that it was the heat that made things happen. It was a   4
summer of empty sidewalks, people I knew drifting in and out of the alley-
ways where trees gave more shade, the dirt there cooler to walk on than any
paved surface. Strangers would walk through the neighborhood seemingly
lost, the dust and the sun's glare making that place look like somewhere else
they were trying to go. Sitting on our porch, I watched people I'd never seen
before walk by seemingly drawn to those rippling pools of heat glistening
above the asphalt, as if something must be happening just beyond where that
warmth quivered down the street. And at night I'd look out from the porch of
our house a few blocks off Eleventh and scan the neighborhood, wanting to
see some change, something besides the nearby rumble of freight trains and
the monotony of heat, something refreshing and new. In heat like that, everyone sat on their porches looking out into the night and hoping for something
better to come up with the sun.

It was during such a summer, my mother told me, that my father got   5
home from the third shift at the bottling plant, woke her with his naked body
already on top of her, entered her before she was able to say no, sweat on her
through moments of whiskey breath and indolent° thrusting, came without
saying a word, and walked back out of our house forever. He never uttered a
word, she said, for it was not his way to speak much when it was hot. My
mother was a wise woman and spoke almost as beautifully as she sang. She
told me he'd left with the rumble of the trains. She told me this with a

---

indolent: Lazy.

smooth, distant voice, as if it were the story of someone else, and it was strange to me that she might have wanted to cry at something like that but didn't, as if there were no need anymore.

She said she lay still after he left, certain only of his sweat, the workshirt   6
he'd left behind, and her body calming itself from the silent insistence of his thrusts. She lay still for at least an hour, aware of two things: feeling the semen her body wouldn't hold slowly leaving her and dripping onto the sheets, and knowing that some part of what her body did hold would fight and form itself into what became me nine months later.

I was ten years old when she told me this. After she sat me down and said,   7
This is how you came to me, I knew that I would never feel like I was ten for the rest of that year. She told me what it was to love someone, what it was to make love to someone, and what it took to make someone. Sometimes, she said, all three don't happen at once. When she said that I didn't quite know what it meant, but I felt her need to tell me. She seemed determined not to hold it from me. It seemed as if somehow she was pushing me ahead of my growing. And I felt uncomfortable with it, the way secondhand shoes are at first comfortless. Soon the pain wasn't as great, just hard to place.

After that she filled my home life with lessons, stories and observations   8
that had a tone of insistence in them, each one told in a way that dared me to let it drift from my mind. By the end of my eleventh year I learned of her sister Alva, who cut two of her husband's fingers off, one for each of his mistresses. At twelve, I had no misunderstanding of why, someday soon, for nothing more than a few dollars, I might be stabbed by one of the same boys that I played basketball with at the rec center. At thirteen I came to know that my cousin Dexter hadn't become sick and been hospitalized in St. Louis, but had gotten a young white girl pregnant and was rumored to be someone's yardman in Hyde Park. And when I was fourteen, through the tree-withering heat of August, during the Watertown Blues Festival, in throngs of sweaty, wide-smiling people, my mother pointed out to me my father.

For the annual festival they closed off Eleventh Street from the downtown   9
square all the way up to where the freight railway cuts through the city, where our neighborhood ends and the land rises up to the surrounding hills dotted with houses the wealthy built to avoid flooding and neighbors with low incomes. Amidst the summer heat were the sizzle of barbecue at every corner, steamy blues from performance stages erected in the many empty lots up and down the street, and of course the scores of people, crammed together, wearing the lightest clothing they could without looking loose. By early evening the street would be completely filled with people and the blues would have dominion over the crowd.

The sad, slow blues songs my mother loved the most. The Watertown   10
Festival was her favorite social event of the year. She had a tight-skinned sort of pride through most days of the year, countered by the softer, bareshouldered self of the blues festival, where she wore yellow or orange-red outfits and deep, brownish-red lipstick against the chestnut shine of her cheeks.

More men took the time to risk getting to know her and every year it was a different man; the summer suitors from past years learned quickly that although she wore that lipstick and although an orange-red skirt never looked better on another pair of hips, never again would she have a man leave his workshirt hanging on her bedpost. With that kind of poise she swayed through the crowds of people, smiling at many, hugging some, and stopping at times to dance with no one in particular.

When I was younger than fourteen, I had no choice but to go. Early in the afternoon she'd make me shower and put on a fresh cotton shirt. You need to hear the blues, boy, a body needs something to tell itself what's good and what's not. At fourteen, my mother approached me differently. She simply came out to the yard where I was watering her garden and said, You going? and waited for me to turn to her and say yes. I didn't know if I liked the blues or not.

We started at the top of Eleventh Street and worked our way downtown over the few hours of the festival. We passed neighbors and friends from church, my mother's boss from Belk's Dry Goods, and Reverend Riggins, who was drinking beer from a paper cup instead of a can. Midway down Eleventh, in front of Macky's Mellow Tone Grill, I bumped into my cousin Wilbert, who had sneaked a tall-boy° of Miller High-Life from a cooler somewhere up the street. A zydeco° band was warming up for Etta James.° We stood as still as we could in the intense heat and shared sips of that beer while we watched my mother — with her own beer — swaying with a man twice her age to the zip and smack of the washboard.

Etta James had already captured the crowd when Wilbert brought back a large plate of ribs and another beer. My mother came over to share our ribs and Wilbert was silent after deftly dropping the can of beer behind his back. I stood there listening, taking in the heat, the music, the hint of beer on my mother's breath. The crowd had a pulse to it, still moving up and down the street but stopping to hear the growl of Etta James's voice. The sense of closeness was almost too much. My mother was swaying back and forth on her heels, giving a little dip to her pelvis every so often and mouthing the words to the songs. At any given moment, one or two men would be looking at her, she seemingly oblivious and lost in the music.

But she too must have felt the closeness of the people. She was looking away from the stage, focusing on a commotion of laughter in front of Macky's, where voices were hooting above the music. She took hold of my shoulders and turned me towards the bar. In a circle of loud men, all holding beer, all howling in laughter — some shirtless and other in work clothes — stood a large man in a worn gray suit, tugging his tie jokingly like a noose, pushing the men into new waves of laughter each moment. His hair was nappy, like

11

12

13

14

tall-boy: 16-ounce can. **zydeco:** Popular music from Louisiana that combines elements of French and Caribbean music with the blues. **Etta James:** Rhythm and blues singer who influenced early rock 'n' roll.

he had just risen from bed. But he smiled as if that was never his main concern anyway, and he held a presence in that circle of people which made me think he had worn that suit for just such an appearance. My mother held my shoulders tightly for a moment, not tense or angry or anxious, just firm, and then let go.

"There's your father," she said, and turned away, drifting back into the music and dancing people. Watching her glide towards the stage, I felt obligated not to follow. When I could see her no longer I looked back to the circle of men and the man that my mother had pointed out. From the way he was laughing he looked like a man who didn't care who he might have bothered with his noise. Certainly his friends didn't seem to mind. Their group commanded a large space of sidewalk in front of the bar. People made looping detours into the crowd instead of walking straight through that wide open circle of drunken activity. The men stamped their feet, hit each other in the arms, and howled as if this afternoon was their own party. I turned to tell Wilbert, but he had gone. I watched the man who was my father slapping his friends' hands, bent over in laughter, sweat soaking his shirt under that suit.

He was a very passionate-looking man, full in his voice, expressively confident in his gestures, and as I watched him I was thinking of that night fourteen years ago and the lazy thrust of his that my mother told me had no passion in it at all. I wondered where he must have been all those years and realized how shocked I was to see the real man to fill the image my mother had made. She had made him up for me, but never whole, never fully graspable. I was thinking of his silence, the voice I'd never heard. And wanting nothing else at that moment but to be closer, I walked towards that circle of men. I walked as if I were headed into Macky's Mellow Tone and they stopped laughing as I split their gathering. The smell of liquor, cheap cologne, and musky sweat hit my nostrils and I was immediately aware not only that I had no reason for going or chance of getting into Macky's, but also that I was passing through a circle of strange people. I stopped a few feet from the entrance and focused on the quilted fake leather covering the door's surface. It was red, faded fabric and I looked at that for what seemed a long time because I was afraid to turn back into the laughter. The men had started talking again, slowly working themselves back into their own good time. But they weren't laughing at me. I turned to face them and they seemed to have forgotten that I was there.

I looked up at my father, who was turned slightly away from me. His mouth was open and primed to laugh, but no sound was coming out. His teeth were large and I could see where sometime before he had lost two of them. Watching him from the street, I had only seen his mouth move and had to imagine what he was saying. Now, so close to him, close enough to smell him, to touch him, I could hear nothing. But I could feel the closeness of the crowd, those unfamiliar men, my father. Then he looked down at me. His mouth closed and suddenly he wasn't grinning. He reached out his hand and I straightened up as my mother might have told me to do. I arced my hand out to slide across his palm, but he pulled his hand back, smiling, a jokester, like he was too slick for my eagerness.

He reached into his suit jacket and pulled out a pair of sunglasses. 18 Watertown is a small town, and when he put those glasses on he looked like he had come from somewhere else. I knew I hadn't seen him before that day. I wondered when in the past few days he must have drifted into town. On what wave of early morning heat had he arrived?

I looked at myself in the reflection of the mirrored lenses and thought, So 19 this is me.

"Them's slick basketball sneakers you got," he said. "You a bad brother on 20 the court?"

I could only see the edge of one eye behind those glasses, but I decided 21 that he was interested.

"Yeah, I am! I'm gonna be like George Gervin, you just watch." And I was 22 sure we'd go inside to Macky's and talk after that. We'd talk about basketball in its entirety and then he'd ask me if I was doing well in school and I'd say, Not too hot, and he'd get on me about that as if he'd always been keeping tabs on me. Then we would toast to something big, something we could share in the loving of it, like Bill Russell's fingerroll layup or the pulled pork sandwich at Ray's Round Belly Ribs or the fact that I had grown two inches that year, even though he wouldn't have known that. We might pause for a moment, both of us quiet, both of us knowing what that silence was about, and he'd look real serious and anxious at the same time, a man like him having too hard a face to explain anything that had happened or hadn't happened. But he'd be trying. He'd say, Hey, brother, cut me the slack, you know how it goes . . . And I might say, It's cool, or I might say nothing at all but know that some-time later on we would spend hours shooting hoop together up at the rec cen-ter and when I'd beaten him two out of three at twenty-one, he'd hug me like he'd always known what it was like to love me.

My father took off his sunglasses and looked down at me for a long, silent 23 moment. He was a large man with a square jaw and a wide, shiny forehead, but his skin looked soft, a gentle light brown. My mother must have believed in his eyes. They were gray-blue, calm and yet fierce, like the eyes of kinfolk down in Baton Rouge. His mouth was slightly open; he was going to speak and I noticed that his teeth were yellow when I saw him face to face. He wouldn't stop smiling. A thought struck me right then that he might not know who I was.

One of his friends grabbed at his jacket. "Let's roll, bro. Tyree's leavin'!" 24

He jerked free and threw that man a look that made me stiffen. 25

The man read his face and then laughed nervously. "Be cool, nigger, break 26 bad someplace else. We got ladies waitin'."

"I'm cool, brother. I'm cool . . . " My father looked back at me. In the mix 27 of the music and the crowd, which I'd almost forgotten about, I could barely hear him. "I'm cold solid." He crouched down, wiped his sunglasses on a shirttail and put them in my pocket. His crouch was close. Close enough for me to smell the liquor on his breath. For him to hug me. Close enough for me to know that he wouldn't. But I didn't turn away. I told myself I didn't care that he was not perfect.

He rose without saying anything else, turned from me, and walked to the corner of Eleventh Street and the alleyway, where his friends were waiting. They were insistent on him hurrying, and once they were sure he was going to join them they turned down the alley. I didn't cry, although I wouldn't have been embarrassed if I had. I watched them leave and the only thing I felt was a wish that my father, on this one day, had never known those men. He started to follow them, but before he left he stopped to look over the scene there on Eleventh Street. He looked way up the street, to where the crowd thinned out and then beyond that, maybe to where the city was split by the train tracks running on a loose curve around our neighborhood to the river, or maybe not as far as that, to just a few blocks before the tracks and two streets off Eleventh, where sometime earlier than fourteen years ago he might have heard the train's early morning rumble when he stepped from our back porch. 28

Questions to Start You Thinking

1. CONSIDERING MEANING: What led the boy to tell himself that "I didn't care that he [his father] was not perfect" (paragraph 27)?

2. IDENTIFYING WRITING STRATEGIES: Lewis relies heavily on sounds, colors, and images to create the moods throughout the selection. Find examples of his use of such sensory detail, and identify the mood created.

3. READING CRITICALLY: The point of view in this piece is that of a man looking back on his childhood. Find some passages written in the voice of the fourteen-year-old boy, and find others written in the voice of the man interpreting what happened to him when he was fourteen. Does this dual voice strengthen or weaken the narration?

4. EXPANDING VOCABULARY: What does Lewis's use of the word *monotony* to describe the heat (paragraph 4) reveal about the boy's state of mind? Find other descriptions of summer heat in the essay. What purpose do they serve?

5. MAKING CONNECTIONS: Lewis and E. B. White ("Once More to the Lake," p. 490) both write about a relationship between a father and son. How are their views similar? How are they different?

Journal Prompts

1. Think about a tense or stressful relationship or situation with a family member that you had to deal with. What was the situation, and how did you handle it?

2. Write a few paragraphs in which you use sounds and colors to create a mood.

Suggestions for Writing

1. Write an essay that explores one aspect of your relationship with a family member as you were growing up. How did you understand the relationship as a child? Has your understanding changed? How? When?

2. Many children are growing up in single-parent families. If the second parent doesn't want to help raise the child, do you think the child should be introduced to that parent? Why, or why not?

Marion Winik *was born in New York and graduated from Brown University in 1978 with a B.A. in history and semiotics. In 1983 she earned her M.F.A. in creative writing from Brooklyn College of the City University of New York. A regular commentator on National Public Radio's* All Things Considered, *Winik received a 1993 National Endowment for the Arts Fellowship in creative nonfiction. Known as both a writer and a spoken-word performer, her works include a volume of poetry,* Nonstop *(1983); a collection of short stories and poems,* Boycrazy *(1986); an essay collection,* Telling: Confessions, Concessions, and Other Flashes of Light *(where this essay first appeared in 1994); and a memoir,* First Comes Love *(1996). Winik is strongly committed to the belief that "building a society where all forms of love are respected and where private prejudices don't make public policy is everybody's business." Through this essay about visiting a brother-in-law, Steven, who has AIDS, Winik explores the nature of her conflicts both with Steven and with herself about confronting the eventual death of someone she loves.*

AS YOU READ: *Try to figure out why Winik felt she had to visit Steven when she did.*

Marion Winik   Visiting Steven

I am walking through Greenwich Village° with Steven again, past the snooty cafés and the democratic delis, the sidewalk montage° of shoes and coats and hairdos and shopping bags. We talked about seeing a movie, about taking the train uptown, but in the end we just put on our coats and walked out the door. We talk and we walk and he smokes, and if he gets mad or upset he walks a little faster and I lag a few steps behind, following the familiar beat-up leather jacket with the sweatshirt hood sticking out of the collar. Now he waits for me to catch up, exhales a drag of the cigarette. Wanna stop for coffee? he says, in that North Jersey tough-guy gravel voice.

We have a lot of things to talk about, none of them easy, and I am in the city for only a couple of days. After a thirteen-year relationship that began when they were still teenagers, my sister, Nancy, left Steven a few years ago. She had her reasons. I've come to accept them. He hasn't. We haven't seen each other much since then, and now we're together for the first time not as part of a threesome or foursome; it's just us. If we're going to be friends now, it's only because we like each other. But somehow, neither of us can leave the past behind: he can't let go of the hurt and I can't stop trying to explain, wanting him to forgive her.

We talk about this so much and are both so passionate and angry, drinking our coffee, eating our omelettes, walking down the street again, buying sunglasses from a Rastafarian,° walking some more, that it might almost seem to be the reason for my visit. I wish it were. But I am here because Steven is sick. He has AIDS.

Greenwich Village: Neighborhood in lower Manhattan.   **montage:** A picture made up of smaller pieces, like a collage.   **Rastafarian:** Member of a Jamaican sect.

511

What has it been — six years? — since the positive HIV test? And until re- 4
cently it didn't slow him down at all. As he had since high school, he worked
as a carpenter, remodeling apartments, building bookshelves for law offices.
In his spare time, he had his painting: suicides and triangles on canvas by day,
pastel T-shirt graffiti slapped on brick walls in the middle of the night. He
took acting classes. He and Nancy traveled to Thailand, India, Italy, Portugal.
Unfortunately, in the midst of this they also did way too many drugs, and by
the time they stopped, he had HIV, she didn't, and they didn't have much of
a marriage left. Soon after the breakup, the HIV moved from the background
to the foreground.

In the past year, Steven's had a bout of AIDS-related pneumonia, a rare 5
disease of the optic nerve, and some mysterious ailment he described as a
"fungus in my brain." Sometime around Christmas he stopped going to work.
Come down and stay here with us for a while, I kept saying on the phone,
standing by the kitchen window of my home in Texas. We'll sit by the pool.
We'll eat Mexican food. It'll be good for you.

Yes, he would say, I want to come. 6

As the months went by, I realized I was being unrealistic. He was on in- 7
travenous medicine for the eye problem, was seeing doctors several times a
week, and sometimes did not have the energy to leave his apartment.

Then one afternoon I was sitting on a friend's porch, talking to a visitor 8
from New York who also knew Steven. At first, we discussed his illness, but
gradually I found myself telling her about the early days of our friendship. The
summer afternoon in '77 when Nancy and Sandye and I met Steven and his
friend Mark at a swimming pool here in Austin, a bunch of born-to-run New
Jersey kids who recognized one another by their accents and the bag of bagels.
How they and their dogs moved into the place we were sharing with two other
girls, and we all paid thirty bucks a month rent until we got thrown out for
having six people and four pets in a two-bedroom house. How Steven and I
went out on a date before he and Nancy ever got together; how we argued the
whole night and basically have been arguing ever since.

It doesn't matter if they've split up, I said, about to cry. I'm still his sister. 9
That was the day I decided to go to New York.

Until the minute I left, I had doubts about the trip. I didn't know whether 10
I'd be seeing him on a good weekend or bad, whether I'd be sitting by his hospital bed or at his kitchen table. Either way, I was nervous about what he
would look like, what toll the illness had taken on the strong, compact body
and the handsome Italian features. And, I worried, does the fact that I'm going
mean he really is dying? And if so — grimly practical now — should I wait
until later? How many trips like this can I afford? Or deal with?

Finally, as I moved through an airport full of business travelers and vaca- 11
tioners, I let my anxiety become anticipation. I hadn't seen Steven in a year; I
missed him. It felt right to go to his side. We are connected, I thought; this is
what being connected means. I slung my carry-on bag over my shoulder and
boarded the plane.

The taxi dropped me off at Steven's building on a busy corner in the West   12
Village. I stepped over the sleeping black man in the foyer, rang the buzzer
with no name on it (Steven would never put his name on a buzzer), and took
the stairs to the second floor, where he was waiting for me, peeking his head
around the door. He looked much better than I'd imagined, almost normal,
really, except for a tiredness around his eyes, a looseness in his muscles. Still,
he was Steven, not Steven's ghost.

He introduced me to his roommate, Ron, and friend Seth, two more   13
sweet, funny, good-looking single New York guys (why couldn't I ever find
one when I needed one?). They were watching *Thelma and Louise* and waiting
for their chicken parmigiana sandwiches to be delivered. I didn't know this
was out on video, I exclaimed.

It wasn't video, these serious film buffs explained to me. It was a laser   14
disc, and furthermore, it was letter-boxed, meaning that the picture was
framed in a black border so that the image on the TV had the same proportions as a movie screen. In fact, the sound and the picture were incredibly rich
and clear. I was impressed. Steven and I subsequently made several trips to the
only store in New York that rents these discs, and the weekend was filled with
movies and sophisticated movie talk. During intermission, I went through
stacks of delivery menus and ordered every kind of ethnic takeout my heart
desired.

Don't you think it's weird how I'm always friends with really smart   15
people? Steven asked, as we tried to decide between the letter-boxed laser disc
versions of *Manhunter* and *The Maltese Falcon*.

That's because you're really smart too, I told him.   16

Nah, he said.   17

Sunday afternoon, Steven dozed off during his two-hour session with the   18
intravenous-medicine pump. Ron was out, and I was looking around the
apartment for something to do. I had been reading Amy Tan's *The Kitchen
God's Wife* on the plane, but at that moment I didn't think I could move my
consciousness all the way to China. I checked out Steven's bookcase, topped
by a jungle of plants and jammed with cassette tapes. I knew without looking
what they were: half ultrahip dance music and half the sweet sexy soul stuff
Steven has such a weakness for. He'd never been a big reader; the only books
I found were an art book on graffiti in SoHo° that included photos of Steve's
T-shirts, and a copy of *Rush*, the novel-turned-film of a lady narc gone astray.
After a few chapters, I realized I'd be better off in China than with IV drug
abusers.

I stared out the window at the people moving in and out of the deli across   19
the street. Newspapers, candy bars, bottles of beer in paper sacks. I found myself thinking back to a call I received from my mother a couple of years ago,

SoHo: Manhattan warehouse loft neighborhood with numerous art galleries.

saying my grandmother was very ill. She said, If you want to see her again, you will have to come soon. I flew up that weekend with my three-month-old son.

Those two days in the hospital room, I found myself talking, talking end- 20 lessly, to the other visitors, even if Gigi wasn't listening. I was there with my baby and my talking, as if I could fill that quiet room with life, that plain, damp, rosewater-smelling room where my grandmother and another woman lay dying.

The first day my grandmother tried to keep up her end of the chatter, as she 21 had all her life, when she was the biggest talker of them all. I brought the baby close to her and she smiled at him, and she reached with her swollen arms to touch his baby skin. She wouldn't kiss him, wouldn't breathe on him, as if what had gone wrong with her insides were contagious, or perhaps just unlucky.

The woman in the next bed, without visitors while my grandmother had 22 six at a time, had a terrible cough. A ragged, harsh cough we winced to hear. I think my grandmother was embarrassed to be subjecting her visitors to this frightening sound, embarrassed that death was so near, that we could not just drink coffee and smoke cigarettes and eat Hershey's Kisses from her candy dish as always. Finally she was too tired to be embarrassed and she closed her eyes. I remember there was a huge box of dried fruit someone had brought — wet figs filled with tiny seeds, tart, shiny apricots, dates dusted with sugar and wrapped in gold paper — and we visitors began to eat the fruit like starving people.

I had never before consciously said good-bye for the last time, never 23 kissed someone I loved, knowing there would not be another chance. Are you scared? I asked her. My voice sounded like a child's.

No, not scared, she said, just sad to leave you all, and then she started to 24 cry, and I did too. I left that day on an airplane and a week later she was gone.

Mar, said Steven. He was sitting up in bed watching me. What are you 25 thinking about?

The last time I saw Gigi, I said, and a look crossed his face. Partly it was 26 because he loved Gigi too, and partly because he knew why I was thinking about it.

It is one thing to lose your eighty-four-year-old grandmother, but it is 27 quite another to face the death of your thirty-four-year-old friend. Maybe that's why I had to go see Steven when I did, to try to begin to accept it, to start mourning while there was still a chance to translate my grief into love and caring for a person who was there to receive it. But to be honest, I didn't accept it that weekend and I don't accept it today. You can make it, Steven, I kept telling him; it's not over till it's over.

Of course he argued with me. 28

I try not to get too excited when I hear he's returned to work, that the eye 29 problem seems to have stabilized, that he's feeling better. I say prayers, I wish on stars and dandelions, and because I don't believe prayers and wishes alone will save all the people who face this merciless disease, I go to rallies, I write letters, and I give money. And every morning when I pick up the newspaper I look for the headline I see in my dreams: AIDS CURE.

**Questions to Start
You Thinking**

1. CONSIDERING MEANING: What does Winik realize about herself during her visit with Steven?

2. IDENTIFYING WRITING STRATEGIES: Although Winik and Steven are related by marriage, she calls herself his "sister" (paragraph 9) and talks about being "connected" (paragraph 11) to him. What details does she use to establish her ties to Steven?

3. READING CRITICALLY: Is Winik's use of emotional appeal in this essay effective? Why, or why not?

4. EXPANDING VOCABULARY: At the end of the essay, Winik calls AIDS a "merciless disease" (paragraph 29). What does *merciless* mean in this context? What does Winik set up in contrast to this mercilessness? Why?

5. MAKING CONNECTIONS: Compare and contrast the remedies for emotional conflicts in Winik's essay and in Phyllis Rose's ("Shopping and Other Spiritual Adventures in America Today," p. 610). How are the writers' solutions similar? How are they different?

Journal Prompts

1. In what ways can essays like Winik's affect the way people interact with those who have AIDS?

2. How is dealing with the death of a young person different from coping with the death of an elderly person?

**Suggestions for
Writing**

1. Write an essay in which you discuss the difficulty you had in coming to terms with the serious illness of a loved one.

2. Write an essay in which you analyze the reasons people often shy away from someone with AIDS, cancer, or other serious illnesses.

Anna Quindlen *was born in 1953 in Philadelphia. After graduating from Barnard College in 1974, she worked briefly as a reporter for the* New York Post *before moving to the* New York Times, *where she wrote the "About New York" column. From 1986 to 1989 Quindlen wrote the syndicated column "Life in the 30s," which drew on her experiences with her family and neighborhood; until 1994, when she left the* Times, *she wrote the syndicated column "Public and Private," which explored more political issues. Quindlen won the Pulitzer Prize for commentary in 1992 for her articles on abortion, the Clarence Thomas hearings, and the Persian Gulf War. In addition to her two collections of columns,* Living Out Loud *(1986) and* Thinking Out Loud *(1993), Quindlen has also written three novels — Object Lessons (1991), One True Thing (1994), and Black and Blue (1998) — and a children's book,* Happily Ever After *(1997). In "Evan's Two Moms," from* Living Out Loud, *Quindlen emphatically argues that gay marriage should be legalized.*

AS YOU READ: *Identify the main points Quindlen uses to support her position.*

Anna Quindlen   Evan's Two Moms

Evan has two moms. This is no big thing. Evan has always had two moms — in his school file, on his emergency forms, with his friends. "Ooooh, Evan, you're lucky," they sometimes say. "You have two moms." It sounds like a sit-com, but until last week it was emotional truth without legal bulwark.° That was when a judge in New York approved the adoption of a six-year-old boy by his biological mother's lesbian partner. Evan. Evan's mom. Evan's other mom. A kid, a psychologist, a pediatrician. A family.   1

The matter of Evan's two moms is one in a series of events over the last year that lead to certain conclusions. A Minnesota appeals court granted guardianship of a woman left a quadriplegic in a car accident to her lesbian lover, the culmination of a seven-year battle in which the injured woman's parents did everything possible to negate the partnership between the two. A lawyer in Georgia had her job offer withdrawn after the state attorney general found out that she and her lesbian lover were planning a marriage ceremony; she's brought suit. The computer company Lotus announced that the gay partners of employees would be eligible for the same benefits as spouses.   2

Add to these public events the private struggles, the couples who go from lawyer to lawyer to approximate legal protections their straight counterparts take for granted, the AIDS survivors who find themselves shut out of their partners' dying days by biological family members and shut out of their apartments by leases with a single name on the dotted line, and one solution is obvious.   3

Gay marriage is a radical notion for straight people and a conservative notion for gay ones. After years of being sledgehammered by society, some gay men and lesbian women are deeply suspicious of participating in an institution that seems to have "straight world" written all over it.   4

But the rads of twenty years ago, straight and gay alike, have other things on their minds today. Family is one, and the linchpin of family has commonly been a loving commitment between two adults. When same-sex couples set out to make that commitment, they discover that they are at a disadvantage: No joint tax returns. No health insurance coverage for an uninsured partner. No survivor's benefits from Social Security. None of the automatic rights, privileges, and responsibilities society attaches to a marriage contract. In Madison, Wisconsin, a couple who applied at the Y with their kids for a family membership were turned down because both were women. It's one of those small things that can make you feel small.   5

Some took marriage statutes that refer to "two persons" at their word and applied for a license. The results were court decisions that quoted the Bible and embraced circular argument: marriage is by definition the union of a man and a woman because that is how we've defined it.   6

bulwark: Strong support.

No religion should be forced to marry anyone in violation of its tenets,° 7 although ironically it is now only in religious ceremonies that gay people can marry, performed by clergy who find the blessing of two who love each other no sin. But there is no secular° reason that we should take a patchwork approach of corporate, governmental, and legal steps to guarantee what can be done simply, economically, conclusively, and inclusively with the words "I do."

"Fran and I chose to get married for the same reasons that any two 8 people do," said the lawyer who was fired in Georgia. "We fell in love; we wanted to spend our lives together." Pretty simple.

Consider the case of *Loving v. Virginia*, aptly named. At the time, sixteen 9 states had laws that barred interracial marriage, relying on natural law, that amorphous° grab bag for justifying prejudice. Sounding a little like God throwing Adam and Eve out of paradise, the trial judge suspended the one-year sentence of Richard Loving, who was white, and his wife, Mildred, who was black, provided they got out of the State of Virginia.

In 1967 the Supreme Court found such laws to be unconstitutional. Only 10 twenty-five years ago and it was a crime for a black woman to marry a white man. Perhaps twenty-five years from now we will find it just as incredible that two people of the same sex were not entitled to legally commit themselves to each other. Love and commitment are rare enough; it seems absurd to thwart them in any guise.

Questions to Start You Thinking

1. CONSIDERING MEANING: According to Quindlen, what is unjust about not allowing gay men and lesbians to marry legally?

2. IDENTIFYING WRITING STRATEGIES: Quindlen ends her essay with a comparison of gay marriage and interracial marriage (paragraphs 9 and 10). How does she use this comparison to support her argument? Do you think it is a valid comparison? Why, or why not?

3. READING CRITICALLY: What kinds of appeals does Quindlen use in her essay? How are they appropriate or inappropriate for addressing her opponents' arguments? (See p. 103 in *A Writer's Guide* for an explanation of kinds of appeals.)

4. EXPANDING VOCABULARY: Define *marriage* as Quindlen would define it. How does her definition of the term differ from the one in the dictionary?

5. MAKING CONNECTIONS: What privileges of the majority culture are gay families, Native American families (Harjo, "Three Generations of Native American Women's Birth Experience," p. 540), and Asian American families (Tan, "Mother Tongue," p. 496) sometimes denied?

Journal Prompts

1. In your opinion, is the dictionary definition of *marriage* no longer adequate? If so, how do you think it should be revised? If you think the dictionary definition is fine, defend it against attack.

tenets: Principles.   **secular:** Relating to nonreligious matters.   **amorphous:** Having no specific shape.

2. Imagine that you have the power to design and create the perfect parents. What would they be like? What criteria would they have to meet to live up to your vision of ideal parents?

Suggestions for Writing

1. Describe the most unconventional family you know. How is this family different from other families? How is it the same?

2. In your opinion, would two people of the same gender help or hurt a child's development? Write an essay comparing and contrasting the possible benefits and disadvantages of this type of family. Use specific examples — hypothetical or gathered from your own observation or reading — to illustrate your argument.

Noel Perrin *was born in 1927 in New York City. He earned degrees at Williams College, Duke University, and Cambridge University and since 1959 has taught English and environmental studies at Dartmouth College. For all his academic credentials, much of his fame as a writer comes from three volumes of essays on part-time farming —* Second Person Rural *(1980),* Third Person Rural *(1983), and* Last Person Rural *(1991). Perrin's most recent book,* A Child's Delight *(1997), is a collection of essays celebrating some of his favorite but underappreciated children's books. In the following essay, first published in the* New York Times Magazine *on September 9, 1984, Perrin satirizes the postdivorce behavior of many middle-class couples and proposes a somewhat unusual remedy for the problems that plague modern marriages. In the paired selection that follows, Stephanie Coontz examines the difficulties of forming new stepfamilies and offers her own solutions.*

AS YOU READ: *Identify the problems with marriage that Perrin addresses in his essay.*

Noel Perrin   A Part-Time Marriage

When my wife told me she wanted a divorce, I responded like any normal college professor. I hurried to the college library. I wanted to get hold of some books on divorce and find out what was happening to me.

Over the next week (my wife meanwhile having left), I read or skimmed about twenty. Nineteen of them were no help at all. They offered advice on financial settlements. They told me my wife and I should have been in counseling. A bit late for *that* advice.

What I sought was insight. I especially wanted to understand what was wrong with me that my wife had left, and not even for someone else, but just to be rid of *me*. College professors think they can learn that sort of thing from books.

As it turned out, I could. Or at least I got a start. The twentieth book was   4
a collection of essays by various sociologists, and one of the pieces took my
breath away. It was like reading my own horoscope.

The two authors had studied a large group of divorced people much like   5
my wife and me. That is, they focused on middle-class Americans of the
straight-arrow persuasion. Serious types, believers in marriage for life. Likely
to be parents — and, on the whole, good parents. Likely to have pillar-of-the-
community potential. But, nevertheless, all divorced.

Naturally there were many different reasons why all these people had di-   6
vorced, and many different ways they behaved after the divorce. But there was
a dominant pattern, and I instantly recognized myself in it. Recognized my
wife, too. Reading the essay told me not only what was wrong with me, but
also with her. It was the same flaw in both of us. It even gave me a hint as to
what my postdivorce behavior was likely to be, and how I might find happiness in the future.

This is the story the essay told me. Or, rather, this is the story the essay   7
hinted at, and that I have since pieced together with much observation, a
number of embarrassingly personal questions put to divorced friends, and to
some extent from my own life.

Somewhere in some suburb or small city, a middle-class couple separate.   8
They are probably between thirty and forty years old. They own a house and
have children. The conscious or official reason for their separation is quite different from what it would have been in their parents' generation. Then, it
would have been a man leaving his wife for another, and usually younger,
woman. Now it's a woman leaving her husband in order to find herself.

When they separate, the wife normally stays in the house they occupied   9
as a married couple. Neither wants to uproot the children. The husband
moves to an apartment, which is nearly always going to be closer to his place
of employment than his house was. The ex-wife will almost certainly never see
that apartment. The husband, however, sees his former house all the time.
Not only is he coming by to pick up the children for visits; if he and his ex-
wife are on reasonably good terms, he is apt to visit them right there, while
she makes use of the time to do errands or to see a friend.

Back when these two were married, they had an informal labor division.   10
She did inside work, he did outside. Naturally there were exceptions: she gar-
dened, and he did his share of the dishes, maybe even baked bread. But
mostly he mowed the lawn and fixed the lawn mower; she put up any new
curtains, often enough ones she had made herself.

One Saturday, six months or a year after they separated, he comes to see   11
the kids. He plans also to mow the lawn. Before she leaves, she says, "That
damn overhead garage door you got is off the track again. Do you think you'd
have time to fix it?" Apartment life makes him restless. He jumps at the
chance.

She, just as honorable and straight-arrow as he, has no idea of asking for   12
this as a favor. She invites him to stay for an early dinner. She may put it

indirectly— "Michael and Sally want their daddy to have supper with them" — but he is clear that the invitation also proceeds from her.

Provided neither of them has met a really attractive other person yet, they 13 now move into a routine. He comes regularly to do the outside chores, and always stays for dinner. If the children are young enough, he may read to them before bedtime. She may wash his shirts.

One such evening, they both happen to be stirred not only by physical de- 14 sire but by loneliness. "Oh, you might as well come upstairs," she says with a certain self-contempt. He needs no second invitation; they are upstairs in a flash. It is a delightful end to the evening. More delightful than anything they remember from their marriage, or at least from the later part of it.

That, too, now becomes part of the pattern. He never stays the full night, 15 because, good parents that they are, they don't want the children to get any false hopes up— as they would, seeing their father at breakfast.

Such a relationship may go on for several years, may even be interrupted 16 by a romance on one side or the other and then resume. It may even grow to the point where she's mending as well as washing his shirts, and he is advising her on her tax returns and fixing her car.

What they have achieved postdivorce is what their marriage should have 17 been like in the first place. Part-time. Seven days a week of marriage was too much. One afternoon and two evenings is just right.

Although our society is even now witnessing de facto part-time arrange- 18 ments, such as the couple who work in different cities and meet only on weekends, we have no theory of part-time marriage, at least no theory that has reached the general public. The romantic notion still dominates that if you love someone, you obviously want to be with them all the time.

To me it's clear we need such a theory. There are certainly people who 19 thrive on seven-day-a-week marriages. They have a high level of intimacy and they may be better, warmer people than the rest of us. But there are millions and millions of us with medium or low levels of intimacy. We find full-time family memberships a strain. If we could enter marriage with more realistic expectations of what closeness means for us, I suspect the divorce rate might permanently turn downward. It's too bad there isn't a sort of glucose tolerance test for intimacy.

As for me personally, I still do want to get married again. About four days 20 a week.

Questions to Start You Thinking

1. CONSIDERING MEANING: How did Perrin's divorce affect him?

2. IDENTIFYING WRITING STRATEGIES: How does Perrin use cause and effect to support the solution he proposes?

3. READING CRITICALLY: What is Perrin's purpose in writing this essay? Do you think he is serious about his proposal for a part-time marriage? What evidence in his essay leads you to your conclusion?

4. EXPANDING VOCABULARY: Notice Perrin's use of the words *straight-arrow, pillar-of-the-community* (paragraph 5), *dominant* (paragraph 6), *self-contempt* (para-

graph 14), *de facto* (paragraph 18), and *glucose tolerance test* (paragraph 19). How does Perrin's vocabulary fit or challenge your expectations of how a college professor writes? Find other examples to support your answer.

5. MAKING CONNECTIONS: Compare and contrast Perrin's role as a father with the father in William Henry Lewis's essay ("Shades," p. 505). How are the children's potential difficulties similar? How are they different?

Journal Prompts

1. Would you prefer a full- or part-time marriage? Why?

2. Sketch out a theory or a plan for part-time marriage. What elements or rules would be needed to make it successful?

Link to the Paired Essay

While Perrin and Stephanie Coontz ("Remarriage and Stepfamilies," p. 522) both discuss a reality of many American families — divorce and remarriage — their essays have very different purposes. Compare and contrast the tones of the two essays. For what purposes might each tone be appropriate? If you as a reader were facing the same problems these writers discuss, how would you respond to the two different tones?

Suggestions for Writing

1. Write an essay explaining how divorce has affected you or those around you.

2. Take a stand on the solution Perrin proposes. In a short essay, agree or disagree with the idea of part-time marriage. Is it a constructive response to problems of marital incompatibility? Why, or why not?

Stephanie Coontz *was born in 1944 in Seattle. She attended the University of California at Berkeley and the University of Washington at Seattle and has taught history and women's studies at Evergreen State College in Olympia, Washington, since 1975. Coontz has explored gender roles and the American family in three books —* Women's Work, Men's Property *(with Peta Henderson, 1986),* The Social Origins of Private Life: A History of American Families 1600–1990 *(1988), and* The Way We Never Were: American Families and the Nostalgia Trap *(1992). In this meticulously researched and documented excerpt from* The Way We Really Are: Coming to Terms with America's Changing Families *(1997), Coontz analyzes sociological, psychological, and historical data to urge a reevaluation of traditional assumptions about how "healthy" families are defined and formed. While Noel Perrin ("A Part-Time Marriage," p. 518) uses his personal experience with divorce to call for an expanded definition of marriage as an institution, Coontz uses an analysis of various statistical studies to recommend ways of handling parent-child relationships after a parent has remarried.*

AS YOU READ: *Identify the reasons Coontz gives for the difficulties stepfamilies often encounter. According to Coontz, what are the rewards of forming a healthy stepfamily?*

Stephanie Coontz　Remarriage and Stepfamilies

The contradictory data on stepfamilies also illustrate the problem with sweeping generalizations about family structure. While remarriage tends to reduce stresses associated with economic insecurity, some studies suggest that children in stepfamilies, taken as a whole, have the same added risks for emotional problems as do children in one-parent families; they are actually *more* likely to repeat a grade than children whose mothers have never married. Yet most stepfamilies work quite well. In a recent long-term, ongoing government study, 80 percent of children in stepfamilies were judged to be doing well psychologically — not a whole lot worse than the 90 percent in intact biological families. The large majority of stepparents and children in one national survey rated their households as "relaxed" and "close," while less than one-third described their households as "tense" or "disorganized." Sibling conflict, found in all types of families, was only slightly more frequent in families with stepfathers.[1]

The trouble with generalizing about stepfamilies is that they are even more complicated and varied than other family types because there are so many possible routes to forming them. Kay Pasley and Marilyn Ihinger-Tallman have identified nine "structurally distinct" types of remarried families, depending on the custody and visitation arrangements of each partner, the presence of children from the new marriage, and whether there are children from one or both of the remarried parents' former families. The challenges of blending a new family mount with the complexity of the combinations that are being put together.[2]

There seem to be two pieces of advice we can confidently give to parents considering remarriage. The first is *not* to marry just to find a mother or father for your child. While remarriage may be helpful for single-parent families experiencing economic distress, those with adequate financial resources may find that their children's adjustment and academic performance are initially set back. Many children take longer to adjust to remarriage than to divorce, especially when they are teens.[3]

But the second piece of advice is not to be scared off. Most stepfamilies do well, and a good relationship with a stepparent does appear to strengthen a child's emotional life and academic achievement.[4]

Although stepfamilies create new stresses and adaptive challenges, write researchers Mavis Hetherington and James Bray, they "also offer opportunities for personal growth and more harmonious, fulfilling family and personal relationships." Children gain access to several different role models, get the chance to see their parents in a happier personal situation than in the past, and can benefit from the flexibility they learn in coping with new roles and relations.[5]

The most important thing to grasp about stepfamilies is that they require people to put aside traditional assumptions about how a family evolves and functions. Since the parent-child relationships predate the marriage, each parent and child brings a history of already formed family values, rules, rituals, and habits to the new household. This situation can lead to conflict and misunderstanding. Research does not support the stereotype that children in stepfamilies normally suffer from conflicting loyalties, but there is often considerable ambiguity° about parenting roles and boundaries. For adolescents, the situation can be particularly tense. Their understandable resentment of the newcomer may cause their age-appropriate distancing from the biological parent to proceed too rapidly.[6]

Another major challenge to stepfamilies lies in the fact that traditional gender roles often conflict with the new family structure. As therapists Monica McGoldrick and Betty Carter put it, "if the old rules that called for women to rear children and men to earn and manage the financing are not working well in first-marriage families, which they are not, they have absolutely no chance at all in a system where some of the children are strangers to the wife, and where some of the finances include sources of income and expenditure that are not in the husband's power to control" — for example, alimony or child support.[7]

For stepfamilies to meet the needs of both adults and children, they have to create a new family "culture" that reworks older patterns into some kind of coherent whole, allowing members to mourn losses from the previous families without cutting off those relationships. The main barriers to doing this include leftover conflict from previous marriages, unrealistic expectations about instant bonding within the new family, and attempts to reproduce traditional nuclear family norms.[8]

As Lawrence Ganong and Marilyn Coleman point out, stepfamilies that try to function like a first-marriage nuclear family "must engage in massive denial and distortion of reality," pretending that former spouses, with their separate family histories, do not exist and cutting members off from important people or traditions in their life. This is not healthy. Nor is it realistic for the biological parent in the household to expect to have sole control over child-rearing decisions. Thus stepfamilies need to have "more permeable° boundaries" than nuclear families usually maintain. And a stepparent-stepchild relationship probably *should* be less emotionally close than a parent-child relationship.[9]

Old-fashioned gender roles pose another problem for stepfamilies. *Stepmother* families have more conflicts, many specialists believe, because both women and men often expect the wife to shoulder responsibility for child care and for the general emotional well-being of the family. A stepmother may therefore try to solve problems between her husband and his children or the children and their biological mother, which sets the stepmother up to be the villain for both the children and the ex-wife. In stepfather families, a woman having trouble with her children may push her new husband to assume a disciplinary role far too early in the marriage, which

ambiguity: Something that is unclear or unspecified.   **permeable:** Able to be passed through; here it means flexible.

tends to set back or even derail his developing relationship with the children.[10]

Therapists recommend that stepfamilies be encouraged to see the problems they face as a consequence of their structural complexities, not of ill will or personal inadequacy. Indeed, many of the difficulties may actually be a result of previous strengths in earlier family arrangements — the woman's desire to make relationships work, for example, or the children's strong commitments to older ties and habits. Hetherington found that sons "who were high in self-esteem, assertiveness, and social competence before the remarriage" were most likely to start out being "acrimonious° and negative toward stepfathers." In the long run, though, these boys were especially likely to accept and benefit from a stepfather's addition to the household. Boys who were close to their mothers in the single-parent family tend to resent the establishment of a strong marital alliance in the new stepfamily. Girls are more likely to welcome a close marital relationship, possibly because it serves as a buffer "against the threat of inappropriate intimacy between stepfathers and stepdaughters."[11]   11

Experts agree that stepfamilies need to develop new norms permitting parental collaboration across household boundaries. They need to facilitate° interactions between children and extended kin on the noncustodial parent's° side of the family. They must let go of romantic fantasies about being able to start over. They also have to become much more flexible about gender roles. The biological parent, whether male or female, should be the primary parent, which means that women must control their tendency to fix everybody's emotional problems and men must control theirs to leave emotional intimacy to women. A new stepfather should resist his wife's desire to have him relieve her of disciplinary duties; similarly, a new wife should resist a husband's pressure to take on maternal roles such as managing schedules, supervising housework, or even making sure the kids remember their lunches on the way to school.[12]   12

What seems to work best is for a stepparent to initially play the role of camp counselor, uncle, aunt, or even sitter — someone who exercises more adult authority than a friend but is less responsible for direction and discipline than a parent. Behaving supportively toward stepchildren is more effective than trying to exercise control, although stepparents should back up their partners' disciplinary decisions in a matter-of-fact manner and help to keep track of children's whereabouts. Stepparents of adolescents have to recognize that even under the best circumstances, resistance to them is likely to continue for some time. If stepparents understand this reaction as normal, they can control their own natural impulse to feel rejected and to back away.[13]   13

Parenting in stepfamilies requires a thick skin, a sensitive ear, and a highly developed sense of balance. A successful stepfamily has to tolerate ambiguous, flexible, and often somewhat distant relationships, without allowing any member to disengage entirely. It has to accept a closer relationship between   14

---

acrimonious: Bitter.   **facilitate:** Help to happen.   **noncustodial parent:** The parent who does not have primary custody of a child.

biological parent and child than between stepparent and child without letting that closeness evolve into a parent-child coalition that undermines the united front of the marriage partners. And effective communication skills are even more important in stepfamilies than they are in other kinds of families.[14]

These tasks are challenging, which may be why stepfamilies take longer to come together as a unified team, are more vulnerable to disruption, and often experience renewed turmoil during adolescence. But Jan Lawton, director of the Stepfamily Project in Queensland, Australia, points out that while the divorce rate among remarried families is high in the first two years, it then slows down. After five years, second marriages are more stable than first ones. And researchers have found that even modest, short-term training in communication and problem solving can dramatically increase the stability of stepfamilies.[15]

Notes

1. Barbara Dafoe Whitehead, "Dan Quayle Was Right," *Atlantic Monthly* (April 1993): 71; "School Dropout Rates for Families," *USA Today,* March 15, 1993; "Stepfamilies Aren't Bad for Most Kids," *USA Today,* August 17, 1992: 10; Frank Mott, "The Impact of Father Absence from the Home on Subsequent Cognitive Development of Younger Children," paper delivered at the American Sociological Association, August 1992; Frank F. Furstenberg Jr. and Andrew J. Cherlin, *Divided Families: What Happens to Children When Parents Part* (Cambridge, Mass.: Harvard University Press, 1991), 89; Andrew J. Cherlin and Frank F. Furstenberg Jr., "Stepfamilies in the United States: A Reconsideration," *Annual Reviews in Sociology* 20 (1994): 372.
2. Kay Pasley and Marilyn Ihinger-Tallman, "Stress and the Remarried Family," *Family Perspectives* 12 (1982): 187.
3. James Bray and Sandra Berger, "Developmental Issues in Stepfamilies Research Project: Family Relationships and Parent-Child Interactions," *Journal of Family Psychology* 7, no. 1 (1993): 86; E. Mavis Hetherington and W. Glenn Clingempeel, *Coping with Marital Transitions: A Family Systems Perspective* (Chicago: Monographs of the Society for Research in Child Development, Serial No. 227, vol. 57, 1992), 205–6; William S. Aquilino, "The Life Course of Children Born to Unmarried Mothers: Childhood Living Arrangements and Young Adult Outcomes," *Journal of Marriage and the Family* 58 (May 1996): 307.
4. E. Mavis Hetherington, "An Overview of the Virginia Longitudinal Study of Divorce and Remarriage with a Focus on Early Adolescence," *Journal of Family Psychology* 7 (1993); Kay Pasley and Marilyn Ihinger-Tallman, *Remarriage and Stepparenting: Current Research and Theory* (New York: Guilford, 1987), 105–9; Bray and Berger, "Developmental Issues in Stepfamilies Research Project," 89.
5. Alan Booth and Judy Dunn, eds., *Stepfamilies: Who Benefits? Who Does Not?* (Hillsdale, N.J.: Lawrence Erlbaum, 1994); Virginia Rutter, "Lessons from Stepfamilies," *Psychology Today* (May–June 1994): 32.
6. Lawrence H. Ganong and Marilyn Coleman, *Remarried Family Relationships* (Thousand Oaks, Calif.: Sage, 1994), 122; Pasley and Ihinger-Tallman, *Remarriage and Stepparenting,* 108; Hetherington and Clingempeel, *Coping with Marital Transitions,* 200–5.

7. Monica McGoldrick and Betty Carter, "Forming a Remarried Family," in McGoldrick and Carter, eds., *The Changing Family Life Cycle: A Framework for Family Therapy,* 3rd ed. (Boston: Allyn and Bacon, 1989).

8. John Visher and Emily Visher, *Therapy with Stepfamilies* (New York: Brunner/Mazel, 1996); McGoldrick and Carter, "Forming a Remarried Family."

9. David Demo and Alan Acock, "The Impact of Divorce on Children," in Alan Booth, ed., 201–2, *Contemporary Families: Looking Forward, Looking Back* (Minneapolis: National Council on Family Relations, 1991); Ganong and Coleman, *Remarried Family Relationships,* 123–37; James Bray and David Harvey, "Adolescents in Stepfamilies: Developmental Family Interventions," *Psychotherapy* 32 (1995): 125; Visher and Visher, *Therapy with Stepfamilies;* McGoldrick and Carter, "Forming a Remarried Family."

10. Lynn White, "Growing Up with Single Parents and Stepparents: Long-Term Effects on Family Solidarity," *Journal of Marriage and the Family* 56, no. 4 (November 1994); Rutter, "Lessons from Stepfamilies," 66; Furstenberg and Cherlin, *Divided Families,* 78; McGoldrick and Carter, "Forming a Remarried Family"; John Visher and Emily Visher, *Old Loyalties, New Ties: Therapeutic Strategies with Stepfamilies* (New York: Brunner/Mazel, 1988).

11. E. Mavis Hetherington, "Presidential Address: Families, Lies, and Videotapes," *Journal of Research on Adolescence* 1, no. 4 (1991): 341, 344.

12. Ganong and Coleman, *Remarried Family Relationships;* James Bray and Sandra Berger, "Noncustodial Father and Paternal Grandparent Relationships in Stepfamilies," *Family Relations* 39 (1990).

13. Mark Fine and Lawrence Kurdek, "The Adjustment of Adolescents in Stepfather and Stepmother Families," *Journal of Marriage and the Family* 54 (1992); Bray and Harvey, "Adolescents in Stepfamilies"; Margaret Crosbie-Burnett and Jean Giles-Sims, "Adolescent Adjustment and Stepparenting Styles," *Family Relations* 43 (October 1994); Hetherington and Clingempeel, *Coping with Marital Transitions,* 10, 200–5; Visher and Visher, *Old Loyalties, New Ties.*

14. McGoldrick and Carter, "Forming a Remarried Family"; Visher and Visher, *Therapy with Stepfamilies;* Nancy Burrell, "Community Patterns in Stepfamilies: Redefining Family Roles, Themes, and Conflict Styles," in Mary Anne Fitzpatrick and Anita Vangelisti, eds., *Explaining Family Interactions* (Thousand Oaks, Calif.: Sage, 1995); Carolyn Henry and Sandra Lovelace, "Family Resources and Adolescent Family Life Satisfaction in Remarried Family Households," *Journal of Family Issues* 16 (1995); Marilyn Coleman and Lawrence H. Ganong, "Family Reconfiguring Following Divorce," in Steve Duck and Julia Wood, eds., *Confronting Relationship Challenges,* vol. 5 (Thousand Oaks, Calif.: Sage, 1995).

15. Rutter, "Lessons from Stepfamilies," 60–62; Phyllis Bronstein, Miriam Frankel Stoll, JoAnn Clauson, Craig L. Abrams, and Maria Briones, "Fathering after Separation or Divorce: Factors Predicting Children's Adjustment," *Family Relations* 43 (October 1994): 478.

Questions to Start You Thinking

1. CONSIDERING MEANING: According to Coontz, what are the traditional expectations about how a family should work that make adjusting to a stepfamily especially difficult? What solutions to these difficulties does Coontz propose?

2. IDENTIFYING WRITING STRATEGIES: Coontz uses cause and effect to explain a stepfamily's problems. Trace the potential causes that she identifies. How effective is the use of cause and effect in Coontz's essay, and why?

3. READING CRITICALLY: Coontz begins her essay by pointing out the logical fallacies of generalizing about stepfamilies. How well does she avoid making generalizations in her own writing?

4. EXPANDING VOCABULARY: In paragraph 8, what does Coontz mean by "family 'culture'"? What does the word *culture* convey that a word like *atmosphere* would not?

5. MAKING CONNECTIONS: Could the solutions that Coontz proposes for stepfamilies' problems be useful for the families in Anna Quindlen's essay ("Evan's Two Moms," p. 516)? Why, or why not?

Link to the Paired Essay

Although Coontz and Noel Perrin ("A Part-Time Marriage," p. 518) explore a similar issue, they use different strategies to develop their different points of view. While Perrin writes about the impact of divorce on a family that is breaking up, Coontz analyzes the new families that form when divorces are followed by second marriages. How are the problems of these two family groups similar? How are they different?

Journal Prompts

1. Think of a complicated situation or difficult problem in your family or the family of a friend. How was the situation handled?

2. Does Coontz's description of what it takes to have a successful stepfamily seem feasible to you? Why, or why not?

Suggestions for Writing

1. Coontz writes that "parenting in stepfamilies requires a thick skin, a sensitive ear, and a highly developed sense of balance" (paragraph 14). What do you think are the primary requirements of good parenting, whether in stepfamilies or first-marriage families? Drawing from your own experience, write an essay explaining your ideal of good parenting.

2. Do you think the family as an institution is deteriorating? Write an essay in which you take a stand — that the family is deteriorating or that the family is not deteriorating — and present evidence to support your position.

Chapter 23

Men and Women

Web Search

Use a search engine such as Yahoo! or InfoSeek that locates Web sites rather than specific documents to find one Web source or publication marketed for women and one marketed for men. Read a few pages of each, and compare and contrast the content. How are they similar? How are they different? Do you think the source stereotypes women and men? How? Why?

Judy Brady was born in 1937 in San Francisco, where she now makes her home. A graduate of the University of Iowa, Brady has contributed to various publications and has traveled to Cuba to study class relationships and education. More recently, she edited the book 1 in 3: Women with Cancer Confront an Epidemic *(1991), drawing on her own struggle with the disease. In the following piece, which has been reprinted frequently since its appearance in* Ms. *magazine in December 1971, Brady considers the role of the American housewife. While she has said that she is "not a 'writer,'" this essay shows Brady to be a satirist adept at taking a stand and provoking attention.*

AS YOU READ: *Ask yourself why Brady says she wants a wife rather than a husband.*

Judy Brady   I Want a Wife

I belong to that classification of people known as wives. I am A Wife. And, not altogether incidentally, I am a mother.

Not too long ago a male friend of mine appeared on the scene fresh from a recent divorce. He had one child, who is, of course, with his ex-wife. He is looking for another wife. As I thought about him while I was ironing one evening, it suddenly occurred to me that I, too, would like to have a wife. Why do I want a wife?

I would like to go back to school so that I can become economically independent, support myself, and, if need be, support those dependent upon me. I want a wife who will work and send me to school. And while I am going to school I want a wife to take care of my children. I want a wife to keep track of the children's doctor and dentist appointments. And to keep track of mine, too. I want a wife to make sure my children eat properly and are kept clean. I want a wife who will wash the children's clothes and keep them mended. I want a wife who is a good nurturant° attendant to my children, who arranges for their schooling, makes sure that they have an adequate social life with their peers, takes them to the park, the zoo, etc. I want a wife who takes care of the children when they are sick, a wife who arranges to be around when the children need special care, because, of course, I cannot miss classes at school. My wife must arrange to lose time at work and not lose the job. It may mean a small cut in my wife's income from time to time, but I guess I can tolerate that. Needless to say, my wife will arrange and pay for the care of the children while my wife is working.

I want a wife who will take care of *my* physical needs. I want a wife who will keep my house clean. A wife who will pick up after my children, a wife who will pick up after me. I want a wife who will keep my clothes clean, ironed, mended, replaced when need be, and who will see to it that my personal things are kept in their proper place so that I can find what I need the minute I need it. I want a wife who cooks the meals, a wife who is a *good* cook.

nurturant: Kind, loving, nourishing.

I want a wife who will plan the menus, do the necessary grocery shopping, prepare the meals, serve them pleasantly, and then do the cleaning up while I do my studying. I want a wife who will care for me when I am sick and sympathize with my pain and loss of time from school. I want a wife to go along when our family takes a vacation so that someone can continue to care for me and my children when I need a rest and change of scene.

I want a wife who will not bother me with rambling complaints about a   5
wife's duties. But I want a wife who will listen to me when I feel the need to explain a rather difficult point I have come across in my course of studies.

I want a wife who will take care of the details of my social life. When my   6
wife and I are invited out by my friends, I want a wife who will take care of the babysitting arrangements. When I meet people at school that I like and want to entertain, I want a wife who will have the house clean, will prepare a special meal, serve it to me and my friends, and not interrupt when I talk about things that interest me and my friends. I want a wife who will have arranged that the children are fed and ready for bed before my guests arrive so that the children do not bother us. I want a wife who takes care of the needs of my guests so that they feel comfortable, who makes sure that they have an ashtray, that they are passed the hors d'oeuvres, that they are offered a second helping of the food, that their wine glasses are replenished when necessary, that their coffee is served to them as they like it. And I want a wife who knows that sometimes I need a night out by myself.

I want a wife who is sensitive to my sexual needs, a wife who makes love   7
passionately and eagerly when I feel like it, a wife who makes sure that I am satisfied. And, of course, I want a wife who will not demand sexual attention when I am not in the mood for it. I want a wife who assumes the complete responsibility for birth control, because I do not want more children. I want a wife who will remain sexually faithful to me so that I do not have to clutter up my intellectual life with jealousies. And I want a wife who understands that *my* sexual needs may entail more than strict adherence to monogamy. I must, after all, be able to relate to people as fully as possible.

If, by chance, I find another person more suitable as a wife than the wife   8
I already have, I want the liberty to replace my present wife with another one. Naturally, I will expect a fresh, new life; my wife will take the children and be solely responsible for them so that I am left free.

When I am through with school and have a job, I want my wife to quit   9
working and remain at home so that my wife can more fully and completely take care of a wife's duties.

My God, who *wouldn't* want a wife?   10

Questions to Start You Thinking

1. CONSIDERING MEANING: How does Brady define the traditional role of the wife? Does she think that a wife should perform all of the duties she outlines? How can you tell?

2. IDENTIFYING WRITING STRATEGIES: How does Brady use observation to support her stand? What other resources does she use?

3. READING CRITICALLY: What is the tone of this essay? How does Brady establish it? Considering the fact that she was writing for a predominantly female — and feminist — audience, do you think Brady's tone is appropriate?

4. EXPANDING VOCABULARY: Why does Brady use such simple language in this essay? What is the effect of her use of such phrases as *of course* (paragraph 2), *Needless to say* (paragraph 3), and *Naturally* (paragraph 8)?

5. MAKING CONNECTIONS: Compare Brady's explanation of the role of wife with Scott Russell Sanders's discussion of the women he observed while growing up ("The Men We Carry in Our Minds," p. 531). What would the women Sanders met at college think of the kind of wife Brady discusses?

Journal Prompts

1. Exert your wishful thinking — describe your ideal mate.

2. Begin with a stereotype of a husband, wife, boyfriend, girlfriend, father, or mother, and write a satirical description of that stereotype.

Suggestions for Writing

1. In a short personal essay, explain what you want or expect in a wife, husband, or life partner. Do your hopes and expectations differ from social and cultural norms? If so, in what way(s)? How has your parents' relationship shaped your attitudes and ideals?

2. How has the role of a wife changed since this essay was written? Write an essay comparing and contrasting the wife of the 1990s with the kind of wife Judy Brady claims she wants.

Scott Russell Sanders *was born in 1945 in Memphis, Tennessee. A graduate of Brown University and Cambridge University, Sanders has taught English at Indiana University since 1971. Although he is the author of more than five children's books, Sanders is best known for his essay collections, including* Paradise of Bombs *(1987),* Staying Put: Making a Home in a Restless World *(1993), and* Terrarium *(1996). Sanders has described his writing as "driven by a deep regard for particular places and voices . . . a regard compounded of grief, curiosity, and love." In the following essay, which first appeared in* Milkweed Chronicle *in 1984, Sanders explains how the experience of growing up in a working-class community made it difficult for him to understand the grievances of women from more privileged backgrounds.*

AS YOU READ: *Identify the privileges Sanders associated with being male when he entered college. How did his perception change?*

Scott Russell Sanders   The Men We Carry in Our Minds

"This must be a hard time for women," I say to my friend Anneke. "They have so many paths to choose from, and so many voices calling them." 1

"I think it's a lot harder for men," she replies. 2

"How do you figure that?" 3

"The women I know feel excited, innocent, like crusaders in a just cause. The men I know are eaten up with guilt." 4

We are sitting at the kitchen table drinking sassafras tea, our hands   5
wrapped around the mugs because this April morning is cool and drizzly.
"Like a Dutch morning," Anneke told me earlier. She is Dutch herself, a writer
and midwife° and peacemaker, with the round face and sad eyes of a woman
in a Vermeer° painting who might be waiting for the rain to stop, for a door
to open. She leans over to sniff a sprig of lilac, pale lavender, that rises from a
vase of cobalt blue.

"Women feel such pressure to be everything, do everything," I say. "Ca-   6
reer, kids, art, politics. Have their babies and get back to the office a week later.
It's as if they're trying to overcome a million years' worth of evolution in one
lifetime."

"But we help one another. We don't try to lumber° on alone, like so many   7
wounded grizzly bears, the way men do." Anneke sips her tea. I gave her the
mug with owls on it, for wisdom. "And we have this deep-down sense that
we're in the *right* — we've been held back, passed over, used — while men feel
they're in the wrong. Men are the ones who've been discredited, who have to
search their souls."

I search my soul. I discover guilty feelings aplenty — toward the poor, the   8
Vietnamese, Native Americans, the whales, an endless list of debts — a guilt in
each case that is as bright and unambiguous as a neon sign. But toward
women I feel something more confused, a snarl of shame, envy, wary tenderness, and amazement. This muddle troubles me. To hide my unease I say,
"You're right, it's tough being a man these days."

"Don't laugh." Anneke frowns at me, mournful-eyed, through the sas-   9
safras steam. "I wouldn't be a man for anything. It's much easier being the victim. All the victim has to do is break free. The persecutor has to live with his
past."

How deep is this past? I find myself wondering after Anneke has left. How   10
much of an inheritance do I have to throw off? Is it just the beliefs I breathed
in as a child. Do I have to scour memory back through father and grandfather?
Through St. Paul? Beyond Stonehenge° and into the twilit caves? I'm convinced the past we must contend with is deeper even than speech. When I
think back on my childhood, on how I learned to see men and women, I have
a sense of ancient, dizzying depths. The back roads of Tennessee and Ohio
where I grew up were probably closer, in their sexual patterns, to the camp-
sites of Stone Age hunters than to the genderless cities of the future into which
we are rushing.

The first men, besides my father, I remember seeing were black convicts   11
and white guards, in the cottonfield across the road from our farm on the outskirts of Memphis. I must have been three or four. The prisoners wore dingy

---

midwife: Someone, usually a woman, who assists in childbirth.   **Vermeer:** Jan Vermeer
(1632–1675), Dutch painter known for interior scenes that masterfully portray light and
color.   **lumber:** Walk or move with heavy clumsiness.   **Stonehenge:** Four-thousand-
year-old arrangement of enormous stones in southern England, thought to have been used
for religious ceremonies and astronomical observations.

gray-and-black zebra suits, heavy as canvas, sodden with sweat. Hatless, stooped, they chopped weeds in the fierce heat, row after row, breathing the acrid dust of boll-weevil° poison. The overseers wore dazzling white shirts and broad shadowy hats. The oiled barrels of their shotguns flashed in the sunlight. Their faces in memory are utterly blank. Of course those men, white and black, have become for me an emblem of racial hatred. But they have also come to stand for the twin poles of my early vision of manhood — the brute toiling animal and the boss.

When I was a boy, the men I knew labored with their bodies. They were   12 marginal farmers, just scraping by, or welders, steelworkers, carpenters; they swept floors, dug ditches, mined coal, or drove trucks, their forearms ropy with muscle; they trained horses, stoked furnaces, built tires, stood on assembly lines wrestling parts onto cars and refrigerators. They got up before light, worked all day long whatever the weather, and when they came home at night they looked as though somebody had been whipping them. In the evenings and on weekends they worked on their own places, tilling gardens that were lumpy with clay, fixing broken-down cars, hammering on houses that were always too drafty, too leaky, too small.

The bodies of the men I knew were twisted and maimed in ways visible   13 and invisible. The nails of their hands were black and split, the hands tattooed with scars. Some had lost fingers. Heavy lifting had given many of them finicky backs and guts weak from hernias. Racing against conveyor belts had given them ulcers. Their ankles and knees ached from years of standing on concrete. Anyone who had worked for long around machines was hard of hearing. They squinted, and the skin of their faces was creased like the leather of old work gloves. There were times, studying them, when I dreaded growing up. Most of them coughed, from dust or cigarettes, and most of them drank cheap wine or whiskey, so their eyes looked bloodshot and bruised. The fathers of my friends always seemed older than the mothers. Men wore out sooner. Only women lived into old age.

As a boy I also knew another sort of men, who did not sweat and break   14 down like mules. They were soldiers, and so far as I could tell they scarcely worked at all. During my early school years we lived on a military base, an arsenal in Ohio, and every day I saw GIs in the guardshacks, on the stoops of barracks, at the wheels of olive drab Chevrolets. The chief fact of their lives was boredom. Long after I left the arsenal I came to recognize the sour smell the soldiers gave off as that of souls in limbo. They were all waiting — for wars, for transfers, for leaves, for promotions, for the end of their hitch — like so many braves waiting for the hunt to begin. Unlike the warriors of older tribes, however, they would have no say about when the battle would start or how it would be waged. Their waiting was broken only when they practiced for war. They fired guns at targets, drove tanks across the churned-up fields of the military reservation, set off bombs in the wrecks of old fighter planes. I knew this was all play. But I also felt certain that when the hour for killing arrived, they

boll weevil: A parasitic insect that bores into cottom bolls and ruins crops.

would kill. When the real shooting started, many of them would die. This was
what soldiers were *for*, just as a hammer was for driving nails.

Warriors and toilers: those seemed, in my boyhood vision, to be the chief   15
destinies for men. They weren't the only destinies, as I learned from having a
few male teachers, from reading books, and from watching television. But the
men on television—the politicians, the astronauts, the generals, the savvy
lawyers, the philosophical doctors, the bosses who gave orders to both soldiers and laborers—seemed as remote and unreal to me as the figures in tap-
estries. I could no more imagine growing up to become one of these cool, potent creatures than I could imagine becoming a prince.

A nearer and more hopeful example was that of my father, who had es-   16
caped from a red-dirt farm to a tire factory, and from the assembly line to the
front office. Eventually he dressed in a white shirt and tie. He carried himself
as if he had been born to work with his mind. But his body, remembering the
early years of slogging work, began to give out on him in his fifties, and it quit
on him entirely before he turned sixty-five. Even such a partial escape from
man's fate as he had accomplished did not seem possible for most of the boys
I knew. They joined the army, stood in line for jobs in the smoky plants,
helped build highways. They were bound to work as their fathers had worked,
killing themselves or preparing to kill others.

A scholarship enabled me not only to attend college, a rare enough feat   17
in my circle, but even to study in a university meant for children of the rich.
Here I met for the first time young men who had assumed from birth that they
would lead lives of comfort and power. And for the first time I met women
who told me that men were guilty of having kept all the joys and privileges of
the earth for themselves. I was baffled. What privileges? What joys? I thought
about the maimed dismal lives of most of the men back home. What had they
stolen from their wives and daughters? The right to go five days a week, twelve
months a year, for thirty or forty years to a steel mill or a coal mine? The right
to drop bombs and die in war? The right to feel every leak in the roof, every
gap in the fence, every cough in the engine, as a wound they must mend? The
right to feel, when the lay-off comes or the plant shuts down, not only afraid
but ashamed?

I was slow to understand the deep grievances of women. This was be-   18
cause, as a boy, I had envied them. Before college, the only people I had ever
known who were interested in art or music or literature, the only ones who
read books, the only ones who ever seemed to enjoy a sense of ease and grace
were the mothers and daughters. Like the menfolk, they fretted about money,
they scrimped and made-do. But, when the pay stopped coming in, they were
not the ones who had failed. Nor did they have to go to war, and that seemed
to me a blessed fact. By comparison with the narrow, ironclad days of fathers,
there was an expansiveness,° I thought, in the days of mothers. They went to

---

expansiveness: Flexibility, openness; also connotes grandness.

see neighbors, to shop in town, to run errands at school, at the library, at church. No doubt, had I looked harder at their lives, I would have envied them less. It was not my fate to become a woman, so it was easier for me to see the graces. Few of them held jobs outside the home, and those who did filled thankless roles as clerks and waitresses. I didn't see, then, what a prison a house could be, since houses seemed to me brighter, handsomer places than any factory. I did not realize — because such things were never spoken of — how often women suffered from men's bullying. I did learn about the wretchedness of abandoned wives, single mothers, widows; but I also learned about the wretchedness of lone men. Even then I could see how exhausting it was for a mother to cater all day to the needs of young children. But if I had been asked, as a boy, to choose between tending a baby and tending a machine, I think I would have chosen the baby. (Having now tended both, I know I would choose the baby.)

So I was baffled when the women at college accused me and my sex of   19
having cornered the world's pleasure. I think something like my bafflement has been felt by other boys (and by girls as well) who grew up in dirt-poor farm country, in mining country, in black ghettos, in Hispanic barrios,° in the shadows of factories, in third world nations — any place where the fate of men is as grim and bleak as the fate of women. Toilers and warriors. I realize now how ancient these identities are, how deep the tug they exert on men, the undertow of a thousand generations. The miseries I saw, as a boy, in the lives of nearly all men I continue to see in the lives of many — the body-breaking toil, the tedium, the call to be tough, the humiliating powerlessness, the battle for a living and for territory.

When the women I met at college thought about the joys and privileges   20
of men, they did not carry in their minds the sort of men I had known in my childhood. They thought of their fathers, who were bankers, physicians, architects, stockbrokers, the big wheels of the big cities. These fathers rode the train to work or drove cars that cost more than any of my childhood houses. They were attended from morning to night by female helpers, wives and nurses and secretaries. They were never laid off, never short of cash at month's end, never lined up for welfare. These fathers made decisions that mattered. They ran the world.

The daughters of such men wanted to share in this power, this glory. So   21
did I. They yearned for a say over their future, for jobs worthy of their abilities, for the right to live at peace, unmolested, whole. Yes, I thought, yes yes. The difference between me and these daughters was that they saw me, because of my sex, as destined from birth to become like their fathers, and therefore an enemy to their desires. But I knew better. I wasn't an enemy, in fact or in feeling. I was an ally. If I had known, then, how to tell them so, would they have believed me? Would they now?

barrios: Spanish-speaking neighborhoods.

Questions to Start You Thinking

1. CONSIDERING MEANING: Why does Sanders call himself an "ally" (paragraph 21) of the women he met in college? Do you agree that he was their ally? Explain.

2. IDENTIFYING WRITING STRATEGIES: Sanders uses recall as a resource in this piece. How does he use the experiences he recalls to support the stand he takes?

3. READING CRITICALLY: What kinds of appeals — emotional, logical, ethical — does Sanders use in his essay? Are the appeals effective? Why, or why not? (For an explanation of kinds of appeal, see pp. 103–04 in *A Writer's Guide*.)

4. EXPANDING VOCABULARY: What qualities do you associate with "warriors" and "toilers" (paragraph 15)? Are the connotations of these terms generally positive or negative? How does Sanders use these connotations to fit the purpose of his essay?

5. MAKING CONNECTIONS: How do the images of men that Sanders acquired in his childhood differ from the images of women that Judith Ortiz Cofer ("The Myth of the Latin Woman," p. 564) acquired in hers?

Journal Prompts

1. Reflect on some of the men and women you knew as a child. How do they compare to the men and women Sanders remembers from his youth?

2. Do you agree that "it's tough being a man these days" (paragraph 8)? Why, or why not? Role-play: if you are female, take a man's point of view; if you are male, take a woman's point of view.

Suggestions for Writing

1. Using recall as a resource, explain the qualities of an important man you "carry in your mind." Who is this man? How did he help shape your views of what masculinity is?

2. Write an essay explaining whether men's or women's roles are more difficult in today's society. Use examples from your own experience as well as from your knowledge of current events.

Emily Prager, *born in 1952, writes fiction featuring a surreal and coldly humorous blend of pop culture slogans and classical allusions. Her novel* Clea and Zeus Divorce *(1987) has been called "a music video in the form of a novel." She is also the author of the novels* A Visit from the Footbinder *(1986) and* Eve's Tattoo *(1991). A former contributing editor to the* National Lampoon, *she has published essays in the* Village Voice *and* Penthouse *and is now a columnist for the* New York Times. *In the following essay, published in* Interview *magazine in December 1991, Prager analyzes what American culture's infatuation with Barbie tells us about ourselves.*

AS YOU READ: *Identify the gender stereotypes that Prager believes Barbie reinforces and the ones Barbie challenges.*

I read an astounding obituary in the *New York Times* not too long ago. It concerned the death of one Jack Ryan. A former husband of Zsa Zsa Gabor, it said, Mr. Ryan had been an inventor and designer during his lifetime. A man of eclectic° creativity, he designed Sparrow and Hawk missiles when he worked for the Raytheon Company, and, the notice said, when he consulted for Mattel he designed Barbie.

If Barbie was designed by a man, suddenly a lot of things made sense to me, things I'd wondered about for years. I used to look at Barbie and wonder, What's wrong with this picture? What kind of woman designed this doll? Let's be honest: Barbie looks like someone who got her start at the Playboy Mansion. She could be a regular guest on *The Howard Stern Show.* It is a fact of Barbie's design that her breasts are so out of proportion to the rest of her body that if she were a human woman, she'd fall flat on her face.

If it's true that a woman didn't design Barbie, you don't know how much saner that makes me feel. Of course, that doesn't ameliorate° the damage. There are millions of women who are subliminally sure that a thirty-nine-inch bust and a twenty-three-inch waist are the epitome of lovability. Could this account for the popularity of breast implant surgery?

I don't mean to step on anyone's toes here. I loved my Barbie. Secretly, I still believe that neon pink and turquoise blue are the only colors in which to decorate a duplex condo. And like many others of my generation, I've never married, simply because I cannot find a man who looks as good in clam diggers° as Ken.

The question that comes to mind is, of course, Did Mr. Ryan design Barbie as a weapon? Because it *is* odd that Barbie appeared about the same time in my consciousness as the feminist movement — a time when women sought equality and small breasts were king. Or is Barbie the dream date of weapons designers? Or perhaps it's simpler than that: perhaps Barbie is Zsa Zsa if she were eleven inches tall. No matter what, my discovery of Jack Ryan confirms what I have always felt: there is something indescribably masculine about Barbie — dare I say it, phallic. For all her giant breasts and high-heeled feet, she lacks a certain softness. If you asked a little girl what kind of doll she wanted for Christmas, I just don't think she'd reply, "Please, Santa, I want a hard-body."

On the other hand, you could say that Barbie, in feminist terms, is definitely her own person. With her condos and fashion plazas and pools and beauty salons, she is definitely a liberated woman, a gal on the move. And she has always been sexual, even totemic.° Before Barbie, American dolls were flat-footed and breastless, and ineffably° dignified. They were created in the image of little girls or babies. Madame Alexander was the queen of doll

---

eclectic: Drawing on various sources.   ameliorate: Make better.   clam diggers: Above-the-ankle pants.   totemic: Symbolic.   ineffably: Indescribably or unspeakably.

makers in the '50s, and her dollies looked like Elizabeth Taylor in *National Velvet*. They represented the kind of girls who looked perfect in jodhpurs,° whose hair was never out of place, who grew up to be Jackie Kennedy before she married Onassis. Her dolls' boyfriends were figments of the imagination, figments with large portfolios and three-piece suits and presidential aspirations, figments who could keep dolly in the style to which little girls of the '50s were programmed to become accustomed, a style that spasm-ed with the '60s and the appearance of Barbie. And perhaps what accounts for Barbie's vast popularity is that she was also a '60s woman: into free love and fun colors, anticlass, and possessed of a real, molded boyfriend, Ken, with whom she could chant a mantra.

But there were problems with Ken. I always felt weird about him. He had   7
no genitals, and, even at age ten, I found that ominous. I mean, here was Barbie with these humongous breasts, and that was O.K. with the toy company. And then, there was Ken with that truncated,° unidentifiable lump at his groin. I sensed injustice at work. Why, I wondered, was Barbie designed with such obvious sexual equipment and Ken not? Why was his treated as if it were more mysterious than hers? Did the fact that it was treated as such indicate that somehow his equipment, his essential maleness, was considered more powerful than hers, more worthy of the dignity of concealment? And if the issue in the mind of the toy company was obscenity and its possible damage to children, I still object. How do they think I felt, knowing that no matter how many water beds they slept in, or hot tubs they romped in, or swimming pools they lounged by under the stars, Barbie and Ken could never make love? No matter how much sexuality Barbie possessed, she would never turn Ken on. He would be forever withholding, forever detached. There was a loneliness about Barbie's situation that was always disturbing. And twenty-five years later, movies and videos are still filled with topless women and covered men. As if we're all trapped in Barbie's world and can never escape.

God, it certainly has cheered me up to think that Barbie was designed by   8
Jack Ryan. There's only one thing that could make me happier, and that's if Gorbachev° would come over here and run for president on the Democratic ticket. If they don't want him in Russia, fine. We've got the capitalist system in place, ready to go; all we need is someone to run it.

Gorbachev for president and Barbie designed by a man. A blissful end to   9
1991.

Questions to Start You Thinking

1. CONSIDERING MEANING: Why was Prager relieved to discover that Barbie was designed by a man?

2. IDENTIFYING WRITING STRATEGIES: How does Prager use the resource of imagination in this essay?

---

jodhpurs: Wide-hipped pants that fit tightly below the knee; typically used for riding horses.   **truncated:** Cut short.   **Gorbachev:** Former president of Russia and winner of the Nobel Peace Prize.

3. READING CRITICALLY: What is the tone of Prager's essay? Would a more formal tone have strengthened her position? Why, or why not?

4. EXPANDING VOCABULARY: Although Prager uses an informal writing style, she also uses some fairly difficult words and concepts. Locate the vocabulary in the article that seems elevated. Is this diction appropriate to her article? Why, or why not?

5. MAKING CONNECTIONS: To what extent do both Prager and Deborah Tannen ("Women and Men Talking on the Job," p. 550) believe that society's expectations of women, instilled in girlhood, can be damaging? Explain.

Journal Prompts

1. Explain the ways in which women are expected to look like Barbie dolls.

2. Do you agree with Prager that in some ways we are "trapped in Barbie's world" (paragraph 7)? What exactly does she mean?

Suggestions for Writing

1. In a brief personal essay, explain how a childhood toy affected the way you learned to view the world and yourself. How did it encourage you to see yourself?

2. Write a counterpart to Prager's essay, analyzing the Ken doll or the G.I. Joe doll as a cultural icon. What problems equivalent to those of Barbie do Ken and G.I. Joe expose about cultural stereotypes of men?

Joy Harjo *was born in 1951 in Tulsa, Oklahoma, and is of Creek (Muscogee) descent. She studied at the Institute of American Indian Arts, the University of New Mexico, and the Iowa Writers' Workshop, where she earned an M.A. in 1978. Harjo now teaches at the University of New Mexico. A poet, essayist, and screenwriter, she writes primarily about social and spiritual themes in Native American life, especially as they relate to Native American women. Her poems and essays often blend myth with current issues, as in her books* She Had Some Horses *(1983),* Secrets from the Center of the World *(1989),* In Mad Love and War *(1990), and* The Woman Who Fell from the Sky *(1994). Harjo coedited* Reinventing the Enemy's Language: Contemporary Native Women's Writing of North America *(1997), a comprehensive anthology that includes more than eighty writers from nearly fifty nations reflecting on what it means to be a Native American woman at the end of the century. In the following essay, which was first published in the July–August 1991 issue of* Ms., *Harjo compares her own experiences giving birth with those of her mother and daughter, using these stories to argue for a return to a birth experience shaped by traditional Native American values.*

AS YOU READ: *Notice how the women in the essay are affected by the loss of their culture. How does this loss affect men? Are the reactions of men and women different?*

Joy Harjo Three Generations of Native American Women's Birth Experience

It was still dark when I awakened in the stuffed back-room of my mother-in-law's small rented house with what felt like hard cramps. At seventeen years of age I had read everything I could from the Tahlequah Public Library about pregnancy and giving birth. But nothing prepared me for what was coming. I awakened my child's father and then ironed him a shirt before we walked the four blocks to the Indian hospital because we had no car and no money for a taxi. He had been working with another Cherokee artist silk-screening signs for specials at the supermarket and making $5 a day, and had to leave me alone at the hospital because he had to go to work. We didn't awaken his mother. She had to get up soon enough to fix breakfast for her daughter and granddaughter before leaving for her job at the nursing home. I knew my life was balanced at the edge of great, precarious change and I felt alone and cheated. Where was the circle of women to acknowledge and honor this birth?

It was still dark as we walked through the cold morning, under oaks that symbolized the stubbornness and endurance of the Cherokee people who had made Tahlequah their capital in the new lands. I looked for handholds in the misty gray sky, for a voice announcing this impending miracle. I wanted to change everything; I wanted to go back to a place before childhood, before our tribe's removal to Oklahoma. What kind of life was I bringing this child into? I was a poor, mixed-blood woman heavy with a child who would suffer the struggle of poverty, the legacy of loss. For the second time in my life I felt the sharp tug of my own birth cord, still connected to my mother. I believe it never pulls away, until death, and even then it becomes a streak in the sky symbolizing that most important warrior road. In my teens I had fought my mother's weaknesses with all my might, and here I was at seventeen, becoming as my mother, who was in Tulsa, cooking breakfasts and preparing for the lunch shift at a factory cafeteria as I walked to the hospital to give birth. I should be with her; instead, I was far from her house, in the house of a mother-in-law who later would try to use witchcraft to destroy me.

After my son's father left me I was prepped for birth. This meant my pubic area was shaved completely and then I endured the humiliation of an enema, all at the hands of strangers. I was left alone in a room painted government green. An overwhelming antiseptic smell emphasized the sterility of the hospital, a hospital built because of the U.S. government's treaty and responsibility to provide health care to Indian people.

I intellectually understood the stages of labor, the place of transition, of birth — but it was difficult to bear the actuality of it, and to bear it alone. Yet in some ways I wasn't alone, for history surrounded me. It is with the birth of children that history is given form and voice. Birth is one of the most sacred acts we take part in and witness in our lives. But sacredness seemed to be far from my lonely labor room in the Indian hospital. I heard a woman screaming in the next room with her pain, and I wanted to comfort her. The nurse used her as a bad example to the rest of us who were struggling to keep our suffering silent.

The doctor was a military man who had signed on this watch not for the 5 love of healing or out of awe at the miracle of birth, but to fulfill a contract for medical school payments. I was another statistic to him; he touched me as if he were moving equipment from one place to another. During my last visit I was given the option of being sterilized. He explained to me that the moment of birth was the best time to do it. I was handed the form but chose not to sign it, and am amazed now that I didn't think too much of it at the time. Later I would learn that many Indian women who weren't fluent in English signed, thinking it was a form giving consent for the doctor to deliver their babies. Others were sterilized without even the formality of signing. My light skin had probably saved me from such a fate. It wouldn't be the first time in my life.

When my son was finally born I had been deadened with a needle in my 6 spine. He was shown to me—the incredible miracle nothing prepared me for—then taken from me in the name of medical progress. I fell asleep with the weight of chemicals and awoke yearning for the child I had suffered for, had anticipated in the months proceeding from his unexpected genesis when I was still sixteen and a student at Indian school. I was not allowed to sit up or walk because of the possibility of paralysis (one of the drug's side effects), and when I finally got to hold him, the nurse stood guard as if I would hurt him. I felt enmeshed in a system in which the wisdom that had carried my people from generation to generation was ignored. In that place I felt ashamed I was an Indian woman. But I was also proud of what my body had accomplished despite the rape by the bureaucracy's machinery, and I got us out of there as soon as possible. My son would flourish on beans and fry bread, and on the dreams and stories we fed him.

My daughter was born four years later, while I was an art student at the 7 University of New Mexico. Since my son's birth I had waitressed, cleaned hospital rooms, filled cars with gas (while wearing a miniskirt), worked as a nursing assistant, and led dance classes at a health spa. I knew I didn't want to cook and waitress all my life, as my mother had done. I had watched the varicose veins grow branches on her legs, and as they grew, her zest for dancing and sports dissolved into utter tiredness. She had been born with a caul over her face, the sign of a gifted visionary.

My earliest memories are of my mother writing songs on an ancient Un- 8 derwood typewriter after she had washed and waxed the kitchen floor on her hands and knees. She too had wanted something different for her life. She had left an impoverished existence at age seventeen, bound for the big city of Tulsa. She was shamed in a time in which to be even part Indian was to be an outcast in the great U.S. system. Half her relatives were Cherokee full-bloods from near Jay, Oklahoma, who for the most part had nothing to do with white people. The other half were musically inclined "white trash" addicted to country-western music and Holy Roller fervor. She thought she could disappear in the city; no one would know her family, where she came from. She had dreams of singing and had once been offered a job singing on the radio but turned it down because she was shy. Later one of her songs would be stolen before she could copyright it and would make someone else rich. She would quit writing songs. She and my father would divorce and she would be forced to work for money to feed and clothe four children, all born within two years of each other.

As a child growing up in Oklahoma, I liked to be told the story of my   9 birth. I would beg for it while my mother cleaned and ironed. "You almost killed me," she would say. "We almost died." That I could kill my mother filled me with remorse and shame. And I imagined the push-pull of my life, which is a legacy I deal with even now when I am twice as old as my mother was at my birth. I loved to hear the story of my warrior fight for my breath. The way it was told, it had been my decision to live. When I got older, I realized we were both nearly casualties of the system, the same system flourishing in the Indian hospital where later my son Phil would be born.

My parents felt lucky to have insurance, to be able to have their children   10 in the hospital. My father came from a fairly prominent Muscogee Creek family. *His* mother was a full-blood who in the early 1920s got her degree in art. She was a painter. She gave birth to him in a private hospital in Oklahoma City; at least that's what I think he told me before he died at age fifty-three. It was something of which they were proud.

This experience was much different from my mother's own birth. She and   11 five of her six brothers were born at home, with no medical assistance. The only time a doctor was called was when someone was dying. When she was born her mother named her Wynema, a Cherokee name my mother says means beautiful woman, and Jewell, for a can of shortening stored in the room where she was born.

I wanted something different for my life, for my son, and for my daugh-   12 ter, who later was born in a university hospital in Albuquerque. It was a bright summer morning when she was ready to begin her journey. I still had no car, but I had enough money saved for a taxi for a ride to the hospital. She was born "naturally," without drugs. I could look out of the hospital window while I was in labor at the bluest sky in the world. I had support. Her father was present in the delivery room — though after her birth he disappeared on a drinking binge. I understood his despair, but did not agree with the painful means to describe it. A few days later Rainy Dawn was presented to the sun at her father's pueblo and given a name so that she will always be recognized as a part of the people, as a child of the sun.

That's not to say that my experience in the hospital reached perfection.   13 The clang of metal against metal in the delivery room had the effect of a tuning fork reverberating fear in my pelvis. After giving birth I held my daughter, but they took her from me for "processing." I refused to lie down to be wheeled to my room after giving birth; I wanted to walk out of there to find my daughter. We reached a compromise and I rode in a wheelchair. When we reached the room I stood up and walked to the nursery and demanded my daughter. I knew she needed me. That began my war with the nursery staff, who deemed me unknowledgeable because I was Indian and poor. Once again I felt the brushfire of shame, but I'd learned to put it out much more quickly, and I demanded early release so I could take care of my baby without the judgment of strangers.

I wanted something different for Rainy, and as she grew up I worked hard to prove that I could make "something" of my life. I obtained two degrees as a single mother. I wrote poetry, screenplays, became a professor, and tried to live a life that would be a positive influence for both of my children. My work in this life has to do with reclaiming the memory stolen from our peoples when we were dispossessed° from our lands east of the Mississippi; it has to do with restoring us. I am proud of our history, a history so powerful that it both destroyed my father and guarded him. It's a history that claims my mother as she lives not far from the place her mother was born, names her as she cooks in the cafeteria of a small college in Oklahoma.

When my daughter told me she was pregnant, I wasn't surprised. I had known it before she did, or at least before she would admit it to me. I felt despair, as if nothing had changed or ever would. She had run away from Indian school with her boyfriend and they had been living in the streets of Gallup, a border town notorious for the suicides and deaths of Indian peoples. I brought her and her boyfriend with me because it was the only way I could bring her home. At age sixteen, she was fighting me just as I had so fiercely fought my mother. She was making the same mistakes. I felt as if everything I had accomplished had been in vain. Yet I felt strangely empowered, too, at this repetition of history, this continuance, by a new possibility of life and love, and I steadfastly stood by my daughter.

I had a university job, so I had insurance that covered my daughter. She saw an obstetrician in town who was reputed to be one of the best. She had the choice of a birthing room. She had the finest care. Despite this, I once again battled with a system in which physicians are taught the art of healing by dissecting cadavers. My daughter went into labor a month early. We both knew intuitively the baby was ready, but how to explain that to a system in which numbers and statistics provide the base of understanding? My daughter would have her labor interrupted; her blood pressure would rise because of the drug given to her to stop the labor. She would be given an unneeded amniocentesis° and would have her labor induced° — after having it artificially stopped! I was warned that if I took her out of the hospital so her labor could occur naturally my insurance would cover nothing.

My daughter's induced labor was unnatural and difficult, monitored by machines, not by touch. I was shocked. I felt as if I'd come full circle, as if I were watching my mother's labor and the struggle of my own birth. But I was there in the hospital room with her, as neither my mother had been for me, nor her mother for her. My daughter and I went through the labor and birth together.

dispossessed: Deprived of ownership.   **amniocentesis:** A test that extracts and analyzes a small amount of the fluid in which a fetus is suspended.   **induced:** Forced to start.

And when Krista Rae was born she was born to her family. Her father was   18
there for her, as were both her grandmothers and my friend who had flown in
to be with us. Her paternal great-grandparents and aunts and uncles had also
arrived from the Navajo Reservation to honor her. Something *had* changed.

Four days later, I took my granddaughter to the Saguaro forest before   19
dawn and gave her the name I had dreamed for her just before her birth. Her
name looks like clouds of mist settling around a sacred mountain as it begins
to speak. A female ancestor approaches on a horse. We are all together.

Questions to Start You Thinking

1. CONSIDERING MEANING: Summarize Harjo's complaints about her first birth experience. How does she feel that her traditional cultural values are damaged by the type of treatment she received at the hospital? How does she regain those values?

2. IDENTIFYING WRITING STRATEGIES: Harjo judges the dominant culture's medical system by contrasting it with the traditions of her Native American heritage. To you, what were the most striking contrasts? Does she convince you that her judgment is correct?

3. READING CRITICALLY: When Harjo compares the experience of giving birth to her son to a "rape" (paragraph 6), how do you respond? Where else does she evoke emotional responses to make her points? How effective for her purpose are these appeals to emotions? (See p. 103 in *A Writer's Guide* for an explanation of emotional appeal.)

4. EXPANDING VOCABULARY: Harjo tells us that her mother "had been born with a caul over her face, the sign of a gifted visionary" (paragraph 7). Define *caul* and *visionary*. Why do you think Harjo provides this detail about her mother?

5. MAKING CONNECTIONS: What traditions of their families' pasts do Harjo and E. B. White ("Once More to the Lake," p. 490) hope to hand down to their children?

Journal Prompts

1. Describe some of the traditions of your family. Which traditions are part of a larger culture, and which are unique to your family?

2. Do you know what your name means? If so, do you think it fits you? If not, can you think of another name for yourself that might better match your personality or identity?

Suggestions for Writing

1. Write an essay describing the cultural traditions of your family. Are there different traditions for women and men? In what ways are you either continuing or breaking these traditions?

2. Harjo says that her "work in this life has to do with reclaiming the memory stolen from our peoples" (paragraph 14). Think of a person you know whose work in life you admire or respect. Drawing examples from reading, observation, or conversation, write an essay in which you describe and analyze this person's lifework. Who benefits from this person's work, and in what way?

Stephen Dunn, *born in 1939, graduated from Hofstra University and teaches writ-*
ing at Richard Stockton College in Pomona, New Jersey. Booklist *has said that*
"Dunn may be incorrect, but he is always right and always ravishingly articulate,"
and Dunn himself writes that "I want to find the cool, precise language / for how
passion gives rise to passion." Celebrated as one of America's foremost poetic voices,
Dunn has received a Guggenheim Fellowship and was awarded the 1995 Academy
Award in Literature from the American Academy of Arts and Literature. His collec-
tions of poetry are Looking for Holes in the Ceiling *(1974),* Full of Lust and
Good Usage *(1976),* A Circus of Needs *(1978),* Between Angels *(1989), and*
Landscape at the End of the Century *(1991). Other works include* Not Dancing
(1984), Local Time *(1986),* Walking Light: Essays and Memoirs *(1993), and*
Loosestrife *(1996). In the following essay, from* In Short: A Collection of Brief
Creative Nonfiction *(1996), Dunn paints dark shades over a lighthearted social*
exchange between men and in the process observes the complicated relationship be-
tween language, emotion, and sexuality.

AS YOU READ: *Consider why Dunn feels conflict about the comments he overhears in*
the locker room.

Stephen Dunn   Locker Room Talk

Having been athletic most of my life, I've spent a fair amount of time in   1
locker rooms and have overheard my share of "locker room talk." For reasons
I couldn't understand for many years, I rarely participated in it and certainly
never felt smug or superior about my lack of participation. In fact, I felt quite
the opposite; I thought something was wrong with me. As a teenager and well
into my twenties I'd heard someone recount his latest real or wishful con-
quest, there'd be a kind of general congratulatory laughter, tacit° envy, but
what I remember feeling most was wonderment and then embarrassment.

There was of course little or no public information about sex when I was   2
growing up in the forties and fifties. The first time I heard someone talk about
having sex was in the school yard (the locker room without walls) when I was
twelve or thirteen. Frankie Salvo, a big boy of sixteen. Frankie made it sound
dirty, something great you do with a bad girl. It was my first real experience
with pornography and it was thrilling, a little terrifying too. My mind conjured its pictures. Wonderment. Not wonderful.

Some years later, after experience, wonderment gave way to embarrass-   3
ment. I wasn't sure for whom I was embarrassed, the girl spoken about, the
storyteller, or myself. Nevertheless, I understood the need to tell. I, too,
wanted to tell my good friend, Alan, but for some reason I never told him very
much. In retrospect, it was my first test with what Robert Frost calls knowing

tacit: Implied.

545

"the delicacy of when to stop short," a delicacy I took no pride in. I felt excessively private, cut off.

I began thinking about all of this recently because in the locker room at   4
college a young man was telling his friend — loud enough for all of us to
hear — what he did to this particular young woman the night before, and
what she did to him. It was clear how important it was for him to impress his
friend, far more important than the intimacy itself, as if the sexual act weren't
complete until he had completed it among other men.

This time I knew something about the nature of my embarrassment. It   5
wasn't just that he had cheapened himself in the telling, but like all things
which embarrass us it had struck some part of me that was complicitous,° to
a degree guilty, the kind of guilt you feel every time there's a discrepancy between what you know you're supposed to feel (correct feelings) and what in
fact you've thought of, if not done. But more than that, I was embarrassed by
the young man's assumption — culturally correct for the most part — that we
other men in the locker room were his natural audience. There were five or six
of us, and we certainly didn't boo or hiss. Those of us who were silent (all of
us except his friend) had given our quiet sanctions.

What did it all mean? That men, more often than not, in a very funda-   6
mental way prefer other men? Or was it all about power, an old story, success
with women as a kind of badge, an accoutrement° of power? Was the young
man saying to the rest of us, "I'm powerful"? I thought so for a while, but then
I thought that he seemed to be saying something different. He was saying out-
loud to himself and to the rest of us that he hadn't succumbed to the greatest
loss of power, yielding to the attractiveness and power of women, which
could mean admitting he felt something or, at the furthest extreme, had fallen
in love.

From Samson, to the knight in Keats's poem "La Belle Dame sans Merci,"°   7
to countless examples in world literature, the warning is clear: women take
away your power. To fall in love with one is to be distracted from the world of
accomplishment and acquisitiveness.° But to have sex and then to talk about
it publicly is a kind of final protection, the ultimate prophylactic against the
dangers of feeling.

"Love means always having to say you're sorry," a friend once said to me.   8
The joke had its truth, and it implied — among other things — a mature love,
a presumption of mutual respect and equality. On some level the young man
in the locker room sensed and feared such a relationship. He had ventured
into the dark and strange world of women and had come out unscathed, literally untouched. He was back with us, in the locker room which was the
country he understood and lived in, with immunity. He thought we'd be
happy for him.

---

complicitous: Participating in or responsible for something by association.   **accou-
trement:** Accessory.   **"La Belle Dame sans Merci":** "The beautiful lady without mercy."
Keats borrowed the title from a medieval poem.   **acquisitiveness:** Desire for material
possessions.

Questions to Start You Thinking

1. CONSIDERING MEANING: According to Dunn, why do men talk with other men about their sexual exploits?

2. IDENTIFYING WRITING STRATEGIES: Find the places in Dunn's essay where he makes a point by referring to something he has read. How do these references support his claims?

3. READING CRITICALLY: What is Dunn's point of view regarding locker room talk? Trace the changes in his reactions.

4. EXPANDING VOCABULARY: Define *delicacy*. What does Dunn mean when he says he felt "a *delicacy* [he] took no pride in" (paragraph 3)?

5. MAKING CONNECTIONS: Dunn and Deborah Tannen ("Women and Men Talking on the Job," p. 550) both write about the ways men talk. How are the authors' observations similar? In what ways are they contradictory?

Journal Prompts

1. Have you ever been in a situation where you felt someone was telling you more than you wanted to hear? Why did you feel that way? What did you do about it?

2. In your own experience, have you found that talking can serve as a form of protection? In what situations?

Suggestions for Writing

1. Write about an experience you have had that you felt you simply had to tell someone. Who did you tell? Did you change or leave out any of the events in the story when you were telling it? Why did you make these choices?

2. Write an essay in which you agree or disagree with Dunn's argument about why men participate in locker room talk.

Matthew Futterman, *born in 1969 in Chevy Chase, Maryland, earned his B.A. in English from Union College in Schenectady, New York, and his master's degree in journalism from Columbia University. Currently a contributing editor for* Swing *magazine, Futterman is also a reporter at the* Star-Ledger *newspaper in New Jersey. His articles have appeared in the* Philadelphia Enquirer *as well. Futterman says, "The best advice for any writer is to marry rich." Here, in an article that originally appeared in* Swing, *he reflects on the possible social implications of the fact that his wife earns more money than he does.*

AS YOU READ: *Identify the stereotypes Futterman responds to in his essay.*

Matthew Futterman   The Gender Gap

As I was sitting in the lofty reaches of Yankee Stadium's upper deck trying to maintain my cool during a playoff game against the Texas Rangers, someone asked me what my wife did for a living. Before I could answer, my friend Ed thrust himself into the conversation. "Like most men these days," he said half-jokingly, "Matt's involved with a woman who is an important executive."

I tried to think of something clever to say to hide the embarrassment that   2
comes with yet another person finding out that your wife could buy you outright.

"I definitely married up," I said with a shrug.   3

The fact is, I am a member of that ever-growing group of men who are   4
outearned by, outworked by, and several rungs down the ladder of success
from their female spouses.

Not that I don't have some impressive company. The year before her hus-   5
band became the leader of the free world, Hillary Rodham Clinton pulled in
a cool quarter of a million in her position at Little Rock's Rose Law Firm. As
governor of Arkansas, old Bill earned a salary of $35,000. Sure, you could
argue that Bill had power over the state. But let's face it, money means power.
And I think we know who makes the final call in the Clinton household.

Sitting in the mostly male crowd at Yankee Stadium, I didn't have to look   6
far to explain this new world order. While I was enjoying a watered-down 24-
ounce beer with a couple of rubberized hot dogs and chanting "Bullshit"
whenever the umpires made a bad call, my wife, Amy, was in the middle of
her second business dinner of the week, at the end of yet another fourteen-
hour day. No twenty-nine-year-old ever got to run her own imprint° at a
major New York publishing house by working 9 to 5.

Now, before I am written off as just another of Newt's angry white men,   7
let me make a few things perfectly clear:

1. I consider myself a feminist (Amy backs me up on that).
2. I think we need more women in positions of power.
3. I couldn't be happier about Amy's success — and not just because she
   writes the rent check every month.

But that doesn't mean I don't feel a little threatened. Knowing that my   8
health insurance depends on her love is a bit unsettling. Growing up in the
suburbs of New York during the '70s and '80s, I learned that fathers put on
suits and took the thirty-two-minute ride to work in the city each morning,
while mothers managed the home front. Even the mothers who worked almost never supported the family. Their jobs usually allowed them more time
to keep the refrigerators full and to make sure we knew that Tuesday meant
Hebrew school and gymnastics and Wednesday meant baseball practice and
a visit to the dentist.

My mother, a psychotherapist, always spent at least two days a week see-   9
ing patients in her home office. My friend's mother turned her basement into
a dance studio so she could teach her classes there. I cannot say I disliked this
arrangement. If our fathers had been responsible for making sure there were
Apple Jacks and Doritos in our cupboards, we would have been a sad lot. And
we never would have made it to Hebrew school.

---

imprint: A division of a publishing company that has an identity separate from the company that owns it.

A few months into my marriage, I can tell those days are gone. As a junior   10
reporter at a major newspaper, I have a slightly unorthodox work schedule.
Some weeks not much happens, and I often don't have to arrive at the office
until after 11 A.M. Amy's in by 9, does business during meals, and rarely arrives
home before 8. Even then, she's usually carrying something to read before
quitting for sleep. I'm off on most Fridays, and I try to spend the time working quietly in our apartment on freelance assignments. By 3 in the afternoon,
Amy is usually about to kill me because I've called her at the office a half
dozen times to report on the status of the dry cleaning and the new coffee
table I have assembled.

"What's doing at work?" I ask, knowing I've crossed the line from atten-   11
tive to annoying.

"*60 Minutes* is interviewing one of my authors, and I think they might   12
also want to talk to me," she says. "I really got to go."

Yeah, me too.   13

I have no idea how all this will play out twenty years down the line. Sta-   14
tistically speaking, women still earn only about three-quarters as much as
men do. And a quick look at the U.S. Senate or America's boardrooms proves
that the glass ceiling is still intact. But from my personal vantage° point, there
is little doubt that the times they are a-changing. So should I still reach for the
check at the end of a romantic Valentine's dinner? Probably. Myths are important to Americans.

Fortunately, God and biology — not to mention Amy — have assured me   15
that at least one of my jobs will not be downsized out of existence. Looks like
I better start putting Apple Jacks and Doritos on my shopping list.

Questions to Start You Thinking

1. CONSIDERING MEANING: How does Futterman feel about his wife's busy and
   successful career?

2. IDENTIFYING WRITING STRATEGIES: Find at least two instances where Futterman
   uses comparison and contrast in his essay. How do his comparisons support
   his observations?

3. READING CRITICALLY: Despite his personal example and his sense that there is
   a "new world order" (paragraph 6) when comparing a husband's and wife's
   careers, Futterman says that the "glass ceiling is still intact" (paragraph 14).
   What does he mean? Does this comment at the end of the essay strengthen
   or weaken his argument? Why, or why not?

4. EXPANDING VOCABULARY: Futterman uses the word *power* three times (paragraphs 5 and 7) in his essay. What are the different kinds of power he is referring to? Which seems most important to the point of his essay?

5. MAKING CONNECTIONS: Compare and contrast the roles that Futterman and
   the wife in Judy Brady's article ("I Want a Wife," p. 529) have in their marriages. How are their situations similar? How are they different?

vantage: View.

Journal Prompts

1. Has a difference in income ever caused a problem between you and a friend or family member? When, why, and how did you deal with it?

2. Futterman says more women should be in positions of power. Do you agree or disagree?

Suggestions for Writing

1. Imagine yourself in a relationship that challenges a cultural stereotype. What difficulties would you encounter? How would you deal with these difficulties? Write an essay in which you explain your choices.

2. Although Futterman uses only the Clintons as an example to support his claim that there are many people in his position, there are other famous couples he could have used as examples. What effect, if any, do these couples' relationships have on the culture at large? Using examples, write an essay that takes a stand on whether famous couples are important in establishing the "new world order" (paragraph 6) Futterman describes.

Deborah Tannen, *born in 1945 in Brooklyn, New York, received her Ph.D. from the University of California at Berkeley in 1979 and is now a professor of linguistics at Georgetown University. Tannen believes that it is her "mission" to make academic linguistic research accessible and interesting, as she has done in her many books for the general public about the way people talk to each other. Her books include* Conversational Style: Analyzing Talk among Friends *(1984),* That's Not What I Meant! How Conversational Style Makes or Breaks Your Relations with Others *(1986), and* You Just Don't Understand: Women and Men in Conversation *(1990). In her most recent book,* The Argument Culture: Moving from Debate to Dialogue *(1998), Tannen takes a penetrating look at the way Americans argue and the sometimes disastrous consequences that follow. This excerpt is from a longer chapter in* Talking from 9 to 5: How Women's and Men's Conversational Styles Affect Who Gets Heard, Who Gets Credit, and What Gets Done at Work *(1994). Here Tannen focuses on both the causes and effects of some key differences in the way men and women negotiate, present their ideas, and express leadership on the job, while in the paired selection that follows, Nicholas Wade addresses broad differences in the ways men and women think.*

AS YOU READ: *Notice what Tannen says accounts for the differences between the ways men and women communicate.*

Deborah Tannen   Women and Men Talking on the Job

Negotiating Styles

The managers of a medium-size company got the go-ahead to hire a human-resources coordinator, and two managers who worked well together were assigned to make the choice. As it turned out Maureen and Harold favored different applicants, and both felt strongly about their preferences. Maureen argued with assurance and vigor that the person she wanted to hire was the most creative and innovative, and that he had the most appropriate experience. Harold argued with equal conviction that the applicant he favored had a vision of management that fit with the company's, whereas her candidate might be a thorn in their side. They traded arguments for some time, neither convincing the other. Then Harold said that hiring the applicant Maureen wanted would make him so uncomfortable that he would have to consider resigning. Maureen respected Harold. What's more, she liked and considered him a friend. So she felt that his admission of such strong feelings had to be taken into account. She said what seemed to her the only thing she could say under the circumstances: "Well, I certainly don't want you to feel uncomfortable here; you're one of the pillars of the place. If you feel that strongly about it, I can't argue with that." Harold's choice was hired.

In this case, the decision-making power went not to the manager who had the highest rank in the firm (their positions were parallel) and not necessarily to the one whose judgment was best, but to the one whose arguing strategies were most effective in the negotiation. Maureen was an ardent and persuasive advocate for her view, but she assumed that she and Harold would have to come to an agreement in order to make a decision, and that she had to take his feelings into account. Since Harold would not back down, she did. Most important, when he argued that he would have to quit if she got her way, she felt she had no option but to yield.

What was crucial was not Maureen's and Harold's individual styles in isolation but how their styles interacted — how they played in concert with the other's style. Harold's threat to quit ensures his triumph — when used with someone who would not call his bluff. If he had been arguing with someone who regarded this threat as simply another move in the negotiation rather than as a nonnegotiable expression of deep feelings that had to be respected, the result might have been different. For example, had she said, "That's ridiculous; of course you're not going to quit!" or "If that's how shallow your commitment to this firm is, then we'd be better off without you," the decision might well have gone the other way.

When you talk to someone whose style is similar to yours, you can fairly well predict the response you are going to get. But when you talk to someone whose style is different, you can't predict, and often can't make sense of, the response. Hearing the reaction you get, if it's not the one you expected, often makes you regret what you said. Harold later told Maureen that he was sorry he had used the argument he did. In retrospect he was embarrassed, even a bit ashamed of himself. His retrospective chagrin was like what you feel if you slam down something in anger and are surprised and regretful to see that it breaks. You wanted to make a gesture, but you didn't expect it to come out with such force. Harold regretted what he said precisely because it caused Maureen to back down so completely. He'd known he was upping the ante° — he felt he had to do something to get them out of the loop of recycling

ante: Cost or stakes.

arguments they were in — but he had not expected it to end the negotiation summarily; he expected Maureen to meet his move with a balancing move of her own. He did not predict the impact that personalizing his argument would have on her. For her part, Maureen did not think of Harold's threat as just another move in a negotiable argument; she heard it as a personal plea that she could not reject. Their different approaches to negotiation put her at a disadvantage in negotiating with him.

"How Certain Are You of That?"

Negotiating is only one kind of activity that is accomplished through talk at work. Other kinds of decision making are also based as much on ways of talking as on the content of the arguments. The CEO of a corporation explained to me that he regularly has to make decisions based on insufficient information — and making decisions is a large part of his work life. Much of his day is spent hearing brief presentations following which he must either approve or reject a course of action. He has to make a judgment in five minutes about issues the presenters have worked on for months. "I decide," he explained, "based on how confident they seem. If they seem very confident, I call it a go. If they seem unsure, I figure it's too risky and nix it."

Here is where the rule of competence and the role of communication go hand in hand. Confidence, after all, is an internal feeling. How can you judge others' confidence? The only evidence you have to go on is circumstantial — how they talk about what they know. You judge by a range of signs, including facial expression and body posture, but most of all, speech. Do they hesitate? Do they speak or swallow half their words? Is their tone of voice declamatory or halting? Do they make bald statements ("This is a winner! We've got to go for it!") or hedge ("Um . . . from what I can tell, I think it'll work, but we'll never know for sure until we try")? This seems simple enough. Surely, you can tell how confident people are by paying attention to how they speak, just as you can tell when someone is lying.

Well, maybe not. Psychologist Paul Ekman has spent years studying lying, and he has found that most people are very sure they can tell when others are lying. The only trouble is, most can't. With a few thus-far inexplicable exceptions, people who tell him they are absolutely sure they can tell if someone is lying are as likely to be wrong as to be right — and he has found this to be as true for judges as for the rest of us.

In the same way, our ability to determine how confident others are is probably quite limited. The CEO who does not take into account the individual styles of the people who make presentations to him will find it difficult, if not impossible, to make the best judgment. Different people will talk very differently, not because of the absolute level of their confidence or lack of it, but because of their habitual ways of speaking. There are those who sound sure of themselves even when inside they're not sure at all, and others who sound tentative even when they're very sure indeed. So being aware of differences in ways of speaking is a prerequisite for making good decisions as well as good presentations.

Feasting on Humble Pie°

Although these factors affecting decision making are the same for men and women, and every individual has his or her own style, it seems that women are more likely to downplay their certainty, men more likely to downplay their doubts. From childhood, girls learn to temper° what they say so as not to sound too aggressive — which means too certain. From the time they are little, most girls learn that sounding too sure of themselves will make them unpopular with their peers. Groups of girls, as researchers who have studied girls at play have found, will penalize and even ostracize a girl who seems too sure she's right. Anthropologist Marjorie Harness Goodwin found that girls criticize other girls who stand out by saying, "She thinks she's cute," or "She thinks she's something." Talking in ways that display self-confidence are not approved for girls. . . .

The expectation that women should not display their own accomplishments brings us back to the matter of negotiating that is so important in the workplace. A man who owned a medium-sized company remarked that women who came to ask him for raises often supported their requests by pointing to a fellow worker on the same level who earned more. He considered this a weak bargaining strategy because he could always identify a different co-worker at that level who earned less. They would do better, he felt, to argue for a raise on the basis of how valuable their own work is to the company. Yet it is likely that many women would be less comfortable "blowing their own horn" than making a claim based on fairness.

Follow the Leader

Similar expectations constrain how girls express leadership. Being a leader often involves giving directions to others, but girls who tell other girls what to do are called "bossy." It is not that girls do not exert influence on their group — of course they do — but, as anthropologists like Marjorie Harness Goodwin have found, many girls discover they get better results if they phrase their ideas as suggestions rather than orders, and if they give reasons for their suggestions in terms of the good of the group. But while these ways of talking make girls — and, later, women — more likable, they make women seem less competent and self-assured in the world of work. And women who do seem competent and self-assured are as much in danger of being negatively labeled as are girls. After her retirement, Margaret Thatcher was described in the press as "bossy." Whereas girls are ready to stick this label on each other because they don't think any girls should boss the others around, it seems odd to apply it to Thatcher, who, after all, was the boss. And this is the rub: standards of behavior applied to women are based on roles that do not include being boss.

Boys are expected to play by different rules, since the social organization of boys is different. Boys' groups tend to be more obviously hierarchical:

humble pie: A colloquial expression for having to admit one is wrong.   **temper:** Here used as a verb meaning to moderate.

someone is one-up, and someone is one-down. Boys don't typically accuse each other of being "bossy" because the high-status boys are expected to give orders and push the low-status boys around. Daniel Maltz and Ruth Borker summarize research by many scholars showing that boys tend to jockey for center stage, challenge those who get it, and deflect challenges. Giving orders and telling the others what to do are ways of getting and keeping the high-status role. Another way of getting high status is taking center stage by telling stories, jokes, and information. Along with this, many boys learn to state their opinions in the strongest possible terms and find out if they're wrong by seeing if others challenge them. These ways of talking translate into an impression of confidence.

The styles typical of women and men both make sense given the context   13
in which they were learned, but they have very different consequences in the workplace. In order to avoid being put in the one-down position, many men have developed strategies for making sure they get the one-up position instead, and this results in ways of talking that serve them well when it comes to hiring and promotion. In relation to the examples I have given, women are more likely to speak in the styles that are less effective in getting recognized and promoted. But if they speak in the styles that are effective when used by men — being assertive, sounding sure of themselves, talking up what they have done to make sure they get credit for it — they run the risk that everyone runs if they do not fit their culture's expectations for appropriate behavior: they will not be liked and may even be seen as having psychological problems.

Both women and men pay a price if they do not behave in ways expected   14
of their gender: men who are not very aggressive are called "wimps," whereas women who are not very aggressive are called "feminine." Men who are aggressive are called "go-getters," though if they go too far, from the point of view of the viewer, they may be called "arrogant." This can hurt them, but not nearly as much as the innumerable labels for women who are thought to be too aggressive — starting with the most hurtful one: bitch.

Even the compliments that we receive are revealing. One woman who   15
had designed and implemented a number of innovative programs was praised by someone who said, "You have such a gentle way of bringing about radical change that people don't realize what's happening — or don't get threatened by it." This was a compliment, but it also hinted at the downside of the woman's gentle touch: although it made it possible for her to be effective in instituting the changes she envisioned, her unobtrusive style ensured a lack of recognition. If people don't realize what's happening, they won't give her credit for what she has accomplished.

Not only advancement and recognition, but hiring is affected by ways of   16
speaking. A woman who supervised three computer programmers mentioned that her best employee was another woman who she had hired over the objections of her own boss. Her boss had preferred a male candidate, because he felt the man would be better able to step into her supervisory role if needed. But she had taken a dislike to the male candidate. For one thing, she had felt

he was inappropriately flirtatious with her. But most important, she had found him arrogant, because he spoke as if he already had the job, using the pronoun "we" to refer to the group that had not yet hired him.

I have no way of knowing whether the woman hired was indeed the bet- 17 ter of these two candidates, or whether either she or the man was well suited to assume the supervisory role, but I am intrigued that the male boss was impressed with the male candidate's take-charge self-presentation, while the women supervisor was put off by it. And it seems quite likely that whatever it was about his way of talking that struck her as arrogant was exactly what led her boss to conclude that this man would be better able to take over her job if needed.

Questions to Start You Thinking

1. CONSIDERING MEANING: According to Tannen, what are the key differences in the way men and women communicate at work? What are the major consequences of these differences?

2. IDENTIFYING WRITING STRATEGIES: Where does Tannen identify the causes and the effects of each gender's style of speech in the workplace? How does she use this cause and effect strategy to make her argument that women are at a cultural disadvantage in the workplace?

3. READING CRITICALLY: Tannen supports her argument with evidence she has apparently gained from personal interviews as well as with studies by a psychologist, an anthropologist, and other scholars. Why does she draw on this wide variety of sources? Is her evidence sufficient to convince you? Why, or why not?

4. EXPANDING VOCABULARY: Define *declamatory, halting,* and *circumstantial* (paragraph 6). Why does a *declamatory* or *halting* tone provide *circumstantial* evidence about a person's level of confidence (paragraph 6)?

5. MAKING CONNECTIONS: Based on Tannen's observations about the differences between the ways men and women talk, would men or women be more likely to succeed in the type of career described by Thomas F. Cawsey, Gene Deszca, and Maurice Mazerolle ("The Portfolio Career as a Response to a Changing Job Market," p. 635)? Why, or why not?

Link to the Paired Essay

Tannen explains that many of the differences between the way men and women talk are learned as children from their peers, while Nicholas Wade ("How Men and Women Think," p. 556) argues that these differences may actually be the result of differences between male and female brains. Compare and contrast Tannen's and Wade's views.

Journal Prompts

1. Analyze your own talking or presentation style at work or in the classroom. Does it conform to Tannen's analysis of how men and women talk?

2. What style of verbal presentation is one expected to use at a job interview? If this expectation did not exist, would you choose a different manner of presenting yourself? Explain.

Suggestions for Writing

1. Analyze the way your boss, co-workers, teachers, or classmates talk to you at work or school. How does their way of talking compare with how Tannen suggests they talk?

2. Are gender differences determined by social forces or biological factors? Write an essay in which you take a stand on this issue, drawing on Tannen's and Wade's arguments as well as other evidence to support your position. Be sure to consider and refute the arguments on the other side of the debate.

Nicholas Wade *was born in 1942 in England. Educated at Cambridge, Wade wrote for* Nature *magazine in London before coming to the United States in 1971. He began his U.S. career writing for* Science *magazine before joining the* New York Times *as an editorial writer. Wade is currently the editor of the* New York Times's *Science section and author of the "Method and Madness" column for the* New York Times Magazine. *His several books include* The Ultimate Experiment *(1977),* The Nobel Duel *(1981), and* A World beyond Healing *(1987). He also coedited* The Environment from Your Backyard to the Ocean Floor *(vol. 2 of* The New York Times Book of Science Literacy, *1994) and* The New York Times Book of Health: How to Feel Fitter, Eat Better, and Live Longer *(1998). "How Men and Women Think" was first published in the* New York Times Magazine *on June 12, 1994. While Deborah Tannen ("Women and Men Talking on the Job," p. 550) believes that behavioral differences between men and women are the result of socialization, Wade suggests that men and women behave differently because of biology.*

AS YOU READ: *Identify the evidence that Wade uses to support his claim that gender differences might have a biological basis.*

Nicholas Wade   How Men and Women Think

The human brain, according to an emerging new body of scientific research, comes in two different varieties, maybe as different as the accompanying physique. Men, when they are lost, instinctually fall back on their in-built navigational skills, honed from far-off days of tracking large prey miles from home. Women, by contrast, tend to find their way by the simpler methods of remembering local landmarks or even asking help from strangers.   1

Men excel on psychological tests that require the imaginary twisting in space of a three-dimensional object. The skill seems to help with higher math, where the topmost ranks are thronged with male minds like Andrew Wiles of Princeton, who proclaimed almost a year ago that he had proved Fermat's Last Theorem° and will surely get around to publishing the proof almost any day now.   2

Fermat's Last Theorem: A problem that has been puzzling mathematicians for 350 years. Since this essay first came out, Wiles *has* published the proof.

Some feminist ideologues° assert that all minds are created equal and   3
women would be just as good at math if they weren't discouraged in school.
But Camilla Benbow, a psychologist at Iowa State University, has spent years
assessing biases like male math teachers or parents who favor boys. She concludes that boys' superiority at math is mostly innate.°

But women, the new studies assert, have the edge in most other ways, like   4
perceptual speed, verbal fluency, and communications skills. They also have
sharper hearing than men, and excel in taste, smell, and touch, and in fine coordination of hand and eye. If Martians arrived and gave job interviews, it
seems likely they would direct men to competitive sports and manual labor
and staff most professions, diplomacy, and government with women.

The measurement of intellectual differences is a field with a long and   5
mostly disgraceful past. IQ tests have been regularly misused, sometimes even
concocted, in support of prevailing prejudices. Distinguished male anato-
mists used to argue that women were less intelligent because their brains
weighed less, neglecting to correct for the strong influence of body weight on
brain weight.

The present studies of sex differences are venturing on ground where self-   6
deception and prejudice are constant dangers. The science is difficult and the
results prone to misinterpretation. Still, the budding science seems free so far
of obvious error. For one thing, many of the field's leading practitioners happen to be women, perhaps because male academics in this controversial field
have had their lives made miserable by militant feminists.

For another, the study of brain sex differences does not depend on just   7
one kind of subvertible measure but draws on several different disciplines, including biology and anatomy. As is described in a new book, *Eve's Rib*, by
Robert Pool, and the earlier *Brain Sex* by Anne Moir and David Jessel, the
foundations of the field have been carefully laid in animal research. Experiments with rats show that exposure in the womb to testosterone indelibly im-
prints a male pattern of behavior; without testosterone, the rat's brain is
female.

In human fetuses, too, the sex hormones seem to mold a male and female   8
version of the brain, each subtly different in organization and behavior. The
best evidence comes from girls with a rare genetic anomaly° who are exposed
in the womb to more testosterone than normal; they grow up doing better
than their unaffected sisters on the tests that boys are typically good at. There's
also some evidence, not yet confirmed, that male and female brains may be
somewhat differently structured, with the two cerebral hemispheres being
more specialized and less well interconnected in men than in women.

If the human brain exists in male and female versions, as modulated in   9
the womb, that would explain what every parent knows, that boys and girls
prefer different patterns of play regardless of well-meaning efforts to impose
unisex toys on both.

---

ideologues: People who believe strongly in a certain theory.   **innate:** Present at birth.
anomaly: Something that is unlike the general rule.

The human mind being very versatile, however, any genetic propensities   10
are far from decisive. In math, for example, the average girl is pretty much as
good as the average boy. Only among the few students at the peak of math
ability do boys predominate.° Within the loose framework set by the genes,
education makes an enormous difference. In Japan, boys exceed girls on the
mental rotation tests, just as in America. But the Japanese girls outscore American boys. Maybe Japanese kids are just smarter or, more likely, just better
taught, Japan being a country where education is taken seriously and parents
and teachers consistently push children to excel.

There are some obvious cautions to draw about the social and political   11
implications that might one day flow from brain sex research. One is that differences between individuals of the same sex often far exceed the slight differences between the sexes as two population groups: "If I were going into
combat, I would prefer to have Martina Navratilova at my side than Robert
Reich,"° says Patricia Ireland, president of the National Organization for
Women. Even if men in general excel in math, an individual woman could
still be better than most men.

On the other hand, if the brains of men and women really are organized   12
differently, it's possible the sexes both prefer and excel at different occupations, perhaps those with more or less competition or social interaction. "In
a world of scrupulous° gender equality, equal numbers of girls and boys
would be educated and trained for . . . all the professions. . . . [Hiring would
proceed] until half of every workplace was made up of men and half,
women," says Judith Lorber in *Paradoxes of Gender*, a new work of feminist theory. That premise does not hold if there are real intellectual differences between the sexes; the test of equal opportunity, when all unfair barriers to
women have fallen, will not necessarily be equal outcomes.

Greek mythology tells that Tiresias, having lived both as a man and a   13
woman for some complicated reason, was asked to settle a dispute between
Zeus and Hera as to which sex enjoyed sex more. He replied that there was no
contest — it was ten times better for women. Whereupon Hera struck him
blind for his insolence and Zeus in compensation gave him the gift of foresight. Like Tiresias, the brain sex researchers are uncovering some impolitic
truths, potent enough to shake Mount Olympus some day.

**Questions to Start
You Thinking**

1. CONSIDERING MEANING: According to Wade, why is it difficult to do valid, reliable studies of sex differences?

2. IDENTIFYING WRITING STRATEGIES: Wade devotes much of the article to summarizing studies on sex differences. Identify the passages where he summarizes others' research as evidence to support his position.

predominate: Be present in greater numbers.   **Robert Reich:** Former Secretary of Labor.
scrupulous: Extremely careful.

3. READING CRITICALLY: Although Wade cites many different expert sources as evidence to support his argument, he makes a number of claims that he does not back up. Reread Wade's essay, noting when he makes a claim without referring to a source. How convincing do you find these claims? Does his lack of evidence damage his argument in any way? Why, or why not?

4. EXPANDING VOCABULARY: Define *impolitic* and *potent* (paragraph 13). Why are the truths that brain sex researchers are uncovering both "impolitic" and "potent"?

5. MAKING CONNECTIONS: Would Michael Shermer ("Abducted! Encounters with Aliens," p. 596) say that Wade is a skeptic? Why, or why not?

Link to the Paired Essay

Both Wade and Deborah Tannen ("Women and Men Talking on the Job," p. 550) suggest that no matter what science is able to prove about the cause, everyday experience shows us that men and women are different. Why do both authors use common sense and everyday examples to help support the scientific research they cite? Do you find examples from everyday life to be convincing as evidence? Why, or why not?

Journal Prompts

1. Do you have any personality traits or intellectual qualities that you feel are typically associated with the opposite sex? How do you feel about these traits?

2. Drawing on your own experience and observations, do you believe there are significant differences in the way men and women think? If so, do you think these differences are innate or the result of socialization? Explain.

Suggestions for Writing

1. Recall your own experience taking aptitude tests. In your opinion, did these tests accurately measure your abilities — or were they unfair because of gender bias? Write an essay explaining your responses to these tests, offering evidence to support your assessment of their fairness and accuracy.

2. Think of a profession that seems to be dominated by either men or women. Using examples from Wade's and Tannen's essays and your own observations, write an essay that examines the possible causes of a gender imbalance in the field you have chosen.

Chapter 24

American Diversity

Web Search

Use a search engine to find the Web site for a political or social organization, such as People for the Ethical Treatment of Animals (PETA), People for the American Way, the National Association for the Advancement of Colored People (NAACP), Empower America, or the Cato Institute. What issues are discussed? Analyze the stand the orgranization takes on one issue that is important to its members. What kinds of evidence does the Web site use to support the organization's position? Are the arguments convincing? Why, or why not? Are they more or less convincing because they are being set forth on the World Wide Web?

Brent Staples, *born in 1951 in Chester, Pennsylvania, earned a Ph.D. in psychology from the University of Chicago and worked for the* Chicago Sun Times *and* Down Beat *magazine before joining the* New York Times *in 1985. A member of the* Times *editorial board, he has contributed to many publications and is the author of the memoir* Parallel Time: Growing Up in Black and White *(1994). In the following essay, published in a slightly different version in* Ms. *magazine in September 1986, Staples reflects on the anxiety his presence arouses in nighttime pedestrians.*

AS YOU READ: *Identify why other pedestrians respond to Staples with anxiety.*

Brent Staples   Black Men and Public Space

My first victim was a woman — white, well dressed, probably in her late twenties. I came upon her late one evening on a deserted street in Hyde Park, a relatively affluent neighborhood in an otherwise mean, impoverished section of Chicago. As I swung onto the avenue behind her, there seemed to be a discreet, uninflammatory distance between us. Not so. She cast back a worried glance. To her, the youngish black man — a broad six feet two inches with a beard and billowing hair, both hands shoved into the pockets of a bulky military jacket — seemed menacingly close. After a few more quick glimpses, she picked up her pace and was soon running in earnest. Within seconds, she disappeared into a cross street.

That was more than a decade ago. I was twenty-two years old, a graduate student newly arrived at the University of Chicago. It was in the echo of that terrified woman's footfalls that I first began to know the unwieldy inheritance I'd come into — the ability to alter public space in ugly ways. It was clear that she thought herself the quarry of a mugger, a rapist, or worse. Suffering a bout of insomnia, however, I was stalking sleep, not defenseless wayfarers. As a softy who is scarcely able to take a knife to a raw chicken — let alone hold one to a person's throat — I was surprised, embarrassed, and dismayed all at once. Her flight made me feel like an accomplice in tyranny. It also made it clear that I was indistinguishable from the muggers who occasionally seeped into the area from the surrounding ghetto. The first encounter, and those that followed, signified that a vast, unnerving gulf lay between nighttime pedestrians — particularly women — and me. And I soon gathered that being perceived as dangerous is a hazard in itself. I only needed to turn a corner into a dicey situation, or crowd some frightened, armed person in a foyer somewhere, or make an errant move after being pulled over by a policeman. Where fear and weapons meet — and they often do in urban America — there is always the possibility of death.

In that first year, my first away from my hometown, I was to become thoroughly familiar with the language of fear. At dark, shadowy intersections, I could cross in front of a car stopped at a traffic light and elicit the *thunk, thunk, thunk, thunk* of the driver — black, white, male, or female — hammering down the door locks. On less traveled streets after dark, I grew accustomed to but

561

never comfortable with people crossing to the other side of the street rather than pass me. Then there were the standard unpleasantries with policemen, doormen, bouncers, cabdrivers, and others whose business it is to screen out troublesome individuals *before* there is any nastiness.

I moved to New York nearly two years ago and I have remained an avid night walker. In central Manhattan, the near-constant crowd cover minimizes tense one-on-one street encounters. Elsewhere — in SoHo, for example, where sidewalks are narrow and tightly spaced buildings shut out the sky — things can get very taut indeed.

After dark, on the warrenlike° streets of Brooklyn where I live, I often see women who fear the worst from me. They seem to have set their faces on neutral, and with their purse straps strung across their chests bandolier-style, they forge ahead as though bracing themselves against being tackled. I understand, of course, that the danger they perceive is not a hallucination. Women are particularly vulnerable to street violence, and young black males are drastically overrepresented among the perpetrators of that violence. Yet these truths are no solace against the kind of alienation that comes of being ever the suspect, a fearsome entity with whom pedestrians avoid making eye contact.

It is not altogether clear to me how I reached the ripe old age of twenty-two without being conscious of the lethality nighttime pedestrians attributed to me. Perhaps it was because in Chester, Pennsylvania, the small, angry industrial town where I came of age in the 1960s, I was scarcely noticeable against a backdrop of gang warfare, street knifings, and murders. I grew up one of the good boys, had perhaps a half-dozen fistfights. In retrospect, my shyness of combat has clear sources.

As a boy, I saw countless tough guys locked away; I have since buried several, too. They were babies, really — a teenage cousin, a brother of twenty-two, a childhood friend in his mid-twenties — all gone down in episodes of bravado played out in the streets. I came to doubt the virtues of intimidation early on. I chose, perhaps unconsciously, to remain a shadow — timid, but a survivor.

The fearsomeness mistakenly attributed to me in public places often has a perilous flavor. The most frightening of these confusions occurred in the late 1970s and early 1980s, when I worked as a journalist in Chicago. One day, rushing into the office of a magazine I was writing for with a deadline story in hand, I was mistaken for a burglar. The office manager called security and, with an ad hoc° posse, pursued me through the labyrinthine halls, nearly to my editor's door. I had no way of proving who I was. I could only move briskly toward the company of someone who knew me.

Another time I was on assignment for a local paper and killing time before an interview. I entered a jewelry store on the city's affluent Near North Side. The proprietor excused herself and returned with an enormous red Doberman pinscher straining at the end of a leash. She stood, the dog ex-

warrenlike: Like a maze.   **ad hoc:** Spur of the moment.

tended toward me, silent to my questions, her eyes bulging nearly out of her head. I took a cursory look around, nodded, and bade her good night.

Relatively speaking, however, I never fared as badly as another black male 10 journalist. He went to nearby Waukegan, Illinois, a couple of summers ago to work on a story about a murderer who was born there. Mistaking the reporter for the killer, police officers hauled him from his car at gunpoint and but for his press credentials would probably have tried to book him. Such episodes are not uncommon. Black men trade tales like this all the time.

Over the years, I learned to smother the rage I felt at so often being taken 11 for a criminal. Not to do so would surely have led to madness. I now take precautions to make myself less threatening. I move about with care, particularly late in the evening. I give a wide berth° to nervous people on subway platforms during the wee hours, particularly when I have exchanged business clothes for jeans. If I happen to be entering a building behind some people who appear skittish, I may walk by, letting them clear the lobby before I return, so as not to seem to be following them. I have been calm and extremely congenial° on those rare occasions when I've been pulled over by the police.

And on late-evening constitutionals° I employ what has proved to be an 12 excellent tension-reducing measure: I whistle melodies from Beethoven and Vivaldi and the more popular classical composers. Even steely New Yorkers hunching toward nighttime destinations seem to relax, and occasionally they even join in the tune. Virtually everybody seems to sense that a mugger wouldn't be warbling bright, sunny selections from Vivaldi's *Four Seasons*. It is my equivalent of the cowbell that hikers wear when they know they are in bear country.

Questions to Start You Thinking

1. CONSIDERING MEANING: How does Staples react to other people's misconceptions about him? What does he feel causes such misconceptions?

2. IDENTIFYING WRITING STRATEGIES: At the end of the essay, how does Staples use comparison to explain his behavior?

3. READING CRITICALLY: What kinds of appeals — emotional, logical, ethical — does Staples use? Are his appeals appropriate for the purpose of his essay? Why, or why not? (For an explanation of kinds of appeals, see p. 103 in *A Writer's Guide*.)

4. EXPANDING VOCABULARY: Define *affluent, uninflammatory* (paragraph 1), *unwieldy, quarry, errant* (paragraph 2), *bandolier, solace* (paragraph 5), *lethality* (paragraph 6), and *bravado* (paragraph 7). Why do you think Staples uses such formal language in this essay?

5. MAKING CONNECTIONS: Staples attempts to counter stereotypes of African American men by whistling "melodies from . . . the more popular classical composers" (paragraph 12). Compare and contrast this response to stereotyping with the one described by Gerald Early in "Black like . . . Shirley Temple?" (p. 502).

berth: Space. **congenial:** Sociable. **constitutionals:** Walks taken for the purpose of pleasure or health.

Journal Prompts

1. Are stereotypes ever useful? Why, or why not?

2. Have you or someone you know ever been wrongfully stereotyped or pre-judged? How did you react?

Suggestions for Writing

1. Staples describes his feelings about being the object of racial fear. Have you ever been the object of such a fear or of other misconceptions based on prej-udice or stereotypes? Write a short personal essay discussing the causes and effects of your experience. What preconceptions were you the victim of? How did you respond?

2. What do you think causes the stereotype of African American men that Staples is addressing? Write an essay that analyzes this stereotype, drawing on several outside sources to support your analysis.

Judith Ortiz Cofer *was born in 1952 in Hormigueros, Puerto Rico, and immi-grated to the United States in 1956. She studied at Augusta College, Florida Atlantic University, and Oxford University and now teaches at the University of Georgia. Her books include the poetry collections* Terms of Survival *(1988) and* Reaching for the Mainland *(1995), the novel* The Line of the Sun *(1989), and the essay col-lection* Silent Dancing *(1990).* The Latin Deli *(1993), includes poetry, fiction, and nonfiction. Ortiz Cofer wrote for young adult readers in her story collection* An Island Like You *(1995); her newest book is* The Year of Our Revolution *(1998). In the following essay from* The Latin Deli, *Ortiz Cofer blends autobiog-raphy with analysis to show how Latin American women are misread within white culture.*

AS YOU READ: *Identify the myths about Latin women that Ortiz Cofer addresses in her essay.*

Judith Ortiz Cofer   The Myth of the Latin Woman: I Just Met a Girl Named María

On a bus trip to London from Oxford University where I was earning some graduate credits one summer, a young man, obviously fresh from a pub, spotted me and as if struck by inspiration went down on his knees in the aisle. With both hands over this heart he broke into an Irish tenor's rendition of "María" from *West Side Story.* My politely amused fellow passengers gave his lovely voice the round of gentle applause it deserved. Though I was not quite as amused, I managed my version of an English smile: no show of teeth, no extreme contortions of the facial muscles — I was at this time of my life prac-ticing reserve and cool. Oh, that British control, how I coveted it. But María had followed me to London, reminding me of a prime fact of my life: you can leave the Island, master the English language, and travel as far as you can, but if you are a Latina, especially one like me who so obviously belongs to Rita Moreno's° gene pool, the Island travels with you.

This is sometimes a very good thing—it may win you that extra minute   2 of someone's attention. But with some people, the same things can make *you* an island—not so much a tropical paradise as an Alcatraz,° a place nobody wants to visit. As a Puerto Rican girl growing up in the United States and wanting like most children to "belong," I resented the stereotype that my Hispanic appearance called forth from many people I met.

Our family lived in a large urban center in New Jersey during the sixties,   3 where life was designed as a microcosm of my parents' casas on the island. We spoke in Spanish, we ate Puerto Rican food bought at the bodega,° and we practiced strict Catholicism complete with Saturday confession and Sunday mass at a church where our parents were accommodated into a one-hour Spanish mass slot, performed by a Chinese priest trained as a missionary for Latin America.

As a girl I was kept under strict surveillance, since virtue and modesty   4 were, by cultural equation, the same as family honor. As a teenager I was instructed on how to behave as a proper señorita. But it was a conflicting message girls got, since the Puerto Rican mothers also encouraged their daughters to look and act like women and to dress in clothes our Anglo friends and their mothers found too "mature" for our age. It was, and is, cultural, yet I often felt humiliated when I appeared at an American friend's party wearing a dress more suitable to a semiformal than to a playroom birthday celebration. At Puerto Rican festivities, neither the music nor the colors we wore could be too loud. I still experience a vague sense of letdown when I'm invited to a "party" and it turns out to be a marathon conversation in hushed tones rather than a fiesta with salsa, laughter, and dancing—the kind of celebration I remember from my childhood.

I remember Career Day in our high school, when teachers told us to come   5 dressed as if for a job interview. It quickly became obvious that to the barrio° girls, "dressing up" sometimes meant wearing ornate jewelry and clothing that would be more appropriate (by mainstream standards) for the company Christmas party than as daily office attire. That morning I had agonized in front of my closet, trying to figure out what a "career girl" would wear because, essentially, except for Marlo Thomas° on TV, I had no models on which to base my decision. I knew how to dress for school: at the Catholic school I attended we all wore uniforms; I knew how to dress for Sunday mass, and knew what dresses to wear for parties at my relatives' homes. Though I do not recall the precise details of my Career Day outfit, it must have been a composite of

---

Rita Moreno: (b. 1931) Latina actress who played María's friend in the movie version of the Broadway musical *West Side Story.*   **Alcatraz:** Federal prison used from 1933 to 1963 and located on a rocky island in San Francisco Bay.   **bodega:** Latino grocery store. **barrio:** Spanish-speaking neighborhood.   **Marlo Thomas:** (b. 1943) Actress who starred in the TV show *That Girl* (1965–71), about an aspiring actress and model.

the above choices. But I remember a comment my friend (an Italian American) made in later years that coalesced° my impressions of that day. She said that at the business school she was attending the Puerto Rican girls always stood out for wearing "everything at once." She meant, of course, too much jewelry, too many accessories. On that day at school, we were simply made the negative models by the nuns who were themselves not credible fashion experts to any of us. But it was painfully obvious to me that to the others, in their tailored skirts and silk blouses, we must have seemed "hopeless" and "vulgar." Though I now know that most adolescents feel out of step much of the time, I also know that for the Puerto Rican girls of my generation that sense was intensified. The way our teachers and classmates looked at us that day in school was just a taste of the culture clash that awaited us in the real world, where prospective employers and men on the street would often misinterpret our tight skirts and jingling bracelets as a come-on.

Mixed cultural signals have perpetuated certain stereotypes — for example, that of the Hispanic woman as the "Hot Tamale" or sexual firebrand. It is a one-dimensional view that the media have found easy to promote. In their special vocabulary, advertisers have designated not only the foods but also the women of Latin America. From conversations in my house I recall hearing about the harassment that Puerto Rican women endured in factories where the "boss men" talked to them as if sexual innuendo was all they understood and, worse, often gave them the choice of submitting to advances or being fired.

It is custom, however, not chromosomes, that leads us to choose scarlet over pale pink. As young girls, we were influenced in our decisions about clothes and color by the women — older sisters and mothers who had grown up on a tropical island where the natural environment was a riot of primary colors, where showing your skin was one way to keep cool as well as to look sexy. Most important of all, on the island, women perhaps felt freer to dress and move more provocatively, since, in most cases, they were protected by the traditions, mores,° and laws of a Spanish/Catholic system of morality and machismo whose main rule was: *You may look at my sister, but if you touch her I will kill you.* The extended family and church structure could provide a young woman with a circle of safety in her small pueblo on the island; if a man "wronged" a girl, everyone would close in to save her family honor.

This is what I have gleaned from my discussions as an adult with older Puerto Rican women. They have told me about dressing in their best party clothes on Saturday nights and going to the town's plaza to promenade with their girlfriends in front of the boys they liked. The males were thus given an opportunity to admire the women and to express their admiration in the form of *piropos*: erotically charged street poems they composed on the spot. I have been subjected to a few piropos while visiting the island, and they can be outrageous, although custom dictates that they must never cross into obscenity. This ritual, as I understand it, also entails a show of studied indifference on

coalesced: Brought together.   **mores:** Customs or norms.

the woman's part; if she is "decent," she must not acknowledge the man's impassioned words. So I do understand how things can be lost in translation. When a Puerto Rican girl dressed in her idea of what is attractive meets a man from the mainstream culture who has been trained to react to certain types of clothing as a sexual signal, a clash is likely to take place. The line I first heard based on the aspect of the myth happened when the boy who took me to my first formal dance leaned over to plant a sloppy overeager kiss painfully on my mouth, and when I didn't respond with sufficient passion said in a resentful tone: "I thought you Latin girls were supposed to mature early" — my first instance of being thought of as a fruit or vegetable — I was supposed to *ripen*, not just grow into womanhood like other girls.

It is surprising to some of my professional friends that some people, including those who should know better, still put others "in their place." Though rarer, these incidents are still commonplace in my life. It happened to me most recently during a stay at a very classy metropolitan hotel favored by young professional couples for their weddings. Late one evening after the theater, as I walked toward my room with my new colleague (a woman with whom I was coordinating an arts program), a middle-aged man in a tuxedo, a young girl in satin and lace on his arm, stepped directly into our path. With his champagne glass extended toward me, he exclaimed, "Evita!"°   9

Our way blocked, my companion and I listened as the man half-recited,   10
half-bellowed "Don't Cry for Me, Argentina." When he finished, the young girl said: "How about a round of applause for my daddy?" We complied, hoping this would bring the silly spectacle to a close. I was becoming aware that our little group was attracting the attention of the other guests. "Daddy" must have perceived this too, and he once more barred the way as we tried to walk past him. He began to shout-sing a ditty to the tune of "La Bamba" — except the lyrics were about a girl named María whose exploits all rhymed with her name and gonorrhea. The girl kept saying "Oh, Daddy" and looking at me with pleading eyes. She wanted me to laugh along with the others. My companion and I stood silently waiting for the man to end his offensive song. When he finished, I looked not at him but at his daughter. I advised her calmly never to ask her father what he had done in the army. Then I walked between them and to my room. My friend complimented me on my cool handling of the situation. I confessed to her that I really had wanted to push the jerk into the swimming pool. I knew this same man — probably a corporate executive, well educated, even worldly by most standards — would not have been likely to regale° a white woman with a dirty song in public. He would perhaps have checked his impulse by assuming that she could be somebody's wife or mother, or at least *somebody* who might take offense. But to him, I was just an Evita or a María: merely a character in his cartoon-populated universe.

Evita: Eva Perón (1919–1952), wife of Juan Perón (1895–1974), the fascist leader of Argentina from 1946 to 1955. The song "Don't Cry for Me, Argentina" is from the Broadway musical *Evita*, based on her life.   **regale:** Entertain.

Because of my education and my proficiency with the English language, I   11
have acquired many mechanisms for dealing with the anger I experience. This
was not true for my parents, nor is it true for the many Latin women working
at menial jobs who must put up with stereotypes about our ethnic group such
as "They make good domestics." This is another facet of the myth of the Latin
woman in the United States. Its origin is simple to deduce. Work as domestics, waitressing, and factory jobs are all that's available to women with little
English and few skills. The myth of the Hispanic menial has been sustained
by the same media phenomenon that made "Mammy" from *Gone with the
Wind* America's idea of the black woman for generations; María, the house-
maid or counter girl, is now indelibly etched into the national psyche. The big
and the little screens have presented us with the picture of the funny Hispanic
maid, mispronouncing words and cooking up a spicy storm in a shiny California kitchen.

This media-engendered image of the Latina in the United States has been   12
documented by feminist Hispanic scholars, who claim that such portrayals
are partially responsible for the denial of opportunities for upward mobility
among Latinas in the professions. I have a Chicana friend working on a Ph.D.
in philosophy at a major university. She says her doctor still shakes his head
in puzzled amazement at all the "big words" she uses. Since I do not wear my
diplomas around my neck for all to see, I too have on occasion been sent to
that "kitchen," where some think I obviously belong.

One such incident that has stayed with me, though I recognize it as a   13
minor offense, happened on the day of my first public poetry reading. It took
place in Miami in a boat-restaurant where we were having lunch before the
event. I was nervous and excited as I walked in with my notebook in my hand.
An older woman motioned me to her table. Thinking (foolish me) that she
wanted me to autograph a copy of my brand new slender volume of verse, I
went over. She ordered a cup of coffee from me, assuming that I was the waitress. Easy enough to mistake my poems for menus, I suppose. I know that it
wasn't an intentional act of cruelty, yet of all the good things that happened
that day, I remember that scene most clearly, because it reminded me of what
I had to overcome before anyone would take me seriously. In retrospect I understand that my anger gave my reading fire, that I have almost always taken
doubts in my abilities as a challenge — and that the result is, most times, a
feeling of satisfaction at having won a convert, when I see the cold, apprais-
ing eyes warm to my words, the body language change, the smile that indicates that I have opened some avenue for communication. That day I read to
that woman and her lowered eyes told me that she was embarrassed at her
little faux pas, and when I willed her to look up at me, it was my victory, and
she graciously allowed me to punish her with my full attention. We shook
hands at the end of the reading, and I never saw her again. She has probably
forgotten the whole thing but maybe not.

Yet I am one of the lucky ones. My parents made it possible for me to ac-   14
quire a stronger footing in the mainstream culture by giving me the chance at
an education. And books and art have saved me from the harsher forms of

ethnic and racial prejudice that many of my Hispanic *compañeras* have had to endure. I travel a lot around the United States, reading from my books of poetry and my novel, and the reception I most often receive is one of positive interest by people who want to know more about my culture. There are, however, thousands of Latinas without the privilege of an education or the entrée° into society that I have. For them life is a struggle against the misconceptions perpetuated by the myth of the Latina as whore, domestic, or criminal. We cannot change this by legislating the way people look at us. The transformation, as I see it, has to occur at a much more individual level. My personal goal in my public life is to try to replace the old pervasive stereotypes and myths about Latinas with a much more interesting set of realities. Every time I give a reading, I hope the stories I tell, the dreams and fears I examine in my work, can achieve some universal truth which will get my audience past the particulars of my skin color, my accent, or my clothes.

I once wrote a poem in which I called us Latinas "God's brown daughters." This poem is really a prayer of sorts, offered upward, but also, through the human-to-human channel of art, outward. It is a prayer for communication, and for respect. In it, Latin women pray "in Spanish to an Anglo God / with a Jewish heritage," and they are "fervently hoping / that if not omnipotent, / at least He be bilingual." 15

Questions to Start You Thinking

1. CONSIDERING MEANING: What does Ortiz Cofer believe are the reasons for the myths about Latin women?

2. IDENTIFYING WRITING STRATEGIES: What examples does Ortiz Cofer use to compare and contrast how Latinas are seen by their own and by other cultures?

3. READING CRITICALLY: Ortiz Cofer states that her personal goal is to "try to replace the old pervasive stereotypes and myths about Latinas with a much more interesting set of realities" (paragraph 14). Does her essay accomplish this purpose? Why, or why not?

4. EXPANDING VOCABULARY: Define *indelibly* and *psyche* (paragraph 11). According to Ortiz Cofer, how has the stereotype of the Hispanic domestic servant been "indelibly etched into the national psyche"?

5. MAKING CONNECTIONS: Ortiz Cofer and Judy Brady ("I Want a Wife," p. 529) both seek to expose stereotypes of women. Compare and contrast Ortiz Cofer's tone with Brady's. Whose approach do you find more effective and why?

Journal Prompts

1. What aspects of your identity are reflected in the clothes you wear?

2. What stereotypes seem particularly difficult to deflate? How would you combat these stereotypes?

entrée: Entrance.

1. Recall a time when you first became aware of a stereotype. What was the stereotype, and what incident triggered your awareness of it? Narrate the incident and your reaction to it.

2. Write an essay analyzing one or two episodes of a television sitcom that you think bases its humor on the use of stereotypes. What are those stereotypes, and how does the show present them? In your opinion, are these stereotypes harmless or destructive? Defend your response.

Steve Olson *was born in 1946 in Rice Lake, Wisconsin. Unaccompanied by the usual list of degrees, awards, and publications, Olson identified himself simply as "a construction worker" when asked for biographical information. Claiming that he writes "mostly for [him]self," he seems to be speaking for the average American. In the following piece, which appeared as a "My Turn" essay in* Newsweek *on November 6, 1989, Olson strives to honor the dialect and ethic of a group of Americans who are often stereotyped but rarely heard from.*

AS YOU READ: *Identify the stereotypes about blue-collar workers that Olson addresses in his essay.*

Steve Olson   Year of the Blue-Collar Guy

While the learned are attaching appropriate labels to the 1980s and speculating on what the 1990s will bring, I would like to steal 1989 for my own much maligned° group and declare it "the year of the blue-collar guy (BCG)." BCGs have been portrayed as beer-drinking, big-bellied, bigoted rednecks who dress badly. Wearing a suit to a cement-finishing job wouldn't be too bright. Watching my tie go around a motor shaft followed by my neck is not the last thing I want to see in this world. But, more to the point, our necks are too big and our arms and shoulders are too awesome to fit suits well without expensive tailoring. Suits are made for white-collar guys.

But we need big bellies as ballast to stay on the bar stool while we're drinking beer. And our necks are red from the sun and we are somewhat bigoted. But aren't we all? At least our bigotry is open and honest and worn out front like a tattoo. White-collar people are bigoted, too. But it's disguised as the pat on the back that holds you back: "You're not good enough so you need affirmative action." BCGs aren't smart enough to be that cynical. I never met a BCG who didn't respect an honest day's work and a job well done — no matter who did it.

True enough, BCGs aren't perfect. But, I believe this: we are America's last true romantic heroes. When some twenty-first-century Louis L'Amour° writes

maligned: Talked badly about.   **Louis L'Amour** (1908–1988): Best-selling author of Westerns.

about this era he won't eulogize the greedy Wall Street insider. He won't commend the narrow-shouldered, wide-hipped lawyers with six-digit unearned incomes doing the same work women can do. His wide-shouldered heroes will be plucked from the ranks of the blue-collar guy. They are the last vestige° of the manly world where strength, skill, and hard work are still valued.

To some extent our negative ratings are our own fault. While we were 4 building the world we live in, white-collar types were sitting on their ever-widening butts redefining the values we live by. One symbol of America's opulent wealth is the number of people who can sit and ponder and comment and write without producing a usable product or skill. Hey, get a real job — make something — then talk. These talkers are the guys we drove from the playgrounds into the libraries when we were young and now for twenty years or more we have endured the revenge of the nerds.

BCGs fidgeted our way out of the classroom and into jobs where, it 5 seemed, the only limit to our income was the limit of our physical strength and energy. A co-worker described a BCG as "a guy who is always doing things that end in the letter 'n' — you know huntin', fishin', workin' . . ." My wise friend is talking energy! I have seen men on the job hand-nail 20 square of shingles (that's 6,480 nails) or more a day, day after day, for weeks. At the same time, they were remodeling their houses, raising children, and coaching Little League. I've seen crews frame entire houses in a day — day after day. I've seen guys finish concrete until 11 P.M., go out on a date, then get up at 6 A.M. and do it all over again the next day.

These are amazing feats of strength. There should be stadiums full of 6 screaming fans for these guys. I saw a forty-year-old man neatly fold a 350-pound piece of rubber roofing, put it on his shoulder and, alone, carry it up a ladder and deposit it on a roof. Nobody acknowledged it because the event was too common. One day at noon this same fellow wrestled a twenty-two-year-old college summer worker. In the prime of his life, the college kid was a 6-foot-3, 190-pound body-builder and he was out of his league. He was on his back to stay in ninety seconds flat.

Great Skilled Work Force

Mondays are tough on any job. But in our world this pain is eased by stories 7 of weekend adventure. While white-collar types are debating the value of reading over watching TV, BCGs are doing stuff. I have honest to God heard these things on Monday mornings about BCG weekends: "I tore out a wall and added a room," "I built a garage," "I went walleye fishing Saturday and pheasant hunting Sunday," "I played touch football both days" (in January), "I went skydiving," "I went to the sports show and wrestled the bear." Pack a good novel into these weekends.

My purpose is not so much to put down white-collar people as to stress 8 the importance of blue-collar people to this country. Lawyers, politicians, and bureaucrats are necessary parts of the process, but this great skilled workforce

vestige: A visible sign left by something vanished or lost.

is so taken for granted it is rarely seen as the luxury it truly is. Our plumbing works, our phones work, and repairs are made as quickly as humanly possible. I don't think this is true in all parts of the world. But this blue-collar resource is becoming endangered. Being a tradesman is viewed with such disdain these days that most young people I know treat the trades like a temporary summer job. I've seen young guys take minimum-wage jobs just so they can wear suits. It is as if any job without a dress code is a dead-end job. This is partly our own fault. We even tell our own sons, "Don't be like me, get a job people respect." Blue-collar guys ought to brag more, even swagger a little. We should drive our families past the latest job site and say, "That house was a piece of junk, and now it's the best one on the block. I did that." Nobody will respect us if we don't respect ourselves.

Our work is hard, hot, wet, cold, and always dirty. It is also often very satisfying. Entailing the use of both brain and body there is a product — a physical result of which to be proud. We have fallen from your roofs, died under heavy equipment, and been entombed in your dams. We have done honest, dangerous work. Our skills and energy and strength have transformed lines on paper into physical reality. We are this century's Renaissance men. America could do worse than to honor us. We still do things the old-fashioned way, and we have earned the honor.

Questions to Start You Thinking

1. CONSIDERING MEANING: Why does Olson feel there should be a "Year of the Blue-Collar Guy"? What would be the purpose of such a year?

2. IDENTIFYING WRITING STRATEGIES: How does Olson support his stand by comparing and contrasting the "blue-collar guy" with "white-collar types"?

3. READING CRITICALLY: What kind of appeal — emotional, logical, or ethical — does Olson use when he suggests that blue-collar workers need to do more bragging to their families about the work they do? Is the appeal an effective one? Why, or why not? (For an explanation of appeals, see p. 103 in *A Writer's Guide*.)

4. EXPANDING VOCABULARY: Define *ballast* (paragraph 2), *eulogize* (paragraph 3), *opulent* (paragraph 4), *disdain* (paragraph 8), and *Renaissance men* (paragraph 9). How does Olson's vocabulary compare to one you might expect from a self-professed "blue-collar guy" (paragraph 1)?

5. MAKING CONNECTIONS: Would Olson consider Scott Russell Sanders ("The Men We Carry in Our Minds," p. 531) an ally or a threat to his cause? Why?

Journal Prompts

1. Has a job ever influenced your self-image? When and how?

2. Does "blue-collar" describe only men? Using observation or imagination as a resource, describe the appearance and identify the leisure activities of a "blue-collar woman."

Suggestions for Writing

1. Identify a group you belong to that you think should have a year of its own (for example, college students, secretaries, parents), and write an essay taking a stand on why your group deserves such an honor.

2. Have attitudes toward blue-collar workers changed since this essay was published in 1989? Why, or why not? Write an essay in which you evaluate this question by analyzing information you gather from media sources and current research.

Toi Derricotte, *born in Detroit in 1941, earned her B.A. in special education from Wayne State University and in 1984 received an M.A. in English and creative writing from New York University. When describing her writing, Derricotte says, "I feel the need to represent what's not spoken. I discover a pocket in myself that hasn't been articulated. Then I have to find a form to carry that." Currently an associate professor of English at the University of Pittsburgh, she has been the recipient of two fellowships from the National Endowment for the Arts, the Distinguished Pioneering of the Arts Award from the United Black Artists, the Lucille Medwick Memorial Award from the Poetry Society of America, a Pushcart Prize, and the Folger Shakespeare Library Poetry Book Award. Her collections of poetry include* The Empress of the Death House *(1978),* Natural Birth *(1983),* Captivity *(1989), and* Tender *(1997). The following selection is from her memoir,* The Black Notebooks: An Interior Journey *(1997). Here Derricotte explores the complicated issue of racial identity by recounting a personal experience with racism.*

AS YOU READ: *Find out why Derricotte refused to pass as white when the opportunity presented itself.*

Toi Derricotte   **Early Memory: The *California Zephyr***

I'm sure most people don't go around all the time thinking about what 1 race they are. When you look like what you are, the external world mirrors back to you an identity consistent with your idea of yourself. However, for someone like me, who does not look like what I am, those mirrors are broken, and my consciousness or lack of consciousness takes on serious implications. Am I not conscious because, like others, I am just thinking of something else? Or is it because I don't want to be conscious? Am I mentally "passing"?

All my life I have passed invisibly into the white world, and all my life I 2 have felt that sudden and alarming moment of consciousness when I remember I am black. It may feel like I'm emerging too quickly from deep in the ocean, or touching an electric fence, or like I'm a deer stuck in the headlights of an oncoming car. Sometimes in conversation with a white person who doesn't know I'm black, suddenly a feeling comes over me, a precursor —though nothing at all has been said about race—and I either wait helplessly for the other shoe to drop, try desperately to veer the conversation in another direction, or prepare myself for painful distinctions. My desire to escape is indistinguishable from my desire to escape from my "blackness," my race, and I am filled with shame and fury. I think the first time I became conscious of this internal state was when I was fifteen, on my way cross-country on a train, the *California Zephyr*.

The first day out, a young white man sat in the seat beside me. We had   3
had a very pleasant conversation, but at night, when I grew tired, I asked him if he would go back to his seat so that I could stretch out. He said, "If you saw what's sitting in the seat beside me, you'd know why I can't go back." Of course, I knew without looking back what he meant, and as I stood up and turned around to see, I felt that now familiar combination of sickening emotions: hope that my sense of the situation was incorrect—in effect preferring to distrust my own perceptions—and fear that it wasn't, that my tender feelings for this man, and his feelings for me, were in mortal danger. If I spoke, I would make myself vulnerable. At the very least, he might categorize me in the same way he had categorized the other black person. If I didn't, I would be a coward, a betrayer of my people.

It seemed to me that even deeper than laws, than institutional practices,   4
it was his invisible thoughts that hurt me. In fact, it seemed that, in a way, it is the combined thoughts, conscious and unconscious, of all of us that hold the machinery of racism in place, and in small remarks such as these, I am able to grasp, because I am allowed entry into it, a world of hatred so deep and hidden that it is impossible to address. This juncture° in communication may seem so small an event in the history of racism, and of such indeterminate origins, that it is hardly worthy of speech. But it is precisely in such moments that I sense the local and engendering° impulse, the twisted heart that keeps us locked in separate worlds of hate. It makes me despair of any real intimacy between blacks and whites.

I turned around and, sure enough, there was a young black man, a sol-   5
dier, sitting in the seat. I said, very softly, "If you don't want to sit next to him, you don't want to sit next to me." I had hoped he'd be too stupid or deaf to understand. But he grew very quiet and said, after a few minutes, in an even softer voice than mine, "You're kidding." "No," I said. "You're kidding," he said again. "No," I said. "You're kidding." Each time he said it, he grew quieter. He excused himself. He may have slept in the bathroom. Every other seat was taken, and when I looked back to see if he was sleeping beside the soldier, the seat was empty.

The next morning, he found me on the way to breakfast and profusely   6
apologized. "Please let me buy you breakfast," he said. I was lonely and wanted company, but I felt I had to punish him. I thought punishment was the only way he would gain respect for black people, and I felt the most effective kind of punishment was not verbal confrontation—which would probably only confirm his stereotypes of hostile blacks—but cool withdrawal. I had to punish myself, too, for I didn't want the pain of loneliness

---

juncture: The moment of coming together.   **engendering:** Causing something to happen.

and alienation. I wanted and needed company, I liked him. But I felt in order to cut myself off from him, I had to cut off my feelings of tenderness and trust.

The last night on board, just before we were to arrive, I looked back and saw him sleeping beside the soldier. Perhaps he had gotten sick of sleeping in the bathroom, or perhaps my suffering had done some good. 7

Questions to Start You Thinking

1. CONSIDERING MEANING: Does confronting the racism of the man who sat next to her on the train help to resolve Derricotte's internal struggle? Why, or why not?

2. IDENTIFYING WRITING STRATEGIES: Where does Derricotte use analysis in her essay? What effect does her analysis have on her story?

3. READING CRITICALLY: Does Derricotte's ethical appeal as an African American woman who appears to be white strengthen or weaken the claims she makes about racism? Why?

4. EXPANDING VOCABULARY: Define *zephyr*. Why does Derricotte use the name of the train in the title of her essay? How may the word *zephyr* be related to the incident?

5. MAKING CONNECTIONS: Compare and contrast Derricotte's situation with the one in which Stephen Dunn finds himself ("Locker Room Talk," p. 545). Do you think the two authors would agree or disagree with each other's responses? Why?

Journal Prompts

1. What determines whether strangers who meet by chance in a public place strike up a conversation?

2. How do you go about trying to change your own way of thinking? Compare and contrast Derricotte's solution with your own.

Suggestions for Writing

1. What factors determine a person's racial identity? Write an essay that uses your own observations and experience to support your position.

2. Derricotte claims that very small events that may seem "hardly worthy of speech" make all the difference in perpetuating racism (paragraph 4). Do you agree? Why, or why not? Write an essay that takes a stand on Derricotte's claim, and support your stand with evidence from the popular media.

Paul Varnell, *born in 1941 in St. Louis, Missouri, earned his B.A. in English from Cornell University in 1963 and his M.A. in English from Indiana University in 1966. He is a writer, reviewer, and columnist whose work has appeared in* Reason *magazine, the* Advocate, *the* Chicago Reader, *and* Lambda Book Report, *among others. His biweekly column for Chicago's* Windy City Times *is syndicated throughout the gay press. Varnell has taught college English, has served on both the Chicago and the Illinois AIDS Advisory Councils, and was named the 1996 Gay Activist of the Year by the Chicago alternative weekly* New City. *In this essay, which appeared with seven of his other essays in* Beyond Queer: Challenging Gay Left Orthodoxy

(1996), Varnell addresses the issue of hate speech and argues that attempts to regulate speech present as many problems as the hate messages themselves.

AS YOU READ: *Identify Varnell's main objections to enforcing civility through legislation.*

Paul Varnell   The Niceness Solution

Sometimes when I have been walking out to my favorite tavern(s) of an 1
evening, I have been yelled at by a group of boys in a passing car.

"Hey, homo," they yell. Or, sometimes, "Faggot!" 2

It is disconcerting, even irritating, as they intend it to be irritating. And, 3
of course, depending on one's mood, it can be felt as vaguely threatening.

So it is hard not to sympathize with the motives of the good citizens of 4
Raritan, New Jersey, whose city council recently passed 5–0 a law banning
rude behavior, including rude speech.

The new law states that anyone found "behaving in a disorderly way . . . 5
by using profane, vulgar, or indecent language, by making insulting remarks
or comments to others" can be fined as much as $500 and jailed for up to
ninety days.

Raritan mayor Anthony De Cicco explained the purpose of the law: "All 6
we, the town fathers, are looking for is to maintain civility and the quality of
our lives."

The idea of enforcing civility is hardly new, of course. Courtesy codes of 7
various sorts have been tried on several college campuses in recent years. But
the earliest example I know of is the one that Michel de Montaigne encountered at the health spa in Plombière during his travels in 1580.

That code read in part, 8

Be it known that in order to secure the repose and tranquility of sundry°
ladies and other notable personages assembling from various religions and
countries at these baths,

All persons, of whatever quality [i.e., social level], condition, region, and
province they may be, are forbidden to provoke one another by insulting language tending to pick a quarrel, to bear arms . . . to give the lie . . . on pain of
being severely punished as disturbers of the peace.

And the code gave special attention to the women of 1580: 9

All persons are forbidden to use toward the ladies, gentlewomen, or other
women and girls who are at the said baths, any lascivious° or shameless
language.

According to Montaigne's journal, the people of Plombière, whom he describes as "good people, free, sensible, and considerate," each year renewed 10

sundry: Various.   lascivious: Sexually charged.

these laws on a tablet in front of the largest bathhouse — in both German and French, since the spa drew patrons from both countries.

There is something deeply touching about these efforts to make people   11 act nice toward one another: it is generous and humane of us to realize that hostile speech can be felt as demeaning to another person's humanity, that it can be psychologically as well as socially harmful. (Although the Plombière bottom line seems to be that rude speech can cause fights.)

But as we keep learning, attempts to force people to behave better gener-   12 ally do not work well, tend to be greatly abused, and equally generally have far greater costs in the long run than benefits.

What Churchill° famously said about democracy being the worst form of   13 government except for all the rest could also be said about speech limitations — that "no limits" is the worst except for all the others — and for about the same reasons.

But there are several serious objections to speech limitations besides the   14 obvious fact that they will be struck down by courts on First Amendment grounds.

For one thing, they assume a much clearer line than actually exists be-   15 tween (a) mere information and discussion of issues, and (b) rude, insulting, or hostile remarks or comments to others. One man's information can be another man's defamation. Antigay religious groups say they are only attacking "homosexuality," not us as people. But to us (as well as heterosexuals) our sexuality is a constitutive element of who we feel we are as people, and the "disagreement" or argument feels like a personal attack.

In the same way, if I disagree with someone's religious beliefs and argue   16 that the beliefs (e.g., reincarnation, virgin birth, the efficacy° of animal sacrifice) are wrong (unscientific, self-contradictory, morally vile, or whatever), devout persons may take offense and claim that their religious beliefs are a constitutive element of their personal identity, of who they are and how they relate to the cosmos. So that when I say their beliefs are false, I am attacking them as a person.

A second problem with speech or niceness codes is that they suffer from   17 a reversal of cause and effect. Whether on a college campus or in society at large, tolerance, understanding, and respect are, to a high degree, the *result* of education and the discussion process, not the precondition or starting point.

No one is born and few grow up with a genuine respect and appreciation   18 for the way others are. Rather it is experience in the world, in the rough and tumble of vigorous and uninhibited discussion, that most people learn how different other people can be and how many interesting and plausible reasons those others can offer for why their way is good or valid. In fact, the whole point of a good old-fashioned liberal education was precisely to try to achieve just such a broad and humane appreciation for the remarkably varied way people have lived and the kinds of greatness of their achievements.

Churchill: Sir Winston Churchill (1874–1965), prime minister of England 1940–45 and 1951–55, noted for his quick wit.   **efficacy:** Usefulness or appropriateness.

A third problem with niceness codes is that they assume everyone is ex- 19
quisitely sensitive to disagreement, rudeness, or being disliked, whether the
response takes the form of "He criticized my report, and I am just devastated
emotionally" or "The dude looked at me wrong, so I wasted him with my
AK-47."

"I fall upon the thorns of life, I bleed," said Shelley's Sensitive Plant. But 20
we do not even try to orient a family to such sensitivities. Rather than preserve
and foster such infirmity, our response should be: Grow a skin. Grow up, for
goodness sake. Why are you overreacting? Why are you letting other people's
speech get to you? Ignore it. Laugh at it.

A final objection to speech codes is that they embody the notion of gov- 21
ernment *in loco parentis* — in the place of parents, as the ultimate "nanny,"
treating "its" citizens as if they were children to be trained and shaped or puppies to be housebroken. The doctrine is as popular on the left, where it is embodied in the utopian dream of creating the "new Socialist man," as it is on
the right, where it is embodied in the title of columnist George Will's book
Statecraft as Soulcraft.

Ultimately, niceness codes express an exasperation with the inevitable 22
tensions among the people and groups that exist in any large and diverse society. They reflect a primitive longing for uniform and placid citizens none of
whom wants anything very much, nor who disagree very strongly about anything only because nothing is very important to them.

Sensibly, Raritan Police Chief Joseph Sferro said he would not enforce the 23
new ordinance.

Questions to Start You Thinking

1. CONSIDERING MEANING: According to Varnell, what do "niceness codes" reveal about a culture that tries to institute them?

2. IDENTIFYING WRITING STRATEGIES: What strategy does Varnell use to show his four main objections to speech codes?

3. READING CRITICALLY: Part of the evidence that Varnell provides is an extended example of an old "courtesy code" (paragraphs 8 to 9)? How well does this evidence support his argument that trying to force people to be nice generally has more costs than benefits?

4. EXPANDING VOCABULARY: Define *constitutive*. What does Varnell mean by a "*constitutive* element" of a person's identity (paragraphs 15 and 16)?

5. MAKING CONNECTIONS: How might Toi Derricotte ("Early Memory: The *California Zephyr*," p. 573) respond to Varnell's claim that it is sensible of the Raritan police chief to refuse to enforce the new law?

Journal Prompts

1. Have you ever been in a situation that caused you to change your opinion about a particular group of people (for example, football players, kindergarten teachers, convenience store owners, members of a particular religious group)? What was your opinion prior to this event? How and why did it change?

2. Do you agree that niceness codes coddle the public? Why, or why not?

Suggestions for Writing

1. Do you think that there should be legal limits to what people can say? Write an essay in which you use examples from your own experience to support your position.

2. Through newspaper archives or Internet sites, research a hate crime that occurred in the last ten years. Was hate speech involved? If so, how? Write an essay that evaluates whether the crime seems typical of other hate crimes and whether legislation might have prevented it.

Nancy Mairs, *born in 1943 in Long Beach, California, earned her B.A. from Wheaton College and attended graduate school at the University of Arizona. She was thirty years old when she developed multiple sclerosis, a disease that would eventually require her to use a wheelchair. In her writing, Mairs says she seeks "to conceptualize not merely a habitable body but a habitable World: a world that wants me in it." An essayist who lives in Tucson, Arizona, with her husband, George, Mairs won the 1995 EDI Media Award for Print Journalism. Her books include* Plaintext *(1986),* Remembering the Bone House *(1989),* Carnal Acts *(1990),* Ordinary Time *(1993), and* Voice Lessons *(1994). The following selection is an excerpt from a longer essay in her most recent book,* Waist-High in the World *(1996), in which she explores intimate personal and volatile political issues that confront people with disabilities. Here Mairs focuses on the ethics of genetic testing of fetuses in order to avoid the birth of babies with disabilities.*

AS YOU READ: *Ask yourself what Mairs means by a "freeing" choice. In what sense are the choices she describes freeing?*

Nancy Mairs   Freeing Choices

A September Sunday morning, still and hot. George and I munch our ritual scones with strawberry jam as we leaf through the *New York Times* and half listen to *Weekend Edition* on NPR. An interview comes on that I begin to heed more closely: a discussion of the increasingly common practice of using amniocentesis° to determine the sex of a fetus, followed by abortion if the parents don't want the sort they've begun. What they generally want, as parents have done from time immemorial, is a boy.

The person being interviewed plainly shares my distaste for sexual selectivity. But the way she articulates it brings me up short. "Sex," she tells her interlocutor° emphatically, "is not a birth defect."

"That sort of statement strikes a chill straight through my heart," I say to George, who has begun to listen more closely, too. He looks puzzled for a mo-

---

amniocentesis: A test that extracts and analyzes a small amount of the fluid in which a fetus is suspended.   interlocutor: Person asking questions.

ment and then responds: "Oh. Yes. I can see how it might. I never thought of it that way."

Not very many people would. The implicit argument appears self-evident: the use of abortion to fulfill the desire for a male (or female) child is impermissible, but the same use to prevent an imperfect one is not merely legitimate but, many would argue, socially responsible. As a defective myself, however, I have some doubts.

Although mine was not a birth defect, some evidence suggests a genetic predisposition° toward MS°, and one day — perhaps even quite soon — this may be detectable. What then? What if, I find myself wondering, such a test had been devised more than half a century ago? Suppose a genetic counselor had said to my mother, "Your baby will be born healthy, and she will probably remain so throughout childhood. But at some point, perhaps in her twenties, she is likely to develop a chronic incurable degenerative disease of the central nervous system. She may go blind. She may not be able to speak. Her bladder and bowels may cease to function normally. She may become incapable of walking or even of moving at all. She could experience tingling, numbness, or intractable° pain. In the end, she might have to be fed, bathed, dressed and undressed, turned over in bed, as helpless as an infant." What would Mother have done then? What should she have done?

I don't know. Morally, I feel a lot more confident asking questions than answering them. What I do know, from my own circumstances, is that I am glad Mother never faced the option to "spare" me my fate, as she might have felt obliged to do. I simply cannot say — have never been able to say, even at my most depressed, when I have easily enough wished myself dead — that I wish I had never been born. Nor do I believe that MS has poisoned my existence. Plenty of people find my life unappealing, I know. To be truthful, it doesn't altogether appeal to me. But a good scone with a cup of hot coffee does much to set things right.

I know I am lucky. There are conditions crueler than MS, including many birth defects, and some of these are already detectable by amniocentesis and ultrasound. Suppose — and I'm being far less speculative here than I was in imagining my own mother — that a woman learns that her fetus has spina bifida. The degree of disability may be impossible to predict, but the risks, she is told, include intellectual impairment, bladder and bowel dysfunction, repeated infections, and the inability to walk. Bright, healthy, and active herself, the woman strains to imagine what quality a life thus impaired might possess. Such a child can adapt to her circumstances, of course, and grow into an energetic and resourceful woman like my friend Martha, now in her sixties, married, the moderator of her own radio show.

Even if persuaded of this potentiality, the mother still must decide whether she is emotionally and financially equipped for such an undertaking, with access to medical care and educational programs, reliable assistance

---

predisposition: Susceptibility.   **MS:** Multiple sclerosis, a degenerative disease that affects the central nervous system.   **intractable:** Stubborn.

from the child's father, a supportive community, a flexible attitude toward surprises and obstacles, and an indefatigable° sense of humor. You can't decide that you're in the middle of a great book, and anyway you're sick unto death of the four-hour catheterization° schedule, and the kid's bladder can damned well wait a couple of hours till you're more in the mood. Caring for children, even undamaged ones, never ceases, and in our society mothers are customarily expected to provide or arrange it. Much as I admire the mothers of variously disabled children I have known — and much as I believe their extraordinary qualities to derive, at least in part, from the rigors of their lives — I could not blame a woman who chose not to test her mettle in this way.

If I make her appear to be choosing in a social vacuum, I do so because, 9 in a society where the rearing of even a healthy child is not viewed as a community undertaking, where much-touted "family values" are always ascribed to the nuclear and not the human family, the parents of a disabled child will find themselves pretty much on their own. If they are lucky enough to have health insurance, the insurer, whose goal is to maximize shareholders' profits rather than the well-being of patients, is not about to spring for a $7,000 power wheelchair that would enable a child with muscular dystrophy to mingle independently with his classmates on an almost equal "footing," though it might provide $425 for a manual wheelchair to be pushed by an attendant (which it would not pay for). A school system, underfunded by screaming taxpayers, is not likely to procure a Kurzweil machine that would permit its blind students to "read" their own textbooks. Unless they are wealthy, Mom and Dad do the pushing, the reading, and whatever other extra duties are required, on top of their jobs and their care for any other children in the family.

"Eric and I plan to have only a couple of children," my daughter tells me, 10 contemplating the start of a family. "Why should we expend our resources on a damaged one?" A plausible point, as I have come to expect from this most clearheaded of young women. And in fact, as she knows, her father and I took great care to avoid conceiving another child after her younger brother was born in distress because of Rh incompatibility. After a couple of blood exchanges, he recovered, but we were told that another baby would likely be damaged, perhaps gravely, by the antibodies in my blood. I was no more eager to raise a deformed or retarded child than Anne is. I might have chosen an abortion if contraception had failed.

But then I think of my godson, the product of contraceptive failure, who 11 shares with his sister a possibly unique genetic condition that has caused severe visual impairment in them both. Many seeing people have a dread of blindness so overwhelming that they might well consider abortion if such a defect could be detected (as it could not in this case). But these are otherwise ideal children — healthy, smart, funny, confident, affectionate — and I think they're going to become terrific adults. The problem is that if you eliminate

---

indefatigable: Unable to be tired.   **catheterization:** Insertion of a tube to drain fluid (often urine) from a patient.

one flaw, you throw out the whole complicated creature, and my world would be a poorer place without Michael and Megan.

Obviously, I don't have an unambiguous answer to this dilemma. I don't   12
think one exists. I do feel certain, in view of the human propensity for ex-
ploiting whatever techniques we can devise with virtually no regard for consequences, that more and more people will choose, either for their own reasons or in response to the social pressure not to produce "unnecessary"
burdens, to terminate pregnancies so as to avoid birth defects (and to select
for sex as well). This development won't eradicate people with disabilities, of
course: birth trauma, accidental injury, and disease will continue to create
them from those who started out as even the healthiest fetuses. What it will
do is to make their social position even more marginal by emphasizing that
no one with the power to choose would ever have permitted them to exist.
Their own choice to survive will seem suspect. *We're doing everything we can to
exterminate your kind*, the social message will read, *and we'd get rid of you too if
only we knew how*. No one will ever say this. No one will have to.

**Questions to Start
You Thinking**

1. CONSIDERING MEANING: Does Mairs think women should be able to choose not to have a baby they know to have birth defects? Why does she feel this way?

2. IDENTIFYING WRITING STRATEGIES: How does Mairs use personal experiences to explain her points?

3. READING CRITICALLY: How does Mairs's discussion of her multiple sclerosis help her make an ethical appeal to her readers? Is this appeal convincing? Why, or why not? (See p. 104 in *A Writer's Guide* for an explanation of ethical appeal.)

4. EXPANDING VOCABULARY: Define *marginal* (paragraph 12)? Why does Mairs believe that the option to abort fetuses with defects will lead to an even more *marginal* social position for the disabled?

5. MAKING CONNECTIONS: How are the difficulties faced by people with disabilities similar to or different from those faced by people with AIDS? What do Mairs and Marion Winik ("Visiting Steven," p. 511) describe as the role of the family in helping to relieve the problems faced by people in these groups?

Journal Prompts

1. What moral and emotional issues would you consider in choosing whether to abort a child that has a known birth defect?

2. How is the impact of technology on human reproduction portrayed by the media? What sort of bias, if any, do you detect?

**Suggestions for
Writing**

1. What limits — if any — do you think should be placed on the way technology is used for purposes of human reproduction? Who should be responsible for setting and monitoring these limits?

2. Mairs compares the choice to abort a child of a particular sex with the choice to abort a child with a birth defect. She makes this comparison to suggest that there is no clear-cut answer to the dilemma of whether to abort a defective fetus. Do you agree or disagree that some abortion choices are "impermis-

sible" while others are acceptable or even "socially responsible" (paragraph 4)? Drawing on Mairs's essay as well as on your own experience for examples, write an essay in which you take a stand on this issue and in which you carefully balance ethical and logical appeals.

Richard Rodriguez, *born in 1944 in San Francisco, could speak only fifty words of English when his parents enrolled him in a Catholic grammar school in Sacramento, California. But Rodriguez proceeded to earn a B.A. at Stanford University in 1967 and an M.A. in philosophy at Columbia University as well as a Ph.D. in English Renaissance literature from the University of California at Berkeley. He now works as an editor at Pacific News Service in San Francisco, as an essayist on* The MacNeil-Lehrer News Hour, *and as a contributing editor for the Opinion section of the* Los Angeles Times *and for* Harper's *magazine, where this selection appeared in March 1984. In his best-known work,* Hunger of Memory: The Education of Richard Rodriguez *(1982), Rodriguez uses his own experience to support his opposition to bilingual education. His book of essays* Days of Obligation: An Argument with My Mexican Father *(1993) was nominated for the Pulitzer Prize in nonfiction. While Jack Kemp uses aspects of America's social and political history to support his evaluation of affirmative action policies ("Affirmative Action: The 'Radical Republican' Example," p. 588), Rodriguez examines the importance of assimilation and diversity to American culture by using examples from his experience as a child of immigrant parents.*

AS YOU READ: *Decide whether Rodriguez answers yes or no to the question, "Does America Still Exist?" Why does he answer the way he does?*

Richard Rodriguez   Does America Still Exist?

For the children of immigrant parents the knowledge comes easier. America exists everywhere in the city — on billboards, frankly in the smell of French fries and popcorn. It exists in the pace: traffic lights, the assertions of neon, the mysterious bong-bong-bong through the atriums of department stores. America exists as the voice of the crowd, a menacing sound — the high nasal accent of American English.

When I was a boy in Sacramento (California, the fifties), people would ask me, "Where you from?" I was born in this country, but I knew the question meant to decipher my darkness, my looks.

My mother once instructed me to say, "I am an American of Mexican descent." By the time I was nine or ten, I wanted to say, but dared not reply, "I am an American."

Immigrants come to America and, against hostility or mere loneliness, they re-create a homeland in the parlor, tacking up postcards or calendars of some impossible blue — lake or sea or sky. Children of immigrant parents are supposed to perch on a hyphen between two countries. Relatives assume the achievement as much as anyone. Relatives are, in any case, surprised when the child begins losing old ways. One day at the family picnic the boy wanders away from their spiced food and faceless stories to watch other boys play baseball in the distance.

There is sorrow in the American memory, guilty sorrow for having left   5 something behind — Portugal, China, Norway. The American story is the story of immigrant children and of their children — children no longer able to speak to grandparents. The memory of exile becomes inarticulate as it passes from generation to generation, along with wedding rings and pocket watches — like some mute stone in a wad of old lace. Europe. Asia. Eden.

But, it needs to be said, if this is a country where one stops being Viet-   6 namese or Italian, this is a country where one begins to be an American. America exists as a culture and a grin, a faith and a shrug. It is clasped in a handshake, called by a first name.

As much as the country is joined in a common culture, however, Ameri-   7 cans are reluctant to celebrate the process of assimilation. We pledge allegiance to diversity. America was born Protestant and bred Puritan, and the notion of community we share is derived from a seventeenth-century faith. Presidents and the pages of ninth-grade civics readers yet proclaim the orthodoxy:° we are gathered together — but as individuals, with separate pasts, distinct destinies. Our society is as paradoxical as a Puritan congregation: we stand together, alone.

Americans have traditionally defined themselves by what they refused to   8 include. As often, however, Americans have struggled, turned in good conscience at last to assert the great Protestant virtue of tolerance. Despite outbreaks of nativist frenzy, America has remained an immigrant country, open and true to itself.

Against pious° emblems of rural America — soda fountain, Elks hall,   9 Protestant church, and now shopping mall — stands the cold-hearted city, crowded with races and ambitions, curious laughter, much that is odd. Nevertheless, it is the city that has most truly represented America. In the city, however, the millions of singular lives have had no richer notion of wholeness to describe them than the idea of pluralism.

"Where you from?" the American asks the immigrant child. "Mexico," the boy   10 *learns to say.*

Mexico, the country of my blood ancestors, offers formal contrast to the   11 American achievement. If the United States was formed by Protestant individualism, Mexico was shaped by a medieval Catholic dream of one world. The Spanish journeyed to Mexico to plunder, and they may have gone, in God's name, with an arrogance peculiar to those who intend to convert. But through the conversion, the Indian converted the Spaniard. A new race was born, the *mestizo*, wedding European to Indian. José Vasconcelos, the Mexican philosopher, has celebrated this New World creation, proclaiming it the "cosmic race."

orthodoxy: Traditional ways.   **pious:** Holy or religious.

Centuries later, in a San Francisco restaurant, a Mexican American lawyer 12
of my acquaintance says, in English, over *salade niçoise*, that he does not intend to assimilate into gringo society. His claim is echoed by a chorus of others (Italian Americans, Greeks, Asians) in this era of ethnic pride. The melting
pot has been retired, clanking, into the museum of quaint disgrace, alongside
Aunt Jemima and the Katzenjammer Kids.° But resistance to assimilation is
characteristically American. It only makes clear how inevitable the process of
assimilation actually is.

For generations, this has been the pattern. Immigrant parents have sent 13
their children to school (simply, they thought) to acquire the "skills" to survive in the city. The child returned home with a voice his parents barely recognized or understood, couldn't trust, and didn't like.

In eastern cities — Philadelphia, New York, Boston, Baltimore — class 14
after class gathered immigrant children to women (usually women) who
stood in front of rooms full of children, changing children. So also for me in
the 1950s. Irish Catholic nuns, California. The old story. The hyphen tipped
to the right, away from Mexico and toward a confusing but true American
identity.

I speak now in the chromium American accent of my grammar school 15
classmates — Billy Reckers, Mike Bradley, Carol Schmidt, Kathy O'Grady. . . .
I believe I became like my classmates, became German, Polish, and (like my
teachers) Irish. And because assimilation is always reciprocal, my classmates
got something of me. (I mean sad eyes; belief in the Indian Virgin; a taste for
sugar skulls on the Feast of the Dead.) In the blending, we became what our
parents could never have been, and we carried America one revolution
further.

"Does America still exist?" Americans have been asking the question for 16
so long that to ask it again only proves our continuous link. But perhaps the
question deserves to be asked with urgency now. Since the black civil rights
movement of the 1960s, our tenuous° notion of a shared public life has de-
teriorated notably.

The struggle of black men and women did not eradicate racism, but it be- 17
came the great moment in the life of America's conscience. Water hoses, bull-
dogs, blood — the images, rendered black, white, rectangular, passed into living rooms.

It is hard to look at a photograph of a crowd taken, say in 1890 or in 1930 18
and not notice the absence of blacks. (It becomes an impertinence° to wonder if America *still* exists.)

In the sixties, other groups of Americans learned to champion their rights 19
by analogy to the black civil rights movement. But the heroic vision faded. Dr.
Martin Luther King Jr. had spoken with Pauline eloquence° of a nation that
would unite Christian and Jew, old and young, rich and poor. Within a

---

Katzenjammer Kids: An early comic strip and silent film series about German children.
tenuous: Fragile.   **impertinence:** Rudeness.   **Pauline eloquence:** Saint Paul's rhetorical power.

decade, the struggles of the 1960s were reduced to a bureaucratic competition for little more than pieces of a representational pie. The quest for a portion of power became an end in itself. The metaphor for the American city of the 1970s was a committee: one black, one woman, one person under thirty . . .

If the small town had sinned against America by too neatly defining who   20
could be an American, the city's sin was a romantic secession. One noticed the romanticism in the antiwar movement — certain demonstrators who demonstrated a lack of tact or desire to persuade and seemed content to play secular protestants. One noticed the romanticism in the competition among members of "minority groups" to claim the status of Primary Victim. To Americans unconfident of their common identity, minority standing became a way of asserting individuality. Middle-class Americans — men and women clearly not the primary victims of social oppression — brandished their suffering with exuberance.

The dream of a single society probably died with *The Ed Sullivan Show.*   21
The reality of America persists. Teenagers pass through big-city high schools banded in racial groups, their collars turned up to a uniform shrug. But then they graduate to jobs at the phone company or in banks, where they end up working alongside people unlike themselves. Typists and tellers walk out together at lunchtime.

It is easier for us as Americans to believe the obvious fact of our separate-   22
ness — easier to imagine the black and white Americas prophesied by the Kerner report° (broken glass, street fires) — than to recognize the reality of a city street at lunchtime. Americans are wedded by proximity° to a common culture. The panhandler at one corner is related to the pamphleteer at the next who is related to the banker who is kin to the Chinese old man wearing an MIT sweatshirt. In any true national history, Thomas Jefferson begets Martin Luther King Jr., who begets the Gray Panthers.° It is because we lack a vision of ourselves entire — the city street is crowded and we are each preoccupied with finding our own way home — that we lack an appropriate hymn.

Under my window now passes a little white girl softly rehearsing to her-   23
self a Motown obbligato.

Questions to Start You Thinking	1. CONSIDERING MEANING: According to Rodriguez, how do ethnic differences affect the way Americans think of themselves?
	2. IDENTIFYING WRITING STRATEGIES: How does Rodriguez use specific examples and sensory details to support his analysis of American culture?
	3. READING CRITICALLY: Rodriguez uses examples of many different national origins, heritages, and names as evidence to support his argument. How effective is this variety in supporting his thesis about cultural diversity and assimilation?

Kerner report: A 1968 report on racial unrest in America by the President's National Advisory Commission on Civil Disorders.   **proximity:** Closeness.   **Gray Panthers:** National organization that promotes the rights and welfare of senior citizens.

4. EXPANDING VOCABULARY: Look up the dictionary definitions of *nativist* (paragraph 8), *pluralism* (paragraph 9), *assimilation* (paragraph 12), and *secession* (paragraph 20). What do these words mean in the context of Rodriguez's essay?

5. MAKING CONNECTIONS: How are Rodriguez's ideas about the assimilation of ethnic minorities into mainstream culture different from those of Judith Ortiz Cofer ("The Myth of the Latin Woman," p. 564)? Where do their arguments support each other?

Link to the Paired Essay

American identity is a central issue in both Rodriguez's and Jack Kemp's essays ("Affirmative Action: The 'Radical Republican' Example," p. 588), although the writers' interests in the issue are different. Compare and contrast the definition of America that Kemp uses to support changes in economic and tax policy with the definition that Rodriguez explores in his essay. How are their definitions shaped by the purpose of their essays?

Journal Prompts

1. At what point does an immigrant to the United States stop being identified by where he or she came from and start being identified as an American?

2. Do you consider the city, the town, or the country most "American"? Compare and contrast the characteristics that make each one American.

Suggestions for Writing

1. Write a brief personal essay explaining how your family's heritage has shaped your experiences of America.

2. Using Rodriguez's ideas as a springboard, write a response to the question "Does America still exist?" How do you define *America*? What, in your opinion, are the most important factors in American culture today? How important are people's national or cultural origins to their participation in American culture?

Jack Kemp, *born in Los Angeles in 1935, earned his bachelor's degree from Occidental College. After thirteen years as a professional football quarterback, Kemp began a career in Republican politics and public service that included nine terms in the U.S. House of Representatives from 1971 to 1989, where he represented the Buffalo area and western New York, and four years as Secretary of Housing and Urban Development. He has also served as chair of the House Republican Leadership Conference, as a Distinguished Fellow at the Heritage Foundation, as a Visiting Fellow at the Hoover Institution, and as a director of Habitat for Humanity, the Opportunities Industrialization Centers, and Howard University. Kemp is currently on the board of directors of Empower America, a public policy and advocacy organization he cofounded in 1993. While Richard Rodriguez supports his examination of America's national identity with personal experience ("Does America Still Exist?" p. 583), Kemp draws on notions of American history and identity to support changes in a specific social policy. Kemp's essay first appeared in the* Washington Post *on August 6, 1995.*

AS YOU READ: *Identify the problems with affirmative action policies that Kemp discusses.*

INTERNET SOURCE: *"Affirmative Action: The 'Radical Republican' Example" was published online at the Empower America Web site (<http://www.townhall.com>). You may want to visit the Web site to understand one context in which this article appeared.*

Jack Kemp   Affirmative Action: The "Radical Republican" Example

The scene is Washington: a Republican president, new to the White   1
House, defiantly throwing down the gauntlet° to a Republican Congress, saying he will veto any bill that proposes to do more for "black Americans" than for "whites." This is not some fast-forward vision of 1997 and the first days of a new Republican White House. It's a flashback to 1866. The agency to be vetoed was the Freedman's Bureau, established in President Lincoln's administration to "affirmatively" assist the recently emancipated African American. The president — Andrew Johnson, Lincoln's successor — worried that any "affirmative action" would hurt the white population by specifically helping "Negroes."

I offer this page from history not to prove once again that, politically,   2
there is not much new under the sun but to illustrate that the issues of race and equality are woven into the essence of our American experience. While our present-day passions on the subject of affirmative action open old wounds, they also summon us to moral leadership of Lincolnesque proportions.

Thus far the summons goes unanswered by both liberals and conservatives alike. The unreconstructed° liberal notion of endless racial reparations   3
and race-based preferences is doubly guilty: wrong in principle and ruinous in practice. President Clinton's much-vaunted° affirmative action review produced more of a bumper sticker than a policy; Clinton's focus-group-fashioned "mend it, not end it" slogan makes a far better rhyme than reason.

The same, however, is true of the new affirmative action "abolitionist" position, which heralds equality but seldom addresses the way to truly give all   4
people an equal footing. Critics are right in asserting that "affirmative action" quotas have contributed to the poisoning of race relations in this country. But critics must offer much more than just opposition and reproach. We know what they are against, but what are they for?

"A colorblind society," comes their response. Of course, the goal of equal   5
opportunity is paramount and a worthy destiny to seek. But to say that we have arrived at that goal is simply not true. My friends on the right call for a colorblind society and then quote Martin Luther King's inspiration "I have a

---

throwing down the gauntlet: Openly challenging.   **unreconstructed:** Resistant to a social change.   **vaunted:** Boasted about.

dream" speech, in which he imagined a nation in which every American would be judged not on the color of his or her skin but on the "content of his character." All too often, though, they neglect to quote the end of his speech, where he describes the painful plight of minority America: "The Negro," King said, "lives on a lonely island of poverty in the midst of a vast ocean of material prosperity."

Much has changed in the thirty years since King stood on the steps of the   6
Lincoln Memorial. Minority enterprises have begun to gain a foothold, although there are far too few of them. But can anyone venture to the crumbling brick and mortar of Cabrini Green Public Housing, or the fear-ridden projects of Bed-Stuy or the streets lined with the unemployed in south Central L.A. or East St. Louis and believe that what he sees there today would pass as progress since Dr. King's day?

This is not to negate the gains made by so many in the black and minor-   7
ity communities. But for large numbers the situation has not only not improved in thirty years; it has grown dramatically worse — with a welfare system that entraps rather than empowers, punishes work and marriage, and prevents access to capital, credit, and property.

Reality requires that we admit two things — difficult admissions for both   8
liberals and conservatives. First, that a race-conscious policy of quotas and rigid preferences has helped make matters worse. Second, and more important, the Good Shepherd reminds all of us that our work is not done, and as we think about moving into the twenty-first century, we must not leave anyone behind.

Sound policy begins with strong principles. Affirmative action based on   9
quotas is wrong — wrong because it is antithetical° to the genius of the American idea: individual liberty. Counting by race in order to remedy past wrongs or rewarding special groups by taking from others perpetuates and even deepens the division between us. But race-based politics is even more wrong and must be repudiated° by men and women of civility and compassion.

Instead, like the "radical republicans" of Lincoln's day, who overrode   10
President Johnson's veto on the Freedman's Bureau, we would honor the past by creating a future more in keeping with our revolutionary founding ideals of equality. In this way, the eventual ending of affirmative action is only a beginning — the political predicate of a new promise of outreach in the name of greater opportunity for access to capital, credit, prosperity, jobs, and educational choice for all.

The time has definitely come for a new approach, an "affirmative action"   11
based not just on gender or race or ethnicity but ultimately based on need. "Affirmative" because government authority must be employed to remove the obstacles to upward mobility and human advancement. "Action" because democratic societies must act positively and create real equality of opportunity — without promising equality of reward.

---

antithetical: Opposite.   **repudiated:** Rejected as untrue.

Affirming opportunity in America begins with education. America's   12
schools, particularly our urban public schools, are depriving minority and
low-income children of the education that may be their passport out of
poverty. Even the poorest parent must have the option more affluent families
enjoy: the right to send their children to the school of their choice. Affirmative effort means ending the educational monopoly that makes poor public
school students into pawns of the educational bureaucracy. And we should be
paving the way to a voucher and magnet school system of public and private
school choice.

Opportunity means an entryway into the job market. That means remov-   13
ing barriers for job creation and entrepreneurship and expanding access to
capital and credit. According to the *Wall Street Journal*, from 1982 to 1987 the
number of black-owned firms increased by nearly 38 percent, about triple the
overall business growth rate during that period. Hispanic-owned businesses
soared by 81 percent. Firms owned by women expanded by 57 percent, and
their sales nearly tripled.

Even so, of the 14 million small businesses in existence across the United   14
States today, fewer than 2 percent are black owned. And of $27 to $28 trillion
of capital in this country, less than one percent is in black ownership. Affirmative effort would take aim at expanding capital and credit as the lifeblood
of business formation and job creation — including an aggressive effort to
end the redlining° of our inner cities and a radical redesign of our tax code to
remove barriers to broader ownership of capital, savings, and credit.

Opportunity means the ability to accumulate property. Affirmative effort   15
would mean an end to every federal program that penalizes the poor for managing to save and accumulate their own assets. An AFDC mother's thrift and
foresight in putting money away for a child's future should not be penalized
by the government welfare system as fraud as is currently the case.

Finally, real opportunity for racial and ethnic reconciliation requires an   16
expanding economy — one that invites the effort and enterprise of all Americans, including minorities and women. A real pro-growth policy must include
policies ranging from enterprise zones in our cities to a commitment to lowering barriers to global trade. It should also offer relief from red tape and regulation and freedom from punitive tax policies. Each is part of an affirmative
action that can "move America forward without leaving anyone behind."

Now that we have opened a somewhat hysterical dialogue on affirmative   17
action, we can never go back — only forward. Our challenge is to put aside the
past — abandon the endless round of recrimination and a politics that feeds
on division, exclusion, anger, and envy. We must reaffirm, as Lincoln did at
his moment of maximum crisis, a vision of the "better angels of our nature,"
a big-hearted view of the nation we were always meant to become and must
become if we are to enter the twenty-first century as the model of liberal
democracy and market-oriented capitalism the world needs to see.

redlining: Refusing to loan money or sell insurance to people who live in certain neighborhoods.

Questions to Start You Thinking

1. CONSIDERING MEANING: What solution does Kemp propose to the problems he sees in current affirmative action policies? How does his solution redefine affirmative action?

2. IDENTIFYING WRITING STRATEGIES: In the beginning of his essay, Kemp sets up his argument by comparing past affirmative action debates to current discussions. Where else in his essay does Kemp use comparison and contrast to make his point?

3. READING CRITICALLY: Reread Kemp's essay, and locate the claims that are not supported with evidence. How do his omissions affect his argument? What do they reveal about whom he considers his audience to be? Do you think such omissions are more excusable or less so when an article appears online? Why?

4. EXPANDING VOCABULARY: What are the origins of the cliché "not much new under the sun"? Why does Kemp use the phrase in paragraph 2?

5. MAKING CONNECTIONS: Why do both Kemp and Jeffrey Obser ("Privacy Is the Problem, Not the Solution," p. 657) use examples from political history? What is each author's purpose? How are their purposes similar? How are they different?

Link to the Paired Essay

Both Kemp and Richard Rodriguez ("Does America Still Exist?" p. 583) address tensions between American mainstream and minority cultures. Compare and contrast the views of Kemp and Rodriguez on the role of education.

Journal Prompts

1. Describe a situation in which you or someone you know has been personally affected by affirmative action policies. What conclusions can you draw from this experience about the effects of such policies on people's lives?

2. Do you agree with Kemp when he says "racial reparations" are "wrong in principle and ruinous in practice" (paragraph 3)? Why, or why not?

Suggestions for Writing

1. Both Rodriguez and Kemp identify religion as a shaping force in American culture and politics. Write an essay in which you explain and illustrate the role you believe religion plays in defining American culture.

2. Research changes or developments in affirmative action policy that have occurred since this article was published in 1995. Do you think these changes have resulted in a better affirmative action policy? Write an essay in which you evaluate these changes in light of the concerns that Kemp raises.

Chapter 25

Popular Culture

Web Search

Look up a Web page about your favorite television show or a movie of interest to you, and analyze the purpose of the page. For example, is the page trying to attract new viewers or to establish a community of loyal fans? Do you think the Web page achieves its purpose? Why, or why not? Could the producers have achieved this purpose through a medium other than the Internet? Why, or why not?

Stephen King was born in 1947 in Portland, Maine, attended the University of Maine at Orono, and now lives in Bangor, Maine, where he writes his best-selling horror novels, many of which have been made into popular movies. The prolific King is also the author of screenplays, teleplays, short fiction, essays, and (under the pseudonym Richard Bachman) novels. His well-known horror novels include Carrie *(1974),* Firestarter *(1980),* Pet Sematary *(1983),* Misery *(1987), and* The Wizard in the Glass *(1997). In the following essay, first published in* Playboy *in December 1981, King draws on his extensive experience with horror to explain the human craving to be frightened.*

AS YOU READ: *Identify the needs that King says horror movies fulfill for viewers.*

Stephen King   Why We Crave Horror Movies

I think that we're all mentally ill; those of us outside the asylums only hide it a little better — and maybe not all that much better, after all. We've all known people who talk to themselves, people who sometimes squinch their faces into horrible grimaces when they believe no one is watching, people who have some hysterical fear — of snakes, the dark, the tight place, the long drop . . . and, of course, those final worms and grubs that are waiting so patiently underground.

When we pay our four or five bucks and seat ourselves at tenth-row center in a theater showing a horror movie, we are daring the nightmare.

Why? Some of the reasons are simple and obvious. To show that we can, that we are not afraid, that we can ride this roller coaster. Which is not to say that a really good horror movie may not surprise a scream out of us at some point, the way we may scream when the roller coaster twists through a complete 360 or plows through a lake at the bottom of the drop. And horror movies, like roller coasters, have always been the special province° of the young; by the time one turns forty or fifty, one's appetite for double twists or 360-degree loops may be considerably depleted.

We also go to reestablish our feelings of essential normality; the horror movie is innately conservative, even reactionary. Freda Jackson as the horrible melting woman in *Die, Monster, Die!* confirms for us that no matter how far we may be removed from the beauty of a Robert Redford or a Diana Ross, we are still light-years from true ugliness.

And we go to have fun.

Ah, but this is where the ground starts to slope away, isn't it? Because this is a very peculiar sort of fun indeed. The fun comes from seeing others menaced — sometimes killed. One critic suggested that if pro football has become the voyeur's° version of combat, then the horror film has become the modern version of the public lynching.

---

province: Area.   **voyeur:** One who takes inordinate pleasure in the act of watching.

It is true that the mythic, "fairy-tale" horror film intends to take away the   7
shades of gray. . . . It urges us to put away our more civilized and adult
penchant° for analysis and to become children again, seeing things in pure
blacks and whites. It may be that horror movies provide psychic relief on this
level because this invitation to lapse into simplicity, irrationality, and even
outright madness is extended so rarely. We are told we may allow our emotions a free rein . . . or no rein at all.

If we are all insane, then sanity becomes a matter of degree. If your in-   8
sanity leads you to carve up women like Jack the Ripper or the Cleveland
Torso Murderer, we clap you away in the funny farm (but neither of those two
amateur-night surgeons was ever caught, heh-heh-heh); if, on the other hand,
your insanity leads you only to talk to yourself when you're under stress or to
pick your nose on your morning bus, then you are left alone to go about your
business . . . though it is doubtful that you will ever be invited to the best
parties.

The potential lyncher is in almost all of us (excluding saints, past and   9
present; but then, most saints have been crazy in their own ways), and every
now and then, he has to be let loose to scream and roll around in the grass.
Our emotions and our fears form their own body, and we recognize that it demands its own exercise to maintain proper muscle tone. Certain of these emotional muscles are accepted — even exalted — in civilized society; they are, of
course, the emotions that tend to maintain the status quo° of civilization itself. Love, friendship, loyalty, kindness — these are all the emotions that we
applaud, emotions that have been immortalized in the couplets of Hallmark
cards and in the verses (I don't dare call it poetry) of Leonard Nimoy.

When we exhibit these emotions, society showers us with positive rein-   10
forcement; we learn this even before we get out of diapers. When, as children,
we hug our rotten little puke of a sister and give her a kiss, all the aunts and
uncles smile and twit and cry, "Isn't he the sweetest little thing?" Such coveted
treats as chocolate-covered graham crackers often follow. But if we deliberately slam the rotten little puke of a sister's fingers in the door, sanctions follow — angry remonstrance° from parents, aunts, and uncles; instead of a
chocolate-covered graham cracker, a spanking.

But anticivilization emotions don't go away, and they demand periodic   11
exercise. We have such "sick" jokes as "What's the difference between a truckload of bowling balls and a truckload of dead babies" (You can't unload the
truckload of bowling balls with a pitchfork . . . a joke, by the way, that I heard
originally from a ten-year-old.) Such a joke may surprise a laugh or a grin out
of us even as we recoil, a possibility that confirms the thesis: if we share a
brotherhood of man, then we also share an insanity of man. None of which
is intended as a defense of either the sick joke or insanity but merely as an ex-

---

penchant: Strong inclination.   status quo: Existing state of affairs.   remonstrance:
Objection.

planation of [how] the best horror films, like the best fairy tales, manage to be reactionary, anarchistic, and revolutionary all at the same time.

The mythic horror movie, like the sick joke, has a dirty job to do. It deliberately appeals to all that is worst in us. It is morbidity unchained, our most base instincts let free, our nastiest fantasies realized . . . and it all happens, fittingly enough, in the dark. For those reasons, good liberals often shy away from horror films. For myself, I like to see the most aggressive of them — *Dawn of the Dead*, for instance — as lifting a trapdoor in the civilized forebrain and throwing a basket of raw meat to the hungry alligators swimming around in that subterranean river beneath.

Why bother? Because it keeps them from getting out, man, it keeps them down there and me up here. It was Lennon and McCartney who said that all you need is love, and I would agree with that.

As long as you keep the gators fed.

Questions to Start You Thinking

1. CONSIDERING MEANING: What does King mean when he says that "we're all mentally ill" (paragraph 1)? Is this a serious statement? Why, or why not?

2. IDENTIFYING WRITING STRATEGIES: How does King use analysis to support his argument?

3. READING CRITICALLY: Why do you think King uses the inclusive pronoun *we* so frequently throughout his essay? What effect does the use of this pronoun have on your response to his argument?

4. EXPANDING VOCABULARY: Define *innately* (paragraph 4). What does King mean when he says horror movies are "*innately* conservative"? Does he contradict himself when he says they are also "*reactionary, anarchistic,* and *revolutionary*" (paragraph 11)? Why, or why not?

5. MAKING CONNECTIONS: King argues that watching violence in horror movies provides a kind of release for viewers. How does this argument support or contradict Ellen Goodman's claims about violence on television ("How to Zap Violence on TV," p. 613)?

Journal Prompts

1. What is your response to "sick" jokes? Why?

2. Recall a movie that exercised your "anticivilization emotions" (paragraph 11). Describe your state of mind before, during, and after the movie.

Suggestions for Writing

1. What genre of movie do you prefer to watch, and why? What cravings does this type of movie satisfy?

2. Do you agree that "the horror film has become the modern version of the public lynching" (paragraph 6)? Write an argument in which you defend or refute this suggestion, citing examples from King's essay and from your own moviegoing experience to support your position.

Michael Shermer   Abducted! Encounters with Aliens

On Monday, August 8, 1983, I was abducted by aliens. It was late at night   1
and I was traveling along a lonely rural highway approaching the small town of Haigler, Nebraska, when a large craft with bright lights hovered alongside me and forced me to stop. Alien creatures got out and cajoled me into their vehicle. I do not remember what happened inside but when I found myself traveling back down the road I had lost ninety minutes of time. Abductees call this "missing time," and my abduction a "close encounter of the third kind." I'll never forget the experience, and, like other abductees, I've recounted my abduction story numerous times on television and countless times to live audiences.

A Personal Abduction Experience
This may seem like a strange story for a skeptic to be telling, so let me fill in   2
the details. . . . For many years I competed as a professional ultra-marathon bicycle racer, primarily focusing on the 3,000-mile, nonstop, transcontinental Race Across America. "Nonstop" means racers go long stretches without sleep, riding an average of twenty-two out of every twenty-four hours. It is a rolling experiment on stress, sleep deprivation, and mental breakdown.

Under normal sleep conditions, most dream activity is immediately for-   3
gotten or fades fairly soon after waking into consciousness. Extreme sleep deprivation breaks down the wall between reality and fantasy. You have severe hallucinations that seem as real as the sensations and perceptions of daily life. The words you hear and speak are recalled like a normal memory. The people you see are as corporeal° as those in real life.

corporeal: Having a body.

596

During the inaugural 1982 race, I slept three hours on each of the first two   4
nights and consequently fell behind the leader, who was proving that one
could get by with considerably less sleep. By New Mexico, I began riding long
stretches without sleep in order to catch up, but I was not prepared for the hallucinations that were to come. Mostly they were the garden-variety hallucinations often experienced by weary truck drivers, who call the phenomenon
"white-line fever": bushes form into lifelike animals, cracks in the road make
meaningful designs, and mailboxes look like people. I saw giraffes and lions,
I waved to mailboxes. I even had an out-of-body experience near Tucumcari,
New Mexico, where I saw myself riding on the shoulder of Interstate 40 from
above.

Finishing third that year, I vowed to ride sleepless in 1983 until I got the   5
lead or collapsed. Eighty-three hours away from the Santa Monica Pier, just
shy of Haigler, Nebraska, and 1,259 miles into the race, I was falling asleep on
the bike so my support crew (every rider has one) put me down for a forty-
five minute nap. When I awoke I got back on my bike, but I was still so sleepy
that my crew tried to get me back into the motorhome. It was then that I
slipped into some sort of altered state of consciousness and became convinced that my entire support crew were aliens from another planet and that
they were going to kill me. So clever were these aliens that they even looked,
dressed, and spoke like my crew. I began to quiz individual crew members
about details from their personal lives and about the bike that no alien
should know. I asked my mechanic if he had glued on my bike tires with
spaghetti sauce. When he replied that he had glued them on with Clement
glue (also red), I was quite impressed with the research the aliens had done.
Other questions and correct answers followed. The context for this hallucination was a 1960s television program — *The Invaders* — in which the aliens
looked exactly like humans with the exception of a stiff little finger. I looked
for stiff pinkies on my crew members. The motorhome with its bright lights
became their spacecraft. After the crew managed to bed me down for another
forty-five minutes, I awoke clear-headed and the problem was solved. To this
day, however, I recall the hallucination as vividly and clearly as any strong
memory.

Now I am not claiming that people who have had alien abduction expe-   6
riences were sleep deprived or undergoing extreme physical and mental stress.
However, I think it is fairly clear that if an alien abduction experience can happen under these conditions, it can happen under other conditions. Obviously
I was not abducted by aliens, so what is more likely: That other people are
having experiences similar to mine, triggered by other altered states and unusual circumstances, or that we really are being visited secretly by aliens from
other worlds? By Hume's criterion of how to judge a miracle — "no testimony
is sufficient to establish a miracle, unless the testimony be of such a kind, that
its falsehood would be more miraculous than the fact which it endeavors to
establish" — we would have to choose the first explanation. It is not impossible that aliens are traveling thousands of light-years to Earth and dropping in
undetected, but it is much more likely that humans are experiencing altered

states of consciousness and interpreting them in the context of what is popular in our culture today, namely, space aliens.

Encounters with Alien Abductees

In 1994 NBC began airing *The Other Side*, a New Age show that explored alien abduction claims, as well as other mysteries, miracles, and unusual phenomena. I appeared numerous times on this show as the token skeptic, but most interesting for me was their two-part program on UFOs and alien abductions. The claims made by the alien abductees were quite remarkable indeed. They state that literally millions of people have been "beamed up" to alien spacecraft, some straight out of their bedrooms through walls and ceilings. One woman said the aliens took her eggs for use in a breeding experiment but could produce no evidence for how this was done. Another said that the aliens actually implanted a human-alien hybrid in her womb and that she gave birth to the child. Where is this child now? The aliens took it back, she explained. One man pulled up his pant leg to show me scars on his legs that he said were left by the aliens. They looked like normal scars to me. Another woman said the aliens had implanted a tracking device in her head, much as biologists do to track dolphins or birds. An MRI° of her head proved negative. One man explained that the aliens took his sperm. I asked him how he knew that they took his sperm, since he had said he was asleep when he was abducted. He said he knew because he had had an orgasm. I responded, "Is it possible you simply had a wet dream?" He was not amused.

After the taping of this program, about a dozen of the "abductees" were going out to dinner. Since I tend to be a fairly friendly, nonconfrontational skeptic in these situations, disdaining the shouting so desired by talk-show producers, they invited me to join them. It was enlightening. I discovered that they were neither crazy nor ignorant, as one might suspect. They were perfectly sane, rational, intelligent folks who had in common an irrational experience. They were convinced of the reality of the experience — no rational explanation I could offer, from hallucinations to lucid dreams to false memories, could convince them otherwise. One man became teary-eyed while telling me how traumatic the abduction was for him. Another woman explained that the experience had cost her a happy marriage to a wealthy television producer. I thought, "What is wrong here? There isn't a shred of evidence that any of these claims are true, yet these are normal, rational folks whose lives have been deeply affected by these experiences."

In my opinion, the alien abduction phenomenon is the product of an unusual altered state of consciousness interpreted in a cultural context replete with films, television programs, and science fiction literature about aliens and UFOs. Add to this the fact that for the past four decades we have been exploring the solar system and searching for signs of extraterrestrial intelligence, and

MRI: Magnetic resonance imaging, produced by a medical scanner that shows images of cells, tissues, and organs.

it is no wonder that people are seeing UFOs and experiencing alien encounters. Driven by mass media that revel in such tabloid-type stories, the alien abduction phenomenon is now in a positive feedback loop. The more people who have had these unusual mental experiences see and read about others who have interpreted similar incidents as abduction by aliens, the more likely it is that they will convert their own stories into their own alien abduction. The feedback loop was given a strong boost in late 1975 after millions watched NBC's *The UFO Incident*, a movie on Betty and Barney Hill's abduction dreams. The stereotypical alien with a large, bald head and big, elongated eyes, reported by so many abductees since 1975, was created by NBC artists for this program. The rate of information exchange took off as more and more alien abductions were reported on the news and recounted in popular books, newspapers, tabloids, and specialty publications dedicated solely to UFOs and alien abductions. As there seemed to be agreement on how the aliens looked and also on their preoccupation with human reproductive systems (usually women are sexually molested by the aliens), the feedback loop took off. Because of our fascination with the possibility of extraterrestrial life, and there is a real possibility that extraterrestrials might exist somewhere in the cosmos (a different question than their arrival here on Earth), this craze will probably wax and wane° depending on what is hot in pop culture. Blockbuster films like *ET* and *Independence Day* and television shows like *Star Trek* and *The X-Files*, as well as best-selling books like Whitley Strieber's *Communion* and John Mack's *Abduction*, continue feeding the movement.

While dining with the abductees, I found out something very revealing: 10 not one of them recalled being abducted immediately after the experience. In fact, for most of them, many years went by before they "remembered" the experience. How was this memory recalled? Under hypnosis. . . . Memories cannot simply be "recovered" like rewinding a videotape. Memory is a complex phenomenon involving distortions, deletions, additions, and sometimes complete fabrication. Psychologists call this *confabulation* — mixing fantasy with reality to such an extent that it is impossible to sort them out. Psychologist Elizabeth Loftus (Loftus and Ketcham, 1994) has shown how easy it is to plant a false memory in a child's mind by merely repeating a suggestion until the child incorporates it as an actual memory. Similarly, Professor Alvin Lawson put students at California State University, Long Beach, into a hypnotic state and in their altered state told them over and over that they had been abducted by aliens. When asked to fill in the details of the abduction, the students elaborated in great detail, making it up as they went along in the story (in Sagan, 1996). Every parent has stories about the fantasies their children create. My daughter once described to my wife a purple dragon we saw on our hike in the local hills that day.

True, not all abduction stories are recalled only under hypnosis, but al- 11 most all alien abductions occur late at night during sleep. In addition to nor-

wax and wane: Enlarge and diminish.

mal fantasies and lucid dreams, there are rare mental states known as *hypno-gogic hallucinations*, which occur soon after falling asleep, and *hypnopompic hallucinations*, which happen just before waking up. In these unusual states, subjects report a variety of experiences, including floating out of their bodies, feeling paralyzed, seeing loved ones who have passed away, witnessing ghosts and poltergeists, and, yes, being abducted by aliens. Psychologist Robert A. Baker presents as typical this subject's report: "I went to bed and went to sleep and then sometime near morning something woke me up. I opened my eyes and found myself wide awake but unable to move. There, standing at the foot of my bed was my mother, wearing her favorite dress — the one we buried her in" (1987/1988, p. 157). Baker also demonstrates that Whitley Strieber's encounter with aliens (one of the more famous in abduction lore) "is a classic, textbook description of a hypnopompic hallucination, complete with awakening from a sound sleep, the strong sense of reality and of being awake, the paralysis (due to the fact that the body's neural° circuits keep our muscles relaxed and help preserve our sleep), and the encounter with strange beings" (p. 157).

Harvard psychiatrist John Mack, a Pulitzer Prize–winning author, gave   12
the abduction movement a strong endorsement with his 1994 book, *Abduction: Human Encounters with Aliens*. Here at last was a mainstream scholar from a highly respectable institution lending credence (and his reputation) to the belief in the reality of these encounters. Mack was impressed by the commonalities of the stories told by abductees — the physical description of the aliens, the sexual abuse, the metallic probes, and so on. Yet I think we can expect consistencies in the stories since so many of the abductees go to the same hypnotist, read the same alien encounter books, watch the same science fiction movies, and in many cases even know one another and belong to "encounter" groups (in both senses of the word). Given the shared mental states and social contexts, it would be surprising if there was not a core set of characteristics of the abduction experience shared by the abductees. And what are we to do with the shared absence of convincing physical evidence?

Finally, the sexual component of alien abduction experiences demands   13
comment. It is well known among anthropologists and biologists that humans are the most sexual of all primates, if not all mammals. Unlike most animals, when it comes to sex, humans are not constrained by biological rhythms and the cycle of the seasons. We like sex almost anytime or anywhere. We are stimulated by visual sexual cues, and sex is a significant component in advertising, films, television programs, and our culture in general. You might say we are obsessed with sex. Thus, the fact that alien abduction experiences often include a sexual encounter tells us more about humans than it does about aliens. . . . Women in the sixteenth and seventeenth centuries were often accused of (and even allegedly experienced or confessed to) having illicit sexual encounters with aliens — in this case the alien was usually Satan

neural: Having to do with the nerves.

himself—and these women were burned as witches. In the nineteenth century, many people reported sexual encounters with ghosts and spirits at about the time that the spiritualism movement took off in England and America. And in the twentieth century, we have phenomena such as "Satanic ritual abuse," in which children and young adults are allegedly being sexually abused in cult rituals; "recovered memory syndrome," in which adult women and men are "recovering" memories of sexual abuse that allegedly occurred decades previously; and "facilitated communication," where autistic° children are "communicating" through facilitators (teachers or parents) who hold the child's hand above a typewriter or computer keyboard reporting that they were sexually abused.

We can again apply Hume's maxim: Is it more likely that demons, spirits, ghosts, and aliens have been and continue to sexually abuse humans or that humans are experiencing fantasies and interpreting them in the social context of their age and culture? I think it can reasonably be argued that such experiences are a very earthly phenomenon with a perfectly natural (albeit unusual) explanation. To me, the fact that humans have such experiences is at least as fascinating and mysterious as the possibility of the existence of extraterrestrial intelligence. 14

Works Cited

Baker, R. A. "The Aliens Among Us: Hypnotic Regression Revisited." *Skeptical Inquirer* 12.2 (1987/1988): 147–62.

Hume, D. *An Enquiry Concerning Human Understanding.* 1758. Great Books of the Western World Series. Chicago: University of Chicago Press, 1952.

Loftus, E. F., and Ketcham, K. *The Myth of the Repressed Memory: False Memories and the Allegations of Sexual Abuse.* New York: St. Martin's, 1994.

Mack, J. E. *Abduction: Human Encounters with Aliens.* New York: Scribner's, 1994.

Sagan, C. *The Demon Haunted World: Science as a Candle in the Dark.* New York: Random, 1996.

Strieber, W. *Communion: A True Story.* New York: Avon, 1987.

Questions to Start You Thinking

1. CONSIDERING MEANING: What is the "positive feedback loop" that Shermer describes (paragraph 9)? How significant is it to his argument?

2. IDENTIFYING WRITING STRATEGIES: Where does Shermer use conversation to support his critique of alien abduction stories? Is this a successful strategy? Why, or why not?

3. READING CRITICALLY: Is Shermer's evidence sufficient to convince you that no one has really been abducted by aliens? Why, or why not?

---

autistic: Having autism, a disease marked by withdrawal from reality.

4. EXPANDING VOCABULARY: Define *skeptic* (paragraph 2). Why does it seem strange for a *skeptic* like Shermer to tell the story of his abduction?

5. MAKING CONNECTIONS: Shermer and Stephen King ("Why We Crave Horror Movies," p. 593) both offer logical explanations for why people are fascinated by stories that seem illogical or beyond the scope of everyday life. How do their arguments support each other? Are there ways in which their arguments are contradictory?

Journal Prompts

1. Are you likely to believe alien encounter stories? Why, or why not?

2. Are you convinced by Shermer's argument against the validity of alien encounter stories told under hypnosis (paragraphs 10 and 11)? Why, or why not?

Suggestions for Writing

1. Is there a type of story or belief, other than tales of alien abductions, that you think might be the result of a "positive feedback loop" in popular culture? Write an essay in which you describe the loop that you think contributes to the popularity of such a story or belief.

2. Find at least three tabloid stories about encounters with aliens. After reading these accounts, do you agree with Shermer's argument that people alter real events into stories that involve aliens? Write an essay in which you evaluate how likely it is that these alien encounter stories are true.

Veronica Chambers, *born in 1970 in the Canal Zone, Panama, was graduated* summa cum laude *with a B.A. in literary studies from Simon's Rock College in Great Barrington, Massachusetts. She is currently an associate editor at* Newsweek *magazine, where she critiques the social significance of music and electronic media for the Arts and Lifestyle section. Formerly a story editor at the* New York Times Magazine, *she has also been a contributing editor at* Glamour *magazine and a senior associate editor of* Premiere *magazine. She is coauthor of* Poetic Justice: Filmmaking South Central Style *(1993) and a contributor to the* Young Feminist Anthology. *Her freelance writing has appeared in publications such as* Essence, *the* New York Times Book Review, *and* Vogue, *and she was awarded a prestigious research fellowship by the Freedom Forum, which she used to analyze news coverage of Asian and African Americans. Her most recent book,* Mama's Girl *(1996), addresses the complexity of African American women and mother-and-daughter relationships. In this selection, published in* Newsweek *in November 1997, Chambers explores the social and historical significance of a Disney television production of* Cinderella, *in which the fairy-tale heroine is played by an actress of African American descent.*

AS YOU READ: *Identify what Chambers claims attracts young girls to the Cinderella story. What criticism of the story does Chambers have?*

For generations, black women have been the societal embodiment of [1] Cinderella. Like Cinderella, black women (and poor white women, too) have often been relegated to the cooking and the cleaning, watching enviously as the women they worked for lived a more privileged life. Think about *Gone with the Wind*. Wouldn't Scarlett O'Hara have laughed, as the evil stepsisters laughed at Cinderella, if Butterfly McQueen had said that *she* wanted to go to the ball, that *she* wanted to dance with Rhett Butler? For years, the idea of a black girl playing the classic Cinderella was unthinkable. But this Sunday, when Brandy, the eighteen-year-old pop singer, stars in the Disney/ABC presentation of Rodgers and Hammerstein's *Cinderella*, reparations will be made. Finally, a sister is getting to go to the ball.

The casting of Brandy as Disney's latest Cinderella is especially significant [2] because for many black women, the 1950 animated Disney Cinderella with her blond hair and blue eyes sent a painful message that only white women could be princesses. "It's hard when you don't fit the traditional view of beauty," says Whoopi Goldberg (who plays the prince's mother in the new version). "I've gotten letters from people that say if I'd just get my nose done or if I wasn't so dark, I'd be OK-looking. That's why I love this Cinderella, because Brandy is a beautiful, everyday-looking black girl."

The Disney/ABC twist on *Cinderella* is to take multiracial casting to the [3] never-never-land extreme: while Whoopi is the queen, the king (Victor Garber) is white; Bernadette Peters is the stepmother with one white daughter and one black. Whitney Houston plays the fairy godmother, in a soulful performance reminiscent of Lena Horne's° in *The Wiz*. Jason Alexander is hilarious as the prince's much maligned valet. And who plays the prince? A Filipino actor, Paolo Montalban.

Even in this postfeminist° era, where a Cinderella waiting to be rescued [4] by a prince can be seen as a wimp, the myth still appeals. There are at least a half dozen other movies in the works, including one starring Drew Barrymore, with Anjelica Huston as the wicked stepmother, for Twentieth Century Fox; Tribeca Productions' *Sisterella*; *Cinderella's Revenge* at Sony, and a Whoopi Goldberg project at Trimark.

Disney's politically correct version is sure to spark controversy in the [5] black community. "I'm genuinely bothered by the subliminal message that's sent when you don't have a black Prince Charming," says Denene Millner, author of *The Sistahs' Rules*. "When my stepson who's five looks at that production, I want him to know he can be somebody's Prince Charming." But this *Cinderella* does mirror, unwittingly, a growing loss of faith in black men by many black women. Just as Brandy's Cinderella falls in love with a prince of

Lena Horne: Blues singer.   **postfeminist:** Relating to the assumption that the goals of the feminist movement have been achieved and that it is no longer necessary to fight actively for them.

another color, so have black women begun to date and marry interracially in record numbers. In 1980 there were 27,000 new marriages between black women and white men. By 1990 that number had doubled, to 54,000. While black men still marry outside the race in greater numbers, interracial marriages involving black women are growing at a faster rate. "Some of it is a backlash because there are a lot of women who feel that black men have done them wrong," says Pulitzer Prize–winning poet Rita Dove. "It's also a way of taking charge and saying, 'I'm waiting for Prince Charming, but the important thing is that he's charming, not that he's black'." There's an irony here: for white women the Cinderella myth is about passivity, but for black women it's about actively seeking a partner who's their equal.

With many black women heading households, the issue isn't necessarily about becoming independent. Estelle Farley is a clinical research scientist in Raleigh, North Carolina. In her thirties, Farley says, "[The man I'm looking for] has to have a salary close to what I make or more. I've gone down the road with someone who didn't, and it's not a good road." bell hooks, author of the new book *Wounds of Passion*, is much more blunt. "Keep this in mind, girlfriend," says hooks. "This generation of black women is growing up in a truly integrated pop culture. Most black women under the age of thirty would rather have a rich white man than a poor black man." 6

Whoopi Goldberg, whose companion is the white actor Frank Langella, has often been under fire for dating white men. "First off, I have dated black men," explains Goldberg. "But a woman with power is a problem for any man, but particularly a black man because it's hard for them to get power. I understand that, but I have to have a life, and that means dating the men that want to date me." 7

Historically, the struggle for racial equality left little room for black women to indulge in Cinderella fantasies. From Reconstruction° through Jim Crow° and through the civil-rights movement, black women devoted their energies to these struggles while secretly hoping that one day their prince would indeed come. Harvard psychiatrist Dr. Alvin Poussaint remembers that during the 1960s, "many of the black women in the movement used to joke —but it was partly serious— that part of why they were fighting was so black men would be able to get good jobs and they would be able to stay at home like white women and have their men take care of them." Furthermore, in the 1970s, many black women were reluctant to embrace feminism because it seemed that just when it was about to be their turn to be Cinderella, white women were telling them that the fantasy was all wrong. "I think there was always more ambivalence about the women's movement on the part of some black women," says Poussaint. "It meant that they were losing out on their chance to be in this dependent role." 8

Reconstruction: The period after the Civil War when the South was rebuilding.   Jim Crow: Laws that legalized segregation by sanctioning "separate but equal" facilities for whites and blacks.

Today Cinderella, for better or worse, is much more accessible to young 9
black women. Disney vice president Anna Perez recalls, "Growing up, I loved
fairy tales. But I never thought someone was going to come along and take
care of me. It sure didn't happen for my mother, who raised six kids by herself." But Brandy says, "I grew up listening to the Cinderella stories; just because she was white didn't mean that I couldn't live the same dream."

What gives Cinderella such staying power is the myth's malleability, the 10
many ways in which it continues to be transformed. Author Virginia Hamilton, a MacArthur "genius" award winner, is partial to a plantation myth called
"Catskinella," which appears in her book, *Her Stories*. In this version Cinderella is strong and wily. The prince wants to marry her, but she makes him
wait until she is good and ready. Hamilton says she loves the story because it
is evidence that "when black women were at their most oppressed, they had
the extraordinary imagination to create stories for themselves, about themselves."

For bell hooks, Zora Neale Hurston's classic novel *Their Eyes Were Watch-* 11
ing God is the best Cinderella story going. "Janie rejects her rich husband for
Tea Cake, the laborer," hooks says of the book, which Oprah Winfrey is developing into a movie. "Janie talks about how there is a jewel inside of her.
Tea Cake sees that jewel, and he brings it out. Which is very different from the
traditional Cinderella myth of the prince holding the jewel and you trying to
get it from him."

In this latest version of Cinderella, Disney makes a subtle — some might 12
say feeble — attempt to give the myth a slightly more feminist slant. When
they first meet, Cinderella tells the prince that she's not sure she wants to get
to know him. She says, "I doubt if this stranger has any idea how a girl should
be treated." He gives her a knowing look and says, "Like a princess, I suppose."
And she looks at him, with her big brown eyes, and says, "No, like a *person*.
With kindness and respect."

Questions to Start You Thinking

1. CONSIDERING MEANING: What does Chambers say is the difference between
   how black and white women interpret the Cinderella myth?

2. IDENTIFYING WRITING STRATEGIES: How does Chambers use cause and effect to
   explain the relationship between America's history of racism and the appeal
   of the Cinderella myth to African American women?

3. READING CRITICALLY: Chambers quotes many different women's opinions of
   the Cinderella myth. How do their credentials and opinions help shape the
   essay? Is this strategy effective for the point Chambers is trying to make? Why,
   or why not?

4. EXPANDING VOCABULARY: Define *malleability*. What does Chambers mean
   when she says that the reason the Cinderella myth has remained appealing for
   centuries is its *malleability* (paragraph 10)? What makes the story malleable?

5. MAKING CONNECTIONS: Would Cinderella as revised by Disney satisfy Ellen
   Goodman's definition of a good television role model for children ("How to
   Zap Violence on TV," p. 613)? Why, or why not?

Journal Prompts

1. What fairy-tale or mythical figure was especially appealing to you as a child? Why? In what way — if any — did it shape your expectations of life as an adult?

2. What change in the Cinderella myth does the end of Chambers's essay suggest? Do you see it as a positive change? Why, or why not?

Suggestions for Writing

1. Does the Cinderella myth represent an ideal for you? Why, or why not?

2. Write an essay in which you analyze the influence of a character from popular culture. Is the character a positive or a negative role model? Why?

James Q. Wilson, *born in 1931 in Denver, Colorado, received his A.B. from the University of Redlands in 1952 and earned his Ph.D. from the University of Chicago in 1959. Considered one of the foremost conservative political thinkers of our time, Wilson is a prolific writer. His works of scholarship include* Varieties of Police Behavior *(1970),* Thinking about Crime *(1975),* American Government *(1987),* Bureaucracy *(1989),* The Moral Sense *(1993),* Political Organizations *(1995), and* Moral Judgment *(1997). He has been elected a member of the American Academy of Arts and Sciences and a fellow of the American Philosophical Society. In 1990 he received the James Madison Award for distinguished scholarhip from the American Political Science Association, and in 1991–92 served as that organization's president. He is currently the James Collins Professor of Management at the University of California at Los Angeles. In this essay, published in the* Utne Reader *in November 1997, Wilson argues that the benefits of the privately owned automobile far outweigh its admittedly high social costs.*

AS YOU READ: *Identify what Wilson says are the major personal benefits of owning a car and the major social benefits of living in a car-dependent society.*

James Q. Wilson In Praise of Asphalt Nation

Imagine the country we now inhabit — big, urban, prosperous — with one exception: the automobile has not been invented. We have trains and bicycles, and some kind of self-powered buses and trucks, but no private cars driven by their owners for business or pleasure. Of late, let us suppose, someone has come forward with the idea of creating the personal automobile. Consider how we would react to such news.

Libertarians° might support the idea, but hardly anyone else. Engineers would point out that such cars, if they were produced in any significant number, would zip along roads just a few feet — perhaps even a few inches — from

Libertarians: People who support a political position of every person for himself or herself.

one another; the chance of accidents would not simply be high, it would be certain.

Environmentalists would react in horror to the idea of automobiles powered by the internal combustion engine, apparently the most inexpensive method. Such devices, because they burn fuel incompletely, would eject into the air large amounts of unpleasant gases, such as carbon monoxide, nitrogen oxide, and sulfur dioxide.

Energy experts would react in horror at the prospect of supplying gasoline stations with the vast quantities of petroleum necessary to fuel automobiles, which, unlike buses and trucks, would be stored at home and not at a central depot and would burn much more fuel per person they carried than some of their mass-transit alternatives.

Big-city mayors would add their own objections, though these would reflect their self-interest as much as their wisdom. If people could drive anywhere, they would be able to live wherever they wished. This would produce a vast exodus from the large cities, led in all likelihood by the most prosperous — and thus the most tax-productive — citizens. People who, being poorer, were less mobile would remain. Money would depart but problems stay.

In short, the automobile, a device on which most Americans rely not only for transportation but also for mobility, privacy, and fun, would not exist if it had to be created today. Of course, the car does exist, and has powerfully affected the living, working, and social spaces of America. But the argument against it persists and dominates the thinking of academic experts on urban transportation and much of city planning. It can be found in countless books complaining of dreary suburban architecture, endless trips to and from work, the social isolation produced by solo auto trips, and the harmful effects of the car on air quality, noise levels, petroleum consumption, and road congestion.

In her recent book *Asphalt Nation: How the Automobile Took Over America and How We Can Take It Back* (Crown, 1997), Jane Holtz Kay, the architecture critic for the *Nation*, assails° the car unmercifully. It has, she writes, "strangled" our lives and landscape, imposing on us "the costs of sprawl, of pollution, of congestion, of commuting." To undo this damage, the massively subsidized automobile will have to be sharply curtailed by heavy investment in public transportation and European-like taxes on gasoline. What is more, people ought to live in cities with high population densities, since "for mass transit," as Kay notes, "you need mass." Housing should be built within a short walk of the corner store and industries moved back downtown.

In Kay's book, hostility toward the car is linked inextricably to hostility toward the low-density suburb. Her view is by no means confined to the political left. Karl Zinsmeister, a conservative, has argued in *American Enterprise* that we have created "inhospitable places for individualism and community life." Suburbs, says Zinsmeister, encourage "rootlessness" and are the enemy of the "traditional neighborhood" and its "easy daily interactions."

assails: Attacks.

Despite the criticisms, automobile use has grown. In 1969, 80 percent of   9
all urban trips involved a car and only 5 percent involved public transportation; by 1990, car use had risen to 84 percent and public transit had fallen to
less than 3 percent. Suppose, however, that the anti-car writers were to win
over the vastly more numerous pro-car drivers. Let us imagine what life would
be like in a carless nation. People would have to live very close together so
they could walk or, for healthy people living in sunny climes,° bicycle to
mass-transit stops. Living in close quarters would mean life as it is now lived
in Manhattan. There would be few freestanding homes, many row houses,
and lots of apartment buildings. There would be few private gardens except
for flowerpots on balconies. The streets would be congested by pedestrians,
trucks, and buses, as they were at the turn of the century before automobiles
became common.

Moving about outside the larger cities would be difficult. People would   10
be able to take trains to distant sites, but when they arrived at some attractive
locale it would turn out to be another city. They could visit the beach, but only
(of necessity) crowded parts of it. They could go to a national park, but only
the built-up section of it. They could see the countryside, but (mostly)
through a train window. More isolated or remote locations would be accessible, but since public transit would provide the only way of getting there, the
departures would be infrequent and the transfers frequent.

In other words, you could see the United States much as most Europeans   11
saw their countryside before the automobile became an important means of
locomotion. A train from London or Paris would take you to "the country" by
way of a long journey through ugly industrial areas to those rural parts where
either you had a home (and the means to ferry yourself to it) or there was a
resort (that would be crowded enough to support a nearby train stop).

All this is a way of saying that the debate between car defenders and car   12
haters is a debate between private benefits and public goods. List the characteristics of travel that impose few costs on society and, in general, walking, cycling, and some form of public transit will be seen to be superior. Noncar
methods generate less pollution, use energy a bit more efficiently, produce
less noise, and (with some exceptions) are safer. But list the characteristics of
travel that are desired by individuals, and (with some exceptions) the car is
clearly superior. The automobile is more flexible, more punctual, supplies
greater comfort, provides for carrying more parcels, creates more privacy, enables one to select fellow passengers, and, for distances over a mile or more,
requires less travel time.

As a practical matter, of course, the debate between those who value pri-   13
vate benefits and those who insist on their social costs is no real debate at all,
since people select modes of travel based on individual, not social, preferences. That is why in almost every country in the world, the automobile has
triumphed, and much of public policy has been devoted to the somewhat inconsistent task of subsidizing individual choices while attemping to reduce
the costs attached to them. In the case of the automobile, governments have

climes: Climates.

attempted to reduce exhaust pollution, make roads safer, and restrict use (by tolls, speed bumps, pedestrian-only streets, and parking restrictions) in neighborhoods that attach a high value to pedestrian passage. Yet none of these efforts can alter the central fact that people have found cars to be the best means for getting about.

A great deal can still be done to moderate the social costs of automobile   14
traffic. More toll roads can be built with variable rates that will allow people to drive — at different prices, depending on the level of congestion — to and from cities. Bridges into cities can charge tolls to ensure that only highly motivated people consume scarce downtown road space. Gasoline taxes can be set much higher. (This will not happen in a society as democratic as ours, but it is a good idea, and maybe someday a crisis will create an opportunity.)

But even if we do all the things that can be done to limit the social costs   15
of cars, the campaign against them will not stop. It will not stop because so many of the critics dislike everything the car stands for and everything that society constructs to serve the needs of its users.

Questions to Start You Thinking

1. CONSIDERING MEANING: What are the main arguments against cars that Wilson outlines? Why does he claim that despite all these drawbacks, cars are still the best way of traveling?

2. IDENTIFYING WRITING STRATEGIES: Where does Wilson acknowledge the opposition's argument in his essay? Does his acknowledgment strengthen or weaken the stand he takes in defending cars as a means of transportation? Why?

3. READING CRITICALLY: What kinds of appeals — emotional, logical, ethical — does Wilson use in the beginning of his essay (paragraphs 1 to 6)? (For an explanation of kinds of appeals, see p. 103 in *A Writer's Guide*.) Is his appeal appropriate? Effective?

4. EXPANDING VOCABULARY: Define *inextricably* (paragraph 8). According to Wilson, why is hostility toward the car often *inextricably* linked to hostility toward the suburb?

5. MAKING CONNECTIONS: Wilson opposes limiting the use of cars, and Paul Varnell argues against restricting speech ("The Niceness Solution," p. 576). How are the issues they address similar? How are they different?

Journal Prompts

1. Would you like to live in a carless society? Why, or why not?

2. Imagine you were in the position of deciding how to limit the problems caused by cars in your city or town. What kinds of solutions would you propose?

Suggestions for Writing

1. In an essay, describe the circumstances in which having or not having access to a car made a difference to you, and explain how the experience affected you.

2. Write an essay in which you analyze a print or television advertisement for a particular kind of car. What image of the car — and its driver — are the advertisers trying to project? What does this image reveal about the value Americans place on cars?

*Phyllis Rose was born in New York City and earned her B.A. from Radcliffe Col-
lege in 1964, her M.A. from Yale University in 1965, and her Ph.D. from Harvard
University in 1970. A distinguished biographer, Rose's works include* Woman of
Letters: A Life of Virginia Woolf *(1978),* Parallel Lives: Five Victorian Mar-
riages *(1983),* Jazz Cleopatra: Josephine Baker in Her Time *(1989),* Writing of
Women *(1985), and* The Year of Reading Proust *(1997). She also recently edited*
The Norton Book of Women's Lives *(1996). Currently a professor of English at
Wesleyan University, she writes frequently for national nonacademic publications,
including the* New York Times Book Review, *the* Sophisticated Traveler, *and*
Civilization. *In this essay, which appeared in* Never Say Goodbye *(1991), a collection of American cultural criticism, Rose argues that the American love of shopping transcends simple materialism and actually serves a valuable social function
that has little or nothing to do with acquiring goods.*

AS YOU READ: *Try to figure out why Rose says that shopping is a "spiritual adventure."*

Phyllis Rose   **Shopping and Other Spiritual Adventures
in America Today**

Last year a new Waldbaum's Food Mart opened in the shopping mall on   1
Route 66. It belongs to the new generation of superduper-markets open
twenty-four hours that have computerized checkout. I went to see the place as
soon as it opened and I was impressed. There was trail mix in Lucite° bins.
There was freshly made pasta. There were coffee beans, four kinds of tahini,°
ten kinds of herb teas, raw shrimp in shells and cooked shelled shrimp, fresh-
squeezed orange juice. Every sophistication known to the big city, even goat's
cheese covered with ash, was now available in Middletown, Connecticut.
People raced from the warehouse aisle to the bagel bin to the coffee beans to
the fresh fish market, exclaiming at all the new things. Many of us felt elevated, graced, complimented by the presence of this food palace in our town.

This is the wonderful egalitarianism° of American business. Was it Andy   2
Warhol° who said that the nice thing about Coke is, no can is any better or
worse than any other? Some people may find it dull to cross the country and
find the same chain stores with the same merchandise from coast to coast, but
it means that my town is as good as yours, my shopping mall as important as
yours, equally filled with wonders.

Imagine what people ate during the winter as little as seventy-five years   3
ago. They ate food that was local, long-lasting, and dull, like acorn squash,
turnips, and cabbage. Walk into an American supermarket in February and
the world lies before you: grapes, melons, artichokes, fennel, lettuce, peppers,
pistachios, dates, even strawberries, to say nothing of ice cream. Have you ever

Lucite: Hard, transparent plastic.   **tahini:** Sesame paste.   **egalitarianism:** Equality.
Andy Warhol: American artist (1930?–1987) known for his depictions of everyday objects,
such as soup cans.

610

considered what a triumph of civilization it is to be able to buy a pound of chicken livers? If you lived on a farm and had to kill a chicken when you wanted to eat one, you wouldn't ever accumulate a pound of chicken livers.

Another wonder of Middletown is Caldor, the discount department store. Here is man's plenty: tennis racquets, panty hose, luggage, glassware, records, toothpaste, Timex watches, Cadbury's chocolate, corn poppers, hair dryers, warm-up suits, car wax, light bulbs, television sets. All good quality at low prices with exchanges cheerfully made on defective goods. There are worse rules to live by. I feel good about America whenever I walk into this store, which is almost every midwinter Sunday afternoon, when life elsewhere has closed down. I go to Caldor the way English people go to pubs: out of sociability. To get away from my house. To widen my horizons. For culture's sake, Caldor provides me too with a welcome sense of seasonal change. When the first outdoor grills and lawn furniture appear there, it's as exciting a sign of spring as the first crocus or robin.

Someone told me about a Soviet émigré° who practices English by declaiming,° at random, sentences that catch his fancy. One of his favorites is, "Fifty percent off all items today only." Refugees from Communist countries appreciate our supermarkets and discount department stores for the wonders they are. An Eastern European scientist visiting Middletown wept when she first saw the meat counter at Waldbaum's. On the other hand, before her year in America was up, her pleasure turned sour. She wanted everything she saw. Her approach to consumer goods was insufficiently abstract, too materialistic. We Americans are beyond a simple, possessive materialism. We're used to abundance and the possibility of possessing things. The things, and the possibility of possessing them, will still be there next week, next year. So today we can walk the aisles calmly.

It is a misunderstanding of the American retail store to think we go there necessarily to buy. Some of us shop. There's a difference. Shopping has many purposes, the least interesting of which is to acquire new articles. We shop to cheer ourselves up. We shop to practice decision-making. We shop to be useful and productive members of our class and society. We shop to remind ourselves how much is available to us. We shop to remind ourselves how much is to be striven for. We shop to assert our superiority to the material objects that spread themselves before us.

Shopping's function as a form of therapy is widely appreciated. You don't really need, let's say, another sweater. You need the feeling of power that comes with buying or not buying it. You need the feeling that someone wants something you have — even if it's just your money. To get the benefit of shopping, you needn't actually purchase the sweater, any more than you have to marry every man you flirt with. In fact, window-shopping, like flirting, can be more rewarding, the same high without the distressing commitment, the material encumbrance.° The purest form of shopping is provided by garage sales.

émigré: A person who has moved to another country permanently.   declaiming: Stating loudly.   encumbrance: Burden

A connoisseur° goes out with no goal in mind, open to whatever may come his or her way, secure that it will cost very little. Minimum expense, maximum experience. Perfect shopping.

I try to think of the opposite, a kind of shopping in which the object is all-important, the pleasure of shopping at a minimum. For example, the purchase of blue jeans. I buy new blue jeans as seldom as possible because the experience is so humiliating. For every pair that looks good on me, fifteen look grotesque. But even shopping for blue jeans at Bob's Surplus on Main Street — no frills, bare-bones shopping — is an event in the life of the spirit. Once again I have to come to terms with the fact that I will never look good in Levi's. Much as I want to be mainstream, I never will be.

In fact, I'm doubly an oddball, neither Misses nor Junior, but Misses Petite. I look in the mirror, I acknowledge the disparity between myself and the ideal. I resign myself to making the best of it. I will buy the Lee's Misses Petite. Shopping is a time of reflection, assessment, spiritual self-discipline.

It is appropriate, I think, that Bob's Surplus has a communal dressing room. I used to shop only in places where I could count on a private dressing room with a mirror inside. My impulse then was to hide my weaknesses. Now I believe in sharing them. There are other women in the dressing room at Bob's surplus trying on blue jeans who look as bad as I do. We take comfort from one another. Sometimes a woman will ask me which of two items looks better. I always give a definite answer. It's the least I can do. I figure we are all in this together, and I emerge from the dressing room not only with a new pair of jeans but with a renewed sense of belonging to a human community.

When a Solzhenitsyn° rants about American materialism, I have to look at my digital Timex and check what year this is. Materialism? Like conformism, a hot moral issue of the fifties, but not now. How to spread the goods, maybe. Whether the goods are the Good, no. Solzhenitsyn, like the visiting scientist who wept at the beauty of Waldbaum's meat counter but came to covet everything she saw, takes American materialism too materialistically. He doesn't see its spiritual side. Caldor, Waldbaum's, Bob's Surplus — these, perhaps, are our cathedrals.

Questions to Start You Thinking	1. CONSIDERING MEANING: What kind of shopping does Rose claim is most fulfilling? What kind is least fulfilling?
	2. IDENTIFYING WRITING STRATEGIES: Where in her essay does Rose write from her imagination? Does this strategy suit her purpose? Why, or why not?
	3. READING CRITICALLY: What is the tone of this essay? How does Rose set the tone? Is it appropriate to her purpose? Why, or why not?
	4. EXPANDING VOCABULARY: Define *materialism*. What is the difference between "a simple, possessive *materialism*" (paragraph 5) and "American *materialism*" as Rose defines it (paragraph 11)?

connoisseur: Expert judge of something.   **Solzhenitsyn:** Aleksandr Solzhenitsyn (b. 1918), Russian writer and cultural critic who won the Nobel Prize for literature.

5. MAKING CONNECTIONS: Both Rose and Steve Olson ("Year of the Blue-Collar Guy," p. 570) make exaggerated claims about American culture. Compare and contrast the effects of the authors' claims. How are the effects similar? How are they different?

Journal Prompts

1. According to your observations, how social is shopping?
2. Do you shop for any reason other than a need to buy particular goods? How do your reasons for shopping compare to those Rose discusses in her essay?

Suggestions for Writing

1. Were you ever particularly aware of an abundance or lack of abundance in your life? Using your experience as evidence, explain why you agree or disagree with Rose's claim that Americans are "used to abundance" (paragraph 5).
2. How might an economist respond to Rose's assessment of superstores? Find two expert views on the cause and effect of the superstore phenomenon in American culture. Write an essay that synthesizes your sources' ideas and evaluates whether Rose's enthusiasm is warranted.

Ellen Goodman, *born in 1941 in Newton, Massachusetts, writes a nationally syndicated column on contemporary American life for the* Boston Globe, *where she is also an associate editor. Before joining the* Globe, *Goodman worked as a researcher, reporter, and feature writer for* Newsweek *and the* Detroit Free Press. *Goodman's newspaper columns are collected in* Close to Home *(1979),* Keeping in Touch *(1985),* Making Sense *(1989), and* Value Judgments *(1993). She won a Pulitzer Prize for commentary in 1980. In this article, first published in the* Globe *on February 15, 1996, Goodman addresses the potential connection between violence on television and violent crime in America and suggests a lack of creativity as a larger, more fundamental problem with television entertainment. In the paired selection that follows, Mike Males ("Public Enemy Number One?" p. 616) takes issue with Goodman's assumption that there is a link between television violence and violence in the culture at large.*

AS YOU READ: *Identify the reasons Goodman believes violence on television is a problem.*

Ellen Goodman   How to Zap Violence on TV

Ed Donnerstein is not a cultural coroner. He doesn't believe that you can understand the problem of violence on television by merely doing a body count. Or a bullet count.

As one of the lead researchers on a study done at . . .[the Santa Barbara] campus of the University of California, he wants to make it perfectly clear that not all the violence on television is equally harmful, nor are all young viewers equally harmed.

No, he would not oppose televising *Romeo and Juliet* despite the bodies in   3
the last act. And no, he does not believe that violence on television is the sole or primary cause of violence in America.

But he says, "We can no longer deny that violence on television con-   4
tributes to the problem." He offers this message slowly and distinctly, as if trying to be heard over the din.

The *National Television Violence Study* that he and his colleagues labored   5
over for three years was released last week into the middle of heated political debate. It made page 1 just as the telecommunications act became law with its controversial provision for a V-chip, a device to help parents block out programs rated too violent. It hit the evening news just as broadcasters were pondering the president's invitation for a February 29 trip to the White House woodshed.

Representative Ed Markey, the man with the V-chip on his mind, imme-   6
diately praised the study as a Perry Mason° Moment, the perfect evidence against an industry in the throes of denial. An NBC executive called the research "ridiculous." *Variety* suggested a lobotomy.°

What the analysis of 2,693 television programs from twenty-three chan-   7
nels showed is that a majority of programs contain what the researchers call "harmful violence." These were programs that posed three distinct threats to public health: "learning to behave violently, becoming more desensitized to the harmful consequences of violence, and becoming more fearful of being attacked."

"The issue for us," Donnerstein says, "is not just that there was violence   8
but how it was presented." In analyzing the plots, images, and programs, the team asked, what makes violence a public health problem? What contexts should we worry about?

For one thing, violence turns out to do a lot of harm when it looks harm-   9
less. One of the lessons children learn watching television is that there are few consequences to the person who commits violence — or to the victim.

In 73 percent of the scenes, the violence went unpunished. In nearly half   10
of the programs with slugfests and shootouts, the victims miraculously never appeared harmed. In 58 percent they showed no pain. In fact, only 16 percent of the programs showed any long-term problems — physical, emotional, or financial.

Add to this "positive" portrayal of negative behavior the fact that chil-   11
dren's programs were least likely to show the bad effects of violence and most likely to make it funny. As Donnerstein says, "We're showing children violence that goes unpunished, is unrealistic and humorous."

Perry Mason: Fictional crime-solving attorney on television and in books. The guilty person is usually revealed during a courtroom trial.   **lobotomy:** Surgery that removes the frontal lobe of the brain to make mentally disturbed people less violent but that also makes them incapable of taking care of themselves.

As for other messages? Only a minuscule 4 percent of violent programs   12
had an antiviolent theme. Or showed any alternative to the gun, the fist, the
fight.

It's not surprising that this study is being touted in Washington as a   13
sound basis for rating television violence. After all, if the V-chip is to become
what Clinton called the "parents' power chip," we need a ratings system that's
more sophisticated than one that counts dead bodies.

Indeed, selling the V-chip to an audience of Virginia parents, Clinton not   14
only quoted the dark facts of the violence research, he promised that "new
technologies can put you back in the driver's seat in your life." It's an appeal
to parents who want to regain some modest control over the messages coming into their houses and to their children.

But the same *National Television Violence Study* also hints at the limits of a   15
technological fix to what is not really a technological problem.

The portrait that emerges from this analysis, after all, is not just of the   16
television environment. It's a profile of an industry that narrowly equates entertainment with violence. It's a profile of a galaxy of broadcasters, producers,
and programmers who have shown more imagination in claiming their programs are harmless than in changing the destructive plots.

The V-chip is a violence block. But the real problem in the television in-   17
dustry is a creative block. Soon we'll have the V-chip. Does anyone know how
to get rid of the C-chip?

Questions to Start You Thinking	1. CONSIDERING MEANING: What solutions does Goodman propose to the prob-lem of violence on television? Which solution does Goodman view as the most important?

1. CONSIDERING MEANING: What solutions does Goodman propose to the problem of violence on television? Which solution does Goodman view as the
   most important?

2. IDENTIFYING WRITING STRATEGIES: How does Goodman evaluate the V-chip in
   her essay? What criteria does she use in her evaluation?

3. READING CRITICALLY: How well does Goodman support her assertion that
   "the real problem in the television industry is a creative block" (paragraph 17)?

4. EXPANDING VOCABULARY: Define *desensitized* (paragraph 7). What does it
   mean to become *desensitized* to violence? What is the difference between
   being *desensitized* and being *insensitive*?

5. MAKING CONNECTIONS: Goodman cites a study that she says "hints at the limits of a technological fix to what is not really a technological problem" (paragraph 15). Could this study apply to Jeffrey Obser's argument ("Privacy Is the
   Problem, Not the Solution," p. 657)? Why, or why not?

Link to the Paired Essay

Goodman and Mike Males ("Public Enemy Number One?" p. 616) take different stands in relation to the issue of violence on television. Compare and contrast the two writers' positions. Do they believe violence in the media *causes* real-
life violence or simply exists alongside it? Why?

Journal Prompts

1. How did you feel when you saw violence in some television shows you've watched recently?

2. How might some people see television violence as giving them persmission to act violently?

Suggestions for Writing

1. Is it ever necessary to show violence on television or in a movie? Why, or why not? Write an essay supporting your position.

2. Research media sources to find out what has happened to the V-chip since the publication of Goodman's article. Write an essay that evaluates whether the V-chip has been an effective tool for parents.

Mike Males, *born in Oklahoma City in 1950, earned his B.A. in political science from Occidental College in 1972 and is currently finishing his dissertation in social ecology at the University of California at Irvine. A writer whose academic work addresses the correspondence between youth and adult behavior, Males has published articles in* Progressive, Adolescence, *the* Lancet, *the* American Journal of Public Health, *the* Journal of School Health, *the* New York Times, *the* Los Angeles Times, *and the* Washington Post. *In 1992 and 1996 he received the Project Censored award for articles about America's "war on drugs." A member of the Advisory Board for the California Wellness Foundation, Males is a frequent speaker at conferences on youth behavior and is the author of* Scapegoat Generation: America's War on Adolescents (1996). *While Ellen Goodman assumes that there is a connection between television violence and violent crime, Males analyzes both media coverage and documented social studies to argue that the economic, social, legal, and domestic violence inflicted on children by adults is far more damaging (and a greater cause of violent crime) than the media representations of violence that children see and hear.*

AS YOU READ: *Identify what Males says is the main problem with television violence.*

Mike Males   **Public Enemy Number One?**

Forget about poverty, racism, child abuse, domestic violence, rape. America, from Michael Medved° to *Mother Jones*° has discovered the real cause of our country's rising violence: television mayhem, Guns N' Roses, Ice-T, and Freddy Krueger.

No need for family support policies, justice system reforms, or grappling with such distressing issues as poverty and sexual violence against the young. Today's top social policy priorities, it seems, are TV lockout gizmos, voluntary restraint, program labeling, and (since everyone agrees these strategies won't work) congressionally supervised censorship. Just when earnest national

Michael Medved: American film critic.   *Mother Jones:* Magazine advocating liberal viewpoints.

soul-searching over the epidemic violence of contemporary America seemed unavoidable, that traditional scapegoat—media depravity—is topping the ratings again.

What caused four youths to go on a "reign of terror" of beating, burning, and killing in a New York City park in August 1954? Why, declared U.S. Senator Robert Hendrickson, chair of the Juvenile Delinquency Subcommittee, the ringleader was found to have a "horror comic" on his person—proof of the "dangers inherent in the multimillion-copy spate° of lurid comic books that are placed upon the newsstands each month."

And what caused four youths to go on a brutal "wilding" spree, nearly killing a jogger in a New York City park in May 1989? Why, Tipper Gore wrote in *Newsweek*, the leader was humming the rap ditty "Wild Thing" after his arrest. Enough said.

Today, media violence scapegoating is not just the crusade of censorious conservatives and priggish preachers, but also of those of progressive stripe—from Senator Paul Simon (D-Illinois) and Representative Edward Markey (D-Maine) to *Mother Jones* and columnist Ellen Goodman. "The average American child," Goodman writes, "sees 8,000 murders and 10,000 acts of violence on television before he or she is out of grammar school." Goodman, like most pundits, expends far more outrage on the sins of TV and rock 'n' roll than on the rapes and violent abuses millions of American children experience before they are out of grammar school.

The campaign is particularly craven° in its efforts to confine the debate to TV's effects on children and adolescents even though the research claims that adults are similarly affected. But no politician wants to tell voters they can't see *Terminator II* because it might incite grownups to mayhem.

Popular perceptions aside, the most convincing research, found in massive, multinational correlational studies° of thousands of people, suggests that, at most, media violence accounts for 1 to 5 percent of all violence in society. For example, a 1984 study led by media-violence expert Rowell Huesmann of 1,500 youth in the United States, Finland, Poland, and Australia found that the amount of media violence watched is associated with about 5 percent of the violence in children, as rated by peers. Other correlational studies have found similarly small effects.

But the biggest question media-violence critics can't answer is the most fundamental one: Is it the *cause*, or simply one of the many *symptoms*, of this unquestionably brutal age? The best evidence does not exonerate celluloid savagery (who could?) but shows that it is a small, derivative influence compared to the real-life violence, both domestic and official, that our children face growing up in '80s and '90s America.

When it comes to the genuine causes of youth violence, it's hard to dismiss the 51 percent increase in youth poverty since 1973, 1 million rapes, and a like number of violently injurious offenses inflicted upon the young every year, a juvenile justice system bent on retribution against poor and minority

spate: Flood.   **craven:** Cowardly.   **correlational studies:** Research studies attempting to establish cause-and-effect relationships between events.

youth, and the abysmal neglect of the needs of young families. The Carter-Reagan-Bush eras added 4 million youths to the poverty rolls. The last twenty years have brought a record decline in youth well-being.

Despite claims that media violence is the best-researched social phenomenon in history, social sciences indexes show many times more studies of the effects of rape, violence, and poverty on the young. Unlike the indirect methods of most media studies (questionnaires, interviews, peer ratings, and laboratory vignettes), child abuse research includes the records of real-life criminals and their backgrounds. Unlike the media studies, the findings of this avalanche of research are consistent: child poverty, abuse, and neglect underlie every major social problem the nation faces.   10

And, unlike the small correlations or temporary laboratory effects found in media research, abuse-violence studies produce powerful results: "Eighty-four percent of prison inmates were abused as children," the research agency Childhelp USA reports in a 1993 summary of major findings. Separate studies by the Minnesota State Prison, the Massachusetts Correctional Institute, and the Massachusetts Treatment Center for Sexually Dangerous Persons (to cite a few) find histories of childhood abuse and neglect in 60 to 90 percent of the violent inmates studied — including virtually all death row prisoners. The most conservative study, that by the National Institute of Justice, indicates that some half-million criminally violent offenses each year are the result of offenders being abused as children.   11

Two million American children are violently injured, sexually abused, or neglected every year by adults whose age averages thirty-two years, according to the Denver-based American Humane Association. One million children and teenagers are raped every year, according to the 1992 federally funded *Rape in America* study of 4,000 women, which has been roundly ignored by the same media outlets that never seem short of space to berate violent rap lyrics.   12

Sensational articles in *Mother Jones* ("Proof That TV Makes Kids Violent"), *Newsweek* ("The Importance of Being Nasty"), and *U.S. News & World Report* ("Fighting TV Violence") devoted pages to blaming music and media for violence — yet all three ignored this study of the rape of millions of America's children. CNN devoted less than a minute to the study; *Time* magazine gave it only three paragraphs.   13

In yet another relevant report, the California Department of Justice tabulated 1,600 murders in 1992 for which offenders' and victims' ages are known. It showed that half of all teenage murder victims, six out of seven children killed, and 80 percent of all adult murder victims were slain by adults over age twenty, not by "kids." But don't expect any cover stories on "Poverty and Adult Violence: The Real Causes of Violent Youth," or "Grownups: Wild in the Homes." Politicians and pundits know who not to pick on.   14

Ron Harris's powerful August 1993 series in the *Los Angeles Times* — one of the few exceptions to the media myopia° on youth violence — details the history of a decade of legal barbarism against youth in the Reagan and Bush   15

myopia: Shortsightedness.

years — which juvenile justice experts now link to the late '80s juvenile crime explosion. The inflammatory, punishment-oriented attitudes of these years led to a 50 percent increase in the number of youths behind bars. Youth typically serve sentences 60 percent longer than adults convicted for the same crimes. Today, two-thirds of all incarcerated youth are black, Latino, or Native American, up from less than half before 1985.

Ten years of a costly "get tough" approach to deter youth violence concluded with the highest rate of crime in the nation's history. Teenage violence, which had been declining from 1970 through 1983, doubled from 1983 through 1991. It is not surprising that the defenders of these policies should be casting around for a handy excuse for this policy disaster. TV violence is perfect for their purposes. 16

This is the sort of escapism liberals should be exposing. But too many shrink from frankly declaring that today's mushrooming violence is the predictable consequence of two decades of assault, economic and judicial, against the young. Now, increasingly, they point at Jason, 2 Live Crew, and *Henry: Portrait of a Serial Killer*. 17

The insistence by such liberal columnists as Goodman and Coleman McCarthy that the evidence linking media violence to youth violence is on par with their linking smoking to lung cancer represents a fundamental misunderstanding of the difference between biological and psychological research. Psychology is not, despite its pretensions, a science. Research designs using human subjects are vulnerable to a bewildering array of confusing factors, many not even clear to researchers. The most serious (but by no means only) weakness is the tendency by even the most conscientious researchers to influence subjects to produce the desired results. Thus the findings of psychological studies must be swallowed with large grains of salt. 18

Consider a few embarrassing problems with media violence research. First, many studies (particularly those done under more realistic "field conditions") show no increase in violence following exposure to violent media. In fact, a significant number of studies show no effect, or even decreased aggression. Even media-violence critic Huesmann has written that depriving children of violent shows may actually increase their violence. 19

Second, the definitions of just what constitutes media "violence," let alone what kind produces aggression in viewers, are frustratingly vague. Respected researchers J. Singer and D. Singer found in a comprehensive 1986 study that "later aggressive behavior was predicted by earlier heavy viewing of public television's fast-paced *Sesame Street*." The Parent's Music Resource Center heartily endorsed the band U2 as "healthy and inspiring" for youth to listen to — yet U2's song "Pistol Weighing Heavy" was cited in psychiatric testimony as a key inspiration for the 1989 killing of actress Rebecca Schaeffer. 20

Third, if, as media critics claim, media violence is the, or even just a, prime cause of youth violence, we might expect to see similar rates of violence among all those exposed to similar amounts of violence in the media, regardless of race, gender, region, economic status, or other demographic differences. Yet this is far from the case. 21

Consider the issue of race. Surveys show that while black and white fam-   22
ilies have access to similar commercial television coverage, white families are
much more likely to subscribe to violent cable channels. Yet murder arrests
among black youth are now twelve times higher than among white, non-
Hispanic youth and increasing rapidly. Are blacks genetically more susceptible to television violence than whites? Or could there be other reasons for
this pattern — perhaps the 45 percent poverty rates and 60 percent unemployment rates among black teenagers?

And consider also the issue of gender. Girls watch as much violent TV as   23
boys. Yet female adolescents show remarkably low and stable rates of violence. Over the last decade or so, murders by female teens (180 in 1983, 171
in 1991) stayed roughly the same, while murders by boys skyrocketed (1,476
in 1983, 3,435 in 1991). How do the media-blamers explain that?

Finally, consider the issue of locale. Kids see the same amount of violent   24
TV all over, but many rural states show no increases in violence, while in Los
Angeles, to take one example, homicide rates have skyrocketed.

The more media research claims are subjected to close scrutiny, the more   25
their contradictions emerge. It can be shown that violent people do indeed
patronize more violent media, just as it can be shown that urban gang members wear baggy clothes. But no one argues that baggy clothes cause violence.
The coexistence of media and real-life violence suffers from a confusion of
cause and effect: Is an affinity for violent media the result of abuse, poverty,
and anger, or is it a prime cause of the more violent behaviors that just happen to accompany those social conditions? In a 1991 study of teenage boys
who listen to violent music, the University of Chicago's Jeffrey Arnett argues
that "[r]ather than being the cause of recklessness and despair among adolescents, heavy metal music is a reflection of these [behaviors]."

The clamor over TV violence might be harmless were it not for the fact   26
that media and legislative attention are rare, irreplaceable resources. Every
minute devoted to thrashing over issues like violence in the media is one lost
to addressing the accumulating critical social problems that are much more
crucial contributors to violence in the real world. In this regard, the media-
violence crusade offers distressing evidence of the profound decline of liber-
alism as America's social conscience, and the rising appeal (even among progressives) of simplistic Reaganesque answers to problems that Reaganism
multiplied many times over.

Virtually alone among progressives, columnist Carl T. Rowan has ex-   27
pressed outrage over the misplaced energies of those who have embraced the
media crusade and its "escapism from the truth about what makes children
(and their parents and grandparents) so violent." Writes Rowan: "I'm appalled that liberal Democrats . . . are spreading the nonsensical notion that
Americans will, to some meaningful degree, stop beating, raping, and mur-
dering each other if we just censor what is on the tube or big screen. . . . The
politicians won't, or can't deal with the real-life social problems that promote
violence in America . . . so they try to make TV programs and movies the
scapegoats! How pathetic!"

Without question, media-violence critics are genuinely concerned about today's pandemic violence. As such, it should alarm them greatly to see policy-makers and the public so preoccupied with an easy-to-castigate° media culprit linked by their research to, at most, a small part of the nation's violence—while the urgent social problems devastating a generation continue to lack even a semblance of redress.°   28

Questions to Start You Thinking

1. CONSIDERING MEANING: What does Males argue are the major causes of real-life violence?

2. IDENTIFYING WRITING STRATEGIES: Where does Males use comparison and contrast to support his point that there are many other violent influences on children besides the media? What other techniques does he use? Are these techniques effective?

3. READING CRITICALLY: Do you detect a politically liberal bias or a conservative bias in Males's argument? On what evidence do you base your conclusion?

4. EXPANDING VOCABULARY: Define *scapegoat*, *censorious*, and *priggish*. What does Males mean when he says that media violence is the *scapegoat* (paragraph 2) of "*censorious* conservatives and *priggish* preachers" (paragraph 5)?

5. MAKING CONNECTIONS: How might Stephen King ("Why We Crave Horror Movies," p. 593) respond to Males's argument that violence on television is a symptom rather than a cause of the escalation of violence in American society?

Link to the Paired Essay

Males and Ellen Goodman ("How to Zap Violence on TV," p. 613) are part of a national conversation about whether violence on television hurts American children. Locate the points in Males's essay where he specifically mentions Goodman. Does Males represent Goodman's arguments accurately? Why, or why not? How might Goodman respond to Males's accusations?

Journal Prompts

1. What was your opinion of the influence of media on real-life violence before you read this essay? Has your opinion changed since reading this essay? Why, or why not?

2. Males explains that many studies on other causes of youth violence do not receive the same publicity as studies about media influences. Why do you think this might be the case?

Suggestions for Writing

1. Write an essay in which you analyze the causes of youth violence. Support your points with your own observations.

2. Males argues that irresponsible government policy is the real cause of the dramatic increase in youth violence and that television, movies, and music are just scapegoats. Within the context of other factors that also influence children, how responsible are the media for real-life violence? Using evidence from both Males and Goodman, write an essay in which you take a stand on this issue.

castigate: Punish or blame.   **redress:** Remedy.

Chapter 26

Technology and Society

Web Search

Evaluate a search engine that you have used more than once, such as Yahoo!, InfoSeek, Excite, or the searching mechanism of a particular archive. What are its strengths and weaknesses? What recommendations would you make for improving it? How is it different from other research tools you have used, such as card catalogs or online catalogs or indexes?

Meghan Daum *was born in Palo Alto, California in 1970. She earned her B.A. in English from Vassar College in 1992 and her M.F.A. in nonfiction writing from Columbia University School of the Arts in 1996. Her writing has appeared in a wide variety of publications, including the* New York Times Book Review, *the* New York Times Magazine, GQ, Self, *the* Bellingham Review, *and* Condé Nast Sports for Women, *among others. She currently lives and works as a freelance writer in New York City. In this essay, which appeared in the August 25–September 1, 1997, issue of the* New Yorker, *Daum traces the evolution of a romance that started via e-mail and offers insightful observations about how personal relationships can be affected by electronic communication.*

AS YOU READ: *Identify the reasons Daum likes to use the computer to communicate with PFSlider.*

Meghan Daum   Virtual Love

It was last November; fall was drifting away into an intolerable chill. I was at the end of my twenty-sixth year and was living in New York City, trying to support myself as a writer and taking part in the kind of urban life that might be construed as glamorous were it to appear in a memoir in the distant future. At the time, however, my days felt more like a grind than like an adventure: hours of work strung between the motions of waking up, getting the mail, watching TV with my roommates, and going to bed. One morning, I logged on to my America Online° account to find a message under the heading "is this the real meghan daum?" It came from someone with the screen name PFSlider. The body of the message consisted of five sentences, written entirely in lowercase letters, of perfectly turned° flattery: something about PFSlider's admiration of some newspaper and magazine articles I had published over the last year and a half, something about his resulting infatuation with me, and something about his being a sportswriter in California.

I was engaged for the thirty seconds that it took me to read the message and fashion a reply. Though it felt strange to be in the position of confirming that I was indeed "the real meghan daum," I managed to say, "Yes, it's me. Thank you for writing." I clicked the "Send Now" icon, shot my words into the void, and forgot about PFSlider until the next day, when I received another message, this one headed "eureka."

"wow, it is you," he wrote, still in lowercase. He chronicled the various conditions under which he'd read my few-and-far-between articles — a boardwalk in Laguna Beach, the spring-training pressroom for a baseball team that he covered for a Los Angeles newspaper. He confessed to having a crush on me. He referred to me as "princess daum." He said he wanted to have lunch with me during one of his two annual trips to New York.

America Online: An online service provider.   **perfectly turned:** Well-written.

623

The letter was outrageous and endearingly pathetic, possibly the practical   4
joke of a friend trying to rouse me out of a temporary writer's block. But the
kindness pouring forth from my computer screen was bizarrely exhilarating,
and I logged off and thought about it for a few hours before writing back to
express how flattered and "touched" — this was probably the first time I had
ever used that word in earnest — I was by his message.

I am not what most people would call a computer person. I have no in-   5
terest in chat rooms, newsgroups, or most Web sites. I derive a palpable thrill
from sticking a letter in the United States mail. But I have a constant low-
grade fear of the telephone, and I often call people with the intention of getting their answering machines. There is something about the live voice that I
have come to find unnervingly organic, as volatile as live television. E-mail
provides a useful antidote for my particular communication anxieties.
Though I generally send and receive only a few messages a week, I take comfort in their silence and their boundaries.

PFSlider and I tossed a few innocuous, smart-assed notes back and forth   6
over the week following his first message. Let's say his name was Pete. He was
twenty-nine and single. I revealed very little about myself, relying instead on
the ironic commentary and forced witticisms that are the conceit° of so many
e-mail messages. But I quickly developed an oblique° affection for PFSlider. I
was excited when there was a message from him, mildly depressed when there
wasn't. After a few weeks, he gave me his phone number. I did not give him
mine, but he looked it up and called me one Friday night. I was home. I
picked up the phone. His voice was jarring, yet not unpleasant. He held up
more than his end of the conversation for an hour, and when he asked permission to call me again I granted it, as though we were of an earlier era.

Pete — I could never wrap my mind around his name, privately thinking   7
of him as PFSlider, "e-mail guy," or even "baseball boy" — began phoning me
two or three times a week. He asked if he could meet me, and I said that that
would be O.K. Christmas was a few weeks away, and he told me that he would
be coming back East to see his family. From there, he would take a short flight
to New York and have lunch with me.

"It is my off-season mission to meet you," he said.   8

"There will probably be a snowstorm," I said.   9

"I'll take a team of sled dogs," he answered.   10

We talked about our work and our families, about baseball and Bill Clin-   11
ton and Howard Stern and sex, about his hatred for Los Angeles and how
much he wanted a new job. Sometimes we'd find each other logged on simultaneously and type back and forth for hours.

I had previously considered cybercommunication an oxymoron,° a fast   12
road to the breakdown of humanity. But, curiously, the Internet — at least in
the limited form in which I was using it — felt anything but dehumanizing.
My interaction with PFSlider seemed more authentic than much of what I ex-

conceit: Extended metaphor or mode.   **oblique:** Indirect.   **oxymoron:** A phrase that
combines contradictory terms.

perienced in the daylight realm of living beings. I was certainly putting more
energy into the relationship than I had put into many others. I also was giving Pete attention that was by definition undivided, and relishing the safety
of the distance between us by opting to be truthful instead of doling out the
white lies that have become the staple of real life. The outside world — the
place where I walked around avoiding people I didn't want to deal with, peppering my casual conversations with half-truths, and applying my motto "Let
the machine take it" to almost any scenario — was sliding into the periphery
of my mind.

For me, the time online with Pete was far superior to the phone. There   13
were no background noises, no interruptions from "call waiting," no long-
distance charges. Through typos and misspellings, he flirted maniacally. "I
have an absurd crush on you," he said. "If I like you in person, you must
promise to marry me." I was coy and conceited, telling him to get a life, bait-
ing him into complimenting me further, teasing him in a way I would never
have dared to do in person, or even on the phone. I would stay up until 3 A.M.
typing with him, smiling at the screen, getting so giddy that when I quit I
couldn't fall asleep. I was having difficulty recalling what I used to do at night.
It was as if he and I lived together in our own quiet space — a space made all
the more intimate because of our conscious decision to block everyone else
out. My phone was tied up for hours at a time. No one in the real world could
reach me, and I didn't really care.

Since my last serious relationship, I'd had the requisite° number of false   14
starts and five-night stands, dates that I wasn't sure were dates, and emphatically casual affairs that buckled under their own inertia. With PFSlider, on the
other hand, I may not have known my suitor, but, for the first time in my life,
I knew the deal: I was a desired person, the object of a blind man's gaze. He
called not only when he said he would call but unexpectedly, just to say hello.
He was protected by the shield of the Internet; his guard was not merely down
but nonexistent. He let his phone bill grow to towering proportions. He told
me that he thought about me all the time, though we both knew that the "me"
in his mind consisted largely of himself. He talked about me to his friends
and admitted it. He arranged his holiday schedule around our impending
date. He managed to charm me with sports analogies. He didn't hesitate. He
was unblinking and unapologetic, all nerviness and balls to the wall.

And so PFSlider became my everyday life. All the tangible stuff fell away.   15
My body did not exist. I had no skin, no hair, no bones. All desire had converted itself into a cerebral current that reached nothing but my frontal lobe.°
There was no outdoors, no social life, no weather. There was only the computer screen and the phone, my chair, and maybe a glass of water. Most mornings, I would wake up to find a message from PFSlider, composed in Pacific
time while I slept in the wee hours. "I had a date last night," he wrote. "And I

---

requisite: Required.   **frontal lobe:** Section of the brain responsible for rational
thought.

am not ashamed to say it was doomed from the start because I couldn't stop thinking about you."

I fired back a message slapping his hand. "We must be careful where we tread," I said. This was true but not sincere. I wanted it, all of it. I wanted un-fettered° affection, soul-mating, true romance. In the weeks that had elapsed since I picked up "is this the real meghan daum?" the real me had undergone some kind of meltdown — a systemic rejection° of all the savvy and indepen-dence I had worn for years, like a grownup Girl Scout badge.

Pete knew nothing of my scattered, juvenile self, and I did my best to keep it that way. Even though I was heading into my late twenties, I was still a child, ignorant of dance steps and health insurance, a prisoner of credit-card debt and student loans and the nagging feeling that I didn't want anyone to find me until I had pulled myself into some semblance of an adult. The fact that Pete had literally seemed to discover me, as if by turning over a rock, lent us an aura of fate which I actually took half-seriously. Though skepticism seemed like the obvious choice in this strange situation, I discarded it pre-cisely because it was the obvious choice, because I wanted a more interesting narrative than cynicism would ever allow. I was a true believer in the urban dream: the dream of years of struggle, of getting a break, of making it. Like most of my friends, I wanted someone to love me, but I wasn't supposed to need it. To admit to loneliness was to smack the face of progress, to betray the time in which we lived. But PFSlider derailed me. He gave me all of what I'd never even realized I wanted.

My addiction to PFSlider's messages indicated a monstrous narcissism, but it also revealed a subtler desire, which I didn't fully understand at the time. My need to experience an old-fashioned kind of courtship was stronger than I had ever imagined. And the fact that technology was providing an av-enue for such archaic discourse was a paradox that both fascinated and re-pelled me. Our relationship had an epistolary° quality that put our commu-nication closer to the eighteenth century than to the impending millennium. Thanks to the computer, I was involved in a well-defined courtship, a neat little space in which he and I were both safe to express the panic and the fas-cination of our mutual affection. Our interaction was refreshingly orderly, noble in its vigor, dignified despite its shamelessness. It was far removed from the randomness of real-life relationships. We had an intimacy that seemed custom-made for our strange, lonely times. It seemed custom-made for me.

The day of our date, a week before Christmas, was frigid and sunny. Pete was sitting at the bar of the restaurant when I arrived. We shook hands. For a split second, he leaned toward me with his chin, as if to kiss me. He was shorter than I had pictured, though he was not short. He struck me as clean-cut. He had very nice hands. He wore a very nice shirt. We were seated at a very nice table. I scanned the restaurant for people I knew, saw none, and couldn't decide how I felt about that.

unfettered: Unrestricted.   **epistolary:** Through letters.

He talked, and I heard nothing he said. I stared at his profile and tried to 20
figure out whether I liked him. He seemed to be saying nothing in particular,
but he went on forever. Later, we went to the Museum of Natural History and
watched a science film about storm chasers. We walked around looking for
the dinosaurs, and he talked so much that I wanted to cry. Outside, walking
along Central Park West at dusk, through the leaves, past the yellow cabs and
the splendid lights of Manhattan at Christmas, he grabbed my hand to kiss
me and I didn't let him. I felt as if my brain had been stuffed with cotton.
Then, for some reason, I invited him back to my apartment. I gave him a few
beers and finally let him kiss me on the lumpy futon in my bedroom. The ra-
diator clanked. The phone rang and the machine picked up. A car alarm
blared outside. A key turned in the door as one of my roommates came home.
I had no sensation at all — only a clear conviction that I wanted Pete out of
my apartment. I wanted to hand him his coat, close the door behind him, and
fight the ensuing emptiness by turning on the computer and taking comfort
in PFSlider.

When Pete finally did leave, I berated myself from every angle: for not 21
kissing him on Central Park West, for letting him kiss me at all, for not liking
him, for wanting to like him more than I had wanted anything in such a long
time. I was horrified by the realization that I had invested so heavily in a
made-up character — a character in whose creation I'd had a greater hand
than even Pete himself. How could I, a person so self-congratulatingly reasonable, have been sucked into a scenario that was more akin to a television
talk show than to the relatively full and sophisticated life I was so convinced
I led? How could I have received a fan letter and allowed it to go this far?

The next day, a huge bouquet of FTD flowers arrived from him. No one 22
had ever sent me flowers before. I forgave him. As human beings with actual
flesh and hand gestures and Gap clothing, Pete and I were utterly incompat-
ible, but I decided to pretend otherwise. He returned home and we fell back
into the computer and the phone, and I continued to keep the real world
safely away from the desk that held them. Instead of blaming him for my disappointment, I blamed the earth itself, the invasion of roommates and ringing phones into the immaculate communication that PFSlider and I had
created.

When I pictured him in the weeks that followed, I saw the image of a 23
plane lifting off over an overcast city. PFSlider was otherworldly, more a concept than a person. His romance lay in the notion of flight, the physics of gravity defiance. So when he offered to send me a plane ticket to spend the weekend with him in Los Angeles I took it as an extension of our blissful
remoteness, a three-dimensional e-mail message lasting an entire weekend.

The temperature on the runway at J.F.K. was seven degrees Fahrenheit. 24
Our DC-10 sat for three hours waiting for deicing. Finally, it took off over the
frozen city, and the ground below shrank into a drawing of itself. Phone calls
were made, laptop computers were plopped onto tray tables. The recirculat-
ing air dried out my contact lenses. I watched movies without the sound and

told myself that they were probably better that way. Something about the plastic interior of the fuselage° and the plastic forks and the din of the air and the engines was soothing and strangely sexy.

Then we descended into LAX.° We hit the tarmac,° and the seat-belt signs   25 blinked off. I hadn't moved my body in eight hours, and now I was walking through the tunnel to the gate, my clothes wrinkled, my hair matted, my hands shaking. When I saw Pete in the terminal, his face seemed to me just as blank and easy to miss as it had the first time I'd met him. He kissed me chastely. On the way out to the parking lot, he told me that he was being se- riously considered for a job in New York. He was flying back there next week. If he got the job, he'd be moving within the month. I looked at him in aston- ishment. Something silent and invisible seemed to fall on us. Outside, the wind was warm, and the Avis and Hertz buses ambled alongside the curb of Terminal 5. The palm trees shook, and the air seemed as heavy and palpable as Pete's hand, which held mine for a few seconds before dropping it to get his car keys out of his pocket. He stood before me, all flesh and preoccupa- tion, and for this I could not forgive him.

Gone were the computer, the erotic darkness of the telephone, the clean,   26 single dimension of Pete's voice at 1 A.M. It was nighttime, yet the combina- tion of sight and sound was blinding. It scared me. It turned me off. We went to a restaurant and ate outside on the sidewalk. We strained for conversation, and I tried not to care that we had to. We drove to his apartment and stood under the ceiling light not really looking at each other. Something was hap- pening that we needed to snap out of. Any moment now, I thought. Any mo- ment and we'll be all right. These moments were crowded with elements, with carpet fibers and automobiles and the smells of everything that had a smell. It was all wrong. The physical world had invaded our space.

For three days, we crawled along the ground and tried to pull ourselves   27 up. We talked about things that I can no longer remember. We read the *Los Angeles Times* over breakfast. We drove north past Santa Barbara to tour the wine country. I felt like an object that could not be lifted, something that se- cretly weighed more than the world itself. Everything and everyone around us seemed imbued° with a California lightness. I stomped around the country- side, an idiot New Yorker in my clunky shoes and black leather jacket. Not until I studied myself in the bathroom mirror of a highway rest stop did I fully realize the preposterousness of my uniform. I was dressed for war. I was dressed for my regular life.

That night, in a tiny town called Solvang, we ate an expensive dinner. We   28 checked into a Marriott and watched television. Pete talked at me and through me and past me. I tried to listen. I tried to talk. But I bored myself and irritated him. Our conversation was a needle that could not be threaded. Still, we played nice. We tried to care, and pretended to keep trying long after we had given up. In the car on the way home, he told me that I was cynical, and I didn't have the presence of mind to ask him just how many cynics he had

---

fuselage: The body of the plane.   **LAX:** Los Angeles International Airport.   **tarmac:** Road or runway surface.   **imbued:** Filled or permeated.

met who would travel three thousand miles to see someone they barely knew.

Pete drove me to the airport at 7 A.M. so I could make my eight-o'clock   29
flight home. He kissed me goodbye — another chaste peck that I recognized from countless dinner parties and dud dates. He said that he'd call me in a few days when he got to New York for his job interview, which we had discussed only in passing and with no reference to the fact that New York was where I happened to live. I returned home to frozen January. A few days later, he came to New York, and we didn't see each other. He called me from the plane taking him back to Los Angeles to tell me, through the static, that he had got the job. He was moving to my city.

PFSlider was dead. There would be no meeting him in distant hotel lob-   30
bies during the baseball season. There would be no more phone calls or e-mail messages. In a single moment, Pete had completed his journey out of our mating dance and officially stepped into the regular world — the world that gnawed at me daily, the world that fostered those five-night stands, the world where romance could not be sustained, because so many of us simply did not know how to do it. Instead, we were all chitchat and leather jackets, bold proclaimers of all that we did not need. But what struck me most about this affair was the unpredictable nature of our demise. Unlike most cyber-romances, which seem to come fully equipped with the inevitable set of mis-representations and false expectations, PFSlider and I had played it fairly straight. Neither of us had lied. We'd done the best we could. Our affair had died from natural causes rather than virtual ones.

Within a two-week period after I returned from Los Angeles, at least seven   31
people confessed to me the vagaries° of their own e-mail affairs. This topic arose, unprompted, in the course of normal conversation. I heard most of these stories in the close confines of smoky bars and crowded restaurants, and we all shook our heads in bewilderment as we told our tales, our eyes focused on some point in the distance. Four of these people had met their correspon-dents, by traveling from New Haven to Baltimore, from New York to Mon-tana, from Texas to Virginia, and from New York to Johannesburg. These were normal people, writers and lawyers and scientists. They were all smart, attrac-tive, and more than a little sheepish about admitting just how deeply they had been sucked in. Mostly, it was the courtship ritual that had seduced us. E-mail had become an electronic epistle,° a yearned-for rule book. It allowed us to do what was necessary to experience love. The Internet was not responsible for our remote, fragmented lives. The problem was life itself.

The story of PFSlider still makes me sad, not so much because we no   32
longer have anything to do with each other but because it forces me to see the limits and the perils of daily life with more clarity than I used to. After I real-ized that our relationship would never transcend the screen and the phone — that, in fact, our face-to-face knowledge of each other had permanently con-taminated the screen and the phone — I hit the pavement again, went through

vagaries: Unpredictable actions, events, or details.   **epistle:** A letter.

the motions of everyday life, said hello and goodbye to people in the regular way. If Pete and I had met at a party, we probably wouldn't have spoken to each other for more than ten minutes, and that would have made life easier but also less interesting. At the same time, it terrifies me to admit to a first-hand understanding of the way the heart and the ego are snarled and entwined like diseased trees that have folded in on each other. Our need to worship somehow fuses with our need to be worshiped. It upsets me still further to see how inaccessibility can make this entanglement so much more intoxicating. But I'm also thankful that I was forced to unpack the raw truth of my need and stare at it for a while. It was a dare I wouldn't have taken in three dimensions.

The last time I saw Pete, he was in New York, three thousand miles away from what had been his home, and a million miles away from PFSlider. In a final gesture of decency, in what I later realized was the most ordinary kind of closure, he took me out to dinner. As the few remaining traces of affection turned into embarrassed regret, we talked about nothing. He paid the bill. He drove me home in a rental car that felt as arbitrary and impersonal as what we now were to each other. 33

Pete had known how to get me where I lived until he came to where I lived: then he became as unmysterious as anyone next door. The world had proved to be too cluttered and too fast for us, too polluted to allow the thing we'd attempted through technology ever to grow in the earth. PFSlider and I had joined the angry and exhausted living. Even if we met on the street, we wouldn't recognize each other, our particular version of intimacy now obscured by the branches and bodies and falling debris that make up the physical world. 34

Questions to Start You Thinking

1. CONSIDERING MEANING: What made it difficult for Daum to sustain a romance with PFSlider?

2. IDENTIFYING WRITING STRATEGIES: How does Daum use cause and effect to explain why she enjoyed exchanging e-mail with PFSlider? Is this use effective?

3. READING CRITICALLY: Daum says, "I was dressed for war. I was dressed for my regular life" (paragraph 27). What evidence does she provide to support the claim that her "regular life" is like "war"? How convincing is this evidence?

4. EXPANDING VOCABULARY: Define *paradox*. What kind of paradox is presented by Daum's use of technology (paragraph 18)?

5. MAKING CONNECTIONS: In paragraph 31, Daum suggests that many people yearn for a traditional "courtship ritual." Does the marriage described by Matthew Futterman ("The Gender Gap," p. 547) necessarily contradict Daum's claim? Why, or why not?

Journal Prompts

1. Daum concludes from her experience that "the heart and the ego are snarled and entwined" (paragraph 32). Do your own observations support this conclusion? Why, or why not?

2. How does living far away from a good friend or close family member affect your relationship? What keeps it going? What makes it difficult?

Suggestions for Writing

1. In an essay, describe a "courtship ritual" that you have observed or experienced. How important is it to the fate of a relationship?
2. Do you think electronic mail has changed social relationships? Compare and contrast letter writing with e-mail writing. Do the different forms encourage people to express themselves differently? Why, or why not? Use examples from three pieces of each kind of correspondence to support your observations.

LynNell Hancock, *born in 1953 in Sioux City, Iowa, received her bachelor's degree from the University of Iowa in 1977. She earned an M.A. in East Asian languages and literature from the Columbia Graduate School of Fine Arts in 1980 and received an M.S. in journalism from Columbia in 1981. Following her dismay at the "chaotic" educational conditions in her child's school, she began to study the public education system in New York City and has been "writing about schools, children, working mothers, curriculum battles, health, and legal issues ever since." Hancock has worked as an assistant editor at Pantheon Books, a writer for the* Village Voice, *an education reporter for the* Daily News *in New York, and an education editor at* Newsweek, *where the following selection appeared on February 27, 1995. In 1993, she joined the Columbia University journalism faculty as assistant professor and currently serves as the director of Columbia's Prudential Fellowship for Children and the* News. *In this essay, Hancock contrasts the situations of two students from markedly different socioeconomic backgrounds and assesses how different people will fare in the information age.*

AS YOU READ: *Identify the factors that Hancock says keep children from having access to the Internet.*

LynNell Hancock   The Haves and the Have-Nots

Aaron Smith is a teenager on the techno track. In America's breathless race to achieve information nirvana, the senior from Issaqua, a middle-class district east of Seattle, has the hardware and hookups to run the route. Aaron and 600 of his fellow students at Liberty High School have their own electronic-mail addresses. They can log on to the Internet every day, joining only about 15 percent of America's schoolchildren who can now forage on their own for documents in European libraries or chat with experts around the world. At home, the eighteen-year-old e-mails his teachers, when he is not prowling the World Wide Web to track down snowboarding conditions on his favorite Cascade mountain passes. "We have the newest, greatest thing," Aaron says.

On the opposite coast, in Boston's South End, Marilee Colon scoots a mouse along a grimy Apple pad, playing a Kid Pix game on an old black-and-white terminal. It's Wednesday at a neighborhood center, Marilee's only chance to poke around on a computer. Her mom, a secretary at the center, can't afford one in their home. Marilee's public-school classroom doesn't have any either. The ten-year-old from Roxbury depends on the United South End Settlement Center and its less than state-of-the-art Macs and IBMs perched on mismatched desks. Marilee has never heard of the Internet. She is thrilled to double-click on the stick of dynamite and watch her teddy-bear creation fly off the screen. "It's fun blowing it up," says the delicate fifth-grader, twisting a brown ponytail around her finger.

Certainly Aaron was born with a stack of statistical advantages over Marilee. He is white and middle class and lives with two working parents who both have higher degrees. Economists say the swift pace of high-tech advances will only drive a further wedge between these youngsters. To have an edge in America's job search, it used to be enough to be well educated. Now, say the experts, it's critical to be digital. Employees who are adept at technology "earn roughly 10 to 15 percent higher pay," according to Alan Krueger, chief economist for the U.S. Labor Department. Some argue that this pay gap has less to do with technology than with industries' efforts to streamline their work forces during the recession. . . . Still, nearly every American business from Wall Street to McDonald's requires some computer knowledge. Taco Bell is modeling its cash registers after Nintendo controls, according to Rosabeth Moss Kanter. The "haves," says the Harvard Business School professor, will be able to communicate around the globe. The "have-nots" will be consigned° to the "rural backwater of the information society."

Like it or not, America is a land of inequities. And technology, despite its potential to level the social landscape, is not yet blind to race, wealth, and age. The richer the family, the more likely it is to own and use a computer, according to 1993 census° data. White families are three times as likely as blacks or Hispanics to have computers at home. Seventy-four percent of Americans making more than $75,000 own at least one terminal, but not even one-third of all Americans own computers. A small fraction — only about 7 percent — of students' families subscribe to online services that transform the plastic terminal into a telecommunications port.

At least in public schools, the computer gap is closing. More than half the students have some kind of computer, even if it's obsolete. But schools with the biggest concentration of poor children have the least equipment, according to Jeanne Hayes of Quality Education Data. Ten years ago schools had one computer for every 125 children, according to Hayes. Today that figure is one for twelve.

Though the gap is slowly closing, technology is advancing so fast, and at such huge costs, that it's nearly impossible for cash-strapped municipalities to catch up. Seattle is taking bids for one company to wire each ZIP code with fiber optics, so everyone — rich or poor — can hook up to video, audio, and other multimedia services. Estimated cost: $500 million. Prosperous Montgomery County, Maryland, has an $81 million plan to put every classroom

consigned: Committed to a final destination or fate.   census: Official population count and demographic information.

online. Next door, the District of Columbia public schools have the same ambitious plan but less than $1 million in the budget to accomplish it.

New ideas — and demands — for the schools are announced every week. 7
The nineties populist° slogan is no longer "A chicken in every pot" but "A computer on every desk." Vice President Al Gore has appealed to the telecommunications industry to cut costs and wire all schools, a task Education Secretary Richard Riley estimates will cost $10 billion. House Speaker Newt Gingrich stumbled into the discussion with a suggestion that every poor family get a laptop from Uncle Sam. Representative Ed Markey wants a computer sitting on every school desk within ten years. "The opportunities are enormous," Markey says.

Enormous, yes, but who is going to pay for them? Some successful school 8
projects have relied heavily on the kindness of strangers. In Union City, New Jersey, school officials renovated the guts of a 100-year-old building five years ago, overhauling the curriculum and wiring every classroom in Christopher Columbus Middle School for high tech. Bell Atlantic provided wiring free and agreed to give each student in last year's seventh-grade class a computer to take home. Even parents, most of whom are South American immigrants, can use their children's computers to e-mail the principal in Spanish. He uses translation software and answers them electronically. The results have shown up in test scores. In a school where 80 percent of the children are poor, reading, math, attendance, and writing scores are now the best in the district. "We believe that technology will improve our everyday life," says principal Bob Fazio. "And that other schools will piggyback and learn from us."

Still, for every Christopher Columbus, there are far more schools like Jor- 9
dan High School in South-Central Los Angeles. Only thirty computers in the school's lab, most of them twelve to fifteen years old, are available for Jordan's 2,000 students, many of whom live in the nearby Jordan Downs housing project. "I am teaching these kids on a system that will do them no good in the real world when they get out there," says Robert Doombos, Jordan's computer-science instructor. "The school system has not made these kids' getting on the Information Highway a priority."

Having enough terminals to go around is one problem. But another im- 10
portant question is what the equipment is used for. Not much beyond rote° drills and word processing, according to Linda Roberts, a technology consultant for the U.S. Department of Education. A 1992 National Assessment of Educational Progress survey found that most fourth-grade math students were using computers to play games, "like Donkey Kong." By the eighth grade, most math students weren't using them at all.

Many school officials think that access to the Internet could become the 11
most effective equalizer in the educational lives of students. With a modem attached, even most ancient terminals can connect children in rural Mississippi to universities in Asia. A Department of Education report last week

---

populist: Having the interests of the general public in mind.   **rote:** Memorization, often without understanding.

found that 35 percent of schools have at least one computer with a modem. But only half the schools let students use it. Apparently administrators and teachers are hogging the info highway for themselves.

There is another gap to be considered. Not just between rich and poor but between the young and the used-to-be-young. Of the 100 million Americans who use computers at home, school, or work, nearly 60 percent are seventeen or younger, according to the census. Children, for the most part, rule cyberspace, leaving the over-forty set to browse through the almanac.   12

The gap between the generations may be the most important, says MIT° guru Nicholas Negroponte, author of the new book *Being Digital*. Adults are the true "digitally homeless, the needy," he says. In other words, adults like Debbie Needleman, forty-three, an office manager at Wallpaper Warehouse in Natick, Massachusetts, are wary of the digital age. "I really don't mind that the rest of the world passes me by as long as I can still earn a living," she says.   13

These aging choose-nots become a more serious issue when they are teachers in schools. Even if schools manage to acquire state-of-the-art equipment, there is no guarantee that trained adults will be available to understand them. This is something that tries Aaron Smith's patience. "A lot of my teachers are quite illiterate," says Aaron, the fully equipped Issaqua teenager. "You have to explain it to them real slow to make sure they understand everything." Fast or slow, Marilee Colon, Roxbury's fifth-grade computer lover, would like her chance to understand everything too.   14

Questions to Start You Thinking

1. CONSIDERING MEANING: According to Hancock, what are the major benefits for children who have access to technology?

2. IDENTIFYING WRITING STRATEGIES: Where does Hancock use comparison and contrast to set up her argument? Why do you think she chose this strategy?

3. READING CRITICALLY: How does Hancock feel about the Internet? How does her position affect her argument?

4. EXPANDING VOCABULARY: Define *digital*. What does Hancock mean by "to be *digital*" in paragraph 3?

5. MAKING CONNECTIONS: How might Richard Rodriguez ("Does America Still Exist?" p. 583) respond to Hancock's call to provide all children equal access to the Internet? Could Internet access help create the kind of national identity Rodriguez envisions? Why, or why not?

Journal Prompts

1. Is "access to the Internet" (paragraph 11) a necessity or a luxury? Why?

2. Find an advertisement either on television or in print that uses the Internet to sell a product. What kind of appeal is the advertiser using? Do you find this appeal effective? Why, or why not?

MIT: Massachusetts Institute of Technology, known for technological research.

Suggestions for Writing

1. What is your background in computers? Are you computer literate? If so, how did you become so? Write an essay that examines your early experience with computers.

2. How necessary do you think it is for children to become computer literate? How necessary is it for adults? Write an essay that examines how important knowledge of electronic culture is for different generations.

Thomas F. Cawsey earned his M.B.A. and Ph.D. degrees in business administration from the University of Western Ontario. Cawsey is the area coordinator of the Management and Organizational Behavior Area in the School of Business and Economics of Wilfrid Laurier University, where he won the Outstanding Teacher Award in 1990. He is the coauthor of Canadian Cases in Human Resource Management. *Gene Deszca earned his Ph.D. in business administration from York University and his M.B.A. from the University of Western Ontario and is currently associate professor and M.B.A. director in the School of Business and Economics of Wilfrid Laurier University.* **Maurice Mazerolle** *received his Ph.D. in industrial relations from the University of Toronto and is an assistant professor at Ryerson Polytechnic University, where he teaches courses in human resource management and organizational behavior. In the following essay, first published in the* Journal of Career Planning and Development *(November 1995), Cawsey, Deszca, and Mazerolle examine changes in the traditional relationship between employers and employees and raise a number of questions about the long-term socioeconomic effects of these changes in a rapidly evolving "knowledge society."*

AS YOU READ: *What is a portfolio career? According to the authors, what are its advantages over a traditional career?*

Thomas F. Cawsey, Gene Deszca, and Maurice Mazerolle
The Portfolio Career as a Response to a Changing Job Market

What comes to mind when we think of careers? Often, we think of patterns: integration around a theme; orderly, sequential development; hierarchical progression in status. Implicit in these images is the metaphor of a ladder or pyramid that symbolizes "career" and "career progress."

For many, this pattern no longer holds, and the metaphor is false. A process called *layoffs* (or *rightsizing, downsizing, resizing, decruitment,* etc.) caused by the recession (or global competition, information technology, shedding of overhead, demands for higher profit performance, etc.), is happening among hundreds of companies worldwide. Their common response to the current economic situation shows that the "normal" assumptions around careers are invalid.

Coming on strong today is a new way of thinking about — and framing   3
relationships among — work, organizations, payment, and value for an individual's effort. Enter "the portfolio career," the concept of an individual having a portfolio of skills that he or she can offer to a portfolio of organizational
clients in support of a work competence for hire.[1] This idea provides a new set
of assumptions to help people cope with the uncertainty and chaos of the job
market.

The Portfolio Career

Webster's Dictionary defines a portfolio variously as "(4) all the securities held   4
for investment," and "(5) a selection of representative works, as of an artist."[2]
This definition suggests that a portfolio comprises a variety of things with
value, held for the purpose of increasing that value.

In a portfolio career, an individual has a portfolio of skills that he or she   5
sells to a portfolio of clients. Like the financial portfolio, its purpose is to
manage risk. The financial portfolio handles risk by holding various stocks
with differing risks for differing parts of the economic cycle. The career portfolio minimizes risks by accumulating skill sets that can produce a variety of
value-adding activities. If one skill is not in demand, another might be. As
well, risk is minimized because the individual deals with several clients; if the
relationship with one client ends, the cost is not extreme. The dependence on
one employer is eliminated. Paradoxically, this nondependence results in job
security being acquired not on the basis of loyalty and commitment but by
detachment and diversification.

The concept of the portfolio career is significant because it provides a new   6
way of viewing our relationship to work. Many of us have the perspective of
"job" equals "career." However, if there are no "jobs" it is easy for us to be
frozen into inaction. Rethinking the structuring of work into projects provides
much more flexibility to the individual and to the organization, with the possibility of mutual gain. For example, the individual can earn his or her way
into contracts requiring increasing higher-skill levels, while at the same time
organizations can have work done — and perhaps even a long-term relationship with the worker — without any long-term commitment.

Skills Risk

With the portfolio career, individuals recognize that their value to organiza-   7
tions comes about because of the skills they hold that can produce results. The
risk of becoming obsolescent is reduced by acquiring proficiency in a variety
of skills and continually developing new ones.

A skill or skill set can be viewed as having a product life cycle akin to that   8
of a consumer good. This is complicated somewhat because the development
of the skill is related to both the expressed and perceived needs of clients.
However, three categories of skills might be considered:

A *developing skill* is a skill or skill set that the individual has decided is   9
worth pursuing and developing. Thus, an individual who is familiar with the

Internet and has international contracts may believe that he or she could conduct market research via the Internet. This skill is not at the stage where the individual feels confident in "selling" it on anything but a results basis — that is, payment would be for results, not for time or effort spent.

A *mature skill* is one that is fully developed and can be sold to organizations. For example, a university graduate could well have excellent skills in report writing. This craft would be of value to organizations in communicating to their internal or external publics.   10

A *postmaturity skill* is one that is either no longer in demand by clients or is subsumed by other, more complex skills of the individual. Thus, skill in using particular computer packages may be valueless because of new software developments. Or the individual's skill levels may grow and this particular skill is a minor one and not worth offering by itself.   11

To reduce skills risk, individuals must begin to see themselves as holders and developers of skills. Skills have a life cycle of usefulness. The process of development, maturity, and decay is essential for the renewal of the individual's skill set and the minimization of risk.   12

Many graduates or managers see themselves as "holders of degrees" or "specialists in . . . ." These perceptions are limiting and block the insights possible from a skills orientation. Thus, most arts or humanities students need to recognize and nurture their abilities in researching, analyzing, synthesizing, writing, etc. — all valuable skills in the new "knowledge society" that author Nuala Beck claims we are moving into.[3] Graduates need to become aware of the value of their skill sets in the knowledge marketplace.   13

Client Risk

The second risk that "career portfolioers" need to manage is their client risk. As one shifts orientation away from "one company and one career" to "many jobs and contracts with many skills," the risk is minimized by having a variety of clients in one's portfolio. With one company and one career, the individual is betting that the organization will continue to view his or her skills as valuable and that the organizational environment will continue to be positive for that organization. In today's world, it is not sufficient merely to add value to the organization; one must also add value to one's self as a means to individual survival. However, even this precaution offers no protection if the organization runs into problems.   14

For maximum protection, an individual must develop a set of clients for his or her portfolio that, in effect, mirror his or her own skill sets. Three types of clients ought to be considered: 15

Money clients provide the money needed to pay the bills. The skills used for these clients are generally not particularly unique or valuable. Individuals have these clients out of necessity, not by choice. Little learning takes place in doing work for money clients.   16

Learning clients provide opportunities to acquire new skills and concepts. In performing these activities the individual learns the skills that will provide him or her with the "next generation" of abilities to market. Generally, con-   17

	LOW PAY	HIGH PAY
HIGH LEARNING	**Attractive:** developing intellectual capital	**Risky:** may not deliver the goods; perhaps some $ gain
LOW LEARNING	Avoid unless necessary	**Attractive:** using intellectual capital for gain

A MATRIX OF CLIENT ATTRACTIVENESS

crete or extrinsic° rewards are not the focus of these skills. If payment is made, it will be for results, since the individual is learning on the job and learning and developing new skills in the process.

Niche clients result from the matching of developed skills with a signifi-   18
cant need. Here, the individual can market or sell his or her skill or skills at an appropriate price. Niche clients also allow one to develop a reputation for skills proficiency and to network for future work.

An alternate way of classifying clients is to do so according to the amount   19
of learning that occurs on the job in context with the amount of pay received. These two conditions are shown as a matrix° in the figure . . . [at the top of this page], which matches high and low learning situations with high and low pay situations. Individuals should strive to work in areas of low pay and high learning, or of high pay and low learning. Areas of low pay and low learning should be avoided whenever possible since the rewards will be minimal or nonexistent. Areas of high pay and high learning appear attractive, but they are also areas of high risk: it is possible that the client will expect more than the individual can deliver since he or she is just in the learning phase. Individuals should seek a pay or learning balance that, for their own circumstances, maximizes income while minimizing risk.

In a similar vein, Handy describes five types of work:[4]   20

- *Wage work* is where payment is for time or effort.
- *Fee work* is where payment is for results.
- *Home work* is that done in the home (e.g., child raising or lawn care).
- *Gift work* is voluntary or charitable work.
- *Learning work* is studying and learning new skills.

In a portfolio career, increasing amounts of work will be done in the   21
learning and fee categories. Learning work creates the next generation of skills

extrinsic: External.   **matrix:** Table or chart showing relationships between factors.

that provide wage or fee work. At times, too, voluntary work will lead to wage or fee work. While many individuals will strive for wage work, this is not the direction being taken by many of today's firms. Instead, as both employers and career portfolioers recognize the value of contract work, a combination of market forces and contract negotiations will assign a value to the task to be performed. Those who are skilled and in high demand will bargain for premium rates — including payment for uncertainty. Those who are low skilled or in the learning phase will suffer from market surpluses and pay the penalty in low wages and dull jobs.

Implications of Portfolio Careers

While organizations have been quick to accept the benefits and inevitability   22
of contracting out and of temporary jobs and part-time employees, perhaps they need to consider if this is going to be beneficial in the long run. In a global context, can U.S. and Canadian firms compete against Japanese and European rivals that often retain the lifelong loyalty and commitment of their employees? How does an employer build a collaborative effort if everyone is working for him- or herself?[5]

Peter Drucker recently pointed out the dramatic power shift that occurs in   23
the knowledge society.[6] For the first time, "the employees — that is, the knowledge workers — own the tools of production." The tools of production become the knowledge held by the individual and the skills to implement that knowledge. While the cry for generalists is often heard, Drucker states that contributions of knowledge workers can only be accessed through their specialties, the skills held in their portfolios. And these skills are best used in teams working together, tapping into the expertise of each.

The paired forces of globalization° and information technology imply an   24
increased likelihood that teams of people will be working together across great distances requiring yet another type of relationship skill. Workers who are able to flourish in this new environment may be so prized by employers that companies will go out of their way to build a new corporate loyalty.[7] Reducing the risks associated with unemployment through longer, more frequent, or more interesting contracts should enable companies to attract creative and productive employees. Furthermore, if training and development are used to teach knowledge that is less firm specific and more generalizable, employees will recognize the value of these skills. Ironically, this may produce more highly committed workers and better performance.

Should companies choose this approach, then there needs to be some re-   25
thinking of the rules concerning both the explicit and implicit psychological employment contracts. For example, here is Apple Computer's written employment contract with every full-time employee:

> Here's the deal Apple will give you; here's what we want from you. We're going to give you a really neat trip while you're here. We're going to teach you stuff you couldn't learn anywhere else. In return we expect you to work like

globalization: Creation of a world economy.

hell, buy the vision as long as you're here. We're not interested in employing you for a lifetime, but that's not the way we are thinking about this. It's a good opportunity for both of us that is probably finite.[8]

If this "New Age" Apple deal is a harbinger of things to come as far as employment contracts go, one has to ask if this is enough. Besides interesting work and the opportunity to learn, how might firms respond to ensure that these highly valued types of individuals are there when needed? The answer, in part, might be found in some of the approaches that so-called New Age firms are bringing to the employment relationship. In a recent *Harvard Business Review* article, Nichols observed that creating meaning may be the true managerial task of the future.[9] Common values and a shared sense of purpose can turn a company into a community where daily work acquires a deeper meaning and sense of satisfaction. But is this really going to be possible, given the emergence of borderless, faceless, nameless groupings of individuals pursuing portfolio careers? 26

In order to overcome this paradox, organizations must recognize the need to form and re-form teams capable of accomplishing great things. And as this team aspect comes to the fore, then "people" skills or process skills become vital. Recruitment systems must be transformed in order to handle the increased volume of contract and temporary work while identifying the critical core employees who form the "permanent" cadre.° Induction° and orientation mechanisms must be revamped so that they quickly and smoothly make newcomers aware of essential information on a need-to-know basis. Outplacement° or ending mechanisms must be reconfigured to provide for intermittent continuity. 27

At the individual level, the career portfolioer must first reframe his or her definition of a job or career along a skills and client basis and answer such questions as "What am I good at?" and "What are organizations willing to pay for?" Each of us must undergo a form of self-assessment in order to know the state of our skills. Once we have taken stock, these skills have to be benchmarked in relation to the marketplace. Self-understanding, determination, and a tolerance for ambiguity will become the basics of portfolio careers. Finally, each person who undertakes a portfolio career must learn to structure uncertainty in order to mitigate° ambiguity. 28

Social researchers Paul Leinberger and Bruce Tucker contend that the communities of the future are going to emerge from far-flung networks of professionals battling time-zone differences.[10] For these authors, true community doesn't grow out of a shared higher purpose but evolves through the pragmatic° need to solve common problems. Can these new "self-careerists" be as committed to the solution of problems and the seizing of opportunities as are the old time "organizational careerists"? Organizations moving to embrace the new portfolio careerists may well ponder this question. 29

cadre: Core group.   **induction:** Bring into or place in an office or position.   **outplacement:** Assistance that helps recently fired or laid off employees to find new employment.   **mitigate:** Relieve.   **pragmatic:** Practical.

Endnotes

1. The term *portfolio career* was first used by Charles Handy in his book *The Age of Unreason.* Our usage here is similar but stresses the match between skills and clients.
2. *Webster's New World Dictionary,* Third College Edition (Simon & Schuster, Inc., 1988).
3. Nuala Beck, *Shifting Gears: Thriving in the New Economy* (Toronto: Harper-Collins, 1992).
4. Charles Handy, *The Age of Unreason* (Boston: Harvard Business School Press, 1989).
5. "I'm Worried about My Job," *Business Week,* October 7, 1991.
6. Peter F. Drucker, "The Age of Social Transformation," *Atlantic Monthly* (November 1994): 53–80.
7. Stratford Sherman, "A Brave New Darwinian Workplace," *Fortune* (January 25, 1993).
8. Barbara Ettorre, "The Contingency Workforce Moves Mainstream," *Management Review* 83(2) (February 1994).
9. Martha Nichols, "Does New Age Business Have a Message for Managers?" *Harvard Business Review* (March–April 1994).
10. Paul Leinberger and Bruce Tucker, *The New Individualists: The Generation after the Organization Man* (New York: Harper Collins, 1992).

Questions to Start You Thinking

1. CONSIDERING MEANING: What changes in the marketplace have given rise to the trend of hiring employees who rely on a portfolio of skills?

2. IDENTIFYING WRITING STRATEGIES: How do Cawsey, Deszca, and Mazerolle set up their proposed solution to a problem they foresee for companies that hire employees with a portfolio of skills? Do you think the solution would be effective? Why, or why not?

3. READING CRITICALLY: Do the authors' credentials lend support to their argument? Why, or why not? Are the appeals they use the ones you might expect from authors with their credentials? Why, or why not? (See p. 103 in *A Writer's Reader* for an explanation of types of appeal.)

4. EXPANDING VOCABULARY: Define *niche* (paragraph 17). Why is a *"niche* client" a desirable client to have?

5. MAKING CONNECTIONS: How might LynNell Hancock ("The Haves and the Have-Nots," p. 631) respond to the solutions Cawsey, Deszca, and Mazerolle propose for workers facing job insecurities in a rapidly changing technology-based marketplace?

Journal Prompts

1. What do you think of the contract that Apple gives its new employees (paragraph 24)? Would you sign it? Why, or why not?

2. Using the authors' guidelines for types of skills and types of clients, how would you sell your skills and to whom?

Suggestions for Writing

1. Write an essay explaining whether or not a portfolio career would suit your needs and ambitions.
2. How is technology changing (or how has it changed) a job you would like? Write an essay based on research in the field.

Leonce Gaiter, *a "refugee" from Los Angeles, is the arts editor of the* Chico News and Review *in Chico, California. His essays have appeared in the* New York Times Magazine, *the* Los Angeles Times, *the* Washington Times, *the* L.A. Weekly, *and elsewhere. The following essay was originally published in June 1997 by* Salon, *an online magazine, to encourage discussion among the magazine's readers about whether racial identity matters in cyberspace. Here Gaiter argues that African Americans may have good reasons for distrusting the Internet but that the Web offers them an opportunity to reinvigorate their political movements and build stronger community ties.*

AS YOU READ: *Identify the obstacles to generating interest about the Internet among African Americans.*

INTERNET SOURCE: *You may want to find* Salon *(<http://www.salonmagazine .com>) to read the essay in its original context or to join a discussion about race and the Internet.*

Leonce Gaiter   Is the Web Too Cool for Blacks?

The surveys aren't very precise, but however you count them, it seems that a significantly smaller percentage of American blacks use the World Wide Web than their white fellow citizens. 1

Why? While everyone from hide-yer-tails white militiamen° to cosmic conspiracy paranoids to lonelyhearts clubbers visit the Web, why do so few black Americans do so? Is it something intrinsic° in the medium? Is the Web somehow racist? Is the issue purely economic? 2

Let me answer with a story: I once had a landlady who thought she was hip. A potter by trade, she dressed in gauzy cottons and attended gallery openings and thus qualified as among L.A.'s liberal arts set. Complaining to me about the black next-door neighbors because they objected to her backyard marijuana plants, she said, "I thought black people were cool." 3

It's a testament to the majority's ignorance of black culture that my landlady probably spoke for a great many with that statement. Yes, black folks brought you jazz. Yes, we are famed in the popular mind for adapting forms of music, speech, and worship to suit our own ends, the rules be damned — and we have historically been demonized in the majority mind for congenital° 4

---

militiamen: Self-proclaimed armed force.   **intrinsic:** Essential   **congenital:** Existing at birth.

lawlessness. Yet in fact we are the product of a culture that is among the most conventional and, yes, even timid in modern America.

For instance, with the clarion call of order and discipline, Louis Farrakhan   5
filled the D.C. streets with nearly one million black men. Can you imagine such stalwart words enticing a million white folks to cross the country? Additionally, only thirty-five years from legalized segregation and enforced second-class citizenship, black Americans still honor the idea of a firm foothold in the middle class, with all of the virtues (and vices) that that implies. A lot of us are still trying to grasp the good old tried-and-true. We haven't necessarily graduated from *The Cosby Show* to *Roseanne*. We are the farthest thing from cool.

The Web, however, is cool. The Web is the antithesis° of middle-class   6
virtues. New, chaotic, shamelessly undisciplined, alternately revolutionary and reactionary, the Web, by nature, butts heads with entrenched Afro-American cultural truths. It mocks some of our fundamental beliefs, our core desires.

Malcolm CasSelle, co-founder of NetNoir, told *USA Today* that "African   7
Americans just don't perceive the value of the Internet." That's because the Web can't help us achieve our '50s and '60s ideals. We still want the corporate American dream — a good steady job with benefits, a shot at the executive suite — while the rest of the country moves on to dreams of entrepreneurship and self-employment.

Suggesting a break with what many consider Afro-American tradition is   8
often greeted with dismay or dismissal. Not only are we outrageously conservative in our cultural outlook; we can be awfully self-righteous about it as well.

On a radio show last year I suggested that black Americans should look   9
beyond marching in the streets to gain political power. After all, the Christian right does not hold street rallies yet has gained political muscle out of all proportion to its numbers. The Web is among the tools the right uses to solidify and mobilize its power base; I suggested that black Americans should do the same.

Another guest, a black reverend, stated flatly that black Americans were a   10
people who relied on mass public demonstrations for political gain. Period. He made the statement as if putting into words an inalterable truth. It was as if he was stating that black Americans are people with dark skin.

This man was so married to the '50s and '60s legacy that he could not see   11
that times had changed. It was as if he believed that we marched in the '50s and '60s and have yet to get what we sought, and so we will keep marching and seeking those same results until we achieve them. (Remember the Million Man March? Does anyone remember the Million Man March?)

We fail to realize, however, that by the time we get the results we seek, they   12
will be what no one else wants, and we will have forgone opportunities like

antithesis: Opposite.

those offered by the Web and other high-tech, chaos-theory-driven engines onto which the majority will have climbed and ridden away.

We are American traditionalists in the extreme — and I am torn between being proud of that fact and being irked by it. On the one hand, it was that traditionalism — our middle-class strivings and solidly Christian social mores° — that kept us from violence while this country's majority made sport of spitting on us. And on the other hand, well . . . that same traditionalism kept us from violence while this country's majority made sport of spitting on us.   13

Another tradition to which we keep, whether out of pride or fear or both, is one of place. The Web is considered a place. We call it cyber*space*. We *visit* a Web site. The Web is presented as a series of landscapes or neighborhoods.   14

Walk into any integrated college dining hall and you will find a majority of the black students sitting together. There is safety in numbers, and we have a long history that makes us crave that safety. Even today, walk down the wrong set of streets and meet the wrong white men and you wind up in a coma.   15

Through decades and generations of cross burnings and redlining° and beatings and bombings and harassment, black Americans are wary of majority space. The Web is no exception to the rule.   16

Some suggest that the Web is the great uncolorizer, the great color barrier dissolver, because in cyberspace, one doesn't know what color one's audience or conversation partner might be. But that's only true in a very narrow sense. True — a black man or woman can do business on the Web without facing what even ideologically pure black conservative Representative Gary Franks (R-Connecticut) called the majority's distaste for "the idea of putting money in a black man's pocket."   17

But suggesting that black Americans would take solace in conversing with those who would not show hatred or bigotry or cultural chauvinism toward them only because the other party didn't know they were black — that's insulting in the extreme. Such a suggestion could only come from a mindlessly, liberally chauvinistic mind, like that of the landlady who thought all black folks were cool.   18

This cyber place is no haven. The hatreds that are part of this nation's very soul live here too, and black Americans know it. Rather than avoid the place, however, instead of retreating to safe ground — familiar territory — we should slough° off our conventionalities and hack some new trails through this principally white territory. We've got to embrace some anarchy° for once in our history — use those Najee and Kenny G CDs for the coasters they are, and slap on some David Murray and Henry Threadgill.°   19

Since the Web is a place, instead of an institution, it holds particular promise. No one's sense of white self and white worth is invested in it. It can   20

mores: Customs or norms.   **redlining:** Refusing to loan money or sell insurance to people who live in certain neighborhoods.   **slough:** Shed.   **anarchy:** Absence of government or political authority.   **Najee and Kenny G, David Murray and Henry Threadgill:** Jazz saxophonists.

truly be, and be seen as, ours as much as anyone else's. There are precious few nationwide places of culture and commerce about which that can be said.

The Web could be an extraordinary disseminator° of Afro-American cul-   21
ture (true Afro-American culture, not the sociopolitical° tics that the majority and too many of us accept as that culture), an extraordinary political tool, and a boon to black business people. But only if we are finally willing to forgo the dreams of terra firma° to which we've hitched our star for all of our postwar history. We must acknowledge that the world into which we so desperately sought entree is dying—and we, like the majority, must embrace new and untested worlds if we are to prosper.

Questions to Start You Thinking

1. CONSIDERING MEANING: What does Gaiter consider "cool" about the Internet? According to Gaiter, how does this hurt the Internet's appeal for African Americans?

2. IDENTIFYING WRITING STRATEGIES: Gaiter uses both his own observations and conversations with others to develop his argument. Find points where he uses each strategy. Are the strategies equally effective? Why, or why not?

3. READING CRITICALLY: This essay originally appeared in the online magazine *Salon*. Why do you think the founders of the magazine chose this name? (You may want to look up the word *salon* in the dictionary.) Does the name of the magazine help to support Gaiter's claim that the Web is a "place" rather than an "institution" (paragraph 20)? Why, or why not?

4. EXPANDING VOCABULARY: Define *clarion* and *stalwart* (paragraph 5). What interpretation of the Million Man March does Gaiter convey with his description of it as a "clarion call" brought about by the "stalwart words" of Louis Farrakhan?

5. MAKING CONNECTIONS: Compare and contrast the way Brent Staples ("Black Men and Public Space," p. 561) participates in "public space" with the way Gaiter recommends African Americans treat cyberspace. How are the spaces similar? How are they different?

Journal Prompts

1. When and where do you feel unwelcome or out of place? How do you deal with it?

2. Do you agree with Gaiter that "the Web is the antithesis of middle-class virtues" (paragraph 6)? Why, or why not?

Suggestions for Writing

1. People often say that race and gender do not matter on the Internet. Do you agree? Why, or why not? Write an essay using your own observations to support your position.

2. Using an Internet search engine such as Yahoo!, Excite, or AltaVista, locate at least three Web sites that address racial identity. Analyze the purpose for each site, and write an essay that evaluates the Internet's usefulness as a disseminator of an ethnic culture.

disseminator: Something that spreads information.   **sociopolitical:** Both social and political.   **terra firma:** Sturdy ground.

Cynthia Joyce was born in 1969 in Columbia, South Carolina, and earned her B.A. in international studies from Duke University in 1991 and her master's in journalism from Northwestern University's Medill School of Journalism in 1993. Currently the music editor for Salon, *an online magazine devoted to cultural, political, and technological issues, she has also researched articles for* Mother Jones *magazine, covered the North American Free Trade Agreement for the* Mexico City News, *and written for* Rolling Stone Online. *Here, Joyce describes her personal experience with a rare illness and uses her quest for medical information on the Internet to explore the larger issues that arise when laypeople attempt to evaluate overwhelming medical information for themselves.*

AS YOU READ: *Identify the kind of medical information that Joyce recommends the Internet be used to find.*

INTERNET SOURCE: *"Six Clicks from Death" was originally published online in* Salon *magazine (<http://www.salonmagazine.com>) in April 1997. You may want to read the essay on the Web to help you answer some of the questions that follow the selection.*

Cynthia Joyce   Six Clicks from Death

I woke up one morning last fall and the entire right side of my face felt like it had been injected with Novocaine. I ran to the mirror to see what was going on and attempted a series of Jim Carrey impersonations to work the numbness out of my face. The left side went along willingly, but the right side stared back at me, unblinking and totally expressionless.

By the time I made it to work, it had gotten worse. The right side of my face now looked like a fallen soufflé, and the right half of my tongue felt like rubber. I tried to downplay how scared I was, offering lame little jokes like, "Is this what they mean by 'self-effacing'?" My jokes didn't have the desired effect of putting my co-workers at ease because by now my speech was so slurred I sounded drunk. By midafternoon, the right side of my face was completely paralyzed — yet, oddly, my hearing on that side was amplified. I felt like a cross between a stroke victim and the Bionic Woman.

My doctor took one look at me and, ruling out the possibility of a stroke (rare for healthy twenty-seven-year-olds), diagnosed me with Bell's palsy — a typically temporary condition resulting from damage to the seventh cranial nerve.° He said no one knows what causes this damage, but most people fully recover in four to six weeks. He didn't tell me what happens to the *other* people, and I didn't ask. Although I understood that I was probably going to look like Bill the Cat for at least a month, I was relieved that my doctor didn't seem overly concerned. As I went to fill his prescription for steroids, I vowed to keep busy, stay away from mirrors for a while, and learn everything I could about my syndrome.

cranial nerve: One of twelve pairs of nerves arising in the brainstem.

As it turned out, staring at my distorted reflection would prove to be far   4
less threatening a pastime than staring into the kaleidoscope of information
on the Web.

The first thing I did when I returned to work the next morning was   5
search the Web for information on Bell's palsy — beginning a series of self-
misdiagnoses that did more lasting damage than the palsy itself. Because I
didn't know where to find reliable health information, I started with a general
search on AltaVista. The first article that turned up was a Healthgate[1] document from the National Library of Medicine's Medline database titled "Management of Bell's palsy." I read the abstract: "The natural history of Bell's palsy
is favorable. Eight-four percent show satisfactory recovery without any treatment; however, 16 percent suffer moderate to severe sequelae."

Sequelae? Good God, what could that be? I'd never heard of it before. I   6
quickly did a new search on sequelae. My heart was beating in my ears as I
waited for the search results. I tried to picture what sequelae might look like.
I imagined myself in scarf and gloves, trying to conceal the sequelae that covered my neck and hands. I pictured friends and co-workers recoiling in horror as sequelae spewed from my right ear. I wondered if sequelae was contagious — would I have to be quarantined?

The sequelae search results finally appeared, barely staving off my hyste-   7
ria. I clicked on an article from the *Journal of Clinical Oncology* titled "Late
Psy-cho-Social Sequelae in Hodgkin's Disease° Survivors: A French Popula-
tion-Based Case-Control Study."° Of course, I'd never suffered from Hodgkin's disease, but it didn't matter. My line of reasoning went something like
this: the incidence of sequelae in French populations must be pretty high to
merit a control study being based on it. My mother's side of the family is
French. As far as I was concerned, this constituted conclusive data. But I was
forced to admit I was probably off-track when I calmed down enough to notice that the dreaded *s* word wasn't even mentioned in the conclusion.

I went back to the original search and followed the second entry, titled   8
simply "Sequelae." It read: "Sequelae . . . may include persistent hypesthesia
and dysesthesia, persistent motor weakness, infection, amputation, and
death. These are the direct result of nerve and muscle injury." The various
-*thesias* didn't mean anything to me, but seeing the words "nerve damage"
and "amputation and death" so close together within the same paragraph
threw me into a panic.

And it didn't end there. By the time I finally bothered to look up *sequelae*   9
in Webster's and found that it means only "something that follows," I had diagnosed myself with a brain tumor, encephalitis, Lyme disease, and two dif-

---

Hodgkin's disease: A degenerative disease that produces inflamed, enlarged lymph nodes,
spleen, liver, and kidneys.   **control study:** An experiment that tests the influence of one
factor in an experiment by keeping other factors constant.

[1]The underlined words in this article appeared as hyperlinks in the original online version of the essay. Hyperlinks are words or images that can take you to related sites elsewhere
on the World Wide Web.

ferent strains of the herpes virus. Whatever Web page I started from, I never seemed to be more than six clicks from a death sentence.

As my doctor predicted, I recovered fully within four weeks. He didn't tell   10
me about the 16 percent who never recover or suffer the dreaded "sequelae" of recurring paralysis because he correctly assumed I'd automatically count myself among them. And since Bell's palsy may be linked to stress, he wisely decided not to give me cause for more. Nonetheless, during those four weeks, I think I found every single one of those 16 percent online.

Although I didn't know it at the time, it's safe to assume that because   11
Bell's palsy usually goes away after several weeks, the people posting in online support groups like the Neurology Web Forum represented a disproportionate segment of those Bell's palsy sufferers whose symptoms never faded. I certainly had no reason to distrust their accounts — but lots of reasons why I didn't need to hear them just then. Still, I opened every one of those links, and needless to say, with subject heads like "SCARED," "10 years later . . . " and "BELL'S STRIKES AGAIN," the stories only added to my hysteria.

Clearly, of course, people with serious illnesses — particularly those who   12
have been properly diagnosed — can greatly benefit from online support groups. Dr. Allison Szapary, a resident at the University of California at San Francisco, believes that although younger residents like herself typically use medical databases like *Medline* "every day, all day," online support groups are far more useful for patients than such data-heavy sites. "I think the Web is better for offering emotional support than for actually giving good factual information," she says. "For people going through serious illnesses, it's important for them to feel connected to others going through the same thing."

One reason it's so useful, especially for people with chronic° or degener   13
ative illnesses, is that people can describe even their most embarrassing health problems without having to look someone in the eye — and in such situations, unlike in other kinds of Web conferences, the anonymity actually encourages more honesty.

As a cancer survivor, health writer, and producer for the popular Ask Dr.   14
Weil alternative medicine site, Steven Petrow knows firsthand both the advantages and dangers of online medical resources.

"When I researched medical libraries like the University of Pennsylvania   15
site, I wound up with more information than I knew how to interpret. When I went to my doctor I was a mess — I thought I was going to die," he says. "I've been a health writer for more than ten years, and when I read a study, I have to read all the footnotes very carefully, and sometimes I still don't understand. So you can only assume your average consumer would be confused some of the time."

Several sites, such as Reuters Health, offer information under two sepa   16
rate categories for consumers and professionals to help alleviate this problem. Patients still have access to medical research but can get it in layman's° terms.

---

chronic: Occurring repeatedly.   **layman:** A nonprofessional in a given field.

Without that option, Petrow points out, having all the latest info "doesn't cure your problems — it could actually create new ones."

The editors of the *Journal of the American Medical Association* attempted to address some of these issues in an April 16 editorial in which they warned that "health care professionals and patients alike should view with equal parts delight and concern the exponential growth of . . . the Web as a medical information delivery tool. Delight because the Internet hosts a large number of high-quality medical resources and poses seemingly endless opportunities to inform, teach, and connect professionals and patients alike. Concern because the fulfillment of that promise remains discouragingly distant."

Part of the problem with the Web, they argue, is that "science and snake oil may not always look all that different on the Net." Petrow agrees that the unregulated proliferation of health information sites on the Web makes it easier for consumers to be duped, especially by sites promoting alternative medicine.

"I think it's easier to scam people online," he says. "Some of us are hoping there will be some kind of oversight in terms of fraud on the Web because right now there isn't. With print magazines, at least you have to have 'advertisement' written on the page if it's an ad. It's hard for someone to tell what's legitimate or not, and part of the problem is when fraud is actually being committed, you don't have an actual physical location where someone could be prosecuted. The consumer law needs to evolve to a national level that incorporates the Web."

The authors of the *JAMA* editorial take a different view. They argue that because the Web is a global and decentralized medium, government regulation isn't the answer. Instead, they favor a standard set of guidelines for authorship, attribution, disclosure, and currency that online resources wishing to establish their reliability would adopt. "Web publishers of all stripes — ourselves included — should be free to post whatever they like and live with the consequences. Let a thousand flowers bloom. We just want those cruising the information superhighway to be able to tell them from the weeds."

But as my doctor, Jesse Dohemann, points out, even by-the-book science can start to smell like snake oil if the doctor-patient relationship is eroded. "I had a guy in here recently who had horrible hives, so I sent him to all the top allergists, and no one could figure out what it was," Dohemann recalls. "He got in touch with a doctor from New York online who prescribed him medication normally used to treat people with Parkinson's disease. The hives did get better, but the guy was now taking a combination of drugs that would have crippled him within ten years. This doctor may have been a real M.D., but he was also a ding-dong."

As the rise of the HMO has put greater emphasis on primary and preventive health care, alternative medical information like that provided by Ask Dr. Weil has become a growth industry. And the kind of general advice to people such sites provide — watch less news, eat more broccoli — would probably keep them out of legal trouble, even without the prominently displayed liability disclaimer, a standard feature of most sites offering free health advice.

But the "free" part of that equation may soon come to an end for the on-   23
line services of more traditional medical institutions. Because many health-
related sites offer interactive elements — like the Internist's Casebook, which
lets you play medical detective — their mix of straight advice and "infotain-
ment" allows them to rely on advertising revenue. But sites that cater more to
health-care professionals, like Medscape, Medline and the Mayo Clinic, may
soon be forced to charge subscription fees. "I think the love affair with free information is going to be coming to an end," Petrow predicts. "And the question seems to be, you pay for this type of information now; why wouldn't you
have to pay for it on the Web?"

Looking back on my experience with Bell's palsy, it wasn't all a nightmare   24
— in retrospect, it even seems pretty funny. And I did, in the end, discover an
entire range of health resources, as well as develop a great new pastime — albeit a rather obsessive one.

For a while there, I was researching my every sneeze online. I no longer   25
needed a *Physician's Desk Reference* to tell me which drugs I couldn't take with
alcohol — I could look it up at PharmInfoNet. I could find out everything I
never wanted to know about the freckles on my shoulders, my receding hair-
line, and why I get leg cramps. I even found an interactive ovulation site —
one of my personal favorites — featuring the What-If Ovulation° Calendar.
Believe me, figuring out the last day of your menstrual cycle has never been so
much fun.

But as my experience showed, too much information can sometimes be a   26
real health hazard. So do the Web a favor: if you've ever suffered a debilitating, embarrassing, or long-lasting illness and been lucky enough to live to tell
about it, then please do. You may not cure anyone of whatever ails them, but
you just might keep them from going crazy.

Questions to Start You Thinking

1. CONSIDERING MEANING: What are the hazards of using the Internet as a medical resource? What are the possible benefits?

2. IDENTIFYING WRITING STRATEGIES: Where does Joyce use evaluation in her
   essay? What are the criteria she uses in her evaluation?

3. READING CRITICALLY: When you read an article online, a word or image on the
   Web page may be highlighted to indicate that it is a hyperlink. Clicking on
   the link takes you to another Web page where you can find more information
   about the topic you were reading about on the previous page on screen. In
   Joyce's essay, the words that were hyperlinks on *Salon*'s Web page are underlined. Look up the Web page where Joyce's article originally appeared
   (<http://www.salonmagazine.com/april97/21st/article.html>) and try to follow the links. Does the information you find on the linked pages help to
   support Joyce's argument? Why, or why not? If the linked information is no
   longer available, what alternative sources do you have? What does this tell
   you about using the Internet as a resource?

ovulation: The release of an egg by the ovaries.

4. EXPANDING VOCABULARY: Define *duped* and *proliferation* (paragraph 18). Why is it possible for people to be "duped" by the "proliferation" of health information on the Internet?

5. MAKING CONNECTIONS: Joyce and Meghan Daum ("Virtual Love," p. 623) both claim that the Internet makes it easier for people to be honest about themselves. How are the explanations they give when making this argument similar? How are they different?

Journal Prompts

1. If you or a family member were seriously ill, what kind of information would you want to know about the condition? Why?

2. What qualities do you look for in a reliable source of information? Why?

Suggestions for Writing

1. Joyce's experience searching for medical information suggests the old saying that "a little knowledge is a dangerous thing." In your own experience, can knowledge be dangerous? Write an essay detailing why, or why not.

2. Research a health-related question on the Internet. Then write an essay that analyzes the steps you took to answer the question and that evaluates the information you found.

Stephanie Brail, *born in 1970 in Camden, New Jersey, earned her B.A. in English and music from the University of Michigan at Ann Arbor in 1992. She is the president and founder of Amazon City (<http://www.amazoncity.com>), "a full-service online community that promotes the success and empowerment of women in a light-hearted and engaging way"and that has won the NetGuide Gold Site Award and the Best of WWWomen Site Award. Brail is a graphic designer, programmer, and writer who lives in Los Angeles. Her articles have appeared in* Computer User, Micro Times, *and* On the Issues: The Progressive Women's Quarterly. *In this essay, which appeared in* Wired Women: Gender and New Realities in Cyberspace *(1996), Brail analyzes the volatile issue of censorship and harassment on the Internet. She then proposes a possible solution to the problem of harassment that leaves intact her strong support for free speech. Both this essay and the next selection, "Privacy Is the Problem, Not the Solution" by Jeffrey Obser, address how the Internet should or should not be regulated.*

AS YOU READ: *Try to discover why Brail values free speech on the Internet.*

Stephanie Brail   The Price of Admission

Online harassment has become a media headliner in the last few years. I should know: I was the target of one of the more sensationalized cases of "sexual harassment" on the Internet. When I wrote about my and others' experiences with online harassment, I found myself inundated by requests for interviews with other reporters writing the same story. I've been quoted in *USA*

Today, interviewed by *Glamour*, pursued by the local ABC news affiliate, and pounced on by editors at *Mademoiselle*, who wanted, I assume, a juicy tale of cyberspace stalking to sell more issues of their magazine.

Online harassment is a tough issue. Finding the fine line between cen-   2
sorship and safety and creating a better environment for women in cyberspace are complex tasks. As I've wrestled with these issues, one of the sharpest
areas of concern for me has become the effect harassment has on our most
precious online commodity: free speech.

Sandy's Story

Sandy,° a polite and friendly forty-year-old woman with a soft Southern ac-   3
cent, loves cats and frequented the newsgroup rec.pets.cats.

In 1993, a gang of people from several newsgroups — alt.tasteless,   4
alt.syntax.tactical, and alt.bigfoot — "invaded" the rec.pets.cats newsgroup.
By the time the invasion had ended, Sandy had received death threats, hate
mail, and harassing phone calls, was having her e-mail monitored at work,
and had almost lost her job.

The incident began when one of the invaders who joined her newsgroup   5
posted a message asking if he could get help destroying his girlfriend's cat. He
said the cat was bothering him, but he didn't want the girlfriend to find out if
he killed it. When he began discussing poison and drowning as options,
Sandy spoke up.

First, she sent e-mail urging him not to kill the cat, but if he insisted, to   6
have it "put to sleep" humanely. When the e-mail didn't help, Sandy became
concerned, then terrified for the cat. She had nightmares. Eventually she
wrote a letter to the police that was subsequently distributed on the Internet.

The flame war° exploded. The request for help in killing the cat was   7
actually a fake. The poster° and his friends had purposefully chosen a quiet
little newsgroup to start a flame war of mythic proportions. Their stated goal
was to inflame the members of the group with their posts. And it worked. But
when Sandy contacted the police, the invaders became ugly and turned their
attention to her.

Soon Sandy found herself on the member list of a Net.Invaderz FAQ (Fre-   8
quently Asked Questions document) that was being passed around Usenet°
and even several computer conventions. Rather than being a victim, Sandy
was singled out as one of the victimizers. "Those of us that opposed the group
coming in and invading us (were added to the list)," she said. "It was
spammed° all over the network as a true document with our names on it."

Sandy was disturbed but tried to ignore the problems as much as possible   9
until she found herself under investigation by her own company. An irate

---

Sandy: A fictitious name. The woman described prefers to remain anonymous.   **flame
war:** Internet term for an angry exchange of e-mail.   **poster:** A person who sends an e-
mail message.   **Usenet:** An Internet-based system of discussion forums, or "newsgroups."   **spammed:** Sent electronically to a large group of people.

"U.S. taxpayer" had written her employer complaining that he didn't want the Internet used for actions such as those described in the Net.Invaderz document. "I'm a twenty-two year employee with this company, with a good reputation which is now in the pooper because of this," she said.

Sandy hasn't prosecuted, but the incident exhausted her and made her fearful. She no longer participates in or even reads rec.pets.cats; concerned friends e-mail her posts of interest privately. She cannot afford her own home computer, so she can only access the Internet through work, where her supervisor now watches her every move.   10

Because she acted (in this case alerting the authorities to what she believed to be cruelty to animals), Sandy became the target of a vicious attack launched by a group of people she had never even met.   11

In part, the wars going on in cyberspace are cultural wars. Who is to decide what is polite and acceptable? Some time ago, I talked with one of the founders of alt.syntax.tactical, who calls himself Antebi. His response to those who suggest his tactics are uncivilized? "Learn to use killfiles,"° he says. "Grow up, welcome to reality."   12

After talking with him, I understood his group to be somewhat like an Internet fraternity, a bunch of young men who like to do virtual "panty raids" on unsuspecting newsgroups. They per se aren't the problem (I do not think alt.syntax.tactical was responsible for the death threats to Sandy), but that kind of mischievous mentality, coupled with a lot of free time, means that certain people can abuse their power in the virtual world.°   13

But should the virtual world be one where war is the only metaphor? An invading army swept through Sandy's village, and when she reached out to protect someone else, they turned their sights on her. She was attacked, accused, harassed, and threatened — with no possible recourse. The army captain merely says she should have armed herself. But perhaps there are other ways to live than by the rule of the strongest? Isn't that what civilization is supposed to be about?   14

Tools, Not Rules

A popular phrase you'll hear on the venerable California-based online service, the WELL, is "Tools, Not Rules." In other words, don't regulate the Internet; train people how to use it and let them decide for themselves what they want to read and see.   15

I'm all for it, since I believe that overregulation would stifle the Internet. Women can and should learn more about their online environment so they can exert more control over their corner of cyberspace. The move of many women to create mailing lists and online services is a positive one. Rather than playing the victim, we can take charge and fight back with the same tools being used against us.   16

killfiles: Software that deletes e-mail messages from certain parties.   **virtual world:** Domain of electronic information, the Internet or World Wide Web.

But the Tools, Not Rules philosophy has its limits. On the WELL, a small   17
cybercommunity of 12,000, where such issues of free speech and community
are cherished and routinely thrashed about, user Preston Stern wrote:

> Like any other good thing, though, embraced wholly with no conditional
> moderation [Tools, Not Rules] can easily be turned over and create effects op-
> posite to those intended. . . . We can insure that everyone has equal access to
> the tools, but we cannot guarantee that everyone will have equal proficiency.
> This means that some people, by virtue of having more expertise, more time
> and/or more experience with the tools, are able to become more powerful, to
> bend the public discourse and agenda toward their own ends.

Stern wasn't writing this in response to a topic about online harassment,   18
but the concern is the same. Tools can empower, but they can also be a barrier. Women, especially, have a greater problem using Internet "tools" — the
typical barriers being lack of time and knowledge and the male domination
of all things technical in our society.

Whose Responsibility?

Harassment isn't just a women's issue. In this kind of free-for-all climate, the   19
only people who will have free speech are those who have the gall to stand up
to threats or frequent requests for sex, and those who have been lucky enough
not to step on the wrong person's toes yet. And while women bear the brunt
of this climate, men can also be affected. The man who spoke up in my case,
Ron, was harassed and at one point challenged to meet his attacker "face-to-
face" — for what, we can only imagine.

Is this the atmosphere that encourages enlightened discourse and free   20
speech? Sandy compares the current atmosphere online to the dark science
fiction movie *Blade Runner*.

> It's like another world, it's like another planet. It's like a totally unregulated
> dirty nasty little underworld. It's got some really nice, great, shining pockets
> of humanity and education and conversation, and then it's got this horrible
> seamy gutter-ridden filth . . . they're spreading like a cancer. As far as how to
> eradicate that without cutting out the good, I don't know what's going to hap-
> pen to it. I really sincerely do not think censorship and government regula-
> tion is the way to go. I just wish people were a little nicer to each other.

So what can be done? Most women will continue to receive wanna   21
fucks,° and many will not even prosecute when they do receive a legitimate
threat.

I don't think a legal remedy is the real answer anyway. Like Sandy, most   22
women I know online are opposed to censorship. I would rather put up with
the harassment than have Uncle Sam reading all my e-mail. But I don't think
that living with harassment should be necessary to enjoy the Internet, nor do
I think the current "everything goes" environment is healthy. I think we can

wanna fucks: E-mail requests for sex.

take steps to make the online world a little more safe. Part of what I would consider to be healthy would be an environment where community responsibility, not rampant individualism, was more the emphasis.

Unfortunately, whenever you so much as mention that you want something done about harassment, you are accused of being procensorship. Certainly, the strict rules you can find on online services such as Prodigy and America Online are double-edged swords. Perhaps these services are a little "safer," but is that truly free speech? Maybe the price of freedom is tolerance. Tolerance of jerks who want to put up a "Rate the Babes Home Page," tolerance of a few unwanted e-mails, tolerance of women online. But sometimes it feels as if the price of freedom also means I must be willing to risk my personal safety for free speech.

In real life, harassment isn't confused with free speech. If I get death threats through regular mail and I report that to the police, am I "censoring" the person who sent the threat? Threats are not free speech. Extortion is not free speech. Defamation° is not free speech. Shouldn't the question be: Do we really have free speech on the Internet in its present form? Isn't the tyranny of vigilante bullies, however rare and arbitrary, the same as tyranny by an officially sanctioned body like a government or corporation? When people tell me the Internet is just words, I can't help but remember checking the locks on my house, looking for a young man who might have decided that words weren't enough.

Easy answers are hard to come by, and extreme positions on either side will do more harm than good. An Internet police state, for example, would undoubtedly not have the freedom of women as its first concern.

Although I would hope that our vigilante friends would take responsibility for their actions and realize that each abuse bodes° ill for their and our future enjoyment of the Internet, the burden of action lies with ourselves. Women must take action. The more of us that speak up, the more of us that exist online, the harder it will be to silence us.

Perhaps there are places that we won't want to go to — if a place offends us, perhaps we should just stay away — but instead of withdrawing totally from the online world, with all its riches and opportunities, we can form our own networks, online support groups, and places to speak. We can support each other in existing online forums. Women cannot be left behind, and we cannot afford to be intimidated.

Questions to Start You Thinking

1. CONSIDERING MEANING: What does Brail argue is the best way for women to deal with the problem of potential harassment on the Internet?

2. IDENTIFYING WRITING STRATEGIES: What strategy does Brail use to support her point that censorship is not the best solution to the problem of harassment on the Internet? Is the strategy successful? Why, or why not?

---

defamation: Slandering someone's character.   **bodes:** Suggests or predicts.

3. READING CRITICALLY: Identify the Internet terms in Brail's essay that were new to you. What does her use of these terms reveal about her assumptions about her audience? How does this affect her argument?

4. EXPANDING VOCABULARY: Define *rampant individualism* (paragraph 22). How does "community responsibility" oppose "rampant individualism"?

5. MAKING CONNECTIONS: How might the solutions that Brail proposes be applied to the concerns that Leonce Gaiter ("Is the Web Too Cool for Blacks?" p. 642) thinks African Americans have about using the Internet?

Link to the Paired Essay

Both Jeffrey Obser ("Privacy Is the Problem, Not the Solution," p. 657) and Brail examine the issue of whether government regulation is appropriate for the Internet. How do the writers rely on the concept of civil liberties in making their arguments?

Journal Prompts

1. Do you worry about being harassed or taken advantage of on the Internet? What do you do to protect yourself?

2. Imagine that you are in Sandy's position and receive an e-mail that describes a crime in the making. How would you handle the situation?

Suggestions for Writing

1. What do you believe is an individual's personal responsibility to his or her community? Write an essay in which you explain what you believe should be your responsibilities to your community.

2. Research the steps that have been taken to regulate the Internet since the publication of Brail's and Obser's ("Privacy Is the Problem, Not the Solution," p. 657) essays. Write an essay that takes a stand on if or how the Internet should be regulated, drawing on Brail's and Obser's arguments as well as other outside sources for evidence to support your position.

Jeffrey Obser, *born in New York, earned his B.A. in Russian studies from the University of California at Berkeley and later wrote his master's thesis on information-age privacy at the University of California–Berkeley Graduate School of Journalism. Formerly an intern at HotWired, his articles have appeared there and in Salon, an online magazine. He is currently a freelance journalist in the San Francisco Bay area. In the selection that precedes this one, Stephanie Brail ("The Price of Admission," p. 651) examines the threat of harassment on the Internet, but here Obser evaluates popular fears and conceptions about threats to privacy. In this article, Obser traces these fears to changing notions of trust in both public and private spheres.*

AS YOU READ: *Ask yourself why Obser thinks Americans value privacy so much.*

INTERNET SOURCE: *"Privacy Is the Problem, Not the Solution" was originally published online in* Salon *magazine (<http://www.salonmagazine.com>) in June 1997. You may want to visit the Web site to read the essay in its original context.*

I wonder what Richard Nixon would have thought of the recently concluded Federal Trade Commission hearings[1] on privacy in the datasphere.°
After all, Nixon suffered the most humiliating privacy loss ever. Surely he
could empathize with all the people who are upset that strangers can find
dossiers° about them on the Web or that their personal information has become an unregulated commodity floating through distant databases. He was
as shocked and confused as we are that a convenient new communications
technology — in his case, audiotape — would turn around and tattle on him.
And, just like us, he reacted by demanding more privacy.

It mystifies us that the man thought he could have it both ways — record
everything, and get away with everything. But curiously, it mystifies nobody
that we all expect to talk freely and shop with convenience through electronic
networks without establishing some sort of reputation for ourselves. In conditions of the utmost anonymity, living in "communities" where neighbors
don't talk to one another, we expect, as Nixon did, to be trusted. And we are
outraged to find that it's not possible, and they're subpoenaing our tapes on
Capitol Hill. Why, we ask, does anyone need to know all this stuff about *me*?

The exploitation of personal data that the FTC hearings took up is plainly
a serious problem. But nobody wants to admit that privacy itself may really
be that problem's root cause rather than its antidote.

Modern life allows us an unprecedented level of physical privacy in real
time and space. This isolated existence not only feeds our paranoia but ne-
cessitates the electronic record keeping that enables us to deal all day with
total strangers. As the scale of interactions and commerce broadens across the
Web, the complexity of that record keeping promises only to deepen.

Want to buy gas on credit? Easy! Even easier than the times when the mechanic down the street knew you personally. The difference is that now the
pump will know your name, a distant computer will make a record, and the
fellow behind the bulletproof glass won't give a damn. He has privacy, you
have privacy. Everyone happy?

It's no coincidence that the jurist Louis Brandeis wrote his often-cited,
groundbreaking "right to be let alone" privacy screed° in 1890, just when the
close-knit scrutiny of real villages began to give way to the anonymity of
urban life. People took privacy for granted until then; in the day before databases, it was not an abstract quality. One's bedroom or backyard was either
private or it wasn't — and one's reputation was rarely more permanent or
widespread than the memory banks of the people one dealt with personally.

---

datasphere: The world of data and communication technology.   **dossiers:** Detailed
summaries of people's lives.   **screed:** A long, monotonous piece of writing.

[1]The underlined words in this article appeared as hyperlinks in the original online version of the essay. Hyperlinks are words or images that can take you to related sites elsewhere
on the World Wide Web.

Over the last fifty years, our journey into suburbs and cars and flickering   7
TV nighttimes behind barred windows has given us extraordinary seclusion in
our personal and home lives. And yet we've only felt more insecure. Only 34
percent of Americans polled by the Louis Harris firm expressed concern about
personal privacy in 1970. By 1995, the figure was up to 80 percent.

What happened? This growing concern doesn't indicate a simple increase   8
in how much we value privacy, any more than the soaring number of lawyers
in the United States means we value justice more. Instead, it's a fearful reaction to the collapse of trust in our culture.

In *The Naked Society* (1964), Vance Packard trembled at the twentieth-   9
century innovations that were draining American life of privacy and auton-
omy: social control by large, impersonal employers; pressure on companies to
scrutinize customer choices in a sophisticated manner in order to compete for
market share; galloping advances in electronic technology; and the McCarthy-
era adoption of a pervasive top-security mentality in both government and
business.

Nearly a decade later, at the dawn of computerized record keeping, James   10
B. Rule pointed out in *Private Lives and Public Surveillance* (1973) that the transition to a society of mobile strangers didn't necessarily increase surveillance
— the prying eyes of small-town neighbors are, he felt, in most cases worse.
But it did lead to more *centralized* surveillance — out of sight and, for practical purposes, beyond the control of the individual.

By 1993, in the book *The Costs of Privacy*, Steven L. Nock attacked privacy   11
itself as the problematic result of systemic social separation. "Privacy grows as
the number of strangers grows," Nock wrote. "And since strangers tend to not
have reputations, there will be more surveillance when there are more
strangers. Privacy is one consequence, or cost, of growing numbers of
strangers. Surveillance is one consequence, or cost, of privacy."

Nock called credit cards, those handy generators of much of the personal   12
data we've lost control over, "portable reputations." In the era of the Internet,
cheap computing, and an increasingly global economy, those portable reputations record more and more of our activities, and more and more strangers
and institutions demand them from us. The trends toward economic consolidation, less face-to-face accountability in our public lives, and faster computing will exert great pressure for ever more elaborate identification and cre-
dentialing schemes. The spread of the use of the social security number to
sixty government agencies is one result of this pressure. Retina and
thumbprint scans, already in pilot testing,° will be the next.

We can complain all we want about Big Brother,° but when we wrested   13
our reputations from human memory and turned them over to far less judgmental computer circuits and phone lines — vanquishing those nasty old village snoops who might keep us from living out our hearts' desires — reputa-

---

pilot testing: Small-scale testing to ensure the usefulness of a planned larger experiment.
Big Brother: Government that closely controls individual activities (from a character in the
George Orwell novel *1984*).

tion remained as important as ever. The difference is that even as we have downplayed its significance — whether out of honest egalitarianism° or excessive individualism — we have consigned it to the banal, impersonal testing ground of supermarket·checkout stands and preemployment background checks.

The only thing a computer ever asks is: Are you approved, or not? And everyone from medical insurers to prospective employers to creditors views us as a potential threat until our data prove otherwise. Setting up new privacy regulations isn't going to alleviate this pressure; it may only lead to more elaborate credentials and invasive identifiers for individuals and increased secrecy for the institutions that manage our reputations. 14

Privacy, particularly when enshrined in law, can protect the corrupt and malign as well as the good and upstanding. But the bulk of breathless newspaper reports issuing forth on this issue since last year have almost universally ignored this, instead focusing on the hypothetical risks of baddies out there finding out where Joe Consumer lives and (gasp!) what his children's names are. Most have taken the same grave, utterly simplistic angle: Privacy good. Stalkers bad. Internet dangerous. Call Congressman. All have invariably repeated the same shopworn top ten privacy-violation horror stories, mostly hypothetical and mostly based on the absurdity of having to hide out from one's HMO, spoon-fed to hungry reporters by a small group of widely quoted privacy activists. James Wheaton, senior counsel of the First Amendment Project, an Oakland, California, group trying to protect and expand the Freedom of Information Act, laments "enormous imprecision" in the concerns raised by some of these activists. 15

By giving government officials the power to deny public-records access to anyone without credentials (i.e., the little guy), Wheaton says, "the privacy activists may inadvertently be helping the moneyed interests and doing nothing for greater security." Even with their good intentions and a laudable° commitment to civil liberties, the professional privacy advocates have little besides fear as a selling point — fear of the stalker, the fraud perpetrator, the government agency run amok. But the fear and paranoia that have become so entrenched in the public mind are the primary cause of all this high-tech surveillance in the first place because nobody wants to deal with anybody in person anymore. 16

Sure, there are legitimate issues of informational privacy, and at their best, the FTC hearings constructively aired them. Businesses that collect personal information from Web browsing should have some regulation against selling it, and anyone can see that companies compiling dossiers on every American are a threat to — well, let's not bring up Hitler again. But the drumbeat of scare stories has focused too much attention on the Internet, even though nobody has explained how the Internet causes the problems in any direct or unique way. Credit-card fraud, costing literally billions of dollars in losses in recent years, was a problem as soon as credit cards were invented — and the Secret 17

egalitarianism: Equality.   **laudable:** Praiseworthy.

Service, which investigates computer crime, has no evidence to date that the resourceful credit-fraud rings have sought or needed help from the Internet.

It's ironic that Americans are asking for privacy protection from the same   18
government that has in the last few years expanded electronic surveillance beyond Richard Nixon's wildest dreams — always with an appeal to public fear and mistrust. Federal agencies are creating centralized databases to track every new job hire in the country (to catch illegal immigrants and deadbeat dads), to make sure that welfare recipients don't overstay their five years by changing states and to provide instant "terrorist" profiling to airport security agents. The country has not hesitated in the last few years to wipe out the civil liberties of whole swaths of the population in futile gropes for greater public security that's never attained.

But as soon as the most minute interest of upper-income people is threat-   19
ened, Congress is shut down with phone calls, as it was during the Lexis-Nexis fiasco last summer and the Social Security Web site controversy this April. Privacy is a vastly different issue to those whose names aren't on anyone's direct-mail list. Ask a homeless person what "privacy" means, and the answer might involve a large appliance box. Once you're on the street, you're a reputation refugee — and no computer is ever going to approve your e-cash transaction.

Simple loss of privacy is not the real problem underlying all the tossing   20
and turning we're going through over the openness the Internet has thrust upon us. The entire experience of Internet use has total privacy as its point of departure — "meatspace" privacy, real-time anonymity, the kind that keeps anyone from knowing you're surfing the Web in your partner's underwear.

No, privacy is only part of the equation. The other part is the basic ques-   21
tion of trust, that elusive property that we've all, in our hearts, given up on. This wide-ranging loss of our electronic virginity was well under way twenty years ago but remained invisible until the Web forced us to confront it. We should be grateful for that. The arrival of the Global Village° could be an opportunity to reevaluate our notions of trust and strangerhood. Maybe it will force us to.

Nixon's demands for privacy were ultimately fruitless and pathetic be-   22
cause there was no longer any trust to base that privacy on. He never understood that — and as privacy-loss hysteria begins to push laws through Congress that may do more harm than good, sadly, neither do we.

Questions to Start You Thinking

1. CONSIDERING MEANING: What are the different kinds of privacy Obser describes? How are they related?

2. IDENTIFYING WRITING STRATEGIES: Where and how does Obser use cause and effect to show that privacy is the root of the problem rather than the solution to the problem?

Global Village: Idea that the cultures and economies of different countries are becoming increasingly interdependent.

3. READING CRITICALLY: What seems to be Obser's purpose in writing this essay? Do you think an online magazine is a good place to try to accomplish this purpose? Why, or why not?

4. EXPANDING VOCABULARY: Define *surveillance*. What are the differences between the kinds of surveillance Obser discusses in paragraph 10?

5. MAKING CONNECTIONS: Would Cynthia Joyce ("Six Clicks from Death," p. 646) agree with Obser that privacy is a problem on the Internet? Why, or why not?

Link to the Paired Essay

Both Stephanie Brail ("The Price of Admission," p. 651) and Obser propose solutions to problems that stem from concerns about privacy on the Internet. How might Brail respond to Obser's claim that upholding trust, not privacy, is the way to prevent the exploitation of personal information online?

Journal Prompts

1. Is privacy without trust possible?

2. If privacy is the problem with society's expectations in an electronic age, what do you think might be the solution?

Suggestions for Writing

1. How do you judge whether a person or source is trustworthy? Write an essay that describes the qualities that gain your trust in either a personal or professional relationship.

2. How might Brail respond to Obser's argument that increasing privacy *causes* problems—like the ones she and Sandy faced? From Brail's perspective, write an essay that evaluates the role of privacy in causing or preventing Internet harassment.

A WRITER'S
RESEARCH
MANUAL

Introduction:
The Nature of Research

Which foods are best for lowering one's risk of cancer?

What are the potential benefits of space exploration as we approach the new millennium?

Why are eating disorders increasingly prevalent among young female athletes?

What steps can law enforcement take to help prevent domestic violence?

How much of an impact do strict death penalty laws have on crime reduction?

Why is baseball exempt from antitrust laws?

You may have asked yourself one or more of these questions. Perhaps you discussed the subject with your friends, asked a teacher about it, or read an article on it. In doing so, you were conducting informal research to satisfy your curiosity.

In your day-to-day life, you are often faced with making a decision that will determine what you are going to do. You may want to buy a CD player or a new automobile, to choose a college or an insurance policy, to decide whether to participate in an innovative medical procedure or go on an exciting vacation to an exotic destination. To be better informed about your decision, you pull together information from talking with friends, get facts from sales personnel, compare prices, read articles in magazines and newspapers, and listen to reports and commercials. You gather and weigh as much information as you can find. By doing so, you are conducting practical research. The more thorough your investigation, the better prepared you are to make a well-informed decision.

To do research is, in a sense, to venture into the unknown — to explore, to experiment, to discover, to constantly revise your thinking, to solve problems.

Whether the object is to probe the mysterious recesses of the human brain or the far galaxies, the causes of earthquakes or the feasibility of using electric automobiles, research can be thrilling. That is why some people devote their entire lives to such investigation — in laboratories, in business, in libraries, in the field.

When one of your college professors assigns you a research paper due in a month or two, you may not be able to make any earthshaking discoveries. You won't be expected to unfold the secrets of the brain or the spiral nebula. Even so, you just might find yourself drawn into the excitement of research as you discover that research isn't merely pasting together information and opinions taken from other people; you use research to draw conclusions and arrive at your own fresh view. The key will be for you to start your investigation as professional researchers do — with a research question that truly interests you and that you really want to find out more about.

Naturally, in doing research and in writing about your discoveries, you'll find yourself taking certain steps ahead of others, just as you do in any composing task. Early on, you'll need to plan your time and block out the work to be done, but you won't follow any inflexible track laid down for you. The process isn't lockstep; it's often recursive: you can backtrack or jump ahead when it makes sense to do so. You might find, in the midst of writing, that you need to reorganize your outline. Or in rewriting, you might find you need more material on a certain point; in that case, back you go to the library, to the Internet, or off to another interview. Like detective work, research sometimes will lead to an insurmountable obstacle. When stopped on one path, you can turn around, go sideways, or set out in another direction altogether.

Whenever you are called on to conduct research to come to a conclusion based on facts and expert opinions — whether in your personal life, for a college class, or on the job — this research manual will provide you with strategies and procedures for conducting efficient, effective research.

Chapter 27, "Forming a Research Question and Finding Sources," introduces you to the basics of dealing with a research assignment: generating ideas, developing your research question, and investigating sources in a library, on the Internet, and in the field. To help you find your own view and express it convincingly, our assignment for a research investigation is fairly simple. If you take our advice and follow several critical steps, you will learn how to do research in different settings and how to use a variety of sources to fill a purpose. Along the way we introduce you to two student researchers — Maria Halloran and Mark Sanchez. Throughout this chapter you will observe the process these students go through in developing a research question and finding sources.

Chapter 28, "Evaluating Sources and Taking Notes," introduces you to the critical process of evaluating, or judging, the information you gather from a variety of sources. To help you determine the *best* evidence for your paper, you will learn what questions to ask of your library, Internet, and field sources. You will also learn how to take accurate, thorough, and useful notes. We encourage you to think of note taking as thinking critically about the ideas and facts you find in your sources.

Chapter 29, "Writing the Research Paper," helps you see how to manage the wealth of information you gather from your diverse sources. In this chapter we show you how to synthesize the information in your sources to answer your research question and bring together your findings in a readable, trustworthy paper. Along the way you will share the experiences of our student researchers as they try to focus and organize all their notes and write coherent research papers that clearly communicate with readers and address their basic research questions. At the end, you will have the opportunity to read their papers — Maria Halloran's final paper using library research skills, "America's Obsession with Sports," and Mark Sanchez's final paper using library, Internet, and field sources, "Into Las Animas and Myself." You can also read another library research paper, "Female Identity in Kate Chopin's 'The Story of an Hour,'" by Chris Robinson. This paper is a literary analysis, as discussed in Chapter 12, "Writing about Literature." Unlike the sample student essay in Chapter 12, this paper uses literary critiques by professional writers and academic scholars as evidence to support the student's own ideas; these sources were uncovered through library research.

Chapter 30, "Documenting Sources," explains and illustrates the MLA and APA documentation styles you will use to indicate the sources of your information. Consult this chapter to see when and how to cite your sources.

The research skills you learn will prove invaluable in your future academic, professional, and personal lives. We hope that you find the research manual helpful as you continue to conduct research in school and beyond.

Chapter 27

Forming a Research Question and Finding Sources

All around us, information keeps exploding. From day to day, television, books, newspapers, and magazines shower us with facts and figures, statements and reports, views and opinions — some of them half-baked, some revealing and trustworthy. College requires you to sort through this massive burst of words, distinguishing between fact and opinion, between off-the-wall claims and sound expert interpretations. Researching a topic and composing a paper based on your findings help you gain such skills.

In Chapter 5, "Reading Critically," if you did the main assignment, you read one or more works by other writers and wrote a paper based on your critical analysis of those pieces. You may want to review that chapter now. Chapter 12, "Writing about Literature," expanded on these skills and showed you how to write a paper analyzing a literary work. When you wrote those papers, you gave credit to other writers in an informal way. That experience will prove good preparation for writing a research paper. This new task, though, will be different in the following ways:

You'll draw from more sources — and from a wider range of sources — in the library, on the Internet, and in the field.

You'll use library, Internet, and field research techniques in ways that complement one another.

You'll use your sources as evidence to support your ideas, rather than as a subject to write about.

You'll do more critical thinking — evaluating, analyzing, and synthesizing of ideas.

You'll learn to cite and list your sources in a form that scholars and professionals follow in writing research reports and articles.

This chapter introduces you to the basic information you will need to carry out a research assignment. You will learn how to find a topic and develop it into a focused and answerable research question. When you are ready to begin answering your research question, you will find here a discussion of how to use, alone or in combination with each other, a rich set of research sources — the library, the Internet, and field research. Armed with these basic skills and tools, you will find yourself prepared to accomplish even the most formidable research task.

To be able to write a research paper is a useful skill. Research writing is essential not only in an academic community but also in business and the professions. Lawyers preparing legal briefs and arguments research previous cases that have a bearing on their own. Engineers rely on research studies when they write feasibility reports. Health-care workers synthesize discoveries from research findings to help them decide on treatment for patients. Business owners depend on market research to sell their products.

Learning from Other Writers: Two Students' Experiences

To give you a sense of what real students encounter in fulfilling typical research paper assignments, we will tell you a couple of stories. They're about students who began their investigation with curiosity and enthusiasm and, although they hit a few snags, continued searching diligently through various research resources until they had some answers to research questions they sincerely wondered about. One story — Maria Halloran's — illustrates a traditional approach to writing a research paper, emphasing sources found primarily in the library. The other story — Mark Sanchez's — illustrates how additional research resources — in particular, resources on the Internet and in field research — can be used along with traditional library resources. We begin with Maria Halloran's story.

Maria Halloran.   Maria Halloran wasn't daunted to find herself taking English 102 that spring, even though it was a course many students dreaded. Its notorious requirement — a research paper — made some people register for it unhappily. Research, however, in her experience hadn't been a cause for despair. Even so, the English 102 assignment presented challenges.

Halloran's professor had centered much of the reading for the composition course on the subject of popular culture in contemporary American society; the research paper, too, was to be on that general subject. Halloran and her classmates were given this assignment:

> Write a paper of at least fifteen hundred words in which you use a variety of sources to answer a question of interest to you. Your research question may be about one of the topics we have discussed in class, or it may address some other aspect of popular culture in the United States. The final paper is due in two months.

Although this assignment told Halloran quite a bit about what her professor expected her to accomplish in her paper, it left the choice of topic wide open. Two months seemed to be a short time to go from the broad subject of "popular culture" to a finished research paper on a focused question.

As Halloran tried to decide on a topic for her research investigation, she thought back over some of the issues the class had discussed—violence in movies, the popularity of video games, the controversy over record labeling, the increasing obsession with TV talk shows. Halloran had grown up in the Philippines, so she viewed American culture differently from the way most of her classmates did. There was one aspect of popular culture that the class had not discussed that puzzled her—sports. Halloran had observed that people in the United States frequently talk about sports and refer to sports. She initially thought she would do her research on sports metaphors in public speeches, such as those used by politicians and newscasters; but she soon discovered that the scope of this subject was overwhelming and that copies of some of the speeches might be difficult to obtain. Next she considered investigating the phenomenon of sports celebrities, but she was not very interested in that angle.

Halloran asked herself what she was most interested to learn about sports in America and realized she wanted to know more about American attitudes toward sports. People aren't as enthusiastic about sports in the Philippines. Perhaps reading and reflecting on what other people said about American attitudes toward sports would help her to understand them better. She decided to do her research paper on the topic of Americans' preoccupation with sports.

Halloran made a preliminary search of her college library's catalog and of some CD-ROM periodical indexes and then did some preliminary reading about the great value Americans place on sports. She found one promising 1984 article in *U.S. News & World Report* in which Richard Weinberg, professor of educational psychology at the University of Minnesota, defended the widespread interest in sports on the basis that "for young people, sports is an important self-esteem builder." But Halloran turned up very little recent material.

Because she was dealing with a contemporary phenomenon, she decided to concentrate her search in newspapers and magazines so that she would have up-to-date information. She expanded her search and began looking in other periodical guides and electronic databases. Using the search engines on the CD-ROMs and databases, she searched for combinations of the terms *sports, society, culture,* and *American.* Her searches revealed a range of sources that might be relevant to her research project. A half hour spent scanning some of the sources quickly helped her distinguish between those that were clearly not on the topic and those that might be relevant.

As she read some of the sources she uncovered during her searches in the library, she grew increasingly interested in connections between sports and violence, crime and suicide. She was particularly intrigued with some of the articles she found in the magazine *Sports Bulletin*. An article by Robert Lipsyte, for instance, seemed to contradict Weinberg's position, arguing that fear of ridicule in playing sports was not good for building self-esteem. Looking through other issues of *Sports Bulletin*, she found still more articles that focused on some of the negative aspects of sports.

Then she read a comment in a *Chicago Tribune* article that amazed her: "There were twenty shootings after the Bulls' game Sunday night, four of which proved fatal. For any given weekend night in Chicago, that toll is high but not shocking." From her perspective, twenty shootings, four of which were fatal, was shocking. Halloran wondered just how prevalent the attitude displayed in this article was. She asked herself if Americans now take sports violence casually.

Halloran was beginning to feel involved personally, and her topic was becoming more focused. Instead of just investigating Americans' fascination with sports, now Maria wanted to research the negative effects of Americans' preoccupation with sports. Could she find enough information to help her better understand the American attitude toward sports? Could she find other recent articles and current statistics? Could she find books on this topic that would give her the in-depth analyses she needed? Could she find enough evidence to make some suggestions for changing the situation? If so, the toil of shuffling note cards, outlining, and citing sources would be justified. She looked forward to the project with enthusiasm.

At this point, Halloran did some early freewriting. She started by stating her topic, as best she could, and then wrote for five minutes without stopping, setting down each thought as it occurred to her.

> *The negative effects of our preoccupation with sports. We don't care if fans get hurt. We don't care if kids get damaged. We just want the thrill. No cost is too high. Maybe the big business behind it is too powerful to stop now. Sports heroes with their endorsements, huge expensive stadiums, big salaries. Lots of money. Lots of power and prestige. It's like a cult. We'll do anything for it, and we want it to fill our lives with meaning. How did this happen? How did some simple games become our national religion? Wait a minute. Is this true? Is sports mania really part of our national identity? Part of who we are? Everywhere? Is America as a whole obsessed with sports?*

Now Halloran had her research question. Although her freewriting turned up some interesting new angles that Halloran would have liked to pursue — the comparison of sports with a cult religion or the effect of big business on the culture of sports — she decided that these would take more time and resources than she had available. Instead, Halloran decided to focus on a more basic question, a question that she actually found more interesting: Is America obsessed with sports?

Because Maria Halloran's research question was focused and meaningful, it served as a good guide through the process of finding sources, gathering evidence, and writing her paper. In this chapter, we share with you some of the experiences Halloran had while conducting her research. We show you some of the library sources she consulted and some of the notes she took. Later, in Chapter 29, we show you how Halloran used her sources to write a convincing paper. Finally, at the end of Chapter 29, you can read Halloran's final research paper, "America's Obsession with Sports."

Mark Sanchez.   Mark Sanchez's story parallels Maria Halloran's in a number of ways. His assignment was to write a research paper about personal identity and family history, drawing on interviews with family members, personal observations, and research in the library and on the Internet. After spending time considering his assignment, he decided to focus on how his sense of identity had been shaped by his family's roots on the plains of southeastern Colorado. Like Halloran, he began his research in the library, starting with a search of his library's online catalog and then expanding the search to periodical indexes and CD-ROM databases. Unlike Halloran, he also made use of resources available on the Internet, such as sites on the World Wide Web, and field resources, including personal interviews with members of his family and faculty at his college and a field trip to learn more about the area in and around Las Animas, Colorado. Later in this chapter, we discuss his research process. In Chapter 29, we show you how Sanchez used his sources to write a paper about the history of his family. At the end of Chapter 29, you can read Sanchez's final research paper, "Into Las Animas and Myself."

Learning by Writing

As a rule, in any composition course a research paper is your most complicated assignment. Some of our advice in this chapter may be old news to you. You may have learned in high school how to take research notes or how to make a working bibliography. At times, as we guide you through writing your paper, we'll pause to explain those special skills. Mastering them, if you haven't mastered them already, will speed you toward that triumphant day when you bang a final staple through your paper.

THE ASSIGNMENT: WRITING FROM SOURCES

Find a topic that intrigues you, and develop a focused research question about it. Answering the question should require you to use one or more of the critical thinking skills you honed in Part Two of this book: reading critically, analyzing, comparing and contrasting, explaining causes and effects, taking a stand, proposing a solution, evaluating. Conduct whatever research is necessary to answer your question, and synthesize the information you assemble to develop your own reasonable answer to the research question. Then write a paper in which you persuasively use a variety of source material to convey your conclusions. Assume that your audience is your instructor and your classmates.

If possible, try to use your paper to benefit a particular cause or group, such as a campus group or a local nonprofit organization. Depending on your topic, your completed paper may benefit your campus administration or your employer. Having a real audience can help you make choices about what information to include and exclude as you write your report. Here's how to proceed, in more or less this order:

1. Choose a general subject that you would like to investigate. (Your instructor may assign one or suggest some suitable possibilities.)
2. Do a little reading in the subject to see exactly what aspects most keenly interest you. Choose one of these aspects as the topic for your research paper.
3. State, in the form of a question about your topic, what you think you want to find out. (This question may change as you read more; its purpose is to guide you in your research.)
4. Make a preliminary search to ascertain that library, Internet, and/or field sources are available to answer your question. If necessary, revise your question.
5. Conduct an initial investigation to learn more about your topic and to find some possible answers to your question. As you develop an answer or answers to your research question, conduct more research to assemble the evidence you'll need to present your ideas persuasively.
6. Then, in a paper of at least fifteen hundred words, set forth the conclusions you have drawn from your study. Give evidence from your research sources to support your ideas.

This paper, as you can see, will be more than a stack of facts. Reading and digesting the ideas of five to ten other writers is just the first step. In the process of writing your paper, you'll also be called on to bring your own intelligence to bear on what you have read.

A Note on Schedules.   Along with the assignment to write a research paper, some instructors will suggest a schedule. Halloran's instructor blocked out the students' obligations over an eight-week period.

February 21: Paper assigned

February 23: Three possible topics due [next class meeting]

February 28: Preliminary research question due [one week]

March 7: Working bibliography due (citations—on cards—of the sources you think will be useful) [one week]

March 21: Note cards due [two weeks]

March 28: Thesis statement (a one-sentence statement of what the paper will demonstrate) and preliminary outline due [one week]

April 11: First draft due [two weeks]

April 18: Completed revised paper due [one week]

If your instructor doesn't give you a series of deadlines, set some for yourself. You can be sure that a research paper will require more time than you expect. You'll find this huge job much more manageable if you break it into a series of small tasks. Writing the final draft, you'll need hours to revise and still more time to cite all your sources accurately. If you procrastinate and try to toss everything together in a desperate all-night siege, you will not be satisfied with the result. Finally, you'll need time to look it over and proofread it. A clear-cut schedule will help.

Generating Ideas and Forming a Research Question

How can we most effectively help long-term prisoners to return to society when their sentences are served?

What are the ethical implications of cloning humans?

What can be done to help the homeless in Dallas, Texas?

Has the charter schools movement resulted in measurably better student learning?

What is the media's role in defining Generation X?

In what ways has intellectual property law changed in response to the growth of the Internet?

If you already have a narrowly defined research question in mind, such as the preceding examples — congratulations. You can just skip to the research checklist on page 678. But if you don't have a question yet, read on.

CHOOSING YOUR TERRITORY

To explore, you need a territory — a subject that interests you. Perhaps, as Maria Halloran found, your work in this very course or in another course will suggest an appropriate territory. Halloran wrote a paper suggested by a theme that ran through all the readings and discussions in her writing course. A psychology course might encourage you to investigate mental disorders; a sociology course, urban renewal; a geography course, tropical forests.

You'll have an easier time from the start if you can make your territory smaller than "mental disorders" or "urban renewal." "Schizophrenia" and "inner-city housing problems" are smaller, more readily explorable territories that will be more manageable as your research leads you to develop a more focused topic. But if you don't feel you can make your topic so narrow and definite at this point in the process, go ahead and start with a broad subject.

The following checklist may help you find a general subject. It sends you back once more to every writer's four basic resources.

**DISCOVERY
CHECKLIST**

Choosing Your Territory

- Can you *recall* an experience from your work or leisure, from your travel or life as a student, that raises interesting questions or creates unusual associations in your mind?
- What have you *observed* recently — perhaps on your way to school or work today, or while running errands — that you could more thoroughly investigate with the aid of books and magazines?
- In recent *conversation* with friends or in class discussions, have you encountered any new perspectives that you'd care to explore?
- Can you *imagine* a solution to a frustration, obstacle, or problem that plagues you?

TAKING AN OVERVIEW

Before launching an expedition into a little-known territory, a smart explorer first makes a reconnaissance flight and takes an overview. Having seen the terrain, the explorer then chooses the very spot to set up camp — the point on the map that looks most promising. Research writers do something like that, too. Before committing themselves to a topic, they first look over a broader territory to see what parts of it look most attractive and then zero in on one small area that seems interesting.

How much time should you devote to your overview? An evening or a few hours should do. How do you take an overview? You might begin by looking up your subject in an encyclopedia and reading the general articles about it — *inner cities* or *urban housing developments, schizophrenia* or *mental illness* or (still more general) *psychiatry.* You are probably a veteran reader of encyclopedias, but for tips on using both general encyclopedias and specialized ones, see the sections on your college library later in this chapter (p. 686). When you write your paper, usually you'll find the information in a general encyclopedia too broad to use as a source, but at this stage it can help orient you within your subject.

In your library's reference room, you might check the *Readers' Guide to Periodical Literature,* an index of recent articles in popular magazines. It will direct you to the latest information and opinion, classified by many subjects. You can also look in a newspaper index such as NewsBank, a computerized index now available in many libraries. Browsing in an introductory textbook, if any seems likely to help, is also a useful early step.

You can spend time on the Internet, visiting sites on the World Wide Web and reading messages posted to newsgroups or Web discussion forums. Searches on some of the leading Web search sites — such as AltaVista, Lycos, and Yahoo! — can lead you to a wide range of Web pages that might be of interest to you. Similarly, searches of the Deja News and Liszt Web sites can help you locate newsgroups and mailing lists that deal with your topic. The number of sources you can locate on the Internet is large — and growing on a daily basis — so you'll need to exercise discipline when it comes to spending time online, especially in this early research stage. Depending on your topic, however, it can be time well spent.

Finally, consider discussing your topic with an expert in the field. If you're interested in a topic such as America's fascination with the automobile, consider meeting with a professor, such as a sociologist or a journalist, who specializes in the area. Or talk with friends or acquaintances who are particularly passionate about their cars. Or spend time at an auto show, carefully observing and talking with the people who attend.

STATING YOUR QUESTION

Once you have zeroed in on part of a territory to explore, you can ask a definite question. Ask what you want to find out, and your task will leap into focus. Having begun with a broad, general interest in (let's say) social problems in large cities, you might then ask, "What happens to teenage runaways on the streets of Manhattan?" Or, if you have started with a general yen to know more about contemporary architecture, a definite question might be "Who in America today is good at designing sports arenas?" Keep in mind that the question you ask should be debatable and of interest to both you and your readers.

Brainstorm.   You might start with a brainstorming session. For fifteen or twenty minutes, let your thoughts revolve, and jot down whatever questions come to mind — even useless ones. Then, looking over your list, you may find one that appears promising. Your instructor also may have some suggestions, but you will probably be more motivated researching a question you select.

Size Up Your Question.   A workable question has to be narrow enough to allow a fruitful investigation in the library. Many interesting questions are too immense, and the research they would require would take years, not the few weeks you have available: "How is the climate of the earth changing?" "Who are the world's best living storytellers?" "Why is there poverty?" "What's going on in outer space?" Restrict your thinking and your topic appropriately. Questions such as the following are more likely to be workable: "How will El Niño affect global climate changes in the next decade?" "How is Irish step dancing a form of storytelling?" "What welfare-to-work programs exist in the southeastern United States?" "What are the most recent discoveries about the atmosphere of Mars?"

A question, however, can be too narrow or too insignificant. If you restrict your topic too far ("How did John F. Kennedy's maternal grandfather influence the decisions he made during his first month as president?"), it may be impossible to find relevant sources. A question may also be so narrow that it becomes uninteresting: avoid questions that can be answered with a simple yes or no or by stating a few statistics ("Are there more black students or white students in the freshman class this year?"). If a mere source or two could answer your research question, the resulting paper will be a thin summary, not a true research paper. Instead, ask a question that will lead you to a lot of meaty books and articles and into the heart of a lively controversy: "How does the ratio of black students to white students affect campus relations?" The best research questions are those about issues that other people take seriously and spend time arguing about. Not only will you find better sources if you focus on a significant, debatable issue, but your paper is more likely to be of real interest to both you and your readers.

A caution: If you pick a topic currently in the news, you may have trouble finding useful material — deep analysis, critical thought, ample historical background, intelligent controversy. For many current topics, the only printed sources may be recent newspapers and newsmagazines, and the only online sources may be messages posted to newsgroups, mailing lists, or Web discussion forums. The topic may be so recent that few qualified experts have done thought-provoking analyses of it. In this case, keep searching periodical guides, electronic databases, and Internet search sites. If your search still doesn't yield any useful analysis or information about your research question, you may need to reconsider your topic.

Hone Your Question.   Try to make the wording of your question specific but simple: identify one thing to find out, not several. A question that reads "How do current art and music reflect the cultural revolution of the 1960s?" is too big. You could split such a question into two parts and then pick one of them: "How does contemporary art reflect the cultural revolution of the 1960s?" or "How does music . . . ?" By qualifying the word *music*, you might further cut the question down to size: "How does rap music reflect the cultural revolution of the 1960s?" Focus on whatever you most keenly wish to learn, as Maria Halloran did.

A well-wrought question will help lead you into your research. Say the question is "What has caused a shortage of low-income housing in northeastern cities?" The wording of the question alone suggests subject headings that may be found in the library catalog or the *Readers' Guide* or NewsBank: *housing, housing shortage, low-income housing, urban housing*. If your question doesn't suggest such leads, try rewording it to make it more concrete and specific.

Some writers find that having not only a *question* but also an *answer* in mind makes the research project easier to tackle. So, for example, if a writer's research question is "Why do people go into the nursing profession?" and he already has an inkling of the likely answer ("People go into nursing out of a strong commitment to caring and a feeling of personal responsibility"), then he might prefer to use the answer to focus the direction of his research. This will allow him to skip all the other possible answers (family background, financial rewards) and to focus on finding evidence that supports or disproves his theory. If you use an answer to your research question in this way, you are using a *working thesis* (see p. 732). At this stage, any answers you have are only tentative: you need to be flexible enough to change your answer or even your question if your research turns up something unexpected. Later, when you are writing your paper, you'll reexamine and revise your working thesis into a final thesis (see "Refining Your Thesis" in Chapter 29, p. 733).

Remember that a working thesis is meant to guide your research, not hinder it. If you find that you're not learning anything new, that you're just finding support for what you already thought was the case, then your working thesis has become too dominant and you're no longer conducting true research. Because of this possibility, many writers prefer to delay formulating a working thesis until they've already done a substantial part of their research — or they might even skip it altogether. Your approach will probably depend on your research assignment, on your instructor's expectations, and on your own work style.

Until you start conducting research, of course, you can't know for certain how fruitful your research question will be. If it doesn't lead you to any definite facts or reliable opinions, if it doesn't start you thinking critically, you'll need to reword it or throw it out and ask a new question. But at the very least, the question you first ask can give you a definite direction in which to start looking.

When you have tentatively stated your question, you can test it by asking these questions about it.

RESEARCH CHECKLIST

Questioning Your Question

* Is the scope of your question appropriate — not too immense and not too narrow?
* Is your question answerable in the time you have? Within the word or page limits you have?
* Can you find sufficient timely information on your question in books and articles?
* Have you worded your question simply, so that you are seeking just one answer, not several?
* Have you worded your question concretely and specifically, so that you understand exactly what you are looking for?
* Is your question of real interest? Does it concern a real issue, about which there is some debate?
* Does your question interest you personally?

MAKING A PRELIMINARY SEARCH

You can quickly test whether your question is likely to lead to an ample research paper by conducting a short, fast, preliminary search that shouldn't take you more than an hour or two. In some ways, this search will be similar to the initial overview you conducted at the beginning of your research process. Your goal then was to discover what interested you most about your topic. Your goal now is to determine whether you'll have enough material to address your question, to identify the most fruitful avenues for research, and to refine your research question.

Check the library catalog to see what books appear under the relevant subject headings. If possible, go into the stacks and look over the shelves. Take a quick check of magazine articles: consult the last annual *Readers' Guide* and an electronic database, looking under the subject headings closest to your special concern. Don't locate and read the articles yet; just see how many there are and whether their titles sound promising. Log on the Internet, and visit some of the leading Web search sites (see p. 707 for a list). Conduct some searches to get a sense of how many Web sites contain information that might be relevant to your topic. Visit some of those sites to see what kind of information they contain.

If the material available looks so skimpy that you won't have anything to choose from, consider asking another question. Similarly, if your first trip into the stacks reveals ten yards of books, alarm bells should start ringing. Instead of asking a question that only two books in your library address or one that a hundred articles directly address, pick a question that a dozen or twenty available sources focus on.

Once you have decided that you can locate enough material to do the job, decide which information sources to concentrate your research efforts on. Some research questions can be addressed through a wide range of information sources. Others are better suited to a narrower range of resources. Part of your preliminary search, as a result, should include a consideration of which sources are most likely to yield the best information.

Using Effective Search Techniques

Your overview and your preliminary search should have given you a rough notion of where your most promising material lies. Most of the remainder of this chapter will give you detailed information on how to identify and locate good research sources in the library, on the Internet, or in the field. Following is some advice on techniques that are useful no matter where your sources are found. A working bibliography is a tool that college writers have used for years: it's a simple way to keep track of where you've been and where you still need to go. The research archive is a more recent innovation, but it's a tremendous advantage when you're faced with having to manage a bewildering number of sources in a variety of formats. These tools may seem like a lot of trouble at first, but if you establish a good system for yourself and spend some effort maintaining it along the way, you will find the final paper much easier to write. Developing a focused set of keywords and using advanced searches are indispensable techniques for any research that you conduct electronically, whether through an online library catalog, a CD-ROM database, or the World Wide Web. By honing your set of keywords and then wielding them intelligently, you can cut through the thousands of possible sources that these electronic resources typically contain and carve out the few that are most relevant to your research question.

STARTING A WORKING BIBLIOGRAPHY

A working bibliography is a detailed list of books and articles you either plan to consult or have consulted. Don't worry about trying to write your final list of sources before you conduct your research. The working bibliography is a tool that will change and grow as you find new sources, eliminate others, and shift the focus of your research. It has two purposes — to guide you in your research by recording which sources you've examined and which you intend to examine and to help you document the final paper by recording detailed information about each source.

Most writers find that a convenient and efficient way to compile such a working bibliography is on 4-by-6-inch note cards, one source to a card. Cards are handy to work with: you can arrange and shuffle them. Other writers keep track of everything in a notebook small enough to fit in a pocket. Still others use a word-processing program or a computer database to keep track of bibliographical information. Whatever method you use, the more care you take in recording your tentative sources, the more time you'll save later, when at the end of your paper you compile a list of works you *actually* used and cited. At that point, you'll be grateful to find all the necessary information about titles, authors, dates, page numbers, and URLs (Internet addresses) at your fingertips. Otherwise, you'll have to make a frantic, time-consuming trip back to the library.

Start a bibliographic card or entry for each source you intend to consult. At this point, your information about the source may be incomplete: "Dr. Edward Denu — cardiologist — interview about drug treatments." Later, once you locate a print or Internet source or conduct field research, you'll be able to fill in the complete bibliographical information. What should each source note in your working bibliography eventually contain? Everything necessary to find the source later as well as to write the final list of sources to be placed at the end of your paper.

BOOKS

1. The library call number
2. The author's full name, last name first
3. The book's title, including its subtitle if it has one, underlined, or in italics if you are using a computer
4. The publication information — place, publisher, and year of publication.
(See Figure 27.1.)

PERIODICALS

1. The author's full name
2. The title of the article, in quotation marks, followed by the name of the publication, underlined or in italics

FIGURE 27.1
A bibliography
card for a
book with
one author,
in MLA style

> *GV*
> *958.P4.7*
> *B57*
> *1990*
>
>   *BISSINGER*
>
> *Bissinger, H. G. Friday Night*
> *   Lights: A Town, a Team,*
> *   and a Dream.*
> *   Reading: Addison, 1990*
>
> *Concrete examples of football*
> *culture. Lots of quotations*
> *from coaches, etc.*

3. For a scholarly journal, the volume number and, for certain journals, the issue number (see Chapter 30 for details)
4. The date of the issue (form varies with the type of journal or magazine; see Chapter 30.)
5. The page numbers of the article (a "+" indicates that the article covers more than one page but not consecutive pages)
(See Figure 27.2.)

ELECTRONIC SOURCES

1. The author's (or editor's) full name, if one is available
2. The title of the site or document
3. The name of the sponsoring organization (if any)
4. The date the source was created or last updated
5. The date you accessed the source
6. The Internet address — or URL (Uniform Resource Locator) — in angle brackets
(See Figure 27.3)

FIGURE 27.2   A bibliography source note recorded on a laptop computer for an article in a monthly magazine, in MLA style

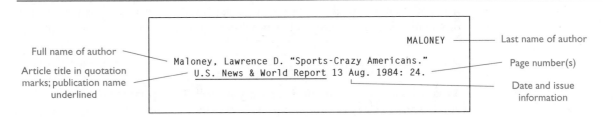

```
                                                  Appel and McCleary

Appel, Robert, and Colleen McCleary. "Cities, Towns and Communities in SE
      Colorado." Southeast Colorado RC&D, Inc. 19 Aug. 1996. 15 Mar. 1998
      <http://www.ruralnet.net/~csn/government/cities.html>.

General information about Bent County and Las Animas.
```

FIGURE 27.3   A bibliography source note recorded on a laptop computer for an Internet site, in MLA style

```
                                                      Octavio Sanchez

Sanchez, Octavio. Personal interview. 2 Mar. 1998.

      Key information on reasons why the family moved to Las Animas from
      New Mexico. Info on buying the farm, losing it, and buying it back.
```

FIGURE 27.4   A bibliography source note recorded on a laptop computer for a personal interview, in MLA style

FIELD SOURCES

1. The name of the person you interviewed or the setting you observed
2. A descriptive title, such as "Personal interview" or "Telephone interview"
3. The date you conducted the interview or observation
   (See Figure 27.4.)

For each source note, you may also want to include a brief annotation to yourself on your impression of the usefulness of the work ("GREAT INFO!" or "Maybe a few gems here" or "Probably not much use"). You may want to update or change your annotation after you have actually consulted the source to indicate the topics or nuggets you found there.

You may list each item of information separately in your source note, but it is wise at this time to put the information in the correct form (see Chapter 30, "Documenting Sources") for a final bibliography entry in your works cited list. This may seem like a lot of record keeping. But it takes less time to jot down all this information in full now than to make future trips to the library.

STARTING A RESEARCH ARCHIVE

As you locate and evaluate sources, you will accumulate information that you'll want to refer to later. If you have ever found yourself staring at a pile of books, photocopied articles, and printouts from databases and Internet sources, wondering which ones contained a particular fact or quotation that you wanted to use, you know how important a good organizational system can be. When writers fail to spend the time needed to organize their information effectively, they spend more time looking for information than they would have if they'd organized it in the first place.

You can organize information from library, Internet, and field sources by creating a research archive. An *archive* is a place in which information is systematically stored. A library, for instance, is an archive, as is a database or a site on the World Wide Web. If you invest the effort to start and maintain a well-organized research archive, you'll benefit by being able to spend more time thinking and writing about your research topic and less time worrying about where you put a useful source.

You can use several techniques to create a research archive. One of the simplest is to use paper copies and standard file folders. To use this method, try to get all important sources in a paper format: photocopy book passages and periodical articles, print out electronic sources, keep copies of questionnaires and other raw information from your field research. Then put the pages for each source in a different file folder, and label the folder according to subject and author. If you take the time to highlight key passages, you'll be able to locate that information even more quickly. Remember, as well, to make sure the name of the source and the page number appear on your copy so that you have the necessary information to connect it to a source note in your working bibliography. If necessary, write the information on the photocopy.

If you find yourself using primarily electronic sources, consider saving each source as a computer file. You can save pages from the World Wide Web, electronic mail messages, posts to newsgroups and mailing lists, transcripts of chat sessions, and records from databases to a floppy diskette, a hard drive, or a network drive. If you take the time to give each file a descriptive name, you'll be able to locate the information quickly later on. If you are dealing with several categories of information, you can also save files into different folders or directories. By giving each folder a descriptive name, you can easily tell what the files in each folder contain.

Regardless of the techniques you use to create an archive, remember two things: copy judiciously and take notes. Some research writers insist that copying (either photocopying or saving to a computer file) has done away with the need to take notes. Indeed, judicious copying can save you time as you gather materials for your paper. But simply copying everything you read with the vague notion that some of it contains material valuable for your essay is likely in the end to waste money and to cost you more time rather than less. Much of the material won't be worth saving. Most important, you won't have digested and evaluated what was on the page; you will merely have copied it. Selecting what is essential, highlighting or transcribing it by hand, perhaps nutshelling or paraphrasing it (see p. 727) helps make it yours. When you start drafting, digesting great amounts of copied material will take you much longer than working from a carefully thought-out set of notes.

RECORDING ELECTRONIC SEARCHES

When conducting Internet research, you will probably benefit from saving the location of a source rather than photocopying it or saving it to a computer file. This technique — called *recording a search* — allows you to locate information quickly and easily when you need it at a later time.

You can save the locations of sites on the World Wide Web within your browser. In Microsoft Internet Explorer, these saved locations are referred to as *favorites*; in Netscape Navigator, they are called *bookmarks*. Once you've recorded the location of a particular site, you can locate it easily using your Web browser. You can also annotate favorites and bookmarks with your browser and organize them into folders, much as you can organize files on a computer.

You can also save the results of a search. If you conducted a search on a database or the Internet that was particularly fruitful, but don't have the time to immediately locate each relevant source, you can make note of the keywords or phrases you used to conduct your search and then conduct it again at a later date. You can also print out the search results or save the results to a computer file. If you do this, you can use the results to locate specific sources without having to rerun the search.

USING KEYWORDS

Keywords are terms or phrases that identify the topic of a research source. When you enter the keywords into an electronic search engine (whether in a library catalog or on the World Wide Web), the engine will return to you a list of all the sources it can find with that keyword. Maria Halloran, for instance, searched her library's online catalog and databases using combinations of the keywords *culture, sports, society,* and *American*.

Finding the best keywords for a given search and a given search engine is essential. When looking for information about the lives of his ancestors in Southeastern Colorado, Mark Sanchez found nothing relevant under *farming* but a wealth of sources under *agriculture*. As you conduct your preliminary search, jot down or print out the keywords you use. Note whether they produce too few or too many results. You are likely to find that some keywords work better than others and that certain combinations of keywords produce the best results. Take the time to write down the combinations that work best: few things are as frustrating as trying to remember how you found those promising sources during your preliminary search.

CONDUCTING ADVANCED ELECTRONIC SEARCHES

Several techniques are available to researchers who want to conduct sophisticated searches of the Web, databases, and library catalogs. Some of these techniques, such as wildcards, can expand the scope of your search. Typically, however, researchers use advanced search techniques to limit the scope of their searches. By limiting the scope of a search, researchers hope to obtain results that are more relevant to their research interests than the results obtained from casting a broad net.

Using Wildcards.   *Wildcards* are symbols that, when used in a search, tell the search engine to look for all possible endings to a word. For instance, if you tell a database, library catalog, or Web search site to search for the keyword *runner*, you'll get every entry containing that word. But you won't get entries that contain only *run, runs,* or *running.* Using a wildcard symbol, typically an asterisk (*), you can search for all words that take the form run*, thus increasing the volume of your search results. The most common wildcard symbols are an asterisk for multiple letters, numbers, or symbols and a question mark (?) for single characters.

Searching for Exact Phrases.   A common technique used by researchers is *searching for an exact phrase.* If you are interested, as Mark Sanchez was, in the *history of Colorado,* you could search for the exact phrase *history of Colorado.* A search of AltaVista using this phrase produced a list of 116 results, far fewer than the keyword search for *history* and *Colorado* on Lycos produced. Depending on the search site you use, you may or may not be required to type quotation marks around a phrase. Consult the online help on a given search site for more information on searching for exact phrases.

Conducting Boolean Searches.   *Boolean search* allows you to specify the relationships between your keywords and phrases. Boolean search is named after the nineteenth-century mathematician George Boole, who developed theories for working with sets of information. The most commonly used Boolean search terms include *AND, OR,* and *NOT.* As the terms imply, *AND* means that all terms linked by *AND* must appear in a result. *OR* means that one or more or the terms must appear. And *NOT* means that one term or more terms can appear, while another must not. The following examples serve as illustrations:

```
Search for: history AND Colorado
```
Result: all entries containing both *history* and *Colorado*

```
Search for: history OR Colorado
```
Result: all entries containing *history* or *Colorado* or both

```
Search for: history NOT Colorado
```
Result: all entries containing *history* but not containing *Colorado*

```
Search for: history AND Colorado NOT Denver
```
Result: all entries containing *history* and *Colorado* but not containing *Denver*

Limiting Searches by Publication Information.   Another widely used technique for limiting a search is *specifying publication information.* Specifying publication information — such as year of publication — and doing a keyword search or a search using other advanced search techniques can help narrow your search. For instance, while searching on the HotBot Web search site, Sanchez learned that he could limit his search by specific date or by time period (for example, to sites indexed in the last two weeks, in the last month, and so on). This technique also works well on library catalogs and databases. Sanchez could also limit his library search of books dealing with the history of Colorado to those published since 1990. This would give him a much smaller set of results, but the books it turned up would take into account more recent events than, for instance, those published in the 1960s or 1970s. Using publication date as a limiting factor is used more often on databases and library catalogs than on the Web, both because the Web is a more recent development and because most Web sites can tell you when they indexed a particular site but not when it was actually created.

Finding Sources in the Library

For the better part of a century, students who have been assigned research papers have spent the majority of their time conducting research in libraries. Although the emergence of the Internet as a major source of information has begun to rival libraries as the premiere repository of information, libraries continue to be your best source of information for most topics. Unlike materials found on the Web, the majority of materials in libraries are carefully reviewed for accuracy and importance.

In addition, libraries are designed to help you locate information easily. Each book, journal, magazine, newspaper, government document, and so on is cataloged, and its location is recorded. You need only consult a map of your library's holdings to learn that Sarah Lindsay's book *Primate Behavior*, with the call letters PS3562.IP75, is located in the north wing of the library's first floor.

Don't think that libraries have ignored the technological advances of the past decade. Although a great deal of the library's information is stored the way it has been for some centuries, on printed pages, the tools for locating these pages and, increasingly, information itself are more and more often in electronic form. That means that the researcher needs to be at home in both the print and electronic worlds. Later in this chapter, we discuss how to search for information on the Internet. In the next chapter, we discuss how to evaluate the information you find.

When you enter a college library for your first research assignment, you may be overwhelmed by everything you see — books, periodicals, microfilm, government documents, videos, and computer terminals — and you may wonder how you can begin to access this wealth of materials. Libraries generally provide some help to get you started. Your library may offer tours, classes on how to use an online catalog, and brochures explaining the library's organization and services. Reference librarians are probably available to help you answer questions, from specifics such as "What is the GNP of Brazil?" to more general queries such as "Where can I find information on the Brazilian economy?" Before you start looking for sources for your paper, it pays to do a little research on the library itself. The following basic questions about your library can start you off.

RESEARCH CHECKLIST

Investigating Your Library

- Does the library have a pamphlet mapping the library's holdings and resources and explaining its services?
- Where is the reference desk, and what hours is it open?
- If the catalog is computerized, is there a brochure explaining its use? Can you search the catalog from your computer at home or from the campus network?
- Where are periodicals kept, and how are they arranged? Where are the indexes or computerized databases for locating articles by subject?
- If the library doesn't have a book or article that you need, can you order it through interlibrary loan?
- Are there quiet places to work on your research?

CONSULTING THE CATALOG

A library catalog provides information about the books, periodicals, videos, databases, and other materials owned by a library. In the past, library catalogs were kept on cards in wooden drawers. Now it is common for the records to be searchable by computer. Whatever the form of access, the function is the same — to describe the materials owned by the library so that a library user can locate them by author, title, or subject. Typically, library catalogs do not provide information about individual articles in periodicals. They do, however, provide you with the periodical's publication information (author, title, publication date, publisher, and so on), call number, location, and in some cases availability.

Searching the Catalog.   When searching your library's catalog, first decide what kind of search you are doing. Are you looking for the works of a particular author? Are you searching for a particular title? Or do you simply want to know what is available on a topic? Some card catalogs file subject cards separately from author and title cards. Most computerized catalogs will ask you to specify what kind of search you are doing, either by making a menu choice or by typing in a command.

If you are searching by subject, you need to decide what to search under. When catalogers put a book into the database, they assign subject headings to it, using a list of standard terms used by many other libraries. The list most college libraries use is found in the *Library of Congress Subject Headings (LCSH)*, a set of large red books that many libraries keep near the card catalog or computer terminals. (See Figure 27.5 for sample entries.) If you are having trouble coming up with an effective term to search under, look in *LCSH*. You may be using different terminology than the catalogers did. For example, rather than use the term *third world*, catalogers use *developing countries*, and because they are loath to change their terms, they continue to use *Afro-American* rather than *African American* and *motion pictures* rather than *movies*.

Most computerized library catalogs give you the additional option of using *free text* or *keyword* searches. You enter whatever term you want, and the computer gives you a list of every item in which the term appears. This is an

Sports   *(May Subd Geog)*
⌐*GN454-GN455 (Ethnology)*¬
⌐*GV561-GV1198.995 (General)*¬
UF Field sports
Pastimes
Recreations
BT Recreation
RT Athletics
Games
Outdoor life
Physical education and training
SA *subdivision* Sports *under military*
services, e.g. United States.   Army
—Sports; *and under ethnic groups*
NT Aeronautical sports
Age and sports
Aquatic sports
Ball games
Bullfights
Discrimination in sports

FIGURE 27.5   Entries from the *Library of Congress Subject Headings*

easy way to find sources relevant to your topic, but keyword searches can also generate lots of irrelevant titles, especially if the term you enter is a common one. Some computer catalogs also have a command for limiting a search by date of publication, a useful function if you need to use only current information.

When Maria Halloran searched her library's online catalog, she used the keywords *sports* and *America*. Her search resulted in fifty-four books, magazines, and academic journals that contained the two words in their catalog entries. The first screen of her search looked like this:

```
You searched for the KEYWORDS: sports America
Found 54 items:

1. 200 years of sport in America : a pageant of a
   nation at pla (1976)
2. American Indian sports heritage / Joseph B. Oxen-
   dine. (1988)
3. The American sporting experience : a historical
   anthology of (1984)
4. Athletics in America. Edited by Arnold Flath.
   (1972)
5. The Caledonian games in nineteenth-century America.
   (1971)
6. Canoeing and rafting : the complete where-to-go
   guide to Ame (1979)
```

```
 7. Champion--Joe Louis : black hero in white America /
    Chris Me (1985)
 8. College guide to athletics and academics in America
    (1984)
 9. Country life.
10. Don't believe the hype : fighting cultural misinfor-
    mation ab (1995)
11. Early American sport : a checklist of books by
    American and (1977)
12. Economic analysis of North American ski areas.
```

Some of the entries weren't relevant to her research paper, but Halloran was pleased to find that her library owned several books that addressed sports in America from a historical perspective. Even if she ended up not using the books in her paper, they would provide her with a better understanding of the role sports had played in the past.

Once you have done a search, you need to sort through your options. The information in each record or on each card can help. In addition to the call number or shelf location and the author and title, the record indicates where the work was published and when. A line of description includes how many pages the work contains, information that may help you decide whether it is going to be helpful. Often there are notes about the contents, and finally subject headings help clarify the scope of the work. (See Figures 27.6, 27.7, and 27.8 for examples of Library of Congress author, title, and subject cards.) Though each system presents information slightly differently, the elements included generally are the same. Use these clues to help you choose your sources wisely.

When Halloran clicked on the third entry in her list of results, she got the following screen:

```
You searched for the KEYWORDS: sports America
Record 3 of 54

Author        Riess, Steven A.
Title         The American sporting experience : a
              historical anthology of sport in America
              / Steven A. Riess.
Publisher     New York : Leisure Press, c1984.
LOCATION      CALL #                      STATUS
MORGAN        GV583.R53 1984              AVAILABLE
Description   400 p. ; 23 cm.
Subject       Sports--United States--History.
Call #        GV583.R53 1984
Bibliography  Bibliography p. 398-400.
ISBN          0880112107 (pbk.) : $17.95
```

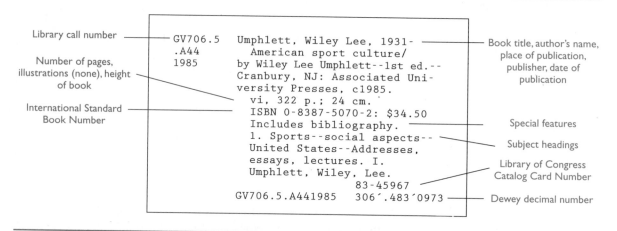

FIGURE 27.6 A Library of Congress author card

The screen gave her more information about Riess's book, including publication information (author, title, publisher, publication city, and publication year), circulation information (the library in which it was located, call number, and availability), and detailed information about the book itself (its page length and whether it contained a bibliography). This information helped her decide to visit the stacks and take a look at the book.

Finding Items on the Shelves. The letters and numbers that tell where a particular item is shelved may seem a random jumble, but the call number is carefully chosen so that books on the same subject end up next to each other on the shelves. College libraries generally use the classification system devised by the Library of Congress. If your library does, you'll find that call letters and numbers direct you to books and other items grouped in subject areas. Other libraries use the older and more

FIGURE 27.7
A Library of
Congress title
card

```
              American sport culture
GV706.5       Umphlett, Wiley Lee, 1931-
.A44            American sport culture/
1985          by Wiley Lee Umphlett--1st ed.--
              Cranbury, NJ: Associated Uni-
              versity Presses, c1985.
                vi, 322 p.; 24 cm.
                ISBN 0-8387-5070-2: $34.50
                Includes bibliography.
                1. Sports--social aspects--
              United States--Addresses, es-
              says, lectures. I. Umphlett,
              Wiley, Lee.
                              83-45967
              GV706.5.A441985  306´.483´0973
```

```
                    ┌──────────────────────────────────────────┐
                    │  SPORTS--SOCIAL ASPECTS--UNITED STATES--   │
                    │       ADDRESSES, ESSAYS, LECTURES.         │
                    │  GV706.5   Umphlett, Wiley Lee, 1931-      │
                    │   .A44          American sport culture/    │
                    │   1985     by Wiley Lee Umphlett--1st ed.--│
                    │            Cranbury, NJ: Associated Uni-   │
                    │            versity Presses, c1985.         │
                    │              vi, 322 p.; 24 cm.            │
                    │              ISBN 0-8387-5070-2: $34.50    │
                    │            Includes bibliography.          │
                    │            1. Sports--social aspects--     │
                    │            United States--Addresses,       │
```

FIGURE 27.8
A Library of
Congress subject
card

```
                    │            essays, lectures. I. Umphlett,  │
                    │            Wiley, Lee.                     │
                    │                                 83-45967   │
                    │  GV706.5.A441985    306´.483´0973          │
                    └──────────────────────────────────────────┘
```

familiar Dewey decimal system, which files items into large categories
by number. Some large libraries have both systems, having changed
from Dewey to the Library of Congress system at some time in the past. In
any case, it can be fruitful to reserve some of your research time for browsing, since you will almost certainly find some materials on the shelf that
are of interest next to the ones you found through the catalog. The two
common classification systems are outlined here. You may notice that certain subjects aren't clearly included in either system: some fields, such as
computer science, mass communications, and environmental studies,
are newer than the classification systems themselves and so have had to be
fit into other related areas.

LIBRARY OF CONGRESS CLASSIFICATION SYSTEM

A General Works
B Philosophy, Psychology, Religion
C–D Foreign History and
        Topography
E–F America
G Geography, Anthropology,
        Sports and Games
H Social Sciences
J Political Science
K Law
L Education

M Music
N Fine Arts
P Language and Literature
Q Science
R Medicine
S Agriculture and Forestry
T Engineering, Technology
U Military Science
V Naval Science
Z Bibliography and Library
        Science

DEWEY DECIMAL CLASSIFICATION SYSTEM

000–099 General Works
100–199 Philosophy
200–299 Religion
300–399 Social Sciences,
        Government, Customs
400–499 Language

500–599 Natural Sciences
600–699 Applied Sciences
700–799 Fine and Decorative Arts
800–899 Literature
900–999 History, Travel,
        Biography

Consulting Catalogs at Other Libraries.   As more and more colleges and universities make their library catalogs available over the Internet, it has become easier for you to consult your own library's catalog from your home or dorm room. It also is easier for you to consult catalogs at other libraries. As a researcher, you can use these catalogs to find books or other materials that you can obtain through interlibrary loan or that you can borrow by visiting a nearby library. Even if you are not sure you want to obtain materials from another library, searching the catalogs at another library can give you a better idea of the range of materials that might be available should you choose to do so. If you're not sure how to access the online catalog at another library, ask a librarian. You may be able to connect directly to other library catalogs via the Internet. If not, you can sometimes access other catalogs through your own library's catalog.

CONSULTING REFERENCE MATERIALS

In any college library the reference collection contains an amazing array of resources. It can be both a good place to start a project, where you can quickly familiarize yourself with a topic, and a place to fine-tune your research by filling in the details of definitions, dates, statistics, or facts. If you are wondering what reference sources relate to your topic, you might want to look at the *Guide to Reference Books*, a directory of sources arranged by discipline. Or you might simply start at the reference desk (or desks, if your library has more than one reference area) and ask the librarian what the reference collection offers on your general topic. Librarians know the library's collection thoroughly and keep up with new publications more effectively than any published guide can hope to do.

Certain basic reference books are worth knowing about for almost any research project. This brief introduction can help you start exploring the reference shelves.

Encyclopedias.   An encyclopedia can give you an overview of your subject and may be especially valuable when you are first casting around for a topic. But when you start investigating more deeply, you will need to go to other sources as well.

General encyclopedias are written for readers who aren't specialists, who want an overview of a topic, or who want some fact they are missing. The *New Encyclopaedia Britannica* is the largest general encyclopedia on the shelves. Because the articles are written by experts, the information is authoritative, and bibliographies are included to point readers to the most important sources for further research. Other general encyclopedias, such as the *Encyclopedia Americana*, can also provide background material quickly. Encyclopedias generally have an index volume and cross-references to help you find what you need to know. Some colleges have access to a computerized version of the *Britannica* in the library or on the campus network.

Specialized encylopedias cover a field of study in much greater depth than general encyclopedias do. You might want to supplement your background reading by consulting one of these works, which often have useful bibliographies of related sources. The following sampling of titles gives you a notion of the variety of specialized encyclopedias:

Dictionary of American History
Encylopedia of Human Biology
Encylopedia of Psychology
Encylopedia of Sociology
Encylopedia of the American Constitution
Encylopedia of World Cultures
McGraw-Hill Encyclopedia of Science and Technology
New Grove Dictionary of Music and Musicians

Some topics are too new or too controversial to be covered in encylopedias. One source that provides overviews of such topics is *CQ Researcher* (formerly called *Editorial Research Reports*). Current topics are covered in magazine-style format, with annual volumes published each year.

Dictionaries. In addition to desk dictionaries like those most college students own, libraries have a variety of large and specialized dictionaries. You'll find dictionaries covering foreign languages, abbreviations, slang, and regionalisms as well as dictionaries for the specialized terminology in a particular field, such as *Black's Law Dictionary*, *Stedman's Medical Dictionary*, or the *Oxford Dictionary of Natural History*. Libraries often have unabridged dictionaries available on dictionary stands, where you can find the most obscure words currently in use and learn what they mean as well as how to pronounce them.

The largest dictionary in any language is the monumental *Oxford English Dictionary* (*OED*), now in its second edition. Its twenty volumes fill a shelf or more and in some libraries are available in a computerized version. It is primarily a historical dictionary that defines each word, tells how the word was used from its earliest appearance in the language to the present, and gives many examples of its use through history. (See Figure 27.9 for a sample entry.) If you simply want a definition, you may find that this source gives you too much information — the entry for the word *play*, for example, fills ten pages — but if you want to establish the significance of a key word in your research, you'll find all the evidence you need here. One student, writing a paper on pollution in the environment, looked up the word *pollution* in the *OED* and as a result was able to reinvigorate the contemporary meaning of the word with earlier meanings of shame and sin. Anytime you ever want to unpack a word and demonstrate its multiple meanings or subtle changes in its interpretation over time, the *Oxford English Dictionary* will help.

sla·pstick. orig. *U.S.* Also **slap-stick.** [f. SLAP *v.*¹ + STICK *sb.*¹] **1.** Two flat pieces of wood joined together at one end, used to produce a loud slapping noise; *spec.* such a device used in pantomime and low comedy to make a great noise with the pretence of dealing a heavy blow (see also quot. 1950).

1896 *N.Y. Dramatic News* 4 July 9/3 What a relief, truly, from the slap-sticks, rough-and-tumble comedy couples abounding in the variety ranks. **1907** *Weekly Budget* 19 Oct. 1/2 The special officer in the gallery, armed with a 'slap-stick', the customary weapon in American theatre galleries, made himself very officious amongst the small boys. **1925** M. W. DISHER *Clowns & Pantomimes* 13 What has caused the playgoers' sudden callousness? The slapstick. Towards the end of the seventeenth century Arlequin had introduced into England the double-lath of castigation, which made the maximum amount of noise with the minimum of injury. **1937** M. COVARRUBIAS *Island of Bali* iv. 77 Life-size scarecrows are erected, but soon the birds become familiar with them... Then watchmen circulate among the fields beating bamboo drums and cracking loud bamboo slap-sticks. **1950** *Sun* (Baltimore) 10 Apr. 3/1 The 50-year-old clown..said that when he bent over another funnyman accidentally hit him with the wrong side of a slap-stick. He explained that a slap-stick contains a blank ·38-caliber cartridge on one side to make a bang. **2. a.** *attrib.* passing into *adj.* Of or pertaining to a slapstick; of or reminiscent of knock-about comedy.

1906 *N.Y. Even. Post* 25 Oct. 10 It required all the untiring efforts of an industrious 'slap-stick' coterie..to keep the enthusiasm up to a respectable degree. **1914** *Photoplay* Sept. 91 (*heading*) Making slap-stick comedy.

1923 *Weekly Dispatch* 4 Mar. 9 He likes good comedies.. but thinks the slapstick ones ridiculous. **1928** *Daily Sketch* 7 Aug. 4/3 The jokes..are rapier-like in their keenness, not the usual rolling-pin or slapstick form of humour. **1936** W. HOLTBY *South Riding* IV. v. 258 She took a one-and-threepenny ticket, sat in comfort, and watched a Mickey Mouse film, a slapstick comedy, and the tragedy of Greta Garbo acting Mata Hari. **1944** [see *POCHO]. **1962** A. NISBETT *Technique Sound Studio* x. 173 Decidedly unobvious effects, such as the cork-and-resin 'creak' or the hinged slapstick 'whip'. **1977** R. L. WOLFF *Gains & Losses* II. iv. 296 The prevailing tone of the book is highly satirical, with strong overtones of slapstick farce.

b. *absol.* Knockabout comedy or humour, farce, horseplay.

1926 *Amer. Speech* I. 437/2 *Slap-stick*, low comedy in its simplest form. Named from the double paddles formerly used by circus clowns to beat each other. **1930** *Publishers' Weekly* 25 Jan. 420/2 The slapstick of 1929 was often exciting. The Joan Lowell episode was regarded as exposing the gullibility of the critics... The popularity of 'The Specialist' made the whole book business look cockeyed. **1955** *Times* 6 June 9/1 A comic parson (Mr. Noel Howlett) is added for good measure, mainly to play on the piano while other people crawl under it. Even on the level of slapstick the farce seemed to keep in motion with some difficulty and raised but moderate laughter. **1967** M. KENYON *Whole Hog* xxv. 253 A contest which had promised..to be short and cruel, had become slapstick. **1976** *Oxf. Compan. Film* 640/1 As it developed in the decade 1910–20..slapstick depended on frenzied, often disorganized, motion that increased in tempo as visual gags proliferated.

FIGURE 27.9   Entry from the *Oxford English Dictionary*, Second Edition.

Handbooks and Companions.   Between dictionaries and encyclopedias lies a species of reference book in which you will find concise surveys of terms and topics relating to a specific subject. The articles are generally longer than dictionary entries but more concise than those found in encyclopedias. Check with a reference librarian to see if specialized handbooks are available for your topic. The following list gives an idea of the variety available:

> *Blackwell Encyclopaedia of Political Thought*
> *Bloomsbury Guide to Women's Literature*
> *Dictionary of the Vietnam War*
> *Halliwell's Filmgoer's Companion*
> *Oxford Companion to English Literature*

Statistical Sources.   For some research, numbers are an essential type of evidence. Many sources for statistics are available in the library. Perhaps the most useful single compilation is the *Statistical Abstract of the United States,* a small volume that contains hundreds of tables of numbers relating to population, social issues, economics, and so on. For public opinion statistics, consult the surveys conducted by the Gallup Poll, published in annual volumes and in a monthly magazine format. The federal government collects an extraordinary amount of statistical data and has recently been releasing much of the data on the World Wide Web at <http://www.census.gov>. If you need more detailed statistics than those available in the *Statistical Abstract,* see if your library has the *U.S. Census of Population and Housing* or *USA Counties* on

CD-ROM. Two other popular sources of statistical information, especially for economic topics, are the *National Trade Data Bank* and the *National Economic Social and Environmental Data Bank,* put out by the U.S. Commerce Department on CD-ROM.

Atlases and Gazetteers.   If your research has a geographical angle, maps and atlases may come into play. In addition to atlases of countries, regions, and the world, there are atlases that cover history, natural resources, ethnic groups, and many other special topics. Gazetteers list place names and give basic information about them, including their location. The *Columbia Lippincott Gazetteer of the World* is one published gazetteer of note. The Geographic Name Server on the Internet at <http://www.census.gov/cgi-bin/gazetteer> gives the precise latitude and longitude of places that you can search for by name.

Biographical Sources.   Directories that list basic information — degrees, work history, honors, addresses — for prominent people include *Who's Who in the United States, Who's Who in Politics,* and *American Men and Women of Science.* For more detailed biographical sketches, try *Contemporary Biography, Contemporary Authors,* or *Politics in America* for elected officials. Several biographical sources contain substantial entries of people who have died: prominent Americans are covered in *The Dictionary of American Biography,* British figures in *The Dictionary of National Biography,* and scientists from all countries and periods in *The Dictionary of Scientific Biography.* To help you locate biographical sources, you can use tools such as *Biography Index* and the *Biographical and Genealogical Master Index.*

CONSULTING PERIODICAL INDEXES AND BIBLIOGRAPHIES

Sometimes students head straight to the catalog and try to find all of their research sources there. Frequently they are disappointed: they may find that the books are too old or that nothing is listed on their specific topic. If this happens to you, you may be looking in the wrong place. Often more information on certain topics — particularly current ones — is published in periodicals than in books. Periodicals are journals, magazines, newspapers, and other publications that are issued at regular intervals. Several indexes — print and electronic — exist to help you locate articles in periodicals. Another option is to use a bibliography (a list of sources on a particular topic) to lead you to relevant sources. Often you will find sources in bibliographies that you would never have thought to look up in a catalog.

Periodical Indexes.   An index is a guide to the material published within other works. In a periodical index, you'll find every article — listed alphabetically by author, title, and subject — for the periodicals and the period covered by the index. The index also includes the source information you'll need to find each article, usually the periodical title, issue number, and page numbers. Indexes are available in print and in electronic form. Electronic indexes — often referred to as *periodical databases* — usually include more information on each article than an index does, such as a short summary.

Electronic indexes, like other databases, are organized as a series of records — or entries on a particular item, such as a newspaper or journal article — that can be searched for and displayed. In many cases, electronic indexes complement or even replace information found in print indexes. For instance, indexes such as *MLA Online, ERIC*, and *PsycLit* are available in both print and electronic forms. Because of the relative ease of searching for information electronically, however, most researchers turn first to the electronic versions to locate information.

Electronic indexes can be stored on CD-ROM, on the Internet, or on commercial sites that are accessible only if your library has a subscription. In some cases, you can access an electronic index only from a computer workstation in your library. In other cases, indexes are available on your campus network or on the Internet. If you have any questions about how to access a particular database, ask a reference or subject-area librarian for help.

Each periodical index includes entries on a specific collection of periodicals, so finding the right article is largely a matter of finding the right index. Before you start looking through a periodical index, ask yourself these questions:

Is my subject covered in this index? Some indexes cover a very specific subject area in depth, and others are more broadly focused.

Does it cover the time period I'm interested in? Most electronic indexes cover only recent publications — no earlier than 1980 — and may not help if you are looking for anything older.

Does it cover articles written for an expert audience or a more general audience? Some indexes focus on highly technical research and scholarship; others lead to articles written for a nonspecialist audience.

Several common indexes can help you if you're looking for magazine or newspaper articles addressed to the general population. The *Readers' Guide to Periodical Literature* is this type of index and is available in print, on CD-ROM, and online. (See Figure 27.10 for sample entries.) The printed version is a good choice if you are doing any historical work. Because it started publication in 1900, you can use older volumes to locate popular press coverage of events happening at any time in the twentieth century — for example, articles about the bombing of Pearl Harbor published days after it happened. The index to the *New York Times* can help you track down that newspaper's coverage of events. Since it goes back to 1851, it is great for historical research. (See Figure 27.11 for a sample entry.) Another popular index is *InfoTrac*, a computerized resource that emphasizes materials written for a fairly general audience. (See Figure 27.12 for a sample entry.)

SPORTS
> *See also*
> Athletes
> Coed sports
> College athletics
> Discrimination in sports
> Gymnastics
> Physical education and training
> Sex discrimination in sports
> Television broadcasting—Sports
> Track and field athletics
> Women—Sports
> > *See also* names of sports
> Ahead of the game [workout tips for the weekend athlete]
> M. Jannot. ii *Men's Health* v9 p42-9 Ap '94
> > **Accidents and injuries**
> > *See also*
> > Automobile racing—Accidents and injuries
> > Football, Professional—Accidents and injuries
> > Running—Accidents and injuries
> The 10 most common sports injuries. M. Fuerst. il
> *American Health* v13 p66-70 O '94

FIGURE 27.10   Entries from the *Readers' Guide to Periodical Literature*

Many libraries also subscribe to *NewsBank*, an index to newspapers that draws on more than five hundred local U.S. newspapers. Updated monthly, *NewsBank* is available both in print and on CD-ROM for computer searching. Your library may have an index to a local newspaper, which can help you track issues that have special importance in your area. Some computerized indexes include abstracts or even the full text of the articles, which you can print out or download for later use.

If you are looking for articles that are aimed at a more specialized audience and provide more analysis than those found in popular magazines, try the *Humanities Index*, the *Social Sciences Index*, the *General Science Index*, the *Business Periodicals Index*, or *PAIS International*, an index focusing on public affairs. These tools index the most important scholarly journals in the fields covered, but they don't include obscure or highly specialized publications. The articles you are likely to find in these indexes will be fairly long, include footnotes, and be based on and give detailed information about research. These are the kinds of indexes you'll want to use if

> Nearly 20 million children under age of 14 participate in nonschool-related sports teams, according to National Youth Sports Coaches Association; despite their initial enthusiasm, many children end up hating sports they used to love largely because their coaches and parents turn children's playing fields into battlefields; Rick Wolff, author of book on parents and children's sports, says adults often destroy children's passion for sports by overemphasizing importance of winning; photos (M), N 18,C,1:3
>   St John's University will drop nickname 'Redmen' in deference to American Indian sensitivities, although name originated with color of football uniforms (S), N 19,B,10:3
>   William C Rhoden Sports of The Times column discusses work of Garry Mendez in studying Sudden Cardiac Disease among athletes; photo (M), N 23,B,13:1

FIGURE 27.11   Entry from the *New York Times Index*

```
InfoTrac * General Periodical Index  1992-Jan 1995

Heading: GELMAN, DAVID
   13.  I'm not a role model: the exploits of Michael Jordan and Charles
        Barkley have stirred a debate about just what pro athletes owe their
        fans. Are kids really that naive? by David Gelman il v121 Newsweek June
        28 '93 p56(2)
          69G0321                                                    71Z1586
        ABSTRACT / HEADINGS
   13.  I'm not a role model: the exploits of Michael Jordan and Charles
        Barkley have stirred a debate about just what pro athletes owe their
        fans. Are kids really that naive? by David Gelman il v121 Newsweek June
        28 '93 p56(2)
          69G0321                                                    71Z1586
        ABSTRACT / HEADINGS
ABSTRACT (6 lines)
  Barkley sparked a debate about the responsibility of professional athletes
for setting examples of appropriate conduct for young fans when he claimed
he was not a role model in a television commercial. The influence of
celebrity athletes on children is discussed.
  -END-
```

FIGURE 27.12   Entry from *InfoTrac* index

you are looking for literary criticism, research on social issues, or scientific or medical research that is only summarized or reported in the popular press.

Bibliographies.   Another way to find good research sources is to take advantage of the research other people have already done on your subject. Bibliographies are lists of sources on particular topics. Researchers compile them after completing their research, and they publish them so that other researchers (including you) won't have to duplicate their work. Bibliographies can give citations for a wide variety of materials — including not only books and articles but also films, manuscripts, letters, government documents, and pamphlets — and they will probably lead you to sources that you wouldn't otherwise find. Remember, though, that a bibliography is not a specialized version of your library catalog: not all the sources will be available in your library or even available through interlibrary loan.

Sometimes you may be able to locate a book-length bibliography on your subject. For example, *Essential Shakespeare* is a bibliography that lists the best books and articles published on each of Shakespeare's works, a wonderful shortcut if you're looking for worthwhile criticism. To find a book-length bibliography in a computerized library, add the word *bibliography* to a subject or keyword search (see p. 684). If you're lucky, such a bibliography will include annotations that describe and evaluate each source.

If there aren't any book-length bibliographies devoted to your subject, you can still take advantage of the work that other researchers have done. Every time you find a good book or article, look at the sources the author draws on; some of these sources may be useful to you, too. An author may record his or her source information in several different places and formats.

A full-length book may have a section labeled "Bibliography" at the back or perhaps a section called "For Further Reading." If the author has quoted or referred to other works, look for a list called "References" or "Works Cited" at the end of the work. If the book or article uses footnotes or endnotes, be sure to check those, too, for possible leads.

How do you find books and articles based on their citations in bibliographies? If the citation gives an author, title, place, publisher, and date, you can search the library catalog by author or title. If a citation lists an author, an article title, the name of a journal, a volume, date, and pages, find out if your library subscribes to that journal, and then look for the particular issue that has the article cited. Some citations are hybrids: they give an author and article title, but instead of journal information, the rest of the citation contains book information. Such a citation refers to an essay published in a collection of essays. In this case you would search the book catalog by the title of the collection and not by the author or title of the essay. If you are having trouble, a librarian can help you interpret a citation and determine whether the source is available in the library or through interlibrary loan. Once you start to use the clues provided in bibliographies and footnotes, those obscure rules you follow for citing sources in your own work begin to make more sense.

USING OTHER LIBRARY RESOURCES

Microform Reference Resources.   Most libraries have some of their resources available on microfilm or microfiche. This technology puts a large amount of printed material — for example, two weeks' worth of the *New York Times* — on a durable strip of film that fits into a small box or on a set of plastic sheets the size of index cards. Machines are used to read microfilm or microfiche, and in many cases full-sized copies of pages can be printed out.

In addition to newspapers and magazines, many libraries have other primary-source material in microform format. For example, the *American Culture Series* reproduces books and pamphlets published between 1493 and 1875 and includes a good subject index. It is one tool for examining colonial-era religious tracts or nineteenth-century abolitionist pamphlets without having to travel to a museum or rare books collection. The *American Women's Diaries* collection reproduces diaries kept by women living in New England and the South and pioneer women traveling west and provides rare first-hand glimpses of the past.

Government Documents.   The federal government of the United States is the most prolific publisher in the world, and, in an effort to make information accessible to citizens all over the country, libraries in many locations serve as depositories for government publications. That is, they are sent a multitude of government publications and, in turn, make them available to the surrounding community. If your college library isn't a depository, there may be one nearby that serves that role. In addition, an increasing number of government documents are available via the World Wide Web.

When most people think of government documents, they think of political information — congressional hearings, presidential papers, and reports from federal agencies — but government documents are not limited to governmental matters. In fact, the government has published something on practically any topic you can think of. The following sampling of government publication titles gives you an idea of what kinds of information you can find:

Ozone Depletion, the Greenhouse Effect, and Climate Change

Placement of School Children with Acquired Immune Deficiency

Policy Implications of U.S. Involvement in Bosnia

Small Business and the International Economy

Strengthening Support and Recruitment of Women and Minorities to Positions in Education Administration

Violence on Television

There are several indexes to government documents, and some are computerized. Among them are the *Monthly Catalog of United States Government Documents,* the most complete index to federal documents; the *CIS Index,* which specializes in congressional documents and includes a handy legislative history index; and the *American Statistical Index,* a detailed index to statistics in government publications. Some large series, like the *Congressional Record,* which reports what happens in Congress each day during each session, have indexes of their own.

Many government publications are now being released on CD-ROM. These make information, particularly statistical data, easier to find than ever before. You can print out a detailed population profile of your hometown, including age groups, income, education level, and ethnic origins, using the *Census on CD-ROM.* You can find *Country Reports on Human Rights Practices, U.S. Industrial Outlook,* and *The Year in Trade* using the *National Trade Data Bank (NTDB).* The *National Economic Social and Environmental Data Bank (NESE)* covers small-business statistics, the cost of pollution abatement programs, regional and state business conditions, and a wealth of other economic data. Every year more and more databases like these are released. If you plan to use government documents in your research, don't be shy about asking a librarian for help. The documents can be difficult to locate on the shelves, and since new computerized sources are coming out all the time, it's wise to get an expert on your side.

Pamphlets and Annual Reports.   When journalists need information, they typically use the telephone to make contact with sources who can send them useful publications. You too can receive pamphlets, brochures, reports, and annual reports by calling organizations or companies directly. The *Encyclopedia of Associations* categorizes organizations by name and subject. For government agencies, try the *United States Government Manual.*

Your library may have already done some of the legwork for you. Many libraries maintain a vertical file in which you can find pamphlets organized by subject. Be sure to evaluate information from such sources: annual reports tend to paint a glowing picture of the companies they cover, and organizations advocating particular points of view tend to present their information in persuasive terms that favor their position.

Interlibrary Loan.   If your library does not have some of the materials that you need for your research project, consider using interlibrary loan. Interlibrary loan allows you to obtain materials from other libraries without having to travel to them. Typically, libraries have an interlibrary loan desk where you can learn how to fill out a request form — either on paper or on a computer.

At some colleges and universities, you can make interlibrary loan requests from a computer in your home or dorm room or from a computer lab. If you've been using a library catalog at another university or college, you may have found materials there that your own library does not have. You can request those materials through interlibrary loan.

Librarians.   One of the most overlooked resources in the library is its staff. Librarians know the library more thoroughly than anyone else. Because they are constantly working with its catalog, reference books, and databases, they are aware of new additions to the library's collections, sometimes even before those materials are entered into the catalog. If you need help locating materials or want to learn how to use the library catalog on a particular database, consult a librarian. They are the most valuable resource available to you.

Finding Sources on the Internet

The Internet contains a startling amount of information — and this amount is growing rapidly. The number of sites on the World Wide Web alone is growing at a phenomenal rate, with most sites containing dozens or hundreds of pages of information, and some sites containing hundreds of thousands of pages. And the World Wide Web is only *part* of the Internet. You can find information in tens of thousands of newsgroups and mailing lists. You can search for information using Gopher, an information distribution system that predates the World Wide Web. And you can use the Internet to interact with other people via electronic mail and real-time discussions.

After Mark Sanchez had spent some time conducting research in his college library, he decided to expand his search to the Internet. He had found some useful sources on the Internet during his overview of his topic and his preliminary search. The Bent County Web site at <http://www.ruralnet.net/~csn/government/bent.html> provided insights into the current social and economic context of the area his parents and grandparents had lived in. Now he returned to the Internet, hoping to find additional information that could help him answer the question "How has my identity been shaped by my family's roots on the plains of southeastern Colorado?"

UNDERSTANDING THE INTERNET

The Internet—a network of computers connected by telephone lines, high-speed fiber-optic networks, microwave relays, and satellite links—was developed by the United States government to maintain communication across the nation in the case of a national emergency, such as a nuclear war or widespread natural disasters. For many years, its primary users were government officials, scientists in colleges and universities, and the military. Over the past decade, however, the Internet has become an increasingly important part of daily life. Today, people use the Internet to send electronic mail to relatives, friends, and co-workers, to learn about and purchase goods and services, to keep up with the latest news in a variety of fields, and to participate in online communities that cross state and national boundaries.

A few years ago, most instructors advised their students to be wary of information found on the Internet. In the early days of the World Wide Web, for instance, relatively little information was available that could help students with their research projects. That has changed, however. Today an increasing amount of high-quality information is available on the Internet—although inaccurate and biased information certainly continues to be published there. Major newspapers and magazines, such as the *New York Times* and *Newsweek*, are publishing on the Internet, as are a growing number of state and government agencies. Similarly, academic journals are springing up all over the World Wide Web, and many print journals are publishing their back issues on the Internet. In addition, a growing number of libraries and museums are providing online access to their collections. If you are interested in the Dead Sea Scrolls, for instance, you can use the Internet to view photos, read documents, and even watch videos about the scrolls. If you want to read about or view photographs of art in the Louvre, you can also find it on the Internet.

Unfortunately, because of the sheer bulk of information on the Internet, searching for materials that are relevant to your topic can be both too easy and too difficult. Searches of the World Wide Web's Yahoo! search site for the keywords *zel* and *miffle*, for instance, produced four and nine items, respectively. You can find almost anything you want on the Internet, even when you're using nonsense words. On the other hand, finding information that is actually useful can be a time-consuming process, just as it is in library and field research. As in those two forms of research, understanding a few basic principles can help a great deal.

When Mark Sanchez began to conduct research on the Internet, he was familiar with some basic search techniques. He knew that you could search for keywords and that you could search for phrases. But he was unaware of some of the advanced techniques that could help him refine his search, such as using wildcard symbols, using Boolean search terms, and limiting searches by publication information. By consulting the online help on some of the popular search sites on the World Wide Web, however, he gained an understanding of how to use these techniques. Soon he was able to carry out searches that were producing higher percentages of sources that appeared relevant to his research question. Given his research interests, the majority of his research efforts on the Internet focused on the World Wide Web. But he also spent some time conducting some searches on Gopher and looking through some of the newsgroups and mailing lists dealing with Chicano culture and history.

You should be aware that information on the Internet generally is not subject to the careful review that is given to most information available through your library. That said, you still can find a great deal of useful information on the Internet. The key issues are knowing where and how to look for information and how to evaluate it once you've found it. In this section, we talk about locating information. In the next chapter, we discuss how to evaluate it.

SEARCHING THE WORLD WIDE WEB

Many people think of the World Wide Web and the Internet as the same thing. But the Web is actually only part of the Internet. What distinguishes information on the Web from other information on the Internet is the way it is formatted. Web pages can be read on virtually any kind of computer that can access the Internet. Bold text or tables, for instance, can be displayed as easily on a Macintosh computer as on a Windows computer or a UNIX workstation. Similarly, computers can read and follow the links between documents on the Web, making it possible for documents to be linked to each other — the characteristic that gives the Web its name. You can use a computer in Dallas, for instance, to read a document stored on a computer in Toronto. By clicking on a link, you can read a document or view a graphic stored on a computer in Zurich or Tel Aviv or Hong Kong.

Web pages are read using programs called *Web browsers*, which are much like word processors. You can open Web pages, search for text on the pages, copy text from them, print them, and save them to your own computer. Most Web browsers, such as Netscape Navigator and Microsoft Internet Explorer, contain built-in electronic mail programs, newsgroup readers, and conferencing software, so that you can converse with other members of the Internet community.

Every page on the World Wide Web has an Internet address, technically known as a *Uniform Resource Locator*, or *URL*. URLs identify the kind of document that is being read, the computer on which the page is stored, the location of the page on the computer, and the name of the file containing the page. The URL of the Web site for Bent County, which Sanchez found on the Web, is <http://www.ruralnet.net/~csn/government/bent.html>. In this URL, *http://* indicates that the page is a Web page, *www.ruralnet.net* is the name of the computer on which the page is stored, *~csn/government/* is the name of the directory in which the file containing the page is located, and *bent.html* is the name of the file containing the page. The *.net* extension on the end of the name of the computer indicates that the computer is in the Internet domain that supports the infrastructure of the Internet. Other domains include .gov (government), .edu (education), .com (commercial), and .org (typically nonprofit organizations but also other organizations that don't fit into the .gov, .com, .net, and .edu domains).

Conducting Searches of the Web.   Searching the Web is similar to searching library catalogs and databases. Sanchez's initial keyword search produced several thousand Web sites that contained the words *history* and/or *Colorado*. Unlike the library catalog or a database, which produce lists of results containing publication and other information about books, periodicals, or government documents, the list produced by the Web search site was live: to read a Web site, Sanchez had only to click on its name in the list.

Unfortunately, Sanchez quickly saw that his search had not produced the kinds of results he had hoped for. It would take hours just to scroll through the list, let alone visit the sites that seemed promising. On top of that, most of the sites he saw in the first few pages of his list were less than promising.

Sanchez decided to try a different tack. Lycos is a *Web index*, which is similar in function to a database or library catalog. Web indexes contain millions of records on Internet sites, much as a database or library catalog contains records on books, periodicals, government documents, or other materials that might be found in a library. By searching an index, he was searching virtually the entire Internet (or at least the part that Lycos had so far found and cataloged) for every site that contained the words *history* and *Colorado*. Instead of working with Lycos, he decided to try Yahoo!, which is a *Web directory*. A *Web directory* contains information that is organized into categories and subcategories. Like Lycos, you can search Yahoo! for all entries that contain a particular set of keywords. But you can also narrow your search by focusing only on entries that belong to particular directories. For instance, Sanchez first tried to look in the directory called Society and Culture. Then he clicked on the subdirectory Cultures and Groups and then on one of its subdirectories — People of Color. The entries he found in this subdirectory were not promising, however, so he returned to the Cultures and Groups subdirectory and checked out some of its other subdirectories.

It didn't take Sanchez long to see that he wouldn't find the information he was seeking in the Society and Culture directory. He returned to the home page of Yahoo! and clicked on another directory, Regional, and then on its subdirectories U.S. States and Colorado. When he was in the directory, he conducted a keyword search for *history*, limiting his search only to those entries classified under the heading Colorado. His search and results are shown in Figures 27.13 and 27.14.

Sanchez found five directories on Yahoo! that dealt in some way with history in Colorado. In addition, he found thirty-two Web sites that appeared to address this topic. This was still more than he cared to examine, but it gave him hope. He decided to check out one of the Web sites, the *Colorado History Page*, but he couldn't find the site at the address listed by Yahoo! He tried some of the other sites listed on his search but still didn't find what he was looking for.

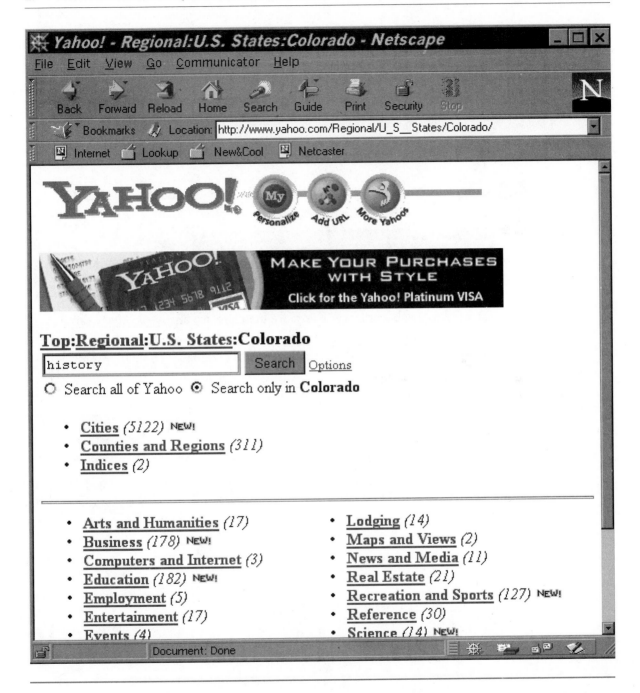

FIGURE 27.13   Sanchez's search for *history* in Yahoo!'s directory, Regional: U.S. States: Colorado

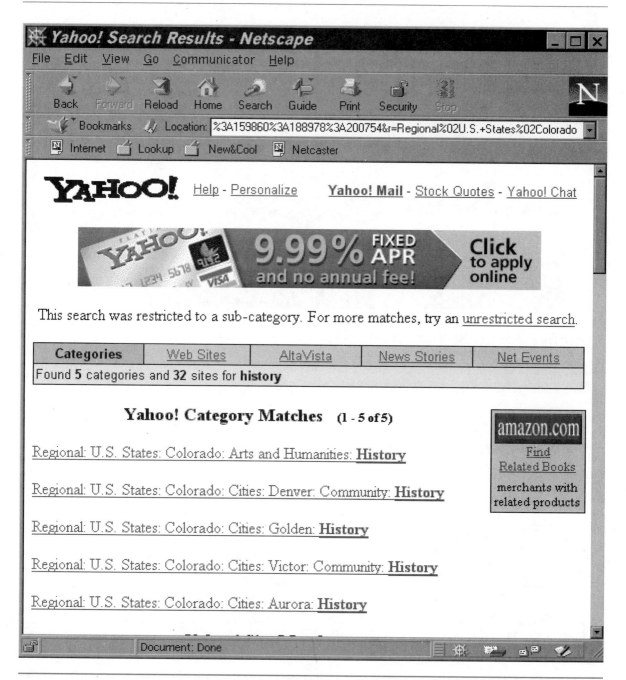

FIGURE 27.14   Results of Sanchez's search on Yahoo!

Sanchez was growing frustrated. He had run into one of the fundamental obstacles to searching for information on the Internet. When you limit your search simply to keywords and broad general categories, you may be overwhelmed with information that is not directly relevant to your topic. In some cases, of course, a keyword search is ideal. If you search for a highly specialized topic, such as interval training for distance runners, you can usually find information that is relevant to your topic. Searches for more general topics however — such as the history of a particular ethnic group in America or even in a single state — can produce seemingly endless lists of results.

Using the Systematic Browsing Technique.   In addition to using Web search sites, researchers can also take advantage of the very nature of the Web to conduct systematic searches. Many sites on the Web are compiled by specialists or people interested in a particular subject area. These sites often contain *links* — comprehensive lists of related sites. Using one of these sites as a starting point, you can often locate a large number of sites that contain information relevant to your research project. These sites, in turn, often contain their own lists of related Web pages. When you exhaust the possibilities in one area, you can return to your starting point (usually by using the Back button or the Go menu on your browser) to begin searching another set of related Web pages. In this way, you can take advantage of the work of others who have pursued their interests in a topic that you want to learn more about.

WRITING WITH A COMPUTER

Leading Internet Search Sites

Web search sites can be categorized into those that are primarily indexes and those that are primarily directories. Web indexes and directories have much in common: they are databases containing millions of records on Internet sites, and they can be searched using a variety of advanced techniques. They differ, however, in the way they organize information. Web indexes simply compile a growing number of records. Web directories, in contrast, organize those records into categories and subcategories.

WEB INDEXES
AltaVista <http://www.altavista.digital.com>
Excite <http://www.excite.com>
HotBot <http://www.hotbot.com>
InfoSeek <http://www.infoseek.com>
Lycos <http://www.lycos.com>
Open Text Index <http://index.opentext.net>

WEB DIRECTORIES
Magellan <http://www.mckinley.com>
WebCrawler <http://www.webcrawler.com>
Yahoo! <http://www.yahoo.com>

SEARCHING GOPHER

The World Wide Web makes it easy to view formatted text, full-color graphics, audio, and video on your computer, regardless of where the document is located on the Internet. But the Web is a relatively recent development in the history of the Internet. Before the Web was developed, the easiest way to view information on the Internet was through a system called *Gopher*. Gopher provides a simple interface that allows you to read unformatted (or plain) text documents on computers connected to the Internet. Like the Web, you can use Gopher to move from a file located on one computer to a file located on another. Unlike the Web, you cannot view formatted text, graphics files, or audio or video files on Gopher.

Although the Web has eclipsed Gopher as the method of choice for viewing information on the Internet, you can still find a great deal of useful information only on Gopher. Fortunately, most Web browsers (such as Netscape Navigator and Microsoft Internet Explorer) can easily read information stored on Gopher.

To search Gopher, visit Veronica (<gopher://veronica.scs.unr.edu>), the leading Gopher search site.

SEARCHING NEWSGROUPS AND MAILING LISTS

Newsgroups and mailing lists are among the oldest forms of communication on the Internet. Their goal is similar — to support discussions of particular topics, such as adult education or immigration, among people connected to the Internet.

Newsgroups and mailing lists generate an enormous amount of text each day. Some of these lists contain detailed analyses of issues and events by contributors who range from interested members of the general public to acknowledged experts in a particular field. If you are working on a research project on a current issue or event, consider consulting the archives of newsgroups and mailing lists. To search newsgroup archives, visit the Deja News Web site at <http://www.dejanews.com> or visit Yahoo!'s directory of newsgroups and newsgroup posts. To search for mailing lists dealing with a particular topic, visit the Liszt Web site at <http://www.liszt.com> or the Catalist Web site at <http://www.lsoft.com/catalist.html>.

Most newsgroups and mailing lists do not maintain archives, but you often can find the most recent postings to newsgroups on the Deja News Web site and Yahoo! subject-directory search tool. If you find a mailing list or newsgroup that is of particular interest to you, consider joining the mailing list or subscribing to the newsgroup. Then try to find a *Frequently Asked Questions* file — or *FAQ* — that might direct you to an archive. If you can't find the FAQ or a FAQ doesn't mention an archive, consider posting a message to the newsgroup or mailing list. A polite message asking whether an archive exists is usually answered promptly.

SEARCHING ONLINE DOCUMENT COLLECTIONS

One of the most useful forms of information on the Internet is the online document collection. Online document collections contain electronic versions of printed texts, often classic texts on which the copyright has expired. Analogous to libraries, online document collections are growing in number and scope. One of the most ambitious online document collections is *Project Gutenberg* at <http://www.gutenberg.net>. Other leading sites include the *Etext Archives* at <http://www.etext.org> and the *New Bartleby Digital Library* at <http://www.bartleby.com>.

USING CHAT AND MOOS

One of the most intriguing sources of information on the Internet — but also among the most confusing — is real-time communication. *Chat programs* allow you to type messages to other people and to record your conversations for later review. *Chat channels*, or *rooms*, are devoted to a variety of subjects, ranging from the mundane to the academic to the erotic. People who participate in chat sessions are not required to reveal their identities, so almost anything goes. As a result, you may not obtain the kind of information you expect to find given the title of a particular chat channel.

That said, chat can be a particularly useful source of information. Major news organizations, such as CNN, use chat to interview public figures or industry leaders. These sessions are advertised and attended by hundreds or even thousands of participants. Similarly, major Web search sites, such as Lycos and Yahoo!, host regular chat sessions on topics including entertainment and finance. Yahoo! also provides transcripts of past sessions for your review. (Everyone who attends these public sessions does not contribute to the discussion, fortunately. Most sessions involving public figures and celebrities are moderated.)

MUDs (Multi-User Domains), MUSHes (Multi-User Shared Hallucinations), and MOOs (MUD, Object-Oriented) are similar to chat in that they allow people to communicate with each other by typing messages. However, these environments are best described as textual spaces that typically use architectural metaphors to organize discussions. When you enter a room in a MOO, for instance, you can receive a detailed description of the room and its inhabitants. These virtual spaces are much more welcoming and easy to use than they probably sound. One way to gain a better understanding of MOOs, MUDs, and MUSHes is to check out Yahoo!'s directory, Recreation:Games: Internet Games:MUDs, MUSHes, MOOs, Etc., where you'll find a number of links to information about these online environments. You can also find information on the Web sites for the Netoric Project's General MOO/ MUD Information Page (<http://bsuvc.bsu.edu/~00gjsiering/netoric/moo .html>) and for Diversity University (<telnet//moo.du.org:8888/>).

Finding Sources in the Field

Conducting field research is an important way to collect information. If you enjoy meeting and talking with people and don't mind what news reporters call *legwork*, you will relish the fun and satisfaction of obtaining ideas and information firsthand. Perhaps you will even investigate matters that few researchers have investigated before. Many rich, unprinted sources of ideas and information lie beyond the library and the Internet.

The goal of field research is the same as that of library and Internet research — to gather the information you need to answer your research question and to marshall the evidence you need to present your conclusions persuasively in your research paper. The only difference is where you conduct the research. Far from being at odds with one another — either philosophically or practically — the three research techniques complement one another. In most cases, an assignment that calls for field research will also benefit from library and Internet research — and vice versa. Mark Sanchez, for example, found that the materials he had collected during his searches of the library and the Internet had not given him all the information he needed to answer his research question "How has my sense of identity been shaped by my family's roots on the plains of southeastern Colorado?" For additional insights, he decided to interview members of his extended family and to observe firsthand the area where his family had settled. He also decided to interview some of the people he met while conducting his site visit, as well as some experts in the area — an anthropology professor at his school and an education professor at a nearby university who had published on the topic of Chicano culture. Finally, he considered corresponding via electronic mail with one or two people who had posted messages to the newsgroup <soc.culture.mexican.american>. He had been intrigued by their posts and thought that they might be willing to share their opinions with him.

Field research is often required in upper-level courses. For a term paper in the social sciences, business administration, or engineering, for example, you may be expected to interview people, gather statistics, or conduct a survey. But almost any paper will be enriched by the inclusion of authentic and persuasive field research sources. And you'll almost certainly learn more about your topic by going out into the field and developing firsthand knowledge of it.

Like library and Internet research, field research should be more than a squirreling-up of facts — or else you may end up with a great heap of rotting acorns and no nourishment. Field research has to be the sensitive, intelligent, and critical selection of *meaningful* ideas and information. In the sections that follow, we'll give you more specific suggestions for picking out what is meaningful from what isn't. Right now, it is sufficient to note that you can expect to change your initial hunches while at work in the field. Just as you do while conducting library and Internet research, you'll be exercising your critical thinking skills — sifting evidence, evaluating, drawing conclusions, revising and correcting your early thoughts, and forming clearer, more valid ideas.

A wide range of field research techniques can be used to extend a research paper. In this section, we focus on techniques that have proven most useful for college students.

OBSERVING

An observational visit may well be essential in field research. Sanchez had noticed during his past visits to southeastern Colorado — as well as during family gatherings — that the family farm played a central role in his family's life. But these were impressions and not something he had taken the time to write down or think about in detail. To obtain firsthand evidence that might support his thesis, he decided to visit Las Animas, Colorado, the area in which his family had settled in the 1920s. His firsthand observations supplied authentic details that he could use in his research paper.

Before making an observational visit, review the suggestions we give in Chapter 2. If you decide to observe a setting such as a private business or a school, you will need to make an appointment. As soon as you arrive, identify yourself and your business. Some receptionists will insist on identification. You might ask your instructor for a statement on college letterhead declaring that you are a bona fide student doing field research. Follow-up field trips may be necessary if, while you are writing, you find gaps in your research or if new ideas occur that you need to test by further observation.

Take notes while conducting an observational visit so that you won't forget any important details when it comes time to incorporate your ideas into your paper. In addition to jotting down any interesting facts you learn, record any telling details or sensory impressions.

You may also want to consider using a still camera or a video camera. Even amateur photographs taken in the field may greatly advance your research. Some photographs may illustrate your paper, whereas others may help you remember details while you write. One student of architecture, making a survey of the best-designed buildings in her city, carried a 35 mm camera and photographed each building she intended to describe. A student of sociology, looking into methods used to manage large crowds, found it effective to carry a video camera to a football game. Later, watching a few crowd scenes in slow motion, he felt better able to write lively and accurate accounts of how police officers and stadium guards performed their jobs.

INTERVIEWING

People in all walks of life are often willing, sometimes even eager, to talk to a college student writing a research paper. Many, you may find, will seem flattered by your attention. Interviews — conversations with a purpose — may prove to be your main source of material. Choose your interview subjects carefully. Whenever possible, try to arrange an interview with an expert in the field you are researching. Or if you are researching a particular group of people, interview a typical member of the group, someone who may or may not have any special knowledge of the field but is representative of the group.

Mark Sanchez, for instance, could have chosen to interview a representative member of his extended family. Similarly, he could choose to interview a professor who had studied the history of Hispanics in the American Southwest. Regardless of your interview subject, preparation is central to conducting a good interview. Chapter 3, "Writing from Conversation," offers advice that may come in handy here.

1. Be sure your prospect is willing to be quoted in writing.
2. If you want to tape-record the interview, ask permission of the interviewee.
3. Plan an appointment for a day when the person will have enough time — if possible, an hour — to have a thorough talk with you.
4. Appear promptly, with carefully thought-out questions to ask.
5. Really listen. Let the person open up.
6. Be flexible, and allow the interview to go in unanticipated directions.
7. If a question draws no response, don't persist; just go on to the next question.
8. Make additional notes right after the interview to preserve anything you didn't have time to record during the interview.

Mark Sanchez followed these guidelines in arranging and conducting his interviews. He interviewed two family members, a resident of Las Animas, Colorado, and two professors who had published scholarship on the history and culture of the American Southwest. He spent forty-five minutes to an hour with each interviewee, and each person he interviewed allowed him to tape-record the conversation. (If you want to use a tape recorder, remember to ask permission of the interviewee.)

In an interview, be sure to take notes so that later when you reconstruct events in your paper, your memory of the interview will be accurate. Even if you use a tape recorder, you should take notes. This will allow you to distill the most important information as you interview. In addition to recording important points and quotations, you should record any telling details that might prove useful later — the interviewee's appearance, the setting, the mood, any notable gestures. All of these details will be useful as you work with your sources to write the paper.

For ease of note taking, we suggest you use a small journalistic notebook with a spiral at the top. Because you will be conducting an interview at the same time you're taking notes, use abbreviations as you take notes. At the end of the interview be sure to *confirm all direct quotations.*

For his own guidance, Sanchez first made lists of questions he wanted to ask his two relatives, the Las Animas resident, and the two professors. Sanchez was careful to phrase his questions so that they would not elicit biased responses. He asked his father and grandfather, for instance, questions that would help reveal details from their experiences with the Sanchez family, in particular, and Las Animas, Colorado, in general.

Where did the family live before settling in Colorado?

When did family members move to Colorado?

Why did they move?

What did they do when they got here?

What difficulties did family members face before and after moving to Colorado?

What are some memorable events that have happened to members of the family?

If you can't talk to an expert in person, your next best resource may be a telephone interview. Make a phone appointment for a time convenient for both you and your interviewee. A busy person may not be able to give you a half hour of conversation on the spur of a moment, and it is polite to ask for a time when you may call again. You will waste the person's time (and yours) if you try to wing your interview; have written questions in hand before you dial. Take notes.

Federal regulations, by the way, forbid recording an interview over the phone without notifying the person who is talking that you are recording his or her remarks and without using a recorder connector with a warning device that emits a beep signal every fifteen seconds.

USING QUESTIONNAIRES

Questionnaires, as you know, are part of contemporary life. You probably filled one out the last time you applied for a job or for college. You may have responded to one in *People* or *Glamour* magazine. As a rule, when researching a particular question, professional pollsters, opinion testers, and survey takers survey thousands of individuals who have been chosen to represent a certain segment of society or perhaps a broad range of the populace (diversified in geography, income, ethnic background, and education).

None of the surveys you conduct for this course is going to be this extensive or thorough, and you should generally avoid deriving statistics from your questionnaire responses and generalizing about these figures as if they were unimpeachable facts. It's one thing to say that "many of the students" who filled out a questionnaire on reading habits hadn't read a newspaper in the past month; it's another to claim that this is true of seventy-two percent of the student population at your school — especially when you gave questionnaires to only those who attended the dining hall the day you were there and when half of *those* students just threw their questionnaires into the trash bins. A far more useful and reliable way for you to use questionnaires is to treat them as group interviews: assume that the information you collect from them is representative, use them to build your overall knowledge of the subject, and cull them for interesting or persuasive details or quotations. Use a questionnaire when you want to collect the same type of information from a large number of people, when you're more interested in what a group thinks as a whole than in what a particular individual has to say, or when an interview that would cover all the questions you're interested in is impossible or impractical.

Mark Sanchez could have gathered more information for his research paper by surveying every member of his family and the Las Animas community. However, he did not have time to conduct such a survey before his research paper was due. Figure 27.15 shows what his questionnaire might have looked like. The questions call for short answers that are easy to supply. This questionnaire asks for information revealing the respondent's personal history, income, education, and years of residence in the community. To maintain the anonymity of his respondents, Sanchez would have given each questionnaire a number and not have asked for the respondent's name.

FIGURE 27.15   A questionnaire about life in Las Animas, Colorado

```
                          Questionnaire

Thank you for completing this questionnaire. All information you sup-
ply will be kept strictly confidential.
1. What is your age? _____
2. How long have you lived in the Las Animas area? _____
3. Please indicate your educational background:
   _____ High school graduate
   _____ Community college courses
   _____ Community college graduate
   _____ Four-year college or university graduate
   _____ Master's degree
   _____ Ph.D.
   _____ Professional degree (lawyer, medical doctor, or other profes-
         sion)
   _____ Vocational/technical school graduate
4. Please describe the kind of work you do:

5. Please indicate your annual income:
   _____ Less than $10,000
   _____ Between $10,000 and $20,000
   _____ Between $20,000 and $30,000
   _____ More than $30,000
6. What do you like best about Las Animas and the surrounding area?

7. What do you like least about Las Animas and the surrounding area?

8. How has Las Animas changed during the time you've lived here?

9. In what ways, if any, do you think Las Animas will change in the
   next twenty years?
```

Know Your Purpose. If you think you want to use a survey to gather information for your paper, ask yourself: What am I trying to discover with this questionnaire? Mark Sanchez's questionnaire would deliver good results because it addresses the questions its author wanted answered and it is directed to the people able to answer them. Define the purpose of your questionnaire and then thoughtfully invent questions to fulfill it.

Keep It Simple. Any questionnaire you design has to be one that people are willing to answer. The main point to remember in writing a questionnaire is to make it easy and inviting to fill out. If you make it too complex and time consuming, the recipient will throw it away. Ask questions that call for a check mark in a list of alternative answers, a simple yes or no, or one word or a few words. Ask yourself as you write each question what information you want to acquire with the question. Then read it over to be sure that it is not ambiguous and will elicit the response you are looking for. It's a good idea to ask for just one piece of information per question.

Ask Open Questions When Appropriate. In addition to simple yes/no questions and multiple-choice questions, you might find it worthwhile to add to your questionnaire some open questions—questions that call for short written responses. Although responses to these questions will be difficult to tally and fewer people are likely to respond, their answers might supply you with something worth quoting or might suggest ideas for you to consider when you mull over the findings.

Avoid Slanted Questions. Write unbiased questions that will solicit factual responses. Do not ask, "How religious are you?" Instead ask, "What is your religious affiliation?" and "How often do you attend religious services?" From the responses to the latter two questions, you could report actual numbers and draw logical inferences about the respondents.

Tally Your Responses. When you get back all your questionnaires, sit down and tally the results. It is easy enough to count short answers ("Republican," "Democrat"), but longer answers to open questions ("What is your goal in life?") will need to be summed up in paraphrase and then sorted into rough categories ("To grow rich," "To serve humanity," "To travel," "To save my soul"). By this means, you can count similar replies and accurately measure the extent of a pattern of responses.

CORRESPONDING

Is there a person whose knowledge or opinions you need but who lives too far away to interview? Write him or her a letter or send an electronic mail message. Make it short and polite, send your questionnaire or ask a few pointed questions, and enclose a stamped, self-addressed envelope for a reply. If you are sending an electronic mail (e-mail) message, insert the questions from the questionnaire into the message.

Large corporations, organizations such as the American Red Cross and the National Wildlife Federation, branches of the military and the federal government, and elected officials are accustomed to getting such mail. In fact, many of them employ public relations officers whose duty it is to answer you. Sometimes they will unexpectedly supply you with a bonus — free brochures, press releases, or other material that they think might interest you.

ATTENDING LECTURES, CONFERENCES, ONLINE FORUMS, AND OTHER PUBLIC DISCUSSIONS

Professionals and special-interest groups sometimes convene for a regional or national conference. Such conferences bring together doctors, lawyers, engineers, scientists, librarians, teachers, and assorted people bound together by some mutual concern. These meetings can be fertile sources of fresh ideas for a student researcher.

Often such conferences are open and free to students and the public, but to gain admission to others you might have to preregister and pay a fee. This drawback might discourage a casual researcher, but if your grade depends on material to be discussed at the conference or if you are thinking of a possible career in that profession, you might find it worthwhile to pay the fee. To attend a professional conference and to meet and talk with speakers and fellow attendees can be an excellent way to learn the language of a discipline. You can take notes on the lectures, which are usually given by experts in the field, and thus obtain some firsthand live opinions. You may even be able to ask questions from the audience or corner a speaker or two later for informal talk. You might also want to record information about who attended the lecture or conference, the reaction of the audience, or any other background details that may prove useful in writing your paper.

In addition, you might obtain a copy of the proceedings of the conference — usually a set of all the lectures delivered, sometimes with accompanying commentary. Unfortunately, many proceedings are published months or even years after a conference, but looking in the library for proceedings of past conferences is another useful research technique.

College organizations frequently bring interesting speakers to campus. Check the schedules of events listed on bulletin boards and in your campus newspaper.

Be on the lookout, as well, for online discussions — such as the chat sessions sponsored by Web search engines such as Yahoo! or Web sites such as CNN Online — that are relevant to your research topic (see "Using Chat and MOOs," p. 709). You can participate in the discussion as an observer or perhaps even ask a question. Remember to use your chat program to record the discussion for later review. You can learn how to record a transcript by consulting the program's online help.

Chapter 28

Evaluating Sources and Taking Notes

How do I know if a source is credible?

How can I tell if information is accurate?

What are the best strategies for keeping track of the information I've collected during my library, Internet, and field research?

What can I do to keep thinking critically while I take notes from my sources?

These are some of the questions you are likely to ask as you begin working with the information you collect during library, Internet, and field research. You will quickly find that locating and collecting information are only two of many activities involved in writing a research paper. You also need to think critically about your sources. (For information on critical thinking and reading strategies, see pp. 93–108.) You need to evaluate them, organize those you decide to keep, and explore the ideas, opinions, facts, and beliefs expressed in your sources. Next to sitting down and writing the research paper itself, these activities pose some of the most significant challenges to writers of research papers. Although locating information requires time, patience, and ingenuity, thinking critically about your sources takes even more thought and energy. Among other challenges, you must decide which of your sources are reliable and relevant to your topic and what information from these sources is most useful for your paper.

In this chapter, you will explore strategies for evaluating and organizing information and for taking notes. As you think about the ideas you encounter in this chapter, remember that these strategies are not necessarily step-by-step activities. Instead, you can use them throughout your research and writing processes. Evaluation, for example, is something you'll want to do from start to finish. Similarly, the ability to organize and reorganize information collected at several points during the writing of a research paper, as well as the ability to scrutinize the ideas, facts, and opinions in a growing collection of information, are critical thinking skills that you'll come to value greatly.

Evaluating Sources

If you go into a library or explore the Internet without knowing how to proceed, you might poke around and think, "There's not much here. Maybe I should change my topic." Once you learn how to use research methods and tools effectively, however, you may have the opposite feeling: "How can I possibly handle all of this information?" Remember that not every source you locate will be equally useful to you. Some sources are weakened by poor reasoning, some are invalidated by strong biases, and some are simply irrelevant to your specific research question. Part of the job of conducting research is thinking critically about sources so that you can select the *best* evidence for your purposes.

How do you know what evidence is best? Experienced researchers have developed a range of techniques for carefully evaluating sources from the field, the library, and the Internet. Learning how to evaluate sources can save you a great deal of time and increase the effectiveness of your papers. In this chapter, we explore the key questions that experienced researchers use to evaluate their sources.

WHAT IS THE PURPOSE?

Understanding the purpose of a source will help you determine whether it might be useful for your research project. A general reference source in a library serves a much different purpose than an editorial in a newspaper, an advertisement in a magazine, or a Web site that provides information about a particular product or service. Asking critical questions is crucial: Is the purpose of this source to explain or inform? To persuade? To offer an alternative viewpoint? To sell a product? Understand the intention behind the source to determine whether the source would make solid *evidence* for your claim.

RESEARCH
CHECKLIST

Evaluating Print Sources

- What is the purpose of the publication? Is it to sell a product or service? To inform? To publish new research? To shape opinion about a particular issue or cause?
- Who is the intended audience? Experts in the field or novices? The general public or people with a particular bias? How does this affect the tone and the evidence?
- Who is the author of your source? Is information provided about the author's credentials and profession? Can you detect the author's bias?
- Is it a primary or a secondary source? If it is a secondary source, does it use sound evidence from primary sources? Would you learn more if you looked at the primary source yourself? Is it available?

- What can you tell about the publisher? Have you heard of this publisher before? Does the publication seem reputable and responsible?
- Is the evidence presented in the source reliable, sufficient, and relevant? Does the argument or analysis leave many questions unanswered?
- What is the date of publication? Is the information contained in the document up-to-date?
- Is the information in the source directly relevant to your research question? Why should you use this source rather than others?

WHO IS THE INTENDED AUDIENCE?

Becoming familiar with the intended audience is a key evaluation step. A source written for an audience of experts in a particular field, for example, is likely to contain different kinds of information than one written for a general audience. Sources written for technical experts are likely to assume that readers possess a great deal of background knowledge about the topic. These sources typically skip general treatments of the topic in favor of detailed discussions tailored to experts. In contrast, sources written for general audiences usually provide background information for readers. For example, for your paper on current treatment plans for HIV patients, you might be considering an article from a well-known medical journal that discusses the most favorable chemical composition for an effective protease inhibitor and is written by a physician for other physicians. Instead, you may be better off beginning with a source that defines *protease inhibitor* and discusses how it helps HIV patients. Think about what kinds of sources might be *most* helpful for your project.

SHOULD I TRUST THIS AUTHOR?

Make every effort to learn about the author of a source before you use his or her words to support a key point in your paper. Investigate the author's credentials, discover the institutions or organizations with which he or she is affiliated, and explore, if you can, the author's reputation among his or her peers. Your overall purpose is to make sure that any author you cite is reliable and trustworthy.

Look for author credentials in the introduction or preface to a book or in a biographical note at the beginning or end of a book or article. If you are still in doubt, check whether the author is listed in the library catalog or whether he or she is included in *Who's Who, Contemporary Authors,* or in specialized reference works such as *American Men and Women of Science.* Inclusion in reference works such as these doesn't guarantee absolute trustworthiness but may give you some insights into the author's background. Ultimately, the best measure of someone's authority is whether his or her work meets the critical demands of other authorities. If your instructor knows the field, ask him or her about the author or whether someone else on campus can answer your questions.

Evaluating Internet Sources

- What can you tell about the purpose of your source? If it is a Web site, is it intended to inform? To shape opinion? To sell a product? Is the information in the source intended for a general or a specialized audience? If you are evaluating posts on a newsgroup or mailing list, what do you know about the purpose of the newsgroup or list? Is a FAQ (Frequently Asked Questions) file available?
- Who is the source intended for? The general Web-browsing public? The members of a small mailing list?
- Who is the author of your source? If it is a Web page, is any information provided about the author? Is an electronic mail address provided so that you can contact the author? If it is a post to a newsgroup or mailing list, what can you tell from the author's electronic mail address and signature file, if one is provided?
- If you're evaluating a Web site that is sponsored by an organization, government agency, or corporation, what do you know about the sponsor? Is a bias clearly evident in the material provided on the site? Is this a commercial site that is trying to sell a product or service? Is this a site that pushes a particular issue or political agenda? Is there a way to contact the sponsor to make further inquiries?
- Can you tell when a Web site was created? Can you determine whether it has been updated recently?
- Are assertions based on evidence? Are sources cited? Would you gain anything by looking at the sources yourself?
- Are the sources of information provided on the Web site, newsgroup, or mailing list provided? Is the information consistent with the information found in print sources, other Web sites, newsgroups, or mailing lists? Is the evidence contained within the source sufficient, reliable, and relevant to your topic?

If your source is a weekly news magazine like *Time, Newsweek,* or *U.S. News & World Report,* the writer of an article is likely to be a reporter who may not have a famous name and probably is not a world-renowned authority. Such magazines do, however, feature some articles by experts, and all such magazines have a good reputation for checking their facts carefully and presenting a range of opinions. Be aware, however, that some magazines *select* facts to mirror the opinions of their editors.

Learning about the credentials of authors of information posted on the World Wide Web, on a newsgroup site, or on certain electronic databases can be difficult. Be tenacious. If no credentials are provided, consider sending electronic mail to the author asking about his or her credentials. If you can't find out anything about the author, it is best not to use the information.

Evaluating Field Sources

- Does your source seem biased or prejudiced? If so, is this bias or prejudice so strong that you have to discount some of the source's information?
- Does the information from your source agree with published accounts in print or Internet sources? If not, can you think of a good reason for the disparity?

- Have you compared different people's opinions, accounts, or evidence? In general, the more viewpoints, the better.
- Is any of your evidence *hearsay* — one person telling you the thoughts of another or telling you about comments or actions that he or she hasn't witnessed? If so, can you support or discount your source's view by comparing it with other evidence?
- If an interviewee or questionnaire respondent has told you about past events, has time or predisposition possibly distorted his or her memory?
- If you have tried to question a random sampling of people, do you feel that they are truly representative? If you have tried to question everyone in a group, have you been thorough enough?

If no author is given, as is sometimes the case with newspaper articles and with sites on the World Wide Web, try to identify the sponsoring organization or publisher. If you're working with a print source that doesn't list an author, consider the nature of the publication: Is the article published in a nationally respected newspaper like the *Wall Street Journal* or in a supermarket tabloid? Is the brochure or pamphlet published by an organization recognized as a leader in its field? On a Web site, look for contact information for the organization or publisher. Sometimes you'll find contact information or a disclaimer on the home page or an "About This Site" page.

If you are conducting field research, you can sometimes select the authors of your information. When you are researching the effectiveness of current standards for infant car seats, for example, a personal interview with a local pediatrician will probably produce different information than an interview with a manufacturer's marketing representative. You can also affect the results of your research by distributing a questionnaire to a particular group of people or observing a particular setting.

Consider, as well, whether the author's bias affects how he or she presents information and opinions in the source. A *bias* is a preference for a particular side of an issue. Since the vast majority of authors have an opinion on the topic they are writing about, you shouldn't ask whether an author is biased. Instead, ask whether the bias has resulted in a source that treats one side of an issue more favorably than another. To explore for bias, consider the author's overall viewpoint on the topic. Where are his or her allegiances? Is the bias hidden or stated? Do you need to look for a balancing viewpoint or approach? Having a strong bias does not mean that everything an author has written is invalid. However, if you recognize such biases early on, you will be better prepared to defend your paper from those who want to challenge your analysis or argument.

IS THIS A PRIMARY OR A SECONDARY SOURCE?

A *primary source* is a firsthand account written by an eyewitness or a participant. It contains raw data and immediate impressions. A *secondary source* is an analysis of the information contained in one or more primary sources. For example, primary sources for a large fire caused by a gas leak would include the statements of victims and witnesses, the article written by a journalist who was at the scene, and the report of the fire chief in charge of putting out the blaze. If another journalist used the first journalist's article as background for a story on industrial accidents, or if a historian used any of these sources in a book on urban life in the twentieth century, these resulting works would be secondary sources.

For most research papers, you need to use both primary and secondary sources. Secondary sources aren't necessarily less trustworthy just because they are not firsthand reports. Eyewitnesses can be prejudiced, self-serving, or simply unable to know as much as a later writer who has synthesized many eyewitness accounts. In writing a history paper on the attitudes of American social workers toward World War I, for example, you might quote a primary source — Jane Addams, founder of Chicago's Hull House, who was a pacifist. If you rely only on Addams's words, though, you might get the idea that social workers were unanimously opposed to the war effort. To put Addams's views into perspective, you also need secondary sources that show that most of her peers did not identify with her unpopular pacifism and publicly disagreed with her.

If, however, you find yourself repeatedly citing a fact or authority as it is quoted in someone else's analysis, go to the primary source of the information itself. For example, statistics are often used by those arguing both sides of an issue: often it's only the interpretation that differs. Going back to the original research (the publication of which is a primary source) will help you to learn where the facts end and the interpretation begins.

WHO IS THE PUBLISHER?

Experienced researchers know that the publisher of a source — the person, organization, government agency, or corporation that prints or electronically distributes a source — plays an important role in shaping its content. Like authors, publishers often have a bias about a particular topic or issue. A corporate publisher, such as Microsoft, which publishes information on one of the largest sites on the World Wide Web, is likely to present its own products and services more favorably than those of its competitors. Similarly, political organizations, such as the Democratic Party or the National Rifle Association, are likely to publish sources that contain information that support policies favored by the organization.

As you evaluate a source, ask critical questions about its publisher. If you are reading a Web site, is it a site created for particular commercial purposes, such as selling a product or service? Is it a site devoted to a particular political cause? Is it a site developed by a particular organization or government agency? If you are reading a newsgroup or mailing list, is it a general-interest group or one devoted to a particular cause? If you are reading a book, is the publisher known for publishing works in a specific field or with a specific political agenda? If you are reading a periodical, does it have a predictable point of view? The *Nation*, a magazine of commentary from a politically liberal point of view, is likely to give you a different picture of the world from that found in the *National Review*, a magazine of conservative commentary. Many of these questions are difficult ones for beginning researchers; consult with a librarian at your college library if you need help finding answers.

More than information from any other kinds of sources, information on Web sites and in periodicals is likely to reflect a publisher's bias. To learn about the publisher of a Web site, try to locate a disclaimer, and also look for a link to "Site Information" or "About This Site." If you are visiting a site sponsored by an organization or agency, find out whether a mission statement is provided. To learn more about the general outlook of a periodical, take a moment to skim through it, noting the following:

> *Editorials* In these, the editors, making no pretense of being impartial, set forth their views. In most magazines and newspapers, editorials will appear in a front section and may not be signed, since the names of the editors are on the masthead, near the table of contents. If you can find an editorial commenting on a familiar issue, you can discover the bias of the editors.
>
> *Featured columnists* Usually, a columnist voices opinions that are congenial to a newspaper's or magazine's editors and publishers. But this test isn't foolproof. Sometimes a dissenting columnist is hired to lend variety.
>
> *Lead stories* The lead story is usually the one placed most prominently in an issue; the cover of a magazine often reflects the lead story. If you don't have time to read the whole story, skim the last paragraph, in which the writer often declares the overall message.
>
> *Letters to the editor* You can often deduce the degree of bias of the letter writers, and this can tell you something about the magazine's readers. A periodical's positions aren't always easy to decipher from letters to the editor since many magazines, such as *Time,* strive to offer space to a diversity of opinions.
>
> *Advertisements* Ads are usually a good guide to a magazine's audience. To whom are its editors trying to appeal? The many ads for office copiers, delivery services, hotels, and expensive vacations in *Newsweek,* for instance, tell you that the magazine is trying to appeal to well-educated professionals.

HOW SOUND IS THE EVIDENCE?

The evidence in a source—the information, opinions, and ideas—can tell you a great deal about its reliability and usefulness for your research project. As you evaluate a source, determine whether evidence is carefully put together, complete, and up-to-date. Understand the thesis, if any, and examine whether it is supported by credible evidence. (See p. 101 for more ideas on testing evidence.) Think critically about the argument or analysis: Is it convincing? Also, is there enough evidence in the source to support the claims being made? If the source leaves you with several important questions unanswered, you might do better by looking for another source.

If you are working with a field source, ask yourself similar questions about the evidence that is provided and the credibility of the source. If you are interviewing someone or attending a public lecture, are the responses provided to questions consistent? Does the interviewee or speaker provide evidence to support or corroborate claims? If you are analyzing responses to a questionnaire, have respondents answered your questions consistently, seriously, and honestly? If you are observing a particular event or setting, are people aware that they are being observed? Often, knowing that they are being observed can change people's behavior.

Finally, continue to question whether each of your sources — print, electronic, and field — is relevant to your topic, your thesis, and your claims. An interesting fact or opinion could be just that — interesting. You need the facts, opinions, information, and quotes that relate directly to the purpose and audience of your research paper.

IS THE INFORMATION UP-TO-DATE?

In most cases, you should strive to use the most current sources possible. In most fields, new information and discoveries come out every year, so the evidence in a source needs to be up-to-date or at least still important. If you cite five-year-old procedures for treating AIDS as if they are still used, for example, you'd be wrong. Use older materials only when their value has held up over time or when your research focuses on a particular period earlier than the recent past.

WHAT WILL I GAIN BY USING THIS SOURCE?

Why use one source rather than another? Is the information it contains useful for your purposes as a writer? Does the source contain strong quotations or hard facts that would be effective in your final paper? Is it relevant in terms of the subject matter and in the way it tackles it? For some papers it may be appropriate to use an article from a popular magazine, and for others you may need to cite the research findings published in the scholarly journal on which the magazine article was based. Remember that you're looking for the best possible sources for your particular paper. Always ask yourself not only "Will this do?" but "Would something else be better?"

Consider, as well, how using this source in your paper will affect the future direction of your research. Does it contain information that challenges your assumptions about the topic? Does it present any strong evidence against your position for which you need to find counterevidence? Does it suggest a new direction that might be more interesting to pursue? It's wise to check in with yourself now and again to make sure you have a clear direction — whether it's the same old direction or a completely new one.

Finally, determine whether a source is directly relevant to your research question. It's surprisingly easy to be sidetracked by a persuasive book, article, or Web site on a topic that is only slightly connected to the direction of your research. Such digressions waste your time and energy.

Taking Notes

Now that you've developed a working bibliography, located some promising source material, and checked it to make sure it's reliable and useful, you're ready to begin taking notes to answer your research question. Your notes are an extremely important part of the research process because you will use them to transfer information from the sources to your research paper. The quality of your notes will contribute to the effectiveness of your paper. As you take notes, think critically about the ideas and facts found in the sources. By selecting information and organizing it for later review, you begin analyzing and evaluating that information. Analysis and evaluation are essential aspects of the research process.

TIPS FOR BETTER NOTE TAKING

As you write your notes, record every fact, idea, and quotation that you might eventually want to use. Make sure your notes are complete and accurate: if you sit down to draft your paper and find you've neglected to jot down that memorable phrase by the most authoritative expert in the field and to make a copy of the source, you'll either have to look it up again or write your paper without it. Remember, though, that your notes are where you start to analyze and synthesize your sources, turning them into the building blocks for your paper. If you copy down everything you read, exactly as it was written, you not only waste time but also postpone the inevitable. If you want your paper to be a sound analysis or argument based on a variety of reliable sources (and not just a place to show off how many sources you looked up), then sooner or later you're going to have to sit down and separate the useful nuggets in each source from all the rest. Your research notes are the best place to do that. A good research note includes three elements:

An *identifier*, usually the last name of the author whose work you're citing, followed by the *location* of the information — a page number or numbers, an Internet address, or a field source. (You should already have a source note in your working bibliography for this source, with complete publication information. If not, make one now.)

A *subject heading*, some key word or phrase you make up yourself to help you decide where in your paper the information will best fit.

The *fact, idea, opinion,* or *quotation* you plan to use in your paper.

You'll need all these elements so that later, when it's time to incorporate your notes into your paper or develop your ideas from multiple sources, you'll have an accurate record of what you found in each source. You'll also know exactly where you found it, so you will be able to cite every source without difficulty.

What will you look for in the source? Facts, ideas, and opinions as well as examples and illustrations of the ideas you're pursuing along with evidence to support them — and to refute them. Avoid making the mistake of looking only for information that supports a preconceived notion. Research should be an opportunity to learn more about a topic, to answer an authentic question, not to collect evidence that tells you only what you want to know.

What follows are several tips that have proven useful for college students. Keep in mind that you have already looked over your source at least once to decide whether to take notes on it. Skim it again to be sure and to decide how extensively. Remember, though, that you can't always know the usefulness of a source in advance. Sometimes a likely article turns out to yield nothing much, and a book that seemed to be a juicy plum shrivels to a prune in your hands.

Use a Sensible Format.   Many writers find that using note cards or a word-processing program works better than taking notes on sheets of notebook paper because when the time comes to organize the material they gathered, they can shuffle and reshuffle cards or computerized notes to arrive at an order that makes most sense to them. If you use cards, roomy 4- by 6-inch or 5- by 8-inch cards will hold more than 3- by 5-inch cards. Even a meaty idea ought to fit on one card.

Use One Card per Idea.   Putting two or more ideas on the same card will complicate your task when you reach the organizing and drafting stages. If you use a computer to take notes, separate your entries clearly so you can move them around easily later.

Take Accurate Notes.   Read the entire article or section of a book before beginning to take notes to help you avoid distorting the meaning. Put exact quotations in quotation marks, and take care not to quote something out of context or change the meaning. Double-check all statistics and lists.

Take Thorough Notes.   Many a writer has come to grief by setting down sketchy jottings and trusting memory to fill in the blanks. A good rule is to make your notes and citations full enough so that once they're written, you are totally independent of the source from which they came. That way you'll avoid having to search the Internet trying to locate again that one-in-a-million (literally) site or having to rush back to the library in a panic trying to find again, in a book or periodical you returned weeks ago, some nugget of material you want to include in your paper.

Bristle While You Work.   While reading the material you are collecting, looking at it a little sourly and suspiciously might be to your advantage because it helps you to remain critical. Mary-Claire van Leunen, author of *A Handbook for Scholars* (New York: Knopf, 1978), has advised researchers who must read much scholarly writing: "Do not smile sweetly as you read through pages of graceless, stilted, maundering bombast. Fume, fuss, be angry. Your anger will keep you up to the mark when you turn to writing yourself." This is also good advice for you as a student writer.

Keep Evaluating. As you take notes, continue to evaluate what you read. Decide whether the stuff is going to be greatly valuable, fairly valuable, or only a little bit valuable. Some note takers put a star at the top of any note they assign great value to and a question mark on a note that might or might not be useful. Later, when they're organizing their material, they can see what especially stands out and needs emphasis. Others write a notation to themselves at the bottom of the card.

Know When to Stop. How many notes are enough? When you find that the sources you consult are mostly repeating what you've learned from previous sources — and aren't any more authoritative or credible — you have probably done enough reading and note taking.

AVOIDING PLAGIARISM

You have an obligation to repay the researchers, scholars, and writers who came before you. Therefore, in doing research, you cite your source materials carefully, mentioning the names of all other writers you get information from. You do so not only for quotations you take but also for ideas, even though you have nutshelled or paraphrased them in your own words (see pp. 728–31). If a writer fails to acknowledge all sources or uses another writer's words without quotation marks, he or she has plagiarized, a very serious offense in the academic, business, and industrial communities. The writer is suspected of a theft, when he or she merely failed to make a debt clear. Chapter 30 offers information about how to cite and list sources so that, like any good scholar, you will know exactly how to pay your debts in full.

QUOTING, PARAPHRASING, NUTSHELLING

When it comes time to draft your paper, you will incorporate your source material in a variety of ways — by quoting, transcribing the author's exact words; by paraphrasing, restating the author's ideas fully but in your own words; or by nutshelling, giving a brief summary of the author's main point. Your notes too, should be in these three forms — and the form you pick for any source should be your best guess as to the form you will use in the final paper.

There are two advantages to deciding whether to quote, paraphrase, or nutshell at the note-taking stage. First, it will save you time. A faithful transcription of a long quotation takes much longer than a quick nutshell, so if you know in advance that you intend to use only a nutshell, you might as well save yourself those extra minutes. Second, weighing each source carefully and deciding how to use it — even while you are reading it — is part of reading critically. As we've tried to stress, research should be a dynamic process, with the researcher thinking critically about sources and their usefulness, not just taking the source material at face value and copying it word for word into the paper. You need to always be thinking about how you will use your sources — otherwise, they'll end up using you.

Of course, you won't always make the correct guess. Sometimes you will find, at the drafting stage, that the wonderful quotation that looked so persuasive back when you were taking notes is just run-of-the-mill rhetoric, and you may prefer to nutshell the author's significant ideas and use them as a single supporting point rather than as the focus of an entire paragraph. Still, it's almost always worth the effort to decide at the note-taking stage how you intend to use a particular source. How do you make the decision? Each method has advantages and disadvantages. Here are some things to consider.

Quoting.   Quoting needs to be done sparingly and only when there is a good reason — to add support and authority to your assertions. Some writers of college research papers do much pointless quoting. Mary-Claire van Leunen in *A Handbook for Scholars* gives cogent advice:

> Quote only the quotable. Quote for color; quote for evidence. Otherwise, don't quote. When you are writing well, your sentences should join each other like rows of knitting, each sentence pulling up what went before it, each sentence supporting what comes after. Quotation introduces an alien pattern — someone else's diction, someone else's voice, someone else's links before and afterward. Even necessary quotations are difficult to knit smoothly into your structure.

That quotation, by the way, seems to us worth quoting. Its words are memorable, worth taking to heart.

If you intend to use a direct quotation, copy the quotation carefully, making sure to reproduce the words, spelling, order, and punctuation exactly, even if they're unusual. Go back over what you've written to make sure that you've copied it correctly. *Put quotation marks around the material* so that when you come to include it in your paper, you'll remember that it's a direct quotation. You might also want to remind yourself in a bracketed note that you intend to use the author's words in a quotation. Maria Halloran extracted a lively quotation for the note card shown in Figure 28.1.

Sometimes it doesn't pay to transcribe a quotation word for word. Parts may fail to serve your purpose, such as transitions, parenthetical remarks, and other information useless to you. If you take out one or more words, indicate the omission in your note by using an ellipsis mark (...).

Paraphrasing.   When paraphrasing, you restate an author's ideas in your own words. A good paraphrase retains the organization and emphasis of the original passage and often many of the details — so it isn't usually much shorter than the original. Why paraphrase? It is especially helpful when the language of another writer is not particularly vivid and memorable, but when you feel it necessary to walk your readers through the points made in the original source. (If you just want to convey the essence of the original passage, use nutshelling.) Remember, when you paraphrase you aren't judging or interpreting another writer's ideas — you are simply trying to restate them fairly and accu-

Children and sports   Leonard 140
"...[in organized sports] children may be subject to
intense emotional stress caused by fear and anxiety,
concern about physical safety, and doubts about
performances and outcomes. This anxiety may emerge if
children are ignored, chastised, or made to feel that they
are no good. Scanlan and Passer's study of
preadolescent male soccer players showed that losing
players evidenced more postgame anxiety than winning
players. Children who experience anxiety in sport competition may try to avoid failure by shying away from active
participation, by developing excuses, or by refusing to try
new things." [Good quote!]

FIGURE 28.1
A sample note card
giving a direct quo-
tation from a source

rately. If Maria Halloran had chosen to paraphrase Leonard, her note card
might have looked like Figure 28.2.

When you paraphrase a passage, be careful not to hover so close to the author's own words that your paraphrase is merely an echo. If your source
writes, "In staging an ancient Greek tragedy today, most directors do not mask
the actors," and you write, "Most directors, in staging an ancient Greek play
today, do not mask the actors," your version is too close to the original. Paraphrasing too close to the source is a form of plagiarism—you must express
each thought in your own words. This would be a good paraphrase: "Few contemporary directors of Greek tragedy insist that their actors wear masks."

FIGURE 28.2   Paraphrasing the quotation from Leonard's book (Figure 28.1)

Paraphrase is about
half the length of origi-
nal passage.

Children and sports   Leonard 140

Stress and anxiety on the playing field can result in
children backing away from participating in sports
because they fear rejection if they perform poorly.
This anxiety and stress is a result of the child's
fears of being hurt or not being good enough. A
study by Scanlan and Passer showing that boys
who lose in soccer have more anxiety after losing a
game than boys who win confirms these findings.

Although emphasis of
original is maintained,
word choice and
order have been re-
worked to avoid the
danger of plagiarism.

No interpretation or
evaluation of original
passage is included.

How do you write a good paraphrase? We suggest that you do the following:

1. Read the entire passage through a couple of times.
2. Divide the passage into its most important ideas or points either mentally or by highlighting or annotating the page. Noting three or four points for an average-length paragraph will make the task manageable.
3. Look away from the original source and restate the first idea in your own words. Summarize the support for this idea. Review the section if necessary.
4. Go on to the next idea and follow the same procedure. Continue in this way until you reach the last point.
5. Go back and reread the entire original passage one more time, making sure you've conveyed its ideas faithfully. Revise your paraphrase if necessary.

Nutshelling. Sometimes even a paraphrase of another author's ideas will take more space than you want to spend on it or will cause more disruption to the flow of your own ideas than is necessary. Often it is sufficient to convey the main point of an original source "in a nutshell." Nutshelling, or summarizing, is a way to let your readers know the most important idea or ideas of a passage by restating those ideas in your own words. This can save a lot of space: a page or more of detailed text can often be distilled into one or two succinct sentences. Be careful, though, that in reducing a long passage down to a brief nutshell you do not distort the original author's meaning or emphasis. Your goal should be to convey as faithfully as possible the meaning of the original. If Mark Sanchez had put into nutshell form the essential ideas from his interview with his father about why his family had moved from New Mexico to southeastern Colorado, his note card might have looked like Figure 28.3.

FIGURE 28.3   Nutshelling, or summarizing, a source

Subject heading	*Reasons for moving to Las Animas* *Aaron Sanchez Interview, 3-11-98*	Identifier: person interviewed and date
Terse, even fragmentary, notes convey gist of key point in the interview	*In 1924, my father Octavio and his family (father, mother, four brothers, three sisters) moved to Las Animas because they couldn't make enough money where they were living in New Mexico. The inheritance from his mother's father went to her brothers, and she got nothing. They moved to the Las Animas region, settling in a <u>colonia</u> (labor camp).*	Main points clearly broken out

How do you write a good nutshell? Try this approach:

1. Read the original passage a couple of times.
2. Without looking at it, state the gist of the passage, the point it makes, the main sense as you remember it.
3. Go back and reread the original passage one more time, making sure you've conveyed its ideas faithfully. Revise your nutshell if necessary.

RESEARCH CHECKLIST

Taking Notes

- Do you identify the source (by last name of author or an important word from the title) and the exact page for each research note? Does each note include a subject heading?
- Have you made a bibliography card or note for each new source you discovered during your reading?
- Does each note contain only one idea? Do you avoid lengthy notes?
- Do you retain the meaning of the original so that you are true to the source?
- Do you quote sparingly — only pithy, striking, short passages?
- When you quote, do you quote exactly? Do you use quotation marks around significant words or phrases as well as longer passages from the original sources? Do you use ellipsis marks as needed?
- Do you take most notes in your own words — summarizing or paraphrasing?
- Do you avoid paraphrasing too close to the source?

Chapter 29

Writing the Research Paper

Planning and Drafting

You began gathering material from library, Internet, and field research sources with a question in mind. By now, if your research has been thorough and fruitful, you know the answer. The moment has come to weave together the material you have gathered. We can vouch for two time-proven methods.

The Thesis Method.   Decide what your research has led you to believe. What does it all mean? Sum up that view in a sentence. That sentence is your thesis, the one main idea your paper will demonstrate. (For more advice on composing such a sentence, see p. 378.) You can then start planning and drafting, including only material that supports your thesis, concentrating from beginning to end on making that thesis clear.

The Answer Method.   Some writers have an easier time if they plunge in and start writing without first stating any thesis at all. If you care to try this method, recall your original question, and start writing with the purpose of answering it, lining up evidence as you go. You may discover what you want to say as you write. (Note that this method usually requires much revising. See p. 432.)

MOVING FROM NOTES TO OUTLINE TO DRAFT

Source notes are only the raw material for the research paper. If they are to end up in a readable, unified whole, they need to be put into the proper setting, carefully shaped, and finely polished. Good, thoughtful notes can sometimes be copied verbatim from note card to first draft. But usually they will take rewriting to fit them in so they don't stand out like boulders in the stream of your prose. Moving from the nuggets of information in your notes to a smooth, persuasive analysis or argument is the most challenging part of the research process — and ironically the part on which we can give the least concrete advice. Every writer's habits of mind are different. Nonetheless, you'll probably find yourself cycling again and again through four basic activities — interpreting your sources, refining your thesis, organizing your ideas, and putting thoughts into the form of a draft. In the end, much of the verbiage in your notes probably won't need to go into your paper. Don't feel that your careful note taking was wasted effort though: your sifted notes are the by-products of a critical process that has carried you to the point where you know what you want to say and are able to say it effectively.

Interpreting Your Sources.   On their own, your source notes are only pieces of information. They need your careful analysis and interpretation to transform them into effective evidence. For her paper on America's obsession with sports, Maria Halloran may have found a reputable statistic indicating that 74 percent of the boys in a certain community play Little League baseball. But what does that number *mean*? Is it surprisingly high? Compared with what? And if it is high, does this fact mean that the town is "sports crazy"? Or does it mean that the promoters have done a good job selling their program? As a researcher and writer, you have to think critically about each fact and decide what it means in the context of your paper. Then you have to make sure that the fact itself is strong enough to bear the weight of the claim you're going to base on it. You may find that you need supplemental evidence to shore up an interesting but possibly ambiguous fact. Halloran, for instance, would have needed statistics on the enrollment in comparable activities in the same community to claim that the Little League enrollment was surprisingly high.

You'll also need to synthesize your sources and evidence, to weave them into a unified whole. If you've been guided throughout your research by a research question or a working thesis, you may find this synthesis fairly easy. You know what the question is; you know what the general answer is; you just need to let the pieces fall into place. Remember too that research questions and working theses change, often because during the research process the researcher unearths persuasive or interesting information that is somewhat at odds with the original direction of the research. In either case, it's important to stop a minute and ask yourself: Taken as a whole, what does all this information mean? What does it really tell me about my topic? What's the most important thing I've learned? What's the most important thing I can tell my readers?

Refining Your Thesis.   A thesis is a clear, precise statement of the point you want to make in your paper. It will help you, as a writer, decide what to say and how to say it. If your thesis is clear to your readers, it will help them interpret the information you present by letting them know in advance the scope of your paper and your general message. Most college papers — especially long, complex papers based on research and analysis — benefit greatly from having a clear thesis presented at the beginning.

Remember that explicitly stating your thesis, right out in the open, as the first or last sentence in your opening paragraph is only one option. Sometimes it is possible to craft your opening paragraph so that your readers know exactly what your thesis is even though you only imply it. Maria Halloran decided to include an explicit thesis statement in the opening paragraph of her paper "America's Obsession with Sports": "The national obsession with sports must end" (see p. 755). But her opening paragraph would also have been effective if she had omitted the thesis statement and ended with the question "Have we as a country gone so overboard on sports that we have learned to take casually whatever comes with this sports obsession, including violence?" Her readers would still have known her answer — her thesis. (Check with your instructor if you're unsure whether an implicit thesis statement will be acceptable.)

If you've been using a working thesis to guide your research, you should take the time to sharpen and refine it now before you start drafting. You may need to change it still further when you encounter unexpected twists in the process of writing, but a clear thesis will help guide you in organizing and expressing your ideas. If you haven't developed a thesis yet, now is the time to write one.

In your thesis, try to be precise and concrete, and don't claim more than you can demonstrate in your paper. If your paper is argumentative — that is, if you take a stand, propose a solution, or evaluate something — then you should make clear what your stand, solution, or appraisal is.

TOPIC	Americans' attitudes toward sports
RESEARCH QUESTION	Is America obsessed with sports?
THESIS	The national obsession with sports must end.

WRITING WITH A COMPUTER

Outlining as a Planning and Drafting Tool

Because of their ability to store, copy, and move information quickly and easily, word processors are well suited to the complex tasks of planning and drafting a research paper. To help organize your ideas, you can write an outline on your word processor. By cutting and pasting parts of the outline, you can experiment with different organizations to find the one that is clearest and most effective.

Many word-processing programs also support a planning and drafting tool called *Outline View*. Once you have a draft in progress, this tool encourages you to think critically about the organization of your paper by allowing you to view parts of your document and move around quickly within your draft. You can view various levels of headings in your paper to begin to evaluate the logic of your argument and the strength of your evidence. Outline View may alert you to gaps you weren't aware of, areas in need of support, and alternative ways of organizing your draft.

Organizing Your Ideas.   In organizing your research information, remember that, as is true of most other kinds of writing, some intuition is called for. It is not enough to relate the steps you took in answering your research question or to string the data together in chronological order. You aren't writing a memoir; you're reporting the significance of what you found out. Try putting your material together in various combinations until you arrive at an organization that seems engaging and clear. If you have trouble, review the patterns of organization in Part Two, "Thinking Critically," and in Chapter 16, "Strategies for Planning."

If your material seems not to want to shape up, you may find it helpful to plan the order of the ideas by writing an outline (see p. 384). You might arrange all your note cards in an order that makes sense. Then the stack of cards becomes your plan, and as you write, turning over card after card, you follow it. Or you can make an informal outline on paper (see p. 385) or on the computer (p. 384). For such a complex writing task, you will probably find writing an outline helpful. That's what Mark Sanchez did first.

Sanchez made a rough preliminary listing of the points he planned to cover.

> *Introduction*
> *History of Las Animas, Colorado*
> *History of my family migrating from New Mexico to Colorado*
> *Examination of works by Gerald Vizenor and Carlos Fuentes*
> *Conclusion*

His early outline was tentative, and it changed as he drafted his ideas. He knew he wanted to start the essay with something gripping—perhaps a concrete description of the town of Las Animas and the old family farm. As he studied his preliminary outline, he wondered whether his own family stories would be more effective than the stories of Vizenor and Fuentes, two contemporary writers who, like Sanchez, explore their family and personal identities. Later, after the first draft, he decided to drop the separate sections on these writers and to integrate the literary connections into the other sections of the paper.

If you begin with a clear, carefully worded research question (see p. 676), you will not have much difficulty selecting and organizing your evidence to answer it. But as we've said so often before, research questions often may change and re-form while you're at work at the library, on the Internet, or in the field. When you begin organizing, don't be afraid to junk an original question that no longer works and to reorganize your material around a newly formed question. In the long run, you'll save both time and toil.

Beginning to Draft.   You'll probably benefit from a formal outline to guide your drafting. But remember that an outline is a skeleton to which you will add flesh (details). Use the outline as a suggested organizational plan and change the subdivisions or the order of the parts if you discover a better way.

When you look over your outline, compare each section with the notes you have on hand for it. If for a certain section you have no notes, or only a single note, your research has a gap, so go back to the library, to the Internet, or into the field again.

When you are satisfied that your notes fall into some kind of order and you have material for every part of your outline, you can start to write. If things don't fall into perfect order, start writing anyway. Get something down on paper so that you will have something to revise. And remember that you don't have to start at the beginning; start wherever you feel most comfortable.

As you write, you should document all the ideas, facts, summaries, and paraphrases you've drawn from your reading or field research. Right after every such borrowing, you refer your readers to the exact source of your material. (In Chapter 30, we show you in detail how to cite your sources.) Although it takes a little extra time to cite your sources, it saves fuss when you're putting your paper into final form. And it prevents unintentional plagiarism (see p. 742).

Note in your draft, right after each borrowed item, the name of the author and the page of the book or article you took it from. If you are quoting a field research source, include the date of the interview or lecture and the name of the person speaking, if any. If you're using two or more works by the same author, you need one more detail to tell them apart: shorten the titles — the first word or phrase will do — and include the shortened title with the author's name.

```
An assassin outrages us not only by his deed but also by
offering an unacceptable reason for violence. Nearly as
offensive as his act of wounding President Reagan was
Hinckley's explanation that he fired in order to impress
screen star Jodie Foster. (Szasz, "Intentionality," 5)
```

The title in parentheses is short for "Intentionality and Insanity," the title of an article by Thomas Szasz, to distinguish it from another work by Szasz that the writer also cites — *The Myth of Mental Illness.*

When in writing a draft you include a direct quotation, you might as well save copying time. Just paste or tape in the whole note card bearing the quotation. Your draft may look sloppy, but who cares? Drafts usually are. You're going to recopy the quotation anyway when you type your final version. If your note is in a computer file, you can just copy the passage from the file and paste it right where you want it in your draft file.

When you lay the quotation into place, add a few words to introduce it. A brief transition might go something like "A more negative view of standardized intelligence tests is that of Harry S. Baum, director of the Sooner Research Center." Then comes Baum's opinion that IQ tests aren't very reliable. The transition announces why Baum will be quoted—to refute a previous quotation in favor of IQ tests. The transition, brief as it is, tells readers a little about Baum by including his professional title. Knowing that he is a recognized authority would probably make readers willing to accept his expert view. (For more suggestions on introducing ideas, see "Achieving Coherence," p. 407.)

If no transition occurs to you as you are placing a quotation or borrowed idea into your draft, don't sit around waiting for it. Make a marginal or mental note that you need a transition, and keep writing while the spirit is moving you along. Later, when you rewrite, you can add connective tissue. Just remember to add it, though: a series of slapped-in summaries and quotations makes rough reading.

INCORPORATING SOURCE MATERIAL

Using Sources (Not Letting Sources Use You).   Sometimes you can be drawn into discussing something that really doesn't have much to do with your investigation, perhaps because the material is interesting and you happen to have a heap of it. When a note has cost you time and toil, it's a great temptation to want to include it at all costs. Resist. Include only material that answers your research question. A note dragged in by force always sticks out like a pig in the belly of a boa constrictor.

Another common danger is for a writer to swagger in triumph over what he or she has discovered. Cultivate a certain detachment. Make no exorbitant claims for what you have discovered ("Thus I have shown that day-care centers deserve the trust of parents in the state of Washington"). You have probably not answered your research question for all time; you need not claim to be irrefutable. Norman Tallent, in his guidebook *Psychological Report Writing* (Englewood Cliffs: Prentice, 1976), quotes a professional reader of reports in the field of psychology: "I have seen some reports which affected me adversely because of a tendency to sound pompous with the implication 'This is the final word!' rather than 'This is an opinion intended to be helpful in understanding the whole.' "

WRITING WITH A COMPUTER

Working with Your Research Archive

The ability of a computer to help you juggle and rearrange is a great advantage when it comes to organizing and managing research material sources. By now, your library, Internet, or field research will probably have generated an abundance of notes. If you have recorded your findings on a computer as you went along, your paper will be easier to organize now.

Use the *Multiple Windows* feature on your word processor to move among your documents — source files, notes, and your draft in progress. Your program allows you to open more than one window — a bordered on-screen space that holds a document — at any given time, so use this to your advantage. (These windows may be tiled, cascaded, or viewed one at a time on your screen.)

Quoting, Paraphrasing, and Nutshelling.   *Quoting* is reproducing an author's exact words. *Paraphrasing* is restating an author's ideas in your own
words. *Nutshelling* is extracting the essence of an author's meaning and stating
it "in a nutshell." These methods of handling source material are also
discussed in Chapter 28 (p. 727). Now you face a similar but different challenge — how to use these methods to incorporate your sources in your actual
paper.

If to save time in the library you made photocopies of long passages or
you took too many notes as direct quotations, you now face the task of selecting from them, boiling them down, and weaving them into your paper.
Nutshell and paraphrase are fine ways to avoid quoting excessively. Both
methods translate another writer's ideas into your own words.

To illustrate once again how nutshelling and paraphrasing can serve you,
let's first look at a passage from historian Barbara W. Tuchman. In *The Distant Mirror: The Calamitous Fourteenth Century* (New York: Knopf, 1978),
Tuchman sets forth the effects of the famous plague the Black Death. In her
foreword to her study, she admits that any historian dealing with the Middle
Ages faces difficulties. For one, large gaps exist in the supply of recorded information. See Tuchman's original wording on the next page.

**WRITING
WITH A
COMPUTER**

Drafting, Shaping, and Developing
Your Research Paper

The word processor also allows you to cut and paste chunks of material between
documents. With a mouse click, you can cut and paste chunks of material among
separate documents. In this way, you can begin to organize your paper by moving
each piece of source information into the appropriate place in your draft. If you've
taken notes on a computer (or if you've transcribed your best material) you can
start to flesh out your paper by moving each piece of source information into the
appropriate place in your outline. After doing this, you may realize that you don't
have enough evidence to support certain claims, or you may decide to shift things
around a bit so that your strongest evidence is in the most prominent position.
Your word processor's *Annotations* feature (sometimes this feature is called *Comments*) can help you to think critically while shaping and developing your research
paper. This tool allows you to annotate, or make comments on, your own document. Use this feature to ask yourself key questions: Is my thesis clear? Have I supported this point well enough? Is this source too biased to be effective?

To develop your draft further, enlist the help of a peer reviewer. He or she can
use the same tool to respond to your questions or to ask additional questions. If
your word processor does not support an Annotation function, ask your reviewer
to make comments within your draft using boldfaced type, square brackets, or
anything else that makes the comments easy for you to locate.

ORIGINAL

A greater hazard, built into the very nature of recorded history, is overload of the negative: the disproportionate survival of the bad side — of evil, misery, contention, and harm. In history this is exactly the same as in the daily newspaper. The normal does not make news. History is made by the documents that survive, and these lean heavily on crisis and calamity, crime and misbehavior, because such things are the subject matter of the documentary process — of lawsuits, treaties, moralists' denunciations, literary satire, papal Bulls. No Pope ever issued a Bull to approve of something. Negative overload can be seen at work in the religious reformer Nicolas de Clamanges, who, in denouncing unfit and worldly prelates in 1401, said that in his anxiety for reform he would not discuss the good clerics because "they do not count beside the perverse men."

Disaster is rarely as pervasive as it seems from recorded accounts. The fact of being on the record makes it appear continuous and ubiquitous whereas it is more likely to have been sporadic both in time and place. Besides, persistence of the normal is usually greater than the effect of disturbance, as we know from our own times. After absorbing the news of today, one expects to face a world consisting entirely of strikes, crimes, power failures, broken water mains, stalled trains, school shutdowns, muggers, drug addicts, neo-Nazis, and rapists. The fact is that one can come home in the evening — on a lucky day — without having encountered more than one or two of these phenomena.

This passage in a nutshell, or summary, might become as follows:

NUTSHELL

Tuchman reminds us that history lays stress on misery and misdeeds because these negative events attracted notice in their time and so were reported in writing; just as in a newspaper today, bad news predominates. But we should remember that suffering and social upheaval didn't prevail everywhere all the time.

As you can see, this nutshell merely abstracts from the original. Not everything in the original has been preserved — not Tuchman's thought about papal bulls, not the specific examples such as Nicolas de Clamanges and the modern neo-Nazis and rapists. But the gist — the summary of the main idea — echoes Tuchman faithfully.

Before you write a nutshell, or summary, an effective way to sense the gist of a passage is to carefully pare away examples, details, modifiers, offhand remarks, and nonessential points.

On the following page is the original quotation from Tuchman as one student marked it up on a photocopy, crossing out elements she decided to omit from her paraphrase.

~~A greater hazard,~~ built into the ~~very~~ nature of recorded history, is ~~over-load of the negative:~~ the disproportionate survival of the bad side — ~~of evil, misery, contention, and harm. In history~~ this is exactly the same as in the daily newspaper. ~~The normal does not make news. History is made by the~~ documents that survive, ~~and these~~ lean heavily on crisis and calamity, crime and misbehavior, because such things are the subject matter of the documentary process — ~~of lawsuits, treaties, moralists' denunciations, literary satire, papal Bulls. No Pope ever issued a Bull to approve of something. Negative overload can be seen at work in the religious reformer Nicolas de Clamanges, who, in denouncing unfit and worldly prelates in 1401, said that in his anxiety for reform he would not discuss the good clerics because "they do not count beside the perverse men."~~

Disaster is rarely as pervasive as it seems from recorded accounts. ~~The fact of being on the record makes it appear continuous and ubiquitous whereas~~ it is more likely to have been sporadic both in time and place. Besides, persistence of the normal is usually greater than the effect of disturbance, as we know from our own times. ~~After absorbing the news of today, one expects to face a world consisting entirely of strikes, crimes, power failures, broken water mains, stalled trains, school shutdowns, muggers, drug addicts, neo Nazis, and rapists. The fact is that one can come home in the eventing — on a lucky day — without having encountered more than one or two of these phenomena.~~

Rewording what was left, she wrote the following nutshell version:

NUTSHELL

```
History, like a daily newspaper, reports more bad than
good. Why? Because the documents that have come down to
us tend to deal with upheavals and disturbances, which
are seldom as extensive and long-lasting as history books
might lead us to believe.
```

In filling her nutshell, you'll notice, the student couldn't simply omit the words she had deleted. The result would have been less readable and still long. She knew she couldn't use Tuchman's very words: that would be plagiarism. To make a good, honest, compact nutshell that would fit smoothly into her research paper, she had to condense the passage into her own words.

Now here is Tuchman's passage in paraphrase. The writer has put Tuchman's ideas into other words but retained her major points. Note that the writer gives Tuchman credit for the ideas.

PARAPHRASE

```
Tuchman points out that historians find some distortion
of the truth hard to avoid, for more documentation
exists for crimes, suffering, and calamities than for
```

the events of ordinary life. As a result, history may
overplay the negative. The author reminds us that we are
familiar with this process from our contemporary newspapers, in which bad news is played up as being of
greater interest than good news. If we believed that
newspapers told all the truth, we would think ourselves
threatened at all times by technical failures, strikes,
crime, and violence--but we are threatened only some of
the time, and normal life goes on. The good, dull, ordinary parts of our lives do not make the front page, and
praiseworthy things tend to be ignored. "No Pope," says
Tuchman, "ever issued a Bull to approve of something."
But in truth, social upheaval did not prevail as widely
as we might think from the surviving documents of medieval life. Nor, the author observes, can we agree with
a critic of the church, Nicolas de Clamanges, in whose
view evildoers in the clergy mattered more than men of
goodwill (xviii).

In this reasonably complete and accurate paraphrase, about three-quarters the length of the original, most of Tuchman's points have been preserved and spelled out fully. Paraphrasing enables the writer to emphasize the ideas important to his or her research and makes readers more aware of them as support for the writer's thesis than if the whole passage had been quoted directly. But notice that Tuchman's remark about papal bulls has been kept a direct quotation because the statement is short and memorable, and it would be hard to improve on her words. In the paraphrase, the writer, you'll observe, doesn't interpret or evaluate Tuchman's ideas — she only passes them on.

When you use the information from a source in your paper, make sure that, like the writer of the nutshell and the paraphrase just given, you indicate your original source. You can pay due credit in a terse phrase — "Barbara W. Tuchman believes that . . ." or "According to Barbara W. Tuchman . . ." — and then give the page number in parentheses after the information you cite.

Often you paraphrase to emphasize one essential point. Here is an original passage from Evelyn Underhill's classic study *Mysticism*:

ORIGINAL

In the evidence given during the process for St. Teresa's beatification, Maria de San Francisco of Medina, one of her early nuns, stated that on entering the saint's cell whilst she was writing this same "Interior Castle" she found her [St. Teresa] so absorbed in contemplation as to be unaware of the external world. "If we made a noise close to her," said another, Maria del

Nacimiento, "she neither ceased to write nor complained of being disturbed." Both these nuns, and also Ana de la Encarnacion, prioress of Granada, affirmed that she wrote with immense speed, never stopping to erase or to correct, being anxious, as she said, to write what the Lord had given her before she forgot it.

Suppose that the names of the witnesses do not matter but that the researcher wishes to emphasize, in fewer words, the celebrated mystic's writing habits. To bring out that point, the writer might paraphrase the passage (and quote it in part) like this:

PARAPHRASE WITH QUOTATION

```
Evelyn Underhill has recalled the testimony of those who
saw St. Teresa at work on The Interior Castle. Oblivious
to noise, the celebrated mystic appeared to write in a
state of complete absorption, driving her pen "with im-
mense speed, never stopping to erase or to correct, being
anxious, as she said, to write what the Lord had given
her before she forgot it."
```

Avoiding Plagiarism.   Here is a point we can't stress too strongly: when you paraphrase, never lift another writer's words or ideas without giving that writer due credit or without transforming them into words of your own. If you do use words or ideas without giving credit, you are plagiarizing. You have seen in this chapter examples of honest nutshelling and paraphrasing. Introducing them into a paper, a writer would clearly indicate that they belong to Barbara Tuchman (or some other originator). Now here are a few horrible examples — paraphrases of Barbara Tuchman's original passage (on p. 739) that lift, without thanks, her ideas and even her very words. Finding such gross borrowings in a paper, an instructor might hear the ringing of a burglar alarm. The first is an egregious example that lifts both thoughts and words.

PLAGIARIZED

```
Sometimes it's difficult for historians to learn the
truth about the everyday lives of people from past soci-
eties because of the disproportionate survival of the bad
side of things. Historical documents, like today's news-
papers, tend to lean rather heavily on crisis, crime, and
misbehavior. Reading the newspaper could lead one to ex-
pect a world consisting entirely of strikes, crimes,
power failures, muggers, drug addicts, and rapists. In
fact, though, disaster is rarely so pervasive as recorded
accounts can make it seem.
```

What are the problems here? The phrase "the disproportionate survival of the bad side" is quoted directly from Tuchman's passage (line 2). The series "crisis, crime, and misbehavior" is too close to Tuchman's series "crisis and calamity, crime and misbehavior" (line 5); only the words "and calamity" have been omitted. The words "lead one to expect a world consisting entirely" is almost the same as the original "one expects to face a world consisting entirely" (lines 16–17). The phrase "strikes, crimes, power failures, muggers, drug addicts, and rapists" simply records — and in the same order — six of the ten examples Tuchman provides (lines 17–18). The last sentence in the plagiarized passage ("In fact, though, disaster is rarely so pervasive as recorded accounts can make it seem") is almost the same — and thus too close to the source — as the first sentence of Tuchman's second paragraph ("Disaster is rarely as pervasive as it seems from recorded accounts"). The student who wrote this attempted paraphrase failed to comprehend Tuchman's passage sufficiently to be able to put Tuchman's ideas in his or her own words.

The second example is a more subtle theft, lifting thoughts but not words.

PLAGIARIZED

```
It's not always easy to determine the truth about the
everyday lives of people from past societies because bad
news gets recorded a lot more frequently than good news
does. Historical documents, like today's newspapers, tend
to pick up on malice and disaster and ignore flat normal-
ity. If I were to base my opinion of the world on what I
see on the seven o'clock news, I would expect to see
death and destruction around me all the time. Actually,
though, I rarely come up against true disaster.
```

By using the first-person pronoun *I*, this student suggests that Tuchman's ideas are his own. That is just as dishonest as quoting without using quotation marks, as reprehensible as not citing the source of ideas.

The next example fails to make clear which ideas belong to the writer and which belong to Tuchman (although none of them belong to the writer).

PLAGIARIZED

```
Barbara Tuchman explains that it can be difficult for his-
torians to learn about the everyday lives of people who
lived a long time ago because historical documents tend to
record only the bad news. Today's newspapers are like that,
too: disaster, malice, and confusion take up a lot more
room on the front page than happiness and serenity. Just as
```

```
the ins and outs of our everyday lives go unreported, we
can suspect that upheavals do not really play so impor-
tant a part in the making of history as they seem to do.
```

After rightfully attributing the ideas in the first sentence to Tuchman, the student researcher makes a comparison to today's world in sentence 2. Then in sentence 3 she goes back to Tuchman's ideas without giving Tuchman credit. The placement of the last sentence suggests that this last idea is the student's whereas it is really Tuchman's.

RESEARCH CHECKLIST

Avoiding Plagiarism

- Remember that taking notes is a process of both writing and understanding what you read.
- Carefully check each paraphrase or summary against the original. Be sure you have not misinterpreted or distorted the meaning of the original.
- When you quote from the original, be sure to quote exactly and use quotation marks. Place significant words from the original in quotation marks.
- Use an ellipsis mark (. . .) to indicate where you have omitted something from the original, and use square brackets ([ ]) to indicate changes or additions you have made in a quotation. When you use these two conventions, take care not to distort the meaning of the original by your omissions or changes.
- Take pains to identify the author of any quotation, paraphrase, or summary. Credit by name the originator of any fact, idea, or quotation you use.
- Make sure you indicate where another writer's ideas stop and yours begin. (You might end your paraphrase with some clear phrase or phrases of transition: " — or so Tuchman affirms. In my own view. . . .")
- If at any place your paraphrase looks close to the exact words of the original, carefully rewrite it in your own words.

EXERCISE

Paraphrasing

Study one of the following passages until you understand it thoroughly. Then using your own words, write a paraphrase of the passage. Compare and contrast your version with that of your classmates in your peer group. With their help, evaluate your own version: What are its strengths and weaknesses? Where should it be revised? In the future when you take notes from library, Internet, or field research, be sure to avoid the problems that you identify in this group activity.

PASSAGE I
Within the next decades education will change more than it has changed since the modern school was created by the printed book over three hundred years ago. An economy in which knowledge is becoming the true capital and the premier wealth-producing resource makes new and stringent demands on the schools for educational performance and educational responsibility. A society dominated by knowledge workers makes even newer — and even more stringent — demands for social performance and social responsibility. Once again we will

have to think through what an educated person is. At the same time, how we learn and how we teach are changing drastically and fast — the result, in part, of new theoretical understanding of the learning process, in part of new technology. Finally, many of the traditional disciplines of the schools are becoming sterile, if not obsolescent. We thus also face changes in what we learn and teach and, indeed, in what we mean by knowledge.

— Peter F. Drucker, *The New Realities*

PASSAGE 2

When I look to the future of humanity beyond the twenty-first century, I see on my list of things to come the extension of our inquisitiveness from the objective domain of science to the subjective domain of feeling and memory. Homo sapiens, the exploring animal, will not be content with merely physical exploration. Our curiosity will drive us to explore the dimensions of the mind as vigorously as we explore the dimensions of space and time. For every pioneer who explores a new asteroid or a new planet, there will be another pioneer who explores from the inside the minds of our fellow passengers on planet Earth. It is our nature to strive to explore everything, alive and dead, present and past and future. When once the technology exists to read and write memories from one mind into another, the age of mental exploration will begin in earnest. Instead of admiring the beauties of nature from the outside, we will look at nature directly through the eyes of the elephant, the eagle, and the whale. We will be able, through the magic of science, to feel in our own minds the pride of the peacock and the wrath of the lion. That magic is no greater than the magic that enables me to see the rocking horse through the eyes of the child who rode it sixty years ago.

— Freeman Dyson, *Infinite in All Directions*

BEGINNING AND ENDING

Perhaps, as we have suggested, you will think of a good beginning and a concluding paragraph or paragraphs only after you have written the body of your paper. The head and tail of your paper might then make clear your opinion of whatever you have found out. But that is not the only way to begin and end a research paper. Maria Halloran initially began her draft with a short summary of her conclusion from her research investigation.

```
America is obsessed with sports, and this national mania is
harmful to children. For their sake and the future of our
country, we should end the national obsession with sports.
```

After reading over this introductory paragraph, she thought it probably wouldn't catch the interest of her readers and might even alienate some who held the opposing point of view. As she drafted and revised her essay, she realized that to bring her readers around to her point of view, she needed to start out slowly and build to a strong finish. Both her opening paragraph and her paper as a whole follow this pattern. For her opening, she starts with a factual account of a real event, something her readers can hardly take issue with.

Only after recounting the event and exploring its implications does she put forth her main idea (her thesis).

```
The national obsession with sports must end.
```

Although her message is clear, Maria Halloran's tone is not yet impassioned. She uses her paper to bombard her readers with evidence about the harmful effects of the U.S. sports mania and then, at the very end of the paper, issues the rousing call to action that she had originally thought to use as her opening.

```
For the sake of our children and the future of our coun-
try, isn't it time that we put the brakes on America's
sports mania? The youth of America have been sold a false
and harmful bill of goods. Let's stop such madness and
step off the carousel now. We owe that to the children of
America and to ourselves.
```

Still another way to begin a research paper is to sum up the findings of other scholars. One research biologist, Edgar F. Warner, has reduced this kind of opening to a formula.

First, in one or two paragraphs, you review everything that has been said about your topic, naming the most prominent earlier commentators. Next you declare why all of them are wrong. Then you set forth your own claim, and you spend the rest of your paper supporting it.

That pattern may seem cut and dried, but it is clear and useful. It is a favorite technique among professional writers because it places the scholar's research and ideas into a historical and conceptual framework. If you browse in specialized journals in many fields — literary criticism, social studies, the sciences — you may be surprised how many articles begin and go on in that very way. Of course, you don't need to damn every earlier commentator. One or two other writers may be enough to argue with. Erika Wahr, a student writing on the American poet Charles Olson, starts her research paper by disputing two views of him.

```
To Cid Corman, Charles Olson of Gloucester, Massachu-
setts, is "the one dynamic and original epic poet
twentieth-century America has produced" (116). To Allen
Tate, Olson is "a loquacious charlatan" (McFinnery 92).
In my opinion, the truth lies between these two extremes,
nearer to Corman's view.
```

Whether or not you have stated your view in your beginning, you will certainly need to make it clear in your closing paragraph. A suggestion: Before writing the last lines of your paper, read back over what you have written earlier. Then, without referring to your paper, try to put your view into writing. (For more suggestions on starting and finishing, see Chapters 17 and 19.)

Revising and Editing

Looking over your evidence and your draft, you may possibly find your essay changing as those of Maria Halloran and Mark Sanchez did. Don't be afraid to make a whole new interpretation, shift the organization, drop a section or add a new one.

When you look over your draft, here are a few points to inspect critically and try to improve.

REVISION
CHECKLIST

Looking Over Your Results

- Have you honestly said something, not just heaped facts and statements by other writers that don't add up to anything? If your answer is no and a mere heap of meaningless stuff is all you've got, then you need to do some hard thinking and revising.
- Is your main idea or thesis clear?
- Have you included only evidence that makes a point? Do all your points support your main idea?
- Does each new idea or piece of information follow from the one before it? Can you see any stronger order in which to arrange things? Have you provided transitions to connect the parts?
- Are your sources of information trustworthy? Do you have lingering doubts about something you read or anything anyone told you? (If so, whom might you consult to verify your information?)
- Do you need more evidence to back up any point? If so, where might you obtain it?
- Are the words that you quote truly memorable? Would you recall them if you hadn't written them down? Would any quotation be better paraphrased or summarized?
- Is the source of every quotation, every fact, every idea you have borrowed made unmistakably clear?
- Do you spend much space announcing what you are going to do or repeating what you demonstrated? (If you do, whittle down these passages or cut them out altogether.)

Once you have done all you can do by yourself to make your paper informative, tightly reasoned, and interesting to read, ask a classmate to read over your draft and give you reactions. When you set about the task of revising, you can start by backtracking at the trouble spots your peer editor has highlighted. If you need to improve connections between parts, try summarizing the previous section of your paper. By doing so, you remind your readers of what you have already said. This strategy can come in handy, especially in a long paper when, after a few pages, readers' memories may need refreshing and a summary of the argument so far will be welcome. Halloran uses this technique effectively in her research paper: "Although these arguments may sound convincing, critics claim that sports can be harmful to children." This type of transition effectively points both back and forward. You might ask your peer editior to answer the questions on the following pages.

Writing from Research

- What is your overall reaction to this paper?
- What do you understand the research question to be? Did the writer answer that question?
- What promises has the writer made that should be met in the paper? Did he or she meet them?
- What changes might the writer make to the introduction that would wake up a sleepy instructor drinking coffee at 3 A.M. and enlist his or her careful attention?
- What do you think about the conclusions the writer has drawn from his or her research? Do they seem fair and logical? Describe any problems you have with the writer's interpretation of the evidence.
- Look carefully at the concluding paragraph of the paper. Does it merely restate the introduction? Is it too abrupt or too hurried? What makes it effective?
- Is the organization logical and easy to follow? Are there any places where the essay becomes hard to follow? Highlight these.
- Do you know which information is from the student writer and which from the research sources? Highlight any facts, opinions, or questions that you think should be documented.
- Does the writer need all the quotations he or she has used? Point out any that puzzled you or that you thought were not well incorporated.
- Do you have any questions about the writer's evidence? Point out areas where the writer has not fully backed up his or her conclusions.
- Did the writer commit any logical fallacies (see p. 104)?
- How interested were you in continuing to read the paper? If you didn't have to, would you have kept on reading? Why or why not?

DOCUMENTING SOURCES

A research paper calls on you to follow special rules in documenting your sources — in citing them as you write and in listing them at the end of your paper. At first, these rules may seem fiendishly fussy, but for good reason professional writers of research papers swear by them and follow them scrupulously. Research papers go by the rules to be easily readable and easily set into type. The rules also ensure that any reader interested in the same subject can use complete and accurate source information to look up the original sources.

In humanities courses and the social sciences, most writers of research papers follow the style of the Modern Language Association (MLA) or the American Psychological Association (APA). Your instructor will probably suggest which style to observe; if you are not told, use MLA. The first time you prepare a research paper according to MLA or APA rules, you'll need extra time to look up just what to do in each situation. (For detailed information about documenting sources, see Chapter 30.)

Quotation Style.   One special manuscript convention for research papers is that for direct quotations. When you use a direct quotation from one of your sources, you must put quotation marks around the words you're using, and you must cite the author and page number. You may include the author's name either in the text of the essay — as in the following example — or in parentheses with the page number at the end of the quotation.

```
Johnson puts heavy emphasis on the importance of "giving
the child what she needs at the precise moment in her
life when it will do the most good" (23).
```

WRITING WITH A COMPUTER

Revising a Research Paper

Writers revise — or "resee" — to strengthen and clarify what they have written. Several tools available within your word-processing program can help you improve your draft. In addition, they can help you by making the revision process more visual.

You can save multiple versions of your paper using the standard *Save As* command or, if your word processor supports it, the *Versions* tool. Either of these allows you to try different beginnings and endings, multiple organizational patterns, and various ways to present evidence — and to save each version as a separate file. Your program may also have a *highlighting* tool. If so, use it to mark key passages in your paper. You could highlight all direct quotes, for instance, to see whether you have overused quotations. You could do the same thing with paraphrasing and nutshelling. Consider highlighting support from different authors in different fonts or colors to determine whether you are relying on one or more authors disproportionately. Finally, many programs include a *Compare Documents* feature, which enables you to track your revisions from draft to draft. This feature can provide you with a concrete revision record.

Using Software to Document Sources

As a responsible researcher, you have carefully noted your sources and maintained your working bibliography. Throughout your paper, you have included in-text citations to indicate any material that comes from a library, Internet, or field source. These citations refer your reader to an alphabetical list of "Works Cited" (MLA style) or "References" (APA style) at the end of your paper. Several bibliographic software programs are available to help you manage your documentation tasks, and some word-processing programs have built-in documentation tools. Citation, EndNote, Reference Manager, and ProCite allow you to build a database of bibliographic information and generate citations in the style required by your instructor. Talk with your instructor, your library staff, or the assistants in your computer lab if you are unfamiliar with such programs.

When you include a quotation longer than four typed lines, set it off in your text by indenting the whole quotation one inch or ten spaces from the left margin if you're following MLA style, five spaces for APA style. Double-space the quotation, just as you do the rest of your paper. Don't place quotation marks around an indented quotation, and if the quotation is a paragraph or less, don't indent its first line. Following is an example, a critic's comment on Emily Dickinson's use of language:

```
Cynthia Griffin Wolff in her biography Emily Dickinson
comments on this nineteenth-century poet's incisive use
of language:
          Language, of course, was a far subtler weapon
          than a hammer. Dickinson's verbal maneuvers
          would increasingly reveal immense skill in
          avoiding a frontal attack; she preferred the
          silent knife of irony to the strident battering
          of loud complaint. She had never suffered fools
          gladly. The little girl who had written of a
          dull classmate, "He is the silliest creature
          that ever lived I think," grew into a woman who
          could deliver wrath and contempt with excruciat-
          ing economy and cunning. Scarcely submissive,
          she had acquired the cool calculation of an
          assassin. (170-71)
```

WRITING WITH A COMPUTER

Editing and Proofreading a Research Paper

Research papers, being rich in names, numbers, and unfamiliar words, invite misspellings and other typographical errors. Proofread your finished research paper carefully. Avoid getting so interested in what you've written that you forget to notice mistakes. Look at spelling, punctuation, and other such mechanical matters. If you've written your paper on a word processor, it's easy to correct all errors right on screen before you print the final draft.

You may use the spell checker during the editing stage also. However, be sure that you understand a spell checker's limitations; this tool cannot guarantee perfect spelling. Grammar checkers are even less reliable than programs that check spelling. Unless you are very familiar with a grammar checker, you shouldn't rely on one for help. (For more on spell checkers and grammar checkers, see p. 473 in Chapter 21.)

Today's high-resolution printers, particularly laser printers, produce attractive documents that resemble professionally typeset writing. Do not be fooled by the slick appearance that these tools can create. There is simply no substitute for attentive, thorough editing and proofreading.

Works Cited.   At the very end of a library research paper, you list all the sources you have cited — books, periodicals, and any other materials. Usually this list is the last thing you write. It is easy to construct this list if your working bibliography includes in each source note all the necessary information (as shown in Figures 28.1 and 28.2). Then you simply arrange the works you used in alphabetical order and type the information about each source, following the MLA or APA guidelines (see Chapter 30). The MLA specifies that you title your list "Works Cited"; the APA, "References." Any leftover parts — notes for sources you haven't used after all — may now be filed for any further writing about the subject you may do in the future. Resist the temptation to use them to lengthen your list. Your list should include only the works you actually referred to in your paper.

MANUSCRIPT FORM

The "Quick Editing Guide" found near the end of *The Bedford Guide* tells you the proper format to use for a final manuscript, whether typewritten or word processed. Its advice on proper formatting applies not only to research papers but to any other college papers you may write. Before you hand in your final revision, go over it one last time for typographical and mechanical errors.

A Completed Library Research Paper

Maria Halloran's lack of understanding of the American preoccupation with sports and her consternation over the eruption of violence following a Chicago Bulls game led her to research the American obsession with sports. Her completed paper is more than a compilation of facts, a string of quotations. Halloran sets forth a problem that troubled her, she provides evidence to support her concern, and she adds her own thoughts to the facts and ideas she gleaned from her research.

Halloran prefaced her paper with a formal *sentence outline*, with each heading stated as a complete sentence. (If your instructor asks for such an outline, see the advice on formal outlines on p. 387.)

Later in college and on her job after graduation, Maria found that the training she acquired as a researcher in her composition course proved valuable.

Although MLA guidelines do not require a title page, you may be asked to prepare one. A title page contains, on separate lines, centered and double-spaced, the title of the paper, the writer's name, the instructor's name, the course number, and the date.

America's Obsession with Sports

Maria Halloran

Professor Sylvia A. Holladay

English 102

April 17, 1998

Type "Outline," centered, one inch from the top. Double-space to the first line of text.

The thesis states the main idea of the paper.

This outline is in sentence form rather than in the shorter topic form. It is a skeleton of the research paper.

Number all pages after the title page in the upper right corner, half an inch from the top. The writer's last name appears before the page number. Number outline pages with small roman numerals (the title page is counted but is not numbered).

Halloran ii

Outline

Thesis: The national obsession with sports must end.

I. The American fervor for sports is running at an all-time high.

   A. Attitudes toward sports figures are overwhelmingly positive.

      1. The image of the sports hero remains untarnished despite unheroic behavior.

      2. The media perpetuate the sports hero myth despite a lack of good role models.

   B. Entire cities sometimes become obsessed with sports.

   C. Sports enthusiasts argue for the benefits of sports.

      1. Sports are fun.

      2. Sports provide exercise.

      3. Sports build character.

II. Critics warn of the harmful effects of organized sports on children.

   A. Sports can actually harm the self-esteem of children.

      1. Little League "cutting" makes children think they have failed.

      2. Ridicule of Little Leaguers' performance makes them think they are being rejected personally.

   B. Obsessed with sports, schools often fail to look out for children's best interests.

      1. Students are held back a year in school to mature for sports teams.

Halloran iii

  2. The American school system is failing
     its students at the expense of
     sports.
  3. Young people are misled into believ-
     ing that they can become professional
     athletes.
C. Young athletes work at their game to the
   exclusion of academics.
  1. Many athletes leave high school func-
     tionally illiterate.
  2. If they don't make it to the pros,
     they have nothing to fall back on.

If you have a title page and an outline, repeat the title on the first page of the text. Double-space to the first line of text.

Number text pages with arabic numerals in the upper right corner, preceded by writer's last name. Place half an inch from the top. Begin the text one inch from the top, and leave one-inch margins at the bottom and sides of the paper.

A citation of a work by two or three authors gives the names of all authors. Halloran includes the page numbers for both pages that she cites from.

The authors' names introduce this quotation, so the parenthetical citation includes only the page number after the quotation.

Use a comma before a quotation if the lead-in text is not a full sentence. Use a colon if the lead-in text is a full sentence.

In the opening paragraph, Halloran recounts a real event and explains its implications before putting forth her thesis statement.

Halloran 1

America's Obsession with Sports

On June 20, 1993, gunplay, violence, and vandalism erupted in Chicago as fans celebrated the Chicago Bulls' 99-98 victory over the Phoenix Suns for the National Basketball Association title. Several innocent bystanders were hit by flying bullets. The police were shot at or assaulted with bottles and bricks, and countless other people suffered minor injuries. Businesses and schools were looted and vandalized, and the damage done to 109 city buses was estimated at $150,000. A total of 682 people were arrested (Recktenwald and Gottesman 1, 6). But across the country hardly any shock or condemnation was expressed over the outrageous behavior of the overzealous fans. Most of the media chose to minimize the shameful eruptions of violence as if they were just something to expect as part and parcel of a victory celebration. In a Chicago Tribune article following the Bulls' victory, William Recktenwald and Andrew Gottesman reported, "There were 20 shootings after the Bulls' game Sunday night, four of which proved fatal. For any given weekend night in Chicago, that toll is high but not shocking" (1). Not shocking? Have we as a country gone so overboard on sports that we have learned to take casually whatever comes with this sports obsession, including violence? Violence is only one of the harmful effects of the American obsession with sports. This mania also has adverse effects on players' self-esteem and on the educational system. The national obsession over sports must end.

Halloran 2

The first section of the body establishes the problem—obsession with sports.

        Despite drug use, sexual assaults, and do-
mestic violence by athletes, the American fervor for sports is running at an all-time high.
The image of sports heroes remains untarnished
despite such questionable behavior. Heavyweight
boxing champion Mike Tyson was convicted of
rape charges, and Pete Rose had to leave
baseball because of his gambling (Sudo 2).

Place citations within the text in parentheses after a sentence and before the period.

Former pro basketball player and Olympian
Michael Jordan also gambled heavily, but his
addiction has not adversely affected his reputation among sports fans. As one twelve-year-
old fan in Lincoln, Nebraska, said in defense
of Jordan: "It was just something he did for
fun, not anything to harm anything" (qtd. in

A direct quotation is used for the exact words of a sports fan. The fan is a secondary source quoted in the article by Gelman, Springen, and Raghavan, so citation reads "qtd. in."

Gelman, Springen, and Raghavan 56). The media
have much to do with the "selling" of these
improper role models, often making them into
celebrities. They are "a product of press
agents and media-hype who are sold to the public, rather than being chosen by the public for

Quotation marks are used around an important word from source.

their heroic qualities" (Crepeau 79). The imma-
ture and sometimes illegal activities of sports
"heroes" have done little to diminish their
standing among those obsessed with sports.

        Not only individuals, but even some cities
as a whole have become sports-crazy. Take
Odessa, Texas, for example. In a book titled
Friday Night Lights, Pulitzer Prize-winning

A transition is made to another aspect of the obsession.

writer H. G. Bissinger portrays the intense
football "win-at-any-cost" mentality of the
community. Football players with broken ankles
and hip pointers received painkillers so they
could keep playing despite injuries (44). Per-

Halloran 3

mian High School spent more on medical supplies for the team than on educational materials for the entire English department. Additionally, tens of thousands more dollars were spent chartering jets for games (145-46). As long as the team won, the coach was well liked, but when the team lost a game, "For Sale" signs appeared on his lawn the next morning (241). Bissinger says that although community pride resulted from the football team's success, Odessa "lost perspective on what a game should be" (qtd. in Herlinger 22). After the release of his book, Bissinger received innumerable threats of physical violence. Those threats, he said, were "an all-too-typical, and disturbing, indication of the increasingly unhealthy influence of sports on American life" (qtd. in Herlinger 23).

Sports enthusiasts argue that sports are beneficial. They claim not only that sports are fun and a superb way to exercise but also that children's experiences in sports can be an effective preparation for life. They argue that sports crystallize the meaning of hard work, self-discipline, teamwork, responsibility, goal setting, competition, fairness, and other positive values that build character. "For young people, sports is an important self-esteem builder," contends Richard Weinberg, professor of educational psychology at the University of Minnesota (qtd. in Maloney 24).

Although these arguments may sound convincing, critics claim that sports can be harmful to children. Little League, for instance, uses a process of "cutting," whereby membership

---

Margin notes (left column):

Halloran uses paraphrase and nutshell rather than direct quotation to discuss Bissinger's findings.

A professional title and credentials establish the source as an authority.

Halloran uses transitional phrases to link this discussion of an opposing viewpoint with previous paragraphs.

Halloran 4

limits are based on quotas and physical ability. As a result of this elimination process,
many children experience rejection. In such a
sports setting, stress and anxiety on the playing field can result in children backing away
from participating in sports because they fear
rejection if they perform poorly (Leonard 140).
Their self-esteem is damaged because they have
been deemed unworthy of the team. At such a
vulnerable age, they have failed to achieve the
approval that matters most to them. Even those
kids who do make the team are likely to have
their self-esteem damaged. As sports columnist
Robert Lipsyte explains, "Children know that
when they're ridiculed for not catching a ball,
they're being ridiculed for their bodies. I
think this is much worse than being laughed at
for reading badly or whatever. You're being
totally rejected as a person." The rejection and
ridicule often leave an indelible mark of unwor-
thiness even on the children who participate.

In an obsession to win games, schools have
sometimes failed to look out for children's
best interests because sports are considered
more important than studying. For instance, it
was common in Texas for junior high school athletes to be "redshirted"--held back a grade--
to give the players more time to mature for
high school competition (Maloney 24). H. G.
Bissinger asserts that, indeed, "we are turning
out a generation of children who can't read or
write or make critical judgments" but that "all
of that takes a backseat to the great god of
high school football" (qtd. in Herlinger 23).

The second section of the essay identifies and provides evidence of the harmful effects of organized sports on children.

Halloran paraphrases valuable ideas that are not worth preserving in the source's original words.

Halloran 5

Instead of making sure the young athletes are trained to become functional citizens, parents and schools concentrate mainly on molding kids to become professional athletes. Dr. Robert Green, dean of the College of Urban Development at Michigan State, describes the training process:

> When a kid as early as the sixth grade shows some potential in athletics, a whole series of events, almost like a piece of machinery, goes into effect to start grooming that kid for the pros.
>
> As he goes through the system and the better he gets, the kid sees he can get away with flunking tests, not handing in papers, skipping classes. Usually his coach will have enough clout so that very few teachers would dare fail that kid. (qtd. in Shapiro and Huff)

Also, young people are often given false hope that if they work hard enough in sports, they can play in the big leagues. But the odds are stacked against them. Studies have shown that only one high school athlete in twelve thousand gets the chance to become a pro (Maloney 24). The American education system responsible for preparing students for life after graduation has been tainted by the sports fervor gripping this country.

It's no wonder that many young athletes work at their game to the exclusion of academics and everything else. The U.S. Department

Halloran 6

of Education reports that "nearly 30% of senior
football and basketball players leave school
functionally illiterate" (Gordon 21). When such
athletes don't make the pros, they have nothing
to fall back on, and their anger and frustration may explode against society. One expert
observes that the federal prison system is full
of people with extraordinary athletic ability,
"but when they found they couldn't make it,
their energies were directed toward anti-
social behavior--crime, drugs, that kind of
thing" (qtd. in Shapiro and Huff).

    Thomas Tutko, a San Jose State psycholo-
gist, summarizes the harmful effects of sports
obsession on youngsters:

> How many millions of youngsters are
> we sacrificing along the way so that
> 10 players can entertain us in a pro
> basketball game? I'm concerned with
> how many good athletes have been
> scarred by injury or burned out psy-
> chologically by the time they were 15
> because they were unable to meet the
> unsatiable needs of their parents,
> their coach, their fans or their own
> personal obsession; or are rejected
> and made to feel ashamed because of
> their limited athletic prowess. We'll
> tolerate almost anything in the name
> of winning--cruelty, insensitivity,
> drugs, cheating and lying....Is it
> any wonder the sports field is over-
> run with neurotic behavior? (qtd. in
> Maikovich 127)

Halloran uses a direct quotation rather than a paraphrase because of the strong, effective language in the original source.

An ellipsis mark indicates that something is omitted from the original.

Halloran 7

The conclusion summa-
rizes the main points
made in the essay and
restates the thesis.

     Sports mania in the United States has cre-
ated a legacy of violence and misplaced values.
Contrary to the popular view, sports are not
inherently beneficial for individuals. The negative effects of the sports fervor gripping the
nation have become harmful to children--affect-
ing their self-esteem, aspirations, and world-
view. For the sake of our children and the future of our country, isn't it time that we put
the brakes on America's sports mania? The youth
of America have been sold a false and harmful
bill of goods. Let's stop such madness and step
off the carousel now. We owe that to the children of America and to ourselves.

Halloran 8

Works Cited

Book title with subtitle

Bissinger, H. G. <u>Friday Night Lights: A Town, a Team, and a Dream</u>. Reading: Addison, 1990.

Chapter in an edited book.

Crepeau, Richard C. "Where Have You Gone, Frank Merriwell? The Decline of the American Sports Hero." <u>American Sports Culture</u>. Ed. Wiley Lee Umphlett. Toronto: Associated Presses, 1985. 76-82.

Article by three authors appearing in a weekly magazine

Gelman, David, Karen Springen, and Suadansan Raghavan. "I'm Not a Role Model." <u>Newsweek</u> 28 June 1993: 56-57.

Gordon, Myles. "Making the Grade?" <u>Scholastic Update</u> 1 May 1992: 20-21.

Herlinger, Chris. "The Young Gods." <u>Scholastic Update</u> 1 May 1992: 22-23.

Works cited in text of paper are listed here alphabetically by authors' last names. Type "Works Cited," centered, one inch from top. Double-space to first entry and double-space within and between entries. Indent second and following lines of each entry five spaces.

Leonard, Wilbert Marcellus, II. <u>A Sociological Perspective of Sport</u>. 3rd ed. New York: Macmillan, 1988.

Lipsyte, Robert. "Peddling Sports Myths: A Disservice to Young Readers." <u>Children's Literature in Education</u> 11.1 (1980): 12. <u>Sports</u>. Vol. 2. Boca Raton: SIRS, 1981. Art. 1.

Maikovich, Andrew J., ed. <u>Sports Quotations</u>. Jefferson, NC: McFarland, 1984.

Maloney, Lawrence D. "Sports-Crazy Americans." <u>U.S. News & World Report</u> 13 Aug. 1984: 23-24.

Newspaper article with two authors. The "1+" indicates that the article begins on page 1 and continues but not on consecutive pages.

Recktenwald, William, and Andrew Gottesman. "Many Agree Violence Not as Bad as '92." <u>Chicago Tribune</u> 22 June 1993, souvenir ed., sec. 2: 1+.

Shapiro, Leonard, and Donald Huff. "The Games Always End." <u>Washington Post</u> 20 Mar.

Halloran 9

1977:D1, D4. <u>Sports</u> Vol. 1. Boca Raton:
SIRS, 1978. Art. 13.

Sudo, Phil. "America at Play." <u>Scholastic Up-</u>
<u>date</u> 1 May 1992: 2-3.

Meaning

1. What is Maria Halloran's thesis?

2. According to Halloran, what are the negative effects of sports? What are the positive effects of sports?

Writing Strategies

3. Does Halloran provide sufficient support to convince you that the national obsession over sports must end? Which of the points that she includes for support of her position are convincing to you? Which are not convincing?

4. Is the example of violence following the Bulls' game effective in the introduction? How is that information related to her main point?

5. If you were Halloran's peer editor, what suggestions would you make for improving the paper?

A Completed Library, Internet, and Field Research Paper

When Professor Mike Palmquist gave Mark Sanchez's class a research assignment to explore personal identity through family history, Sanchez knew he would have many resources from which to draw information. His story is that of a Chicano family that migrated to southeastern Colorado in the early part of the twentieth century. He knew he could find material in the library on the history of this part of the country. In addition, he could use library resources to link his exploration of identity and family history with similar explorations by contemporary authors Gerald Vizenor and Carlos Fuentes. Since Sanchez had an Internet account at his school, his investigation could include online searches for additional information. Finally, conducting interviews with family members and local professors and making a trip to Las Animas, Colorado, would give his research project the authentic spark it needed.

Early in his process, Mark Sanchez formed his preliminary research question: "How has my identity been shaped by my family's roots on the plains of southeastern Colorado?" After making a preliminary search to assess the availability of relevant sources, he spent weeks collecting, evaluating, and organizing information in preparation for developing a draft. He found along the way that access to a variety of sources strengthened his essay. As you read this paper, see if you agree.

To document his sources, Sanchez used MLA style. He was especially glad to have access to MLA's newest guidelines for citing Internet sources (see p. 808 for these guidelines).

Into Las Animas and Myself
Mark Sanchez
Professor Mike Palmquist
English 101
April 2, 1998

Mark Sanchez turned in an outline with the final draft of his paper. This outline provides a brief overview of the paper's organization.

Outline

Thesis: By understanding our past, we gain insight into ourselves.

I. Learning about Las Animas, Colorado, helps me to understand my family history.
   A. At one time it was a bustling town.
   B. Today it is no longer a thriving place.

II. Knowing about my paternal ancestors helps me to understand my family and myself.
   A. My great-grandfather's grandfather homesteaded in Corazon, New Mexico.
   B. My grandfather's family moved to Las Animas to find work.
   C. My grandfather Octavio Sanchez had a difficult life.
   D. My father Aaron grew up on the farm.

III. Remembering stories of my maternal ancestors deepens my understanding of myself.
   A. My grandmother Sandra Torrez was a strong-willed woman in a tough world.
   B. My mother Jessica was adopted.

IV. Knowing about my parents Aaron and Jessica adds to my self-identity.
   A. They married in 1964.
   B. I was born in 1967.
   C. Both worked hard at a variety of jobs.
   D. They were divorced in 1974.

V. I try to put the pieces together to understand myself.
   A. I suffered an identity crisis.
   B. I explore my self through my writing.

Sanchez 1

Into Las Animas and Myself

"My tribal grandfather and my father were related to the leaders of the crane; that succession . . . is celebrated here in the autobiographical myths and metaphors of my imagination, my crossblood remembrance." (Vizenor 3) Many contemporary writers, such as Gerald Vizenor and Carlos Fuentes, are concerned with self and self-identification through connection to the past. In contrast, many young people do not see the past as something to hold on to, cherish, and identify with. Instead, people constantly find ways to separate themselves from the past and create a new self. Like Vizenor, I want to reconcile my self with my family's past and my Chicano heritage. By looking at the history of mi familia, I want to explore my personal identity--to examine and take pride in my family stories. By understanding our past, we gain insight into ourselves.

To begin my journey into the past and into myself, I must go into Las Animas, the location of much of my family history. Spring has yet to wrestle its way into the landscape of this southeastern Colorado town. Las Animas, Colorado, thirteen miles east of Bents Old Fort along the Arkansas River (Appel and Appel), is the place where my father grew up. It is the town my grandfather grew up in and the place his father moved to in the early 1900s. The family farm is vacant now. I walk the old farm, kick old tires, and pull on an old piece of baling wire in search of those memories that helped shape who I am. Ghosts of eleven chil-

---

Sanchez uses an epigraph to establish a literary context for his own family's story. An ellipsis mark indicates that part of the original is omitted.

Sanchez presents his thesis at the conclusion of his opening paragraph.

The writer cites the two authors of material that he found on a Web site.

Sanchez 2

dren, numerous dogs, horses, and cattle tumble
with the wind that rattles skeletonized cotton-
woods. Lost stories have faded into yellowed
paint that crumbles with the sagging barn.
Glimpses of rabbit hunts along the Arkansas
River and walks through itchy corn fields flash
through my mind. In the middle of all these
memories stands my grandfather, a man who
squeezed my fingers so hard shaking hands that
I'd cry, a man who would show us how to care
for horses and how to avoid being kicked, a man
my father says could load hay bales for hours
(A. Sanchez). However, those days are gone. My
grandfather, Octavio Sanchez, hasn't lived on
the farm for nine years now.

As settlers moved west down the Santa Fe
Trail, Las Animas, Colorado, was the first Spanish town they encountered (Sween). Las Animas
was named after El Rio de Las Animas Perdidas
en Purgatorio (The River of Lost Souls in Pur-
gatory), a group of Spaniards who died in a
flood along the Purgatoire River (Taylor 57).
There is disagreement about exactly who the
Spaniards were. My grandfather says that a
group of settlers perished along the river,
while another story has it that Spanish soldiers "died somewhere along its course without
[proper burial]" (Taylor 58). At one time, Las
Animas was a bustling town of between three and
four thousand people (United Banks 25). "At its
height it had three banks, a JC Penny, a local
grocery story, and a theater, and its largest
employer was Ft. Lyon Veterans Administration
Hospital," my grandfather told me. According to

Print, Internet, and field sources are used in this paragraph.

The writer uses brackets to add information or to make changes within a direct quotation.

The writer cites a corporate author by shortening the name, but the reader can refer to the full citation in the list of works cited.

Sanchez 3

Gene Stuart, a native of the town, "Numerous ranchers and farmers frequented Las Animas's busy diners, gossiping and talking about cattle, corn, and beets. Kids would go to the movies or swim down at the public swimming pool."

Las Animas is still the center of many activities--Santa Fe Trail Day and the Bent County Fair and Rodeo, for example--and historical markers--the Kit Carson Museum, the restored town of Boggsville, and Bents Old Fort (Appel and McCleary). But now the JC Penney building, long empty, is a deathly yellow where weeds, time, and a blistering southeastern sun have eaten away its paint. At night, kids bored for fun can be heard driving its streets or setting off fireworks. Once bustling farms, like my grandfather's, are quiet. Tractors and barbed-wire fences are black from summer and winter rusting away at metal. Tumbleweeds bunch up at barn doors and bury shovels and hoes. Revisiting this place helps me to feel my roots in the earth.

I realize I want to continue my journey into the past by talking with my grandfather. Ever since those days on the farm, I have tried to be the man that my grandfather was. I always offer a firm handshake like he did. I learned from him the value of hard work and perseverance. This man's blood runs through my bones; he and his past, I realize, have helped to create who I am. Today at eighty-one my grandfather lives in Cañon City, where I visit him. He lies covered by an old Navajo blanket. His once

Sanchez mentions his source's name in the body of his paper, so he does not repeat the source information in parentheses. This direct quote came from a personal interview.

Personal observations made in the field inform this descriptive passage.

Sanchez 4

strong hands shake uncontrollably due to
Parkinson's disease. Resting on his back, peeking out from dark eyes, he does his best to answer questions about the past.

I had always imagined that my great-grandfather, Premitivo Sanchez, was a victim of the
Treaty of Guadalupe Hidalgo and that his grandfather and father lost their land when the
United States annexed land that once belonged
to Mexico ("Treaty"). I had always imagined
that much of the fight in me and in my father
stemmed from the days my ancestors fought alongside Emiliano Zapata (Welker). But actually,
they were simply Spanish settlers who, looking
for some place to call their own, homesteaded
in Corazon, New Mexico.

In 1924, when my grandfather was a boy,
his family--father, mother, four brothers, and
three sisters--left New Mexico and moved to Las
Animas because there wasn't enough opportunity
for steady work and income in New Mexico. According to Noberto Valdez, professor of anthropology at Colorado State University, low agriculture prices forced many people in the region
to move and find work elsewhere. The family
moved into a colonia, or labor camp, and worked
hard in the fields hoeing and harvesting sugar
beets and onions (A. Sanchez).

My grandfather Octavio's life as a young man
was never easy. In 1937 he worked in Civilian
Conservation Corps, an organization that re-
cruited men between the ages of seventeen and
twenty-one. The men performed various jobs including building roads through the national for-

This Web document with
no author listed is cited in
the text, and a brief version of the title is given in
quotations within paren-
theses.

Including this source's title
establishes the source as
an authority.

In this reference to a personal interview, the first
initial distinguishes the
source from another with
the same last name.

Sanchez 5

Sanchez builds on his thesis by telling four family stories.

est (Cordova). My grandfather remembers working at Mesa Verde, where he excavated and painted "things to look old." In 1938 he was married, and the first of his eleven children was born later that year. By the time he was drafted into World War II, he had five children and a farm in Las Animas. During the war he served on the USS ROI CV 103 as a third-class metalsmith. Octavio returned home from time to time on leave, but he lost his farm in 1944 because the family could not pay to keep it up. After the war, he returned to Las Animas and was able to repurchase the farm.

My father, Aaron Sanchez, born in 1945, was one of the eleven children raised on that farm. Much of farm life was tough and trying. Mixed in between the hardships, however, were times of fun and horseplay. Aaron and Pablo Sanchez, my uncle, did a lot together because only one year separated them. One time, their older brother, Cesar Sanchez, fresh from the navy, taught his younger brothers how to tie a hangman's noose. The two, "Sheriff Pablo" and "Deputy Aaron," took their sister Maria outside to a three-hundred-year-old cottonwood tree. They made their noose and secured it. My aunt stood on a rusted galvanized bucket and helped her brothers slip the noose around her neck. Before she knew it, the bucket was sent flying with a swift kick. She passed out, and the two boys, realizing their horseplay was no longer playful, ran for help. Fortunately for my aunt, Cesar happened around the corner, saw feet dangling, and ran to take her down.

Sanchez 6

As I listen to my grandfather, I recall stories of my mother and maternal grandmother, who also played a role in shaping who I am. My grandmother, Sandra Torrez, was born in 1907 in New Mexico. She was married at fifteen and lived in an adobe home. In 1927 she divorced her first husband and three years later moved to Las Animas and married my mother's father, Roberto Rodriguez, a railroad worker who was a quiet man, smoked cigars, and enjoyed bottles of beer at the local bar. The legend around Las Animas was that when she found her first husband with another woman, he was so scared that he broke through a window and ran for hours. The woman, Rosario Hernandez, wasn't fast enough. Sandra, six feet tall and one hundred eighty pounds, caught Rosario by the hair and dragged her outside screaming and kicking in all her nakedness. Rosario had a bloody nose and a boot print where Sandra had kicked her in the ribs. Rosario, knees bloodied, tufts of hair missing, finally escaped Sandra's grasp and ran for the woods. Years later, Sandra and Roberto adopted my mother, Jessica, from Sandra's sister, who was too poor to support another child.

Perhaps Sandra should have watched Jessica and young Aaron Sanchez a little more closely because when Aaron was seventeen, he and Jessica decided to leave Las Animas and get married. Three years later, on December 19, 1967, I was born to Aaron and Jessica Sanchez. Jessica worked at a pharmacy in La Junta, and Aaron worked at the railroad. Two and a half years later, in July of 1970, Aaron was trans-

Sanchez 7

ferred to Pueblo, where he could work and go to college. Aaron finished school in 1972 and was hired by Public Service in Loveland, Colorado. We moved, farther from the farm, farther from the family, and within two years, he and Jessica divorced.

This transition moves the reader into the final part of the paper—the author's connection of present with past.

As I sit listening to my grandfather and remembering stories about my family, my mind shifts to thinking about my self again. Like my grandfather and my father, I married and became a father at a young age. My daughter was born with eyes like mine--large dark eyes that dart back and forth. Our skin color is the same; her hair is even strangely layered and unmanageable like mine. There are many similarities between us, which makes me wonder about the similarities between other members of my family and me. Throughout my first twenty-one years, I never really considered my biological history--never thought about mi familia and where "we" had been. I never took pride in being Chicano. I had no Chicano friends or education that taught me the value of identification with my historical roots. Over time, I developed an identity crisis. Who am I? I asked. Mexican? Chicano? American? Would I speak better Spanish if I had been raised in the southwest or on a farm like my dad? Would I understand my past better if I, too, worked in a colonia? Today, as I expand my mind through education and writing, opportunities that other family members had fewer or none of, I explore these questions by putting myself into stories I've written about my family. I am my father irrigating fields next to

Sanchez 8

his father. I am his father clipping horse
hooves. And I am his father loading up a wagon
and leaving New Mexico. I am my grandmother
kicking the woman who slept with her husband. I
am my Aunt Maria with a noose around her neck.
I am all of these people. I am Chicano, and as
my grandfather and Las Animas slip toward
death, both live on in me.

A writer--a creator--I am trying to reconcile my biological and historical selves. I've
learned that the creation of the new stems from
one's ability to wade through the past and combine it with the present. Like my mentors Carlos Fuentes and Gerald Vizenor, I have used my
writing to chart the tangled legends of mi familia and my heritage. As I write, the paths of
the old ancestral roadways become clearer and
the figures become more distinct, until finally
I see my individual self--tenacious, ambitious,
strong-willed--standing at a crossroad and know
that my story is the collective story of my
family. Even though this is a country that
values and encourages individualism and self-
reliance, one can better understand oneself by
making connections to, not severing ties with,
the past. The United States had Carlos Fuentes
believing for a time that "we live only for
the future," but he came to understand that we
can "make present the past as well as the future" (8).

My grandfather is tired from talking. It
is eight at night, and I can see he is ready
for bed. I put my pencil and note pad away and
help him sit up. My wife and daughter hug him

Sanchez reinforces his
thesis with a realization of
what he has learned, and
then he moves to a final
concrete description of
leaving his grandfather.

and walk to the door. When I hug him and shake his hand to leave, his firm grip is gone. His skin drapes on old bones, and I'm not sure how fast to move away. Finally, I leave him there. Driving home, I think about myself, about my father, us at eighty-one. And I wonder how often we will revisit the memories that shape who we are.

Electronic citations always include both the publication date and the access date. The URL (online address) is enclosed in angle brackets.

Book with title and subtitle

Citations for personal interviews include the person interviewed, the title "Personal interview," and the date the interview was conducted.

Web site with no author listed

Citation for a corporate author

Sanchez 10

Works Cited

Appel, Robert, and Katie Appel. "Welcome to Bent County, Colorado, U.S.A.!" Southeast Colorado RC&D, Inc. 24 Jan. 1996. 25 Feb. 1998 <http://www.ruralnet.net/~csn/government/bent.html>.

Appel, Robert, and Colleen McLeary. "Cities, Towns and Communities in SE Colorado." Southeast Colorado RC&D, Inc. 19 Aug. 1996. 25 Feb. 1998 <http://www.ruralnet.net/~csn/government/cities.html>.

Cordova, Jose. Personal interview. 22 Feb. 1998.

Fuentes, Carlos. Myself with Others: Selected Essays. New York: Farrar, 1988.

Sanchez, Aaron. Personal interview. 11 Mar. 1998.

Sanchez, Octavio. Personal interview. 2 Mar. 1998.

Stuart, Gene. Personal interview. 12 Mar. 1998.

Sween, Nancy. "States, Towns, Forts, and Rest Stops along the Santa Fe Trail." CyberTrail (SFT). 15 Mar. 1998. 16 Mar. 1998 <http://raven.cc.ukans.edu/heritage/research/sft/sft-cities.html>.

Taylor, Morris F. Pioneers of the Picketwire. Pueblo: O'Brien Printing & Stationery, 1964.

"The Treaty of Guadalupe Hidalgo." Library of Congress Online. 2 Feb. 1998. 15 Mar. 1998 <http://lcweb.loc.gov/exhibits/ghtreaty>.

United Banks of Colorado, Inc. Las Animas, Colorado: An Economic Overview. Denver: United Banks of Colorado, 1979.

Sanchez 11

Valdez, Noberto. Personal interview. 28 Feb. 1998.

Vizenor, Gerald. Interior Landscapes. Minneapo-
    lis: University of Minnesota, 1990.

Welker, Glenn. "Emiliano Zapata." American Indian
    Heritage Foundation. 7 Jan. 1996. 19 Feb.
    1998 <http://www.indians.org/welker/
    zapata.html>.

Questions to Start
You Thinking

Meaning

1. Why does Sanchez visit Las Animas? Why does he visit Octavio, his grand-father?

2. According to Sanchez, why did many families leave the Southwest in the 1920s?

Writing Strategies

3. For a research paper, Sanchez's opening is fairly nontraditional. What is his purpose in opening like this? Is his opening effective?

4. Where in the essay is Sanchez's thesis? How are the main points in the essay related to the thesis?

5. How does Sanchez integrate library, Internet, and field research? Does he integrate the information from these varied types of research effectively?

A Completed Literary Research Paper

The following is a literary research paper that Chris Robinson wrote for a composition class with a focus on literature. When Professor Whitney gave Robinson's class a research assignment to write a critical analysis with secondary sources on a work that they had read that semester, he was at a loss about where to begin. He considered some of the stories that he had enjoyed reading in class but was unable to come up with an interesting angle to analyze or a question that would benefit from further research.

Then Robinson remembered a discussion in his composition class about a short story by Kate Chopin, "The Story of an Hour" (p. 311). He had thoroughly enjoyed the story and remembered the heated discussion about the story. The issues raised by Chopin were intriguing to Robinson. He wondered what life was really like for Victorian women, why Chopin had written this story, and why some of his classmates had reacted so strongly to it. After rereading the story, conducting some preliminary research, and doing a little more thinking, he formulated a research question: "Why did Chopin write this story, and what was its impact on her society?" He realized that this was a two-pronged topic but decided that he would work on unifying it after he had done his research. As you read his paper, notice how he fuses these two aspects of his investigation to form a unified essay.

To guide the drafting of his paper, Chris Robinson prepared an outline of his paper (see p. 779). (Later he turned it in with the final draft of his paper.) Robinson compared each section of his outline with his research notes to make sure that he had enough sources to support each part of his paper. As he went through his notes, he discovered that the section on Chopin's commentary about the effect of marriage and love on a woman's sense of self was lacking sufficient sources, so he went back to the library and added an additional source to bolster this section. In the formal sentence outline that Robinson prepared, each heading is stated as a complete sentence (for advice on formal outlines, see p. 387).

Outline

Thesis: Through the portrayal of Louise Mallard in "The Story of an Hour," Kate Chopin sets forth the universal theme of the importance of a woman's individual identity.

I. Chopin portrays Louise Mallard as a traditional wife who changes into a New Woman who values individual freedom.

   A. One of Chopin's literary techniques is the names of the main character.

      1. Before her realization of freedom and personal identity, she is referred to as "Mrs. Mallard."

      2. After her awakening, she is called "Louise."

   B. Another technique is physical description.

      1. Before her realization, she is sickly and vulnerable.

      2. After she changes, she is vibrant and victorious.

   C. The main techniques are actions and thoughts.

      1. Before gaining self-knowledge, she is passive and silent.

      2. After her self-understanding, she is free and fully alive.

II. Through Louise's realization, Chopin offers a commentary about the effect of marriage and love on a woman's sense of self, ideas against traditional beliefs of Victorian society.

   A. Chopin suggests that marriage can kill love.

Robinson ii

B. Chopin implies that freedom is a natural state that the institution of marriage upsets, yet such freedom is unrealistic for Victorian women.

C. Chopin suggests that life for the woman who dares to be different is difficult.

In researching and writing his paper, Robinson drew not only on the library research techniques described in this *Research Manual* but also on the strategies for writing about literature that his class had been studying. (For more on writing about literature, see Chapter 12, p. 271)

Robinson's paper, according to his instructor's specifications, is in MLA style. Notice how Robinson cites his secondary research sources as well as his primary source, "The Story of an Hour," in his essay.

MLA guidelines do not require a title page. Instead, include the writer's name, instructor's name, course number, and date on separate, double-spaced lines one inch from the top of the first page flush with the left margin. Double-space to title.

A direct quotation from literary critics in the opening paragraph lends credibility and provides background information. Indent quotations of more than four typed lines one inch (or ten spaces) and double-space with no quotation marks. Citation of source is in parentheses following the end punctuation of the quotation. Authors' names are included in the citation following the quotation because they are not given in the text leading up to the quotation.

Robinson 1

Chris Robinson

Professor MaryJane Whitney

English 101

March 23, 1998

Female Identity in Kate Chopin's
"The Story of an Hour"

In the nineteenth century males were clearly dominant and authoritarian, while females were subservient and passive. Slowly, women began to question their assigned role and responded to the battle between the sexes in a variety of new ways--withdrawal, revolt, and action to change society:

> Significantly, as the hope for a new future merged with revulsion against a contaminated past, and as the vision of a New Woman fused with horror at the traditional woman, much female-authored literature oscillated between extremes of exuberance and despair, between dreams of miraculous victory and nightmares of violent defeat. (Gilbert and Gubar 81)

Such are the characters in the fiction of Kate Chopin, American author of the late nineteenth century. In fact, literary critics Sandra Gilbert and Susan Gubar claim that this oscillation "is perhaps most brilliantly depicted in Kate Chopin's terse, O. Henry-like 'The Story of an Hour'" (81).

When Kate Chopin tried to publish "The Story of an Hour" in 1894, she met with resistance from various magazines, who found the story too radical and feminist for the times.

Robinson 2

Robinson paraphrases to lead in to a memorable quotation.

R. W. Gilder, the editor of the popular magazine Century, rejected the story because he
felt it was immoral. Gilder's opposition to
Chopin's tale of a woman freed by her husband's
apparent death is not surprising, since Gilder
"had zealously guarded the feminine ideal of
self-denying love, and was that very summer
publishing editorials against women's suffrage
as a threat to family and home" (Ewell 89).

The thesis states the main idea of the paper.

To understand the radical nature of
Chopin's message, readers must recognize the
traditional Victorian society in which Chopin
lived, a society in which gender roles were
very traditionally defined. In the character of
Louise Mallard, the author creates a woman who
through the death of her husband comes to the
profound realization of a new life and a self
that she didn't know existed. But ironically,
Chopin also shows Louise's feeling of independence to be a doomed fantasy, because in actuality such a vision of freedom outside of
marriage was an unrealistic goal for nineteenth-
century women. Through this narrative Chopin
sets forth the universal theme of the importance
of a women's individual identity outside of marriage, outside of her role as a man's wife.

The first section of the essay analyzes Chopin's depiction of the evolution of Louise Mallard from a traditional wife to a woman who values indi-vidual freedom outside the confines of marriage.

Chopin portrays Louise Mallard as a typical nineteenth-century wife--fragile, feminine,
and dependent--who changes into a self-assured,
independent individual when she mistakenly
thinks she is freed by her husband's death. One
of Chopin's subtle techniques for this portrayal is the way she names the protagonist.
Early in the story, the character is known as

Robinson 3

"Mrs. Mallard," a title that defines her as
Brently's wife rather than her own person.
Only after Mrs. Mallard realizes her freedom is
she addressed as "Louise" by her sister
Josephine. Critic Mary Papke notes that the
reader comes to learn the difference between
her "social self--Mrs. Mallard--and private female self--Louise" (74). Through the difference
in how the heroine is addressed, Chopin clearly
indicates Louise's awakening female identity.
She has claimed an identity and a life for herself, a life beyond the confines of marriage.

Another effective technique Chopin uses to
depict Mrs. Mallard/Louise is physical description. At the beginning of the story, Mrs. Mallard is very much the traditional Victorian
ideal of a fragile, feminine being. The author
describes her as a delicate creature who is
likely to fall ill at any moment. For example,
Josephine and Richard take great care to "break
[the news of Mallard's death] to her as gently
as possible" because she is believed to have "a
heart trouble" (Chopin 311). Another description of Mrs. Mallard's fragility occurs when,
after she locks herself in her room and exposes
herself to the cold air from the open window,
Josephine begs her to "open the door--you will
make yourself ill" (312). Other physical details portray her as passive. She sits with a
"dull stare" (312) and "a suspension of intelligent thought" (312). In a particularly
telling passage, Chopin describes Mrs. Mallard
as "young, with a fair, calm face, whose lines
[bespeak] repression and even a certain

A transition identifies the source as a recognized authority and leads to a direct quotation, included for the strong, effective language in the original source. The name of the author is mentioned in the text, so the citation gives only the page number.

Robinson uses a transition word to indicate that he will list other examples.

Parenthetical references cite page numbers for both paraphrases and di-rect quotations in primary source, the short story.

Robinson uses narrative details from the plot of the story to support his analysis.

Robinson 4

strength" (312). This description suggests that
she doesn't express her own desires and instead
follows the role prescribed for her by her
society--that of the stoic, silent wife.

While Chopin's early physical description
of Mrs. Mallard conforms to traditional notions
of the "weaker sex," the author gradually provides glimpses of Mrs. Mallard's newfound identity as she emerges from her shell and directly
challenges the prevailing notions of female
identity. Chopin provides physical details
to indicate that a change has occurred in
Louise and she is no longer passive or frightened:

> The vacant stare and the look of ter-
> ror that had followed it went from
> her eyes. They stayed keen and
> bright. Her pulses beat fast, and the
> coursing blood warmed and relaxed
> every inch of her body. (312)

She is fully alive and at ease for the
first time in her life because she is free, and
she is "drinking in a very elixir of life" (312).
There is "a feverish triumph" in her eyes
(313). As she descends the stairs at the ironic
ending, she carries herself like a "goddess of
Victory" (313), suggesting that at that moment
she feels triumphant in her battle for self.

The major evidence of the change in Louise
Mallard is in her actions and thoughts.
Through the shock of her grief Louise Mallard
experiences an awakening of her self and ultimately rejoices in her newfound female identity. Immediately after she hears of her hus-

A transition summarizes
and points forward.
Robinson emphasizes
analysis and interpreta-
tion, not the plot of the
story.

Robinson 5

band's death, she experiences a "storm of
grief" (311), weeping "at once, with sudden
wild abandonment" (311). Then she enters the
first stage of self-discovery by locking herself
in her room alone. This act is her first moment
of stubborn self-assertion, as "she would have
no one follow her" (311). But at this stage,
she has not quite found her independent self.
She seems suspended, sitting "quite motionless"
except when a sob racks her, as a "child who
has cried itself to sleep continues to sob in
its dreams" (312). When she starts to feel some
"thing" or strange feeling, something "too
subtle and elusive to name," coming over her
(312), she waits for it "fearfully" (312). She
tries to "beat it back with her will" but finds
herself "as powerless as her two white slender
hands would have been" (312). Her response to
this newly discovered emotion is like that of a
child who is willful but has no power. According to literary critic Peggy Skaggs, her bewilderment and confusion over her emotions are
typical of Chopin's female characters, who
often "seem to lack a clear concept of their
own roles and purpose in life, a constant grop-
ing for such self-knowledge shaping their personalities and actions" (312). By allowing
these feelings merely to wash over her, Mrs.
Mallard indicates that she is still playing the
passive role of Brently's wife.

      As these conflicting emotions overtake her,
however, Mrs. Mallard realizes the power that
she now holds because of her husband's death.
This "thing that was approaching to possess

Robinson combines his
own ideas with the critic's
comments and supporting
details from the story.

Robinson 6

her" (312) turns out to be a joyous realization that she is free from her husband. Over and over again, she says the words "Free, free, free!" and feels a "monstrous joy" (312) that she can live the rest of her life for herself. She imagines the years "that would belong to her absolutely" (312).

Through Louise's realization, Chopin offers a commentary about the effect of marriage and love on a Victorian woman's sense of self. First, she suggests that marriage can kill love. The reader learns that Louise has loved her husband only "sometimes" because he has often imposed his "private will" on her (312). Even though she knows that Brently loved her, she realizes that his kind intentions were nonetheless cruel because they restricted her independence and identity. She realizes that love is not as strong a need as is "self-assertion, which she suddenly [recognizes] as the strongest impulse of her being" (312). Literary critic Barbara Ewell writes of the recurrence of this theme in Chopin's work: "as Chopin often insists, love is not a substitute for selfhood; indeed, selfhood is love's pre-condition" (89). Louise couldn't really love her husband because she didn't have a sense of her own identity; she didn't know herself. Chopin seems to be saying that by squelching individual identity, especially in women, marriage can squelch love. Love can flourish only if both partners are free. This idea was quite radical at the turn of the century.

A transition sentence leads to the second section of the essay, which claims that the story can be read as a commentary on the effect of marriage and love on a woman's sense of self.

Robinson 7

Even further, Chopin suggests that freedom is a natural thing that the social institution of marriage upsets. When Louise is having her moment of revelation in her room, she communes with nature, the blue sky and "the tops of trees that were all aquiver with the new spring life" (311). Her sister Josephine wants her to shut the window, but Louise refuses because she is "drinking in a very elixir of life through that open window" (312). Women at this time were usually confined to a domestic role, but Louise wants a different role. The open window and the natural images are symbolic of her desire to be free. As Ewell notes, Chopin's story suggests that freedom is a "human right--as natural as generation, spring, or even death" (90). Through the ironic end of Louise's short-lived vision of freedom, Chopin suggests that freedom as an individual, freedom outside of marriage, is unfortunately unrealistic for a nineteenth-century woman. When she sees her husband alive, Louise dies of a heart attack, an attack the doctor calls "joy that kills" (313). The irony of the ending is that she is not overjoyed at finding her husband alive; rather, the "monstrous joy" she has felt at experiencing her own freedom is actually the source of her death. Now that she has found herself, she can't go back to the inequality of marriage, and the only way out is death.

Mary Papke argues that the conclusion of the story both "informs and warns" that if an individual changes but the world around her remains constant, then self-oblivion and death

Robinson paraphrases to avoid quoting excessively. He uses quotation marks around important words from the source.

Robinson 8

may result for a woman who dares to be different (76). Louise's family and friends, however, misinterpret the cause of her death, implying that Victorian society cannot comprehend the joy of a woman outside the confines of marriage. In fact, Chopin's readers at the time the story was first published may not have understood the irony of the ending. Elizabeth McMahan notes that "women in [Chopin's] day did not seek self-determination, did not question whether they had any identity outside of marriage" (34). The tragic ending of "The Story of an Hour" underscores the irony that only through her husband's death, and therefore the death of her marriage, can Louise see the possibilities in life for herself. When she realizes he is alive, she can be free only in death. As Emily Toth suggests, "The Story of an Hour" is "a criticism of the ideal of self-sacrifice that still haunted women at the end of the century" (252).

Chopin's fable of female self-assertion and identity was misunderstood and criticized in her time, but modern readers can find important messages in her story. In a sense, Louise Mallard died because her society could not accept that a married woman could have a self outside of her role as wife. A similar situation brought tragedy to many women in the nineteenth century, and "The Story of an Hour" still carries an important warning for women today: find yourself before you marry.

Brackets indicate an added or altered word in a quotation.

The conclusion suggests that Chopin's story still resonates for contemporary women.

Works cited in the text of a paper are listed here alphabetically by authors' last names. Type "Works Cited," centered, one inch from top. Double-space to first entry, and double-space within and between entries. Indent the second and following lines of each entry five spaces.

The primary source is from a book by three authors.

Multivolume work

Journal article with pagination by issue

Essay in an edited collection

Book by one author

Robinson 9

Works Cited

Chopin, Kate. "The Story of an Hour." The Bedford Guide for College Writers, with Reader, Research Manual, and Handbook. 5th ed. By X. J. Kennedy, Dorothy M. Kennedy, and Sylvia A. Holladay. Boston: Bedford, 1999.

Ewell, Barbara C. Kate Chopin. New York: Ungar, 1986.

Gilbert, Sandra M., and Susan Gubar. The War of the Words. New Haven: Yale UP, 1988. Vol. 1 of No Man's Land: The Place of the Woman Writer in the Twentieth Century. 3 vols. 1988-89.

McMahan, Elizabeth. "Nature's Decoy: Kate Chopin's Presentation of Women and Marriage in Her Short Fiction." Turn of the Century Women 2.2 (1985): 32-35.

Papke, Mary E. "Chopin's Stories of Awakening." Approaches to Teaching Chopin's The Awakening. Ed. Bernard Koloski. New York: MLA, 1988.

Skaggs, Peggy. Kate Chopin. Boston: Twayne, 1985.

Toth, Emily. Kate Chopin. New York: Morrow, 1990.

Questions to Start You Thinking

Meaning

1. What did you learn about the role of Victorian women from reading Chris Robinson's essay?

2. According to Robinson, why did Kate Chopin write "The Story of an Hour"? How was it received by her society?

3. What does Robinson point out as the relevance of this story for modern women and men today? Do you agree with him?

4. What is his thesis?

Writing Strategies

5. How effectively does Robinson unify the two prongs of his original research question in his final research essay?

6. How does Robinson integrate information from the plot of the story with the information he gleaned from his research?

Other Assignments

Using library, Internet, and field sources, write a short research paper, under 2,000 words (Halloran's paper is 1,500 words; Sanchez's is 1,850; Robinson's is 1,900), in which you give a rough survey of the state of knowledge on one of the following topics or on another that you and your instructor agree offers promising opportunities for research. Proceed as if you had chosen to work on the main assignment that is described on page 672.

1. Investigate the career opportunities in a line of work that interests you. Include data from interviews conducted with people in the profession.

2. Write a paper discussing the progress being made in the prevention and cure of a disease or syndrome. Investigate Internet and electronic sources for current data.

3. Discuss the treatment of drug abuse or the rehabilitation methods being used for substance abusers. Analyze the effectiveness of these methods.

4. Discuss the recent political or economic changes occurring in a European, Asian, or African country.

5. Compare student achievement in schools with no (or limited) computer and Internet access with that of those having computer and Internet access in every classroom.

6. Survey the effects of banning advertisements for tobacco products.

7. Study the growth of telecommuting, the tendency of people to work in their own homes, keeping in touch with the main office by phone, fax, e-mail, and wide-area networking.

8. Write a portrait of life in your town or neighborhood as it was in the past, using as sources articles in the local newspaper and interviews with senior citizens. Any photographs or other visual evidence you can gather might be valuable to include. Try to verify any testimony you receive by comparing it with old newspapers or by talking with a local historian.

9. Write a short history of your immediate family, drawing on interviews, photographs, scrapbooks, old letters, written but unpublished records, and any other sources.

10. Study the reasons students today give for going to college. Gather your information from actual interviews with and possibly filled-out questionnaires from students at your college. Try to contact a variety of types of students for your research.

11. Investigate a current trend you have noticed on television (collecting evidence by observing news programs, other programs, or commercials).

12. Write a survey of recent films of a certain kind (detective movies, horror movies, science fiction movies, comedies, love stories), making generalizations that you support with evidence from your own film watching.

Applying What You Learn: Some Uses of Research

In many courses beyond your English course you will be asked to write papers from research — library, electronic, and field research. The more deeply you move into core requirements and specialized courses for your major, the more independent research and thinking you will do. At some colleges, a long research paper is required of all seniors to graduate. Beyond college, the demand for writing based on research is evident. Scholars explore issues that absorb and trouble them and the community of scholars to which they belong. In the business world, large companies often maintain their own specialized libraries since information and opinions are worth money, and decisions have to be based on them. If you should take an entry-level job in the headquarters of a large corporation, don't be surprised to be told, "We're opening a branch office in Sri Lanka, and Graham [the executive vice president] doesn't know a thing about the place. Can you write a report on it — customs, geography, climate, government, state of the economy, political stability, religion, lifestyle, and all that?" If you should decide to start your own business, plan to spend time investigating a variety of resources to determine market segment, growth trends, budgeting, strategic planning, and product development. At a large city newspaper, reporters and feature writers continually do library and Internet research as well as field research, and the newspaper's library of clippings on subjects covered in the past (the "morgue") is in constant use.

As one of the ways they become prominent in their disciplines, academics and professionals in many fields — law, medicine, English, geography, sociology, art history, physics — write and publish papers in specialized journals and whole books based on research. Anthropologists and psychologists study how people live, archaeologists dig up evidence of how people lived in the past, biologists and students of the environment collect evidence about the behavior of species of wildlife — and all of them publish their findings so that other people can learn from them. In an exciting study of urban architecture, *Spaces: Dimensions of the Human Landscape* (New Haven: Yale UP, 1981),

Barrie B. Greenbie draws connections between our notion of "self" — a personal universe bounded by the skin — and our sense of the kind of dwelling we feel at home in. In exploring this relationship (and the need to build dwellings that correspond to our psychic needs), Greenbie brings together sources in psychology, architecture, economics, and literature (the poetry of

FOR GROUP LEARNING

Collaborating on a Research Assignment

To write a collaborative essay from library research is a complex job, and we recommend that you attempt it only if your writing group has already had some success in writing collaboratively. If you embark on such an endeavor, you will find that working as a research team can make your project advance with alacrity. After consulting with your instructor and getting a go-ahead, your group might develop a research paper following one of the assignments in this chapter.

You will need to fix a series of deadlines, parcel out the work, and meet faithfully according to a schedule. Everyone must do his or her share of the work. Here is a sample schedule that one group followed for an eight-week research project:

Week 1: Members individually seek a topic for the group project.

Week 2: The members of the group meet and agree on a topic — a research question. They choose a coordinator to keep the project moving — someone willing to make phone calls to keep in touch with people when necessary. They clear the topic with the instructor.

Weeks 3–4: Assisted by two people, the coordinator makes a preliminary search and compiles a tentative bibliography. The group members meet to divide up responsibilities — who will collect what material. Then, without further meetings, all members begin work.

Week 5: Each member continues his or her assigned portion of the research, reading and taking relevant notes.

Week 6: The group meets to evaluate the material and to see where any further information may be needed. Members collaborate on a rough plan or outline.

Week 7: Three writers divide up the outline, and each writes part of a draft (if possible, with the aid of a word processor). The other group members read over the writing during this week and help solve any problems in it.

Week 8: All group members meet for one long evening session and carefully review the draft. All write comments and corrections on it. Then two fresh writers divide the criticized draft and type it up smoothly. One person in the group who is good at proofreading is designated to do that job for the group. The coordinator gives the whole paper another, final proofreading.

Obviously such a plan can succeed only if your group can work in a close, friendly, and responsible fashion. No one should enter into such an arrangement without first making sure he or she has enough unobstructed time to meet all assigned responsibilities — or else the whole project can bog down in an awful mess. But if it succeeds, as it probably will, your research will generate excitement. You'll know the pleasure of playing your part on a dynamic, functioning team. Many of you will do this type of writing on jobs in the future.

Emily Dickinson). This passage from the beginning of his book may give you a sense of his way of weaving together disparate materials:

> The psychoanalyst Carl Jung placed great emphasis on the house as a symbol of self, and many others have elaborated this idea.[1] Of course Jung considered "self" both in a social as well as individual sense, and in fact the concept of *self* has no meaning except in the context of *others*. Most of us share our houses with some sort of family group during most of our lives, and while parts of an adequately sized house may belong primarily to one or another individual, the boundaries of the home are usually those of a cluster of selves which form a domestic unit. Even people who by choice or circumstance live alone express in their homes the images and traditions formed at one time in a family group.
>
> The architects Kent C. Bloomer and Charles W. Moore view buildings as the projection into space of our awareness of our own bodies. Fundamental and obvious as this relationship might seem, it has been to a great extent ignored in contemporary architecture. Bloomer and Moore sum up the personal situation very well in their book, *Body, Memory, and Architecture:*
>
>> One tell-tale sign remains, in modern America, of a world based not on a Cartesian abstraction, but on our sense of ourselves extended beyond the boundaries of our bodies to the world around: that is the single-family house, free-standing like ourselves, with a face and a back, a hearth (like a heart) and a chimney, an attic full of recollections of *up*, and a basement harboring implications of *down*.[2]
>
> Many North American tract houses fit this characterization less adequately than they might. But whatever the deficiencies of domestic and other kinds of contemporary architecture may be, they are as nothing compared to the shortcomings of most urban design. . . . This book will focus on the hierarchical structures that extend from the "skin" of the family home to the street and beyond.

Notice that Greenbie uses endnote form because the amount of information he has to put in his notes might have interrupted the flow of his prose. Endnote 1, for instance, reads:

> [1] Carl G. Jung, *Memories, Dreams, and Reflections* (London: Fontana Library Series, 1969). For an exceptionally good summary and elaboration, see Clare Cooper, "The House as Symbol of the Self," *Designing for Human Behavior*, ed. J. Lang et al. (Stroudsburg: Dowden, 1974).

You may never do research extensive enough for writing a book, but the techniques you have learned in this chapter will serve you well in other college courses and on the job.

Chapter 30

Documenting Sources

When writers use information from other sources — written or spoken — they *document* those sources. That is, in the text of their paper they cite the exact source (book or article with page number, person interviewed, television program, Web site) for every fact or idea, paraphrased or quoted, from their research. At the end of their paper, they list the sources cited. The purpose of citing and listing sources is twofold: (1) to give proper credit to the original writer or speaker and (2) to enable any interested reader to look up a source for further information. The mechanics of documentation may seem fussy, but the obligation to cite and list sources keeps research writers truthful and responsible.

Writers of college research papers most often follow the rules for citing sources from either of two handbooks — one compiled by the Modern Language Association (MLA) and the other by the American Psychological Association (APA). The documentation style of the MLA is generally observed in English composition, literature, history, foreign language courses, and other humanities. APA documentation style usually prevails in the social sciences and business. If your research takes you into any scholarly or professional journals in those special areas, you will probably find all the articles following a recognizable style.

In other disciplines, other handbooks prescribe style: the *Scientific Style and Format: The CBE Style Manual for Authors, Editors, and Publishers* of the Council of Biology Editors (1994), for instance, is used in the biological sciences and medicine. You will need to familiarize yourself with it, or with other manuals, if you ever do much research writing in those or other disciplines.

You need not memorize any of the documentation styles. Instead, you should understand that you will use different styles in different disciplines, and you need to practice using at least one style to become accustomed to scholarly practices. For the purpose of the papers you write in your composition course, more than likely your instructor will ask you to use the MLA style. Maria Halloran's, Mark Sanchez's, and Chris Robinson's papers in Chapter 29 illustrate the use of this style.

This chapter is here for handy reference. We try to tell you no more than you will need to know to write a freshman research paper. Knowing MLA style or APA style will be useful at these moments:

Citing while you write You'll need to use a documentation style any time you want to document (often on a note card or in your paper) exactly where you obtained a fact, statistic, idea, opinion, quotation, graph, or chart.

Listing all your sources You'll need to use a documentation style when you type a final bibliography (a list entitled "Works Cited" or "References").

Citing Sources: MLA Style

As you write, you need to indicate in the text of your paper or in a parenthetical reference what you borrowed and where you found it. For complete information about your source, readers can then turn to the end of your paper and refer to your list titled "Works Cited" (see p. 802). The *MLA Handbook for Writers of Research Papers,* 4th ed. (New York: MLA, 1995) has extensive and exact recommendations. If you want more detailed advice than that given here, you can purchase a copy of the *MLA Handbook* or see a copy in the reference room of your college library.

CITING PRINTED SOURCES: NONFICTION BOOKS

To cite a book in the text of a paper, you usually place in parentheses the author's last name and the number of the page containing the information cited.

SINGLE AUTHOR

One reason we admire Simone de Beauvoir is that "she lived the life she believed" (Morgan 58).

At least one critic maintains that Dean Rusk's exposure to Nazi power in Europe in the 1930s permanently influenced his attitude toward appeasement:

> In contrast to Acheson, who had attended Groton, Yale, and Harvard despite his family's genteel poverty, Rusk was sheer Horatio Alger stuff. He had grown up barefoot, the son of a tenant farmer in Georgia's Cherokee County, and had worked his way through Davidson. . . . Then came the moment that transformed his life and

```
his thinking. He won a Rhodes scholarship to
Oxford. More important, his exposure to Europe
in the early 1930s, as the Nazis consolidated
their power in Germany, scarred his mind, lead-
ing him to share Acheson's hostility to ap-
peasement in any form anywhere. (Karnow 194)
```

Notice that a direct quotation longer than four lines is indented one inch (or ten spaces) and needs no quotation marks to set it off from the text of your paper.

TWO OR MORE AUTHORS

For the sake of readability and transition, you'll sometimes want to mention an author or authors in your text, putting only the page number in parentheses.

```
Taylor and Wheeler present yet another view (25).
```

MULTIPLE WORKS BY THE SAME AUTHOR

If you have used two or more works by the same author (or authors), you need to indicate with an abbreviated title which one you are citing in your text. In a paper that uses as sources two books by Iona and Peter Opie, *The Lore and Language of Schoolchildren* and *The Oxford Nursery Rhyme Book*, you would cite the first book as follows:

```
The Opies found that the children they interviewed were
more straightforward when asked about their "magic prac-
tices" or their "ways of obtaining luck or averting ill
luck" than when asked about their "superstitions" (Lore
210).
```

A MULTIVOLUME WORK

For a work with multiple volumes, provide the author's name and the volume number followed by a colon and the page number.

```
In ancient times, astrological predictions were sometimes
used as a kind of black magic (Sarton 2: 319).
```

INDIRECT SOURCE

Whenever possible, cite the original source. If that source is unavailable to you (as often happens with published accounts of spoken remarks), use the abbreviation "qtd. in" (for "quoted in") before the secondary source you cite in parentheses.

```
Zill says that, psychologically, children in stepfamilies
most resemble children in single-parent families, even if
they live in a two-parent household (qtd. in Derber 119).
```

CITING PRINTED SOURCES: LITERATURE

NOVEL OR SHORT STORY

```
In A Tale of Two Cities, Dickens describes the aptly
named Stryver, who "had a pushing way of shouldering him-
self (morally and physically) into companies and conver-
sations, that argued well for his shouldering his way up
in life" (110; bk. 2, ch. 4).
```

PLAY

For classic plays, leave out page numbers and include the act, scene, and line numbers, separating them with periods.

```
Love, Iago says, "is merely a lust of the blood and a
permission of the will" (Othello 1.3.326).
```

```
In Equus, Dora says, "What the eye does not see, the
heart does not grieve over, does it?" (1.7).
```

POETRY

When you cite poetry, use the word *line* or *lines* in the first reference, and cite only numbers in subsequent references, as in the following examples from William Wordsworth's "The World Is Too Much with Us." The first reference:

```
"The world is too much with us; late and soon / Getting
and spending, we lay waste our powers" (lines 1-2).
```

The subsequent reference:

```
"Or hear old Triton blow his wreathed horn" (14).
```

A WORK IN AN ANTHOLOGY

For works in an anthology, use the author of the selection, not the editor of the collection, in your text or in the parentheses.

```
In the opening lines of Julio Marzán's "The Ingredient,"
Vincent finds himself looking down on his neighborhood
from a rooftop and realizing that "there was a kind of
beauty to the view" (145).
```

CITING PRINTED SOURCES: REFERENCE BOOKS AND PERIODICALS

ARTICLE IN A REFERENCE BOOK

In citing a one-page article from a work with entries arranged alphabetically, include the author's name in your text or in the parenthetical reference and omit the page number.

> Some intellectuals have offered unusual definitions of
> love, with one calling it the force that enables individ-
> uals to "understand the separateness of other people"
> (Havell).

If a reference article is long, give the page number.

> Gordon discusses Carver's "implosive" technique of ending
> stories just before epiphany (176).

If the article is unsigned, include a brief title in your text or in the parenthetical citation.

> She alienated many feminists with her portraits of women
> "who seemed to accept victimization" ("Didion").

JOURNAL ARTICLE

If the author is named in the text, cite just the page number(s) in the parenthetical reference.

> Mueller notes that Arthur's quest "aims at a goal that
> is, suggestively, beyond the immediate context of the
> narrative" (751).

If the author is not named in the text, provide the name in the reference.

> Arthur's quest "aims at a goal that is, suggestively, be-
> yond the immediate context of the narrative" (Mueller
> 751).

MAGAZINE OR NEWSPAPER ARTICLE

In citing a one-page magazine or newspaper article, include the author's name in your text or in a parenthetical reference. Do not include the page number, which will be noted in the list of works cited at the end of the paper.

```
Vacuum-tube audio equipment is making a comeback, with
aficionados praising the warmth and glow from the tubes,
as well as the sound (Patton).
```

When citing articles longer than one page, provide the specific page number(s) in the parenthetical reference.

```
Some less than perfect means have been used to measure
television viewership, including a sensor that scans
rooms for "hot bodies" (Larson 69).
```

When citing an anonymous magazine article, put the first few words of the title of the article in parentheses, beginning with the word by which it is alphabetized in the list of works cited.

```
At least one former gang member has gone on to write
about his experiences ("Other Side").
```

THE BIBLE

```
The Bible speaks of the sacrifice God made to save the
world (John 3.16).
```

No entry is necessary in the list of works cited.

CITING ELECTRONIC AND OTHER NONPRINT SOURCES

WEB SITE

You should document your electronic and nonprint material — such as interviews or tapes — as faithfully as you credit books, newspapers, and periodicals. Treat a World Wide Web site the same as you would treat a print source, indicating the author (or, if no author, a brief title) in parentheses.

```
Survival of breast cancer depends a lot on early detec-
tion before the cancer has a chance to spread. The
five-year survival rate for a woman with localized breast
cancer is 93 percent (Bruckheim).
```

ONLINE ARTICLE

You may also gracefully weave your mention of each source into the body of your paper. In your list of works cited you give complete information about each source.

Robert S. Boynton's article on <u>The Atlantic Monthly On-line</u> explored the recent achievements and popularity of the new African American intellectuals.

INTERVIEW

In a recent interview, nutritionist Christina Diaz revealed that eating disorders among teens, especially teenage girls, are mainly triggered by control issues.

RECORDING

Hearing Yeats reading "The Song of the Old Mother" on tape sheds new light on several lines in the poem.

For more about incorporating material gracefully, see the suggestions in Chapter 29, page 737.

Listing Sources: MLA Style

At the end of your paper, you will provide a list of the sources from which you have cited ideas or information in your text. If you indicated the work and page number on each of your source notes while doing your research, you will have little trouble compiling this list. For most English courses, you will follow the guidelines set forth by the Modern Language Association (MLA).

The list of sources is called "Works Cited," includes only those sources actually used in your paper, and is placed at the end of your paper. Center the title at the top of a new page. Double-space the list, and alphabetize the entries by authors' last names or, for works with no author, by title. When an entry exceeds one line, indent the second and subsequent lines one-half inch (or five spaces).

LISTING PRINTED SOURCES: BOOKS

Notice that the information about each source is divided into three sections, each followed by a period — author or agency's name (if there is one), title, and publishing information. Give the author's name, last name first, and the title in full as they appear on the title page. (If a work has more than one author, all names after the first are given in normal order.) If the publisher lists more than one city, include just the first. Use just the first name of a publisher with multiple names: not Holt, Rinehart and Winston, but simply Holt. Omit initials too. For J. B. Lippincott Co., simply write Lippincott.

SINGLE AUTHOR

>Bolton, Ruthie. <u>Gal: A True Life</u>. New York: Harcourt, 1994.

TWO OR THREE AUTHORS

>Phelan, James R., and Lewis Chester. <u>The Money: The</u>
>   <u>Battle for Howard Hughes's Billions</u>. New York:
>   Random, 1997.

FOUR OR MORE AUTHORS

>Roark, James L., et al. <u>The American Promise</u>. Boston:
>   Bedford, 1998.

MULTIPLE WORKS BY THE SAME AUTHOR

List the works alphabetically by title.

>Gould, Stephen Jay. Full House: <u>The Spread of Excellence</u>
>   <u>from Plato to Darwin</u>. New York: Harmony, 1996.

>---, ed. <u>Questioning the Millennium</u>. New York: Harmony,
>   1997.

CORPORATE AUTHOR

>Student Conservation Association. <u>The Guide to Graduate</u>
>   <u>Environmental Programs</u>. Washington: Island, 1997.

UNKNOWN AUTHOR

><u>Alcoholism and You</u>. Pearl Island: Okra, 1986.

EDITED BOOK

If your paper focuses on the work or its author, cite the author first.

>Hardy, Thomas. <u>Tess of the D'Urbervilles</u>. Ed. Scott
>   Elledge. 3rd ed. New York: Norton, 1991.

If your paper focuses on the editor or the edition used, cite the editor first.

>Elledge, Scott, ed. <u>Tess of the D'Urbervilles</u>. By Thomas
>   Hardy. 3rd ed. New York: Norton, 1991.

TRANSLATED WORK

> Hoeg, Peter. <u>Tales of the Night</u>. Trans. Barbara Haveland.
> New York: Farrar, 1998.

If your paper focuses on the translation, cite the translator first.

> Haveland, Barbara, trans. <u>Tales of the Night</u>. By Peter
> Hoeg. New York: Farrar, 1998.

MULTIVOLUME WORK

> <u>Out of Many: A History of the American People</u>. 2 vols.
> Englewood Cliffs: Prentice, 1994.

> Ford, Boris, ed. <u>The Age of Shakespeare</u>. New York: Pen-
> guin, 1982. Vol. 2 of <u>The New Pelican Guide to</u>
> <u>English Literature</u>. 8 vols. 1982-84.

REVISED EDITION

> Starke, Mary C. <u>Strategies for College Success</u>. 3rd ed.
> New York: Prentice, 1997.

BOOK IN A SERIES

> Berlin, Jeffrey B., ed. <u>Approaches to Teaching Mann's</u>
> <u>Death in Venice</u>. <u>Approaches to Teaching World Lit</u>.
> 43. New York: MLA, 1992.

LISTING PRINTED SOURCES: PARTS OF BOOKS

When documenting parts of books give the author of the book first. The editor of the book should follow the title. Following the publication information
give the page numbers of the selection.

CHAPTER OR SECTION IN A BOOK

> Greene, Evarts B. "The Revolutionary Generation, 1763-
> 90." <u>A History of American Life</u>. Ed. Arthur M.
> Schlesinger, Jr. New York: Scribner, 1996. 289-408.

ESSAY, SHORT STORY, POEM, OR PLAY IN AN EDITED COLLECTION

> Sandor, Marjorie. "You with Your Nose in a Book." <u>The</u>
> <u>Most Wonderful Books</u>. Eds. Michael Dorris and Emilie
> Buchwald. Minneapolis: Milkweed, 1997. 219-21.

TWO OR MORE WORKS FROM THE SAME EDITED COLLECTION

The following examples show citations for articles in the collection *Growing Up Latino: Memoirs and Stories* as well as the citation for the collection itself.

> Alvarez, Julia. "Daughter of Invention." Augenbraum and
>   Stavans 3-15.
>
> Augenbraum, Harold, and Ilan Stavans, eds. Growing Up
>   Latino: Memoirs and Stories. Boston: Houghton, 1993.
>
> Colón, Jesús. "Kipling and I." Augenbraum and Stavans
>   155-58.

AN INTRODUCTION, PREFACE, FOREWORD, OR AFTERWORD

> Godwin, Mike. Foreword. High Noon on the Electronic Fron-
>   tier. Ed. Peter Ludlow. Cambridge: MIT, 1996. xiii-
>   xvi.

LISTING PRINTED SOURCES: REFERENCE BOOKS

It is unnecessary to supply the editor, publisher, or place of publication for well-known references such as *Webster's, The Random House Dictionary, World Book Encyclopedia,* and *Encyclopaedia Britannica.* Omit volume and page numbers when citing an entry from a reference that is arranged alphabetically.

SIGNED DICTIONARY ENTRY

> Turner, V. W. "Divination." A Dictionary of the Social
>   Sciences. Ed. Julius Gould and William L. Kolb. New
>   York: Free, 1964.

UNSIGNED DICTIONARY ENTRY

> "Organize." Webster's Third New International Dictionary.
>   1993 ed.

SIGNED ENCYCLOPEDIA ARTICLE

> Binder, Raymond C., et al. "Mathematical Aspects of Phys-
>   ical Theories." Encyclopaedia Britannica: Macropae-
>   dia. 15th ed. 1993.

UNSIGNED ENCYCLOPEDIA ARTICLE

> "Jellyfish." Encyclopaedia Britannica: Micropaedia. 1993 ed.

LISTING PRINTED SOURCES: PERIODICALS

JOURNAL ARTICLE WITH SEPARATE PAGINATION

To list an article from a journal that paginates each issue of a volume separately, provide the volume number and issue number, separated by a period.

```
Ferris, Lucy. "'Never Truly Members': Andre Dubus's Pa-
     triarchal Catholicism." South Atlantic Review 62.2
     (1997): 39-55.
```

JOURNAL ARTICLE WITH CONTINUOUS PAGINATION

In journals with continuous pagination, page numbers run continuously through all issues of a volume. To cite these journals, give the volume number, year, and page numbers.

```
Daly, Mary E. "Recent Writing on Modern Irish History:
     The Interaction between Past and Present." Journal
     of Modern History 69 (1997): 512-33.
```

SIGNED MAGAZINE ARTICLE

```
Weschler, Lawrence. "Artist in Exile." New Yorker 5 Dec.
     1994: 88-106.
```

If the article does not appear on consecutive pages, list the starting page number followed by +.

```
Lemley, Brad. "The Underground Architect." New Age
     Jan.-Feb. 1995: 66+.
```

UNSIGNED MAGAZINE ARTICLE

```
"Other Side of Cool." Mother Jones May-June 1992: 19.
```

SIGNED NEWSPAPER ARTICLE

```
Kolata, Gina. "Men and Women Use Brain Differently, Study Dis-
     covers." New York Times 16 Feb. 1995, natl. ed.: A1+.
```

```
Wilkie, Curtis. "Mississippi Flogging Debate Opens Old
     Wounds." Boston Globe 21 Feb. 1995: 1.
```

UNSIGNED NEWSPAPER ARTICLE

```
"U.S. Seeks Broader NATO Ties for Russia." Boston Globe
     21 Feb. 1995: 4.
```

SIGNED EDITORIAL

> Schrag, Peter. "When Government Goes on Autopilot."
>   Editorial. New York Times 16 Feb. 1995, natl.
>   ed.: A27.

UNSIGNED EDITORIAL

> "Budget Fudge." Editorial. Nation 27 Feb. 1995: 259-60.

PUBLISHED INTERVIEW

> Kallen, Ben. "Freeing Your Inner Artist." New Age Journal
>   Feb. 1995: 53+.

LETTER TO THE EDITOR

> Freeland, Edward P. Letter. Atlantic Feb. 1995: 10.

REVIEW

> Passaro, Vince. "The Unsparing Vision of Don DeLillo."
>   Rev. of Underworld, by Don DeLillo. Harper's Nov.
>   1997: 72-75.

LISTING OTHER PRINTED SOURCES

GOVERNMENT DOCUMENT

> U.S. Bureau of the Census. Statistical Abstract of the
>   United States: 1997. Washington: U.S. Department of
>   Commerce, 1997.

PAMPHLET

> Association of American Publishers. An Author's Primer to
>   Word Processing. New York: Assn. of Amer. Publish-
>   ers, 1983.

UNPUBLISHED DOCTORAL DISSERTATION

> Beilke, Debra J. "Cracking Up the South: Humor and Iden-
>   tity in Southern Renaissance Fiction." Diss. U. of
>   Wisconsin--Madison, 1997.

PERSONAL LETTER

> Finch, Katherine. Letter to the author. 15 Jan. 1998.

ADVERTISEMENT

> Marriott. Advertisement. <u>Sports Illustrated</u> 9 Mar. 1998:
> 37.

LISTING INTERNET AND ELECTRONIC SOURCES

With an increasing amount and variety of information available to you through the Internet, it is critical that you document electronic sources in a consistent and responsible way. The following documentation models are consistent with MLA's most recent guidelines, which can be found in *The MLA Style Manual* (2nd ed., 1998) or at <http://www.mla.org>.

Here are the basic elements of an Internet or electronic citation:

Name of the author (if known)
Title of the site or document
Name of the sponsoring organization (if any)
Date of publication or of latest update
Date of access
URL (online address), in angle brackets

Notice that since most Internet sources do not have page numbers, these are not required.

PROFESSIONAL OR PERSONAL WEB SITE

If the author's name is unknown, begin with the site title.

> <u>EPA Laws and Regulations Page</u>. United States Environmen-
> tal Protection Agency. 6 Mar. 1998. 11 Mar. 1998.
> <http://www.epa.gov/epahome/rules.html>.

If no title is available, include a description such as *Home page*.

> Watson, Chad J. Home page. 27 Jan. 1998. 10 Mar. 1998
> <http://cc.usu.edu/~slypx/index.html>.

ONLINE SCHOLARLY PROJECT OR REFERENCE DATABASE

For an online source accessed from within a larger scholarly project or reference database, begin your citation with the author (if any) and title of the source, followed by any editors or translators. Continue with electronic publication information, including version number (if relevant and available), date of electronic publication or of the latest update, name of the sponsoring organization, date of access, and URL.

> <u>The Einstein Papers Project</u>. Ed. Robert Schulmann.
> 18 Feb. 1998. Boston U. 10 Mar. 1998 <http://
> albert.bu.edu>.

```
"Osteoporosis." Britannica Online. Vers. 98.1. Sept. 97.
    Encyclopaedia Britannica. 10 Mar. 1998
    <http://www.eb.com:180/cgi-bin/g?DocF = micro/
    443/47.html>.
```

ARTICLE IN AN ONLINE PERIODICAL

When citing articles from online journals, magazines, and newspapers, follow the guidelines for citing print articles (see pp. 806–07), modifying them as necessary. Be sure to end the citation with the date of access and the URL.

```
Kongshem, Lars. "Censorware: How Well Does Internet Fil-
    tering Software Protect Students?" Electronic School
    Jan. 1997. 10 Mar. 1998 <http://www.electronic
    -school.com/0198f1.html>.
```

```
Loker, William M. "'Campesinos' and the Crisis of Modern-
    ization in Latin America." Journal of Political
    Ecology 3.1 (1996). 13 Mar. 1998 <http://
    www.library.arizona.edu/ej/jpe/volume_3/
    ascii-lokeriso.txt>.
```

AN ONLINE POSTING

To cite a newsgroup posting, provide the author's name, followed by the title of the posting (the subject line) in quotation marks, the posting date, the words *Online posting*, the date of access, and the name of the newsgroup, with the prefix *news*.

```
Cowan, Cheryl. "Eating Disorders." 23 Feb. 1998. Online
    posting. 16 Mar. 1998 <news:alt.arts.ballet>.
```

To cite a posting to an e-mail discussion list, provide the author's name, followed by the title of the posting (the subject line) in quotation marks, the posting date, the words *Online posting*, the name of the forum (if known), the date of access, and the list's Internet site (if available) or the list moderator's e-mail address.

```
Royar, Robert D. "Internet Linked Courses." 28 Feb. 1998.
    Online posting. Alliance for Computers and Writing.
    3 Mar. 1998 <acw-l@ttacs6.ttu.edu>.
```

GOPHER, FTP, AND TELNET SITES

To cite Internet documents retrieved by protocols other than http, follow the guidelines for World Wide Web documents presented earlier in this section.

Lovelace, Dean, and Gordon Welty. "Community Policing in
Dayton: More Flash Than Substance?" <u>Dayton Daily
News</u> 29 May 1992. 16 Mar. 1998 <ftp://ftp.etext.org/
pub/Politics/Essays/community.policing>.

ELECTRONIC MAIL

Wirth, Eric. E-mail to the author. 12 Mar. 1998.

A PUBLICATION ON CD-ROM

Sheehy, Donald, ed. <u>Robert Frost: Poems, Life, Legacy</u>.
CD-ROM. New York: Holt, 1997.

COMPUTER SOFTWARE

<u>Electronic Supplements for Real Writing: 1. Interactive
Writing Software</u>. Vers. 1. Diskette. Boston: Bedford, 1998.

MATERIAL ACCESSED THROUGH AN ONLINE COMPUTER SERVICE

Cite the print information first, followed by the online information and
the date of access.

Boynton, Robert S. "The New Intellectuals." <u>Atlantic
Monthly</u> Mar. 1995. <u>Atlantic Monthly Online</u>. Online.
America Online. 3 Mar. 1995.

LISTING OTHER NONPRINT SOURCES

AUDIOTAPE OR RECORDING

Begin with the name of the speaker, the writer, or the production director, depending on what you want to emphasize.

Byrne, Gabriel. <u>The James Joyce Collection</u>. Dove Audio,
1996.

Yeats, William Butler. "The Song of the Old Mother." <u>The
Poems of William Butler Yeats</u>. Read by William But-
ler Yeats, Siobhan McKenna, and Michael MacLiammoir.
Audiotape. Spoken Arts, 1974.

TELEVISION OR RADIO PROGRAM

<u>The Windsors: A Royal Family</u>. PBS. WGBH, Boston. 12 Mar.
1995.

"A Dangerous Man: Lawrence after Arabia." Perf. Ralph
    Fiennes and Siddig el Fadil. Great Performances.
    PBS. WNET, New York. 6 May 1992.

FILM

Primary Colors. Dir. Mike Nichols. Universal, 1998.

If you cite a person connected with the film, start with his or her name.

Nichols, Mike, dir. Primary Colors. Universal, 1998.

PERFORMANCE

Whale Music. By Anthony Minghella. Dir. Anthony
    Minghella. Perf. Francie Swift. Theater Off Park,
    New York. 23 Mar. 1998.

A WORK OF ART

Botticelli, Sandro. The Birth of Venus. Uffizi Gallery,
    Florence.

SPEECH OR LECTURE

Hurley, James. Address. Opening Gen. Sess. Amer. Bar
    Assn. Convention. Chicago, 17 Jan. 1987.

BROADCAST INTERVIEW

Haffner, Robert. Interview. WBUR, Boston. 16 Mar. 1998.

PERSONAL INTERVIEW

Boyd, Dierdre. Personal interview. 5 Feb. 1994.

Ladner, John. Telephone interview. 20 Oct. 1995.

Citing Sources: APA Style

The American Psychological Association (APA) details the style most commonly used in the social sciences in its *Publication Manual*, 4th ed. (Washington: APA, 1994). As in MLA style, APA citations are placed in parentheses in the body of the text.

CITING PRINTED SOURCES

To cite a work in the APA style, you usually place in parentheses the author's last name, a comma, and the year the source was published. Place this information as close as possible to the information you have borrowed. Give a page number in parentheses only for a direct quotation from the source.

SINGLE AUTHOR NOT CITED IN TEXT

A number of experts now believe that cognitive development begins much earlier than Piaget had thought (Gelman, 1978).

AUTHOR CITED IN TEXT

If the author's name appears in the body of the text, give only the date in parentheses.

> As Gelman (1978) points out, a number of experts now be-
> lieve that cognitive development begins much earlier than
> Piaget had thought.

If you are citing ideas from a long work, you can refer to a specific page so your readers can easily find the reference. Use the abbreviation *p.* (or *pp.*).

> Dean Rusk's exposure to Nazi power in Europe in the 1930s
> seems to have permanently influenced his attitude toward
> appeasement (Karnow, 1991, p. 194).

When the author's name appears in the text, put the page number in parentheses after the cited material.

> Karnow (1991) maintains that Dean Rusk's exposure to Nazi
> power in Europe in the 1930s "scarred his mind" (p. 194).

QUOTATION FORMAT

If you quote more than forty words from your source, indent the whole quotation five spaces. Put the author's name, the publication year, and the page number in parentheses following the quotation with no additional period.

> At least one critic maintains that Dean Rusk's exposure
> to Nazi power in Europe in the 1930s permanently influ-
> enced his attitude toward appeasement:
>> Then came the moment that transformed his life and
>> his thinking. He won a Rhodes scholarship to Ox-
>> ford. More important, his exposure to Europe in the
>> early 1930s, as the Nazis consolidated their power
>> in Germany, scarred his mind, leading him to share
>> Acheson's hostility to appeasement in any form any-
>> where. (Karnow, 1991, p. 194)

TWO AUTHORS

Refer to coauthors by their last names, in the order in which they appear in the book or article you cite. Join the names by *and* if you mention them in the body of your text and by an ampersand (&) if the citation is in parentheses.

```
Ex-mental patients released from institutions but given
no follow-up care will almost surely fail to cope with
the stresses of living on their own (Bassuk & Gerson,
1978).
```

```
Bassuk and Gerson (1978) hold out little hope for ex-
mental patients who are released from institutions but
are given no follow-up care.
```

THREE TO FIVE AUTHORS

When a book or article you cite has three to five authors, include all the last names in your first reference only. In referring to the same source again, use the first author's name only, followed by *et al.* (for "and others"), whether in text or in parentheses.

```
In one study, the IQs of adopted children were found to
correlate more closely with the IQs of their biological
mothers than with those of their adoptive mothers (Horn,
Loehlin, & Wellerman, 1975).
```

CORPORATE AUTHOR

```
There are three signs of oxygen deprivation (American Red
Cross, 1984).
```

GOVERNMENT DOCUMENT

In the first citation in your text, identify the document by originating agency, followed by its abbreviation (if any) and year of publication (and page number, if appropriate).

```
Clearly, it is of paramount importance to stop the spread
of mosquito-borne diseases (Department of Health and
Human Services [DHHS], 1986, p. 25).
```

In later citations use just the abbreviation for the agency and the date: (DHHS, 1986).

UNKNOWN AUTHOR

When you cite an anonymous work, identify it with a short title and a date.

```
There are questions people can ask themselves if they
suspect their drinking has gotten out of hand
(Alcoholism, 1986).
```

MULTIPLE WORKS BY THE SAME AUTHOR

```
One nuclear energy proponent for years has insisted on
the importance of tight controls for the industry (Wein-
berg, 1972)....He goes so far as to call on utility com-
panies to insure each reactor with their own funds (Wein-
berg, 1977).
```

CITING OTHER SOURCES

PERSONAL COMMUNICATIONS

Personal communications — including personal interviews, letters, memos, and electronic mail — are not listed in the references in APA style. But in the text of your paper, you should include the initials and surname of your communicator, with the date of the communication.

```
C. G. Sherwood (personal communication, September 29,
1986) has specific suggestions about the market in
Belgium.
```

```
It is important to keep in mind the cultural differences
between countries, especially the differences between the
United States and Belgium (C. G. Sherwood, personal com-
munication, September 29, 1986).
```

WEB SITE

Treat a World Wide Web site the same as you would treat a print source, indicating the author's last name and year of publication in parentheses.

```
Survival of breast cancer depends a lot on early detec-
tion before the cancer has a chance to spread. The five-
year survival rate for a woman with localized breast can-
cer is 93 percent (Bruckheim, 1998).
```

Listing Sources: APA Style

If you're using APA guidelines, each entry should contain most of the same information given in an MLA citation, but the format is slightly different. In the APA style, the list of works cited is called "References" and appears at the end of the text. For entries that run past the first line, indent subsequent lines five spaces.

Organize your list alphabetically by authors' last names. The year appears immediately following the authors' names, in parentheses. In the titles of books and articles, capitalize only the first word, proper names, and the first word following a colon. Underline book titles, but use no quotation marks or underlining for article titles. Underline journal names and capitalize all important words. For the authors' first and middle names, only initials are used. Note that APA style uses a more complete name for a publisher (including *Press*) than does MLA style.

LISTING PRINTED SOURCES: BOOKS

SINGLE AUTHOR

> Karnow, S. (1991). <u>Vietnam: A history.</u> New York: Viking.

TWO OR MORE AUTHORS

> Abelson, R., & Friquegnon, M. (1982). <u>Ethics for modern life.</u> New York: St. Martin's Press.

CORPORATE AUTHOR

> American Red Cross. (1984). <u>Lifesaving: Rescue and water safety.</u> New York: Doubleday.

UNKNOWN AUTHOR

> <u>Alcoholism and you.</u> (1986). Pearl Island: Okra Press.

MULTIPLE WORKS BY THE SAME AUTHOR

Arrange the titles by date, the earliest first:

> Gould, S. J. (1996). <u>Full house: The spread of excellence from Plato to Darwin.</u> New York: Harmony.

> Gould, S. J. (Ed.). (1997). <u>Questioning the millennium.</u> New York: Harmony.

CHAPTER OR SECTION OF A BOOK

> Galbraith, J. K. (1984). The military power. In Gwyn Prins (Ed.), <u>The nuclear crisis reader</u> (pp. 197-209). New York: Vintage Books.

INTRODUCTION, PREFACE, FOREWORD, OR AFTERWORD

> Godwin, M. (1996). Foreword. In P. Ludlow (Ed.), <u>High noon on the electronic frontier</u> (pp. xiii-xvi). Cambridge: MIT Press.

WORK IN AN EDITED COLLECTION

> Tollifson, J. (1997). Imperfection is a beautiful thing:
> On disability and meditation. In K. Fries (Ed.),
> Staring Back (pp. 105-112). New York: Plume.

EDITED BOOK

> Schneir, M. (Ed.). (1994). Feminism in our time: Essen-
> tial writings, World War II to the present. New
> York: Vintage Books.

TRANSLATED WORK

> Ishinomori, I. (1988). Japan inc.: Introduction to Japan-
> ese economics (B. Schneiner, Trans.). Berkeley: Uni-
> versity of California Press. (Original work pub-
> lished 1986.)

REVISED EDITION

> Starke, M. (1997). Strategies for college success (3rd
> ed.). New York: Prentice Hall.

LISTING PRINTED SOURCES: PERIODICALS

ARTICLE FROM A JOURNAL PAGINATED BY ISSUE

> Meyer, D. S. (1992). Star wars, Star Wars, and American
> political culture. Journal of Popular Culture,
> 26(2), 99-115.

ARTICLE FROM A JOURNAL PAGINATED BY VOLUME

> Martin, J. (1997). Inventing sincerity, refashioning
> prudence: The discovery of the individual in Renais-
> sance Europe. American Historical Review, 102, 1309-
> 1342.

MAGAZINE ARTICLE

> Lankford, K. (1998, April). The trouble with rules of
> thumb. Kiplinger's Personal Finance Magazine, 52,
> 102-104.

SIGNED NEWSPAPER ARTICLE

> Brody, J. E. (1995, February 21). Health factor in veg-
> etables still elusive. New York Times, p. C1.

UNSIGNED NEWSPAPER ARTICLE

> Stimulation seen to hurt babies' sleeping habits. (1995,
> February 21). Boston Globe, p. 13.

SIGNED EDITORIAL

> Kass, R. (1998, March 23). Wanted: An official state jan-
> itor. [Editorial.] Boston Globe, p. A15.

UNSIGNED EDITORIAL

> Military mischief in Indonesia. (1998, March 23). [Edito-
> rial.] New York Times, p. A20.

LETTER TO THE EDITOR

> Beeman, R. H. (1994, September). Time travel [Letter to
> the editor]. Scientific American, 271, 10.

REVIEW

> Rose, T. (1998, February 24). Blues sisters [Review of
> the book Blues legacies and black feminism: Gertrude
> "Ma" Rainey, Bessie Smith, and Billie Holliday].
> Village Voice, 8, 139-141.

LISTING OTHER PRINTED SOURCES

GOVERNMENT DOCUMENT

Start with the name of the department and then give the date of publication, the title (and author, if any), identifying number, and publisher.

> Department of Health and Human Services. (1986). Mosquito
> control measures in Gulf Coast states (DHHS Publica-
> tion No. F 82-06000). Washington, DC: U.S. Govern-
> ment Printing Office.

UNPUBLISHED DOCTORAL DISSERTATION

> Beilke, D. (1997). "Cracking up the south: Humor and
> identity in southern Renaissance fiction." Unpub-
> lished doctoral dissertation. University of
> Wisconsin--Madison.

LISTING INTERNET AND ELECTRONIC SOURCES

For Internet and electronic sources, provide as much of the following information as available:

> Name of the author or editor (if known)
>
> Date of publication or of latest update, in parentheses
>
> Document title
>
> Periodical or Web site title, Web site producer, or database name, followed by the designation *[Online]*
>
> URL (online address)
>
> Date of access, in square brackets

For further information on formatting online sources using APA style, visit Xia Li and Nancy B. Crane's "Bibliographic Formats for Citing Electronic Information" at <http://www.uvm.edu/~ncrane/estyles/apa.html>.

WEB SITE

> Schulman, R. (Ed.). (1998). The Einstein papers project
> [Online]. Boston University. Available: http://
> albert.bu.edu [1998, March 10].

ONLINE ARTICLE

> Kongshem, L. (1997, January). Censorware: How well does
> Internet filtering software protect students?
> Electronic School [Online]. Available:
> http://www/electronic-school.com/0198f1.html
> [1998, March 10].

> Loker, W. M. (1996). "Campesinos" and the crisis of mod-
> ernization in Latin America. Journal of Political
> Ecology [Online], 3.1. Available: <http://
> www.library.arizona.edu/ej/jpe/volume_3/
> ascii-lokeriso.txt>.

DISCUSSION LIST MESSAGE

> ROYAR. (1998, February 28). Internet linked courses. Al-
> liance for Computers and Writing [Online]. Available
> E-mail: ACW-L@ ttacs6.ttu.edu [1998, March 3].

ELECTRONIC MAIL

> Palmquist, Mike (mpalmquist@vines.colostate.edu). (1998,
> March 19). Bibliographic software. E-mail to
> Michelle Clark (dclark4@worldnet.att.net).

COMPUTER SOFTWARE

> Microsoft Excel (Version 5.0) [Computer software].
> (1993). Redmond, WA: Microsoft.

MATERIAL ACCESSED THROUGH A COMPUTER NETWORK OR SERVICE

> Boynton, R. S. (1994, March 3). The new intellectuals [3
> parts]. The Atlantic Monthly Online: [Online ser-
> ial]. Available America Online: Directory: The At-
> lantic Monthly Online: Main Menu: Newsstand: Folder:
> The Atlantic Monthly 40-99669: File: The New Intel-
> lectuals: Article: The New Intellectuals Parts 1-3.

LISTING OTHER NONPRINT SOURCES

AUDIOTAPE OR RECORDING

> Byrne, G. (1996). The James Joyce collection (Audiotape).
> Hollywood: Dove Audio.

TELEVISION OR RADIO PROGRAM

> Braithwaite, D., & Jimenez, S. (1995). Murder, rape and
> DNA. In: P. Aspell (Executive Producer), Nova.
> Boston: WGBH.

FILM

> Castle Rock Entertainment (Producer). (1995). Othello
> [Sound film].

PERSONAL INTERVIEW

APA guidelines suggest omitting personal interviews from the reference list because they do not provide recoverable data. You would, of course, mention such sources in the text of your paper (see p. 815).

A WRITER'S
HANDBOOK

Contents

Introduction: Grammar, or The Way Words Work

Shoe

EVERY AMERICAN HAS THE RIGHT TO VOTE FOR WHOEVER OR, INDEED...

WHOMEVER HE OR SHE WANTS,

DEPENDING ON GRAMMATICAL ORIENTATION...

Reprinted by permission: Tribune Media Services

One way to view grammar is as a set of rules for using language, like chalk-drawn lines that writers and speakers of English must toe. This approach is *prescriptive*: there are right and wrong ways to use the English language.

An alternative is a *descriptive* approach: **grammar** is that study of language concerned with the regular, systematic, and predictable ways in which words work together. How do speakers of English create sentences? How do they understand each other's sentences? In the last fifty years grammarians haven't been laying down strict rules so much as they have been listening, observing, and trying to describe the way language is used.

Every speaker of English, even a child, commands a grammatical system of tremendous complexity. Take the sentence "A bear is occupying a telephone booth while a tourist impatiently waits in line." In theory, there are nineteen billion different ways to state the idea in that sentence.[1] (Another is "A tourist fumes while he waits for a bear to finish yakking on a pay phone.") How do we understand a unique sentence like that one? For we do understand it, even though we have never heard it before — not in those very same words, not in the very same order.

To begin with, we recognize familiar words and we know their meanings. Just as significantly, we recognize grammatical structures. As we read or hear the sentence, we know that it contains a familiar pattern of *syntax,* or word order. This meaningful order helps the sentence make sense to us.

Ordinarily we aren't even conscious of such an order, for we don't need to think about it; but it is there. To notice it, all we need do is rearrange the words of our sentence:

> Telephone a impatiently line in waits tourist bear a occupying is a booth while.

The result is nonsense: it defies English grammar. The would-be sentence doesn't follow familiar rules or meet our expectations of order.

Hundreds of times a day, with wonderful efficiency, we perform tasks of understanding and of sentence construction more complex than any computer can even try. Indeed, linguist Noam Chomsky has suggested that the human brain probably contains some kind of language-grasping structure. Certainly some such ability is part of our makeup. For we can understand and create sentences even as toddlers, before we know anything about "grammar."

Why, then, think about grammar in college? Isn't it entirely possible to write well without contemplating grammar at all? Yes. If your innate sense of grammar is reliable, you can write clearly and logically and forcefully without knowing a predicate nominative from a handsaw. Many of the writers featured in current magazines and newspapers would be hard pressed to name all the parts of speech they use. Most successful writers, though, have been practicing for so many years that grammar has become second nature to them. Few students we know have a built-in sense so infallible. Those who speak English as a second language must work especially hard to develop a sense of English grammar. When you doubt a word or a construction, a glance in a handbook can clear up your confusion and restore your confidence — just as referring to a dictionary can help your spelling.

However, merely following accepted practices doesn't guarantee good writing. The so-called grammatical conventions you'll find in this handbook are not mechanical specifications, but accepted ways in which skilled writers and speakers put words together to convey meaning efficiently and clearly. They come from observations of what educated, accomplished users of English actually do — how they utilize the language to communicate their ideas successfully. The amateur writer can learn by following their example, just as an amateur athlete, artist, or even auto mechanic can learn by watching the

---

[1] Richard Ohmann, "Grammar and Meaning," *American Heritage Dictionary* (Boston: Houghton, 1979), pp. xxxi–xxxii.

professionals. Knowing how the English language works, and how its parts get along together, is of enormous value to you as a writer. Once you understand what goes on under the hood, so to speak, you will have a keener sense of words and of why at times they won't go — so that when you write, you drive smoothly to your destination.

This handbook is divided into nine chapters, which fall into three groups:

31 BASIC GRAMMAR	The first chapter lays the groundwork for those that follow by reviewing the basic building blocks of English grammar: parts of speech, sentence structure, and types of sentences.
32 GRAMMATICAL SENTENCES	
33 EFFECTIVE SENTENCES	Chapters 32–36 contain complete information on all important rules and conventions of standard written English. Exercises are provided so you can practice putting the information to use.
34 WORD CHOICE	
35 PUNCTUATION	
36 MECHANICS	At the end of the handbook are convenient resources that you will find indispensable when editing your writing: you can find them quickly by looking for the blue band that runs down the edges of the pages. The "Quick Editing Guide" is a brief discussion of the most common and troublesome grammar, style, punctuation, and mechanics problems found in college writing. It serves both as a convenient grammar reference and as a tool to help you edit more effectively. It contains useful tables and lists, editing checklists, computer tips, and cross-references to the fuller chapters that precede it. "A Glossary of Troublemakers" lists words and phrases that trouble student writers. Turn here when you have questions about which of two words to use or when you're not sure you're using a word correctly. The "Answers for Lettered Exercises" are excellent tools for self-study. To test yourself on a particular skill, simply try to answer the lettered exercise sentences, and then turn to the answers to see how you did.
QUICK EDITING GUIDE	
A GLOSSARY OF TROUBLEMAKERS	
ANSWERS FOR LETTERED EXERCISES	

At times your instructor may refer you directly to a section in the handbook, but more often you will probably find yourself looking up information to answer your own questions. With practice, you will be able to find the answers to your questions on your own. To get you started, we want to alert you to a number of quick and easy ways to find information in this book. The most obvious way is to use the *table of contents* at the beginning of the handbook (p. H-2). If you were looking for help with quotation marks, for instance, you would first look under the chapter titled "Punctuation." By scanning the list of topics, you would quickly find the section and page number you needed (section 29, "Quotation Marks," p. H-160). Another quick way to find information is the alphabetically arranged *index* located at the back of the book. Here you will find all of the key terms used in the handbook followed by the exact page that you should turn to. For those of you who are speakers of English as a second language, near the back of the book is an *ESL index* listing all the ESL boxes in the handbook.

We hope that you find the handbook a useful tool both in and out of the classroom. With time and practice, you will be able to quickly find the answers to the questions that arise as you are writing for your composition class, your major, and beyond.

Chapter 31

Basic Grammar

1. *Parts of Speech*

Grammar deals with the elements that make up sentences. These elements may be single words or whole phrases and clauses. Let's look first at the simplest building blocks of sentences: words.

We sort words into eight classes: the ***parts of speech.*** We tell them apart by their functions (the jobs they do in sentences), by their forms, and by their meanings. Like most classifications, the parts of speech are a convenience: it is easier to refer to "an adjective modifying a noun" than "that word there that tells something about that thing." Here is a quick review of the celebrated eight.

1a. Nouns

A ***noun*** names. A ***common noun*** names a general class of person (*clergyman, believer*), place (*town, dormitory*), thing (*car, dog*), or concept (*freedom, industrialization*). A ***proper noun*** names a specific person, place, thing, or concept: *Billy Graham, Milwaukee, Cadillac, New Deal.*

1b. Pronouns

A ***pronoun*** stands in place of a noun. Without pronouns, most writing would be top-heavy with repeated nouns. Imagine writing an essay on Martin Luther King Jr. in which you had to say "Martin Luther King Jr." or "the clergyman and civil rights leader" every time you mentioned your subject. Instead, you can handily use *personal pronouns* (*he* and *him*) and the *possessive pronoun* (*his*).

There are nine types of pronouns.

1. *Personal pronouns* (*I, you, it*) stand for nouns that name persons or things. "Mark awoke slowly, but suddenly *he* bolted from the bed."
2. *Possessive pronouns* (*his, our/ours*) are a form of personal pronoun showing ownership. They are used in place of nouns or as adjectives modifying nouns. "*His* trophy is on the left; *hers* is on the right."
3. *Intensive pronouns* (*yourself, themselves*) emphasize a noun or another pronoun. "Michael Jackson *himself* opened the door."
4. *Relative pronouns* (*who, that, which*) start a subordinate clause (see p. H-31) that functions as an adjective modifying a noun or pronoun in another clause. "The gift *that* you give them ought to be handsome."
5. *Reflexive pronouns* have the same form as intensive pronouns but are used as objects referring back to subjects. "She helped *herself*."

Pronouns

	SINGULAR	PLURAL
PERSONAL PRONOUNS		
First person	I, me	we, us
Second person	you	you
Third person	he, she, it, him, her	they, them
POSSESSIVE PRONOUNS		
First person	my, mine	our, ours
Second person	your, yours	your, yours
Third person	his, her, hers, its	their, theirs
INTENSIVE AND REFLEXIVE PRONOUNS		
First person	myself	ourselves
Second person	yourself	yourselves
Third person	himself, herself, itself	themselves

RELATIVE PRONOUNS
that, what, whatever, which, who, whoever, whom, whomever, whose

INTERROGATIVE PRONOUNS
what, which, who, whom, whose

INDEFINITE PRONOUNS
all, another, any, anybody, anyone, anything, both, each, either, everybody, everyone, everything, few, many, neither, nobody, none, no one, nothing, one, several, some, somebody, someone, something

DEMONSTRATIVE PRONOUNS
such, that, these, this, those

RECIPROCAL PRONOUNS
each other, one another

---

6. *Interrogative pronouns* (*who, what*) ask or introduce questions. *"What did you give them?"*
7. *Indefinite pronouns* (*any, no one*) stand for persons or things not specified. *"No one ran because of the rain."*
8. *Demonstrative pronouns* (*this, those*) point to nouns. *"That is the man, Officer!"*
9. *Reciprocal pronouns* (*each other, one another*) express relationship between two or more nouns or other pronouns. *"Joe and Donna looked at each other with complete understanding."*

EXERCISE 1–1

Identifying Nouns and Pronouns

Underline the nouns and pronouns in the following sentences. Identify each noun as common or proper. Identify the type of each pronoun (personal, possessive, relative, and so on). Answers for the lettered sentences appear in the back of the book. Example:

Edwards High School may lose its principal.

Edwards High School [proper noun] may lose <u>its</u> [possessive pronoun] principal [common noun].

a. She is among the most creative artists working in Hollywood.
b. His failure to pay the rent resulted in a fine.
c. She poured herself a tall glass of water after running five miles.
d. The money was given to us to use as we wished.
e. Tenants at Castlegate Towers are not allowed to keep pets in their apartments.

1. Students must ask themselves what they want out of their educations.
2. A good poem cannot be reduced to a simple message or moral.
3. The man who owns the store is from the Dominican Republic.
4. Toni Morrison, a novelist, received the Nobel Prize for literature.
5. The shoes, which were made in Taiwan, cost slightly less than the other brands.

1c. Verbs

A *verb* shows action ("The cow *jumped* over the moon") or a state of being ("The cow *is* brown," "The cow *felt* frisky").

Verbs like *is* or *felt* often show a state of being by linking the sentence's subject with another word that renames or describes the subject, as in the last two examples. Such verbs are called *linking verbs*. (See also 5a.)

A verb that shows action is called *transitive* when it has a direct object.

      VT   DO
Jim *hit* the *ball* hard.

         VT   DO
Does she *resemble* her *mother?*

A transitive verb must have an object to complete its meaning. You can't write just *Jim hit* or *Does she resemble?* But if a verb is complete in itself and needs no object, we call it **intransitive**.

The surgeon *paused*.

Sally *lives* on Boilermaker Street.

If you look up a verb in your dictionary, you will find it classified *vt* (for "verb, transitive") or *vi* (for "verb, intransitive"). Many verbs can work either way.

The bus *stopped*. [Intransitive]

The driver *stopped* the bus. [Transitive]

Not all verbs consist of just one word. The **main verb** in a sentence identifies the central action (*hit, stopped*). We can show variations on this action by adding **helping verbs,** such as *do, can, have,* or *will.* The main verb with its helping verbs is the **complete verb** or **verb phrase.**

HV   MV
Alan *did* not *hit* the ball.

┌─HV─┐ MV
The bus *will have stopped* six times before we reach Main Street.

Helping Verbs

There are twenty-three helping verbs in English. Fourteen of them can also function as main verbs:

be, is, am, are, was, were, being, been
do, does, did
have, has, had

The other nine can function only as helping verbs, never as main verbs:

can, could, should, would, may, might, must, shall, will

EXERCISE 1–2

Identifying Verbs

Underline the verbs in the following sentences. Identify each one as transitive (VT), intransitive (VI), linking (LV), or helping (HV). Answers for the lettered sentences appear in the back of the book. Example:

Marie released the ball too early, and it rolled into the gutter.

VT   VI
Marie <u>released</u> the ball too early, and it <u>rolled</u> into the gutter.

a. When Jorge goes to Providence, Jim will accompany him.
b. Sylvia prefers television shows that are educational.
c. Never give yellow roses to a friend: they symbolize infidelity.
d. The president should have spent more time on our proposal.
e. Harry dreams of becoming a famous novelist, but he rarely reads fiction.

1. People watched helplessly as the fire destroyed their homes and neighborhood.
2. Louise introduced herself to Leon while he was walking his dog.
3. Ian is the musician whose band she likes so much.
4. Woodpeckers must have a padded lining inside their skulls.
5. If Hitler had become an artist as he had wished, perhaps the course of history would be very different.

1d. Adjectives

An *adjective* describes, or modifies, a noun or a pronoun. In doing so it often answers the question Which? or What kind? Usually an adjective is a single word.

War is a *primitive* activity.

Young men kill other *young* men.

The *small brown* cow let out a *lackluster* moo.

Articles.   In the preceding examples, some grammarians would classify *the* and *a* as adjectives. Others would call them by a special name: *articles. The* is called the *definite article* because it indicates one particular item.

I need to borrow *the* car.

A and *an* are the *indefinite articles* because they indicate any one of many possible items.

I need to borrow *a* car.

1e. Adverbs

An *adverb* modifies a verb, an adjective, or another adverb.

The cow bawled *loudly*. [The adverb *loudly* modifies the verb *bawled*.]

The cow bawled *very loudly indeed*. [Three adverbs in a row: *loudly* modifies the verb *bawled*, while *very* and *indeed* modify the adverb *loudly*.]

Adverbs often flesh out thoughts by showing how, when, or where an action happens.

The cow *quickly* [how] galloped *outside* [where] and *immediately* [when] kicked the farmer.

EXERCISE 1–3

Identifying Adjectives and Adverbs

Underline and identify the adjectives, definite articles, indefinite articles, and adverbs in the following sentences. For each adverb, draw an arrow to the word it modifies and mark that word as a verb, adjective, or adverb. Answers for the lettered sentences appear in the back of the book. Example:

The opera was too long, but Judith sang beautifully.

DA   ADV   ADJ   V   ADV

The opera was <u>too</u> <u>long</u>, but Judith sang <u>beautifully</u>.

a. After a mild winter, the environmental experts greatly fear a drought.
b. James's young cousins are incredibly mature.
c. The wildly handsome Jake often made wise women act foolishly.
d. She had a very difficult message to relate, so she chose her words carefully.
e. We were absolutely delighted to get tickets to the lovely play.

1. The character of Mercutio is not bad; the actor just played him badly.
2. The part of Juliet, in contrast, was remarkably well acted.
3. With someone so young in the role of Juliet, Romeo probably should have been younger.
4. The tragic end invariably makes me sad.
5. In an ethnically and economically divided world the play will always have a strong appeal.

1f. Prepositions

A *preposition* is a transitional word that leads into a phrase. The preposition and its object (a noun or pronoun), plus any modifiers, form a *prepositional phrase*: *in the bar, under a rickety table, with you.*

A prepositional phrase can function as an adjective or an adverb. When it modifies a noun or pronoun, a prepositional phrase is called an *adjective phrase*.

> I want a room *with a view.* [The adjective phrase *with a view* modifies the noun *room.*]

> Everybody *in Hillsdale* knows Big Jake. [The adjective phrase *in Hillsdale* modifies the pronoun *Everybody.*]

When it modifies a verb, an adjective, or an adverb, a prepositional phrase is called an *adverb phrase.*

> Jarvis, the play reviewer, always leaves *after the first act.* [The adverb phrase *after the first act* modifies the verb *leaves.*]

> Alice is miserable *without you.* [The adverb phrase *without you* modifies the adjective *miserable.*]

> Ken works far *from home.* [The adverb phrase *from home* modifies the adverb *far.*]

There are dozens of prepositions in English. The chart below includes the most common ones. Notice that some prepositions consist of more than one word. Also, some prepositions occasionally play other roles: *since*, for example, can be a preposition (*I've known him since childhood*), or an adverb (*He has since left town*), or a subordinating conjunction (*Let's go, since there's nothing to do here*).

Common Prepositions

about	below	except for	on	to
above	beneath	for	onto	toward
according to	beside	from	opposite	under
across	besides	in	out	underneath
after	between	in addition to	outside	unlike
against	beyond	inside	over	until
along	but (except)	in spite of	past	up
among	by	instead of	plus	upon
around	concerning	into	regarding	with
as	considering	like	since	within
at	despite	near	than	without
because of	down	next to	through	
before	during	of	throughout	
behind	except	off	till	

EXERCISE 1–4

Identifying Prepositional Phrases

Underline each prepositional phrase in the following sentences, and identify it as an adjective or adverb phrase. Circle the preposition. Answers for the lettered sentences appear in the back of the book. Example:

In the distance, you can see the tornado.

(In) the distance, you can see the tornado. [Adverb phrase]

  a. Rarely has anyone ever behaved so rudely to me.
  b. The bright light in the sky was a supernova.
  c. Ann warned us before the meeting that her proposal might cause trouble.
  d. She presented her sculpture strictly according to the rules.
  e. My belief is that all but a few troublemakers will be reasonable once they understand the new rules.

  1. The politicians at City Hall would welcome a chance to intervene.
  2. Napoleon's soldiers were decimated by the Russian winter.
  3. Luis wants to go to the arcade.
  4. From his seat beyond the foul pole he can hardly see the batter.
  5. We drove to a house at the edge of a lake.

1g. Conjunctions

A *conjunction* links words or groups of words and connects them in sense.

A *coordinating conjunction* is a one-syllable word that joins elements with equal or near-equal importance: "Jack *and* Jill," "Sink *or* swim."

A word used to make one clause dependent on, or subordinate to, another is called a *subordinating conjunction*. (See 3e–3g.)

Before we left the party, six people had fainted.

They passed out *because* Roger had spiked the punch.

I heard *that* they went looking for him the next day.

ESL GUIDELINES

In, On, At: Prepositions of Location and Time

The prepositions *in, on,* and *at* are frequently used to express location.

Maria lives *in* the United States.

Elaine lives *at* a swanky address *on* Fifth Avenue.

- *In* means "within" or "inside of" a place, including geographical areas, such as cities, states, countries, and continents.

  I packed my books *in* my knapsack.

  I left my bags *in* the train station.

  My cousins live *in* Canada, but my uncle lives *in* Texas.

  Brazil is *in* South America.

- Whereas *in* emphasizes *location* only, *at* is often used to refer to a place when a specific *activity* is implied: *at the store* (to shop), *at the office* (to work), *at the theater* (to see a play), and so on.

  Angelo parked his bicycle *in* the bike rack.

  He left the bicycle there while he was *at* school, and then he rode it home.

- *On* means "on the surface of" or "on top of" something and is used with floors of buildings and planets. It is also used to indicate a location *beside* a lake, river, ocean, or other body of water.

  The service department is *on* the fourth floor.

  Mardi Gras in New Orleans is the greatest free show *on* earth.

  The raft floated *on* calm water.

We have a cabin *on* Lake Michigan.

- *In, on,* and *at* can all be used in addresses. *In* is used to identify a general location, such as a city or neighborhood. *On* is used to identify a specific street. *At* is used to give an exact address.

    We live *in* Boston.

    We live *on* Medway Street.

    We live *at* 20 Medway Street.

- *In* and *at* can both be used with the verb *arrive*. *In* indicates a large place, such as a city, state, country, or continent. *At* indicates a smaller place, such as a specific building or address. (*To* is never used with *arrive*.)

    Joel's plane arrives *in* Alaska tomorrow; he will arrive *in* Fairbanks the day after that.

    Alanya arrived *in* Asia yesterday.

    She will arrive *at* the airport soon.

The prepositions *in, on,* and *at* are also used in many time expressions.

- *In* indicates the span of time during which something occurs or a time in the future; it is also used in the expressions *in a minute* (meaning "shortly") and *in time* (meaning "soon enough"). *In* is also used with seasons, months, and periods of the day.

    He needs to read this book *in* the next three days. [During the next three days]

    I'll see you *in* two weeks. [Two weeks from now]

    We'll be leaving *in a minute*; I hope to get there *in time* to see the first act.

    My birthday is *in* April.

    We usually exercise *in* the morning.

- *On* is used with the days of the week, with the word *weekend,* and in the expression *on time* (meaning "punctually").

    Let's have lunch *on* Friday.

    The train arrived in the station *on time.*

    I like to travel *on weekends.*

- *At* is used in reference to a specific time on the clock as well as a specific time of the day (*at night, at dawn, at twilight*).

    We'll meet again next Monday *at* 2:15 P.M.

    The office is cleaned *at night.*

Coordinating Conjunctions

and, but, for, nor, or, so, yet

Common Subordinating Conjunctions

after	even if	since	when
although	even though	so	whenever
as	how	so that	where
as if	if	than	wherever
as soon as	in order that	that	while
as though	once	though	why
because	provided that	unless	
before	rather than	until	

Correlative Conjunctions

as . . . as	just as . . . so	not only . . . but also
both . . . and	neither . . . nor	whether . . . or
either . . . or	not . . . but	

Common Conjunctive Adverbs

accordingly	furthermore	moreover	then
also	hence	nevertheless	thereafter
anyway	however	next	therefore
as	incidentally	nonetheless	thus
besides	indeed	now	undoubtedly
certainly	instead	otherwise	
consequently	likewise	similarly	
finally	meanwhile	still	

Some conjunctions consist of paired words, such as *either . . . or*, that appear separately but work together to join elements of a sentence. Such a pair is called a ***correlative conjunction.***

Augustus courted Serena *not only* for her money *but also* for her cooking.

Neither his friends *nor* hers thought the marriage would last.

When you use a correlative conjunction, remember to complete the pair.

INCOMPLETE   *Not only* was Robert saving money for his college tuition, he was saving for a new car.

REVISED   *Not only* was Robert saving money for his college tuition, *but* he was *also* saving for a new car.

Certain adverbs also can function as conjunctions. Called ***conjunctive adverbs,*** these linking words connect independent clauses and show a relationship between two ideas, such as addition (*also, besides*), comparison (*likewise, similarly*), contrast (*instead, however*), emphasis (*namely, certainly*), cause and effect (*thus, therefore*), or time (*finally, subsequently*).

> Armando is a serious student; *therefore,* he studies every day.

1h. Interjections

An *interjection* inserts an outburst of feeling at the beginning, middle, or end of a sentence.

> I'd go, but, *oh,* I don't want to.

> *Ow!* What torture it was to read that essay!

> There are pigeons on the grass, *alas.*

An entire phrase can work as an interjection.

> Who *the dickens* are you?

> What *in the world* is my term paper doing in the wastebasket?

EXERCISE 1–5

Identifying Conjunctions and Interjections

Underline and identify the conjunctions and interjections in the following sentences. Mark each conjunction as coordinating, subordinating, or correlative. Answers for the lettered sentences appear in the back of the book. Example:

> Do we have to eat liver and onions again, for heaven's sake?

>   COORD CONJ   INTERJ
> Do we have to eat liver <u>and</u> onions again, <u>for heaven's sake?</u>

a. Oh, well, the team will do better when Smoots gets back in the game.
b. According to Polonius and many others, neither borrowing nor lending is wise.
c. Steve and Matt could not decide whether to leave town or work on their apartment over vacation.
d. Holy mackerel, what a big fish!
e. Although time and tide wait for no man, Juan is taking hours to launch his boat.

1. I'll dive in if you will, but, oh, that water's cold!
2. Neither Larry's father nor Kevin's is tall, yet both boys grew up to be over six feet tall.
3. How in the world are you and Elwood going to patch up your differences if neither of you will talk to the other?

4. Even though he seemed both weakened and depressed in the hospital, in a few weeks he had regained his strength.
5. Athens and the other Greek city-states were bitter rivals; nevertheless, they put aside their differences in the face of the Persian threat.

EXERCISE 1–6

Identifying Parts of Speech

Identify the part of speech of each underlined word in the following passages. Answers for the lettered words appear in the back of the book. Example:

> We live by our imaginations, by our admirations, by our sentiments.
>
> — Ralph Waldo Emerson, "Illusions," in *The Conduct of Life*

We: pronoun; live: verb; our: pronoun; sentiments: noun

A. It is a mellow day, very (a) gentle (b). The ash has lost its leaves and when (c) I went out to get the mail and (d) stopped to look up (e) at it, (1) I rejoiced (2) to think that soon everything (3) here will be honed down to structure. It is all a rich farewell (4) now to leaves, to color. I think of (5) the trees and how simply (6) they let go, let fall the riches of a season, how without (7) grief (it seems) they can (8) let go and go deep (9) into their (10) roots for renewal and sleep.

> — May Sarton, *Journal of a Solitude*, October 6, 1977

B. The other day (a) I rowed in my boat a free, even (b) lovely young lady, and as (c) I plied the oars, she (d) sat in the (e) stern, and there was nothing (1) but (2) she between (3) me and the sky. So might all our (4) lives be picturesque (5) if (6) they were free enough, but mean relations and prejudices intervene (7) to shut out the sky, and we never (8) see a man as simple and distinct as the man-weathercock (9) on (10) a steeple.

> — *The Journals of Henry David Thoreau*, 1840

2. *Sentence Structure*

PARTS OF SENTENCES

Every sentence has two basic parts: a subject and a predicate. The *subject* names something — a person, an object, an idea, a situation. The *predicate* makes an assertion about the subject. Any word group that is missing either of these elements is not a complete sentence.

Both subject and predicate may consist of either one word or a group of words. A one-word subject is always a noun or pronoun; a one-word predicate is always a verb.

> ### Sentence Parts at a Glance
>
> The *subject* of a sentence identifies some person, place, thing, activity, or idea.
> The *predicate* of a sentence makes an assertion about the subject.
> An *object* is the target or recipient of the action described by a verb.
> A *complement* renames or describes a subject or object.
>
> *For basic sentence patterns, see page H-24.*

SUBJ   PRED
Birds fly.

Many subjects and most predicates contain other elements as well, such as modifiers, objects, and complements. A modifier (such as an adjective or adverb) provides more information about the subject or some part of the predicate. A *direct* or *indirect object*, which always appears in the predicate, is the target or recipient of the action indicated by the verb. A *complement*, which also appears in the predicate, renames or describes the sentence's subject or object.

Let's look more closely at subjects, predicates, objects, and complements. Then we can explore the various ways of combining these elements in sentences.

2a. Subject

The *subject* of a sentence identifies some person, place, thing, activity, or idea. Often the subject is the agent of the action identified by the predicate ("*Jill* hit the ball"). Sometimes the subject is the receiver of the action of the predicate ("The *ball* was hit by Jill"; "*Baseball* came up for discussion"). Because the subject names something, it almost always is (or includes) a noun or pronoun. That noun or pronoun is the *simple subject.*

Queen Elizabeth waved to the crowd.

I waved back.

Often a subject includes additional nouns or pronouns, modifiers, or both. A subject that consists of two or more nouns or pronouns linked by a conjunction is called a *compound subject.*

The Queen and I exchanged waves.

My mother, my father, and my sister just stood and stared.

The *complete subject* consists of the simple or compound subject plus any words that modify it.

The imposing, world-famous Queen smiled at me.

Prince Charles on her left and Princess Anne on her right didn't notice me.

Occasionally a subject is a phrase or clause that contains no nouns at all.

Whether or not to smile back was the question.

In a command, the subject is understood to be *you*, even though the word does not appear in the sentence.

Don't [*you*] stand so close to me.

2b. Predicate

The ***predicate*** of a sentence makes an assertion about the subject. This assertion can involve an action ("Birds *fly*"), a relationship ("Birds *have* feathers"), or a state of being ("Birds *are* warm-blooded"). The ***simple predicate*** consists of the main verb plus any helping verbs that accompany it (*will fly, should have flown*). (For a full list of helping verbs, see 1c.) The ***complete predicate*** consists of the verb plus any other words that help it make its assertion, such as modifiers, objects, and complements.

Geese normally *can fly* more gracefully than chickens. [Simple predicate]

Geese *normally can fly more gracefully than chickens.* [Complete predicate]

Hiram *showed* me a goose that bites. [Simple predicate]

Hiram *showed me a goose that bites.* [Complete predicate]

In many sentences, the subject appears between two parts of the predicate.

When I visited his farm, Hiram *showed* me a goose that bites. [Simple predicate]

When I visited his farm, Hiram *showed me a goose that bites.* [Complete predicate]

You can tell that the opening clause *When I visited his farm* is part of the predicate because it modifies the verb (*showed*), not the subject (*Hiram*).

Just as a sentence may have a compound subject, a sentence may also have a compound predicate.

The child *screamed, cried, and kicked* until he got his way. [Simple compound predicate]

The child *screamed, cried, and kicked until he got his way.* [Complete compound predicate]

The receiver *intercepted* the pass *and ran* for a touchdown. [Simple compound predicate]

The receiver *intercepted the pass and ran for a touchdown.* [Complete compound predicate]

Identifying Subjects and Predicates

Identify each simple subject (ss), complete subject (cs), simple predicate (sp), and complete predicate (cp) in the following sentences. Answers for the lettered sentences appear in the back of the book. Example:

Does your brother George really dye his hair?

```
          ┌──────── CS ────────┐ ┌──── CP ────┐
   SP  ┌       SS          ┌┌        SP        ┐
Does your brother George really dye his hair?
```

a. Several coyotes have been seen recently in this area.
b. War, that curse of the human race, has plagued civilization throughout history.
c. Even after he became deaf, the composer Beethoven continued to write music.
d. One cup of coffee in the morning keeps me awake all day.
e. John Updike's mother, who had been a writer herself, always encouraged her son's literary aspirations.

1. Until the 1850s, the city now known as San Francisco was a tiny outpost with few human inhabitants.
2. San Francisco, like many California cities, was given its name by Spanish missionaries.
3. The Golden Gate Bridge was named after the harbor entrance, long known as the Golden Gate.
4. The introduction of the telegraph enabled San Franciscans to find out when a ship was approaching the city.
5. It was the Gold Rush that brought a flood of easterners and other outsiders to northern California.
6. Today people still flock to California, but few expect to get rich by finding gold.
7. During the 1989 World Series, an earthquake hit the San Francisco area and caused millions of dollars of damage.
8. Buildings burned, roads buckled, and bridges collapsed.
9. Frightened people called for help, ran into the streets, and cried when they saw the devastation.
10. Immediately after the earthquake the number of visitors to San Francisco decreased; however, the slump in tourism did not last long.

2c. Objects

An *object* is the target or recipient of the action of a verb. Whereas the subject of a sentence does something, the object has something done to it or for it. Objects, like subjects, usually are (or include) nouns or pronouns.

Some geese bite *people.*

A sentence can have two types of objects: direct and indirect. A *direct object* completes the action performed by the subject or asserted about the subject;

it is the verb's target. (Not all verbs take direct objects. Those that do are called *transitive verbs*; see 1c.)

> She sells *seashells* by the seashore.
>
> Birds have *feathers*.
>
> Give me *your tired, your poor*. . . .

An **indirect object** names a person or other entity that is affected by the subject's action. Usually an indirect object is the recipient of the direct object, via the action indicated by the verb. Only certain transitive verbs take indirect objects. Among them are *ask, bring, buy, get, lend, offer, pay, promise, sell, show, tell,* and *write.*

> She sells *the tourists* seashells.
>
> Give *me* your tired, your poor. . . .

As you can see, the word *to* is implied before an indirect object: "She sells seashells [*to*] *the tourists*," "Give your tired, your poor *to me*. . . ."

2d. Complements

A *complement* renames or describes a subject or object. It consists of a word or group of words in the predicate that completes the assertion in a sentence.

A complement that renames or describes the subject of a sentence is called a **subject complement**. It always follows a linking verb such as *be, am, were, seem, feel* (see 1c, 5a). A subject complement can be a noun, an adjective, or a group of words that functions as a noun or adjective.

>   S   SC
> That *dog* looks *friendly.* [Describes]

> ┌— S —┐   ┌————— SC —————┐
> *Manute Bol* must have been *the tallest basketball player in the NBA.* [Renames]

A complement that renames or describes a direct object is called an **object complement.** Like a subject complement, an object complement can be a noun, an adjective, or a group of words that functions as a noun or adjective.

>   DO ┌——— OC ———┐
> Leroy calls *Julie the hostess with the mostest.* [Renames]

>   ┌— DO —┐ OC
> This new computer will keep *Professor Mutt happy.* [Describes]

Sentence Patterns

With a subject, a verb, an object or two, a complement or two, and some modifiers, you can build virtually any English sentence. As complex as our language is, most sentences that we recognize as grammatical follow one of five patterns. Sometimes the order of the ingredients changes, and sometimes

ESL GUIDELINES

Indirect Objects and Prepositions

These two sentences mean the same thing:

> I sent the president a letter.

> I sent a letter to the president.

In the first sentence, the phrase *the president* is the **indirect object**: it receives the direct object (*a letter*), which was acted on (*sent*) by the subject of the sentence (*I*). In the second sentence, the same idea is expressed by using a **prepositional phrase** beginning with *to* (see 3a).

- Some verbs can either have an indirect object or use the preposition *to*: *give, send, lend, offer, owe, pay, sell, show, teach,* and *tell*. Some verbs can use either an indirect object or the preposition *for*: *bake, build, buy, cook, find, get,* and *make*.

  > I paid *the travel agent* one hundred dollars.

  > I paid one hundred dollars *to the travel agent*.

  > Margarita cooked *her family* some chicken.

  > Margarita cooked some chicken *for her family*.

- Some verbs cannot have an indirect object; they must use a preposition. The following verbs must use the preposition *to*: *describe, demonstrate, explain, introduce,* and *suggest*.

  | INCORRECT | Please explain me indirect objects. |
  | CORRECT | Please explain indirect objects *to me*. |

- The following verbs must use the preposition *for*: *answer* and *prepare*.

  | INCORRECT | He prepared me the nonalcoholic punch. |
  | CORRECT | He prepared the nonalcoholic punch *for me*. |

- Some verbs must have an indirect object; they cannot use a preposition. The following verbs must have an indirect object: *ask* and *cost*.

  | INCORRECT | Sasha asked a question to her. |
  | CORRECT | Sasha asked her a question. |

the pattern is obscured by modifying words and phrases. Here are the five basic sentence patterns, with examples. (Only simple subjects, verbs, objects, and complements are marked.)

1. *subject/verb*

      S   V
The *king lives.*

          S   V
The former *king* now *lives* in a cottage on the palace grounds.

      V   S
Long *live* the *king*!

2. *subject/verb/subject complement*

      S   V   SC
This *plum tastes ripe.*

                S   V   V   V   SC
When this plum was picked, *it* probably *would* not *have tasted ripe.*

      SC V   S   V
How *ripe does* this *plum taste* to you?

3. *subject/verb/direct object*

 S   V   DO
I photographed the *sheriff.*

 S V   V   DO
I did not, however, *photograph* the *deputy.*

   V S V   V   DO
Would I have photographed Sheriff Brown if he were a kinder man?

4. *subject/verb/indirect object/direct object*

      S   V IO   DO
Charlene asked you a *question.*

    V IO   DO
Ask me no more *questions* than you wish to hear answered. [The subject of the verb *Ask* is *you*, understood.]

     V   S   V IO   DO
Didn't Charlene ask you a *question?*

5. *subject/verb/direct object/object complement*

      S   V   DO   OC
The *judges rated Hugo* the best *skater.*

       S   V   V   DO   OC

Last year's *judges had rated Hugo* second *best* of all the skaters.

     V   S   V   DO   OC

Will the *judges rate Hugo first* again next year?

EXERCISE 2–2

Identifying Objects and Complements

Underline and identify the subject complements (SC), indirect objects (IO), direct objects (DO), and object complements (OC) wherever they appear in the following sentences. Mark the whole complement or object, not just its key noun or pronoun. Answers for the lettered sentences appear in the back of the book. Example:

> Venus, the goddess of love, considered Adonis her equal.

                                                DO   OC

> Venus, the goddess of love, considered <u>Adonis</u> <u>her equal</u>.

a. You are an educated person; how can you believe such a story?
b. King Lear gave his daughters his kingdom.
c. Elizabeth, a cynical observer, believes that the president is an evasive man.
d. Holography is an interesting art, but it requires expensive equipment.
e. Many people call Chicago the Windy City.

1. The outfielder's agent negotiated him a new contract.
2. The scorers named Shaquille O'Neal most valuable player in last week's game.
3. Her uncle left Maria a fortune.
4. The Empire State Building was once the tallest building in the world.
5. My friend Alicia calls her yellow Volkswagen "Buttercup."

3. *Phrases and Clauses*

Grammar deals not only with single words but also with groups of words known as phrases and clauses. A *phrase* consists of two or more related words that work together: *my uncle Zeke, in the attic, will have been*. Words that do not work together do not make up a phrase: *Zeke uncle my, in attic the, been have will*.

Notice that a phrase doesn't make complete sense the way a sentence does. Useful as it may be, it is lacking. It may lack a subject (*will have been*), a verb (*my uncle Zeke*), or both (*in the attic*).

A *clause* too is a group of related words that work together. However, it has more going for it than a phrase: it contains both a subject and a verb. Clauses come in two forms: main and subordinate. A *main clause* needs only end punctuation to make it a complete sentence.

                    S   V
Uncle Zeke likes solitude.

A *subordinate clause* contains a subject and a verb, but it cannot stand alone; it depends on a main clause to help it make sense.

                    S   V
who plays the oboe

Only in combination with a main clause does a subordinate clause work in a sentence.

Uncle Zeke, *who plays the oboe,* likes solitude.

TYPES OF PHRASES

Phrases, being incomplete by themselves, are versatile. They can function as nouns, verbs, adjectives, or adverbs. Every compound subject or object is a phrase by definition: *Zeke and Jake, my father and I.* So is every verb that consists of more than one word: *will have played, sang and danced.* Other types of phrases can play varied roles in sentences.

Playing the oboe is Uncle Zeke's favorite pastime. [Noun phrase — subject]

He really enjoys *making music.* [Noun phrase — object]

Uncle Zeke plays an oboe *custom-made for him.* [Adjective phrase modifying *oboe*]

My music teacher says he plays *like a professional.* [Adverb phrase modifying *plays*]

To determine whether a phrase functions as a noun, an adjective, or an adverb in a sentence, you can ask yourself what question the phrase answers. If it answers the question Who? or What?, it is a noun phrase. If it answers the question What kind?, it is an adjective phrase. If it answers the question When? or Where? or How?, it is usually an adverb phrase.

We can name phrases by the roles they play in a sentence: noun phrase, adjective phrase, adverb phrase. We can also name them by their form: prepositional phrase, verbal phrase, absolute phrase, appositive phrase. Because the form of a phrase determines the roles it can play, our discussion of phrases will classify them by form.

3a. Prepositional Phrases

What do the following sentences have in common?

Doesn't Lew have other friends besides Pat?

Over the next sand dune lies the ocean.

To understand his comments you must read between the lines.

Each sentence contains a *prepositional phrase,* so named because it starts with a preposition: *besides Pat, Over the next sand dune, between the lines.* (See the prepositions chart in 1f.)

Prepositional phrases are a common and very useful sentence ingredient. Most often, they function as adjectives or adverbs. When a prepositional phrase does the work of an adjective — that is, when it modifies a noun — it is an *adjective phrase.*

> Joyce wanted to live in a city *without smokestacks.* [Adjective phrase modifying *city*]

> Tyrone is a man *of honor.* [Adjective phrase modifying *man*]

When a prepositional phrase does the work of an adverb — that is, when it modifies a verb, an adjective, or another adverb — it is an *adverb phrase.*

> She writes *with vigor.* [Adverb phrase modifying the verb *writes*]

> Jake feels indebted *to his coach.* [Adverb phrase modifying the adjective *indebted*]

> Mr. Francis phoned early *in the morning.* [Adverb phrase modifying the adverb *early*]

Some prepositional phrases function as nouns; they are *noun phrases.*

> *Over the river and through the woods* is the long way to Grandmother's house.

3b.   Verbal Phrases

A *verbal* is a form of a verb that cannot function as a simple predicate in a sentence. Verbals include infinitives (*to live, to dream*), present participles (*falling, dancing*), and past participles (*lived, fallen*).

A verbal and its modifiers, if any, constitute a *verbal phrase.* The three types of verbal phrases are infinitive phrases (*to live alone, to dream vividly*); participial phrases (*falling behind, written in stone*); and gerund phrases (*smoking in the boys' room, slow dancing*). Verbal phrases (and verbals) can operate as nouns, adjectives, and adverbs.

Infinitive Phrases

An *infinitive phrase* consists of the infinitive form of a verb preceded by *to* (*to quit*) plus any modifiers or objects (*to quit suddenly; to quit the job*). Infinitive phrases function as nouns, adjectives, and adverbs.

> *To err* is human. [Noun phrase used as subject]

> Their goal is *to stop the pipeline project.* [Noun phrase used as subject complement]

> Jennifer is the candidate *to watch.* [Adjective phrase modifying *candidate*]

Melvin lives *to eat.* [Adverb phrase modifying *lives*]

He is too fat *to play tennis.* [Adverb phrase modifying *fat*]

Phrases at a Glance

A *prepositional phrase* contains a preposition and its object(s) and any modifiers: "*In the old mansion* we found a stack *of books* hidden *behind the fireplace.*" (3a)

A *verbal phrase* consists of a verbal and its modifiers: "All she wanted was *to attend college someday*" [*infinitive phrase*]; "*Swimming in cold water,* we hardly noticed that the air temperature was 101 degrees" [*participial phrase*]; "*Combing the dog's hair* took at least thirty minutes every other day" [*gerund phrase*]. (3b)

An *absolute phrase* does not modify any one word in a sentence but modifies the entire sentence. It usually consists of a noun followed by a participial phrase: "*The 12:30 bus having already passed,* Arturo waited in the hot sun for the next one." (3c)

An *appositive phrase* is a group of words that adds information about a subject or object by identifying it in a different way: "Magali, *a student from France,* learned colloquial English by living with an American family." (3d)

An infinitive phrase is easy to distinguish from a prepositional phrase starting with *to*: in an infinitive phrase, *to* is followed first by a verb (*to row*) and only then by an object, if any (*to row a boat*). In a prepositional phrase, *to* is followed directly by its object, a noun or pronoun (*to me, to the lighthouse, to the boat*).

Participial Phrases

A *participial phrase* is an adjective phrase that opens with the present or past participle of a verb. Here are examples of the infinitive and participial forms of a few common verbs:

INFINITIVE	PRESENT PARTICIPLE	PAST PARTICIPLE
(to) find	finding	found
(to) fly	flying	flown
(to) go	going	gone
(to) see	seeing	seen
(to) walk	walking	walked

All participial phrases share two characteristics: they start with participles, and they function as adjectives.

Leading the pack, Michael sprinted into the final straightaway. [Modifies *Michael*]

He made the most of the few seconds *remaining in his race.* [Modifies *seconds*]

Worn out by the intensity of his effort, Michael fell. [Modifies *Michael*]

Gerund Phrases

A *gerund phrase* is a noun phrase that begins with the present participle of a verb. It can serve as the subject of a sentence, a direct object, a subject complement, or the object of a preposition.

Giving blood is a valuable public service. [Subject]

Audrey loves *performing in plays.* [Direct object]

Phil's job is *making doughnuts.* [Subject complement]

My mother is nervous about *traveling by herself.* [Object of a preposition]

3c. Absolute Phrases

An *absolute phrase* usually consists of a noun followed by a participle. It does not modify any one word; rather, it modifies an entire clause or sentence. It can appear anywhere in the sentence.

The stallion pawed the ground, *nostrils flaring, chestnut mane and tail swirling in the wind.*

Nostrils flaring, chestnut mane and tail swirling in the wind, the stallion pawed the ground.

3d. Appositive Phrases

An appositive is a word that adds to what we know about a subject or object simply by identifying it in a different way ("my dog *Rover,*" "Harvey's brother *Fred*"). An *appositive phrase* is a group of words that provides the same kind of amplification.

Bess, *the landlord's daughter,* had long black hair.

I walked across the field, *a golden sea of wheat flecked with daisies,* to the stone wall.

ESL GUIDELINES

Using Participles, Infinitives, and Gerunds

A *verbal* is a form that does not function as the main verb in a sentence. Verbals can function as adjectives, adverbs, and nouns. There are three types of verbals: *participles*, *gerunds*, and *infinitives*.   *(continued)*

Using Participles

- *Participles* end in either *-ing* (the present participle) or *-ed* or *-d* (the past participle).
- When used as an adjective, the *-ing* form expresses cause, and the *-ed* and *-d* forms express effect or result.

  The movie was *terrifying to the children.* [The movie caused terror.]

  The children were *terrified by the movie.* [The movie resulted in terrified children.]

Using Verbs with Gerunds and Infinitives

- A *gerund* is a form of a verb ending in *-ing* that functions as a noun (*going, playing*). An *infinitive* is the base form of the verb preceded by *to* (*to go, to play*). Some verbs are followed by gerunds, while other verbs are followed by infinitives.
- Verbs that are followed by infinitives include *decide, expect, pretend, refuse,* and *want.*

  My mother decided *to eat* at McDonald's for dinner.

- Verbs that are followed by gerunds include *appreciate, avoid, consider, discuss, enjoy, finish, imagine, practice,* and *suggest.*

  My family enjoys *going* to the beach.

- Some verbs, including *continue, like, love, hate, remember, forget, start,* and *stop,* can be followed by either a gerund or an infinitive.

  I like *going* to the museum.

  I like *to go* to the movies.

NOTE: Some verbs, such as *stop, remember,* and *forget,* have significantly different meanings according to whether they are followed by a gerund or an infinitive.

  I stopped *smoking.* [I don't smoke anymore.]

  I stopped *to smoke.* [I stopped so that I could smoke.]

- Be careful to distinguish between *used to* (meaning "did in the past") and *be used to* or *get used to* (meaning "be or become accustomed to"). *Used to* is followed by the basic form of the verb; *be used to* or *get used to* is followed by a gerund.

  I *used to live* in Rio, but now I live in New York. [I lived in Rio in the past.]

  I *am used to living* in the United States. [I am accustomed to living in the United States.]

  I *got used to living* in the United States. [I became accustomed to living in the United States.]

EXERCISE 3–1

Identifying Phrases

Underline and identify the prepositional, verbal (infinitive, participial, and gerund), absolute, and appositive phrases in the following sentences. For each prepositional and verbal phrase, also identify its role in the sentence (noun, adjective, adverb). Answers for the lettered sentences appear in the back of the book. Example:

> Reading about global poverty can be depressing.

> <u>Reading about global poverty</u> can be depressing. [Gerund phrase, noun]

     a. The heat from the wood stove warmed the entire cabin.
     b. The team's goal is to win the district championship.
     c. The fire raged throughout the night.
     d. Despite a mighty effort, the firefighters could not control the blaze.
     e. Drinking a little red wine each day may have positive health effects.

     1. Lacking money and broad support, the candidate withdrew.
     2. The troops endured heavy losses during the first two weeks.
     3. The watch was a gift from his brother.
     4. The superintendent, exhausted from his work, will soon resign.
     5. To last that long is a notable achievement.

TYPES OF CLAUSES

The main difference between a clause and a phrase is that a clause has both a subject and a verb. Some clauses, indeed, can stand alone as complete sentences. They are called *main clauses* (or *independent clauses*).

> My sister has a friend.

> The flowers were beautiful.

Clauses that cannot stand alone are called *subordinate clauses* (or *dependent clauses*).

> who comes from Lebanon

> that Dan gave Nicola

A subordinate clause begins with a subordinate word, either a subordinating conjunction (H-14) or a relative pronoun (H-8), and must be linked with a main clause for its meaning to be entirely clear.

> My sister has a friend *who comes from Lebanon.*

> The flowers *that Dan gave Nicola* were beautiful.

Subordinate clauses, like phrases, are versatile: they can function as nouns, adjectives, and adverbs. A clause that answers the question What? or Who? is a noun clause. One that answers the question What kind? or Which one? is an adjective clause. One that answers the question When? or How? or Where? is usually an adverb clause.

3e. Noun Clauses

A subordinate clause that serves as a sentence subject, object, or complement is called a *noun clause.* Usually a noun clause begins with a subordinating conjunction — *how, when, where, whether, why* — or with a relative pronoun — *what, who, whom, whoever, whomever,* or *that.*

What I believe is none of their business. [Noun clause as subject]

James doesn't know *whom he should blame.* [Noun clause as direct object]

> ### Subordinate Clauses at a Glance
>
> A *noun clause* serves as a sentence subject, object, or complement. It answers the question What? or Who? (3e)
>
> An *adjective clause* serves as an adjective by modifying a noun or pronoun. It answers the question What kind? or Which one? (3f)
>
> An *adverb clause* plays the role of an adverb, modifying a verb, an adjective, or another adverb. It answers the question When? or How? or Where? (3g)

In both of these examples, the relative pronoun that opens the subordinate clause (*What, whom*) is followed by the subject and verb of the clause. In both cases, the pronoun serves as the direct object within the subordinate clause.

DO S V
What I believe is none of their business.

DO S V
James doesn't know *whom he should blame.*

Sometimes, however, the relative pronoun that opens the subordinate clause also serves as the subject of the clause.

S V
James doesn't know *who did it.* [Noun clause as direct object]

S V
Sarah gave *whoever walked* through the door a coupon for a free meal. [Noun clause as indirect object]

3f. Adjective Clauses

Subordinate clauses can serve as adjectives modifying nouns or pronouns. Usually an adjective clause is introduced by one of the relative pronouns: *who, which,* or *that.* Sometimes the relative pronoun is implied: "I got the letter [*that*] you sent me." You can tell an adjective clause from a noun clause by its function in a sentence.

> I like people *who are optimistic.* [Adjective clause modifying *people*]

> I plan to major in psychology, *which I have always found fascinating.* [Adjective clause modifying *psychology*]

> Science is a tide *that can only rise.* — Jonathan Schell [Adjective clause modifying *tide*]

3g. Adverb Clauses

An adverb clause plays the role of an adverb in a sentence, modifying a verb, an adjective, or another adverb.

> Larry left *before I could explain my mistake.* [Adverb clause modifying the verb *left*]

> He was sure *that I had insulted him.* [Adverb clause modifying the adjective *sure*]

> He loses his temper faster *than most people do.* [Adverb clause modifying the adverb *faster*]

Generally, subordinate clauses acting as adverbs are introduced by one of the common subordinating conjunctions, such as the following:

after	before	than	until	wherever
although	if	that	when	while
as	since	though	whenever	why
because	so that	unless	where	

(For a complete list of subordinating conjunctions, see 1g.) As with adjective clauses, the subordinating conjunction in an adverb clause sometimes is implied rather than stated: "You paint so well [*that*] you could be a professional."

EXERCISE 3–2

Identifying Clauses

Underline the subordinate clauses in the following sentences, and identify each one as a noun, an adjective, or an adverb clause. Answers for the lettered sentences appear in the back of the book. Example:

The man whose toe Susan had stepped on yelped in pain.

The man <u>whose toe Susan had stepped on</u> yelped in pain. [Adjective clause]

a. My grandfather was a rolling stone; wherever he lived at the moment was his home.
b. While we were still arguing about its value, the statue was removed from the gallery.
c. The shirt that I took to the cleaners came back with a ripped sleeve.
d. Ann did so badly on the exam that she may fail the course.
e. He won't know what hit him.

1. Although many had tried, none could pull the sword from the stone.
2. The man who was so charming has been arrested for fraud.
3. Sailing, which is Charlie's favorite summer pastime, has been banned in Rock Harbor.
4. There before them lay more gold than they had ever seen.
5. Blame John's death on the cocaine he refused to give up.

ESL GUIDELINES

Adjective Clauses and Relative Pronouns

Be sure to use relative pronouns (*who, which, that*) correctly in sentences with adjective clauses.

- Do not omit the relative pronoun when it is the subject within the adjective clause.

    INCORRECT   The woman *gave us directions to the museum* told us not to miss the Picasso exhibit.

    CORRECT   The woman *who gave us directions to the museum* told us not to miss the Picasso exhibit. [*Who* is the subject of the adjective clause.]

- In speech and informal writing, you can imply (not state) a relative pronoun when it is the object of a verb or preposition within the adjective clause. In formal writing, you should use the relative pronoun.

    FORMAL   Jose forgot to return the book *that I gave him.* [*That* is the object of *gave.*]

    INFORMAL   Jose forgot to return the book *I gave him.* [The relative pronoun *that* is implied.]

    FORMAL   This is the box *in which we found the jewelry.* [*Which* is the object of the preposition *in.*]

    INFORMAL   This is the box *we found the jewelry in.* [The relative pronoun *which* is implied.]

NOTE: The preposition moves to the end of the sentence when the relative pronoun is omitted. The preposition must not be left out, even when the relative pronoun is omitted.

- **Whose** is the only possessive form of a relative pronoun. It is used with persons, animals, and things. No other form may be used as a possessive introducing an adjective clause.

INCORRECT   I sat on a chair *that its* legs were wobbly.

CORRECT   I sat on a chair *whose* legs were wobbly.

NOTE: If you are not sure how to use a relative pronoun, try rephrasing the sentence more simply.

I sat on a chair *that had wobbly legs* [or *with wobbly legs*].

4. *Types of Sentences*

What is a *sentence*? There is more than one answer. In conversation, the single word *Where?* can be a sentence. But in striving to write clear, readable prose, you will find it useful to think of a sentence as the expression of a complete thought containing at least one *main clause.* (See pp. H-25–H-35 on types of clauses.) Sentences come in four varieties according to their structure.

4a. Simple Sentences

Any sentence that contains only one main clause is a *simple sentence,* even if it includes modifiers, objects, complements, and any number of phrases in addition to its subject and verb.

Even amateur stargazers can easily locate the Big Dipper in the night sky.

George Washington exhibited courage and leadership during a crucial period in our country's history.

Fred and Sandy have already applied for summer jobs.

The spectators laughed and cried at the same time.

Notice in the last two examples that a simple sentence may have a compound subject (*Fred and Sandy*) or a compound verb (*laughed and cried*). Still, it remains a simple sentence, for it contains only one main clause. Sometimes the subject of a simple sentence is not stated but is clearly understood. In the command "Run!," the understood subject is *you.*

4b. Compound Sentences

A *compound sentence* consists of two or more main clauses joined by a coordinating conjunction such as *and, but,* or *for* or by a semicolon. Sometimes the semicolon is followed by a conjunctive adverb such as *however, nevertheless,* or *therefore.* (For complete lists of coordinating conjunctions and conjunctive adverbs, see 1g.)

      MAIN CLAUSE   MAIN CLAUSE
I would like to accompany you, but I can't.

MAIN CLAUSE   MAIN CLAUSE
Two's company; three's a crowd.

      MAIN CLAUSE   MAIN
Henry Kissinger was born in Europe; therefore, he cannot be a candidate for
CLAUSE
the presidency of the United States.

4c. Complex Sentences

A *complex sentence* consists of one main clause and one or more subordinate clauses.

     MAIN   SUBORDINATE
     CLAUSE   CLAUSE
I will be at the airport when you arrive.

     SUBORDINATE   MAIN
     CLAUSE   CLAUSE
Since Amy bought a computer, she has been out of circulation.

     SUBORDINATE   MAIN
     CLAUSE   CLAUSE   SUBORDINATE
Because George has to travel widely, he is grateful whenever his far-flung ac-
CLAUSE
quaintances invite him to a home-cooked meal.

In some sentences, the relative pronoun linking the subordinate clause to the main clause is implied rather than stated.

     MAIN   SUBORDINATE
     CLAUSE   CLAUSE
I know [that] you saw us.

4d. Compound-Complex Sentences

As its name implies, a *compound-complex sentence* shares the attributes of both a compound sentence (it contains two or more main clauses) and a complex sentence (it contains at least one subordinate clause).

     SUBORDINATE   MAIN
     CLAUSE   CLAUSE   MAIN
Where politics is concerned, Michael seems indifferent and Joanne seems
CLAUSE
ill informed.

     MAIN   SUBORDINATE   SUBORDINATE   MAIN
     CLAUSE   CLAUSE   CLAUSE   CLAUSE
I'd gladly wait until you're ready; but if I do, I'll miss the boat.

EXERCISE 4–1

Identifying Sentence Types

Identify each of the following sentences as simple, compound, complex, or compound-complex. Also label each clause of the sentence. Answers for the lettered sentences appear in the back of the book. Example:

> If a bullfrog had wings, he wouldn't bump his tail so much, but he'd have a hard time swimming.

SUBORDINATE CLAUSE   MAIN CLAUSE   MAIN

If a bullfrog had wings, he wouldn't bump his tail so much, but he'd have CLAUSE

a hard time swimming. [Compound-complex]

a. Not only women but also men and children benefit from society's increasing resistance to sex-role stereotypes.
b. To become a doctor, you know how hard you must study.
c. Biology is interesting, but I prefer botany as it is taught in our department.
d. Do you prefer bacon and eggs or cereal and toast for breakfast this morning?
e. Most people believe that poverty begets poverty; however, recent studies have shown that, more often than not, when children from welfare families reach adulthood, they achieve economic independence.

1. Geraldine believes that the sexual revolution, without compensating women for their losses, has robbed them of all the advantages automatically bestowed by old-fashioned marriage.
2. Just before the earthquake, the animals became agitated.
3. Do you want to join us, or are you just going to lie there like a slug?
4. Since Jennifer moved to the city, her attendance at concerts, plays, and museum shows has increased markedly; and she dines out at least once a week.
5. As a boy, Mike couldn't wait to qualify for the Little League team; a few weeks after joining, he wanted only to quit.
6. Executives who promote incompetent workers can drive a corporation to the brink of disaster.
7. In the Virgin Islands the sun shines every day, the temperature drops to a comfortable level every night, and the breeze rustles through the palm trees at all hours.
8. Because of the flood, traffic was rerouted, and flights were delayed.
9. At some point in the long and surprisingly complex history of popular music, rock 'n' roll acquired its present identity as the music of youth and rebellion.
10. If a man makes a better mousetrap, the world will beat a path to his door.
— Ralph Waldo Emerson

Chapter 32

Grammatical Sentences

5. *Verbs*

Most verbs show action (*swim, fight, eat, hide, pay, sleep, win*). Some verbs indicate a state of being by linking the subject of a sentence with a word that renames or describes it; they are called *linking verbs* (*is, become, seem*). A few verbs work with a main verb to give more information about its action; they are called *helping verbs* or *auxiliary verbs* (*have, must, can*). Editing for verb usage is also covered in the "Quick Editing Guide." (For more help, see A1.)

VERB FORMS

5a. Use a linking verb to connect the subject of a sentence with a subject complement.

A *linking verb* indicates what the subject of a sentence *is* or *is like*. Some common linking verbs are *be, appear, feel,* and *grow*. A linking verb creates a sort of equation, either positive or negative, between the subject and its complement (see 2d). The subject complement can be a noun, a pronoun, or an adjective.

             LV   SC
Julia will *make* a good *doctor.* [Noun]

         LV   SC
George *is* not the *one.* [Pronoun]

               LV   SC
London weather *seems foggy.* [Adjective]

A verb may be a linking verb in some sentences and not in others.

I often *grow* sleepy after lunch. [Linking verb with subject complement *sleepy*]

I often *grow* tomatoes in my garden. [Transitive verb with direct object *tomatoes*]

If you pay attention to what the verb means, you can usually tell whether it is functioning as a linking verb.

Common Linking Verbs

Some linking verbs tell what a noun is, was, or will be.

be, become, remain
grow: The sky *is growing* dark.
make: One plus two *makes* three.
prove: His warning *proved* accurate.
turn: The weather *turned* cold.

Some linking verbs tell what a noun might be.

appear, seem, look

Most verbs of the senses can operate as linking verbs.

feel, smell, sound, taste

5b.   Use helping verbs to add information about the main verb.

A *helping* or *auxiliary verb* can add essential information about a main verb's action or state of being. Adding a helping verb to a simple verb (*go, shoot, be*) allows you to express a wide variety of tenses and moods (*am going, did shoot, would have been*). (See 5g–5l and 5n–5p.)

All the forms of *be, do,* and *have* can function as helping verbs. The other helping verbs are *can, could, may, might, must, shall, should, will,* and *would.* These last nine can function only as helping verbs, never as main verbs.

A main verb plus one or more helping verbs is called a *verb phrase.* The parts of a verb phrase need not appear together but may be separated by other words.

I probably *am going* to France this summer.

You *should* not *have shot* that pigeon.

This change *may* well *have been* seriously *contemplated* by the governor even before the election.

5c. Use the correct principal parts of the verb.

The **principal parts** are the forms the verb can take — alone or with helping verbs — to indicate the full range of times when an action or state of being does, did, or will occur. Verbs have three principal parts: the infinitive, the past tense, and the past participle.

The **infinitive** is the simple or dictionary form of the verb (*go, sing, laugh*) or the simple form preceded by *to* (*to go, to sing, to laugh*). (See 3b.)

The **past tense** signals that the verb's action is completed (*went, sang, laughed*).

The **past participle** is combined with helping verbs to indicate action occurring at various times in the past or future (*have gone, had sung, will have laughed*). It is also used with forms of *be* to make the passive voice. (See 5m.)

In addition to the three principal parts, all verbs have a present participle, the *-ing* form of the verb (*going, walking*). The present participle is used to make the progressive tenses. (See 5k and 5l.) It also can modify nouns and pronouns ("the *leaking* bottle"); and, as a gerund, it can function as a noun ("*Sleeping all day* pleases me"). (See 3b.)

5d. Use *-d* or *-ed* to form the past tense and past participle of regular verbs.

Most verbs in English are *regular verbs*: they form the past tense and past participle in a standard, predictable way. Regular verbs that end in *-e* add *-d* to the infinitive; those that do not end in *-e* add *-ed*.

INFINITIVE	PAST TENSE	PAST PARTICIPLES
(to) smile	smiled	smiled
(to) act	acted	acted
(to) please	pleased	pleased
(to) trick	tricked	tricked

5e. Use the correct forms for the past tense and past participle of irregular verbs.

The English language has at least two hundred *irregular verbs,* which form their past tense and past participle in some other way than by adding *-d* or *-ed.* Most irregular verbs are familiar to native English speakers and pose no problem, although they can be a torment to people trying to learn the language. A chart of principal parts that lists just the most troublesome irregular verbs can be found on pages R-4–5.

5f. Use the correct forms of the principal parts of *lie* and *lay* and *sit* and *set*.

Among the most troublesome verbs in English are *lie* and *lay*. If you have difficulty choosing between them, you can forever eliminate confusion by taking two easy steps. The first is to memorize the principal parts and present participles of both verbs (see the chart on this page).

The second step in deciding whether to use *lie* or *lay* is to fix in memory that *lie*, in all its forms, is intransitive. *Lie* never takes a direct object: "The island *lies* due east," "Jed *has lain* on the floor all day." *Lay*, on the other hand, is a transitive verb. It always requires an object: "*Lay* that pistol down."

The same distinction exists between *sit* and *set*. Usually, *sit* is intransitive: "He *sits* on the stairs." *Set*, on the other hand, almost always takes an object: "He *sets* the bottle on the counter." There are, however, a few easily memorized exceptions. The sun *sets*. A hen *sets*. Gelatin *sets*. You *sit* on a horse. You can *sit* yourself down at a table that *sits* twelve.

Principal Parts and Present Participles of *Lie* and *Lay*, *Sit* and *Set*

lie: recline

PRESENT TENSE		PAST TENSE	
I lie	we lie	I lay	we lay
you lie	you lie	you lay	you lay
he/she/it lies	they lie	he/she/it lay	they lay

PAST PARTICIPLE
lain   (We have *lain* in the sun long enough.)

PRESENT PARTICIPLE
lying   (At ten o'clock he was still *lying* in bed.)

lay: put in place, deposit

PRESENT TENSE		PAST TENSE	
I lay	we lay	I laid	we laid
you lay	you lay	you laid	you laid
he/she/it lays	they lay	he/she/it laid	they laid

PAST PARTICIPLE
laid   (Having *laid* his clothes on the bed, Mark jumped into the shower.)

PRESENT PARTICIPLE
laying   (*Laying* her cards on the table, Lola cried, "Gin!")

(*continued*)

Principal Parts and Present Participles of *Lie* and *Lay, Sit* and *Set (continued)*

sit: be seated

PRESENT TENSE		PAST TENSE	
I sit	we sit	I sat	we sat
you sit	you sit	you sat	you sat
he/she/it sits	they sit	he/she/it sat	they sat

PAST PARTICIPLE
sat   (I have *sat* here long enough.)

PRESENT PARTICIPLE
sitting   (Why are you *sitting* on that rickety bench?)

set: place

PRESENT TENSE		PAST TENSE	
I set	we set	I set	we set
you set	you set	you set	you set
he/she/it sets	they set	he/she/it set	they set

PAST PARTICIPLE
set   (Paul has *set* the table for eight.)

PRESENT PARTICIPLE
setting   (Jerry has been *setting* pins at the Bowl-a-drome.)

EXERCISE 5–1

Using Irregular Verb Forms

Underline each incorrectly used irregular verb in the following sentences, and substitute the verb's correct form. Some sentences may be correct. Answers for the lettered sentences appear in the back of the book. Example:

> We have already <u>drove</u> eight hundred miles, and we still have a long way to go to reach Oregon.

> We have already driven eight hundred miles, and we still have a long way to go to reach Oregon.

a. In those days, Benjamin wrote all the music, and his sister sung all the songs.
b. After she had eaten her bagel, she drank a cup of coffee with milk.
c. When the bell rung, darkness had already fell.
d. Voters have chose several new representatives, who won't take office until January.
e. Carol threw the ball into the water, and the dog swum after it.

1. He brought along two of the fish they had caught the day before.
2. By the time the sun set, the birds had all went away.
3. Teachers had spoke to his parents long before he stole the bicycle.

4. While the cat laid on the bed, the mouse ran beneath the door.
5. For the past three days the wind has blew hard from the south, but now the clouds have began to drift in.

TENSES

The *tense* of a verb is the *time* when its action did, does, or will occur. With the *simple tenses* we can indicate whether the verb's action took place in the past, takes place in the present, or will take place in the future. The *perfect tenses* enable us to narrow the timing even further, specifying that the action was or will be completed by the time of some other action. With the *progressive tenses* we can indicate that the verb's action did, does, or will continue.

5g. Use the simple present tense for an action that takes place once, recurrently, or continuously in the present.

The simple present tense is the infinitive form of a regular verb plus *-s* or *-es* for the third-person singular.

I like, I go	we like, we go
you like, you go	you like, you go
he/she/it likes, he/she/it goes	they like, they go

Notice that some irregular verbs, such as *go*, form their simple present tense following the same rules as regular verbs. Other irregular verbs, such as *be* and *have*, are special cases for which you should learn the correct forms.

I am, I have	we are, we have
you are, you have	you are, you have
he/she/it is, he/she/it has	he/she/it is, he/she/it has

You can use the simple present tense for an action that is happening right now ("I *welcome* this news"), an action that happens repeatedly in the present ("Judy *goes* to church every Sunday"), or an ongoing present action ("Wesley *likes* ice cream"). In some cases, if you want to ask a question or intensify the action, use the helping verb *do* or *does* before the infinitive form of the main verb.

I *do think* you should take the job.

Does Andy *want* it?

Besides present action, you can use the simple present for future action: "Football season *starts* Wednesday."

Use the simple present for a general truth, even if the rest of the sentence is in a different tense:

Columbus proved in 1492 that the world *is* round.

Mr. Hammond will argue that people *are* basically good.

> ### Verb Tenses at a Glance
>
> Note: the examples show first person only.
>
> | SIMPLE TENSES | REGULAR | IRREGULAR |
> |---|---|---|
> | *Present* | *Past* | *Future* |
> | I cook | I cooked | I will cook |
> | I see | I saw | I will see |
> | **PERFECT TENSES** | | |
> | *Present perfect* | *Past perfect* | *Future perfect* |
> | I have cooked | I had cooked | I will have cooked |
> | I have seen | I had seen | I will have seen |
> | **PROGRESSIVE TENSES** | REGULAR | IRREGULAR |
> | *Present progressive* | *Past progressive* | *Future progressive* |
> | I am cooking | I was cooking | I will be cooking |
> | I am seeing | I was seeing | I will be seeing |
> | *Present perfect progressive* | *Past perfect progressive* | *Future perfect progressive* |
> | I have been cooking | I had been cooking | I will have been cooking |
> | I have been seeing | I had been seeing | I will have been seeing |

5h. Use the simple past tense for actions already completed.

Indicate the simple past tense with the verb's past tense form. Regular verbs form the past tense by adding *-d* or *-ed* to the infinitive; the past tense of irregular verbs must be memorized. (See 5e.)

> Jack *enjoyed* the party. [Regular verb]
>
> Suzie *went* home early. [Irregular verb]

In the past tense, you can use the helping verb *did* (past tense of *do*) to ask a question or intensify the action. Use *did* with the infinitive form of the main verb for both regular and irregular verbs.

I went.	I did go.	Why did I go?
You saw.	You did see.	What did you see?
She ran.	She did run.	Where did she run?

NOTE: In some cases, spoken language may interfere with written language, causing problems with forming the past tense. Although speakers may not always pronounce the *-d* or *-ed* ending clearly, standard written English requires that you add the *-d* or *-ed* on all regular past tense verbs.

> NONSTANDARD   I *use* to wear weird clothes when I was a child.
>
> STANDARD   I *used* to wear weird clothes when I was a child.

5i. Use the simple future tense for actions that are expected to happen but have not happened yet.

> George *will arrive* in time for dinner.

> *Will* you please *show* him where to park?

To form the simple future tense, add *will* to the infinitive form of the verb.

I will go	we will go
you will go	you will go
he/she/it will go	they will go

You can also use *shall* to inject a tone of determination: ("We *shall over-come!*") or in polite questions ("Shall we dance?").

Although the present tense can indicate future action ("We *go* on vacation next Monday"), most actions that have not yet taken place are expressed in the simple future tense ("Surely it *will snow* tomorrow").

5j. Use the perfect tenses for an action completed at the time of another action.

The present perfect, past perfect, and future perfect tenses consist of a form of the helping verb *have* plus the past participle. The tense of *have* indicates the tense of the whole verb phrase.

The action of a ***present perfect*** verb was completed before the sentence is uttered. Its helping verb is in the present tense: *have* or *has*.

> I *have* never *been* to Spain, but I *have been* to Oklahoma.

> Mr. Grimaldi *has gone* home for the day.

> *Have* you *seen* John Sayles's new film?

You can use the present perfect tense either for an action completed before some other action ("I *have washed* my hands of the whole affair but I am watching from a safe distance") or for an action begun in the past and still going on ("Max *has worked* in this office for twelve years").

The action of a ***past perfect*** verb was completed before some other action in the past. Its helping verb is in the past tense: *had*.

> The concert *had ended* by the time we found a parking space.

> Until I met her, I *had* not *pictured* Jenna as a redhead.

> *Had* you *wanted* to clean the house before Mother arrived?

The action of a ***future perfect*** verb will be completed by some point (specified or implied) in the future. Its helping verb is in the future tense: *will have*.

> The builders *will have finished* the house by June.

The Simple Tenses

Present Tense: base form of the verb (+ -s or -es for **he, she, it**)

- Use the simple present tense to express general statements of fact or habitual activities or customs. Although it is called "present," this tense is really *general* or "timeless."

    You *make* wonderful coffee.

    Henry *goes* to the movies every Sunday afternoon.

- To form negatives and questions, use **do** or **does** 1 base form.

    Henry *does not* (*doesn't*) *go* to the movies during the week.

    Do you still *make* wonderful coffee?

Past Tense: base form 1 -d or -ed for regular verbs (for irregular verbs, see 5e.)

- Use the simple past tense to express an action that occurred at a specific time in the past. The specific time may be stated or implied.

    The package *arrived* yesterday.

    They *went* to San Juan for spring break.

- To form negatives and questions, use **did** 1 base form.

    They *did not* (*didn't*) *go* to Fort Lauderdale.

    Did the package *arrive* yesterday?

Future Tense: **will** or **be going to** 1 base form

- Use the simple future tense to express an action that will take place in the future. Also use **will** to imply promises and predictions.

    The students *will study* hard for their exam.

    The students *are going to study* hard for their exam.

    We *will help* you move. [Promise]

    Computers *will* soon *replace* most typewriters. [Prediction]

- To form negatives and questions, use **will** 1 base form.

    Jose *will not* (*won't*) *graduate* this year.

    Will computers *replace* typewriters?

NOTE: Use the simple present, not the future, to express future meaning in clauses beginning with **before, after,** or **when.**

INCORRECT   When my mother *will get* home from work, we will make
            dinner.

CORRECT   When my mother *gets* home from work, we will make dinner.

Use the simple present to show a future action when other words in the sentence
make the future meaning clear.

The bus *departs* in five minutes.

We *leave* for Chicago in the morning and *return* next Wednesday.

ESL
GUIDELINES

The Perfect Tenses

Present Perfect Tense: *has* or *have* 1 past participle (*-ed* or *-en* form for regular
verbs; for irregular verbs, see 5e.)

- Use the present perfect tense when an action took place at some unspecified
  time in the past. The action may have occurred repeatedly.

  I *have traveled* to many countries.

  The dog *has bitten* my aunt twice.

- Use the present perfect tense with *for* and *since* to indicate that an action began
  in the past, is occurring now, and will probably continue.

  I *have gone* to school with Jim and Susan since fifth grade.

  Jenny *has lived* next door to the Kramers for twelve years.

Past Perfect Tense: *had* 1 past participle

- Use the past perfect tense to indicate an action was completed in the past before some other past action.

  Josef *had smoked* for many years before he decided to quit.

  We got rid of the dog because he *had bitten* my aunt twice.

- Particularly in speech or informal writing, the simple past may be used instead
  of the past perfect when the relationship between actions is made clear by a
  conjunction such as *when, before, after,* or *until.*

  Observers *saw* the plane catch fire *before* it landed.

Future Perfect Tense: *will* 1 *have* 1 past participle

- Use the future perfect tense when an action will take place before some time in
  the future.

  The package *will have* already *arrived* by the time we get home from work.

  By June, the students *will have studied* ten chapters.

When you get the Dutch Blue, *will* you *have collected* every stamp you need?

The store *will* not *have closed* by the time we get there.

5k. Use the simple progressive tenses for an action in progress.

The present progressive, past progressive, and future progressive tenses consist of a form of the helping verb *be* plus the present participle (which is formed by adding *-ing* to the infinitive). The tense of *be* determines the tense of the whole verb phrase.

The *present progressive* expresses an action that is taking place now. Its helping verb is in the present tense: *am, is,* or *are.*

I *am thinking* of a word that starts with *R.*

Is Joe *babysitting* while Marie *is* off *visiting* her sister?

You can also express future action with the present progressive of *go* plus an infinitive phrase.

I *am going to read* Tolstoy's *War and Peace* someday.

Are you *going to sign up* for Professor Blaine's course on the sixties?

The *past progressive* expresses an action that took place continuously at some time in the past, whether or not that action is still going on. Its helping verb is in the past tense: *was* or *were.*

The old men *were sitting* on the porch when we passed.

Lucy *was planning* to take the weekend off.

The *future progressive* expresses an action that will take place continuously at some time in the future. Its helping verb is in the future tense: *will be.*

They *will be answering* the phones while she is gone.

Will we *be dining* out every night on our vacation?

5l. Use the perfect progressive tenses for a continuing action that began in the past.

Use the present perfect progressive, the past perfect progressive, or the future perfect progressive tense for an action that started in the past and did, does, or will continue.

The *present perfect progressive* indicates an action that started in the past and is continuing in the present. Form it by adding the present perfect of *be* (*has been* or *have been*) to the present participle (the *-ing* form) of the main verb.

All morning Fred *has been singing* the blues about his neighbor's wild parties.

Have you *been reading* Janine's postcards from England?

The *past perfect progressive* expresses a continuing action that was completed before another past action. Form it by adding the past perfect of *be* (*had been*) to the present participle of the main verb.

By the time Dave finally arrived, I *had been waiting* for twenty minutes.

The *future perfect progressive* expresses an action that is expected to continue into the future beyond some other future action. Form it by adding the future perfect of *be* (*will have been*) to the present participle of the main verb.

**ESL
GUIDELINES**

The Simple Progressive Tenses

Present Progressive Tense: present tense of *be* 1 present participle (-*ing* form)

- Use the present progressive tense when an action began in the past, is happening now, and will end at some time in the future.

    The students *are studying* for their exam.

    My sister *is living* with us until she graduates from college.

- You can also use the present progressive tense to show a future action when other words in the sentence make the future meaning clear.

    Maria *is flying* to Pittsburgh on July 8.

NOTE: Linking verbs (such as *be, seem, look*), verbs that express an emotional or mental state (such as *trust, like, guess, realize*), and verbs without action (such as *belong, have, need*) are not generally used in the present progressive tense. For these verbs, use the present tense to express a continuous state.

> INCORRECT   I think I *am liking* you very much.

> CORRECT   I think I *like* you very much.

Past Progressive Tense: *was* or *were* 1 present participle

- Use the past progressive tense when an action began and continued at a specific time in the past.

    Maria *was watching* the news when I arrived.

    The students *were studying* for their exam all day.

Future Progressive Tense: *will be* 1 present participle; or present tense of *be* + *going to be* 1 present participle

- Use the future progressive tense when an action will begin and will continue in the future.

    Hans *will be wearing* blue jeans to the party.

    The students *are going to be studying* until midnight.

By 1999 Joanne *will have been attending* school longer than anyone else I know.

Studying tenses can improve your writing by making you aware of the variety of verb forms at your disposal and by giving you practice at using them effectively. An important thing to remember about verb tenses is to avoid changing from one to another without reason. (See 11a.)

EXERCISE 5–2

Identifying Verb Tenses

Underline each verb or verb phrase and identify its tense in the sentences at the top of the next page. Answers for the lettered sentences appear in the back of the book. Example:

> John is living in Hinsdale, but he prefers Joliet.

> John <u>is living</u> [present progressive] in Hinsdale, but he <u>prefers</u> [simple present] Joliet.

ESL GUIDELINES

The Perfect Progressive Tenses

Present Perfect Progressive Tense: *have* or *has been* 1 present participle (*-ing* form)

- Use the present perfect progressive tense when an action began at some time in the past and has continued to the present. The words *for* and *since* are often used in sentences with this tense.

> She *has been answering* questions all day.

> The students *have been studying* for a long time.

Past Perfect Progressive Tense: *had been* 1 present participle

- Use the past perfect progressive tense when an action began and continued in the past and then was completed before some other past action.

> We *had been studying* for three hours before we took a break.

> Miguel *had been ringing* the bell for five minutes when we got home.

Future Perfect Progressive Tense: *will have been* 1 present participle

- Use the future perfect progressive tense when an action will continue in the future for a specific amount of time and then end before another future action.

> The students *will have been studying* for twenty-four hours by the time they take the exam tomorrow.

> The captain *will have been sailing* for ten days when she arrives in Jamaica.

a. Yesterday Joan broke her leg because she was skiing too fast.
b. Bill sleeps for nine hours every night; even so, he is always yawning.
c. Until last weekend, Josh had never seen a whale, except on those nature specials the public television station runs.
d. The upcoming tour represents the first time the band will have performed together since they split up.
e. I have heard that if you spend the night alone on the summit of Mount Snowdon, you will climb down either mad or a poet.

1. After they had burned the dead on funeral pyres, the Greeks turned back to the siege of Troy.
2. As of December 1, Ira and Sandy will have been going together for three years.
3. I was thinking about all the fun we've had since we met in third grade.
4. Dan will have embarked on his career by the time his brother starts college.
5. She will be working in her study if you need her.
6. By the time they have counted the last votes, you will have heard so much about the candidates that you won't be looking forward to an election campaign for a long time.
7. Have you been hoping that Carlos will come to your party?
8. I know that he will not yet have returned from Chicago.
9. His parents had been expecting him home any day until they heard that he was still waiting for the bus.
10. Probably he is sitting in the depot right now, unless he has switched to the train.

VOICE

Intelligent students read challenging books.

Challenging books are read by intelligent students.

These two statements convey similar information, but their emphasis is different. In the first sentence, the subject (*students*) performs the verb's action (*read*); in the second sentence, the subject (*books*) receives the verb's action (*are read*). One sentence states its idea directly, the other indirectly. We say that the first sentence is in the *active voice* and the second is in the *passive voice*.

5m.   Use the active voice rather than the passive voice.

Verbs in the *active voice* consist of principal parts and helping verbs. Verbs in the *passive voice* consist of the past participle preceded by a form of *be* ("you *are given*," "I *was given*," "she *will be given*"). Most writers prefer the active to the passive voice because it is clearer and simpler, requires fewer words, and identifies the actor and the action more explicitly.

ACTIVE VOICE   *Sergeants give* orders. *Privates obey* them.

Some writers use a verb in the passive voice when the active voice would be more effective. Normally the subject of a sentence is the focus of the readers' attention. If that subject does not perform the verb's action but instead receives the action, readers may wonder: What did the writer mean to emphasize? Just what is the point?

PASSIVE VOICE   *Orders are given* by sergeants. *They are obeyed* by privates.

Other writers misuse the passive voice to try to lend pomp to a humble truth (or would-be truth). The nervous student, trying to impress the profes-

---

ESL
GUIDELINES

The Passive Voice

Passive Voice: form of *be* + past participle (-*ed* or -*en* form for regular verbs; for irregular forms, see 5e.)

- In a passive voice sentence, the grammatical subject *receives* the action of the verb instead of performing it.

    ACTIVE   The university *awarded* Hamid a scholarship. [The subject (*university*) performs the action of *awarding*.]

    PASSIVE   Hamid *was awarded* a scholarship by the university. [The subject (*Hamid*) receives the action.]

- Often the identity of the action's performer is not important or is understood, and the *by* phrase is omitted.

    PASSIVE   Automobiles are built in Detroit. [It is understood that they are built *by people.*]

- When forming the passive, be careful to use the appropriate tenses of *be* to maintain the tense of the original active sentence.

    ACTIVE   Bongo the clown *entertains* children. [Present tense]

    PASSIVE   Children *are entertained* by Bongo the clown. [Present tense]

    ACTIVE   Bongo the clown *entertained* the children. [Past tense]

    PASSIVE   The children *were entertained* by Bongo the clown. [Past tense]

NOTE: Intransitive verbs are not used in the passive voice (see 1c for more on intransitive verbs).

    INCORRECT   The plane *was arrived.*

    CORRECT   The plane *arrived.*

NOTE: The future progressive and future perfect progressive tenses are not used in the passive voice.

    INCORRECT   The novel *will be being read* by John.

    CORRECT   John *will be reading* the novel.

sor, says, "Your help is greatly appreciated by me." When the airplane needs repairs, the flight attendant tells the passengers, "Slight technical difficulties are being experienced."

Some writers use the passive voice deliberately to obscure the truth — a contradiction of the very purpose of writing. One of the witnesses in the congressional Iran-Contra hearings tried to dodge a key question by replying, "Whether full knowledge had been attained by us at that time is uncertain." If he had answered in the active voice — "I don't know whether we knew everything then or not" — his listeners easily would have recognized an evasion.

You do not need to eliminate the passive voice entirely from your writing. In some contexts the performer of the verb's action in a sentence is unknown or irrelevant. With a passive voice verb, you can simply omit the performer, as in "Many fortunes were lost in the stock market crash of 1929" or "The passive voice is often misused." It's a good idea, though, as you comb through a rough draft, to substitute the active voice for the passive unless you have a good reason for using the passive.

EXERCISE 5–3

Using Active and Passive Voice Verbs

Revise the following passage, changing the passive voice to the active voice in each sentence, unless you can justify keeping the passive. Example:

The Galápagos Islands were reached by many species of animals in ancient times.

Many species of animals *reached* the Galápagos Islands in ancient times.

The unique creatures of the Galápagos Islands have been studied by many scientists. The islands were explored by Charles Darwin in 1835. His observations led to the theory of evolution, which he explained in his book *On the Origin of Species*. Thirteen species of finches on the islands were discovered by Darwin, all descended from a common stock; even today this great variety of species can be seen by visitors to the islands. Each island species has evolved by adapting to local conditions. A twig is used by the woodpecker finch to probe trees for grubs. Algae on the ocean floor is fed on by the marine iguana. Salt water can be drunk by the Galápagos cormorant, thanks to a salt-extracting gland. Because of the tameness of these animals, they can be studied by visitors at close range.

MOOD

Still another characteristic of verbs is mood. Every verb is in one of three *moods*: the *indicative,* the *imperative,* or the *subjunctive.* The indicative mood is the most common. The imperative mood and subjunctive mood add valuable versatility to the English language.

5n. Use the indicative mood to state a fact, to ask a question, or to express an opinion.

The vast majority of verbs in English are in the indicative mood.

FACT	Pat *left* home two months ago.
QUESTION	*Will* she *find* happiness as a belly dancer?
OPINION	I *think* not.

5o. Use the imperative mood to make a request or to give a command or direction.

The understood but usually unstated subject of a verb in the imperative mood is *you.* The verb's form is the infinitive.

REQUEST	Please *be* there before noon. [*You* please be there. . . .]
COMMAND	*Hurry!* [*You* hurry!]
DIRECTION	To reach my house, *drive* east on State Street. [. . . *you* drive east. . . .]

5p. Use the subjunctive mood to express a wish, a requirement, a suggestion, or a condition contrary to fact.

The subjunctive mood is used in a subordinate clause to suggest uncertainty: the action expressed by the verb may or may not actually take place as specified. In any clause opening with *that* and expressing a requirement, the verb is in the subjunctive mood and its form is the infinitive.

Professor Avery requires that every student *deliver* his or her work promptly.

She asked that we *be* on time for all meetings.

When you use the subjunctive mood to describe a condition that is contrary to fact, use *were* if the verb is *be;* for other verbs, use the simple past tense. Wishes, whether present or past, follow the same rules.

If I *were* rich, I would be happy.

If I *had* a million dollars, I would be happy.

Elissa wishes that Ted *were* more goal-oriented.

Elissa wished that Ted *knew* what he wanted to do.

For a condition that was contrary to fact at some point in the past, use the past perfect tense.

If I *had been* awake, I would have seen the meteor showers.

If Jessie *had known* you were coming, she would have cleaned her room.

Although use of the subjunctive mood has grown scarcer over the years, it still sounds crude to write "If I *was* you...." If you ever feel that the subjunctive mood makes a sentence sound stilted, you can rewrite it, substituting an infinitive phrase.

Professor Avery requires every student *to deliver* his or her work promptly.

EXERCISE 5–4

Using the Correct Mood of Verbs

Find and correct any errors in mood of verbs in the following sentences. Identify the mood of the incorrect verb as well as of its correct replacement. Some sentences may be correct. Answers for the lettered sentences appear in the back of the book. Example:

The law requires that each person files a tax return by April 15.

The law requires that each person *file* a tax return by April 15. [Incorrect *files*, indicative; correct *files*, subjunctive]

 **ESL GUIDELINES**

Conditionals

Conditional sentences usually contain an *if* clause, which states the condition, and a result clause.

- When the condition is true or possibly true in the present or future, use the present tense in the *if* clause and the present or future tense in the result clause. The future tense is not used in the *if* clause.

  If Jane *prepares* her composition early, she usually *writes* very well.

  If Maria *saves* enough money, she *will buy* some new software.

- When the condition is not true in the present, for most verbs use the past tense in the *if* clause; for the verb *be*, use *were*. Use *would, could,* or *might* + infinitive form in the result clause.

  If Carlos *had* a computer, he *would need* a monitor, too.

  If Claudia *were* here, she *could do* it herself.

- When the condition was not true in the past, use the perfect past tense in the *if* clause. If the possible result was in the past, use *would have, could have,* or *might have* + past participle (*-ed* or *-en* form) in the result clause. If the possible result is in the present, use *would, could,* or *might* + infinitive form in the result clause.

  If Claudia *had saved* enough money last month, she *could have bought* new software. [Result in the past.]

  If Annie *had finished* law school, she *might be* a successful lawyer now. [Result in the present.]

    a. Dr. Belanger recommended that Juan flosses his teeth every day.

    b. If I was you, I would have done the same thing.

    c. Tradition demands that Daegun shows respect for his elders.

    d. If they had given him the time off, he would have been free to do as he wished.

    e. Diane wishes that choosing a college was quicker and easier.

    1. If she was slightly older, she could stay home by herself.

    2. If they have waited a little longer, they would have seen some amazing things.

    3. If Pamela ran the restaurant, she would insist that the chef receive a raise.

    4. Emilia's contract stipulates that she works on Saturdays.

    5. If James invested in the company ten years ago, he would have made a lot of money.

    6. The job requires that John is in Italy three months of every year.

6. *Subject-Verb Agreement*

What does it mean for a subject and a verb to agree? Practically speaking, it means that their forms are in accord: plural subjects take plural verbs, third-person subjects take third-person verbs, and so forth. Creating agreement in a sentence is like making sure that all the instruments in a song are playing in the same key. When your subjects and verbs agree, you prevent a discord that could distract readers from your message. Editing for subject-verb agreement is also covered in the "Quick Editing Guide." (For more help, see A2.)

6a. A verb agrees with its subject in person and number.

Subject and verb agree in person (first, second, or third):

> *I write* my research papers on a typewriter. [Subject and verb in first person]

> *Jim writes* his research papers on a word processor. [Subject and verb in third person]

Subject and verb agree in number (singular or plural):

> *Susan has enjoyed* college. [Subject and verb singular]

> *She and Jim have enjoyed* their vacation. [Subject and verb plural]

The present tense of most verbs is the infinitive form, with no added ending except in the third-person singular. (See 5g–5l.)

I enjoy	we enjoy
you enjoy	you enjoy
he/she/it enjoys	they enjoy

Forms of the verb *be* vary from this rule.

I am	we are
you are	you are
he/she/it is	they are

6b. A verb agrees with its subject, not with any words that intervene.

> My *favorite* of O. Henry's short stories *is* "The Gift of the Magi."

> *Dollars,* once the dominant currency in international trade, *have fallen* behind the yen.

A singular subject linked to another noun or pronoun by a prepositional phrase such as *along with, as well as,* or *in addition to* remains a singular subject and takes a singular verb.

> My cousin *James* as well as his wife and son *plans* to vote for the Democratic candidate.

6c. Subjects joined by *and* usually take a plural verb.

Two or more nouns or pronouns linked by *and* constitute a *compound subject.* (See 2a.) In most cases, a compound subject counts as plural and takes a plural verb.

> *"Howl" and "Gerontion" are* Barry's favorite poems.

> *Sugar, salt, and fat* adversely *affect* people's health.

However, for phrases like *each man and woman* or *every dog and cat,* where the subjects are considered individually, use a singular verb.

> *Each man and woman* in the room *has* a different story to tell.

Use a singular verb for two singular subjects that refer to the same thing.

> *Lime juice and soda quenches* your thirst.

6d. With subjects joined by *or* or *nor,* the verb agrees with the part of the subject nearest to it.

> Either they or *Max is* guilty.

> Neither Sally nor *I am* willing to face the truth.

Subjects containing *not . . . but* follow this rule also.

> Not we but *George knows* the whole story.

You can remedy the awkwardness of such constructions by rephrasing the offending sentences.

Either they are guilty or Max is.

Sally and I are unwilling to face the truth.

We do not know the whole story, but George does.

6e. Most collective nouns take singular verbs.

What do you do when the number of a subject is not obvious? Collective nouns, such as *committee, congregation, family, group, jury,* and *trio,* represent more than one person. When a collective noun refers to a group of people acting in unison, use a singular verb.

The *jury finds* the defendant guilty.

My *family upholds* traditional values.

When the members act individually, use a plural verb.

The *jury do* not yet *agree* on a verdict.

Alice's *family* rarely *eat* together.

If you feel that using a plural verb with a collective subject results in an awkward sentence, reword the subject so that it refers to members of the group individually. (Also see 9e.)

The *jurors do* not yet *agree* on a verdict.

The *members* of Alice's family rarely *eat* together.

6f. Most indefinite pronouns take a third-person singular verb.

The indefinite pronouns *each, either, neither, anyone, anybody, anything, everyone, everybody, everything, one, no one, nobody, nothing, someone, somebody,* and *something* are considered singular and take a third-person singular verb.

Someone is bothering me.

Even when one of these subjects is followed by a phrase containing a noun or pronoun of a different person or number, use a singular verb.

Each of you *is* here to stay.

One of the pandas *seems* dangerously ill.

6g. The indefinite pronouns *all, any,* and *some* use a singular or plural verb depending on their meaning.

I have no explanation. *Is any* needed?

Any of the changes that really needed to be made *have* been made already.

All is lost.

ESL GUIDELINES

Count Nouns and Articles

Nouns that refer to items that can be counted are called *count* (or *countable*) nouns. Count nouns can be made plural.

> *table, chair, egg*   two *tables*, several *chairs*, a dozen *eggs*

- Singular count nouns must be preceded by a *determiner*. The class of words called determiners includes *articles* (*a, an, the*), *possessives* (*John's, your, his, my*, and so on), *demonstratives* (*this, that, these, those*), *numbers* (*three, the third*, and so on), and *indefinite quantity words* (*no, some, many*, and so on).

> *a* dog, *the* football, *one* reason, *the first* page, *no* chance

- The choice between using an indefinite article (*a, an*) or the definite article (*the*) before a singular count noun depends on context and meaning. Use the indefinite article when the noun is unspecific or when you are introducing something not previously known to the reader or you the writer.

> She likes to have *a* milkshake every day. [Any milkshake, not a specific one]

> I saw *a* dog in my backyard this morning. [The dog is not known to the writer.]

- Use the definite article when a noun is mentioned for the second time.

> She likes to have *a* milkshake every day. *The* milkshake must be cold.

> I saw *a* dog in my backyard this morning. *The* dog was black.

- Use the definite article before a specific count noun mentioned the first time when the reader or listener is given enough information to identify what is referred to, usually in a phrase or clause after the noun.

> *The* young woman wearing blue is my sister. [*Wearing blue* identifies the particular woman.]

- Use the definite article before a singular count noun to make a generalization.

> *The* dog has been humans' favorite pet for centuries. [All dogs]

- Use the definite article before some geographical names.

> ***Collectives:*** the United States, the United Kingdom
> ***Groups of islands:*** the Bahamas, the Canary Islands
> ***Large bodies of water (except lakes):*** the Atlantic Ocean, the Dead Sea
> ***Mountain ranges:*** the Rocky Mountains, the Himalayas

- When plural count nouns are used to name a general group, they are not preceded by an article. When they are used to name a definite or specific group they must be preceded by *the* or another determiner.

> *Horses* don't eat meat, and neither do *cows*.

> Hal is feeding *the horses* in the barn, and he has already fed *his cows*.

All of the bananas *are gone.*

Some of the blame *is* mine.

Some of us *are* Democrats.

None—like *all, any,* and *some*—takes a singular or a plural verb, depending on the sense in which the pronoun is used. (See also 9d, 9f.)

None of you *is* exempt.

None of his wives *were* blond.

ESL GUIDELINES

Noncount Nouns and Articles

Nouns that cannot be counted are called ***noncount*** (or ***uncountable***) nouns. Noncount nouns cannot be made plural.

> INCORRECT   I need to learn more *grammars.*
>
> CORRECT   I need to learn more *grammar.*

- Common categories of noncount nouns include types of ***food*** (*cheese, meat, bread, broccoli,* and so on), ***solids*** (*dirt, salt, chalk*), ***liquids*** (*milk, juice, gasoline*), ***gases*** (*methane, hydrogen, air*), and ***abstract ideas*** including emotions (*democracy, gravity, love, jealousy*).
- Another category of noncount nouns is ***mass*** nouns, which usually represent a large group of countable nouns, such as *furniture, equipment, luggage, mail,* and *clothing.*
- The only way to count noncountable nouns is to use a countable noun with them; these countable nouns usually indicate a quantity or a container.

  one *piece* of furniture

  two *quarts* of water

  an *example* of jealousy

- Noncount nouns are never preceded by an indefinite article; they are often preceded by *some.*

> INCORRECT   She gave us *a* good advice.
>
> CORRECT   She gave us good advice.
>
> CORRECT   She gave us *some* good advice.

- When noncount nouns are *general* in meaning, no article is required, but when the context makes them specific (usually in a phrase or a clause after the noun), the definite article is used.

> GENERAL   Deliver us from *evil.*
>
> SPECIFIC   The *evil* that humans do lives after them.

6h. In a subordinate clause with a relative pronoun as the subject, the verb agrees with the antecedent.

When you are writing a subordinate clause that modifies a noun, the subject may be a relative pronoun: *who, which,* or *that.* To determine the person and number of the verb in the clause, look back at the pronoun's antecedent, the word to which the pronoun refers. (See 9a–9f.) The antecedent is usually (but not always) the noun closest to the relative pronoun.

> I have a friend *who studies* day and night. [The antecedent of *who* is the third-person singular noun *friend.* Therefore, the verb in the subordinate clause is third-person singular, *studies.*]

> Unfortunately, I bought one of the two hundred recently manufactured cars *that have* defective upholstery. [The antecedent of *that* is *cars,* so the verb is third-person plural, *have.*]

> This is the only one of the mayor's new ideas *that has* any worth. [Here *one,* not *ideas,* is the antecedent of *that.* Thus, the verb in the subordinate clause is third-person singular, *has,* not *have.*]

6i. A verb agrees with its subject even when the subject follows the verb.

A writer need not necessarily place the subject of a sentence before the verb. In some sentences, an introductory phrase or a word such as *there* or *here* changes the ordinary subject-verb order. If a sentence opens with such a phrase or word, look for the subject after the verb. Remember that verbs agree with subjects and that *here* and *there* are never subjects.

> Here *is* a *riddle* for you.

> There *are* forty *people* in my law class.

> Under the bridge *were* a broken-down *boat and* a worn *tire.*

6j. A linking verb agrees with its subject, not its subject complement.

In some sentences, a form of the verb *be* is used to link two or more nouns ("Matthew *is* the composer"). The linking verb's subject is the noun that precedes it. Nouns that follow the linking verb are subject complements. (See 2d.) Take care to make a linking verb agree with the subject of the sentence, not with the subject complement.

> *Jim is* a gentleman and a scholar.

> Amy's *parents are* her most enthusiastic audience.

6k. When the subject is a title, use a singular verb.

When I was younger, *James and the Giant Peach* by Roald Dahl *was* my favorite book.

"Memories" sung by Barbra Streisand *is* my favorite song.

6l. Singular nouns that end in *-s* take singular verbs.

Some nouns look plural even though they refer to a singular subject: *news, measles, logistics, mathematics, physics, electronics, economics.* Such nouns take singular verbs.

The *news is* that *economics has become* one of the most popular majors.

EXERCISE 6–1

Making Subjects and Verbs Agree

Find and correct any errors of subject-verb agreement in the following sentences. Some sentences may be correct. Answers for the lettered sentences appear in the back of the book. Example:

Addressing the audience tonight is the nominees for club president.

Addressing the audience tonight *are* the nominees for club president.

a. Our foreign policy in Cuba, Nicaragua, El Salvador, and Panama have not been as successful as most Americans had hoped.
b. The large amount of metal and chlorine in our water makes it taste funny.
c. I read about a couple who is offering to trade their baby for a brand-new Chevrolet.
d. A shave, a haircut, and a new suit has turned Bill into a different person.
e. Neither the guerrillas nor the government are willing to negotiate.

1. Each of us, including Alice, want this to be a successful party.
2. The police force, after the recent rash of burglaries, have added more patrols in this neighborhood.
3. More disturbing than John's speech was the gestures that accompanied it.
4. One of Korea's most fascinating cities are Kyongju.
5. Nearly everybody who traveled by air during the last six weeks was aware of increased security precautions.
6. The bad news about interest rates have been widely publicized.
7. Most of the class believed that both the private sector and the government was taking appropriate action on homelessness.
8. Jane Austen, along with George Eliot and Charles Dickens, are still popular today.
9. Ron Wood is not the only member of the Rolling Stones who have played in the band Faces.
10. Beside the cottage was a small barn and a well.

7. *Pronoun Case*

As you know, pronouns come in distinctive forms. The first-person pronoun can be *I*, or it can be *me, my, mine, we, us, our,* or *ours*. Which form do you pick? It depends on what job you want the pronoun to do. Filling these jobs may sound easy, but now and again every writer has a hard time hiring the pronoun that is properly qualified.

To choose correctly, it may help you to know the three *cases* used to classify pronouns. Depending on a pronoun's function in a sentence, we say that it is in the **subjective case,** the **objective case,** or the **possessive case.**

Some pronouns change form when they change case and some do not. The personal pronouns *I, he, she, we,* and *they* and the relative pronoun *who* have different forms in the subjective, objective, and possessive cases. Other pronouns, such as *you, it, that,* and *which,* have only two forms: the plain case (which serves as both subjective and objective) and the possessive case.

We can pin the labels *subjective, objective,* and *possessive* on nouns as well as on pronouns. Like the pronouns *you, it, that,* and *which,* nouns shift out of their plain form only in the possessive case (*teacher's pet*, the *Joneses'* poodle).

Beware, when you are not sure which case to choose, of the temptation to fall back on a reflexive pronoun (*myself, himself*). Reflexive pronouns have limited, specific uses in writing (see 1b). They do not take the place of subjective or objective pronouns. If you catch yourself writing, "You can return the form to John or *myself*" or "John and *myself* are in charge," replace the reflexive pronoun with one that is grammatically correct: "You can return the form to John or *me*"; "John and *I* are in charge."

Editing for pronoun case is also covered in the "Quick Editing Guide." (For more help, see A3.)

7a.   Use the subjective case for the subject of a sentence or clause.

I ate the granola.

Who cares?

Mark recalled that *she* played jai alai.

Election officials are the people *who* count.

Sometimes a compound subject will lead a writer astray: "Jed and *me* ate the granola." *Me*, an objective pronoun, is the wrong one for this job. Use the subjective form, *I*, instead: "Jed and *I* ate the granola."

A pronoun serving as subject for a verb is subjective even when the verb isn't written but is only implied:

Jed is hungrier than *I* [am].

Don't be fooled by a pronoun that appears immediately after a verb, as if it were a direct object, but that functions as the subject of a clause.

The pronoun's case is determined by its role in the sentence, not by its position.

The judge didn't believe *I* hadn't been the driver.

We were happy to interview *whoever* was running. [Subject of *was running*]

7b. Use the subjective case for a subject complement.

A pronoun can function as a subject complement after a linking verb such as *is, seems,* or *appears*. (See 2d for more on subject complements, 5a for more on linking verbs.) Because it plays essentially the same role as the subject, the pronoun's case is subjective.

The phantom graffiti artist couldn't have been *he*. It was *I.*

7c. Use the subjective case for an appositive to a subject or subject complement.

A pronoun placed in apposition to a subject or subject complement is like an identical twin to the noun it stands beside. It has the same meaning and the same case. (See also 3d.)

The class *officers* — Jed and *she* — announced a granola breakfast.

7d. Use the objective case for a direct object, an indirect object, the object of a preposition, or a subject of an infinitive.

The custard pies hit *him* and *me*. [Direct object]

Mona threw *us* towels. [Indirect object]

Mona threw towels to *him* and *us*. [Object of a preposition]

We always expect *him* to win. [Subject of an infinitive]

7e. Use the objective case for an appositive to a direct or indirect object or the object of a preposition.

Mona helped *us* all — Mrs. Van Dumont, *him,* and *me*. [*Him* and *me* are in apposition to the direct object *us.*]

Binks gave his favorite *students,* Tom and *her,* an approving nod. [*Her* is in apposition to the indirect object *students.*]

Yelling, the persistent pie flingers ran after *us* — Mrs. Van Dumont, Mona, *him,* and *me*. [*Him* and *me* are in apposition to *us,* the object of the preposition *after.*]

7f.   Use the possessive case to show ownership.

Possessive pronouns can function as adjectives or as nouns. The pronouns *my, your, his, her, its, our,* and *their* function as adjectives by modifying nouns or pronouns.

> *Their* apartment is bigger than *our* house.

> *My* new bike is having *its* first road test today.

Notice that the possessive pronoun *its* does not contain an apostrophe. *It's* with an apostrophe is not a possessive pronoun, but a contraction for *it is,* as in "*It's* a beautiful day." If you want to write about the day and *its* beauty, be sure to omit the apostrophe.

The possessive pronouns *mine, yours, his, hers, ours,* and *theirs* can discharge the whole range of noun duties. These pronouns can serve as subjects, subject complements, direct objects, indirect objects, or objects of prepositions.

> *Yours* is the last vote we need. [Subject]

> This day is *ours*. [Subject complement]

> Don't take your car; take *mine*. [Direct object]

> If we're honoring requests in chronological order, give *hers* top priority. [Indirect object]

> Give her request priority over *theirs*. [Object of a preposition]

7g.   Use the possessive case to modify a gerund.

A possessive pronoun (or a possessive noun) is the appropriate escort for a gerund, a form of verb that functions as a noun: *griping, being, drinking.* (See 3b.) As a noun, a gerund requires an adjective, not another noun, for a modifier.

> Mary is tired of *his griping*. [The possessive pronoun *his* modifies the gerund *griping*.]

> I can stand *their being* late every morning but not *his drinking* on the job. [The possessive pronoun *their* modifies the gerund *being*; the possessive pronoun *his* modifies the gerund *drinking*.]

Gerunds can cause confusion when you edit your writing because they look exactly like present participles. (See 5c.) Whereas a gerund functions as a noun, a participle often functions as an adjective modifying a noun or pronoun.

> Mary heard *him griping* about work. [The participle *griping* modifies the direct object *him*.]

If you are not sure whether to use a possessive or an objective pronoun with a word ending in *-ing,* look closely at your sentence. Which word — the pronoun or the *-ing* word — is the object of your main verb? That word functions as a noun; the other word modifies it.

> Mr. Phipps remembered *them* smoking in the boys' room.

> Mr. Phipps remembered *their* smoking in the boys' room.

In the first sentence, Mr. Phipps's memory is of *them,* those naughty students. *Them* is the object of the verb, so *smoking* is a participle modifying *them.* In the second sentence, Mr. Phipps remembers *smoking,* that nasty habit. The gerund *smoking* is the object of the verb, so the possessive pronoun *their* is the right choice to modify it.

In everyday speech, the rules about pronoun case apply less rigidly. Someone who correctly asks in conversation, "To whom are you referring?" is likely to sound pretentious. You are within your rights to reply, as did the comic-strip character Pogo Possum, "Youm, that's whom!" Say, if you like, "It's *me,*" but write "It is *I.*" Say, if you wish, "*Who* did he ask to the party?" but write "*Whom* did he ask?"

EXERCISE 7–1

Using Pronouns Correctly

Replace any pronouns that are used incorrectly in the following sentences. (Consider all these examples as written — not spoken — English, and so apply the rules strictly.) Explain why each pronoun was incorrect. Some sentences may be correct. Answers for the lettered sentences appear in the back of the book. Example:

> In the photograph, that's him at the age of seven.

> In the photograph, that's *he* at the age of seven. [*He* is a subject complement.]

a. She can run faster than me.
b. Mrs. Van Dumont awarded the prize to Mona and I.
c. Judy laughed at both of us — she and I.
d. I am sure that I overheard that rude man speaking of we.
e. Jerry, myself, and the pizza chef regard you and she as the very people who we wish to get acquainted with.

1. I like to watch them swimming in the hotel pool.
2. Lee and me would be delighted to serenade whomever will listen.
3. The waiters and us busboys are highly trustworthy.
4. The neighbors were driven berserk by him singing.
5. Strictly platonic affairs suit us — Biff, the Flipper, and me.
6. Dean Fitts and them, who I suspect of being the pie throwers, flung crusty missiles at Stan, he, and myself.
7. Have you guessed the identity of the person of who I am speaking?
8. I didn't appreciate you laughing at her and I.
9. They — Jerry and her — are the troublemakers.

10. It was him asking about the clock that started me suspecting him.
11. Juliana isn't as old-fashioned in her views as them.
12. The Jeffersons invited Martha and I over for dinner.
13. There is a lack of communication among you and he and Dean.
14. The counterattack was launched by Dusty and myself.
15. Whomever this anonymous letter writer is, I resent him lying about Jules and me and the cabbages.

8. *Pronoun Reference*

Look hard at just about any piece of writing — this discussion, if you like — and you'll find that practically every pronoun in it points to some noun. This is the main use of pronouns: to refer in a brief, convenient form to some *antecedent* that has already been named. A pronoun usually has a noun or another pronoun as its antecedent. Often the antecedent is the subject or object of the same clause in which the pronoun appears.

Josie hit the *ball* after *its* first bounce.

Smashing into *Greg,* the ball knocked off *his* glasses.

The antecedent also can appear in a different clause or even a different sentence from the pronoun.

Josie hit the *ball* when *it* bounced back to *her.*

The *ball* smashed into *Greg. It* knocked off *his* glasses.

A pronoun as well as a noun can be an antecedent.

My *dog* hid in the closet when *she* had *her* puppies. [*Dog* is the antecedent of *she; she* is the antecedent of *her.*]

8a.   Name the pronoun's antecedent: don't just imply it.

In editing, in combing over what you write, be sure you have identified clearly the antecedent of each pronoun. A writer who leaves a key idea unsaid is likely to confuse readers.

VAGUE   Ted wanted a Norwegian canoe because he'd heard that *they* produce the lightest canoes afloat.

What does *they* refer to? Not to *Norwegian,* which is an adjective; the antecedent of a pronoun has to be a noun or pronoun. We may guess that this writer has in mind Norwegian canoe builders, but no such noun has been mentioned. To make the sentence work, the writer must supply an antecedent for *they.*

CLEAR   Ted wanted a Norwegian canoe because he'd heard that Norway produces [*or* Norwegians produce] the lightest canoes afloat.

Watch out for possessive nouns. They won't work as antecedents.

> VAGUE   On William's canoe *he* painted a skull and bones. (For all we know, *he* might be some joker named Fred.)
>
> CLEAR   On his canoe William painted a skull and bones.

8b. Give the pronoun *it, this, that,* or *which* a clear antecedent.

Vagueness arises, thick as fog, whenever *it, this, that,* or *which* points to something a writer assumes he or she has said but indeed hasn't. Is the reference of a pronoun fuzzy? Might a reader get lost in the fog? Often the best way out of the fog is to substitute a specific noun or phrase for the pronoun.

> VAGUE   I was an only child, and *it* was hard.
>
> CLEAR   I was an only child, and my solitary life was hard.
>
> VAGUE   Ruth majored in economics and applied for a job in a broker's office, *which* caused her father to exult. Still, *it* was not what she desired.
>
> CLEAR   Ruth's deciding to major in economics and applying for a job in a broker's office pleased her father. Still, a career in finance was not what she desired.
>
> VAGUE   Judy could not get along with her younger brother. *This* is the reason she wanted to get her own apartment.
>
> CLEAR   Because Judy could not get along with her younger brother, she wanted to get her own apartment.

8c. Make the pronoun's antecedent clear.

Confusion strikes if the antecedent of a pronoun is ambiguous — that is, if the pronoun seems to point in two or more directions. In such a puzzling situation, there's no lack of antecedent; the trouble is that more than one antecedent looks possible. Baffled, the reader wonders which the writer means.

> CONFUSING   Rob shouted to Jim to take off his burning sweater.

Whose sweater does *his* mean — Jim's or Rob's? Simply changing a pronoun won't clear up the confusion. The writer needs to revise the sentence drastically enough to move the two antecedents out of each other's way.

> CLEAR   "Help, Rob!" Jim shouted. "My sweater's on fire! Take it off!"
>
> CLEAR   "Jim!" shouted Rob. "Your sweater's on fire! Take it off!"
>
> CLEAR   Flames were shooting from Jim's sweater. Rob shouted to Jim to take it off.

As you can tell from that first fogbound sentence, pronouns referring to nouns of the same gender are particular offenders. How would you straighten out this grammatical tangle?

CONFUSING   Linda welcomed Lee-Ann's move into the apartment next door.
            Little did she dream that soon she would be secretly dating her
            husband.

Let meaning show the way. If you had written these sentences, you would
know which person is the sneak. One way to clarify the antecedents of *she* and
her is to add more information.

CLEAR   In welcoming Lee-Ann to the apartment next door, Linda didn't
        dream that soon her own husband would be secretly dating her for-
        mer sorority sister.

Instead of *her own husband,* you can identify that philanderer by name if
you have previously identified him as Linda's husband: "Ned would be secretly dating. . . ." (Grammatical tangles are easier than human tangles to
straighten out.)

8d.   Place the pronoun close to its antecedent to keep the
          relationship clear.

Watch out for distractions that slip in between noun and pronoun. If your
sentence contains two or more nouns that look like antecedents to a pronoun, your readers may become bewildered.

CONFUSING   Harper steered his dinghy alongside the polished mahogany
            cabin cruiser that the drug smugglers had left anchored under
            an overhanging willow in the tiny harbor and eased it to a stop.

What did Harper ease to a stop? By the time readers reach the end of the sentence, they are likely to have forgotten. To avoid confusion, keep the pronoun
and its antecedent reasonably close together.

CLEAR   Harper steered his dinghy into the tiny harbor and eased it to a stop
        alongside the polished mahogany cabin cruiser that the drug smug-
        glers had left anchored under an overhanging willow.

Never force your readers to stop and think, "What does that pronoun
stand for?" You, the writer, have to do this thinking for them.

EXERCISE 8–1

Making Pronoun Reference Clear

Revise each sentence or group of sentences so that any pronoun needing an antecedent clearly points to one. Possible revisions for the lettered sentences appear in the back of the book. Example:

I took the money out of the wallet and threw it in the trash.

I took the money out of the wallet and threw *the wallet* in the trash.

a. Bill's prank frightened Josh and made him wonder why he had done it.
b. Korean students study up to twenty subjects a year, including algebra, calculus, and engineering. Because they are required, they must study them year after year.
c. Roger Clemens signed a baseball for Chad that he had used in a game.
d. When the bottle hit the windshield, it shattered.
e. My friends believe they are more mature than many of their peers because of the discipline enforced at their school. However, it can also lead to problems.

1. I could see the moon and the faint shadow of the tree as it began to rise.
2. Katrina spent the summer in Paris and traveled to several other countries, which broadened her awareness of language and culture.
3. Most managers want employees to work as many hours as possible. They never consider the work they need to do at home.
4. I worked twelve hours a day and almost never got enough sleep, but it was worth it.
5. Kevin asked Mike to meet him for lunch but forgot that he had class at that time.

9. Pronoun-Antecedent Agreement

A pronoun's job is to fill in for a noun, much as an actor's double fills in for the actor. Pronouns are a short, convenient way for writers to avoid repeating the same noun over and over. The noun that a pronoun stands for is called its *antecedent*.

The sheriff drew a six-shooter; he fired twice.

This action-packed sentence unfolds in a familiar order. First comes a noun (*sheriff*) and then a pronoun (*he*) that refers back to it. *Sheriff* is the antecedent of *he*.

Just as verbs need to agree with their subjects, pronouns need to agree with the nouns they stand for. A successful writer takes care not to shift number, person, or gender in midsentence ("The *sheriff* and the *outlaw* drew *their* six-shooters; *he* fired twice"). Rather, the writer starts each sentence with nouns clearly in mind and picks appropriate pronouns to refer to them.

Editing for pronoun-antecedent agreement is also covered in the "Quick Editing Guide." (For more help, see A4.)

9a. Pronouns agree with their antecedents in person and number.

A pronoun matches its antecedent in person (first, second, or third) and in number (singular or plural), even when a string of intervening words separates the pronoun and its antecedent. (See the pronoun chart in 1b.)

FAULTY   All *campers* should bring *your* knapsacks.

Here, noun and pronoun disagree in person: *campers* is third person, but *your* is second person.

FAULTY   Every *camper* should bring *their* knapsack.

Here, noun and pronoun disagree in number: *camper* is singular, but *their* is plural.

REVISED   All *campers* should bring *their* knapsacks.

REVISED   Every *camper* should bring *his or her* knapsack. (See also 9f.)

9b. Most antecedents joined by *and* require a plural pronoun.

What if the subject of your sentence is two nouns (or a noun and a pronoun) connected by *and*? Such a *compound subject* is plural; use a plural pronoun to refer to it.

George, who has been here before, *and Susan*, who hasn't, should bring *their* knapsacks.

However, if the nouns in a *compound subject* refer to the same person or thing, they make up a singular antecedent. In that case, the pronoun too is singular.

The *owner and founder* of this camp carries *his* own knapsack everywhere.

9c. A pronoun agrees with the closest part of an antecedent joined by *or* or *nor*.

If your subject is two or more nouns (or a combination of nouns and pronouns) connected by *or* or *nor*, look closely at the subject's parts. Are they all singular? If so, your pronoun should be singular.

Neither *Joy* nor *Jean* remembered *her* knapsack last year.

If *Sam, Arthur, or Max* shows up, tell *him* I'm looking for *him*.

If the part of the subject closest to the pronoun is plural, the pronoun should be plural.

Neither *Joy* nor *her sisters* remembered *their* knapsacks last year.

If you see *Sam, Arthur, or their friends*, tell *them* I'm looking for *them*.

9d. An antecedent that is an indefinite pronoun takes a singular pronoun.

An indefinite pronoun is one that does not refer to any specific person, place, or thing: *anybody, each, either*. (For a complete list, see the pronoun chart in

1b.) Indefinite pronouns are usually singular in meaning, so a pronoun referring to one of them is also singular.

Either of the boys can do it, as long as *he's* on time.

Warn *anybody* who's still in *her* swimsuit that a uniform is required for dinner.

Sometimes the meaning of an indefinite pronoun is plural. To avoid awkwardness, avoid using such a pronoun as an antecedent.

Tell *everyone* in Cabin B that I'm looking for *him*.

This sentence works better if it is phrased differently.

Tell *all the campers* in Cabin B that I'm looking for *them*.

(See also 6f, 9f.)

9e. Most collective nouns used as antecedents require singular pronouns.

A collective noun is a singular word for a group of people or items: *army, band, committee, jury*. When the members of such a group act as a unit, use a singular pronoun to refer to them.

The *cast* for the camp play will be posted as soon as our theater counselor chooses *it*.

When the group members act individually, use a plural pronoun.

The *cast* will go *their* separate ways when summer ends.

(See also 6e.)

9f. A pronoun agrees with its antecedent in gender.

If *one of your parents* brings you to camp, invite *him* to stay for lunch.

While technically correct (the singular pronoun *he* is used to refer to the singular antecedent *one*), this sentence overlooks the fact that some parents are male, some female. To make sure the pronoun refers to both, a writer has two choices. (See 22a, 22c, 22d.)

If *one of your parents* brings you to camp, invite *him or her* to stay for lunch.

If your *parents* bring you to camp, invite *them* to stay for lunch.

EXERCISE 9–1

Making Pronouns and Antecedents Agree

If any nouns and pronouns disagree in number, person, or gender in the following sentences, substitute pronouns that agree with the nouns. If you prefer, strengthen any sentence by rewriting it. Some sentences may be correct. Possible revisions for the lettered sentences appear in the back of the book. Example:

> A cat expects people to feed them often.
>
> A *cat* expects people to feed *it* often.
>
> *Cats* expect people to feed *them* often.

a. All students are urged to complete your registration on time.
b. When a baby doesn't know their own mother, they may have been born with some kind of vision deficiency.
c. Each member of the sorority has to make his own bed.
d. If you don't like the songs the choir sings, don't join them.
e. Young people should know how to protect oneself against AIDS.

1. Many architects find work their greatest pleasure.
2. Neither Melissa nor James has received their application form yet.
3. He is the kind of man who gets their fun out of just sipping one's beer and watching his Saturday games on TV.
4. Many a mother has mourned the loss of their child.
5. When one enjoys one's work, it's easy to spend all your spare time thinking about it.

EXERCISE 9–2

Making Pronouns and Antecedents Agree

Revise the following passage so that all nouns and pronouns agree in number, person, or gender. If you prefer, strengthen any sentence by rewriting it. Some sentences may be correct. Example:

> Ken, a physics major, and Elaine, who is studying chemistry, work hard at her job.
>
> Ken, a physics major, and Elaine, who is studying chemistry, work hard at *their jobs*.

It isn't easy juggling the responsibilities of school and work. All working students know how difficult it is to keep his eyes open in class after an exhausting day at his job. Ken Tucker, a student at Boston College, and Elaine Vierra, a student at Northeastern University, agree that she doesn't know how she finds the time to balance her responsibilities. With most of their time spent at work or in class, neither Ken nor Elaine has much time to devote to their friends. Ken, a quarterback with Boston College, complains that he is often unable to join his team as they celebrate their victories after the game. Elaine adds that if any of her old friends comes to visit, she does not have much time to spend with her. Neither Ken, Elaine, nor their working friends see his student life as ideal and advise all those entering college to budget her time and finances carefully.

10.   *Adjectives and Adverbs*

An *adjective* is a word that modifies a noun or pronoun. (See 1d.) A phrase also can function as an adjective. (See 3a, 3b, 3f.) An adjective's job is to provide information about the person, place, object, or idea named by the noun or pronoun. The adjective typically answers the question Which? or What kind?

> Karen bought a *small red* car.

> The radios *on sale* are an *excellent* value.

An *adverb* is a word (or a phrase) that modifies a verb, an adjective, or another adverb. (See 1e, 3a, 3b, 3g.) An adverb typically answers the question How? or When? or Where? Sometimes it answers the question Why?

> Karen bought her car *quickly.*

> The radios arrived *yesterday;* Max put them *in the electronics department.*

> Karen needed her new car *to commute to school.*

The most common problems that writers have with adjectives and adverbs involve mixing them up: sending an adjective to do an adverb's job or vice versa. Editing for adjectives and adverbs is also covered in the "Quick Editing Guide." (For more help, see A5.)

10a.   Use an adverb, not an adjective, to modify a verb, adjective, or another adverb.

> FAULTY   Karen bought her car *quick.*

> FAULTY   It's *awful* hot today.

Although an informal speaker might be able to get away with these sentences, a writer cannot. *Quick* and *awful* are adjectives, so they can modify only nouns or pronouns. To modify the verb *bought* we need the adverb *quickly;* to modify the adjective *hot* we need the adverb *awfully.*

Adjectives and Adverbs at a Glance

ADJECTIVES
1. Typically answer the question Which? or What kind?
2. Modify nouns or pronouns

ADVERBS
3. Answer the question How? When? Where? or sometimes Why?
4. Modify verbs, adjectives, and other adverbs

REVISED   Karen bought her car *quickly*.

REVISED   It's *awfully* hot today.

10b. **Use an adjective, not an adverb, as a subject complement or object complement.**

If we write, "Her old car looked awful," *awful* is a *subject complement*: it follows a linking verb and modifies the subject, *car*. (See 2d, 5a.)

FAULTY   Her old car looked *awfully*.

REVISED   Her old car looked *awful*.

An *object complement* is a word that renames a direct object or completes the sentence's description of it. (See 2d.) Object complements can be adjectives or nouns, but never adverbs.

Early to bed and early to rise makes a man *healthy, wealthy,* and *wise*. [Adjectives modifying the direct object *man*]

When you are not sure whether you're dealing with an object complement or an adverb, look closely at the word's role in the sentence. If it modifies a noun, it is an object complement and therefore should be an adjective.

The coach called the referee *stupid* and *blind*. [*Stupid* and *blind* are adjectives modifying the direct object *referee*.]

If it modifies a verb, you want an adverb instead.

In fact, though, the ref had called the play *correctly*. [*Correctly* is an adverb modifying the verb *called*.]

10c. **Use *good* as an adjective and *well* as an adverb.**

A common adjective-adverb mix-up occurs when writers confuse *good* and *well* as subject complements. *Good* is almost always an adjective; *well* is almost always an adverb.

This sandwich tastes *good*. [The adjective *good* is a subject complement following the linking verb *tastes* and modifying the noun *sandwich*.]

Heloise's skin healed *well* after surgery. [The adverb *well* modifies the verb *healed*.]

Only if the verb is a linking verb (see 5a) can you safely follow it with *good*. Other kinds of verbs do not take subject complements. Instead, they need adverbs to modify them.

FAULTY   That painting came out *good*.

REVISED   That painting came out *well*.

Complications arise when we write or speak about health. It is perfectly correct to say *I feel good,* using the adjective *good* as a subject complement after the linking verb *feel.* However, generations of confusion have nudged the adverb *well* into the adjective category, too. A nurse may speak of "a well baby"; and greeting cards urge patients to "get well" — meaning, "become healthy." Just as *healthy* is an adjective here, so is *well.*

What, then, is the best answer when someone asks, "How do you feel?" If you want to duck the issue, reply, "Fine!" Otherwise, in speech either *good* or *well* is acceptable; in writing, use *good.*

ESL GUIDELINES

The Definite Article *(the)*

- Use the definite article, *the,* with a specific count or noncount noun when both the writer and the reader know the identity of what is referred to or when the noun has been mentioned before. (See p. H-60 for examples of count and noncount nouns.)

   Did you feed *the* baby? [Both the reader and the writer know which baby is referred to.]

   The coffee tastes strong today. [Both the reader and the writer know which coffee is referred to.]

   She got a huge box in the mail. *The* box contained oranges from Florida. [*The* is used the second time the noun (*box*) is mentioned.]

- Use the definite article, *the,* before specific count or noncount nouns when the reader is given enough information to identify what is being referred to.

   The furniture in my apartment is old and faded. [Specific furniture]

   The young woman wearing blue is my sister. [Specific young woman]

- Use the definite article, *the,* before a singular count noun to make a generality.

   The dog has been humans' favorite pet for centuries. [*The dog* here refers to all dogs.]

- Use the definite article before some geographical names.

   Collectives: the United States, the United Kingdom

   Groups of Islands: the Bahamas, the Canary Islands

   Large Bodies of Water (except lakes): the Atlantic Ocean, the Dead Sea, the Monongahela River, the Gulf of Mexico

   Mountain Ranges: the Rockies, the Himalaya Mountains

10d. Form comparatives and superlatives of most adjectives with *-er* and *-est* and of most adverbs with *more* and *most*.

Comparatives and superlatives are special adjective and adverb forms that allow us to describe one thing in relation to another. You can put most adjectives into their comparative form by adding *-er* and into their superlative form by adding *-est*.

The budget deficit is *larger* than the trade deficit.

This year's trade deficit is the *largest* ever.

We usually form the comparative and superlative of long adjectives with *more* and *most* rather than with *-er* and *-est*, to keep them from becoming cumbersome.

Our national debt is *enormous*.

It may become *more enormous* over the next few years.

For short adverbs that do not end in *-ly*, usually add *-er* and *-est* in the comparative and superlative forms. With all other adverbs, use *more* and *most*. (Also see 10f.)

ESL GUIDELINES

The Indefinite Article *(a, an)*

- Use the indefinite article, *a* or *an*, with a nonspecific, singular count noun when it is not known to the reader or to either the reader or the writer. (See p. H-60 for examples of count nouns.)

  My brother has *an* antique car. [The car's identity is unknown to the reader.]

  I saw *a* dog in my back yard this morning. [The dog's identity is unknown to the writer.]

- Use the indefinite article (*a, an*) when the noun is mentioned for the first time. Use the definite article (*the*) when the noun is mentioned again.

  I saw *a* car that I would love to buy. *The* car was red and had a leather interior.

- Use *some* or no article instead of *a* or *an* with noncount nouns or plural nouns used in a general sense. (See p. H-60 for examples of noncount nouns.)

  INCORRECT I am going to buy *a* furniture for my apartment.

  CORRECT I am going to buy *some* furniture for my apartment.

  CORRECT I am going to buy furniture for my apartment.

Spending *faster* than one earns will plunge a person into debt *sooner* than any other way I know.

The *more indiscriminately* we import foreign goods, the *more rapidly* the trade deficit grows.

It grows *fastest* and *most uncontrollably* when exports are down and imports remain high.

For negative comparisons, use *less* and *least* for both adjectives and adverbs.

Michael's speech was *less interesting* than Louie's.

Paulette spoke *less interestingly* than Michael.

Bud's speech was the *least interesting* of all.

The comparative and superlative forms of irregular adjectives and adverbs (such as *bad* and *badly*) are also irregular and should be used with special care.

Tom's golf is *bad*, but no *worse* than George's.

Tom plays golf *badly*, but no *worse* than George does.

10e. Omit *more* and *most* with an adjective or adverb that is already comparative or superlative.

Some words become comparative or superlative when we tack on *-er* or *-est*. Others, such as *top*, *favorite*, and *unique*, mark whatever they modify as one of a kind by definition. Neither category requires further assistance to make its point. To say "a *more worse* fate" or "my *most favorite* movie" is redundant: "a *worse* fate" or "my *favorite* movie" does the job.

FAULTY   Lisa is *more uniquely* qualified for the job than any other candidate that submitted a résumé.

REVISED   Lisa is *better* qualified for the job than any other candidate that submitted a résumé.

REVISED   Lisa is *uniquely* qualified for the job.

10f. Use the comparative form of an adjective or adverb to compare two people or things, the superlative form to compare more than two.

No matter how fantastic, wonderful, and terrific something is, we can call it the *best* only when we compare it with more than one other thing. Any comparison between two things uses the comparative form (*better*), not the superlative (*best*).

FAULTY   Their chocolate and vanilla are both good, but I like the chocolate *best.*

REVISED   Their chocolate and vanilla are both good, but I like the chocolate *better.*

FAULTY   Of his two dogs, he treats Bonzo *most affectionately.*

REVISED   Of his two dogs, he treats Bonzo *more affectionately.*

ESL GUIDELINES

Cumulative Adjectives

Cumulative adjectives are two or more adjectives used directly before a noun and not separated by commas or the word *and* (see 25d). They usually have a specific order of placement before a noun. Use the following chart as a guideline for writing sentences with adjectives, but keep in mind that the order can be varied.

1. Articles or determiners
   a, an, the, some, this, these, his, my, two, several

2. Evaluative adjectives
   beautiful, wonderful, hardworking, distasteful

3. Size or dimension
   big, small, huge, obese, petite, six-foot

4. Length or shape
   long, short, round, square, oblong, oval

5. Age
   old, young, new, fresh, ancient

6. Color
   red, pink, aquamarine, orange

7. Nation or place of origin
   American, Japanese, European, Bostonian, Floridian

8. Religion
   Protestant, Muslim, Hindu, Buddhist, Catholic

9. Matter or substance
   wood, gold, cotton, plastic, pine, metal

10. Noun used as an adjective
    telephone (as in *telephone operator*), *computer* (as in *computer software*)

Cumulative adjectives do not require commas when used in a series.

She is an *attractive older French* woman.

His *expressive large brown* eyes moved me.

Using Adjectives and Adverbs Correctly

Find and correct any improperly used adjectives and adverbs in the following sentences. Some sentences may be correct. Answers for the lettered sentences appear in the back of the book. Example:

> The deal worked out good for both of us.

> The deal worked out *well* for both of us.

a. The sun shone bright the whole afternoon.
b. Ted finished the race more strongly than he started it.
c. Jennifer eats good when she visits her grandmother.
d. The boy who delivers our newspaper is more reliably than we thought.
e. The cost of health care increased significant in the early 1990s.

1. The builder finished the house quicker than expected.
2. It was a real difficult test, and none of the students did very well.
3. The candidate who was overwhelming elected has fairly moderate views.
4. The owners stood proud in front of their new home, as if they were having their picture taken.
5. The boat rose and fell rapidly, and the crew held on tightly to the railings.

11. *Shifts*

When you look at a scene, you view it from a particular position in time and space. If you go to your favorite spot at the beach at dawn, at noon, at twilight, and at midnight, the scene will appear different each time. If you look at the scene standing on a sand dune, lying flat on the sand, or swimming in the surf, it will appear different from each location. Your perspective or point of view determines the details of the scene.

Similarly, when you perceive a subject in a sentence, you may consider it from various positions. If the time or the actor changes, your writing should reflect the change. However, writers sometimes shift point of view unconsciously or unnecessarily, causing ambiguity and confusion for readers. Such shifts are evident in grammatical inconsistencies.

11a. Maintain consistency in verb tense.

When you write a paragraph or an essay, keep the verbs in the same tense unless the time changes.

INCONSISTENT	Football *is* a favorite spectator sport in my hometown. When the quarterback *threw* for a touchdown, everyone in the bleachers *stood* up and *cheered*.
CONSISTENT	Football *is* a favorite spectator sport in my hometown. When the quarterback *throws* for a touchdown, everyone in the bleachers *stands* up and *cheers*. [All verbs are present tense.]

INCONSISTENT	The driver *yelled* at us to get off the bus, so I *ask* him why and he *tells* me it *is* none of my business.
CONSISTENT	The driver *yells* at us to get off the bus, so I *ask* him why and he *tells* me it *is* none of my business. [All verbs are present tense.]
CONSISTENT	The driver *yelled* at us to get off the bus, so I *asked* him why and he *told* me it *was* none of my business. [All verbs are past tense.]

ESL GUIDELINES

Negatives

You can make a sentence negative by using either *not* or another negative adverb.

- With *not*: subject + helping verb + *not* + main verb

  Regina has *not* driven across the country before.

  Jerry did *not* go to the concert.

  They will *not* call again.

- For questions: helping verb + *n't* (contraction for *not*) + subject + main verb

  Hasn't Regina driven across the country before?

  Didn't Jerry go to the concert?

  Won't [for *Will not*] they call again?

Negative adverbs besides *not* include **seldom, rarely, never, hardly, hardly ever,** and **almost never.**

- With a negative adverb: subject + negative adverb + main verb; *or* subject + helping verb + negative adverb + main verb

  My son *seldom* watches TV.

  John may *never* see them again.

  Maxine is *rarely* in a bad mood.

- With a negative adverb at the beginning of a clause: negative adverb + helping verb + subject + verb

  Not only does Emma play tennis well, but she also excels in golf.

  Never before have I been so happy.

  Seldom have I experienced the satisfaction I felt when we finished the design project.

11b. If the time changes, change the verb tense.

Tense indicates time. Shifts in tense should indicate an actual change in time. If you are writing about something that occurred in the past, use past tense verbs. If you are writing about something that occurs in the present, use present tense verbs. If the time shifts, change the verb tense.

> I *do* not *like* the new television programs this year. The situation comedies *are* too realistic to be amusing, the adventure shows *don't have* much action, and the courtroom dramas *drag* on and on. Last year the television programs *were* different. The sitcoms *were* hilarious, the adventure shows *were* action-packed, and the courtroom dramas *were* fast-paced. I *prefer* reruns of last year's programs to new episodes of this year's choices.

The time and the verb tense change appropriately from present (*do like, are, do have, drag*) to past (*were, were, were, were*) back to present (*prefer*), indicating contrast between this year's *present* programming and last year's *past* programming and ending with *present* opinion.

NOTE: When writing papers about literature, the accepted practice is to use present tense verbs to summarize what happens in a story, poem, or play. When discussing other aspects of a work, use present tense for present time, past tense for past, and future tense for future.

> John Steinbeck *wrote* "The Chrysanthemums" in 1937. [Past tense for past time]

> In "The Chrysanthemums," John Steinbeck *describes* the Salinas Valley as "a closed pot" cut off from the world by fog. [Present tense]

11c. Maintain consistency in the voice of verbs.

In most writing, active voice is preferable to passive voice (see 5m). Shifting unnecessarily from active to passive voice causes confusion for readers.

> INCONSISTENT   My roommates and I *sit* up late many nights talking about our problems. Grades, teachers, jobs, money, and dates *are discussed* at length.

> CONSISTENT   My roommates and I *sit* up late many nights talking about our problems. We *discuss* grades, teachers, jobs, money, and dates at length.

11d. Maintain consistency in person.

Person indicates the perspective from which an essay is written. First person (*I, we*) establishes a personal, informal relationship with readers. Second person (*you*) is also informal and personal, bringing the readers into the writing. Third person (*he, she, it, they*) is more formal and objective than the other two persons. (See 7.) In a formal scientific report, first person and second person are seldom appropriate. In a personal essay, using *he, she,* or *one* to refer to yourself sounds stilted. Choose the person appropriate for your purpose and stick to it.

INCONSISTENT	In *my* composition class is a divorced woman returning to school after fifteen years of raising her children. Watching her, *you* can tell she is uncertain about her decision to enter college.
CONSISTENT	In *my* composition class is a divorced woman returning to school after fifteen years of raising her children. Watching her, *I* can tell she is uncertain about her decision to enter college.
INCONSISTENT	Today college *students* need transportation, but *you* need a job to pay for the insurance and the gasoline.
CONSISTENT	Today college *students* need transportation, but *they* need jobs to pay for the insurance and the gasoline.
INCONSISTENT	*Anyone* can go skydiving if *you* have the guts.
CONSISTENT	*Anyone* can go skydiving if *he or she* has the guts.

11e. Maintain consistency in the mood of verbs.

Closely related to shift in person is shift in the mood of the verb, usually from the indicative to the imperative. (See 5n–5p.)

INCONSISTENT	Counselors *advised* the students to register early to choose the best professors. Also *pay* tuition on time to avoid being dropped from classes. [Shift from indicative to imperative]
CONSISTENT	Counselors *advised* the students to register early to choose the best professors. They also *advised* them to pay their tuition on time to avoid being dropped from classes. [Both verbs in indicative]

11f. Maintain consistency in level of language.

Attempting to impress readers, writers sometimes inappropriately use inflated language or slip into slang or a too informal tone. The level of language should be appropriate to your purpose and your audience throughout an essay.

If you are writing a personal essay, use informal language.

INCONSISTENT	I felt like a typical tourist. I carried an expensive camera with lots of gadgets I didn't quite know how to operate, and I had brought as much film as I could carry. But I was in a quandary because there was such a plethora of picturesque tableaus to record for posterity.

The sudden shift to formal language is inappropriate. The writer could end the passage simply: *But there was so much beautiful scenery all around that I just couldn't decide where to start.*

If you are writing an academic essay, use formal language.

INCONSISTENT   Puccini's final work *Turandot* is set in a China of legends, riddles, and fantasy. Brimming with beautiful melodies masterfully orchestrated — including the famed tenor aria "Nessun dorma" — this opera is music drama at its most spectacular. Man, I dig this gig!

The shift from formal language to slang is unnecessary. The last sentence can be cut without weakening the rest of the paragraph.

EXERCISE 11–1

Maintaining Grammatical Consistency

Revise the following sentences to eliminate shifts in verb tense, voice, mood, person, and level of language. Possible revisions for the lettered sentences appear in the back of the book. Example:

> I needed the job at the restaurant, so I tried to tolerate the insults of my boss, but a person can take only so much.

> I needed the job at the restaurant, so I tried to tolerate the insults of my boss, but *I could* take only so much.

a. Sometimes late at night, I hear stereos booming from passing cars. The vibrations are so great you can feel your house shake.
b. Dr. Jamison is an erudite professor who cracks jokes in class.
c. The audience listened intently to the lecture, but the message was not understood.
d. It was in the Near East that people first began to grow crops and city-states were established.
e. Most of the people in my psychology class are very interesting, and you can get into some exciting discussions with them.

1. Scientists can no longer evade the social, political, and ethical consequences of what they did in the laboratory.
2. To have good government, citizens must become informed on the issues. Also, be sure to vote.
3. Good writing is essential to success in many professions, especially in business, where ideas must be communicated in down-to-earth lingo.
4. Our legal system made it extremely difficult to prove a bribe. If the charges are not proven to the satisfaction of a jury or a judge, then we jump to the conclusion that the absence of a conviction demonstrates the innocence of the subject.
5. Before Morris K. Udall, Democrat from Arizona, resigns his seat in the U.S. House of Representatives, he helped preserve hundreds of acres of wilderness.
6. When Washington, D.C., was redesigned in the early twentieth century, many critics objected that the Mall would separate the government center from the residential city, and time has proved them dead right.
7. Anyone can learn another language if you have the time and the patience.

8. The immigration officer asked how long we planned to stay, so I show him my letter of acceptance from Tulane.

9. Many people do not like the accelerating pace of modern life. In the last century, people have time to relax with their friends and families instead of rushing back and forth to work.

10. Archaeologists spent many months studying the site of the African city of Zimbabwe and many artifacts were uncovered.

12. *Sentence Fragments*

A **complete sentence** is one that has both a subject and a predicate and can stand alone. (See 2a, 2b.) A **fragment** lacks a subject or a predicate or both or for some other reason fails to express a complete thought. We all use fragments in everyday speech, where their context and the way they are said make them understandable and therefore acceptable.

That bicycle over there.

Good job.

Not if I can help it.

In writing, fragments like these fail to communicate complete, coherent ideas. Notice how much more effective they are when we turn them into complete sentences.

I'd like to buy that bicycle over there.

You did a good job sanding the floor.

Nobody will steal my seat if I can help it.

Some writers purposefully use fragments. For example, advertisers are fond of them because short, emphatic fragments command attention, like a series of quick jabs to the head.

Seafood special. Every Tuesday night. All you can eat. Specially priced at $6.95. For seafood lovers.

Professional writers use fragments, too, especially in journals, descriptions, and fiction — often to good effect, as in this passage from the beginning of Vladimir Nabokov's novel *Lolita*:

Lolita, light of my life, fire of my loins. My sin, my soul. Lo-lee-ta: the tip of the tongue taking a trip of three steps down the palate to tap, at three, on the teeth. Lo. Lee. Ta.

In your college writing, though, it is good practice to express your ideas in complete sentences. Writing a paper or a report is a more formal, less experimental activity than writing fiction. Besides, complete sentences usually convey more information than fragments — a big advantage in expository writing. Sprinkling fragments through your work, unless you do so with great skill and style, tends to make readers wonder whether you completely thought through your ideas.

If you sometimes write fragments without recognizing them, learn to edit your work. Luckily, fragments are fairly easy to correct. Often you can attach a fragment to a neighboring sentence with a comma, a dash, or a colon. Sometimes you can combine two thoughts without adding any punctuation at all.

Editing for sentence fragments is also covered in the "Quick Editing Guide." (For more help, see A6.)

12a. If a fragment is a phrase, link it to an adjoining sentence or make it a complete sentence.

A freestanding phrase is a fragment because it lacks a subject or a verb or both. You have two choices for revising a fragment if it is a phrase: (1) link it to an adjoining sentence using punctuation such as a comma or a colon or (2) add a subject or a verb to the phrase to make it a complete sentence.

FRAGMENT   Malcolm has two goals in life. *Wealth and power.*

FRAGMENT   Schmidt ended his stories as he mixed his martinis. *With a twist.*

FRAGMENT   *To stamp out the union.* That was the bosses' plan.

FRAGMENT   The students taking the final exam in the auditorium.

Wealth and power is a phrase rather than a sentence because it has no verb. *With a twist* has neither a subject nor a verb. *To stamp out the union* has a verbal, which cannot be used as the main verb of a sentence, and it has no subject. *Taking* is not a complete verb: it is a participle and requires a helping verb to make it complete. You can make each of these phrases express a complete thought by linking it with a neighboring sentence or by adding the missing element. In each case there are several ways to complete the thought. Here is one set of possibilities:

REVISED   Malcolm has two goals in life: wealth and power. [A colon links *wealth and power* to *goals.*]

REVISED   Schmidt ended his stories as he mixed his martinis, with a twist. [The prepositional phrase *with a twist* is connected to the main clause with a comma.]

REVISED   To stamp out the union was the bosses' plan. [The infinitive phrase *To stamp out the union* becomes the subject of the sentence.]

REVISED   The students were taking the final exam in the auditorium. [The helping verb *were* completes the verb and thus makes a sentence.]

REVISED   The students taking the final exam in the auditorium were interrupted by the fire alarm. [The predicate *were interrupted by the fire alarm* completes the sentence.]

12b. If a fragment is a subordinate clause, link it to an adjoining sentence or eliminate the subordinating conjunction.

Some fragments are missing neither subject nor verb. Instead, they are subordinate clauses, unable to express complete thoughts unless linked with main clauses. (See 3e–3g, 4c.) As you examine your writing for sentence fragments, be on the lookout for *subordinating conjunctions*. (Some of the most common subordinating conjunctions are *although, because, if, since, unless, until,* and *while*; for a complete list, see 1g.) When you find a subordinating conjunction at the start or in the middle of a word group that looks like a sentence, that word group may be a subordinate clause and not a sentence at all.

FRAGMENT   The new law will stem the tide of inflation. *If it passes.*

FRAGMENT   Wealth doesn't guarantee happiness. *Whereas poverty does guarantee unhappiness.*

FRAGMENT   George loves winter in the mountains. *Because he is an avid skier.*

If you find that you have treated a subordinate clause as if it were a complete sentence, you can correct the problem in one of two ways: (1) you can combine the fragment with a main clause nearby or (2) you can make the subordinate clause into a complete sentence by dropping the subordinating conjunction.

REVISED   The new law will stem the tide of inflation, if it passes.

REVISED   Wealth doesn't guarantee happiness, whereas poverty does guarantee unhappiness.

REVISED   George loves winter in the mountains. He is an avid skier.

A sentence is not necessarily a fragment just because it opens with a subordinating conjunction. Some perfectly legitimate complex or compound-complex sentences have their conjunctions up front instead of in the middle. (See 4c, 4d.)

If you leave early, say good-bye.

Because of rain, the game was canceled.

12c. If a fragment has a participle but no other verb, change the participle to a main verb or link the fragment to an adjoining sentence.

A participle (the *-ing* form of the verb, such as *being, writing, looking*) can serve as the main verb in a sentence only when it is accompanied by a form of *be* ("Jeffrey *is working* harder than usual"). When a writer mistakenly uses a participle alone as a main verb, the result is a fragment.

FRAGMENT   *Sally being the first athlete on the team to compete in a national contest.* She received many congratulatory telegrams.

FRAGMENT Jon was used to the pressure of deadlines. *Having worked the night shift at the daily newspaper.*

One solution is to combine the fragment with an adjoining sentence.

REVISED Being the first athlete on the team to compete in a national contest, Sally received many congratulatory telegrams.

REVISED Jon was used to the pressure of deadlines, having worked the night shift at the daily newspaper.

Another solution is to turn the fragment into a complete sentence by choosing a form of the verb other than the participle.

REVISED Sally *was* the first athlete on the team to compete in a national contest. She received many congratulatory telegrams.

REVISED Jon was used to the pressure of deadlines. He *had worked* the night shift at the daily newspaper.

12d. If a fragment is part of a compound predicate, link it with the complete sentence containing the rest of the predicate.

FRAGMENT In spite of a pulled muscle, Jeremy ran the race. *And won.*

A fragment such as *And won* sounds satisfyingly punchy. Still, it cannot stand on its own. *Ran…and won* is a compound predicate — two verbs with the same subject. You can create a complete sentence by linking the verbs.

REVISED In spite of a pulled muscle, Jeremy *ran* the race *and won.*

If you want to keep more emphasis on the second verb, you can turn the fragment into a full clause by adding punctuation and another subject.

REVISED In spite of a pulled muscle, Jeremy ran the race — and *he* won.

(For a review of the rules about punctuating linked phrases and clauses, see 18a.)

EXERCISE 12–1

Eliminating Fragments

Find and eliminate any fragments in the following examples. Some sentences may be correct. Possible revisions for the lettered sentences appear in the back of the book. Example:

Bryan hates parsnips. And loathes squash.

Bryan hates parsnips *and* loathes squash.

a. Polly and Jim plan to see the new Woody Allen movie. Which was reviewed in last Sunday's *New York Times.*

b. For democracy to function at all, two elements are crucial. An educated populace and a firm collective belief in people's ability to chart their own course.

c. Scholastic achievement is important to Alex. Being the first person in his family ever to attend college.

d. Does our society rob children of their childhood? By making them aware too soon of adult ills?

e. No one would ever forget that night. The half-empty lifeboats. The useless flares. The band playing hymns as the ship slid under.

1. If the German people had known Hitler's real plans. Would they have made him führer?

2. Lisa advocated sleeping no more than four hours a night. Until she started nodding through her classes.

3. You must take his stories as others do. With a pinch of salt.

4. Jack seemed well qualified for a career in the air force. Except for his tendency to get airsick.

5. Illness often accompanies stress. Catching a cold after the death of a loved one, for example.

6. None of the board members objected to Butch's proposal at the time. Only afterward, when they realized its implications.

7. Michael had a beautiful southern accent. Having lived many years in Georgia.

8. Richard III supposedly had the young princes murdered. No one has ever found out what really happened to them.

9. They met. They talked. They fought. They reached agreement.

10. Pat and Chris are determined to marry each other. Even if their families do not approve.

EXERCISE 12–2

Eliminating Fragments

Rewrite the following paragraph, eliminating all fragments. Explain why you made each change. Example:

> Little league baseball damaged my self-esteem. And turned me off to organized sports forever.

> Little league baseball damaged my self-esteem, *and* turned me off to organized sports forever.

When I was about eleven years old. I played on a Little League baseball team. Played, that is, when I wasn't sitting on the bench. Which was most of the time. I got into the lineup only because the rules said every kid had to get a chance at bat. A rule my coach didn't like. Because he wanted our team to win every game. I rarely got to play in the field. Only when a shortage of players made my presence there necessary. Then always right field. Unless there were a lot of lefties coming up to bat on the opposing team. Believe me when I say that for me Little League baseball was no fun.

13. *Comma Splices and Fused Sentences*

Splice two ropes, or two strips of movie film, and you join them into one. Splice two main clauses by putting only a comma between them, however, and you get an ungainly construction called a *comma splice.* (See p. H-31 on main clauses.) Here, for instance, are two perfectly good main clauses, each separate, each able to stand on its own as a sentence:

> The detective wriggled on his belly toward the campfire. The drunken smugglers didn't notice him.

Now let's splice those sentences with a comma.

> COMMA SPLICE   The detective wriggled on his belly toward the campfire, the drunken smugglers didn't notice him.

The resulting comma splice makes for difficult reading.

Even more confusing than a comma splice is a *fused* (or *run-on*) *sentence:* two main clauses joined without any punctuation.

> FUSED SENTENCE   The detective wriggled on his belly toward the campfire the drunken smugglers didn't notice him.

Lacking clues from the writer, a reader cannot tell where to pause. To understand the sentence, he or she must halt and reread.

Even writers who know better can fall at times into fusing and comma splicing. Temptation may overwhelm them when, having written one sentence, they want to add some further thought. Either they simply jam the two thoughts together, or they push in a comma, like a thumbtack, to stick on the second thought.

Here are five simple ways to eliminate both comma splices and fused sentences. Your choice depends on the length and complexity of your main clauses and the effect you want to achieve.

Editing for comma splices and fused sentences is also covered in the "Quick Editing Guide." (For more help, see A7.)

13a. Write separate complete sentences to correct a comma splice or a fused sentence.

> COMMA SPLICE   Sigmund Freud has been called an enemy of sexual repression, the truth is that he is not a friend of free love.
>
> FUSED SENTENCE   Sigmund Freud has been called an enemy of sexual repression the truth is that he is not a friend of free love.

Neither sentence yields its meaning without a struggle. To point readers in the right direction, separate the clauses.

> REVISED   Sigmund Freud has been called an enemy of sexual repression. The truth is that he is not a friend of free love.

13b. Use a comma and a coordinating conjunction to correct a comma splice or a fused sentence.

Is it always incorrect to join two main clauses with a comma? No. If both clauses are of roughly equal weight, you can use a comma to link them — as long as you add a coordinating conjunction (*and, but, for, nor, or, so, yet*) after the comma.

COMMA SPLICE   Hurricane winds hit ninety miles an hour, they tore the roof from every house on Paradise Drive.

REVISED   Hurricane winds hit ninety miles an hour, *and* they tore the roof from every house on Paradise Drive.

13c. Use a semicolon or a colon to correct a comma splice or a fused sentence.

A semicolon can keep two thoughts connected while giving full emphasis to each one.

COMMA SPLICE   Hurricane winds hit ninety miles an hour, they tore the roof from every house on Paradise Drive.

REVISED   Hurricane winds hit ninety miles an hour; they tore the roof from every house on Paradise Drive.

If the second thought clearly illustrates or explains the first, add it on with a colon.

REVISED   The hurricane caused extensive damage: it tore the roof from every house on Paradise Drive.

Remember that the only punctuation powerful enough to link two main clauses single-handedly is a semicolon, a colon, or a period. A lone comma won't do the job.

13d. Use subordination to correct a comma splice or a fused sentence.

If one main clause is more important than the other, or if you want to give it more importance, you can subordinate the less important clause to it. Using subordination helps your reader more than simply dividing a fused sentence or comma splice into two sentences does. When you make one clause subordinate, you throw weight on the main clause. In effect, you show your reader how one idea relates to another: you decide which matters more.

FUSED SENTENCE   Hurricane winds hit ninety miles an hour they tore the roof from every house on Paradise Drive.

REVISED   *When hurricane winds hit ninety miles an hour,* they tore the roof from every house on Paradise Drive.

REVISED   Hurricane winds hit ninety miles an hour, *tearing the roof from every house on Paradise Drive.*

For a rundown of different ways to use subordination, see 3e to 3g and 18d to 18f.

13e.   Use a conjunctive adverb with a semicolon and a comma to correct a comma splice or a fused sentence.

A writer who is sharp enough to beware of fused sentences and comma splices but who still wants to cram more than one clause into a sentence may join two clauses with a *conjunctive adverb.* Some common conjunctive adverbs are *also, besides, consequently, even so, finally, furthermore, however, indeed, moreover, nevertheless,* and *therefore.* (See 1g.) These transitional words and phrases can be a useful way of linking clauses — but only if used with the right punctuation.

COMMA SPLICE   Sigmund Freud has been called an enemy of sexual repression, however the truth is that he is not a friend of free love.

The writer might consider a comma plus the conjunctive adverb *however* enough to combine the two main clauses; but that glue won't hold. Stronger binding is called for.

REVISED   Sigmund Freud has been called an enemy of sexual repression; however, the truth is that he is not a friend of free love.

A writer who fuses and comma splices sentences is like a man trying to join two boards. If he comma splices, he tries to put them together with only one nail; if he fuses, he puts them together with no nail at all. But most thoughts, to hang together, need plenty of hammering.

EXCEPTION: Certain very short, similar main clauses can be joined with a comma. Only if you now feel sure that you can tell a comma splice or a fused sentence when you see one, read on: here comes a fine point. We hate to admit it, lest it complicate life, but once in a great while you'll see a competent writer joining main clauses with nothing but a comma between them.

Jill runs by day, Tom walks by night.

I came, I saw, I conquered.

Commas are not obligatory with short, similar clauses. If you find this issue confusing, you can stick with semicolons to join all main clauses, short or long.

Jill runs by day; Tom walks by night.

I came; I saw; I conquered.

EXERCISE 13–1

Revising Comma Splices and Fused Sentences

In the following examples, correct each comma splice or fused sentence in two ways and decide which way you believe works best. Be creative: don't correct every one in the same way. Some sentences may be correct as written. Possible revisions for the lettered sentences appear in the back of the book. Example:

> The castle looked eerie from a distance, it filled us with nameless fear as we approached.

> The castle looked eerie from a *distance*; it filled us with nameless fear as we approached.

> *Or*

> The castle, *which looked eerie from a distance,* filled us with nameless fear as we approached.

a. Everyone had heard alarming rumors in the village about strange goings-on, we hesitated to believe them.
b. Bats flew about our ears as the carriage pulled up under a stone archway an assistant stood waiting to lead us to our host.
c. We followed the scientist down a flight of wet stone steps at last he stopped before a huge oak door.
d. From a jangling keyring Dr. Frankenstein selected a heavy key, he twisted it in the lock.
e. The huge door gave a groan it swung open on a dimly lighted laboratory.

1. Our guide turned, with a lopsided smile, silently he motioned us into the room.
2. Before us on a dissecting table lay a form with closed eyes to behold it sent a quick chill down my spine.
3. With glittering eyes the scientist strode to the table, he lifted a white-gloved hand.
4. The form lying before us seemed an obscenely large baby in disbelief I had to rub my eyes.
5. It resembled no human child instead it seemed constructed of rubber or clay.
6. With a hoarse cry Frankenstein flung a power switch, blue streamers of static electricity crackled about the table, the creature gave a grunt and opened smoldering eyes.
7. "I've won!" exclaimed the scientist in triumph he circled the room doing a demented Irish reel.
8. The creature's right hand strained, the heavy steel manacle imprisoning his wrist groaned in torment.
9. Like a staple wrenched from a document, the manacle yielded.
10. The creature sat upright and tugged at the shackles binding his ankles, Frankenstein uttered a piercing scream.

Revising Comma Splices and Fused Sentences

Revise the following passage, using subordination, a conjunctive adverb, a semicolon, or a colon to correct each comma splice or fused sentence. You may also write separate complete sentences. Some sentences may be correct. Example:

> Ancient Rome is an ambiguous political symbol, it has come to represent freedom and slavery, dictatorship and democracy, law and cruelty.

> Ancient Rome is an ambiguous political symbol: it has come to represent freedom and slavery, dictatorship and democracy, law and cruelty.

The classical world of Greece and Rome is the foundation of Western art and thought, it has also provided the modern world with much of its political imagery. In the eighteenth century, French revolutionaries believed they were restoring the democracies of ancient Athens and of republican Rome, they modeled themselves on those ancient Roman heroes who had resisted the authority of kings. In the United States, Jefferson and the nation's founders established a new system of government that revived the terminology and symbols of ancient Rome, the United States was to be represented by a Roman eagle, and a *Senate* was to meet in a *Capitol,* a word derived from the early meeting place of the ancient Roman Senate on the Capitoline hill. Both the American and the French revolutionaries saw the Roman republic as the model for their new democratic states, however, in the early nineteenth century, a dictator like Napoleon was more interested in the imperial phase of Roman power. Napoleon advertised himself as the new Caesar, he believed he was destined to restore Roman peace and unity to Europe. Although Napoleon failed in his bid to revive the Roman empire, the myth of a powerful centralized state endured, it influenced the political imagery and ideology of the totalitarian governments of the twentieth century. The use of Roman political symbols by governments from all shades of the ideological spectrum is significant in itself, it indicates the powerful grip that Rome still exerts on the Western imagination.

Revising Comma Splices and Fused Sentences

Write six fused sentences and comma splices. Then trade papers with a classmate, and revise each other's deliberate errors. You may want to revise each sentence in several ways and then confer with your partner to decide which revision works best.

Chapter 33

Effective Sentences

14. *Misplaced and Dangling Modifiers*

The purpose of a modifier is to give readers additional information. To do so, the modifier must be linked clearly to whatever it is meant to modify. If you wrote, "We saw a stone wall around a house on a grassy hill, beautiful and distant," your readers would be hard put to figure out whether *beautiful* and *distant* modify *wall, house,* or *hill.* When you finish writing, double-check your modifiers — especially prepositional phrases and subordinate clauses — to make sure each one is in the right place. Editing for misplaced or dangling modifiers is also covered in the "Quick Editing Guide." (For more help, see B1.)

14a. Keep modifiers close to what they modify.

Misplaced modifiers — phrases and clauses that wander away from what they modify — produce results that are more likely to amuse your readers than inform them. To avoid confusion, place your modifiers as close as possible to whatever they modify.

MISPLACED   She offered handcrafted toys to all the orphans in colorful packages. [Does the phrase *in colorful packages* modify *toys* or *orphans*?]

CLEAR   She offered handcrafted toys in colorful packages to all the orphans.

MISPLACED   Today's assignment is to remove the dishes from the crates that got chipped. [Does the clause *that got chipped* modify *dishes* or *crates*?]

CLEAR   Today's assignment is to remove from the crates the dishes that got chipped.

Sometimes when you move a misplaced modifier to a better place, an additional change or two will help you to clarify the sentence.

MISPLACED   Jim offered cream and sugar to his guests in their coffee.

CLEAR   Jim offered his guests cream and sugar in their coffee. [When *guests* is made an indirect object, *to* is cut.]

14b.   Place each modifier so that it clearly modifies only one thing.

A *squinting modifier* is one that looks two ways, leaving the reader uncertain whether it modifies the word before it or the word after it. Don't let your modifiers squint. Make sure each modifies only one element in a sentence. A good tactic is to place your modifier close to the word or phrase it modifies and away from any others that might cause confusion.

SQUINTING   The best-seller that appealed to Mary *tremendously* bored Max.

CLEAR   The best-seller that *tremendously* appealed to Mary bored Max.

CLEAR   The best-seller that appealed to Mary bored Max *tremendously*.

EXERCISE 14–1

Placing Modifiers

Revise the following sentences, which contain modifiers that are misplaced or squinting. Possible revisions for the lettered sentences appear in the back of the book. Example:

Patti found the cat using a flashlight in the dark.

Using a flashlight in the dark, Patti found the cat.

a. The bus got stuck in a ditch full of passengers.
b. He was daydreaming about fishing for trout in the middle of a staff meeting.
c. The boy threw the airplane made of folded-up paper through an open window with a smirk.
d. I reached for my sunglasses when the glare appeared from the glove compartment.
e. High above them, Sally and Glen watched the kites drift back and forth.

1. In her soup she found a fly at one of the best French restaurants in town.
2. Andy learned some tips about building kites from the pages of an old book.
3. Alex vowed to return to the island sometime soon on the day he left it.
4. The fish was carried in a suitcase wrapped in newspaper.
5. The reporters were informed of the crimes committed by a press release.

14c.   Have something in the sentence for each modifier to modify.

Generally we assume that a modifying phrase that appears at the start of a sentence will modify the subject of the main clause to follow. If we encounter a modifying phrase midway through a sentence, we assume that it modifies something just before or (less often) after it.

> *Feeling sick to his stomach, Jason* went to bed.

> *An early bird by nature, Felix* began at eight o'clock.

> *Alice, while sympathetic,* was not inclined to help.

Occasionally a writer will slip up by allowing a modifying phrase to dangle. A *dangling modifier* is one that, on close inspection, is found to be shirking its job: it doesn't modify anything in its sentence.

> DANGLING   *Noticing a slight pain behind his eyes,* an aspirin seemed like a good idea. [The introductory phrase cannot be said to modify *aspirin.* In fact, it doesn't modify anything.]

> DANGLING   *To do a good job,* the right tools were needed.

To correct a dangling modifier, recast the sentence. First, figure out what noun, pronoun, or noun phrase the modifier is meant to modify, and then make that word or phrase the subject of the main clause.

> CLEAR   *Noticing a slight pain behind his eyes, he* decided to take an aspirin.

> CLEAR   *To do a good job, the plumber* needed the right tools.

Another way to correct a dangling modifier is to turn the dangler into a clause that includes the missing noun or pronoun.

> DANGLING   Her progress, *although talented,* has been slowed by poor work habits.

> CLEAR   *Although she is talented,* her progress has been slowed by poor work habits.

Sometimes a bit of rewriting will clarify what the modifier modifies and improve the sentence as well.

> CLEAR   *Although talented, she* has been handicapped by poor work habits.

EXERCISE 14–2

Revising Dangling Modifiers

Revise any sentences that contain dangling modifiers. Some sentences may be correct. Possible revisions for the lettered sentences appear in the back of the book. Example:

> Angry at her poor showing, geology would never be Joan's favorite class.

> *Angry at her poor showing, Joan* knew that geology would never be her favorite class.

   a. After working for six hours, the job was done.
   b. Unable to fall asleep, a warm bath relaxes you.
   c. To compete in the Olympics, talent, training, and dedication are needed.
   d. It's common, feeling lonely, to want to talk to someone.
   e. Having worried all morning, relief flooded over him when his missing son returned.

1. Once gripped by the urge to sail, it never leaves you.
2. Further information can be obtained by calling the specified number.
3. Passing the service station, the bank will appear on your right.
4. Having created strict ethical standards, there should be some willingness on Congress's part to live up to them.
5. Recalling Ben Franklin's advice, "hanging together" became the club members' new policy.
6. Short-tempered and irritable, his paintings reveal a passionate love of humanity.
7. To get the job, his portfolio had to be meticulously assembled.
8. Pressing hard on the brakes, the car spun into a hedge.
9. Showing a lack of design experience, the architect advised the student to take her model back to the drawing board.
10. When deep in concentration, interruptions are unwelcome.

15. *Incomplete Sentences*

A fragment fails to qualify as a sentence because it lacks a subject or a predicate or both (see 12). However, a sentence can contain these two essentials and still miss the mark. If it lacks some other key element — a crucial word or phrase — the sentence is *incomplete*. Often the problem is carelessness: the writer sets down too few words to cover a whole idea. The resulting incomplete sentence is likely to lose readers. Like a bridge open to the public, it invites us to cross; but it has unexpected gaps that we topple through.

Incomplete sentences catch writers most often in two writing situations: comparisons and the abbreviated type of parallel structure called elliptical constructions.

COMPARISONS

15a. Make your comparisons clear by stating fully what you are comparing with what.

> INCOMPLETE   Roscoe loves spending time with a computer more than Diane.

What is the writer of this sentence trying to tell us? Does Roscoe prefer the company of a keyboard to the company of his friend? Or, of these two people, is Roscoe (and not Diane) the computer addict? We can't be sure because the writer has not completed the comparison. Adding a word would solve the problem.

REVISED   Roscoe loves spending time with a computer more than Diane *does.*

REVISED   Roscoe loves spending time with a computer more than *with* Diane.

In editing what you write, double-check your comparisons to be sure they are complete.

INCOMPLETE   Miami has more newcomers from Havana than New York.

REVISED   Miami has more newcomers from Havana than New York *has.*

REVISED   Miami has more newcomers from Havana than *from* New York.

15b.   When you start to draw a comparison, finish it.

The unfinished comparison is a favorite trick of advertisers — "Our product is better!" — because it dodges the question "Better than what?" A sharp writer (or shopper) knows that any item being compared must be compared *with* something else.

INCOMPLETE   Scottish tweeds are warmer.

REVISED   Scottish tweeds are warmer *than any other fabric you can buy.*

15c.   Be sure the things you compare are of the same kind.

The saying "You can't compare apples and oranges" makes a useful grammatical point. A sentence that draws a comparison should assure its readers that the items involved are similar enough for comparison to be appropriate. When you compare two things, be sure the terms of the comparison are clear and logical.

INCOMPLETE   The engine of a Ford truck is heavier than a Piper Cub airplane.

What is being compared? Truck and airplane? Or engine and engine? If we consider, we can guess: since a truck engine is unlikely to outweigh an airplane, the writer must mean to compare engines. Readers, however, should not have to make the effort to complete a writer's incomplete thought.

REVISED   The engine of a Ford truck is heavier than *that of* a Piper Cub airplane.

REVISED   A Ford truck's engine is heavier than a *Piper Cub's.*

In this last example, parallel structure (*Ford truck's* and *Piper Cub's*) helps to make the comparison concise as well as clear. (See 17a and 17c for more on parallel structure.)

15d. To compare an item with others of its kind, use *any other*.

A comparison using *any* shows how something relates to a group without belonging to the group.

> Alaska is larger than *any* country in Central America.

> Bluefish has as much protein as *any* meat.

A comparison using *any other* shows how one member of a group relates to other members of the same group.

> Death Valley is drier than *any other* place in the United States.

> Bluefish has as distinctive a flavor as *any other* fish.

EXERCISE 15–1

Completing Comparisons

Revise the following sentences by adding needed words to any comparisons that are incomplete. (There may be more than one way to complete some comparisons.) Some sentences may be correct. Possible revisions for the lettered sentences appear in the back of the book. Example:

> I hate hot weather more than you.

> I hate hot weather more than you *do.*

> I hate hot weather more than I *hate* you.

a. She plays the *Moonlight Sonata* more brilliantly than any pianist her age.
b. Driving a sports car means more to Jake than his professors.
c. People who go to college aren't necessarily smarter, but they will always have an advantage at job interviews.
d. I don't have as much trouble getting along with Michelle as Karin.
e. Annapolis, Maryland, has more colonial brick houses than any city in the United States.

1. The crime rate in the United States is higher than Canada.
2. A more sensible system of running the schools would be to appoint a school board.
3. A hen lays fewer eggs than any turtle.
4. The town meeting form of government doesn't function as efficiently as a mayor.
5. Singing is closer to prayer than a meal of Chicken McNuggets.

ELLIPTICAL CONSTRUCTIONS

A well-known poem by Robert Frost begins with this line:

Some say the world will end in fire, some say in ice.

When Frost wrote that sentence, he avoided needless repetition by implying certain words rather than stating them. The result is more concise and more effective than a complete version of the same sentence would be:

Some say the world will end in fire, some say the world will end in ice.

This common writer's tactic — leaving out (for the sake of concision) an unnecessary word — produces an *elliptical construction.* Readers can easily fill in the words that, although not written, are clearly understood. Elliptical constructions can create confusion, however, if the writer gives readers too little information to fill in those missing words accurately.

15e. When you eliminate repetition, keep all words that are essential for clarity.

An elliptical construction saves repeating what a reader already knows. But whenever you use this strategy, make sure to omit only words that are stated elsewhere in the sentence. Otherwise, your reader may fill the gap incorrectly.

> INCOMPLETE   How can I date her, seeing that she is a senior, I a mere freshman?

This elliptical construction won't work. A reader supplying the missing verb in the last part of the sentence would get "I *is* a mere freshman." Although the writer means *am,* the verb *is* has already been stated.

> REVISED   How can I date her, seeing that she is a senior and I *am* a mere freshman?

Leaving out a necessary preposition also can produce a faulty elliptical construction.

> INCOMPLETE   The train neither goes nor returns from Middletown.

Without a *to* after *goes,* readers are likely to fill in an extra *from* to complete the verb's action. Write instead:

> REVISED   The train neither goes *to* nor returns from Middletown.

15f. In a compound predicate, leave out only verb forms that have already been stated.

Compound predicates are especially prone to incomplete elliptical constructions. Writing in haste, we accidentally omit part of a verb that is needed for the sentence to make sense. When you write a sentence with a compound predicate, check your verbs most carefully if they are in different tenses. Be sure that no necessary part is missing.

INCOMPLETE	The committee never has and never will vote to raise taxes.
REVISED	The committee never has *voted* and never will vote to raise taxes.

15g. If you mix comparisons using *as* and *than,* include both words.

To contrast two things that are different, we normally use the comparative form of an adjective followed by *than: better than, more than, fewer than.* To show a similarity between two things that are alike, we normally use the simple form of an adjective sandwiched between *as* and *as: as good as, as many as, as few as.* Often we can combine two *than* comparisons or two *as* comparisons into an elliptical construction.

The White House is smaller [than] and newer than Buckingham Palace.

Some corporate executives live in homes as large [as] and as grand as the White House.

If you want to combine a *than* comparison with an *as* comparison, however, an elliptical construction won't work.

INCOMPLETE	The White House is smaller but just as beautiful as Buckingham Palace.
REVISED	The White House is smaller *than* but just *as* beautiful *as* Buckingham Palace.
INCOMPLETE	Some corporate executives live in homes as large and no less grand than the White House.
REVISED	Some corporate executives live in homes *as* large *as* and no less grand *than* the White House.

EXERCISE 15–2

Completing Sentences

Revise the following sentences by adding needed words to any constructions that are incomplete. (There may be more than one way to complete some constructions.) Some sentences may be correct. Possible revisions for the lettered sentences appear in the back of the book. Example:

President Kennedy should have but didn't see the perils of invading Cuba.

President Kennedy should have *seen* but didn't see the perils of invading Cuba.

a. Eighteenth-century China was as civilized and in many respects more sophisticated than the Western world.
b. Pembroke was never contacted, much less involved with, the election committee.
c. I haven't yet but soon will finish my term paper.

    d. Ron likes his popcorn with butter, Linda with parmesan cheese.
    e. George Washington always has been and will be regarded as the father of his country.

1. You have traveled to exotic Tahiti; Maureen to Asbury Park, New Jersey
2. The mayor refuses to negotiate or even talk to the civic association.
3. Building a new sewage treatment plant would be no more costly and just as effective as modifying the existing one.
4. You'll be able to tell Jon from the rest of the team: Jon wears white Reeboks, the others black high-tops.
5. Erosion has and always will reshape the shoreline.

16. *Mixed Constructions and Faulty Predication*

Sometimes a sentence contains all the necessary parts and still doesn't work. Reading it, we feel uneasy, although we may not know why. The problem is a discord between two or more parts of the sentence: the writer has combined phrases or clauses that don't fit together (a *mixed construction*) or mismatched a verb and its subject, object, or modifier (*faulty predication*). The resulting tangle looks like a sentence at first glance, but it fails to make sense.

16a. Link phrases and clauses logically.

A *mixed construction* results when a writer connects phrases or clauses (or both) that don't work together as a sentence.

> MIXED   In her efforts to solve the tax problem only caused the mayor additional difficulties.

The prepositional phrase *In her efforts to solve the tax problem* is a modifier; it cannot function as the subject of a sentence. The writer, however, has used this phrase as a noun — the subject of the verb *caused*. To untangle the mixed construction, the writer has two choices: (1) rewrite the phrase so that it works as a noun or (2) use the phrase as a modifier rather than as the sentence's subject.

> REVISED   Her efforts to solve the tax problem only caused the mayor additional difficulties. [With *in* gone, *efforts* becomes the subject of the sentence.]

> REVISED   In her efforts to solve the tax problem, the mayor created additional difficulties. [The prepositional phrase now modifies the verb *created*.]

To avoid mixed constructions, check the links that join your phrases and clauses — especially prepositions and conjunctions. A sentence, like a chain, is only as strong as its weakest link.

MIXED   Jack, although he was picked up by the police, but was not charged with anything.

Using both *although* and *but* gives this sentence one link too many. We can unmix the construction in two ways.

REVISED   Jack was picked up by the police but was not charged with anything.

REVISED   Although he was picked up by the police, Jack was not charged with anything.

16b. Relate the parts of a sentence logically.

Faulty predication refers to a skewed relationship between a verb and some other part of a sentence.

FAULTY   *The temperature of water freezes* at 32 degrees Fahrenheit.

At first glance, that sentence looks all right. It contains both subject and predicate. It expresses a complete thought. What is wrong with it? The writer has slipped into faulty predication by mismatching the subject and verb. The sentence tells us that *temperature freezes,* when science and common sense tell us it is *water* that freezes. To correct this error, the writer must find a subject and verb that fit each other.

REVISED   *Water freezes* at 32 degrees Fahrenheit.

Faulty predication also can result from a mismatch between a verb and its direct object.

FAULTY   Rising costs *diminish college* for many students.

Costs don't *diminish college.* To correct this predication error, the writer must change the sentence so its direct object follows logically from its verb.

REVISED   Rising costs *diminish the number of students who can attend college.*

Subtler predication errors result when a writer uses a linking verb to forge a false connection between the subject and a subject complement.

FAULTY   *Industrial waste* has become *an important modern priority.*

Is it really *waste* that has become a *priority*? Or, rather, is it *working to solve the problems caused by careless disposal of industrial waste*? A writer who says all that, though, risks wordiness. Why not just replace *priority* with a closer match for *waste*?

REVISED   *Industrial waste* has become *a modern menace.*

Predication errors tend to plague writers who are too fond of the passive voice. Mismatches between a verb and its subject, object, or another part of the sentence are easier to avoid (and to spot during editing) when the verb is active than when it is passive. To improve your sentences, cast them in the active voice whenever possible. (See 5m.)

> FAULTY   The idea of giving thanks for a good harvest *was not done* first by the Pilgrims.

> REVISED   The idea of giving thanks for a good harvest *did not originate* with the Pilgrims.

16c.   Avoid starting a definition with *when* or *where.*

Many inexperienced writers slip into predication errors when they define terms. A definition, like any other phrase or clause, needs to fit grammatically with the rest of the sentence.

> FAULTY   Dyslexia is when you have a reading disorder.

> REVISED   Dyslexia is a reading disorder.

> FAULTY   A lay-up is where a player drives in close to the basket and then makes a usually one-handed, banked shot.

> REVISED   To shoot a lay-up, a player drives in close to the basket and then makes a usually one-handed, banked shot.

16d.   Avoid using *the reason is because . . .*

Anytime you start an explanation with *the reason is,* what follows *is* should be a subject complement: an adjective, a noun, or a noun clause. (See 2d.) *Because* is a conjunction; it cannot function as a noun or adjective.

> FAULTY   *The reason* Gerard hesitates *is because* no one supported him two years ago.

> REVISED   *The reason* Gerard hesitates *is simple*: no one supported him two years ago.

> REVISED   *The reason* Gerard hesitates *is that no one supported him two years ago.*

> REVISED   *The reason* Gerard hesitates *is his lack of support two years ago.*

EXERCISE 16–1

Correcting Mixed Constructions and Faulty Predication

Correct any mixed constructions and faulty predication you find in the following sentences. Possible revisions for the lettered sentences appear in the back of the book. Example:

The storm damaged the beach erosion.

The storm worsened the beach erosion. *Or*
The storm damaged the beach.

a. The cost of health insurance protects people from big medical bills.
b. In his determination to prevail helped him finish the race.
c. The AIDS epidemic destroys the body's immune system.
d. The temperatures are too cold for the orange trees.
e. A recession is when economic growth is small or nonexistent and unemployment increases.

1. The opening of the new shopping mall should draw out-of-town shoppers for years to come.
2. The reason the referendum was defeated was because voters are tired of paying so much in taxes.
3. In the glacier's retreat created the valley.
4. A drop in prices could put farmers out of business.
5. The researchers' main goal is cancer.

17. *Parallel Structure*

An important tool for any writer is **parallel structure,** or parallelism. You use this tool when you create a series of words, phrases, clauses, or sentences with the same grammatical form. The pattern created by the series — its parallel structure — emphasizes the similarities or differences among the items, which may be things, qualities, actions, or ideas.

My favorite foods are roast beef, deep-dish apple pie, and linguine with clam sauce.

Louise is charming, witty, intelligent, and talented.

Jeff likes to swim, ride, and run.

Dave likes movies that scare him and books that make him laugh.

Each series is a perfect parallel construction, composed of equivalent words: nouns in the first example, adjectives in the second, verbs in the third, and adjective clauses in the fourth. Editing for parallel structure is also covered in the "Quick Editing Guide." (For more help, see B2.)

17a. In a series linked by a coordinating conjunction, keep all elements in the same grammatical form.

Whenever you connect items with a coordinating conjunction (*and, but, for, or, nor, so,* and *yet*), you cue your readers to expect a parallel structure. Whether your series consists of single words, phrases, or clauses, its parts should balance one another.

AWKWARD   The puppies are *tiny, clumsily bumping* into each other, *and cute.*

Two elements in this series are parallel one-word adjectives (*tiny, cute*) but the third is a verb phrase (*clumsily bumping*). The writer can improve this awkward sentence by making the series consistent.

PARALLEL   The puppies are *tiny, clumsy, and cute.*

Don't mix verb forms in a series. Avoid, for instance, pairing a gerund and an infinitive.

AWKWARD   Switzerland is a good place for a winter vacation if you like *skiing and to skate.*

PARALLEL   Switzerland is a good place for a winter vacation if you like *skiing and skating.*

PARALLEL   Switzerland is a good place for a winter vacation if you like *to ski and to skate.*

 **ESL GUIDELINES**

Mixed Constructions, Faulty Predication, and Subject Errors

Mixed constructions result when phrases or clauses are joined even though they do not logically go together. Combine clauses with either a coordinator (*and, but, so,* and so on) or a subordinator (*although, because,* and so on). Never use both a coordinator and a subordinator to join two clauses.

INCORRECT   *Although* baseball is called "the national pastime" of the United States, *but* football is probably more popular.

CORRECT   *Although* baseball is called "the national pastime" of the United States, football is probably more popular.

CORRECT   Baseball is called "the national pastime" of the United States, *but* football is probably more popular.

Faulty predication results when a verb and its subject, object, or modifier do not match. Do not use a noun as both the subject of the sentence and the object of a preposition.

INCORRECT   *In my neighborhood has* several good restaurants.

CORRECT   *My neighborhood has* several good restaurants.

CORRECT   *In my neighborhood, there are* several good restaurants.

Avoid also these common errors that may occur with the subject of a clause.

• Do not omit *it* used as a subject. A subject is required in all English sentences except imperatives.

INCORRECT   *Is* interesting to visit museums.

CORRECT   *It is* interesting to visit museums.

• Do not repeat the subject of a sentence with a pronoun.

INCORRECT   *My brother-in-law, he* is a successful investor.

CORRECT   *My brother-in-law* is a successful investor.

In a series of phrases or clauses, be sure that all elements in the series are similar in form, even if they are not similar in length.

AWKWARD The fight in the bar happens after the two lovers have their scene together but before the car chase. [The clause starting with *after* is not parallel to the phrase starting with *before*.]

PARALLEL The fight in the bar happens after the love scene but before the car chase.

AWKWARD You can take the key, or don't forget to leave it under the mat. [The declarative clause starting with *You can* is not parallel to the imperative clause starting with *don't forget*.]

PARALLEL You can take the key, or you can leave it under the mat.

17b. In a series linked by correlative conjunctions, keep all elements in the same grammatical form.

When you use a correlative conjunction (*either . . . or, neither . . . nor, not only . . . but also*), follow each part of the conjunction with a similarly structured word, phrase, or clause.

AWKWARD I'm looking forward *to either attending* Saturday's wrestling match *or to seeing* it on closed-circuit TV. [Parallel structure is violated because *to* precedes the first part of the correlative conjunction (*to either*) but follows the second part (*or to*).]

PARALLEL I'm looking forward *either to attending* Saturday's wrestling match *or to seeing* it on closed-circuit television.

AWKWARD Take my advice: try *neither to be first nor last* in the lunch line. [Parallel structure is violated because *to be* follows the first part of the correlative conjunction but not the second part.]

PARALLEL Take my advice: try to be *neither first nor last* in the lunch line.

17c. Make the elements in a comparison parallel in form.

A comparative word such as *than* or *as* cues the reader to expect a parallel structure. This makes logical sense: to be compared, two things must resemble each other, and parallel structure emphasizes this resemblance. (See also 15g.)

AWKWARD Philip likes *fishing* better than *to sail*.

PARALLEL Philip likes *fishing* better than *sailing*.

PARALLEL Philip likes *to fish* better than *to sail*.

> AWKWARD   *Maintaining* railway lines is as important to our public transportation system as *to buy* new trains.
>
> PARALLEL   *Maintaining* railway lines is as important to our public transportation system as *buying* new trains.

17d.   Reinforce parallel structure by repeating rather than mixing articles, conjunctions, or prepositions.

When you write a series involving articles, conjunctions, or prepositions, be consistent. Try to repeat rather than to vary the word that begins each phrase or clause.

> "The time has come," the Walrus said,
> "To talk of many things:
> Of shoes — and ships — and sealing-wax —
> Of cabbages — and — kings — "

In this famous rhyme from *Through the Looking-Glass,* Lewis Carroll builds a beautiful parallel structure on three *of*'s and three *and*'s, each followed by a noun. The repetition of preposition and conjunction makes clear the equivalence of the nouns.

Sometimes the same lead-in word won't work for all elements in a series. In such cases you may be able to preserve a parallel structure by changing the order of the elements to minimize variation.

> AWKWARD   The new school building is large but not very comfortable, and expensive but unattractive.
>
> PARALLEL   The new school building is large and expensive, but uncomfortable and unattractive.

17e.   In a series of clauses, repeat lead-in words to emphasize parallel structure.

Parallel structures are especially useful in complex sentences expressing equivalent ideas. Whenever you write a sentence containing a series of long, potentially confusing clauses, try to precede each clause with *that, who, when, where,* or some other connective, repeating the same connective every time. To do so not only helps you to keep your thoughts in order as you write but helps readers to follow them with ease.

> No one in this country needs a government that aids big business at the expense of farmers and laborers; that ravages the environment in the name of progress; that slashes budgets of health and education; that turns its back on the unemployed, the illiterate, the mentally ill, the destitute; that constantly swaggers and rattles its sabers; that spends billions piling up missiles it would be insane to use.

Repeating an opening phrase can accomplish the same goal in a series of parallel sentences, as the graceful example on the following page shows.

The Russian dramatist is one who, walking through a cemetery, does not see the flowers on the graves. The American dramatist is one who, walking through a cemetery, does not see the graves under the flowers.

EXERCISE 17–1

Making Sentences Parallel

Revise the following sentences by substituting parallel structures for awkward ones. Possible revisions for the lettered sentences appear in the back of the book. Example:

> Not only are you wasting your time but also mine.

> You are wasting not only your time but also mine.

a. Linda loves to watch soccer and tennis and playing squash.
b. Better than starting from scratch would be to build on what already has been done.
c. Her apartment needed fresh paint, a new rug was a necessity, and Mary Lou wished she had a neater roommate and that she had chosen quieter friends.
d. All my brothers are blond and athletes.
e. For breakfast the waiter brought scrambled eggs, which I like, and kippers, although I don't like them.

1. The United States must start either focusing more attention on education or we must accept a future as a second-rate power.
2. Not only were they homeless but sick as well.
3. The best teachers are kind, firm, are smart, and have a sense of humor.
4. Students can write either a term paper or give a presentation.
5. The twentieth century was not an age of progress, but violence and brutality on a scale unknown since ancient times.
6. Melrose would rather carry his battle to the Supreme Court than he would be willing to give up without a fight.
7. My landlady is tidy, generous, easygoing, and a talker.
8. Are problem novels for the young really good for children or merely exploit them by making life appear more burdensome, chaotic, more wretched, and evil than it really is?
9. When you first start out, running halfway around the track is as big a challenge as to complete several circuits.
10. Her excuses were the difficulty of the task, the instructions were awkwardly worded, and having only four hours to complete the assignment.
11. In my drama class so far we've read a Shakespearean tragedy, another by Marlowe, and one of Webster's.
12. When you are broke and unemployed and your friends have deserted you, while you have nowhere to sleep but under a bridge, then and only then should you call this number.
13. Giving is better than to receive.
14. Not only should we accept Marinda's kind offer, but thank her for making it.
15. How often Reuben has done this kind of work is less important than the quality of his output.

18. *Coordination and Subordination*

A good piece of writing is greater than the sum of its parts. Links between sentences help readers to see how one thought relates to another and to share the writer's overview of the topic.

When you write, you can use coordination and subordination to bring out the relationships between your ideas. Coordination clarifies the connection between thoughts of equal importance; subordination shows how one thought affects another. These two techniques will help you produce sentences, paragraphs, and essays that function as a coherent whole.

18a. Coordinate clauses or sentences that are related in theme and equal in importance.

> The car skidded for a hundred yards. It crashed into a brick wall.

These two clauses make equally significant statements about the same subject, a car accident. Because the writer has indicated no link between the sentences, we can only guess that the crash followed from the skid; we cannot be sure.

Suppose we join the two with a conjunction.

> The car skidded for a hundred yards, and it crashed into a brick wall.

Now the sequence is clear: first the car skidded, then it crashed. That's coordination.

Another way to coordinate the two clauses is to combine them into a single sentence with a compound verb. The second main clause, losing its subject, becomes a phrase.

> The car skidded for a hundred yards and crashed into a brick wall.

Now the connection is so clear we can almost hear screeching brakes and crunching metal.

Once you decide to coordinate two clauses, there are three ways you can do it: with a conjunction, with a conjunctive adverb, or with punctuation.

1. Join two main clauses with a coordinating conjunction (*and, but, for, or, nor, so,* or *yet*).

UNCOORDINATED	George does not want to be placed on your mailing list. He does not want a salesperson to call him.
COORDINATED	George does not want to be placed on your mailing list, nor does he want a salesperson to call him.
COORDINATED	George does not want to be placed on your mailing list or called by a salesperson.

2. Join two main clauses with a semicolon and a conjunctive adverb such as *furthermore, however, moreover,* or *therefore.* (See 1g.)

| UNCOORDINATED | The guerrillas did not observe the truce. They never intended to. |
| COORDINATED | The guerrillas did not observe the truce; furthermore, they never intended to. |

3. Join two main clauses with a semicolon or a colon. (For details on when to use which punctuation mark, see 26 and 27.)

UNCOORDINATED	The government favors negotiations. The guerrillas prefer to fight.
COORDINATED	The government favors negotiations; the guerrillas prefer to fight.
UNCOORDINATED	The guerrillas have two advantages. They know the terrain, and the people support them.
COORDINATED	The guerrillas have two advantages: they know the terrain, and the people support them.

18b. Coordinate clauses only if they are clearly and logically related.

Whenever you hitch together two sentences, make sure they get along. Will the relationship between them be evident to your readers? Have you chosen a coordinating conjunction, conjunctive adverb, or punctuation mark that accurately reflects this relationship?

| FAULTY | The sportscasters were surprised by Easy Goer's failure to win the Kentucky Derby, but it rained on Derby day. |

The writer has not included enough information for the reader to see why these two clauses are connected.

| COORDINATED | The sportscasters were surprised by Easy Goer's failure to win the Kentucky Derby; *however, he runs poorly on a muddy track,* and it rained on Derby day. |

Another route to faulty coordination is a poorly chosen link between clauses.

| FAULTY | The sportscasters all expected Easy Goer to win the Kentucky Derby, and Sunday Silence beat him. |

The conjunction *and* implies that both clauses reflect the same assumptions. This is not the case, so the writer should choose a conjunction that expresses difference.

| COORDINATED | The sportscasters all expected Easy Goer to win the Kentucky Derby, *but* Sunday Silence beat him. |

18c. Coordinate clauses only if they work together to make a
coherent point.

When a writer strings together several clauses in a row, often the result is excessive coordination. Trying to pack too much information into a single sentence can make readers dizzy, unable to pick out which points really matter.

> EXCESSIVE   Easy Goer was the Kentucky Derby favorite, and all the sportscasters expected him to win, but he runs poorly on a muddy track, and it rained on Derby day, so Sunday Silence beat him.

What are the main points in this passage? Each key idea deserves its own sentence so that readers will recognize it as important.

> REVISED   Easy Goer was the Kentucky Derby favorite, and all the sportscasters expected him to win. However, he runs poorly on a muddy track, and it rained on Derby day; so Sunday Silence beat him.

Excessive coordination also tends to result when a writer uses the same conjunction repeatedly.

> EXCESSIVE   Phil was out of the house all day, so he didn't know about the rain, so he went ahead and bet on Easy Goer, so he lost twenty bucks, so now he wants to borrow money from me.

> REVISED   Phil was out of the house all day, so he didn't know about the rain. He went ahead and bet on Easy Goer, and he lost twenty bucks. Now he wants to borrow money from me.

One solution to excessive coordination is subordination: making one clause dependent on another instead of giving both clauses equal weight. (See 18d.)

EXERCISE 18-1

Using Coordination

Revise the following sentences, adding coordination where appropriate and removing faulty or excessive coordination. Possible revisions for the lettered sentences appear in the back of the book. Example:

> The wind was rising, and leaves tossed on the trees, and the air seemed to crackle with electricity, and we knew that a thunderstorm was on the way.

> The wind was rising, leaves tossed on the trees, and the air seemed to crackle with electricity. We knew that a thunderstorm was on the way.

a. Congress is expected to pass the biotechnology bill. The president already has said he will veto it.
b. Mortgage rates have dropped. Home buying is likely to increase in the near future.
c. The earth trembled. The long-dreaded cataclysm had begun.
d. I left the house in a hurry and ran to the bank so I could cash a check to buy lunch, but it was the bank's anniversary, and the staff was busy serving cof-

fee and cake, so by the time I left, after chatting and eating for twenty minutes, I wasn't hungry anymore.

e. The U.S. Postal Service handles millions of pieces of mail every day. It is the largest postal service in the world.

1. The rebels may take the capital in a week. They may not be able to hold it.
2. If you want to take Spanish this semester, you have only one choice. You must sign up for the 8 A.M. course.
3. Peterson's Market has raised its prices. Last week tuna fish cost $.89 a can. Now it's up to $1.09.
4. Joe starts the morning with a cup of coffee, which wakes him up, and then at lunch he eats a chocolate bar, so that the sugar and caffeine will bring up his energy level.
5. The *Hindenburg* drifted peacefully over New York City. It exploded just before landing.

18d. Subordinate less important ideas to more important ideas.

Subordination is one of the most useful of all writing strategies. By subordinating a less important clause to a more important one, you show your readers that one fact or idea follows from another or affects another. You stress what counts, thereby encouraging your readers to share your viewpoint — an important goal, whatever you are writing.

When you have two sentences that contain ideas in need of connecting, you can subordinate one to the other in any of the following three ways.

1. Turn the less important idea into a subordinate clause by introducing it with a subordinating conjunction such as *although, because, if,* or *when.* (See 1g for a list of subordinating conjunctions.)

Jason has a keen sense of humor. He has an obnoxious, braying laugh.

From that pair of sentences, readers don't know what to feel about Jason. Is he likable or repellent? The writer needs to decide which trait matters more and to emphasize it.

Although Jason has a keen sense of humor, he has an obnoxious, braying laugh.

The revision makes Jason's sense of humor less important than his annoying hee-haw. The less important idea is stated as a subordinate clause opening with *Although,* the more important idea as the main clause.

The writer could reverse the meaning by combining the two ideas the other way around:

Although Jason has an obnoxious, braying laugh, he has a keen sense of humor.

That version makes Jason sound fun to be with, despite his mannerism.

Which of Jason's traits to emphasize is up to the writer. What matters is that, in both combined versions of the original two separate sentences, the writer takes a clear stand by making one sentence a main clause and the other a subordinate clause.

2. Turn the less important idea into a subordinate clause by introducing it with a relative pronoun such as *who, which,* or *that.* (See 1b for a list of relative pronouns.)

Jason, *who has an obnoxious, braying laugh,* has a keen sense of humor.

Jason, *whose sense of humor is keen,* has an obnoxious, braying laugh.

3. Turn the less important idea into a phrase.

Jason, *a keen humorist,* has an obnoxious, braying laugh.

Despite his obnoxious, braying laugh, Jason has a keen sense of humor.

18e. Express the more important idea in the main clause.

Sometimes a writer accidentally subordinates a more important idea to a less important idea and turns the sentence's meaning upside down.

FAULTY   Although the Algonquin Round Table lives on in spirit, the
SUBORDINATION   writers who created it are nearly all dead now.

This sentence is factually accurate. Does the writer, however, really want to stress death over life? This is the effect of putting *are nearly all dead* in the main clause and *lives on* in the subordinate clause. Recognizing a case of faulty subordination, the writer can reverse the two clauses.

REVISED   Although the writers who created it are nearly all dead now, the Algonquin Round Table lives on in spirit.

18f. Limit the number of subordinate clauses in a sentence.

The cause of excessive subordination is usually that a writer has tried to cram too much information into one sentence. The result is a string of ideas in which readers may not be able to pick out what matters.

EXCESSIVE   Debate over the Strategic Defense Initiative (SDI), which
SUBORDINATION   was originally proposed as a space-based defensive shield
                that would protect America from enemy attack, but which
                critics have suggested amounts to creating a first-strike ca-
                pability in space, has to some extent focused on the wrong
                question because it concentrates on the plan's technologi-
                cal flaws and thus fails to consider adequately whether SDI
                would in fact lower or increase the odds of nuclear war.

In revising this sentence, the writer needs to decide which are the main points and turn each one into a main clause. Lesser points can remain as subordinate clauses, arranged so that each of them gets an appropriate amount of emphasis.

REVISED   Debate over the Strategic Defense Initiative (SDI) has to some extent focused on the wrong question. The plan was originally proposed as a space-based defensive shield that would protect America from enemy attack; but critics have suggested that it amounts to creating a first-strike capability in space. However, most arguments about SDI have concentrated on its technological flaws and thus have failed to consider adequately whether SDI would in fact lower or increase the odds of nuclear war.

EXERCISE 18–2

Using Subordination

Revise the following sentences, adding subordination where appropriate and removing faulty or excessive subordination. Possible revisions for the lettered sentences appear in the back of the book. Example:

> Some playwrights like to work with performing theater companies. It is helpful to hear a script read aloud by actors.

> Some playwrights like to work with performing theater companies *because* it is helpful to hear a script read aloud by actors.

a. Although we occasionally hear horror stories about fruits and vegetables being unsafe to eat because they were sprayed with toxic chemicals or were grown in contaminated soil, the fact remains that, given their high nutritional value, these fresh foods are generally much better for us than processed foods.

b. English has become an international language. Its grammar is filled with exceptions to the rules.

c. Some television cartoon shows have become cult classics. This has happened years after they went off the air. Examples include *Rocky and Bullwinkle* and *Speed Racer.*

d. At the end of Verdi's opera *La Traviata,* Alfredo has to see his beloved Violetta again. He knows she is dying and all he can say is good-bye.

e. Violetta gives away her money. She bids adieu to her faithful servant. After that she dies in her lover's arms.

1. Cape Cod is a peninsula in Massachusetts. It juts into the Atlantic Ocean south of Boston. The Cape marks the northern turning point of the Gulf Stream.

2. The developer had hoped the condominiums would sell quickly. Sales were sluggish.

3. Tourists love Italy. Italy has a wonderful climate, beautiful towns and cities, and a rich history.

4. Although bank customers have not yet begun to shift their money out of savings accounts, the interest rate on NOW accounts has gone up.

5. I usually have more fun at a concert with Rico than with Morey. Rico loves music. Morey merely tolerates it.

EXERCISE 18–3

Using Coordination and Subordination

Revise the following passage, adding coordination and subordination where appropriate and removing faulty or excessive subordination. Example:

> The car plays an essential but destructive role in American consumer society. It requires the maximum consumption of resources and energy. It contributes to the disintegration of community.

> The car plays an essential but destructive role in American consumer society: it *not only* requires the maximum consumption of resources and energy *but also* contributes to the disintegration of community.

> The invention of the automobile transformed society in one profound way. It offered everyone unlimited freedom of movement. It is true that the car has allowed the population greater mobility, and the cost to the landscape and the environment has been devastating. The reliance on the car has created sprawling suburbs, miles of ugly strip malls and acres of parking lots, and it has destroyed farmland, wetland, and wildlife habitat, while it continues to pollute the environment, poisoning the air we breathe, and discouraging walking, a traditional fat-burning activity, thus contributing directly to our personal health problems. In addition to ecological damage, the obsessive reliance on the automobile has had serious social consequences and has accentuated social and racial polarization, separating the suburban middle classes from the urban poor and has also intensified the social isolation of the individual. The car owner spends a great deal of his or her time alone in the car, driving to and from shopping and living zones, so with shopping malls far from the centers of towns and cities, consumers no longer patronize town centers and thus contribute to the destruction of traditional American community life. The car is here to stay. We must find a way to limit its destructive power.

19. *Sentence Variety*

Just as the special-effects experts in movies use the unexpected to shock or to please, writers may combine sentence elements in unexpected ways to achieve special effects. Writers use some patterns more than others to express ideas directly and efficiently, but sometimes they vary the normal expectations in sentences to emphasize ideas and surprise readers.

19a. Normal Sentences

In a *normal sentence,* a writer puts the subject before the verb at the beginning of the main clause. This pattern is the most common in English because it expresses ideas in the most straightforward manner.

> Most college *students* today *are* not interested in reading.

> *Franklin sighed* because he was frustrated over his inability to solve the quadratic equation.

19b.   Inverted Sentences

In an *inverted sentence,* a writer inverts or reverses the subject-verb order to emphasize an idea in the predicate.

NORMAL   *My peers are uninterested* in reading.

INVERTED   How *uninterested* in reading *are my peers!*

19c.   Balanced Sentences

In a *balanced sentence,* a writer purposefully repeats key words and uses parallel sentence patterns to emphasize ideas.

In studying the heavens, we are debarred from all senses except sight. *We cannot* touch the sun *or* travel to it: *we cannot* walk around the moon *or* apply a foot-rule to the Pleiades.

19d.   Cumulative Sentences

In a *cumulative sentence,* a writer piles details at the end of a sentence to help readers visualize a scene or understand an idea.

They came walking out in heavily brocaded yellow and black costumes, the familiar "toreador" suit, heavy with gold embroidery, cape, jacket, shirt and collar, knee breeches, pink stockings, and low pumps.

— Ernest Hemingway, "Bull Fighting a Tragedy"

19e.   Periodic Sentences

The positions of emphasis in a sentence are the beginning and the end. In a *periodic sentence*, a writer suspends the main clause for a climactic ending, emphasizing an idea by withholding it until the end.

Leaning back in his chair, shaking his head slowly back and forth, frustrated over his inability to solve the quadratic equation, Franklin scowled.

EXERCISE 19–1

Increasing Sentence Variety

Revise the following passage, adding sentence variety to create interest, emphasize important ideas, and strengthen coherence.

We are terrified of death. We do not think of it, and we don't speak of life. We don't mourn in public. We don't know how to console a grieving friend. In fact, we have eliminated or suppressed all the traditional rituals surrounding death.

The Victorians coped with death differently. Their funerals were elaborate. The yards of black crepe around the hearse, hired professional mourners, and its solemn procession leading to an ornate tomb is now only a distant memory. They wore mourning jewelry. They had a complicated dress code for the grieving process. It governed what mourners wore, and it governed how long they wore it. Many of these Victorian rituals may seem excessive or even morbid to us today. The rituals served a psychological purpose in helping the living deal with loss.

EXERCISE 19–2

Generating Varied Sentences

Try your hand — either alone or with classmates — at composing each of these types of sentences: a normal sentence, an inverted sentence, a balanced sentence, a cumulative sentence, and a periodic sentence.

Chapter 34

Word Choice

20. *Appropriateness*

When you talk to people face to face, you can gauge how they are reacting to what you say. Often their responses guide your tone of voice and your choice of words: if your listener chuckles at your humor, you go on being humorous; if your listener frowns, you cut the comedy and speak more seriously.

When you write, you cannot gauge your readers' reactions as easily because you cannot see them. To know whether your comments will be successful, you must imagine yourself in a reader's place. Although you may consider your readers from time to time as you gather material and as you write, you probably focus most closely on their responses when you reread your writing to determine how to revise.

20a. Choose a tone appropriate for your topic and audience.

Like a speaker, a writer may come across as warm and friendly or cool and aloof, furious or merely annoyed, playful or grimly serious. This attitude is the *tone* of the piece of writing, and, like the tone of the speaking voice, it strongly influences the audience's response. A tone that seems right to a reader comes when you have written with an awareness of and concern for how the reader may react. If you ignore or are unaware of your reader, then your tone will be inappropriate. For instance, taking a humorous approach to a disease such as cancer or AIDS probably would yield an inappropriate tone. The reader, not finding the topic funny, is likely to reject what you say.

To help you convey your tone, you may use sentence length, level of language, vocabulary, and other elements of style. You may choose formal or informal language, colorful or bland words, coolly objective words, or words loaded with emotional connotations ("You pig!" "You angel!").

20b. Choose a level of formality appropriate for your tone.

Being aware of the tone you want to convey to your audience helps you choose words that are neither too formal nor too informal. By *formal* language, we mean the impersonal language of educated persons, usually written. In general, formal language is marked by relatively long and complex sentences and by a large, often esoteric, vocabulary. It doesn't use contractions (such as *doesn't*), and the writer's attitude toward the topic is serious.

Informal language more closely resembles ordinary conversation. Its sentences tend to be relatively short and simple. Informal language is marked by common words and may include contractions, slang, and references to everyday objects and activities (cheeseburgers, T-shirts, car repair). It may address the reader as *you*, and the writer may use *I*.

The right language for most college essays lies somewhere between formal and informal. If your topic and your tone are serious (say, for an expository paper on the United Nations), then your language is likely to lean toward formality. If your topic is not weighty and your tone is light and humorous (say, for a narrative paper about giving your dog a bath), then your language can be informal.

EXERCISE 20–1

Choosing an Appropriate Tone and Level of Formality

Revise the following passages to ensure that both the tone and the level of formality are appropriate for the topic and audience. Example:

I'm sending you this letter because I want you to meet with me and give me some info about the job you do.

I'm writing to inquire about the possibility of an interview.

1. Dear Senator Crowley:
   I think you've got to vote for the new environmental law, so I'm writing this letter. We're messing up forests and wetlands — maybe for good. Let's do something now for everybody who's born after us.
   Thanks,
   Glenn Turner

2. The new Holocaust Museum in Washington, D.C., is a great museum dedicated to a real bad time in history. It's real hard not to get bummed out by the stuff on show. Take it from me, it's an experience you'll never forget.

3. Dear Elaine,
   I am so pleased that you plan on attending the homecoming dance with me on Friday. It promises to be a gala event and I am confident that we will enjoy ourselves immensely. I understand a local recording act by the name of Acid Bunny will be providing the musical entertainment. Please call me at your earliest convenience to let me know when I should pick you up.
   Sincerely,
   Bill

20c. Choose common words instead of jargon.

Whatever your tone and your level of formality, certain types of language are best avoided when you write an essay. **Jargon** is the name given to the specialized vocabulary used by people in a particular field. Nearly every academic, professional, and even recreational field — music, carpentry, the law, computer programming, sports — has its own jargon. In baseball, pitcher Dennis Eckersley says that when he faces a dangerous batter, he thinks: "If I throw him *the heater*, maybe he *juices it out* on me" (emphasis added). Translation: "If I throw him a fastball, he might hit a home run."[1]

To a specialist addressing other specialists, jargon is convenient and necessary. Without technical terms, after all, two surgeons could hardly discuss a patient's anatomy. To an outsider, though, such terms may be incomprehensible. If your writing is meant (as it should be) to communicate information to your readers and not to make them feel excluded or confused, you should avoid unnecessary jargon.

Commonly, we apply the name *jargon* to any private, pretentious, or needlessly specialized language. Jargon can include not only words but ways of using words. Some politicians and bureaucrats like to make nouns into verbs by tacking on suffixes like *-ize*.

JARGON	Let us *prioritize* our objectives.
CLEAR	Let us *assign priorities to* our objectives.
CLEAR	Let us *rank* our objectives *in order of urgency*.

JARGON	The government intends to *privatize* federal landholdings.
CLEAR	The government intends to *sell* federal landholdings *to private buyers*.

Although *privatize* implies merely "convert to private ownership," usually its real meaning is "sell off" — as might occur, say, were a national park to be auctioned to developers. *Privatize* thus also can be called a *euphemism*, which is any pleasant term that masks an unpleasant meaning (see 20d).

Besides confusing readers, jargon is likely to mislead them. Recently, high technology has made verbs of the familiar nouns *access*, *boot*, and *format*. Other terms that have entered the popular vocabulary include *interface*, *x amount of*, *database*, and *parameters*. Such terms are useful to explain technical processes; but when thoughtlessly applied to nontechnical ideas, they can obscure meaning.

JARGON	A democracy needs the electorate's *input*.
CLEAR	A democracy needs the electorate *to vote and to express its views to elected officials*.

[1] Quoted by Mike Whiteford, *How to Talk Baseball* (New York: Dembner, 1983) 51.

Here's how to avoid needless jargon.

1. Beware of choosing any trendy new word when a perfectly good old word will do.
2. Before using a word ending in *-ize, -wise,* or *-ism,* count to ten. This will give you time either to think of a clearer alternative or to be sure that none exists.
3. Avoid the jargon of a special discipline — say, psychology or fly-fishing — unless you are writing of psychological or fly-fishing matters and you know for sure that your reader, too, is familiar with them. If you're writing for an audience of general readers about some field in which you are an expert — if, for instance, you're explaining the fundamentals of hang gliding — define any specialized terms. Even if you're addressing fellow hang-gliding experts, use plain words and you'll rarely go wrong.

EXERCISE 20–2

Avoiding Jargon

Revise the following sentences to eliminate the jargon. If you see a need to change a sentence extensively, go ahead. If you can't tell what a sentence means, decide what it might mean and rewrite it so that its meaning is clear. Possible revisions for the lettered sentences appear in the back of the book. Example:

The proximity of Mr. Fitton's knife to Mr. Schering's arm produced a violation of the integrity of the skin.

Mr. Fitton's knife cut Mr. Schering's arm.

a. The driver education course prepares the student for the skills of handling a vehicle on the highway transportation system.
b. We of the State Department have carefully contexted the riots in Lebanon intelligencewise, and after full and thorough database utilization, find them abnormalling rapidly.
c. Certain antinuclearistic and pacifistic/prejudicial factions have been picketing the missile conference in hopes of immobilizing these vital peacekeeping deliberations.
d. In the heart area, Mr. Pitt is a prime candidate-elect for intervention of a multiple bypass nature.
e. Within the parameters of your insurance company's financial authorization, he can either be regimed dietwise or be bypass prognosticated.

1. The study will examine the negative ramifications of toxic nonbiodegradable manufactured waste products.
2. Engaging in a conversational situation with God permits an individual to maximally interface with God.
3. The deer hunters number-balanced the ecological infrastructure by quietizing x amount of the deer populace.
4. "I am very grateful that we have education up where it is, high on the educational agenda of this country." — Secretary of Education T. H. Bell, in a speech, June 1983
5. A noninterventionist policy has been adopted by the government with respect to the situation in Bosnia.

20d.   Use euphemisms sparingly.

Euphemisms are plain truths dressed in attractive words, sometimes hard facts stated gently and pleasantly. To say that someone *passed away* instead of *died* is a common euphemism — useful and humane, perhaps, in breaking terrible news to an anxious family. In such shock-absorbing language, an army that retreats *makes a strategic withdrawal;* a poor old man becomes a *disadvantaged senior citizen.* But euphemisms aren't always oversized words. If you call someone *slim* who you think *underweight* or *skinny,* you use a euphemism, though it has only one syllable.

Because they can bathe glum truths in a kindly glow, euphemisms are beloved by advertisers — like the *mortician (undertaker)* who offered *preneed arrangements.* Euphemisms also can make ordinary things sound more impressive. Some acne medications treat not *pimples* but *blemishes.* In Madison, Wisconsin, a theater renamed its candy counter the *patron assistance center.*

Euphemisms may serve grimmer purposes. During World War II, Jewish prisoners sent to Nazi extermination camps carried papers stamped *Rückkehr Unerwünscht* (Return Unwanted). In 1984, the Doublespeak Award of the National Council of Teachers of English went to the U.S. State Department for its announcement that it would no longer use the word *killing* in its official reports but would substitute *unlawful or arbitrary deprivation of life.*

Even if you aren't prone to using euphemisms in your own writing, be aware of them when you read, especially when collecting evidence from biased sources and official spokespersons.

EXERCISE 20–3

Avoiding Euphemisms

Revise the following sentences to turn euphemisms into plainer words. Possible revisions for the lettered sentences appear in the back of the book. Example:

> I am temporarily between jobs, so I am currently experiencing a negative cash flow.

> I'm *out of work* and therefore *in debt.*

a. After the Rodney King trial, Los Angeles was engulfed in a riot, during which many innocent people passed away.
b. The ship sank because of loss of hull integrity.
c. The new K27 missile will effectively depopulate the cities of any aggressor nation.
d. In our town, sanitation engineers must wear professional apparel when making their rounds.
e. Freddie the Rocker has boarded a first-class flight for the great all-night discotheque in the sky.

1. Our security forces have judiciously thinned an excessive number of political dissidents.

2. The soldiers were victims of friendly fire during a strategic withdrawal.
3. To bridge the projected shortfall between collections and expenditures in next year's budget, the governor advocates some form of revenue enhancement.
4. Saturday's weather forecast calls for extended periods of shower activity.
5. We anticipate a downturn in economic vitality.

20e. Avoid slang in formal writing.

Poet Carl Sandburg once said, "Slang is language that takes off its coat, spits on its hands, and gets to work." Clearly, Sandburg approved. Probably even the purists among us will concede that slang, especially when new, can be colorful ("She's not playing with a full deck"), playful ("He's wicked cute!"), and apt (*ice* for diamonds, a *stiff* for a corpse).

The trouble with most slang, however, is that it quickly comes to seem quaint, even incomprehensible. We don't hear anyone say *groovy* anymore except on reruns of *The Brady Bunch*. *Bad vibes*, ubiquitous in the 1960s, today wear spiderwebs. Even the more recent *bummer* and *grody to the max* already seem as old and wrinkled as the Jazz Age's favorite exclamation of glee, *twenty-three skidoo!*

In the classroom and out of it, your writing communicates your thoughts. To be understood, your best bet is to stick to Standard English. Most slang is less than clever. The newest of it, apt though it may seem, like any fad is in danger of being quickly tossed aside in favor of something newer still. Seek words that are usual but exact, not the latest thing, and your writing will stay young longer.

EXERCISE 20–4

Avoiding Slang

Revise the following sentences to replace slang with Standard English. Possible revisions for the lettered sentences appear in the back of the book. Example:

The public health office hopes that smoking cigs won't be considered a cool thing to do anymore.

The public health office hopes that smoking *cigarettes* will no longer be *socially acceptable*.

a. A lot of consumers get ripped off when they buy a new set of wheels.
b. Lately, she's been dissing all her friends.
c. Most of the people at the clinic are boozers or dopeheads.
d. The weed being toked nowadays is stronger than in the past.
e. They don't want to go out; they just want to veg.

1. At three hundred bucks a month, the apartment is a steal.
2. Churchill was a wicked good politician.
3. The president's health care plan was toast; there was no way that Congress would approve it.

4. The course was a joke; the prof passed everyone and didn't even grade the stuff we turned in.
5. The caller to the talk-radio program sounded totally wigged out.

21. *Exact Words*

What would you think if you read in a newspaper that a certain leading citizen is a *pillow of the community?* How would you react to a foreign dignitary's statement that he has no children because his wife is *inconceivable?* Good writing — that is, effective written communication — depends on more than good grammar. Just as important are knowing what words and phrases mean and using them precisely.

21a. Choose words for their connotations as well as their denotations.

The *denotation* of a word is its basic meaning — its dictionary definition. *Stone*, for instance, has the same denotation as *rock*. *Excited, agitated,* and *exhilarated* all denote a similar state of physical and emotional arousal. When you look up a word in a dictionary or thesaurus, the synonyms you find have been selected for their shared denotation.

The *connotations* of a word are the shades of meaning that set it apart from its synonyms. We say *Phil's house is a stone's throw from mine*, not *a rock's throw*. You might be *agitated* by the prospect of exams next week, but *exhilarated* by your plans for a vacation afterward. When you choose one out of several synonyms listed in a dictionary or thesaurus, you base your choice on connotation.

Paying attention to connotation helps a writer to say exactly what he or she intends, instead of almost but not quite.

IMPRECISE   Advertisers have given light beer a macho image by showing football players *sipping* the product with *enthusiasm*.

REVISED   Advertisers have given light beer a macho image by showing football players *guzzling* the product with *gusto*.

IMPRECISE   The cat's eyes *shone* as she *pursued* the mouse.

REVISED   The cat's eyes *glittered* as she *stalked* the mouse.

21b. Avoid clichés.

A *cliché* is a trite expression, worn out from too much use. It may have glinted once, like a coin fresh from the mint, but now it is dull and flat from years of passing from hand to hand. If a story begins, "It was a dark and stormy night," and introduces a *tall, dark, and handsome* man and a woman who is *a vision of loveliness,* then its author is obviously using worn coins.

A cliché isn't just any old dull expression: it is one whose writer mistakenly assumes is bright. "Let's run this up the flagpole and see if anyone salutes," proposes the executive, while his or her colleagues yawn at this effort to sound clever. Stale, too, is the suggestion to put an idea *on the back burner.* Clichés abound when writers and speakers try hard to sound vigorous and colorful but don't trouble themselves to invent anything vigorous, colorful, and new.

George Orwell once complained about prose made up of phrases "tacked together like the sections of a prefabricated henhouse." If you read newspapers, you are familiar with such ready-made constructions. A strike is usually settled after *a marathon bargaining session* that *narrowly averts a walkout,* often *at the eleventh hour.* Fires customarily *race* and *gut.* Some writers use clichés to exaggerate, giving a statement more force than they feel. The writer to whom everything is *fantastic* or *terrific* arouses a reader's suspicion that it isn't.

No writer can entirely avoid clichés or avoid echoing colorful expressions first used by someone else. You need not ban from your writing all proverbs ("It takes a thief to catch a thief"), well-worked quotations from Shakespeare ("Neither a borrower nor a lender be"), and other faintly dusty wares from the storehouse of our language. "Looking for a needle in a haystack" may be a time-worn phrase, yet who can put that idea any more memorably?

Nor should you fear that every familiar expression is a cliché. *Just in time, more or less, sooner or later* — these are old, familiar expressions, to be sure; but they are not clichés, for they don't try to be vivid or figurative. Inevitably, we all rely on them.

When editing your writing, you will usually recognize any really annoying cliché you'll want to eradicate. If you feel a sudden guilty desire to surround an expression with quotation marks, as if to apologize for it —

> In his campaign speeches for his fourteenth term, Senator Pratt shows that he cannot "cut the mustard" any longer.

— then strike it out. Think again: What do you want to say? Recast your idea more clearly, more exactly.

> At age seventy-seven, Senator Pratt no longer can hold a crowd with an impassioned, hour-long speech, as he could when he first ran for Congress.

By what other means can you spot a cliché? One way is to show your papers to friends, asking them to look for anything trite. As you go on in college, your awareness of clichés will grow with reading. The more you read, the easier it is to recognize a cliché on sight, for you will have met it often before.

Meanwhile, here is a list of a few clichés still in occasional circulation. If any is a favorite of yours, try replacing it with something more vivid and original.

above and beyond the call of
  duty
Achilles' heel
acid test
add insult to injury
apple of one's eye
as American as apple pie
an astronomical sum
beyond a shadow of a doubt
born with a silver spoon in one's
  mouth
bosom companions, bosom
  buddies
burn one's bridges
burn the midnight oil
busy as a beaver (or a bee)
But that's another story.
come hell or high water
cool as a cucumber
cream of the crop
cut like a knife
dead as a doornail
do your own thing
dressed fit to kill
eager beaver
easy as falling off a log
easy as taking candy from a baby
a face that would stop a clock
feeling on top of the world
few and far between
fine and dandy
fly in the ointment
from (or since) time immemorial
golden years
greased lightning
hands-on learning experience
hard as a rock
high as a kite
holler bloody murder
honest as the day is long

In conclusion, I would like
  to say . . .
in my wildest dreams
last but not least
little did I dream
make a long story short
natural inclination
neat as a pin
nutty as a fruitcake
old as the hills
on the ball
on the brink of disaster
pay through the nose
piece of cake
point with pride
proud as a peacock
pull the wool over someone's
  eyes
salad days
sell like hotcakes
a sheepish grin
since the dawn of time
skating on thin ice
a skeleton in the closet
slow as molasses
smell a rat
a sneaking suspicion
stab me in the back
stack the deck
stagger the imagination
stick out like a sore thumb
sweet as honey
That's the way the ball bounces.
through thick and thin
time-honored
tip of the iceberg
too little and too late
tried but true
You could have knocked me over
  with a feather.

21c. Use idioms in their correct form.

Every language contains *idioms,* or *idiomatic expressions:* phrases that, through long use, have become standard even though their construction may defy logic or grammar. Idioms can be difficult for a native speaker of English to explain to someone just learning the language. They sound natural, however, to those who have heard them since childhood.

Many idiomatic expressions require us to choose the right preposition. We say we live *in* the city, but vacation *at* the seashore, even though we might be hard-pressed to explain why we use *in* in one phrase and *at* in the other. To pause *for* a minute is not the same as to pause *in* a minute. We work *up* a sweat while working *out* in the gym. We argue *with* someone but *about* something. We can also argue *for* or *against* it.

For some idioms we must know which article to use before a noun — or whether to use any article at all. We can be *in motion,* but we have to be *in the swim.* We're occasionally in *a tight spot* but never in *a trouble.* Certain idioms vary from country to country: in Britain, a patient has an operation *in hospital*; in America, *in the hospital.* Idioms can involve choosing the right verb with the right noun: we *seize* an opportunity, but we *catch* a plane. We *break* a law but *explode* a theory.

Sometimes even the best writers draw a blank when they confront a common idiomatic expression. Is *compared with* or *compared to* the right phrase? Should you say *agree to, agree on,* or *agree with*? *Disgusted at* or *disgusted with*? *Smile about, smile at, smile on,* or *smile over*?

Depending on what you mean, sometimes one alternative is correct, sometimes another. When you're at work on a paper, the dictionary can help you choose. Look up *agree* in *The American Heritage Dictionary,* for instance, and you will find *agree to, agree with, agree about, agree on,* and *agree that* illustrated with sentence examples that make clear just where and when each combination is appropriate. You can then pick the idiom that belongs in the sentence you are working on. In the long run, though, you learn to use idioms accurately in your writing by reading the work of careful writers, by absorbing what they do, and by doing likewise.

EXERCISE 21–1

Selecting Words

Revise the following passage to replace inappropriate connotations, clichés, and faulty idioms. Example:

The Mayan city of Uxmal is a common tourist attraction. The ruins have stood alone in the jungle since time immemorial.

The Mayan city of Uxmal is a *popular* tourist attraction. The ruins have stood alone in the jungle since *ancient times.*

We spent the first day of our holiday in Mexico arguing around what we wanted to see on our second day. We finally agreed to a day trip out to some Mayan ruins. The next day we arrived on the Mayan city of Uxmal, which is as old as the hills. It really is a sight for sore eyes, smack dab in a jungle stretching as far as the eye can see, with many buildings still covered in plants and iguanas moving quickly over the decayed buildings. The view from the top of the Sooth-sayer's Temple was good, although we noticed storm clouds gathering in the distance. The rain held up until we got off of the pyramid, but we drove back to the hotel in a lot of rain. After a day of sightseeing, we were so hungry that we could have eaten a horse, so we had a good meal before we turned in.

22. *Bias-Free Language*

The words we use reveal our attitudes — our likes and dislikes, our preferences and prejudices. Favorable or unfavorable connotations help us to express how we feel. A *brat* is quite different from a *little angel,* a *childish prank* from an *act of vandalism,* a *jalopy* from a *limousine.*

Language with unfavorable connotations has the power to insult or hurt someone. Thoughtful writers attempt to avoid harmful bias in language. They respect their readers and don't want to insult them or make them angry. They realize that discriminatory language can impede communication. According to Rosalie Maggio, "Ordinary people have chosen to replace linguistic pejoration and disrespect with words that grant full humanity and equality to all of us."[2] You may not be able to eliminate discrimination from society, but you can eliminate discriminatory language in your writing. Be on the lookout for words that insult or stereotype individuals or groups by gender, age, race, ethnic origin, sexual preference, or religion.

Accept your inability to change the English language overnight, single-handedly. As more people come to regard themselves as equals, the language will increasingly reflect the reality. Meanwhile, in your writing, try to be fair to all individuals without succumbing either to clumsiness or to grammatical error.

22a. To eliminate sexist language, use alternatives that make no reference to gender.

Among the prime targets of American feminists in the 1960s and 1970s was the male bias built into the English language. Why, they asked, do we talk about *prehistoric man, manpower,* and *the brotherhood of man,* when by *man* we mean the entire human race? Why do we focus attention on the gender of an accomplished woman by calling her a *poetess* or a *lady doctor*? Why does a letter to a corporation have to begin "Gentlemen:"?

[2] *The Dictionary of Bias-Free Usage: A Guide to Nondiscriminatory Language* (Phoenix: Oryx, 1991) vii.

Early efforts to provide alternatives to sexist language often led to awkward, even ungrammatical solutions. To substitute "Everyone prefers their own customs" for "Everyone prefers *his* own customs" is to replace sexism with bad grammar. "Everyone prefers his or her [*or* his/her] own customs" is correct but sometimes clumsy. Even clumsier is "Was it George or Jane who submitted his or her [his/her] resignation?" *Chairperson, policeperson, businessperson, spokesperson,* and *congressperson* do not flow easily from tongue or pen; and some people object to *chairwoman, policewoman,* and similar words because they call attention to gender where gender ought not to matter. *Male nurse* or *female supervisor* elicits the same objection.

Some writers try to eliminate sexual bias by alternating between the masculine and feminine genders every few sentences. Dr. Benjamin Spock, when referring to babies in recent revisions of his well-known *Baby and Child Care,* uses *he* and *she* in roughly equal numbers. Some readers find this approach refreshing. Why should we, after all, think of every baby as a boy, every parent as a woman? Other readers find such gender switches confusing.

Well-meaning attempts to invent or borrow neutral third-person pronouns (*thon asks* instead of *he asks* or *she asks,* for instance) have not gained general acceptance. How then can we as sensitive writers minimize the sexist constraints that the English language places in our path? Although there are no hard-and-fast rules, no perfect solutions, we can be aware of the potholes and try to steer around them as smoothly as possible.

22b. Avoid terms that include or imply *man*.

We all know from experience that the most obvious way to neuter *man* or a word starting with *man* is to substitute *human*. The result, however, is often clumsy.

SEXIST   Mankind has always been obsessed with man's inhumanity to man.

NONSEXIST *Humankind* has always been obsessed with *humans'* inhumanity to other humans.

Adding *hu-* to *man* alleviates sexism but weighs down the sentence. When you run into this problem, think for a moment. Usually you can find a more graceful solution.

REVISED   *Human beings* have always been obsessed with *people's* cruelty to one another.

Similarly, when you face a word that ends with *-man,* you need not simply replace that ending with *-person*. Take a different approach: think about what the word means and find a synonym that is truly neutral.

SEXIST   Did you leave a note for the mailman?

REVISED   Did you leave a note for the *mail carrier*?

The same tactic works for designations with a male and a female ending, such as *steward* and *stewardess.*

SEXIST   Ask your steward [or stewardess] for a pillow.

REVISED   Ask your *airline attendant* for a pillow.

22c.   Use plural instead of singular.

Another way to avoid sexist language is to use the plural rather than the singular (*they* and *their* rather than *he* and *his*). This strategy sometimes has the additional benefit of avoiding an unintentional stereotype, which is always a danger when writers let a single individual stand for a large and diverse group.

SEXIST   Today's student values his education.

REVISED   Today's students value *their* education.

STEREOTYPE   The Englishman drives on the left-hand side of the road.

REVISED   *English people* drive on the left-hand side of the road.

22d.   Where possible, omit words that denote gender.

If you find yourself using words that denote gender, stop and ask yourself if the words are really necessary. You can make your language more bias-free by omitting pronouns and other words that needlessly indicate gender.

SEXIST   For optimal results, there must be rapport between a stockbroker and his client, a teacher and her student, a doctor and his patient.

REVISED   For optimal results, there must be rapport between stockbroker and *client*, teacher and *student*, doctor and *patient.*

SEXIST   My uncle is a male nurse and my aunt is a woman doctor.

REVISED   My uncle is a *nurse* and my aunt is a *doctor.*

You should also be careful to treat men and women equally in terms of description or title.

SEXIST   I now pronounce you man and wife.

REVISED   I now pronounce you *husband* and wife.

SEXIST   Please call Mr. Pease, Mr. Mankodi, and Susan Brillantes into the conference room.

REVISED   Please call Mr. Pease, Mr. Mankodi, and *Ms.* Brillantes into the conference room.

22e.   Avoid condescending labels.

A responsible writer does not call women *chicks, coeds, babes, woman drivers,* or any other names that imply that they are not to be taken seriously. Nor should an employee ever be referred to as a *girl* or *boy.* Avoid any terms that put down individuals or groups because of age (*old goat, the grannies*), race or ethnic background (*Indian giver, Chinaman's chance*), or disability (*amputee, handicapped*).

CONDESCENDING	The girls in the office bought President Schmutz a birthday cake.
REVISED	The *secretaries* bought President Schmutz a birthday cake.
CONDESCENDING	My neighbor is just an old fogy.
REVISED	My neighbor *has old-fashioned ideas*.
CONDESCENDING	I heard that the cripple who lives around the corner won the lottery.
REVISED	I heard that the *disabled person* who lives around the corner won the lottery.

When describing any group, try to use the label or term that the members of that group prefer. While the preferred label is sometimes difficult to determine, the extra effort will be appreciated.

POSSIBLY OFFENSIVE	Alice is interested in learning about Oriental culture.
REVISED	Alice is interested in learning about *Asian* culture.
POSSIBLY OFFENSIVE	Many of the Hispanics at our school speak Spanish at home.
REVISED	Many of the *Latino students* at our school speak Spanish at home.

22f.   Avoid implied stereotypes.

Sometimes a negative stereotype is linked to a title or designation indirectly. Aside from a few obvious exceptions such as *mothers* and *fathers*, never assume that all the members of a group are of the same gender.

STEREOTYPE	Pilots have little time to spend with their wives and children.
REVISED	Pilots have little time to spend with their *families*.

Sometimes we debase individuals or groups by assigning a stereotypical descriptor to them. Be alert for these widespread biases. Stereotypes that seem positive should also be avoided if they assume that all people of a certain group share a certain characteristic.

STEREOTYPE	Roberto isn't very good at paying his rent on time, which doesn't surprise me because he is from Mexico.
REVISED	Roberto isn't very good at paying his rent on time.
STEREOTYPE	I assume Ben will do very well in medical school because both of his parents are Jewish.
REVISED	I assume Ben will do very well in medical school.

22g. Use *Ms.* for a woman with no other known title.

Ms. is a wonderfully useful form of address. Comparable to *Mr.* for a man, it is easier to use than either *Miss* or *Mrs.* for someone whose marital status you don't know. Now that many married women are keeping their original last names, either professionally or in all areas of their lives, *Ms.* is often the best choice even for someone whose marital status you do know. However, if the woman to whom you are writing holds a doctorate, a professional office, or some other position that comes with a title, use that title rather than *Ms.*

Ms. Jane Doe, Editor. Dear Ms. Doe:
Professor Jane Doe, Department of English. Dear Professor Doe:
Senator Jane Doe, Washington, D.C. Dear Senator Doe:

EXERCISE 22–1

Avoiding Bias

Revise the following sentences to eliminate bias words. Possible revisions for the lettered sentences appear in the back of the book. Example:

A fireman needs to check his equipment regularly.

Firefighters need to check *their* equipment regularly.

a. My cousin volunteered as a candy striper at the old folks' home.
b. The television crew conducted a series of man-on-the-street interviews on the new tax proposal.
c. Whether the president of the United States is a Democrat or a Republican, he will always be a symbol of the nation.
d. The senator was highly regarded by voters in her district even though she was a spinster.
e. Simon drinks like an Irishman.

1. Dick drives a Porsche because he likes the way she handles on the road. He gets pretty upset at the little old ladies who slow down traffic.
2. Like most Asian Americans, Soon Li excels at music and mathematics.
3. The new doctors on our staff include Dr. Scalia, Anna Baniski, and Dr. Throckmorton.
4. Our school's extensive athletic program will be of particular interest to Black applicants.
5. The diligent researcher will always find the sources he seeks.

23. *Wordiness*

Writers who try to impress their audience by offering few ideas in many words rarely fool anyone but themselves. Concision takes more effort than wordiness, but it pays off in clarity. (For more on how to unpad your prose, see "Cutting and Whittling," p. 439.)

The following list contains common words and phrases that take up more room than they deserve. Each has a shorter substitute. If this list contains some of your favorite expressions, don't worry. Not even the best professional writer is perfectly terse. Still, being aware of verbal shortcuts may help you avoid rambling. The checklist can be useful for self-editing, particularly if you ever face a strict word limit. When you write an article for a college newspaper where space is tight, or a laboratory report that you must squeeze into a standard worksheet, or an assignment limited to six hundred words, use this list to pare your prose to the bone.

CHECKLIST OF WINDY WORDS AND PHRASES

WORDY	CONCISE
adequate enough	adequate
a period of a week	a week
approximately	about
area of, field of	[Omit.]
arrive at an agreement, conclude an agreement	agree
as a result of	because
as far as . . . is concerned	about
as to whether	whether
as you are already well aware	as you know
at an earlier point in time	before, earlier
at a later moment	after, later
join together	join
kind of, sort of, type of	[Omit.]
large in size, large-sized	large
a large number of	many
lend assistance to	assist, aid, help
make contact with	call, talk with
members of the opposition	opponents
merge together	merge
numerous	many
on the occasion of	on
on a daily basis	daily
other alternatives	alternatives
past experience, past history	experience, history
persons of the female gender	women
persons of the homosexual persuasion	homosexuals, gays, lesbians
persons of the Methodist faith	Methodists
pertaining to	about, on
plan ahead for the future	plan
prior to	before
put an end to, terminate	end
rarely ever, seldom ever	rarely, seldom
strongly urge	urge
sufficient amount of	enough
the reason why	the reason

WORDY	CONCISE
refer to by the name of	call, name
refer back to	refer to
remarks of a humorous nature, remarks on the humorous side	humorous remarks
repeat again	repeat
resemble in appearance	look like
respective, respectively	[Omit.]
returning back	returning
similar to	like
subsequent to	after
subsequently	later, then
sufficient number (or amount) of	enough
true facts	facts, truth
until such time	until
utilize, make use of	use
very	[Omit unless you need it.]
way in which	way
whether or not	whether

EXERCISE 23–1

Eliminating Wordiness

Revise the following passage to eliminate wordiness. Example:

> At this point in time, a debate pertaining to freedom of speech is raging across our campuses.

> A debate *about* freedom of speech is raging across our campuses.

The media in recent times have become obsessed with the conflict on campuses across the nation between freedom of speech and the attempt to protect minorities from verbal abuse. Very innocent remarks or remarks of a humorous nature, sometimes taken out of context, have got a large number of students into trouble for the violation of college speech codes. Numerous students have become very vocal in attacking these "politically correct" speech codes and defending the right to free speech. But is the campaign against the politically correct really pertaining to freedom of speech, or is it itself a way in which to silence debate? Due to the fact that the phrase "politically correct" has become associated with liberal social causes and sensitivity to minority feelings, it now carries a very extraordinary stigma in the eyes of conservatives. It has become a kind of condemnation against which no defense is possible. To accuse someone of being politically correct is to refute their ideas before hearing their argument. The attempt to silence the members of the opposition is a dangerous sign of our times and suggests that we are indeed in the midst of a cultural war.

Chapter 35

Punctuation

24. *End Punctuation*

Three marks can signal the end of a sentence: the period, the exclamation point, and the question mark.

24a. Use a period to end a declarative sentence, a directive, or an indirect question.

Most English sentences are *declarative*, meaning simply that they make a statement. No matter what its topic, a declarative sentence properly ends with a period.

> Most people on earth are malnourished.

> The Cadillac rounded the corner on two wheels and careened into a newsstand.

A period is also used after a *directive*, a statement telling someone to do something.

> Please send a check or money order with your application.

> Put down your weapons, and come out with your hands up.

Some readers are surprised to find a period, not a question mark, at the end of an *indirect question*. But an indirect question is really a kind of declarative sentence: it states that a question was asked or is being asked. Therefore, a period is the right way to end it.

The counselor asked Marcia why she rarely gets to class on time.

I wonder why George didn't show up.

If those sentences were written as *direct questions*, they would require a question mark.

The counselor asked, "Marcia, why do you rarely get to class on time?"

Why, I wonder, didn't George show up?

24b. Use a period after most abbreviations.

A period within a sentence shows that what precedes it has been shortened.

Dr. Hooke's plane arrived in Washington, D.C., at 8:00 P.M.

The names of most organizations (YMCA, PTA), countries (USA, UK), and people (JFK, FDR) are abbreviated without periods. Other abbreviations, such as those for academic degrees and designations of time, use periods. (See 32e.)

When an abbreviation that uses periods falls at the end of a sentence, follow it with just one period, not two.

Jim hopes to do graduate work at UCLA after receiving his B.A.

24c. Use a question mark to end a direct question.

How many angels can dance on the head of a pin?

The question mark comes at the end of the question even if the question is part of a longer declarative sentence. (See 29a for advice about punctuating indirect quotations and questions.)

"What'll I do now?" Marjorie wailed.

Only if the question is rewritten into indirect form does it end in a period.

Marjorie, wailing, wanted to know what she should do now.

You can use a question mark, also, to indicate doubt about the accuracy of a number or date.

Aristophanes, born in 450(?) B.C., became the master comic playwright of Greece's Golden Age.

Usually, however, the same purpose can be accomplished more gracefully in words:

Aristophanes, born around 450 B.C., became the master comic playwright of Greece's Golden Age.

In formal writing, avoid using a question mark to express irony or sarcasm: *her generous (?) gift*. If your doubts are worth including, state them directly: *her meager but highly publicized gift*.

24d.   Use an exclamation point to end an interjection or an urgent command.

An exclamation point signals strong, even violent, emotion. It can end any sentence that requires unusually strong emphasis.

We've struck an iceberg! We're sinking! I can't believe it! This is horrible!

It may mark the short, emphatic structure known as an *interjection*. (See 1h.)

Oh, no! Fire!

Or it may indicate an urgent directive.

Hurry up! Help me!

Because most essays appeal to readers' reason more than to their passions, you will rarely need this punctuation mark in expository writing. In newspaper parlance, exclamation points are *astonishers*. Although they can grab a reader's attention, they cannot hold it. Tossing in an exclamation point, as if it were a firecracker, is no substitute for carefully selected emphatic words and syntax.

EXERCISE 24–1

Using End Punctuation

Where appropriate, correct the end punctuation in the following sentences. Give reasons for any changes you make. Some sentences may be correct. Answers for the lettered sentences appear in the back of the book. Example:

Tom asked Cindy if she would be willing to edit his research paper?

Tom asked Cindy if she would be willing to edit his research paper. [Not a direct question]

a. The question that still troubles the community after all these years is why federal agents did not act sooner?
b. We will ask him if he will help us build the canoe.
c. I wonder what he was thinking at the time?

   d. One man, who suffered a broken leg, was rescued when he was heard screaming, "Help me. Help me."
   e. If the suspect is convicted, will lawyers appeal the case?

   1. What will Brad and Emilia do if they can't have their vacations at the same time.
   2. When a tree falls in a forest, but no one hears it, does it make a sound.
   3. If you have a chance to see the new John Sayles film, you should do so. The acting is first-rate!
   4. What will happen next is anyone's guess.
   5. On what day does the fall term begin.

25. *The Comma*

Speech without pauses would be hard to listen to. Likewise, writing without commas would make hard reading. Like a split-second pause in conversation, a *comma* helps your readers to catch the train of your thought. It keeps them, time and again, from stumbling over a solid block of words. A comma can direct readers' attention, pointing them to what you want them to notice. And a well-placed comma can prevent misreading: it keeps your audience from drawing an inaccurate conclusion about what you are trying to tell them.

Consider the following sentence:

Lyman paints fences and bowls.

From this statement, we can deduce that Lyman is a painter who works with both a large and a small brush. But add commas before and after *fences* and the portrait changes:

Lyman paints, fences, and bowls.

Now our man wields a paintbrush, a sword, and a bowling ball. What the reader learns about Lyman's activities depends on how the writer punctuates the sentence. Carefully placed commas prevent misreading and ensure that readers meet the real Lyman.

Editing for comma usage is also covered in the "Quick Editing Guide." (For more help, see C1.)

25a.   Use a comma with a coordinating conjunction to join two main clauses.

The joint between main clauses has two parts: a coordinating conjunction (*and, but, for, or, nor, so,* or *yet*) and a comma. The comma comes after the first clause, right before the conjunction.

The chocolate pie whooshed through the air, and it landed in Lyman's face.

The pie whooshed with deadly aim, but the agile Lyman ducked.

If your clauses are short and parallel in structure, you may omit the comma.

Spring passed and summer came.

They urged but I refused.

Or you may keep the comma. It can lend your words a speechlike ring, throwing a bit of emphasis on your second clause.

Spring passed, and summer came.

They urged, but I refused.

CAUTION: Don't use a comma with a coordinating conjunction that links two phrases or that links a phrase and a clause.

FAULTY   The mustangs galloped, and cavorted across the plain.

REVISED   The mustangs galloped and cavorted across the plain.

25b.   Use a comma after an introductory clause, phrase, or word.

Weeping, Lydia stumbled down the stairs.

Before that, Arthur saw her reading an old love letter.

If he knew who the writer was, he didn't tell.

Placed after any such opening word, phrase, or subordinate clause, a comma tells your reader, "Enough preliminaries: now the main clause starts." (See 3 for a quick refresher on phrases and clauses.)

EXCEPTION: You need not use a comma after a single introductory word or a short phrase or clause if there is no danger of misreading.

Sooner or later Lydia will tell us the whole story.

EXERCISE 25–1

Using Commas

Add any necessary commas to the following sentences, and remove any commas that do not belong. Some sentences may be correct. Answers for the lettered sentences appear in the back of the book. Example:

Your dog may have sharp teeth but my lawyer can bite harder.

Your dog may have sharp teeth, but my lawyer can bite harder.

a. When Verity gets to Paris I hope she'll drop me a line.
b. Beethoven's deafness kept him from hearing his own music yet he continued to compose.
c. Adrian plans to apply for a grant, and if her application is accepted, she intends to spend a year in Venezuela.
d. The cherries are overripe for picking has been delayed.

e. Antonio expected Minnesota to be cold, but was unprepared for the frigid temperatures of his first winter there.

1. During the summer of the great soybean failure Larry took little interest in national affairs.
2. Unaware of the world he slept and grew within his mother's womb.
3. While across the nation farmers were begging for mortgages he swam without a care.
4. Neither the mounting agricultural crisis, nor any other current events, disturbed his tranquillity.
5. In fact you might have called him irresponsible.

25c.   Use a comma between items in a series.

When you list three or more items, whether they are nouns, verbs, adjectives, adverbs, or entire phrases or clauses, separate them with commas.

Country ham, sweet corn, tacos, bratwurst, and Indian pudding weighted Aunt Gertrude's table.

Joel prefers music that shakes, rattles, and rolls.

In one afternoon, we rode a Mississippi riverboat, climbed the Matterhorn, voyaged beneath the sea, and flew on a rocket through space.

Notice that no comma *follows* the final item in the series.

NOTE: Some writers (especially Britons and journalists) omit the comma *before* the final item in the series. This custom has no noticeable advantage. It has the disadvantages of throwing off the rhythm of a sentence and, in some cases, obscuring the writer's meaning. Using the comma in such a case is never wrong; omitting it can create confusion.

I was met at the station by my cousins, brother and sister.

Who are these people? Are they a brother-and-sister pair who are the writer's cousins or a group consisting of the writer's cousins, her brother, and her sister? If they are in fact more than two people, a comma would clear up the confusion.

I was met at the station by my cousins, brother, and sister.

25d.   Use a comma between coordinate adjectives but not between cumulative adjectives.

Adjectives that function independently of each other, even though they modify the same noun, are called **coordinate adjectives.** Set them off with commas.

Ruth was a clear, vibrant, persuasive speaker.

Life is nasty, brutish, and short.

CAUTION: Don't use a comma after the final adjective before a noun.

FAULTY   My economics professor was a wonderful, brilliant, caring, teacher.

REVISED   My economics professor was a wonderful, brilliant, caring teacher.

To check whether adjectives are coordinate, apply two tests. Can you re-arrange the adjectives without distorting the meaning of the sentence? (*Ruth was a persuasive, vibrant, clear speaker.*) Can you insert *and* between them? (*Life is nasty and brutish and short.*)

If the answer to both questions is yes, the adjectives are coordinate. Removing any one of them would not greatly affect the others' impact. Use commas between them to show that they are separate and equal.

NOTE: If you choose to link coordinate adjectives with *and* or another conjunction, omit the commas.

New York City is huge and dirty and beautiful.

Cumulative adjectives work together to create a single unified picture of the noun they modify. Remove any one of them and you change the picture. No commas separate cumulative adjectives.

Ruth has two small white poodles.

Who's afraid of the big bad wolf?

If you rearrange cumulative adjectives or insert *and* between them, the effect of the sentence is distorted (*two white small poodles; the big and bad wolf*).

EXERCISE 25–2

Using Commas

Add any necessary commas to the following sentences, remove any commas that do not belong, and change any punctuation that is incorrect. Some sentences may be correct. Answers for the lettered sentences appear in the back of the book. Example:

Mel has been a faithful hardworking consistent pain in the neck.

Mel has been a faithful, hardworking, consistent pain in the neck.

a. Mrs. Carver looks like a sweet, little, old lady, but she plays a wicked electric guitar.
b. Her bass player, her drummer and her keyboard player all live at the same rest home.
c. They practice individually in the afternoon, rehearse together at night and play at the home's Saturday night dances.
d. The Rest Home Rebels have to rehearse quietly, and cautiously, to keep from disturbing the other residents.
e. Mrs. Carver has two Fender guitars, a Stratocaster and a Telecaster, and she also has an acoustic twelve-string Gibson.

1. When she breaks a string, she doesn't want her elderly crew to have to grab the guitar change the string and hand it back to her, before the song ends.
2. The Rest Home Rebels' favorite bands are U2, the Talking Heads and Lester Lanin and his orchestra.
3. They watch a lot of MTV because it is fast-paced colorful exciting and informative and it has more variety than soap operas.
4. Just once, Mrs. Carver wants to play in a really, huge, sold-out, arena.
5. She hopes to borrow the rest home's big, white, van to take herself her band and their equipment to a major, professional, downtown, recording studio.

25e.   Use commas to set off a nonrestrictive phrase or clause.

A *nonrestrictive modifier* adds a fact that, while perhaps interesting and valuable, isn't essential. You could leave it out of the sentence and still make good sense. When a word in your sentence is modified by a nonrestrictive phrase or clause, set off the modifier with commas before and after it.

> Potts Alley, *which runs north from Chestnut Street,* is too narrow and crowded for cars to get through.

> At the end of the alley, *where the street fair book sale was held last summer,* a getaway car waited.

A *restrictive modifier* is essential. Omit it and you significantly change the meaning of both the modified word and the sentence. Such a modifier is called *restrictive* because it limits what it modifies: we are talking about this specific place, person, action, or whatever, and no other. Because a restrictive modifier is part of the identity of whatever it modifies, no commas set it off from the rest of the sentence.

> They picked the alley *that runs north from Chestnut Street* because it is close to the highway.

> Anyone *who robs my house* will regret it.

Leave out the modifier in that last sentence — write instead *Anyone will regret it* — and you change the meaning of your subject from potential robbers to all humankind.

Here are two more examples to help you tell a nonrestrictive modifier, which you set off with commas, from a restrictive modifier, which you don't.

> Germans, who smoke, live to be 120.

> Germans who smoke live to be 120.

See what a difference a couple of commas make? The first sentence declares that all Germans smoke, but they nevertheless live to old age. The second sentence singles out smokers from the rest of the population and declares that they reach age 120.

NOTE: Use *that* to introduce (or to recognize) a restrictive phrase or clause. Use *which* to introduce (or to recognize) a nonrestrictive phrase or clause.

The food *that I love best* is chocolate.

Chocolate, *which I love,* is not on my diet.

25f. Use commas to set off nonrestrictive appositives.

An ***appositive*** is a noun or noun phrase that renames or amplifies the noun it follows. (See 3d.) Like the modifiers discussed in 25e, an appositive can be either restrictive or nonrestrictive. If it is nonrestrictive — if the sentence still makes sense when the appositive is omitted or changed — then set it off with commas before and after.

My third ex-husband, *Hugo,* will be glad to meet you.

We are bringing dessert, *a blueberry pie,* to follow your wonderful dinner.

Hugo created the recipe for his latest cookbook, *Pies! Surprise!*

If the appositive is restrictive — if you can't take it out or change it without changing your meaning — then include it without commas.

Of all the men I've been married to, my ex-husband *Hugo* is the best cook.

His cookbook *Pies! Surprise!* is selling better than his beef, wine, and fruit cookbooks.

EXERCISE 25–3

Using Commas

Add any necessary commas to the following sentences, and remove any commas that do not belong. You may have to draw your own conclusions about what the writer meant to say. Some sentences may be correct. Possible revisions for the lettered sentences appear in the back of the book. Example:

Jay and his wife the former Laura McCready were high school sweethearts.

Jay and his wife, the former Laura McCready, were high school sweethearts.

a. The aye-aye which is a member of the lemur family is threatened with extinction.
b. The party, a dismal occasion ended earlier than we had expected.
c. Secretary Stern warned that the concessions, that the West was prepared to make, would be withdrawn if not matched by the East.
d. Although both of Don's children are blond, his daughter Sharon has darker hair than his son Jake.
e. Herbal tea which has no caffeine makes a better after-dinner drink than coffee.

1. The colony, that the English established at Roanoke disappeared mysteri-ously.
2. If the base commanders had checked their gun room where powder is stored, they would have found several hundred pounds missing.
3. Brazil's tropical rain forests which help produce the air we breathe all over the world, are being cut down at an alarming rate.
4. Senator Edward Kennedy's late brothers, Joe and Jack, were older than his third brother, Bobby.
5. Excavations have revealed that Paris which was a thriving Roman town de-veloped on the Île de la Cité an island in the Seine.

25g. Use commas to set off conjunctive adverbs.

A key function of the comma, as you probably have noticed, is to insert ma-terial into a sentence. To perform this service, commas work in pairs. When you drop a conjunctive adverb such as *furthermore, however,* or *nevertheless* into the middle of a clause, set it off with commas before and after it. (See 1g for a full list of conjunctive adverbs.)

Using lead paint in homes has been illegal, *however*, since 1973.

Builders, *indeed*, gave it up some twenty years earlier.

25h. Use commas to set off parenthetical expressions.

Use a pair of commas around any parenthetical expression — that is, a transi-tional expression (*for example, as a result, in contrast*) or any kind of aside from you to your readers.

Professional home inspectors, *for this reason*, are often asked to test for lead paint.

The idea, *of course*, is to protect small children who might eat flaking paint.

The Cosmic Construction Company never used lead paint, *or so their spokesperson says*, even when it was legal.

25i. Use commas to set off a phrase or clause expressing contrast.

It was Rudolph, *not Dasher*, who had a red nose.

EXCEPTION: Short contrasting phrases beginning with *but* need not be set off by commas.

It was not Dasher but Rudolph who had a red nose.

25j. Use commas to set off an absolute phrase.

An *absolute phrase* modifies an entire clause rather than a single word. (See 3c.) The link between an absolute phrase and the rest of the sentence is a comma, or two commas if the phrase falls in midsentence.

Our worst fears drawing us together, we huddled over the telegram.

Luke, *his knife being the sharpest,* slit the envelope.

EXERCISE 25–4

Using Commas

Add any necessary commas to the following sentences, and change any punctuation that is incorrect. Answers for the lettered sentences appear in the back of the book. Example:

> The officer a radar gun in his hand gauged the speed of the passing cars.
>
> The officer, a radar gun in his hand, gauged the speed of the passing cars.

a. The university insisted however that the students were not accepted merely because of their parents' generous contributions.
b. This dispute in any case is an old one.
c. It was the young man's striking good looks not his acting ability that first attracted the Hollywood agents.
d. Gretchen learned moreover not to always accept as true what she had read in textbooks.
e. The hikers most of them wearing ponchos or rain jackets headed out into the steady drizzle.

1. The lawsuit demanded furthermore that construction already under way be halted immediately.
2. It is the Supreme Court not Congress or the president that ultimately determines the legality of a law.
3. The judge complained that the case was being tried not by the court but by the media.
4. The actor kneeling recited the lines with great emotion.
5. Both sides' patience running thin workers and management carried the strike into its sixth week.

25k. Use commas to set off a direct quotation from your own words.

When you briefly quote someone, distinguish the source's words from yours with commas (and, of course, quotation marks). When you insert an explanation into a quotation (such as *he said*), set that off with commas.

> Shakespeare wrote, "Some are born great, some achieve greatness, and some have greatness thrust upon them."

> "The best thing that can come with success," commented the actress Liv Ullmann, "is the knowledge that it is nothing to long for."

Notice that the comma always comes *before* the quotation marks. (For more on how to use other punctuation with quotation marks, see 29h and 29i.)

EXCEPTION: Do not use a comma with a very short quotation or one introduced by *that*.

Don't tell me "yes" if you mean "maybe."

Jules said that "Nothing ventured, nothing gained" is his motto.

Don't use a comma with any quotation that is run into your own sentence and that reads as part of your sentence. Often such quotations are introduced by linking verbs.

Her favorite statement at age three was "I can do it myself."

It was Shakespeare who originated the expression "my salad days, when I was green in judgment."

25l. Use commas around *yes* and *no,* mild interjections, tag questions, and the name or title of someone directly addressed.

YES AND NO	*Yes,* I would like to own a Rolls-Royce, but, *no,* I didn't place an order for one.
INTERJECTION	*Well,* don't blame it on me.
TAG QUESTION	It would be fun to drive down Main Street in a Silver Cloud, *wouldn't it?*
DIRECT ADDRESS	Drive us home, *James.*

25m. Use commas to set off dates, states, countries, and addresses.

On June 6, 1969, Ned Shaw was born.

East Rutherford, New Jersey, seemed like Paris, France, to him.

Shortly after his tenth birthday his family moved to 11 Maple Street, Middletown, Ohio.

NOTE: Do not use a comma between a state and a zip code: *Bedford, MA 01730.*

EXERCISE 25–5

Using Commas

Add any necessary commas to the following sentences, remove any commas that do not belong, and change any punctuation that is incorrect. Some sentences may be correct. Answers for the lettered sentences appear in the back of the book. Example:

When Alexander Graham Bell said "Mr. Watson come here, I want you" the telephone entered history.

When Alexander Graham Bell said, "Mr. Watson, come here, I want you," the telephone entered history.

a. On October 2 1969 the future discoverer of antigravity tablets was born.
b. Corwin P. Grant entered the world while his parents were driving to a hospital in Costa Mesa California.
c. The car radio was playing that old song "Be My Baby."
d. Today ladies and gentlemen Corwin enjoys worldwide renown.
e. Schoolchildren from Augusta Maine to Azuza California can recite his famous comment "It was my natural levity that led me to overcome gravity."

1. Yes I was born on April 14 1973 in Bombay India.
2. Move downstage Gary, for Pete's sake or you'll run into Mrs. Clackett.
3. Vicki my precious, when you say, "great" or "terrific," look as though you mean it.
4. Perhaps you have forgotten darling that sometimes you make mistakes, too.
5. Well Dotty, it only makes sense that when you say, "Sardines!," you should go off to get the sardines.

25n. Do not use a comma to separate a subject from its verb or a verb from its object.

FAULTY   The slim athlete driving the purple Jaguar, was the Reverend Mr. Fuld. [Subject separated from verb]

REVISED   The slim athlete driving the purple Jaguar was the Reverend Mr. Fuld.

FAULTY   The new president should not have given his campaign manager, such a prestigious appointment. [Verb separated from direct object]

REVISED   The new president should not have given his campaign manager such a prestigious appointment.

25o. Do not use a comma between words or phrases joined by correlative or coordinating conjunctions.

Be careful not to divide a compound subject or predicate unnecessarily with a comma.

FAULTY   Neither Peter Pan, nor the fairy Tinkerbell, saw the pirates sneaking toward their hideout. [Compound subject]

REVISED   Neither Peter Pan nor the fairy Tinkerbell saw the pirates sneaking toward their hideout.

FAULTY   The chickens clucked, and pecked, and flapped their wings. [Compound predicate]

REVISED   The chickens clucked and pecked and flapped their wings.

25p. Do not use a comma before the first or after the last item in a series.

> FAULTY   We had to see, my mother's doctor, my father's lawyer, and my dog's veterinarian, in one afternoon.

> REVISED   We had to see my mother's doctor, my father's lawyer, and my dog's veterinarian in one afternoon.

25q. Do not use a comma to set off a restrictive word, phrase, or clause.

A restrictive modifier is essential to the definition or identification of whatever it modifies; a nonrestrictive modifier is not. If you are not sure whether an element in your sentence is restrictive, review 25e.

> FAULTY   The fireworks, that I saw on Sunday, were the best ones I've ever seen.

> REVISED   The fireworks that I saw on Sunday were the best ones I've ever seen.

25r. Do not use commas to set off indirect quotations.

When *that* introduces a quotation, the quotation is an indirect one and requires neither a comma nor quotation marks.

> FAULTY   He told us that, we shouldn't have done it.

> REVISED   He told us that we shouldn't have done it.

This sentence also would be correct if it were recast as a direct quotation, with a comma and quotation marks.

> FAULTY   He told us that, "You shouldn't have done it."

> REVISED   He told us, "You shouldn't have done it."

EXERCISE 25–6

Comma Review

Revise the following passage, adding any necessary commas, removing any commas that do not belong, and changing any punctuation that is incorrect. Example:

Everyone knows the myth of Atlantis the island, that sank beneath the waves.

Everyone knows the myth of Atlantis, the island that sank beneath the waves.

Like many old legends, the myth of Atlantis may be a distant memory of a historical event — the volcanic eruption of Thera a Greek island in 1628 B.C.E. Thera which is located in the eastern Mediterranean had trading connections with Crete the center of Minoan civilization. The Minoans had created one of the most sophisticated, affluent and influential civilizations in the world. Minoan influence and trade reached, Egypt, Cyprus and the Levant and the people of Thera where the eruption occurred also had important trading links with the Minoans. With plenty of warning of the coming explosion the inhabitants of Thera fled the island never to return. The eruption of Thera, resulted in the decline of Minoan civilization or so it is believed because of the tidal waves that damaged Minoan ports. The fame of Minoan power however endured. The civilization that dominated the Mediterranean became legendary and out of these myths developed the story of Atlantis the sophisticated wealthy and powerful island that sank beneath the sea.

26. *The Semicolon*

A semicolon is a sort of compromise between a comma and a period: it creates a stop without ending a sentence.

26a. Use a semicolon to join two main clauses not joined by a coordinating conjunction.

Suppose, having written one statement, you want to add another. You could start a new sentence, but let's say that both statements are closely related in sense. You decide to keep them both in a single sentence.

> Shooting clay pigeons was my mother's favorite sport; she would smash them for hours at a time.

A semicolon is a good substitute for a period when you don't want to bring your readers to a complete stop.

> By the yard life is hard; by the inch it's a cinch.

> I never travel without my diary; one should always have something sensational to read in the train.

Remember that usually when you join two statements with a coordinating conjunction (*and, but, for, or, nor, so, yet*), no semicolon is called for: just use a comma. (For exceptions to this general rule, see 26d.)

26b. Use a semicolon to join two main clauses that are linked by a conjunctive adverb.

When the second of two statements begins with (or includes) a conjunctive adverb, you can join it to the first statement with a semicolon. Common conjunctive adverbs include *also, consequently, however, indeed, nevertheless, still, therefore,* and *thus.* (For a complete list, see 1g.)

> Bert is a stand-out player; *indeed,* he's the one hope of our team.

> We yearned to attend the concert; tickets, *however,* were hard to come by.

Note in the second sentence that the conjunctive adverb falls within the second main clause. No matter where the conjunctive adverb appears, the semicolon is placed between the two clauses.

26c. Use a semicolon to separate items in a series that contain internal punctuation or that are long and complex.

The semicolon is especially useful for setting off one group of items from another. More powerful than a comma, it divides a series of series.

> The auctioneer sold clocks, watches, and cameras; freezers of steaks and tons of bean sprouts; motorcycles, cars, speedboats, canoes, and cabin cruisers; and rare coins, curious stamps, and precious stones.

If the writer had used commas in place of semicolons in that sentence, the divisions would have been harder to notice.

Commas are not the only internal punctuation that warrants the extra force of semicolons between items.

> The auctioneer sold clocks and watches (with or without hands); freezers of steaks and tons of bean sprouts; trucks and motorcycles (some of which had working engines); and dozens of smaller items.

26d. Use a semicolon to separate main clauses that are long and complex or that contain internal punctuation.

The semicolon also separates the clauses in a long sentence of two or more clauses, at least one of which contains internal punctuation.

> Though we had grown up together, laughing and playing like brother and sister, I had never regarded Spike as a possible lover; and his abrupt proposal took me by surprise.

In that sentence, an important break between clauses needs a mark stronger than a comma to give it impact. A semicolon is appropriate, even though it stands before a coordinating conjunction — where, ordinarily, a comma would suffice.

You can see the difference between a compound sentence joined with a comma and one joined with a semicolon in these examples:

> Captain Bob planned the hog-riding contest for Thursday, but it rained.

> Captain Bob, that old cynic, planned the hog-riding contest for Thursday despite a ban by the city council; but it rained.

You would not be wrong if you kept the original comma between clauses in the second sentence. The sentence is easier to read, however, with a semicolon at its main intersection.

A semicolon can do the same job for clauses that contain internal punctuation other than commas.

Captain Bob—that cynical crowd assembler—planned the hog-riding contest for Thursday (although the city council had banned such events); but it rained.

You also can use a semicolon with a coordinating conjunction to link clauses that have no internal punctuation but that are long and complex.

The powers behind Her Majesty's secret service occasionally deem it advisable to terminate the infiltrations of an enemy agent by ending his life; and in such cases they generally call on James Bond.

26e. Use a comma, not a semicolon, to separate a phrase or subordinate clause from the rest of a sentence.

Remember that a semicolon has the force of a period; its job is to create a strong pause in a sentence, especially between main clauses. When your purpose is simply to add a phrase to a clause, use a comma, not a semicolon.

FAULTY   The road is long; winding through many towns.

REVISED   The road is long, winding through many towns.

Similarly, use a comma, not a semicolon, to join a subordinate clause to a main clause.

FAULTY   Columbus sailed unknowingly toward the New World; while Ferdinand and Isabella waited for news from China.

REVISED   Columbus sailed unknowingly toward the New World, while Ferdinand and Isabella waited for news from China.

EXERCISE 26–1

Using Semicolons

Add any necessary semicolons to the following sentences, and change any that are incorrectly used. Some sentences may be correct. Answers for the lettered sentences appear in the back of the book. Example:

They had used up all their money, they barely had enough left for the train trip home.

They had used up all their money; they barely had enough left for the train trip home.

a. By the beginning of 1993, Shirley was eager to retire, nevertheless, she agreed to stay on for two more years.
b. In 1968 Lyndon Johnson abandoned his hopes for reelection; because of fierce opposition from within his own party.
c. The committee was asked to determine the extent of violent crime among teenagers, especially those between the ages of fourteen and sixteen, to act as a liaison between the city and schools and between churches and volunteer organizations, and to draw up a plan to significantly reduce violence, both public and private, by the end of the century.

   d. The leaves on the oak trees near the lake were tinged with red, swimmers no longer ventured into the water.

   e. The football team has yet to win a game, however, the season is still young.

1. Although taking the subway is slow, it is still faster than driving to work.
2. When the harpist began to play; the bride and her father prepared to walk down the aisle.
3. The Mariners lost all three games to Milwaukee, worse yet, two star players were injured.
4. There was nothing the firefighters could do; the building already had been consumed by flames.
5. Chess is difficult to master; but even a small child can learn the basic rules.

27. *The Colon*

A colon introduces a further thought, one added to throw light on a first. In using it, a writer declares: "What follows will clarify what I've just said."

> Her Majesty's navy has three traditions: rum, sodomy, and the lash.
> — Winston Churchill

Some writers use a capital letter to start any complete sentence that follows a colon; others prefer a lowercase letter. Both habits are acceptable; but whichever you choose, be consistent. A *phrase* that follows a colon always begins with a lowercase letter.

27a. Use a colon between two main clauses if the second exemplifies, explains, or summarizes the first.

Like a semicolon, a colon can join two sentences into one. The chief difference is this: a semicolon says merely that two main clauses are related; a colon says that the second clause gives an example or explanation of the point made in the first clause. You can think of a colon as an abbreviation for *that is* or *for example.*

> Mayor Curley was famed as a silver-tongued orator: it is said that, with a few well-chosen words, he could extract campaign contributions from a mob intent on seeing him hanged.

> She tried everything: she scoured the library, made dozens of phone calls, wrote letters, even consulted a lawyer.

27b. Use a colon to introduce a list or a series.

A colon can introduce a word, a phrase, or a series as well as a second main clause. Sometimes the introduction is made stronger by *as follows* or *the following.*

The dance steps are as follows: forward, back, turn, and glide.

Engrave the following truth upon your memory: a colon is always constructed of two dots.

When a colon introduces a series of words or phrases, it often means *such as* or *for instance*. A list of examples after a colon need not include *and* before the last item unless all possible examples have been stated.

On a Saturday night many different kinds of people crowd our downtown area: gamblers, drifters, bored senior citizens, college students out for a good time.

27c.   Use a colon to introduce an appositive.

An *appositive* is a noun or noun phrase that renames another noun. A colon can introduce an appositive when the colon is preceded by an independent clause.

I have discovered the key to the future: plastics.

27d.   Use a colon to introduce a long or comma-filled quotation.

Sometimes you can't conveniently introduce a quoted passage with a comma. Perhaps the quotation is too long or heavily punctuated; perhaps your prefatory remarks demand a longer pause than a comma provides. In either case, use a colon.

God told Adam and Eve: "Be fruitful, and multiply, and replenish the earth, and subdue it."

27e.   Use a colon when convention calls for it.

AFTER A SALUTATION	Dear Professor James: Dear Sir or Madam:
BIBLICAL CITATIONS	Genesis 4:7 [The book of Genesis, chapter four, seventh verse]
BOOK TITLES AND SUBTITLES	*Convergences: Essays on Art and Literature* *In the Beginning: Creation Stories from around the World*
SOURCE REFERENCES	Welty, Eudora. *The Eye of the Story: Selected Essays and Reviews.* New York: Random, 1978.
TIME OF DAY	2:02 P.M.

27f.   Use a colon only at the end of a main clause.

In a sentence, a colon always follows a clause, never a phrase. Avoid using a colon between a verb and its object, between a preposition and its object, and before a list introduced by *such as*. Any time you are in doubt about whether to use a colon, first make sure that the preceding statement is a complete sentence. Then you will not litter your writing with unnecessary colons.

FAULTY   My mother and father are: Jill and Jim.

REVISED   My mother and father are Jill and Jim.

FAULTY   Many great inventors have changed our lives, such as: Edison, Marconi, and Hymie Glutz.

REVISED   Many great inventors have changed our lives, such as Edison, Marconi, and Hymie Glutz.

REVISED   Many great inventors have changed our lives: Edison, Marconi, Hymie Glutz.

Use either *such as* or a colon. You don't need both.

EXERCISE 27–1

Using Colons

Add, remove, or replace colons wherever appropriate in the following sentences. Where necessary, revise the sentences further to support your changes in punctuation. Some sentences may be correct. Possible revisions for the lettered sentences appear in the back of the book. Example:

Yum-Yum Burger has franchises in the following cities; New York, Chicago, Miami, San Francisco, and Seattle.

Yum-Yum Burger has franchises in the following cities: New York, Chicago, Miami, San Francisco, and Seattle.

a. The Continuing Education Program offers courses in: building and construction management, engineering, and design.
b. The interview ended with a test of skills, taking dictation, operating the switchboard, proofreading documents, and typing a sample letter.
c. The sample letter began, "Dear Mr. Rasheed, Please accept our apologies for the late shipment."
d. Constance quoted Proverbs 8, 18: "Riches and honor are with me."
e. A book that profoundly impressed me was Kurt Vonnegut's *Cat's Cradle* (New York, Dell, 1963).

1. The following rhyme was written in the eighteenth century for the collar of the king's dog at Kew Gardens, London, "I AM his Highness' Dog at Kew; / Pray, tell me Sir, whose Dog are you?"
2. If you go to the beach this summer, remember these three rules: wear plenty of sunscreen, eat plenty of fruit to replace lost fluids, and avoid exposure during the hottest hours of the day.
3. These are my dreams, to ride in a horse-drawn sleigh, to fly in a small plane, to gallop down a beach on horseback, and to cross the ocean in a sailboat.
4. In the case of *Bowers v. Hardwick*, the Supreme Court decided that: citizens had no right to sexual privacy.

5. Paris at night presents an array of characters; sidewalk artists, jugglers, and dancers; rap musicians and one-man bands; hippies, bohemians, and amazed tourists.
6. He ended his speech with a quotation from Homer's *Iliad*, "Whoever obeys the gods, to him they particularly listen."
7. To get onto Route 6: take Bay Lane to Old Stage Road, turn right, and go straight to the end.
8. Professor Bligh's book is called *Management, A Networking Approach*.
9. George handed Cynthia a note, "Meet me after class under the big clock on Main Street."
10. Rosa expected to arrive at 4.10, but she didn't get there until 4.20.

28. *The Apostrophe*

Use apostrophes for three purposes: to show possession, to indicate an omission, and to add an ending to a number, letter, or abbreviation. Editing for apostrophe usage is also covered in the "Quick Editing Guide." (For more help, see C2.)

28a. To make a singular noun possessive, add -'s.

The *plumber's* wrench left grease stains on *Harry's* shirt.

Even when your singular noun ends with the sound of *s*, form its possessive case by adding -'s.

Felix's roommate enjoys reading *Henry James's* novels.

Some writers find it awkward to add -'s to nouns that already end in an -s, especially those of two syllables or more. You may, if you wish, form such a possessive by adding only an apostrophe.

The Egyptian king *Cheops'* death occurred more than two thousand years before *Socrates'*.

28b. To make a plural noun ending in -s possessive, add an apostrophe.

A *stockbrokers'* meeting combines *foxes'* cunning with the noisy chaos of a *boys'* locker room.

28c. To make a plural noun not ending in -s possessive, add -'s.

Nouns such as *men, mice, geese,* and *alumni* form the possessive case the same way as singular nouns: with -'s.

What effect has the *women's* liberation movement had on *children's* literature?

28d. To show joint possession by two people or groups, add an apostrophe or -'s to the second noun of the pair.

> I left my *mother and father's* house with our *friends and neighbors'* good wishes.

If the two members of a noun pair possess a set of things individually, add an apostrophe or -'s to each noun.

> *Men's* and *women's* marathon records are improving steadily.

28e. To make a compound noun possessive, add an apostrophe or -'s to the last word in the compound.

A compound noun consists of more than one word (*commander in chief, sons-in-law*); it may be either singular or plural. (See 37a–5 for plurals of compound words.)

> The *commander in chief's* duties will end on July 1.

> Esther does not approve of her *sons-in-law's* professions, but she is glad to see her daughters happily married.

28f. To make an indefinite pronoun possessive, add -'s.

Indefinite pronouns such as *anyone, nobody,* and *another* are usually singular in meaning, so they form the possessive case the same way as singular nouns: with -'s. (See 28a.)

> What caused the accident is *anybody's* guess; but it appears to be *no one's* fault.

28g. To indicate the possessive of a personal pronoun, use its possessive case.

The personal pronouns — *I, me, he, she, it, him, her, we, us, they, them,* and *who* — are irregular; each has its own possessive form. No possessive personal pronoun contains an apostrophe. If you are ever tempted to make a personal pronoun possessive by adding an apostrophe or -'s, resist the temptation.

NOTE: If you learn nothing else this year, learn when to write *its* (no apostrophe) and when to write *it's* (with an apostrophe). *Its* is always a possessive pronoun.

> I retreated when the Murphys' German shepherd bared *its* fangs.

It's is always a contraction.

> *It's* [It is] not our fault.

> *It's* [It has] been a memorable evening.

28h. Use an apostrophe to indicate an omission in a contraction.

They're [They are] too sophisticated for me.

I've [I have] learned my lesson.

Pat *didn't* [did not] finish her assignment.

Bill's [Bill has] been in jail for a week.

Americans grow up admiring the Spirit of *'76* [1776].

It's nearly eight *o'clock* [of the clock].

When you are presented to the Queen, say "Your Majesty"; after that, say "*Ma'am*" [Madam].

28i. Use an apostrophe to form the plural of an abbreviation and of a letter, word, or number mentioned as a word.

ABBREVIATION Do we need I.D.'s at YMCA's outside our hometown?

LETTER How many *n*'s are there in *Cincinnati*?

WORD Try replacing all the *should*'s in that sentence with *could*'s.

NUMBER Cut out two *3*'s to sew on Larry's shirt.

NOTE: A letter, word, or number named as a word is usually italicized (underlined).

EXCEPTION: To refer to the years in a decade, simply add *-s* without an apostrophe.

The 1980s differed greatly from the 1970s.

Apostrophes and Plural Nouns

Using apostrophes with plural nouns may cause confusion for writers because both plural nouns and possessive nouns often end with *-s*. To avoid confusion in your writing, remember that *plural* means more than one (two *dogs*, six *friends*) but *possessive* means ownership (the *dogs'* biscuits, my *friends'* cars). If you can substitute the word *of* instead of the *-s* and apostrophe (the biscuits *of* the dog, the cars *of* my friends), you need the plural possessive with an apostrophe after the *-s*. If you cannot substitute *of*, you need the simple plural with no apostrophe (the *dogs* are well fed, my *friends* have no *money for gas*).

Using the Apostrophe

Correct any errors in the use of the apostrophe in the following sentences. Some sentences may be correct. Answers for the lettered sentences appear in the back of the book. Example:

> Youd better put on you're new shoes.
>
> *You'd* better put on *your* new shoes.

a. Its not easy to be old in our society.
b. I dont understand the Jameses's objections to our plans for a block party.
c. Its not fair that you're roommate wont help with the cleaning.
d. Is this collection of 50's records your's or your roommates?
e. Alas, Brian got two Ds on his report card.

1. Joe and Chucks' fathers were both in the class of 53.
2. They're going to finish their term papers as soon as the party ends.
3. It was a strange coincidence that all three womens' cars broke down after they had picked up their mothers-in-law.
4. Dont forget to dot you're is and cross you're ts.
5. Mario and Shelley's son is marrying the editor's in chief's daughter.
6. The Hendersons' never change: their always whining about Mr. Scobee farming land thats rightfully their's.
7. Its hard to join a womens' basketball team because so few of them exist.
8. I had'nt expected to hear Janice' voice again.
9. Don't give the Murphy's dog it's biscuit until it's sitting up.
10. Isnt' it the mother and fathers' job to teach kid's to mind their *p*s and *q*s?

29. *Quotation Marks*

Quotation marks always come in pairs: one at the start and one at the finish of a quoted passage. In the United States, the double quotation mark (") is preferred over the single one (') for most uses. Use quotation marks to set off a quoted or highlighted word or words from the rest of your text.

> "Injustice anywhere is a threat to justice everywhere," wrote Martin Luther King Jr.

29a. Use quotation marks around direct quotations from another writer or speaker.

You can enrich the content, language, and authority of your writing by occasionally quoting a source whose ideas support your own. When you do this, you owe credit to the quoted person. If you use his or her exact words, enclose them in quotation marks.

> The Arab concept of community is reflected in Egyptian leader Anwar al-Sadat's comment "A man's village is his peace of mind."

Minnesota-born songwriter Bob Dylan told an interviewer, "When I was growing up in Hibbing, home was a place to run away from."

(See 33j for correct capitalization with quotation marks.)

In an indirect quotation, you report someone else's idea without using his or her exact words. Do not enclose an indirect quotation in quotation marks. Do, however, name your source; and stay as close as you can to what the source actually said.

> Anwar al-Sadat asserted that a person's community provides a sense of well-being.

(For punctuation of direct and indirect questions, see 24a, 24c, and 25r.)

29b.   Use single quotation marks around a quotation inside another quotation.

Sometimes a source you are quoting quotes someone else or puts a word or words in quotation marks. When that happens, use single quotation marks around the internal quotation (even if your source used double ones), and put double quotation marks around the larger passage that you are quoting.

> "My favorite advice from Socrates, 'Know thyself and fear all women,' " said Dr. Blatz, "has been getting me into trouble lately."

29c.   Instead of using quotation marks, indent a quotation of more than four lines.

Suppose you are writing an essay about Soviet dissidents living in the United States. You might include a paragraph like this:

```
          In a June 1978 commencement address at Harvard Uni-
     versity, Aleksandr Solzhenitsyn commented:
                    I have spent all my life under a Communist
               regime, and I will tell you that a society
               without any objective legal scale is a terrible
               one indeed. But a society with no other scale
               but the legal one is not quite worthy of man
               either.
```

Merely by indenting the quoted passage, you have shown that it is a direct quotation. You need not frame it with quotation marks. Simply double-space above and below the passage, indent it ten spaces from the left margin, and double-space the quoted lines.

Follow the same practice if your quoted material is a poem of more than three lines.

```
    Phillis Wheatley, the outstanding black poet of
colonial America, expresses a sense that she is condemned
to write in obscurity and be forgotten:
        No costly marble shall be reared,
            No Mausoleum's pride--
        Nor chiselled stone be raised to tell
            That I have lived and died.
```

Notice that not only the source's words but her punctuation, capitalization, indentation, and line breaks are quoted exactly. (See also 33j.)

ESL GUIDELINES

Direct and Indirect Quotations

Avoid the problems that arise when a direct quotation (someone else's exact words) is changed into an indirect quotation (when you report someone else's idea without using his or her exact words). Be sure to change the punctuation and capitalization.

DIRECT QUOTATION   Sasha said, "Dallas is in Texas."

INDIRECT QUOTATION   Sasha said that Dallas is in Texas.

• In addition to the punctuation and capitalization, you may need to change the verb tense.

DIRECT QUOTATION   Pascal said, "The assignment is on Chinua Achebe, the Nigerian writer."

INDIRECT QUOTATION   Pascal said that the assignment was on Chinua Achebe, the Nigerian writer.

• If the direct quotation is a question, you must change the word order in the indirect quotation.

DIRECT QUOTATION   Jean asked, "How far is it to Boston?"

INDIRECT QUOTATION   Jean asked how far it was to Boston.

NOTE: Use a period, not a question mark, with questions in indirect quotations.

• Very often, you must change pronouns when using an indirect quotation.

DIRECT QUOTATION   Antonio said, "I think you are mistaken."

INDIRECT QUOTATION   Antonio said that he thought I was mistaken.

29d. In dialogue, use quotation marks around a speaker's words, and mark each change of speaker with a new paragraph.

> Randolph gazed at Ellen and uttered a heartfelt sigh. "What extraordinary beauty."
>
> "They are lovely," she replied, staring at the roses, "aren't they?"

29e. Use quotation marks around the titles of a speech, an article in a newspaper or magazine, a short story, a poem shorter than book length, a chapter in a book, a song, and an episode of a television or radio program.

> The article "An Updike Retrospective" praises "Solitaire" as the best story in John Updike's collection *Museums and Women*.
>
> In Chapter 5, "Expatriates," Schwartz discusses Eliot's famous poem "The Love Song of J. Alfred Prufrock."
>
> My favorite episode of *The Brady Bunch* is the one in which they sing "Sunshine Day" at the variety show audition.

(Most other types of titles are underlined or italicized. See 35a.)

29f. Avoid using quotation marks to indicate slang or to be witty.

Quotation marks should not be used around slang or would-be witticisms. By "quoting" them, you make them stand out like the nose of W. C. Fields; and your discomfort in using them becomes painfully obvious.

INADVISABLE	Liza looked like a born "loser," but Jerry was "hard up" for companionship.
REVISED	Liza looked like a born loser, but Jerry was hard up for companionship.

Stick your neck out. If you really want to use those words, just go ahead.

Some writers assume that, by placing a word in quotation marks, they wax witty and ironic.

INADVISABLE	By the time I finished all my chores, my long-awaited "day off" was over.
REVISED	By the time I finished all my chores, my long-awaited day off was over.

No quotation marks are needed after *so-called* and other words with similar meaning.

FAULTY	Call me "a dreamer," but I believe we can win.
REVISED	Call me a dreamer, but I believe we can win.

29g.   Put commas and periods inside quotation marks.

A comma or a period always comes before quotation marks, even if it is not part of the quotation.

> We pleaded and pleaded, "Keep off the grass," in hope of preserving the lawn.

(Also see 25k.)

29h.   Put semicolons and colons outside quotation marks.

> We said, "Keep off the grass"; they still tromped onward.

29i.   Put other punctuation inside or outside quotation marks depending on its function in the sentence.

Parentheses that are part of the quotation go inside the quotation marks. Parentheses that are your own, not part of the quotation, go outside the quotation marks.

> We said, "Keep off the grass (unless it's artificial turf)."

> They tromped onward (although we had said, "Keep off the grass") all the way to the road.

If a question mark, exclamation point, or dash is part of the quotation, place it inside the quotation marks.

> She hollered, "Fire!"

> "Marjorie?" he called. "I thought you — "

If any of these marks is not part of the quoted passage, place it after the closing quotation marks.

> Who hollered "Fire"?

> "Marjorie" — he paused for breath — "we'd better go."

As these examples show, don't close a sentence with two end punctuation marks, one inside and one outside the quotation marks. If the quoted passage ends with a dash, exclamation point, question mark, or period, you need not add any further end punctuation. If the quoted passage falls within a question asked by you, however, it should finish with a question mark, even if that means cutting other end punctuation (*Who hollered "Fire"?*).

EXERCISE 29–1

Using Quotation Marks

Add quotation marks wherever they are needed in the following sentences, and correct any other errors. Answers for the lettered sentences appear in the back of the book. Example:

Annie asked him, Do you believe in free will?

Annie asked him, "Do you believe in free will?"

a. What we still need to figure out, the police chief said, is whether the victim was acquainted with his assailant.
b. A skillful orator, Patrick Henry is credited with the phrase Give me liberty or give me death.
c. I could hear the crowd chanting my name — Jones! Jones! — and that spurred me on, said Bruce Jones, the winner of the 5,000-meter race.
d. The Doors' The End is a disturbing ballad about parricide.
e. In his essay Marrakech, George Orwell writes, All people who work with their hands are partly invisible, and the more important the work they do, the less visible they are.

1. That day at school, the kids were as "high as kites."
2. Notice, the professor told the class, Cassius's choice of imagery when he asks, Upon what meat doth this our Caesar feed, / That he is grown so great
3. "As I was rounding the bend," Peter explained, "I failed to see the sign that said Caution: Ice.
4. John Cheever's story The Swimmer begins with the line It was one of those midsummer Sundays when everyone sits around saying, I drank too much last night.
5. Who coined the saying Love is blind?

30. *The Dash*

A *dash* is a horizontal line used to separate parts of a sentence — a more dramatic substitute for a comma, semicolon, or colon. To type a dash, hit your hyphen key twice. When using a pen, make your dashes good and long, so that readers can tell them from hyphens.

30a. Use a dash to indicate a sudden break in thought or shift in tone.

The dash signals that a surprise is in store: a shift in viewpoint, perhaps, or an unfinished statement.

Ivan doesn't care which team wins — he bet on both.

I didn't even pay much attention to my parents' accented and ungrammatical speech — at least not at home.

30b. Use a dash to introduce an explanation, an illustration, or a series.

When you want the kind of preparatory pause that a colon provides, but without the formality of a colon, try a dash.

My advice to you is simple — stop complaining.

You can use a dash to introduce an appositive (a noun or noun phrase that renames the noun it follows) if the appositive needs drama or contains commas.

Elliott still cherishes the pastimes of the '60s — sex, drugs, and rock 'n' roll.

Longfellow wrote about three young sisters — grave Alice, laughing Allegra, and Edith with golden hair — in "The Children's Hour."

30c. Use dashes to set off an emphatic aside or parenthetical element from the rest of a sentence.

It was as hot — and I mean *hot* — as a seven-dollar pistol on Fourth of July in Death Valley.

If I went through anguish in botany and economics — for different reasons — gymnasium work was even worse.

Dashes set off a phrase or clause with more punch than commas or parentheses can provide. (Compare commas, 25, and parentheses, 31a–31b.)

30d. Avoid overusing dashes.

Like a physical gesture of emphasis — a jab of a pointing finger — the dash becomes meaningless if used too often. Use it only when a comma, a colon, or parentheses don't seem strong enough.

EXCESSIVE   Algy's grandmother — a sweet old lady — asked him to pick up some things at the store — milk, eggs, apples, and cheese.

REVISED   Algy's grandmother, a sweet old lady, asked him to pick up some things at the store: milk, eggs, apples, and cheese.

EXERCISE 30–1

Using the Dash

Add, remove, or replace dashes wherever appropriate in the following sentences. Some sentences may be correct. Possible answers for the lettered sentences appear in the back of the book. Example:

Stanton had all the identifying marks, boating shoes, yellow slicker, sunblock, and an anchor, of a sailor.

Stanton had all the identifying marks — boating shoes, yellow slicker, sunblock, and an anchor — of a sailor.

a. I enjoy going hiking with my friend John — whom I've known for fifteen years.
b. Pedro's new boat is spectacular: a regular seagoing Ferrari.
c. The Thompsons devote their weekends to their favorite pastime, eating bags of potato chips and cookies beside the warm glow of the television.

d. We were running the rapids when — WHAM!
e. "A rock!" I cried. "Anthony, I'm afraid we're"

1. The sport of fishing — or at least some people call it a sport — is boring, dirty — and tiring.
2. Ancient Egypt had just the right geographic features, a warm climate, a fertile soil along the Nile, and a protective periphery of desert, to allow the development of civilization.
3. At that time, three states in the Sunbelt, Florida, California, and Arizona, were the fastest growing in the nation.
4. The refugees have been forced to build a village if you can call it that out of boxes, rusting cars, and planks.
5. LuLu was ecstatic when she saw her grades, all A's!

31. Parentheses, Brackets, and the Ellipsis Mark

Like quotation marks, parentheses (singular, *parenthesis*) work in pairs. So do brackets. Both sets of marks usually surround bits of information added to make a statement perfectly clear. An ellipsis mark is a trio of periods inserted to show that some bit of information has been cut.

PARENTHESES

31a. Use parentheses to set off interruptions that are useful but not essential.

FDR (as people called Franklin D. Roosevelt) won four presidential elections.

In fact, he occupied the White House for so many years (1933 to mid-1945) that babies became teenagers without having known any other president.

The material within the parentheses may be helpful, but it isn't essential. Were the writer to omit it altogether, the sentence would still make good sense. Use parentheses when adding in midsentence a qualifying word or phrase, a helpful date, or a brief explanation — words that, in conversation, you might introduce in a changed tone of voice.

31b. Use parentheses around letters or numbers indicating items in a series.

Archimedes asserted that, given (1) a lever long enough, (2) a fulcrum, and (3) a place to stand, he could move the earth.

You need not put parentheses around numbers or letters in a list that you set off from the text by indentation.

EXERCISE 31–1

Using Parentheses

Add, remove, or replace parentheses wherever appropriate in the following sentences. Some sentences may be correct. Possible answers for the lettered sentences appear in the back of the book. Example:

> The Islamic fundamentalist Ayatollah Khomeini — 1903–1989 — was described as having led Iran forward into the fifteenth century.

> The Islamic fundamentalist Ayatollah Khomeini (1903–1989) was described as having led Iran forward into the fifteenth century.

a. In *The Last Crusade*, archaeologist Indiana Jones, who took his name from the family dog, joins his father in a quest for the Holy Grail.
b. Our cafeteria serves the four basic food groups: white — milk, bread, and mashed potatoes — brown — mystery meat and gravy — green — overcooked vegetables and underwashed lettuce — and orange — squash, carrots, and tomato sauce.
c. The hijackers will release the hostages only if the government, 1, frees all political prisoners and, 2, allows the hijackers to leave the country unharmed.
d. When Phil said he works with whales (as well as other marine mammals) for the Whale Stranding Network, Lisa thought he meant that his group lures whales onto beaches.
e. Actually, the Whale Stranding Network, WSN, rescues whales that have stranded themselves.

1. The new pear-shaped bottles will hold 200 milliliters, 6.8 fluid ounces, of lotion.
2. The letter from Agatha — not her real name — told a heart-wrenching story of abandonment and abuse.
3. Al's policeman clown was a fantastic success (even his mother was fooled).
4. World War I, or "The Great War," as it was once called, destroyed the old European order forever.
5. The Internet is a mine of fascinating, and sometimes useless, information.

BRACKETS

Brackets, those open-ended typographical boxes, work in pairs like parentheses. They serve a special purpose: they mark changes in quoted material.

31c. Use brackets to add information or to make changes within a direct quotation.

A quotation must be quoted exactly. If you need to add or alter a word or a phrase in a quotation from another writer, place brackets around your changes. When is it appropriate to make such a change? Most often the need arises when you weave into your own prose a piece of someone else's, and you want to get rid of dangling threads.

Suppose you are writing about James McGuire's being named chairman of the board of directors of General Motors. In your source, the actual words are these: "A radio bulletin first brought the humble professor of philosophy the astounding news." But in your paper, you want readers to know the professor's identity. So you add that information, in brackets.

> "A radio bulletin first brought the humble professor of philosophy [James McGuire] the astounding news."

Be careful never to alter a quoted statement any more than you have to. Every time you consider an alteration, ask yourself: Do I really need this word-for-word quotation, or should I paraphrase?

31d. Use brackets around *sic* to indicate an error in a direct quotation.

When you faithfully quote a statement that contains an error and you don't want your reader to blame you for it, follow the error with a bracketed *sic* (Latin for "so" or "so the writer says").

> "President Ronald Reagan foresaw a yearly growth of 29,000,000,000 [*sic*] in the American populace."

Of course, any statement as incorrect as that one is not worth quoting. Usually you're better off paraphrasing an error-riddled passage than pointing out its weaknesses. The writer who uses *sic* is like someone who goes around with a mean dog, siccing it on fellow writers. Never unleash your dog unless your target truly deserves a bite.

THE ELLIPSIS MARK

31e. Use the ellipsis mark to signal that you have omitted part of a quotation.

Occasionally, in quoting a passage of prose, you will want to cite just those parts that relate to your topic. It's all right to make judicious cuts in a quotation, as long as you acknowledge them. To do this, use the *ellipsis mark*: three periods with a space before and after each one (. . .).

Let's say you are writing an essay, "Today's Children: Counselors on Marital Affairs." One of your sources is Marie Winn's book *Children without Childhood*, in which you find this passage:

> Consider the demise of sexual innocence among children. We know that the casual integration of children into adult society in the Middle Ages included few sexual prohibitions. Today's nine- and ten-year-olds watch pornographic movies on cable TV, casually discourse about oral sex and sadomasochism, and not infrequently find themselves involved in their own parents' complicated sex lives, if not as actual observers or participants, at least as advisers, friendly commentators, and intermediaries.

You want to quote Winn's last sentence, but it has too much detail for your purposes. You might shorten it by omitting two of its parts.

> Today's nine- and ten-year-olds . . . not infrequently find themselves involved in their own parents' complicated sex lives, . . . at least as advisers, friendly commentators, and intermediaries.

If you want to include parts of two or more sentences, use a period plus the ellipsis mark—four periods altogether. The period that ends the first sentence appears in its usual place, followed by the three spaced periods that signal the omission.

> Consider the demise of sexual innocence among children. . . . Today's nine- and ten-year-olds [and the rest].

31f. Avoid using the ellipsis mark at the beginning or end of a quotation.

Even though the book *Children without Childhood* keeps on going after the quoted passage, you don't need an ellipsis mark at the end of your quotation. Nor do you ever need to begin a quotation with three dots. Save the ellipsis mark for words or sentences you omit *inside* whatever you quote.

Anytime you decide to alter a quotation, with an ellipsis mark or with brackets, pause to ask yourself whether the quoted material is still necessary and still effective as changed. A passage full of ellipsis marks starts to look like Swiss cheese. If you plan to cut more than one or two sections from a quotation, think about paraphrasing instead.

EXERCISE 31–2

Using Brackets and the Ellipsis Mark

The following are two hypothetical passages from original essays. Each one is followed by a set of quotations. Adapt or paraphrase each quotation, using brackets and ellipsis marks, and splice it into the essay passage.

I. ESSAY PASSAGE

Has evil lost its capacity to frighten us? Today's teenagers use words like *wicked*, *bad*, and *evil* not to condemn another person's behavior or style but to show that they approve of it. Perhaps the declining power of organized religion has allowed us to stop worrying about evil. Perhaps the media's coverage of war, genocide, and murder has made us feel impotent against it. Perhaps the worldwide spread of nuclear weapons has made evil too huge and uncontrollable for our imaginations to grapple with.

QUOTATIONS

a. It was as though in those last minutes he was summing up the lessons that this long course in human wickedness had taught us—the lesson of the fearsome, word-and-thought-defying *banality of evil*.
> — Philosopher Hannah Arendt, writing about the Nazi official Adolf Eichmann

b. I am not a pessimist; to perceive evil where it exists is, in my opinion, a form of optimism.

— Filmmaker Roberto Rossellini

c. The world has achieved brilliance without conscience. Ours is a world of nuclear giants and ethical infants.

— General Omar Bradley

2. ESSAY PASSAGE

Every human life is touched by the natural world. Before the modern industrial era, most people recognized the earth as the giver and supporter of existence. Nowadays, with the power of technology, we can (if we choose) destroy many of the complex balances of nature. With such power comes responsibility. We are no longer merely nature's children, but nature's parents as well.

QUOTATIONS

a. A land ethic for tomorrow should be as honest as Thoreau's *Walden*, and as comprehensive as the sensitive science of ecology. It should stress the oneness of our resources and the live-and-help-live logic of the great chain of life. If, in our haste to "progress," the economics of ecology are disregarded by citizens and policymakers alike, the result will be an ugly America.

— Former Secretary of the Interior Stewart Lee Udall

b. The overwhelming importance of the atmosphere means that there are no longer any frontiers to defend against pollution, attack, or propaganda. It means, further, that only by a deep patriotic devotion to one's country can there be a hope of the kind of protection of the whole planet, which is necessary for the survival of the people of other countries.

— Anthropologist Margaret Mead

c. The survival of our wildlife is a matter of grave concern to all of us in Africa. These wild creatures amid the wild places they inhabit are not only important as a source of wonder and inspiration but are an integral part of our natural resources and of our future livelihood and well-being.

— Former President of Tanzania Julius Nyerere

d. [Religion] is a force in itself and it calls for the integration of lands and peoples in harmonious unity. The lands wait for those who can discern their rhythms. The peculiar genius of each continent, each river valley, the rugged mountains, the placid lakes, all call for relief from the constant burden of exploitation.

— Native American leader Vine Deloria Jr., a Standing Rock Sioux

EXERCISE 31–3

Punctuation Review

Punctuate each of the following sentences correctly, changing punctuation and capitalization if necessary. Example:

The English language, is all around us we speak it read it and hear it constantly.

The English language is all around us; we speak it, read it, and hear it constantly.

The English language, that we speak today, has a long history. During the fifth century C.E. Germanic tribes emigrated to Britain from Denmark, Germany and Holland and they brought their languages with them. These languages the ancestors of modern English were closely related and formed the basis for the language that we speak today. The Viking invasions which began in 793 C.E. also influenced the development of Old English however it was the Norman invasion of 1066 that had the greatest impact on the language. The Normans brought French and Latin words into Britain, and contributed to the evolution of the next linguistic phase Middle English. The most famous writer of this Middle English period is of course Geoffrey Chaucer. Chaucer's achievement was widely acknowledged at the time and by subsequent generations. In the seventeenth century the poet Dryden wrote, ". . . He must have been a Man of a most wonderful comprehensive Nature, because, as it has been truly observed of him, he has taken into the compass of his *Canterbury Tales* the various Manners and Humours (as we now call them) of the whole *English* Nation" . . .

In the late sixteenth century emerged the greatest writer in the English language William Shakespeare. Shakespeare, was the first to demonstrate the flexibility of the language and its great range of expression. It was also during this time that British colonists began carrying English to distant parts of the world. In America words from Native American languages were absorbed and as the British Empire expanded so did English vocabulary. By the late nineteenth century English speakers, were using words from languages as different as: Algonquian and Hindi as well as from almost every European language French, German, Dutch, Danish Yiddish, Swedish, Italian and Spanish. As Ralph Waldo Emerson wrote "The English language is the sea which receives tributaries from every region under heaven".

The English language is always changing like the world itself it is in a constant state of flux. In the late twentieth century English is no longer the language of the British Empire and its colonies. As Salman Rushdie writes:

"English, no longer an English language, now grows from many roots; and those whom it once colonized are carving out large territories within the language for themselves. The Empire is striking back."

In India there are now more speakers of English than there are in Britain about seventy million according to some estimates. Some writers have compared the state of modern English in the former colonies to the vitality of the language during Shakespeares' time. Whereas the grammar police patrol British and American English, other forms of English: such as Indian, Caribbean and African English are developing relatively unrestrained. Anthony Burgess has commented with admiration that "It (Indian English) is not pure English, but it's like the English of Shakespeare, Joyce, and Kipling — gloriously impure." The language will continue to change under the influence of many factors cultural, technological and historical far from its original, island home.

Chapter 36

Mechanics

32. *Abbreviations*

Abbreviations are a form of shorthand that enables a writer to include certain necessary information in capsule form. In your writing, limit abbreviations to those that are common enough for readers to recognize and understand without pausing. When a reader has to stop and ask, "What does this mean?," your writing loses impact.

If ever you're unsure about whether to abbreviate a word, remember: when in doubt, spell it out.

32a. Use abbreviations for some titles with proper names.

Abbreviate the following titles:

Mr. and Mrs. Hubert Collins   Dr. Martin Luther King Jr.
Ms. Martha Reading   St. Matthew

Write out other titles in full:

General Douglas MacArthur   Senator Nancy L. Kassebaum
President Bill Clinton   Professor Shirley Fixler

Titles that are unfamiliar to readers of English, such as *M.* (for the French *Monsieur*) or *Sr.* (for the Spanish *Señor*), should be spelled out.

Spell out most titles that appear without proper names.

FAULTY   Fred is studying to be a dr.

REVISED   Fred is studying to be a doctor.

H-173

When an abbreviated title (such as an academic degree) follows a proper name, set it off from the name and from the rest of the sentence with commas.

> Alice Martin, C.P.A., is the accountant for Charlotte Cordera, Ph.D., and John Hoechst Jr., Esq.

> Lucy Chen, M.D., and James Filbert, D.D.S., have moved their offices to the Millard Building.

An academic degree that appears without a proper name can be abbreviated, but it is not set off with commas.

> My brother has a B.A. in economics.

Avoid repeating different forms of the same title before and after a proper name. You can properly refer to a doctor of dental surgery as either *Dr. Jane Doe* or *Jane Doe, D.D.S.*, but not as *Dr. Jane Doe, D.D.S.*

32b. Use *a.m., p.m.,* B.C., A.D., and $ with numbers.

> 9:05 a.m.   3:45 p.m.
> 2000 B.C.   A.D. 1066

The words we use to pinpoint years and times are so commonly abbreviated that many English speakers have forgotten what the letters stand for. In case you are curious: *a.m.* means *ante meridiem*, Latin for "before noon"; *p.m.* means *post meridiem*, "after noon." A.D. is *anno domini*, Latin for "in the year of the Lord" — that is, since the official year of Jesus' birth. B.C. stands for "before Christ." You may also run into alternative designations such as B.P., "before present," and B.C.E., "before the common era." If you think your readers may not know what an abbreviation stands for, spell it out or add an explanation.

> The ruins date from 1200 B.P. (before present).

For exact prices that include cents and for amounts in the millions, use a dollar sign with numbers (*$17.95, $10.52, $3.5 billion*).

Avoid using an abbreviation together with a word or words that mean the same thing: write *$1 million*, not *$1 million dollars*. Write *9:05 a.m.* or *9:05 in the morning*, not *9:05 a.m. in the morning*.

32c. Avoid abbreviating names of months, days of the week, units of measurement, or parts of literary works.

Many references that can be abbreviated in footnotes or citations should be spelled out when they appear in the body of an essay.

NAMES OF MONTHS AND DAYS OF THE WEEK

FAULTY   After their meeting on 9/3, they did not see each other again until Fri., Dec. 12.

REVISED   After their meeting on September 3 [*or* the third of September], they did not see each other again until Friday, December 12.

UNITS OF MEASUREMENT

FAULTY   It would take 10,000 lbs. of concrete to build a causeway 25 ft. × 58 in. [*or* 259× 58].

REVISED   It would take 10,000 pounds of concrete to build a causeway 25 feet by 58 inches.

PARTS OF LITERARY WORKS

FAULTY   Von Bargen's reply appears in vol. 2, ch. 12, p. 187.

REVISED   Von Bargen's reply appears in volume 2, chapter 12, page 187.

FAULTY   Leona first speaks in act 1, sc. 2.

REVISED   Leona first speaks in act 1, scene 2 [*or* the second scene of act 1].

32d. Use the full English version of most Latin abbreviations.

Unless you are writing for an audience of ancient Romans, translate Latin abbreviations into English and spell them out whenever possible.

COMMON LATIN ABBREVIATIONS

ABBREVIATION	LATIN	ENGLISH
et al.	*et alia*	and others, and other people, and the others (people)
etc.	*et cetera*	and so forth, and others, and the rest (things)
i.e.	*id est*	that is
e.g.	*exempli gratia*	for example, such as

Latin abbreviations are acceptable, however, for source citations and for comments in parentheses and brackets. (See also 31d.)

32e. Use abbreviations for familiar organizations, corporations, and people.

Most sets of initials that are read as letters do not require periods between the letters (CIA, JFK, UCLA). You will not be wrong if you insert periods (C.I.A., J.F.K., U.C.L.A.), as long as you are consistent.

A set of initials that is pronounced as a word is called an *acronym* (NATO, AIDS, UNICEF) and never has periods between letters.

To avoid misunderstanding, write out an organization's full name the first time you mention it, followed by its initials in parentheses. Then, in later references, you can rely on initials alone. (With very familiar initials, such as FBI, CBS, and YMCA, you need not give the full name.)

32f. Avoid abbreviations for countries.

When you mention the United States or another country, give its full name, unless the name is repeated so often that it would weigh down your paragraph.

> The president will return to the United States [*not* U.S.] on Tuesday from a trip to the United Kingdom [*not* U.K.].

EXCEPTION: Although it is not advisable to use *U.S.* as a noun, you can use it as an adjective: *U.S. Senate, U.S. foreign policy.* For other countries, find an alternative: *British ambassador.*

EXERCISE 32–1

Using Abbreviations

Substitute abbreviations for words and vice versa wherever appropriate in the following sentences. Correct any incorrectly used abbreviations. Answers for the lettered sentences appear in the back of the book. Example:

> Please return this form to our office no later than noon on Wed., Apr. 7.

> Please return this form to our office no later than noon on *Wednesday, April 7.*

a. The Temple in Jerusalem was destroyed by the Romans in the year 70 anno domini.
b. Mister Robert Glendale, a C.P.A. accountant, is today's lucky winner of the daily double.
c. A.I.D.S. has affected people throughout U.S. society, not just gay men and IV-drug users.
d. Pres. Bush and Clinton must share the blame for the tragedy of Bosnia.
e. The salmon measured thirty-eight in. and weighed twenty-one lbs.

1. Hamlet's famous soliloquy comes in Act III, sc. one.
2. The red peppers are selling for three dollars and twenty-five cents a lb.
3. In 1995, Sen. Helms became chair of the Sen. Foreign Relations Committee.
4. The end of the cold war between the U.S. and the Soviet Union complicated the role of the U.N. and drastically altered the purpose of N.A.T.O.
5. Emotional political issues, e.g., abortion and capital punishment, cannot be settled easily by compromise.

33. *Capital Letters*

The main thing to remember about capital letters is to use them only with good reason. If you think a word will work in lowercase letters, you're probably right. Editing for capital letter usage is also covered in the "Quick Editing Guide." (For more help, see D1.)

33a. Capitalize proper names and adjectives made from proper names.

Proper names designate individuals, places, organizations and institutions, brand names, and certain other distinctive things.

Miles Standish	University of Iowa
Belgium	a Volkswagen
United Nations	a Xerox copier

Any proper name can have an adjective as well as a noun form. The adjective form too is capitalized.

Australian beer	a Renaissance man
Shakespearean comedy	Machiavellian tactics

33b. Capitalize a title or rank before a proper name.

Now in her second term, Senator Wilimczyk serves on two important committees.

In his lecture, Professor Jones went on and on about fossil evidence.

In formal writing, titles that do not come before proper names are not capitalized.

Ten senators voted against the missile research appropriation.

Jones is the department's only full professor.

EXCEPTION: The abbreviation for the full name of an academic or professional degree is capitalized, whether or not it accompanies a proper name. The informal name of a degree is not capitalized.

Dora E. McLean, M.D., also holds a B.A. in music.

Dora holds a bachelor's degree in music.

33c. Capitalize a family relationship only when it is part of a proper name or when it substitutes for a proper name.

Do you know the song about Mother Machree?

I've invited Mother to visit next weekend.

I'd like you to meet my aunt, Emily Smith.

33d. Capitalize the names of religions, their deities, and their followers.

Christianity	Muslims	Jehovah	Krishna
Islam	Methodists	Allah	the Holy Spirit

33e. Capitalize proper names of places, regions, and geographic features.

Los Angeles	the Black Hills	the Atlantic Ocean
Death Valley	Big Sur	the Philippines

Do not capitalize *north, south, east,* or *west* unless it is part of a proper name (*West Virginia, South Orange*) or refers to formal geographic locations.

Drive south to Chicago and then east to Cleveland.

Jim, who has always lived in the South, likes to read about the mysterious East.

A common noun such as *street, avenue, boulevard, park, lake,* or *hill* is capitalized when part of a proper name.

Meinecke Avenue	Hamilton Park
Sunset Boulevard	Lake Michigan

33f. Capitalize days of the week, names of months, and holidays, but not seasons or academic terms.

By the Monday after Passover I have to choose between the January study plan and junior year abroad.

At Easter we'll be halfway through the spring term.

33g. Capitalize historical events, periods, and documents.

Black Monday	the Roaring Twenties
the Civil War [*but* a civil war]	Magna Carta
the Holocaust [*but* a holocaust]	Declaration of Independence
the Bronze Age	Atomic Energy Act

33h. Capitalize the names of schools and colleges, department names, and course titles.

West End School, Central High School [*but* elementary school, high school]

Reed College, Arizona State University [*but* the college, a university]

Department of Geography [*but* geography department, departmental meeting]

Feminist Perspectives in Nineteenth-Century Literature [*but* literature course]

33i. Capitalize the first, last, and main words in titles.

When you write the title of a paper, book, article, work of art, television show, poem, or performance, capitalize the first and last words and all main words in between. Do not capitalize articles, conjunctions, or prepositions unless they come first or last in the title or follow a colon.

ESSAY	"Once More to the Lake"
NOVEL	*Of Mice and Men*
VOLUME OF POETRY	*Poems after Martial*
POEM	"A Valediction: Of Weeping"
BALLET	*Swan Lake*

(For advice about using quotation marks and italics for titles, see 29e and 35a.)

33j. Capitalize the first letter of a quoted sentence.

Oscar Wilde wrote, "The only way to get rid of a temptation is to yield to it."

Only the first word of a quoted sentence is capitalized, even when you break the sentence with words of your own.

"The only way to get rid of a temptation," wrote Oscar Wilde, "is to yield to it."

If you quote more than one sentence, start each one with a capital letter.

"Art should never try to be popular," said Wilde. "The public should try to make itself artistic."

(For advice about punctuating quotations, see 29g–29i.)

If the beginning of the quoted passage blends in with your sentence, use lowercase for the first word of the quotation.

Oscar Wilde wrote that "the only way to get rid of a temptation is to yield to it."

EXERCISE 33–1

Using Capitalization

Correct any capitalization errors you find in the following sentences. Some sentences may be correct. Answers for the lettered sentences appear in the back of the book. Example:

"The quality of mercy," says Portia in Shakespeare's *The Merchant Of Venice*, "Is not strained."

"The quality of mercy," says Portia in Shakespeare's *The Merchant of Venice*, "is not strained."

a. At our Family Reunion, I met my Cousin Sam for the first time, and also my father's brother George.

b. I already knew from dad that his brother had moved to Australia years ago to explore the great barrier reef.

c. At the reunion, uncle George told me that he had always wanted to be a Marine Biologist.

d. He had spent the Summer after his Sophomore year of college in Woods Hole, Massachusetts, on cape cod.

e. At the Woods Hole oceanographic institution he studied Horseshoe Crabs.

1. "These crabs look like armored tanks," he told me. "They have populated the Northeast for millions of years."

2. "I'm writing a book," he said, "Entitled *Horseshoe Crabs are Good Luck.*"

3. I had heard that uncle George was estranged from his Mother, a Roman catholic, after he married an Atheist.

4. She told George that God created many religions so that people would not become Atheists.

5. When my Uncle announced that he was moving to a Continent thousands of miles Southwest of the United States, his Mother gave him a bible to take along.

6. My Aunt, Linda McCallum, received her Doctorate from one of the State Universities in California.

7. After graduation she worked there as Registrar and lived in the San Bernardino valley.

8. She has pursued her interest in Hispanic Studies by traveling to South America from her home in Northeastern Australia.

9. She uses her maiden name — Linda McCallum, Ph.D. — for her nonprofit business, Hands across the Sea.

10. After dinner we all toasted grandmother's Ninetieth Birthday and sang "For She's A Jolly Good Fellow."

34. *Numbers*

When do you write out a number (*twenty-seven*) and when do you use figures for it (*27*)? Unless your essay relies on statistics, you'll want in most cases to use words. Figures are most appropriate in contexts where readers are used to seeing them, such as times and dates (*11:05 P.M. on March 15*).

34a. In general, write out a number that consists of one or two words, and use figures for longer numbers.

Short names of numbers are easily read (*ten, six hundred*); longer ones take more thought (*two thousand four hundred eighty-seven*). So for numbers of more than a word or two, use figures.

> More than two hundred suckers paid twenty-five dollars apiece for that cheap plastic novelty item.

> A frog's tongue has 970,580 taste buds, one-sixth as many as a human being's.

EXCEPTION: For multiples of a million or more, you can use a figure plus a word.

The earth is 93 million miles from the sun.

The Pentagon has requested a $3.4 billion increase.

34b. Use figures for most addresses, dates, decimals, fractions, parts of literary works, percentages, exact prices, scores, statistics, and times.

Using figures is mainly a matter of convenience. If you think words will be easier for your readers to follow, you can always write out a number.

NOTE: Any number that precedes *o'clock* should be in words, not figures.

(For pointers on writing the plurals of figures [*6's, 1960s*], see 28i.)

34c. Use words or figures consistently for numbers in the same category throughout a passage.

Switching back and forth between words and figures for numbers can be distracting to readers. Choose whichever form suits like numbers in your passage and use that form consistently for all numbers in the same category.

Figures at a Glance

ADDRESSES	4 East 74th Street; also, One Copley Place; 5 Fifth Avenue
DATES	May 20, 1992; 450 B.C.; also, Fourth of July
DECIMALS	98.6° Fahrenheit; .57 acre
FRACTIONS	3½ years ago; 1¾ miles; also, half a loaf; three-fourths of voters surveyed
PARTS OF LITERARY WORKS	volume 2, chapter 5, page 37; act 1, scene 2 (*or* act I, scene ii)
PERCENTAGES	25 percent; 99.9 percent
EXACT PRICES	$1.99; $200,000; also, $5 million; ten cents; a dollar
SCORES	a 114–111 victory; a final score of 5 to 3
STATISTICS	men in the 25–30 age group; odds of 5 to 1 (*or* 5–1 odds); height 5'7"; also, three out of four doctors
TIMES	2:29 P.M.; 10:15 tomorrow morning; also, three o'clock, half past four

Ten years ago, only 25 percent of the land in town was developed; now, all but 15 percent is occupied by buildings.

Of the 276 representatives who voted, 97 supported a 25 percent raise, while 179 supported an amendment that would implement a 30 percent raise over five years.

34d. Write out a number that begins a sentence.

Readers recognize a new sentence by its initial capital; however, you can't capitalize a figure. When a number starts a sentence, either write it out or move it deeper into the sentence. If a number starting a sentence is followed by other numbers in the same category, write them out, too, unless to do so would make the sentence excessively awkward.

Five percent of the frogs in our aquarium ate sixty-two percent of the flies.

Ten thousand people packed an arena built for 8,550.

Using Numbers

Correct any inappropriate uses of numbers in the following sentences. Some sentences may be correct. Answers for the lettered sentences appear in the back of the book. Example:

As Feinberg notes on page 197, a delay of 3 minutes cost the researchers 5 years' worth of work.

As Feinberg notes on page 197, a delay of *three* minutes cost the researchers *five* years' worth of work.

a. Wasn't it the 3 Musketeers whose motto was "One for all and all for one"?
b. In the 1970s, there were about ninety-two million ducks in America, but in the last 4 years their number has dropped to barely sixty-nine million.
c. Of the 3 pyramids built at Giza, Egypt, between two thousand five hundred and eighty and two thousand four hundred and ninety B.C.E., the largest pyramid is four hundred and fifty feet high.
d. Forty days and 40 nights would seem like 40 years if you were sailing on an ark with two of every kind of animal.
e. I doubt that I'll ever bowl a perfect 300, but I hope to break 250 if it takes me till I'm eighty.

1. If the murder took place at approximately six-twenty P.M. and the suspect was ½ a mile away at the time, he could not possibly have committed the crime.
2. A program to help save the sea otter transferred more than eighty animals to a new colony over the course of 2 years; however, all but 34 otters swam back home again.
3. 1 percent or less of the estimated fifteen to twenty billion pounds of plastic discarded annually in the United States is recycled.

4. The 1983 Little League World Series saw the Roosters beat the Dusters ninety-four to four before a throng of seven thousand five hundred and fifty.

5. In act two, scene nine of Shakespeare's *The Merchant of Venice*, Portia's 2nd suitor fails to guess which of 3 caskets contains her portrait.

6. *Fourscore* means 4 times 20; a *fortnight* means 2 weeks; and a *brace* is two of anything.

7. 50 years ago, traveling from New York City to San Francisco took approximately 15 hours by plane, 50 hours by train, and almost 100 hours by car.

8. The little cottage we bought for fifty-five thousand dollars in the nineteen-seventies may sell for $2,000,000 today.

9. At 7 o'clock this morning the temperature was already ninety-seven degrees Fahrenheit.

10. Angelica finished volume one of Proust's *Remembrance of Things Past*, but by the time she got to page forty of volume two, she had forgotten the beginning and had to start over.

35. *Italics*

Italic type — as in this line — slants to the right. Slightly harder to read than perpendicular type, it is usually saved for emphasis or for special use of a word or phrase. In handwriting or typewriting, indicate italics by underlining.

35a. Italicize the titles of magazines, newspapers, and long literary works (books, pamphlets, plays); the titles of films; the titles of paintings and other works of art; the titles of long musical works (operas, symphonies); the titles of CDs and record albums; and the names of television and radio programs.

We read the story "Araby" in James Joyce's book *Dubliners*.

The Broadway musical *My Fair Lady* was based on Shaw's play *Pygmalion*.

Pete read reviews in the *Washington Post* and *Newsweek* magazine of the Cleveland Philharmonic's recording of Beethoven's *Pastoral* Symphony.

I saw a *Melrose Place* episode that featured cuts from R.E.M.'s album *Monster*.

The names of the Bible (King James Version, Revised Standard Version), the books of the Bible (Genesis, Matthew), and other sacred books (the Koran, the Rig-Veda) are not italicized.

(For titles that are put in quotation marks, see 29e.)

35b. Italicize the names of ships, boats, trains, airplanes, and spacecraft.

The launching of the Venus probe *Magellan* was a heartening success after the *Challenger* disaster.

The *Concorde* combines the elegance of an ocean liner like the *Queen Mary* with the convenience of high-speed air travel.

Italics at a Glance

TITLES

MAGAZINES AND NEWSPAPERS
Ms.　　the *London Times*

LONG LITERARY WORKS
Heart of Darkness (a novel)　　*The Less Deceived* (a collection of poems)

FILMS
Notorious　　*Black Orpheus*

PAINTINGS AND OTHER WORKS OF ART
Four Dancers (a painting)　　*The Thinker* (a sculpture)

LONG MUSICAL WORKS
Aïda　　Handel's *Messiah*

CDS AND RECORD ALBUMS
Crash　　*Disciplined Breakdown*

TELEVISION AND RADIO PROGRAMS
I Love Lucy　　*All Things Considered*

OTHER WORDS AND PHRASES

NAMES OF AIRCRAFT, SPACECRAFT, SHIPS, AND TRAINS
the *Orient Express*　　the *Challenger*

A WORD OR PHRASE FROM A FOREIGN LANGUAGE IF IT IS NOT IN EVERYDAY USE
The Finnish sauna ritual uses a *vihta*, a brush made of fresh birch branches tied together.

A LETTER, NUMBER, WORD, OR PHRASE WHEN YOU DEFINE IT OR REFER TO IT AS A WORD
There were two *5*'s on the door, and she guessed that a *4* had fallen off between them.

What do you think *fiery* is referring to in the second line?

NOTE: See 29e for titles that need to be placed in quotation marks.

When you give a synonym or a translation — a definition that is just one or two words long — italicize the word being defined and put the definition in quotation marks.

The word *orthodoxy* means "conformity."

Trois, drei, and *tres* are all words for "three."

35c. Italicize a word or phrase from a foreign language if it is not in everyday use.

Gandhi taught the principles of *satya* and *ahimsa:* truth and nonviolence.

Although there is no one-word English equivalent for the French *chez,* we can translate *chez Bob* simply as "at Bob's."

Foreign words that are familiar to most American readers need not be italicized. (Check your dictionary to see which words are considered familiar.)

After being declared passé several years ago, détente is making a reappearance in East-West politics.

I prefer provolone to mozzarella.

35d. Italicize a word when you define it.

The rhythmic, wavelike motion of the walls of the alimentary canal is called *peristalsis.*

35e. Italicize a letter, number, word, or phrase used as a word.

George Bernard Shaw pointed out that *fish* could be spelled *ghoti: gh* as in *tough, o* as in *women,* and *ti* as in *fiction.*

Watching the big red *8* on a basketball player's jersey, I recalled the scarlet letter *A* worn by Hester Prynne.

Psychologists now prefer the term *unconscious* to *subconscious.*

35f. Use italics sparingly for emphasis.

When you absolutely *must* stress a point, use italics; but watch out. Frequent italics can make your writing look hysterical. In most cases, the structure of your sentence, not a typographical gimmick, should give emphasis where emphasis is due.

He suggested putting the package *under* the mailbox, not *into* the mailbox.

People committed to saving whales, sea otters, and baby seals may not be aware that *forty thousand children per day* die of starvation or malnutrition.

EXERCISE 35–1

Using Italics

Add or remove italics as needed in the following sentences. Some sentences may be correct. Answers for the lettered sentences appear in the back of the book. Example:

Hiram could not *believe* that his parents had seen *the Beatles'* legendary performance at Shea Stadium.

Hiram could not believe that his parents had seen the Beatles' legendary performance at Shea Stadium.

a. Hiram's favorite Beatles album is "Sergeant Pepper's Lonely Hearts Club Band," but his father prefers "Magical Mystery Tour."
b. Hiram named his rowboat the "Yellow Submarine."
c. He was disappointed when I told him that the play *Long Day's Journey into Night* is *definitely not* a staged version of the movie "A Hard Day's Night."
d. I had to show him the article "Eugene O'Neill's Journey into Night" in "People" magazine to convince him.
e. We ate *spaghetti* and *tortellini* in the new Italian restaurant.

1. Is "avocado" Spanish for "lawyer"?
2. During this year's *First Night* celebrations, we heard Verdi's Requiem and Monteverdi's Orfeo.
3. You can pick out some of the best basketball players in the *NBA* by the 33 on their jerseys.
4. It was fun watching the passengers on the Europa trying to dance to *Blue Moon* in the midst of a storm.
5. In one episode of the sitcom "Seinfeld," Kramer gets a job as an underwear model.
6. *Eye* in France is *oeil,* while *eyes* is *yeux.*
7. "Deux yeux bleus" means "two blue eyes" in French.
8. Jan can never remember whether Cincinnati has three n's and one t or two n's and two t's.
9. My favorite comic bit in "The Pirates of Penzance" is Major General Stanley's confusion between "orphan" and "often."
10. In Tom Stoppard's play "The Real Thing," the character Henry accuses Bach of copying a *cantata* from a popular song by *Procol Harum.*

36. *The Hyphen*

The hyphen, that Scotch-tape mark of punctuation, is used to join words and to connect parts of words. You will find it indispensable for the following purposes.

36a. Use hyphens in compound words that require them.

Compound words in the English language take three forms:

1. Two or more words combined into one (*crossroads, salesperson*)
2. Two or more words that remain separate but function as one (*gas station, high school*)
3. Two or more words linked by hyphens (*sister-in-law, window-shop*)

Compound nouns and verbs fall into these categories more by custom than by rule. When you're not sure which way to write a compound, refer to your dictionary. If the compound is not listed in your dictionary, write it as two words.

Use a hyphen in a compound word containing one or more elements beginning with a capital letter.

> Bill says that, as a *neo-Marxist* living in an *A-frame* house, it would be politically incorrect for him to wear a Mickey Mouse *T-shirt*.

> Bubba doesn't mind being labeled a *pre-Neanderthal*, but he'll break anyone's neck who calls him *anti-American*.

There are exceptions to this rule: *unchristian*, for one. If you think a compound word looks odd with a hyphen, check your dictionary.

36b. Use a hyphen in a compound adjective preceding a noun but not following a noun.

> Jerome, a devotee of *twentieth-century* music, has no interest in the classic symphonies of the *eighteenth century*.

> I'd like living in an *out-of-the-way* place better if it weren't so far *out of the way*.

In a series of hyphenated adjectives with the same second word, you can omit that word (but not the hyphen) in all but the last adjective of the series.

> Julia is a lover of eighteenth-, nineteenth-, and twentieth-century music.

The adverb *well*, when coupled with an adjective, follows the same hyphenation rules as if it were an adjective.

> It is *well known* that Tony has a *well-equipped* kitchen, although his is not as *well equipped* as the hotel's.

Do *not* use a hyphen to link an adverb ending in *-ly* with an adjective.

> FAULTY   The sun hung like a newly-minted penny in a freshly-washed sky.
>
> REVISED   The sun hung like a newly minted penny in a freshly washed sky.

36c. Use a hyphen after the prefixes *all-*, *ex-*, and *self-* and before the suffix *-elect*.

> Lucille's *ex-husband* is studying *self-hypnosis*.

> This *all-important* debate pits Senator Browning against the *president-elect*.

Note that these prefixes and suffixes also can function as parts of words that are not hyphenated (*exit, selfish*). Whenever you are unsure whether to use a hyphen, check a dictionary.

36d. Use a hyphen in most cases if an added prefix or suffix creates a double vowel, triple consonant, or ambiguous pronunciation.

It is also acceptable to omit the hyphen in the case of a double *e*: *reeducate*.

> The contractor told us that his *pre-estimate* did not cover any *pre-existing* flaws in the building.

> The recreation department favors the *re-creation* of a summer activities program.

36e. Use a hyphen in spelled-out fractions and compound whole numbers from twenty-one to ninety-nine.

> When her sister gave Leslie's age as six and *three-quarters*, Leslie corrected her: "I'm six and *five-sixths*!"

> The fifth graders learned that *forty-four* rounds down to forty while *forty-five* rounds up to fifty.

36f. Use a hyphen to indicate inclusive numbers.

> The section covering the years 1975-1980 is found on pages 20-27.

36g. Use a hyphen to break a word between syllables at the end of a line.

Words are divided as they are pronounced, by syllables. Break a hyphenated compound at its hyphen and a nonhyphenated compound between the words that make it up. For a noncompound word, saying it out loud usually will give you a good idea where to break it; if you still are not sure, check your dictionary.

> FAULTY   Bubba hates to be called an-
>   ti-American.

> REVISED   Bubba hates to be called anti-
>   American.

> FAULTY   Francis will not be home until dinn-
>   er.

> REVISED   Francis will not be home until din-
>   ner.

Don't split a one-syllable word, even if keeping it intact makes your line come out a bit too short or too long.

FAULTY   I'm completely drench-
          ed.

REVISED   I'm completely drenched.

FAULTY   Arnold is a tower of stren-
          gth.

REVISED   Arnold is a tower of
          strength.

Don't split a word after a one-letter syllable or before a one- or two-letter syllable.

FAULTY   What's that up the road a-
          head?

REVISED   What's that up the road
          ahead?

FAULTY   I am proud to be an Americ-
          an.

REVISED   I am proud to be an Ameri-
          can.

Don't split a word after a segment that looks like a whole word, even if a dictionary puts a syllable break there.

CONFUSING   The lusty sailor aimed his sex-
            tant at the stars.

CLEAR   The lusty sailor aimed his
            sextant at the stars.

CONFUSING   He is addicted to her-
            oin.

CLEAR   He is addicted to heroin.

EXERCISE 36–1

Using Hyphens

Add necessary hyphens and remove incorrectly used hyphens in the following sentences. Some sentences may be correct. Answers for the lettered sentences appear in the back of the book. Example:

Her exhusband works part-time as a short order cook.

Her *ex-husband* works part-time as a *short-order* cook.

a. The strong smelling smoke alerted them to a potentially life threatening danger.
b. Burt's wildly-swinging opponent had tired himself out before the climactic third round.
c. Tony soaked his son's ketchup and mustard stained T shirt in a pail of water mixed with chlorine bleach.

    d. The badly damaged ship was in no condition to enter the wide-open waters beyond the bay.

    e. Tracy's brother in law lives with his family in a six room apartment.

1. Do you want salt-and-pepper on your roast beef sandwich?
2. Health insurance companies should not be allowed to exclude people on account of preexisting conditions.
3. Heat-seeking missles are often employed in modern day air-to-air combat.
4. *The Piano* is a beautifully crafted film with first-rate performances by Holly Hunter and Harvey Keitel.
5. Nearly three fourths of the money in the repair and maintenance account already has been spent.

37. *Spelling*

English spelling so often defies the rules that many speakers of the language wonder if, indeed, there *are* rules. You probably learned to spell — as most of us did — mainly by memorizing. By now you remember that there's a *b* in *doubt* but not in *spout*, a *k* in *knife* but not in *nine*. You know that the same sound can have several spellings, as in *here, ear, pier, sneer,* and *weird*. You are resigned to the fact that *ou* is pronounced differently in *four, round, ought,* and *double*. Still, like most people, you may have trouble with the spelling of certain words.

How many times have you heard someone say "ath-uh-lete" for *athlete*, "gov-er-ment" for *government*, or "nuc-yu-lar" for *nuclear*? Get the pronunciation right and you realize that the spelling has to be *arctic* (not *artic*), *mischievous* (not *mischievious*), *perform* (not *preform*), *surprise* (not *suprise*), *replenish* (not *replentish*), *similar* (not *similiar*).

The trouble is that careful pronunciation is only sometimes a reliable guide to English spelling. Knowing how to pronounce *psychology, whistle, light, gauge,* and *rhythm* doesn't help you spell them. How, then, are you to cope?

Editing for spelling is also covered in the "Quick Editing Guide." (For more help, see D2.)

37a. Follow spelling rules.

Fortunately, there are a few rules for spelling English words that work most of the time. Learning them, and some of their exceptions, will give you a sturdy foundation on which to build.

EI or IE?

The best way to remember which words are spelled *ei* and which ones *ie* is to recall this familiar jingle:

> *I* before *e* except after *c*,
> Or when sounded like *a*, as in *neighbor* and *weigh*.

Niece, believe, field, receive, receipt, ceiling, beige, and *freight* are just a few of the words you'll be able to spell easily once you learn that rule. Then memorize a few of the exceptions:

counterfeit	foreign	kaleidoscope	protein	seize
either	forfeit	leisure	science	weird
financier	height	neither	seismograph	

Also among the rule breakers are words in which *cien* is pronounced "shen"; *ancient, efficient, conscience, prescience.*

Homonyms

Words that sound the same, or almost the same, but are spelled differently are called **homonyms.** See page R-21 in the "Quick Editing Guide" for some of the most commonly confused homonyms, briefly identified, with examples of how to use them. (Also see the Glossary of Troublemakers following the "Quick Editing Guide.")

Plurals

1. To form the plural of most common nouns, add *-s.* If a noun ends in *-ch, -sh, -s,* or *-x,* form its plural by adding *-es.*

attack, attacks	umbrella, umbrellas
ridge, ridges	zone, zones
boss, bosses	trellis, trellises
sandwich, sandwiches	crash, crashes
tax, taxes	church, churches

2. To form the plural of a common noun ending in *-o,* add *-s* if the *-o* follows a vowel and *-es* if it follows a consonant.

radio, radios	video, videos
hero, heroes	potato, potatoes

3. To form the plural of a common noun ending in *-y,* change the *y* to *i* and add *-es* if the *y* follows a consonant. Add only *-s* if the *y* follows a vowel.

baby, babies	sissy, sissies
fly, flies	wallaby, wallabies
toy, toys	monkey, monkeys
guy, guys	day, days

4. To form the plural of a proper noun, add *-s* or *-es* without changing the noun's ending.
Proper nouns follow the same rules as common nouns, with one exception: a proper noun never changes its spelling in the plural form.

Mary Jane, Mary Janes	Dr. Maddox, the Maddoxes
Mr. Curry, the Currys	Saturday, Saturdays
Professor Jones, the Joneses	

5. To form the plural of a compound noun, add -*s* or -*es* to the chief word, or to the last word if all the words are equal in weight.

brother-in-law, brothers-in-law	actor-manager, actor-managers
aide-de-camp, aides-de-camp	tractor-trailer, tractor-trailers

6. Memorize the plural forms of nouns that diverge from these rules. Certain nouns have special plurals. Here are a few:

alumna, alumnae	man, men
alumnus, alumni	medium, media
child, children	mouse, mice
half, halves	self, selves
goose, geese	tooth, teeth
leaf, leaves	woman, women

Suffixes

The -*s* added to a word to make it plural is one type of *suffix*, or tail section. Suffixes allow the same root word to do a variety of jobs, by giving it different forms for different functions. Keeping a few basic rules in mind will help you to use suffixes successfully.

1. Drop a silent *e* before a suffix that begins with a vowel.

move, mover, moved, moving
argue, arguer, argued, arguing
accrue, accruing, accrual

EXCEPTION: If the *e* has an essential function, keep it before adding a suffix that begins with a vowel. In *singe*, for instance, the *e* changes the word's pronunciation from "sing" to "sinj." If you dropped the *e* in *singeing*, it would become *singing*.

singe, singed, singeing
tiptoe, tiptoed, tiptoeing

2. Keep a silent *e* before a suffix that begins with a consonant.

move, movement
hope, hopeless

EXCEPTION: In a word ending in a silent *e* preceded by a vowel, sometimes (but not always) drop the *e*.

argue, argument
true, truly

3. Change a final *y* to *i* before a suffix if the *y* follows a consonant but not if the *y* follows a vowel.

cry, crier, cried
joy, joyous, joyful

happy, happiest, happily
hurry, hurried
pray, prayed, prayer

EXCEPTION: Keep the *y* whenever the suffix is *-ing.*

hurry, hurrying
pray, praying

Drop a final *y* before the suffix *-ize.*

deputy, deputize
memory, memorize

4. Double the final consonant of a one-syllable word before a suffix if (1) the suffix starts with a vowel *and* (2) the final consonant follows a single vowel.

sit, sitter, sitting
flop, flopped, floppy
rob, robbed, robbery

Don't double the final consonant if it follows two vowels or another consonant.

fail, failed, failure
stack, stacking, stackable

Don't double the final consonant if the suffix starts with a consonant.

top, topless
cap, capful

5. Double the final consonant of a word with two or more syllables if (1) the suffix starts with a vowel *and* (2) the final consonant follows a single vowel *and* (3) the last syllable of the stem is accented once the suffix is added.

commit, committed, committing
rebut, rebuttal
regret, regretted, regrettable

Don't double the final consonant if it follows more than one vowel —

avail, available
repeat, repeating

— or if it follows another consonant —

accent, accented
depend, dependence

— or the suffix starts with a consonant —

commit, commitment
jewel, jewelry

— or, when the suffix is added, the final syllable of the stem is unaccented.

> confer, conference (*but* conferred)
> travel, traveler

Prefixes

The main point to remember when writing a word with a **prefix** (or nose section) is that the prefix usually does not alter the spelling of the root word it precedes.

dis + appear = disappear	mis + understand = misunderstand
dis + satisfied = dissatisfied	with + hold = withhold
mis + step = misstep	un + necessary = unnecessary

(For guidelines on when to use a hyphen to attach a prefix, see 36c and 36d.)

37b. Develop spelling skills.

Besides becoming familiar with the rules in this chapter, you can use several other tactics to teach yourself to be a better speller.

1. *Use mnemonic devices.* To make unusual spellings stick in your memory, invent associations. *Weird* behaves *weirdly.* Would you rather study *ancient science* or be an *efficient financier*? Using such *mnemonic devices* (tricks to aid memory) may help you not only with *ie* and *ei* but with whatever troublesome spelling you are determined to remember. Rise ag*ai*n, Brit*ai*n! One *d* in *dish*, one in *radish*. Why isn't *mathe*matics like *athle*tics? You write a let*ter* on station*ery*. Any silly phrase or sentence will do, as long as it brings tricky spellings to mind.

2. *Keep a record of words you misspell.* Buy yourself a little notebook in which to enter words that invariably trip you up. Each time you proofread a paper you have written and each time you receive one back from your instructor, write down any words you have misspelled. Then practice pronouncing, writing, and spelling them out loud until you have mastered them.

3. *Check any questionable spelling by referring to your dictionary.* Keep a dictionary at your elbow as you write. In matters of spelling, that good-as-gold book is your best friend. Use it to check words as you come up with them and to double-check them as you proofread and edit your work.

4. *Learn commonly misspelled words.* To save you the trouble of looking up every spelling bugbear, the "Quick Editing Guide" has a list of words frequently misspelled, beginning on page R-23. This list will serve to review our whole discussion of spelling, for it contains the trickiest words we've mentioned. Check-mark those that give you trouble — but don't stop there. Spend a few minutes each day going over them. Pronounce each one carefully or have a friend read the list to you. Spell every troublesome word out loud; write it ten times. Your spelling will improve rapidly.

Everybody has at least ten or twenty bugbears. Shoot down yours.

Spelling

Edit the following passage to correct misspelled words. You may want to consult the list of commonly misspelled words on pages R-23 through R-25.

> There are alians living among us, who are commited to enslaveing the human race.

> There are *aliens* living among us, who are *committed* to *enslaving* the human race.

They are mysterios beings of devious inteligence who qietly govern our lives. They are all around us, in our homes and our streets. When you come home exausted after a disasterous day at work, they are there waiting for you, and if you do not feed them immediatly, there behavior becomes barberous: now begins the theatrical nibbling of plants and other iritable antics devised to harrass you until you finally either lose your mind or open the can of tuna fish. They will flaunt their power before your very eyes by tormenting flys, or assasinating moths. Their senses are tuned to a world beyond human perception. Strange, explosive sprints into ajoining rooms suggest involvment with the imaginery Olympics, while imperceptable air currents on the ceiling will keep them amused indefinitly. They have a passion for shredding favorite chairs and enjoy decorating with fur balls. Despite thier destructive habits, we need fear no personal injury, for they look on us compasionately as thier pets.

Quick Editing Guide

Proofreading and editing occur at the very end of the writing process. Once you are satisfied that you have your ideas down on paper in words that express them well, you should go over every sentence and word carefully to make sure that each is concise, clear, and correct. The difference between a college paper that has been carefully edited and one that has not is often the difference of a full letter grade.

Proofreading and editing are needed because writers — *all* writers — find it difficult or even impossible to write error-free sentences the very first time they try. Sometimes as a writer you pay more attention to what you want to say than to how you say it. Sometimes you have inaccurate, insufficient, or faulty information in your memory, possibly about spelling or grammar or punctuation. At other times you are distracted from your writing by something happening around you or by an unrelated thought that comes into your head. And sometimes you make errors in typing or keyboarding. Proofreading and editing are necessary to find and correct mistakes arising from all these causes.

This "Quick Editing Guide" provides an overview of the most troubling grammar, style, punctuation, and mechanics problems typical of college writing. Certain common errors in Standard Written English are like red flags to careful readers: they send the message that the writer is either ignorant or careless. Use the "Quick Editing Guide" to check your paper for these problems and to make changes if you find any errors. An editing checklist at the beginning of the chapter gives you an overview of the problems you should check for; additional editing checklists in each section help you focus on and correct errors in your writing. And Editing with a Computer tips give advice on how your word processor can (or cannot) help you edit.

For more information on each of the problems covered here — as well as complete coverage of other grammar, style, punctuation, and mechanics issues that apply to college writing — turn to the relevant sections in any complete reference handbook. Learning and using good proofreading techniques is an important part of completing a well-polished paper; for more help with proofreading, see Chapter 19, "Strategies for Revising and Editing."

EDITING CHECKLIST

Common and Serious Problems in College Writing

- Have you used the correct form for all verbs in the past tense? (See A1.)
- Do all verbs agree with their subjects? (See A2.)
- Have you used the correct case for all pronouns? (A3.)
- Do all pronouns agree with their antecedents? (See A4.)
- Have you used adjectives and adverbs correctly? (See A5.)
- Have you avoided writing sentence fragments? (See A6.)
- Have you avoided writing comma splices or fused sentences? (See A7.)
- Does each modifier clearly modify the appropriate sentence element? (See B1.)
- Have you used parallel structure where necessary? (See B2.)
- Have you used commas correctly? (See C1.)
- Have you used apostrophes correctly? (See C2.)
- Have you used capital letters correctly? (See D1.)
- Have you spelled all words correctly? (See D2.)
- Have you used correct manuscript form? (See D3.)

A. *Editing for Common Grammar Problems*

A1. Check for correct past tense verb forms.

The *verb* is the word in a sentence that shows action ("Tom *hit* the ball") or a state of being ("He *is* tired now"). The *form* of a verb — the way it is spelled and pronounced — changes depending on exactly how it is used in a particular sentence. The *tense* of a verb is the time when its action did, does, or will occur (whether it is in the past, the present, or the future). The form of verb changes to indicate the tense of the verb. In other words, a verb about something in the present will often be spelled and pronounced differently than a verb about something in the past.

PRESENT   Right now, I *watch* only a few minutes of television per day.

PAST   Last month, I *watched* television shows every evening.

Many writers fail to use the correct form for past tense verbs. In general, there are two different problems, depending on whether the verb is regular or irregular. *Regular verbs* are verbs for which the forms follow standard rules; they form the past tense by adding *-ed* or *-d* to the end of the present tense form: *watch/watched, look/looked, hope/hoped*. Check all regular verbs in the past tense to be sure you have used one of these endings.

FAULTY   I *ask* my brother for a loan yesterday.

CORRECT   I *asked* my brother for a loan yesterday.

FAULTY   Nicole *finish* her English theme.

CORRECT   Nicole *finished* her English theme.

TIP: If you learn to enunciate the final -*d* sound when you talk, you may find it easier to remember the final -*d* or -*ed* when you write past tense regular verbs.

Irregular verbs do not follow standard rules to make the different forms. There is no way to predict what the past tense forms will look like, so they have to be memorized: *eat/ate, see/saw, get/got.* Irregular verbs can also use different forms for the past tense and the past participle (a form of the verb used with a helping verb): "She *ate* the whole pie; she *has eaten* two pies this week." The most troublesome irregular verbs are actually very common, so if you take the effort to learn and use the correct forms, you will quickly improve your writing. Check all irregular verbs that are in the past tense or that use a past participle to be sure you have used the correct form; use the chart on pages R-4 to R-5 or a standard dictionary for any verbs you are unsure of.

FAULTY   My cat *laid* on the tile floor to take her nap.

CORRECT   My cat *lay* on the tile floor to take her nap.

FAULTY   I *have swam* twenty laps every day this month.

CORRECT   I *have swum* twenty laps every day this month.

**EDITING
CHECKLIST**

Past Tense Verb Forms

- Have you identified the main verb in the sentence?
- Is the sentence about the past, the present, or the future? Does the verb reflect this sense of time?
- Is it a regular verb or an irregular verb?
- Have you used the correct form to express your meaning?

**EDITING WITH
A COMPUTER**

You can use your word processor's Search or Find function to locate all instances of irregular verbs you have particular trouble with. For example, if you routinely type *brung* instead of *brought*, you can have the computer locate all examples of *brung* and change them to *brought*. Consider keeping track of your verb tense form errors so that you can take advantage of this feature to simplify your editing.

Grammar checkers catch some, but not all, problems with verbs, and they rarely suggest suitable substitutions for an error. They only sometimes catch missing -*ed* endings for the past tense of regular verbs; for example, most would ignore the missing -*ed* ending in *Derek has turn down several job offers.* You will need to consider the grammar checker's suggestions carefully before accepting them.

Principal Parts of Common Irregular Verbs

INFINITIVE	PAST TENSE	PAST PARTICIPLE
be	was	been
become	became	become
begin	began	begun
blow	blew	blown
break	broke	broken
bring	brought	brought
burst	burst	burst
catch	caught	caught
choose	chose	chosen
come	came	come
do	did	done
draw	drew	drawn
drink	drank	drunk
drive	drove	driven
eat	ate	eaten
fall	fell	fallen
fight	fought	fought
freeze	froze	frozen
get	got	got, gotten
give	gave	given
go	went	gone
grow	grew	grown
have	had	had
hear	heard	heard
hide	hid	hidden
know	knew	known
lay	laid	laid
lead	led	led
let	let	let
lie	lay	lain
make	made	made
raise	raised	raised
ride	rode	ridden
ring	rang	rung
rise	rose	risen
run	ran	run
say	said	said
see	saw	seen
set	set	set
sing	sang	sung
sit	sat	sat
slay	slew	slain
slide	slid	slid
speak	spoke	spoken
spin	spun	spun
stand	stood	stood
steal	stole	stolen

(*continued*)

Principal Parts of Common Irregular Verbs *(continued)*

INFINITIVE	PAST TENSE	PAST PARTICIPLE
swim	swam	swum
swing	swung	swung
teach	taught	taught
tear	tore	torn
think	thought	thought
throw	threw	thrown
wake	woke, waked	woken, waked
write	wrote	written

For the appropriate form of any irregular verb not on this list, consult your dictionary. (Some dictionaries list principal parts for all verbs, some just for irregular verbs.)

A2.   Check for correct subject-verb agreement.

The *verb* is the word in a sentence that shows action ("Tom *hit* the ball") or a state of being ("He *is* tired now"). The **subject** is who or what performed the action or existed in the state of being (*Tom, he*). The *form* of a verb — the way it is spelled and pronounced — changes depending on exactly how it is used in a particular sentence. The form can change to show **number** — whether the subject is singular (one) or plural (more than one). It can also change to show *person* — whether the subject is *you* or *she*, for example.

SINGULAR	Our instructor *grades* every paper very carefully.
PLURAL	Most instructors *grade* papers using a standard scale.
SECOND PERSON	You *write* well-documented research papers.
THIRD PERSON	She *writes* good research papers, too.

A verb must match (or *agree with*) its subject in terms of number and person. For *regular verbs* (those that follow a standard rule to make the different forms), this rule causes problems only in the present tense. Regular verbs have two present-tense forms: one that ends in *-s* or *-es* and one that does not. The subjects *he, she, it,* and singular nouns use the verb form that ends in *-s* or *-es*. Plural pronouns and nouns use the verb form that does not end in *-s* or *-es*.

I like	we like
you like	you like
he/she/it likes	they like

The verbs *be* and *have* do not follow the *-s/no -s* pattern to form the present tense; they are irregular verbs, so their forms must be memorized. The verb *be* is also irregular in the past tense. (See the chart on p. R-6.)

Check to make sure that every verb agrees in number with its subject. Problems often occur when the subject is difficult to find, is an indefinite pronoun, or is confusing for some other reason. In particular, make sure that you

---

Forms of *Be* and *Have*

THE PRESENT TENSE OF *BE*

I am	we are
you are	you are
he/she/it is	they are

THE PAST TENSE OF *BE*

I was	we were
you were	you were
he/she/it was	they were

THE PRESENT TENSE OF *HAVE*

I have	we have
you have	you have
he/she/it has	they have

THE PAST TENSE OF *HAVE*

I had	we had
you had	you had
he/she/it had	they had

---

have not left off any *-s* or *-es* endings and that you have used the correct form for irregular verbs.

FAULTY   Jim *write* his research papers on a computer.

CORRECT   Jim *writes* his research papers on a computer.

FAULTY   The students *has* difficulty understanding the physics professor.

CORRECT   The students *have* difficulty understanding the physics professor.

FAULTY   All of the football players *was* jubilant that the team won the game.

CORRECT   All of the football players *were* jubilant that the team won the game.

FAULTY   Every one of the cakes *were* sold at the church bazaar.

CORRECT   Every one of the cakes *was* sold at the church bazaar.

**EDITING
CHECKLIST**

Subject-Verb Agreement

- Have you correctly identified the subject and the verb in the sentence?
- Is the subject singular or plural? Does the verb match?
- Have you used the correct form of the verb?

**EDITING WITH
A COMPUTER**

You can use your word processor's Search or Find function to locate some habitual problems with subject-verb agreement. For example, if you routinely make mistakes with the verb *be*, have the computer locate all instances of *was* and *were*; then you can check to make sure you have used each one correctly. Since indefinite pronouns as subjects often cause difficulties with subject-verb agreement, you can search for all instances of *each* or *few* (or whatever your particular bugaboo is) and make sure you've used the correct form of the verb. (For a list of indefinite pronouns, see p. R-9.) Consider keeping track of your subject-verb agreement errors so that you can take advantage of this feature to simplify your editing.

Grammar checkers attempt to catch problems with subject-verb agreement, but they are frequently unable to identify the subject and the verb accurately. As a result, they often mistakenly flag correct sentences and overlook errors. You will need to understand the principles discussed in this section and consider the grammar checker's advice carefully before you make changes.

A3. Check for correct pronoun case.

A *pronoun* replaces a noun or another pronoun in a sentence so that you do not have to repeat it. Depending on the role a pronoun plays in a sentence, it is said to be in the *subjective case, objective case,* or the *possessive case*. Use the subjective case if the pronoun is the subject of a sentence, the subject of a subordinate clause, or a subject complement (after a linking verb). Use the objective case if the pronoun is a direct or indirect object of a verb or the object of a preposition. Use the possessive case to show possession.

SUBJECTIVE   *I* will argue that our campus needs more parking.

OBJECTIVE   This issue is important to *me*.

POSSESSIVE   *My* argument will be quite persuasive.

There are many types of pronouns, but only some change form to show case. The personal pronouns *I, you, he, she, it, we,* and *they* and the relative pronoun *who* each have at least two forms.

There are two frequent errors in pronoun case. First, writers often use the subjective case when they should use the objective case—sometimes because they are trying to sound formal and correct. Find all personal pronouns in a sentence, and determine whether they are functioning as subjects, objects, or possessives. Then choose the correct form based on the pronoun's function in the sentence.

FAULTY   My company gave my husband and *I* a trip to the Cayman Islands.

CORRECT   My company gave my husband and *me* a trip to the Cayman Islands.

Pronoun Cases

SUBJECTIVE	OBJECTIVE	POSSESSIVE
I	me	my, mine
you	you	your, yours
he	him	his
she	her	hers
it	it	its
we	us	our, ours
they	them	their, theirs
who	whom	whose

FAULTY   The argument occurred because my uncle and *me* had different expectations.

CORRECT   The argument occurred because my uncle and *I* had different expectations.

FAULTY   Jack is taller than *me*.

CORRECT   Jack is taller than *I*.

A second common error with pronoun case involves gerunds (the *-ing* form of a verb used as a noun). Whenever you need a pronoun to modify a gerund, use the possessive case.

FAULTY   Our supervisor disapproves of *us* talking in the hallway.

CORRECT   Our supervisor disapproves of *our* talking in the hallway.

EDITING CHECKLIST

Pronoun Case

- Have you identified all the pronouns in the sentence?
- For each one, is it functioning as a subject, an object, or a possessive?
- Given the function for each one, have you used the correct form?

EDITING WITH A COMPUTER

You can use your word processor's Search or Find function to help you edit pronoun case. If you often misuse *I* in place of *me* or vice versa, have the computer locate all instances of both *I* and *me* so that you can be sure you've used them correctly. Or if you want to be sure you've used *who* and *whom* correctly, search for every instance of each of these words.

A4. Check for correct pronoun-antecedent agreement.

A *pronoun* replaces a noun or another pronoun in a sentence so that you do not have to repeat it. The *form* of a pronoun — the way it is spelled and pronounced — changes depending on exactly how it is used in a particular sentence. The form can change to show *number* — whether the subject is singular (one) or plural (more than one). It can also change to show *gender* — masculine or feminine, for example.

SINGULAR   My brother took *his* coat and left.

PLURAL   My brothers took *their* coats and left.

MASCULINE   I talked to Steven before *he* had a chance to leave.

FEMININE   I talked to Stephanie before *she* had a chance to leave.

In most cases, a pronoun refers to a specific noun or pronoun mentioned nearby; that word is called the pronoun's *antecedent*. The connection between the pronoun and the antecedent must be clear so that readers know what the pronoun means in the sentence. One way to make this connection clear is to ensure that the pronoun and the antecedent match (or *agree*) in terms of number and gender.

A common error in pronoun agreement is using a plural pronoun to refer to a singular antecedent. This often crops up when the antecedent is difficult to find, when the antecedent is an indefinite pronoun, or when the antecedent is confusing for some other reason. When editing for pronoun-antecedent agreement, look carefully to find the correct antecedent, and then make sure you know whether it is singular or plural. Make the pronoun match its antecedent.

FAULTY   Each of the boys in the Classic Club has *their* own rebuilt car.

CORRECT   Each of the boys in the Classic Club has *his* own rebuilt car.

[The word *each*, not *boys*, is the antecedent. *Each* is an indefinite pronoun and is always singular, so any pronoun referring to it must be singular as well.]

FAULTY   Everyone in the monastery had *their* own cell.

CORRECT   Everyone in the monastery had *his* own cell.

[*Everyone* is an indefinite pronoun that is always singular, so any pronoun referring to it must be singular as well.]

FAULTY   Neither Juanita nor Paula has received approval of *their* financial aid yet.

CORRECT   Neither Juanita nor Paula has received approval of *her* financial aid yet.

[*Neither Juanita nor Paula* is a compound subject joined by *nor*. Any pronoun referring to it must agree with only the nearest part of the compound. In other words, *her* needs to agree with *Paula*, which is singular, not with *Juanita and Paula*.]

Indefinite pronouns as antecedents are troublesome when they are grammatically singular but create a plural image in the writer's mind. Fortunately, most indefinite pronouns are either always singular or always plural.

Indefinite Pronouns

ALWAYS SINGULAR			ALWAYS PLURAL
anybody	everyone	no one	any
anyone	everything	nothing	both
anything	much	one (of)	few
each (of)	neither (of)	somebody	many
either (of)	nobody	someone	several
everybody	none	something	

EDITING CHECKLIST

Pronoun-Antecedent Agreement
- Have you identified the antecedent for each pronoun?
- Is the antecedent singular or plural? Does the pronoun match?
- Is the antecedent masculine, feminine, or neuter? Does the pronoun match?
- Is the antecedent in the first person, second person, or third person? Does the pronoun match?

EDITING WITH A COMPUTER

You can use your word processor's Search or Find function to locate some habitual problems with pronoun-verb agreement. Since indefinite pronouns as subjects often cause difficulties with subject-verb agreement, you can search for all instances of *each* or *few* (or whatever your particular bugaboo is) and make sure you've used the correct form of the verb. (For a list of indefinite pronouns, see p. R-9.) Consider keeping track of your pronoun-antecedent agreement errors so that you can take advantage of this feature to simplify your editing.

Grammar checkers do not catch problems with pronoun-antecedent agreement. A computer program can identify a pronoun, but it takes a human reader to recognize which word, if any, the pronoun refers to. As a result, grammar checkers miss even obvious errors.

A5. Check for correct adjectives and adverbs.

Adjectives and *adverbs* describe or give more information about (*modify*) other words in a sentence. Many adverbs are made by adding -*ly* to adjectives: *simple, simply; quiet, quietly*. Because adjectives and adverbs resemble one another, writers sometimes make the mistake of using one when they should use the other. To edit, find the word that the adjective or adverb modifies. If that word is a noun or pronoun, use an adjective. If it is a verb, adjective, or another adverb, use an adverb.

FAULTY Kelly ran into the house *quick*.
CORRECT Kelly ran into the house *quickly*.

FAULTY Michelle looked *terribly* after her bout with the flu.
CORRECT Michelle looked *terrible* after her bout with the flu.

Adjectives and adverbs that have similar comparative and superlative forms can also cause trouble. Take special care when using these: always ask whether you need an adjective or an adverb in the sentence, and then use the correct word.

FAULTY His scar from surgery healed so *good* that it was barely visible.
CORRECT His scar from surgery healed so *well* that it was barely visible.

Comparison of Irregular Adjectives and Adverbs

	POSITIVE	COMPARATIVE	SUPERLATIVE
ADJECTIVES	good	better	best
	bad	worse	worst
	little	less, littler	least, littlest
	many, some, much	more	most
ADVERBS	well	better	best
	badly	worse	worst
	little	less	least

EDITING CHECKLIST

Finding and Correcting Problems with Adjectives and Adverbs

- Have you identified which word the adjective or adverb modifies?
- If the word modified is a noun or pronoun, have you used an adjective?
- If the word modified is a verb, adjective, or adverb, have you used an adverb?
- Have you used the correct comparative or superlative form?

EDITING WITH A COMPUTER

You can use your word processor's Search or Find function to help you edit for correct adjective and adverb use. If you have difficulty with the irregular adjectives and adverbs listed on this page, have the computer find every instance so that you can check your usage. Or you can have the computer search for *-ly* at the ends of words to make sure that you have used adverb forms correctly. (This won't help with the instances where you should have used an *-ly* adverb but did not.) Since these common modifiers often cause problems, consider having the computer search for *quick(ly), slow(ly), real(ly),* and *slow(ly)*. Consider keeping track of your adjective and adverb errors so that you can take advantage of this feature to simplify your editing.

Grammar checkers are useful for identifying some perennial adjective and adverb problems, such as the confusion of *good* and *well*. At the very least, they can flag your use of these words and ask whether you have used them correctly. However, aside from these few troublesome modifiers, grammar checkers are relatively useless for identifying adjective and adverb problems.

A6.   Find and correct any sentence fragments.

A complete sentence is one that has a subject, has a predicate, and can stand on its own. A *sentence fragment* lacks a subject, a predicate, or both, or for some other reason fails to convey a complete thought. It cannot stand on its own as a sentence.

Although they are used frequently in advertising and fiction, fragments are usually ineffective in college writing because they do not communicate coherent thoughts. The cause of a fragment is often a pause or interruption in thought as you are writing. To edit for fragments, examine each sentence carefully to make sure it has a subject, a verb, and expresses a complete thought. To correct a fragment, either make it into a complete sentence or join it to a complete sentence nearby, depending on which would make more sense.

FAULTY   Bob has two sisters. Denise and Leasa.

CORRECT   Bob has two sisters, Denise and Leasa.

FAULTY   The children going to the zoo.

CORRECT   The children were going to the zoo.

CORRECT   The children going to the zoo were caught in a traffic jam on the interstate.

FAULTY   Last night when we saw Jack Nicholson's most recent movie.

CORRECT   Last night we saw Jack Nicholson's most recent movie.

EDITING CHECKLIST

Finding and Correcting Fragments

- Does the sentence have a subject?
- Does the sentence have a complete verb?
- If the sentence contains a subordinate clause, does it contain a complete main clause too?
- If you have a fragment, is it a phrase? If so, link it to an adjoining sentence.
- If you have a fragment, is it a clause? If so, link it to an adjoining sentence or eliminate its subordinating conjunction.

EDITING WITH A COMPUTER

If you have a serious problem with sentence fragments, you may need to find a way to focus on each individual sentence in your writing rather than reading through your paper quickly. A word processor can help. Make a duplicate of your document. Then use the Replace function to find each period and replace it with a period followed by two returns. This technique will put each sentence (or each group of words punctuated as a sentence) on its own line. Now you should go through each sentence and make sure you can find a subject and verb. Starting from the end of the paper, read each one aloud to see if it makes sense on its own. Be on the lookout for any "sentences" that are especially short; they may lack essential sentence elements. These techniques may help you locate sentence fragments in your writing.

Grammar checkers can catch some, but not all, sentence fragments. For example, some programs correctly flag the sentence fragment *Ella and Louis going to the Cotton Club*, yet they ignore *Ella going to the Cotton Club*. Grammar checkers also ignored the following fragments: *As the curtain rose and the actors took the stage. The stars twinkled in the heavens, but the moon.* Moreover, some grammar checkers will incorrectly identify a complete sentence as a fragment, such as *The campers curled up inside their sleeping bags to stay warm.* If you have a problem with sentence fragments, learn to proofread for them.

A7. Find and correct any comma splices or fused sentences.

A complete sentence has a subject, has a predicate, and can stand on its own. Sometimes two sentences are joined together to form one sentence (each sentence within the larger sentence is called an *independent clause*). However, there are rules for joining independent clauses, and when writers fail to follow these rules, they create serious sentence errors — comma splices or fused sentences. A *comma splice* is two independent clauses joined with only a comma. A *fused sentence* is two independent clauses joined with no punctuation at all. These errors often occur because the writer's mind is running faster than the pen (or fingers on the keyboard) can move.

COMMA SPLICE	I went to the mall, I bought a CD of my favorite jazz group.
FUSED SENTENCE	I went to the mall I bought a CD of my favorite jazz group.

To find comma splices and run-on sentences, examine each sentence to be sure it is a complete sentence. If it has two independent clauses, make sure they are joined correctly. If you find a comma splice or run-on sentence, correct it in one of these four ways, depending on which makes the best sense.

ADD A PERIOD	I went to the mall. I bought a CD of my favorite jazz group.
ADD A SEMICOLON	I went to the mall; I bought a CD of my favorite jazz group.
ADD A COMMA AND A COORDINATING CONJUNCTION	I went to the mall, and I bought a CD of my favorite jazz group.
ADD A SUBORDINATING CONJUNCTION	I went to the mall where I bought a CD of my favorite jazz group.

EDITING CHECKLIST

Correcting Comma Splices and Fused Sentences
- Can you make each main clause a separate sentence?
- Can you link the two main clauses with a comma and a coordinating conjunction?
- Can you link the two main clauses with a semicolon or, if appropriate, a colon?
- Can you subordinate one clause to the other?

EDITING WITH A COMPUTER

If you have a serious problem with comma splices and fused sentences, you may need to focus on each individual sentence in your writing rather than reading through your paper quickly. A word processor can help. Make a duplicate of your document. Then use the Replace function to find each period and replace it with a period followed by two returns. This technique will put each sentence (or each group of words punctuated as a sentence) on its own line. Now you should go through each sentence and make sure either that it has only one independent clause — or that, if it has two independent clauses, they are joined correctly. Starting from the end of the paper, read each sentence aloud to see if it sounds correct; your inner ear is often a good resource. Be on the lookout for any "sentences" that are especially long; they may be two sentences incorrectly joined. These techniques may help you locate comma splices and fused sentences in your writing.

Grammar checkers can catch some comma splices and fused sentences, but they frequently overlook such errors. For example, most programs would miss the comma splice in this sentence: *In those days I was earning just enough money to pay the rent, new clothes were a luxury I could not afford.* And programs that can identify a comma splice may not be able to suggest correct punctuation. You will need to judge for yourself whether a flagged sentence needs correcting and how best to repair the problem.

B. *Editing to Ensure Effective Sentences*

B1. Find and correct any misplaced or dangling modifiers.

Modifiers are words or word groups that describe or give more information about other words in a sentence. For the sentence to be clear, the connection between the modifier and the thing it modifies must be obvious. Usually, a modifier should be placed right before or right after the sentence element it modifies. If the modifier is placed too close to some other sentence element, it is a *misplaced modifier*. If there is nothing in the sentence that the modifier can logically modify, it is a *dangling modifier*. Both of these errors cause confusion for readers — and they sometimes create unintentionally humorous images. As you edit, be sure that a modifier is placed directly before or after the word modified and that the connection is clear.

MISPLACED   George found some leftover chicken when he visited in the refrigerator.

CORRECT   George found some leftover chicken in the refrigerator when he visited.

[In the faulty sentence, *in the refrigerator* seems to modify George's visit, when obviously it is the chicken that is in the refrigerator.]

MISPLACED   The movie that Barb enjoyed a great deal bored Sharon.

CORRECT   The movie that Barb enjoyed bored Sharon a great deal.

[This type of problem, where a modifier (*a great deal*) can plausibly modify either of two things (Barb's enjoyment or Sharon's boredom) is sometimes called a *squinting modifier*. Edit by moving the modifier to make the correct relationship clear.]

DANGLING   Looking out the window, the clouds were beautiful.

CORRECT   Looking out the window, I saw that the clouds were beautiful.

[In the faulty sentence, *looking out the window* should modify *I*, but *I* is not in the sentence. The modifier is left without anything logical to modify—a dangling modifier. To correct this, the writer has to edit so that *I* is in the sentence.]

EDITING CHECKLIST

Finding and Correcting Misplaced and Dangling Modifiers

- For each modifier in the sentence, what is it meant to modify? Is the modifier as close as possible to that sentence element? Is any misreading possible?
- If there is a misplaced modifier, can you move the modifier to clarify the meaning?
- What noun, pronoun, or noun phrase is a dangling modifier meant to modify? Can you make that word or phrase the subject of the main clause?
- Can you turn the dangling modifier into a clause that includes the missing noun or pronoun?

EDITING WITH A COMPUTER

A word processor can help you focus on the sentence elements that often hide misplaced or dangling modifiers. Go through your paper, and highlight (with boldface or underlining, for example) all introductory phrases; these are at the beginning of sentences and are usually followed by a comma. Then go back and look at each one. If it is a modifier, does it clearly point to the sentence element it modifies? Could the relationship be made clearer?

Grammar checkers cannot flag misplaced or dangling modifiers. Only a human reader can recognize this kind of ambiguity.

B2.   Check for parallel structure.

A series of words, phrases, clauses, or sentences with the same grammatical form are said to possess *parallel structure* or *parallelism*. Using parallel structure for elements that are parallel in meaning or function helps readers grasp the meaning of a sentence more easily. A lack of parallelism can confuse readers: at the very least, it will distract and annoy them.

To use parallelism, use similar structures to express similar ideas. Put nouns with nouns, verbs with verbs, and phrases with phrases. Parallelism is particularly important in a series, with correlative conjunctions (*both . . . and; either . . . or; neither . . . not; not only . . . but also; rather . . . than*), and in comparisons using *than* or *as*.

FAULTY   I like to go to Estes Park for skiing, ice skating, and to meet interesting people.

CORRECT   I like to go to Estes Park to ski, to ice skate, and to meet interesting people.

FAULTY   The proposal is neither practical, nor is it innovative.

CORRECT   The proposal is neither practical nor innovative.

FAULTY   When dealing with a small child, a parent should have a few firm rules rather than having many flimsy ones.

CORRECT   When dealing with a small child, a parent should have a few firm rules rather than many flimsy ones.

Take special care to reinforce parallel structures by repeating articles, conjunctions, prepositions, or lead-in words as needed.

AWKWARD   His dream was that he would never have to give up his routine enjoyments but he would nonetheless find time to explore new frontiers.

PARALLEL His dream was that he would never have to give up his routine enjoyments but *that* he would nonetheless find time to explore new frontiers.

 **EDITING CHECKLIST**

Parallel Structure

- Are all the elements in a series in the same grammatical form?
- Are the elements in a comparison parallel in form?
- Are the articles, conjunctions, or prepositions between elements repeated rather than mixed or omitted?
- In a series of clauses, are lead-in words repeated?

 **EDITING WITH A COMPUTER**

You can use your word processor's Search or Find function to help you locate some sentences that may have problems with parallelism. Have the computer find the first word in correlative conjunctions (for a list, see page R-15). Then read each sentence carefully to make sure that the second word is present and that parallel structure is used.

Grammar checkers cannot catch faulty parallelism because they cannot judge whether ideas have parallel meanings. It takes a human reader, able to understand the meaning of words, to identify faulty parallelism.

C. *Editing for Common Punctuation Problems*

C1. Check for correct use of commas.

The *comma* is a punctuation mark indicating a pause. By setting some words apart from others, commas help clarify relationships; they prevent the words on the page and the ideas they represent from becoming a meaningless jumble. There are many conventional uses of commas; here are some of the most important.

1. Use a comma after an introductory clause, phrase, or word group.

    After the war, the North's economy developed rapidly.

2. Use commas to separate the items in a series of three or more items.

    The chief advantages will be *speed,* *durability,* and *longevity.*

3. Use a comma before the coordinating conjunction (*and, but, for, or, so, yet, nor*) joining two independent clauses in a compound sentence.

    The discussion was brief, *so* the meeting was adjourned early.

4. Use commas to set off an appositive; an appositive comes directly after a noun or pronoun and renames it.

    Sheri, *my sister,* has a new job as an events coordinator.

5. Use commas to set off parenthetical expressions, conjunctive adverbs, and other interrupters.

    The proposal from the mayor's commission, however, will not be feasible.

6. Use commas to set off an adjective clause if it is nonrestrictive — that is, if it can be taken out of the sentence without completely changing the meaning of the sentence. (An adjective clause is a group of words with a subject and a verb that begins with *who, which,* or *that* and describes a noun immediately before it in a sentence.)

    Good childcare, *which is difficult to find,* should be provided by the employer.

    Good childcare *that is reliable and inexpensive* is the right of every employee.

EDITING CHECKLIST

Using Commas Correctly

*   Is there a comma after each introductory clause, phrase, or word?
*   Are items in a series separated by commas?
*   Do two main clauses joined by a coordinating conjunction have a comma between them?
*   Is there a comma before and after each nonrestrictive phrase or clause?
*   Have you used commas to set off parenthetical expressions, conjunctive adverbs, and other interrupters?
*   Have you avoided putting commas before the first item in a series or after the last?
*   Have you avoided using commas around a restrictive word, phrase, or clause?

EDITING WITH A COMPUTER

If you have a problem with using too many commas, you may want to use the computer's Search or Find function to identify every comma in your writing. Then you can examine each one to make sure it is necessary and used correctly. (Be warned! The average paper can contain quite a few commas, so prepare yourself for a few minutes of editing time.)

Grammar checkers can flag some punctuation errors, but because they cannot understand the meaning of sentences, they ignore many more than they catch. Grammar checkers can remind you that a comma is often required before or after certain words, such as *which* or *therefore*, but they ignore most other misused or missing commas.

C2. Check for correct use of apostrophes.

An apostrophe is a punctuation mark that either shows possession (*Sylvia's*) or indicates that one or more letters have intentionally been left out to form a contraction (*didn't*). Since apostrophes are so small and easy to overlook, careless writers often either omit a necessary apostrophe, use one where it is not needed, or put the apostrophe in the wrong place. Learn how to use apostrophes correctly, and proofread for them carefully. Remember that an apostrophe is never used to create the possessive form of a pronoun; use the possessive pronoun form instead.

FAULTY   *Mikes* car was totaled in the accident.

CORRECT   *Mike's* car was totaled in the accident.

FAULTY   The principles of the *womens'* liberation movement are still controversial to some people.

CORRECT   The principles of the *women's* liberation movement are still controversial to some people.

FAULTY   The dog wagged *it's* tail happily.

CORRECT   The dog wagged *its* tail happily.

FAULTY   *Its* raining.

CORRECT   *It's* raining.

FAULTY   Che *did'nt* want to stay at home and study.

CORRECT   Che *didn't* want to stay at home and study.

Possessive Case of Personal Pronouns

PERSONAL PRONOUN	POSSESSIVE CASE
I	my, mine
you	your, yours (*not* your's)
he	his
she	her, hers (*not* her's)
it	its (*not* it's)
we	our, ours (*not* our's)
they	their, theirs (*not* their's)
who	whose (*not* who's)

EDITING CHECKLIST

Using Apostrophes Correctly

- Have you used apostrophes to show letters left out in a contraction?
- Have you used apostrophes to create the possessive form of nouns?
- Have you used the possessive case—rather than an apostrophe—to show that pronouns are possessive?
- Have you used *it's* correctly (to mean *it is*)?

EDITING WITH A COMPUTER

If you often put apostrophes where they don't belong (by misspelling contractions or using *it's* where you mean *its*, for example), you may want to use the computer's Search or Find function to identify every apostrophe in your writing. Then you can examine each one to make sure it is necessary and used correctly. (Be warned! The average paper can contain quite a few apostrophes, so prepare yourself for a few minutes of editing time.) If you often misuse *its* and *it's*, you may want to have the computer locate every instance of each word so that you can make sure you have used it correctly.

Grammar checkers can flag some punctuation errors, but because they cannot understand the meaning of sentences, they ignore many more than they catch. Grammar checkers can flag missing apostrophes in common contractions, such as *won't* and *didn't*, and can catch some, but not all, problems with possessives.

D. *Editing for Common Mechanics Problems*

D1. Check for correct use of capital letters.

Capital letters are used in three general situations: at the beginning of a new sentence; at the beginning of names of specific peoples, places, dates, and things (proper nouns); and at the beginning of important words in titles. Careless writers often use capital letters where they are not needed; a common error is to use capital letters for emphasis. Sometimes writers also fail to use capital letters where they are needed. Both problems can cause confusion to readers, so check your capitalization carefully.

FAULTY   During my Sophomore year in College, I took World Literature, Biology, History, Psychology, and French — courses required for my Major in English.

CORRECT   During my sophomore year in college, I took world literature, biology, history, psychology, and French — courses required for my major in English.

FAULTY   Desdemona, who was raised in the Southern part of Alabama and did not travel out of the southeast until she was twenty years old, has a distinct Southern drawl.

CORRECT   Desdemona, who was raised in the southern part of Alabama and did not travel out of the Southeast until she was twenty years old, has a distinct southern drawl.

EDITING
CHECKLIST

Capitalizing Correctly

- Have you used a capital letter at the beginning of each complete sentence, including sentences that are quoted?
- Have you used capital letters for proper nouns and pronouns?
- Have you avoided using capital letters for emphasis?
- Have you used a capital letter for each important word in a title, including the first word and the last word?

EDITING WITH
A COMPUTER

Grammar checkers can remind you that sentences should start with capital letters. And spell checkers may flag words that you have lowercased but that most dictionaries usually spell with a capital letter: they would recommend using *France* instead of *france*, for example. Many words, however, should be capitalized only in certain contexts, according to how they are used in a sentence. And both spell checkers and grammar checkers may miss many more errors than they find. Use these tools, but use them with care.

Capitalization at a Glance

Capitalize the following.

THE FIRST LETTER OF A SENTENCE, INCLUDING A QUOTED SENTENCE
She called out, "Come in! The water's not cold."

PROPER NAMES AND ADJECTIVES MADE FROM THEM
Marie Curie   Cranberry Island   Smithsonian Institution
a Freudian reading

RANK OR TITLE BEFORE A PROPER NAME
Ms. Olson   Professor Harvey

FAMILY RELATIONSHIP ONLY WHEN IT SUBSTITUTES FOR OR IS PART OF A PROPER NAME
Grandma Jones   Father Time

RELIGIONS, THEIR FOLLOWERS, AND DEITIES
Islam   Orthodox Jew   Buddha

PLACES, REGIONS, AND GEOGRAPHIC FEATURES
Palo Alto   the Berkshire Mountains

DAYS OF THE WEEK, MONTHS, AND HOLIDAYS
Wednesday   July   Labor Day

HISTORICAL EVENTS, PERIODS, AND DOCUMENTS
the Boston Tea Party   the Middle Ages   the Constitution

SCHOOLS, COLLEGES, UNIVERSITIES, AND SPECIFIC COURSES
Temple University   Introduction to Clinical Psychology

FIRST, LAST, AND MAIN WORDS IN TITLES OF PAPERS, BOOKS, ARTICLES, WORKS OF ART, TELEVISION SHOWS, POEMS, AND PERFORMANCES
The Decline and Fall of the Roman Empire

D2. Check spelling.

Misspelled words are difficult to spot in your own writing. You usually see what you think you wrote, and often pronunciation or faulty memory may interfere with correct spelling. When you proofread for spelling, check especially for words that sound alike but are spelled differently (*accept* and *except*, for example), words that are spelled differently than they are pronounced, words that do not follow the basic rules for spelling English words (*judgment*, for example), and words that you habitually confuse and misspell. On pages R-21 to R-25 are two useful lists: words that are commonly confused and words that are often misspelled. Consult them as a reference; use a dictionary whenever you still have questions.

 **EDITING CHECKLIST**

Finding and Correcting Misspellings

- Have you checked for the words you habitually misspell?
- Have you checked for commonly confused or misspelled words?
- Are you familiar with the standard spelling rules, including their exceptions?
- Have you checked a dictionary for any words you are unsure about?

 **EDITING WITH A COMPUTER**

If you know which words you habitually misspell, you can use your word processor's Search or Find functions to locate all instances and check their spelling. Consider keeping track of misspelled words in your papers for a few weeks so you can take advantage of this feature to simplify your editing.

Spelling checkers offer a handy alternative to the dictionary, but writers need to be aware of their limitations. A spelling checker program compares the words in your text to the words listed in its dictionary, and it flags words that do not appear there. (The size of computer spelling dictionaries varies greatly, but most contain fewer entries than a typical college-level dictionary in book form.) A spelling checker cannot help you spell words that its dictionary does not contain, including most proper nouns. Spelling checkers ignore one-letter words; for example, they will not flag a typographical error such as *s truck* for *a truck*. Nor will spelling checkers flag words that are misspelled as different words, such as *except* for *accept*, *to* for *too*, or *own* for *won*. Always check the spelling in your text by eye *after* you've used your spelling checker software.

Grammar checkers can flag some commonly confused homonyms (see below), but they often do this even when you have used the correct form. Use a dictionary to decide whether to accept the grammar checker's suggestion.

COMMONLY CONFUSED HOMONYMS

accept (v., receive willingly); **except** (prep., other than)

Mimi could *accept* all of Lefty's gifts *except* his ring.

affect (v., influence); **effect** (n., result)

If the new rules *affect* us, what will be their *effect*?

COMMONLY CONFUSED HOMONYMS (continued)

allusion (n., reference); **illusion** (n., fantasy)

Any *allusion* to Norman's mother may revive his *illusion* that she is upstairs, alive, in her rocking chair.

capital (adj., uppercase; n., seat of government); **capitol** (n., government building)

The *Capitol* building in Washington, D.C. (our nation's *capital*), is spelled with a *capital C*.

cite (v., refer to); **sight** (n., vision or tourist attraction); **site** (n., place)

Did you *cite* Mother as your authority on which *sites* feature the most interesting *sights*?

complement (v., complete; n., counterpart); **compliment** (v. or n., praise)

For Lee to say that Sheila's beauty *complements* her intelligence may or may not be a *compliment*.

desert (v., abandon); **dessert** (n., end-of-meal sweet)

Don't *desert* us by leaving before *dessert*.

elicit (v., bring out); **illicit** (adj., illegal)

By going undercover, Sonny should *elicit* some offers of *illicit* drugs.

formally (adv., officially); **formerly** (adv., in the past)

Jane and John Doe-Smith, *formerly* Jane Doe and John Smith, sent cards *formally* announcing their marriage.

led (v., past tense of *lead*); **lead** (n., a metal)

Gil's heart was heavy as *lead* when he *led* the mourners to the grave.

principal (n. or adj., chief); **principle** (n., rule)

The *principal* problem is convincing the media that our school *principal* is a person of high *principles*.

stationary (adj., motionless); **stationery** (n., writing paper)

Hubert's *stationery* shop stood *stationary* for twenty years until a flood swept it down the river.

their (pron., belonging to them); **there** (adv., in that place); **they're** (contraction of *they are*)

Sue said *they're* going over *there* to visit *their* aunt.

to (prep., toward); **too** (adv., also or excessively); **two** (n. or adj., numeral: one more than one)

(continued)

COMMONLY CONFUSED HOMONYMS (continued)

Let's not take *two* cars *to* town — that's *too* many unless Lucille and Harry are coming *too*.

who's (contraction of *who is*); **whose** (pron., belonging to whom)

Who's going to tell me *whose* dog this is?

your (pron., belonging to you); **you're** (contraction of *you are*)

You're not getting *your* own way this time!

COMMONLY MISSPELLED WORDS

absence	appreciate	characteristic
academic	appropriate	chief
acceptable	arctic	choose
accessible	arrest	(present tense)
accidentally	argument	chose (past tense)
accommodate	ascend	climbed
achievement	assassinate	column
acknowledgment	assistance	coming
acquaintance	association	commitment
acquire	athlete	committed
across	athletics	committee
address	attendance	comparative
advertisement	attractive	competent
advice	audience	competition
advise	average	complement
aggravate	awkward	compliment
aggressive	basically	conceive
aging	beginning	condemn
allege	believe	congratulate
alleviate	beneficial	conscience
all right	benefited	conscientious
all together (all in	breath (noun)	conscious
one group)	breathe (verb)	consistent
a lot	bureaucracy	controlled
already	business	controversy
although	cafeteria	criticism
altogether (entirely)	calendar	criticize
amateur	candidate	cruise
analysis	careful	curiosity
analyze	casualties	curious
answer	category	deceive
anxiety	ceiling	decision
apology	cemetery	defendant
apparent	certain	deficient
appetite	changeable	definite
appearance	changing	dependent

(continued)

COMMONLY MISSPELLED WORDS (continued)

descendant
describe
description
desirable
despair
desperate
develop
development
device (noun)
devise (verb)
diary
difference
dilemma
dining
disappear
disappoint
disastrous
discipline
discussion
disease
dissatisfied
divide
doesn't
dominant
don't
drawer
drunkenness
efficiency
eighth
either
eligible
embarrass
emphasize
entirety
environment
equipped
equivalent
especially
exaggerate
exceed
excel
excellence
exercise
exhaust
existence
experience
explanation
extremely

familiar
fascinate
February
fiery
finally
financial
foreign
foresee
forth
forty
forward
fourth (number
    four)
frantically
fraternities
friend
fulfill
fulfillment
gaiety
gauge
genealogy
generally
genuine
government
grammar
grief
guarantee
guard
guidance
harass
height
heroes
humorous
hurrying
hygiene
illiterate
illogical
imitation
immediately
incidentally
incredible
indefinite
independence
indispensable
infinite
influential
intelligence
intentionally

interest
interpret
interrupt
irrelevant
irresistible
irritable
island
its (possessive)
it's (it is, it has)
jealousy
judgment
knowledge
laboratory
led (past tense of
    lead)
library
license
lightning
literature
loneliness
loose (adjective)
lose (verb)
lying
magazine
maintenance
marriage
mathematics
medicine
miniature
mischievous
misspell
misstep
muscle
mysterious
necessary
neither
nickel
niece
ninety
ninth
noticeable
notorious
nuclear
nucleus
numerous
obstacle
occasion
occasionally

(continued)

COMMONLY MISSPELLED WORDS (continued)

occur	quizzes	successful
occurrence	realize	suddenness
official	rebelled	supersede
omission	recede	suppress
omitted	receipt	surprise
opinion	receive	suspicious
opportunity	recipe	technical
originally	recommend	technique
outrageous	reference	temperature
paid	referring	tendency
pamphlet	regrettable	therefore
panicky	relevance	thorough
parallel	relief	thoroughbred
particularly	relieve	though
pastime	religious	thought
peaceable	remembrance	throughout
perceive	reminisce	tragedy
perform	reminiscence	transferred
performance	repetition	traveler
perhaps	representative	traveling
permanent	resistance	truly
permissible	restaurant	twelfth
persistence	review	tyranny
personnel	rhythm	unanimous
persuade	ridiculous	unnecessary
physical	roommate	unnoticed
playwright	sacrifice	until
possession	safety	useful
possibly	scarcely	usually
practically	scarcity	vacuum
precede	schedule	valuable
predominant	secretary	vengeance
preferred	seize	vicious
prejudice	separate	view
preparation	sergeant	villain
prevalent	shining	warrant
privilege	siege	weather
probably	similar	Wednesday
procedure	sincerely	weird
proceed	sophomore	whether
professor	source	wholly
prominent	specifically	who's (who is)
pronounce	sponsor	whose (possessive of
pronunciation	strategy	*who*)
pursue	strength	withhold
quantity	strenuous	woman
quiet	stretch	women
quite	succeed	writing

D3. Check for correct manuscript form.

Some instructors are sticklers in specifying how your paper ought to look; others maintain a benign indifference about form. In writing for an instructor of either school, you would do well to turn in a paper easy to read and to comment on.

In case you have received no particular instructions for the form of your paper, here are some general, all-purpose specifications.

General Manuscript Style for Essays, Articles, and Reports

1. If you handwrite your paper, make sure your handwriting is legible. If you type, keep your typewriter keys clean, or make sure you have a fresh ribbon or toner in your printer. If you use a word processor, don't format your paper entirely in italics or extra-fine characters. Pick a conventional, easy-to-read typeface such as Courier, Times Roman, Helvetica, or Palatino.

2. Use dark blue or black ink if you write and a black ribbon or ink if you type or use a computer.

3. Write, type, or print on just one side of standard letter-size paper (8½ inches by 11 inches).

4. If you handwrite your paper, use 8½-by-11 inch paper with smooth edges (not torn from a spiral-bound notebook). If you type or use a computer, use a smooth bond paper. Erasable typing paper, however helpful to a mistake-prone typist, may be irksome to an instructor who needs to write comments. The paper is easily smeared, and it won't take certain kinds of ink.

5. For a paper without a separate title page, place your name, together with your instructor's name, the number and section of the course, and the date in the upper left or right corner of the first page, each item on a new line. (Check to see whether your instructor has a preference for which side.) Double-space and center your title. Don't underline the title, don't put it in quotation marks or type the title in all capital letters, and don't put a period after it. Capitalize the first and last words, the first word after a colon or semicolon, and all other words except prepositions, coordinating conjunctions, and articles. Double-space between the title and the first line of your text. (Most instructors do not require a title page for short college papers. If your instructor does request one but doesn't give you any guidelines, see number 1 under "Additional Suggestions for Research Papers" on the following page.)

6. Number your pages consecutively, including the first page. For a paper of two or more pages, put your last name in the upper right corner of each sheet along with the page number. Do not type the word *page* or the letter *p* before the number, and do not follow the number with a period or parenthesis.

7. Leave ample margins — at least an inch — left and right, top and bottom.

8. If you type or use a word processor, double-space your manuscript; if you handwrite, use wide-ruled paper or skip every other line.

9. Indent each new paragraph five spaces or one-half inch.

10. Long quotations should be double-spaced like the rest of your paper but indented from the left margin — ten spaces (one inch) if you're following MLA (Modern Language Association) guidelines, five if you're using APA (American Psychological Association) guidelines. Citations appear in parentheses immediately after the final punctuation mark of the block quotation. (For more about citing sources, consult a style manual.)

11. Place a comma or period inside closed quotation marks.

12. Try not to break words at the ends of lines. If you must break a word, divide it between syllables. If you're uncertain about where a syllable ends, check a dictionary.

13. Label all illustrations, and make sure they are bound securely to the paper.

14. Staple the paper in the top left corner. Don't use any other method to secure the pages.

15. For safety's sake and peace of mind, make a copy of your paper.

Additional Suggestions for Research Papers

For research papers, the format is the same as recommended in the previous section, with the following additional specifications.

1. Type a title page, with the title of your paper centered and double-spaced about a third of the way down the page. Then go down two to four more spaces and type your name, then the instructor's name, the number and section of the course, and the date, each on a separate line, double-spaced.

2. Do not number your title page; number your outline, if you submit one with your paper, with small roman numerals (ii, iii, and so on). Number consecutively all subsequent pages in the essay, including your "Works Cited" or "References" pages, using arabic numerals (1, 2, 3, and so on) in the upper right corner of the page.

3. Double-space your works cited or references list, if you have one.

How to Make a Correction

Although you will want to make any large changes in your rough draft before you produce your final copy, don't be afraid to make small corrections in pen when you give your paper a last once-over. No writer is error-free; neither is any typist. In making such corrections, you may find it handy to use certain symbols used by printers and proofreaders.

A transposition mark (⌒) reverses the positions of two words or two letters:

The nearby star Tau Ceti closely resmebles our sun.

Close-up marks (⌒) bring together the parts of a word accidentally split. A separation mark (|) inserts a space where one is needed:

```
The nearby star Tau Ceti closely re sembles our sun.
```

To delete a letter or a punctuation mark, draw a line with a curlicue through it:

```
The nearby star Tau Ceti closely ressembles our sun.
```

When you insert a word or letter, use a caret (∧) to indicate where the insertion belongs:

```
                                       s
The nearby star Tau Ceti closely reembles our sun.
                                     ∧
```

The symbol ¶ before a word or a line means "start a new paragraph":

```
But lately, astronomers have slackened their efforts to
                           ¶
study dark nebulae. That other solar systems may support

life as we know it makes for still another fascinating

speculation.
```

To make a letter lowercase, draw a slanted line through it. To make a letter uppercase, put three short lines under it:

```
i read it for my History class.
=
```

You can always cross out a word neatly, with a single horizontal line, and write a better one over it (*never* type a correction right over a mistake).

```
                            closely
The nearby star Tau Ceti somewhat resembles our sun.
```

Finally, if a page has many handwritten corrections on it, type or write it over again.

A Glossary of Troublemakers

Usage refers to the way in which writers customarily use certain words and phrases. It includes matters of accepted practice or convention. To incorporate appropriate usage in your writing, you can observe (as dictionary makers carefully do) the practices followed by a majority of admirable writers.

This glossary lists words and phrases whose usage troubles student writers. Not every possible problem is listed — only some that frequently puzzle students. This brief list is meant to help you pinpoint a few sources of difficulty and wipe them out. Look it over; refer to it when you don't remember the preferred usage. It may clear up a few problems for you.

For advice on getting rid of long-winded expressions (*in the field of, in regards to*), see page H-134. For advice on spelling, see Chapter 36.

a, an   Use *an* only before a word beginning with a vowel sound. "*An* asp can eat *an* egg *an* hour." (Note that some words, such as *hour* and *honest*, open with a vowel sound even though spelled with an *h*.)

above   Using *above* or *below* to refer back or forward in an essay is awkward and may not be accurate. Less awkward alternatives: "the *preceding* argument," "in the *following* discussion," "on the *next* page."

accept, except   *Accept* is a verb meaning "to receive willingly"; *except* is usually a preposition meaning "not including." "This motel *accepts* all children *except* infants under two." Sometimes *except* is a verb, meaning "to exempt." "The rate of $20 per person *excepts* children under twelve."

adverse, averse   *Adverse* means "unfavorable or antagonistic" and is used to modify things, not people. *Averse* means "reluctant or strongly opposed" and is followed by *to*. "Because of the *adverse* winds, the captain is *averse* to setting sail."

advice, advise   *Advice* is a noun, *advise* a verb. When someone *advises* you, you receive *advice*.

affect, effect   Most of the time, the verb *affect* means "to act on" or "to influence." "Too much beer can *affect* your speech." *Affect* can also mean "to put on airs." "He *affected* an Oxford accent." *Effect*, a noun, means "a result": "Too much beer has a numbing *effect*." But *effect* is also a verb, meaning "to bring about." "Beer *effected* his downfall."

aggravate   Although in speech people often use *aggravate* to mean "to annoy," in formal writing use *aggravate* to mean "to make worse." "The noise of the jackhammers *aggravated* her headache."

agree to, agree with, agree on   *Agree to* means "to consent to"; *agree with*, "to be in accord." "I *agreed to* attend the New Age lecture, but I didn't *agree with* the speaker's views." *Agree on* means "to come to or have an understanding about." "Chuck and I finally *agreed on* a compromise: the children would go to camp but not overnight."

ain't Don't use *ain't* in writing; it is nonstandard English for *am not, is not* (*isn't*), and *are not* (*aren't*).

allusion, illusion An *allusion* is a reference to history, literature, music, science, or some other area of knowledge. In the statement "Two by two we hurried aboard Flight 937 as though the waters of the flood lapped at our heels," the writer makes an allusion to the biblical story of Noah's ark. An *illusion* is a misleading appearance ("an optical illusion") or a mistaken assumption. "He labors under the *illusion* that he's Romeo" (to give an example with an allusion in it).

a lot Many people mistakenly write the colloquial expression *a lot* as one word: *alot*. Use *a lot* if you must; but in writing, *much* or *a large amount* is preferable. See also *lots, lots of, a lot of.*

already, all ready *Already* means "by now"; *all ready* means "set to go." "At last our picnic was *all ready,* but *already* it was night."

altogether, all together *Altogether* means "entirely." "He is *altogether* mistaken." *All together* means "in unison" or "assembled." "Now *all together* — heave!" "Inspector Trent gathered the suspects *all together* in the drawing room."

among, between *Between* refers to two persons or things; *among*, to more than two. "Some disagreement *between* the two superpowers was inevitable. Still, there was general harmony *among* the five nations represented at the conference."

amoral, immoral *Amoral* means "neither moral nor immoral" or "not involved with moral distinctions or judgments." "Some people think children are *amoral* and should not be held accountable for their actions." *Immoral* means "violating moral principles, morally wrong." "Stealing from the poor is *immoral.*"

amount, number Use *amount* to refer to quantities that cannot be counted or to bulk; use *number* to refer to countable, separate items. "The *number* of people you want to serve determines the *amount* of ice cream you'll need."

an, a See *a, an.*

and/or Usually use either *and* or *or* alone. "Tim *and* Elaine will come to the party." "Tim *or* Elaine will come to the party." If you mean three distinct options, write, "Tim *or* Elaine, *or both,* will come to the party, depending on whether they can find a babysitter."

ante-, anti- The prefix *ante-* means "preceding." An *antechamber* is a small room that leads to a larger one; *antebellum* means "before the Civil War." *Anti-* most often means "opposing": *antidepressant.* It needs a hyphen in front of *i* (*anti-inflationary*) or in front of a capital letter (*anti-Marxist*).

anxious, eager Although the meanings of these two words overlap to some extent, in writing reserve *anxious* for situations involving anxiety or worry. *Eager* denotes joyous anticipation. "We are *eager* to see him, but we're *anxious* about his failing health."

anybody, any body When *anybody* is used as an indefinite pronoun, write it as one word: "*Anybody* in his or her right mind abhors murder." (*Anybody* is singular; therefore it is wrong to say "Anybody in *their* right mind." See 22 for acceptable alternatives.) *Any body,* written as two words, is the adjective *any* modifying the noun *body.* "Name *any body* of water in Australia."

anyone, any one *Anyone* is an indefinite pronoun written as one word. "Does *anyone* want dessert?" The phrase *any one* consists of the pronoun *one* modified by the adjective *any* and is used to single out something in a group: "Pick *any one* of the pies — they're all good."

anyplace *Anyplace* is colloquial for *anywhere* and should not be used in formal writing.

anyways, anywheres These are nonstandard forms of *anyway* and *anywhere* and should not be used in writing.

apt Usually, *apt* means "likely." "That film is *apt* to bore you." "Jack's big feet make him *apt* to trip." *Apt* can also mean "fitting" and "quick to learn": "an *apt* nickname," "an *apt* student of French." See also *likely, liable.*

as Sometimes using the subordinating conjunction *as* can make a sentence ambiguous. "*As* we were climbing the mountain, we put on heavy sweaters." Does *as* here mean "because" or "while"? Whenever using *as* would be confusing, use a more specific term instead, such as *because* or *while.*

as, like   Use *as, as if,* or *as though* rather than *like* to introduce clauses of comparison. "Dan's compositions are tuneful, *as* [not *like*] music ought to be." "Jeffrey behaves *as if* [not *like*] he were ill." *Like,* because it is a preposition, can introduce a phrase but not a clause. "My brother looks *like* me." "Henrietta runs *like* a duck."

as to   Usually this expression sounds stilted. Use *about* instead. "He complained *about* [not *as to*] the cockroaches."

at   See *where . . . at, where . . . to.*

averse   See *adverse, averse.*

bad, badly   *Bad* is an adjective; *badly* is an adverb. They are commonly misused after linking verbs (*be, appear, become, grow, seem, prove*) and verbs of the senses (*feel, look, smell, sound, taste*). Following a linking verb, use the adjective form. "I feel *bad* that we missed the plane." "The egg smells *bad.*" (See 10a, 10b.) The adverb form is used to modify a verb or an adjective. "They played so *badly* they lost to the last-place team." "It was a *badly* needed victory that saved the cellar-dwellers from elimination."

being as, being that   "*Being as* I was ignorant of the facts, I kept still" is a nonstandard way to say "*Because* I was ignorant" or "*Not knowing* the facts."

beside, besides   *Beside* is a preposition meaning "next to." "Sheldon enjoyed sitting *beside* the guest of honor." *Besides* is an adverb meaning "in addition." "*Besides,* he has a sense of humor." *Besides* is also a preposition meaning "other than." "Something *besides* shyness caused his embarrassment."

between, among   See *among, between.*

between you and I   The preposition *between* always takes the objective case. "Between *you* and *me* [not *I*], that story about the dog's eating Joe's money sounds suspicious." "Between *us* [not *we*], what's going on between Chris and *her* [not *she*] is unfathomable."

bi-, semi-   These prefixes are often confused. *Bi-* means "two." *Semi-* means "half of." Thus, *semiautomatic* means "partly automatic," and *semiannual* means "happening every half year." *Biaxial* means "having two axes." Although sometimes people also use *bi-* to mean "happening twice in," avoid that use

because it can be confusing (for example, it's difficult to know whether the person using *biweekly* means "twice a week" or "every two weeks").

but that, but what   "I don't know *but what* [or *but that*] you're right" is a wordy, imprecise way of saying "Maybe you're right" or "I believe you're right."

can, may   Use *can* to indicate ability. "Jake *can* bench-press 650 pounds." *May* involves permission. "*May* I bench-press today?" "You *may,* if you *can.*"

capital, capitol   A *capital* is a city that is the center of government for a state or country. *Capital* can also mean "wealth." A *capitol* is a building in which legislators meet. "Who knows what the *capital* of Finland is?" "The renovated *capitol* is a popular tourist attraction."

censor, censure   *Censor* as a verb means "to evaluate and remove objectionable material." As a noun, it means "someone who censors." "All mail was *censored* before it left the country." *Censure* as a verb means "to find fault with, criticize." As a noun, it means "disapproval." "The governor's extreme actions were met with public *censure.*"

center around   Say "Class discussion *centered on* [or *revolved around*] her paper." In this sense, the verb *center* means "to have one main concern" — the way a circle has a central point. (Thus, to say a discussion centers *around* anything is a murky metaphor.)

cite, sight, site   *Cite,* a verb, means "to quote from or refer to." *Sight* as a verb means "to see or glimpse"; as a noun it means "a view, a spectacle." "When the police officer *sighted* my terrier running across the playground, she *cited* the leash laws and told me I'd be fined." *Site,* a noun, means "location." "Standing at the *site* of his childhood home, he wept tears of nostalgia. He was a pitiful *sight.*"

climatic, climactic   *Climatic,* from *climate,* refers to meteorological conditions. Saying "climatic conditions," however, is wordy — you can usually substitute "the climate": "*Climatic* conditions are [or "The *climate* is"] changing because of the hole in the ozone." *Climactic,* from *climax,* refers to the culmination of a progression of events. "In the *climactic* scene the hero drives his car off the pier."

compare, contrast   *Compare* has two main meanings. The first, "to liken or represent as similar," is followed by *to.* "She *compared* her room *to* a jail cell." "He *compared* me *to* a summer's day." In its second meaning, *compare* means "to analyze for similarities and differences" and is generally followed by *with*. "The speaker *compared* the American educational system *with* the Japanese system."

Contrast also has two main meanings. As a transitive verb, taking an object, it means "to compare or analyze to emphasize differences" and is generally followed by *with*. "The speaker *contrasted* the social emphasis of the Japanese primary grades *with* the academic emphasis of ours." As an intransitive verb, *contrast* means "to exhibit differences when compared." "The matted tangle of Sidney's fur *contrasted* sharply *with* its usual healthy sleekness."

complement, compliment   *Compliment* is a verb meaning "to praise" or a noun meaning "praise." "The professor *complimented* Sarah on her perceptiveness." *Complement* is a verb meaning "to complete or reinforce." "Jennifer's experiences as a practice teacher *complemented* what she learned in her education class."

continual, continuous   *Continual* means "often repeated." "Mike was in *continual* conflict with his neighbors." *Continuous* means "uninterrupted." "Lisa's *continuous* chatter made it impossible for Debbie to concentrate on her reading."

could care less   This is nonstandard English for *couldn't care less* and should not be used in writing. "The cat *couldn't* [not *could*] *care less* about which brand of cat food you buy."

could of   *Could of* is colloquial for *could have* and should not be used in writing.

couple of   Write "a *couple of* drinks" when you mean two. For more than two, say "a *few* [or *several*] drinks."

criteria, criterion   *Criteria* is the plural of *criterion*, which means "a standard or requirement on which a judgment or decision is based." "The main *criteria* for this job are attention to detail and good typing skills."

data   *Data* is a plural noun. Write "The data *are*" and "*these* data." The singular form of *data* is *datum* — rarely used because it sounds musty. Instead, use *fact, figure,* or *statistic.*

different from, different than   *Different from* is usually the correct form to use. "How is good poetry *different from* prose?" Use *different than* when a whole

clause follows. "Violin lessons with Mr. James were *different than* I had imagined."

disinterested, uninterested   *Disinterested* means "impartial, fair, objective." "The defendant hoped for a *disinterested* judge." *Uninterested* means "indifferent." "Suzanne was *uninterested* in world news."

don't, doesn't   *Don't* is the contraction for *do not,* and *doesn't* is the contraction for *does not.* "They *don't* want to get dressed up for the ceremony." "The cat *doesn't* [not *don't*] like to be combed."

due to   *Due* is an adjective and must modify a noun or pronoun; it can't modify a verb or an adjective. Begin a sentence with *due to* and you invite trouble: "*Due to* rain, the game was postponed." Write instead, "*Because of* rain." *Due to* works after the verb *be*. "His fall was *due to* a banana peel." There, *due* modifies the noun *fall*.

due to the fact that   A windy expression for *because.*

eager, anxious   See *anxious, eager.*

effect, affect   See *affect, effect.*

either   Use *either* when referring to one of two things. "Both internships sound great; I'd be happy with *either*." When referring to one of three or more things, use *any one* or *any*. "*Any one* of our four trained counselors will be able to help you."

elicit, illicit   *Elicit*, a verb, means "to bring or draw out." *Illicit*, an adjective, means "unlawful" or "not permissible." "Try as he might, Gus could not *elicit* details from Bob about his *illicit* nighttime activities."

emigrant, immigrant   An *emigrant* has left a country or region; an *immigrant* has moved into a country or region. The verb forms reflect the same distinction: *emigrate from, immigrate to.* "Even in the United States, *immigrants* often hold the lowest-paying positions." "Anders *emigrated* from Norway."

eminent, imminent   *Eminent* means "distinguished or outstanding"; *imminent* means "about to happen." "The *eminent* novelists shyly announced their *imminent* marriage."

enormity, enormousness, enormous   *Enormity* means "monstrous evil"; *enormousness* means "vastness or immensity"; and *enormous* means "vast or huge." "The *enormity* of the convicted woman's crimes baffled her acquaintances." "The *enormousness* of the lake impressed them."

enthuse   Good writers shun this verb. Instead of "The salesman *enthused* about the product," write, "The salesman *was enthusiastic* about the product."

et cetera, etc.   Replace *et cetera* (or its abbreviation, *etc.*) with exact words, and you will sharpen your writing. Even translating the Latin expression into English is an improvement: *and other things.* Rather than announcing an athletic meet to feature "high-jumping, shot-putting, *etc.*," you could say, "high-jumping, shot-putting, and other field events."

everybody, every body   When used as an indefinite pronoun, *everybody* is one word. "Why is *everybody* on the boys' team waving his arms?" Keep in mind that *everybody* is singular. It is a mistake to write, "Why is *everybody* waving *their* arms?" (See 9d and 22a for acceptable alternatives.) *Every body* written as two words refers to separate, individual bodies. "After the massacre, they buried *every body* in *its* [not *their*] own grave."

everyone, every one   Used as an indefinite pronoun, *everyone* is one word. "*Everyone* has *his or her* own ideas." Remember that *everyone* is singular. Therefore it is wrong to write, "*Everyone* has *their* own ideas." (See 9d and 22a for acceptable alternatives.) *Every one* written as two words refers to individual, distinct items. "I studied *every one* of the assigned exercises."

except, accept   See *accept, except.*

expect   In writing, avoid the informal use of *expect* to mean "suppose, assume, or think." "I *suppose* [not *expect*] you've heard that half the class flunked."

fact that   This is an expression that, nearly always, you can do without. "*The fact that* he was puny went unnoticed" is wordy; write, "That he was puny went unnoticed." "Because [not *Because of the fact that*] it snowed, the game was canceled."

famous, infamous   Do something that attracts wide notice and you become celebrated, or *famous*: "Marcia dreamed of growing up to be a *famous* inventor." But if your deeds are detestable, you may instead become notorious, or *infamous*, like Bluebeard, the *infamous* wife killer.

farther, further   In your writing, use *farther* to refer to literal distance. "Chicago is *farther* from Nome than from New York." When you wish to denote additional degree, time, or quantity, use *further*: "Sally's idea requires *further* discussion."

fewer, less   *Less* refers to general quantity or bulk; *fewer*, to separate, countable items. "Eat *less* pizza." "Salad has *fewer* calories."

field   In a statement such as "He took courses *in the field of* economics," leave out *the field of* and save words.

firstly   The recommended usage is *first* (and *second*, not *secondly*; *third*, not *thirdly*; and so on).

flaunt, flout   To *flaunt* is to show off. "She *flaunted* her wealth by buying much more than she needed." To *flout* is to defy. "George *flouted* the law by refusing to register for the draft."

former, latter   *Former* means "first of two"; *latter*, "second of two." They are an acceptable but heavy-handed pair, best done without. Too often, they oblige your reader to backtrack. Nine times out of ten, your writing will be clearer if you simply name again the persons or things you mean. Instead of writing, "The *former* great artist is the master of the flowing line, while the *latter* is the master of color," write, "Picasso is the master of the flowing line, while Matisse is the master of color."

further, farther   See *farther, further.*

get, got   *Get* has many meanings, especially in slang and colloquial use. Some, such as the following, are not appropriate in formal writing:

To start, begin: Let's start [not *get*] painting.

To stir the emotions: His frequent interruptions finally started annoying [not *getting to*] me.

To harm, punish, or take revenge on: She's going to take revenge on [not *get*] him. Or better, be even more specific about what you mean. She's going to spread rumors about him to ruin his reputation.

good, well   To modify a verb, use the adverb *well*, not the adjective *good*. "Jan dives *well* [not *good*]." Linking verbs (*be, appear, become, grow, seem, prove*) and verbs of the senses (such as *feel, look, smell, sound, taste*) call for the adjective *good*. "The paint job looks *good*." *Well* is an adjective used only to refer to health. "She looks *well*" means that she seems to be in good health. "She looks *good*" means that her appearance is attractive. (See 10b, 10c.)

hanged, hung   Both words are the past tense of the verb *hang*. *Hanged* refers to an execution. "The murderer was *hanged* at dawn." For all other situations, use *hung*. "Jane *hung* her wash on the clothesline to dry."

have got to In formal writing, avoid using the phrase *have got to* to mean "have to" or "must." "I *must* [not *have got to*] phone them right away."

he, she, he or she Using *he* as a matter of course to refer to an indefinite person is considered sexist; so is using *she* with reference to traditionally female occupations or pastimes. However, peppering your writing with the phrase *he or she* can seem wordy and awkward. For alternatives, see 22.

herself See *-self, -selves.*

himself See *-self, -selves.*

hopefully *Hopefully* means "with hope." "The children turned *hopefully* toward the door, expecting Santa Claus." In writing, avoid *hopefully* when you mean "it is to be hoped" or "let us hope." "I *hope* [not *Hopefully*] the posse will arrive soon."

if, whether Use *whether,* not *if,* in indirect questions and to introduce alternatives. "Father asked me *whether* [not *if*] I was planning to sleep all morning." "I'm so confused I don't know *whether* [not *if*] it's day or night."

illicit See *elicit, illicit.*

illusion, allusion See *allusion, illusion.*

immigrant, emigrant See *emigrant, immigrant.*

imminent See *eminent, imminent.*

immoral See *amoral, immoral.*

imply, infer *Imply* means "to suggest"; *infer* means "to draw a conclusion." "Maria *implied* that she was too busy to see Tom. As their conversation proceeded, Tom *inferred* that Maria had lost interest in him."

in, into *In* refers to a location or condition; *into* refers to the direction of movement or change. "The hero burst *into* the room and found the heroine *in* another man's arms." "Hiroko decided to go *into* banking."

individual Don't use *individual* for *person.* "What kind of *person* [not *individual*] would do that?" Save *individual* to mean "one" as opposed to "many": "an *individual* thinker in a conforming crowd."

infamous, famous See *famous, infamous.*

infer, imply See *imply, infer.*

ingenious, ingenuous *Ingenious* means "clever." "The *ingenious* inventor caught the mouse unharmed." *Ingenuous* has two related meanings: "naive, unsophisticated" and "frank, candid." "Little Lord Fauntleroy's *ingenuous* remarks touched even his ill-tempered grandfather."

in regards to Write *in regard to, regarding,* or *about.*

inside of, outside of As prepositions, *inside* and *outside* do not require *of.* "The students were more interested in what was going on *outside* [not *outside of*] the building than in what was happening *inside* [not *inside of*] the classroom." Do not use *inside of* to refer colloquially to time or *outside of* to mean "except." "I'll finish the assignment *within* [not *inside of*] two hours." "He told no one *except* [not *outside of*] a few friends."

irregardless *Irregardless* is a double negative. Use *regardless.*

is because See *reason is because.*

is when, is where Using these expressions results in errors in predication. "Obesity *is when* a person is greatly overweight." "Biology *is where* students dissect frogs." *When* refers to a point in time, but *obesity* is not a point in time; *where* refers to a place, but *biology* is not a place. Write instead, "Obesity is the condition of extreme overweight." "Biology is a laboratory course in which students dissect frogs." (See 16b.)

its, it's *Its* is a possessive pronoun, never in need of an apostrophe. *It's* is a contraction for *it is.* "Every new experience has *its* bad moments. Still, *it's* exciting to explore the unknown."

it's me, it is I Although *it's me* is widely used in speech, don't use it in formal writing. Write "It is *I,*" which is grammatically correct. The same applies to other personal pronouns. "It was *he* [not *him*] who started the mutiny." (See 7.)

kind of, sort of, type of When you use *kind, sort,* or *type* — singular words — make sure that the sentence construction is singular. "That *type* of show *offends* me." "Those *types* of shows *offend* me." In speech, *kind of* and *sort of* are used as qualifiers. "He is *sort of* fat." Avoid them in writing. "He is *rather* [or *somewhat* or *slightly*; not *sort of*] fat."

latter, former See *former, latter.*

lay, lie The verb *lay*, meaning "to put or place," takes an object. *Lie*, meaning "to rest or recline," does not. Their principal parts are *lay, laid, laid* and *lie, lay, lain.* "*Lay* that pistol down." "*Lie* on the bed until your headache goes away." (See 5f.)

leave, let *Leave* means "to go away." *Let* means "to permit." "I'll *leave* on a jet plane." "*Let* the child run — she needs the exercise."

lend, loan Although *lend* and *loan* are used interchangeably in speech, avoid using *loan* as a verb. "Can you *lend* (not *loan*) me some money?"

less, fewer See *fewer, less.*

let, leave See *leave, let.*

liable, likely Use *likely* to mean "plausible" or "having the potential." "Jake is *likely* [not *liable*] to win." Save *liable* for "legally obligated" or "susceptible." "A stunt man is *liable* to injury."

lie, lay See *lay, lie.*

like, as See *as, like.*

likely, liable See *liable, likely.*

literally Don't sling *literally* around for emphasis. It means "strictly according to the meaning of a word (or words)"; if you are speaking figuratively, it will wreck your credibility. "Professor Gray *literally* flew down the hall to the chairman's office" means that Gray traveled on wings. "Rick was *literally* stoned out of his mind" means that someone drove Rick insane by pelting him with mineral specimens. Save *literally* to mean that, by everything holy, you're reporting a fact. "Chemical wastes travel on the winds, and it *literally* rains poison."

loan, lend See *lend, loan.*

loath, loathe *Loath* is an adjective meaning "reluctant." *Loathe* is a verb meaning "to detest." "We were *loath* to say good-bye." "We *loathed* our impending separation."

loose, lose *Loose*, an adjective, most commonly means "not fastened" or "poorly fastened." *Lose*, a verb, means "to misplace" or "to not win." "I have to be careful not to *lose* this button — it's so *loose.*"

lots, lots of, a lot of Use these expressions only in informal speech. In formal writing, use *many* or *much*. See also *a lot.*

mankind This term is considered sexist by many people. Use *humanity, humankind, the human race,* or *people* instead.

may, can See *can, may.*

media, medium *Media* is the plural of *medium* and most commonly refers to the various forms of public communication. "Some argue that of all the *media*, television is the worst for children because it leaves so little to the imagination."

might of *Might of* is colloquial for *might have* and should not be used in writing.

most Do not use *most* when you mean "almost" or "nearly." "*Almost* [not *Most*] all of the students felt that Professor Chartrand should have received tenure."

must of *Must of* is colloquial for *must have* and should not be used in writing.

myself See *-self, -selves.*

not all that *Not all that* is colloquial for *not very*; do not use it in formal writing. "The movie was *not very* [not *not all that*] exciting."

number, amount See *amount, number.*

of See *could of, might of, must of, should of.*

off of *Of* is unnecessary with *off*. Use *off* alone, or use *from*: "Cartoon heroes are forever falling *off* [or *from*] cliffs."

O.K., o.k., okay In formal writing, do not use any of these expressions. *All right* and *I agree* are possible substitutes.

one Like a balloon, *one*, meaning "a person," tends to inflate. One *one* can lead to another. "When *one* is in college, *one* learns to make up *one's* mind for *one-self*." Avoid this pompous usage. Whenever possible, substitute *people* or a more specific plural noun. "When *students* are in college, *they* learn to make up their minds for *themselves*." Also see *you* and 22c.

ourselves See *-self, -selves.*

outside of, inside of See *inside of, outside of.*

percent, per cent, percentage When you specify a number, write *percent* (also written *per cent*). "Eight *percent* of the listeners responded to the offer." The only time to use *percentage*, meaning "part," is with an adjective, when you mention no number. "A high *percentage* [or *a large percentage*] of listeners responded." *A large number* or *a large proportion* sounds better yet, and we urge you to strike *percentage* from your vocabulary.

per se Translate this Latin expression into English and you'll sound less stiff. Write "Getting a good education is important *in itself* [or *by itself*; not *per se*]."

phenomenon, phenomena *Phenomena* is plural for *phenomenon*, which means "an observable fact or occurrence." "I've read about many mysterious supernatural *phenomena*." "Clairvoyance is the strangest *phenomenon* of all."

pore over, pour over *Pore over* a book and you study it intently; *pour over* a book and you get it wet.

precede, proceed *Precede* means "to go before or ahead of"; *proceed* means "to go forward." "The fire drill *proceeded* smoothly; the children *preceded* the teachers into the safety of the yard."

principal, principle *Principal* means "chief," whether used as an adjective or as a noun. "Marijuana is the *principal* cash crop of Colombia." "Our high school *principal* frowns on pot." Referring to money, *principal* means "capital." "Investors in marijuana earn as much as 850 percent interest on their *principal*." *Principle*, a noun, means *rule* or *standard*. "Let's apply the *principle* of equality in hiring."

proved, proven Although both forms can be used as past participles, *proved* is recommended. Use *proven* as an adjective. "They had *proved* their skill in match after match." "Try this *proven* cough remedy: lemon, honey, whiskey, and hot water blended into a toddy."

quote, quotation *Quote* is a verb meaning "to cite, to use the words of." *Quotation* is a noun meaning "something that is quoted." "The *quotation* [not *quote*] next to her yearbook picture fits her perfectly."

raise, rise *Raise*, meaning "to cause to move upward," is a transitive verb and takes an object. *Rise*, meaning "to move up (on its own)" is intransitive and does not take an object: "I *rose* from my seat and *raised* my arm, but the instructor still didn't see me."

rarely ever *Rarely* by itself is strong enough. "George *rarely* [not *rarely ever*] eats dinner with his family."

real, really *Real* is an adjective, *really* an adverb. Do not use *real* to modify a verb or another adjective, and avoid overusing either word. "*The Ambassadors* is

a *really* [not *real*] fine novel." Even better: "*The Ambassadors* is a fine novel."

reason is because, reason . . . is *Reason . . . is* requires a clause beginning with *that*. Using *because* is nonstandard. "The *reason* I can't come *is that* [not *is because*] I have the flu." But *reason . . . is* is a wordy construction that can usually be rephrased more succinctly. It is simpler and more direct to write, "I can't come because I have the flu."

respectfully, respectively *Respectfully* means "with respect, showing respect." *Respectively* means "each in turn" or "in the order given." "They stopped talking and stood *respectfully* as the prime minister walked by." "Joan, Michael, and Alfonso majored in history, sociology, and economics, *respectively*."

rise See *raise, rise*.

seldom ever Let *seldom* stand by itself. "Martha *seldom* [not *seldom ever*] attends church."

-self, -selves Don't use a pronoun ending in *-self* or *-selves* in place of *her, him, me, them, us,* or *you*. "Nobody volunteered but Jim and *me* [not *myself*]." Use the *-self* pronouns to refer back to a noun or another pronoun and to lend emphasis. "We did it *ourselves*." "Sarah *herself* is a noted musician." (See 1b.)

semi- See *bi-, semi-*.

sensual, sensuous Both words have to do with stimulation of the senses, but *sensual* has more blatantly carnal overtones. "Gluttony and lust were the *sensual* millionaire's favorite sins." *Sensuous* pleasures are more aesthetic. "The *sensuous* beauty of the music stirred his soul."

set, sit *Set*, meaning "to put or place," is a transitive verb and takes an object. *Sit*, meaning "to be seated," is intransitive and does not take an object. "At the security point we were asked to *set* our jewelry and metal objects on the counter and *sit* down." (See also 5f.)

shall, will; should, would The helping verb *shall* formerly was used with first-person pronouns. It is still used to express determination ("We *shall* overcome"; "They *shall* not give in") or to ask consent ("*Shall* I let the cat out?"). Otherwise *will* is commonly used with all three persons. "I *will* enter medical school in the fall." "They *will* accept the bid if the terms are clear." *Should* is a helping verb that expresses obligation; *would*, a helping verb that expresses a hypothetical condition. "I *should* wash the dishes before I watch TV." "He *would* learn to speak English if you *would* give him a chance."

should of   *Should of* is colloquial for *should have* and should not be used in writing.

sight   See *cite, sight, site.*

since   Sometimes using *since* can make a sentence ambiguous. "*Since* the babysitter left, the children have been watching television." Does *since* here mean "because" or "from the time that"? If using *since* might be confusing to your readers, use an unambiguous term (*because, ever since*).

sit   See *set, sit.*

site   See *cite, sight, site.*

sort of   See *kind of, sort of, type of.*

stationary, stationery   *Stationary,* an adjective, means "fixed, unmoving." "The fireplace remained *stationary* though the wind blew down the house." *Stationery* is paper for letter writing. To spell it right, remember that *letter* also contains *-er.*

suppose to   Write *supposed to.* "He was *supposed to* appear for dinner at eight o'clock."

sure   *Sure* is an adjective, *surely* an adverb. Do not use *sure* to modify a verb or another adjective. If by *sure* you mean "certainly," write *certainly* or *surely* instead. "He *surely* [not *sure*] is crazy about cars."

than, then   *Than* is a conjunction used in comparisons; *then* is an adverb indicating time. "Marlene is brainier *than* her sister." "First crack six eggs; *then* beat them."

that, where   See *where, that.*

that, which   Which pronoun should open a clause — *that* or *which*? If the clause adds to its sentence an idea that, however interesting, could be left out, then the clause is nonrestrictive and should begin with *which* and be separated from the rest of the sentence with commas. "The vampire, *which* had been hovering nearby, leaped for Sarah's throat."

If the clause is essential to your meaning, it is restrictive and should begin with *that* and should not have commas around it. "The vampire *that* Mel brought from Transylvania leaped for Sarah's throat." The clause indicates not just any old vampire but one in particular. (See 25e.)

Don't use *which* to refer vaguely to an entire clause. Instead of "Jack was an expert drummer in high school, *which* won him a college scholarship," write: "Jack's skill as a drummer won him . . . ." (See 8b.)

that, who, which, whose   See *who, which, that, whose.*

themselves   See *-self, -selves.*

then, than   See *than, then.*

there, their, they're   *There* is an adverb indicating place. *Their* is a possessive pronoun. *They're* is a contraction of *they are.* "After playing tennis *there* for three hours, Lamont and Laura went to change *their* clothes because *they're* going out to dinner."

to, too, two   *To* is a preposition. *Too* is an adverb meaning "also" or "in excess." *Two* is a number. "Janet wanted to go *too*, but she feared she was still *too* sick to travel in the car for *two* days. Instead, she went *to* bed."

toward, towards   *Toward* is preferred in the United States, *towards* in Britain.

try and   Use *try to.* "I'll *try to* [not *try and*] attend the opening performance of your play."

type of   See *kind of, sort of, type of.*

uninterested, disinterested   See *disinterested, uninterested.*

unique   Nothing can be *more unique, less unique, really unique, very unique,* or *somewhat unique. Unique* means "one of a kind."

use to   Write *used to.* "Jeffrey *used to* have a beard, but now he is clean-shaven."

wait for, wait on   Write *wait for* when you mean "await." *Wait on* means "to serve." "While *waiting for* his friends, George decided to *wait on* one more customer."

well, good   See *good, well.*

where, that   Although speakers sometimes use *where* instead of *that,* you should not do so in writing. "I heard on the news *that* [not *where*] it got hot enough to fry eggs on car hoods."

where at, where to   The colloquial use of *at* or *to* after *where* is redundant. Write "*Where* were you?" not "*Where* were you *at*?" "I know *where* she was rushing [not *rushing to*]."

whether   See *if, whether.*

which, that   See *that, which.*

who, which, that, whose   *Who* refers to people, *which* to things and ideas. "Was it Pogo *who* said, 'We have met the enemy and he is us'?" "The blouse, *which* was lime green embroidered with silver, accented her dark skin and eyes." *That* refers to things but can also be used for a class of people. "The team *that* puts in the most overtime will get a bonus." Using *of which* can be cumbersome; use *whose* even to refer to things. "The mountain, *whose* snowy peaks were famous world over, was covered in a dismal fog." See also *that, which.*

who, whom   *Who* is used as a subject, *whom* as an object. In *"Whom do I see?" Whom* is the object of *see.* In *"Who goes there?" Who* is the subject of "goes." (See also 7a, 7d.)

who's, whose   *Who's* is a contraction for *who is* or *who has.* "*Who's* going with Phil?" *Whose* is a possessive pronoun. "Bill is a conservative politician *whose* ideas are unlikely to change."

whose, who, which, that   See *who, which, that, whose.*

will, shall   See *shall, will.*

would, should   See *shall, will; should, would.*

would of   *Would of* is colloquial for *would have* and should not be used in writing.

you   *You,* meaning "a person," occurs often in conversation. "When *you* go to college *you* have to work hard." In writing, use *one* or a specific, preferably plural noun. "When *students* go to college *they* have to work hard." But see *one* for some cautions. And see 22c.

your, you're   *Your* is a possessive pronoun; *you're* is the contraction for *you are.* "*You're* lying! It was *your* handwriting on the envelope."

yourself, yourselves   See *-self, -selves.*

Answers for Lettered Exercises

EXERCISE 1–1   IDENTIFYING NOUNS AND PRONOUNS, p. H-9

a. Nouns: artists (common), Hollywood (proper); pronoun: She (personal);   **b.** Nouns: failure (common), rent (common), fine (common); pronoun: His (possessive);   **c.** Nouns: glass (common), water (common), miles (common); pronouns: She (personal), herself (reflexive);   **d.** Noun: money (common); pronouns: us (personal), we (personal);   **e.** Nouns: Tenants (common), Castlegate Towers (proper), pets (common), apartments (common); pronoun: their (possessive)

EXERCISE 1–2   IDENTIFYING VERBS, p. H-10

a. Transitive: accompany; intransitive: goes; helping: will;   **b.** Transitive: prefers; linking: are;   **c.** Transitive: give, symbolize;   **d.** Transitive: spent; helping: should have;   **e.** Transitive: reads; intransitive: dreams

EXERCISE 1–3   IDENTIFYING ADJECTIVES AND ADVERBS, p. H-12

a. Adjectives: mild, environmental; indefinite articles: a, a; definite article: the; adverb: greatly, modifying verb *fear*;   **b.** Adjectives: young, mature; adverb: incredibly, modifying adjective *mature*;   **c.** Adjectives: handsome, wise; definite article: The; adverbs: wildly, modifying adjective *handsome*; often, modifying verb *made*; foolishly, modifying verb *act*;   **d.** Adjective: difficult; indefinite article: a; adverbs: very, modifying adjective *difficult*; carefully, modifying verb *chose*;   **e.** Adjectives: delighted, lovely; definite article: the; adverb: absolutely, modifying adjective *delighted*

EXERCISE 1–4   IDENTIFYING PREPOSITIONAL PHRASES, p. H-13

a. to me; preposition: to; adverb phrase;   **b.** in the sky; preposition: in; adjective phrase;   **c.** before the meeting; preposition: before; adverb phrase;   **d.** according to the rules; preposition: according to; adverb phrase;   **e.** but a few troublemakers; preposition: but; adjective phrase

EXERCISE 1–5   IDENTIFYING CONJUNCTIONS AND INTERJECTIONS, p. H-17

a. Conjunction: when (subordinating); interjection: Oh, well;   **b.** Conjunctions: and (coordinating), neither . . . nor (correlative);   **c.** Conjunctions: and (coordinating), whether . . . or (correlative);   **d.** Interjection: Holy mackerel;   **e.** Conjunctions: Although (subordinating), and (coordinating)

EXERCISE 1–6   IDENTIFYING PARTS OF SPEECH, p. H-18

A. a. adverb;   **b.** adjective;   **c.** subordinating conjunction;   **d.** coordinating conjunction;   **e.** adverb;   **B. a.** noun;   **b.** adverb;   **c.** subordinating conjunction;   **d.** pronoun;   **e.** adjective (article)

EXERCISE 2–1   IDENTIFYING SUBJECTS AND PREDICATES, p. H-21

a. Simple subject: coyotes; complete subject: Several coyotes; simple predicate: have been seen; complete predicate; have been seen recently in this area;   **b.** Simple subject: War; complete subject: War, that curse of the human race; simple predicate: has plagued; complete predicate: has plagued civilization throughout history;   **c.** Simple subject: composer; complete subject: the composer Beethoven; simple predicate: continued; complete predicate: Even after he became deaf . . . continued to write music;   **d.** Simple subject: cup; complete subject: One cup of coffee in the morning; simple predicate: keeps; complete predicate: keeps me awake all day;   **e.** Simple subject: mother; complete subject: John Updike's mother, who was a writer herself; simple predicate: encouraged; complete predicate: encouraged her son's literary aspirations

EXERCISE 2–2   IDENTIFYING OBJECTS AND COMPLEMENTS, p. H-25

a. Subject complement: an educated person; direct object: such a story;   **b.** Direct object: his kingdom; indirect object: his daughters;   **c.** Subject complement: an evasive man;   **d.** Subject complement: an interesting art; direct object: expensive equipment;   **e.** Direct object: Chicago; object complement: the Windy City

EXERCISE 3–1   IDENTIFYING PHRASES, p. H-31

a. from the wood stove: prepositional phrase, adjective;
b. to win the district championship: infinitive phrase, noun;
c. throughout the night: prepositional phrase, adverb;
d. Despite a mighty effort: prepositional phrase, adverb;
e. Drinking a little red wine each day: gerund phrase, noun

EXERCISE 3–2   IDENTIFYING CLAUSES, p. H-33

a. wherever he lived at the moment: noun clause;
b. While we were still arguing about its value: adverb clause;
c. that I took to the cleaners: adjective clause;   **d.** that she may fail the course: adverb clause;   **e.** what hit him: noun clause

EXERCISE 4–1   IDENTIFYING SENTENCE TYPES, p. H-37

a. Simple sentence. Compound subject: Not only women but also men and children; verb: benefit;   **b.** Complex sentence. Infinitive phrase: To become a doctor; main clause: you know; subordinate clause: how hard you must study; **c.** Compound-complex sentence. Main clauses: Biology is interesting; I prefer botany; subordinate clause: as it is taught in our department;   **d.** Simple sentence. Subject: you; verb: Do prefer; compound direct object: bacon and eggs or cereal and toast;   **e.** Compound-complex sentence. Main clauses: Most people believe; recent studies have shown; subordinate clauses: that poverty begets poverty; that they achieve economic independence; when children from welfare families reach adulthood

EXERCISE 5–1   USING IRREGULAR VERB FORMS, p. H-42

a. In those days, Benjamin wrote all the music, and his sister *sang* all the songs.
b. Correct
c. When the bell *rang*, darkness had already *fallen*.
d. Voters have *chosen* several new representatives, who won't take office until January.
e. Carol threw the ball into the water, and the dog *swam* after it.

EXERCISE 5–2   IDENTIFYING VERB TENSES, p. H-50

a. broke: simple past; was skiing: past progressive;
b. sleeps: simple present; is yawning: present progressive;
c. had seen: past perfect; runs: simple present;   **d.** represents: simple present; will have performed: future perfect; split: simple past;   **e.** have heard: present perfect; spend: simple present; will climb: simple future

EXERCISE 5–4   USING THE CORRECT MOOD OF VERBS, p. H-55

a. Dr. Belanger recommended that Juan *floss* his teeth every day. (Incorrect *flosses*, indicative; correct *floss*, subjunctive)
b. If I *were* you, I would have done the same thing. (Incorrect *was*, indicative; correct *were*, subjunctive)
c. Tradition demands that Daegun *show* respect for his elders. (Incorrect *shows*, indicative; correct *show*, subjunctive)
d. Correct

e. Diane wishes that choosing a college *were* quicker and easier. (Incorrect *was*, indicative; correct *were*, subjunctive)

EXERCISE 6–1   MAKING SUBJECTS AND VERBS AGREE, p. H-62

a. Our foreign policy in Cuba, Nicaragua, El Salvador, and Panama *has* not been as successful as most Americans had hoped.
b. Correct
c. I read about a couple who *are* offering to trade their baby for a brand-new Chevrolet.
d. A shave, a haircut, and a new suit *have* turned Bill into a different person.
e. Neither the guerrillas nor the government *is* willing to negotiate.

EXERCISE 7–1   USING PRONOUNS CORRECTLY, p. H-66

a. She can run faster than I. (I is the subject of the implied verb *can run*.)
b. Mrs. Van Dumont awarded the prize to Mona and me. (*Me* is an object of the preposition *to*.)
c. Jud laughed at both of us — her and me. (*Her* and *me* are appositives to *us*, the object of the preposition.)
d. I am sure that I overheard that rude man speaking of us. (*Us* is the object of the preposition *of*.)
e. Jerry, the pizza chef, and I regard you and her as the very people *whom* we wish to get acquainted with. (*I* is a subject of the verb *regard*; *her* is a direct object of the verb *regard*; *whom* is the object of the preposition *with*.)

EXERCISE 8–1   MAKING PRONOUN REFERENCE CLEAR, p. H-69

Suggested revisions:

a. Bill's prank frightened Josh and made Bill wonder why he had done it. *Or* Bill's prank frightened Josh and made Josh wonder why Bill had done it.
b. Korean students study up to twenty subjects a year, including algebra, calculus, and engineering. Because these subjects are required, students must study them year after year.
c. Roger Clemens signed a baseball for Chad that Clemens had used in a game.
d. The bottle shattered when it hit the windshield.
e. My friends believe they are more mature than many of their peers because of the discipline enforced at their school. However, the emphasis on discipline can also lead to problems.

EXERCISE 9–1   MAKING PRONOUNS AND ANTECEDENTS AGREE, p. H-72

Suggested revisions:

a. All students are urged to complete *their* registration on time.
b. *Babies* who don't know *their* own mothers may have been born with some kind of vision deficiency.

c. Each member of the sorority has to make *her* own bed.

d. If you don't like the songs the choir sings, don't join *it*.

e. Young people should know how to protect *themselves* against AIDS.

EXERCISE 10–1   USING ADJECTIVES AND ADVERBS CORRECTLY, p. H-80

a. Change *bright* to *brightly;*   b. Correct;   c. Change *good* to *well;*   d. Change *reliably* to *reliable;*   e. Change *significant* to *significantly.*

EXERCISE 11–1   MAINTAINING GRAMMATICAL CONSISTENCY, p. H-84

Suggested revisions:

a. Sometimes late at night, I hear stereos booming from passing cars. The vibrations are so great *I* can feel *my* house shake.

b. Dr. Jamison is an erudite professor who *tells amusing anecdotes in class.* (Formal) *Or* Dr. Jamison is a *comical* teacher who cracks jokes in class. (Informal)

c. The audience listened intently to the lecture but *did not understand* the message.

d. It was in the Near East that people first began to grow crops and *establish* city-states.

e. Most of the people in my psychology class are very interesting, and *I* can get into some exciting discussions with them.

EXERCISE 12–1   ELIMINATING FRAGMENTS, p. H-88

Suggested revisions:

a. Polly and Jim plan to see the new Woody Allen movie, which was reviewed in last Sunday's *New York Times.*

b. For democracy to function at all, two elements are crucial: an educated populace and a firm collective belief in people's ability to chart their own course.

c. Scholastic achievement is important to Alex, being the first person in his family ever to attend college.

d. Does our society rob children of their childhood by making them aware too soon of adult ills?

e. No one would ever forget that night: the half-empty lifeboats, the useless flares, and the band playing hymns as the ship slid under.

EXERCISE 13–1   REVISING COMMA SPLICES AND FUSED SENTENCES, p. H-93

Suggested revisions:

a. Everyone had heard alarming rumors in the village about strange goings-on. We hesitated to believe them.
Although everyone had heard alarming rumors in the village about strange goings-on, we hesitated to believe them.

b. Bats flew about our ears as the carriage pulled up under a stone archway. An assistant stood waiting to lead us to our host.

Bats flew about our ears as the carriage pulled up under a stone archway, where an assistant stood waiting to lead us to our host.

c. We followed the scientist down a flight of wet stone steps. At last he stopped before a huge oak door.
We followed the scientist down a flight of wet stone steps, until at last he stopped before a huge oak door.

d. From a jangling keyring Dr. Frankenstein selected a heavy key; he twisted it in the lock.
From a jangling keyring Dr. Frankenstein selected a heavy key, which he twisted in the lock.

e. The huge door gave a groan and swung open on a dimly lighted laboratory.
The huge door gave a groan; it swung open on a dimly lighted laboratory.

EXERCISE 14–1   PLACING MODIFIERS, p. H-96

Suggested revisions:

a. The bus full of passengers got stuck in a ditch.

b. In the middle of a staff meeting, he was daydreaming about fishing for trout.

c. With a smirk, the boy threw the airplane made of folded-up paper through an open window.

d. When the glare appeared, I reached for my sunglasses from the glove compartment.

e. Sally and Glen watched the kites high above them drift back and forth.

EXERCISE 14–2   REVISING DANGLING MODIFIERS, p. H-97

Suggested revisions:

a. After working for six hours, they finished the job. *Or* After they worked for six hours, the job was done.

b. When you are unable to fall asleep, a warm bath relaxes you.

c. To compete in the Olympics, you need talent, training, and dedication.

d. It's common for a person feeling lonely to want to talk to someone.

e. Having worried all morning, he felt relief flood over him when his missing son returned.

EXERCISE 15–1   COMPLETING COMPARISONS, p. H-100

Suggested revisions:

a. She plays the *Moonlight Sonata* more brilliantly than any *other* pianist her age.

b. Driving a sports car means more to Jake than *it does to* his professors. *Or* Driving a sports car means more to Jake than his professors *do.*

c. People who go to college aren't necessarily smarter *than those who don't,* but they will always have an advantage at job interviews.

d. I don't have as much trouble getting along with Michelle as *I do with* Karin. *Or* I don't have as much trouble getting along with Michelle as Karin *does.*

e. Annapolis, Maryland, has more colonial brick houses than any *other* city in the United States.

EXERCISE 15–2   COMPLETING SENTENCES, p. H-102

a. Eighteenth-century China was as civilized *as* and in many respects more sophisticated than the Western world.
b. Pembroke was never contacted *by,* much less involved with, the election committee.
c. I haven't yet *finished* but soon will finish my term paper.
d. Ron likes his popcorn with butter; Linda *likes hers* with parmesan cheese.
e. Correct

EXERCISE 16–1   CORRECTING MIXED CONSTRUCTIONS AND FAULTY PREDICATION, p. H-105

Suggested revisions:

a. Health insurance protects people from big medical bills.
b. His determination to prevail helped him finish the race.
c. AIDS destroys the body's immune system.
d. The temperatures are too low for the orange trees.
e. In a recession, economic growth is small or nonexistent, and unemployment increases.

EXERCISE 17–1   MAKING SENTENCES PARALLEL, p. H-110

Suggested revisions:

a. Linda loves to watch soccer and tennis and to play squash.
b. Better than starting from scratch would be building on what already has been done.
c. Her apartment needed fresh paint and a new rug, and Mary Lou wished she had a neater roommate and quieter friends.
d. All my brothers are blond and athletic.
e. For breakfast the waiter brought scrambled eggs, which I like, and kippers, which I don't like.

EXERCISE 18–1   USING COORDINATION, p. H-113

Suggested revisions:

a. Congress is expected to pass the biotechnology bill, but the president already has said he will veto it.
b. Mortgage rates have dropped, so home buying is likely to increase in the near future.
c. The earth trembled; the long-dreaded cataclysm had begun.
d. I left the house in a hurry and ran to the bank so I could cash a check to buy lunch. But it was the bank's anniversary, and the staff was busy serving coffee and cake. By the time I left, after chatting and eating for twenty minutes, I wasn't hungry anymore.
e. The U.S. Postal Service handles millions of pieces of mail every day; it is the largest postal service in the world.

EXERCISE 18–2   USING SUBORDINATION, p. H-116

Suggested revisions:

a. We occasionally hear horror stories about fruits and vegetables being unsafe to eat because they were sprayed with toxic chemicals or were grown in contaminated soil. The fact remains that, given their high nutritional value, these fresh foods are generally much better for us than processed foods.
b. English has become an international language although its grammar is filled with exceptions to the rules.
c. Some television cartoon shows, such as *Rocky and Bullwinkle* and *Speed Racer,* have become cult classics years after they went off the air.
d. At the end of Verdi's opera *La Traviata,* Alfredo has to see his beloved Violetta again, even though he knows she is dying and all he can say is good-bye.
e. After giving away her money and bidding adieu to her faithful servant, Violetta dies in her lover's arms.

EXERCISE 20–2   AVOIDING JARGON, p. H-123

Suggested revisions:

a. The driver education course teaches the student how to drive.
b. We the State Department staff have investigated the riots in Lebanon, and all our data indicate that they are rapidly becoming worse.
c. Antinuclear protesters have been picketing the missile conference in hopes of stalling the negotiations.
d. I recommend multiple bypass heart surgery for Mr. Pitt.
e. If your insurance company will pay for it, he can be scheduled for bypass surgery; if not, he should go on a strict diet.

EXERCISE 20–3   AVOIDING EUPHEMISMS, p. H-124

Suggested revisions:

a. After the Rodney King trial, Los Angeles was engulfed in a riot, during which many innocent people died.
b. The ship sank because of a hole in the hull.
c. The new K27 missile will kill everyone in the cities of any nation that attacks us.
d. In our town, trash collectors must wear uniforms at work.
e. Freddie the Rocker is dead.

EXERCISE 20–4   AVOIDING SLANG, p. H-125

Suggested revisions:

a. A lot of consumers pay too much when they buy a new car.
b. Lately, she has been insulting all her friends.
c. Most of the people at the clinic are drug or alcohol abusers.
d. The marijuana being smoked nowadays is stronger than in the past.
e. They don't want to go out; they just want to sit around doing nothing.

EXERCISE 22–1   AVOIDING BIAS, p. H-134

Suggested revisions:

a. My cousin volunteered as an aide at the retirement home.
b. The television crew interviewed a number of average passersby about the new tax proposal.

c. Whether the president of the United States is a Democrat or a Republican, he or she will always be a symbol of the nation.

d. The senator was highly regarded by voters in her district.

e. Simon drinks quite a bit.

EXERCISE 24–1   USING END PUNCTUATION, p. H-139

a. The question that still troubles the community after all these years is why federal agents did not act sooner.

b. Correct

c. I wonder what he was thinking at the time.

d. One man, who suffered a broken leg, was rescued when he was heard screaming, "Help me! Help me!"

e. Correct

EXERCISE 25–1   USING COMMAS, p. H-141

a. When Verity gets to Paris, I hope she'll drop me a line.

b. Beethoven's deafness kept him from hearing his own music, yet he continued to compose.

c. Correct

d. The cherries are overripe, for picking has been delayed.

e. Antonio expected Minnesota to be cold but was unprepared for the frigid temperatures of his first winter there.

EXERCISE 25–2   USING COMMAS, p. H-143

a. Mrs. Carver looks like a sweet little old lady, but she plays a wicked electric guitar.

b. Her bass player, her drummer, and her keyboard player all live at the same rest home.

c. They practice individually in the afternoon, rehearse together at night, and play at the home's Saturday night dances.

d. The Rest Home Rebels have to rehearse quietly and cautiously to keep from disturbing the other residents.

e. Correct

EXERCISE 25–3   USING COMMAS, p. H-145

Suggested revisions:

a. The aye-aye, which is a member of the lemur family, is threatened with extinction.

b. The party, a dismal occasion, ended earlier than we had expected.

c. Secretary Stern warned that the concessions that the West was prepared to make would be withdrawn if not matched by the East.

d. Although both of Don's children are blond, his daughter, Sharon, has darker hair than his son, Jake.

e. Herbal tea, which has no caffeine, makes a better after-dinner drink than coffee.

EXERCISE 25–4   USING COMMAS, p. H-147

a. The university insisted, however, that the students were not accepted merely because of their parents' generous contributions.

b. This dispute, in any case, is an old one.

c. It was the young man's striking good looks, not his acting ability, that first attracted the Hollywood agents.

d. Gretchen learned, moreover, not to always accept as true what she had read in textbooks.

e. The hikers, most of them wearing ponchos or rain jackets, headed out into the steady drizzle.

EXERCISE 25–5   USING COMMAS, p. H-148

a. On October 2, 1969, the future discoverer of antigravity tablets was born.

b. Corwin P. Grant entered the world while his parents were driving to a hospital in Costa Mesa, California.

c. Correct

d. Today, ladies and gentlemen, Corwin enjoys worldwide renown.

e. Schoolchildren from Augusta, Maine, to Azuza, California, can recite his famous comment "It was my natural levity that led me to overcome gravity."

EXERCISE 26–1   USING SEMICOLONS, p. H-153

a. By the beginning of 1993, Shirley was eager to retire; nevertheless, she agreed to stay on for two more years.

b. In 1968, Lyndon Johnson abandoned his hopes for re-election because of fierce opposition from within his own party.

c. The committee was asked to determine the extent of violent crime among teenagers, especially those between the ages of fourteen and sixteen; to act as a liaison between the city and schools and between churches and volunteer organizations; and to draw up a plan to significantly reduce violence, both public and private, by the end of the century.

d. The leaves on the oak trees near the lake were tinged with red; swimmers no longer ventured into the water.

e. The football team has yet to win a game; however, the season is still young.

EXERCISE 27–1   USING COLONS, p. H-156

Suggested revisions:

a. The Continuing Education Program offers courses in building and construction management, engineering, and design.

b. The interview ended with a test of skills: taking dictation, operating the switchboard, proofreading documents, and typing a sample letter.

c. The sample letter began, "Dear Mr. Rasheed: Please accept our apologies for the late shipment."

d. Constance quoted Proverbs 8:18: "Riches and honor are with me."

e. A book that profoundly impressed me was Kurt Vonnegut's *Cat's Cradle* (New York: Dell, 1963).

EXERCISE 28–1   USING THE APOSTROPHE, p. H-160

a. It's not easy to be old in our society.

b. I don't understand the Jameses' objections to our plans for a block party.

c. It's not fair that your roommate won't help with the cleaning.

d. Is this collection of '50s records yours or your roommate's?

e. Alas, Brian got two D's on his report card.

EXERCISE 29–1   USING QUOTATION MARKS, p. H-164

a. "What we still need to figure out," the police chief said, "is whether the victim was acquainted with his assailant."

b. A skillful orator, Patrick Henry is credited with the phrase "Give me liberty or give me death."

c. "I could hear the crowd chanting my name — 'Jones! Jones!' — and that spurred me on," said Bruce Jones, the winner of the 5,000-meter race.

d. The Doors' "The End" is a disturbing ballad about parricide.

e. In his essay "Marrakech," George Orwell writes, "All people who work with their hands are partly invisible, and the more important the work they do, the less visible they are."

EXERCISE 30–1   USING THE DASH, p. H-166

Suggested revisions:

a. I enjoy going hiking with my friend John, whom I've known for fifteen years.

b. Pedro's new boat is spectacular — a regular seagoing Ferrari.

c. The Thompsons devote their weekends to their favorite pastime — eating bags of potato chips and cookies beside the warm glow of the television.

d. Correct

e. "A rock!" I cried. "Anthony, I'm afraid we're —"

EXERCISE 31–1   USING PARENTHESES, p. H-168

Suggested revisions:

a. In *The Last Crusade*, archaeologist Indiana Jones (who took his name from the family dog) joins his father in a quest for the Holy Grail.

b. Our cafeteria serves the four basic food groups: white (milk, bread, and mashed potatoes), brown (mystery meat and gravy), green (overcooked vegetables and underwashed lettuce), and orange (squash, carrots, and tomato sauce).

c. The hijackers will release the hostages only if the government (1) frees all political prisoners and (2) allows the hijackers to leave the country unharmed.

d. Correct

e. Actually, the Whale Stranding Network (WSN) rescues whales that have stranded themselves.

EXERCISE 32–1   USING ABBREVIATIONS, p. H-176

a. The Temple in Jerusalem was destroyed by the Romans in the year 70 A.D.

b. Mr. Robert Glendale, a C.P.A., is today's lucky winner of the daily double.

c. AIDS has affected people throughout U.S. society, not just gay men and intravenous-drug users.

d. Presidents Bush and Clinton must share the blame for the tragedy of Bosnia.

e. The salmon measured thirty-eight inches and weighed twenty-one pounds.

EXERCISE 33–1   USING CAPITALIZATION, p. H-179

a. At our family reunion, I met my cousin Sam for the first time, and also my father's brother George.

b. I already knew from Dad that his brother had moved to Australia years ago to explore the Great Barrier Reef.

c. At the reunion, Uncle George told me that he had always wanted to be a marine biologist.

d. He had spent the summer after his sophomore year of college in Woods Hole, Massachusetts, on Cape Cod.

e. At the Woods Hole Oceanographic Institution he studied horseshoe crabs.

EXERCISE 34–1   USING NUMBERS, p. H-182

a. Wasn't it the Three Musketeers whose motto was "One for all and all for one"?

b. In the 1970s, there were about 92 million ducks in America, but in the last four years their number has dropped to barely 69 million.

c. Of the three pyramids built at Giza, Egypt, between 2580 and 2490 B.C.E., the largest pyramid is 450 feet high.

d. Forty days and forty nights would seem like forty years if you were sailing on an ark with two of every kind of animal.

e. Correct

EXERCISE 35–1   USING ITALICS, p. H-185

a. Hiram's favorite Beatles album is *Sergeant Pepper's Lonely Hearts Club Band*, but his father prefers *Magical Mystery Tour*.

b. Hiram named his rowboat the *Yellow Submarine*.

c. He was disappointed when I told him that the play *Long Day's Journey into Night* is definitely not a staged version of the movie *A Hard Day's Night*.

d. I had to show him the article "Eugene O'Neill's Journey into Night" in *People* magazine to convince him.

e. We ate spaghetti and tortellini in the new Italian restaurant.

EXERCISE 36–1   USING HYPHENS, p. H-189

a. The strong-smelling smoke alerted them to a potentially life-threatening danger.

b. Burt's wildly swinging opponent had tired himself out before the climactic third round.

c. Tony soaked his son's ketchup-and-mustard-stained T-shirt in a pail of water mixed with chlorine bleach.

d. Correct

e. Tracy's brother-in-law lives with his family in a six-room apartment.

ACKNOWLEDGMENTS (continued from p. ii)

Toi Derricotte, "Early Memory: The *California Zephyr.*" From *The Black Notebooks: An Interior Journey* by Toi Derricotte. Copyright © 1997 by Toi Derricotte. Reprinted by permission of W. W. Norton & Company, Inc.

Stephen Dunn, "Locker Room Talk." From *In Short: A Collection of Brief Nonfiction* (1996). Copyright © 1996 by Stephen Dunn. Reprinted by permission of the author.

Gerald Early, "Black like . . . Shirley Temple?" Copyright © 1992 by *Harpers Magazine.* From the February issue. Reprinted by permission of the author.

David L. Evans, "The Wrong Examples." From *Newsweek*, March 1, 1993. Reprinted by permission of the author.

James Fallows, "'Throwing like a Girl!'" From *The Atlantic Monthly*, volume 278 No. 2 (August 1996). Copyright 1996 by James Fallows. Reprinted by permission of *The Atlantic Monthly* and the author.

Kurt M. Fischer and Arlyne Lazerson. From *Human Development* by Kurt M. Fischer and Arlyne Lazerson. Copyright © 1984 by W. H. Freeman & Company. Reprinted by permission.

Robert Frost, "Putting in the Seed," "The Road Not Taken," and "Stopping by Woods on a Snowy Evening." From *The Poetry of Robert Frost*, edited by Edward Connery Lathem. Copyright © 1916, 1969 by Henry Holt and Co. Reprinted by permission of Henry Holt and Company, Inc.

Matthew Futterman, "The Gender Gap." From *Swing Magazine* (February 1997). Reprinted by permission of the author.

Leonce Gaiter, "Is the Web Too Cool for Blacks?" This article first appeared in the June 1997 edition of *Salon Magazine*, an online magazine, at http://www.salonmagazine.com. Reprinted with permission.

Melina Gerosa, "Jodie Loses Her Cool." Copyright © 1995 by the Meredith Corporation. All rights reserved. Reprinted with permission from *Ladies' Home Journal* Magazine.

Ellen Goodman, "How to Zap Violence on TV." From *Globe* (February 1996). Copyright 1996 by Ellen Goodman. Reprinted with permission.

Stephen Jay Gould, "Sex and Size." From *The Flamingo's Smile: Reflections in Natural History* by Stephen Jay Gould. Copyright © 1985 by Stephen Jay Gould. Reprinted by permission of W.W. Norton & Company, Inc.

Kelly Grecian, "Playing Games with Women's Sports." From *Colby Community College 1996 Collection.* Copyright 1997 by Kelly Grecian. Reprinted by permission of the author.

Barrie B. Greenbie. Excerpt from *Spaces: Dimensions of the Human Landscape* by Barrie B. Greenbie. Copyright © 1981 by Barrie B. Greenbie. Reprinted by permission of the publisher, Yale University Press.

LynNell Hancock, "The Haves and the Have-Nots." From *Newsweek* (February 27, 1995). Copyright © 1995 by Newsweek, Inc. All rights reserved. Reprinted by permission.

Garrett Hardin. Excerpt from *Naked Emperors: Essays of a Taboo-Stalker*, by Garrett Hardin. Copyright © 1982 by William Kaufmann, Inc., Los Altos, CA 94023. Reprinted by permission. All rights reserved.

Joy Harjo, "Three Generations of Native American Women's Birth Experience." From *Ms.* Magazine, 1991. Copyright © 1991 by Ms. Magazine. Reprinted by permission of the author and Ms. Magazine.

Suzan Shown Harjo. "Last Rites for Indian Dead." From the *Los Angeles Times*, September 16, 1989. Copyright 1989 by Suzan Shown Harjo. Reprinted by permission.

Shirley Jackson, "The Lottery." From *The Lottery* by Shirley Jackson. Copyright © 1948, 1949 by Shirley Jackson. Copyright renewed © 1976, 1977 by Laurence Hyman, Barry Hyman, Mrs. Sarah Webster and Mrs. Joanne Schnurer. Reprinted by permission of Farrar, Straus & Giroux, Inc.

Cynthia Joyce, "Six Clicks from Death." This article first appeared in the April 1997 edition of *Salon Magazine*, an online magazine, at http://www.salonmagazine.com. Reprinted with permission.

Michiko Kakutani, "'Paradise': Worthy Women, Unredeemable Men." From *The New York Times Book Review.* Copyright 1998 by The New York Times Company. Reprinted by permission of The New York Times Company, Inc.

Jack Kemp, "Affirmative Action: The 'Radical Republican' Example." From *Washington Post* (Empower America online, August 6, 1995). Copyright 1995 by Jack Kemp. Reprinted with permission.

Stephen King, "Why We Crave Horror Movies." Copyright © by Stephen King. Reprinted with permission. All rights reserved.

Elisabeth Kübler-Ross, excerpt from *On Death and Dying* by Elisabeth Kübler-Ross. Copyright © 1969 by Elisabeth Kübler-Ross. Reprinted with the permission of the Macmillan Publishing Company.

Ron A. Larsen, "Put Me Out of My Misery, Shoot Me!" From *Gateway*, The University of Nebraska. Copyright 1997 by The Gateway. Reprinted by permission of The Gateway.

William Henry Lewis, "Shades." From *Ploughshares* (Fall 1995), ed. Ann Beattie. Copyright 1995 by William Henry Lewis. Reprinted by permission of the author.

Nancy Mairs, "Freeing Choices." From *Waist-High in the World* by Nancy Mairs. Copyright © 1996 by Nancy Mairs. Reprinted by permission of Beacon Press, Boston.

Mike Males, "Public Enemy Number One?" From *In These Times*, Chicago. Reprinted by permission.

Charles C. Mann and Mark L. Plummer, "The Butterfly Problem." Copyright © 1992 by Charles C. Mann and Mark L. Plummer, as originally published in *The Atlantic*, January 1992. Reprinted by permission.

N. Scott Momaday, "To the Singing, to the Drums." Reprinted with permission from *Natural History*, 2/75. Copyright © 1975 the American Museum of Natural History.

Jeffrey Obser, "Privacy Is the Problem, Not the Solution." This article first appeared in the June 1997 edition of *Salon Magazine*, an online magazine, at http://www.salonmagazine.com. Reprinted with permission.

Steve Olson, "Year of the Blue-Collar Guy." From *Newsweek*, November 6, 1989. Copyright © 1989 by Steve Olson. Reprinted with permission of the author.

Judith Ortiz Cofer, "The Myth of the Latin American Woman." From *The Latin Deli: Prose and Poetry* by Judith Ortiz Cofer. Reprinted with permission of the University of Georgia Press.

Cynthia Ozick, "The Shock of Teapots." From *In Short: A Collection of Brief Creative Nonfiction*, ed. Judith Kitchen and Mary Paumier Jones. Copyright 1996 by Judith Kitchen and Mary Paumier Jones. Reprinted by permission of W. W. Norton & Company, Inc.

Noel Perrin, "A Part-Time Marriage." From the About Men column in the September 9, 1984 issue of *The New York Times Magazine.* Copyright © 1984 by The New York Times Company. Reprinted by permission.

Sylvia Plath. Excerpt from *The Journals of Sylvia Plath*, edited by Ted Hughes and Francis McCullough. Copyright © 1982 by Ted

Hughes and Francis McCullough. Reprinted by permission of Doubleday, a division of Bantam, Doubleday Dell Publishing Group, Inc.

Emily Prager, "Our Barbies, Ourselves, " retitled from "Major Barbie." Originally published in *INTERVIEW*, Brant Publications, Inc., December 1991. Reprinted by permission of INTERVIEW.

Anna Quindlen, "Evan's Two Moms." From the February 5, 1992 issue of the *New York Times*. Copyright © 1992 by The New York Times Company. Reprinted by permission.

Howell Raines, from an interview with Franklin McCain in *My Soul is Rested.* Copyright © 1977 by Howell Raines. Reprinted by permission of the Putnam Publishing Group.

Mary Ann Raywid, excerpt from "Power to Jargon, for Jargon is Power." From *Journal of Teacher Education*, September/October 1978, p. 95. Reprinted by permission.

Wilbert Rideau, "Why Prisons Don't Work." From *Time*, March 21, 1994. Copyright © 1994 by Time, Inc. Reprinted by permission.

Richard Rodriguez, "Does America Still Exist?" Copyright 1984 by Richard Rodriguez. Reprinted with permission.

Phyllis Rose, "Shopping and Other Spiritual Adventures in America Today." From *Never Say Goodbye* (1991). Copyright © 1991 by Phyllis Rose. Reprinted with permission.

Scott Russell Sanders, "The Men We Carry in Our Minds." Copyright © 1984 by Scott Russell Sanders. First appeared in *Milkweed Chronicle.* Reprinted with permission.

Michael Shermer, "Abducted! Encounters with Aliens." From *Why People Believe Weird Things: Pseudoscience, Superstition, and Other Confusions of Our Time* by Michael Shermer. Copyright © 1997 by Michael Shermer. Used with permission of W.H. Freeman and Company.

Brent Staples, "Black Men and Public Space." From *Harper's*, December 1987. Copyright © 1987 by Brent Staples. Reprinted by permission of the author.

Ann Swidler. From *Habits of the Heart: Individualism and Commitment in American Life* by Robert N. Bellah, Richard Madsen, William M. Sullivan, Ann Swidler, and Steven M. Tipton. Copyright © 1985, 1996 Regents of the University of California. Reprinted by permission of the University of California Press.

Amy Tan, "Mother Tongue." Copyright © 1990 by Amy Tan. As first appeared in *The Threepenny Review.* Reprinted with permission.

Deborah Tannen, "Women and Men Talking on the Job." From pp. 32–36 and 39–41 of *Talking from 9 to 5* by Deborah Tannen. Copyright © 1994 by Deborah Tannen, Ph.D. Reprinted by permission of William Morrow & Company, Inc.

Lillian Tsu, "A Woman in the White House." From *Cornell Political Forum.* Copyright 1997 by Lillian Tsu. Reprinted with permission of the author.

Charles Van Riper. Excerpt from *A Career in Speech Pathology* by Charles Van Riper. Copyright © 1979 by Allyn & Bacon. All rights reserved. Granted by permission of Allyn & Bacon.

Paul Varnell, "The Niceness Solution." From *Beyond Queer* (1996), originally from *Windy City Times,* November 3, 1994. Copyright © 1994 by Paul Varnell. Reprinted by permission of the author.

Nicholas Wade, "How Men and Women Think." From the June 12, 1994 issue of *The New York Times Magazine.* Copyright © 1994 by The New York Times Company. Reprinted by permission.

Thaddeus Watulak, "Affirmative Action Encourages Racism." From the *Johns Hopkins Newsletter*, March 26, 1998. Copyright 1998 by Johns Hopkins University. Reprinted with permission.

Bruce Weigl, "Song of Napalm." From *Song of Napalm*, Atlantic Monthly Press, 1988. Reprinted by permission of the author.

Gerald Weissmann, M.D., excerpt from "Foucault and the Bag Lady." From *The Woods Hole Cantata: Essays on Science and Society.* Reprinted by permission of Dr. Gerald Weissmann and the Watkins/Loomis Agency.

E. B. White, "Once More to the Lake." From *Essays of E. B. White.* Copyright 1944 by E. B. White. Reprinted by permission of Mr. Joel White.

George F. Will, "The 'Decent' against the 'Street.'" From *The Woven Figure.* Copyright 1997 by George F. Will. Reprinted by permission of Scribner, a division of Simon & Schuster.

James Q. Wilson, "In Praise of Asphalt Nation." From *Commentary*, July 1997. Copyright 1997 by James Q. Wilson. Reprinted with permission of the author and Commentary. All rights reserved.

Marion Winik, "Visiting Steven." From *Telling* (1994). Copyright © 1994 by Marion Winik. Reprinted by permission of Random House.

Art and Photograph Credits

Page 489: Photo "Family in Kitchen" by Ron Chapple. © 1986 Ron Chapple/FPG International LLC

Page 528: Photo "Pregnant Lady in Meeting" by David De Lossy. © David De Lossy/Image Bank.

Page 560: Photo by Ulli Stelzer from p. 82 of *The New Americans.* Published by NewSage Press, 1988. © 1988 by Ulli Stelzer.

Page 592: Photo from *Aliens.* Reprinted courtesy of Photofest. © 1986 Twentieth Century Fox Film Corp.

Page 622: Photo "MIT Student" by Webb Chappell. © 1995 by Webb Chappell Photography.

Figure 27.9: Entry from *The Oxford English Dictionary*, 2nd ed. Copyright 1989 by Oxford University Press. Reprinted with permission.

Figure 27.10: *Reader's Guide to Periodical Literature*, entries under "Sports" from January 1995, Volume 94 No. 11, page 289. Copyright 1995 by the H. W. Wilson Company. Material reproduced with the permission of the publisher.

Figures 27.13 and 27.14: Text and artwork copyright © 1998 by Yahoo! Inc. All rights reserved. YAHOO! and the YAHOO! logo are trademarks of Yahoo! Inc.

"Shoe" cartoon. Reprinted by permission of Tribune Media Services.

Index

Rhetorical Index

(*in order of appearance*)

Definition

Description

Division and Classification

Evaluation

Example

PROOFREADING SYMBOLS

Use these standard proofreading marks when making minor corrections in your final draft. If extensive revision is necessary, type or print out a clean copy.

∿	Transpose
≡	Capitalize
/	Lowercase
#	Add space
⌒	Close up space
ℓ	Delete
‾.....	Stet (undo deletion)
∧	Insert
⊙	Insert period
⋏	Insert comma
;/	Insert semicolon
:/	Insert colon
⋎	Insert apostrophe
⋎ ⋎	Insert quotation marks
|=|	Insert hyphen
¶	New paragraph
no ¶	No new paragraph

CORRECTION SYMBOLS

Many Instructors use these abbreviations and symbols to mark errors in student papers. Refer to this chart to find out what they mean.

Boldface numbers refer to sections of the handbook and the Quick Editing Guide.

abbr	faulty abbreviation **32**	om	omitted word **15**
ad	misuse of adverb or adjective **10, A5**	p	error in punctuation **24–31, C**
agr	faulty agreement **6, 9, A2, A4**	$\wedge$	comma **25, C1**
appr	inappropriate language **20, 22**	no ,	no comma **25n–r**
awk	awkward	;	semicolon **26**
cap	capital letter **33, D1**	:	colon **27**
case	error in case **7, A3**	$\check{v}$	apostrophe **28, C2**
coord	faulty coordination **18**	" "	quotation marks **29**
cs	comma splice **13, A7**	. ? !	period, question mark, exclamation point **24**
dm	dangling modifier **14, B1**	– ( ) [ ] . . .	dash, parentheses, brackets, ellipsis **30–31**
exact	inexact language **21**	par, ¶	new paragraph
frag	sentence fragment **12, A6**	pass	ineffective passive **5m**
fs	fused sentence **13, A7**	ref	error in pronoun reference **8, A4**
gl	see glossary of trouble-makers	rev	revise
gr	grammar **1–4, A**	sp	misspelled word **37, D2**
hyph	error in use of hyphen **36**	sub	faulty subordination **18**
inc	incomplete construction **15**	t	error in verb tense **5c, g–l, A1**
irreg	error in irregular verb **5e, A1**	v	voice **5m**
ital	italics (underlining) **35**	vb	error in verb form **5, A1, A2**
lc	use lowercase letter **33, D1**	w	wordy **23**
mixed	mixed construction **16**	//	faulty parallelism **17, B2**
mm	misplaced modifier **14a–b, B1**	^	insert
mood	error in mood **5n–p**	x	obvious error
ms	manuscript form **D3**	#	insert space
nonst	nonstandard usage **20, 21**	$\cup$	close up space
num	error in use of numbers **34**		

Directory to MLA Documentation Models

Directory to APA Documentation Models

Index to ESL Guidelines

A Guide to the Handbook